The Jewish Question

The Jewish Question

Biography of a World Problem

ALEX BEIN

TRANSLATED BY
HARRY ZOHN

A Herzl Press Publication
•
Rutherford • Madison • Teaneck
Fairleigh Dickinson University Press
London and Toronto: Associated University Presses

Associated University Presses
440 Forsgate Drive
Cranbury, NJ 08512

Associated University Presses
25 Sicilian Avenue
London WC1A 2QH, England

Associated University Presses
P.O. Box 488, Port Credit
Mississauga, Ontario
Canada L5G 4M2

Herzl Press
515 Park Avenue
New York, NY 10022

The paper used in this publication meets the requirements
of the American National Standard for Permanence of Paper
for Printed Library Materials Z39.48-1984.

Library of Congress Cataloging-in-Publication Data

Bein, Alex, 1903–1988
    [Judenfrage. English]
    The Jewish question : biography of a world problem / Alex Bein ;
translated by Harry Zohn.
    p. cm.
    Translation of: Die Judenfrage.
    Includes bibliographical references and index.
    ISBN 0-8386-3252-1 (alk. paper)
    1. Antisemitism—History. 2. Christianity and antisemitism.
3. Jews—History—70– 4. Holocaust, Jewish (1939–1945) 5. Judaism—
Relations. I. Title.
DS141.B3813   1990
909'.04924—dc19   87-46422
                                             CIP

Printed in the United States of America

In remembrance of my late wife, Betty (née) Bildstein
For the generations of my children and grandchildren to
remember

Contents

Part 1: The Jewish Question

Part 2: Notes and Excursuses

The Jewish Question

PART 1
The Jewish Question

Preface

This book, the first drafts of which go back more than four decades, is not really a historical work but one oriented toward the present and the future. By means of historical presentation and interpretation it attempts to understand a problem that has been occupying the Jews and the nations for more than two thousand years, although not under the same name. It will be shown that the Jewish question, the term and the concept, are of relatively recent date, but the problem concealed behind it has been in existence at least since the dispersal of the Jews among the nations.

The history of this problem, as we understand it, is by no means identical with the nature and the history of the persecutions of the Jews with which it is often equated, nor with hatred of Jews as such, and still less with the special form of the organized hatred and persecution of the Jews for which—under circumstances that are to be detailed in this book—the word anti-Semitism was coined three generations ago. It will be the task of the historical analysis attempted here to trace the reasons why hatred and persecution of the Jews have come into being and keep arising anew, and to ascertain the effects and repercussions produced by them. In the widest sense it is thus a problem of the Jews living with the nations and the nations with the Jews. We shall have to ask this question: How were the opinions, images, and stereotypical notions of the Jews formed, along with the fearful or hateful accusations against them with all their ramifications and repercussions, the reactions they produced on the part of those concerned—that seemingly inextricable tangle of prejudices and fears, often by no means onesided, which we regard as the core of the Jewish question?

As will be shown, this involves a many-layered problem that came into being over a period of centuries. The various layers must be laid bare through historical analysis, and not only to satisfy the urge for research and knowledge; it seems to me that there is a deeper meaning. History is not something singular and transient; it is basically ever-present. Past times live on in all kinds of forms: in languages and customs, traditions and ideals, forms of organization, ideological movements, and special-interest groups, in pictures and buildings, in the atmosphere of countries and cities, in the cultural values and valuations that we receive and pass on as a matter of course, and above all in the contents of con-

13

sciousness and the subconscious in which layers of past cultural epochs have often accumulated in archaic form. Every era builds on the foundations of past ages, externally and internally, and layers are covered by fresh layers without the effects of the old strata being thereby fully obliterated. The present is, so to speak, the topmost layer of an earth-formation under which many geologic strata from earlier times are concealed. In turbulent times of crises and upheavals geologic disturbances occur for the sake of survival. At such times originally deep-seated layers are suddenly propelled to the surface by volcanic forces, and layers from various eras intermingle, producing new, unexpected phenomena of the present. In the layers of consciousness the process is similar to that of geological reality.

Thus it must be the task of this examination of the Jewish question to expose the layers of this problem, to trace its origin, its growth, and its mutual influences, and in this way to make the ground on which we stand transparent, as it were.

We shall, then, attempt to view the present from the vantage point of the past and the past from the vantage point of the present to the extent that it concerns the coexistence of the Jews and the nations. Only from such viewpoints will facts and events be mentioned or ignored, discussed in detail or only referred to in passing. The decisive events of the last few decades—the destruction of the majority of European Jewry and the founding of the State of Israel—are of course a focal point for anyone who concerns himself with the Jewish question today.

In this context the new situation created by the founding of Israel must be acknowledged. We have to ask certain questions: What effect has this foundation had and what effect is to be expected of the existence of the Jewish State for the further development of our problem? After all, the Zionist movement arose with the claim that the Jewish question would be solved through the founding of a Jewish State. To what extent have these claims and hopes been fulfilled, or is there a prospect that they are on their way to fulfillment?

This book was not conceived as a scholarly work but is intended for a wider readership. It has the advantages and disadvantages of one author's survey of historical developments spanning more than two thousand years. It is only natural that one author cannot be an expert on every period and base his discussion on only primary sources in each case. I will frequently have to rely on citations and digests of these sources in the scholarly literature about ages and specialized problems; this is, after all, the purpose of this literature. It is also possible that I will make errors in details here and there. On the other hand, such a book has the advantage that it offers a uniform survey of the entire historical development.

As in my earlier books, I have not striven to present new information, but to find the truth and to be a guide to understanding and appreciation. Thus the emphasis is not on a retelling of generally known facts and events about which the reader's memory need only be refreshed, but on illuminating them and integrating them into a comprehensive historical picture. Whether this approach will give researchers and scholars food for thought and ideas for further research as well, only they can judge. I can only hope so.

This book makes no claim to being "objective" in the sense of those writers who have no point of view and adopt a *laissez-faire* attitude of so-called neutrality. It is written by a Zionist who has been living in Jerusalem for more than fifty years. This vantage point and angle are unmistakable. But within this natural limitation, of which I am fully aware, I have done all I could to present the problem *sine ira et studio* and to appeal to the readers' intelligence rather than to their emotions and moods. In my presentation of events and developments I have striven to do as much justice to all sides as is possible for a person who has definite views of the rightness and wrongness of a path and who, unlike so many today, does not regard it as permissible to show everywhere only the problems and to provide everything with question marks.

Another admission to be made is that this book has not been written for any specific readership. Like any genuine artistic and scholarly work, like any more searching historical investigation, it was born of a personal need and quest, but I assume that these are not mine alone. This justifies its publication. In contrast to the effort of many people, particularly our youth, to free themselves from the pressure of the past by ignoring it, I agree with those like the historian and philosopher of history Benedetto Croce who believe that one frees oneself from the past by raising it to the status of an intellectual problem and experiencing it as such. May a concern with this book and its cluster of subjects have the same effect on the readers as it has had on me. Since I began to concern myself with the Jewish question, there has been a change in the way the world around us sees and expresses things. In the realm of the Jewish question there have been many changes as well; for this reason I have often stopped and asked myself whether my subject was still timely. But I have always returned to it and felt that I would not be true to myself if I abandoned it altogether. Chance conversations with people close to me as well as strangers repeatedly convinced me that this problem is not seen very clearly. Thus this book is intended to contribute to a further clarification of the Jewish question.

I have purposely chosen *Biography of a World Problem* as the subtitle of this book. Biography means the story of a life in all its relationships, in the interplay of idea and reality, of action and thought, of idea, will, and deed. It is the story of a problem that has occupied the world for many centuries, down to our time, and that, beyond its singularity and uniqueness as a totality, contains a great deal of the universally and problematically human.

The book is divided into two parts. Part 1 begins with an introductory chapter that outlines the fundamentals and approaches and then presents and analyzes the historical development of the problem from ancient times to the present. Part 2 contains notes, documentations, and excursions—many things that might have unduly impeded or sidetracked the flow of the narrative in the first part. These observations about and discussions of specific problems, personalities, concepts, and methodological questions often assume the dimensions of independent treatises or essays. Even though as supplements and nuances they are closely connected with the text of the first part, they can be read independently of it. Hence they purposely have not been distinguished by reference marks or numbers, but are identified only by the page number and the pertinent key word to which they apply in Part 1. This leaves the reader free to decide whether he wishes to read them and at what point; the text portion is comprehensible even without reference to them. Only where I deemed it especially desirable to read them have I included an express reference in the text to pertinent excursions or notes in the second part.

Repetitiveness in mentioning facts and events cannot be avoided in a book of these dimensions. Often they are necessary as a summary and anamnesis, and thus this is a deliberate device for bringing out theses and developments and easing the task of the reader, who normally would not read such a voluminous study in one sitting, by referring him to what has been and is to be presented. The same purpose is served by the chronological table at the end of Part 2 and the index of persons and places. With the aid of this index it is easy to make cross connections between persons, ideas, events, and problems that often could not be fully demonstrated in the historical presentation and in the excursions.

As already stated, the book evolved over a period of decades, and its sections have been formulated in ever-revised versions. It assumed its definitive form between 1972 and 1977. It is in the nature of this evolution that I was not able to take due cognizance of research results and publications that did not come to my attention until after the completion of the book or individual chapters. For this failing I can only ask for the understanding of readers and the indulgence of colleagues and critics.

Finally, to whom shall I express my thanks? This book and its author are obliged to so many for their (witting or unwitting) help: to my teachers, friends, colleagues, and partners in dialogue of every kind and origin; to the reviewers, the positive and encouraging ones and no less the critical ones, who pointed out deficiencies in my earlier publications, virtually all of which are in some way connected with the subject of this book; to the archives, libraries, scholarly institutions, and book dealers in many countries and cities in which I became acquainted with the source material on which I could base myself; to those who helped with the production of this book. To name them all is impossible, and to attempt it would probably be unfair to many whose share I am no longer aware of. Thus I must limit myself to a few people who had a direct part in the preparation of the manuscript and the printing of this book: Grete Marx, to whom I dictated the first draft and who can no longer receive my thanks; Mrs. Chanah Gurevitz, who copied the major portion of the manuscript in its often all but illegible versions; Abraham Tobias, who gave the entire manuscript a critical reading, and Moshe Schaerf, who helped me read the proofs; Ruth Liepman in Zurich, whose experience and friendship procured the publishers for me. My most profound thanks are owed my late wife Betty (née) Bildstein. With her unshakable love and her understanding indulgence for all that may have been missing in her life because of this study she accompanied the growth of this book, with its joys and inner crises, until years of grave illness and death took her from me. It is almost symbolic that she died on the evening of the day on which I wrote the last pages. It is to her memory that I dedicate this book as well as to the insight of my children and grandchildren, whose love and will to understand are my constant companion and support. May it be granted to them to lead lives of rectitude and integrity, without the tragic entanglements that really opened the eyes of many members of past generations—and in particular of mine, to the extent that it was able to survive the tragedy—to the problem and induced them to attempt its solution. This book is intended as a contribution to an understanding of this problem.

Jerusalem, November 1986   Alex Bein

1
Introduction

"The Jewish Question": The Term and the Concept

What is involved when we speak of the "Jewish Question"? Responses of many kinds have been given. In 1909 Martin Buber cited in the first of his *Three Addresses on Judaism* (published in 1911) with emphatic agreement the definition of his friend, the Jewish writer Moritz Heimann: "What a Jew marooned on a desert island still recognizes as The Jewish Question—that is all it is." In this identification with himself, in each Jew's decision about what he recognizes and affirms in himself as his Jewish self and substance, "in the choice between environment and substance," he sees "the root of all Jewish questions." Today, after the experiences of the past fifty years, we are, to say the least, dubious about such an esoteric definition. In contrast to this, Moritz Güdemann, a historian and chief rabbi of Vienna, who had been one of the first to read Herzl's *The Jewish State: An Attempt at a Modern Solution of the Jewish Question* in 1895, as late as 1917 regarded the Jewish question as "nothing but a construct designed for material business purposes of the anti-Semites, who adopted this name like a registered firm, as it were, for the conduct of the 'Jewish Question' they had raised."

In 1945 the French writer and philosopher Jean-Paul Sartre expressed a rather similar view. "What makes the Jew," according to him, is "his 'concrete situation,' what unites him to other Jews is the identity of their situations. . . . The Jewish problem is born of anti-Semitism; thus it is anti-Semitism that we must suppress in order to resolve the problem." By contrast, the Declaration of Independence of the State of Israel of 14 May 1948 speaks of the solution of the problem of the homeless Jewish people through the reestablishment of the Jewish State in the Land of Israel.

These are only a few examples from the definitions of the last two generations; many others, equally antithetical, could easily be added. Perhaps we can make some progress by asking ourselves when and how the term and the concept "Jewish Question" originated and became common usage. After all, the history of the term and of its reception is itself part of the history of the Jewish question.

One would expect the term to have had a long etymological and semantic history, to go back to antiquity or the Middle Ages. After all, in our consciousness there is involved a problem that is as old as the existence of the Jews, or at least as their life in the Diaspora among other nations. In point of fact, however, the term "Jewish Question" is of relatively recent date; the word *Judenfrage* seems to have come into being in Germany around 1840. Thus the public did not become aware of the Jewish question as an extensive problem until then, though its roots go back to the beginnings of Jewish history and its development extends over many centuries, more than two thousand years. Theoretically, however, the problem did not exist as long as the Jews were regarded by their environment and by themselves as a religious and national community and as such occupied their legitimate place as one nation among others. As long as Christianity in particular was the predominant power, there was no real Jewish problem for the part of mankind that was organized in its faith and claim to power. In the Christian philosophy the Jews had their place—not a very honorable or agreeable one, but one legitimated by dogma and the secular order based on it. And it was similar from the Jews' own standpoint: As long as they clung to their faith and the religious laws and customs based on it, they did not regard themselves as a problem, however insecure and perilous their lives might be.

Only when at the turn of the eighteenth to the nineteenth century these premises were increasingly shaken and crumbled among the Jews themselves and in their environment, when the Jews left the ghettos and the Jewish districts, entered the economic, social, and political life around them, and demanded equal status with the other citizens, did people begin to regard their existence as a problem requiring a solution, as a question that demanded an answer. People spoke of problems of "toleration," "civil improvement," "equal rights," and the "emancipation" of the Jews, also of the "Jewish cause," until around 1842 the concept of the "Jewish Question" crystallized from all this. The term *Judenfrage* was coined in Germany, but it soon spread to other countries as well. One of the first independent works that used the word as a title was written by the neo-Hegelian Bruno Bauer; it appeared in 1842 as an essay in a journal ("Die Juden-Frage") and was published as a pamphlet *(Die Judenfrage)* a year later. By the Jewish question Bauer meant the problem of integrating the Jews in the states and societies of the Christian peoples of Europe. Bauer's attitude toward it was a negative one; his essay placed it in question. The word *Judenfrage* received its first dissemination in the positive or negative reviews of this essay (among them the article "Zur Judenfrage" by the young Karl Marx, known for its cutting vehemence and for its equation of the Jews with capitalism), in the polemics prompted by it and similar writings, and in the public discussion of the implementation of the emancipation of the Jews that was carried on in the 1840s. The question mark that the term contained was perceptible for a long time, and thus it was at first used more by the opponents of the emancipation of the Jews than by its proponents. The latter used it with a certain restraint—by way of protest, as it were.

Public discussion of the concept and the problems of the Jewish question was resumed and intensified by the so-called anti-Semitic movement that arose around 1880 (cf. chap. 6). With his work *Die Judenfrage als Racen-, Sitten- und Culturfrage* [The Jewish question as a question of race, morals, and culture], published in 1881, Eugen Dühring set the new tone. In the large number of writings that appeared at that time, the concept "Jewish Question" was again primarily used by foes of the Jews, to whom the existence of the Jews and their conduct appeared at least problematic and perhaps even dangerous. The Jews occasionally used it in their polemics, though reluctantly. In their view, or at any rate in the view of their leading strata and their spokesmen, the Jewish question existed only in the imagination or through the activities of the Jew-baiters; the real problem was the full implementation of the legally decreed equal rights. Similar points of view were enunciated in the rekindled debate at the beginning of the 1890s.

On the Jewish side, the word *Judenfrage* and its substance were taken seriously by the founders of the Zionist movement and their adherents. The Russian-Jewish physician Leon Pinsker began his fundamental work *Auto-Emancipation*, published anonymously in 1882, with these words: "The age-old problem of the Jewish Question is causing emotions to run high today, as it has over the ages. Like the quadrature of the circle, it is an unsolved problem, but unlike it, it remains the burning question of the day." In 1893 Nathan Birnbaum published in Vienna his work *Die Nationale Wiedergeburt des jüdischen Volkes in seinem Land als Mittel zur Lösung der Judenfrage* [The national rebirth of the Jewish people in its country as a means toward the solution of the Jewish question], and in 1896 there appeared Theodor Herzl's basic booklet *Der Judenstaat: Versuch einer modernen Lösung der Judenfrage*, which was soon translated into many languages. This work in particular made the *Judenfrage*, the word and the concept, a subject of discussion among the Jews— between the proponents, who acknowledged the existence of a problem designated by the word, and the opponents, who denied it (cf. chap. 8). The discussion of the Jewish question reached its zenith—particularly in Germany but also in other countries, though not with the same intensity and vehemence—in the period following World War I and especially since the rise and accession to power of the National Socialist movement. Everyone remembers its endeavor to bring about the so-called final solution to the Jewish Question through the systematic extermination of European Jewry (cf. chap. 9).

In one form or another, with a positive or negative rating, the term and the concept have been disseminated down to the present time, sometimes in connection with other attempts at a solution of the problem, such as communism. The discussion about the nature of the Jewish question and its possible solution continues unabated across countries and continents and in multifarious variations, interpretations, and reinterpretations—from America to Israel and from the Arab states to Soviet Russia.

The Nature of the Jewish Question

The discussion of the history of the concept "Jewish Question" yields the insight that the word and the idea were created by non-Jews to characterize an existing problem. Thus the complex of problems called "Jewish Question" is viewed from both a non-Jewish and a Jewish viewpoint. Both sides are affected by the problem but view it from different angles, seeing it in different ways at different times. The founding of the State of Israel gave it a fresh impetus, and we are in the midst of a historical transformation that has probably changed and is changing the premises and the impact of the problem more radically than other events have done in the last nineteen hundred years.

Nietzsche once said that only things without history are definable. Since the Jewish question is an eminently historical problem, it is hard to give a brief outline of its nature and its manifestations. If we nevertheless attempt to do so as a necessary point of departure, we can give only very tentative definitions and characterizations to which we shall subsequently have to add substance, form, and color.

Viewed from the non-Jewish and the Jewish aspects, and for the time being without reference to the Jews living in Israel, one could generally define the Jewish question as the problem of the existence of the Jews among the nations. The first characteristic of this existence would be that this existence frequently arouses displeasure both among the nations and among the Jews. Among the non-Jewish population this displeasure frequently grows into hatred of the Jews and violent eruptions of this hatred, eruptions that reached their zenith in the systematic extermination of European Jewry by the German National Socialists.

If we take a closer look at the special nature of this Jewish existence, we may characterize it as follows: We are dealing with the existence of a group of people dispersed over almost all inhabited countries of the earth, people who are for the most part recognizable as members of this group by external characteristics and who are somehow kept together by bonds of descent, religion, history, and tradition, even though in language, customs, and culture they are largely separated from one another and assimilated to their countries of domicile. The members of this group who reside in various countries—their number is not insignificant and reached its zenith around 1933—usually constitute a small minority everywhere, Israel being the sole exception. As regards its professional and social stratification, this minority differs from the rest of the population in that it has an above-average representation in certain occupations, but a below-average or virtually nonexistent one in others. Even where the Jews have completely adopted the language and the culture of a nation and fulfill all the duties of citizenship, they are generally regarded by the majority of the population as members of a special group and often as foreign bodies, even though their fellow citizens have no clear notion of what constitutes the special nature of this Jewish existence. For this reason the Jews are somehow shrouded in mystery and exposed to suspicions, accusations, and animosity against which they must constantly defend themselves, both toward the outside and in their own eyes. Hence there is almost no place where there is a correspondence between their formal equal rights and their social equality.

The peculiar position of the Jews among the nations is also reflected by the fact that their positive achievements, their contributions to the development of the economy, the civilization, and culture are usually credited to the peoples in whose midst they live. On the other hand, every negatively perceived action of Jews is generally debited only to the account of the Jews, at least in their countries of residence. If people say of someone that he is a Jew, this is usually not done merely to state a fact, as it is with members of other nations; it usually involves a positive or a negative evaluation, and the very mention of a person's Jewishness expresses such an evaluation. The special existence and life-style of the Jews in the Diaspora are almost never regarded by their surroundings as something natural, legitimate in itself, and thus of equal value; therefore the Jews too, hardly ever consider it as natural, justified, and independent of the judgment of their environment. We might even say that the existence of non-Jews is recognized by their simply being and living, but the existence of Jews only if they accomplish something. That is why they strive for special achievements and distinctions; they have to stand out to be recognized. The economic, social, and cultural rise of the Jews above the average of the population is generally viewed with suspicion by this population. In times of political and social unrest and upheaval this tension between the Jews and their surroundings often intensifies, leading to hostile behavior and the eruption of violence. These conditions have repeatedly made life barely endurable or impossible for considerable parts of the Jewish population and caused them to leave their places of residence and set out in search of others.

Even this (provisional and crude) characterization of the Jewish question establishes that we are here dealing with a unique problem for which no real parallels can be found. There are, to be sure, parallels to some manifestations of the problem. Members of other religious communities have also been scattered throughout the world and have from time to time had to endure discord and persecution because of their faith. No religion with millions of adherents, however, has been so indissolubly connected with an ethnic entity in a history of 4,000 years as the Jews. Larger or smaller parts of other ethnic groups (nations) also live in a Diaspora and constitute ethnic minorities in a variety of countries. With the sole exception of the gypsies, who should probably be numbered among the nomadic rather than the settled part of humanity, all of them possess a common motherland from which they or their ancestors emigrated a few generations ago and to which they inwardly remain tied with manifold bonds. This living connection sustains and strengthens them in their existence as an ethnic minority—even if (as is the case with the Irish) these minority groups surpass in number those living in the motherland.

Until the founding of the State of Israel the Jews of the Diaspora had no such center in the almost nineteen hundred years since the destruction of their state by the Romans in 70 C.E. Other peoples, too, were driven out of their original domiciles and forced to go wandering; but this wandering always came to a natural end before very long. Either the people conquered another country and turned it into a new national domicile or it became completely assimilated and absorbed by the nation among which it had been scattered. In the latter eventuality the people ceased to exist as a separate ethnic entity with the consciousness, the historical tradition, and the will to live of a separate national group. Other nations, too, lost their political independence in struggles with other, more powerful peoples and regained it only after a shorter or longer period of political and cultural subjugation, often after centuries. All of these, however, remained in their domicile during the period of their political dependence, stayed on their soil, and somehow continued their national life in their natural environment. But there is no other people that, like the Jews, after hundreds of years of spatial separation from their original homeland and of dispersion over all continents and in groups of varying size, returned to their original homeland by the hundreds of thousands and there reestablished its own state, successfully defended it, secured it economically and politically, and thus turned it into a recognized national homeland.

Thus, even though there are certain parallels to some aspects of Jewish existence, there is nothing comparable for the phenomenon as a whole; it is a problem *sui generis*. Hence one can approach a comprehension of the Jewish question only if one eschews hasty generalizations and analogies and tries to understand it as the unique problem that it is. This is why any monistic attempts at explanation are bound to fail. Nowhere more than here does Jacob Burckhardt's warning against the *terribles simplificateurs* apply, for a scholarly and pseudo-scholarly examination is all too apt to lead to a one-sided evaluation with corresponding social and political conclusions. The Jewish question cannot be reduced to a common denominator without doing violence to it, be it the common denominator of religion, race, ethnic unity, culture and civilization, economy and society, or whatever. Any attempts to present and explain the Jewish question exclusively from one of these aspects without considering the others can at best produce partial results, but not a comprehensive understanding of the problem. It is precisely the many-faceted character, the intermingling and opposition of different forces and currents, the multiplicity of phenomena and approaches that make the existence of the Jews such a peculiar, uncomprehended, and mystery-shrouded phenomenon in the eyes of the world around the Jews and often in their own eyes as well.

This dooms to failure the attempts that are repeatedly made, and often with scientific lavishness, to analyze and generalize about the situation and problems of Jewish existence in all its nuances with what may be called a horizontal approach, as pure problems of the present, with the methods of sociology and psychology. Being a problem whose roots lie deep in the earth of the past, the Jewish question cannot be understood even by a very careful and systematic analysis of the present situation, valuable though its results may be. After all, the so-called present is only a transition from the past to the future, a narrow border region between these main periods, provided one wishes to subdivide the continuous flow of evolution and action by limitations in the first place. In general, any present time can be grasped properly only if one includes in it the continuing effects of the past with all its manifestations and structures. This is particularly the case with the Jewish present time, which has developed over the course of at least two and a half thousand years of documented history to produce the present situation from an intertwinement of events and views, effects and countereffects of all kinds, in the Jewish and non-Jewish worlds.

Hence our point of departure will be the present, and through a historical review and analysis we shall try to clarify the foundations as well as the inner and outer fources that have affected and are still affecting the Jewish question. In doing so we are more interested in the actual situations and the interplay of the various factors than in the question whether the Jews and the nations acted and reacted properly in certain historical situations or whether other courses of action and decisions would have been more appropriate. Our presentation cannot do without judgments, but it does not presume to reveal in the concurrence of natural dispositions and so-called chance events laws of a higher "destiny" that may govern the lives of men and groups of people. In a presentation of conflict-laden situations there is no avoiding accusations and justifications; often these are indissolubly bound up with the account of what happened. It is, however, not the aim of this presentation to accuse or to justify, but to contribute to the understanding and thus to the solution of the world problem that is called the Jewish question.

Number and Dissemination of the Jews in Our Time

It has been said that "history without demography is an enigma, just as is demography without history." Let us therefore try to get a general idea of some demographic foundations of Jewish existence, especially the number and dissemination of Jews all over the earth.

This is no easy task, particularly for the time before the eighteenth century, for which almost all statistics are unsystematic and lack scientific precision. But even for our time we are in large measure dependent on estimates and calculations, because in many countries, particularly those with Jewish mass settlement, there is no reliable information about the religion or descent of the inhabitants. Often an official census does not gather that information as a matter of principle. Thus the figures may not be very accurate in detail, but they do convey an approximate picture and enable us to make comparisons within a certain period and with the situation in other periods.

Let us use *our* time as a point of departure. Around the middle of our century, and in the course of one generation, there has been one of those great demographic transformations in the life of the Jews that are rather frequent in their history—perhaps the greatest since the destruction of the Second Temple and State. Two decisive events have left their mark on this population shift: the systematic mass murder of European Jewry by Hitler's National Socialists in World War II and the foundation of the State of Israel after its end (1948). These two events and their consequences have decisively changed the face of Jewry, the distribution of the Jews over continents and countries, and the weight and the influence of the Jews of certain countries on Jewry as a whole.

It has been calculated, or estimated, that in 1939, before the outbreak of World War II, the Jewish population amounted to 16.25 to 16.75 million.* In absolute terms this was the greatest number ever attained by the Jews, and with it the Jews constituted 0.78 percent of the population of the earth at that time (2.15 billion), or a bit less than 2 percent of the population in those countries that had a significant Jewish population and in which the influence of a European population and culture predominated—which excluded Central Africa, as well as Cen-

---

*After Arthur Ruppin, *Jewish Fate and Future* (London, 1940) and *American Jewish Year Book* 1939, pp. 583–90.

tral and East Asia. In 1946 the number of Jews was estimated at 11 million, in 1976 (probably too high) at more than 14.* These 14 million constituted 0.356 percent of the total population of the earth (over 4 billion), or about 1 percent in countries with an appreciable Jewish population. Thus in the course of one generation there was a radical change in the absolute number of Jews and their percentage of the total population.

These changes appear even more radical if we look at the distribution of the Jews over continents and countries. At the outbreak of the war in 1939, 9.5 to 9.75 million Jews lived in Europe, i.e., far more that half (58%) of the total Jewish population of the world; in Europe they constituted 1.8 percent of the total population of 515 million. There has been a fundamental change in this, largely due to the mass murders during the war years. The number of Jews living in Europe today [1979] is estimated at 4 million; thus they constitute only half of the former percentage—about 29 percent of the Jews worldwide and 0.54 percent of the total population of Europe (including Soviet Russia). Even before World War I the Jews of (North and South) America constituted the largest percentage of the total population. The Jews living there—at that time about 5.34 million, today 6.7 million (i.e., a bit more than a third before the war, today almost half, of the total Jewish population)—constituted 2.2 percent of the total population (250 million) then and 1.2 percent (of 558 million) today (in North America 6.12 million, or 2 percent of the total population of 300 million).

There has been a marked change in the number of Jews in Asia. In 1939 900,000 Jews lived there—i.e., only about 5½ percent of the total Jewish population, or 0.8 percent of the total population of the continent. Thirty-one years after the foundation of the State of Israel the Jewish population of Asia had risen to more than 3 million, or more than 22 percent of the Jews in the world (0.16% of the population of the continent). The Jewish population of Africa has declined from 600,000 (0.78% of the total population) to 177,000 (ca. 1.5% of the Jewish population of the world). The Jewish population of Australia and New Zealand has increased from 32,000, or 0.13 of the total population, to ca. 75,000 (0.52 of the Jews in the world, 0.45 of the population of these countries).

Even though the Jews number no more than 2 percent of the population in any continent, their share in the total population of certain countries and groups of countries is substantially larger.

The Jews of the State of Israel occupy a special position. In 1939, when Palestine was British mandated territory, 475,000 Jews lived there—31 percent of the total population (and less than 3% of world

*American Jewish Year Book 1978, p. 517, gives the figure 14,259,525.

Jewry!) By the time the State of Israel was established in 1948, their number had increased to 650,000. Today three and a half million Jews live in Israel, which has a total population of more than 3.6 million, or over 21 percent of the Jewish population of the world.

The countries in the Diaspora with the greatest density of Jews before the war were those of Central and Eastern Europe—namely, the area east of Germany that included Poland, Western Russia and White Russia, the Ukraine and the Crimea, Lithuania, Latvia, Danzig, Hungary, and Czechoslovakia. The approximately 7.5 million Jews living there constituted 5.64 percent of the total population of those countries. The relative percentage of Jews in individual countries or regions was substantially higher, however; in Poland it amounted to almost 10 percent (in the Polish district of Lodz it was 14.4 percent), in the Ukraine to 5.4 percent, in Lithuania 7.6 percent, in Hungary 5.1 percent, in the Carpatho-Russian area belonging to Czechoslovakia 14.1 percent (while the Jews constituted only a little over 1 percent of the total population of Czechoslovakia). In the meantime there has been a substantial change. It is true that even today more than 2.6 million Jews live in the lands of the Soviet Union—that is, almost 19 percent of world Jewry and about 1 percent of the Soviet Union's total population. However, while the Jewish population of Central and Eastern Europe was the most important Jewish group in the Diaspora in cultural terms as well, this role has today passed to the Jews of America, particularly the United States. In the Eastern and Central European countries other than the Soviet Union there live today only larger or smaller remnants of the once-great Jewish settlements. In Poland, formerly a main area of settlement, there are about 6,000 Jews (as compared to the former figure of 3 million); in Bulgaria there are 7,000 (out of 50,000), in Czechoslovakia 12,000 (formerly 380,000), in Hungary 80,000 (as compared to 600,000 in 1939), in Rumania 60,000 (of 800,000 in 1939), and in Yugoslavia 6,000 (as compared to 75,000 in 1939).

In today's largest area of Jewish settlement, the United States, there are now around 6 million Jews, or 2.7 percent of the total population. In most other countries the number of Jews never exceeded 2 percent, and often it was much less than that. Even in such a numerically and culturally significant Jewish population as that of Germany, the Jews constituted less than 1 percent of the total population (today 0.04 percent); in Great Britain there were about 0.75 percent and in France a bit over 0.5 percent. Today France (with 650,000 Jews) and England (with over 400,000) have replaced Germany as the Western European countries with the largest Jewish communities. In addition to the United States, Argentina (500,000 Jews) and Canada (280,000) are American countries with a substantial Jewish population.

As we have pointed out, the percentage of the Jewish population of the various countries was by no means of uniform size. We have already given some examples. The uneven distribution of the Jews in the United States is particularly striking. In 1976 more than 85 percent of the Jewish population of the United States lived in nine states (New York, New Jersey, Massachusetts, Pennsylvania, Maryland, Illinois, Ohio, Florida, California), 67 percent in eleven cities (New York, Los Angeles, San Francisco, Chicago, Philadelphia, Boston, Baltimore, Miami, Washington, Cleveland, Detroit), and 35 percent in metropolitan New York. It is similar with the concentration of Jews in the cities, and increasingly in the big cities, in almost all countries of the Diaspora, while fewer and fewer Jews live in the country and have rural occupations. Before the war the Crimea and Carpatho-Russia constituted exceptions. It follows that the Jews living in the countries of the Diaspora have predominantly urban occupations; hence their percentage in the urban populations and occupations in those countries is substantially higher than their ratio in the total population. Here are some particularly striking instances: In the Polish industrial city of Lodz the 192,000 Jews constituted almost one-third of the total population in 1939; in the Ukrainian city of Chernovtsy—until 1918 part of Austria-Hungary (Czernowitz) and from 1919 to 1940 belonging to Rumania (Cernauti)—the 43,700 Jews living there in 1919 constituted 47.4 percent of the population; and in New York, with its more than two million Jews, they amounted to around 28 percent. In the State of Israel, too, the Jewish population is increasingly concentrated in the cities—over 73 percent in 27 larger cities, 16 percent in rural towns. The remaining 11 percent are distributed over 700 rural settlements and have predominantly rural occupations.

Number and Distribution of the Jews in Earlier Times

Let us compare the number of the Jews and their distribution over continents and countries in our time with the comparable numbers of earlier times. In 1880, before the beginning of the great migration from Eastern Europe to America, 6.7 million Jews (or over 88% of the total Jewish population) lived in Europe, 5.7 million (almost 75%) in Eastern Europe, and only 250,000 (3.3%) in America. By contrast, of the estimated 2.5 million Jews (0.42% of the population of the world) toward the end of the eighteenth century, 40 percent, or one million, probably lived in the Orient and about one-third in Eastern Europe. A century and a half before that, in 1650, there were only 650,000 or 700,000 Jews in Europe and at most about 2.75 million in the whole world.* At that time

*This is Ruppin's estimate of the total number. In his *Social and Religious History of the Jews* (2: 165), Salo W. Baron's estimate of the total Jewish population at the middle of the seventeenth century is only 900,000, with 650,000 of these in Europe—probably the smallest number since the earliest history of the Jews as a people. According to this estimate, at that time the Jews constituted only 0.2 percent of the European population.

at least two-thirds of European Jewry (about half a million) lived in Eastern Europe. Around 1500, after the expulsion of at least 120,000 Jews from Spain and Portugal, about half the total Jewish population lived in European Turkey, Asia Minor, and North Africa; around the middle of the twelfth century the overwhelming majority of the Jews still lived in the Orient.

Thus, in the course of the centuries there have been great changes in the number of the Jews and great shifts in their distribution over the earth. All peoples have experienced great changes in population and dissemination over a definite area in the course of their history. However, migrations from continent to continent and country to country are a special feature of Jewish history, and so are the frequent wanderings from place to place within a country.

The Migrations of the Jews

The main lines of these mass migrations are generally known: the transplantation and emigration of large groups to the Assyrian and Babylonian empires since the eighth century B.C.E. and to Egypt in the Hellenistic period; the migration over areas of the Roman empire since the middle of the first pre-Christian century and particularly since the destruction of Judea's temple and state (70 C.E.) and the suppression of the Bar Kochba rebellion (135 C.E.); the migration to West Africa, Spain, and Southern France in consequence of the Arab expansions between the seventh and tenth centuries; the migrations to Eastern Europe from the twelfth to the sixteenth century, which reached their zenith in the second half of the fourteenth century; the wanderings of the Spanish and Portuguese Jews to Southern Europe and Holland, particularly in the area of the Ottoman Empire, since the end of the fifteenth century; the return from Eastern Europe to Central and Western Europe since the second half of the seventeenth century; the mighty migration to the western overseas countries (America) since the end of the nineteenth century and the immigration to Palestine since then, particularly during the past sixty years. These are only the great streams of migration, not the numerous migrations from country to country, region to region, or place to place.

If we trace the roots of these migrations, we find a multiplicity of causes. Almost invariably the migrations had an economic background, at least as far as the destination was concerned. It stands to reason that no large-scale immigration is possible where the material basis is lacking. Not infrequently the impetus for emigration was economic in nature, particularly for migration within a country. In this respect the Jewish migrations were no different from those of other peoples and ethnic groups, for they too were in large measure influenced by shifts in political and economic power, in traffic routes and centers, and by similar factors. In the Jewish migrations, however, there were almost always other intensifying factors: persecutions and expulsions, flight from actual or feared violence and thought control, and so forth, such as hardly occurred among other nations to this extent and in such numerous instances.

But what most radically distinguished the Jewish migrations in the past from those of other peoples is the fact that they seemed to take place without a destination and without an end. In general, the migrations of other peoples end with the immigrating people settling in a new area of domicile, whether it be through displacement of the resident population or their subjugation, through integration with it, or through that population's assimilation to the immigrating elements. When only relatively small groups emigrated, as happened in the overseas migrations of the European peoples, to the extent that they preserved their identity they still felt as members of a distant homeland or motherland, at least spiritually and for a more or less extended period of time. In the course of Jewish history, however, there were a number of complete shifts in their centers of residence without any discernible goal of colonization—that is, without this shift in the center of gravity producing any political results and without the new immigrants imposing their stamp on their new domicile politically, ethnically, or culturally. The new place of residence always remained temporary; even if it often lasted for many centuries, its permanence was repeatedly placed in doubt and its recognition was determined by the will of the resident non-Jewish population. Only since the founding of the State of Israel has there been a radical change in this respect as well.

Even this initial and cursory survey of the statistics and the migrations of the Jews raises a number of questions which have been asked, in one form or another, over and over again and will concern us as well: How was the Jewish people, scattered over the world and repeatedly visited by catastrophes, able to maintain itself? Why did it not perish as an ethnic group because of persecution, adverse circumstances, and especially assimilation to other cultures and mingling with other peoples? How has it preserved its identity and its coherence despite all adversity? But these questions can be asked in reverse as well: How many losses must the Jews have suffered in their Diasporal history of almost two thousand years if in more than sixty generations they did not grow from a few million in Roman times to a people numbering hundreds of millions, but remained a small people that constitutes only a tiny percentage of mankind? What accounts for the fact that the members of such a small, dispersed people have such an unusually high share in great and supremely great achievements in the most varied fields of culture and civilization? And how did it come about that the existence and way of life of such a people, such a widely scattered group which usually constitutes an infinitesimal minority in all countries of the Diaspora, was and still is regarded as an international problem, one about which more has been written and argued than about the problems of other religious communities and peoples far superior to the Jews in number and power?

The Jews—a People?

At this point the reader may ask a basic question that has been asked time and time again since the epoch of the French Revolution and the beginning of the emancipation of the Jews (though no earlier than that!), especially in Jewish circles: Can the Jews still be regarded as a people, or did they not permanently lose the character of a people when their state was vanquished by superior Roman forces? For many people, Jews and non-Jews alike, this question apparently received an answer with the foundation of the State of Israel. Let us, however, leave it in abeyance for the time being; it is, after all, more or less a matter of semantics and concerns the conceptual definition more than the real nature of the special destiny of the Jews. Surely there can be no doubt that the Jews lived as a people until the year 70 of the Common Era and that a new chapter in their history began with the destruction of the Temple in Jerusalem and of the remnants of their independent political life: the history of their statelessness. This event and its consequences not only produced a decisive change in the situation of the Jews in Palestine but gave a special permanent character to the Jewish Diaspora as well. Thus it may be appropriate to make a thorough assessment of this event and its consequences and to examine the nature of its influence on the development of the Jewish question. From this point of departure we shall have to trace the further development of the Jewish problem down to our day and to draw from the insights gained from our historical survey conclusions for the present and the future.

2

Foundations and Conditions: Jews and Environment in Ancient Times

The Jewish Diaspora

As we have already indicated, the dispersal of the Jews among the nations is the first phenomenon that strikes any observer of the Jewish question. This dispersion is of a special kind, has certain features peculiar only to it, and is probably the most characteristic element of the Jewish question. Thus anyone who wishes to understand this question must before all else examine its origin and its nature. Though it runs counter to the idea anchored in the traditional historical consciousness of the Jews and of the religions based on Judaism, one thing must be clearly stated at the outset: The Jewish Diaspora as such, the dispersal of the Jews over many countries, did not come into being after the destruction of the Temple and the Jewish State by the Romans in the year 70. It existed much earlier, alongside and in connection with the homeland. But—and this is the foundation and the inner truth-content of the traditional historical consciousness—it received from the development that began at that time its special character as the "exile" of a homeless people that is designated by the Hebrew word *galut* or *golah*. Only the reestablishment of the State of Israel in 1948 provided the impetus for a new development in this respect as well.

THE ORIGIN OF THE JEWISH DIASPORA

The beginnings of the Jewish Diaspora go back many centuries before the year 70 C.E. Some of its causes were peaceful and others violent in nature. Like members of other nations, Jews probably left their country in hard times, when wars devastated the land or there was a drought, and settled temporarily or permanently in neighboring countries. The trade route from Egypt to Syria and Mesopotamia, that went through Palestine, may also have caused Palestinian Jews to settle in Egypt and Syria, even though at that time the Jews in Palestine were essentially a people of farmers. In addition, at the end of the eighth century B.C.E.

there began large-scale forcible shifts in the population. In 733 B.C.E. the Assyrian king Tiglat Pileser IV conquered the major portion of the northern state of Israel and in accordance with the method used in other conquered states banished the upper classes (ca. 6,000 people) to Mesopotamia. Twelve years later, in 721 B.C.E., his successor Sargon II did likewise with the small remnant state Samaria and its population (around 27,000 deported people). One hundred thirty years after that (597–586 B.C.E.) the Babylonian king Nebuchadnezzar II, after capturing Jerusalem and destroying the Temple, deported the political and economic leadership of the southern state of Judea to Babylonia. On the basis of what little reliable information we have about the fate of those forcibly deported we can assume that it was particularly the Jewish exiles in Babylonia who established flourishing, predominantly agricultural settlements, some of which might have been able to attach themselves to nuclei of settlements of those deported from Israel earlier. It seems that more than a few of the resettled people achieved prosperity and respect. Thus it was logical that only a minority of the Jews living in Babylonia at the time availed themselves of the permission to return to their homeland granted by the Persian king Cyrus after his conquest of the Babylonian empire fifty years later (538 B.C.E.). After all, the procession of thousands of remigrants made unusual physical and mental demands on all participants, involving a months-long trek comparable to the biggest army marches of the time. Settlement in Egypt, too, increased after the destruction of the First Temple—first because of the fugitives (of whom the prophet Jeremiah was a reluctant member), later through the settlement of combat-ready Jewish soldiers who even received permission to build their own temple in their military colony in Elephantine, at the southern border of Egypt, probably around the middle of the sixth century B.C.E.

With the voluntary or involuntary creation of settlement centers in the surrounding countries, particularly Mesopotamia and Egypt, as well as the religious and later also political recovery and expansion of the regenerated center in Palestine there presumably developed a steady intercourse between this center and the Jewish settlements in the Diaspora, and, depending on circumstances, this led to immigration or emigration. Like any flourishing settlement, the Jewish Diaspora settlements attracted new immigrants, no matter how they had come into being. A variety of factors, both positive and negative, promoted this development: the growth of the population of Palestine; the wars in and around the country during Persian rule and particularly in the era of Alexander the Great and the Diadochi empires, followed by deportations, military settlements, slave trading, and emigration because of economic hardships; the founding of cities in Egypt by Alexander (Alexandria!) and his successors (e.g., Antiochia in Syria), which promoted the immigration of colonists from the neighboring countries; the increasing commercial relations between Palestine and the neighboring countries, in which the Jews of the Diaspora naturally assumed particular importance; and finally, the ever-increasing inclusion of the Near East in the power structure of the Roman Empire since the second century B.C.E., along with the natural population increase and the acceptance of numerous proselytes recruited by the Jews, at that time still quite ready to make converts, in the Hellenic world, whose belief in gods had been shaken. All these factors caused a steady increase in the numbers and extent of the Jewish Diaspora in the ensuing centuries, even though for lack of reliable sources we are unable to trace this development in detail. In any case, as early as the beginning of the Common Era the Jewish Diaspora seems to have extended over all areas of the Roman Empire and beyond (Babylonia, Mesopotamia) and to have far surpassed the Jewish settlement in Palestine in population as well as in economic importance.* Nevertheless, this Diaspora, whose relationship to the surrounding world will be discussed later, was not abnormal in nature; it was the Diaspora of a people with a natural homeland.

PALESTINE AND THE JEWISH DIASPORA

The Jewish Diaspora was tied to Judea** with a variety of bonds. Jerusalem was the religious center of all of Jewry, and since the religious and national realms were not separated at that time, it was the national center as well. The books of Jewish history, of halachic precepts, of prophetic plaints, exhortations, warnings, and consolations, of religious exhortation, faith, and hope, all of which had in Judea been gradually integrated into the canon of "Holy Writ" in the centuries after the return from Babylon, were regarded as the basic writings of the Jewish religion in the Jewish Diaspora as well. Translated from the original Hebrew for the Jews linguistically assimilated to their surroundings, first orally and then in writing as well, into the languages of the various countries

---

*Estimates of the number of Jews at that time range from 4.5 to 8 million. The 4.5 to 6 million Jews in the Roman Empire probably constituted 8–10 percent of the total population. The number of those residing in Palestine is a matter of dispute. Estimates range from 700,000 to 5 million, but the general assumption is a figure of one or two million. (See also the notes in Part 2.)

**This (Land of Yehuda, Judea) is what the country was generally called after the return of the Jews from Babylonia. Later the name Eretz Yisrael (Land of Israel) became customary among the Jews, while the Romans used the name Palestine after the suppression of the Bar Kochba uprising (135 C.E.; cf. also pp. 47f.). Here I use the word Palestine synonymously with Judea and Eretz Yisrael as a geographical designation widely used today, though its use is really anachronistic for periods prior to the second century C.E. It appears to have been first used by Emperor Hadrian in 139.

(Aramaic, Greek, Syrian, Latin), they became "The Books" *(Biblia),* "The Book" for all Jews. The history of the ancestors—from the creation of the entire world as an act of God, the covenant of Noah, Abraham's recognition of one God, the exodus from Egypt as liberation from oppressive servitude, the wilderness wanderings and the divine revelation on Mount Sinai, the conquest and settlement of the "Promised Land" up to the destruction of the First Temple, exile and return from Babylonia, rebuilding of the Temple and the Jewish community in Judea, all under the religious aspect of the people's chosenness to fulfill a divine mission and the covenant between God and the people chosen to carry out his will, and with everything presented with earthy naturalness and color—viewed in this light the past was always kept alive in the hearts of all Jews as the history of the world, the holy history, and at the same time their own history. The religious laws and customs (rituals), which by their nature preserved the religious substance in the national ritual form of the mother country and encompassed all areas of daily life, were just as binding for the Jews of the Diaspora as for those of Palestine, even though some special customs developed among the former. It was not merely for symbolic reasons that Jews residing in other countries faced Palestine when they prayed. The Temple in Jerusalem, which had been rebuilt and splendidly renovated under Herod I (73–74 B.C.E.), was the focal point and center of all religious life and the communal life connected with it. No matter were he lived, every Jewish adult was obligated to contribute to the maintenance of the central place of worship by paying an annual temple tax, the half-shekel, and, as Mommsen established, these voluntary tax monies, which were collected by emissaries from Jerusalem who regularly traveled to the lands of the Diaspora, were paid more willingly than the obligatory state taxes in the countries of residence, with many added donations. In the Diaspora the beginning of the month and the holidays were celebrated at the times established by the synhedrion in Jerusalem and communicated to the Jewish settlements, and every year thousands of pilgrims from all countries of Jewish domicile came to Jerusalem for the appropriate festivals, particularly Passover, the festival commemorating the time when the Jews were liberated and became a people. When they returned, they bore living witness to the land, its life, its customs, and its problems, thus deepening the spiritual connection between the Diaspora and the center in Jerusalem. All in all, Palestine and the Diaspora constituted, so to speak, one national-religious entity. To everyone, Jewish history meant essentially the history of Palestine. Jews and non-Jews regarded the scattered Jewish settlements as a kind of "colonies" of the motherland. For all—the Diaspora, Palestine, and the non-Jewish world—Jerusalem was the metropolis, with everything that in antiquity was connected with the concept of "mother city" and "mother state." No matter how precarious the political existence of Palestine might be, even though it was dependent on the policies of the ruling great powers, to the last it remained the heart and head of the Jewish body politic, its history-making center. Despite its political weakness, Jerusalem was, as it were, the capital of an empire, albeit a special kind of empire. The letter written in 40 C.E. by Agrippa I, the later Jewish king (by Rome's grace), to the Roman emperor Gaius Caligula is revealing in this regard. This is what he says about the "holy city" of Jerusalem: "As I have said, it is my home town and the capital not only of the one Jewish state but also of the Jews in all the many countries in which we have settled in the course of time—in the neighboring countries Egypt, Phoenicia, and Syria as well as in the Near Eastern countries and in Greece. However, not only the mainland but also the most famous islands (Euboea, Cyprus, and Crete) are full of Jewish settlements. I am disregarding the lands on the other side of the Euphrates; Babylon and the other fertile satrapies have, with the exception of few areas, a Jewish population. If, then, my native city finds favor in your eyes, this will benefit not only one place but thousands of cities in all continents."*

Hence the political collapse of this metropolis of Jerusalem as a consequence of the Jewish uprising against Rome and of the Roman-Jewish war of 66–70 was bound to have profound effects on all members of the Jewish body politic. The destruction of Jerusalem and its Temple was tantamount to its decapitation.

The Consequences of the Destruction of Jerusalem and Its Temple

Jewish tradition had established the day of the destruction of the Temple as a day of fasting for all time.** In a real sense it regards this day as the beginning of the *galut*, the period of banishment and forcible dispersion, of the Jewish people's homelessness and life in exile. However, in modern times doubts have been expressed, often from diametrically opposed theological, historical, political, and philosophical standpoints, as to whether the fall of Jerusalem and of the Jewish State

---

*We have the text of this letter in a report by Philo of Alexandria, the Jewish philosopher and historian who wrote in Greek, about a delegation of Alexandrian Jews to Emperor Caligula of Rome of which he was a member. Thus the characterization of the status of Jerusalem probably corresponded with the views of the assimilated Greek Jews of Alexandria. This view was formulated by Agrippa even though Caesarea was formally the capital of the Roman province of Judea.

**It consolidated the dates of the destruction of the First and the Second Temple, a few days apart, into one date, the ninth of Av (Tisha b'Av), and later it dated other unfortunate events in Jewish history, from the fall of the last stronghold (Betar) in the Bar Kochba rebellion (135) to the expulsion of the Jews from Spain (1492), from that day.

really has such decisive significance as a caesura in Jewish history, as a watershed between two fundamental epochs, and if it has, whether the transformation that it initiated should be evaluated as negatively as the traditional national consciousness of the Jews has done. In his lecture of 1919 about "The Spirit and Epochs of Jewish History" Franz Rosenzweig, the philosophical, historical, and theological thinker and quester, contrasts the Zionist-nationalist view with the liberal-assimilationist kind. Both see in the events of the year 70 a basic historic watershed, but they evaluate them differently. Some people interpret them negatively and therefore endeavor to rescind the events, as it were, by working toward a return to Palestine and the reestablishment of the Jewish State. Others regard the subsequent development toward dispersion among the nations, denationalization, cosmopolitanism, and intellectualization as the "will of fate or providence" and hence evaluate it positively. In the face of this Rosenzweig points to the strange fact that Heinrich Graetz, the Jewish historian who laid the groundwork for modern Jewish historiography, began his great history with volume 4, which covers the Talmudic period. According to Rosenzweig, with the creation of the great didactic and legal work that for many centuries regulated the Jewish way of life all over the world, this period not only provided a bridge over the epochs but, as it were, wiped out the year 70 as a watershed. "The spirit of Judaism goes beyond it; it is both older and younger than it. It brooks no epochs. But this means that it brooks no history. . . . The Jewish spirit breaks the bonds of epochs. . . . No wonder that history and what lives in it resent this spirit." Rosenzweig's presentation of 1919 sounds basic themes of the Jewish question in the euphoric atmosphere of an epoch which after the bitter experiences of World War I lived with the Messianic hope for a regeneration of the world by the spirit and ended fourteen years later with the organized barbarism of German National Socialism that led to the destruction of European Jewry in World War II and after its end to the foundation of the third Jewish State.

From the vantage point of the new State of Israel, too, the question has been raised whether the year 70 really was the decisive turning point in the history of the Jews. As has been pointed out, decades before the great Jewish rebellion Judea had been turned into a Roman province that was governed by Roman procurators and had retained only a certain autonomy. Only for a short time, from 41 to 44, had it been politically independent once more under Agrippa I, a king of its own by the grace of Rome. Moreover, a hundred years before that, beginning with the bloody conquest of Jerusalem by Pompey (63 B.C.E.) and the integration of Judea into the Roman empire, the independence of the Jewish political structure erected by the Maccabees in the course of their uprising against Hellenization (from 165 B.C.E. on) had, for all practical purposes, come to an end. There can be no doubt that in 70 C.E., following the victory over the Jewish rebels, Titus and Vespasian eliminated the last vestiges of Judea's Jewish statehood and political freedom, and with the Temple the center and symbol of the Jewish state religion and its rituals for Judea and the Diaspora had fallen. But it may justifiably be argued that despite this the Roman victors did not keep the vanquished from observing their religious customs, no matter how incomprehensible these might have seemed to them. Nor did they for the time being make any significant changes in the legal position of the Jews in Judea and the extensive Roman Diaspora; instead, they permitted the Jews to continue as a recognized national-religious community. More than that, the Romans did not prevent this community from replacing the destroyed Temple with a new religious-national center in the school of the Judean coastal town of Jabneh (south of Jaffa), or from establishing there in place of the Jerusalem synhedrion a new, recognized, almost monarchical authority, which exerted a profound influence on the life of the Jews in Palestine and in the Diaspora. This authority was established in the hereditary patriarchate ("Nessiut") under the descendants of the scholar and patriarch Hillel (I), who laid the foundation for the Jewish legal tradition and was presumed to be descended from the royal lineage of David. Thanks to the influx of Jews who were fleeing or had been ransomed from slavery, the Jewish population of the Diaspora remained so strong that forty-five years later (115–17) it was able to utilize Emperor Trajan's campaign against the Parthians to mount bloody uprisings against their suppressors in Libya, Egypt, and Cyprus. Despite all devastations, executions, and expropriations the Jewish settlement in Judea had remained so strong, or had recovered so quickly, that fifteen years after that (132–35) it was able to risk the great rebellion under the leadership of Bar Kochba; Emperor Hadrian had to send his best general to put it down. It has been established that the Jewish settlement in the country did not start its constant decline until the succeeding centuries. The decisive caesura in the history of Palestine as a Jewish country is its conquest (in 637) and its settlement by the Arabs beginning in the second third of the seventh century. Only from that time on did Palestine cease to be the history-making center of the Diaspora and did the epoch of *golah* begin in the real sense of the word.

All these facts are indisputable, and there can be no doubt about their significance for the history of the Jewish people. They carry less weight, however, for the problem that concerns us here, the history of the Jewish *question*—that is, the origin and development of the complex problem of Jewish existence among the nations. Here these and similar arguments skirt decisive questions.

After all, what makes an event in our judgment and consciousness one of world-historical significance is often not the immediate consequences but developments that continue to affect, directly or indirectly, distant times, even the present. In his well-known essay on "Causalities and Values in History" the celebrated German historian Friedrich Meinecke distinguishes among three different kinds of causality—the mechanical, the biological, and the spiritual-moral. Only the effect of the first, the mechanical kind, can be demonstrated without difficulty; here the effect directly follows the cause, as in accordance with a physical law. It is different with biological causality; there it is a matter of consequences that far transcend what may immediately be expected according to physical-mechanical laws and that may be compared with the laws of biological growth from roots and germs. The intensity, the extent, the form, and the duration of the continued effectiveness are in no foreseeable relationship to the causal event that triggers other occurrences and produces new, often unexpected developments. The third historical causality, the spiritual-moral kind, goes far beyond the other two, being closely linked with them, just as they are interconnected with each other; it revalues tradition and creates new values and evaluations, which in turn affect occurrences and create new causalities of all kinds. Viewed and evaluated in this light, the catastrophe of 70 surely was an epochal event in the truest sense of the word.

In assessing the situation in the two generations following the fall of Jerusalem, we should add the well-known fact that the formal-legal regulations in force are often by no means tantamount to the real situation of a population. Legal regulations that determine or regulate the legal status of a population or population group in a country come into being through the legal fixation of certain views shaped or influenced by traditions or political, economic, and social interests and relationships. Changes in these views often are not given their formal-legal expression until a long time later, when they have become more or less common property. Even then political or economic considerations may keep the powers that be from immediately taking juridical cognizance of this change in public opinion. However, once the new conceptions have finally been reflected in revised legislation, the newly created legal conditions again affect the mood and opinion of the people, to whom the views underlying the new laws now appear to be the only legitimate, "right," "just," and normal ones. In any case, as we know only too well from the experience of our immediate past and our present, the formal-legal equality of a population group often tells us very little about its real situation and the actual tensions between it and other parts of the population.

Thus the questions we have to ask in our examination are three: What was the actual relationship between the Jews and their environment, how was it reflected in the eyes of the Jews and the world around them, and how did the breakdown of 70 and its consequences affect this relationship? This is always the important factor in our presentation if we want to understand the origin and development of the Jewish question.

The Jews and Their Environment Prior to the Destruction of the Jewish State

In point of fact, even *before* the breakdown the situation of the Jews in the lands of the Roman Empire was anything but unproblematical. To be sure, in accordance with the views generally prevailing in the Roman-Hellenic world the Jews shared in the right of religious-national autonomy in their settlements outside Palestine, which means that they were free of certain civic duties connected with pagan sacrifices. As far as their civil rights were concerned, in the big urban centers of the Diaspora (such as the Greco-Egyptian capital Alexandria, where two out of five districts had a Jewish population) they occupied a position midway between the privileged Greeks (and naturally, at a later date, the Romans as well) and the underprivileged indigenous population (such as the Egyptians). Only in the parts of Palestine that were thickly settled by Jews were they the truly native, fully privileged, and thus also opinion-making population. In certain areas of the Palestinian cities founded by Greeks and Romans (e.g., the important seaport Caesarea, the capital of the Roman administration of the country), and particularly in the countries of the Diaspora, they were actually regarded as aliens—even where they had been domiciled for centuries (as in Alexandria) and constituted a large percentage of the total population. That is how they were viewed by their adversaries among the population as well as by their Roman protectors, who guarded their traditional rights from encroachments by the population as long as this was in their interest. Thus the same Emperor Claudius who confirmed the rights of the Alexandrian Jews that had been granted them by Augustus admonished the Jews, in a letter to the citizens of Alexandria written in 41, not to aspire to an extension of their rights in a city that was "not theirs"—and this three hundred and fifty years after the first Jewish settlement in the city!

The roots of this mutual estrangement and the resulting tensions, which not infrequently led to bloody clashes, were certainly not primarily economic, as more recent observers influenced by modern anti-Semitic or Marxist doctrine have stated. To be sure, there were economically influential families that attracted attention and excited envy, for example in the Egyptian Diaspora and especially in Alexandria. The Jewish masses, however, who engaged in all occupations were, if anything, mocked because of their poverty. Particularly in Palestine, but in large measure in the Diaspora as well, the Jews were primarily farmers and engaged in all trades. The first thing that aroused opposition to them since the time of their dissemination and the expansion of the Hellenistic world was their hostile and negative attitude toward

Hellenism and their struggle against its penetration of Palestine since the second century before Christ. While the entire Near East succumbed to the advance of Greek culture and blended its modes of faith and thinking with its own, unaccountably this small people resisted the world civilization that bound the nations together and insisted on its own national-religious way of life with its monotheistic belief in one invisible God without idols or depictions—ideas that were utterly incomprehensible to a world that delighted in deities and images. Even philosophical thinkers who saw in the idols only symbolic representations of natural forces or the all-encompassing power of nature and fate were not able to understand how thinking people could engage in a life-and-death struggle for the undepictability of their God, the consumption or nonconsumption of certain foods, or the sanctification of the seventh day of the week instead of joining in the customary ritual acts, which everyone could interpret as he pleased. Individuals and peoples always regard what is alien and incomprehensible to them as uncanny;* in what is different they sense and fear something inimical and menacing, and thus they react defensively and with hostility—viewed subjectively, with a defense mechanism against the alien thing that is outside their familiar and hallowed customs. This defensive movement born of fear and timidity not infrequently finds its rational solution and expression in mockery and defamation.

Thus anti-Jewish canards came into being as a weapon and justification of the fight against the Jews in connection with the Maccabees' struggle against the forcible attempts at Hellenization by Antiochus Epiphanes and his successors (and apparently no earlier than that; there is, in any case, no earlier documentation). According to these stories, Antiochus Epiphanes found in the sanctuary of the Jerusalem Temple, which he had desecrated in 170 and robbed of its greatest treasures, a golden donkey's head; so this was what what the Jews actually worshiped, even though they spoke of their invisible God! More than that, in the Jerusalem Temple he had liberated a Greek whom the Jews had fattened up so that later they might slaughter and consume him, as was their custom, "amidst frightful oaths of feuds against all Hellenes."

This is the first appearance of the legend of ritual murder, which later was directed more against the Christians and in the Middle Ages was used by the Christians against the Jews in all sorts of variants. In the struggle for legal status and power in Alexandria, Egyptian writers told other anti-Jewish tales. In the third century B.C.E. the Egyptian priest Manetho told a story which, as we know from Flavius Josephus's polemic against him, the Jew-baiter Apion had in the first century C.E. disseminated in his writings, in addition to other anti-Jewish canards, with an

---

*The German word *unheimlich* (*un-heim-lich*, i.e., not homelike or homey) clearly indicates the close connection between something alien and something feared.

anti-Jewish twist that had evidently not existed before him and which then recurred, in one form or another, in almost all ancient reports about the Jews. According to this story, a people of impure and leprous individuals that had for a time ruled over Egypt and then had been expelled from the country by the Egyptians had gone to Palestine after its expulsion and there founded Jerusalem. The Jews were the descendants of these unclean outcasts who mocked at all that was holy to the Egyptians.

This, then, is how the Jews appeared to their environment, which never took the trouble to read the Greek translations of the basic Hebrew writings. The Jews' unbending, self-assured clinging to the one invisible God who refused to show himself in any depictable form, the monotheistic faith for whose dissemination the Jews regarded themselves as chosen, for which they gave their lives and with whose preservation in the struggle with the ruling powers they initiated a new era in the religious and intellectual history of mankind was regarded by the surrounding world as an arrogant superstition, godlessness, or even a deliberate deception. The strict observance of the Sabbath as a day of rest, the social character of which was completely misinterpreted by the ancient world, seemed to be evidence of the Jews' deep-rooted indolence. All the institutions and practices that were designed to isolate the Jews from their polytheistic environment and keep them pure and "holy,"* or that simply had that effect, were all too easily misunderstood by a world much more tolerant in its faith and religious activities. These practices included nonparticipation in the meals of non-Jews, as decreed by the religious ritual, in their religious services, and in all forms of pagan ritual that were indissolubly linked to the political and social life of the ancient community; refusal to marry non-Jews if these did not convert to Judaism; and all national-religious precepts and customs, from circumcision to the celebration of different festivals and the annual donation to the central Temple in Jerusalem. All this was interpreted as an expression of the hostility and hatred that the Jewish people harbored toward everything alien and non-Jewish. *Odium generis humani*, hatred of all mankind: in the literature this is the most frequent reproach that has since Tacitus** been leveled against the people that has set down

---

*On the close connection, in language and content, found in traditional Jewish writings between the words and concepts of "holiness" (in the sense of fulfilling God's commandments) and the "separation" (from the pagan peoples and their rituals) that is necessary because of it, see Leo Baeck, *The Pharisees*.

**It is impossible to overestimate the influence of the great Roman historian Tacitus (ca. 55–120), who in his *Histories* described the war of the Romans under Vespasian and Titus against Judea from the viewpoint of a Roman aristocrat and also gives a historical-ethnographic account of the life of the Jewish people. This account is based on the sources and literary traditions known at that time, though strangely enough these did

and preached the love of one's neighbor as one of the foundations of its religious views.

Beginning with the time of Roman rule, political conflicts were added with ever-increasing severity to these religious-social differences between the Jewish and the Hellenic worlds. Only this one small nation had offered any protracted and serious resistance to the Greek hegemony in the Near East; now it also resisted the Romans, the great world power which no one could withstand and which therefore seemed to have been chosen as the ruler by the gods themselves. This people offered resistance even though the Romans treated it with unusual gentleness—a kindness that many a Roman might have regarded as an unworthy concession. The Romans did not meddle with the Jews' religion; they did not enter their Temple; with the exception of a few years under Gaius Caligula, they exempted the Jews in general from recognizing the divinity of the emperor and even from serving in the army and in civil offices if that violated their orthodox faith, thus giving them a privileged position envied by other parts of the population; they granted them a large measure of autonomy in their country and comprehensive communal rights in their domiciles outside the country. And yet this people rebelled again and again, using every opportunity to do so and repeatedly jeopardizing the road from Egypt to Syria and Mesopotamia that was of such strategic importance for the Roman legions. In their striving for freedom from the Roman yoke the Jews were thus bound to appear to the Romans, who were convinced of their right to world domination, and to the nations that recognized this domination as a people that was rebellious, recalcitrant, and malign by nature, a people that placed itself outside the laws of power and the fortunes of war (*fortuna*) and that struggled against the beneficial peaceful reign of *pax Romana* with its chimera of an invisible God who was supposed to have chosen for himself this small, powerless nation, this superstitious people of xenophobes and Sabbath loafers. This is the image of the Jews in the Roman writers Cicero, Horace, Seneca, and Tacitus.

The National Breakdown of the Jews as Viewed by Their Environment

Consequently, the non-Jewish world, and the Romans in particular, were bound to view the war waged by Vespasian and Titus against Judea

---

not include the Septuagint, the Greek translation of the Bible that had been in existence for a long time. Tacitus was regarded as an authority not only in antiquity and the early Middle Ages but since the European Renaissance as well. Anti-Jewish writers like to quote his judgment on the Jews and Judaism to this day. Because of the great influence of this account we are reprinting it in Part 2.

as an all too justified punitive expedition by Rome against the rebellious Jewish people, and the collapse of its State and the burning of its Temple as the just punishment for its overweening pride. In accordance with this view, the political power of the Jews could be regarded as broken. It seemed that with the devastation of its country and the destruction of its capital the Jewish people had dropped out of history forever. As far as could be foreseen, the Jews scattered all over the world and now deprived of their national-political and religious center would sooner or later have to go under—if not through extermination, then through the natural process of assimilation to the life-styles of their surroundings and their interbreeding with the populations of their countries of domicile.

The religious adversaries of the Jews were able to hail the fall of the Temple with the same feeling of triumph. The arrogant belief of this strange people in its invisible God, who refused to be depicted, seemed unmasked once and for all as heresy and superstition. What kind of God might that be who not only left his "chosen" people in the lurch but was even unable to save from the flames his own house, this miracle of splendor and beauty? In this sense the Romans surely welcomed the destruction of the Temple, even if one wants to believe the report by Flavius Josephus that Titus, the general and later emperor (79–81), did not intend the conflagration. After all, so the reasoning went, the fall of the Temple and the religious-political metropolis had to demonstrate even to the Jews in Palestine, and particularly in the powerful Diaspora, how senseless their rigid adherence to their vanquished chimera of a God was and thereby break their imprudent resistance against the Roman world domination and world culture.

Accordingly, the triumphal arch erected in Rome after the victory celebrated Titus in the flattering style of the time, one that stretched truth somewhat. Through it the proud general, "as it were, the embodiment of victorious Jupiter," led masses of captured Jews along with his victorious army in a triumphal procession hallowed by ritual and martial tradition—as the first man who "destroyed the city of Jerusalem which before him had been besieged in vain or not even attacked by all generals, kings, and peoples." The commemorative coins issued on the occasion of this victory depicted, in addition to Emperor Vespasian's likeness on the obverse, the fall of Judea as symbolized by the figure of a woman prostrate in mourning under a palm tree as well as the proud figure of a victorious Roman warrior, with the caption reading *Judaea capta* (captured Judea).* The triumphal arch in Rome, preserved as the

*There are other versions of the coin. One shows in place of the warrior the victory goddess Nike (Fortuna) stepping on a helmet and writing on a shield; this is similar to a coin with a picture of Titus on which she writes on a shield the Greek words *Ioudaias Ealokyas*, the fall of Judea. A coin with Vespasian's picture on one side shows on the obverse a captured Judean under a palm tree, the symbol of Judea, and the inscription

so-called Titus arch, which was erected by Titus's brother, Emperor Domitian, in 84 after Titus's early death and dedicated to the memory of Titus, shows in plastic relief the ritual objects stolen from the burned sanctuary of the defeated god as symbols of his ritual and his vanquished religion: the seven-armed candelabrum, the golden shewbread table, and the silver trumpets carried in a triumphal procession by laurel-wreathed Roman warriors. A people struck down in its devastated land, a god beaten, dethroned, and expelled from his burned domicile—the fate of both seemed to be sealed for all time.

An Anti-Jewish Special Law

There was another way to express the stigmatization of the nation that had been misunderstood and treated with hostility even before that and which now was hated all the more as a people of vanquished rebels. As already mentioned, up to that time the Jews of Palestine and of the Diaspora had voluntarily paid an annual tax for the maintenance of the Temple in Jerusalem. This tax and the emissaries from Jerusalem who traveled through the countries of the Diaspora in order to collect it had served as one of the most essential links between the center and the periphery. Now, after his victory, Emperor Vespasian transformed this voluntary tax into a statutory head tax for all Jews in Palestine and the Diaspora. This *Fiscus Judaicus*, the Jewish tax collected by Roman officials—and sometimes by force, particularly under Domitian (81–96)—now served as a "bitter parody" (Mommsen) of the construction and maintenance of the temple of Jupiter Capitolinus in Rome, the Roman holy of holies that had burned down one year before the fall of Jerusalem—strangely enough coinciding with the Jewish rebellion and its initial success. The collapse of Judea with its enormous loss of life and property, the burning of its capital and its Temple, the elimination of the high priesthood and the synhedrion as the religious-national authority of the Jews, the sale of masses of cheap Jewish slaves in all countries under Roman rule, who were often ransomed and freed by the Jews living there—all this would have sufficed to degrade the Jews in the eyes of the nations. Now there was added the disgrace that they were made tributaries of the god and "divine" emperor whose laws, dominion, and divinity they had so vehemently denied and opposed. More than that,

---

Judea devicta (conquered Judea), and yet another shows a captive sitting under a victory trophy, with the inscription *Judea*. The above-named coin was newly minted in 1948, after the founding of the State of Israel. In place of Vespasian's likeness it shows on the obverse the same palm, but on the left a mother proudly lifting up her newborn child and on the right an Israeli planting a tree. The surrounding inscription reads *Israel Liberata* and in Hebrew *Israel Lacherut*, Liberated Israel.

for the first time in their history the Jews—and not only those residing in Palestine but all Jews in the Roman Empire—were subject to a special tax that removed them from the community of the other residents of the empire by imposing upon them special obligations toward the state and giving the state special rights over them. Beyond that, this law, which of necessity defamed the Jews in the eyes of the non-Jews, created a dangerous precedent that was in the course of the centuries to be frequently exploited by the lawgivers. All subsequent special legislation against the Jews in the "Holy Roman Empire" during the Middle Ages was able to build on this Jewish tax as a symbol and legal basis for the enslavement and tributary exploitation of the Jews, and often the powers that be did not fail to use this logical argument.

The Attitude of the Jews

This, then, is how the world reacted to the collapse of Judea. Convinced of the right of the victor in an armed conflict, a right recognized by gods and men, it could regard the Jewish people as destroyed, and in accordance with the laws and rules of history the Jews should also have had to accept this defeat as a national death sentence and regard their life as a people finished after the fall of their state. This would have been a logical process, at least in the Diaspora. In the homeland the preservation of the national tradition was something more natural during the succeeding centuries, when it was still predominantly settled by Jews, at least in the north. There the continuation of a national existence was more comprehensible on the basis of experience with other nations. Only the conquest and settlement of the land by the Arabs in the seventh century could be regarded as a decisive turning point here. It was different in the Diaspora. There all experience indicated that the Jews would sooner or later give up their national and religious special existence. After all, many peoples were eliminated from national life after being crushed in battle. They mingled with the new population that had entered their country as victors. At best they preserved their national identity for a few generations as captives, expellees, or emigrants, only to be absorbed by other peoples. This is how the expellees of the Israelite northern empire eight hundred years previously must have been absorbed by the population of their surroundings—even if popular beliefs and legends did not accept this, dreaming and hopefully talking of the existence and future return of the "ten lost tribes" in distant countries.

Here, however, something mysterious happened that has always proved thought-provoking and in a very real sense prepared the ground for the problem called the Jewish question: The Jewish people refused to recognize the universally valid "rules" of the history of nations, just as earlier it had not recognized the dominion of the Greek world of gods and the Roman power based on martial law. Despite the complete breakdown of their political existence and their religious and national center, despite what appeared to be crystal-clear evidence of their own powerlessness and the impotence of their God, the Jews as a totality did not accept the power-based decision as a national death sentence and even less as a judgment on the worth and right to exist of their religion and the way of life based upon it.

This strange decision ran counter to all practices to such an extent that world opinion and international historiography have really not come to terms with it to this day. It made the Jews even more incomprehensible to the nations and, as it were, placed them outside the prevailing world order and the natural laws of national life. The world has never forgiven the Jews for this infraction of the "rules" of world history.*

The later legends about the "Eternal Jew" in which the Jew appears as an uncanny, demonic figure outside normal human terms also have their deepest roots in this behavior of the Jews.

At first the Jews did not even come to terms with the terrible military defeat as a definitive decision based on power. The Jews defied the Roman military power and engaged in armed struggle for the restoration of their political independence in numerous smaller revolts, particularly in the big uprising of the Jewish Diaspora in Africa and Asia—from Cyrenaica to Mesopotamia under Emperor Trajan (115–17) and then (132–35) under his successor Hadrian, in Judea's great national fight for liberation which is connected with the names Bar Kochba and Rabbi Akiba and (according to Mommsen) was "unparalleled in intensity and duration in Roman imperial history." Naturally, all these heroic attempts inspired by faith and despair were crushed in streams of blood by the superior forces of Rome.

Consequences of the Bar Kochba Uprising

These defeats had two consequences. The first, external one was a significant worsening in the situation of the Jews, particularly in Pal-

---

*In almost all works on world history the existence of the Jewish people as a historical collective ends with the fall of Jerusalem, and certainly with the victory of Christianity (see pp. 63ff.). From then on the Jews are mentioned, if at all, only in connection with great murders of Jews or, after the French Revolution, with the fight for their emancipation. In his *History of the Jews* (1925) Simon Dubnow rightly remarks: "To all these historians the downfall of the Jewish nation for the sake of the triumph of deeply religious individuals seems to be natural and desirable. But they disregard one thing: the development laws of the collective-individual who constitutes a product of history and is not at all prepared to give up his life when the scholars think it is time to do so." Only in recent decades, particularly since the foundation of the State of Israel, does there seem to be a change in this as well.

estine, but in the *golah* as well. Only after the suppression of the Bar Kochba rebellion was Jerusalem completely taken away from the Jews; their former capital now became a Roman colony. The new city, crowned by a shrine of the victorious supreme god of the Romans, "Jupiter Capitolinus," and an equestrian statue of Hadrian, was given the name Aelia Capitolina—in honor of the reigning emperor Publius Aelius Hadrianus and the Capitoline triad Jupiter, Juno, and Minerva. The Jews were barred from entering the city on pain of death. One must consider what dishonor for the Jews resided in this prohibition, even though it might not always have been strictly enforced. After all, for the Jews Jerusalem—in the Roman view, as a metropolis identical with the land itself—continued to remain the capital. Having been destroyed and desecrated as a Jewish city, it was bound to rise all the higher in the memory and estimation of the Jews, and as the "holy city" it became the goal and the focus of yearning for religious and national regeneration. Only now did Judea become desolate; those of its Jewish inhabitants who had escaped death or slavery fled to Galilee or one of the neighboring countries. The name Judea now disappeared from the maps as a valid political concept, and in its place the land was given by the Roman victors and masters the name of the erstwhile oppressors, the Philistines. The "Syria of the Philistines," "Syria-Palestine," later shortened to "Palestine," was the new designation of the country, and via the Arab "Falestin" it has survived to this day.* As a consequence of this uprising the feelings of hatred and contempt toward the vanquished people of stubborn rebels were bound to be exacerbated and deepened. The combination of national struggle for liberation with religious expansion over the areas of the Roman world empire increasingly stamped the Jews in the eyes of the Romans as a people of misanthropes and dangerous conspirators against the foundations of the Roman empire—that is, against the order of the world as they knew it. This is approximately the depiction of the Jews thirty years before the Bar Kochba rebellion by so authoritative a Roman conservative historian as Tacitus, a man with what for his time was a comprehensive education and knowledge of the world, and the picture painted by him became the foundation of educated people's knowledge and opinion of the Jews. In an effort to root out the Jewish rebellious spirit the Romans turned, after more bloody fights, against the practice of Jewish religious precepts and customs as well. Circumcision, Sabbath rest, and instructional meetings were prohibited on pain of death, and from time to time these prohibitions were very strictly enforced.

---

*Even the British mandatory government (1920–48) retained this name and only added in parentheses the abbreviation of the Hebrew name of the land, E[retz]-Y[srael], the Land of Israel.

The Jews Refrain from Further Armed Struggle

The second important consequence of the repeated military breakdown was internal. Ever widening circles began to realize that the continuation of military power struggles with the Roman empire was hopeless for the Jews as a totality and therefore pointless for the Jewish people. This insight prevailed in the course of time, though isolated uprisings down to the seventh century prove that it did not do so completely for centuries (see p. 161).

The Jews as individuals were able to draw various conclusions from this realization. Refraining from armed struggle could be tantamount to the recognition of Rome as the mistress in all areas, in the sphere of power and dominion as well as that of life, faith, and thought. Part of Jewry surely came to this conclusion, then as well as in later conflicts between the Jews and the ruling powers. People have everywhere and at all times regarded the permanently victorious and ruling elements as the better ones, and their recognition has been thought to be the natural and proper thing under the circumstances. These elements appear to have demonstrated their higher viability and *raison d'être* through struggle and victory. But even without this quasi-"moral" foundation, which is active even in modern historiography and its evaluations, recognition of the victor is the normal thing. People want to live, and so they bow to actualities; not everyone is cut out to be a hero or a martyr even if he intones hymns to martyrdom. The average person seeks a quiet everyday life and not the heroic, unquiet life of a "historic" epoch.

Thus the Jews who were becoming alienated from their people and embracing apostasy drew the normal conclusion that individuals and peoples generally draw from the victory of arms. For them there no longer existed a Jewish problem, at least in the second or third generation. In the absence of any statistical source material it is impossible to gauge whether it was a majority or a minority of Jews who at various times took the normal path, joined the victor, and were absorbed by the ruling people with loss of their Jewish identity.

Even among those who did *not* recognize the power and intellectual-religious superiority of Rome and did not succumb to the indolence of the masses, there surely were quite a few who turned their backs on Judaism. Disappointment at the fall of the Temple, which had been regarded as well-nigh indestructible as the dwelling place of God, and at the collapse of religious-national hopes for the future, which had assumed a Messianic coloration at that time, widened the gulf between the official, Pharisee-led Judaism and the Jewish sect of Christians, of respectable size at that time. The latter, which will be discussed in detail elsewhere,* had seen in the fall of the Temple a divine punishment of

*About this and the Messianic-apocalyptic mood of that generation, see p. 60.

the Jews for their failure to recognize the divine mission of Jesus; that is why they did not participate in the uprisings against the Romans. They now increasingly separated themselves from the fate of the beaten Jewish people and were joined by disappointed people for whom the new faith meant rescue from despair, support, and fresh hope.

As we have said, it is impossible to estimate the number of those who removed themselves from the Jewish national fate in one of those ways at that time, but it would be strange if their number was not very significant.* After all, the Jews were human beings like everyone else. Nevertheless, one thing is clear: At all times and in all places a core was preserved that regarded itself as the real representative of the people, maintained its identity, and continued the historical life of the people. The tradition-bound masses did so with the naturalness and perseverance that results from the law of inertia of the mass**—the more perceptive people with the conscious realization of a fate and a mission as well as the readiness to make sacrifices and the will to keep faith with the past and to prepare the future.

If, however, this part of the Jewish people, its real core, which henceforth was identified with the Jewish people by the outside world as well, gradually came to realize that any further armed conflict with the Roman power was senseless, this was by no means tantamount to these Jews giving up their existence as a people and an independent religious community. On the contrary, both were affirmed more strongly than before.

Basically, there was no conflict between this new attitude of passive obedience to God and the earlier attitude of active struggle. After all, even martial resistence to Rome had received its deepest impetus from religious forces—from the certain expectation of the impending Messianic end of time which the struggle was to bring about, therefore from the belief that the fighters were serving as God's tools. Thus quite a few had to the last harbored the profound hope for a miracle and believed in the miracle by means of which God would save his city and his Temple. The defeat now seemed to them as a proof that God no longer desired this kind of struggle. Refraining from the senseless use of armed force against superior worldly forces thus meant for the Jews submission to the evident will of God, but certainly not the recognition of power as justice, and even less an admission of the powerlessness of the Jewish God in the face of the other gods or the worthlessness of the Jewish people as compared to other nations. The Jews refused to acknowledge

---

*A mathematical-statistical observation leads to this conclusion. If this assumption were not correct, the number of Jews living today would have to be many times what it is—even if one takes into consideration the enormous losses through wars, mass murder, and crises and catastrophes of all kinds.

**In a conversation with me held in 1949, my teacher Friedrich Meinecke described the *vis inertiae* as the most important force, one without which nothing would exist.

that the victory of arms was tantamount to a judgment on the rightness or wrongness of religions and peoples. They recognized the fact of their outward impotence, but not the higher right which other peoples and nations derived from this for themselves, the more powerful ones.

But what was really astonishing and incomprehensible and therefore uncanny to the ancient world was this: How could a people ignore a clear judgment on its God in such a way that even after the fall of its Temple and capital it regarded its God, more arrogantly than ever, as more powerful than all other gods, even calling these victorious gods chimeras, and that even after the most abject defeat it successfully propagated this absurd religion among the nations?

Religion, Nation, and Homeland

This brings us to what may be the most profound question that concerns us in this study: How can one explain this loyal or stubborn adherence of the Jews to their traditional view of God, an adherence that defied even the most adverse circumstances? Why did not the Jews, like other nations of antiquity, see in their national defeat the defeat of their God? And finally, what is the relationship between the adherence of the Jews to their faith and their loyalty to their peoplehood and their homeland, or putting it more succinctly: What connection is there between the religious and the national elements in Judaism, and how do these two elements relate to the Jews' relationship to Palestine as their own land, Eretz Yisrael, the Land of Israel?

These questions must be posed here, for without these peculiar decisions and interrelationships there might hardly be any Jews or a Jewish question today. Let us therefore try to pursue this cluster of problems even if it takes us to the apparently remote fields of the history of religion and theology, areas in which we may rightly be judged to be incompetent. The Jewish question is a problem that encompasses all areas of life and transcends the boundaries of specialized fields. We must thus dare to evade no questions, even at the risk of not satisfying all detailed scholarly demands in our attempts to find answers.

The Historical Development of the Problem

Basically, the problems with which the Jews were confronted by the final destruction of their Temple and capital were not new. Six and a half centuries earlier, when the First Temple fell and the considerable numbers of their people were exiled by Babylonia, the Jews had faced the same question: Who was responsible for their defeat—God or the gods of their adversaries? At that time the Jews had definitely embraced a view that contrasted with the Persians' dualistic view of the deity—namely, that God, the only God, was responsible for everything, good as well as bad, and that everything that happened in the world followed a divine cosmic plan in which nothing was accidental and peoples and powers had their tasks assigned to them by the one and all-powerful God.

This one God, however, who recognized the existence of no other gods, was for the Jews identical with that God of their fathers who had revealed himself to Israel, and only to Israel, through the mouths of Moses and the prophets, and who at the beginning of the people's history, and actually even before the Jews became a people, had made a covenant with his people and his country, the Land of Israel. He chose this one people to serve him and this one land and its capital, Jerusalem, for his and his people's country.

Thus three factors combined in the consciousness of the Jews from the beginning: the one God as the God of Israel, the people of Israel, and the land of Israel. They concluded an eternal covenant, were made for each other, and were thus in the final analysis inseparable. Together they constitute a unit, and their separation is almost like a cosmic process, a temporary interference with the prestabilized world order. If the people is sinful, God can separate it from its country; he can call in enemies to chastise his people if it has been disloyal to his service and its mission; he can drive it from its land, or, to put it another way, the land can spew out its inhabitants if the people does not guard, cultivate, and administer in justice its land, the property entrusted it by God, thus proving unworthy of the covenant with God and the land. At all times, however, the divine promise remains in force: The people and the land will never be permanently separated; there is a return of the people or of the "remnant," purified by banishment and fresh wilderness wanderings, that will "hallow" the land and consecrate itself in serving the land—that is, live righteously in the land and in the spirit of God's commandments.

Viewed in this way, the defeat of the state in the struggle with its enemies and even the destruction of the Temple could be regarded as a punishment for the people's sins, and that is how it was actually understood. To regard it as the success of a rival god was out of the question, for as a matter of principle there was no other god for a pious Jew. There was only one God, *his* God, and beside him all other gods were only sham and illusion, idols rather than gods, "the work of human hands": "They have a mouth and cannot speak, they have eyes and cannot see . . . ," mocks the Psalmist. Thus the question as to who brought about victory or defeat was really no problem for the Jews. Since there is only one God and this God is all-powerful, both defeat and victory can only be *his* work.

(This, of course, does not mean that there was no superstition among the plain folk, including the worship of idols such as were used by old established neighbors and neighboring nations. Even among the tone-setting elite belief in the one God was not always free from the influences of superstition and surely not from anthropomorphisms, of which no human mode of thought and faith is, and perhaps cannot be, free.)

Prophecy as a Nationality-Preserving Element

That the above-mentioned view was able to prevail among the people to an ever-increasing extent, and particularly in times of crises and defeats, was due to the prophets. They had predicted the downfall as punishment for the disloyalty of the people chosen for service—disloyalty to God and to the God-given commandment of righteous living in the land. In light of the prophets' admonishments and warnings the current catastrophe appeared to the contemporaries not as a weakness and failure of God but as a sign of his omnipotence. It was he who had called in the enemies and given them victory in order to chastise his people and put it on the right path. As a chosen people the Jews have been selected for a higher duty—and for harsher chastisement if they do not fulfill this priestly duty.

This is the meaning of the much-quoted and much-misunderstood "chosenness" of the Jewish people, which has so often been interpreted as arrogance by non-Jews and occasionally even by Jews. It does not mean capricious favoritism, but chosenness for greater duties—service to God and the consecration of life.

But the nations who have done bad things to God's chosen people will also fall when they have fulfilled their duty as chastisers, and Israel will return to serve its God in its own country, more faithfully than before. Moreover, Israel's return—and this is the faith that increasingly permeated the people from the time of Isaiah on—will be the beginning and the symbol for the turning of all mankind. The nations will peacefully gather around Israel and its newly rebuilt Temple, and eventually they will all attain to a proper recognition of God, the one God, the God of Israel.

This brought a new conception of history and of God into the world. Universalistic in nature, it is oriented toward the future and far above local deities and their conflicts. But because of the way it originated, through the religious preservation of the fact that it was revealed solely to the people of Israel, and finally through the confirmation it received from the experiences of the people this universalistic view of God, strangely enough, had a solidifying effect on the national cohesiveness of the Jewish exiles in Babylon and on the Jews in many other countries and at many other times. To be sure, among the Jews it also laid the foundation for that often presumptuous self-assurance and conviction of their special chosenness and closeness to God against which the prophets had inveighed and which has at all times provoked or exacerbated the criticism, resistance, and hatred of other peoples. For the Jews the revelation on Mount Sinai of the monotheistic theology and its ethical demands has always been the foundation of their religious consciousness, but it has at the same time been part of their national history, the first and greatest communal experience of the people, and it is preserved as such for all time in the Scriptures. In a real sense it was this revelation and vocation that created the people, at least according to the Scriptures and their teachers and believers; in any case, it first gave the existence of the people a justification that transcended what was natural. Because of it the people and the doctrine soon could not be separated conceptually; the universalistic and the national factors had become intermeshed, and so were the past and the future, with the present as a transition.*

The conviction of the truth of the doctrine and of the chosenness of the Jewish people for the embodiment and propagation of this truth was bound to become solid certainty when after the prophecies of doom the prophetic proclamations of the redemption and return of the people became reality as well. Hence the permission given the exiles to return from Babylon to Judea meant to the Jews of that period more than the rebuilding of their religious and national homeland. This occurrence, which had been foretold by the prophets, was at the same time the definitive proof of the divine truth of the words of the prophets and of the veracity of the prophetic view of God in general. By implication it also proved that the Messianic period proclaimed by the prophets would come by the will of God when the time and mankind were ripe for it.

Democratization of the Doctrine of God

The leaders of those who had returned from Babylon and their descendants now made this view the predominant doctrine in Judaism. The Temple was rebuilt, and the splendor of the Herodian edifice surpassed that of the Solomonian. But the development that had begun under the Judean king Josiah (640–609 B.C.E.)** with the centralization of the sacrificial service in Jerusalem as the only permissible place of sacrifice and that was intensified and accelerated by the interruption of the sacrifices since the destruction of the First Temple continued after

---

*It may not be accidental that in the Hebrew language only the past tense and the future have independent grammatical forms, while the present tense is formed with the aid of a participle. In German and in English, the imperfect and the present have independent forms, while the future is formed with an auxiliary verb.

**The author of II Kings says about Josiah (23:25), under whom the people was pledged to observe the recovered Torah, that there was no king before and after him who had returned to God like him and had upheld the teachings of Moses with all his heart and soul.

the rebuilding of the Temple. Next to or in place of the sacrifices in the Temple the religious services in the meeting house of the local community assumed increasing importance, and within them prayer, "that original creation of Judaism" (Wellhausen, *Israelitische und jüdische Geschichte*, 200), as a form of union with God that was equal or superior to the sacrifices—a form that was later taken over by Christianity and Islam. Acting righteously, that true essence of the prophetic demand, is placed on an equal footing with, or in a privileged position beside, the expiatory sacrifice. Beyond its status as a day of rest, the Sabbath increasingly becomes the day of public religious service. On every Sabbath, and later on the market days Monday and Thursday as well, chapters from the Torah—the Book of Creation, peoplehood, law-giving, and promise—are read in the synagogue of the community, followed by readings from the books of the prophets. The reading and interpretation of the Holy Scriptures, a collection with ever more marked canonical character of the books of history, of teaching and admonishment, and of praise and consolation, increasingly took the place of the prophetic words proclaimed in person or the sacred sacerdotal acts. Knowledge and dissemination of the doctrine thus ceased to be the secret and privilege of a caste of priests. They became the business of the whole people and the teachers and Bible scholars growing out of it, of the "sages" whose records, teaching, debates, and decisions produced the Talmud—from Ezra to the Pharisees* and the later exegetes of the written and oral teachings in the Middle Ages and down to our day.

There was a democratization of religious knowledge and activity such as had been developed by no other religion. This democratization of doctrine is one of the main reasons why the masses of the people remained loyal to Judaism even when those of the highest social status, who were most strongly exposed to the seductive glamor of the surrounding cultures, were lost to it.

The Community and Its National-Religious Function

The knowledge and interpretation of Scripture, the learning of the commandments and their practice was not a theoretical, unworldly occupation remote from daily life. The community gathered around the

---

*We need hardly emphasize here that the Pharisees (etymologically, the word probably denotes those who isolate themselves to lead pious lives) in actuality had nothing to do with the distorted picture the New Testament paints of them. There may well have been hypocrites among them, as there are among all groups, but these surely were not representative of the far-reaching religious movement that under the leadership of the Pharisees and at the time of the Second Temple laid the foundation for the preservation and development of the Jewish religion in the Hellenic and Roman world and in the world of their heirs.

religious service; if it constituted itself on alien soil and in alien surroundings, it became at the same time the preserver of the home tradition and the national elements. The meeting-house—called *Bet Haknesset* in Hebrew, translated into Greek as "synagogue" and taken over by European languages in that form—constituted the center of the life of the community in all its aspects, from the religious to the legal and social. With its Bible readings, prayers, and religious instruction for young and old, the synagogue and the community around it coalesced into a unit, both in Palestine and in the Diaspora; eventually one was not conceivable without the other. Jewish life means communal life, Jewish settlement—and especially outside Palestine, communal settlement without the house of God as its center—Jewish religion with a belief in chosenness and Messianic redemption despite all "temporary" adversities of the present, communal living as a people, mutual aid through social institutions that developed early, a legal system based on religious laws, economic interests, and a feeling of being sheltered and at home in a familiar atmosphere. In other words, religious, national, and economic-social elements gradually coalesced into an inseparable unit and supported one another. Even though every crisis might confront the leaders, the intellectuals, with spiritual decisions that defeated them or that they overcame by means of interpreting and developing their religious heritage, the masses of the people found their way through simple faith and the preservation of the traditional forms without struggling with problems and decisions in every case. Tradition, custom, and faith became one, the only right and normal course, the homelike and God-given way. This became a support in the present and a guarantor of a better future.

The emergence of this new way of faith and life had saved the Jews from religious, national, and cultural disintegration in the period of the Babylonian exile. The development and creation of firm traditions kept them together during the succeeding centuries of expansion beyond the borders of Palestine and made them resistant to threats from within and without. This condition is the main reason why the final collapse of the state and the Temple, as well as the defeats under Titus, Trajan, and Hadrian, did not lead to the dissolution of the Jewish people or the loss of its national and religious identity.

As was the case at the fall of the First Temple, in the catastrophes of 70 to 135 the Jews did not regard defeat and exile as evidence of the impotence of their God but as proof of the truth of his word as proclaimed by the prophets, both in execration and in promise. "We were driven from our land because of our sins"—this is the teaching that gradually prevailed and was impressed upon the people every day in the liturgy that was establishing itself. Two conclusions were drawn from this teaching: First, that it was the foremost duty of a Jew to live in strict accordance with the laws of the Torah; and second, as a consistent development of this idea, that armed resistance to the superior power of "Edom" (this image was now replaced by Rome) was not only senseless but blasphemous. Punishment, expiation, and the coming of the Messianic period were in God's hand, and a Jew could hasten this coming only by faithfully serving God, fulfilling the commandments, and leading a pious life. To "force" the secure and good end, to try to bring it about with human means more quickly than had been decided, meant to "tempt God."

Talmud and Messianism

The Jewish people's will to live thus expresses itself in two different ways whose seeming inner antithetical nature has often been misunderstood. One is the assurance of a mystical belief in the coming of the Messiah, "soon, in our days"; the other is the development of Talmudic Judaism—originally intended as preparation for the Messianic last days, which may come at any moment, and not, as often falsely assumed, as a guide to life in the Diaspora.

In the Talmud the so-called "oral teachings" have been written down—formally as an interpretation of the biblical laws, actually as their continuation and adaptation to the new realities of the present. This was first done in the Mishnah (teaching) around the year 200. In the succeeding three centuries new traditional material was gathered in the discussions of the academies in Palestine and Babylonia. The authoritative collection of these decisions about the right way of living (Halakhah) and the statements, debates, narratives, and pious interpretations of these were written down around 500 in the so-called Gemara (completion). The entire Talmud has furnished the foundation for the Jewish way of life for sixty generations down to the present day. The way of life of an individual Jew and of the community as a whole is thus fixed down to every detail by commandments, prohibitions, and customs, and it is distinguished and shielded from the life-style of any non-Jewish surroundings: from rising in the morning through the vicissitudes of the day to bedtime; in the regular rhythm of working days and weekly days of rest, days of festive joy and of remorseful soul-searching and fast days of atonement; from the cradle to the grave, through all stages of life, which thus receive their regulation and consecration. The religious world of the Jews in Palestine and in the Diaspora, which seemed so strange and even misanthropic to the outside world, is cast into ever firmer orders and delimitations. This only made it even more alien, more suspicious, more uncanny, more unfamiliar, and therefore more untrustworthy to the surrounding world, which hardly knew the biblical background, let alone the oral and written extensions and "fences." Yet this screening off certainly did not mean that the Jews separated themselves from their surroundings in all things. On the contrary; at that time, and in all preceding and subsequent periods, the Jews adopted many things from their surroundings: dwellings and clothing, working methods, forms of organization, language and writing, the entire outward life-style as well as important cultural forms of seeing, thinking, and believing. They always remained separate, however, in everything concerning religious beliefs and rituals, and this precluded close communal living in the most intimate spheres of daily life—for example, communal eating and drinking, which unites people amicably and often affectionately and which occupies an important position in the ritually consecrated public functions of the communal organizations of the state, the city, and allied associations. By refusing to participate in such festive actions of the recognized representatives of the state or other public institutions, or by staying away from the banquets and sacrifical feasts associated with these, the Jews furnished, as it were, daily confirmation of the traditional view, based on hearsay, of their misanthropy—or, more accurately, their hostility toward all those who did not belong to their own society with its mysterious rites. Balaam's curse-blessing over Israel, the people that lives in isolation and does not mingle with other nations, became reality, so to speak, in both of its components, the blessing and the curse.

Palestine Remains the Center

For centuries Palestine remained for the Jews of the Diaspora as well the supreme authority in all questions of religious activities and the legal decisions profoundly influenced by it. The academies there (in Hebrew, *batei midrash, yeshivot*) had developed into institutions that had academic functions and at the same time the authority to make religious and civil decisions, thus laying the foundation for a system of education and self-government that has been preserved to our day and is probably unequaled in its continuity. To a great degree it is due to this system that despite their dispersion the Jews have preserved themselves as a people of culture, intelligence, and practical wisdom. The head of the central academy, which was first located in the Judean coastal town Jabneh, after the suppression of the Bar Kochba rebellion was transferred farther north, finally being situated in the Galilean towns Tzippori (Sepphoris) and Tiberias, acquired the rank of a Patriarch (Nassi) recognized by the Romans. He fixed the calendar of religious festivals and conveyed it every year to the communities in Palestine and the *golah* through emissaries. In addition to appointing officers of the community, he had the last word in legal questions.

Palestine's central position in the Jews' feelings and thoughts as the

"Land of Israel" was preserved even when the definitive determination of the beginning of the months and the holidays (by Patriarch Hillel II, from 344 on) made the communities of the Diaspora more independent and when—under the pressure of Christian Rome and Byzantium and finally through the Arab conquest of the seventh century—the Jewry of Palestine, which steadily declined in numbers and culture, gradually lost its influence upon the Jews of the Diaspora to the Babylonian center. This was accomplished, in addition to the Bible, by the religious order of the liturgy, which had since the end of the fourth century become ever firmer and was valid for all congregations. It was not only on the specially created fast day, the ninth of Av, in commemoration of the destruction of the two Temples that Jews remembered this destruction, and in addition to mourning it also expressed hope for the speedy rebuilding of the Temple. In the principal prayers, the *Shmoneh Esreh* (Eighteen Benedictions), which was recited before the assembled congregation three times a day, and the confession of faith, *Shema* ("Hear, O Israel"), there recurred the supplication for leading the dispersed back "from the four corners of the earth" and for the rebuilding of Jerusalem and its holy Temple as well as the coming of the Messiah "soon, in our days." And the same supplication is repeated in many prayers of the congregation, including those that an individual speaks for himself in place of, or in addition to (like grace), the communal prayer. The hope for return to the homeland was given particularly memorable form in the celebration of the Passover evening (Seder). There the living memory of the beginnings of national history, the exodus from Egypt, was combined in narrative and drama, exegesis, song, and prayer with the everlasting hope for return to the homeland in the near future. Every Jew should at every age feel—this is how integration into the chain of the generations is taught—as though he himself had participated in the exodus from Egypt. The hopeful statement at the close of the Seder evening, "Next year in Jerusalem!" constituted, as it were, a living bridge from a bright past to a bright future over a dark present in which, if this was God's will, the Messianic future could begin at any time.

As was already mentioned, the same purpose, bringing about the Messianic period expected in the near future, was to be served by the collection of the oral teachings, their editing and writing down in the Mishnah and Gemara. The authoritative codification of the teachings and their application in the present was intended to prepare the people, "hallow" every daily activity, and thus make possible and perhaps hasten the arrival of the anointed one in the near future. The Mishnah was not created for life in a long period of dispersion, the *golah*, but for the near future in Palestine, the reestablishment of the Jewish State, and the imminently expected beginning of the Messianic period. When this expected time did not come, however, the Palestinian precepts and practices set down in the Mishnah and the Talmud could constitute the foundation for the religious and national particular life of the Jews during the long centuries of their homelessness in the *golah*.

The Nature of Jewish Messianism

Thus, as has frequently been stated, paraphrasing Heine,* the Bible and the Talmud with its precepts based on national life in Palestine constituted a sort of "portable state" for the Jews who had been deprived of their real state. Messianic faith was the soul of the people, so to speak. It afforded the people the certain hope for a better future even when it threatened to sink into misery or rigidify in ritualism, and gave the existence of the people its real meaning for the present as well as its goal for the future. It was the inner driving force of its whole life, the inner meaning of its existence. As a goal-oriented vital force it could almost be described in the Aristotelian concept *entelechy*.

Since its origin in prophetic times, the Messianic idea in Judaism has undergone many changes and transformations. At all times, however, the universal and national elements remained indissolubly linked in it. The redemption of Israel is the prelude to the redemption of mankind, or tantamount to it, and initially both were understood as earthly salvation.

Even the forcible dispersion was given its place in this conception of Messianism. To be sure, the Jews were driven out of their country because of their sins, their deficient loyalty to God, and their insufficient actualization of the righteous life commanded by God. But just as every happening has its deeper meaning in the divine plan of the world, so does the dispersion of the Jews; through it the pure theology is disseminated among the nations. Once this has been done and the Jews have atoned for their sins through their God-fearing life amidst the sufferings of the Diaspora, the Messianic period will begin.

The greater the sufferings of the present, the more firmly was faith in the future linked with the sufferings of the present. It was believed that the coming of the Messiah would have to be preceded by times of violence, injustice, and sorrow; with reference to words of the Prophet Hosea, they were regarded as "birth-pangs of the Messiah" (*chevleh Mashiach*). From this viewpoint, any time of need that otherwise would have to lead to despair could now be interpreted as a time of hope. The greater the sufferings were, the greater the proof that the coming of the Messiah was imminent. They were his footprints *Ikvot Hamashiach*), so to speak the shadow that his figure cast before it. Wars—were they not

---

*In his "Confessions" Heine calls the Bible a "portable fatherland." Cf. also "The Shameless Heine" in Part 2.

the struggles of Gog and Magog as narrated by later tradition on the basis of Ezekiel's prophecy (chaps. 38–39)? The certain fall of these barbaric forces would demonstrate the strength of God, the God of Israel! After the collapse of the State and the Temple, as in all subsequent persecutions and times of need down to the present, this belief in the close connection between chastisement and redemption has helped large parts of the Jewish people to overcome despair.

For, as we have said, this day of redemption can come at any time; its determination is solely a matter of God's decision. A person can hasten its coming only by living in a manner that is pleasing in the sight of God. To try to do so by force of arms is not only senseless, but—raising the actual balance of power to the sphere of doctrine and faith—a blasphemous interference with God's decision.

It took centuries for the doctrine to be finally established in this form. For centuries there still were a number of uprisings and the utilization of political situations, the last in the seventh century when the Palestinian Jews participated in the armed struggle for Palestine between Byzantium and Persia and Byzantium and Islam—fights that were interpreted eschatologically, like the struggle with Rome many generations before that. From then on, after the victory of Islam which dashed all hopes for the recovery of Palestine in the foreseeable future, "the nation definitely submitted to the admonitions of its teachers. God had made his will manifest; it was his will that the Jews should bear the yoke of foreign nations. The Jews left the ranks of warring nations and put their fate altogether in the hands of God" (Yitzhak F. Baer, *Galut* [New York, 1947], p. 19).

Changes in the Image of the Messiah

In keeping with this change in the constellation of power and in the realization that any earthly struggle for homeland, return, and freedom was hopeless, the image of the Messiah changed to an ever-increasing extent as well. From the outset we may distinguish between two different Jewish conceptions of the Messiah: on the one hand, the figure of an earthly, natural savior and ruler from the house of David who liberates and gathers the people and leads it back into its country, and on the other the idea of a supernatural being, a divine Messiah at the end of time who brings about the heavenly kingdom with the Last Judgment and the resurrection of the dead. At almost all times both elements have been present and have overlapped; the heavenly and the earthly spheres have not always been clearly separated and have not infrequently coalesced. But an eminently real idea of the people's return to its homeland, the rebuilding of the State and the Temple, and of a human Messiah working with human means was always preserved as long as realistic hope for self-help was alive in the people. In subsequent periods, however, the image of the Messiah became increasingly removed from earthly reality and for the faithful reached the heights of fantasy and pure miracle. "Beginning in the seventh century, the same scene is imagined generation after generation. On some fine day all the Jews of the world will pack their baggage and prepare themselves in holiday clothes to be transported to their home—on clouds or by the hands of angels" (Baer, *Galut*, 19).

The change in the Messianic image and faith in return and redemption was a reflection of actual conditions; it was an escape to supernatural heights in an effort to preserve religious faith and national hopes even though the realities on earth offered no prospect that these hopes would be fulfilled in the foreseeable future, for in the meantime the political and religious situation of the world had changed substantially in the Jews' disfavor.

The victory of Christianity in the early fourth century, and subsequently that of Islam in the seventh—of those monotheistic world religions which conveyed to the world the basic teachings of Judaism in more general form and with certain particular additions and variations—created a completely new psychic and ideological atmosphere for Judaism. The fall of the Roman Empire, the rise of new barbaric states in Europe, and finally the creation of the Islamic-Arabic empire provided new economic and social foundations for the actual life of the Jews. Under these changed circumstances the Jewish question assumed the form in which it continued to persist for many centuries, in a multiplicity of transformations and variants, and has actually survived to recent times.

Judaism and Christianity

One of the consequences of the fall of the Jewish Temple and State was, as is well known, that the Jewish sect of the "Nazarenes" definitively broke away from Judaism and that Christianity, with its doctrine that was inimical to its mother religion, constituted itself as an independent religious community and church. The believers in the Jewish preacher and prophet Jesus of Nazareth, who had been executed by the Romans as the Messiah and King of the Jews almost forty years before the great war and the destruction of the Temple, also regarded the defeat in the struggle as punishment for the sins of the Jews. Up to that point they, as Jewish believers in God, shared the view of the misfortune held by the Pharisees and other Jewish scholars and leaders. However, they parted company with them in their conviction that this disaster was God's punishment for the Jews' refusal to recognize Jesus as the Messiah proclaimed by the prophets and sent by God, as the Son of God incarnate. In their eyes the destruction of the Temple was a visible sign that God had rejected the Jews because of this failure. In the Roman wars of 68–70 they had at best adopted an attitude of neutrality,* but now they completely removed themselves from the fate of the Jewish people. In the great Jewish uprisings against the Romans fifty and sixty years later under Trajan and Hadrian they were, if anything, on the side of the adversaries and certainly not in the Jews' corner. Therefore it is only logical that they were not ready to bear the stigma of belonging to the "rebellious" Jewish nation with which they were identified by the Romans—all the less so because in the decisive shift connected with the activities and teachings of the Apostle Saul/Paul they had turned away from the "stubborn" Jews and toward the heathens, who proved to be more open and receptive to their doctrine. Hence they increasingly emphasized in their propaganda that which divided them from Judaism, while they sought to blur the elements that both faiths had in common and that the pagan world was most apt to see. With this detachment from the Jews, who were decried as a rebellious, vanquished, destroyed people, Christianity made its way as a world religion that was at first persecuted and later became dominant.

Why the Jews Rejected Christianity

Again and again the question has been raised why the Jews as a totality did not adopt the Christian doctrine or later that of Islam— religions which, after all, gave worldwide dissemination to the specific ideas of Judaism in more general form, thus fulfilling the task for which the Jewish people regarded itself as chosen. Did this not show—so people were able to ask—that the Jews did not really care about what they professed to believe? And did not the pagans, in adopting Christianity, demonstrate a more honest and more far-sighted recognition of the requirements, a greater readiness to disseminate the pure religion than the Jews, who "narrow-mindedly" clung to the connection of their religion with their national ideals and goals?

The first reply to these questions is that they are unhistorical; they do not emanate from a consideration of that crisis period in which the Jewish people fought for its existence as a people and Christianity for

---

*During the siege of Jerusalem they had fled from the city, but so had other religious leaders who disagreed with the radical line in the struggle against the Romans—first and foremost Yohanan ben Zakkai, later the founder of the yeshiva at Jabneh. This became the center of the movement for religious-national regeneration, which in the course of the ensuing centuries created the Mishnah, the Talmud, and the supplementary homiletic literature of legends and myths (Midrash, Aggada). The important thing thus was not participation or nonparticipation in the armed struggle, but identification with the fate of the people or removal from it.

recognition and expansion. The heathens living toward the end of the ancient Greco-Roman world had long since begun to doubt their own faith, even though they retained their rituals in family life and the public activities of the community, and the foundations of their life had been shaken. They were thus hungry and ready to adopt a religious doctrine of unity and redemption such as had already been prefigured in many existing philosophies and religions imported from the East. In this situation the pagans embraced Judaism and Christianity in equal measure. The communities of Jewish proselytes were the soil in which the seeds of Christian propaganda bore the first fruits. Only with the proscription of the Jews as rebels and losers (particularly after the Bar Kochba uprising), the strict ban on the circumcision of proselytes* (that is, the prohibition of their complete integration into Judaism), the facilitation of the adoption of the Christian faith through the Pauline reforms (the abolition of the Jewish ritual commandments and prohibitions in the young Christian community) did Christian propaganda gain the upper hand over Jewish propaganda. The Jews, for their part, had developed their monotheistic doctrine for centuries and increasingly purged it of idolatrous admixtures. Whatever monotheistic teachings existed in Christianity the Jews recognized as their own. A Jew did not need to convert to Christianity in order to receive the teachings passed on for many generations from father to son to grandson, to be given his own sacred writings in an interpretation that he was bound to reject as a falsification. He had to regard the doctrine of the Trinity as a deviation from pure monotheism, as a throwback to idolatry, especially later, when Christianity made compromises with the religious services of the pagan peoples and incorporated many elements from the pagan religious world into its own religious rituals or customs, as a cult with saints or a belief in demons, or at least tolerated them there. Moreover, all the elements of national consciousness and hopes for the future that were alive in the Jewish people, particularly at the time of the decisive struggles with Rome for the continued existence or disappearance of this people, had to resent the fact that the members of this sect, who in the eyes of the Jews were primarily Jews like all other Jews, distanced and separated themselves in words and deeds from the common national fate and even scornfully capitalized on the misfortune by presenting it as proof that their adversaries in mainstream Judaism were in the wrong. The Jews, who then and later were not ready to commit national suicide for the sake of a heavenly hope, were bound to regard the Christians as traitors

---

*Circumcision, the mark of the Jews' covenant, was forbidden in Hadrian's reign under pain of death. His adopted son and successor Antoninus Pius (emperor from 138 to 161) rescinded this prohibition for those born as Jews but continued it for non-Jews (including proselytes).

to the Jewish nation and falsifiers of the Jewish faith. It is not fair to blame the Jews for this loyalty to their God and homeland as well as to the religion with its laws and traditions that is connected with this people and homeland, which is what Christian theology and historiography and the thinking of peoples that have been influenced by both have in effect done to this day, despite all polite mitigations.

In any case, this will to live as nation that was closely connected with belief in the Messiah effectively constituted a dividing line between Jews and Christians. We have already seen how indissolubly national and religious elements, acceptance of the current lot and hopes for the future, the fate of the individual and the fate of the people were bound up with one another in the consciousness of a Jew and in his daily life and actions, how greatly universal substances and national forms had coalesced into a unit in his faith. Being pressed from without and within in their struggle for the existence of their people, with all the actual and ideal elements this encompassed, the Jews could not believe the Christian claim that the Messiah had already appeared. How could that be if God's people suffered so—in contrast to all prophecies and all hallowed national beliefs in which the redemption of the Jewish people and of mankind went hand in hand? So respected a believer and scholar as Rabbi Akiba (ca. 50–135) was more likely to recognize the Messiah in the Jewish warrior and popular leader Bar Kochba, who called for rebellion against Rome in 132, than in Jesus, who had been crucified one hundred years earlier. But he surely could not see the Messiah in the figure into which Christian doctrine and legend had in the meanwhile shaped the image of Jesus.

Judaism now had to fashion a response to this antithesis: complete separation from Christianity. By inserting a curse against heretics and Christians, apostates and informers into the basic prayer said three times daily (the so-called *Shemoneh esreh*, the eighteen benedictions),* admittance to the synagogues was rendered impossible for the Jewish Christians who had hitherto still used the synagogues for prayer and dissemination of the Christian doctrine. The Jewish leaders could have no interest in continuing to give the Christians an outlet for a propaganda that was intended to deprive the Jewish people of the last thing it possessed: a worthy past and the prospect of a worthy future. For that seemed to be the aim of the new religion.

---

*The text appears in Part 2. The benediction against heretics, Christians, apostates, and informers—probably inserted into the liturgy by Rabbi Gamaliel Raban II in the period between the destruction of the Temple and the Bar Kochba uprising—was, logically enough, deleted at a later date when the separation was final and Christianity had become the dominant power, leaving only the imprecations against the heretics and the informers. In the Reform synagogues of the nineteenth century even these were eliminated.

Jews and Judaism in the Christian Doctrine

Let us examine the image of Jews and Judaism in the Christian doctrine, how the Jew was viewed by Christians in that period of decision and separation. Here we must distinguish between the way in which this image of the Jews was reflected in the sacred writings of the "New Covenant" (Testament), composed in this period of national struggle, and the way it appears in the authoritative Christian teachers, the Church Fathers, whose books were written during the polemics between Christians and Jews in the succeeding three centuries. An acquaintance with these views is important not only because it affords a better understanding of the resistance of the Jews against the adoption of Christianity and its dissemination; in the final analysis, this would be of interest only to historians. The importance of these views of the Jews resides in the fact that they became part of Christian religion and even of Christian dogma. Anchored in the sacred books of Christianity and thus elevated to the status of God-given, unassailable truth and established as such by Council decisions, they were bound to be of the greatest influence on the feeling and thinking of all believing Christians in succeeding ages and to shape their ideas of the nature of the Jewish religion and the life of the Jews. Through the victory of Christianity and its rise as the dominant power in the course of the fourth century, this dogmatic image of the Jews increasingly affected the legislation and the social life of the Christian states and countries as well.

The basis of all Christian views and teachings about Judaism and the Jewish people is the dogma that the Jews have been cursed and cast out by God because they did not recognize Jesus as the Messiah and caused him to be crucified. The question as to the Jews' share in the crucifixion of their fellow Jew Jesus has not been clearly answered to this day, despite constant attempts to interpret Christian traditions and conclusions on the basis of the legal, religious, and social conditions of the period. No contemporary sources exist, and those that claim to be are accounts of faithful disciples and teachers that were written down long after the events, probably toward the end of the first century. There is only one definite fact, and it is reported by the Roman historian Tacitus (*Annals* 15. 44): Jesus was executed in the reign of Emperor Tiberius (14–37 C.E.) by the Roman governor Pontius Pilate, probably around the year 30. In the Christian literature, which originated as a polemic against Jews and pagans, as a defense of the Christian faith and a demonstration of its correctness, and which finally received canonical character as the New Testament, probably at the end of the second century, the blame of the Jews for Christ's sentencing and crucifixion was increasingly emphasized. It was depicted in ever more expansive and venomous terms as the Christians, disappointed at the Jews' "obstinacy" and endeavoring to free themselves from their ties to the land and fate of the vanquished Jewish nation, successfully turned to the pagans and Romans under the leadership of the Pharisaic Jew Saul/Paul of Tarsus and supported them in their struggle against Judea. Correspondingly, the Romans were increasingly exculpated from the blame for the sentence and the execution. Pilate, who was described in a contemporary letter as "by nature unyielding, self-willed, and hard,"* is finally permitted to say in the gospels that he was "innocent of this man's blood"—a righteous man who resigns himself to the popular rage of the depraved Jews. Into the narrative of the life of Jesus, which is expanded on the basis of Jewish legends and prophecies abut the Messiah, into his simple teachings and dialogues there are inserted curses on the Temple and the priesthood, against the Pharisees, who are depicted as hypocrites, and against the Jews of the time, who take everlasting responsibility for the crucifixion with the cry, "His blood be on us!" All this was evidently not done as a deliberate falsification; rather, believing disciples here continued to speak and write on the basis of experiences of a present marked by the catastrophe of the Temple and the State as well as by God's curse which had, as it were, manifested itself through death, enslavement, and destruction.

The Bible as a Weapon against the Jews

From this aspect of God's curse and rejection of the Jewish people as well as its dispersion and enslavement the entire Jewish Bible, which is built into the foundation of the church as the "Old Covenant" (Old Testament), is reinterpreted for Christianity, the "New Covenant." To be sure, this made the Bible a world book and the history of the Jewish people, the lives and teachings of its admonishers and proclaimers, a model and example for the European world. But this national book of the Jews, the autobiography of the Jewish people and testimony of its dialogue with itself and with God, its admonisher and consoler, its guarantor of a happier future, was at the same time wrested from the Jews, as it were, and annexed by the Christian church. More than that, in the hands of the Christian church, in its falsifying reinterpretation, the Jewish Bible became the most fearful weapon against Judaism.

In this interpretation of the Bible, Christianity is regarded as preexistent, secretly existing long before the appearance of Christ. The great figures of Jewish history mentioned in the Bible, the pious and pure

---

*In a letter from the Jewish king Herod Agrippa I to Emperor Caligula (37–41 C.E.) that was cited (and possibly drafted) by the Jewish-Alexandrian philosopher Philo ("Of the Proofs of God's Power"). The letter names as known misdeeds of Pilate's administration bribery, violence, robbery, ill-treatment, insults, constant executions without judgments, "endless and insufferable cruelties."

before God, belong to *it* and the spiritual Israel is its precursor. As for the bad, "human, all too human" things that the Bible, a narrative of unique integrity in the religious literature of the world, reports—that is the earthly Judaism, the actual Jewish people! The blessing contained in the Bible applies to the preexistent Christianity or refers to the Christianity of the future. All Messianic prophecies are taken away from the Jewish people and related to Jesus and Christianity; thus the Jews are denied the right to hope for a better future. But the evil deeds related in the Bible—defection from God, unfaithfulness, falseness, murder—are the actual history of the Jewish people, the case history of its atrocious deed, the rejection of Jesus and his crucifixion, the history and legal basis of God's rejection and cursing of the Jews. "A fugitive and wanderer over the earth"—this curse of Cain is now transferred to the Jewish people to the end of time. James Parkes, the Christian historian of this conflict, rightly remarks that "no people has ever paid so high a price for the greatness of its own religious leaders and for the outspoken courage with which they held up an ideal and denounced whatever seemed to them to come short of it." If, according to Parkes, the prophets had known how maliciously their words of threat and benediction would be misused so that these words finally contained a benediction for all nations and a malediction only for the Jews, they might have (according to a sarcastic remark made in the second century by Christian Church Father Irenaeus, Bishop of Lyon) burned their own scriptures.

In this way the Christian view and doctrine change all positive aspects of Judaism into something negative as far as the Jewish people is concerned. Just as the pagan gods lived on as demons in the Christian view of life, so did the Jewish Messiah. His positive realization is Jesus, but the image of the Messiah in Jewish hearts appears to the Christians as the arch-fiend, the Antichrist, Satan. To many the Jews themselves appeared as creatures of the devil, as Satan's brood. According to the Gospel of St. John (8:44), the Jews are not the children of God but of Satan.

The Jewish Type of the Christian Church

Something dreadful came into being in this manner. The church created the ideal type of the accursed Jew—the depraved Jew whose thinking and scheming only concerned evil, who constantly proved unworthy of divine grace and of human love, who rejected God in favor of the Golden Calf, who gambled away his bliss for the sake of the nearest earthly advantage, the "Judas" (the gospels may have given this name to the traitor intentionally)* who again and again betrays Jesus for

---

*In any case, the name mingled with the idea of the Jew, assumed Satanic character, and became synonymous with Jews and traitors. See also Part 2.

thirty pieces of silver, the murderer of the Savior and the one accursed by him.

The Jew is worse than any heathen, for he knows the truth. Christians convinced of their truth increasingly believed that in his heart of hearts a Jew knew that Jesus was the Savior; that therefore the Christian, Christological interpretation of Holy Writ was the correct one; that everything in it was aimed at the appearance of Jesus; that it was Jesus whom the prophets had proclaimed as the Messiah and redeemer of mankind. If the Jews, against their better knowledge, nevertheless denied Jesus as they did at the time of his earthly existence, if despite everything they stuck with their "limited" interpretation of Scripture, unyieldingly clung to their Law (which the Christian teachers often turned into virtual devil's work) and their belief in the divine chosenness of the Jews, of all peoples, after all the obvious proofs of their accursedness—then that was further evidence of the falseness, corruption, and innate devilish malice of the Jews. As has rightly been observed, the existence of the Jews was in Christian eyes "like a continued crucifixion of Christ."

The Significance of the Christian Image of the Jews for the Development of the Jewish Question

The importance of this image of the corrupt Jew that was created by the saints and teachers of the Christian church and incorporated into their religious teachings and dogmas cannot be overestimated, for it became the basis of all later animosity. The hatred of Jews found its first classic expression here.

Even earlier, accusations and feelings of hatred toward the Jews had accumulated in the ancient world. As already stated, because of their religious and national segregation the Greeks and Romans regarded the Jews as inhospitable xenophobes and, because of their belief in the oneness of their invisible God and their chosenness and calling for his service, as arrogant, conceited, intolerant, and even godless. In their struggle with the Roman Empire there was added (as the second stratum in the geology of feelings, as it were) their bad reputation as rebels and after their defeats the odium of the vanquished. Aside from the defeat itself, the vanquished are still the target of the hatred and contempt of the victor and all those who served him. Sold on the markets of the Roman Empire as cheap slaves and contemptuously singled out by the special tax imposed upon them, the Jews surely enjoyed little social respect in connection with everything that had preceded it, even though they had possessed Roman citizenship since Emperor Caracalla's well-known edict of 212 that bestowed the full rights of Roman citizens on all free inhabitants of the Roman world empire.

All these opinions, dislikes, and hatreds were, of course, preserved in the consciousness of the people as a bedrock. Hatred and scorn of what is different can be passed on. These feelings were transmitted from generation to generation as tradition even if the causes of those views and feelings were in the remote past and hence long forgotten. If the real reason is no longer relevant, people devise reasons for the adopted feelings of hatred and contempt, for the justification of their aggressions in legends, jokes, and anecdotes. Legends of hate and contempt are most easily fashioned around those who are weak, vanquished, and beaten down. Those have always been the objects of vengeance not only by victors but by everyone who would like to play the role of the victor and therefore flatters him and is all too eager to document his agreement with him in the safe gesture of kicking the person who is lying prostrate.

But all these feelings of dislike and hatred still were on natural, earthly grounds. *Fatum* and *Fortuna*, the fate and fortune predestined by the gods, somehow played a part with supernatural claims, but no more than in everything experienced by the ancient world. The emphasis always remained on the human elements; after all, it was more of a struggle of human forces, and the decision in the contest between Rome and Judea had been rendered on earth.

Now, however, Christianity elevated the curse and contempt of the Jews, their enslavement and dispersion, to an expression of divine judgment, a sacred act, a supernatural verdict. A Jew was damned not as a human being and by human beings, but as one sentenced, rejected, and damned by God.* Jew-hatred and revulsion against the Jews were justified on supernatural grounds; more than that, they were virtually mandated. God was said to have spoken, and a man was only executing on earth the judgment that God had made in heaven.

As James Parkes and other researchers have shown, the interesting thing about this is that when these teachings against the Jews and Judaism came into being, everyday relationships between Jews and Christians were entirely normal. The accusations of the Church Fathers against the Jews hardly ever contained arguments from the economic and social life of the time. It was not the social reality that spawned the hatred, as people later thought under the influence of modern racial and social doctrines, but the dogma, the theological necessity. Originally the objects of hatred were not the real-life Jews as encountered by real-life Christians, but the typical Jew, the evil caricature of the Jew that was hallowed by the dogma.** This distorted image of the Jew was handed

---

*Epithets like "damned Jew" are to be understood on that basis; the original meaning was "damned by *God*."

**Hence dogmatic and anti-Jewish writings tend to speak of "the Jew" or "the Jews"— that is, the stereotypical Jew as imagined—rather than of individual Jews with their good and bad qualities.

down from generation to generation, and as the tradition became older it became a stereotype that was unquestioningly accepted and believed as the true picture of the Jew.

Thus it happened that as Christianity spread to various countries, the hatred of the Jews preceded their settlement there. This also explains why to our day individual Jews are usually regarded as exceptional cases by non-Jews, even those known as Jew-baiters, with whom they happen to come into close contact. As compared to the image of the typical Jew which a Christian has derived from tradition and hence regards as a true image, the real-life Jew, as a person of flesh and blood, is bound to be an exception to the "rule" if he is a half-way decent person.

To be sure, as we shall see, the church did everything in its power to make the real-life Jew as like the stereotype sketched by it as possible.

The Future of the Jews According to the Christian Dogma

The Church Fathers certainly did not agree on the future of the Jews. The ideas of St. Augustine (354–430), the Church Father most influential in the development of the official doctrine, increasingly prevailed as the official view. He, the African Roman Aurelius Augustinus, Bishop of the Numidian city of Hippo, has been called the most wide-ranging spirit of late antiquity, a man who absorbed and assimilated the traditions and cultures of the Roman-Hellenic world, the Orient, and Christianity. Like everyone else he faced the problem of trying to explain the continued existence of the Jewish people when, according to church doctrine, it had been damned by God hundreds of years before because it bore the blame for the crucifixion. Because St. Augustine wanted to incorporate this fact into his view of the world, and possibly also because he felt inwardly obligated and beholden to the Jews for the heritage of which they had been deprived, he attained to a somewhat forced harmony between curse and blessing in the fate of the Jews.

For him, as for St. Paul, the Jews remained God's people. To be sure, they have forfeited their chosenness until the return at the end of time; they are accursed, scattered over the earth, enslaved, condemned to serve the new religion that has inherited their chosenness, and subjected to the princes and peoples in political servitude. But they should be kept alive as eternal witnesses to their own guilt and also to bear witness to the truth of the prophecies in their writings in favor of the Christians and to Christianity's triumph over them. "But the Jews who rejected Him," says St. Augustine in his *City of God*, probably the most comprehensive work of early Christian theology (book 18, chapter 46),

and slew Him (acording to the needfulness of His death and resurrection), after that were miserably spoiled by the Romans, under the domination of strangers, and dispersed over the face of the whole earth. For they are in all places with their testament, to show that we have not forged those prophecies of Christ. . . . But that suffices us which we have from the books of our enemies, which we acknowledge in that they preserve it for us against their wills, themselves and their books being dispersed as far as God's Church is extended and spread, in every corner of the world. . . . And therefore He [God] slew them not, that is, He left them their name of Jews still, although they be the Romans' slaves, lest their utter dissolution should make us forget the law of God concerning his testimony of theirs. So it were nothing to say, "Slay them not," but that He adds, "Scatter them abroad"; for if they were not dispersed throughout the whole world with their scriptures, the Church would lack their testimonies concerning those prophecies fulfilled in our Messiah.

Similar statements may be found in other writings of St. Augustine, particularly his "Sermon about the Jews."

Thus the Jews, the bearers of a mission who are still accursed by God, will be enslaved and dispersed to the end of days. Then God's grace will enlighten them as well, they will be converted to Jesus as the true Savior, they will be freed of the curse, and they too will share in salvation again.

The Effects on Popular Opinion

This view of the fate of the Jews, which conceded to them a certain place in the Christian conception of the world, albeit a negative one, became the official view of the Church. Its attitude toward the Jews during the Middle Ages was shaped by this view, both negatively and positively, in condemnation and proscription as well as in their preservation from complete destruction. But at the same time the Church disseminated the stereotypical image of the typical Jew that it had created and was increasingly vulgarized by the lower clergy. It was to influence and shape popular opinion more strongly than the ingenious, seemingly paradoxical harmony of St. Augustine's view of the world in which the Jewish people remains God's people, with a claim to salvation despite being accursed.

If any part of St. Augustine's doctrine reached the people and somewhat modified the cruder interpretation of the Scriptures in the Jews' disfavor, this probably only intensified the fear of the Jews. The mystery that had surrounded the Jews since Roman times because of their strange customs, their hopeless obstinacy, and their absence from common meals and ritual acts now assumed mystical dimensions and thus became even more demonic and incomprehensible. The curse that, in the Christians' view, God laid upon the Jews thus redounded to their disadvantage all the more strongly. If the Jews are to be spared despite being deicides, this is done, in the popular view, less for the sake of the divine grace that, according to St. Augustine, is in store for them as well than because of the curse that lies on them as it did on Cain, the fratricide. In this way it was possible to bring out even more markedly the demonic character of the Jews and the devilish, uncanny elements that the Christian world discerned in them. In more peaceful periods St. Augustine's more harmonious picture of the Jews' position in God's cosmic scheme might have exerted control over the minds of people, but in times of political and social turbulence, when desires and instincts were stirred up, the image of the demonic Jewish deicide was all too apt to show the masses how to give full vent to their instincts.

To understand this process one must realize that down to modern times the overwhelming majority of the nations were illiterate, people with primitive drives and ideas. They did not read the Bible and form an opinion on the basis of its contents, but heard about it in church. Its official version was Greek (the Septuagint) or Latin (the Vulgate of St. Jerome). The lower clergy shaped the opinion of the plain people, reading, translating, and interpreting the Bible and the gospels to the faithful, who became acquainted with the text, or parts thereof, only together with the interpretation. If the Jews were discussed—which was bound to happen very often, particularly during the major festivals of the Passion, the Resurrection, etc.—there naturally was less, if any, talk of the Pauline-Augustine doctrine and the eventual redemption of even the Jews than of the curse lying upon them because of their "impenitence" and deicide. Again and again, the picture of the evil Jew was redrawn as a deterrent and prototype of the sinner and blasphemer and provided with new hues. Children absorbed it with the catechism and adults through the sermons in church. Every sculpture and painting of the crucifixion and the passion of the Savior and the martyrs with which the churches were adorned reminded people of it and clarified it for them. In songs, fairy tales, and soon in mystery plays about the old and New Testaments—everywhere this image of the Jews recurred until it became self-evident and almost part of a person's unconscious. No wonder, then, if in times of excitement the accumulated zeal vented itself in bloody deeds.

Laws of Church and State Dealing with Jews

The effect of these stereotypes of Jews was bound to become stronger when the Church no longer confined itself to disseminating them as teachings. Once it had come to power, the Church mercilessly translated its views of the fate deserved by the Jews into action. It did everything to bring the situation of the Jews into line with what it had decreed for a rejected, dispersed, and enslaved people and to make real-life Jews resemble the stereotype it had devised by defaming, degrading, and disenfranchising them.

For this the Church had two means at its disposal: ecclesiastic legislation and influence on the legislation of the state. Since the official recognition of the Christian Church by Emperor Constantine (313) and its elevation to state church in the Roman Empire under Emperor Theodosius I (prohibition of all non-Catholic rituals in 392) it was able to proceed on both paths. The decisions of the general ("ecumenical") Councils since the meeting of the first one in 325 in the imperial summer palace at Nicaea sooner or later became state laws, and subsequently those state laws that affected the ecclesiastical sphere received sacral character by being ratified by the Councils. As a natural consequence of the ideological premises both the church edicts and the state laws served to make the Jews in reality what they appeared to be in the dogmatic-stereotypical image of the church, and to demonstrate over and over again by means of the reality thus created that the teachings of the Church were correct.

Jerusalem—a Christian Metropolis

Only now was Jerusalem completely wrested from the Jews. The Romans had destroyed it, turned it into a Roman colony, erected a Jupiter temple there, and barred the Jews from staying in their former capital. They had also abolished the name Judea for the Jewish land and given it the name of their enemies, the Philistines (Palestine). But for the world, as for the Jews, Jerusalem nevertheless remained the metropolis of the Jews, albeit a fallen one. After all, the hope for the reconstruction of this destroyed Jerusalem remained closely bound up with all Jewish hopes for the future, and the Jews prayed for this reconstruction every day. Starting with the time of Constantine, Jerusalem *was* rebuilt, though not as the capital of the Jews but as a symbol of their accursedness, an emblem and trophy of the "New Israel," the Christian Church. As the city of the redeemer Jerusalem was made a center of Christian worship through the erection of magnificent churches, and there was an ever mightier stream of Christian pilgrims who sought edification and sanctification at the places in Jerusalem and other cities of Palestine that, according to history or legend, were the sites of the life and death of Jesus and his disciples. This was yet another way in which the Jewish people was declared to have forfeited its land and its capital; Christianity took them over as an inheritance.

At the same time the Jews were increasingly driven from the soil of Palestine through the chicanery of legal decrees and persecution by Christian authorities—this, too, in consonance with the prophecies and in belated demonstration thereof. Under these conditions the Jewish population of Palestine decreased, and so did the living influence of the country upon the Jews of the Diaspora. As a consequence of this attitude of Christianity the Palestinian patriarchate was abolished in 425; up to that time it had been recognized as the supreme authority of Jewry, and by virtue of a number of important authorities it had also affected the life of the Jews outside Palestine. The center in Babylon increasingly took its place. In this way the progressive dispersion of the Jews was increasingly turned into reality—here, too, so to speak as a fulfillment of the curse embedded in Christian dogma.

The Influence of Christianity on the Situation of the Roman-Jewish Diaspora

At the same time the dominance of Christianity increasingly affected the situation of the Jews in the countries of the Roman Diaspora.

It would have been logical to expect that Emperor Constantine's Edict of Toleration would create more favorable conditions for the Jews as well. The worship of the gods, the foundation and apex of which was the deification of the emperor, ceased to be the official cult of the Roman Empire, and thus its recognition and practice no longer were requirements for civil service. This removed a barrier between the pagan and the nonpagan population. In point of fact, however, Christianity used this bridge of tolerance to become the dominant religion. Since the church was convinced of the divine truth and exclusive correctness of its own doctrine and imbued with the resultant obligation to use every means to make this only true doctrine the only recognized and valid one, it had to strive to suppress all other religions as heresies. It was bound to oppose Judaism with particular vehemence, because it initially threatened to be the strongest competition, and perhaps also to keep the Romans from confusing the Church with Judaism.

In the fourth century the Church was, after all, still in a state of consolidation, both dogmatically and organizationally. From the adherents of the Jewish religion to the believers in the orthodox church there were a number of transitions, intermediary views, and sects of all kinds. Some of them were close to Judaism, others to Christianity, and they were subject to all sorts of influences from East and West, philosophies and religious currents. Thus it was always possible to "stray" from the true Christian faith if the boundary lines were not clearly drawn. This is why in the laws relating to the Jews that were issued by the Church and by the state in the period following the recognition of Christianity there was a clear tendency to isolate Judaism and Christianity, or Jews and Christians, from one another and to deprive the Jews of the opportunity to convert Christians (or pagans) to Judaism. The celebration of the Christian festivals was definitely scheduled on different days so that these might not coincide with the festivals of the Jews, hitherto celebrated at the same time.* The Jews were prohibited from circumcising Christians, even Christian slaves, and from proselytizing those of other faiths; transgressors faced severe punishment. At the same time the Jews were barred from persecuting or disinheriting Jews who had converted to Christianity.

Defamatory Laws

To an ever greater extent the laws assumed a character defamatory of the Jews. The legislation of the state was increasingly pervaded by an ecclesiastical spirit. Except for brief atavistic episodes (particularly under Emperor Julian, 361–63, an admirer of Hellenic-pagan culture and hence called The Apostate by the Christians), the view developed that the Roman emperor was the God-appointed defender of the Christian faith. Hence it was one of his main tasks to make Christianity the sole ruler and to eradicate heretics and infidels who did not recognize the true faith or deviated from it, or at least to subject them to the Christian-Catholic Church. In this way popular belief and Christian dogmas invaded the official legislation and served as justification for the defamatory laws. Thus a law passed at the beginning of the fifth century excluded the Jews from military and court service, and a short time thereafter they were barred from all government service. Other anti-Jewish laws followed.

All these laws and decrees promulgated since the rise of Christianity under Constantine were collected in the fifth century under Theodosius II (408–50); some of them were supplemented and made more severe, and in 438 they were published in the great collection of the valid Roman laws, the Codex Theodosianus, named after the emperor. This elevated them to the status of state laws for the entire Roman Empire. In the sixth century (528–36) they were included in the *Corpus juris*, the great authoritative collection of Emperor Justinian, and supplemented with newer laws. With the adoption of Roman law they became the legal basis of the successor states to the Roman Empire.

The extent to which the dogmas of Christianity had already been incorporated into state legislation is shown by the motivation given by

---

*The text of the decision of the Council of Nicaea not to celebrate the Christian Easter at the same time as the Jewish Passover from which it had originated, reads as follows: "It would be unworthy for us to follow for this holy feast the custom of the Jews who soiled their hands with the most monstrous crimes and remained spiritually blind. Henceforth we wish to have nothing more in common with the people of the Jews, who are hostile to us, for our Savior has shown us another way." (Quoted after Werner Keller, *Diaspora* [New York, 1969], p. 94.) The Church Father and historian Eusebius has Emperor Constantine speak these words.

the Theodosian Edict of 438 for some of the anti-Jewish decrees. If the ban on the building of a synagogue is renewed or the inducement of a slave or free man to become an apostate from Christianity is made punishable by death or the confiscation of property, the general justification for this is the emperor's duty to take action against heathens and heretics, as well as the "blindness" and "obstinacy" of the Jews, which make them impervious to improvement through the law and unworthy of divine grace. In particular, their exclusion from government service is motivated by saying that the enemies of the Heavenly Majesty and the Roman law cannot be permitted to gain dominance over Christians and even high Christian clergymen by letting them execute the laws. But they ought to bear the burdens connected with participation in the local civil administration and from which they had earlier been exempted on religious grounds. The privilege of exemption was abolished, but at the same time the Jews were barred from attaining to higher honors.

The most stringent economic measures were the laws against the ownership of Christian slaves, which were virtually tantamount to a ban on the owning of slaves. Considering that the economy of the time was based on slave labor, the enforcement of such laws was bound to lead to an ever-increasing extent to the elimination of the Jews from certain branches of the economy and in particular from farm work and the ownership of landed property.

However, the question of the economic situation of the Jews in this transitional period is not relevant here. We are not writing the history of the Jews, and for our purposes it does not matter whether the decrees and the views on which they were based had an economic effect immediately or after a period of time, and to what extent. Depending on the place and the time, this was determined by local conditions, events, and personalities, and thus one cannot speak of a uniform effect. Even without specific documentation there can be no doubt, however, that in the long run these decrees were bound to have a profound effect in the social sphere on the assessment of the Jews by the non-Jews. If the state declared people to be inferior, unworthy of higher government positions, and not even entitled to have Christian slaves (or any other kind, for that matter) because as deicides and obstinate adherents of a heresy they could not be allowed to rule over those loyal to God, the Christians, and not even over Christian slaves, this was bound to affect the position of the Jews in the eyes of their surroundings. To be sure, formally and legally the Jews continued to be Roman citizens, but they were second-class ones. This is how they entered the world of the early Middle Ages wherever Christian-Roman law extended. However, for as long as the Roman law embodied in the Theodosian Code was valid, its positive part, legal protection for Roman citizens, applied to the Jews as well. But wherever in Europe the Roman law was replaced by the laws of the newly developing states, this legal protection vanished, leaving only the restrictions which canon law had long since made the common property of the legal systems of all Christian countries.

Summary Survey

If we take another look at the development of the Jewish question since the clash of the Jews with the Romans, we see that the catastrophe of the year 70 and the subsequent unsuccessful uprisings under Trajan and Hadrian constituted the decisive turning point in the fate of the Jews. True, even before the destruction of the Temple and the capital there was an extensive Diaspora, with tensions between the Jews and their surroundings and only a very limited political independence in the country, and the defeats in the struggles with the Roman world empire did not immediately lead to a complete dispersal of the Jews. For centuries a very considerable Jewish population lived in Palestine, and it took centuries for Palestine to decline (or, if you will, rise) from its position as the real religious and national-political center of the people to an unreal position as the land of its longing and dreams. However, the consequences of a great historic event cannot be measured only by its immediate effects; rather, the real significance of decisive historical events often lies in their impetus to further developments that can hardly be foreseen by their contemporaries. Just as a germ cell gradually permits blossoms, fruits, and seeds to ripen that were prefigured in it without being discernible to the eye in form and size, decisive historical events lead to far-reaching consequences and effects in all spheres of human existence that far surpass the event itself in scope and significance.

A historic event of this kind was the collapse of the State and the Temple of the Jews and the suppression of the most decisive attempt to reverse the defeat, the Bar Kochba uprising. As we have tried to show, the blow thus dealt to the position of the Jews and their standing among the nations had profound and far-reaching consequences. That marked the beginning of the national and social defamation of the Jews. The national breakdown produced a definitive split between Judaism and Christianity—between the Jewish people, which did not give up on itself and its national hopes for the future, and the daughter religion, which now finally turned away from Judaism and adopted a hostile stance toward it. From the fourth century on, Rome and Christianity, the two enemies of Judaism, joined forces to systematically drive the Jews out of Palestine and defame them in the Diaspora. They gave to the Jewish concept of *galut* (exile) the Christian stamp of everlasting dispersion among all nations as punishment for deicide. They created the real conditions that increasingly corresponded to this idea, and constructed the dogmatic distortion of the rejected and rejectable Jew, disseminating it among the people as a stereotype wherever their dominion extended. By the end of antiquity the non-Jews had thus created the spiritual basis (as well as the makings of the economic, legal, and social basis) for the history of the Jews in the Middle Ages as well as for the development of the Jewish question in the forms in which we know it.

Counteractions within Jewry

We must consider, however, that all this would not have happened if the Jews had given themselves up as a people and a religious community. After all, the Jewish question—that is, the problem of the life of the Jews among the nations and the interrelationship between them— was and is not determined only by these nations. Its basis was and is the Jewish people's special conception of God and the world, which an environment with different modes of faith and thought was not able to comprehend. The blessings and curses of Balaam that are reported in the Bible from the beginnings of the people of Israel—"a people that dwells apart, not reckoned among the nations" (Num. 23:9) remains characteristic of its further history as well. The Jewish question would not have arisen without this will to self-preservation, without the struggle of the Jewish people, even *after* the loss of its national political independence, with the factors threatening its religious-national existence. Like history in general, the history of the Jews and of the Jewish question is a contest between forces from without and other forces resisting from within, between inert and dynamic forces, economic factors, and cultural aspirations. It is the interweaving of all these forces and factors that produces historical reality. We must therefore ask ourselves: What reactions within Judaism were produced by the attitude of the outside world, and how did these new factors and circumstances affect the relationship of the Jews to the outside world?

The parting of Christianity from Judaism and the anti-Jewish legislation of the Christian church that had attained to political power were, of course, bound to have profound effects on the Jews.

Up to that time, and after a period of inner concentration in the fifth century B.C.E., in the era of the return from Babylonia after Ezra and Nehemiah, the Jews had proselytized among the pagans to a large extent and with great success. For example, the author of the Gospel according to St. Matthew expressly warns against the Jewish propagandists who move over the lands and the seas to make a proselyte.* A convert who assumed the obligations of the Jewish religion was accepted into the

---

*The warning taken from a speech of Jesus (Matthew 23:15) reads as follows: "Woe unto you, scribes and Pharisees, hypocrites! for ye compass sea and land to make one proselyte, and when he is made, ye make him twofold more the child of hell than yourselves!"

Jewish fold with equal rights, including marriage, and in general there was no legal distinction between him and those who belonged to the Jewish people by virtue of their descent and tradition. The expansion of the Jewish Diaspora in the first century before and after the Common Era was probably due in no small measure to the making of proselytes. At a later date the Roman ban on circumcision—first decreed even for Jews, then maintained for non-Jews—as well as numerous other anti-Jewish laws and measures after the Bar Kochba uprising combined with the opprobrium of the defeat of the prostrate people to impede proselytism and limit its success, though it was by no means abandoned. Proof of the continued appeal of Judaism are the countermeasures that Christianity found it necessary to take soon after its assumption of power. The Council decisions made from the first decades of the fourth century on in order to effectuate the complete separation between Christianity and Judaism, as well as the state laws in the spirit of these decisions, imposed severe punishments for propagandizing Judaism and in particular "seducing" Christians—that is, converting them to Judaism, something that was still feared, and evidently with justification. By virtue of the greater inducements to convert offered to the pagans by the victor's religion (as opposed to the religion of a vanquished, dispersed, powerless people), the lesser demands it made on daily living, and—when even that did not suffice—by threats of severe punishments, the Christian church achieved what the Roman swords had not attained to anything like the same extent: Large-scale Jewish proselytism was blocked in all areas of Christian rule and Christian influence.

Judaism and Islam

The same is true of the areas which Islam began to penetrate from the Arab peninsula as a religion and conquering power—from Persia and Mesopotamia to Syria and Palestine, from North Africa to Spain. This was a complex of countries and territories in which the majority of Jews lived for centuries to come.

Judaism served as the basis for Islam as it had for Christianity, albeit in a different form of reception.* The patriarchs and prophets of the Jews, particularly Abraham** and Moses, are also the patriarchs and

---

*In contrast to Christianity, Islam did not adopt the Hebrew Bible as the basic book (the Old Testament of Christianity); rather, it incorporated into the Koran figures, tales, legends, and interpretations from the Bible and other Jewish writings in the form it deemed appropriate. It continued to regard the Bible as the highly respected sacred book of the Jews, and in its eyes the Jews were the "People of the Book," which, however, did not put its doctrine into practice, as taught by Mohammed as the last successor of the prophets.

**Particular respect is enjoyed by Abraham as the father of Ishmael, from whom the Arabs regard themselves as descended. He is mentioned seventy times in thirty-five suras of the Koran (Philip K. Hitti, *Islam and the West* [1962], p. 16).

prophets of the new monotheistic religion; Mohammed, its founder and prophet, is the continuator and completer of his predecessors, among whom Jesus is counted as a prophet. And Islam joined Christianity in adopting a hostile attitude toward Judaism when the majority of the Jews with whom Mohammed and his adherents and successors came into contact refused to recognize the new doctrine as the continuation and crowning of their own and Mohammed as the creator of Islam, as the prophet and executor of the biblical prophecies.

Even though Christianity and Islam were hostile toward each other, they agreed on the principle that in the countries dominated by them only the predominant religion, the only true one, had a right to proselytize and convert those of other faiths, and this view was reflected in the religious and civil legislation. Hence Judaism was a religion permitted by law only for those born as Jews in the countries under Islamic rule as well. It was the tolerated tribal religion of the Jewish people. Here, too, conversion to the Jewish religion carried the most severe penalties for adherents of Islam, those who had been educated in the state religion. To be sure, there was a difference between Islam's attitude toward Judaism and the Christian attitude. While Islam also discriminated against the Jewish "infidels" economically and socially and often subjected them to degrading special regulations (in clothing and the like), unlike the Christian dogma Islam did not regard the Jews as deicides rejected by God and men, and Jews shared the status of second-class "infidels" with the Christians, who were regarded by Islam as equal unbelievers and often were hated more bitterly than the Jews as more powerful adversaries and thus as a more threatening danger.

The Indissoluble Connection between the Jewish Religion and the Jewish People

There is, in any case, one clear result of these developments: The domination of the two world religions nourished by Jewish thought over all countries in which Jews lived in appreciable numbers permanently blocked the path into the open of the Jewish mother religion. The strict prohibition of the two monotheistic world religions would have made large-scale conversions to Judaism of people of other faiths impossible even if Judaism had aspired to do this. This meant that Judaism as a religion and Jewry as an ethnic entity indissolubly coalesced with each other because of pressure from without as well. Hence it mattered even less than before whether or not they were referred to as a religious community or as a people, a nation, as documents of the time usually did. One was no longer conceivable without the other, and it is only a question of terminology and semantics, or religious or legal logic, or of the purpose inherent in the choice of words whether henceforth one term or the other was used.

Development of the Jewish "Racial Type"

More than that, this blockage of Judaism from the influx of ethnically alien elements significantly strengthened the homogeneity of the Jewish national character (we shall not use the dubious term "racial character" that was created in the nineteenth century), though this blockage was never so complete that blood mixtures did not take place on a smaller or larger scale. After all, nature always asserts itself, and at least in bad times—rather than in times of peace and harmony—attacks and rapes produced an infusion of some alien blood into the Jewish body politic. Despite all prohibitions there were at all times conversions to Judaism, though not to any great extent. Along with the influence of climate and life-style, this explains the development of special Jewish types in the large areas of Jewish mass settlement where the Jewish population was always bent on inbreeding (termed *Engzuchtgebiete*, endogamous areas, by Ruppin)—such as the Babylonian-oriental type in Babylon from the seventh to the eleventh centuries, the Sephardic type from the eleventh to the fifteenth centuries in Spain and North Africa, and the Ashkenazic-East European type that developed between the twelfth and the sixteenth centuries from the convergence in Poland of the Jewish migratory streams from the West and the East.

Influence of the Talmud

In the succeeding centuries the Babylonian Talmud, which had been completed around 500, became a guide for the people who had been herded together by their environment and were united by shared memories of their past and a hallowed tradition, people of the same type and nature who were bound together by a shared fate in the present and the same Messianically tinged hope for a better future. Its influence intensified the tendency toward an increasingly uniform development of the national character by seeking to approximate each individual to the national-religious Jewish ideal type, by popularizing these teachings, and especially by the precise regulation of daily life in the spirit of these teachings. To be sure, the "fence around the Torah" erected by the Talmud was not tantamount to the blockage of Jewry from all non-Jewish secular knowledge, at least not in periods when the national power was still unbroken. But the barriers did bring it about that alien elements were assimilated to the Jewish core rather than Judaism being absorbed by alien elements, as happened at the time of Hellenism and even more markedly from the nineteenth century on.

Here, too the Talmud served as a kind of substitute for a normal national life based on a territory. Complete assimilation to the language and culture of the surrounding world with partial abandonment of

Hebrew even in the religious services, as happened in the Hellenic period, was unthinkable under the new conditions. To be sure, even now the vernacular was adopted for everyday purposes both in religious and secular writings (particularly in the Arabic sphere of influence), and it was only natural that along with the language and daily intercourse quite a bit of the surrounding culture entered the Jewish realm, often enriching and fructifying it. But at the same time there was a renascence of Hebrew as the exclusive language of prayer and in the widest measure also as the official language of justice and all internal affairs of the Jewish community (to the extent that they were subject to the ever-maintained Jewish communal autonomy). These bonds of a religious-national and traditional-customary nature were so firm, and faith in them and their unbreakableness was so deep, that even after forced conversions to the dominant religion of a country thousands still clung to the old, familiar customs and continued to practice them secretly, living on as pseudo-Christians or pseudo-Mohammedans—from the time of the Visigoths in Spain in the seventh century to the centuries of the Inquisition (not to mention the Communist state ideologies of our days). There developed that loyalty of the Jews to Judaism that was woven of many strands and made them prefer being burned at the stake and committing suicide "for the sanctification of the Holy Name" to conversion to Christianity and the betrayal of the past and the future—that often almost pathological fanaticism of faith and creed that, strangely enough, remained incomprehensible to the Christian-European world, with its glorification of its own martyrs to the point of worship and even appeared as blasphemous obstinacy to Christians, hence exacerbating their dislike and hatred of the Jews.

Added to these conflicts deriving from the religious sphere as well as the national sphere connected with it were now economic factors, some of which were fed from the same roots but later worked independently as additional factors exacerbating the relationship between the Jews and the surrounding world. We shall next have to concern ourselves with the ways in which these disparate elements combined in the Middle Ages and influenced the development of the Jewish question.

3

The Development of the Jewish Question
in the Christian-European Middle Ages

Time and Place

When we speak of the Jewish question in the Middle Ages,* we usually mean its development in Western and Central Europe from about the tenth century on, for this is the geographical and temporal site of events and developments that have shaped the modern Jewish question. This epoch was preceded by a transitional period that German historians generally refer to as the Early Middle Ages and Anglo-Americans as the Dark Ages. We regard it as dark primarily because of the lack of reliable and continuous sources—generally and for Jewish history in particular, and this is why it poses problems for our investigation.** It is safe to say, however, that in the first centuries of this transitional period from ancient times to the rise of the modern western world the majority of the Jews were still living in the East, in Asia and North Africa, in the Christian-Byzantine (Eastern Roman) empire, and in the Islamic empires that spread vigorously from Arabia and were far superior to metamorphosing Christian Europe in civilization and culture. Between eighth and twelfth centuries, however, there occurred a complete shift of Jewish settlement from East to West, from Asia to Europe, though it is impossible for us to trace the detailed course of this movement. The only certain thing is that from the twelfth century, the majority of the Jewish people lived and worked in Christian Europe, and since the second half of the nineteenth century, more and more worked in Christian America as well. This is where the economic, social, religious, and intellectual battles were fought and the achievements were produced that henceforth determined the existence and the image of the Jews in the surrounding world. As Central and Western Europe, in antiquity only an

*See Part 2 for a discussion of the concept "Middle Ages" in the periodization of general and Jewish history and of its use in our presentation.
**We shall have more to say about all decisive events of this transitional period at points where their influence on later developments in the Jewish question in the European-Christian world can be discerned and ascertained.

84

unknown "barbaric" appendage to the Mediterranean world and the Afro-Asian empires, moved into the center of the political, economic, and cultural world and became the dominant historical power, so did the Jews and the Jewish question in this geographic-historical area.

Economy and Society As Viewed in the Middle Ages

If we want to understand the economic and legal-social position of the Jews in the Middle Ages, we must abandon certain views that have developed in the course of recent centuries, particularly the nineteenth century. Our modern world has divided human life and activity in the state and society into various distinct spheres. The economy, the legal system, religion, ethics, science, art, literature, and so forth—today these are distinct, more or less autonomous fields in which input from other spheres is not automatically recognized. It was different in the Christian Middle Ages up to the Reformation, and to a certain extent far beyond that. That world and society were essentially shaped by religious belief.* As late as the Renaissance, before the secularization of political and economic thought began and gradually prevailed in the course of the following two centuries, there basically were no separate spheres of life and of thought. Economics was regarded as part of ethics and ethics as part of theology. The Church, that embodiment of divine will and divine dominion on earth, controlled—at least theoretically—the view of the economy and society, and of right and wrong in all areas. The more the views and the power of the Church prevailed in political life, the more far-reaching did its influence on the economic thought of the nations become.

In that world of the Middle Ages earthly things were not separated from divine matters, and the divine was not sundered from the Satanic, the demonic. Everything was simultaneous reality—the earthly, primitive, crude, and cruel as well as the heavenly and demonic.

Immigration of the Jews into Christian Europe

The Jews now increasingly came into this European world of transformations, migrations, and conquests of tribes and peoples, of the downfall and reconstruction of states and empires, of the spread of Christianity (and at first of Islam as well) in changing versions, interpretations, and combinations of power. In general they came from afar across the Mediterranean, the Alps and Pyrenees, along the old trade routes and rivers through the valleys of the Rhone, the Rhine, and the

---

*In this the Moslem world was not essentially different from the Christian world. In fact, this medieval view remained valid in the Islamic realm down to modern times.

Danube. Even in antiquity there had been significant European Jewish settlements in the areas of Hellenic influence and particularly of the Roman Empire—in Greece and the Aegean islands, Italy and Spain, in the Roman colonial cities on the Rhine, and in Southern France. However, a very considerable part of these settlements had foundered in the early Middle Ages and been rendered insignificant after the irruption of conquering, destructive hordes or because of forced conversions by the pagan peoples, themselves recently converted to Christianity and thus particularly radical in their religious zeal. This is what happened in the seventh century in the Spain of the Visigoths, and it was similar in France, Northern Italy, and presumably in other places as well. Thus a very considerable part of the Jewish settlements that we find in Christian Europe from the tenth century on probably came into being through immigration, and these were founded by Jews who came from distant foreign countries: Catholic Spain, the areas of Eastern Roman-Byzantine and especially Islamic domination and culture—a world regarded by the Christian Europe of the early Middle Ages as surrounded by an aura of the strange, uncanny, alien, and hostile.

Modes of Jewish Settlement

As descendants of an ancient people with the knowledge and the memory as well as the spiritual and practical experience of a people that had absorbed the accomplishments of historical, highly developed civilized areas, the Jews spread among the young peoples of Europe. As a guide they had a sacred book of their teachings and history, and this book constantly kept alive in them the consciousness of their being different—"a people that dwells alone"—and with its interpretations and elaborations shaped their lives down to the daily details. They did not come with the deliberate intention of remaining strangers. On the contrary; despite all those memories that continued to be alive in them, despite the deviant religious-traditional customs and usages that, as it were, confined them to a territory of their own, they endeavored to integrate themselves economically and culturally into the life of their countries of domicile. However, religion and customs—their own as well as those of the world around them—did not permit full integration. Their way of life did not comport with the regulations of the other existing societies. This singularity in a world that was different was the Jews' fate—and their guilt in the eyes of the ever more conformist populations among which they lived.

After all, unlike members of other nations, the Jews did not come as conquerors and colonizers bent on transforming a foreign country into their own; they were not leaving a fatherland to which they could return at any time. True, inwardly they did not abandon Palestine, which they regarded as their religious home in the present and as their actual home in the near or distant future. This relationship to Palestine as their real homeland prevented them from fully regarding the new countries of settlement as their new home and a complete substitute for Palestine. At the same time, however, this old homeland was able to offer them only spiritual support and not the actual, truly potent kind that a homeland normally offers a migrant or a settler. There was thus no state or political center to guide the Jews' steps, support them, and direct them to concerted action. They came as individuals. To be sure, they generally settled in smaller or larger groups and lived in close proximity to one another on one street or in one section of town; like all strangers, they felt more at home and more sheltered in the vicinity of their fellow Jews. An additional factor was that this was the only way for them to preserve their religious services, which were based on communal prayer. Only in this way were they able to make it possible for their children to learn their religion in school, something that was of the greatest importance to them, to develop their religious-national autonomy, and to keep in force their Biblical-Talmudic laws which always kept alive the memory of their national life in Palestine. They had their own laws and courts based on the Bible and the Talmud, and for both the sacred and the profane (to the extent that the latter concerned justice and social life) they had their own language, Hebrew. All this, however, they regarded as applicable only to themselves, and they had no desire to force it upon their non-Jewish environment (though conversions to their religion never completely ceased) or the slightest ambition to dominate their environment economically, ethnically, or linguistically, or to make it conform with their practices. The Jews founded settlements, but these invariably were only an appendage to the settlements of others rather than independent nuclei and centers of more extensive colonization. Yeheskel Kaufmann has called this kind of Jewish settlement "ghetto colonization." And one thing at least is clear: this mode of settlement of the Jews laid the foundation for their later forcible confinement in ghettos.

This Jewish style of settlement reflected the fact that they were settling as strangers. As with the other aspects of the Jewish question, it is not important to determine whether the Jews were always and everywhere regarded as aliens, formally and legally; we shall deal with this later. From the viewpoint of national psychology, they were definitely strangers—both in their own consciousness and in that of the nations. To his non-Jewish environment a Jew appeared as an alien in many respects: on the basis of his religion, as a member of an alien tribe and people, and as an alien as far as his right (or, rather, his lack thereof) to the land on which he settled was concerned. All peoples of the earth who adopted the Bible as the foundation of their religion always regarded the Jews as really being at home in Palestine, a country from which they had been expelled, and currently staying in alien lands as aliens. The teaching of the Christian Church, and the belief of the people, that this loss of their own home was a punishment for the nonrecognition and murder of the Savior added an uncanny element to this foreignness. And in certain places this could all too readily lead to the suspicion that the Jews were even now in league with the enemies of the Christians, with the adherents of Islam (ever more widely known as "Saracens") from whose territory most of them had come and with whom they continued to have trade relations.

Basically, the Jews viewed themselves in a similar light. Even in the Middle Ages they might in everyday parlance describe countries and cities in which they had lived for a long time, sometimes generations, as their home; they might feel inwardly close to their countries of domicile and speak their languages in everyday life. In the final analysis, however, their country of residence remained the country of others. It was possible for the Jews to settle down in some fashion, to have offspring, earn a living, become prosperous, set up places of worship and cultural institutions, and adopt many customs and practices from the neighboring world. Yet they never forgot that they were not really living on their own soil even if they had acquired it by purchase. Even in times of outward well-being it remained alien soil in the national consciousness, at best good till the arrival of the Messiah who would gather the Jews from all ends of the earth and lead them back to their land.

This socio-psychological foreignness and otherness was now intensified by the economic function of the Jews in medieval Europe. In a world in which the majority of the population lived in the country and was bound up with the ownership of land and the tilling of the soil, the Jews appeared as city-dwellers, as merchants, as dealers in merchandise and later in money. How did this come about?

Displacement of the Jews from Rural Areas

By the first centuries of transition to the Middle Ages there probably was no substantial difference in occupational categories between the Jews and the nations among which they lived. They were farmers cultivating the soil, as they had done in their State; they were artisans, and in the upper classes merchants as well. Their tendency toward commerce may have increased with the expansion of the Diaspora, but the Jews certainly did not occupy an unusual position as tradesmen in the economy of waning antiquity. A number of circumstances had to combine to push the Jews into a special occupational position among the western peoples.

The first stage in this development was the increasing displacement of the Jews from agriculture and land ownership. As already stated, in

Palestine this was done by a systematic policy of the Byzantine emperors and the Christian Church, a policy that was then continued by the Arabic conquerors. In the countries of the Diaspora the main factor was the anti-Jewish legislation enacted by the Roman emperors under the influence of the Church and embodied in the codes of Theodosius and Justinian. These laws excluded the Jews from engaging in certain professions (e.g., military and civil service), especially those involving a greater measure of prestige and authority. For dogmatic reasons the members of the people accursed by God were to be prevented from rising above Christians, God's faithful servants, let alone dominating them. For the same reasons the Jews were prohibited from owning Christian slaves; pagan slaves who converted to Christianity had to be freed by the Jews, with or without compensation. In antiquity and the early Middle Ages, however, agriculture was almost entirely carried on with slave labor, for otherwise the ownership and cultivation of larger tracts of land were not profitable. After all, in those days slaves had the same function as machines in the modern world. This discrimination was bound to cause the Jews to abandon agricultural work to an ever-increasing extent.

There were other factors as well. In the new barbarian states of Europe the laws permitted land ownership only to members of the indigenous ethnic group, excluding the Jews as members of an alien tribe. The displacement of the Jews was intensified with the rise and development of feudalism in the medieval European economy and society, for now a Christian oath of fealty was required for the acceptance of a fief, and of course a Jew could not take such an oath. Then, too, the unsafety of remote farmsteads and the difficulty of practicing the communal religious customs in isolated rural life increasingly caused the Jews to leave the country and move to the cities. This tendency was, of course, intensified when persecution became rampant. A person could have no interest in hard-to-sell immovable property when he could at any time be confronted with the necessity to leave the place and the country. Nevertheless, until well into the Middle Ages there still were Jews in rural settlements, and even beyond the period of the Crusades Jews owned lands, vineyards, and fields here or there in the small country towns and even cultivated them; our chief source for this is the Responsa. The overwhelming majority of the Jews, however, were concentrated in the cities, and to an ever-increasing extent the Jews became a people of city-dwellers.

Jews and Trade

As city-dwellers the Jews mainly turned to trade, but certainly not exclusively so. In many places, particularly the East, the Jews worked as artisans in substantial numbers. In the upper classes there were not a few who made a name for themselves as physicians, but the Jews' share in trade became ever more significant. People have tried to attribute the Jews' active participation in trade to a racial characteristic of theirs, to their natural disposition toward trade and the excessive development of their intellect by their laws and the concomitant discussions of Talmudic literature. Jews have frequently countered such arguments, which have been adduced mostly by non-Jews, particularly the German sociologist Werner Sombart, by saying that their occupation with trade was caused less by their disposition than by the force of circumstances. It is probably safe to say that, viewed in isolation, neither argument does justice to the historical truth, and these views have frequently been influenced by anti-Jewish or anticapitalistic valuations, or else by pro-Jewish apologetics. If the Jews had been able to continue living as a normal people on their own soil, everything we know about their history before the destruction of their State leads us to assume that they would not have developed into a people of tradesmen, even though surely part of the population always took advantage of the location of the country on the route from Africa to Asia, with its natural incentive to trading. In ancient times Asian trade was primarily in the hands of the "coastal peoples," the Greeks, Syrians, and Phoenicians. On the other hand, the Jews' greater age as a civilized nation, their experience in various countries and under various cultures, and their intellectual acuity and alertness shaped by centuries of persecution and mental concentration gave them an advantage over the peoples of Europe with less history. Added to this were their life in the Byzantine and Islamic realm with a highly developed urban culture and an appreciation of trade, as well as their knowledge of foreign languages and of Hebrew as a language of contact with the Jews in other countries. Without these actualities the Jews might have sought and found other ways out of their difficult situation, but as things were, activity as dealers necessarily presented itself to them as an appropriate occupation in the early medieval world.

In that world, which had for centuries regressed almost completely from the highly developed money economy of antiquity to the stage of a household and barter economy, the Jews filled a place that others had not been able to occupy. Despite the odium that attached to them, this was the basis for their acceptance in the various countries. They were the logical mediators, particularly in the Mediterranean region, which with the spread of anti-Christian Islam was for some centuries virtually closed to Christian merchants, at least in its Islamic part. Thus until around the middle of the tenth century the trade from Europe to the Orient and from the Orient to Europe was in the hands of Jewish merchants—not exclusively, but to a great extent. In those centuries trade was so closely connected with the life of the Jews, at least in the eyes of the environment, that in the documents of the time the terms *Judaei* and *mercatores* were used all but synonymously. The caravans of Jewish merchants, who were called Radanites, brought to Europe particularly Oriental spices and delicacies; from Eastern Europe they exported to the Orient slaves and furs, from Western Europe silk and arms. They filled a gap in European economic life, but the products that they brought to Europe were designed more for the upper classes and the Church's need for luxuries than for the people in general.

If the Jews occupied a special position among the population of the European countries as merchants and dealers, the people were again struck primarily by the special nature of the Jews, their deviation from the life-style of the others, and at the same time the great profits that accrued to them from their commercial activities. Their usefulness to the national economy remained concealed, however, because they benefited only a small part of the population.

Around the turn from the tenth to the eleventh centuries the burgeoning Italian cities successfully challenged the Saracens' sovereignty over the sea routes in the western Mediterranean. As a consequence the Jews increasingly lost their preferential position as commercial mediators between East and West. Now that this great earning opportunity attracted competitors—first the Upper Italian cities, later the burgeoning German ones—it became obvious how precarious the situation of the Jews vis-à-vis these non-Jewish merchants was. Behind the non-Jewish competitors was the power of the city or the state, as well as customs and society. The non-Jewish merchants were *eo ipso* regarded as privileged, and indeed as the only legitimate ones. Those who were powerful enough managed with the aid of the state and the Church to shake off the burdensome competitors and bar them from trade routes and means of transportation. In this competition there was handy ammunition: the arguments transmitted by the Church and long since hallowed by convention against the reprobate people of deicides that must not be helped to augment its property and its influence. As happened so often before and since, it was easy to establish a close connection between religion and economic competition.

People were free to do so, for as is generally known, there was no state, no city, and no organized church behind the Jews. They were weak, and hence there was no need to be considerate of them—unless they happened to be needed. For example, in 945 Arso Participazio, the Doge of Venice, was able to prohibit seafarers without any fear of countermeasures from taking Jewish tradesmen on board. Similarly, a Venetian law of 960 was able to bar slaves belonging to Jews from being transported on Venetian ships, and in 992 the Byzantine emperors Basilius and Constantine granted the Venetians special privileges on condition that they did not transport Jewish merchandise on their ships.

The Role of the Jews in the Non-Jewish Economy

Thus the Jews were forced out of direct wholesale trading across the Mediterranean. They had to buy oriental goods from the Italians or find new trade routes, such as that leading via Germany and the Slavic countries to the Caspian Sea and from there to Central Asia. Again and again the Jews had to find a gap in economic life that had not yet been filled by the natives and privileged ones, that had not yet been blocked by society, the state, and the Church. Thus they always filled a gap in the economy of a country. The very fact that they were accepted and tolerated as aliens and non-Christians is proof that in the eyes of the ruling class they fulfilled an important function. One does not take in a stranger if he does not prove useful, and surely this was true of the Jews in the Christian society of the Middle Ages. If the Jews had been only "parasites," as they were later described by their enemies, they would surely not have been admitted everywhere and provided with special privileges for carrying on their trading activities.

But since a Jew is an alien and never loses this status in the consciousness of the people and the powers that be, he is tolerated in his position in the economy only for as long as he is truly indispensable to it. His very success creates competitors who, as is only natural, envy him his good earnings and big profits and by virtue of their more "indigenous" privilege and power push him from a secure position into an insecure one. Thus the Jews gradually declined in the economic scale and at the same time in social standing. As in wartime, in an economic power struggle the weaker and the vanquished must endure, in addition to the defeat, the dislike and contempt of the victor and all those who adhere to him and serve him.

Economic Decline

Since we are not writing the history and economic history of the Jews, we can refrain from describing this decline in all its stages and varieties depending on the time, the degree, the situation, and the developmental stages of the economy and society in the various countries, states, and cities. Here we can be concerned only with showing the *typical* development and its consequences for the position of the Jews in the world around them.

In the course of this development in Europe, particularly in Central and Western Europe, the Jews' sphere of activity was progressively narrowed. They were increasingly crowded out of overseas trade and limited to domestic trade, but with the rise of the European cities after the eleventh century they were cut off from this occupation as well. The guild system that developed there and in which there was legal room only for natives and those of the true Christian faith largely kept the Jews from engaging in those skilled trades that were designed not only for Jewish needs. Then, too, the merchants banded together in guilds and trading companies from which the Jews were barred as non-Christians and aliens and with which the Jews could not compete in the long run.

The activity of the Jews in trading in goods had always been combined to a certain extent with trading in money—in the form of credit, the participation of foreign capital in certain commercial transactions, the lending of money to princes and cities, etc. With the development outlined above Jewish trading activities increasingly turned away from merchandise and to financial transactions (with or without pawnbroking).

The high point and turning point of this development was reached with the Crusades. They brought to light the problems of Jewish life among the nations that we call the Jewish question, with all their complex manifestations, expressions, and effects, and they clearly mark the downward direction of the further development of these problems in the Middle Ages.

The Crusades

The collective term *Crusades* is generally used to designate the martial enterprises that were carried on as "holy wars" by European Christianity from the end of the eleventh century (1096) to the late thirteenth (1270) for the conquest of Palestine as the "Holy Land" of Christendom. The cross as the religious symbol of Christianity was to be restored to power in Jerusalem, where Jesus had taught and suffered, and serve also to symbolize the victory of the only legitimate faith over all non-Christian infidelity. Contemporaries at first regarded the Crusade movement as a continuation of the pious pilgrimages to the Holy Land and described the crusaders as pilgrims, as they did the medieval fighters who later determined the character and the actions of the seven organized Crusades. When Pope Urban II, formerly a monk and abbot in the French monastery of Cluny, the center of the Christian movement of regeneration against the secularization of the Church, issued a call for the First Crusade at Clermont in 1095, he regarded it as the fulfillment of God's desire *("deus lo vult")* to raise Christianity to domination over the infidels and bring about the reunification of the Roman-Latin Christians of Europe with the Byzantine-Greek Church of the Near East. After all, emperors and patriarchs of Constantinople had turned to him for aid against the advance of the conquering Turkish-Islamic Seljuks.

As happens with all religious and political movements, all sorts of motives, tendencies, and interests, often antithetical in nature, mingled with this Christian religious movement. From the outset, and to an ever-increasing extent, economic-political endeavors as well as all longings and desires of the contemporaries were added to the ecclesiastic-religious impetus. With its endeavors to organize the Crusades, the Church not only pursued aims in the distant Orient, but also strove to strengthen its power over the faithful both in the struggle against unbelief and heresy and the fight for hegemony over the state, emperors, and princes. As for the Crusaders, they were impelled to participate in the Crusades by a great variety of motives: religious fanaticism and altogether secular adventurism, striving for spiritual atonement (promised by the Church as a reward), and a desire for material disencumbrance (starting with the Second Crusade, loans did not have to be repaid, nor interest paid on them, for the duration). To the great trading cities of Italy, headed by Venice, and to the great merchants there beckoned profit from the Mediterranean trade, now forcibly placed in European hands, and the knights and princes looked forward to the spoils of victory and the rule over conquered areas in Palestine and Syria. For many participants in the Crusades it was an escape from the confining European country life to the legendary spaciousness and fullness of the Orient, an escape from the strict discipline of the laws and customs of their own country to an untrammeled life and a less inhibited indulgence of their drives and desires.

At first the movement had nothing to do with the Jews; the Holy Sepulchre in Jerusalem was to be wrested away from Islam, not from the Jews. But since the Jews occupied a central place in the religious philosophy of Christendom, since they were present everywhere and played a visible and perceptible role in the economic life as tradesmen, property owners, and money-lenders, various tendencies, endeavors, and aims of the movement (as of many earlier and later religious and political movements) were all too apt to redound to the Jews' disadvantage, and they did in fact have a deleterious effect on them.

From the outset, the religious zeal stirred up to fever heat was disastrous for the Jews. The Christian Church's doctrine that the Jews were deicides had been sown into believing hearts for a millenium, and now it bore bloody fruit. On 15 July 1099, when after a short siege the Christian Crusaders from Franconia entered Jerusalem as conquerors through the Jewish quarter (which defended itself), their fighting and religious fury were directed not only against the Islamic population; the Jews also were its victims, being killed or sold into slavery. In his book on the Roman popes Leopold Ranke described this strange mixture of faith and cruelty as follows: "When they caught sight of Jerusalem the Crusaders dismounted and bared their feet in order to arrive at the sacred walls as true pilgrims; in the fiercest fight they thought they experienced the help of the saints and the angels in visible form. No sooner had they scaled the walls, however, than they rushed off to pillage and kill. At the site of Solomon's Temple they strangled many thousands of Saracens, and they burned the Jews in their synagogue. . . ."

But it is understandable that the religious zeal, once stirred up, did not wait for a chance to vent itself at the destination of the Crusades—legally, as it were. Actually, it was only logical to proceed against the infidels in their own countries and on the way to the Holy Land. The foreignness of the Jews, their isolation from the Christian population by virtue of their religion, way of life, dwelling, and to a great extent their activities as well—all this suddenly was seen in a new and clearer light. For Christian religious fanatics this was the varied expression of the one basic fact, the one original guilt: the Jews' murder of Christ and their accursedness as deicides.

The Persecution of the Jews in Europe

The persecution of Jews in Europe nearly coincided with the beginning of the Crusades, and on a scale unprecedented for centuries. To be sure, there had been violence against Jews prior to the Crusades, but apart from those by the Visigoths in Spain centuries previously, these persecutions had been aimed at individual Jews or Jewish communities. To be sure, the degradation of the Jews by the Church had weakened people's moral consciousness toward the Jews before the Crusades. For example, as early as the beginning of the tenth century a Council in Mainz had to impress upon the faithful that killing a Jew was also murder and not a minor offense. In general, however, the relationship of the Jews to the non-Jews was a peaceful one, at least in the cities. For the most part, the Jews still felt so secure at the beginning of the First Crusade that they could not believe any harm would come to them. When the French Jewish communities, in whose vicinity the Crusade movement and with it the persecution of the Jews (Rouen, Metz) began, appealed to the Jews in the Rhineland, described how they were threatened by the Crusaders, and asked them to fast for their brethren in France, the Mainz Jews replied that all Rhenish communities had arranged a fast for their French brethren, about whose fate they were greatly concerned, and that they wanted to help in any way they could, but they did not have the least reason to fear for their own safety and had not even heard any rumors about any threatening misfortune.

It is a strange phenomenon that almost all periods of great violence, at least since the Middle Ages, have caught the Jews by surprise and found them unprepared. Generally speaking, the persecutions began with particular severity and intensity especially when Jews believed their position was so secure and their relationship to their environment so well ordered that there was no thought of attacks and major violence—at least not in *their* country, *their* house. The Jews of Mainz in 1096 are only a first example; fifty years later, during the Second Crusade, the Jews of Würzburg acted the same way, and so did the Jews in many other countries at later dates: the Polish Jews in the face of Chmielnicki's onslaught in 1648–49, the Russian Jews during the pogroms of 1881, the German Jews in 1933, and all of European Jewry in the years 1940 to 1944. Precisely those involved have never believed that they were in imminent danger. At all times there prevailed a strange feeling of safety that must almost be called frivolous, a feeling born of an optimism that cannot believe in evil because this evil runs counter to everything on which according to Jewish beliefs the world and the fate of the Jews are founded. Faith in the eternal existence of the Jewish people and its chosenness for the future of the world probably is part of it. This optimism, which often seems incomprehensible and arrogant and is blind to the threatening danger, has cost the Jewish people many victims in its procession through the centuries, but in critical times it probably preserved the people from the despair to which it could otherwise easily have fallen prey.

Thus the disaster of the Crusades caught Western and Central European Jewry by surprise. Thousands of Jews became victims of the mass murders in the countries participating in the crusading movement and in the areas through which the fanatical crusaders, composed of all sorts of people, passed. Numerous important communities, particularly in France, the Rhineland, Southern Germany, and Bohemia, were destroyed. Jewish blood marked the paths of the crusaders, particularly during the First Crusade, but to a considerable extent in the two following ones as well. The persecution and murder of Jews became a general Christian-European phenomenon.

The Consequences of the Crusades for the Jewish Question

Two consequences of the Crusades affected the development of the Jewish question. Jerusalem and Palestine as the seat of a numerically and intellectually significant Jewish *yishuv* were eliminated from the actual life of the Jews for centuries; Palestine remained the land of longing, but an increasingly distant and unreal longing. At the same time the economic foundations of Jewish life were profoundly shaken in the countries of the European Diaspora as well—more accurately, not only the basis of the Jews' economic existence but the very foundation of their lives.

For the destruction of many Jewish communities had more far-reaching effects. Even when after the Crusades those who had escaped the persecutions returned to their home communities and rebuilt them, or when they settled in different places, this did not mean a restoration of the earlier situation. There had been one decisive change since the events of the First Crusade among Jews as well as non-Jews: In most countries of Europe, and for centuries to come, a Jew could no longer feel really secure.

At first this was most evident in a Jew's economic activity. Considering the constant threat of despoilment, expulsion from his domicile, and perhaps even murder, not to mention the unsafe trade routes, it was only natural that Jews increasingly turned away from trading in merchandise, more and more the domain of Christian merchants, and engaged in financial transactions, something that could be done without constantly making long journeys. The accumulation of wealth in money and jewels was the only means of averting threatening dangers through the payment of "fines" (which were really blackmail). Often persecutions were staged under religious and other pretexts only to make the Jews ransom themselves from threatening peril. Money and valuables could also be taken along more easily when the Jews were forced to leave their residences hastily in the face of threatening danger. Thus the development from trading in goods to trading in money that had already started now continued in intensified form under the influence of the Crusades.

The economic development of Europe also pushed the Jews in that direction. The flourishing of the Christian Mediterranean trade, which was in part a corollary and permanent result of the Crusades, as well as the rise of the cities with their native merchants, meant that one could do without the Jews in the merchandise trade; there they were only unnecessary and burdensome competitors of the local, native, orthodox merchants. On the other hand, in the money-poor economy of the time, which increasingly developed from a static one based on autarkic principles and payment in kind into an economy based on money and commerce, the position of the Jews as financiers became important. Once again they had to fulfill an economic function that was only inadequately perceived by others but gave them a new *raison d'être* in the altered economic system of the time. This existence, however, was at all times a precarious one, and it had profound consequences for the position of the Jews in the world around them and for their environment's evaluation of them.

The Development of the Image of the "Typical" Jew

As it was, the Crusades brought about a change in the non-Jewish world's attitude toward the Jews. Christian Europe became more "Jew-conscious" than it had previously been; the existence of the Jews impinged upon the consciousness of their surroundings more strongly. Even before the Crusades the Church had disseminated in words and

pictures the Christian-dogmatic image of the Jews as deicides and reprobates. Now the Christian propaganda in connection with the Crusades
disseminated it ever more widely among the people, and the experiences of the time gave it even more real form and tangible substance. In
their struggle against the unbelievers the people saw the real-life Jew
ever more graphically as the prototype of the misbeliever and even of the
anti-Christian, the murderer of the Christian God, the person "cast out"
in every respect. It was no accident that at that time, from the middle of
the twelfth century on, the legends of Jewish ritual murder were created
and given credence. The image of the Jews became so closely interwoven with the idea of the Christian God's murder that people's imagination easily developed this notion to the point where the yearly
murder of Christians became a ritual necessity. Starting with the middle
of the thirteenth century this led to the accusation of the infamous
desecration of the Host, no matter how illogical the idea that the Jews,
whose biblical precepts forbade even the consumption of animal blood,
should use human blood for their matzos, or that they, who as non-
Christians did not believe in the holiness or miraculous powers of the
Host, should want to make Christ's body bleed and suffer again by
desecrating and injuring these Hosts. But logic was not something one
could expect of that religiously roiled time—and of course even less a
scientific explanation of the red spots on the consecrated wafers that
were caused by a bacterium, the so-called *bacillus prodigiosus*.

This notion of the reprobate Jew now increasingly combined with the
image of the Jew as money-lender and usurer. This image, too, had
really been prefigured in the dogmas. Had Jesus not driven the Jewish
money-changers out of the Temple (Matthew 21:12–13, John 2:13ff.),
had Judas not betrayed the Savior for thirty pieces of silver (Matthew
26:15)? It was easy to see a prototype in this despicable money-Jew
when the Jew whom one met every day really concerned himself mainly
with financial dealings.

Money-Lending and Usury in the Economic System of the Middle Ages

This image of the Jew as money-lender and usurer has actually survived among the people to this day, for among the plain people a stigma
attaches to the occupation of someone who lends money at interest, even
if this interest is moderate. A farmer or workingman who lives by the
labor of his hands always feels that a money-lender collects money to
which he has no right, that he derives profit from the toil of others
without working himself. If such a climate of opinion and sentiment
against money-lending and interest are still common among the people
at a time of a highly developed money economy and an economic science

in which a credit system and payment of interest occupy a central place, one can imagine what great animosity it evoked in the Middle Ages. For in that age credit was not organically integrated into the economic system, and in medieval economics, which was dominated by Christian dogma, there was no room for money-lending at interest—more accurately, no legal place. This economic system, whose theory derived from natural law and the idea of "fair price," did not recognize any justification for interest on credit, even if this credit was given for economic purposes and helped to produce profits. It did approve of financial investment with a share in the profits and risks of the enterprise; in fact, many loans took this form in an effort to circumvent existing prohibitions. Loans to needy persons were, in accordance with the Christian view, subsumed under the concept of *caritas;* they were charitable deeds that carried their own reward and could be rewarded by God with well-being in this world and in the next, but they must not be degraded to a business or the exploitation of one's neighbor's need for one's own profit. Profit cannot accrue from money but only from honest work; interest is a dishonest gain, a kind of payment for time that is deemed to be not for sale.

These ethical principles, however, were in conflict with the demands of the developing economy. In this burgeoning European economy, which was given a strong impetus by the Crusades, money was needed in all strata and occupations. A farmer needed it in years of crop failure, when his masters, both ecclesiastic and secular, mercilessly demanded their tithe, regardless of ethical postulates. An artisan often lacked ready money for the purchase of raw materials. A merchant in the city needed money for his profit-bearing enterprises. A nobleman or a knight needed money to equip himself for a fight that promised rich booty if successful. Finally, in largest measure money was needed by the potentates who did not regularly receive from any system of taxation and administration, no matter how well developed, sufficient income for the upkeep of their courts and for extraordinary enterprises. Money was indispensable for all branches of the economy, but it circulated only in relatively small quantities. Loans were needed and utilized by all circles, but generally in exceptional cases and for special expenditures. The regular credit system had no natural place in the economic system and was not recognized as a need. This is why the Church strictly adhered to its negative attitude toward loans and interest and through a series of Council decisions impressed upon the faithful this prohibition, which of course was constantly violated even by ecclesiastical institutions out of economic necessity.

In line with its condemnation of any profit from money-lending the Church regarded all interest as usury, that is, illicit gain, Whenever medieval people spoke of interest, particularly the demand for interest, they used the expression "usury," no matter what the interest rate might be. There was no word for interest on money; the German word *Zins* (from Latin *census*) originally designated only payment for services, dwellings, plots of land, etc.* Anyone who lent money at interest was thus a usurer, no matter whether he took moderate or high interest. Since a usurer was violating the prohibitions of God and the Church, he placed himself outside the ecclesiastic-human community. He might become rich, but the Church and society regarded his wealth as unlawfully acquired, "shady," a gift from Satan. Actually, this is how even a Christian usurer viewed it when he looked back on his life.

The Church based its prohibition of usury on the Gospel according to St. Luke (6:35), Aristotle's *Politics* (1. 10. 1258b), and particularly on the well-known passages in the Bible (Exodus 22:2; Lev. 25:35–37; Deut. 23:20–21). In accordance with the often-quoted passage from Deuteronomy, taking interest from one's brother, one's fellow countryman, was forbidden, but it was allowed from a foreigner. As the Church interpreted this verse, Christians were prohibited from charging interest, but Jews were permitted to do so. This represented a way out of the conflict between the ethical doctrine and the requirements of an unethical reality. There was no need to rescind the condemnation of usury if this usury was practiced only by Jews, who were in any case outside the Christian community. On the contrary, this role of the Jew as the executor of proscribed actions that were prohibited and accursed by God and by his representative, the Church, comported quite well with the task that according to Church doctrine a Jew performed: By performing it the demand acquired ever new damnation.

The Jew as Usurer

Thus the Jews were assigned the position of money-lenders and "usurers" by the economy on the one hand and the Church on the other. The fact that they were tolerated and even encouraged in this occupation indicates that they were needed to fulfill an economic function and also that they were outside the Christian society. This once again documented and emphasized that they were outsiders and as aliens subject to other orders and laws. Disregarding for the moment the legal and social relationships connected with these regulations, one thing should be borne in mind: The image of the Jews in the consciousness of the people increasingly blended with the image of the usurer. Under the constant influence of Christian dogma, this image developed into the conviction that the Jew was a usurer not because of the force of circumstances but because his whole Satanic inclination and disposition im-

*See the remarks "On Terminology" in the notes on this chapter in Part 2.

pelled him to take advantage of other people's plight, to suck others dry, and to appropriate the fruits of their diligence. He may do this because he is outside the Christian world order, which is the only valid and just one. Because he is a reprobate, he is allowed to do depraved things. The notions of the Jew and the usurer became so closely connected in people's minds and this connection was so enduringly transmitted through legends, sagas, jokes, verses, and caricatures that this equation has not substantially changed to this day. (This manifests itself particularly when people are enraged or intoxicated—that is, when emotions or drugs remove their inhibitions. We can perhaps go still further and ask whether the theories of modern sociologists from Roscher to Sombart, from Max Weber to the present are not in effect secularized versions and paraphrases of this accusation, according to which a basic disposition drives the Jew into money trade, even though the evaluation of this disposition— which is viewed as being intimately bound up with a Jew's nature—varies according to each author's philosophy, education, and attitude to Judaism and to the modern world.)

To be sure, in that period of an undeveloped credit system this image of the Jewish usurer constantly received fresh fuel from reality. In the nature of things, interest rates were driven up by the lack of money on the one hand and the great risk involved in money-lending in those days of insecurity (and particular insecurity for the Jews!) on the other. From a purely economic point of view one can probably justify the interest rates in most instances, even though by the standards of today's economy they often appear unduly high. If they had been unfounded, they would not have been generally demanded and accepted. Contemporary documents agree that Christian money-lenders certainly did not charge lower rates and frequently demanded even higher ones. This does not alter the fact, however, that the payment of such interest was a heavy burden on those concerned and that they were bound to regard such rates as unfair. No matter how much a debtor may have been helped by a loan, one can never expect him to consider the payment of interest at a high rate as justified. He will view the money-lender who helps him out of his difficulties but receives in return a sum considerably higher than the one he lent him as an exploiter and oppressor who utilizes his advantage as a moneyed person, who often earns far more on the sole basis of this "unjustified" advantage than the worker who has borrowed money earns with his "honest labor."* And if we are permitted to take the risk into account, who can guarantee that in setting the interest rate this risk is

---

*In *Das Schicksal des deutschen Kapitalismus* (Berlin, 1930), pp. 16f., M. I. Bonn speaks of "the age-old conflict between debtors and creditors that has pervaded all social revolutions of the past. . . . The debtor is productive, a man who toils to produce goods for the benefit of the community. The creditor is the vermin that feeds on his blood. . . . The debtor is the bee, the creditor is the drone."

not really overestimated or used only as an excuse to exploit the impecunious person's plight to the full? The Jews were as human as anyone
else; in addition, they were often persecuted and stripped of their
belongings, and almost always they were vilified and despised. Was it
fair to expect them always to be morally so great as to treat the borrowers
with social understanding and a sense of fairness that people did not
deem appropriate in their own dealings with the Jews? Can one be
honestly surprised or indignant that the Jews perhaps not infrequently
exploited their special position as damned usurers and, since they had to
bear the stigma of dishonorableness, really practiced usury to the best of
their ability? Their teachers and leaders always admonished them not to
do so and warned against the deleterious consequences of unfair practices.

Exploiting the demand for money made all the more sense because
the acquisition of wealth became a prerequisite for the existence of the
Jews. Only their money could save them from persecution, avert threatening danger, and prevent expulsion, forced baptism, and murder. Only
through wealth were they able to gain and maintain a *raison d'être* in the
eyes of the rulers in whose domain they lived and on whose protection
they depended.

On the other hand, it would not be fair to expect the people or those
affected by high rates of interest to come to the defense of usurious
money-lenders or to base their moral evaluation on psychology and
history. The borrower who paid high interest was dealing with the Jews
as exploiters and not with the exploiters of the Jews, whom he did not
know and of whom he did not need to take cognizance even if he was told
about them. All he was sure of was that Jews often treated him usu-
riously, for whatever reason.

Therefore, if contempt for the Jews and their persecution had hitherto
been motivated only dogmatically with their nature as deicides, unbelievers, and damned people,* their everyday conduct as money-
lenders and usurers furnished in increasing measure ever new arguments for the existing repugnance and created fresh hatred that mingled
with the at least latently ever-present dislike of the Jews as aliens and
people damned by God. Now the Church, the rulers, competitors, and
booty-hungry people were able to use the economic and social reality as
ever stronger and more conclusive arguments against the Jews.** The

---

*In the anti-Jewish writings of the Lyon bishop Agobard (779–840) there is no accusation
that the Jews practiced usury; if anything, he complains about the good relations
between the unbelieving Jews and the Christians. Even during the attacks at the
beginning of the First Crusade no reproaches were leveled at the economic and social
behavior of the Jews; the persecutions were motivated only with religious arguments
("deicides").

**This has been pointed out with particular incisiveness by James Parkes (*The Jew in the*

Jew as economic exploiter could now always be put forward when people wanted to hit the deicides and religious opponents, and the deicide and unbeliever could be adduced when they wanted to destroy the usurer and economic competitor. Thus the economy and religion, which in any case were not separate spheres in the Middle Ages, could substitute for and supplement each other in the argumentation against the Jews. They coalesced in the consciousness of the people; in each of the arguments the other played at least an emotional part, even when it was not specifically mentioned. Jew and deicide, Jew and usurer became almost identical concepts, and in the minds of the people the Jew became harmful to God and to men. The Jewish question received a new dimension: Justified or unjustified complaints about bad economic and social conditions worked as moral arguments against the Jews. Thus old prejudices based on ancient tradition and religious dogmas were greatly intensified.

Jewish Usury as a System of Taxation

This amalgamation and mingling of the religious and secular spheres made even insightful people lose sight of the fact that the Jews actually were in a predicament that had been created by the economy, the Church, and the secular rulers—often in open struggle with one another and yet in hidden harmony. Their money often provided protection for the Jews, but at the same time it brought persecution upon them. Not infrequently their protectors stripped them of all their possessions when they needed money, and even in normal times they levied high taxes on them. For the rulers the Jews were an ever-copious source of taxes, and more than that, a kind of tax system that, given the poorly developed administrative and transportation system of the time, was easier to handle than the collection of other taxes. Hence they were glad to have the Jews make a big profit on money-lending and did not even mind if they really engaged in usury—provided that the people's resentment did not become too vehement and the attacks of the Church, which was here able to appear as the protector of the people, were not voiced too harshly. For the more a Jew acquired, the more easily and profitably he could be fleeced, and in return for this one could even tolerate popular rage and violence to some extent—as long as the indignation of the exploited people turned against the Jews, who were damned in any case and not against the princes, the real beneficiaries as well as the real

---

Medieval Community, pp. 386ff.): "For the first time it became possible to use the contemporary behaviour of the Jew as an argument against him, as justification for the hatred of him. Hatred of the usurer came in the minds of the Christian public to justify the killing of the deicide."

exploiters of the people. When the excitement had reached its zenith and Jewish property threatened to be destroyed by the people, it was appropriate to intervene as "protectors" and to place the endangered property in the good Christian hands of the ruler—by expelling the Jews, leveling taxes or fines against them, or in some other way. Less frequently, perhaps by remission of a debt, the "exploited" were the beneficiaries. In this cruel game the world tested for the first time a quality of the Jews that has so often been demonstrated since then. Because as a numerically small minority they were weak, had no state of their own to defend them, and were outside the legitimate Christian world, thus really belonging to the realm of Satan and the demons, they could all too easiuly serve as scapegoats for any misfortune and in times of unrest to distract the masses from the real evils, the real evil-doers and evil-minded people.

Degradation and Defamation of the Jews by the Church

The reason why the Jews could be used in this way was their degradation in the consciousness of the entire Christian world in connection with the First Crusade. As far as dogma was concerned, the First Crusade created nothing new. What was new was the more general dissemination and definitive acceptance of the teachings about the Jews by the European-Christian world. The greater strength of the papacy and its dominion over Europe as well as the Crusades, repeatedly organized for this purpose, created in Europe a Christian feeling of unity that had not previously existed.

From the time of Hellenism to that of National Socialism, it was always diastrous for the Jews when the world became all too unified intellectually, religiously, or politically, when a single "totalitarian" power embraced and controlled all areas of life. The special quality of the Jews as expressed in their religion, tradition, and general view and way of life, their will (which at least to them appears as a religious commandment) to preserve this special nature under all circumstances, can be legally exerted only in a world that respects individualities or at least benevolently tolerates special qualities, in what today is thought of as a "pluralistic" world. Where a totalitarian-dogmatic system strives to come to power, it must necessarily come into conflict with Judaism, which is not prepared for the sake of any unitary system to abandon its philosophy and its national aspirations for the future. (Often the persecutions of Jews are only the harbingers of persecutions of other minorities—so to speak, the seismographic warnings before greater and more general upheavals in consequence of a doctrinaire-totalitarian will to power.) Thus arose the great conflicts of Judaism with Hellenism and the Roman Empire. In the world of the manifold developments after the fall of this Empire there always was room and a way out for the Jews somehow and somewhere. With the victory of Christianity over the chaotically pluralistic Europe this way out threatened to be blocked. Therein lies the great significance of the era of the Crusades for the Jewish question. Hating, despising, and persecuting the Jews now became common property. During its entire existence the Catholic Church had by means of its dogmas and Councils, as well as the power of its clergymen over the hearts of the Christians, influenced the life of the Jews among the nations in line with Church doctrine. Now, however, as the victor and almost undisputed ruler, it increasingly used canon law to impose its view of the Jewish question upon all of Europe.

The high point of this legislation was the decisions of the Fourth Lateran Council of November 1215.

The Fourth Lateran Council of 1215

We have already shown that the Church did its best to make the real picture of the Jew conform as much as possible to the picture shaped by Church doctrine. The Lateran Council of 1215 was one of the most decisive steps in that direction, comparable only to the codification of the anti-Jewish legislation by the Christian Roman emperors Theodosius and Justinian in the fifth and sixth centuries. As had happened then, the Church's teachings about the Jews now had far-reaching consequences that were disseminated throughout the civilized Christian world with the force of law.

The Jewish policies of Innocent III, the Pope who raised respect for the Church and its power to its highest level, were the consistent continuation of the policies of his predecessor and the consistent expression of the Church's policies toward the Jews in general. Along with all responsible leaders of Christendom, he was convinced, on the basis of the Augustinian teachings, that the Jews should be preserved. Like his predecessors, he issued an edict for the protection of the Jews soon after his election to the papacy (September 1199). In accordance with a tradition of eighty years' standing, it guaranteed the Jews their traditional rights for the practice of their religion. They were not to be subject to forced baptism or disturbed during their festivals by whipping or stoning; their cemeteries were to be respected and their corpses were not be be exhumed and desecrated; no Christian was to have the right to kill or rob them. How necessary such a bull was in the face of the true situation of the Jews is indicated by the fact that this papal bull for the protection of the Jews had to be renewed no less than ten times from the beginning of the twelfth century to the middle of the thirteenth.

The preamble that Innocent added to the customary text is characteristic of him. It reiterated the Church doctrine according to which the

Jews were to be preserved despite their unbelief and damnation for the sake of the witness that they continued to bear to the Christian doctrine in their writings. This once again impressed upon the people that at bottom the preservation of the Jews was senseless, that they were to be protected from being killed and robbed not as human beings like all others but solely by virtue of their peculiar position in the Christian doctrine of salvation. It is safe to assume that the people all too readily understood the negative rather than the positive elements in this view—all the more so because the negative aspects were legally embodied in the decrees of the Lateran Council.

Unlike what one might conclude from Jewish historiography, the Fourth Lateran Council of 1215 did not concern itself exclusively or even primarily with the Jewish question. In the struggle against the far more threatening Christian heretics—at the conclusion of a cruel crusade against the heresy of the Cathars (Albigenses) in Southern France, which endangered the unity of the Church—it made important decisions for the inner reformation of the church, its organization, its resistance to "false doctrines," and its attitude toward secular powers. Of its seventy decisions, only the last four deal with the Jews, but these profoundly affected Jewish life.

Paragraph 70 seems relatively harmless; it decreed that Jews who had voluntarily converted to Christianity should be obliged to remain Christians, practice Christian rites, and be forcibly prevented from observing Jewish rites. Even if one does not apply the principle of true freedom of thought and faith, which was totally unknown at the time, one must always ask oneself how "voluntarily" Jews had been baptized in times of persecution. Among the Jews who had themselves baptized there surely were then, as there have always been, weaklings, swindlers, and opportunists of all kinds who utilized the advantages that were often connected with a "conversion." Nevertheless, we may be certain that when it was feared that the baptized Jews might "relapse" into their old "unbelief," most of them had really been baptized by force, as had happened earlier and would happen later. It was only natural that the decision made in the fight against Christian heretics to prevent the apostates under all circumstances from continuing to observe Jewish rites had to lead to ever more severe persecution of such not truly devout pseudo-Christians. This was the point of departure for the establishment twenty years later (in 1238) of the Courts of Inquisition against Christian heretics, among whom were now included the baptized Jews who had been too weak to remain loyal to their religion even in the face of mortal danger but who were too closely bound to Judaism by origin, belief (including superstition!), and custom for them to abandon it altogether.*

Another decision (Paragraph 67) dealt with usury. This decree was a consequence of the official ban on the taking of interest by Christians

*About these Jews, later called Marranos in Spain, see pp. 132ff. below.

that the Third Lateran Council of 1179 had ordained. This had, as it were, given the Jews a monopoly on the charging of interest, but it was now feared that like all holders of a monopoly the Jews would take unfair advantage of it. Thus the powers that be attempted to keep the Jews from demanding high interest on pain of punishment by the Church, but though the decision officially stated that this was done to protect the ordinary people, whom the Church liked to look after, from being cheated, this was not the only reason. (It was, incidentally, by no means established what a fair rate of interest was; thus *any* rate could be regarded as unduly high.) The authorities wanted and needed to prevent the Jewish reprobates from acquiring too much respect, importance, and prosperity by virtue of this right to exact interest. The peculiar position of the Jews between ecclesiastical and secular power is reflected in the last sentence of this decree, which admonishes the princes not to resent the Christians because of this decision limiting the interest rate.

Another decision (Paragraph 69) indicates that concern about the rise of Jewish power played a part in the usury decree. It prohibits the Jews from holding any public office that might give them power over Christians. By way of motivating this decision, which was based on a decision of the Third Spanish-Visigothic Council of Toledo in 589, it was stated— entirely in the spirit of the Church Fathers—that it was absurd for the blasphemous Jews to exert power over Christians, for they would use this power only to the detriment of the Christians. If a Jew nevertheless accepted an office, he was to be forced to give it up without compensation.

The "Yellow Badge"

The best-known and most far-reaching decree of the Fourth Lateran Council concerning the Jews (Paragraph 68) was the introduction of special garb or special badges for the Jews, intended to identify them as such outwardly as well. The Church did not create anything new there but simply took over laws that had on a number of occasions been passed in the Moslem world against infidels, Christians as well as Jews, in order to make a visible distinction between believers and unbelievers. Similarly, the Church Council now decreed that Jews and Saracens should be distinguished from Christians by special clothing. By way of motivation the decision states that sameness of dress occasionally led to sexual intercourse between Jews and Christians; after all, Moses had already bidden Jews to wear special attire.* The decree says nothing about the way in which Jewish apparel had to differ from the clothing of believers,

---

*The reference is to the four-cornered garment with fringes, the so-called *Tallit Katan* or *Arba Kanfot*, that the Jews were bidden to wear (in accordance with a later interpretation of Num. 15:38–41 and Deut. 22:12), as a constant admonition to lead a pure life by observing God's commandments.

but left this up to the local authorities. It only laid down the principle, as it were, that a dividing wall should be erected between Jews and Christians not only inwardly but outwardly as well, that Jews should be excluded from civilized Christian society not only through their way of thinking, doctrine, and economic activities but also through their appearance and conduct. The accursed, unsettled, and fugitive people were to bear the mark of Cain visibly.

For our investigation it is not very important to state that like most anti-Jewish regulations this decree was not enforced immediately and everywhere; rather, its introduction differed in place, time, and form, and often individual Jews or the Jewish populations of certain towns and areas were exempted by the payment of special taxes or bribes, or for other reasons that will be discussed later. But at some point this decree was in force almost everywhere in the course of the ensuing decades. Where it was not enforced from time to time—out of negligence or in return for economic services—it always hung over the Jews' heads like a Damoclean sword. "Henceforth," writes Graetz in his *History of the Jews,* "provincial Councils, diets, and princely cabinets concerned themselves, in addition to the exclusion of the Jews from all honors and offices, with the Jewish badge in order to determine its color, form, length, and width with pedantic thoroughness. Whether it was square or round, saffron-yellow or some other color, worn on the hat or the outer garments, the Jewish badge was an invitation to the street urchins to mock its wearers and to fling mud at them, a cue for the stultified rabble to pounce on them and beat or even kill them, and an opportunity even for the upper classes to regard them as the scum of humanity, plunder them, or deport them." The *yellow* badge became the prevalent mark of shame and stigma of the Jews; that color had already been used by the Moslems to identify infidels, particularly Jews.

Persecutions as Justification for More Persecutions

There was an additional factor that must be noted here and throughout this study: The elimination of the Jews from civilized Christian society that caused them to be despised and persecuted created a new argument for persecutions. If the Jews were despised and persecuted everywhere, surely they must be wickedness personified! Where the teachings of the Church did not reach directly, this simple and at first glance eminently logical argumentation effectively substituted for them—even among the Jews and down to the Nazi period and even the present.

In any case, in the years of the Crusades and the religious incitement the people understood one thing very well: that robbing or killing Jews entailed no great risk, at least in times of unrest. A despised person was at the same time an envied one; as his contemporaries saw it, his money and property might be disrespectable and ill-gotten, but everyone could see that he was prosperous and privileged. What was there to prevent anyone from stripping him at any time of the money that he had extorted from the people?

In this defenseless state of the Jews, which had been caused by the doctrines and legal system of the Church, their own economic position, and popular opinion, secular powers came to the rescue. We have already indicated that an excessively totalitarian world always was dangerous for the Jews. Thus they were now saved only by the fact that the secular powers set limits to the power of the Church, which from time to time wielded an almost untrammeled power over souls and minds, and that finally these by no means uniform secular powers also smashed the uniform spiritual realm of the Church. Through the rule of the worldly powers the Jews did endure a great deal of suffering and injustice. However, the opposition of these secular powers to the Church as well as the multiplicity and diverse attitudes of these worldly rulers, which in times of persecution and expulsion from one territory usually enabled the Jews to reach a neighboring territory, saved them from complete destruction even in times of the worst persecution.

"Protected Jews"

This rescue of the Jews by worldly powers was, to be sure, at the same time a further step toward their degradation and humiliation. They were afforded protection under certain conditions, and the greater the threat and the greater the Jews' dependence on the secular powers, the more debasing the conditions under which they were granted protection.

We have already mentioned in passing what the basis of the Jews' relationship to the secular powers in the Middle Ages was. The Jews entered the European world of the early Middle Ages as foreigners—which meant, after the abolition of the Roman legal system (in which the Jews had citizenship), that they had no rights. To safeguard their lives and their economic activity they needed special permission from their sovereign, and it was only logical that they were given rights and protection only when this was beneficial to the ruler. They either had to be good tax payers or perform an economic function that was important to him. Thus the fact that they were placed under the protection of a potentate proved *eo ipso* their importance to the ruler or the ruling class of a country, but certainly not their importance or usefulness to other parts of the population. On the contrary; to the people the Jews usually appeared only in connection with the seamy side of their ruler—as collectors of money, accumulators of wealth, and purveyors of fancy goods—without sharing in his authority based on tradition and age-old respect. Though they were officially not even entitled to be masters of Christian slaves, by virtue of their economic position, which was supported by privileges, they often wielded actual power that appeared to go considerably beyond their legal and formal status. This duality of their position endangered their existence from the beginning.

At first the Jews were granted protection through privileges—that is, special rights—in the same form as other merchants were, usually as merchants in accordance with their economic function in Western and Central Europe. The earliest known privileges of this kind were issued in the early ninth century in the chancellery of the Carolingian emperor Louis the Pious (around 828). With the increase in Jewish settlements it became necessary to grant to entire Jewish communities privileges regulating the position of the community toward its environment, as well as its rights and duties. The first known privilege of this kind is the one granted to the community of Speyer in the Rhineland in 1084. The First Crusade highlighted the increasing need of the Jews for protection as non-Christians; hence the emperor specifically included them in the general peace agreement of 1103, giving official expression to their need for protection.

The Jews as *Kammerknechte* (*Servi Camerae*, Servants of the Treasury)

This already manifested the view that the protection of the Jews was the responsibility of the sovereign, which placed the Jews directly under him. Thus they were distinguished from the rest of the populace, which was subordinated to definite lower local authorities depending on status and economic function and had only a loose and very indirect connection with the sovereign by way of these in hierarchical or feudal gradation and rank. From the outset the concept of the protection of the Jews was based on this direct relationship of the Jews to the sovereign, who extended his protection only in return for taxes and economic services. As early as 846 Archbishop Amulo of Lyon described the Jews as "servants and tributaries" of the princes. J. F. Baer (in *EJ* 1:257) rightly remarks that "this already characterizes the legal situation of the Jews with its substance that was characteristic for the entire Middle Ages. It is clearly formulated in the legal documents of the 12th century. The Jews and all their property belong to the king. . . . They belong to the chamber of the sovereign, the *fiscus* [treasury]. . . . They are slaves of the king and permanently relegated to the *fiscus*. . . . Thus the designation *servi camerae* (servants of the royal treasury), customary in German documents particularly from the 13th century on, was new neither as a term nor in its substance."

In this concept of the Jews as *Kammerknechte* the medieval view of the legal position of the Jews found its characteristic expression. Again, for our examination it does not matter whether the conditions under which the Jews were given the emperor's protection here or there were more or less oppressive; that concerned only the physical and economic well-being of the Jews. What was decisive for their position within the Christian world, however, was the view underlying this concept of *servi camerae*. The Jews' actual lack of rights was clearly expressed in this form of "certified, paid, and temporary protection" (H. Fischer in *EJ* 9:861). In the view of the people, which reflected the teachings of the Church, it was a consequence of the Jews' decisive defeat in their struggle with the Romans. As reported in the Sachsenspiegel (1221–24) and the Schwabenspiegel (ca. 1275), fundamental and widely recognized collections of laws compiled in Saxony and Swabia in the thirteenth century, after the fall of Jerusalem in 70 Josephus obtained peace for the Jews from Emperor Vespasian as a reward for curing the gout of his son Titus. According to legend, Titus turned the vanquished and enslaved Jews over to the Roman emperor's treasury. There the *fiscus Judaicus*, the tax levied on the Jews after the fall of Jerusalem, seems to have served as the basis for the concept of the Jews' status as *Kammerknechte*. In any case, one thing is clear: In accordance with ecclesiastical and secular thinking, official doctrine, and popular belief, a Jew was a creature outside the Christian and human order, a person ordained by God and men to be a slave and to be tolerated only by special grace or in return for special achievements.

Thus the protection granted the Jews by the secular powers from the second third of the thirteenth century on (1238) was more and more widely described as *Kammerknechtschaft* (servitude to the imperial chamber, or treasury) and was always only a conditional and temporary protection. It could be rescinded at any time, and its continuance or renewal could always entail new conditions or higher taxes. Like other rights and properties, the patents of protection as well as the rights and taxes accruing to the ruler from it could be transferred to other authorities, and they were indeed transferred from higher to lower powers with increasing frequency. Emperors transferred their powers over certain Jewish populations, and especially the right to levy taxes and assessments on them, to territorial rulers and cities, and these lower authorities could in turn sell or pledge their Jews to others in case of need or for the sake of profit. In the general thinking of the times, which is expressed in such practices, Jews had essentially no rights; they were the property of princes, for sale like any other property.

During the thirteenth century this status of the Jews was definitively sanctioned by ecclesiastical and secular legal authorities. We have already mentioned the Sachsenspiegel and the Schwabenspiegel with their derivation of *Kammerknechtschaft* from the servitude into which the Jews had been plunged by the collapse of their State. Similar motivations occur in other legal books, and even where they do not, the view prevailed that the Jews were basically slaves of the princes and possessed any rights only by special dispensation and only for its duration and under definite conditions. The fact that the privileges granted the Jews (as a reward for their financial services) often made them appear freer and more privileged than the members of many other classes only made their status in the eyes of the populace more incomprehensible and more "unjustified."

The Jews in the Teachings of Thomas Aquinas

This view of the Church was given authoritative expression in the doctrine of Thomas Aquinas (1225–74), the great Church teacher who was canonized as early as the beginning of the fourteenth century. His work was based on the teachings of the Church Fathers and increasingly supplanted the writings of St. Augustine. In his general conception of the position of the Jews in the Christian world he follows the teachings of Augustine and ecclesiastical tradition: The Jews should be preserved as eternal witnesses to the truth of Christianity; they should be converted to Christianity by persuasion and not by force, and in general they should not be disturbed in the practice of their customs.

As concerns the legal position of the Jews, however, Thomas followed the prevailing philosophy of law, both ecclesiastical and secular, and by his approval lent it higher authority and greater permanence. According to him, because of their own guilt the Jews have been assigned to the princes for eternal servitude. Hence the potentates are entitled to appropriate the Jews' property, provided that they leave the Jews enough to live on. This is a clear illustration of the idea that the Jews are unfree serfs, which means that their masters and not they are entitled to their acquisitions. To be sure, Thomas immediately qualifies this, for its strict application would have rendered the economically necessary function of the Jews as money-lenders impossible. Since, however—he goes on to say—in accordance with the words of the apostle the members of the Christian Church have to conduct themselves nobly even toward unbelievers, no higher taxes should be levied on the Jews than they have traditionally paid. To be sure, this statement, too, is qualified. Since the Jews' money has usually been acquired by usury and thus illegitimately, a ruler has the right to confiscate these ill-gotten gains. However, the money taken from the Jews should as far as possible be returned to the rightful owners. If the persons from whom the Jews have extorted interest can no longer be located, their money can be used for pious purposes or, if necessary, for public ones. In line with tradition, fresh taxes may be levied upon the Jews for such purposes. Caro rightly notes in his *Sozial- und Wirtschaftsgeschichte der Juden* (1:312f.): "The final result of his deliberation is a justification of any financial burden on the Jews. . . . The views presented by Thomas Aquinas were indeed theoretical ones; but when the doctrines of the Church were given a logical interpretation by the theologians, they exerted the greatest influence not only on the thinking of the contemporaries but on their actions as well. The Jews were serfs of the princes, and their possessions, which had been acquired by usury, could be handled by the rulers as they wished. Such principles were bound to have a very significant effect on the fate of the Jews in France, England, and Germany during the 13th century and later." With the acceptance of the Aquinist doctrine the position of the Jews as merely tolerated people who were really condemned to eternal servitude was definitively established.

The Jews in Comparison with Other Oppressed Groups

It would, however, be quite wrong to lament, in self-pitying fashion, the lot of the Jews in the Middle Ages as though they had been the only persecuted and oppressed people at the time. They certainly were not. After all, in that period there were large-scale persecutions of unbelievers and heretics, tens of thousands of whom were mercilessly massacred, cruelly tortured, and burned alive. We only need to remind the reader of the abovementioned persecution and annihilation of the Albigenses. In the social order the Jews were by no means on the lowest end of the scale. Social equality of the kind that is increasingly demanded by the modern world was really alien to the medieval world, even as a postulate. Medieval society was founded on inequality. As R. H. Tawney noted in his *Religion and the Rise of Capitalism*, it was a society of unequal classes with diverse functions, organized for a shared goal. There was no uniform law but a plethora of special laws for strata, classes, corporations, estates, and individuals. In this society, which was based on entitlements of all kinds, the Jews even had privileges of a religious, autonomous-legal, and economic nature that far transcended the rights of many another class and stratum. For this reason and also because of their wealth--whether actual or presumed, often wrongly so—they were at once despised and greatly envied. A peasant, for example, who was an illiterate serf had a far worse economic and social position than most Jews, but of course his position was traditionally "built into" the great economic and social system and he was "at home." The Jews, on the other hand, were often people of a very high cultural level who really had no rights—at once settled and homeless, economically influential and powerless.

The differences between their position and that of other oppressed groups and social strata was to come out clearly later, in the Age of

Emancipation, when the legal inequalities were officially abolished. The peasants and workers were in their homeland, fighting for their rights. While higher social classes might put up barriers against them and look down upon them, no one doubted that they were part of their people. The road to social advancement was open to them, and when they fought for status, the legitimacy of this struggle was recognized. It was different with the Jews. The special nature of their struggle and the reaction of their surroundings to their demands once again demonstrated that the Jews were viewed differently from other underprivileged people. They did not really belong, but were and remained aliens. This difference between the Jews and other underprivileged classes already became apparent in the waning Middle Ages in the persecutions to which the Jews were subject as Jews.

Persecutions and Expulsions of Jews in the Waning Middle Ages: The "Black Death"

The logical consequence of the conditions described above was the persecutions, expulsions, and wholesale massacres that befell the Jews for two long, bitter centuries, from the end of the thirteenth to the end of the fifteenth, destroyed or undermined the foundations of Jewish settlement in Western and Central Europe, decimated the number of the Jews, and led to a change in the distribution of the Jews over Europe and in their legal and social position.

Many factors combined in these persecutions. The general foundation was the crisis of the medieval economy since the beginning of the fourteenth century, and in consequence thereof the fight of the urban lower classes for social advancement, as well as the struggle of the cities with the princely powers for freedom and dominance. To these economic crises must be added the natural catastrophes and epidemics that were sometimes the cause of these, the years of crop failure and famine that often killed thousands, or the plague which spread unimpeded from Asia and Africa over large parts of the inhabited world and reached its zenith in Europe around the middle of the fourteenth century, in 1348–49. In those years the so-called "Black Death" is said to have destroyed one-third of the population of Europe; in some regions and places the losses were even far greater than that. Europe had not been visited by an epidemic of such proportions since the time of Justinian—that is, in eight hundred years. The economic consequences of these catastrophes was, of course, a rise in prices and hence an increase of poverty among the people. This produced or exacerbated political and social unrest. Italy was wracked by civil war and constant fighting among the numerous local governments. In Germany political anarchy became rampant with the decline of the empire. Large parts of France were laid waste by the so-called Hundred Years' War with England (1339–1453), and this war ruined England's economy as well. Thus the stage was set for the incitement of popular rage and for outbursts of violence from the masses. After all that had happened, was it any wonder that popular excitement turned in particular measure against the Jews?

In times of crises whose cause they do not understand, the people seek the guilty party in the sphere of the incomprehensible. To some degree this is true of every period, but it was so in particular measure in the Middle Ages. Somehow the devil must be involved; secret forces have produced the misfortune! What was more logical than to identify the Jews with these secret forces? From the beginning the founders and teachers of the Church closely connected them with "Satan," the "Antichrist," the will to evil, and this status as reprobates was given terse expression once again in the Conciliar decisions of the thirteenth century. Their exclusion from the Christian community by means of visible badges, their special legal and economic position—all this gave the Jews the stamp of the uncanny and increasingly heightened this impression. From such a viewpoint their customs could also assume a devilish, uncanny character. After all, people have always regarded anything deviating from the norm as suspicious; an alien is always a potential enemy. A minority that is regarded as foreigners can exist relatively undisturbed in times of peace or prosperity, but it is always endangered in times of unrest and want. Such times are always bound to become disastrous for members of such a minority if their own activities involve them in the crises of the economy and of social welfare, if they appear as partisans of one side or another in a struggle or are regarded as such. Such times of general crisis can and must be particularly pernicious for a minority that has all the characteristics of a scapegoat and whose destruction promises valuable spoils and hardly any punishment for the destroyers. In those days the Jews assumed all qualities of such a minority. They were at hand everywhere; they could be "sent out into the desert" with impunity, with no one to avenge them; and it made sense to impute sin to them, for by their entire being and existence they were sinners, minions of the devil, accursed by God and because of their actions by men as well. Thus it was possible for the naive rage of the superstitious and frightened people, the lust for loot of the rabble, and the cupidity of the rulers to turn against them, and in times of crisis the cognoscenti have always been able to divert the hate instincts of the masses to them.

All these factors were encountered again in the persecutions of the ensuing centuries; at various times one or the other predominated, but almost invariably the various motives and currents intermingled: the usury of the Jews and their profanation of the Christian faith; their wealth and their alleged practice of ritual slaughter of Christian children; their position as a source of taxes for the potentates and their alleged desecration of the Host in order to murder Christ's body over and over again; the poisoning of the souls and spirits that the Church discerned in the dissemination of Jewish teachings; and the poisoning of the wells that people imputed to them at the time of the Black Death and occasionally had confirmed by confessions made under torture. All this combined and produced a well-nigh endless chain of persecutions in Southern, Western, and Central Europe, particularly in Germany.

In many respects these persecutions were basically different from those of the first Crusades. In those days religious fanaticism had still been the strongest impetus, though not the only one. What became increasingly common now was the mingling of religious superstition with lust for loot; of mortal fear and the fanatical sadomasochistic penitential orgies of the bloody flagellants with bestial bloodthirstiness; of threats, robbery and arson with the extortion of taxes, the cancellation of debts, and the burning of promissory notes.

What was also new was the complete expulsion of Jews from larger or smaller territories for longer or shorter periods of time. The expulsion of the Jews from England at the end of the thirteenth century (1290) marked the beginning. It was followed by the expulsion from the major part of France by Philip the Fair in 1306 (this became final in 1394), as well as the massacre and destruction of about three hundred communities in Germany and the expulsion of the survivors in the horrible period of the Black Death (1348–49). At the end of the fourteenth century (1391) there began with the "Holy War" against the Jews the great tragedy of Spanish Jewry that ended a century later with the expulsion of the Jews from Spain (1492) and from Portugal (1496). In between there were the expulsions from Prague (1400), Vienna (1421), Cologne (1424), Mainz (1438), Augsburg (1440), and the Tyrol (1493); immediately following were the expulsions from Nuremberg (1499), Provence (1498–1506), and finally from the old Jewish settlement of Regensburg (1519), to mention only a few stations on this road of suffering without enumerating the many persecutions in individual communities and districts, the mass murders, expulsions, resettlements, and renewed expulsions.

Migrations

In this era of the late Middle Ages, which was in everything a consequence and development of the preceding centuries, there was a decisive change in the situation of the Jews in Europe, A substantial part of European Jewry perished—of diseases, like the non-Jews, and of persecution, a special Jewish fate. The Jews were expelled, permanently or for a considerable period of time, from a number of countries and towns in which they had lived for many centuries, places whose Jewish settlements were sometimes as old as or older than the settlements of the "native" non-Jews. England and France were to have no major Jewish settlements for centuries; Spain, which had since the eleventh century become one of the great centers of Jewish life and culture, remained permanently closed to the Jews from now on (1492)—if one disregards the Jewish Marranos, who will be discussed later. The Jewish migratory movement, which had never ceased, now became a mighty stream, and there was a tremendous shift in the distribution of Jewry over the earth. Large numbers of Jews streamed from Western and Central Europe to the East, to Poland, where the Jews were permitted to perform for a few more centuries the economic function that they had in large measure already performed in the more western countries of Europe. The Jews driven out of Spain and Portugal—the Sephardim, as they have been called after a region mentioned in the Bible (Obadiah 1:20)—strengthened the Jewish settlements in Northern Italy. They laid the foundation for Jewish settlements in Holland and migrated especially to the regions of the Turkish-Ottoman empire that were open to them and of which Palestine had also been part since 1517. The Jewish population of Palestine now began to grow again in number and cultural importance.

In addition to the migrations from country to country and across the Mediterranean to the Orient there was also an increase in the internal migration in those areas of Central Europe from which the Jews had not been completely expelled. In this settlement area, which was split up into small and tiny territories, the mass outbreaks against the Jews at the time of the Black Death around the middle of the fourteenth century constituted a decisive turning point. In the torturings, the mass burnings, and the expulsions of the Jews of those years there may be discerned all elements of the Jewish question that had crystallized in the preceding centuries and coalesced into an ever more inextricable complex. Poverty, social revolutions, and the fear of death, as well as the tradition of religious and economic hatred of Jews and their social ostracism and isolation, now concentrated into mass eruptions against which even the influence of the Pope remained ineffectual. His admonitions to clergymen and laymen, his threats of excommunication, his appeals to reason that the plague had also appeared in regions in which there were no Jews and that thus the Jews could not possibly have poisoned the wells there, and that in other areas the Jews themselves had been afflicted with the plague—all this fell on deaf ears. The sower cannot command the fruit that grows from the seed. The ecclesiastical image of the devilish Jew who is capable of all evil had been so deeply

embedded in the people's faith by the propaganda of the Church itself
and particularly that of the mendicant orders serving it that no reason
availed against it anymore.

The Destruction of the Strassburg Jewish Community as a Model

A contemporary account of the destruction of the Jewish community
of Strassburg (February 1349) is very instructive as one example among
many of the amalgamation of religious fanaticism and lust for loot, the
Jewish question and the social question in those days. That account was
thirteen years later included by the chronicler Friedrich Closener in his
Strassburger Deutsche Chronik. According to this report, the ruling
patricians of the city wanted to protect the Jews. The city had borrowed
money from the Jews and given them patents of protection, and the
reigning mayors wanted to honor these pledges, but the people objected. The high interest which the Jews were entitled to take are given
as the reason for the people's hatred of the Jews. This right, so the
chronicler says, has made the Jews "arrogant in spirit" and unyielding.
In addition, the Jews were accused of having poisoned the wells and the
[flowing] waters. "The people grumbled about this and said the Jews
should be burned." The council of the patricians to which the people
were opposed—opposition to the Jews was combined with a power
struggle against the old patrician families—demanded proof of this accusation or confessions on the part of Jews. Thereupon a number of Jews
were tortured; in order to escape the torment they admitted to some
offenses, "and for these they were broken on the wheel, but they never
confessed that they were guilty of poisoning [wells]." The Jewish quarter
was now blocked, and people continued to demand of the Council that
the Jews be annihilated. Since the Council and the three mayors did not
bow to the will of the people, the mayors were accused of having taken
bribes from the Jews. People refused to believe "that they did it only out
of justice," for that seemed all too improbable toward the Jews. In an
armed uprising of the artisans the mayors and the magistrate were
deposed and expelled from the city, although it is expressly stated that
there was no proof that they had accepted bribes from the Jews. Then
the constitution was changed in the spirit of the craftsmen, and now the
persecution of the Jews started. The people gave free rein to their
avarice but exempted from their pillaging those who had themselves
baptized and did other things "pleasing to God" by snatching children
away from their parents and having them baptized by force. We shall let
the source himself speak: "On Friday the Jews were caught, on Saturday
they were burned—approximately two thousand of them. But those who

were willing to be baptized were allowed to live. Many young children were taken from the fire against the will of their fathers and mothers and baptized. All debts to the Jews were canceled and all pledges and promissory notes were returned. The Council took the Jews' cash and distributed it among the artisans' guilds. That money was also the poison that killed the Jews."

Short-Term Settlement

The catastrophical years 1348 and 1349 were a decisive turning point also for the few Jews in Central Europe who had escaped the persecutions and had not left the country—and not only in their inner experience, which will be discussed later. They did not regain their former legal position. To be sure, the solemn vows of the people and the city government never to admit Jews to the city again, or not during the next hundred years, were broken almost immediately after the events. The surviving Jews were admitted again to many of the German cities from which they had been expelled, for evidently the economy could not get along without them. Every effort was made, however, to make them dispensable in short order; hence they were expressly admitted for only a very limited period of time. It was declared openly and unabashedly that their readmittance was serving only a limited economic purpose, and they were admitted for no more than ten or twelve years. Fixing the duration of the contract enabled the powers that be to tighten the conditions when the contract was renewed by increasing the admission fees and annual taxes. Hence it was possible legally to expel the Jews over and over again without coming into conflict with other authorities, the sovereign, or the emperor. All that needed to be done was not to renew the short-term contract.

At the same time the right to settle was no longer granted to the Jews in general, to a Jewish settlement of indeterminate size; rather, admittance was granted only to individuals and individual families, to a limited number of Jews. In general Jews were now no longer able to acquire real property. The houses inhabited by Jews were no longer their property, as had usually been the case earlier; they belonged to the town and were only rented to the Jews. In earlier centuries Jews had been free to live where they pleased and Jewish quarters had arisen more from personal predilection than from outside compulsion and restriction. The Jews inhabited a street or streets that were deemed most appropriate by the citizens; they were surrounded by walls with gates that were closed at night and fenced off from the Christian population—for the protection of the Jews from the people and the protection of the Christians from the Jews. Only now did there come into being in a very real sense what was to be called "ghetto" in the sixteenth century (apparently the first instance was in Venice; see chapter 4 and the excursus in Part 2).

This isolation, which was practiced with increasing strictness, was intended not only to impede or eliminate any social relations between Jews and Christians such as had repeatedly been demanded by the Church; it was also intended to be an expression of the Jews' degradation. True, frequently documents still referred to the Jews as "citizens," because they were legally included in the municipal corporation, but they were second- or third-class citizens. They were not permitted to use the municipal dance hall and bathhouse, and their right to buy food was limited to certain hours—allegedly to avoid an undue rise in prices. With a great deal of pedantry ever-changing dress regulations for the Jews were formulated, specifying exactly what the Jews were or were not permitted to wear so they could be distinguished from the Christians with sufficient clarity. Even Christian whores and municipal bordellos were *verboten* for the Jews.

The Jew—A Utilitarian Object

That period constituted the logical conclusion of the development since the Crusades in the Jews' economic activity for Central Europe and increasingly for the western and southern European countries as well.* Under the pressure of circumstances the Jews had in ever-increasing measure turned to financial dealings since the twelfth century, but now they were expressly permitted to settle only for this purpose. Medicine is the only other occupation that is documented for Jews; they were expressly barred from all other occupations, crafts, and trades, at least in German cities. When they were admitted, it was because they were needed as financiers or as a source of taxes. At any rate, both Christians and Jews clearly realized that Jews were admitted to German towns only for practical, functional reasons. "Their treatment," writes I. Elbogen, "was determined not by human rights but solely by their utility."

This utility also was the sole determinant of their position within the empire. The concept of *Kammerknechtschaft*, being part of the royal *fiscus*, that had developed by the thirteenth century had contained a contractual relationship. True, since the days of Vespasian the Jews had been slaves of the emperor and their property legally belonged to the emperor, who could give it away or pawn it like any other property, and who did so when it was to his advantage. But in return the emperor also

---

*This development was slower in Italy and Spain with their old-established Jewish populations, some of them artisans, because it ran counter to an old tradition.

had to give the Jews his personal protection; they were included in the emperor's peace, and anyone who harmed them violated the emperor's rights. Now only the *Knechtschaft* part of the *Kammerknechtschaft* remained. In the persecutions of 1348–49 Emperor Charles IV (1346–78) never seriously attempted to protect the Jews. He was largely concerned with his own share in the booty taken from the Jews—to the extent that cities like Frankfurt, Augsburg, and Nuremberg were a priori assured impunity if the people attacked, burned, or drove out the Jews. The only bone of contention between the emperor on the one hand and the sovereigns and towns on the other was the extent to which each of them could exploit the Jews without violating the rights of the others. They all agreed that Jews existed to be exploited. In the so-called Golden Bull of 1356, in which the emperor generally and formally transferred his right to the Jews, who had already been pledged on frequent other occasions, to the electoral princes, this transfer was characteristically lumped together with the transfer of the right to mineral resources.* There could be no more trenchant expression of the assessment of the Jews by the ruling powers.

The Image of the Jews at the End of the European Middle Ages

This, then, was the position of the Jews at the end of the Middle Ages: isolated, defamed, a poison that in small doses might be a stimulant to the economic health of the country as well as to the passions of the rulers and thus was often in demand, but always a poison that had to be treated with caution and had to be isolated in the poison cabinet of the ghetto. As far as the ordinary people were concerned, even before any personal encounter with a Jew they knew him from the liturgy, sermons, sculptures, and pictures of the Church as a Judas and deicide, as a Satan and Antichrist, and thus the Jews had long since been removed from the world of the human and the familiar. A Jew was not a human being but closer to the mystical-demonic forces, for good as well as evil: as a physician, as a breaker of evil spells and charmer of fields in years of crop failure as well as a usurer, poisoner of wells, desecrator of Hosts and murderer of Christians, or as a secret accomplice of the enemy. And he was strange, for he was virtually the prototype of the alien: he did not have the right of domicile anywhere; he was everywhere tolerated for only a short time, he was always migrating from town to town and from country to country as dictated by the economy, the political situation, or conditions of some kind. Now the people developed the image of the

---

*In chapter 9, which consists of a single sentence of eighteen printed lines and is headed *De auri, argenti et aliarum specierum mineris* (Of gold mines, silver mines, and other mines).

Jew as the "wandering Jew" (Romance and English-speaking countries) or the "eternal wanderer" (Germany), and it is no accident that the legend of the "Eternal Jew" now assumed more graphic form. It was based on old oriental legends that were transferred to the Jew, and on the basis of the biblical legend of Cain with its Christian interpretation it was applied to Jewish fate. This legend was made vibrant and colorful by real life in which Jews were killed everywhere and yet appeared in living form as peculiar wanderers. And finally it embodied the uncanny and devilish elements that seemed to surround the Jews and the curse that had pursued them since the crucifixion and the destruction of the Temple. The Jew mocked Jesus, and by way of punishment Jesus cursed him so that he was not able to die; he has to roam the earth until the Savior's return. In the fifteenth and sixteenth centuries people claimed to have seen Ahasver, the eternally wandering Jew, in the flesh in various places and under different names, and conversations with him were recorded. When the legend appeared in print for the first time as a chapbook at the beginning of the seventeenth century (see the next chapter and excursus in Part 2), the pamphlet immediately became a bestseller and was repeatedly reprinted in ever new versions. It was the classic expression of the people's idea of the Jew since the late Middle Ages. The old legend about a man pledging a pound of flesh from his own body for a loan was transferred to a Jew in 1378 by the Italian writer Ser Giovanni Fiorentino. It was given its classic expression in the sixteenth century in Shakespeare's figure Shylock (see the following chapter).

This equation of Jews with the nonhuman and demonic in the eyes of the people (though not in official Church doctrine) may also explain numerous inhuman cruelties toward the Jews. In killing Jews people did not kill human beings but Jewish specters and demons. But the extent to which the murder of a Jew, though from the basest motives, was regarded as meritorious even in the ruling circles is illustrated by the fact that Duke Albrecht of Austria had his glorious deed, the burning of the Jews in 1421, expressly recorded on his gravestone.

The Reaction of the Jews

Let us emphasize once more that we are not writing a history of the Jews but wish to trace the development of the Jewish question, pursuing the formation of the complex relationships between Jews and non-Jews, of their attitudes toward one another, and of the image that they had of one another. It is in the nature of things that these relationships between Jews and non-Jews were not determined only by the world around them. As we have tried to show, the Jewish question of the Middle Ages was determined by many factors, but the religious basis remained constant. Even in times of mass pillaging by the rabble, even in persecutions when it was obvious that the persecutors cared more about Jewish property than about the salvation of their souls, a Jew could as a rule immediately escape persecution if he converted to Christianity and severed his relationship with his accustomed religious-national community. In this respect, therefore, his fate was not merely passive, not just forced upon him by his surroundings, but depended on his own decision, and he had the option of evading it. The Jews' will to live as a distinct community and religion thus basically remained the ultimate cause of what happened to them. To that extent the history of the Jews was never merely the story of their sufferings, though it has long been presented as such, but also a history of their daily active and passive decisions.

There was another factor. What the Jews experienced in the Middle Ages, the persecutors and persecutions to which they succumbed or which they escaped, the contemporary conditions under which they lived—all those things naturally evoked reactions on the part of the Jews, and of course these reactions again affected the attitude of the world toward the Jews. It is this continued effect and countereffect of the various elements that gradually gave the Jewish question its modern form, that hard-to-unravel complex of relationships and estrangements, of attractions and repulsions that we are attempting to illuminate here.

To complete the picture of the position of the Jews in the medieval world we must therefore ask the question: How did the Jews react to the persecutions that befell them from the time of the Crusades on, particularly in the waning Middle Ages? In the Middle Ages, as in all other periods, they reacted as people of flesh and blood, as members of an ethnic community, as professors of a religious idea and tradition, and as believing bearers of a mission.

Let us first consider the purely human and everyday aspect. The Jews wanted to live and had to live. The laws of the Church and of the state made material and religious life difficult in every way, often rendering it well-nigh impossible. The authorities added everyday, petty, bureaucratic harassment, and the people and frequently the rulers as well practiced despotism and used violence. No one can blame the Jews for often defending their lives and activities against their powerful, unscrupulous enemies with equally dubious means, with the methods of the powerless: feigned submissiveness, secret circumvention of laws, bribery, and fraud. This was done in an endeavor to preserve their existence, and surely sometimes out of the equally understandable resentfulness of the oppressed and the vindictive feelings of the unfairly beaten. Frequently the persecutors almost took this element of resentment and vengeance for granted, probably also because they had a bad conscience, and not infrequently (e.g., at the time of the Black Death) this caused them to extort from the Jews "confessions" of misdeeds out of vengefulness that they had never committed.

Confusion of Moral Principles

No socially oppressed person is morally improved by oppression, and this was true of the Jews. But there were profound inward effects as well. When there is a shift in moral principles and they become blurred, this confusion generally does not stop at a certain limit, especially if it prevails for a long time. It is only too natural for it to spread to areas that people have tried hard to save from it. Circumvention of the law by interpreting it, as well as by fraud and bribery; inward contempt for the laws of the state as an institution basically invented only for the torture of the Jews; seeming submissiveness to a powerful person and secret mockery of him; outward inferiority and an inner feeling of superiority to the goy (who, in the spirit of the ancients, is basically regarded as a barbarian)—all this was bound to bring a dichotomy into the life and thought of the Jews. These tendencies were intensified by the necessity to adapt the Jewish laws to changing conditions through exegetic methods that in effect often came very close to a circumvention of these laws. Thus a Jew became a more and more complex creature. In his daily life, in and outside his own community, morality and immorality were often so closely connected that it was hard to distinguish between them.

This, of course, affected the world around him. The Jews appeared ever more uncanny and reprehensible to it. In this way the ecclesiastical expressions *perfidia* and *perversitas*, originally applied to the Jews in official documents only in the religious sense of disloyalty to God and his emissary and of reprobacy, could with increasing ease and with the appearance of justification be applied to the everyday conduct of the Jews.

But no matter how earnestly the Jews preached and fought against infractions of morality in their own ranks—both for ethical reasons and out of concern for reactions of the world around them—in the final analysis this "flexibility" of thought and action was necessary for a Jew who wanted to make his way in the world and maintain himself and his family. The only other alternative was the secluded existence of an ascetic, something that Jews never accepted as an ideal. Even a scholar did not despise the world of commerce and human activities but often participated in these and expressed himself about problems that arose for observant, orthodox Jews in a non-Jewish environment.

The Community as a Substitute for a Homeland

The second consequence of this "constant life in enemy country" (to use a later formulation by Herzl) was the Jews' ever-increasing adherence to their own community. There is one important achievement that the Jews have preserved for themselves in all periods (down to the nineteenth century) and under the most adverse circumstances: self-government. To a certain extent the Jewish community—with its religious and secular functions, from religious services to the right of taxation down to its own jurisdiction founded on biblical-Talmudic law—served the Jews as a substitute for the feeling of being at home that their surroundings never vouchsafed them.

In addition to the will of the Jews, there were various reasons why Jewish self-government was able to survive in the medieval period. One of its roots was the teaching of official Christianity that while the Jews should be kept in bondage, they should be preserved to the end of time. If the Jews' right to exist was recognized, they also had to be given an opportunity to live in accordance with the precepts and customs of their religion. People were all the more ready to do so because they wanted to isolate the Jews from the Christians. Added to this was the fact that the Jews had already had extensive communal rights in ancient times and in the Islamic world. Medieval Europe took over the tradition of antiquity, and since the medieval world respected tradition, it was repeatedly confirmed by the rulers as a legal foundation.

The framework and the possibility for these regulations was provided by the corporate organization of the medieval state. In contrast to the modern state since the rise of absolutism and the development of modern nationalism, the medieval state had no interest in uniformity. Every estate had its particular laws and customs and was judged in accordance with them. Hence it was not difficult to integrate the Jewish communal system organically into the corporative structure of the medieval world.

This, however, exacerbated the estrangement between the Jews and the rest of the population, for there was a difference between the special rights of the Jews and those of all other recognized corporations and estates. All other special rights were based on Christianity; despite all individual differences, the loyalty oath of all special groups was a Christian oath. Beyond the religious aspects, the people sensed the strangeness behind the special customs of the Jews; long before there was a clear sense of nationalism and it had been translated into organized movements, it was a living force in the emotional life of the people. Somehow the Jewish quarter was always shrouded in mystery. It may have been partly due to a reluctance to explore this mystery, and the strange customs of divine or devilish provenance, that even in times of persecution people did not interfere in internal Jewish matters any more than was deemed necessary for the collection of taxes and the like. After all, the medieval world was a superstitious world, and the world of the ordinary people has been one to this day. One never knew what the consequences might be if one got too close to those strange, unfamiliar customs and practices . . .

One thing is certain, in any case: The persecutions impelled the Jews to band ever more closely together. When the outside world was gloomy, cold, and dangerous, when their lives and existence were threatened every day, the Jews fled to their own houses, which offered a bit more security and above all gave them warmth and a feeling of being at home. That solidly built world of their own was regarded as a kind of independent Jewish urban community not only by the law; its independence and otherness were expressed to an even greater extent by the entire lifestyle and the consciousness of its members. There was first of all the regular sequence of weekdays and the Sabbath, of working days and holidays that gave form and substance to life, structured it, and provided it with meaning and rhythm. It must have seemed rather strange to the surrounding world that the Jews celebrated the spring festival of trees when it was still winter in Europe, that harvest festivals were celebrated at times that did not coincide with the harvest times in their countries of residence by people whose only concern with the yield of the harvest was as dealers or as estimators of a pawn for money loaned on it—and all this only because ages ago the festivals had been celebrated in that way in distant Palestine. But no matter what the world around them might think, the Jews found it proper that way; it hardly occurred to them to doubt or modify the rightness of these times that had been ordained by God and were oriented toward their sacred homeland. To them these times and festivals were as firmly founded as laws of nature. It was possible to discuss their meaning and importance, one could reinterpret them and explain them—but there was no gainsaying that they had from the beginning been the basis of every Jew's life and would be till the end of time. One could not question them any more than one could doubt the laws of nature, which, after all, might be transcended by miracles in accordance with God's will.

The more the Jews strayed from a life bound to nature, the more their interpretation of it and endowing it with meaning became removed from nature to a sphere of the intellect, allegory and symbolism, and finally mysticism. The earthly background of the festivals receded into the background, and intellectual interpretation and references to the history of the people came to the fore: the liberation from Egypt and the receiving of the law, which every generation should experience anew as though this had happened to *it;* expiation and atonement, the annual mourning of the destruction of the Temple, and the ever renewed joy when a yearly cycle of Torah readings was completed and a new one began—under these aspects the people experienced the festive times of the year which had once been connected with natural phenomena. Characteristically, the festival of the Maccabees was now only the festival of the miraculous light; it was not renewed as a national festival of liberation from Syrian-Hellenistic rule until the end of the nineteenth century under the influence of the Zionist movement. At the same time Jews clung to every commandment and prohibition, to every practice that had been hallowed by age and persecution and thus was almost equated in holiness and legal force with the commandments and sometimes even prized above them. This was done out of heightened love for what was threatened and had been preserved amidst danger. People also believed that the pedantically strict observance of all commandments and rituals was an important step on the road to atonement and liberation that could be attained only if God forgave his people.

The Meaning of Life in the Diaspora

There was one conviction to which the Jews of the Middle Ages adhered as they had adhered to it after the destruction of their Temple and State: Nothing happens without God's will. Their own lives, too, were governed by laws and not simply shaped by their enemies; they were controlled by God. The harder a life is, the more necessary it is to find a meaning for it; if it is not endowed with meaning, it is unbearable. Least of all can a Jew, given his entire tradition and education, live without asking about the meaning of his life. In times of the worst persecutions individual Jews may have asked this bitter question of God: Hast Thou forgotten Thy people? Such questions occasionally are contained in elegies that were included in the liturgy of the synagogues. But the people cannot seriously believe in the justification of such doubts; these are only appeals to God to remember the sufferings of his people. One cannot seriously doubt that all this—banishment, dispersion, sorrow, and death—must have a meaning in God's cosmic design.

The only question is this: What is their meaning? The answer to this question was relatively simple in the first centuries after the destruction. The fall of the Temple and the State as well as life in the Diaspora could be regarded as a punishment of the kind predicted long ago by the Torah and the prophets. After all, according to the peculiar Jewish view of history the victorious enemy is the executor of God's will—and at the same time he remains the depraved person to whom punishment is sure to be meted out for his outrage against God's people. That was a simple, somehow naive belief, and as long as there was hope for a speedy return and retribution, it sufficed. From the seventh century on, however, the Messianic faith was increasingly raised to the realm of miracle. But it was preserved, and in the twelfth century Maimonides, the great teacher and codifier of Judaism who in his time was opposed as a rationalist, included it among his Thirteen Articles of Faith. At all times there was preserved the consciousness of the special nature of Jewish fate that appeared to have been raised above natural causality. The Christian adversaries adduced the long period of dispersion as proof that the Jews were reprobates for all time, and they cited the Jews' adherence to their faith and law despite this obvious proof as an expression of their malign obduracy. The Jews, on the other hand, regarded their preservation despite all the miseries of the *galut* as a miracle and proof that their chosenness continued. To use the argument of Judah Halevi, the great Spanish-Jewish poet (1086–1141), otherwise they would long since have succumbed to the persecution. Just as the preservation of the Jews is a miracle of God, their redemption will also occur through a miracle, and only a miracle. In times of need, which under the aspect of the *hevle mashiach,* the birthpangs of the Messianic period, were regarded as proof that the end of time was approaching, there always appeared people who believed, or pretended to believe, that they were the Messiah or at least his proclaimer or precursor, and the greater the need, the greater the number of the believing, enthusiastic, desperate people who were ready to follow them.

At the same time efforts were made to gain a deeper understanding of the nature of *galut* as the exile of the Jewish God's people and to motivate it. Judah Halevi spoke from the heart of his people when (in his philosophical-apologetic book of dialogue *Kuzari*) he assigned to Jewish life in the Diaspora the task of freeing themselves and the world from sin. Thus the idea of sacrificing oneself for one's faith, in line with the sacrificing of Isaac, led to veritable epidemics of suicide from his time, the age of the Crusades, on. The Jews regarded themselves as expiatory sacrifices, as it were, if they slaughtered themselves and their families by the thousands or, as in the days of the Black Death, set their houses on fire or jumped singing and dancing into the fires prepared for them to escape falling into the hands of the "idolaters," as they regarded the Christians with their icon cult. The more cruel and degenerate Christianity seemed to them, the more the best and most naively pious among the Jews believed in their task to bear witness, even through voluntary death, to the preservation of the pure monotheistic religion and to the "sanctification of God's name" *(kiddush hashem).* In so doing they also believed that their dispersion over all countries and their testimony would serve everywhere for the dissemination of the true doctrine and thus hasten the approach of the Messianic period in which they, liberated as a people, would be a model and a focus for the other nations.

Palestine in the Faith of Medieval Jewry

Even though every Jew and Jewry as a whole could contribute through penance and "sanctification of (the ineffable) God's name" while living and dying *(kiddush hashem)* to the hastening of the last days, that time of redemption could really be brought about only by God himself—in supernatural fashion, as was now generally believed, and not gradually but suddenly. In this faith there was a consolation: the "catastrophe" of redemption could come at any moment. But at the same time this faith indicated how distant the real Palestine had become in the actual life of the Jews, particularly since the almost complete eradication of the Jewish population of Palestine by the Crusaders. Only now did Palestine become for the Jewish masses entirely and exclusively the "Holy Land," the land that really had little in common with the earthly world anymore. Every day—morning, noon, and night—the Jews prayed for return to their "own country"; they believed that this return would become reality some day, and an entire "science" endeavored to calculate the date of this final period of history. However, the commandment to move to Palestine, as contained in the Talmud, had long since ceased to have any validity. At the end of time the Jews would be taken by God and his Messiah to the Holy Land, the land of God and his people of Israel, in some wondrous way, on subterranean paths or on angels' wings. Only very few Jews, impelled by excessive longing for the old homeland, dared to overcome all obstacles of medieval roads and borders and make a pilgrimage on foot to Palestine for a temporary or permanent stay; these, to be sure, included such greats as Judah Halevi, Maimonides, and Rabbi Moses ben Nahman (Nahmanides). For the others, mysticism attempted to build a bridge between the gaping misery of the present and the hoped-for bright future by interpreting everything earthly as a secret reference to hidden divine things. The lower the Jews sank in their status and in the spatial narrowness of the world, the more they were inclined to let mystical speculations transport them to heights and distances.

From the vantage point of mysticism the minutely observed traditional customs received a new interpretation and a new splendor. But this also bathed all of life in an unreal, ghostly light; basically, everything was only a symbol for other, more real things, and for that reason it was not worthwhile to take matters in hand and devise real ways out of the *galut*. The strange combination of faith, tradition, and mysticism that surrounded the Jews' love of Palestine and their inner connectedness with it thus produced—in addition to a practical attitude toward all everyday matters—a quietistic, fatalistic stance of devout, expiatory temporization that viewed and condemned any political activity aimed at a radical change in the Jews' national destiny and the abolition of the *galut* as a reprehensible interference in God's reign. The time of penance in the exile of the Diaspora must not be arbitrarily shortened. This peculiar reversal of the Messianic idea of redemption has survived among certain circles of pious Jews to this day. From its very beginnings,

the Zionist movement has had difficulties combating this piously fatalistic attitude . . .

The Historical Consciousness of the Jews

One thing, however, was always preserved for the Jews: an unbroken
historical consciousness. As long as they lived in their own settlements,
no matter whether these were called *Judengasse* or (later) ghetto, with
awe or with contempt, they had no doubt that they were a people with a
God-given past and an equal future. To them the present was not
"history" in the real sense; it was exile, something that happened and
that they allowed to happen to them which was hardly worth recording
for the sake of remembrance—unless it was to remember the martyrs
and "saints" who had sealed their loyalty to God with their deaths. At
bottom they felt superior to the "idolatrous" peoples who were enslaving
them, who only used violence and remained enmeshed in a cheerless
present because according to their "foolish" misbelief the Messiah had
already appeared. This conviction of their own superiority as a chosen
people in the service of the one God precluded the Jews from viewing
themselves as the pariahs that the nations saw in them and treated them
as.* No matter how degrading their outward position might be, in their
own eyes they were, as God's people and believers in pure monotheism,
far above the other nations, and in their daily prayers they thanked God
for not creating them in the pattern of the others. When their sins and
those of their fathers were expiated and their tasks in the *galut* were
completed, then the outward relationship between them and the nations
would also change in their favor. The Christians regarded this attitude as
arrogance, obstinacy, and hatred of Christians, and it intensified their
dislike of the Jews and their hostility toward them.

The thought and actions of the leaders concentrated on keeping the
Jewish people alive during this difficult and extremely long transitional
period. They supported the people spiritually by faithfully preserving
the Jewish teachings and adapted their interpretations to the conditions
prevailing in given places and at given times; these teachings almost
became a substitute for the territorial basis of a normal national life. The
communal autonomy with its own judicial system and its necessarily
severe measures against any outsider who was endangering the unity,
and even more severe action against traitors and harmful persons, always
created a rather homelike atmosphere. Charity for the poor, which was

*The Jews did not begin to refer to themselves as pariahs until the eighteenth century,
when under the influence of the Enlightenment they began to strive for equality and
began to view themselves through the eyes of their environment. We shall have more to
say about this at a later point. (See the literature in Part 2 and on p. 265.)

organized in exemplary fashion for those times, protected the community from social disintegration even in hard times, and frequently the utilization of acquired wealth in negotiations with the enemy (or the "friendly" protecting powers) provided the necessary protection from the outside. In the second half of the twelfth century the Jewish world traveler Benjamin of Tudela (Spain) expressed the typical attitude of the Jews toward their persecutions as follows: "The Greeks [he meant the Byzantines] hate the Jews no matter whether they are good or bad. They impose a heavy yoke upon them, they beat them in the streets and enslave them on the roads. But the Jews are rich and good people, charitable and pious, and they bear the yoke of the *galut* with equanimity."

Valuation of Wealth

In this ghetto community there increasingly developed, almost of necessity and in a formally democratic manner, a rule of the rich. Their wealth was regarded as a sign that they were especially favored by God, for this wealth, which evidently was a reward for leading lives pleasing in the sight of God, served to maintain the Jews inwardly and outwardly. By means of this charity, which was increasingly regarded not only as a wealthy man's duty ordained and recognized by God but also as a right of the receiver, as indicated by the Hebrew terms *tzeddakah* (justice) and *mitzvah* (duty, commandment), the rich protected the poor from ruin. At the same time the influence of the rich inclined the rulers in favor of the Jews in times of hardship and danger. A wealthy man was the rescuer and protector and therefore the leading force. Especially since the end of the Middle Ages and in the ensuing centuries up to the period of emancipation Jews were frequently permitted to settle in the cities only as helpers or relatives of the few wealthy men whose help was desired and who were therefore granted the right of settlement. The more difficult the terms were, the more the influence of the rich was bound to rise. There developed an unhealthy situation whose aftereffects could be felt long after the granting of equal rights: In the Jewish settlements a few powerful rich people were effectively in control, particularly because not infrequently the authorities put them in charge of raising the Jewish taxes and sometimes gave them an appropriate title ("*magister judaeorum*," "master of the Jews").

The natural consequence was that striving for wealth became more and more common. That was the only way to protect oneself from one's enemies, and it was also the road to social standing within one's own community. The scholar on the one hand and the rich man on the other constituted the elite of the ghetto community, and not infrequently one person managed to combine both virtues in himself. The greater the poverty and the oppression became, the more did the wealthy rise in esteem. When it was hard to make a living, scholarship naturally had to decline; in the hopeless conditions of the Central European ghetto there was less and less room for it after the period of the Black Death.

The Problem of the Apostates

That was how things developed inside the ghetto walls. Of course, not all Jews withstood the attacks, threats, and seducements and remained loyal to Judaism, for the price of such loyalty often was slight from long-time domiciles, sufferings and humiliations of all kinds, or even death. All that was demanded of the Jews, at least theoretically, was baptism—a meaningless ceremony to them, a sprinkling with a few drops of holy water. It is understandable that many took this road—some out of the ordinary motive of the will to live and immediate advantage, others because they lacked the power of resistance, and many because they feared rape, torture, and death; all of these motives are humanly comprehensible. Surely some, and not the worst ones, did it out of desperate conviction. After all, it was always possible to conclude from pressure and catastrophes that one's adversaries were in the right, and actually this was much more in line with both medieval and ancient thought. God had provided visible evidence that he had rejected his people and that the victorious Christian faith was the right one. To this day many people have regarded victory as an expression of justice. Hence it is entirely understandable that often despair over the fate of their people caused especially truth-seekers rather than shallow persons to have inner doubts and to leave the Jewish fold. Others did so to facilitate their career or in an unheroic submission to force. When these conversions involved individuals, that was a normal loss to Judaism and did not really pose a problem. Individuals have always converted to the predominant religions and faiths. One cannot expect everyone to become a martyr in defiance of persecution or to resist the temptations of a more comfortable life, especially when the preservation of human life is regarded as a value and commandment of the first order, as it is in Judaism. Nor can one impose limits on a thinking person who is inwardly shaken and keep him from drawing conclusions that are different from what his tradition and his environment permit him. Again and again we must emphasize that the Jews were as human as anyone else and behaved like other people; they acted as resolute and weak, heroic and cowardly, unflinching and wavering, convinced and doubting persons. When this involved individuals and these individuals were absorbed by other nations, it had little to do with the Jewish question. However, the fact that such individuals who severed their connection with Judaism occasionally became foes and persecutors of the Jews does show that frequently matters did not end with a conversion as far as both the apostates and their surroundings were concerned. This problem became particularly severe after mass baptisms, and then it turned into a general problem that is of interest to us in connection with the Jewish question. We can observe this problem in all the great forced conversions of the Jews to another faith that was the dominant one—in the territories of Islam, in the Christian Europe of the Middle Ages, and down to the countries of the Communist compulsory faith in our day. This problem found its most striking expression in fifteenth-century Spain.

The Problem of the Marranos

The origin of this problem in Spain is well known. Since the forced conversions of the Jews by the Christian Visigoths in the sixth and seventh centuries, the beginning of the Christian *"reconquista"* in the eleventh century, and the development of the Islamic–North African sect of the Almohades in the twelfth, in that land of religious fanaticism there had repeatedly been neophytes, new believers about whose true faith and religious activities the old believers had doubts, and rightly so. This became a religious and national mass problem at the end of the fourteenth century. The religious persecutions of 1391, led by the fanatical priest Martinez and fueled by a mixture of religious frenzy and lust for loot, had caused many communities in Christian Spain to convert and submit to baptism. The compulsory public disputation at Tortosa in the years 1413 and 1414 had led additional large numbers of Jews from all walks of life who could not withstand the terrible spiritual and physical pressure to the baptismal font. All the abovementioned motives played a part in these conversions. Here, too, there were many martyrs who were ready to sacrifice themselves, as well as thousands who fell victim to brute force. But the number of Jews who simply yielded to force and went to the baptismal font to save themselves from immediate danger to life and limb was far greater than it had been in the persecutions in Germany during the Crusades. What was involved here was not a minority of the Jews but a majority, tens of thousands. Many of them may have regarded this only as a formality and a submission to force without any intention of letting it affect their lives; others may have been ready to convert to Christianity in earnest. In contrast to the Jews of Germany, a large part of the Jews of Spain, at least the upper class of Court Jews, the wealthy, and the intelligentsia who were leaders and models to the others, had a close connection with Spanish culture in language, thought, and action, with all the inner bonds that such an assimilation involves. However, the large numbers of voluntary and compulsory baptisms created a problem with which neither side, the Christians or the forcibly converted "New Christians," was able to cope.

The problem of the forced converts, called *anusim* (forced or violated ones) by the Jews and *marranos* (swine) by the Spaniards, shows to what extent the Jewish problem had by then become an almost inextricable complex on both sides.

The majority of the baptized Jews were not able to abandon Judaism entirely. This clinging to Judaism was not merely a question of religious convictions or doubts; since ancient times, and increasingly as time went on, Judaism had been far more than that: a whole world. It was, above all, a way of life, traditions and customs passed on from generation to generation and thus almost hereditary, a growing up in social and economic circumstances that usually did not change even if the faith was officially changed. Thus ties with Judaism remained despite baptism, and in the nature of things there still were ties to Jewish friends and companions among whom the convert still lived for the time being. This attachment of the Jews to their Jewishness, however, was bound to evoke mistrust and anxiety among the non-Jews who had, as it were, taken their erstwhile enemies into their own camp. In the view of the Church it was impossible to permit the Jews to return to the Jewish fold, at least where it could not be clearly demonstrated that a forced baptism had taken place; but there were many nuances of compulsion and fear of force, so that one could always interpret a baptism as having been voluntary. But there might be a real danger to the purity of the Christian-Catholic faith if the New Christians, who were inwardly inclined toward Judaism and secretly practiced their accustomed rituals, were allowed to do as they pleased. After all, they often constituted a considerable part of the middle class, and as financiers, courtiers, physicians, and even high clergymen they were more influential than their number and background warranted. Why should the Old Christians—so one might ask—be obliged to observe the Christian commandments more strictly than the New Christians, who observed Jewish customs or, under the influence of their forced conversion and the inner untruthfulness of their lives, derided both Judaism and Christianity and accordingly had to be irreligious scoffers, rationalistic theists, or unbelieving atheists? It was certainly not out of mere envy of the privileged positions of many New Christians if people refused to accept this situation, though of course this envy played a significant part. It was a justified concern from the standpoint of Christianity and a strict Christian morality.

But people did not consider that the Christians themselves were to blame for this situation, nor did they realize that the methods used to remedy this deplorable state of affairs—anti-Jewish agitation in speech and writing, spying, and finally the dreadful and cruel activities of the tribunals of the Inquisition with their insidious system of physical and mental torture—were not designed to present Christianity to the New

Christians in a more ideal light. These methods were bound to be particularly repulsive to the best among the Jewish Christians—until they were even ready to die on the stake for their faith *(auto da fé)* in order to escape lies and psychic torment. As for those still wavering, such treatment could cause only the inferior, the timid, or the religiously indifferent among them to embrace Christianity completely—those who did not mind feigning piousness when that seemed indicated. But when such Jews entered Christian society, this was only bound to intensify the true Christians' dislike of pseudo-Jews and even real Jews and to provide fresh fuel for suspicion, revulsion, and hatred.

The Christians now identified with the Jews everything that they disliked about the New Christians and Jewish Christians, with whom they now had closer contact than they had had with the Jews as Jews. In this way the traditional, dogma-shaped image of the depraved Jew received new features that were derived from reality and seemed to be constantly confirmed by daily contact. Thus there arose for the first time in the polemics against the New Christians an anti-Jewish literature that did not stop at the traditional Christian teachings about the Jews with their excesses (blood libel, desecration of the Host, etc.) or the accusations from the economic and social sphere (usury, wealth, etc.). The corruption of the Jews was anchored in the blood, which was similar to what happened in the anti-Semitic teachings four hundred years later, though without the pseudo-scientific basis of the latter. What was demanded was purity of the Spanish blood *("limpieza de sangre")* without foreign pollution. The image of the "typical" Jew received a further elaboration and already approximated the stereotype that was to become common in the anti-Jewish literature of the nineteenth and twentieth centuries (in part on the basis of similar experiences). In this Spanish polemic a Jew's character and actions were characterized as follows (in the worlds of the greatest expert on this period): "He is nihilistic and libertine in matters of religion; he espouses that religion which brings in the most money; he plots to subvert and destroy the Christian community; he pollutes the pure Spanish blood; he lives as a parasite in Spain and emigrates to Palestine with the money he has taken from Christians" (Y. F. Baer, *Galut* [New York, 1947], pp. 57–58). The picture thus drawn of the Jew influenced the non-Jews who occupied themselves with the Jewish question far beyond that place and that time; this was one of the effects on the further development of the Jewish question.

The immediate effect was more far-reaching. The door was opened wide to mutual suspicion. Even those who were willing to detach themselves from Judaism completely were rebuffed time and time again and constantly reminded of their origin. The world around them viewed them with almost more suspicious eyes than the Jews who were loyal to

Judaism and whom the Inquisition, too, left unmolested. It became obvious that Judaism could no longer be shed like a garment, that the historical events and experiences of a millenium had so welded it to the entire personality of a Jew, his activities, his behavior, his thinking, his belief, and his supersititions, that a period of one or two generations did not suffice for him really to detach himself from it. For a Jew to be completely integrated into his surroundings, the world around him would have had to be patient and forbearing for a much longer period of time—but have people anywhere ever shown understanding patience with a minority that was different? This mistrust of the world around them was imparted to the true converts and went a long way toward explaining, then as later, the behavior of those apostates who adopted a hostile stance toward the Jewish society from which they had come. Viewing themselves through the eyes of their surroundings, they were full of self-hatred and hatred of their background. They wanted to prove to themselves and to the world that they had completely detached themselves from Judaism—and yet to insightful persons they showed only how dubious this proof was and what an effort it took for them to break away and "cleanse" themselves completely. As many of those "completely" de-Judaized people endeavored to do so, they developed into the bitterest persecutors of the Jews.

In Spain, and soon thereafter in Portugal, the Marrano problem demonstrated that the Jewish question could not be solved in this way, through compulsory conversion. Then and at any time, individuals could be integrated into their environment through conversion to another faith, but it was impossible to absorb the Jews and make them disappear as a whole in this fashion. In the European world as it had developed in the Middle Ages it was possible, if one feared the harmful influence of the Jews, to destroy them, expel them, or let them lead in the ghetto a life as isolated from the surrounding world as possible. There was no other choice. This is how the Jewish question stood at the turn of the European Middle Ages to the modern period.

4

The Development of the Jewish Question in the Modern Age up to the French Revolution

The Jewish Question at the Beginning of the Modern Age

It is common knowledge that the era in European history that we are used to calling the modern age did not begin suddenly; rather, as in any historical epoch, conditions changed gradually and with many transitional phenomena. Thus it is clear from the outset that at the turn of the fifteenth to the sixteenth century the situation of the Jews and the world's relationship to the Jews—what we call the Jewish question—did not suddenly assume another character and new forms.

Yet there was something different about this particular transition to a new age. The world around the Jews began to change in important ways. The so-called Renaissance brought—first in Italy and soon in northern Europe as well—a revival of art and scholarship; there was a new sense of life, at least in a leading stratum of society. People had the feeling of being new-born as personalities; at the same time they felt as though after a dark night the golden age of antiquity was illuminated for them once more and could be integrated into the life of the present again. They began to ask fresh questions of the reality of existence and dared to give answers that deviated from the religiously determined dogmatism of the Christian Middle Ages. The unity of Christian faith was broken, and Protestantism in its various forms of expression successfully struggled for a *raison d'être* within a Christianity that had hitherto been dominated solely by the Pope. It, too, was based on ancient sources—the Bible and the Gospels, which were being studied in the Hebrew and Greek original as well as being translated into the vernacular, making them accessible and comprehensible to everyone in contrast to the Vulgate, the Latin Bible, the only one that had hitherto been valid. New geographical and intellectual worlds were discovered, and new states and a new political science came into being. Despite all wars, sufferings, and defects the temper of the times may have found its most typical expression in the words of the German humanist and chivalric activist Ulrich von Hutten: It is a joy to live in this century.

All this, however, had initially little influence on the life of the Jews and the problems of their existence. If anything, the estrangement of Jewish life in Europe from the surroundings increased. It was as though Jewish history and general history were being enacted on different planes and at different times, as though there were an ever-increasing gulf between them, and as if the Jews were being cast out and spewed forth by that which contemporary consciousness regarded as human history (and what in reality was Christian-European history). Yet there were of course closer connections than there appeared to be, and mutual influences certainly were no less effective than before. The Bible in its original language and its medieval Jewish exegetes as well as Jewish mysticism (kabbalah) were studied by the Humanists and the religious reformers and absorbed in Christian reinterpretations of all kinds. The Jews, for their part, certainly did not ignore these new manifestations of a more liberal way of thinking, for these gave rise to many real and Messianic hopes. For the time being, however, the relations between Jews and Christians did not change for the better. It was as if the world were changing and progressing in all matters but one: in the way the Jews were viewed, in the attitude of the world to the Jews and of the Jews to the world. On the contrary: the modes of behavior that had developed at the end of the Middle Ages received their most enduring form in the very decades and centuries of the greatest transformations in the world. The laws pertaining to the Jews, which had been decisively formulated by the Lateran Council of 1215, were enforced with particular harshness in this period.

Luther's Attitude toward Judaism and the Jewish Question

At first it did appear as though the representatives of the new faith, especially Luther and his adherents, had greater understanding for Judaism. Beginning in 1509 the German Humanist Johannes Reuchlin's stalwart defense of Jewish writings against attacks by the Jewish renegade Pfefferkorn, who was supported by the Cologne Dominicans—the so-called *Talmudstreit* (a dispute about the Talmud)—gave rise to much hope among the Jews, and after 1517 these hopes were intensified by Luther's public stand against the absolute rule of the papal-ecclesiastic dogmas and the corruptness of their propagators. Did it not seem as though the representatives of the new humanistic mentality who fought the cult of saints and image-worship as the Jews had always done, who based themselves on the Hebrew Bible and even let themselves be influenced by the written and spoken words of Jewish exeges, were coming closer to the Jewish point of view in their religious beliefs?

Luther, too, had been heard to speak many a critical word against the Church's hostility to the Jews, and in 1523 he had published a widely disseminated and often reprinted pamphlet entitled "That Jesus Christ Was Born a Jew." It seemed to contain the sharpest condemnation of Jew-hatred and past Christian policy toward the Jews that had been voiced by the Christian side. "The fools, popes, bishops, sophists, and monks, those coarse dunderheads," says Luther in his blunt language, "have hitherto dealt with the Jews in such a way that anyone who was a good Christian would have preferred to become a Jew. . . . The Jews have been treated like dogs; they have been cursed and robbed of their possessions. . . . And yet they are blood-kin cousins and brothers of the Savior. God has distinguished them like no other people, and he entrusted the Holy Writ to their hands."

The structure of this work and the context of these words did indicate that Luther hoped to convert the Jews to Christianity as he viewed and preached it. He thought that if they were treated more lovingly and prudently, they could be convinced of the truth of his religion, but he expressed this in formulations to which one was not accustomed from zealous Christians. They sounded like a defense of the Jews and almost like the kind of complaint against the Christians that the Jews had voiced since time out of mind. "But if we only use force against them, if we maintain that unless they have Christian blood they stink, and I know not what other kinds of foolishness . . . what good would that be? Also, if we forbid them to work among us and have the kind of human intercourse that would not drive them to usury, how should that improve them? If we want to help them, we must make the laws more Christian and not more papal, show them love, give them a friendly reception, and let them carry on trades and labor so that they can come to know the teachings and the lives of Christians from their own observation."

These words surely contain the seeds of something new, and they *were* noticed. They made many Jewish leaders—among them Josel of Rosheim, the recognized spokesman for the German Jews of his time—hope that they marked the beginning of a change in the relationship between the Christians and the Jews—though such a change did not come to a certain extent until two and a half centuries later, in the period of the Enlightenment and the French Revolution, and more under the influence of the ideas of the Renaissance than of those of Protestantism. At the time of the Reformation, however, the Jews were bitterly disappointed, just as Luther was deeply disappointed that his words of peace appeared to be ignored by the Jews. To his astonishment they did not lead Jews to convert to Christianity in appreciable numbers. And now it turned out that even the words that were regarded as praise and defense actually did not reflect any change of heart but were only tactical and missionary in nature, with no change for the better in the theological and spiritual attitude toward the Jews. If anything, the opposite was the case; even the so-called defense of the Jews had really been written in Luther's own defense. Archduke Ferdinand, the brother of Emperor Charles V, had accused Luther of calling Christ the seed of Abraham, thus evidently denying his birth by the pure virgin Mary. He wanted to combine his defense against the reproach of Christological heresy, which he regarded as folly, with "something useful" and formulate his avowal of Christ in such a way as to "perhaps also induce some Jews to accept the Christian faith."

When these hopes were dashed, in the ensuing years Luther increasingly made anti-Jewish private and public remarks in his "Table Talks" and numerous publications that did not directly deal with the Jewish question. He could not comprehend the "obstinacy" of the Jews in the face of all biblical and historical evidence against them which to him were so evident that their nonrecognition could only spring from ill will* and devilish influences.

These increasingly venormous attacks reached their zenith in two works expressly directed against the Jews which Luther published in 1543, twenty years after his first writings on the Jews, *Von den Juden und ihren Lügen* (Of the Jews and Their Lies) and *Vom Shemhamphoras und vom Geschlecht Christi* (On Shemhamphoras and the lineage of Christ). In these words the ancient hatred of the Jews, derived from tradition, education, and environment and intensified by occupation with the Bible, politics, and the religious currents of the time, is expressed with such elemental force that despite everything that has happened since then we can only take cognizance of it with astonishment and revulsion.

In the crudest manner and in a vulgar language which even in that period of unbridled, ruffianly polemics even in humanistic circles exceeds any permissible bounds, Luther approvingly repeats all the accusations against the Jews that had accumulated during the Middle Ages. Even the canards about the poisoning of wells, ritual murder, and Jewish sorcery that Luther had earlier opposed are now described as plausible or at least as typical of the Jewish character. Luther now says that it is no longer the purpose of his publications to convert the Jews— "which is no more possible than it is to convert the Devil"—but to show the Jews and their lies as they are "so that we Germans might know what a Jew is on the basis of history and to warn our Christians against the Jews as against the devils themselves. . . ." (*On Shemhamphoras . . .*) The comparison with the Devil and even the equation of the Jews with him keeps recurring,** though we must remember that Luther, like

*Here is one example of many: "Those desperate scoundrels know full well that the New Testament is a book about our Lord Jesus Christ, God's son, and yet they pretend and claim not to know what the New Testament is" (*Of the Jews and Their Lies*).
**For example, in this passage from the same work: "All right, maybe one of the merciful

many of his contemporaries, increasingly saw the earthly world full of devils and identified other adversaries, down to the Pope, with the Devil as well.

In Luther's view, the Jews have been cursed and cast out by God because of their wickedness and especially because they did not recognize Jesus as the Savior and crucified him."*

The best proof of this is their almost fifteen hundred years of exile from their country. "For such cruel wrath of God shows all too clearly that they must surely be on the wrong track; even a child can grasp that. . . . That is why this wrathful act proves that they have surely been rejected by God, no longer are his people, and that he is not their God any more."

The arrogance of the Jews is thus all the more shocking; even now they regard themselves as superior to the Christians, against their better knowledge deny Christ's divinity and Messianic mission, and deride God's son and his virginal mother with obscene epithets.

All they are striving and scheming to do is to torment, exploit, and destroy the Christians. Dominance over the Christians is also the meaning and purpose of their Messianic belief. "Therefore know, dear Christian, and do not doubt that next to the Devil you have no more bitter, venomous, and violent enemy than a real Jew who is serious about wanting to be a Jew. . . . That is why in the histories they are often blamed for poisoning wells and stealing and mutilating children, as at Trent, Weissensee, etc. They do deny it. However, be that as it may, I know full well that they do not lack the will or readiness to do such deeds either secretly or publicly if they have a chance. Be sure to understand that and govern youself accordingly" (*Of the Jews and Their Lies*).

Elsewhere in this work Luther writes: "I know that they deny such things and everything. But it all agrees with Christ's judgment that they

---

saints among us Christians might think I am too indelicate and too rough on the poor Jews if I treat them with such contempt and scorn. Oh my Lord, I am much too lowly to mock such devils, though I would gladly do so. But they are too far superior to me in mockery and also have a god who is a master at mockery and is called the accursed devil and the evil spirit."

*In one of his Table Talks from the same period (spring 1543) we read: "Then someone said: 'Is it written that the Jews shall be threatened by the Day of Judgment?' Doctor Martin Luther said: "Where is is written? I know of no specific reference. There is a passage in Rom. 9, but it cannot be proved by that" (*Kampfschriften gegen das Judentum*, ed. Walter Linden [Berlin, 1936], p. 69). This answer is typical of the style of argumentation in which Luther always based himself on Bible verses which for him contained the absolute truth. But like many Christian theologians before and after him, he could of course have cited the Epistle of Paul to the Romans, chapter 11, verses 25 and 26, which speaks of the salvation of Israel: "Blindness in part is happened to Israel, until the fulness of the Gentiles be come in. And so all Israel shall be saved." (Here Paul based himself on Isaiah 59:20 and 31:33.)

are venomous, bitter, rapacious, insidious snakes, assassins, and children of the Devil that strike and do damage secretly because they are unable to do so openly. . . . It is a lie that the Jews are being held in captivity by the Christians; in reality they dominate and mock the Christians. They make the Christians work, suck them dry, and lead comfortable lives, and yet they are hostile to their Christian hosts,* curse them, and harm them in every way. . . . Besides, no one is holding them back now; the countryside and the roads are open to them, so let them go to their own country whenever they wish; we shall be glad to give them gifts to be rid of them, for they are a heavy burden on us, like a plague, a pest, and pure misfortune in our country."

Luther asks: "What shall we Christians now do with this cast-out, condemned Jewish people?" He counsels a "severe mercy" as expressed in the following proposals: "First, that their synagogues or schools be set afire; whatever will not burn should be covered with earth so that no one will ever see a stone or a cinder. . . .** Second, that their houses be similarly razed and destroyed. . . . For this purpose they should be put under some roof or in some stable like the gypsies to make them realize that they are not the masters in our country. . . . Third, that there be taken from them all prayer books and Talmudic writings in which such idolatry, lies, curses, and blasphemy are taught. Fourth, that henceforth their rabbis be forbidden on peril of their lives to teach. Fifth, that safe-conduct and the right of the roads be entirely taken away from them, for they have no business being abroad. Sixth, that usury be forbidden them and all money and precious things in gold and silver be taken from them and put away for safekeeping . . . (for the use of needy converts). Seventh, that the young and strong Jews and Jewesses be given flails, axes, hoes, spades, sticks, and spindles and made to earn their bread by the sweat of their brow, as has been imposed on Adam's children. . . ."

Luther counsels the clergymen to warn incessantly against the wickedness of the Jews and the rulers not to have any more dealings with them but to expel them from their countries: "If we are to remain free of the Jews' blasphemy, we have to part company with them and drive them out of our country. Let them remember their fatherland; then they must no longer scream about us before God and lie that we are keeping them imprisoned, and we must no longer complain that they are bur-

---

*Luther seems to be the source of the terms *host nation* and *guest nation* that have kept recurring in the anti-Semitic and even the general literature about the Jewish question since Treitschke and have even been unthinkingly adopted by Jewish historians and politicians: "The Jews, our guests, are doing the same to us; we are their hosts." We shall have more to say about this in chapters 6 and 9.
**Here is another passage: ". . . that their synagogues be burned with fire and that whoever is able throw sulphur and tar into the flames; it would be good if someone could add hellfire."

dening us with their blasphemy and usury. This is the most logical and best advice which in such a case safeguards both parts." In even stronger language Luther writes elsewhere: "If this does not avail, we must cast them out like mad dogs so that we shall not share in their horrible blasphemy and all vices, deserve God's wrath along with them, and be damned."

Thus hatred of Jews is preached in the crudest language. In his sermons and table talks Luther keeps coming back to it and demands that the Jews be expelled and destroyed, sometimes adding that they could return to their old fatherland Palestine—an addition that under the prevailing political circumstances was probably intended to be more of a mockery than serious advice. If the Jews will not listen to reason and accept baptism, if they are in league with the Devil (and probably also with the Mohammedan Turks, the enemies of Christianity who were a serious threat to Europe at the time) and virtually embody the Devil, what other solution is there except expulsion and destruction?

The Nature and Effects of Luther's Hostility to the Jews

If in the face of these views and demands, which four hundred years later were to become horrible reality in Nazi Germany and on the European continent dominated by it, we want to be fair to Luther—a man whom Nietzsche called the most eloquent and immodest peasant Germany had ever had as.well as the protest of the Middle Ages against the Renaissance and the revival of learning—we must take several factors into consideration. The first and most important of these is the anti-Jewish tradition of Christianity that had developed over a period of fifteen hundred years and was anchored in the Christian dogmas. This led even the defenders of the Jews to reject only certain untruths and false accusations, as for example in the question of the preservation or burning of their religious writings, particularly the Talmud, or the estimate of the benefit or harm to the economic prosperity of a Christian area. At the same time such defenders did not want to be regarded as friends of the Jews, if only because they might be suspected of being heretics. Even Humanists of the stature of an Erasmus, a Reuchlin, or an Ulrich von Hutten were no exceptions. Added to this was the fact that the economic and social position of the Jews made it hard, almost impossible, to love them. That was the tragic situation into which the Jews had been forced: Even if they were of the purest character, the world around them perceived them as religious, economic, and social troublemakers.

For someone like Luther, whom a religious crisis had impelled to protest against the ecclesiastic Establishment, the decisive thing was the religious-dogmatic element; other things, derived from daily life, were added later. In his quest for religious release from his monastic-Christian guilt feelings and in his return to the theological wellsprings of Christianity, from the Bible and the basic Christian writings of the New Testament to the Church Fathers, he kept reverting to the fundamental dogmas and the basic conflict between Judaism and Christianity. He once more fought the Pauline fight with the Jewish God as he perceived him—the God of avenging "justice" and the empty sacredness of good works—and escaped from him, as it were, through the principle of grace which Jesus had vouchsafed the faithful without their having merited it.

His hatred of the Jews and fight against them may be understood as a continuation transposed to earthly reality of his inner struggle against the Jewish God of the Old Testament, who as a devil threatens the new God's people, the Christians, to which the chosenness and vocation have been transferred. In this fight there can be no mercy, for as Luther sees it, it is a struggle of truth against lies and of God against the Devil. And this contest is no longer merely one between dogmatics and the Roman-Christian system of order; it is now situated in the human soul, in the German psyche, and becomes a daily and hourly struggle of the individual conscience. Thus there can be no compromise here, no doctrinal edifice like the Catholic one that damns and yet with Romance-theological finesse concedes a right to live and leaves hope for future redemption.

Thus Lutheran Protestantism basically brought no easement in the Jewish question, but on the contrary exacerbated it. In the Catholic doctrine that had dominated the Middle Ages the fate of the Jews had despite execration and damnation been incorporated into a doctrine of salvation according to which the Jews were to be degraded and enslaved, but also to be preserved as witnesses to the truth of Christianity and its redemption at the end of time. All that was left now was the execration—irrevocable and expressed in the crudest terms.

This is not the place for a detailed documentation of the effect that Luther's anti-Jewish statements and writings had on his contemporaries and on posterity. This has probably not yet been sufficiently investigated for such a documentation. But it is safe to say that in the states where the new teachings were accepted, either promptly or eventually, the anti-Jewish attitude of the populace remained at least unchanged. Luther's coarse fulminations sounded so beautiful to many that in 1523 the popular Nuremberg poet Hans Sachs could bring himself to write a poem about the "Wittenberg Nightingale."

But the effect of these writings and the view of the Jewish question contained in them was more profound and more far-reaching. After all, the new doctrine appealed to the conscience of individuals, of persons motivated by their faith. It demanded that everyone read the Bible in Luther's translation and concern himself with the doctrine as laid down in his writings and interpretations of the Bible. Time and time again, for centuries and down to our day, Luther's speeches and writings have been and are being read, and any kind of anti-Semitism can be justified on their basis. Hence they can be used to motivate the most vicious attacks against the Jews and justify any excess against them, and not infrequently they have been so used. To be sure, many a person of goodwill can base himself on the words of Luther's early work of 1523, but his far more frequent and increasingly sharp words *against* the Jews can be used to prove that the young Luther simply knew little about the true nature of the Jews and that the more mature man regretted and renounced all the good things he had said about the Jews in his youthful trust and exuberance. As soon as his anti-Jewish writings appeared, they once and for all dashed the hope that with the religious revolution against the Catholic Church and its doctrines its teachings about the Jews would be invalidated and its horrifying image of the Jews would be replaced by a friendlier one. As far as the Jewish question was concerned, Luther's appeal for independent thought and belief was immediately directed into the wrong channels.

Other currents in the Reformation did not substantially differ from Luther in their rejection of the Jews and their persecution of all "Judaizing" tendencies—particularly Calvinism, which in one form or another took hold in Switzerland and Western Europe. In the various countries all these new currents within Christianity were organized into churches that incorporated a bit of the national spirit that was coming to the fore since the waning Middle Ages and which frequently surpassed the Catholic Church in their absolute demands for religious obedience and compulsion. In the sixteenth century these churches were still a long way from the kind of principled tolerance toward those of different thought and faith that was to develop in the course of the succeeding centuries after bloody fights.

Intensification of Anti-Jewish Sentiment in the Catholic World

At the same time the attitude of the Catholic world toward the Jews hardened, and not only because the Catholic Church—which was defending itself against attacks from without and within, reforming itself, and mounting a counterattack—naturally intensified its militant measures against heretics and infidels. In 1540 Pope Paul III ratified the fighting order of the Jesuits that had been founded a few years earlier by Loyola; in 1542 the establishment of the Inquisition was renewed and concentrated in Rome; and 1545 brought the opening of the general Church Council of Trent that met with several interruptions until the end of 1583 and marked the beginning of the so-called Counter Reformation. This countermovement was bound to redound to the disadvantage of the Jews, for a considerable influence on the development of the great evangelical heretic movements was attributed to them. Had not the originators of the new currents and the founders of the new sects gone back to the original Hebrew Bible, and had they not used Jews for linguistic instruction and an interpretation of its contents instead of using the Latin Vulgate of St. Jerome (347–420), which had hitherto been regarded as the only authoritative and sacred text and which the Council of Trent had in 1546 again confirmed as the only accredited translation of the Bible? Everybody knows what a revolutionary influence these new Bible translations had. Thus the medieval ecclesiastical laws concerning the Jews with their degrading character were preserved in the countries that remained Catholic or were regained for Catholicism during the century of religious struggles; in fact, they were now frequently enforced more strictly than before. Actually, in Italy, and particularly in the papal territories, they now became full reality for the first time.

The Ghetto

It is surely no accident that the word and the concept *ghetto* came into being at this particular time and increasingly became common usage—first in Italy and for Italian conditions, and in the course of the following centuries in other countries as well. The first use of the concept dates from 1516, the year before Luther's public appearance, when the Venetian Republic established a separate, isolated quarter for the Jews who had been admitted again after a lengthy banishment. This section probably received its name from a nearby foundry (Italian *geto*).* In 1562, shortly before the close of the Council of Trent, the designation appeared for the first time in a papal bull of 1556 for the Jewish quarter of Rome, located on the left bank of the Tiber. At the beginning of the seventeenth century it was gradually used in other countries (e.g., Germany and England) and languages. New words come into being, solidify into definite concepts, and are ever more universally accepted when the phenomena they designate have assumed a more or less uniform and generally valid character and hence have been recognized in their specificity and universality. Once this happens, the existence and acceptance of the concept often lead to a wider dissemination and generalization of its substance.

In point of fact, closed ghettos were not established in Italy until the sixteenth century. But even in the European countries in which they had existed earlier, e.g., Germany and Southern France,** the ghetto as

---

*About the origin, etymology, dissemination, and change in meaning of the term *ghetto* see the detailed discussion and bibliography in Part 2.
**On the development of special Jewish quarters in medieval cities, see pp. 86ff.

a compulsory institution for the Jews was developed with full severity and in systematic and pedantic fashion only now, in the first two centuries of the modern age.

What a far cry from the privileges of 1084 and 1090 for the settlement of the Jews in Speyer, the first known privileges for a Jewish settlement in Germany, to the ghettos of the waning Middle Ages and the first three centuries of the modern age! The privileges for the Jewish settlement in Speyer granted special rights to a guild of merchants. In the Privilege of 1084 Bishop Rüdeger, who turned his village bishopric into a town, expressly declared that he had invited the Jews and given them rights that were better than what the Jewish people possessed in any other city of the German Reich "in order to augment the honor of our region." He said he had made them settle outside the residential district of the other citizens and had surrounded their settlement with a wall "so they would not be bothered by the mischief of the rabble." The Jews were given the right to "freely change gold and silver and buy and sell anything they pleased," to govern themselves, employ Christian servants, and keep Christian slaves. Six years later Emperor Henry IV confirmed and expanded these rights. His Privilege of 1090 expressly enjoins people from "depriving the Jews of any of their possessions, their land, buildings, gardens, vineyards, fields, slaves, or other movable and immovable property." They were to be free to "honestly trade their possessions with any person and to move about freely and peacefully in our territory, to engage in commerce and business, to buy and sell, without anyone demanding duty on merchandise and imposing any public or private taxes upon them." Compulsory conversion, as well as torture to extort confessions, was forbidden, and killing or injuring Jews was to be severely punished. As we have repeatedly pointed out, the fact that it was necessary to give the Jews such special rights was due to their special position as aliens; these rights were an expression of their existence as aliens of a special kind. But on the whole, the separate settlements of the Jews were similar in structure to the "colonies of foreign merchants who lived under their own government and in accordance with their own laws. . . . These constituted a very desirable privilege of the merchants, and the potentates of less developed states used it in an endeavor to attract foreign merchants" (Franz Oppenheimer).

It was downhill all the way from there—what with the Crusades beginning in 1096; the establishment of the ecclesiastical-papal dominance of Christianity, which found its most drastic expression in the decisions of the Fourth Lateran Council of 1215; the consequences of the plague around the middle of the fourteenth century, with the expulsion of the Jews and permission for short-term residence; the transformations of the European economy and society, and so forth. This finally led to the confinement of the Jews in cramped districts, with walls whose gates were closed at night and were not opened on Christian holidays. The clear intention was to isolate the Jews from the Christian population as disruptive foreign bodies, almost like nidi spreading disease and pestilence. Their districts were kept to a minimum and generally not expanded even if there was an increase in the population. To create more living space it was necessary to make additions to the point where the structure of the houses became unsafe; these ells and extensions narrowed and darkened the lanes even more and made it more and more difficult to keep them clean and sanitary. Moreover, in general Jews were not permitted to purchase the houses but had to rent them from Christian owners. Everything was done to make the Jews' dwellings as unlivable as possible and, in accordance with the commandments of Christian charity (which people liked to cite), to make the position of their inhabitants as degrading as was proper for the slaves of the church and of the secular authorities who were accursed by God and by men.*

This intent to degrade and isolate the Jews is expressed in the preface to the bull *Cum nimis absurdum* (1555) with which Pietro Caraffa, who had just ascended to the throne of St. Peter as Paul IV, justified the confinement of the Jews to the ghetto in Rome. This acknowledgment that all earlier ecclesiastical laws and decrees had not fully reached that goal begins with these words: "Since it appears utterly absurd and impermissible that the Jews, whom God has condemned to eternal slavery because of their guilt, should enjoy our Christian love and toleration only to repay our graciousness with base ingratitude and insults and, instead of being humbly submissive, to strive for power; moreover, in view of the fact that their impudence, which has been brought to our attention, goes so far in Rome and other places lying within the domains of the Holy Roman Church that Jews venture to show themselves in the midst of Christians and even the immediate vicinity of churches without wearing any badge, rent lodgings in the finest sections of the city, acquire immovable property, employ Christian nurses and other servants in their households, and in many other ways trample Jewish honor underfoot, we find ourselves obliged to institute

---

*Anyone who would like to get an idea of how a typical ghetto appeared to an observer from the outside should read the description of the Jewish ghetto of Rome that the East Prussian writer and historian Ferdinand Gregorovius published three hundred years after its opening. (Yes, it was written in 1855, and the ghetto was not abolished until the occupation of Rome and the elimination of the Papal States in 1870.) The well-known Christian theologian and historian of religion Travers Herford (1860–1950) writes in *The Legacy of Israel* (1927, p. 122): "Legal compulsion to reside there made the Jews' quarter a ghetto. . . . Within the narrow enclosure thus marked out the Jews of the city were compelled to live, and however much their numbers increased they were not allowed to extend their boundary. For unsanitary conditions and over-crowding the worst slum of a modern city would be preferable to a medieval ghetto. Under some such conditions the majority of the Jews in Europe were forced to exist during three centuries (ca. 1400–ca. 1700), the dreariest period in all Jewish history."

the following measures. . . ." There follow fifteen paragraphs of regulations: the Jewish quarter was to be walled off; the Jews were forbidden to purchase houses and parcels of land and ordered to sell those in their possession to Christians; they were enjoined from having more than one synagogue in each district; the men were ordered to wear a yellow hat and the women a yellow bonnet; Jews were forbidden to employ Christian servants or to eat, play, and bathe with Christians; they were prohibited from trading in foodstuffs and new clothing, and permitted to be only junk dealers; Jewish physicians were forbidden to treat Christians and to be addressed by Christians as "sir."

This is what the statutes and regulations for many similar ghettos and Jewish districts were like. In some places they were a bit easier or harder, and the regulations were more specific or somewhat less pedantically defined, but they were always carefully surrounded by a wall composed of special interests and religious and human aversion. This wall of condescending and degrading bureaucracy supplemented the stone walls and regulated everything animate and inanimate within them.

Reasons for the Fixation of the Ghetto

1. TRANSITIONAL PERIODS

Why—so one might ask—were the anti-Jewish laws of the Middle Ages more strictly enforced and fixed in the institution of the ghetto precisely in such a dynamic age, in contrast to the more static nature of the Middle Ages, at a time of changes in all areas, of religious conflict and a struggle of the emerging scientific-rationalistic thought with the ecclesiastical powers, of profound economic and social transformations, and of a lessening of religious influence at least among some of the educated classes? To find an answer to this question we must first of all abandon the notion that mankind follows a straight upward path from darkness to light, from prejudice to a scientifically unprejudiced mode of thinking and a comparable life-style. (This notion became part of the liberal view of history of the nineteenth century, via the Enlightenment of the eighteenth century, including the philosophy of history of many Jews.) The new never prevails over the old immediately and in a straight line; the dominant powers resist it. For a long transitional period the old and the new exist side by side, against and within each other. There is another factor as well:

2. FEAR OF THE DEVIL AND WITCHES

Great watersheds of history give rise to anxieties; we are experiencing this in our time, which W. H. Auden has characterized as "The Age of

Anxiety." The world—that is, our familiar, accustomed world—seems to be threatened by demonic forces and going under. Everything adverse, whether old or new, is viewed from this aspect of anxiety which threatens to choke off all life. When everything changes, when there is a revaluation of values and today's right is tomorrow's wrong, then there must be something fishy about it, to use a colloquial phrase. Hence everything that diverted one from the right path, everything seductive, everything that faith and morality forbade—heresy, women and sensuality, Jews and usury—was in that age regarded as the devil's work. We know about Luther's constant fight with the devil; his doctrine of grace is basically an escape from the anxiety of a man with guilt feelings to the grace of the Redeemer. In this, as in much else, Luther was the strongest embodiment and proclaimer of a general Zeitgeist. Catholics, Lutherans, and Calvinists agreed that the age viewed the world from the aspect of the threatening dominance of the Devil. Satanic forces were lurking everywhere; everything evil and hostile, all the "discontents" of civilization (to use Freud's cautious formulation) were a work of the Devil and his helpers, the demons (who often assumed some familiar and inscrutable human form and shape), the sorcerers, and especially the witches. The two centuries from the late fifteenth to the late seventeenth were a period of great witch-hunts. Catholic and Protestant countries vied in the persecution, the most cruel torture (which caused many to make the most absurd "confessions"), and the burning of witches. In those days many tens of thousands of people (according to other, probably more dubious estimates, hundreds of thousands) fell victim to this obsessive belief in witches—doctors and magicians and sorcerers, old bewitched and bewitching women, and young women whose "enchanting" beauty seemed uncanny to the frightened faithful and hence could only be satanic in nature. Of course this anxiety could also be exploited, and it often was—by vengeful people, spurned lovers who became haters, base interests of all kinds, and every kind of malicious person. This is bound to happen with hysterical persecutions and inquisitorial courts from which there is no legal protection or system of legal defense. However, from this viewpoint of fear of the uncanny and devilish most judges probably acted with a subjectively good conscience even in the most cruel tortures. After all, the salvation of the world in its struggle with Satan was at stake.

3. THE JEWS AND THE DEMONIC FORCES

Popular belief established a close connection between these demonic forces and the Jew as physician and sorcerer, denier of the basic truths of the Christian world, Antichrist and the embodiment of the Devil in human form. These notions had been taken over from antiquity and the

Middle Ages and were part of the stereotypical image of the Jew, but in the atmosphere of the struggle against the Devil and Antichrist, against sorcerers and witches a glaring spotlight was again turned on the Jew. Were they not the originators, the teachers or propagators of this devilish magic? They were known as physicians; in those days that profession was still closely related to the position of the medicine man in primitive society, just as astronomers had not yet been sundered from astrologers, and chemists and physicians often were still at the same time alchemists. Science had not yet freed itself of religious belief and superstition. We have already pointed out that learned humanists and religious reformers had sought out Jews to teach them to understand the Hebrew Bible, and their new translations of the Bible into the vernacular had led to rebellion against the dominance of the Catholic Church and often also that of new, moderately reformed churches. A number of Humanists, such as Reuchlin or Pico della Mirandola, had also learned from Jewish mystics; the kabbalah, the mystic secret teachings of the Jews (the development and dissemination of which will be discussed later), attracted many Christians who were seeking an explanation of the mysterious existence that was now being questioned. The existing anti-Jewish laws, including the prescribed Jewish badge, had not kept Jews from establishing contact with Christians and influencing them with their teachings. These laws were not enforced at all times and in all places; often the needs of economic life and the seductive power of money were too powerful. If, therefore, the powers that be wanted to prevent further infection by the Jewish bacillus and further damage from the Jewish poison, they had to try to isolate the Jews everywhere as strictly as possible—not only as individuals but in their totality—and to reduce their contact with the Christian world to a minimum.

4. OFFICIAL REGULATION AND BUREAUCRATIZATION OF GHETTO LIFE

In addition, this time of intellectual movements, religious transformations and conflicts that spread over all of Europe and mingled with the wars of interest of states that were becoming increasingly secularized and of their rulers, this epoch of dynamism and unrest was at the same time a period in which there evolved a system of documents and a bureaucracy that developed in all areas, both ecclesiastical and secular. It is in the nature of things that in times of radical change the bureaucracy always has an important task. It is virtually conditioned by constant change, representing the steady element in the face of such change, pitting its principle of order against threatening chaos, and constituting in the face of arbitrariness a legal order and regulation to the point of pedantry. Almost paradoxically, the new principles of streamlining found their first expression in this. Even the cruel court proceedings and tortures of the Inquisition and witchcraft trials were conducted in accordance with precise regulations and handbooks which thanks to the new technique of printing were disseminated everywhere and guaranteed the bureaucratic uniformity and quasi-logical systematic nature of the deliberations and actions. The principle of order was adopted as well by the Catholic and Protestant churches in all their different persuasions. Everywhere there developed a new orthodoxy with clearly defined bureaucratic forms that shielded it from any threat of heterodoxy and infidelity. In the Catholic Church this principle of order in faith and action found its pithiest expression in the new order of the Jesuits with its commandment of unconditional obedience, but everywhere there developed similar orders with precise regulations that distinguished them from opposing currents. All this now shaped the solution of the Jewish question which was deemed appropriate by that period: locking the Jews up in ghettos.

Aversion to the Jews as deicides, religious seducers, and demonic accomplices of the Antichrist on the one hand and their necessity for certain financial transactions officially forbidden to Christians (though often practiced by them) on the other, as well as the evaluation of the Jews according to their utility to the rulers and the ruled, had been taken over as a heritage of the Middle Ages and were already tradition. All accusations against the Jews, as well as people's perception and fear of them, had long since become axiomatic. It was no longer necessary to investigate their origin, for these things were part of that period's general view of the world. But like everything else, the life of the Jews among the Christians was also subjected to the regulating principle of order, organization, and bureaucratization. The aim of these precise regulations was to decrease the danger of the Jews' harmfulness and to enhance their utilitarian value.

As a consequence the regulations governing the clothing of the Jews, particularly the attire or the badges intended to distinguish them from the surrounding world, as well as their life in the ghetto, now increasingly occupied the attention of the central or local bureaucracy. Every detail was fixed, changed, and fixed again. As before, Jewish settlement was legally permitted only in certain predetermined numbers; this was enforced more and more strictly, and later a natural increase was controlled by imposing limits on marriages. Even in the Age of Enlightenment, during the eighteenth century, often only the oldest son was legally permitted to marry in many Austrian, German, and Italian towns, or the number of marriages was made dependent upon the number of deaths. In an effort to prevent competition with Christian merchants as much as possible, Jewish trading outside the ghetto was often limited to dealing in used articles. For the same reason, Jews were forbidden to keep shops in Christian districts, and so their commercial activity was increasingly channeled into peddling. Thus the

Jew who roamed the countryside with a sack on his back in order to sell the products made in the cities became such a familiar figure that in the popular imagination he became almost identical with the perception of the Jew in general. The frequent expulsions from the cities and the consequent settlement in villages made the Jews dealers in agricultural products from grain to cattle. To the extent that they managed to accumulate wealth, the Jews also remained dealers in precious stones and jewels as well as financiers and pawnbrokers. In fact, Jews were admitted to Italian cities only under the condition that they establish such money-lending institutes ("Monti di Pietà") for the poor. Jews crossing the borders of the hundreds of small and tiny territories and customs districts in Germany, Austria, Alsace, and other countries had to pay a special toll, the so-called *Leibzoll*, for themselves as for their cattle; this toll seems to have been collected for the first time in Thuringia in 1368, but with the expulsion of the Jews from the towns in the fifteenth and sixteenth centuries it increasingly became the general practice. In short, the Jews were regarded and valued as human beings even less than they had been in the Middle Ages. As life became better organized, this process of degradation was intensified. The Jews were objects that one imported, exported, and paid duty on, whose permission to live somewhere depended entirely on whether in the opinion of the powers that be their usefulness outweighed their harmfulness, or vice versa. Exceptions that were occasionally made in the case of individual Jews (something to be discussed later) cannot change this general picture, which was decisive for the history of the Jewish question.

Typification of the Image of the Jew in Caricature

Just as the life-style of the Jews in the ghetto was systematized by minute regulations that sometimes even extended to the religious realm, now the image of the Jew as it existed among the people was typified to an ever-increasing extent and disseminated in its standardized form. The living space of the Jews was narrow, and it seemed even more so as compared to a world that was expanding spatially and intellectually. A Jew jutted out into the transforming non-Jewish world like a fossil from times long gone by. Caricature which, as Eduard Fuchs has pointed out, is usually an expression of a conflict between certain persons and things and "the prevailing general condition of society," took hold of the Jews. To be sure, in the late Middle Ages caricatured Jewish types had already been displayed as works of art on churches and secular buildings. However, the new art of printing, woodcuts, and the use of movable type for books from the second half of the fifteenth century on gave caricature an entirely different dissemination and effectiveness, and the new techniques could immediately be used against the Jews. Printed broadsides illustrated with woodcuts and a bit later also with copper engravings flooded the countryside, and the pictures and satirical verses that caricatured Jews in never-changing fashion went from hand to hand. A Jew who "stellt sein synne nacht und tag/ wie er den christen verderben mag" [keeps scheming day and night/ to ruin a Christian with all his might]; the Jewish usurer who makes all others work hard so he can pocket the profits; the Jewish migrant in his two manifestations, the eternally unstable wanderer across countries and times and the little Jewish domestic peddler with a cane in his hand and a pack of junk on his back—these were the types that became ever more deeply engrained in the popular consciousness.* Added to these caricatures were pictures and verses about desecrations of the Host (particularly those of Trent, 1475), and so forth, and the pornographic mockery of the Jews in the absurd picture of the "Judensau" that had since the thirteenth century been affixed as a sculpture to churches and public buildings (e.g., in Magdeburg, Regensburg, Cologne, and even Uppsala in Sweden) and now received general dissemination in the form of numerous woodcuts. Basing himself on the sculpture on the parish church at Wittenberg (dating from 1440), Luther gave a detailed description of it in his *Von Schemhamphoras und vom Geschlecht Christi*,** a description that reflects his and his time's vulgar delight in the bawdy. According to Fuchs, a representation of the "Jew's sow" was among the first known nonreligious woodcuts. The image of the corrupt Jew that was transmitted to every Christian with the Christian doctrine and the reading of the Old and New Testament and that now reached ever wider circles with the translations of the Bible into the vernacular and the dissemination by book dealers of these translations, which were often illustrated with woodcuts—this image now increasingly mingled in the popular consciousness with the Jewish types that were disseminated in those broadsides and caricatures.

The "Eternal Jew"

The extent to which the image of the eternally wandering Jew was in keeping with the popular image is indicated by the fact that the *Kurtze Beschreibung und Erzelung von einem Juden mit Namen Ahasverus* (Brief description and story of a Jew named Ahasuerus), the first printing

---

*Details of these and the following statements may be found in Part 2.
**Instead of describing this insufferably crude pictorial defilement ourselves, we shall let Luther do so: "On our parish church here in Wittenberg there is a sow hewn in stone. Young piglets and Jews lie under it, sucking away. Behind the sow stands a rabbi who lifts up the sow's right leg. With his left hand he pulls the sow's ass toward himself, stoops and with great zeal looks through the sow's ass into the Talmud as if he wanted to glimpse and read something sharp and special there. Surely this is where the Jews get their *shemhamphoras* [the secret name of God]. . . ." Could this abusive picture be the derivation of the abusive term *Saujud* that was later generally used against the Jews?

of the legend of the Eternal (or Wandering) Jew, which appeared in 1602 in an as yet primitive literary form and went through eight different printings that same year, was in the following years translated into other European languages and then reprinted in ever new editions and versions. In 1694 the "Wandering Jew" (since 1609 "Juif Errant") was also called "Ewiger Jude" (Eternal Jew) in German editions, and he retained this name in German-speaking countries and others under their influence. At the beginning of the eighteenth century (Schudt, 1714) the strange figure of this individual Jew (who was probably interwoven symbolically-theologically with Judaism as such) was identified with the fate of the entire Jewish people. Due to the delight in exotic things from distant times and countries, the inclination to typify the characters of peoples and epochs, and the struggle for the emancipation of the Jews in the ages of Romanticism and modern nationalism the figure began to assume an increasingly symbolic, uncanny, and universal character at the end of the eighteenth century and the beginning of the nineteenth centuries, and the phrase "The Eternal Jew" became a synonym for Jewish fate. As is almost indicated by the full title,* even the first versions contained all the elements that enabled this material to become

*The full title of this first known edition, long-winded in the style of the time, is (in continuation of the above): "Welcher bey der Creutzigung Christi selbst Persönlich gewesen, auch das Crucifige uber Christum hab helffen schreyen unnd umb Barnabam bitten, hab auch nach der Creutzigung Christi nimmer gen Jerusalem können kommen, auch sein Weib und Kinder nimmer gesehen; unnd seithero im Leben geblieben, und vor etlich Jahren gen Hamburg kommen, auch anno 1599 Im December zu Dantzig ankommen./ Es hat auch Paulus von Eitzen der heil[igen] Schrift D[octor] und Bischoff von Schlesswig beneben dem Rector der Schulen zu Hamburg, mit jhme conferirt: von den Orientalschen Landen, nach Christi was sich verloffen, hatt er solchen guten Bericht davon gegeben, das sie sich nicht genug darüber verwundern können./ Matthei am 16.: Warlich ich sage euch, es stehen all hier etliche, die werden den Tod nicht schmecken, biss das sie dess Menschen Sohn kommen sehen inn sein Reich./ Gedruckt zu Leyden bei Christoff Creutzer. Anno 1602." (Who was personally present at the crucifixion of Christ, also helped cry "Let him be crucified" and ask for Barabbas. After Christ's crucifixion he was not able to return to Jerusalem or see his wife and children again. He has remained alive since then, came to Hamburg a few years ago and arrived in Danzig in December 1599. Paul von Eitzen, Doctor of Holy Scriptures and Bishop of Schleswig, as well as the director of the Hamburg schools conferred with him. He gave such a good report about the oriental countries, where he fled after Christ, that their wonderment knew no end. In Matthew 16:28 [Jesus says]: Verily I say unto you, there be some standing here which shall not taste of death till they see the Son of man coming in his kingdom./ Printed at Leyden by Christoff Creutzer, anno 1602.)

The first French translation, published in 1609 at Bordeaux, has a shorter and more general title: "Discours véritable d'un Juif Errant, lequel maintient avec parolles probables avoir esté présent à voir crucifier Jésus-Christ, et est demeuré en vie jusque à présent. Avec plusieurs beaux Discours de diverses personnes sur ce mesme subject." (True discourse about a Wandering Jew who maintains plausibly that he was present at the crucifixion of Jesus Christ and who has remained alive to the present. With several fine discourses by various persons about the same subject.) On the history and dissemination of the legend and its literary treatment, see my remarks in Part 2.

one of the most frequently treated themes of literature as well as popular material for the graphic arts, particularly drawing and painting. In addition to the dozens of older woodcuts, especially the pictures by Gustave Doré (nineteenth century) became generally known, and in our time many are probably familiar with the ink drawing of Alfred Kubin, the eccentric artist of the uncanny, grotesque, and fantastic.

Shylock

The crude, uncomprehending, disparaging caricature of the Jews in the picture of the "Judensau" and the figure of Ahasuerus, the "Eternal Jew" or "Wandering" Jew that uncannily symbolized the Jew as the eternal stranger who did not belong in the Christian-human society, were now joined by a third figure, one that typified the Jew in the real world of beginning modern capitalism, the figure of the cruel, anti-Christian money-Jew who had no regard for any human considerations. This figure is crystallized most impressively in Shakespeare's Venetian Jew Shylock, and at the turn of the sixteenth century to the seventeenth century it entered world literature.*

As is well known, the figure of the Jew who lends a respected Christian merchant a large sum of money under the condition that a pound of flesh from the Christian's body serve as a guarantee for timely repayment, who then insists on the literal enforcement of this stipulation in his legally valid contract and is formally accorded his rights but in the end has to leave duped, despised, impoverished, and forcibly baptized amidst the mockery of his noble Christian enemies, has a long history. The main motif—human flesh for money, in a bet or stipulated in a business contract—was first encountered in medieval stories and then applied to a Jew by an Italian storyteller of the fourteenth century (see p. 122 above). That made sense to readers of such tales, for around that time (1378), thirty years after the Black Death with its accusations, mass persecutions, and mass expulsions of the Jews, a Jew was the logical satanically cruel hero of such a story. Somehow it came to Shakespeare's attention in this form, though it apparently had not been translated into English when he wrote *The Merchant of Venice*.

When stories of this kind are in tune with the times, however, they

---

*Shakespeare's play *The Merchant of Venice*, in which the Jew Shylock figures as a prominent counterplayer of the "royal merchant" Antonio, is generally called a comedy. It seems to have been performed for the first time in 1595, was first mentioned officially and in the literature in 1598, and two years later appeared in print in two editions. The title there is *The excellent History of the Merchant of Venice. With the extreme cruelty of Shylocke the Iew toward the saide Merchant, in cutting a iust pound of his flesh. And the obtaining of Portia, by the choyse of three Caskets. Written by W. Shakespeare. Printed by J. Roberts, 1600*. See also the supplementary remarks in Part 2.

spread rapidly over lands and eras without our being able to follow all traces at all times. For example, we know a *Meistergesang* with similar contents from the end of the fifteenth century (Bamberg, 1493). In 1584 the story appears in Paris in a collection of tales and legal cases; it is set in Turkey and contains a detailed debate about the law: as in Shakespeare, the Jew argues in favor of his rights and the validity of the law in general. In Elizabethan England the story was disseminated in ballads as well; these came into being before or after the performance of Shakespeare's play and tended to be accepted by the people as plausible.*

It is doubtful whether Shakespeare ever saw a Jew or had a closer acquaintance with one. No Jews had officially been admitted to his England for three hundred years, though some Marranos probably lived there as physicians, and English merchants (and perhaps also politicians) may have been in contact with Marrano merchants on the European continent or in the Levant. But the very fact that no real-life Jews were seen who might have served as a comparison with the image of the Jew disseminated over the Christian world made it all the easier for the Shylock image to take particular hold in its stereotypical form. We read of some plays about Jews that were on English stages at the time. The best-known among these, and the only one whose text has been preserved, is Christopher Marlowe's drama *The Jew of Malta*, first performed in 1591. Its hero, the Jew Barabas,** introduced in the Prologue by Machiavelli himself, is a devil in human form and does everything of which a Christian believes a Jewish devil to be capable: He is a usurer, a brewer of poisons, a hater and killer of Christians, a hypocrite and a traitor, an imperious person who is capable of appearing submissive. The only positive qualities he has are his love of his daughter and his loyalty to Judaism, though Christians naturally regarded the latter as arrogant obduracy.

There was a topical element as well. At the end of January 1594 Rodrigo Lopez, a respected doctor of Marrano origin, physician-in-ordinary to Queen Elizabeth, who also served as an interpreter and diplomatic agent at her court, was accused of high treason and the intention of poisoning the queen. Having confessed under torture to all

*In Shakespeare's comedy *The Winter's Tale* (4. 4) a peddler sells, among other things, printed ballads. A shepherdess says, with the respect of plain people for the printed word that has survived to this day: "Pray now buy some. I love a ballet [ballad] in print a-life, for then we are sure they are true." A similar tale has been reported, as a true story from the time of Pope Sixtus V, who was on the whole kindly disposed toward the Jews, but there the roles are reversed: The Jew bets a piece of flesh from his body and the Christian wants to cut it.

**This name, of course, immediately makes one think of the Jewish rebel Bar-Abbas, called a criminal in Matthew 27 : 16ff., whom Pilate proposed to the Jews for crucifixion in place of Jesus, and whom the Jews in turn asked to be reprieved in Jesus' stead.

the things he was accused of, he was sentenced to death in February 1594. Queen Elizabeth, who evidently was not convinced of his guilt, hesitated for a long time but confirmed the sentence a few months later, whereupon Lopez was publicly executed in early June of that year. At the trial and in the accounts of it Lopez was characterized as "that vile Jew . . . a perjured and murdering villain and Jewish doctor, worse than Judas himself." When Lopez attempted to address the people from the gallows, he was shouted down: "A Jew, a Jew!"

The sentencing and public execution of the Jew Rodrigo Lopez was widely discussed, written about, and sung about in ballads heard in streets and taverns. This, of course, created a big market for plays about Jews in the theater. Marlowe's drama was restored to the repertory and had a number of successful performances. It was in this atmosphere that Shakespeare's play *The Merchant of Venice* came into being.

The tenor of the play and its denouement were surely influenced by it. The Jew had to be sentenced, he had to be guilty, and all Christians express their contempt for him. Shakespeare was a child of his time, and he adopted its image of the Jew, the general and the topical one. One should not be surprised at this; the astonishing thing is what he made of it, for he was not only a child of his age but the kind of genius that always transcends his age and, in fact, all ages. Thus it has always been felt that *The Merchant of Venice* is a play without uniformity, with illogical arguments and a dichotomous character. In this it is the typical expression of a transitional period and the inner contradictions in the thinking and feeling of its most important writer. Hence it is not surprising that more has been said and written from opposite points of view about this play and especially its most outstanding figure, the Jew Shylock, than about most other plays and dramatic figures. The ambiguity of the play and the figure of Shylock can be explained only on the basis of the clash of the *Zeitgeist* with the greatest dramatic genius. Thus there came into being in the figure of Shylock a stereotype of the Jew turned flesh and blood with humanly moving features.

The structure of the play, the plot, and the denouement are entirely in the spirit of the time and of tradition. Shakespeare called his play a comedy—that is, he conceived of it as one. His main figures are Renaissance people of the highest social class and the beneficiaries of this class—as friends, wooers of rich heiresses, cultured *bons vivants*, and seducers of attractive women. The dark world of the Jew Shylock is the counterpole; he was probably first conceived of as a satanically grotesque, blasphemously ludicrous figure enmeshed in the uncultured, joyless reality of mere material profit. But as Shakespeare started to develop this figure, it turned into a human figure (one is tempted to say: almost against the will of its creator), a more human Jewish figure than had ever been drawn by a Christian.

Shylock hates Christians, but he has a right to do so. Shakespeare lets him motivate his hatred of the "royal merchant" Antonio in verse and prose. Antonio, the Christian, has always treated him with contempt, kicked him, spat at him, and reviled him. Should he now—"for suff'rance is the badge of all our tribe"*—"bend low, and in a bondman's key,/ With bated breath, and whisp'ring humbleness,/ Say this: 'Fair sir, you spet on me on Wednesday last,/ You spurned me such a day, another time/ You called me dog, and for these courtesies/ I'll lend you thus much moneys'?" And later there is an even more bitter complaint about Antonio's shameful treatment of him, the humiliations, the mockery, the harm he has done him as a businessman in these proud, much-quoted prose words in which he identifies his fate with that of the Jewish people and, almost scornfully, identifies Antonio's behavior with the Christians' feeling of hate and revenge: "And what's his reason? I am a Jew. Hath not a Jew eyes? Hath not a Jew hands, organs, dimensions, senses, affections, passion? . . . If you prick us, do we not bleed? If you tickle us, do we not laugh? If you poison us, do we not die? And if you wrong us, shall we not revenge? If we are like you in the rest, we will resemble you in that. If a Jew wrong a Christian, what is his humility? Revenge! If a Christian wrong a Jew, what should his sufferance be by Christian example? Why revenge! The villainy you teach me I will execute, and it shall go hard but I will better the instruction."

He appears in court and claims his right to enforce the contract, will accept no greater amount of money as a substitute; he insists on his rights. And to the admonition to temper justice with mercy he responds with a reproachful reference to the master's rights exercised by his merciful Christian admonishers over their slaves and by invoking the law as a foundation of society: "You have among you many a purchased slave,/ Which like your asses and your dogs and mules/ You use in abject and in slavish arts,/ Because you bought them. Shall I say to you,/ 'Let them be free! Marry them to your heirs!/ Why sweat they under burdens? Let their beds/ Be made as soft as yours, and let their palates/ Be seasoned with such viands'? You will answer,/ 'The slaves are ours.' So do I answer you:/ The pound of flesh which I demand of him/ Is dearly bought, is mine, and I will have it./ If you deny, fie upon your law!/ There is no force in the decrees of Venice./ I stand for judgment. Answer; shall I have it?"

No doubt about it—Shylock is inhuman in his hatred, and he is to be shown to the public as a monster. But the arguments with which the counterfigure Portia, who is disguised as a legal scholar and is supposed

---

*In the thirteenth century (and till their expulsion) English Jews had to wear a Jewish badge. Englishmen of Shakespeare's time knew it from caricatures of Jews. For pictures of Jewish badges in England, see *EJJ* 4:63.

to personify a socially, culturally, and morally higher social stratum, trips up the Jew are juridically untenable (as the German legal scholar Ihering pointed out with sharp words in 1872). One could call this sheer trickery. The judge could have declared the contract null and void because it contained an inhuman, immoral provision. If, however, all the provisions of the contract were declared valid, as happened during the trial, the Jew, who had been granted his rights, should not have been impeded in their exercise by the impossible stipulation that he could not shed one drop of Christian blood. Nor should he have been punished for his intention to endanger a Christian's life with the loss of half his possessions or have had forced baptism imposed upon him in place of being sentenced to death. "When I saw this play performed at the Drury Lane theater," wrote Heinrich Heine in 1838, "a pale British woman stood in the box behind me, who cried bitterly at the end of the fourth act, and kept exclaiming 'The poor man is wronged!' . . . I have never been able to forget those big dark eyes that wept for Shylock!"

These are the judgments of a Jew who had experienced German Romanticism and of a German jurist in the second half of the nineteenth century who was violently attacked because of this view of his. There is no doubt that Shakespeare's contemporaries and the Bard himself thought differently. To them this very conclusion, which gave the Jew an apparent victory but then made him plunge all the more deeply because of his arrogance and vindictiveness and finally vouchsafed him the "grace" of the Christian faith, was the desirable one. This way the Jew was caught in the net of his own casuistic argumentation, vanquished and done for, and in the last act there is sheer joy, music, and satisfaction, as befits the end of a Renaissance comedy.

Shylock's Significance for the Jewish Question

The question we must ask here is this: What is the significance of this play in the history of the Jewish question? It seems to us that it is of extraordinary significance. The stereotypical image of the Jew as a usurer, a vengeful hater of Christians, and a cruel formalist whose antihuman Jewish-Pharisaic principle of law and justice was in glaring contrast to the humane Christian principle of compassion and mercy was here given living form and a classic expression. Just as the word Jew was used in everyday parlance in English and a number of other western European languages as a synonym for usurer and cheat (and also as a verb), the cruel Jewish usurer now received a lexicographically registered name as well: Shylock, which was comparable to the earlier Judas for a traitorous Jew and Cain and Ashasuerus for the restlessly wandering Jew. At the same time new notes were now sounded—audible but still largely drowned out by other, louder voices—which 150 or 200 years later were to cause other strings to join in and vibrate in purer chords.

In Shakespeare's Shylock the stereotypical image of the Jew was given human form; even its repellent, inhuman elements were motivated psychologically and historically. But for this very reason—and this is the other side of the human understanding shown here—it now had a more far-reaching effect in space and time, and it entered heads and hearts more deeply and more dangerously than the figure of Barabas, Marlowe's satanic-Machiavellian caricature of a Jew. He has broken free of the stiff medieval cliché and has stepped out of the ecclesiastic-religious sphere into the secular human sphere—but precisely for this reason he will see to it that even among classes of people in which religious bonds recede in the face of a freer, more secularly oriented education and lifestyle the old image of the Jew is not forgotten and undergoes a fresh, "living development as a stamped form" in Goethe's sense. As a sibling of the figure of the "Eternal Jew" Shylock will wander through the ages on the stage and in world literature, inspire ever new reflections in his combination of myth and reality and in his eerily iridescent ambiguity, and invite people to have understanding for the fate of the Jews or to rebel against the repulsive, hateful figure. Even though this may not have been intended when it was chosen, the name Shylock will evoke associations of the shy and suspicious glance of the Jew with his earlocks *(peot)* whom one might meet in the street tomorrow.

The Effect of Isolation on the Inner Life of the Jews

The increasing exclusion of the Jews from participation in the life of the surrounding world through the forcible ghettos, the bureaucratic enforcement of the laws governing the Jews, etcetera, naturally had far-reaching effects on their psyche as well. The Jews grew accustomed to the life that was forced upon them and almost regarded it as normal. After all, their tight confinement behind ghetto walls was often their only protection, and it was accepted as such with something resembling gratitude. Considering that the Jews were always prone to humiliations and often compelled to seek sustenance with bent backs it is no wonder that often their bearing remained physically and spiritually warped even when circumstances did not require it, or no longer required it. In contrast to popular opinion about the wealth of the Jews the great majority of them were poor; in the seventeenth and eighteenth centuries beggary became more and more common among them. Increasingly driven out of the big cities and relegated to small towns, villages, and hamlets in the vicinity they were itinerant mediators between the urban and the rural economy. This dispersal among small settlements and communities, the necessity to concentrate all their efforts on the acquisition of money, the sufferings and losses in wars with their wild bands of mercenary soldiers, and the isolation and lack of any outside stimulation caused their intellectual level to decline. The study of the Talmud fell into disuse in the ghettos and small rural settlements of Central Europe. Joseph Caro's *Shulhan Arukh* (The Prepared Table), a collection of religious precepts, appeared at just the right time (1564).

The *Shulhan Arukh*

Joseph (ben Ephraim) Caro (1488–1575) was born in Toledo (or in Portugal) four years before the expulsion of the Jews from Spain. Like many other Spanish-Portuguese (Sephardic) Jews, he fled to Turkey (Adrianopolis, Nicopolis, Salonika) with his parents in 1497, after the expulsion of the Jews from Portugal. Living in the small Palestinian-Galilean town Safed from 1536 on, he became a leading scholar and kabbalist of this flourishing Jewish settlement and wrote the *Shulhan Arukh* as an extract from a great learned commentary on which he had worked for twenty years. In this larger work he had given detailed citations of authorities and different opinions; in the short version he gave only his findings: all the religious precepts—commandments, prohibitions, and practices deemed equivalent to commandments (*"minhagim"*)—that were still valid in his time (and thus not dependent on the existence of the Temple). They were clearly arranged in chapters and paragraphs (*"seiphim"*), reflecting some of the scholarly-encyclopedic atmosphere of the humanistic culture of Renaissance Europe. Caro's work was intended to serve as a textbook or a review for anyone seeking knowledge; and such a person was to be able to cover it in a month of daily lessons without years of study, as with multi-volume compendiums. The first edition appeared in late November 1564 (the 18th of Kislev 5325) in Venice—that is, about fifty years after the establishment of the first compulsory ghetto (1516). In the third edition, which appeared two years later, the book was divided into thirty chapters for the purpose of completing it in a month. The sixth edition (Venice, 1574) appeared as a pocket book, and on the title page it was explicitly stated that this format was chosen to enable a person to carry it in his breast pocket and use it easily at any time and in any place, at home or on a journey. It was the author's intention to facilitate the absorption of the teachings as well as the making of quick decisions on all important matters in accordance with Jewish law and custom—and in this respect the work was entirely successful. In a short time the book went through a number of editions, aroused much discussion and was enthusiastically received but also rejected by some because of its very brevity and the assurance of the rulings, which seemed to be in conflict with the accustomed method of commentary, the citing of many authorities, and the careful weighing of the various opinions. Many others objected that the rulings of the *Shulhan Arukh* were essentially in keeping with the views and customs of Sephardic Jewry and hardly took cognizance of the substantially different decisions, customs, and practices of Central and East European Jewry. Was this so-called Ashkenazic Jewry whose centers of life and research in that period were increasingly concentrated in Poland instead of, as earlier, in Central and Western Europe, supposed to subject itself to what was in many ways the alien tradition of the formerly Spanish and Portuguese Jews, whose centers were now in Turkey and particularly in Palestine (Safed)? But despite all conflicts the inner unity of Jewry manifested itself here, and any opposition was short-lived. Both western and eastern authorities came to the defense of Caro's decisions and demonstrated that they were based on a great deal of knowledge, on the critical analyses and reflections of the author's great learned works. One of the most respected rabbinical authorities of Poland, Rabbi Moshe ben Israel Isserles of Cracow (Rama), a man whose extensive Jewish-religious and secular knowledge led his contemporaries to call him the Maimonides of Polish Jewry, had a positive attitude toward Caro's works in general and their compact version in the *Shulhan Arukh* in particular. Despite individual criticisms he recognized their importance as a unifying force and added in his commentaries the customs and recognized rulings of Ashkenazic (and particularly Polish) Jewry. His supplement *("Hagahot")* to the *Shulhan Arukh*, which frequently contradicted Caro's decisions, appeared fifteen years after the first Venetian printing of the Cracow edition of 1579–81 under the title *Ha-Mappa* (i.e., "The Tablecloth" for Caro's "Prepared Table"). It made Caro's codification acceptable to Central and Eastern European Jews as well, and together with a number of additional commentaries and supplements by other authors it paved the way for the general acceptance of the *Shulhan Arukh* as the authoritative codification of the Jewish religious laws and the practices deemed to be of equal significance and binding force (though this of course caused it to go far beyond the framework of a pocket book). In this way the *Shulhan Arukh* became something like a written constitution for the life of the Jews, both private and public, their conduct in the Jewish community, and their relations to the non-Jewish world. For Jewry as a whole it remained this until the slackening of the religious unity in the Age of Emancipation (beginning with the late eighteenth century), and from then on for the "Orthodox" part of world Jewry, which continued to adhere to the religious laws. The importance of this work from the Renaissance for the preservation, cohesion, and unification of the Jewish life-style in the following two or three centuries cannot be overestimated. The authoritative codification of all precepts and practices in a (relatively) clear presentation eased the religiously regulated life of generations that often found it hard or even impossible to concern themselves with the Talmudic sources and the subsequent commentaries, interpretations, and rulings. This summarization, authorization, and transmission of religious practices as a general order about which one no longer had to inquire also intensified a development that had started long before it and had been promoted by the forced isolation of the Jews from the outside world. It also made the inner life in the ghetto more and more stereotypical and the valuations more and more uniform. Basic commandments and comparatively unimportant practices, profound ethical teachings and the painstaking execution of some detail in the traditional order—their observance appeared equally important and their violation equally reprehensible. Everything transmitted by tradition was regarded as sacred; clothing and customs, superstitions and languages that might have been adopted from the surrounding world in ancestral times—all this became as holy as a divine commandment. At all times and in all places a people overvalues what belongs to it, what it has taken over from its fathers. Here, however, in the European ghetto, it assumed an even greater significance because it was the only thing that completely belonged to the people, that could not easily be stolen from it, and bound the individual to the community.*

The Lurianic Kabbalah

A current that seemed to be diametrically opposite in nature nevertheless worked toward the same end, the unification of faith and action. It was the renewal of the kabbalah, and it emanated around the same time from Safed in Galilee and in the succeeding two or three generations spread through the Jewish population of the entire world. In earlier chapters we became acquainted with the mystical currents among the Jews of ancient times and the Middle Ages, and we noticed that in general the antithesis between the observant Jews living in accordance with the Law and the pious Jews absorbed in mysticism was more the work of later observers than it was present in reality. Jewish mysticism was based on the biblical-Talmudic law, illuminated it, interpreted it, motivated, deepened and enlivened it—and in essence without going beyond the religious precepts and prohibitions and their strict regulation of daily living. This applied in particular measure to the regeneration of the kabbalah that took place in Safed in the sixteenth century. At all times mystical interpretations of catastrophic events served to preserve the people from despair, unbelief, and nihilism whenever the terrible events of the time and consequently the opinion

*Concerning the literature on the *Shulhan Arukh* and its position in the later polemics on the Jewish question and in anti-Semitism, see the excursus in Part 2.

of the world threatened to shake their faith and abandon the faithful to doubt and even despair.

Under the impact of the catastrophes of the waning Middle Ages—particularly the expulsion of the Jews from Spain and Portugal, Marranism, the wanderings, and the ghettoization—the Jewish settlement of Safed, which expanded primarily because of Spanish exiles, developed into a center of Judaism that produced a renewal and an expansion of Jewish mysticism alongside and in supplementation of the codification and strict observance of the laws and customs—and in a form that was able to extend across times and places. The central personality of this renewal was Isaac ben Solomon Luria (1534–72), whom his disciples later called Ha-Ari*—that is, the (sacred) Lion, based on the abbreviation of the initials of his name that were given an allegorical-symbolic interpretation. He must have been a fascinating personality; even in his lifetime he was surrounded by legends that were further expanded in the decades following his early death. He lived on in that world of legends, which does not yield much accurate information about his real life. His father, who also died at an early age, was apparently a native of Germany or Poland who had emigrated to Jerusalem and married into a Sephardic family there, yet the Ashkenazic origin of both father and son was preserved in the memory of their contemporaries.** Isaac evidently lived with his mother in Egypt for a time. His historically significant activities in Safed were limited to the last three years of his life. He flashed like a meteor in the circle of kabbalists that had formed there near the tomb of Rabbi Simeon bar Yohai (second century) at Meron, who was venerated as the recipient of the divine message of the Zohar. This book was probably written in Spain around 1300, but it first appeared in print around that time (1558–59) and developed from a work known only to a small group of initiates into the basic book of the kabbalists that was next to the Bible and Talmud in holiness. Even though Luria and his disciples strictly observed the commandments, prohibitions, and customs that had most recently been established by Caro, who in turn was indebted to the kabbalah and its basic text, the lives and teachings of Caro and Luria express almost symbolically the polarity of Jewish existence—the pole and counterpole between which flows the vital current of Jewish being. Caro began his activities long before Luria, published his major work ten years before Luria's arrival in Safed, and outlived his younger contemporary, who was carried off by

*Ha-Ari—the initials of the words Ha-Elohi (The Divine, the Divinely Favored, The Saint) Rabbi Isaac. His disciples seem to have seen in him the "Mashiach ben Joseph," i.e., a precursor of the real Messiah ("Maçhiach ben David"), and perhaps this is the way he viewed himself.

**In his lifetime he was called "Ha-Riash," i.e., Rabbi Isaac Ashkenazi, or "Ha-Rial," an abbreviation of Rabbi Isaac Ashkenazi Luria.

the plague at age thirty-eight, by three years. He died at a ripe old age in 1575, recognized as an authority by the entire Jewish world. Caro has gone down in history as the preserver of a venerable tradition, as the codifier of laws, as the solidifier of the dividing wall that separates Jews from the non-Jewish world, surrounding them in their nationally and religiously determined daily activities, on their days of rest and festivals, even where and when there is no wall of stone or wood to do so. On the other hand, Luria seemed to live on in eternal youth in the circle of his pupils and disciples, who were dazzled by the luster of a legendary life lived ascetically, and ecstatically wandering in nature, hearing the inaudible and seeing the invisible, conversing with the living and the spirits of those deceased long ago, mystically interpreting the traditional laws, and receiving revelations that transcended his life and harbored the risk of some day shattering the traditional material that these revelations attempted to grasp more deeply and more vibrantly at their source. Luria was beset by visions, ideas, and illuminations; they evidently gushed out of him in such a way that he could pass them on only in conversation and perhaps in song, ready to make any sacrifice for the sake of redemption. Like many other religiously inspired men, this ecstatic, who was blessed and blessed others, left behind hardly any written works or systematic formulations. And yet he originated a new system of kabbalistic mysticism which his pupils transmitted and developed, a system that profoundly shaped the life and thought of Jews all over the world for centuries.

It cannot be our task, and is beyond our competence, to present here the Lurianic kabbalah in its religious substance or its gnostic-theosophic foundations. In his publications, which are accessible even to non-specialists, Gershom Scholem, who rediscovered Jewish mysticism for all of us, investigated its many-sided foundations and analyzed its widely ramified effects, giving everyone a chance to inform himself in competent fashion. The only question we have to ask here is what the new element was that affected the history of the Jewish question.

It is the task of any movement of religious regeneration to give an answer to the weighty questions of the time. Mysticism tried to do this in various ways at different times, but in accordance with its nature it was always limited to narrow circles. What was new and revolutionary about the Lurian kabbalah was that here a lonely Godseeker projected his and his people's experiences and upheavals upon the universe and its Creator, thereby creating a doctrine that established a causal and cosmological connection between the fate of an individual and that of the totality, between the fate of the totality of the Jewish people and that of the world, and between the fate of the world and the nature and perfection of the divine entity. In this context everything had its place; everything personal and national-communal had its parallel and correspondence in cosmic events. This gave a new meaning to the life of individuals and of the people: it depends on each individual, on his life, on his painstaking observance of all commandments, and on each individual's highly concentrated direction toward God in prayer *(kavvanah)* whether the sparks of divine splendor that have been removed from their center by man's sinfulness and banished to the fragmentary coverings of earthly or devilish existence will be released from their banishment and freed to return to their source. The banishment of the people of Israel and its dispersion over the world is a parallel, a symbol, and more than that: an instrument in the banishment and redemption of particles of divine light. It is the task of the Jewish people and each individual Jew (and this is the meaning of their dispersion throughout the world) to aid the world in the restoration *(tikkun)* and completion of these particles. Just as after the destruction of the Temple prophecy was able to give meaning to the catastrophe (see pp. 53f. above), the new mysticism gave meaning and justification to the catastrophical recent past as well as the present and assigned them their tasks in the divine world order. The Messiah for whom people were waiting and hoping will not come out of the blue. His coming must be prepared; sinfulness and the rift in the original unity and perfection of the world must be healed through exemplary living. Only when all scattered divine sparks have thereby been redeemed and brought home—then and only then will the Messiah appear and lead God's people, too, back into its homeland as the conclusion and crowning of the restored perfect world order.

This doctrine transformed many traditional elements, but it also included much from the contemporary world: the endeavor to place the cosmos, whose laws of motion were newly investigated in those days (when astronomy was still closely connected with astrology), in the context of what was happening on earth; belief in evil forces as well, in the devil and the threatening torments of hell, in evil spirits that take possession of man and can be exorcised from him with the proper symbol of faith (the cross there, the holy name of God—*shem mephorash*—here) and the right religious courage; the association with specters, the ghostlike wandering souls of the dead; and other things of that sort. At the same time this doctrine contained a new version of the consciousness of the Jewish people's chosenness. Its dispersal had a mission to fulfill and its return was dependent on the completion of this mission—ideas that were later able to serve as a stimulus or support for both reformatory and Messianic currents.

These basic moods and multifarious redemptive tendencies that lent justification, meaning, and direction to an almost unbearable existence were probably the reason for the wide dissemination of the new doctrine. After all, the reception of books, ideas, and religious doctrines is frequently an even more far-reaching historical act than their conception; only its willing reception makes a formulated thought an effective force. The new codification of Jewish life, as well as the new inner meaning in the light of the kabbalah, shaped life behind the ghetto walls in such a way that it became spiritually endurable.

But this very development turned a Jew, wherever he lived, into an ever more uniform type that was increasingly sundered from the surrounding world. It is in keeping with this that Judaism now adopted an increasingly negative attitude, to the point of prohibiting them under threat of anathematization, toward the profane sciences which the creators of the new teachings had still absorbed. All secular means of leading the people back to its homeland were now rejected. It was thought that soul-searching, penance, and good deeds would have to pave the way for that, but only God could and would decide when the perfection had been reached that made the appearance of the Messiah possible.

This is how the fate of the Jews looked from the inside. But at the same time there were developments in the surrounding world that served to transform the life of the Jews and their relationship to that world.

Changes in the Relations between the Jews and the Surrounding World

The fate of the Jews in the world, their relationship to it, and its relationship to them—all the factors that we call the "Jewish question"—has always depended on what happened in the world. Even a people that stays in its country cannot permanently isolate itself from what happens in other countries. Much less can the members of a people that is interspersed among the nations remain unaffected.

This surrounding world underwent ever more far-reaching transformations in its economic, political, religious, and intellectual structure. For a certain period of time it was possible to exclude the Jews more or less from these changes in the surrounding world's mode of thought and way of life, changes that were initiated by the Renaissance and Humanism. As we have seen, the general development was impeded by the Counter Reformation and the ensuing wars and crises. Medieval notions and traditions also continued to be operative for a long time everywhere. However, when the new ideas in economics (mercantilism), politics (absolutism), and the general view of life (rationalism and Enlightenment) prevailed after the second half of the seventeenth century and definitively in the eighteenth, this also marked a turning point in the Jewish question, and changes became apparent in the nineteenth century.

The exclusion of the Jews, as a matter of principle, from the general economy, the assignment or toleration of a special position within it, and the complete social isolation of the Jews from the surrounding world were based on the fixed economy of the Middle Ages, in which every class and profession had a definite place based on origin and convention. This economic constraint was eased in the first centuries of the modern period. The conquest of Constantinople by the Turks, the discovery of a direct sea route to India, and the discovery of America caused great shifts in international trade. The economic center shifted from the southern, Mediterranean countries to the northern ones. Whether the expulsion of the Jews from Spain and Portugal contributed as materially to this shift of trade from the South to the North, as Sombart claimed,* or whether this shift was primarily caused by the abovementioned objective factors is open to argument, but it is certain that in the newly developing commercial centers of the Netherlands Jewish merchants from Spain and Portugal played an important role. In Europe and in the American colonies, particularly South America, the Jews also occupied an important place in the colonial trade that increasingly expanded in connection with the new discoveries and conquests.

A considerable number of the Jews who were active there as tradesmen and financiers, often amassing substantial fortunes, had originally been Marranos. This gave the Marranos an important function in the development of the Jewish question.

The Marranos as Pioneers

The Marranos were the only Jews who had never lived in a ghetto or had long since shed the fetters of the ghetto. True, in Spain and Portugal they had presumably been able to practice their Judaism only in secret, and this dual life turned many of them into diplomats and actors and in many cases probably spoiled their purity of character. On the other hand, the Marranos had in this fashion gained access to the cultural world of their homelands, a culture to which at least the upper-class Jews of Spain had always been close. From economics to art, literature, and philosophy they were conversant with everything that occurred in their homeland; its language and life-styles had become their own. As the persecution of the pseudo-Christians mounted, many escaped danger by emigrating, often under adventurous circumstances. In Amsterdam, where they created a new center of Judaism at the end of the sixteenth century, they openly returned to the Jewish fold; in fact, they often observed the Jewish commandments and customs, for the preservation of which they had suffered so much, with particular strictness. At

---

*Concerning Sombart and his views of the Jews and the Jewish question, see the excursus in Part 2.

the same time they took both the material and the intellectual Spanish-Portuguese culture with them and continued them in their lives.

The non-Jews in their new countries of domicile saw in them a new type of Jew that seemed to bear little resemblance to the type familiar to them and that differed from the stereotypical image of the European Jew formed since the Middle Ages. These Jews were freer, prouder human beings; they had an appreciation of style; their language and culture might not have been those of the countries in which they lived, but they were at least European; they were modern people. For centuries these "Sephardic" Jews, wherever they appeared, were regarded by the surrounding world and by themselves as aristocratic types, not to be confused with the "degenerate" Ashkenazic Jews of Central Europe.

Another difference between them and the garden variety of Jew was that many of them were prosperous or wealthy and did not share in the decline of the Central European Jews to the status of junk dealers and pawnbrokers. Equipped with the economic experience they had acquired in Spain and Portugal, they soon played an important role as financiers and large-scale dealers. Holland, a state that had secured its religious and political independence after many years of struggling against the Catholic monarchy Spain, granted them a large measure of toleration as people persecuted by the "Papists" and was glad to utilize their abilities and wealth. They were soon followed by other Jews not of Spanish-Portuguese origin; the respect enjoyed by the Spaniolic (Sephardic) Jews gained admission and toleration for other Jews as well, and not only in Holland. In other countries and areas, too, their influence paved the way for the readmittance of the Jews, particularly in Cromwell's England and in the German city-state Hamburg, the "Free and Hanseatic City." Beyond that, they called the attention of states and cities to the importance of the Jews for the promotion of commerce and manufacturing. People rightly asked themselves why only Holland, a country to which all impecunious potentates of Europe applied for loans in the seventeenth and eighteenth centuries, should profit from the Jews. Was it not better to utilize their abilities to develop commerce and industry in one's own country?

The Jews in the Mercantile System

In other respects, too, the development of states and economies tended in this direction. The state headed by an absolutistic prince that came into being in Europe in the seventeenth and eighteenth centuries and became ever more dominant was no longer guided by church interests, or at any rate to a far lesser extent than previously. The basic principle of its Machiavellian policy was reason of state (*raison d'état*), the interest of the state and its ruler, who was thought of as identical with it.* For the preservation and strengthening of the state in the world of states the interest of the state demanded the development of its instruments of power, above all the creation of a dependable standing army instead of temporary mobilizations or sporadically serving troops of mercenaries as well as the development of civil servants completely devoted to the state. This required money, and preferably funds that were derived from new sources of taxation and did not have to be approved by the estates in each instance, for these old estates resisted the new development that disregarded their privileges and was designed to make the state and its ruler omnipotent, freed from all traditional or legalistic ties, and "absolute" as well as establishing direct contact between him and his subjects without the intervention of other powers. The means for this was the promotion of commerce and industry in every possible way in the large workshops *(manufactures)*, in which there was division of (manual) labor and which were the forerunners of mechanical industry.

The most characteristic feature of this new economic system, mercantilism—the term with its emphasis on trading in merchandise was coined by its opponents, the physiocrats and Adam Smith—was the high value placed on money and foreign trade. Occupations with which the Jews had been closely identified for centuries but which were deemed inferior by the economists of the Middle Ages were now regarded by the leaders of the new economic policy of the state as important occupations that a state had to promote and encourage if it properly understood its interest. In line with this economic policy foreigners were invited into the country if they had special expertise in commerce and industry or money and connections that could be exploited for the promotion of foreign trade.

It was logical to use the Jews as particularly suitable helpers toward that end. Everyone knew that they were closely tied to money and trade; after all, since the Middle Ages "Jew" and "dealer" or "financier" had become virtually synonymous concepts. Beginning with the late fifteenth century people used the expressions "mit dem Judenspiess rennen" (Sebastian Brant, 1494), "mit dem Judenspiess laufen" (1541) [both "to run with the Jews' spear"], and "mit dem Judenspiess fechten" [to fight with the Jews' spear], familiar images in those martial times, to denote trade and usury. The Jews as such had no rights and for that very reason were more readily available for the new purposes and needs of the state; their fortunes were, for better or for worse, more closely tied to the state and its administration than the estates and guilds with their old traditional rights were. Hence it was possible to make fewer con-

---

*This is how "L'état c'est moi" (*I* am the state), a statement attributed to Louis XIV, the most representative ruler of the epoch, is to be understood.

cessions to the Jews and to keep tighter reins on them, since their usually very temporary rights were granted directly by the state and only under certain conditions. For these reasons there was less fear that the Jews would participate in factional opposition to the state and its potentate.

Thus the powers that be did not hesitate to use the Jews who appeared qualified for the furtherance of the new economic policies even in places and countries from which they had frequently been banned for centuries. During the Thirty Years' War the Jews, with their connections beyond the shifting boundary lines, had proved useful to the princes and military commanders as suppliers of war materials, messengers, and intelligencers; they had frequently served officers and soldiers as buyers and sellers of booty. Many Jews had again accumulated considerable fortunes in this way. Their services became particularly desirable after the Peace of Westphalia that ended the Thirty Years' War in 1648, when the German princes did their utmost to settle their devastated, depopulated, and impoverished lands again, to strengthen their economy, and to organize them systematically and in politically more progressive fashion. On this foundation arose the institution of the so-called Court Jew.

The "Court Jew"

The Court Jew was not a new institution that came into being in the sixteenth or seventeenth century; its history goes back to the early Middle Ages. Whenever rulers needed financial help to make themselves independent from competing political and economic forces, to expand their sphere of power, to develop the economy of their territory, or to satisfy their own needs for luxury they relied, whenever possible, on foreigners and members of minorities (e.g., the Huguenots expelled from France in the seventeenth century). The Jews, who were everywhere a foreign minority without rights, were always suitable in this regard. Owing to the special situation in Europe, the institution of the Court Jew became so common from the end of the sixteenth century on, and in particular in the seventeenth and eighteenth centuries (with aftereffects beyond the French Revolution well into the nineteenth century), that the concept is usually identified with that period. People customarily think of the Court Jews at the great royal or princely courts from whom sprang banking families like the Hirsches, Rothschilds, or Mendelssohns, or of figures like Jud Süss Oppenheimer who have captured and occupied the popular imagination down to our time with their rise, their power, and love of splendor as well as their precipitous downfall. However, the position of the Jews as helpers of the powers that be in this epoch of the rising absolutistic state and an economy on the way to modern capitalism is far more extensive and complex than that.

In those days Jews were admitted by rulers, great and small, in all sorts of functions, frequently even if Jews in general were barred from their territories; in fact, they were often brought in and encouraged. In the seventeenth and eighteenth centuries the institution of the Court Jew became common—not only in Poland, "where every nobleman had his Jewish factor" (Priebatsch), but particularly in Germany, where there were countless almost wholly independent territories after the Thirty Years' War, and even in areas where Jews were otherwise forbidden to live. These Jews were frequently mint-masters; they were the most important suppliers of war material as well as sellers and exploiters of booty taken in the numerous wars of the time; they were heads of workshops and the most frequent attenders of fairs. Their connections opened up foreign markets for the products of their country, and domestically they were mediators between the city and the country. They stimulated the economy, and by virtue of this and also because of the various taxes and contributions with which they had to buy their right to stay, to travel, and to trade, they were the state's most lucrative single source of revenue.

Basically, this produced no change in the legal status of the Jews as a whole. Even where Jews had de facto equality with the other subjects in their economic activities or where they even enjoyed a privileged position by virtue of special considerations, they were not recognized as citizens with equal rights. The Frankfurt "Judenstättigkeit" (Statute for the Jews) of 1617, for example, in which the conditions of their sojourn were legally established, forbade the Jews expressly and under pain of punishment to call themselves "citizens of Frankfurt" since they were only "under the protection of an honorable council." Everywhere Jews were entitled to permanent residence and activities only if they received express permission, a special privilege, for it and thereby were extended the protection of a state or a city. Of course, the granting of this often temporary right involved the payment of certain taxes, and the privilege, including the right to marry as well as certain trading rights, could often be transferred to only one child. Documents addressed to the Jews emphasized the fact that they were far from being citizens like any others and that they were "protected Jews" dependent on the favors of the rulers. This was recognized by the Jews themselves in their petitions and official signatures, though we must remember that the servility of the subjects toward their rulers was the general style of the Baroque Age. As before, the Jews did not have a right to exist per se but only to the extent that the interest of a prince, a state, or a city made it seem desirable. As late as 1750 a Prussian law relating to the Jews declared that the settlement of foreign Jews was forbidden. The royal decree issued in the state of the "enlightened" absolutistic king Frederick II (the Great) continues characteristically: "However, if such a Jew really has 10,000 reichsthaler in his possession and brings this sum into the country, an inquiry should be addressed to Us."

The Absolutistic State and the Jews

Even though the legal situation of the Jews remained basically unchanged, their position toward the state (or, more accurately, the position of the state and its organs toward the Jews) did change in that epoch of absolutism and mercantilism. After all, the absolutistic state was substantially different from the medieval state, which essentially governed in indirect fashion. All strata of the population had their particular organization and structure, their special rights and duties; the national law was the totality of these diverse legal relationships. By contrast, the absolutistic state of modern times—from a historical point of view, the precursor of the modern national state—endeavored to establish direct contact with each individual citizen. All special rights of estates and economic corporations were repugnant to it, no matter how greatly they might be hallowed by tradition. The ruler and the civil servants submissive to him were engaged in a constant struggle with these corporate forces. In this struggle of the state and its ruler against traditional rights, and in particular in the state's struggle against the middle classes, which clung to the organization of the trades in the guilds, the Jews were on the side of the state. From the outset this position was dictated by their obligations toward the state. After all, one reason why the rulers and the civil servants submissive to them had admitted the Jews was to make the state more independent in its revenue and thus strengthen it in its struggle against the forces resisting its policy of unification. In the nature of things, the government's economic interests also pointed it in the same direction. Only when the firm organization of the medieval urban economy and division into estates was shattered, only when the economy was freed of the many traditional fetters and restrictions was there a place in it for the Jews. Thus the Jews served voluntarily and also under coercion by the state as a kind of shock troops against the conventional methods of the economy. This had both positive and negative consequences.

The Urban Citizenry and the Jews

This position of the Jews as pioneers of a new economic and political structure naturally also affected the relationship of the citizenry to them. As we have shown, the medieval hatred of the Jews had, as it were, gradually taken the form of several "geologic" strata, and now a new stratum was added. The traditional stereotypical notions about the Jew and the fearful accusations against the Jews as demonic corrupters of Christianity—notions and accusations that were ever more widely disseminated by the modern printing of books and pictures, increasingly took hold of the people, and were exacerbated by the period's belief in witches—were now joined by the hatred of the old established burghers of the city who were accustomed to their tradition and naturally defended their rights and the economic foundations of their existence. To such a person a Jew was, in a handy generalization, the corrupter of the "good old" customs, the destroyer of a hallowed tradition, and the violator of venerable conventions. At the same time he viewed the Jews primarily as economic competitors, more zealous than Christian merchants and quicker, more adroit, and more unscrupulous in the employment of all resources of the modern world. A Jew was quicker and more unscrupulous because he was bound by no tradition of a guild, because he had to get ahead at all costs if he did not wish to go under, because this revolutionary pushing ahead in the economy was, so to speak, the condition for his admittance, and because his economic activity was shaped by the customs and education of many generations. For centuries a Jew had been constrained to find gaps in the firmly established economy of the Middle Ages and of the modern age which he, the man without rights and without protection, could fill, relying only on his abilities, his instincts, and his feel for economics. This constraint made him more pliant and more flexible, quicker to seize and utilize any economic opportunities that presented themselves. There is no need for us to decide the much-discussed question to what extent the Jews were the founders or co-founders of the new economic forms that arose now and captured the world. For our investigation it does not matter whether the Jews created, as Sombart claims, or helped to create, the new economy; what is certain is that this economy seemed to have been created for them. In the now highly valued branches of commerce and industrially organized large-scale business enterprises they were the more experienced persons, and in some branches of the economy they could even be regarded as instructors.

As we have pointed out, these conditions enhanced the Jews' economic value in the eyes of the rulers and those who did their bidding. In many instances, however, they exacerbated the gulf between the Jews and the middle class, which viewed them as a threat to its economic position. If the Jews now began to use their connections with Jews in neighboring countries to import goods more cheaply, if more skillful organization and a freer conduct of their businesses enabled them to offer merchandise to buyers at lower prices than "honorable" merchants with an old tradition as well as master tradesmen and guildsmen, they naturally incurred the hatred of such groups. In this way economic interest was elevated to the sphere of morality. With economic and moral arguments the citizenry defied higher powers by defending its right to bar Jews from the cities.

This conflict of interest gave rise to a fresh reproach against the Jews, one that has since then appeared whenever Jews have tried to immigrate and create a place for themselves in the economy of a country: The Jew is the "immoral" undercutter; through the frivolous cheapness of his offers he endangers the existence of noble tradesmen, honest businessmen, and old established workingmen. Be on your guard against him!

Popular Sentiment against the Jews as Representatives of the Rulers

The Jews fared similarly when, upon orders from the rulers, they performed functions that were unpopular with the people. When Jews administered the estates of noblemen as their representatives in Poland, in German territories, or elsewhere, or if they collected the state's taxes as tax farmers (in return for loans they made), it was only natural that the displeasure of the people should be primarily directed not against the ruler, who remained in the background, but against the Jews, the executors of the unpopular measures and the objects of traditional dislike. During the Seven Years' War, fought between 1756 and 1763 for the possession of Silesia, Frederick the Great engaged in large-scale currency devaluation to improve his financial situation—a common practice in those days and one comparable to today's inflationary devaluations of currency—and for this purpose he used a consortium of Jewish financiers, Veitel Ephraim and his sons and Daniel Itzig. When these men used Jewish peddlers to bring in large quantities of good currency from neighboring countries and had the debased currency disseminated there, the people called the inferior new coins "Ephraimites" and devised these satiric verses; "Von aussen schön, von innen schlimm, von aussen Friederich, von innen Ephraim" (Outside fine, inside bad, outside Frederick, inside Ephraim). How deep-seated the hatred of the Jews was is indicated by the popular rejoicing when Court Jews, who had under certain circumstances risen to enjoy great respect and wield great power, were suddenly toppled by intrigues of their enviers, the overextension of their power, or changing circumstances. We need only recall the fate of Jew Süss Oppenheimer, familiar through broadsides, stories, narratives, and biographies, who became the most powerful man in Württemberg and was hanged as a symbol of demonic evil in Stuttgart on 4 February 1738, with the joyous participation of the court and the rabble.

Lessing's Play "Die Juden"

On that occasion the medieval doctrine, deeply rooted in the popular consciousness, that Jews must not rule over Christians was cruelly triumphant. Gotthold Ephraim Lessing surely reproduced this atmosphere quite correctly in his comedy *Die Juden* (The Jews), written eleven years later, in 1749, in which he makes an unmannerly and unprincipled Christian servant indignantly address his master, of whose Jewishness he has just learned: "What, you are a Jew and had the heart to employ an honest Christian as a servant? *You* should have been *my* servant; that would have been proper in accordance with the Bible. In me you have insulted all of Christendom." In this play, which is little known today, Lessing makes another person, a hypocritical cheat, say this about the Jews: "All of them are, without exception, cheats, thieves, and highwaymen. That is why they are a people accursed by God. . . . If the Good Lord did not hate them, why did almost twice as many Jews as Christians perish in the recent disaster in Breslau? Our pastor very wisely pointed this out in his last sermon. . . . Oh, my good master . . . guard against the Jews more than you do against the plague." And the high-minded nobleman, whose life has been saved by a Jew, tells his rescuer (whose Jewishness he is not aware of) his opinion of the Jews in the following words: "A people that is so intent upon profit does not really care whether it gets it lawfully or unlawfully, by trickery or by force. The Jews seem to have been made for trading or—to come right out with it—for cheating. Courtesy, freedom, enterprise, discretion— these are qualities that would make them estimable if they did not use them so much for our misfortune. . . . Oh, they are the most malicious and the meanest people." Their very physiognomy, he goes on to say, predisposes people against them. "Their insidiousness, unscrupulousness, selfishness, deceitfulness, and perjuriousness can, I should think, be read very clearly in their eyes."

Physiocratic Economics and Its Influence on the Evaluation of the Jews

This hostile attitude toward the Jews was greatly intensified and "scientifically" legitimized by the new economic doctrine that came into vogue around the middle of the eighteenth century. The doctrine of the so-called physiocrats, originated by the French physician F. Quesnay, rejected the overvaluation of commerce and merchandise that had been a feature of the system of mercantilism. The "natural system" of the economy that they wanted to produce contained both elements favorable to the Jews and views that could work in their disfavor. The

principle of *"Laissez faire, laissez passer,"* first formulated by the physiocrats and then adopted by the liberalistic economy of the mid-nine-
teenth century, as well as their view that the natural productive forces
should be given the greatest possible chance at unimpeded development—what could be better for the Jews than to have such views prevail
in economic and political life? It was different, however, with the revaluation of the branches of the economy that also was part of the
physiocratic doctrine. If under the influence of natural law and probably
also of early Romanticism the peasant class was now regarded as the only
productive one and trade and commerce, which had been at the top in
the value system of mercantilism, were declared to be a *"classe sterile,"*
the Jews were numbered among the unproductive economic forces, as
had happened in the Middle Ages. This gave fresh sustenance to the
traditional opinion that the Jews were basically nothing but parasitic
exploiters; the view of the Jews' unproductivity was here scientifically
reinforced, as it were. By way of this evaluation of the branches of the
economy as taught by the physiocrats, the evaluation of the Jews as
unproductive forces in the economy became part of the scholarship and
thought of its teachers. A contemporary reaction may be found in the
judgmental and condemnatory words with which the German theologian, poet, and philosopher Johann Gottfried Herder concludes the
chapter "Hebrews" in his *Ideen zur Philosophie der Geschichte der
Menschheit* (Thoughts on the Philosophy of the History of Mankind):
"God's people to which heaven itself once gave its fatherland has for
millenia, and almost since its origin, been a parasitic plant on the stems
of other nations, a species of crafty transactors in almost every part of the
world that despite all suppression nowhere yearns for its own honor, a
domicile of its own, or a fatherland." Since then the Jews have never
freed themselves from the stigma of this accusation, a stigma that in the
nature of things plain people have always attached to them and that in
the cruder form of later anti-Semitism was to be concentrated in the
doctrine that the Jews are parasites on the body politic of their host
nations.

Here we see the "hereditary handicap" of the Jewish question, and
something similar was to appear over and over again: From every new
intellectual current and every new doctrine popular opinion (and to a
large extent that included even the thin upper crust of the so-called
intellectuals) adopted as a matter of course primarily the ideas that
confirmed anew old prejudices and traditional views of the Jews. In
general, the physiocratic doctrine did not at first lead to the logical
insight that it might be better to enable even the Jews to develop their
energies freely; instead, the stigma attaching to them was now seen all
the more clearly: the occupational structure with which they were
reproached, occupations that were different and thus always evaluated as

"abnormal" and "unhealthy," though people actually knew that they themselves had barred the Jews from all other occupations and often continued to do so. And this critical and negative opinion of the Jews' economic activities was preserved even though the physiocrats' view of agriculture as the only productive branch of the economy was embraced by the public to only a minor extent and economics instead tended to a freer play of forces in which the Jews were able to display their abilities in trade and industry.

In any case, under the influence of these currents the more "humanely" oriented people first conceived the idea that the Jews should be turned into better people so that they might be granted more rights in the future. Beginning in the eighteenth century, this gave rise to endeavors in Germany and Eastern Europe to train the Jews for different occupations, particularly in agriculture and handicrafts. In modified form and with a different emphasis these efforts later occupied an important place in the teachings and endeavors of Zionism and Jewish Socialism.

The Attitude of the Enlightenment toward Judaism

These attempts at an occupational restructuring of the Jews in order to turn them into "normal" and "better" people and citizens were, of course, part of the movement aimed at the "education of the human race" (to use G. E. Lessing's phrase) to ever higher types of humaneness, the movement that termed itself "Enlightenment."* In our investigation we have already repeatedly encountered the beginnings and effects of this pan-European, primarily Western European, movement in the changes of the economy and society, but here we must consider it in somewhat greater detail as a comprehensive phenomenon. Its roots were multifarious and deeply embedded in the past, and it was composed of currents and endeavors since the late Middle Ages, the Renaissance, Humanism, the religious reformations, the rise of the natural sciences and of the urban middle class, the development of the universities, and the founding of the scholarly academies. The basic tendency of the Enlightenment, even if it was not able to prevail fully against the forces of tradition, was, to use Kant's formulation toward the end of the epoch (1784), "man's freeing of himself from his self-inflicted immaturity."** This meant a struggle against the forces of the church as well as a striving for mutual "tolerance" (*Toleranz* was the catchword) toward

---

*On the attitude of the Jews toward the Enlightenment, see p. 202 below.
**"Immaturity," Kant goes on to say in his famous essay "What Is Enlightenment?" "is the inability to use one's intellect without someone else's guidance. This immaturity is a person's own fault if it is not caused by a lack of intellect but by a lack of resoluteness and courage to use it without guidance."

other religions and modes of thought. After all, the religious wars of the seventeenth century (which were increasingly transformed into fights between dynasties and political powers with which they had been closely connected from the beginning) had shown that in the long run there hardly were real winners and losers and that one would have to learn not to regard one's own opinion as the only correct and justified one, or at least not to force it upon others. Originating in England and Holland, the principle of tolerance made its way via the minds of thinking people—unless organized religions with their dogmas were rejected altogether and people contented themselves with a general belief in an undefined deity in the spirit of the English deists or in the pantheistic form of the Spinozan equation of God and nature,* though most of them regarded this as reprehensible atheism. Rationalism increasingly prevailed in the thinking about God, the world, the economy, and society, and it was based on a believing optimism that the human spirit would soon succeed in truly freeing itself of prejudices and superstitions as well as the doctrines, legal systems, and institutions based on them—and despite the resistance of the churches, the privileged classes, and conservative economic circles. This transformation of the general intellectual atmosphere surely produced fertile soil for a better understanding of Judaism, for a normalization of Jewish existence, and for the integration of the Jews into the lives of the nations. Beginning, at the latest, with the publication of John Toland's work *Reasons for Naturalising the Jews in Great Britain and Ireland on the same foot with all other Nations. Containing also a Defence of the Jews against all vulgar Prejudices in all Countries* (London, 1714)** there were an increasing number of voices that pleaded for a new treatment of the Jewish problem—for economic reasons, on grounds of a humanitarianism that could not exclude the Jews, and also out of the conviction that all problems of human communal existence could be solved only through human understanding and mutual toleration and only on the basis of a legal order applying to everyone. Another factor that may have contributed to a friendlier attitude toward the Jews was the return of British and later North American Puritanism, as well as Geneva and Dutch Calvinism, to the Old Testament, which led to an evaluation of the Mosaic-Israelitic legislation as the right basis for modern constitutions as well. In the seventeenth century this was one of the motives for the admittance of the Spanish-Portuguese Jews to Holland and for the permission granted to Jewish merchants to settle in Cromwell's England (though this permission was at first given only tacitly and not embodied in the law).

But even the Enlightenment, with its emphasis on natural right and

*On Spinoza and Judaism, see the excursus in Part 2.
**About John Toland and his defense of the Jews, see the excursus in Part 2.

human dignity and its striving for freedom from prejudices and a humanitarianism founded on rational insights, did not, as one might assume from these ideological premises, redound only to the benefit of the Jews. Here, too, it turned out that the forces of conservatism and tradition were usually stronger than the optimistic proponents of new modes of thought assumed—in fact, that these proponents of new ideas frequently could not shed the old prejudices themselves and that the traditional notions, which the enlighteners normally fought with all their might, continued to dominate thoughts and feelings in the Jewish question. More than that: Precisely at this turn of an era, when educated people increasingly abandoned not the Christian faith but the orthodox observance of the Christian precepts in favor of a free-thinking, deistically or pietistically deepened faith,* the Jews with their clinging to traditional customs, their loyalty to the old festivals, and their study of the ancient books from the Bible to the Talmud and kabbalah, appeared more obdurate and peculiar than ever. Their strangeness in the face of modern culture, as determined by Christianity and the regenerated heritage of the ancients, became more striking than ever, and their peculiar otherness aroused at the same time that period's interest in exotic things and stimulated observation. It was, after all, the time when distant China began to be part of people's conception of the world and the national customs of the nearby gypsies began to be studied. Whereas people had once timidly shunned the ghettos and Jewish districts, now many educated people established closer contact with the Jews beyond the usual business connections—and not only with the "exceptional Jews," the Court Factors and bankers who were often privileged to live among non-Jews, built sumptuous houses for themselves, and vied with the surrounding world in secular education. Many a Christian now visited the Jewish quarter and saw with his own eyes the dirty streets, the inhabitants crammed together in the high boxlike buildings, and their strange customs that were sometimes captured in pictures and writings—and the visitors did not always view this with the pious astonishment of a Rembrandt, who found the models for his biblical figures there and drew and painted them in ever new versions. In many visitors knowledge of these conditions inspired an endeavor to fight for their improvement; in others it only intensified their dislike, and the unpleasant impression of the "dirty Jew" that was gained from such actual encounters was then often projected into the past—in some cases consciously, in others surely unconsciously. Added to this was the belief of the enlighteners that man as such basically always remains the same.

In any case, the fact that under the influence of the Enlightenment

---

*Concerning pietism and Judaism, see the excursus in Part 2.

educated people no longer saw the Jews only through the eyes of the Church definitely did not mean that they were now more favorably disposed toward them. To be sure, there were personalities who freed themselves from the fetters of prejudices and received opinions, viewed the Jews with unprejudiced eyes, attempted to understand their situation in the present as a product of historical conditions, and endeavored to gain a deeper understanding of both the past and the present. While the Jews themselves under the influence of the teachings of sin, punishment, and future redemptions showed no real interest in their own history since the destruction of the Temple and State until well into the nineteenth century and did not go beyond chronicle-like listings of the most important events and apologetic writings in defense of Judaism, the non-Jewish world now began to concern itself more seriously with Jewish history in the countries of the Diaspora after the downfall of the Jews' state. At the beginning of the eighteenth century (1706–11) there appeared as the most important result of such endeavors J. C. Basnage's history of post-biblical and contemporary Jewry under the title *L'Histoire et la religion des Juifs depuis Jésus-Christ jusqu'à présent*. The author, a Huguenot clergyman in Rouen and after the rescission, in 1685, of the Nantes Edict of Toleration (1598) by Louis XIV, in Holland as well, and also respected as a diplomat, attempted for the first time to write the history of the Jews in the long centuries about which historiography had been silent. It was his intention to continue the historical work of Flavius Josephus beyond the destruction of the State, and in so doing he freed himself from the Church's view (which had in one form or another been adopted by nonecclesiastical circles as well) that the history of the Jewish people after the crucifixion of Christ was no real history but only a curse and an absurdity. Until well into the nineteenth century Basnage's work served as a foundation for all who seriously concerned themselves with the fate of the Jews.

There were also others who strove to deal with the Jews and Judaism in as unprejudiced a fashion as possible. We need to think only of Herder's abovementioned writings about the poetry of the Jews,* of Lessing's magnificent appeal for religious and human tolerance in his verse drama *Nathan the Wise* (first printed in May 1779, one year after Voltaire's death),** and especially of the work *Über die bürgerliche Verbesserung der Juden* (Concerning the amelioration of the civil status of the Jews) by the thirty-year-old Prussian Kriegsrat (military councillor) Christian Wilhelm von Dohm.

Dohm's book was written at the suggestion of Moses Mendelssohn

*Concerning Herder's somewhat ambiguous attitude toward Judaism, see the excursus in Part 2.
**See the excursus in Part 2.

and appeared in two parts in 1781–82 and in a new, improved edition in
1783. This book, which aroused a great deal of attention, is typical of the
benevolent circles of the enlightened class of civil servants. Dohm
certainly does not take a rosy view of the Jews, "those unfortunate Asian
fugitives," but under Basnage's guidance he seeks to explain the decline
of the Jews on the basis of their history, as a result of oppression and
persecution. In the spirit of Tacitus, Dohm writes that as early as the
later years of their own State the Jews overestimated their own qualities
and developed "hatred and scorn of other people"; gradually their noble
pride degenerated into "an antisocial separation from other men." In
Dohm's opinion, traces of this have remained in the Jews of his own
time. That their religion was preserved despite all persecutions was
bound to appear to them as an even greater distinction than they had
received in all their previous history. The pressure and the unfair
treatment by the nations are bound to keep creating and intensifying
feelings of hatred among the Jews, and thus many of them may regard it
as permissible to hate non-Jews like Canaanites. "But such feelings are
indubitably only conclusions from their ancient laws. . . . Certainly the
present religion of the Jews contains no commandment to hate and
insult members of other faiths."

From such arguments it is clear how friends of the Jews had to
contend with resistance from without but also with their own inner
attitude if they wanted to prove that differences in their religion and
historical origin did not have to make worse citizens of the Jews. Dohm
attacks the generally prevailing opinion that the Jews were too corrupt
and too filled with hatred of the non-Jews to be granted equal civil
rights. He does not deny that the Jews of his time might be worse than
most Christian citizens. "I can admit," he expressly states, "that the
Jews may be morally more corrupt than other nations, that they are
guilty of a relatively greater number of infractions than the Christians,
that on the whole their character is more designed for usury and
deception in trade and their religious prejudices are more divisive and
antisocial. But I must add that this greater corruption of the Jews, which
is taken for granted, is a necessary and natural consequence of the
condition of oppression under which they have lived for so many centuries."

The situation of the Jews that he describes admits of only one logical
conclusion for Dohm: The exceptional conditions under which the Jews
have to live must be eliminated. He demands that the Jews be granted
civil equality and that all professions and economic activities be opened
to them. However, they should not be allowed to hold public office until
their aptitude for this is recognized on the basis of this new development. The state should take care of their education and enlightenment;
it should also grant them free exercise of their religion, autonomy, and

their own court system for minor private disputes, though the prerogatives of the rabbis should be restricted. At the same time the Christians ought to be educated to respect the Jews and practice religious tolerance.

We can see that at bottom enemies and friends of the Jews agreed that the Jews of their time were corrupt, though they drew different conclusions from this. The latter were optimistic, regarded the Jews as capable of improvement, and hence wished to demonstrate "how the Jews could become more useful members of civil society" and what could make them "happier and more useful to our states" (Dohm). The former regarded them as fundamentally so corrupt that a change and improvement in their living conditions would not ennoble their character and their behavior toward other people. Let us demonstrate by two examples how the same intensive concern with the Jews that turned men like Toland, Lessing, or Dohm into friends of the Jews could also produce enmity toward the Jews and how this could engender in the same era of Enlightenment not only fundamental works in justification of the Jews and pleading for their equality, but also equally fundamental writings in substantiation of modern Jew-hatred.

Fundamental Anti-Jewish Writings in the Epoch of the Enlightenment

One example is Johann Eisenmenger's *Entdecktes Judentum* (Judaism uncovered). This work, consisting of two fat tomes, was first printed in Frankfurt in 1700, but it was not released for general dissemination until the new Berlin printing of 1711, seven years after the author's death. Eisenmenger certainly did not approach his task lightly; his book evidences a thorough knowledge of Hebrew and extensive occupation with Talmudic and Rabbinic literature. After all, the learning of Hebrew, the reading of the basic Jewish writings, and their exegesis in the original language was by no means rare among Christian scholars since leading Humanists like Reuchlin, the Buxtorfs, and others had started this praiseworthy pursuit. Since then it had been part of the education of any scholar who dealt with the Bible and Judaism. It is not clear whether the author occupied himself with Jewish subjects only with anti-Jewish intentions. It may be that he was initially motivated by a scholarly thirst for knowledge, an eagerness to become more closely acquainted with that peculiar people, and the desire to distinguish himself by means of this study as a Christian Oriental scholar. He himself said that in the final analysis, anti-Christian remarks by his Jewish teacher, as well as the impression made upon him by the conversion of three Christians to Judaism, had induced him to write his work. Be that as it may, the prejudices he had absorbed from tradition and education evidently gave his studies an anti-Jewish tendency from the beginning, so that in his interpretation of the sources and his selection of quotations (which he usually gave first in the original Hebrew and then in German translation) he primarily emphasized what was detrimental to the Jews. The tendency of the entire work is already expressed in its full title: *Entdecktes Judentum oder gründlicher und wahrhaftiger Bericht, welcher Gestalt die verstockten Juden die Hochheilige Dreieinigkeit Gottvater, Sohn und Heil. Geist erschrecklicherweise lästern und verunehren, die Heilige Mutter Christi schmähen, das Neue Testament, die Evangelisten und Aposteln, die christliche Religion spöttisch durchziehen und die ganze Christenheit auf das Äusserste verachten und verfluchen,* etc. (Judaism Uncovered or thorough and truthful report of the way in which the obdurate Jews terrifyingly blaspheme and dishonor the very holy trinity, the Father, the Son, and the Holy Spirit, revile the holy mother of Christ, mockingly go through the New Testament, the Evangelists, the Apostles, and the Christian religion, and despise and curse all of Christianity in the extreme, etc.) In this title as well as in many statements by Eisenmenger one can perceive a strong influence of Luther's anti-Jewish writings.

The entire organization of the book with its copious quotations from Jewish religious literature, from the Bible and the Talmud down to the tosaphists and contemporary commentators, and particularly from the *Shulhan Arukh* shows that the author had an extensive knowledge of the Hebrew language and literature and also associated with Jewish scholars, whom he seems to have told that he was going to convert to Judaism. There can be no doubt about his extensive knowledge, though he misunderstood, misinterpreted, or falsely translated many passages—particularly when he took them out of context to support his theses. Here, too, one should not be too ready to assume that he always had evil intentions, for he was only reproducing the doctrines that had been prevalent for centuries, and this Christian tradition had from the outset steered his reading of Jewish books in an anti-Jewish direction. This was the characteristic feature of occupation with Jewish affairs (and actually still is today): A non-Jew had to have outstanding judgment and exceptional moral courage to express more just opinions about the Jews and to maintain them in the face of prevailing views. Eisenmenger was not such a person. He was an outstanding student of Jewish writings who wanted to warn the Christians against the Jewish danger and protect them from it. His scholarship actually served to create one of the fundamental books of modern anti-Jewish movements. It contains every one of the well-known accusations against the Jews, down to the killing of Christians and the poisoning of the wells. Hence there was hardly an anti-Semitic writer of the nineteenth and twentieth centuries who did not avail himself of this treasure trove of anti-Jewish sources and misinterpretations that had been compiled with a scholarly apparatus and thus were often taken all too seriously even by people without an anti-Jewish orientation. In addition to purely religious-dogmatic questions, the author was particularly enraged by the arrogance of the Jews. According to him, they still regarded themselves as chosen, superior to all nations, and the goal of earthly creation, even though, as everyone knew, they had been rejected by God. The author also repeats in great detail and documents copiously the accusation, raised at least since Tacitus, that the Jews hate all non-Jews and have a particularly hostile attitude toward the Christians. On the strength of his so very scholarly work Eisenmenger received the chair for oriental languages at the University of Heidelberg, but the influence of his book extended far beyond the time and place of his teaching activities.

Voltaire's Attitude toward Judaism

Another example is Voltaire's attitude toward Judaism. There is no need to discuss here Voltaire's importance as a central figure of the Enlightenment and the overwhelming influence that he exerted during his long life (1694–1778) on the origin and development of modern literature, as a fighter for freedom of thought and belief, as a founder of cultural historiography and the philosophy of history (a term coined by him), and as an opponent of the domination of the Christian church. This importance is universally known; here we are concerned only with his attitude toward Judaism and his influence on the Jewish question.

Voltaire's critical occupation with Jewish history and the Jews of his time stemmed from his struggle against Christianity and dogmatic religions generally, which he, like so many of his contemporaries of the Enlightenment, regarded as the main preservers and disseminators of antirational prejudices. For this reason he endeavored to devalue their literary basis, the Bible, as a historical document or as revealed wisdom, as Spinoza and others had done before him. He attempted to demonstrate that Christianity was not foretold in the Old Testament and that the Jews had not been a holy people or one chosen in any way. On the contrary, he said; the pagans were superior to them in culture. As he made a decisive break with the Judeocentric and Christological presentation of ancient history that had been prevalent up to that time, he delighted in presenting "the vagabond horde of Arabs called Jews"* as an insignificant barbarian people and in documenting this with a one-sided selection from biblical sources.

---

*"*La horde vagabonde des Arabes, appelés Juifs*" (*Dictionnaire philosophique*, ed. Benda and Naves [Paris, 1961], p. 5). This is one of the bases for the "discoveries" of Oswald Spengler and Toynbee in which the Jews are regarded only as an appendage to an Arab or Syrian culture. (See chap. 9 below.)

But all this could have been done without the crude vilifications of Judaism and the Jews that are found in many of his writings. After all, Basnage, too, had taken a critical view of many things in his history of the Jews without disparaging the Jews, but in this respect Basnage was an exception. It was the customary thing—and in this even "enlightened" and enlightening spirits were not free from the *Zeitgeist*—to apply the prevalent opinion of contemporary Jewry to the past, provided that one deviated from the Christian-dogmatic doctrines about Jewish history. It was certainly no longer necessary to be a devout Christian to adopt anti-Jewish theories from ancient and Christian tradition as well as from the contemporary opinion of the environment. The literature and daily intercourse provided ample opportunities for this.

This explains why Voltaire denies the Jews any economic and intellectual independence. According to him, they have from the beginning been nothing but agents and thieves, economically and intellectually. Their religious services, their Bible, and everything for which the world and the Jews themselves give them credit as special cultural achievements they have for the most part adopted from other nations and, as with their dealing in old clothes, sold as newly refurbished. In ancient times even their language was only a jargon—a mixture of Phoenician and Arabic, just like their present Judeo-German gibberish.

An example of the great extent to which Voltaire always proceeds from the present are his remarks about hygienic regulations in the military camp (Deut. 23:13ff.). "The Jewish people," he writes, "was so gross, and even today the masses of this nation are so unclean and smelly, that its law-givers were forced to stoop to the tiniest and lowest details [in order to regulate them]." The people were so filthy, he writes elsewhere, that frequent washing had to be imposed upon them as a religious precept—and this was then called "hallowing oneself."

In this and numerous other remarks Voltaire, the freethinker, the fighter against prejudices, and the foe of the Church, continues the ancient and Christian-dogmatic interpretation of the Bible that may be found in non-Jewish Bible criticism to this day, not to mention the deliberately anti-Jewish kind. In biblical laws or prophetic philippics such critics see less the moral power and the will to lead a pure and righteous life that is documented in them than they interpret the human weakness, shared by all nations, which the legal regulations and exhortations try to combat, as specifically Jewish vices.

In Voltaire's eyes the Jews of antiquity were more or less identical with the Jews of his time as he saw them; this was in keeping with his general view of the fixed nature of individuals and peoples. From the beginning their law made usurers out of them, virtually imposed usury upon them as a sacred duty. In the Babylonian captivity they were brokers, money-changers, and junk dealers. In Alexandria, too, they were usurers, and so they remained in the ensuing periods. On the other hand, they were never much good in the military and political realms. Their scholarly abilities are slight, but superstition has always flourished among them. Artistically they are quite untalented. Their morality is extremely low. After all, their own sacred writings describe them as cruel toward their enemies, cruel and rapacious even toward their fellow Jews, and frequently the driving force of this cruelty is their religious fanaticism. They have always been perfidious, crafty, dishonest, and avaricious.

The only positive qualities Voltaire discerns in the Jews are their physical fruitfulness and their economic thriftiness. He regards their belief in their chosenness as reprehensible arrogance that has caused the Jews to strive for dominance over the entire world. This striving for world domination that has been instilled in them by the Bible is the reason for the xenophobia which he, like many others since Tacitus, rebukes them for. They regard the land of a stranger as basically their property. In keeping with this, their morality is limited to their relations with their coreligionists. The other peoples hated them not because they were monotheists but because of their own xenophobia and their whole barbaric way of life. According to Voltaire, the Jews were not even superior to the other peoples in their concept of God, which does not include belief in immortality. From this brief outline we can see that Voltaire presented to his contemporaries the entire arsenal of anti-Jewish criticism that had accumulated since antiquity and since Spinoza. The explosive force of these half-truths was dangerously intensified by his excellent style and the brilliance and irony of his language.

Voltaire's relationship to the Jews of his time was bound to be in keeping with his attitude toward the Jews of history. He derided the attempts at conversion that were frequently being made by well-meaning Christians and pietistic believers. After all, this was the period in which the modern mission to the Jews was organized. As an Enlightener, however, Voltaire was of course against any religious persecution as a matter of principle, and that included the persecution of the Jewish religion. He regarded it as absurd for the Christian religion, which was based on the Jewish religion, to hate the latter. But for him the Jews were "an ignorant and barbaric people that has long combined the most sordid avarice with the most detestable superstition and an invincible hatred of all peoples that tolerate and enrich it." Instead of continuing to lead such a reprehensible life, the Jews ought to abandon their isolation, their superstitious laws, and so forth, and become pure Deists (like himself); then they could be admitted to the community of the Deists.

But to those Jews who despite everything cling to their superstitious beliefs he proposes—half in jest, half seriously—that they return to Palestine. "Do not reproach me," he addresses the Jews, "for not loving you; I love you so much that I wish you were in Jerusalem instead of the Turks, who are devastating your whole country. . . ." And a bit later he wrote: "Return to Judea as soon as you can." With his accustomed self-irony (which we later find in Jewish form in Heine) he adds: "I would only like two or three Hebrew families to stay here in order to establish a bit of necessary trade on the estate where I live." Shortly thereafter he gave the Jews this general advice for their life-style: "You were cruel and fanatical monsters in Palestine, and that is what you have been in our Europe. . . . You have been calculating animals; try to become thinking animals."

According to Voltaire, it was not their merits or their good qualities but the idea of tolerance which demanded that the Jews not be persecuted. Jews and Christians ought to abandon their reprehensible traditions and superstitious notions and then live together in peace. But as far as Voltaire was concerned, this certainly did not mean that the Jews should be granted equal civil rights.

If one considers how widely disseminated and respected Voltaire's writings were in his lifetime and for a long time afterwards, and to a certain extent are even today, how they reached the people with their wit and their clear, lively style, one can gauge the great influence of his estimate of the Jews. His *Essai sur les moeurs* and his *Dictionnaire philosophique*, works that contain deprecatory and venomous judgments about the Jews and Judaism, were veritable primers for educated people. Then, too, in many of Voltaire's widely disseminated stories (e.g., in *Zadig*, where he has the Jews' God solemnly give thanks for a successful fraud) there are barbs against the Jews. Voltaire's conception and presentation of the Jewish question clearly show how hard it was even for a person with a comprehensive education, who in accordance with the principles of the Enlightenment wished to free himself from any kind of prejudice, to arrive at a fair judgment about the Jews.*

It is certainly not necessary to cite Voltaire's bad personal experiences with Jewish financiers as the main (or even contributory) reason for his attitude toward Judaism, as has frequently been done. Surely Voltaire had bad experiences with other people without making a devastating judgment about the group to which they belonged. Even a philosopher with such revolutionary judgments about recognized doctrines as Immanuel Kant (1724–1804),** a man who was unprejudiced in his personal associations with Jews and even was friends with a few (such as Markus Herz), had no understanding of Judaism and not approaching it with an

---

*To be sure, at the same time he acknowledges the social importance of unexamined notions (prejudices) taken over from childhood and points to the continued presence of old notions in language (e.g., the rising and setting sun) even after their scholarly refutation. (Cf. the article "Préjugés" in the *Dict. phil.*, pp. 351ff.)

**See the excursus on Kant and the Jewish question in Part 2.

open mind made derogatory statements about it that had a negative effect as "philosophical truths" beyond his place and his time. Other intellectually and humanly outstanding persons of his time behaved just as he did, some of them under his influence: writers and philosophers, historians of the stature of a Gibbon,* classic writers of German literature and other literatures. Here we are evidently dealing with general developments that tended to have a negative effect when the Jewish question was evaluated.

The increasing secularization of scholarship and its detachment from ecclesiastic thought stripped the Jewish question of its superhuman character, both for good and evil. The curse of the Church was lifted from the Jews, but so was the mercy which according to the Augustinian view would be theirs again at the end of time. The Bible criticism that had been founded by the Jew Baruch Spinoza** (*Theologico-Political Treatise*) and emerged in the philosophical struggle for freedom of thought within and without Judaism regarded the Jews as a people like any other and the Bible as a historical and literary document like other literary monuments. In the eyes of the Enlighteners—from Spinoza to the Encyclopedists around Diderot and Holbach and down to German Classicism—this invalidated all claims that the Jews were accustomed to deriving from the Bible as God's people and bearers of a divine mission. There remained only the bare reality, which usually did not appear very likable.

As we have repeatedly pointed out, the revival of classical literature also brought a revival of the image of the Jews that was embodied in Greek and Roman literature. At the same time the Christian dogmatic views, as religious doctrines or secularized in ethical-philosophical form, remained the foundation of European thought. As the Christian "religious truths" were given greater depth and made the basis of a spiritualized life-style, as happened in German Pietism from the late seventeenth century on, *** the wrongs of the Jews that had caused the sufferings of God's son became a sin that was felt as a personal hurt, and the desire to convert the Jews, who were continuing on their wrong track, through the newly organizing mission to the Jews became all the stronger.

From all these viewpoints the actual life of the Jews and their traditionalism, which outsiders found increasingly incomprehensible, was apt to evoke merciless criticism—all the more so because large numbers of educated Jews in Central and Western Europe began to doubt the meaning of their existence and inclined toward the critical views of the

*Cf. Part 2.
**See the excursus in Spinoza in Part 2.
***See the excursus on German Pietism in Part 2.

Enlighteners (see pp. 196f. below). Thus the Enlightenment was both a curse and a blessing for the Jews, with a close connection between its good and bad elements.

Both the Jewish self-image and the non-Jews' views of the Jews were understandably greatly influenced by the events and changes in Jewish life since the middle of the seventeenth century.

Eastern and Western Europe

Thus far we have mainly traced the development in Central and Western Europe, and we must keep reverting to it because there (and particularly in Germany) the Jewish question, the exploration of which is the sole purpose of this book, developed in its basic social, economic, and ideological forms. This is why in a presentation of the nature and the history of the modern Jewish question the conditions in that area occupy more space than they would merit on the basis of its numerical share in the total Jewish population—that is, from a "quantitative-historical" point of view. But we must remember one thing: In Central Europe, and especially in Germany, where the modern theories about the Jewish question originated, there lived only a small fraction of the Jewish people as a whole* and even of the Jewish population of Europe. Since the persecutions of the Crusades, and particularly since the fourteenth century, the majority of European Jewry had been concentrated in Poland. This great center of European Jewry in Poland, however, experienced around the middle of the seventeenth century a catastrophe that affected all of Jewry.

THE JEWS OF POLAND

We have already mentioned (p. 117 above) the immigration of Jews in Poland since the Crusades and especially since the thirteenth and fourteenth centuries, when the situation of the Jews in Western and Central Europe worsened to the point of intolerability and, on the other hand, the Polish rulers were interested in bringing in German and Jewish settlers for the development of their decayed land. The Jewish settlers received privileges that guaranteed them personal safety, the right to practice their religion freely, a great measure of self-government, freedom of movement, unlimited trade in money and merchandise, and even the right to own land. Under the prevailing circumstances their legal situation could be regarded as satisfactory. Thus enterprising Jews in particular, who often had considerable re-

---

*Cf. also the remarks about the distribution of the Jews over the world in various eras in the introductory chapter, p. 25 above.

sources at their disposal, had an incentive to settle and to gain a livelihood by developing the land. Under what appeared to be economically sound conditions there could develop a cultural center as well that was to serve as a guide for European Jewry.

However, here too, it turned out that even the most favorable privileges and laws could not help the Jews in the long run if they were opposed by other, native, societal forces. As they had been in Western Europe, the Jews in Poland were, formally and legally, *Kammerknechte* (servants of the treasury) of the king. Their taxes went to him, and formally they were subordinate only to him. In the societal reality, however, there were of course other significant forces as well: the burgeoning cities, the lower nobility with its decisive influence on the election of the king and the administration of the country, and finally the clergy, an increasingly strong political force since the sixteenth century. All these forces were interested in pushing the Jews out of certain economic areas. Beginning with the sixteenth century, a concentric pressure was exerted on the economic position originally assigned to the Jews. The Sejm, the chamber that represented the Polish nobility, deprived them of the lease of state revenues that had been one of their functions in the Middle Ages. The magistrates took away their freedom to trade within the city limits; the Sejm sanctioned and extended their trading prohibition. In the Council of Piotrkow (1538) the Church demanded the exclusion of the Jews from any trade.

Therefore, while the Jews retained the rights in their inner realm, freedom of religion and communal autonomy, their economic activities were increasingly restricted. They maintained themselves in foreign trade; they flocked to the handicrafts, establishing their own Jewish guilds because they were barred from the Christian ones; and they engaged extensively in the administration of the estates of Polish magnates (of the higher nobility). With the expansion of Polish colonization in the sixteenth and seventeenth centuries they also went to the Ukraine as estate administrators for the aristocratic landed proprietors, as leaseholders (according to the so-called Arenda System), as tavern owners, dealers, and artisans. This was their situation when the catastrophe of 1648 befell them.

THE POLISH-UKRAINIAN CATASTROPHE OF 1648–1649

The events of 1648 in Poland are a classic example of the complicated and peculiar nature of the Jewish question and of the tragic situations into which the Jews have again and again been plunged by developments that occurred through no fault of their own and in which they became disastrously involved through the circumstances of their life.

Actually, the uprising of the Cossacks under their leader Bogdan

Chmielnicki, who raised a wrong done him to a universal plane and thus became a popular leader, was not directed against the Jews but against the Poles, against the national, religious, and social suppression of the (Greek-Orthodox) Ukrainian people by the (Roman-Catholic) Polish nobility. The Jews were the middlemen and executive organs of the nobility; Chmielnicki himself employed a Jew as a tavern keeper. Hence a Ukrainian peasant or Cossack often did not even know his real oppressor, a Polish nobleman, but only the Jew who administered the estates, collected the taxes, and demanded money for his schnapps in the tavern. In these positions and functions the Jews behaved hardly better or worse than their employers. Even the Ukrainian folk song about the "Cleaned-out Cossack" presents the Jew essentially as a manager concerned with the profit of his Polish master,* even though it also expresses indignation at the arrogance with which the Jewish unbeliever in this position presumes to lord it over the Christian peasants and Cossacks.

The decisive feature of that situation was this: The rage at the Jew was all the more grim because the hatred of him as a representative of the Polish oppressor was exacerbated by the "primal hatred" of the Jew, the traditional Christian hatred of the unbeliever and perfidious person, the deicide who is accursed and thus ought to be a servant, yet in defiance of all divine and human laws presumes to exercise a lord's rights over the orthodox Christian. This gave the attack on the Jews the particular bestiality that is most impressively documented in Nathan Hannover's memorable chronicle of those bloody events, *Yeven Matzula.*** That, and not only fear and cowardice, led the resident Polish population in many places to join with the attacking enemies of the country against the Jews, who, after all, were oppressors and competitors to those outsiders as well. But that always gave the Jews a chance, albeit one used by only very few, to save their lives, despite all political and social sins committed as Polish leaseholders and economic competitors, by having themselves baptized and becoming good, believing Christians.

The most tragic thing about the catastrophe was that the Jews carried on a struggle—often bearing arms in the joint defense of the cities—that was senseless for them and lost it. Polish, Ukrainian, and Russian history can report victory or defeat in this struggle as a meaningful event. Russian and Ukrainian historiography celebrates Chmielnicki as a national hero and his fight and victory as an important step in the development of the Russian state and the Ukrainian nation. A monument was erected in Kiev to this national hero. In Polish history the event marks

---

*"The heroic Ukrainian cossack rides past the inn, but the Jew takes hold of him and won't let go. 'Rest, my little cossack, my little cossack, come in, for how else can I pay my master, the Pole, his rent?'"
**The title of the chronicle means "Deep Mire" or "Slimy Deep" (Ps. 69:3). The first word (*Yeven*) is similar to *Yavan* (Greek), to designate the Greek-Orthodox Ukrainians.

the end of colonizing expansion, a decisive stage in the decline of the Polish-Lithuanian state. As far as the Poles and the Russians were concerned, the fate of the Jews did not matter in the least; usually historians did not even consider it necessary to mention them. For the Jews, however, who really were not a party to this struggle and were involved in it only because their existence as Jews pushed them between the contending forces, this event means one of the greatest catastrophes of their history in the Diaspora; the Jewish contemporaries regarded it as the third destruction of their existence as a people. Hundreds of Jewish communities in the Ukraine and Poland were destroyed between 1648 and 1656 during the Cossack rebellions and the subsequent Polish-Swedish war. According to contemporary accounts, about one hundred thousand Jews lost their lives and thousands were sold into slavery by the Tatars. The great Jewish center in Poland was struck at its root. It did continue to exist and grow, but it never recovered from this blow inwardly and in its relation to the outside world. The era of Polish-Jewish history that has been called the "golden age" (probably with as much exaggeration as in the case of medieval Spanish-Jewish history) was irretrievably past.

REMIGRATION FROM EAST TO WEST

The consequences of this shock were felt far beyond the Polish realm; all of Jewry was affected by it, and in many respects. At a moment in history when Central Europe, exhausted by the recently finished Thirty Years' War, dared to hope for a period of peace, a healing of the wounds of war, and a reconstruction of what had been destroyed and devastated, the Jews were once again reminded of their singular fate. A flightlike remigration from Poland began. The country that had for centuries admitted Jews from Central and Western Europe and given them a chance to exist economically and culturally now began to be a country from which they emigrated. Jews emigrated from Poland in large numbers immediately after the events, and thereafter without interruption, with the numbers fluctuating according to the political, economic, and social situation. They went west, south, and north, to Germany, Central Europe, and Italy, to Holland and all other countries in which they had a chance to earn a living. The wars in Poland and Lithuania, the economic decline of the steadily increasing Jewish population, as well as religious, economic, and social persecutions and worries, gave the Jews ever new impulses to leave the country and seek other domiciles.

This never-ending trek from East to West had far-reaching consequences. It kept reminding the Jews of other countries—often when they, rightly or wrongly, regarded their situation as particularly secure—of the catastrophic character of their existence in the Diaspora. It brought back memories of their past and thereby impeded their complete assimilation to their surroundings precisely at a time when this complete absorption by the environment threatened to endanger the existence of the Jewish people through collective forgetting and repression. To be sure, it also was capable of producing a feeling of aloofness and arrogance toward the Jews immigrating from the East who had developed differently under the influence of other environments in their appearance, their life-style, and their views.

The remigration of the Ashkenazic Jews from Poland affected the surrounding world in the same way. Over and over again it served to display to this world the unity of world Jewry. The world saw how the Jews in all countries concerned themselves with their newly arriving coreligionists and aided them with money, clothing, and work even when these immigrants appeared alien to them and differed from the native Jews in their customs and often their language as well. Thus the "Wandering Jew" became an everyday phenomenon, the "Eternal Jew" even in places where Jews had resided for a long time and felt at home among the population of the country.

Messianic Mysticism

The immediate consequence of the catastrophe of 1648 was even more far-reaching. Jews have never admitted that a misfortune that befell them could be accidental in nature; they have always asked about the reason and the meaning of the occurrence. The Jews of that period were not interested in the historical conditions—such an examination would not have been in keeping with their view of history nor with that of their contemporaries—or in the connection of their fate with the national and social situations of other peoples. The actual conditions of the period did not answer the great basic question that they asked, as Jews had always asked before: What meaning, what significance does this catastrophe have in the course of Jewish history? To the Jews of the seventeenth century the course of Jewish history still meant what it had to the Jews of the Middle Ages as well as to the Spanish and Portuguese exiles of the sixteenth century: the history of salvation, of the banishment and redemption of the Jewish people. Elsewhere (see p. 000 above) we have discussed the origin of the idea of the Messianic period and the struggles and catastrophes that were to precede it as "birthpangs of the Messiah." It is in this light that the Jews always viewed the events that befell them when, in desperate piousness, they asked about the meaning of their sufferings. The more grievous these sufferings were, the more far-reaching the catastrophes and the greater the number of the Jews affected by them, the more audible and the closer the footsteps of the Messiah seemed to be. The Spanish exiles were profoundly convinced that the time of redemption was imminent; otherwise the catastrophe of Spanish-Portuguese Jewry would have been meaningless, and for devout Jews, as for any true believer, meaninglessness of an occurrence was inconceivable. Hence it was no accident that in the sixteenth century figures like Solomon Molcho and David Reubeni, pious Messiah figures and adventurous visionaries, were given credence and found adherents when they spoke of the imminent hour of redemption. Nor was it accidental that Lurianic mysticism, with its integration of the idea of redemption into cosmic happenings (see pp. 164ff. above), spread from Safed to world Jewry and became the dominant factor in the religious world of the Jewish Diaspora in the early decades of the seventeenth century, after hopes for a rapid redemption through the appearance of the Messiah had repeatedly been dashed. By means of mortification of the flesh, a life truly pleasing in the eyes of God, self-absorption, and mystical union of an individual soul with the divine source of all being, Jews hoped and strove to gather the scattered sparks of God's glory (*Shekhina*) and thereby bring about the gathering and redemption of Jewry and of mankind that was expected at any moment.

The Popular Messianic Movement of Sabbatai Tzevi and Its Consequences

Naturally, the Polish catastrophe too, had to be endowed with meaning in this image of the Diaspora's history, in this salvation story of banishment, suffering, and redemption. In the view of the pious, it was the last stage in the ongoing process of redemption. A catastrophe of this dimension in which such a considerable part of Jewry perished under such shameful circumstances was comprehensible only as the last and deepest humiliation before the liberation and redemption. This is the only explanation for the influence exerted by the appearance of a pathological zealot like Sabbatai Tzevi as the Messiah not only on contemporary Jewry but also on the Jews and the Jewish question far beyond his time.

After all we have already said, it is not so astonishing for the history of our problem that an obviously manic-depressive, faith-possessed personality like Sabbatai Tzevi should have laid claim to being the expected Messiah. Such "believing liars of their own destiny," as a biographer (Kastein) has called them, had frequently appeared in the history of the Jewish Diaspora, though not under comparable dramatic circumstances. It was more significant that at the same time there appeared a prophet (Nathan of Gaza) who assigned to Sabbatai Tzevi a position in the history of salvation, and that this seemed to revive prophecy. The really decisive thing, however, was the response of the Jews and the non-Jewish world: It marked the beginning of a worldwide Jewish popular movement with considerable consequences for the development of the Jewish question. The facts are generally known; many of them are well documented by contemporary accounts, documents, and Messianic-theological writings. Despite all the modern critical investigation of the sources (especially by G. Scholem), in the case of personalities like Sabbatai Tzevi, the circumstances of whose life are all too easily spun into legends, it is difficult to distill facts and actual occurrences from fables and stories of miracles. Added to this is the fact that after the shameful failure and the apostasy of the "Messiah" interested parties destroyed many sources that testified to their belief in the "false Messiah."

It is certain that Sabbatai Tzevi was born in 1626 at Smyrna (Izmir), but the (possibly manipulated) date of his birth remains in doubt—the ninth of Av, the day of the destruction of the Temples and date which religious tradition liked to use for major misfortunes and which for that very reason might have seemed suitable for the birth of the Messiah. He was the son of a merchant who was probably of Ashkenazic origin and, like many other local Jews (including his two younger brothers), had soon become prosperous when the Turkish-Venetian war of 1645–64 quickly caused Smyrna to flourish as a trade center. This status of his birthplace as a new eastern trade center goes a long way toward explaining the speed with which news of the Messiah and miracle worker spread through all countries: by means of circular letters, diplomatic representatives, commercial agents, travelers, and emissaries. Not so the news about his first attempt (or, as Scholem put it, manic eruption), that is, Sabbatai Tzevi's first public avowal of his Messianic mission, the first utterance (permitted only to the high priest in the Temple—and to the Messiah) of the full name of God *(Shem amephorash)*, which is usually expressed only paraphrastically *(Adonai,* my master, or *Shem,* name). That had happened in 1648 at the latest when news of the terrible massacres of the Jews by Chmielnicki's hordes in Poland reached Smyrna. This appearance did not evoke any positive response as yet; on the contrary, as a consequence Sabbatai was banned from Smyrna by the Jewish authorities in the early 1650s. He then led an unstable itinerant life, one of religious-mystical asceticism that oscillated between spiritual elation, depression, and fresh illuminations that were believed and accepted by a growing circle of adherents, until the decisive turning point came in 1665–66: Jewish and Christian mystics had determined that 1666 was the year of the great divine world change.

In 1662 Sabbatai had gone to Jerusalem for a year, and in the fall of 1663 he had been sent from there as an emissary to Cairo, at that time an important Jewish and kabbalistic center. There he married (after two divorces) in 1664 amid fantastic and pompous celebrations an Ashkenazic girl of dubius reputation who had been orphaned by the Polish massacres of 1648 (which was of symbolic importance to him). This girl had come to Cairo via Amsterdam and Mantua, either summoned by him or on her own initiative. When her dubious reputation was mentioned, he answered that the prophet Hosea had also married a prostitute at the behest of God. Replies of this sort certainly did not decrease his stock among his adherents. If anything, they helped to place him in the lineage of strangely saintly predecessors and convey a picture of the atmosphere that surrounded him.

When he received news of a prophet and faith-healer named Nathan who lived in Gaza, Sabbatai went to see him in the spring of 1665. The twenty-one-year-old devout visionary Nathan of Gaza, who in February of that year had in a "vision" seen Sabbatai as the Messiah, finally convinced Sabbatai Tzevi, who was beset by shifting psychic states and whose belief in his chosenness was wavering, that he was the expected Messiah. From then on Nathan acted as the prophet of this Messiah and as a proclaimer of his doctrine. Its theological structure, to be sure, was not created by Sabbatai Tzevi (by whom we have nothing in writing and little authentic verbal material), but by Nathan Elisha Chaim Ashkenazi of Gaza. He remained Sabbatai's adherent, prophet, and theologian even when everything spoke against his messiahship: his public transgression of religious precepts; his willful change of feasts that transformed fast days into joyous festivals; Sabbatai's imprisonment upon his arrival in Constantinople (8 February 1666), which his adherents had expected to mark the beginning of his rule in place of the Sultan. Unless one regards copious bribes in addition to political sagacity as the motivation of the Turkish authorities, it strikes one as strange that they permitted his prison to be transformed into a place of pilgrimage where he received his faithful like a king. This was repeated and even intensified after 14 April 1666, the eve of Passover, when Sabbatai was transferred for security reasons (in connection with the war for Crete) to the Turkish fortress for important political prisoners in Gallipoli (on the European side of the Dardanelles). To his adherents this prison henceforth became a *Migdal Oz* (tower of strength).* Then came the catastrophic reversal after July and August, which had been expected to be the climactic period of the crowning of the Messiah, after Sabbatai had transformed the day of the destruction of the Temple (the ninth of Av) into the liturgical-religious celebration of his own birthday: In mid-September of 1666 Sabbatai Tzevi, who had been taken to Adrianople a few days earlier, converted to Islam in a festive meeting of the royal divan attended by Sultan Mohammed IV and received the name Aziz Muhammed Effendi as well as an honorary post with an honorary stipend ("Doorkeeper of the Seraglio"). His wife and his most devoted adherents followed his example.

*Prov. 18:10: "The name of the Lord is a tower of strength to which the righteous man runs and is safe."

This chronicle-like compilation of the most important generally known biographical facts was given here because their very confusion sheds the proper light on the response that Sabbatai Tzevi's appearance evoked. No matter how strange and well-nigh incomprehensible it may appear to later observers, Sabbatai's life and work were, after initial doubts, accepted by his surroundings with ever-increasing belief. Hopes rose high in Jewry all over the world and produced a popular Messianic movement such as the Jews had not experienced since the days of Bar Kochba more that fifteen hundred years previously and the Jews of the Diaspora had never experienced to such as extent. In Turkey, Poland, Italy, Holland, and Germany many Jews—not only the impoverished and afflicted but also the prosperous and wealthy, not only the simple and uneducated but also students of the Talmud, learned kabbalists, rabbis, and notables—prepared to depart. Among these were people who rushed to sell their real property so they could leave the moment the call came. Many packed provisions for the journey. Entire communities were drawn into this vortex of hectic expectations and preparations. In his novel *Die Juden von Zirndorf* Jakob Wassermann depicted the atmosphere of that period in a Jewish community in Franconia; it is only one artistically presented example of what happened in many other communities. A considerable number of Jews later were ashamed of their rash trustfulness and destroyed the traces of it in protocols and other archival documents; yet plenty of documents have remained. As "enlightened" a theologian and diplomat as Heinrich Oldenburg (Bremen) inquired from London in early December 1665 of his friend Baruch Spinoza what he thought "of the rumor that the Jews, who have been scattered for more than 2,000 years, are returning to their fatherland," a rumor discussed by everyone in London; "few people here believe it, but many desire it." He wants to know what the Amsterdam Jews have heard about it and "what impression this news is making upon them which, if confirmed, will probably revolutionize everything in this world. . . ." Even those who cautiously adopted a wait-and-see attitude did not doubt the possibility that redemption from the *galut* was imminent, though they were not sure whether Sabbatai Tzevi was indeed the redeemer. For this reason, and frequently also because they feared thought control from the many "believers," only few Jews dared to take a public stand against the general hope and enthusiasm, particularly on the part of religious plain people. In her memoirs the highly intelligent simple Jewish woman Glückel of Hameln writes as follows about the Hamburg community: "The joy when letters were received [that contained news about Sabbatai Tzevi] cannot be described. Most of the letters were received by the Portuguese. They always took them to their synagogue and read them aloud there. The Germans, young and old, also went to the Portuguese synagogue. The young Portuguese lads put on their best clothes, and each tied a green silk ribbon around his waist—that was the livery of Sabbatai Tzevi. . . . Many people sold their house and home and all their belongings, expecting redemption any day. My father-in-law, peace unto him, who lived in Hameln, moved from there, leaving his house, his hearth, and all the good household utensils, and transferred his residence to Hildesheim." From there he sent two barrels with clothes and food that would not go bad for a long time. "For the old man thought that they would leave from Hamburg for the Holy Land without further ado." After a year the foodstuffs were taken out of the barrels to keep them from spoiling. But the clothes were in readiness for another two years—until the first reports about Sabbatai Tzevi's failure were confirmed with ever greater frequency and people became increasingly convinced that the redemption was not as imminent as had been expected. Even though hopes for imminent salvation had been dashed, however, for the time being this had little effect on the belief in the coming of the Messianic redeemer when the time was ripe. Glückel von Hameln closes her report with an expression of her simple faith: "We know well that the Almighty has promised it to us, and if we were pious and not so evil to the bottom of our hearts, I know for sure that God would have mercy on us. If only we obeyed His commandment 'Love thy neighbor as thyself.' . . . Yet, dear Lord, what you have promised us you will royally and graciously fulfill. Even if it is delayed for so long because of our sins, we shall surely have it when your appointed time has come." The desire to believe in the imminent Messianic liberation from all troubles was so strong that many kept faith with their "Messiah" even when he became an apostate from Judaism and converted to Islam. From the Jewish point of view this was the utmost degradation, but to the desperate dreamers it was only the ultimate evidence that the end of time had really come.

The Consequences of the Failure of Sabbatean Messianism

The majority of the Jews were not willing to go that far, and certainly not their official leaders, the heads of congregations, the rabbis and scholars—those who enjoyed any respect. To them Sabbatai Tzevi became a "false Messiah" like many of his predecessors whose "name and memory should be expunged," whose appearance and deception should be forgotten as completely as possible, or who at best should be remembered as a deterrent and an object lesson that it was not in the power of one mortal man to redeem the Jewish people. All subsequent movements of national regeneration down to Herzl have had to contend with this image of the failed, "false" Messiah. It was this figure that was warningly referred to when adherents gathered around a popular leader and when all too extreme hopes and expectations seemed to crowd out rational deliberations.

It was only natural that excessive hopes should give way to disillusionment. If even a catastrophe of the dimension of 1648, such an all-embracing popular movement as that of Sabbatai, and devout yearning of such intensity had not been able to bring about redemption, then redemption in supernatural fashion still had to be a long way off, and it would be necessary to try new ways to bring about redemption. After all, if all of life was not to be meaningless, even failure had to have some meaning.

It was possible to draw various conclusions from this. As after any dashed hope for redemption, it was possible to leave the Jewish fold, and a considerable number of people did take that step. Mass conversions to the dominant religion have taken place after every breakdown of national-religious hopes. The remarkable thing on that occasion was that some of these conversions still took place under the aegis of the redemption movement—as a step of the deepest degradation that was to promote the final liberation. In this belief some of Sabbatai Tzevi's adherents embraced Islam, and a hundred years later many adherents of the Polish "Messiah" Jakob Frank (1726–91), the last offshoot of the continuing underground Sabbatean movement, converted to Christianity.

Even before its failure, Sabbatai Tzevi's Messianic movement had shaken people's loyalty to the traditional commandments and customs. The Messiah preached freedom from the commandments, whose validity would cease with the beginning of the Messianic period. The consequence was religious anarchy among a considerable number of adherents. Scholars like Yitzhak Baer and Gershom Scholem have rightly characterized the Sabbatai Tzevi movement as a kind of rebellion against the ghetto and its way of life. Even after the failure of the movement the weakening of the solid structure of traditional Judaism continued in the form of nihilism and indifference toward tradition, though the official guardians of Judaism now mandated the pedantic observances of all forms and practices with particular strictness and took stringent measures against excessive occupation with the books of mysticism.

This, then, was the situation of Jewry beginning with the late seventeenth century: On the one side we see the old Jewry as it had developed in the course of the Middle Ages, increasingly isolated inwardly and outwardly in the ghetto, representatives of an unbroken historical view of chosenness, exile, redemption, and return to the old homeland—not through a gradual development but through a sudden miracle when this was God's will. The great majority of Jews continued to live by this view; like any mass with the gravity peculiar to it, these Jewish masses were the real preservers of tradition. But this magnificently simple view of Judaism and Jewish history was now shaken from two sides. One was "the self-refutation of the messianic idea" (Baer, *Galut*), the sobriety that followed the mystic-Messianic rapture. Once the Messianic fervor had been aroused, it could no longer simply be relegated to the solid rabbinical teaching about the Messiah, who would have to demonstrate his reality and truth through miracles. This often gave rise to a skepticism toward the traditional faith which could easily lead to a rejection of any kind of faith.

This intellectual attitude was now able to combine with the current of the *Enlightenment*, whose attitude to the Jews and Judaism has already been discussed (see p. 179 above). Beginning with the Renaissance and particularly the eighteenth century it had an increasingly powerful direct effect on the firmly established world of Judaism. The Messianic tenor of Judaism could be very well combined with it. After all, Enlightenment meant not only the application of reason to everything traditional and to the phenomena of life; this rationalistic-critical attitude was a method and a means but not the goal. The real substance of the Enlightenment was humanism, belief in the possibility of a cosmopolitan coexistence of all men in accordance with the laws of nature, which had, particularly since Rousseau, been viewed in a highly idealized light. Like Judaism and Christianity, the Enlightenment had a Messianic ideal of its own, but with a more resolute devoutness it localized it in the present. Here and now it was a matter of bringing about, through the elimination of superstition and hatred and through tolerance and humanitarianism, the better times that the faithful believed would come at the end of time.

When Jews of the upper classes, shaken by the sudden failure of their Messianic hopes and brought into closer contact with non-Jews by life under the mercantile system, approached the world of Enlightened circles, it might have seemed to them like the realization, albeit in different form, of things that Jews had always striven and yearned for with their demand for the hallowing of life. These Enlightened circles might have wondered whether it was still appropriate to maintain the inner separation between the Jews and the surrounding world if the external economic and social barriers were gradually modified and beyond utilitarian business contacts there began to be encounters between Jews and unprejudiced non-Jews in the neutral or semineutral sphere of academicians and the intelligentsia. If, as had just been proved again, every attempt to return to the old homeland failed, would it perhaps be possible to be freed from the homelessness of the Diaspora through becoming integrated into the surrounding world and gaining a home in the *golah*? Thus, religious faith (or unbelief) and national hopes for the future were able to be separated (for the first time in Judaism!) Perhaps—so people were able to argue—the old ideals could be realized in different form and in other countries, provided one did not already view these values with skepticism under the influence of the ideas of rationalism and "cosmopolitanism."

Thus it came about that the Jews of a higher economic or intellectual level began to regard the world surrounding them as a model. Disappointment at the hopelessness of reaching their national goal, fragmentation as a consequence of integration in the mercantile economic system of early capitalism, and the attraction of the ever more glamorous culture of the Enlightenment and Classicism weakened among those Jews their sense of unity with Jewry and their will to maintain national and social ties with the Jews scattered over so many national boundaries. The florescence of modern scholarship and philosophy in the European world, which coincided with an intellectual weariness and rigidification in the Jewish world, was too great a temptation for intellectually and socially advanced European Jews not to succumb to it. The roots of the movements of assimilation, emancipation, and religious reform, which attracted ever-increasing numbers of Jews from the end of the eighteenth century on, and particularly in the nineteenth, may be found in this development within Judaism and without.

Striving for Equal Rights and Assimilation

From the Jewish point of view, the decisive thing about this development was that the Jews desired to emerge from their isolation. They were no longer content to live in their own circles; they wanted to participate in the general culture. However, when viewed through the eyes of this humanistically enlightening outside world, their legal, and also cultural, situations appear even bleaker than they actually were. Earlier the Jews had not really cared what non-Jews thought of them, even though they might have wanted non-Jews to think well of them for utilitarian reasons, in order to be able to live. It was far more important what they thought of themselves and what they, God's people, thought of the goyim, who were outwardly more fortunate but simply not chosen by God. Now the Jews adopted new, alien standards from the outside and used them to evaluate Jewish conditions as well. This increasingly inspired them to strive for equal rights with the non-Jewish population—an endeavor that had been completely foreign to medieval Jewry. The natural consequence of this was an attempt to assimilate to the surrounding world, and it often led to baptism in an effort to identify completely with that world, its history and culture, and to be absorbed by it.

Assimilation in a similar sense had hitherto existed only among the

Alexandrine Jews and an upper crust of medieval Spanish Jewry. In general, Jews with an unbroken national instinct had absorbed and appropriated from the surrounding world what appeared appropriate and useful to them, but they had adapted to their environment only to the extent required by their economic activity. Now there prevailed a tendency to adapt to the surrounding world with its values and standards, to "assimilate." For the first time, assimilation to the surrounding world became not only a reality but an ideologically motivated program as well. The tendency of absolutism toward standardization had borne its fruit. The Jews no longer wanted to be different from their environment; they wanted the same rights as the other citizens of the state, and they also wished to integrate themselves into its culture, language, and customs, into the appreciation and enjoyment of its art and literature. Under no circumstances did they want to be isolated from the surrounding world either outwardly or inwardly. Earlier the ghetto had, despite all its defects, given them a feeling of being sheltered and at home during the waiting period till the final redemption and return to their own land. Despite all its flaws and adversities it had remained the domicile of the "holy community" of God; now the Jews saw in this ghetto only its narrowness and uncleanness, its dark isolation and its remoteness from the culture of the world around it. Their striving for union with that world, for legal and social integration, was a revolt against the ghetto, its actual walls and the intellectual narrowness and limitation that had developed inside these walls. "The pressure under which we have been living for so many centuries," wrote Moses Mendelssohn bitterly in January 1770 in a well-known letter to "a man of standing," "has robbed our spirit of all *vigueur*. It is not our fault; however, we cannot deny that the natural drive to freedom has become inactive in us. It has been transformed into a monk's virtue and manifests itself merely in prayer and suffering, not in activity."

Moses Mendelssohn (1729–1786)

Thus Mendelssohn expressed discouragement about the Jews of his time when a plan for a Jewish state was presented to him by a non-Jew. At the same time he attempted to bring the two worlds, the traditional Jewish one and the culture of the surrounding world, into accord. This was the basis for the powerful impression that his personality made on his contemporaries. That someone was able to absorb his period's literary and philosophical culture so comprehensively, express it so purely in thoughts and in the language of the German world around him, and that he nevertheless belonged to this despised Jewish people with its strange customs and its Judeo-German speech, in fact professed his loyalty to this people with a certain pride and publicly demonstrated that the teaching and religious laws of Judaism were in full accord with the philosophy of the century—that was something completely new. It caused many a benevolent and insightful person to revise his opinion of this people that had found such a wise and worthy spokesman. This was the basis for the profound impression that Mendelssohn made on the outside world; as the prototype for Lessing's "Nathan the Wise" he demonstrated, as it were, the possibility of cultural communication as a preliminary stage of political and social understanding, even though most people regarded him only as an exceptional case and regarded his arguments in favor of Judaism as more of a skillful apologia than a fully valid proof of the ethical justification of Judaism.

In point of fact, anyone who concerns himself today with Mendelssohn's personality and his views will immediately notice that the two worlds in which he lived were really unconnected. Their union in him, something that astonished his admiring contemporaries, was actually not accomplished in an intellectual synthesis but in the spiritual uniqueness of his personality. Despite all his interest in the philosophy and literature of his time, which he had a leading role in shaping as a representative and popularizer of the Enlightenment, Mendelssohn was devoutly rooted in Judaism and its tradition, and he aimed at preserving the complete structure of ancient Judaism. He did this by explaining the religious precepts and ceremonies of Judaism as a code of laws given to the Jews by God through revelation, a code the validity of which could be abrogated or changed in its substance only by God through a new revelation.

Those Jews of his time and the ensuing generation who did not reject him but regarded him as a model and leader generally adopted only one aspect of his effectiveness: his own entry into European culture and his introduction of the Jews to that culture. To most Jews, however, it appeared illogical and inconsistent to preserve at the same time all precepts of traditional Judaism. Hardly anyone among Mendelssohn's pupils and none of his children emulated his life as a union of the two worlds. The educated Jews in Western and Central Europe walked out on Judaism, with more or less straight steps and with furled flags or flying colors, and went over to the other camp. It even came about that his closest relatives cited Mendelssohn himself as they completely turned their backs on Judaism. Salomon Bartholdy wrote to his brother-in-law Abraham Mendelssohn (the son of Moses Mendelssohn and father of the composer Felix Mendelssohn-Bartholdy), who was hesitating to have his children baptized: "You say that you owe it to the memory of your father. Do you think you will be doing something bad if you give your children the religion that you regard as the better one? It is virtually a tribute that you and all of us pay to your father's efforts in behalf of true Enlightenment."

The Jewish Question and the Image of the Jew at the End of the Eighteenth Century

Never before had the existence of the Jews in the European world been as ambivalent as it was at the end of the eighteenth century. To be sure, their legal restrictions had been eased here and there, but almost nowhere had there been a fundamental change in them, and the Jews' pride rebelled against them more than ever. In economic life individual Jews had attained to a high level, but the great majority of Jews were poorer than ever. Here and there Jews had made their way into the highest strata of society and made a name for themselves in the economy and in cultural life. But the garden variety of Jew as encountered by the surrounding world did not resemble figures like the "Jewish Socrates" Moses Mendelssohn, the Court Jew and banker Meyer Amschel Rothschild (and his sons), or queens of sociability like Rahel Levin Varnhagen or Henriette Herz with their salons. Rather, the Jew ordinarily encountered was a peddler or beggar with threadbare clothes and a language that seemed equally sleazy, a "jargon" produced by an admixture of Hebrew words and expressions, often with strange inflections, adaptations, and emphases. Here and there the strict isolation of the Jews in the ghetto and the Jewish districts was actually broken and modified by exceptional rights of individuals, though it had not been formally eliminated anywhere. In almost all German and many other European states the Jews still had to pay body taxes and numerous other special taxes; even Mendelssohn had to do so when he traveled to Dresden. In the Spanish and Portuguese countries the Inquisition was still in force, at least formally.

Shifts in Political Boundaries and their Influence on the Jewish Question

At the same time the Jewish question, with its tensions between the Jews and the surrounding world, had become more topical than it had been at the beginning of the seventeenth century. In 1648 the bishopric and city of Metz and especially Alsace had definitively become part of France, and so had the Jewish population that had lived there for a long time. Thus France, which had tolerated no Jews in the country since the end of the fourteenth century, received a considerable number of Ashkenazic Jews. In addition there were a small number of Marranos in southern France who had returned to the Jewish fold as well as four Sephardic communities around Avignon. Without the Alsatian Jews there probably would have been no debate about the Jewish question in France before and during the great Revolution, a debate that ushered in their emancipation in all of Europe.

In Eastern Europe the political decline of the Polish state and the division of the Polish territories among the great powers Russia, Austria, and Prussia between 1772 and 1795 had decisive consequences for the Jewish question as well. The incorporation of Polish Galicia into Austria brought an increase in the Jewish population of the Austrian national territory. In Prussia, where a limited number of Jews had been admitted since 1670 in connection with the expulsion of the Jews from Vienna, the incorporation of Western and Southern Prussia, Posen, and Neuschlesien increased the Jewish percentage of the population considerably. Most importantly, however, the division of Poland created a tremendous Jewish problem in Russia. To be sure, the incorporation of the Eastern Ukraine in 1667 had added an area with what was probably not a very great number of Jews to Russia, a country that had up to then prohibited any Jewish settlement. Now, however, the annexation of the Polish heartland meant that great masses of Jews became Russian subjects. The Jew as a type in Christian dogma, legend, and saga had always and everywhere been present in the folk consciousness. Now the living embodiment of this image appeared, in different and thus very confusing forms, even in countries where the Jew had hitherto existed almost only as a threatening, repulsive vision or as a memory from the past. On the one hand, this created new problems for the countries and states, and on the other, it placed the Jews involved under new and unaccustomed sovereignties with the most diverse views and traditions.

The Jewish question was full of such tensions and unsolved problems when the French Revolution broke out.

5

Emancipation and the Jewish Question (1789–1880)

The Position of the French Revolution in the History of the Jewish Question

The French Revolution of 1789 marks the beginning of a new era in the history of the Jewish question. Up to that time the Jews and the nations had endeavored to regulate in some fashion the coexistence between the Jews and the world around them in accordance with their needs. If they admitted Jews, the nations and the states wanted to derive the maximum benefit from them and to reduce to a minimum the dangers this posed from the asocial, strange, and sinister people, whether in reality or only in their fearful imagination. Until the Enlightenment took hold of them, the Jews, for their part, had in essence striven for a secure life that would enable them to earn a decent and proper living and to continue to practice their own life-style unimpeded, in accordance with religious precepts and hallowed usage, in their places of domicile—until the Messiah would lead them back to their own country, the Land of Israel. For the sake of this religious, national, legal, and social autonomy they were ready to put up with a certain measure of intolerance on the part of their environment, accommodate themselves to compromises of all kinds, and become accustomed to averting threatening misfortune through the intervention of one of their influential big-wigs as well as through ad hoc contracts and the financial contributions that these involved. By contrast, the French Revolution of 1789 and the liberal freedom movement based on it attempted a radical solution of the Jewish question by giving the Jews equal rights and eliminating all barriers existing between them and the surrounding world. The struggle for special rights and mutual toleration was now replaced by a fight for equal rights and a striving for conformity in all areas. In the struggle for the implementation of equal rights for the Jews, as proclaimed by the French Revolution, the Jewish question received its modern form.*

*Cf. the remarks in chap. 1 about the history of the concept "Jewish question" as well as the notes and excursuses in Part 2.

The Emancipation of the Jews

Since the French Revolution the point of departure for the Jewish question has been the integration of the Jews into the modern state and the modern society and culture in all its forms to which the state has given shape and which has shaped it—the problem that has customarily been summed up as "the emancipation of the Jews." This term derives from a concept of Roman civil law which the French Revolution applied to public law and which, after 1828 and beginning with Germany, became widely used in the discussion of the Jewish question. It referred to the liberation of the Jews from all limitations embodied in special laws and their being granted the same rights enjoyed by all citizens of the state. The striving for these rights—in contrast to the medieval system of special rights for the estates and classes of society—had different roots. One of the most important of these was the Enlightenment's philosophy of natural right. In many other respects, too, the French Revolution was the executor of the rationalistic clear thinking of the eighteenth century. The guiding principles of the American Declaration of Independence (1776) were already based on the conviction of the equality of all human beings. The Declaration of the Rights of Man and of the Citizen of 1789 gave worldwide dissemination to this view, and the French Revolution's abolition of the estates and privileges put these principles into practice in France. The emancipation of the Jews was the logical consequence of the Declaration of the Rights of Man. This solemn declaration, like the American one that had preceded it, said that all men were free and equal by nature and hence must be treated as equal human beings and citizens, and that this was the foundation and task of any government. There was no denying that the Jews were human beings. The logical conclusion to be drawn from this was that as human beings the Jews must be put on an equal footing with all other human beings and citizens. It was, as it were, the result of a mathematical equation. In this spirit Max Nordau was able to say, a hundred years later, in his famous speech at the First Zionist Congress (1897) and in his characteristic exaggerated aphoristic style that the Jews had been emancipated out of "*Prinzipienreiterei*" (a pedantic adherence to principles).

There were, of course, other factors as well that made the application of these principles possible. The religious indifference or the monistic belief in a deity without denomination (deism, theism) in leading circles of the late eighteenth century facilitated the inclusion of the Jews among the non-Jewish citizens, at least to a certain extent. The ever-rising capitalistic economy created a legal place for the occupations in which the Jews were predominantly engaged, and in the eyes of greater numbers of people (though surely not in those of the population as a whole) this removed some of the opprobrium that had hitherto been attached to their economic activities. With the growing influence of the bourgeoisie and the rising importance of commerce in general and the money market in particular the Jews as a social caste were increasingly released from their isolation and integrated into the general economic life. Added to this was the fact that the French state of the revolutionary period, and also the modern states since then, adopted from the absolutistic state the striving for centralization and the most uniform organization possible. The modern state wanted to have direct contact with all citizens; no social or religious special groups, no classes and privileges were to come divisively between it and the citizenry. It desired no "state within a state," as we say now, no "nation within the nation," which is the common synonymously intended formulation in French.

All these factors led to the "emancipation" of the Jews—that is, as human beings and citizens they were placed on an equal footing formally and legally with the other citizens of the state, and at the same time it was demanded that as individuals they be completely integrated into the political and social life of the nations among which they lived. In the very first great debate about civil equality for the Jews, which was held in the French National Assembly from 21 to 24 December 1789, and, characteristically enough, ended with the postponement of a decision for almost two years, Count Clermont-Tonnère, one of the most active proponents of the emancipation of the Jews, made this unmistakable declaration on 23 December: "The Jews should be denied everything as a nation and granted everything as individuals; in the state they must form neither a political body nor an order; they shall be citizens as individuals. It is said [so he continued emphatically] that they do not want to be that. Then let them say so and be banished; there must be no nation within the nation." On 28 September 1791, three days before the dissolution of the constituent assembly, the French National Assembly definitively decided to grant equal civil rights to all French Jews—that is, to the Ashkenazic, primarily the Alsatian, Jews as well; the Sephardic ones had already been granted them in January 1790. At the same time it logically rescinded all special rights and privileges of the Jews and even asked that by taking a civil oath (which had replaced the Christian one that had been unacceptable to the Jews and other non-Christians) every Jew expressly recognize this rescission of the special rights with which the Jews had hitherto lived. Thus it was only natural that the assembly of Jewish notables convened by Napoleon as a kind of parliament gave the emperor in August 1806 the answer that he evidently wanted to hear and whose substance seemed to be the prerequisite for the recognition of the Jews as French citizens: "Nowadays the Jews no longer constitute a nation, since they have had the distinction of being incorporated into the structure of the 'great nation' in which they see their political redemption." In a similar formulation the "Great Sanhedrin" that met in Paris from 9 February to 9 March 1807, evidently having been convoked by Napoleon for the solemn sanctioning of the decisions of the Assemblée des Notables, expressly mentioned in its decisions the French Jews' renunciation of a separate national-political existence as well as their willingness to be completely integrated into the French nation. It was stated that the Jewish religious laws contained religious and political precepts that must be carefully separated; only the religious precepts were binding and timeless, but the political provisions were dated and no longer applicable since the Jews had ceased to constitute a national body *("un corps de nation")*. In the following years similar declarations by Jewish corporate bodies and individuals were repeatedly made and published in France and other countries.

In other words, through the emancipative actions of the French Revolution, and equally through the corresponding legislation in other countries that ensued,* the Jews did obtain equality before the law as individuals, as human beings, as citizens, and as members of other nations. This equality, however, was not for the Jews as a totality, as the Jewish people. On the contrary; the emancipation of the Jews was really a last, decisive blow against the existence of the Jewish people as a collective individuality. What force had not managed to achieve was to be accomplished by the seduction of peace, as it were: The Jewish people as a totality was to be dissolved and buried once and for all, with its members scattered among the nations as individuals. The only difference between them and the other citizens of the state was to be that some went to church and others to synagogue. Even this difference, so many hoped, would disappear in time—through the elimination and disappearance of religion as an important factor in modern life, or through the conversion of the Jews to a less dogmatic, diluted Christianity, which would eliminate the last vestiges of the separate existence of the Jews. According to the old legend discussed above, the fate of the Jew damned by God is eternal homeless wandering and the inability to die. This curse of the "Eternal" or "Wandering" Jew was to be removed, in both its parts, by emancipation. The Jew was to be made to feel at home in the states in which he lived and no longer be *unheimisch-unheimlich* (homeless and therefore uncanny/sinister)—and at the same time he was to die as a Jew. He was no longer to have any home other than the country that had accepted him among its citizens. No Messiah should have to come to free the Jews from their feeling of homelessness by leading them back to their old ancestral land. Revolution, freedom, and equal rights as properly domiciled citizens in a liberal state were to constitute the modern version of Messianic redemption.

Dissemination of the Emancipative Ideology

In the excitement of the early stage of the Revolution these ideas found wide acceptance both among the nations and the Jews. The

*Cf. pp. 212f. below, as well as the chronology in Part 2.

victorious sounds of the Marseillaise, the booming footsteps of the Napoleonic armies, and the rattling and clattering of the machines that were beginning to transform the bourgeois world in the age of the first industrial revolution caused the walls of the ghettos to collapse. Light and air streamed into the cramped quarters of the Jews. The inspiration of the new ideas caused the inner world of many Jews to collapse along with the outer barriers. As the Jews were integrated into the economic life of the nations and increasingly included in the civil order as citizens with equal rights or as individuals aspiring to these, the Jews also became part of the cultural life of the nations. They strove very hard, and with astonishingly quick success, to collaborate on the cultural development of the nations,* and in the course of a few decades they became so acclimated to their cultural world that they regarded themselves as an integral part of it. In the Jewish upper classes of Western and Central Europe more and more people endeavored to forget their past as one people, and along with this past they also lost the dreams and hopes for the national future that had once enabled them to keep up their courage amid sufferings and persecutions. These Jewish citizens believed and declared that the Jews were no longer a people but were part of the nations among which they lived and whose destiny they now shared both actively and passively. Beyond that, the only thing that tied them to the Jews of other countries was their religion, which means that there were no deeper ties than those of a French Catholic to an Italian or a German one. The logical conclusion was that many Jews accepted baptism and thus severed their last ties to the Jewish community.

This development was slower in the Jewish mass settlements of Eastern Europe—for one thing, because of the inertia necessarily caused by great numbers, and for another, because of the backwardness of the political surroundings in the East that by its nature made assimilation seem less attractive. Despite these circumstances, however, the tendencies were the same. Even in Russia (and Poland, which it had incorporated), the upper classes emulated their more "advanced" brethren in the West and made the greatest possible assimilation to their surroundings as well as the abandonment of their own peoplehood part of their program. The educated Jews, those who had attended Russian schools, increasingly began to feel as Russians, spoke and wrote Russian, and fought for the prospective emancipation that would enable them to be completely absorbed by Russian culture.

It may very well be that if this emancipative movement had continued undisturbed for several generations, the Jews would have been more fully absorbed by their countries of domicile than by any previous

*For examples of this, see pp. 261ff. below.

violent attack on their existence as a people. This, however, did not happen, and could not happen because neither the Jews nor the nations among which they dwelled live without history and memory. Revolutions, like wars, cannot eliminate the products of long development at one blow. They do overthrow what is obsolete, and with quicker thrusts and harder strikes they make use of previous changes in the social realities and of the ideas and ideologies as whose executors they appear, thus providing the impetus for new developments. But the forces that press forward through or with them also arouse the resistance of the old powers, the conservative forces and interests. They do not change the instincts and deep-rooted feelings; at most they very slowly modify the traditional notions and reactions. Only such a generation of rational thinkers as that of the late eighteenth century, only a generation with such joyous faith in the Enlightenment, could believe that the foundations of society could be changed overnight by decreeing some law. (The fact that this did not happen, something that radical innovators cannot comprehend, is probably one of the foundations of the Jacobin reign of terror.)

The political movement for the emancipation of the Jews that was introduced to the political world by the French Revolution did lay new foundations for the relationship of the Jews to the nations and of the nations to the Jews; it did set up new principles, even applied some of them, and created new conditions for the relationship between Jews and non-Jews. It attempted to make amends for old injustices, to make peace, and to awaken fruitful forces. In so doing, however, it created new problems that were as severe as the old ones. The struggle for emancipation and its implementation actually marked the development of the modern Jewish question, the return of the Jews to the cultural life of the nations, the regeneration of the Jewish people and the founding of its state, and the frightful catastrophe of the Hitler period.

Legal Emancipation and Social Reality

In Western and Central Europe the legal equality of the Jews became reality within two generations, though not all at once. The movement to emancipate the Jews and to gain for them full rights and equal status with all other citizens took the form of revolutionary thrusts in connection with the social and national transformations in the European countries—in the course of the extension of the French Revolution after 1791, in particular the creation of the Napoleonic empire and its legislation, through the reforms in many countries in connection with the liberal and democratic tendencies in the revolutionary movements of 1830 and 1848–49, and in the national movements for independence and unification in the nineteenth century. At any event, by the late 1870s the legal and formal equality of the Jews had been attained in all European states except Russia and the eastern states incorporated into it or under its domination (Poland, Lithuania, etc.). There the emancipation of the Jews was not accomplished until a generation later in the revolutionary transformations of 1917.

The fact that it repeatedly took revolutionary impulses to advance the movement and to gain political acceptance for the idea and the promotion of legal equality for the Jews shows how strong the forces opposing its realization really were.

The "Jewish Question" in the Public Consciousness

In point of fact, the Jewish question has played a certain role in almost all peace conferences since the Congress of Vienna (1814–15), and it dominated numerous debates of the parliaments of various countries. The columns of the ever-developing press were full of articles, arguments, and counterarguments; numerous leaflets, pamphlets, and books were printed and distributed. Only around 1840 was the word *Judenfrage* created in connection with these discussions and became a general concept—that is, only then did people become fully aware of the problem of the existence of the Jews in the modern world of states and nations.* But once the idea of equality for the Jews had been expressed, it made its way despite all kinds of resistance. It reached the point where in 1878 the Congress of Berlin granted recognition to the newly formed Balkan states (particularly Rumania) only on condition that these states grant the Jews equal rights before the law. To be sure, this stipulation— recognition of equality of rights without reference to religion—was not fully observed anywhere.

From a superficial point of view it is possible to say that the advocates of the emancipation of the Jews secured complete victory for this idea within two to four generations. However, in most places social reality and equality of rights were not the same thing. Despite all efforts by the Jews to be completely absorbed by their environment, to preserve their Jewishness only as a religion, and to be no different in all other areas from the surrounding world as human beings and citizens, they were not accepted as equals by the majority of the population in their countries of domicile. The Jews adopted the languages and the customs of their surroundings. In their clothing, the practices of daily life, the fulfillment of duties toward the state, and formally also in the rights granted them by the state, they could hardly be distinguished from the rest of the

---

*Cf. the section about the "Jewish question," the term and the concept, in the introductory chapter.

population in the western states, at least in the cities and in the second or third generation. At the same time, however, they were in some way increasingly isolated from their surroundings and faced with accusations and animosity. Precisely when the emancipative movement seemed to have won a decisive victory in the Congress of Berlin, the opposing forces began to close ranks and under the new name "anti-Semitism" started an anti-Jewish movement, the significance of which was at first greatly underestimated but which was to become a popular and political movement that assumed enormous dimensions and was catastrophical in nature.*

Many kinds of forces and factors combined to create this glaring contrast between the legal framework and the social reality. The first and foremost reason was that, as we have already indicated, both the Jewish and the non-Jewish proponents of emancipation and complete assimilation of the Jews to the surrounding world underestimated the resistance of the old forces and the inertia of tradition. The bearers of the pre-revolutionary political order, the nobility and especially the Church, retained their power to a large extent even in the nineteenth century. The image of the typical Jew and the views of the position of the Jews within the European Christian society that had evolved in the Middle Ages on the basis of ancient and Christian notions, had developed futher in modern times, and had been popularized by printing were thus kept alive in all strata of the population. This image of the Jew had been painted in more secular colors and in particularly detailed and influential fashion by Voltaire in the eighteenth century, and we find a similar outline of it in many figures in contemporary literature.** It was this image that even haunted the debates of the French National Assembly.

The Debates in the French National Assembly

The representatives of the old forces had one advantage over the well-meaning ideological champions of the emancipation of the Jews: Their more realistic view of the Jews and the Jewish question was often more correct than that of the philo-Semites. In the face of the theory that the Jews would henceforth be only a religious community they pointed to the national nature of Judaism and the Jewish religion, and in so doing they were able to base themselves on important Jewish and non-Jewish thinkers. On 23 December 1789, Abbé Maury, one of the most principled and most eloquent clerical opponents of emancipation, said in the big debate on the Jews of the French National Assembly that over a

*This is treated in greater detail in chaps. 6 and 9.
**Cf. chap. 4.

period of seventeen centuries the Jews had not intermingled with other nations; they were not a religious sect but a people with laws of their own. To give them civil equality would be like permitting an Englishman to become a citizen of France without giving up his British citizenship.* He said that the Jews had never had any other occupation than dealing in money; they were the scourge of the agricultural provinces. How can we—asked another speaker in the same debate— take in an alien tribe whose eyes are incessantly on its own distant fatherland? J.-F. Rewbell, the Jacobin delegate from Alsace and one of the most determined opponents of emancipation, added another very important argument, saying that dislike and hatred of the Jews because of their behavior in all ages were so deeply rooted in the people that it would not be wise to place them on an equal footing with the other citizens. He mixed semiracist and disparaging arguments from the school of Voltaire and antiquity with contemporary ones. Every opponent found telling arguments in the complaints of the deputies from Alsace about the Jews' usury. According to many reports, the rural population had been completely enslaved by the Jews. This was yet another repetition of the accusations, surely often not groundless, with which Dohm had concerned himself ten years earlier (see p. 184 above), although they were now increasingly formulated as secular ideology.

These debates of 1789 to 1791 already contain *in nuce* the whole problematic nature of the Jewish question in recent times. Here there was intoned, as it were, the fugue theme which during the entire nineteenth century resounded again and again in parliaments, in the press, and in all discussions. The accompanying voices changed and the basic theme was varied in one form or another, but it could always be clearly recognized as the real theme: Are the Jews really only individuals who espouse another religion than the Christian population, or are they the distinct people that they have always been? Is it not just a subterfuge if they assure us that there is no other connection between them and the Jews of other countries than religion? After all, reality seems to offer a definite refutation of this asseveration. Are the Jews really serious about being fully absorbed by the rest of the population, about regarding their countries of domicile as their real, only, and definitive homelands, and

---

*It is interesting to note how absurd that seemed at the time. Today many states, among them Israel, permit dual citizenship. It is revealing that Abbé Maury came from a town without Jews; thus he was representing views stemming from the Christian tradition. Under Napoleon he later became cardinal-archbishop of Paris. An anonymous clergyman who identified himself as the teacher of Abbé Grégoire, a champion of emancipation, answered him in a pamphlet, saying, among other things, that the Jews were no longer a nation but only the remnants of a destroyed nation. (Cf. Arthur Hertzberg, *The French Enlightenment and the Jews* [New York, 1968], pp. 351, 362.)

about abandoning the idea of national redemption and return to their own country? Finally, people asked whether the Jews' economic activity, which was generally viewed only in negative terms, was a consequence of conditions given permanence by history, as presented by the Jews' well-meaning defenders, or whether it had been an expression of their corrupt character from the very beginning. Depending on the evaluation arrived at, the influence of the Jews on the cultural life of their countries of domicile was evaluated as a positive contribution or—whether consciously or unconsciously—a destructive element in the life of the nations.

The Jews in the Economy

As we have already stated, among the arguments with which hostility against the Jews was motivated in the debates the economic argument played a prominent role. Down to the middle of the nineteenth century, with particular stridency in the struggle for emancipation but afterwards as well, the anti-Jewish pamphlets and treatises repeatedly sounded a call against the Jews as usurers. Before a banking system and agricultural credit unions were organized in response to a need, the Jews were the chief financiers for the rural population. That was true in the Middle Ages and, as we have seen, in modern times, particularly after the fourteenth century, when the Jews had increasingly been forced out of the larger cities. One can probably give credence to the numerous reports of local officials to their central offices in which they complain that not infrequently the Jews made improper use of their monopoly. Anyone would have done the same in a similar position. It is only human nature if people derive the utmost advantage from their superiority in a certain field, and only individuals of greater nobility and moral fiber can resist the temptation to make use of greater economic or political power. But even when entirely normal financial transactions were involved— and that was true of most of these economic dealings—some of the rural population became economically dependent on the Jews. In this way the image of the Jewish usurer that the Middle Ages, in keeping with the prevalent economic mentality, had fashioned from legend and reality remained alive, and the conditions of the time added new hues. People indignantly spoke of the Jew as the real master of a rural population dependent on him; this happened in the Alsace before and during the French Revolution, under Napoleon, and even after him in Western and Southern Germany during the debates about emancipation and in election campaigns, in Poland and other countries. With the growth of Jewish influence in the banking and financial system of the nineteenth century there was an increase in the hateful and at the same time fearful accusations that the Jew, the ecclesiastic and secular slave of yesterday, was now the real ruler and was striving to keep expanding his dominion over the non-Jews.

It was entirely natural that the Jews should have gained great influence over the development of the modern financial system, for they had served European society as financiers and money-traders for centuries.* In the increasingly flourishing capitalistic economy, in the modern age of worldwide trade in merchandise and money and of communication transcending all borders, the Jews had by virtue of their centuries of experience a tremendous advantage over their non-Jewish fellow citizens. Their mental acuity and ingenuity derived from the persecutions and adversities of their fate, situations in which only the adroit could stand their ground. Thus the Jews were better able to utilize the new conditions than many others and to adapt to the rapidly changing times. Their newly acquired freedom of movement in a number of countries and the utilization of new means of conveyance enabled them to choose the most favorable places, principally the big cities, for their economic activity, and in this quest they were often aided by Jewish relatives in other countries. Hence it is understandable that the non-Jewish merchants tried everything to stave off this growing competition of the Jews. Beginning with the eighteenth century, and particularly in the nineteenth, the Rothschilds became a dominant financial power, and many other Jews exerted a decisive influence on the economy as big bankers and financiers of all kinds and thus also on the policies of the states whose financial policy was often dependent on these big Jewish financiers to some extent (though this has often been greatly overestimated or deliberately exaggerated). Because of these developments the discomfort of the population culminated in the fearful accusation that the Jews were the real rulers of the world and that, in fact, the domination of the world was their real goal and the meaning of their much-discussed belief in their divine chosenness.

This accusation seemed to make sense, being close to the popular belief about the demonic character of Jewish existence, and it received ever new sustenance when people heard of the Jews' great influence on the stock exchange, that institution of international finance and commerce dating from the sixteenth century, an instrumentality that assumed increasing importance in the nineteenth century and for the first time attracted popular attention then. Because of its newness and the evident unpredictability of its transactions, with the unexpected rise and fall of the rates, the stock exchange all too easily assumed a sinister and reprehensible character in the eyes of the people—all the more so because many small speculators saw their hopes for quick profits dashed

*Cf. pp. 168f. above and the excursus in Part 2.

when the rates suddenly fell and then were quick to ascribe the catastrophic consequences to an institution whose nature they had never
really understood. The historical development had of necessity given the
Jews a far greater share in the money economy than their percentage of
the population warranted; therefore their share in the speculative economic enterprises of the time and in bankruptcies in times of crisis was
also far greater than average and thus attracted attention. As we have
seen in our discussion of earlier periods, the Jews have by nature been a
dynamic element in the economy. Since they did not have to abandon
traditional practices or the regulations of a guild, they were quicker to
see and utilize all opportunities of the ever-expanding capitalistic economy. They soon rose to a leading position in those branches of the
economy with which they had long been associated; in addition to
dealing in money and jewels, this was particularly the clothing industry
in which the Jews had since days of old been active as silk and wool
dealers between East and West, and since the mercantile system as
founders of factories and industries. They quickly and skillfully used
innovations in retail trading, as for example the department store, which
enabled them to sell all kinds of products. On the other hand, they
usually stayed away from heavy industry, because it developed from
trades united in guilds that were closed to the Jews. Hence it was all too
easy for people in economic circles to regard the Jews once again as
destroyers of existing and accustomed things, and at the same time as
people who were acting in urban and rural places only as middlemen far
removed from the original production, thus apparently performing no
vital function.* This perception, and particularly the Jews' connection
with money trade and the speculative enterprises of the time, made it all
too easy for people to regard and represent the convulsions of the
capitalistic economy that accompanied its florescence as the work of the
Jews that was designed to slip money out of non-Jewish hands and put it
into Jewish pockets. Here something became evident that was to be
confirmed in many other areas: Real tensions and difficulties were
particularly exacerbated by the fact that the traditional notions about the
Jewish character were melded with the disagreeable aspects of the new
conditions. Warding off a burdensome competitor is understandable and
legitimate. Here, however, the arguments repeatedly went beyond the
economic sphere and included universally human elements. The same
thing happened in other spheres of economic life. When Jewish intellectuals strove to free themselves from an association with money and
commerce and, since higher government positions were closed to them

*The productive role of the middleman or go-between and the negotiator making
compromises as one of the most essential elements of business life is generally underestimated in comparison with the role of the producer, who actually cannot work creatively
without them.

(legally until the second half of the nineteenth century, in practice far beyond that), turned to the professions and attempted to become doctors, lawyers, journalists, writers, or scholars, this aroused more than the understandable, normal, in this sense legitimate resistance on the part of those who were facing new competitors. At the same time this awakened memories of the "perfidious" Jew of Christian dogma, of the deceitful and hostile Jew of legend. The Jew with his Talmud-trained mind would surely use his rights only to translate his anti-Christian tendencies into action. Behind the Jews' arguments in the press and their often excessive critique of existing conditions, people were all too ready to sense the devilish intentions of people whom they had always presumed to be in close contact with Satan.

The Jew Becomes Visible

Added to this was the fact that the emancipation made the Jew as a real being (and not merely as a dogmatic concept or legendary figure) more visible as a person living in the present. While the Jews were living in the ghetto, only a comparatively small part of the population had had any contact with them. The Jew was known as a trader, but as such he came from another world, as it were; he met with the Christian world only for certain purposes and then returned to his own. The Jews remained an alien phenomenon; in individual cases they might be respected or (starting with the Enlightenment) studied as an ethnographic peculiarity. But apart from exceptional cases people had no contact with them beyond the immediate purpose, nor did they desire any. The Jew came as a member of a group outside legitimate society and returned to that group. Any contact was and basically remained collective rather than individual, and the tensions between Jews and non-Jews were essentially those between two groups. But now the Jews entered the world surrounding them as individuals and became visible as such. To the natural tension between the groups, which continued to some degree despite all assurances and frequently legal efforts as well, there was added the tension between each member of the group and the surrounding world. In chapter 7 we shall consider the way in which this relationship affected the inner life of the Jews. Suffice it to say here that this immensely expanded the fields of tension and that the opportunities for friction between the Jews and their environment were increased many times.

It is true that personal contacts helped to overcome many a prejudice. This is what the champions of emancipation had hoped for, and in many cases they had reason to hope. When Jews and non-Jews established really close contact, the result was sometimes personal appreciation, mutual respect, and even friendship and love.* For this to happen, however, great inner resistance had to be overcome, for the new visibility of the Jews made the alien elements in their daily life more evident. In general, an instinctive inclination to preserve one's own makes the psyche of the people more prone to identify what is alien to it and to disassociate itself from it than to see and stress shared elements. As the Jews became part of the life of their surroundings, they did not change overnight, of course. A person's origin, the tradition of long centuries, a common way of life and a common fate leave an indelible mark on him, on his way of moving, thinking, reacting, speaking, and writing. Hence the Jews retained their alien character in the eyes of the surrounding world even if they did not differ, or seem to differ, from it in their clothing, language, and external deportment—even if, in an effort to eliminate all that separated them, they ceased to observe their religious precepts and to celebrate their festivals. And even if a non-Jew had become accustomed to the longtime Jewish resident of his town and wanted to forget that he did not have the same origin, tradition, and history of his Christian fellow citizens, he kept being reminded of this fact by the increasing immigration of indigent or culture-hungry Jews from the Jewish mass settlements of Eastern Europe to the western countries with their better opportunities for making a living and getting an education. These Jewish immigrants from Eastern Europe since the latter part of the seventeenth century** who hoped to escape material and spiritual want kept arousing in both the Jews and their new surroundings an awareness of their otherness and renewed it whenever it seemed to be fading.

Avoidance of the Word "Jew"

It availed little that from the end of the eighteenth century on people tried to replace the word *Jew*, which had become disreputable, with other words that had not acquired a dishonorable connotation through long use and abuse. Jews as well as well-disposed non-Jews increasingly used "Israelite" or "citizens of the Mosaic faith" in place of "Jew", thus only degrading that word further and turning it into an epithet. The new terms gradually were used in government records and official documents. But this official avoidance of "Jew," a word in daily use among non-Jews and commonly used in both religious and secular writings, was apt to have the opposite effect: Surely the Jews must have something to

*Where amorous relationships with sexual contacts came about, this often aroused the old group feelings of rejection and revived the traditional views.
**Cf. p. 191 above and chapters 6, 7, and 9.

hide if they so obviously wish to change their name; there must be many objectionable things in their past if they want to shed the old established name that all of them used to bear with pride. The common people— and who is not to some extent part of them in this regard?—do not stop to investigate why a person has acquired a bad reputation or why his name has received a disreputable connotation. Hence they will never realize that they themselves, their ancestors, and their tradition may be to blame for this devaluation. They judge phenomena on the basis of the present, without realizing the decisive part played in this judgment by historical and traditional elements. Thus many people are convinced that to be ashamed of one's name means that one has something to hide and wants to be something different from what one actually is.

Increase in the Jewish Population

Entering the living sphere of their surroundings was not the only thing that made the Jews more visible and more perceptible; they occupied more room numerically as well. Around the middle of the seventeenth century the Jews, whose number has been estimated from 900,000 (Baron) to 1,750,000 (Ruppin), constituted 0.2 to 0.4 percent of the world population and .65 to 1.2% of the European population. They were rather evenly divided between the Orient and the Occident. Two hundred years later (around 1850) the number of Jews in Europe had increased much faster than that of the Orient, especially because of the better hygienic conditions; it had risen to 4 million, or 1.5% of the European population (86.6% of the total Jewish population). Of these about one-sixth (almost 700,000) lived in Western and Central Europe, the rest in Eastern Europe. This rising tendency continued until the end of the nineteenth century and became even more evident in the population statistics of certain countries. The increase in the percentage of Jews within the European population slowed from the end of the nineteenth century; in a number of countries the percentage remained the same, and in some there even was a decrease. However, the 16 million Jews in 1938, before the Hitlerian catastrophe, did constitute 0.8 percent of the total population of the world, with the 10 million European Jews forming 2 percent of the population of Europe.

The Jews multiplied more rapidly than the surrounding world, and presumably this came about through the combination of their still unbroken relationship to the biblical commandment of natural multiplication with their ever-increasing concentration in the cities. Thanks to the advances of modern hygiene, the city, which Rousseau had still called the grave of the population, offered in the nineteenth century better conditions for raising children than the country. The mortality rate kept declining, at least among the more affluent population. As stated above, in the nineteenth century the Jews moved in ever greater numbers from the villages and small country towns to the larger cities, particularly the capitals, which offered them the best opportunities for their advancement and their striving for culture. Hence their share in the composition of the population in the larger cities—the centers of economic, political, and cultural life—increased far beyond their percentage of the total population of the country. The consequence of this was that their existence suddenly attracted much more attention and was noticed precisely by the leading circles in the intellectual and political life of the nation. Thus the fear of being threatened by the Jews as a foreign element was always given fresh sustenance. In the psyche of the non-Jews the actual increase in the Jewish population was often exaggerated beyond recognition, and the same was true of the actual influence of the Jews as compared to the notion that people had of it.

Modern Nationalism

Added to all this was modern nationalism. The nineteenth century has rightly been called the century of national movements. The first wave came in the awakening and crystallization of nationalism; in the twentieth century this was to be followed by a second wave that affected the peoples of Asia and Africa. This essentially Western European nationalism of the nineteenth century was a complex phenomenon; it grew from a variety of roots and underwent many changes in the course of the decades. It was more than the continuation of a quest for uniformly organized states that originated in the seventeenth and eighteenth centuries; it was not merely informed by the romantic longing of the early nineteenth century for a closer connection with one's own past, its traditions and formations that had developed in ever more differentiated form in the late Middle Ages. One of its important foundations was the idea of the sovereignty of the people that had gained acceptance since the American Revolution and especially since the French one. It spurred the French armies that went to war for the fatherland beginning in 1792 just as it later inspired the oppressed peoples in their uprising against Napoleon. This idea, part of the intellectual heritage of antiquity and the Middle Ages, had been taken up again and renewed in the seventeenth and eighteenth centuries, initially for the protection of the individual, whose rights it was intended to safeguard from the encroachments of the all-powerful state. Actually, however, as the people began to take an active part in political life under the banner of national sovereignty, they took over the state's striving for power and gave it a broader basis and a greater impact. In this way the liberal idea of sovereignty of the people gradually gave rise to an illiberal idea of a nation-state. According to this idea, the people constituting the majority of a state's population were to have the sole right to dominion in all areas. This right included the claim to deprive smaller nations and politically nonautonomous parts of the population of their cultural autonomy and to adapt and integrate them into the ruling people in any way—by force or by the outwardly more peaceful but inwardly often more stringent methods of a systematic cultural policy, as well as through propaganda, language, and schooling.

In the nature of things the idea of the sovereignty of the people caused ever greater population groups to ally themselves with the state and share the responsibility for political life. In the eighteenth century it had been essentially the upper classes that concerned themselves with questions of political life. Toward the end of that century, and primarily because of the French Revolution and its aftereffects, the bourgeoisie began to take an active part in politics. By the end of the nineteenth century universal suffrage had been adopted by almost all countries, at least in the western world, and established ever closer contact between the state and the population, albeit often with many restrictions based on class and property. If earlier the state and the people had confronted each other, there now was increasing interpenetration. The people adopted the state's striving for power, and the state was increasingly formed by forces from the people. In theory and increasingly in practice as well, the state and the people blended into an indissoluble entity. This brought a formidable power into being, and woe to the external or internal adversary that it opposed.

Romanticism, Historiography, and the Theory of Evolution

This idea of liberal-democratic nationalism based on the sovereignty of the people now combined with all the other currents prevailing in the world of the nineteenth century. In the early part of that century it was primarily Romanticism, alongside and in opposition to the liberal ideas of the Enlightenment and the French Revolution. It led to a transfiguring revival of the Middle Ages and its bonds hallowed by tradition. It inspired new love and understanding for Christianity and enhanced and solidified its influence on political and social life. In contrast to the revolutionary and secular tendencies of the revolutionary periods, the state was again understood as a Christian state, and despite all formal-legal equality between the citizens irrespective of their religion, in decisive questions Christianity was regarded as the obvious basis for the governance of the state and the understanding of its cultural values. Romanticism often combined with the teleological or Darwinistic ideas of development and progress to prepare the ground for the blossoming science of historiography, for that historical perception of all phenomena of human life and even of nature that is so characteristic of nineteenth century thought. In the further course of the century, nationalism to an ever-increasing extent intermingled with economic endeavors and interests. The liberalistic free-trade policy was replaced by the demarcation of states through protective tariffs, and these demarcations often transcended the economic sphere. The idea of imperialism, of the control of underdeveloped countries and their capitalistic exploitation, made itself felt ever more crudely both internally and externally. At the same time the participation in political life of the masses crowded together in the factories and cities also gave ever greater currency and power to the idea that a social reorganization on a revolutionary or reformatory basis was necessary. And finally, the national idea combined with natural science, which blossomed especially in the second half of the nineteenth century, developing new branches like biology, daring to offer an unambiguous explanation of the evolution of the world and its inhabitants on the basis of the theory of evolution adopted from history and monistically developed by Darwin, and also embracing history and philosophy with a claim to absolute validity. The idea of race that was created or scientifically undergirded by it was particularly important and momentous for its connection with nationalism.*

By way of summing up, it is safe to say that the nationalist movement gradually gained the place in the emotional life of the nations that religion had previously occupied, though the power of the latter continued to be widely exerted and often managed to establish a close connection with the idea of a nation-state.

The Jew as an Anomaly and Hostile Outsider

For the Jewish question this development had one far-reaching consequence: The Jew was—still or again—regarded as an alien in ever new ways and by ever greater parts of the population. The populace became increasingly aware of this status, and in it the Jews were in ever greater measure looked upon with suspicion and animosity in addition to being socially isolated. The Jews could have no place in the *Weltanschauung* of Romanticism, with its revival of the past, tradition, and old customs. As in the Middle Ages, they could be integrated into that movement only as a less respected special group with special privileges. If the non-Jews considered Jewish history in its interconnection with the history of other nations, they were bound to perceive the Jews as a historical phenomenon that conflicted with everything accustomed and legitimate—a peo-

*These currents and influences, which are only sketched here, are treated in greater detail in the following chapters and the excursuses in Part 2.

ple that continued to exist visibly, in strange fashion and in multifarious guises and fragments, even though (and therein the view of the Christian historians and philosophers scarcely differs from that of the Christian theologians) it had lost its *raison d'être* long ago. Only recently had Hegel's philosophy of history,* which to some degree shaped the historical thought of the time, renewed the Christian-dogmatic view of the Jewish people's fate in secularized form: The historical existence of a people is the state—that is, with the destruction of its state its existence is over. Every people has to perform a task given it by the spirit of history; once it has performed it, it leaves the stage of world history and loses any justification for its historical existence. By producing Christianity—which, for Hegel, as for Kant, was the most perfect embodiment of divine reason—the Jewish people fulfilled its mission. But the Jewish people existed, running counter to this historical prophecy; the Jews existed, their numbers were growing, their power was assuming seemingly immeasurable proportions, especially in the economy but also in culture and society, and increasingly in political life as well. The Jews were what they had always been since their dispersion: an anomaly. If a Jew was viewed in the mythic form in which the people perceive and process phenomena, the image of a hydra with many heads arose. The Romanticists' image of the Jew as Ahasuerus, the eternal, deathless wanderer through the world, also became popular at that time and a much-used literary figure. If people wanted to find a rational explanation for the anomalous existence of the Jews, they could presume only malevolent intentions behind the various forms of their growing influence: These were only disguises, diverse expressions of their own tendency—their all-encompassing will to power, to dominion over the non-Jews. Literature, too, scarcely managed to present a contemporary Jew as an individual; he remained an evil, malevolent, money-hungry stereotype.** Under the spell of an imperialistic idea of the nation-state, directed toward the inside as well as the outside, people suspected behind all Jewish manifestations of life a nationalistic-imperialistic idea. Under the influence of the continuing traditional image of the demonic, anti-Christian Jew this idea was all too apt to coalesce with the notion of the Jew striving for world dominion who was amassing mammon in order to subjugate the Christian peoples (which is how the Messianic promises were understood). This also involved secret guilt feelings as

---

*Concerning Hegel's position (ambivalent to negative) toward historical Judaism and his positive attitude toward the emancipation of contemporary Jewry, see the excursus in Part 2. Hegel's attitude exemplified the inner conflict of many of the best people of his generation; they rejected the Jews as Jews but accepted them as human beings and therefore wished to grant them civil rights.

**Concerning the image of the Jew in the literature of the period of emancipation, see the excursus in Part 2.

well as an obscure fear that the people freed from the coercive ghetto not long ago (who, as Herzl later frankly stated, behaved like freed slaves rather than free men) might take revenge on their former masters for a bondage endured for centuries. And this fear born of a bad conscience now mingled with hurt feelings because a slave of yesterday was to have the rights of a master today.*

This irrational background exacerbated the antagonisms in the economic and social sphere and made both sides more sensitive. Frequently the accusations were disproportionate to the actual occasion. The special existence of the Jews was again perceived by the entire population and given a definite emphasis. In the economic sphere the Jews as proponents and exponents of capitalism aroused the resistance and the hostility of those whom the new economic forms caused suffering. The Jews were identified with capitalism—not only by the people but even by scholars.** Thus, in the eyes of the craftsmen and the tradition-bound petite bourgeoisie the Jews were, even more than in the eighteenth century, the smashers of tradition, of everything that was professional, right, and proper. The bourgeoisie regarded them with animosity, and even though in individual cases the nobility liked to use the services of the Jews or gild its coats of arms by marrying wealthy Jewish girls, it thought of them as upstarts who undermined the nobility's inherited feudal rights with their financial power or as leaders and adherents of revolutionary movements—from liberalism to socialism—who were undermining and shaking up the existing social order. The fourth estate, finally, frequently regarded the Jews as a symbol of the capitalism that amassed money and enslaved the workers. Hence it was anything but accidental that early socialists like Fourier and especially his pupil Alphonse Toussenel opposed the Jews as representatives of trade and financial power, as the "kings of the present" (1845), that a number of other socialists joined them in their hostility toward, or at least dislike of, the Jews, and that even the founders of modern materialistic socialism, Marx and Engels, as well as many of their leading adherents, were not free from prejudice and contemptuous rejections of the Jews.***

All these currents combined with modern nationalism as well as the anti-Jewish tradition of many centuries, which permeated even literature and linguistic usage, and caused the Jews eventually to be regarded as *the* enemy. The fact that the Jews were really trail-blazers in many areas**** afforded them no protection, because a trail-blazer is

---

*Cf. the quotation from Lessing's play, *The Jews*, p. 177 above.
**Sombart's book about the Jews and economic life, which has already been discussed, appeared at the end of this epoch, three years before the outbreak of World War I. It was a scientific expression of this *Zeitgeist*.
***Cf. the excursus in Part 2.
****Cf. chap. 7.

always a destroyer, too. Under these conditions the Jews as aliens could
be blamed for everything unwholesome in the world and all the short-
comings connected with the decline of old conditions and the rise of new
forms of economic, political, and social life in the nineteenth century.

Anti-Jewish Movements and Riots

Hence the nations regarded the very visible Jews as a likely point of
departure and outlet for their feelings of hatred, unless these could be
vented more "naturally" through the common effort of a war against an
external enemy. These feelings could be triggered by local occasions
connected with economic or social realities or they could have general,
ideologically founded causes rooted in a religious and historical tradition. In an atmosphere charged with tension, seemingly insignificant
quarrels, inequities, indiscretions, or teasing on either part were apt to
turn into uncontrollable tempests that had a deleterious effect on large
areas as a chain reaction, with no one being aware of the harmless
occasion. Such an outburst was immediately placed in a context familiar
from tradition and ideologically motivated with seeming rationality. This
is the explanation for the anti-Jewish riots in many towns in Germany
and some neighboring countries in 1819, with plundering, threats,
beatings, temporary expulsions, and the battlecry "*Hepp, hepp, Jude
verreck'!*"—a cry that resounded in this form and in a number of variants
for the first time in the modern age and in the choice of the epithet
verreck'! (croak!), usually employed only in reference to animals, fore-
shadowed the most horrible developments.* In the revolutionary years
1830 and 1848, and also in some purely local political or social conflicts
around that time, there was further violence against the Jews in which
the same or similar threats were uttered. Thus the blood libel against the
Jews was revived, first in the Rhineland in 1834, and it was believed,
though the optimistic rationalists had thought it had finally disappeared
together with the Middle Ages. When, in 1840, the accusation of ritual
murder was made by the French counsel in Damascus, the French
government in Paris (under Adolphe Thiers) vacillated, and only public
opinion and the intervention of Jewish leaders in England (Moses Mon-
tefiore), France (Adolphe Crémieux), and in other countries called a halt
to the medieval torture of the Jewish suspects in Damascus, the Jews
and the surrounding world realized all over again how deeply rooted the
fearful mistrust of the Jews still was in the people and how insecure their
position among the nations was. In the final analysis, this is the explana-

*Cf. the excursus in Part 2.

tion for the great response to the anti-Jewish movement that originated in Germany in the late 1870s and claimed the Jews were to blame for all the misfortune in the world. This movement, which organized around the new watchword *anti-Semitism* was to become a political force of menacing dimensions.

Modern Anti-Semitism and Its Place in the History of the Jewish Question

"Anti-Semitism," the Word and the Concept

In the history of the Jewish question the origin of modern anti-Semitism in the 1870s marks the conclusion of centuries of development and at the same time the beginning of a new epoch.

The very fact that a specific term for the hatred of Jews now came into being shows that the Jewish question had entered a new phase. It is no accident if a collective concept arises for a societal movement. In general, such concepts are created when a movement has reached a stage at which its diverse currents combine into a collective idea and the movement, as it were, attains self-knowledge—or, to put it less abstractly, when its leaders become aware of the novel and special aspects of the ideas and aims of the movement. From there the road usually leads to a more rational, more purposeful, and more systematic realization of its goal. The modern anti-Jewish movement reached this stage in the late 1870s.

Hence the word *Antisemitismus*, first used in Germany around 1879, gained acceptance by all groups in all languages in a very short time. It was probably used in 1860 by the Jewish scholar Moritz Steinschneider in a polemic against Ernest Renan and first employed as a political term in 1879 by the German pamphleteer Wilhelm Marr.*

There were various reasons for the increasing use of the term *anti-Semitism* to designate the new anti-Jewish movement instead of having a catchy term say clearly that a movement directed against Jews and Judaism was involved. First of all, it was a kind of concession to the prevailing *Zeitgeist*, liberalism, which no one could simply ignore. As "anti-Semites" people denied, so to speak, that they were indulging in a "medieval" hatred of the Jews that an "enlightened" modern period proscribed. In this they were actually following the example of the philo-Semites. As we have already said, these had increasingly become ac-

*Concerning the history of the word *Antisemitismus*, see the excursus for this section in Part 2.

customed to using the terms "Israelites" and "adherents of the Mosaic faith," terms that had an Old Testament ring and were less burdened by gloomy associations, in place of *Jude*, a word that sounded corrupted by prolonged misuse in the medieval Christian tradition. By so doing they also tried to prove that they regarded the Jews only as a religious community and not as a separate nation. In similar fashion the nationalistic and racist antagonists of the Jews now chose the concept "Semites" instead of "Jews."* Yet in general it was quite clear that "Semites" usually referred only to the Jews and not also the Arabs, with whom people in the European cultural sphere had hardly any dealings. This made hating Jews respectable, as it were. At the same time it was given a scientific veneer by taking the *terminus technicus* from modern science, even the most modern of modern sciences, natural science— biology and its most modern offshoot, ethnology, the study of race. The new name also gave clear expressiion to the new conception of the Jewish question—its consideration as a question of *race*. At the same time the suffix -*ism* raised antagonism toward the Jews to the sphere of modern philosophical-political doctrines and concepts.

The Development of Anti-Semitic Racial Theory

GOBINEAU

The origin of this racial theory and its antagonistic application to the Jewish question is well known in its basic features. All modern anti-Jewish racial theories are based on the work of Joseph Arthur, Comte de Gobineau (1816–82), the scion of an old aristocratic family who became a writer and diplomat after Alexis de Tocqueville (1805–59) appointed him chief of his cabinet in the Foreign Ministry. In his *Essai sur l'inégalité des races humaines* (Paris, 1853–55) Gobineau had made the epoch-making attempt to give history a basis freed from subjectivity by integrating it into the natural sciences. "What matters," he wrote in the conclusion of his *magnum opus*, "is to get history admitted to the family of the natural sciences and to give it all the exactitude of this type of knowledge . . . finally removing it from the arbitrariness of interested

*Eugen Dühring, the first and most consistent theoretician of racial anti-Semitism (see p. 236 below), sensed this and therefore rejected the term as a matter of principle: "Even if one means the race, one should simply say *Jude* and not *Semit*. . . . The term *semitisch* tends to become a euphemism, and even the Jews themselves may prefer it to the appellation of well-known significance. . . . What concerns our modern culture and society is not the whole Semitic race but a tribe that has developed the characteristics of a race in marked contrast to the rest of mankind." (E. Dühring, *Die Judenfrage als Racen-, Sitten- und Culturfrage* [Karlsruhe and Leipzig, 1881], p. 3.) Concerning the differentiation from the Arabs, see the remark in Part 2. In later editions Dühring abandoned his resistance to the term.

jurisdiction which the political parties have imposed upon it to this day."
Gobineau thought he had found the cause of all historical events in race.
According to him, it was not the individual qualities of important personalities nor the free will, creative impulse, or individual interest of
people that produced the actions of history and brought about changes
in the historical life of mankind. He thought that history was dominated
by an iron law and that the decisive and indeed only essential factor was
the one determined by nature: race. As compared to race as the fundamental element all other influences were deemed to be of secondary
importance. According to Gobineau, this law of nature controls everything that happens in history; no will or faith, no matter how beautiful,
can rescind this autocratic rule of a fate determined by the law of nature,
a law the expression of which is race.

This theory of the dominant influence of race on historical events was
able to be a valuable corrective to other theories of history that over-
emphasized the intellectual or economic factors, or that let individuals
act too independently of the natural origin from which they sprang. In
that sense attention had already been paid, certainly since Montesquieu's *Esprit des lois,* to the influence of racial premises on historical
life. In Gobineau's view, however, that was totally inadequate; in his
writings race appears with a totalitarian claim. In the face of it all other
values lose at least their independent significance. "The god of race, as
proclaimed by Gobineau," rightly remarks Ernst Cassirer (*The Myth of
the State* [New Haven, 1946], p. 232), "is a jealous god. He does not
allow other gods to be adored beside himself. Race is everything, all the
other forces are nothing."

It is clear that even this monistic-fatalistic-naturalistic foundation of
Gobineau's theory of history could have deleterious effects. There were,
however, a number of additional elements that aggravated its effect and
in particular facilitated its disastrous exploitation in the dispute about
the nature and the solution of the Jewish question, even though
Gobineau himself pursued no political goals, and certainly none relating
to a policy toward the Jews, with his writings.* The science of anthropology was still in its infancy, and thus the arbitrary, subjective
determination and interpretation of races and racial characteristics could
proceed unchecked. Modern linguistics had just taken the basic steps
toward the identification of language families, their connections, and
differences. Toward the end of the eighteenth century the term "Semitic
languages" as a grouping of related languages had been used for the first
time (by J. G. Eichhorn, 1787) in place of "Oriental languages" and since
then had gradually gained currency, particularly in connection with the

*Cf. also the quotation from the dedication of the first edition (in Part 2).

critical study of the Old Testament. In the middle of the nineteenth century the young German philologist and mythologist Friedrich Max Müller (1823–1900), a son of Wilhelm Müller (1794–1827, a poet whose poems became famous through Schubert's musical settings) and a resident of England since 1846, had used the Sanskrit word *Aryan* to designate an Indo-European group of languages, terming the speakers of these languages "Aryan race." This concept was immediately taken up by writers and scientists of all kinds who coarsened it naturalistically. The concept "Aryan" had originally been intended only as a designation for a group of languages, but now a primordial race of people was constructed from it.*

As the very title of Gobineau's book indicates, the doctrine of the inequality of the races occupied an important place in his race theory. According to him, there are higher and lower races; the former are destined to rule, the latter have been chosen by racial fate to serve the higher races. The white race is most creative—indeed, the only creative one. Within the white race the "Aryans" are the most gifted branch, and the Teutons are closest to them in blood, which makes them the noblest race in the world.

Gobineau now contrasted this tall, blond, and blue-eyed Germanic race (also called "Nordic race" since the end of the century) with the small, dark-haired Semites as uncreative, unoriginal, parasitic elements.** His successors put this antithesis in ever cruder terms. With an early work on the Semitic language that appeared around that time (1855) the famous French philologist and historian Ernest Renan (1823–92) contributed to having this confrontation of racial characteristics come out in disfavor of the "Semitic" race. To be sure, in his foreword he warned against the application of his theory to the Jews of his time, many of whom, despite their direct descent from the former inhabitants of Palestine, had been purged of their Semitic character by modern civilization. Renan later repeated these warnings when he became aware of the diastrous effect of the racial doctrine. But of what consequence is

---

*There is much evidence that language and script definitely do not permit one to draw conclusions about the biological origin and composition of peoples. For example, the Arabic language was disseminated by the Arabs among the nations of North Africa in the course of their campaign of conquest, starting with the middle of the seventh century, and Arabic script was adopted, among others, by the Persians and Turks—peoples who are not related to the Arabs either linguistically or ethnically. Concerning F. M. Müller's position on this intermingling of linguistic and ethnographic concepts, see the note in Part 2.

**Gobineau himself certainly did not deny that the Semites and Jews had any creative character. He even had a certain respect for the Jews because they attached great importance to the factor of race in their own lives. His successors increasingly stressed the uncreativity of their racial disposition.

that foreword in the face of all generalizations contained in the book itself as well as in later publications?* Generalizations always do violence to historical life in its individual variety. They become dangerous when on the basis of inadequate observation they reduce the colorful, ever-changing life of individuals and peoples to seemingly fixed types and then make a value judgment by placing these types into a frame of reference that claims validity for every individual case of the present. This is precisely what happened here. In Renan's opinion, the peoples of the Semitic language family actually constitute a group of people with definite, racially rooted psychic qualities. The races are by no means equal. In comparison with the Indo-European race, the Semitic race is inferior in nature. It lacks original talent and does not create culture; its monotheism is an unimaginative desert religion without a close connection with the morality of everyday life. It goes without saying that such views and formulations gave the anti-Jewish theoreticians valuable material for the development of their theory.

In the prevailing anti-Jewish atmosphere these new "scientific" arguments were eagerly adopted. As already mentioned, works about the Jewish question, especially anti-Jewish writings, had appeared in great numbers since the end of the eighteenth century in connection with the controversial question of emancipation for the Jews. All political groups, from the conservatives to the socialists, and all literary currents, from Classicism to Realism, and particularly Romanticism, had made a contribution. In general the arguments were a rehash of the traditional anti-Jewish material that had accumulated, on the basis of religious dogma, since the rise of Christianity to the dominant western religion and that had repeatedly been confirmed and intensified. The nineteenth century had added as a new element in the complex of the anti-Jewish tradition accusations that derived principally from contemporary economic and social problems and were connected with evolving capitalism. Beginning with the 1840s, or even earlier, the principle of race was also employed, or at least hinted at.** All this as well as the "instinctive" dislike of the Jews rooted in nationalism had already been given expression in Richard Wagner's essay *Das Judentum in der Musik* which first appeared pseudonymously in 1850 and was reprinted in 1869—a sign of the times!—under Wagner's own, by then quite well-known name.*** Now all these anti-Jewish currents were given what seemed like an objective foundation by the argument of race, which claimed to be scientific.

*The polemics against Renan's disparaging remarks about the racial characteristics of the Semites probably led to the coining of the word *anti-Semitic*. See p. 230 above as well as the excursus about *Antisemitismus*, the word and the concept, in part 2.
**Concerning this see the notes in Part 2.
***On Richard Wagner's place in the history of the Jewish question see the excursus in Part 2.

As early as 1861 there appeared an essay entitled *Die Juden und der deutsche Staat* which opposed full equality for the Jews. It was first published anonymously and then under the pseudonym D. H. Naudh, but the real author was the ever-radical anti-Jewish writer J. Nordmann.* In this work the new "scientific" argument of race was combined with all the old accusations against the Jews from Manetho to Voltaire: "Thousands of years of isolation and inbreeding have solidified the all-encompassing dominance of the racial type and made mentality part of it. Jewish blood and Jewish mentality have become inseparable, and we must think of Judaism not only as a religion and a church but also as the expression of a racial peculiarity." By reviving the account of the Egyptian priest Manetho from the third century C.E. about the origin of the Jews from an unclean and leprous people expelled by the Egyptians (see p. 42 above) and combining it with the impressions and opinions of the world around him, he comes to the conclusion that the Jews were produced by the refuse of all sorts of peoples, by the rotten, vice-ridden, and leprous elements. Their physical constitution is that of shirkers, and their conception of God is in keeping with their inferior racial character. The author varies the theses renewed and systematized by Bauer and Marx and repeatedly cited by others as follows: "The world of the Jew revolves around material advantage. He has chosen his god for profit, he tests him for profit, and be obeys him for the sake of profit. His religion is the religion of advantage. No higher point of view may be found in it anywhere." The author considers it highly unlikely that the Jews will assimilate; the intermingling of nations is possible only "through suppression and intermixture." Never before has an Indo-European tribe intermingled with a Semitic one—let alone with the Jews! "The Germans are the most ideal part of the Indo-Europeans, and even within the Semitic group of predators the Jews are regarded as the lowest branch of the family."

WILHELM MARR

In 1879 there appeared the first work of Wilhelm Marr, whose share in the early dissemination of the word *Antisemitismus* has already been mentioned. This was toward the end of the so-called *Gründerjahre* in Germany, the boom after the victorious Franco-Prussian War and the establishment of the German Reich, a period in which great numbers of both legitimate and phony businesses and institutions were founded and Jewish names frequently appeared among the flourishing, foundering, and fraudulent enterprises. The title of this work already says everything that is important to know about its contents: *Der Sieg des Judentums*

*Concerning the question of authorship see the notes and quotations in Part 2.

über das Germanentum, vom nicht-konfessionellen Standpunkt aus be-trachtet (The victory of the Jews over the Germans as seen from a nonsectarian point of view). In Marr's view, the Jews—or, as he puts it at first occasionally and then more and more frequently, the "Semites"—whose great talents he acknowledges, have already achieved world dominion; according to him, the Jews are convinced that the Semites deserve to rule the world and the Germans are close to succumbing to them. Hence Marr, in this work as well as in his later writings, calls upon the Germans to brace themselves, join the battle, and thereby avert the threatening defeat.

EUGEN DÜHRING

The first and most significant attempt to establish a scientific foundation—through philosophy, biology, and history—for the nascent political anti-Semitic movement (whose ups and downs and multifarious organizational ramifications cannot be detailed here) was made in 1881 by the Berlin philosopher and economist Eugen Dühring (1833–1921) with his work *Die Judenfrage als Racen-, Sitten- und Culturfrage* (The Jewish question as a question of race, morality, and culture). This ominous promise is appended to the title: *Mit einer weltgeschichtlichen Antwort* (With an answer based on world history). Dühring deals with the Jewish question with the consistency, the straightforwardness, and the narrow-mindedness that one often finds in discoverers of new "truths" and that characterizes him elsewhere as well: as a question of *race*.

To present it as a question of religion would, in Dühring's opinion, be a deliberate deception and obfuscation. "The plain people and the middle class have allowed neither the priests nor the religious enlighteners to trick them out of all their natural instincts and feelings" (p. 2). Even baptism would not change their aversion; even if all Jews converted to the dominant religions, as desired by the liberals, this would not solve the Jewish question. On the contrary; this would only increase the danger and threat to the nations: "The baptized Jews are the very people who penetrate unimpeded deepest into all channels of society and political communal life" (p. 3). "The insertion of members of the Jewish race into the crevices and columns of our national domiciles" in connection with emancipation and baptism was bound to be counterproductive. Dühring is certain that people will come to realize "how incompatible with our best instincts the implantation of the qualities of the Jewish race into our conditions is. Until then the Jewish question will be less behind us than before us" (p. 4).

In light of the racial foundation the religious or philosophical shadings within Jewry are of no importance. As among the animals, human habits, customs, qualities, thought, and faith are only consequences of the natural, racial basis (though on a higher level): "Thus the approach of natural science is appropriate here as well." The Jewish religion is practically an expression of the Jews' bad racial character. The religious monism of which the Jews are so proud is only an expression of their will to dominate the nations. "The Jewish god is as intolerant as his people. He must definitely have a monopoly; other gods must not exist beside him. The Jews are the chosen people, and he is the one god. The Jews are his servants, but in return they shall be the lords of the world. . . . The Jewish god is the embodiment of the Jews' quest" (p. 30).

The Jews are uncreative and the Jewish race is without any cultural value. They are "one of the lowest and most botched products of nature"; their stock has "for thousands of years been a select, deeply ingrained egotism" (p. 109). A Jew can only steal and exploit the fruits of other nations and cultures; as a "parasite" he feels best in an already somewhat corrupted society: "Wherever a Jew feels most confortable after his fashion in the flesh of the nations, check and see whether it is still healthy" (p. 8).

For thousands of years the Jews have been waging a "war of oppression and exploitation" against the nations, and these have to defend themselves. True, at present the focus of the struggle is Germany, but by nature the Jewish question is an international one. "The hostility which the Jews have since time immemorial displayed toward humankind," says Dühring in continuation of Tacitus, "has an international character." Hence—and this idea is emphasized—the solution must be international as well. A single nation can make a beginning, but true success can be attained only through similar measures taken by all civilized nations. A "social and political solution of the Jewish question" must begin with the "social unfitness of the Jews" (p. 94).

According to Dühring, it would be misleading to speak of tolerance in this connection, for it is not a matter of tolerating religious customs: "The Jewish religion is a racial religion, just as Jewish morality is a racial morality." Thus people would actually be demanding "tolerance toward a race with morally bad and antisocial qualities that are hostile to the rest of humanity" (p. 99). Even the religious institutions of the Jews are in reality political structures. Under the guise of religion, for which tolerance is demanded, the Jews are undeservedly enjoying greater political privileges than any other political association. In the Middle Ages the Jews were admitted by the European nations as "tolerated and protected foreigners." In light of their pernicious qualities it was a mistake to admit them in the first place, even with lesser rights, and in this sense (and not in that asserted by the Jews) the present is, as it were, suffering "from a piece of the Middle Ages" (p. 107). There is nothing to improve or tolerate here. "Jewishness can be eliminated . . . only with the Jews themselves" (p. 108). Their tribal nature is incorrigible and biologically unalterable, at least in the foreseeable future (p. 112). The solution must be sought on the basis of this fact of nature.

What solution? The author did not dare to suggest the logical consequences, the expulsion of the Jews from "our countries of high culture to other regions of the earth." "For the time being this is still too remote from surveyable reality and practice"; hence it must be postponed "to a more distant and more energetic future." For the rest, the Jews have created "a Jewish question wherever they appeared, for many thousands of years" (p. 110). Hence an expulsion would mean only a relocation of the problem.

A proposal to be more seriously considered would be "internment under international law" by concentrating the Jews in certain areas—or, in other words, by founding a Jewish state. "Nomadism," however, is too much part and parcel of the Jews' nature for them to be capable of founding a state of their own; history has rendered a definitive judgment on that score. Besides, there is a danger that "for the scattered masses the Jewish state, which at first would be isolated but would nevertheless prevent seclusion—a Palestine that might be newly settled by Jews—would in the end become the head" (p. 111).*

On the other hand, coexistence between the Jews and the nations would in the long run be rendered impossible by the rise of national consciousness among the latter. What would happen then, where the Jews would have to move and settle, was a matter for the Jews themselves. "For the time being, only great collective crimes, such as collective treason, might lead people to get rid of whole groups of Jews that were involved. But that would not be an internment but a real deportation" (p. 11).

Until such radical solutions were possible, people would have to content themselves with provisional measures to be taken in countries with a Jewish population. The Jews would have to be separated from the nations, their emancipation would have to be rescinded, and they would have to be subjected to special regulations. Their influence on public affairs, education, and the press would have to be completely eliminated, and their property would have to be placed under the control of the state. Marriage to Jews should be proscribed.

But all these measures should be regarded only as transitional measures, as means to an end. "Once race has been properly recognized," says Dühring, clearly hinting at the future, "a further goal will be kept in mind from the beginning, a goal that can be reached only if the strongest measures are taken. The Jews . . . are an inner Carthage whose power

---

*In the sixth edition, still prepared by Dühring but not published until 1930, nine years after his death, Zionism, which had in the meantime taken shape as a political movement, was expressly rejected for this reason.

the modern nations must break if they do not want it to destroy their moral and material foundations."

Dühring's work, supplemented in 1883 by a further publication entitled *Ersatz der Religion durch Vollkommeneres und die Ausscheidung des Judentums durch den modernen Völkergeist* (Replacement of religion by something more perfect and the elimination of Jewry through the modern spirit of the nations), collected—but now consistently and on the basis of the racial principle—all the accusations against the Jews which had been leveled at them over the ages; at the same time it already contained in embryonic form everything that the later literature treated and popularized in greater detail. Hence one can call his book the classic, fundamental work of anti-Semitism based on the principle of race. This is how Dühring himself viewed it and how his successors and executors evaluated it two generations later.

EDOUARD DRUMONT

Even the real founder of modern anti-Semitism in France, Edouard Drumont (1844–1917), added nothing fundamentally new to Dühring's remarks. The only thing in his book *La France juive*, published in two fat tomes in 1886 and immediately translated into German, that went beyond them was the historical foundation on which he placed the anti-Semitic doctrine. This gifted writer, who was even able to apply for admission to the Academy, gave his readers a unified system of anti-Semitism, as it were. A survey of Jewish characteristics—"All major and even the minor discoveries are to be attributed to the Aryans . . . a Semite knows only how to exploit the inventiveness and the labor of the Christians"—is followed in his *magnum opus* by a treatise on the Jews in French history from the beginnings to his time. Drumont views the entire history from the standpoint of anti-Semitism: an expedition of conquest on the part of the Jews for the domination of France and the grafting of a foreign body onto the hitherto healthy organism of the French nation. Hence the author also justifies, among other things, the Inquisition as Spain's self-defense against the foreigners who tried to destroy it through the poisoning of wells, treason, and political agitation. The author was originally a Voltairean and became a devout Catholic; thus he could derive anti-Jewish arguments both from the tradition of the Church and from secular Enlightenment. All the appurtenances of the medieval hatred of the Jews appear in his work; he even believed in the blood libel. The emancipation of 1791 was a mistake; despite what they assert, the Jews are not Frenchmen but a people of guests who only exploit the courtesy of the host nation in order to squeeze it dry, rule it, and extend Jewish world domination, the central organ of which is the Alliance Israélite Universelle. As representatives of an anonymous capitalism the Jews, whose trading mentality is rooted in race, use their large concerns to destroy the Christian middle class and get hold of all the property of the nations (see the Rothschild banking house). With their inferior racial character they corrupt French civilization, and they are to blame for the decadence of France. Their assimilation is impossible, and because of their pernicious racial influence their radical absorption through intermarriage is undesirable. Their emancipation ought to be rescinded and their property should be confiscated and used to purchase capital goods for the exploited workers.

Drumont's book, the publication of which was advocated by the well-known novelist Alphonse Daudet, was one of the greatest commercial successes of the nineteenth century. In 1886, the year of its publication, more than 100,000 copies were sold, 60,000 of these within two months of its appearance—proof of the extent to which its ideas were in keeping with the temper of the times.

ADOLF WAHRMUND

Of the numerous later writings that developed the anti-Semitic theory in one direction or another without adding anything substantially new, we shall mention as typical the book of the German Orientalist Adolf Wahrmund (1827–1913, in Vienna from 1853 on), *Das Gesetz des Nomadentums und die heutige Judenherrschaft* (The law of nomadism and present-day Jewish domination, 1887). The book is typical of the way in which scientific and semiscientific assumptions were frivolously generalized, applied to the Jewish question, and used in support of the anti-Semitic racial doctrine. The author began his foreword to the first edition as follows: "This little book joins the large number of writings already published in Austria-Hungary, Germany, and France which combat the domination of the Jews in those countries. However, by pointing out the workings of deeper developmental laws it aims primarily at promoting among us that new view of history which alone can serve as an ideational basis for the reformation of Central Europe, a reformation that is indispensable for a successful averting of the dangers posed to Europe and Christian western culture by the Asiatic spirit and nomadism. The Asiatic spirit is represented in Europe particularly by the Jews, who as nomads embody a revolutionary principle that tends to dissolve and destroy the accomplishments of the established farmers, as Semites a principle hostile to the Aryans, as heirs and representatives of the Punic spirit a principle that transforms free labor into bondage, and as a pre-Christian and ethnic (pagan) religious association—i.e., one based on national exclusivity—an anti-Christian principle" (p. 3).

According to the author of this book, which the editor of the second edition (1919) called "the fundamental treatise about the psychology of the Jews," the eternally wandering Jews are a race of nomads and Bedouins, in contrast to the Aryan or Indo-Germanic nations, who have been living as settled farmers. "What a husbandman has created with patience and diligence over a long period of time, a nomad can only plunder and lay waste in the predatory attacks" (p. 10). The Jews live in accordance with the law of the desert on predatory incursions on the farms of others to which they bring destruction and moral corruption. They wage a constant holy war against all those of another faith (= "infidels"). "According to rabbinic thought, a Jew, strictly speaking, transgresses his law if he does not kill any infidel that he can safely kill" (p. 45). Like the Arabs, the constant point of departure and generalization of the Arabist Wahrmund, the Jews have always been parasites remote from real work. Their ideal is the domination of others and of the world, which they want to be at their feet, slavelike.

HOUSTON STEWART CHAMBERLAIN

All previous anti-Semitic literature, however, was far surpassed in influence by the two-volume work of the British-born German-by-choice Houston Stewart Chamberlain (1855–1927), *Die Grundlagen des 19. Jahrhunderts* (Foundations of the nineteenth century), first published in 1899 and subsequently reissued in numerous editions, including popular ones. The very intention of the book, to reveal the foundations of the age at the end of a century that had seen such pioneer work in all areas, was bound to elicit a great response. Added to this was Chamberlain's treatment of his subject. In the brilliant style of a gifted writer and with equally brilliant generalizations of half-truths and scientifically amateurish "insights" and experiences, the author presented a generation that had doubts about itself with a view of history that attributed everything great and culturally creative over the ages to the Aryans, the Teutons, while the Semites, the Jews, were depicted as having brought into the world only inferior and harmful things.

The book avoided excessively sharp attacks on the Jews as well as the crude naturalistic interpretations of the principle of race. Precisely because of this and also because it attempted to interpret race from a spiritual and intellectual point of view and to show its effect on the events of world history and particularly culture, the book managed to gain acceptance even in circles that indignantly rejected the radically anti-Semitic literature. Hence no other book contributed as much to the dissemination of the anti-Semitic racial doctrine as this work, with its harmless title referring to cultural history. It was part of the reading and library of every educated person, Christian as well as Jew, just like Spengler's *The Decline of the West* a generation later and subsequently Toynbee's *A Study of History*. Written by a person with supersensitive nerves, a man enthusiastic about Wagner (whose biography he wrote), his *Gesamtkunstwerk* (synthesis of the arts) and his views on cultural policy, it evidently met in the greatest measure the needs of a time that had begun to doubt itself and its advances and was searching for a guide through the shrubbery of the ever more specialized sciences and the contradictory crosscurrents of cultural and social life, as well as politics. The book gave the Germans (and people of "Aryan" origin) an awareness of their own importance as creators of culture—and, as has been rightly emphasized, a good conscience if under the sign of "imperialism" they treated other nations to the culture-carrying domination of Teutonism and Aryanism. In the "non-Aryans," on the other hand, it aroused a feeling of inferiority; these included many Jews, something that will be discussed later.

This was so even though almost no statement and valuation could really stand up to serious examination and many things seem downright absurd to us today (and seemed so to critical observers at the time). A few examples should suffice. Chamberlain gives various definitions and quasi-historical-anthropological surveys of the development of races, acknowledging Gobineau's towering significance for modern racial doctrine as well as his basic principle that the races are dynamic, dissimilar, and unequal basic forces of history. On the other hand, he rejects Gobineau's theory of the superior quality of the "pure" races, saying that all races have come about through mixing and, as in the breeding of horses and dogs, their quality is determined by the good or bad elements composing them. At the same time, Chamberlain's concept of race is increasingly removed from the purely anthropological realm and shifted to the psychological sphere. The decisive thing is not the findings of ethnologists and anthropologists, for they often arrive at antithetical observations and conclusions. "To make a judgment on the basis of the state of scientific knowledge at any given time is as if a painter [what a comparison!] wanted to view the world not with his eyes but through a transparent, constantly changing kaleidoscope." Rather, life as such is "different from systematic knowledge, a far more stable, firmly founded, more comprehensive entity—simply the quintessence of all reality."

This philosophy of life and reality is followed by apodictic doctrines. "What is immediately convincing is the presence of 'race' in one's own consciousness. Anyone who belongs to an absolutely pure race feels this every day. . . . Race lifts a person beyond himself and lends him extraordinary, I would almost say supernatural, faculties." Yet this awareness is not the only thing that determines the presence of the superior Aryan race; necessity for the future does too. "Even if it were proved that no Aryan race ever existed in the past, we want one to exist in the future; for men of action this is the decisive point of view."

In Chamberlain's view, then, every important person must be an Aryan or at least have a strong admixture of Aryan blood; this view is at first frequently presented as a hypothesis with the words *perhaps* or *probably,* but, as is characteristic of hypothetical assumptions, it gains greater assurance with every repetition. This is then applied to the kings David and Solomon, not to mention Jesus, who simply cannot have been a Jew.

Chamberlain praises the Jews for their exemplary observation of the principle of race, and he regards the racially much more noble Sephardim as far superior to the Ashkenazim. However, he always combines this praise with a warning against the Jewish world domination for which all Jews are striving. When they got ready to conquer the nations in the age of Emancipation, they used their racial law, which seemed to have been broken by assimilation and baptism, for their purposes of conquest. "Notice with what mastery they are using the law of blood for the extension of their domination; the main stock remains untainted, with not a drop of alien blood entering it . . . Meanwhile, however, thousands of little offshoots are cut off and used to infect the Indo-Europeans with Jewish blood. If this continued for a few centuries, there would be only one racially pure people in Europe, the Jews; all others would be a herd of pseudo-Hebrew half-breeds, undoubtedly a physically, intellectually, and morally degenerate people." Similar, almost identical formulations may be found twenty-five years later in Chamberlain's pupils Hitler and Rosenberg.

With H. S. Chamberlain the anti-Semitic racial doctrine transcends the often rather provincial sphere of the one-sided ideologists of race and enters the realm of cultural history, cultural policy, and general education. Whether people accepted it, dissociated themselves from parts of it, or rejected it in toto, from then on it was, in any case, a theory that was taken seriously and widely discussed as one discussed other doctrines of the natural sciences, philosophy, and history. It increasingly became a constituent element of the consciousness of the time, and in various forms of expression: those pertaining to natural science, anthropology, politics, and even mythical belief.

The Significance of the Anti-Semitic Racial Doctrine

Modern anti-Semitism and its anti-Jewish theories have frequently been regarded as a variant and new version of the age-old hatred of the Jews. There may be a great deal of truth in such a view, but it overlooks the fundamentally new elements by virtue of which anti-Semitism marks a decisive turning point in the development of the Jewish question. It is true that anti-Semitism was based on earlier developments and theories pertaining to the Jewish question which have been treated here in detail, and that, viewed in this way, it was a new expression of the old hostility toward the Jews. The anti-Semitic doctrine, however, went farther than that, and it did not merely sum up everything that preceded it and find a common denominator for it. By introducing racial theory and gaining acceptance for it, it established entirely new foundations for the Jewish question and its solution, at least theoretically.

In judging and evaluating this theory it would be quite erroneous to deny the existence and historical significance of ethnic groups with similar hereditary characteristics, whether one refers to them as a "race," a term widely used since Gobineau, or, more cautiously, as a "tribe," an "ethnic group," and so forth. An individual is a product of genotype, history, environment, and the concurrence of unique events, and so is a human group. The identification of certain characteristics of Jews that is made on this basis is not in itself an expression of hostility toward the Jews; only some assimilated Jews who (quite understandably) are overly nervous and anxious because they feel threatened in their social position will feel that such identification is *eo ipso* an expression of hatred of the Jews.

If human groups are different in *nature*, this does not mean that they are different in *value*. One can recognize the diversity of human groups of common descent and history as well as the special nature of their achievements and above all their similar reactions as facts without adopting at the same time the valuations that many people automatically connect with them. Of course, the evaluation of the nature of human groups and their achievements, like the assessment of the nature and the achievements of individuals, depends on the observer's point of view. It is entirely normal for such an observer to tend to measure the life and the achievements of others by the positive image that he has of himself (provided that his self-esteem is sound). Danger arises only if one regards one's own subjective viewpoint as the only possible, objective, and legitimate one and makes it the standard for everything else. This is precisely what the anti-Semitic racial doctrine did: it came to view what was different as something of different and inferior value.

Actually, the condemnation of the Jews as inferior, bad, and harmful was nothing really new. After all, as we have shown in the preceding sections of this book, in the course of their long history from antiquity to modern times the Jews had been condemned from all sorts of viewpoints and all sorts of motives: as negators of the faith and the customs of the ancient world; as rebels against the sovereignty of a powerful individual whom Fortuna had rewarded with victory; as deicides, infidels, and eternal nonconformists; as usurers and dealers; as economic competitors and interlopers in all occupations; as revolutionary, rootless, sinister destroyers of everything traditional, rooted, and homelike. All these and many other arguments against the Jews, deriving from different periods and deposited in ever new layers of the people's conscious and sub-conscious, return in anti-Semitic literature in all variations.

The Rootedness in Nature of God's Curse and Its Perpetuation

The truly decisive thing about the anti-Semitic racial theory is that it rooted these negative judgments of the Jews in nature. Christianity had based on the ancients' hatred of the Jews its dogmatic image of the perfidious and perverted Jew.* The Jew who has denied and murdered God has been cursed by God, sentenced to servitude, and scattered over the world. However, the Jews as a totality remain God's people under that curse and will return to God's grace at the end of time. Each individual Jew can personally free himself from the curse at any time if he gives up his "obduracy" and adopts the Christian faith. Accordingly, the salvation of his soul and in many threatening situations even the saving of his physical life in this world are left to his free will. The curse can cease and be lifted, the danger to life and property can be eliminated. All it takes is a person's decision to will his salvation by believing in the Christian redeemer. Baptism expiates, redeems, and liberates. It is not only the life in the next world that it channels in the direction of promise; in general it gives security, a livelihood, and social respect to a persecuted Jew even in this world.

As we have already mentioned, this doctrine and reality had prevailed in Christian Europe as long as the rule of Catholic Christendom was unbroken. Since the beginning of the modern age its validity had not remained unchallenged and its sphere of validity had been restricted. Luther already regarded the execration of the Jews as a totality and their rejection by God as final,** even though an individual Jew still had a chance to redeem himself through the act of baptism. The Jews as a whole remained accursed in all eternity, but an individual could escape the curse if he abandoned his people and his religion by converting to Christianity. The secularization of the modern world and its values further diminished the validity of the Christian-dogmatic teaching about the Jew and his position before God and the world. With increasing self-evidence the Jews were regarded as people of flesh and blood, both in their history and in their present life. We have already discussed the origins and foundations of biblical criticism that began in the seventeenth century (Spinoza) and reached its zenith in the nineteenth. It

---

*It should be noted that the terms *Judaeus perfidus* and *Judaeus perversus* originally were used in a purely religious-dogmatic sense and meant "unbelieving," that is, "incorrect" or "wrong" only in this sense. Only later did they assume the current meanings, "perfidious" and "perverse".

**Cf. pp. 143ff. above.

tended in the same direction by secularizing the "sacred" Old Testament and breaking it down into a number of "literary" sources that were put together with definite theological intentions. It regarded the Jews of biblical times as human beings like any others, but it was often unconsciously influenced by the Christian, New Testament reinterpretation of the Old Testament as well as by the conditions of the time, and thus it tended to paint the seamy sides of Jewish life, the all-too-human elements which the prophets and religious leaders of the Jews had themselves most severely scourged, with particular harshness as a true picture of the Jews.* It also recognized that the history of the Jews in Palestine could only be understood within the framework of the history of the ancient Orient and that of the peoples now designated as "Semitic." It was logical to compare the characteristics of the Jews as familiar from life and literature with those of the nations related to them by language and descent and to attempt to find common dispositions and types of reaction. At the same time the scientific approach substantially retained the historical view (philosophically recast by Hegel) according to which the historical goal of Judaism had been reached with the creation of Christianity and the further development of Judaism ran counter to the sense of history.

The Enlightenment added its own ideas to this explanation. With its tendency toward secularization and rationalism it mitigated the curse of Christian dogma and restricted its sphere of validity, but it also eliminated the claim to salvation and took the ghetto Jew of the nearest Jewish quarter as the prototype of the Jew as he had always been. To be sure, it added to this often harsh picture the gentle light of its new faith—its belief that men can be improved through enlightenment, culture, knowledge, and education. This belief, which constituted a counterpoise to the increasingly predominant realistic approach of the natural sciences, was adopted by political liberalism, which had at the same time been the basis for the emancipation of the Jews. It was hoped that under the influence of the emancipation the Jews would "improve" in accordance with the educational standards of their surroundings and rise from the low state of morality, about the existence of which even most of their defenders had no doubt.

The racial doctrine of anti-Semitism broke completely with this faith, more decisively than any of its predecessors in the dispute about emancipation. If race is the decisive, only authoritative and determining factor in the life of nations and people, the optimistic belief in the ennoblement of a person through his individual desire no longer has any foundation. Good and bad, superior and inferior, culturally creative and destructive—all this is a mark of race. Race—that is the ironclad, un-

*Cf. p. 67 above.

shakable law, more unalterable than any decree of God. Here, in this wrongly or half understood and frivolously deified scientific doctrine, there was no change and no grace; salvation and curse remained unalterably ingrained in nature.

The consequence for the Jewish question was clear: In continuation of the idea of religious execration which in one form or another continued to be active in the subconscious or the hearts of the people, the Jews were now declared to be inferior from the very beginning to the end of time on the basis of their racial character. Christianity had regarded the Jews as a people cursed by God, and racial anti-Semitism gave expression to this belief, which the tradition of many centuries had long since made part of the instinctual life of the people, on the scientific basis that was appropriate for the nineteenth and twentieth centuries. The inferiority of the race—that was God's curse which now became absolutely permanent. The *Judaeus perversus* of Christian doctrine became the perverse racial type in the modern caricatures of Jews.

In this racial kind of modern caricature the Jewish type as created by Christian dogmatism and developed further under the influence of changing circumstances and doctrines was given perfect expression. Medieval caricature knew no physical Jewish type as yet; it placed the mark of Cain inside, on the character and the action of the Jews. When pictorial representations gave outward features for the Jews, these were generally the Jewish hat and the Jewish beard. Only from the seventeenth century on was the crooked nose emphasized as a Jewish characteristic in isolated instances. This was done, on the one hand, under the influence of the increasingly realistic view or representation of the world, and on the other, probably with the transference of the caricature of the devil to the Jewish face, it was intended to emphasize the evil in the Jewish character. Starting with the end of the eighteenth and the beginning of the nineteenth century, but especially since the rise of anti-Semitism as an anti-Jewish racial movement, the Jewish nose became the most striking characteristic of the Jew in caricatures—a visible mark of Cain, as it were. The Jew was now no longer a vague idea, a dogmatic concept, a synonym for everything bad and reprehensible; he was now also physical reality, a fixed human type, racially determined, with definable characteristics and measurable physical properties, and able to be depicted in his gestures, his typical appearance, his facial features, and his bodily structure.

The Logical Conclusions

In this image of the Jew it was possible to include everything that past epochs as well as the present had established as Jewish characteristics and found disturbing about them. The motivation was the only one possible for a time of unbelief (or at least a shaken belief in God): it was a fact of nature. *This is what the Jews are like*—from the beginning or through a natural development over long periods of time that go beyond historical memory and antedate the beginning of recorded history. Their character is unalterable and seems all the more so the more natural science embraces the neo-Darwinian theory that acquired qualities are not inheritable. In the dispute about emancipation it was still possible to argue whether the Jews should be given equal rights in order to improve them or whether their "improvement" should be made the prerequisite for equal rights. The liberalistic-humanistic views of those who believed in the possibility of the Jews' improvement and their full integration into the surrounding world had prevailed over the skeptics.

On the basis of this assumption, equal rights for the Jews had been proclaimed in Western and Central Europe, though certainly not in Eastern Europe, where there were special situations. In the years and decades following the emancipation it was repeatedly asked whether the Jews had fulfilled this condition, whether they had sufficiently "improved" and adapted to their environment. If, however, the anti-Semitic racial doctrine was followed to its logical conclusion, these questions were meaningless. If all qualities were determined by nature, if the nature of this Jewish "race" was bad, corrupt, and harmful to all who came in contact with it, if racial characteristics were unalterable in all eternity and the qualities acquired through influence and education could not improve the racial character, what good was emancipation? This would mean only that a bad element was permanently admitted to one's own national body. Complete assimilation, baptism, mixed marriages—things that many Christian champions of emancipation considered and demanded as solutions of the Jewish question—could under the influence of the racial doctrine all too easily be interpreted as an exacerbation of the problem. This meant only that a pernicious element was infiltrated into the noble blood of the "Aryans" as a hereditary factor and that the pure "Nordic" race was threatened with decline and disintegration down to its core. If one unabashedly drew the full logical conclusion from these premises, there no longer was a place for the Jews among the nations. There was logically no way out but the removal of the Jews from the midst of the nations—by concentrating them in a territory of their own or, even better, by destroying them.

J. G. FICHTE

These two ways out were not infrequently hinted at in the literature that led to modern anti-Semitism and later in the anti-Semitic literature itself. Sometimes they were mentioned together, with the emphasis on one or the other; at other times only one was mentioned; and on still other occasions it was left up to the reader to consider the consequences.

The merciless destruction of the Jews or their expulsion to Palestine had, as we have seen, already been demanded by Luther, and many of his successors followed suit. In an anonymously published essay on the French Revolution (1793) the German philosopher Johann Gottlieb Fichte (1762–1814) referred to Judaism as a "powerful, hostile state that is engaged in constant warfare with all others." The reason this state was so "fearsome" was that it was "built upon hatred for the entire human race." Fichte said that he did not personally hate the Jews and that as human beings they ought to be granted all human rights even though they denied these rights to others. It was different with their rights as citizens: "But I see only one way to give them civil rights: to cut off all their heads in one night and put others on them in which there is not a single Jewish idea. To protect ourselves against them I see no other way but to conquer their Promised Land for them and send them all there."

VON HUNDT-RADOWSKY

The extermination of the Jews or at least their expulsion was demanded by the demagogue Hartwig Hundt (von Hundt-Radowsky) at the time of the Teutomaniacs' hatred of the Jews and the Hepp-Hepp movement. "Even though I personally," he wrote, "regard the killing of a Jew as neither a sin nor a crime but merely as a drastic police action, I shall never counsel . . . their condemnation or punishment without a hearing." He proposed that the Jews be sold to the English, who could use them on their Indian plantations in place of the blacks. To keep them from multiplying, the men should be emasculated and their wives and daughters placed in houses of ill repute. It would be best, however, to "cleanse the country completely of this vermin," and this could be accomplished either by "exterminating all of them or, as the Pharaoh and the people of Meiningen, Würzburg, or Frankfurt have done, drive them from the country."

If such statements and demands made by a Hundt-Radowsky in the early nineteenth century could be dismissed as the words of an irresponsible rabble-rouser, they had to be taken much more seriously when, beginning with the late 1870s, they appeared, in one form or another, in the writings of highly educated personalities—university professors, philosophers, Orientalists, economists, and historians. We have already discussed the fundamental importance of the philosopher and economist Eugen Dühring for the formulation of the anti-Semitic racial doctrine. His conclusions also anticipated in more or less clear words all subsequent excrescences. As early as 1881 he counted on the "powerful awakening of healthy popular instincts" that would have a decisive effect on the Jewish question: "Once the people's energies have been properly emancipated in their national consciousness, it will be impossible for them and the Jews to stay together on the same soil. *Where* the Jews will go is their own problem."

LAGARDE

Paul de Lagarde (1827–91), the famous Orientalist and cultural philosopher, was less narrow-minded and rigid in his view of the racial doctrine and its application to the Jewish question, but he was sometimes even more racial in his conclusions. He regarded himself as a prophet, and in the 1870s and 1880s he concerned himself repeatedly and ever more passionately with the Jewish question.

His demands were at first not as one-sided as those of Eugene Dühring. Lagarde demanded the complete absorption of the Jews by the nations or their transplantation to Palestine, but he had serious doubts about both possibilities. "The most thorough way to cure the Jews of Judaism," he said in a lecture of 1853, "is to force them to be for once nothing but Jews. This will make them scared of themselves, and this scare as well as the need to work hard for a living will cause them to transcend themselves." In his *Deutsche Schriften* his criticism of the Jews' conduct in economic and cultural life became more and more severe. In the end he saw in the Jews as "aliens nothing but carriers of putrefaction" that ought to be eliminated from the body of the European nations. In his work *Juden und Indogermanen* (1887) he condemned the "atavism" of the Jews, their racial arrogance, their close national cohesiveness, their international solidarity in dealing with other nations, and especially their usury. In this work we find such formulations as the following: "It takes a heart as hard as crocodile skin not to feel pity for the poor, fleeced Germans and—which is the same thing—not to hate the Jews, not to hate and despise those who—out of humaneness!— speak up for those Jews or are too cowardly to crush this proliferous vermin. One does not negotiate with trichinae and bacilli; trichinae and bacilli are not educated either; they are destroyed as quickly and completely as possible" (p. 339). In the same work Lagarde says: "Where such a mass of putrefaction has accumulated as in the Israel of Europe, internal medicaments can be effective only after surgery has removed the pus that has built up" (p. 347). As his subsequent statements indicate, Lagarde meant that the Jews ought to be deprived of the money on which their power was based. But what if his images of putrescence and canker, bacilli, trichinae, vermin, and the other favorite images of the Jews as parasites and pestilence were taken seriously? What if the decline of liberalism also discredited the humanism which Lagarde and a number of his contemporaries mentioned in disparaging terms? What if the general cultural climate changed and "nature" and "matter" rose God-like to direct world history? What if in the further development of this process humane, religious, philosophical, or moral inhibitions were eliminated? Could the images and valuations taken from biology not then become naturelike reality, turning the words into scourges and the demands into commandments and orders that were carried out with mathematical logic and straightforwardness?

THE TREITSCHKE POLEMIC

In the 1880s things had not reached such a point, and as Dühring himself noted at the time, such radical consequences were rejected and the sheer crudeness of demagogic Jew-baiters was condemned. However, in more refined form those ideas entered literature and art and were discussed in essays, pamphlets, and books by persons of the highest standing. They were made fit for polite society by removing their radical sting. A comprehensive historical study like Heinrich Treitschke's *Deutsche Geschichte im 19. Jahrhundert* (German history of the nineteenth century, 5 vols., 1879–94), a work widely disseminated and read with (generally deserved) admiration, probably contributed more to the spread of anti-Jewish tendencies than the radical anti-Semitic literature, and in this way it helped the more radical teachings to fall on fertile soil. It was similar with Treitschke's polemical works on the Jewish question that were written in a formally moderate tone. If a Treitschke, at that time one of the most respected professors at the University of Berlin and perhaps its best orator and journalist, at the beginning of the modern anti-Semitic movement published *Ein Wort über unser Judentum* (A word about our Jewry) as an essay in 1879 and in pamphlet form in January 1880, talking about a "group of ambitious young pants salesmen" who streamed year after year from the inexhaustible Polish cradle across the eastern German border and "whose children and grandchildren are to dominate Germany's stock-exchanges and newspapers some day" (p. 2), this made even educated people sit up and take notice. And they did so even more when he hailed the anti-Semitic movement, while rejecting its radical demands, with the following words: "If one surveys all these conditions . . . the loud agitation of the movement appears only as a brutal and hateful but natural reaction of the Germanic popular feeling against an alien element that has taken up too much room in our life. . . . Let us not deceive ourselves: the movement is very deep and strong; it will take more than some jokes about the wise remarks of Christian Social stump speakers to vanquish it. Up to the sphere of the highest culture, among men who would reject with repugnance any thought of ecclesiastical intolerance or nationalistic arrogance, these words are spoken as if in chorus nowadays: 'The Jews are our misfortune'" (p. 4).

In December of 1880, when the polemic concerning Treitschke's work was gradually subsiding,* Theodore Mommsen rightly stated in a polemical pamphlet entitled *Auch ein Wort über unser Judentum* (Another word about our Jewry) that what Treitschke himself had foreseen had come to pass: his words had been misunderstood.

> Surely they were well-meant; surely there is much truth behind the individual complaints made there; surely harsher complaints against the Jews have gone unheard a thousand times. But if the perception of the differences between this part of the German citizenry and the great majority had hitherto been kept in bounds by the strong sense of duty of the better part of the nation, which not only knew that equal duties also demanded equal rights but also acted on that basis, this perception has now seen itself proclaimed by Herr von Treitschke as the "natural reaction of the German people's national feeling against an alien element" and as "the outburst of a deep-seated, long pent-up anger." This was said by Herr von Treitschke, the man to whom the German nation in its recent great crises has been more indebted than to any of its other writers. . . . This made what *he* said respectable. Hence the tremendous effect of those articles which we have all witnessed. The bridle of shame has been removed from this "deep and strong movement," and now the breakers are surging and the foam is spurting.

Anti-Semitism as a Political Movement

As we have seen, with the development of the anti-Semitic theory anti-Semitism also appeared as an organized political movement—at first particularly in Germany. From there it soon spread to other states, to the area of the Austro-Hungarian monarchy with its increasingly critical nationality problems and struggles, to France, England, and the United States of America. In Eastern Europe the movement assumed special forms; this will be discussed later. The center of the movement, however, continued to be Germany with its long tradition of hatred of the Jews; with its open eastern border across which, to a steadily increasing degree, Jews entered the country, and particularly since the early 1880s, settling there or going on to the western countries; and with its never fully solved national problems, as well as its economic upheavals and social crises that followed its belated entry into world politics. The pioneer of anti-Semitism as a political movement (though at first not under the new name) was the Protestant court preacher and

*Its participants were primarily Jews, from the well-known historian Heinrich Graetz, whose *History of the Jews* (vol. 11, covering the period of emancipation up to 1848) had particularly aroused Treitschke's ire, to the philosopher Hermann Cohen. Cf. the notes on this polemic in the next chapter and in Part 2.

popular orator Adolf Stoecker (1835–1909). The interesting thing about this is that the idea of race was by no means the foundation of Stoecker's struggle; to him the Jewish question was primarily an economic and social problem. He fought the Jews as prototypes of liberalism and as social parasites. His "Christian Social" movement made an appeal to the declining class of craftsmen, and by combining Christian conservative and modern social sentiments it tried to take the wind out of the sails of the up-and-coming Social Democrats. In this the Jews were a symbol and a logical means of channeling the rage and the cupidity of the people into the desired direction. Stoecker's weapons were primarily his sermons that he delivered from the pulpit in the most popular style as well as in large, tumultuous public assemblies. Like the writings of Treitschke, they made anti-Semitism respectable. As a man of the people and popular orator Stoecker carried it as a popular movement to wide circles of the bourgeoisie, and as a court preacher he presented it to the Prussian court and government circles, even though these found themselves obliged to disapprove of his overabusive attacks on the Jews and capitalists (as on Bismarck's financial adviser, the Jewish banker Bleichröder).

The first anti-Jewish organization that was consciously created on the basis of racial anti-Semitism was Wilhelm Marr's "Anti-Semites' League." It first acquainted the general public with the term "anti-Semites." The *Antisemitenliga* named as its goals the combating of the Jewish spirit, the elimination of Jewish domination by raising the German national consciousness, the commercial and social isolation of the Jews, and their elimination from parliament and public life. In September 1882 the "First International Anti-Jewish Congress" met in Dresden at the initiative of Hungarian anti-Semites. At this Congress racial anti-Semitism prevailed as the majority view over Stoecker's Christian Social hatred of the Jews.

The Significance of Anti-Semitism as a Political Movement

The immediate political effect of this movement was insignificant at the time, and there is no point in detailing here the development of these anti-Semitic groups and organizations, their ups and downs, and their internal disputes and conflicts. We are interested only in fundamental matters affecting the development of the Jewish question. The decisively new thing was that the fight against the Jews and the hostility toward them for the first time constituted the substance of a political movement. If earlier the fight against the Jews and Judaism had played a part in religious, political, or social movements, it had—viewed objectively—always been a secondary role, even though the Jews may have viewed themselves as the main target of that hostility. Now parties and movements appeared with the sole, publicly declared aim of combating the Jews and Judaism. The movement quickly went beyond the national plane; Hungarian anti-Semitic leaders promptly proclaimed as their goal the founding of an anti-Semitic league of nations. These movements were at first still weak, but they do have an ominous historical significance as a symptom, a stimulus, and the germ cells if not the vanguard of mightier movements that were to be formed later with similar programs.

In the discussions of the period, in the vulgar disputes of the anti-Semitic party, and in the more civilized discussions of the intelligentsia one may note how the most varied motives and arguments blended in the justification of hatred of the Jews. After all, eras do not completely succeed each other; in a certain sense they always continue to coexist in the various strata of the population whose mode of thought and way of life also keep preserving the heritage of bygone epochs. Thus the earlier forms of hatred of the Jews continued to exist alongside the ever more widely accepted racial anti-Semitism: the Christian religious dogma with its anti-Jewish tendency and mysticism that had been part of a person's mental makeup from early childhood on; the pseudo-economic doctrine of the Jewish parasite who shirks work and feeds on the sweat and blood of his Christian fellow citizen—analogies and images that were all too apt to combine disastrously with the ideas of the Christian blood libel and the newer images of Jews as racially harmful persons and bacilli in the body of another people. Added to this was, of course, the struggle of people against economic competitors and the will to preserve their own economy, customs, and culture from what seemed like a threatening infiltration by alien elements. All arguments resound with the fear of being dominated, dominated by someone who yesterday was still suppressed, whose dominance harbors the humiliating elements of the upstart and the foreign conqueror—and perhaps also vengefulness toward the former hard master.

As its opponents always rightly remarked, the anti-Semitic movement was surely exploited by all sorts of interests. In this, however, it was not substantially different from other currents. Political parties, economic interests, demagogues, people feeling ill-used by fate, and many others utilize existing currents, conditions, and tendencies for their own purposes. One can virtually gauge the strength of a current by the extent to which it is employed for the furtherance of intersts, for advertising and propaganda. The fact that anti-Semitism could be so strikingly used for all sorts of purposes and interests is yet another indication of how deeply rooted in the people the sentiments underlying it were; Treitschke and other antagonists of the Jews had seen this quite correctly.

A political theory that is incapable of appealing to such deep layers in the popular consciousness is easy to shake; any intelligent argument can cause its foundations to waver. This is basically different with movements that are anchored in deeper strata of the folk psyche. Their organization may be temporarily shattered, their advocates may be convicted of intellectual dishonesty and their leaders of moral corruption, but all this will touch only the most superficial layers of people's consciousness. The roots embedded in deeper psychic strata will remain unaffected by rational arguments, and they will always produce fresh growths—a cultivated plant or proliferous weeds, depending on the circumstances and the care.

As far as the Jewish question was concerned, the peoples were so full of fears, prejudices, religious notions, historical memories, and mythical images, and the multifarious experiences of real life were so closely bound up with these psychic contents or could so easily be connected with them that no objective argument could seriously shake anti-Semitism. If one pillar fell, enough were always left standing to support the beams. Only in this way can the flourishing of anti-Semitism in the last quarter of the nineteenth century and its spread throughout the world be understood—despite the absurdities of its arguments, the personal and intellectual conflicts among its often questionable leaders, and the most contradictory conclusions that its adherents drew from it.

Conclusions and Demands

The demands made of the Jews and the surrounding world as a consequence of the analysis of the Jewish question were antithetical in nature, and not only because of the variety of the arguments. Often the same accusations produced contradictory conclusions and demands. The most radical racial anti-Semites (though by no means all), for the time being still a small though very vocal minority, were already demanding the most extreme solution: the consistent elimination of the Jews as troublesome foreign bodies from the organism of the nations—through rescission of the emancipation, expulsion, and perhaps even worse things that for the time being were hinted at rather than specified (see pp. 238f. and 246f. above). By contrast, the most general demand was the complete intermingling of the Jews with the nations, the self-abandonment of the Jews as Jews, their complete integration into the surrounding world until every special characteristic disappeared. On this demand, which seemed as logical as it was radical, the adversaries of the Jews not infrequently agreed with their defenders. Even such an indisputable defender of the Jews as Theodor Mommsen could bring himself to advise the Jews at the end of his polemical pamphlet, using words somewhat similar to those of his adversary Treitschke, to draw the logical conclusion from their equal rights and unite without reservation with the people in whose midst they lived. He said that the Jews themselves were partly to blame for the fact that they were foreign bodies within the people and were treated accordingly by the majority. "The word 'Christianity' no longer fully means what it once meant; but it is still the only word that sums up the character of today's international civilization and that makes millions upon millions feel they are standing together on this very populous globe. To remain outside these borders and yet within a nation is possible but difficult and dangerous. Anyone whom his conscience, be it positive or negative, forbids to renounce Judaism and to embrace Christianity will act accordingly and bear the consequences. . . . but it is a well-known fact that a great number of people are being kept from converting not by scruples but only by quite different feelings that I can understand but not approve of. . . . Entry into a great nation has its price."

Conversion to Christianity was here urged as a way to enter the European cultural realm, which is what had been demanded again and again since the beginning of the emancipation movement. At the same time, however, the ever-latent Christian anti-Jewish traditions were deliberately revived and activated by the leaders of the Christian religious and political movements. After all, this was the period of the struggle between the recently unified Italian kingdom and the Papal States, of the dispute about the infallibility dogma of the Pope (1870), and of Bismarck's *Kulturkampf* against the power of the Catholic Church. In connection with this Pope Pius IX sharply attacked Jewish liberalism and journalism in the early 1870s. In Germany, France, Austria, and other countries the traditional Christian ideas combined with modern social ones to produce anti-Jewish ideologies and movements. As we have already mentioned, beginning in 1879 Adolf Stoecker acted as leader and representative of such a Christian Social movement, and so did Karl Lueger, who was in 1895 elected Mayor of Vienna, though the initial opposition of the government meant that he could not assume office until two years later. In this atmosphere it was possible to revive the accusation of ritual murder which had been thought to have been laid to rest forever after the dismissal of the charges of Damascus (1840; see p. 228 above). In 1882 a ritual murder trial was held in Tisza Eszlár (Hungary), and the same charge was made in 1891 at Xanten (Rhineland), in 1899 at Polna (Bohemia, the Hilsner affair), in 1891 at Corfu (Greece), in 1900 at Konitz (Western Prussia) and Vilna (Poland), and between 1911 and 1913 at Kiev (the Ukraine, the Beilis trial). Scholarly authorities testified about the question whether the Jews (who are forbidden by the Bible to consume even animal blood) had been commanded to use Christian blood for their religious sacrifices. The books and pamphlets of anti-Jewish "experts" revived such classic anti-Jewish writings as Eisenmenger's. The refutations of true experts, both Christians and Jews, carried weight in court but not with popular opinion. Despite all evidence to the contrary, inflammatory pamphlets like Rohling's *Der Talmudjude* continued to be widely disseminated and believed. Where the new anti-Semitic movement could lead was shown by events in Russia, though these were rudimentary by comparison with what happened in our time.

The Russian Pogroms

We have already briefly discussed the origin of the Jewish question in Russia (see p. 207 above). The problem differed from that of the western countries in various respects. Russia was a more backward country, and the ideas of equality, freedom of movement, and personal independence of the eighteenth and nineteenth centuries were very slow in coming to this large country that was autocratically ruled and was just freeing itself from economic feudalism. Owing to historical circumstances and policies of the government, the Jews were concentrated in definite parts of Russia, the western and southern provinces. Half of the Jewish population of the world—more than five million in 1897—lived in Russia, crowded together in the few districts of the so-called Pale, while the other parts of the Russian Empire, whose large undeveloped territories would have offered sufficient room, were absolutely closed to the Jews. In the Jewish Pale, an area that became ever more crowded with the steady natural increase in the population, large numbers of Jews lived under the most wretched conditions. Since the catastrophes of the seventeenth century, which we have already discussed, the economic situation of the Polish Jews had steadily worsened, and in that condition they had become Russian subjects through the partition of Poland toward the end of the eighteenth century. Barred from many occupations and forcibly concentrated in the cities, many eked out a living as small craftsmen or by engaging in petty trading, always worried about feeding their large families. In a speech at the Fourth Zionist Congress (1900) Max Nordau coined the bitter word *Luftmenschen* (people who live on air) for them. There was, however, another side to this life in close quarters: United by their own language, Yiddish, these people clung more tenaciously to the tradition-bound life whose forms and substance remained familiar to them from generation to generation and which gave them a feeling of security in their materially difficult life. Thus they offered more determined resistance to the European and Jewish "Englightenment," the disintegrative tendencies that had so severely shaken the existence of the Jewish people in the West. The ideas and forms of earlier epochs lived on in them and could be conveyed by them to the Jews of western countries in the constant westward migratory movement that became a veritable flood in the 1870s, and especially in the 1880s.

Naturally, this situation impeded the integration of the Jews into the population of the Russian Empire, though the government and the ruling classes did not seriously pursue that. Even in the countries of Western and Central Europe, where the Jews were only a small minority, the acceptance of the Jews as economic and legal equals caused resistance and strife, but the problem in Russia was far more difficult to solve. The question that had repeatedly occupied the western states in the struggle for emancipation—whether the Jews should be given equal rights immediately in order to effect their "improvement" or whether they should first be trained to be good citizens before they were freed from their disadvantaged special status—would have been still harder to decide for a responsible Russian statesman even if the general economic and political conditions and the influence of the Christian churches— particularly the predominant Greek-Orthodox one—had not from the outset prevented a radical solution in the Jews' favor. In any case, beginning with the middle of the nineteenth century it was attempted to induce the Jews to assimilate to the language and culture of their surroundings by gradually releasing privileged, educated groups from the ghettos of the Pale and granting them permanent residence in the entire area of the state. At first, from 1859 on, this privilege was extended to the wealthiest Jews—wholesale dealers, bankers, especially industrialists; then, from the 1870s, to trained craftsmen, army veterans, all persons with a university education, and all medical personnel. It was hoped that those less entitled would try to emulate the more highly placed persons and would gradually prove worthy of similar concessions by acquiring a secular education and giving up their own religious and national tradition.

This policy had mixed consequences. The masses greeted the attempt at Russianization with that resistance which any mass by its nature offers to change; after all, the law of gravity and inertia rules communal life as well. Added to this was the well-founded worry that education in the general state schools might alienate the pupils from their own religion and bring them into the Christian fold. The resistance of the Jewish masses was bound to intensify the government's reservations about equality for the Jews and their admittance to other areas of settlement. The "obduracy" of the Jews did not seem to justify more liberal measures. On the other hand, many members of the upper classes of Russian Jewry and also some young people reacted to the lure of the wider world opening up to them with hardly less zeal than the western Jews, who were in this respect two generations ahead of them. The privileged circles of Russian Jewry, too, made assimilation to their environment and the abandonment of their own peoplehood and special life-style part of their program. The more advanced among them already began to feel completely as Russians; they spoke and wrote Russian and fought for the complete emancipation that would enable them to become absorbed by

Russian culture. Instead of this emancipation, however, these progressive elements emancipating themselves from Judaism encountered resistance on the part of the Christian groups—merchants and professional people—whom they were confronting as unwanted competitors and from the governing circles, who regarded the Jews as undesirable intruders.

A variety of factors then combined to produce anti-Jewish outbursts of popular rage, with a brutality that had hitherto not been thought possible: the traditional Christian hatred of the Jews among the masses; competition among the upper classes; the resistance of the people against financial dependence on and exploitation by Jewish leaseholders, retail dealers, and saloonkeepers; the visible increase in wealth in the hands of some Jewish bankers and wholesalers, something that socialistic and anarchistic currents found it all too easy to exploit demagogically; the struggle against the Jews as rebels when in their disappointment at conditions they joined revolutionary movements—a struggle that was encouraged by the government; and in time also the influence of the new anti-Semitic racial doctrine imported from the West.

In May 1881 there began in southern Russia the bloody persecutions of the Jews that have since been designated by the Russian word *pogrom* (hitherto unknown, at least in the West). Twenty years later these were continued in intensified form in the pogroms of Kishinev and Homel (1903), as well as the October pogroms after the failure of the Russian revolution of 1905, and they finally came to a climax in the Ukrainian pogroms of 1917 to 1920. Hundreds, thousands, and finally hundreds of thousands of Jews were brutally murdered; many others were beaten, raped, and robbed of their homes and property. Henceforth the survivors, both those who had been directly affected and those who had been spared, lived under the constant threat of further violence.

Since that time we have learned that these pogroms, which appeared to the Jews of Russia and to the civilized liberal western world in general as surprising and incomprehensible events that were conceivable only in the uncivilized Czarist empire, were almost idyllic by comparison with what happened in the center of Europe in our days. Measured by what happened later, they were like rehearsals for a great drama. In 1910 Leo Motzkin, as their historian the greatest authority on them, characterized the first pogroms as follows:

> The shape of the first pogroms also contained the germs of the more sophisticated ones of recent years. A pogrom starts with a relatively insignificant group of people but it usually snowballs, and the process of destruction is performed in a definite order: Shop by shop, flat by flat, street after street— and so it goes on and on. Windowpanes rattle, ordinary objects or heavy pieces of furniture are ripped apart and smashed, but anything of value is

pocketed, put on, wrapped around, taken home. The work becomes more and more jolly and free. What was yesterday regarded as theft is today a vested right. . . . In those days there were sinister forces that used to work in the background to make sure that the process was carried out normally. But once the pogrom had been skillfully started, it went like clockwork. The Jew-baiting went on for hours and even days, filling the air with the wild shouts of the active troublemakers, the cheering and howling of the crowd, the cries of the terrified Jews, and the moaning of those who have been beaten, mocked, and raped. The street is covered with more and more junk and debris; clumsy hands that cannot find anything better grab these, too, but more respectable and circumspect persons are there with carts and snatch up what they need. Inside, however, in some cellar, in an attic or some other hiding place, sit the owners of what is being smashed or stolen and keep waiting for the moment when their possessions will have been destroyed and the danger to their lives may have passed. If worst comes to worst, their ordeal lasts for days, but for them it transcends time and extends reality by centuries facing backward and centuries facing forward. . . . But even a Jewish pogrom comes to an end, be it because the Jew-baiters have had enough or because the so-called government has intervened. Then the persecuted Jews climb out of their holes, and, feeling absolutely powerless, they realize only now the full misery that human hands have created for them.*

Similar and increasingly gruesome descriptions of the later pogroms exist. There is hardly a Jewish poet or writer from the East in whose works they have not been given expression in one form or another. They were a fundamental experience of two generations.

---

*Leo Motzkin, "Prototyp des Pogroms in den achtziger Jahren," in *Die Judenpogrome in Russland* [Cologne and Leipzig, 1910], vol. 1, pp. 18–20.

7

The Reaction of the Jews to the Renewed Jew-Baiting and Anti-Semitism

For the Jews striving for emancipation—and even more for those already emancipated—the recrudescence of hatred of the Jews, as reflected in the press and in literature, in excesses and administrative measures, finally condensing into the ideology and political organization of "anti-Semitism", was a surprise and a bitter disappointment. This movement, the extent and emotional vehemence of which remained incomprehensible to most of them, forced them to make new decisions and confronted them with problems whose meaning and magnitude became apparent only after a long period of confusion. Their reaction to the new hostility varied according to the degree of their emancipation and their social stratum, the firmness of the tradition that bound them to their ancestors, the honesty and straightforwardness with which they viewed their situation, and the courage with which they dared to accept the consequences.

The Entry of the Jews into the Economic and Cultural Life of the Nations

In order to arrive at a proper assessment of the problems confronting the Jews, we must once more visualize the situation in which the emancipation movement placed the Jews. Before they entered the political, social, and cultural life of the surrounding world the Jews had despite their spatial dispersion been kept together in various respects by their way of life. As far as their faith and their *Weltanschauung* were concerned, they had been bound together by their religious precepts with their exact determination of what was forbidden, allowed, and commanded. It had had a unifying effect on their life-style and their way of reacting. Beyond that, their religious tradition had given them a common historical consciousness. True, in religious practices and in the liturgy of the synagogue this tradition had to a certain extent taken cognizance of local peculiarities and the special historical destinies of countries and communities—perhaps through special prayers and songs

261

or through locally dictated customs and living habits. Basically, however, the emphasis was on what was common to all and typical of Jewish fate in all countries. Thus the past and the future had been linked to the present in trusting harmony despite all daily cares and hardships.

To be sure, great economic and social contrasts had existed within Jewry, but viewed as a totality vis-à-vis the other nations, the Jews also constituted an economic and social stratum whose function in the life of the nations was more or less clearly defined. They were regarded as an entity by the nations and viewed themselves as one; even the small group of Court Jews with their multifarious special privileges was really part of that picture. Added to this was communal life in the close quarters of the ghetto or in ghettolike districts, a life that despite all its hardships had the inestimable advantage of giving the Jews a home, a homelike environment with age-old customs and practices hallowed by tradition as well as a common language. This language—which they called *Taitsch, Juden-Deutsch, Unsere Sprache*, and not until much later, especially in Eastern Europe, *Jiddisch*—might be regarded as a jargon by outsiders, an impure, seemingly ludicrous, and often derided mixture of the German vernacular and Hebrew. For the Ashkenazic Jews, however, this language had, up to the time of the Enlightenment and the nineteenth century (in rural regions even longer), the autonomy, familiarity, and intimacy of a national language of their own, even in Germany and the adjoining regions (and not only, as later, in the eastern European countries and the countries to which they emigrated).

This common possession fell apart with emancipation. In nineteenth-century Europe, which was becoming more secular and which the Jews entered or into which they were pushed, the influence of religion and religious laws on Jewish life, a force that had once bound all Jews together, steadily diminished. All sorts of religious gradations, from agnosticism to strict Orthodoxy, resulted. Unity was replaced by the struggle of individuals with themselves and others for new substances, forms of faith, and religious activities that would be more in tune with the changed living conditions.

As far as their occupations and their social status were concerned, the Jews tried very hard to break out of the narrow confines that had been set in the Middle Ages by Christian dogma and economic development. When they left the ghetto and entered the life of the surrounding world, it was only natural for them to try in many instances to transcend the earlier framework of commercial or social life and to choose those occupations that were most suited to their talents and abilities, seemed to be socially more respected, and thus meant a social advancement for them. Hence they no longer confined themselves to the retail or even the wholesale trade, nor to banking and related occupations in which they had been increasingly active since the eighteenth century, though their influence did rise tremendously even in these branches of the economy. The Jews entered all areas of the intellectual and cultural life of the nations, pursuing all occupations that did not remain closed to them by law or administrative practice. They did so with a vehemence that can only be explained by the release of long-pent-up energies and that almost frightened the surrounding world. The Jews' participation in agricultural labor and in industrial primary production was and remained insignificant. This was particularly true of heavy industry, which had originated from craftsmanship, and there the Jews' slight inclination combined with strong opposition from those occupations. In industries that grew out of commerce (especially the clothing industry) or were based on new inventions (e.g., electrical industry, railroad construction), the Jews often occupied leading positions.* In political life, the positions of greatest power and prestige were closed to them in most countries until recent times, for large groups opposed the idea of Jews filling positions that involved substantial power and decision-making authority. Here the Christian view of the God-ordained bondage of the Jews operated consciously or unconsciously. Hence the Jews entered the professions that gave greater latitude to individual activity. They became lawyers (though only seldom judges); parliamentarians (but only seldom high officials); physicians, often highly respected ones with a large private practice or with leading positions in hospitals; and researchers in all areas of the natural sciences and the humanities, often first-rate scholars, though their accpetance by the universities was a far cry from the legally mandated equality. The Jews' influence on the cultural life of the nations was often characterized more by breadth than by depth. This influence was exerted through literature and especially through the press, for the development, organization, and revitalization of which they displayed particular ability.** In these and other ways they freed themselves from the spell of their own tradition and entered the cultural life of the Christian people. They had been repeatedly told that a condition for their legal equality before the law was their wholehearted participation in the life of the nation and their identification with its cultural values, traditions, and goals for the future. Among the Jews cultural conditions had reached such a low point by the beginning of the eighteenth century that the cultural life of the surrounding world was bound to appear as an ideal worth striving for. In general, people assimilate to what is deemed to be of higher value. Thus the demands of the nations and the endeavors of a large part of the Jewish population

*See chap. 5 (pp. 208ff.) and the note in Part 2.
**Cf. the notes and excursuses in Part 2.

coincided in an effort to denationalize the Jews as Jews and to amalgamate them with the national and cultural way of life and thought of the nations.

Completed Dispersion: The Denationalization of the Jews

This had profound consequences for the Jews; only now was their dispersion complete, and not only in space. As the Jews left the ghetto as well as their common religious-cultural tradition and obligations, there began a new kind of dispersion. The Jews in the various countries declared that they were members of the nations in whose midst they lived; they identified with the cultural life of these nations and their national aspirations for the future, and they even attempted to identify with their historical consciousness, although it was based on different premises of origin, destiny, and religious and national traditions. In the wars of the nations the Jews served as soldiers in opposing armies. At earlier times individual Jews had supported the fighting parties of various camps as advisers, financiers, or purveyors, but never before had the Jews of various countries fought against other Jews for the sake of those nations. Never before had they had such close ties to the lands in which they lived as to make them forget the unity of Judaism—the unity of religious and national consciousness as well as the community of interest of a persecuted people. Now this sense of community faded, at least among the upper classes of central and western European Jewry. Deep abysses opened up: The Jews in the central and western European countries and those in Eastern Europe were divided by the degree of their emancipation, and they looked upon one another with suspicion, but they agreed that the Jews of the Oriental areas were culturally backward and hardly equal partners.

In this way a Jewry united in its basic concepts and ultimate goals gave way to many Jewries who declared that they were nationally and culturally members of all sorts of nations. The Jews who were emancipated or aspiring to emancipation no longer wanted to be Jews living in certain countries by destiny or by accident; they wanted to be Frenchmen, Englishmen, Germans, and Hungarians and perceive their Jewishness merely as a fact or characteristic that concerned only their private life and no one else. They no longer were Jews living in France (or some other country) and hardly French Jews any more; they preferred to call themselves Jewish Frenchmen or, even better, Israelite Frenchmen or Frenchmen of the Mosaic faith. Even this distinction, if expressed in public, was regarded as a curtailment of emancipation and almost a personal insult, for it lifted the Jews out of the entity of the other citizens as a special group.

This endeavor not to remain singled out is only partly explained by a desire for economic advancement and access to, or progress in, certain occupations. Especially among the best Jews we discern a more deeply rooted aspiration and a higher goal: They really wanted to denationalize themselves as Jews to the very limit set by loyalty and faith (to individually varying degrees) and unite fully with the nations whose cultural life they had entered. The Jews desired a *homeland* with all their heart, and they hoped and wished and believed that through emancipation they had found that homeland, or would soon find it, in their countries of domicile. The new, free, expansive homeland among the nations was to take the place of the homelike feeling that had developed through the communal life of the ghetto and of the hope for a return to the old homeland Palestine.

The Jews' Adoption of Other Nations' Standards of Value

The opposition of the surrounding world to full acceptance into their society, the hostility and the excesses, and finally the rejection and enmity that were organized as a political movement caught precisely this leading stratum within Jewry by surprise and confronted these leaders with a difficult situation. Had they abandoned their tradition and history, given up their memories and hopes, repressed the consciousness of their national unity, and attempted to integrate themselves fully into the national life of their adoptive countries only to be uprooted, rebuffed, and declared to be aliens? Had they acquired the languages of their new homelands, attended their schools and universities, absorbed their culture, and given up their own language only to be reproached with having no share in the national culture that they had so lovingly embraced? And those who had, along with schooling and education, adopted the values of their surroundings were especially stung by every attack on their honor, their conduct, and their entire nature.

After all, the decisive transformation that had taken place in the leading class of Jewry under the influence of the Enlightenment and the emancipation movement manifested itself in their ceasing to derive their standards from their own national tradition and historical experiences and instead acknowledging those of the surrounding world as their own. This adoption of alien standards of value should not be thought of as something superficial, as a simple act of will on the part of the Jews or even as a deliberate change of heart. With the entry of the Jews into the life of the nations, with the voluntary or forcible attendance at the general schools, through daily life, evenings at the theater (the great educational institution of the nineteenth century), and conversations with non-Jewish fellow citizens the Jews adopted the values of their surroundings rather unconsciously, actually without being aware of it. In the eyes of the law, they were, after all, Germans, Frenchmen, and so on, and as Germans and Frenchmen by law and education they learned to view the world with non-Jewish eyes. More than that: they increasingly viewed even themselves with the eyes and standards of the surrounding world. No wonder, then, that they often did not come off well in their own eyes and that feelings of their own "inferiority" were aroused and constantly confirmed in them.

No human being can live without contact with his environment; he lives within its customs, and in the long run he can develop a positive self-image only if he feels recognized by his surroundings. A person in constant conflict with his environment cannot lead a spiritually and intellectually healthy life.* That is why it is a normal procedure for a person to adapt to his surroundings in many ways. Such an adaptation brings about a harmonious adjustment between a person and his surroundings, between an individual and the community, provided that there are enough preconditions for this.

This is one of the main reasons why people belonging to the same group settle and act jointly. Communal feeling has many components: community of background, destiny, historical memory, life-style and life-goals, community of language, faith, and mode of expression down to gestures—which means that communal feeling contains many elements of the unconscious that make possible communication without special explanations. Where everything needs to be explained to be understood, life is deprived of its naturalness and the self-evident and comfortable are replaced by constant inner compulsion. One's mind has to remain too active; there can be no well-being, and the natural joy of creation cannot develop.

This is precisely what characterized the situation of the Jews from the early nineteenth century on. They believed they were entering a world that would welcome them and unite with them harmoniously, but in reality they faced a world that looked at them critically and treated them with extreme mistrust.

The Inner Insecurity of the Jews and Its Consequences

As the Jews learned to view themselves with the eyes of the world around them, in whose scale of values they usually did not rank high, they became insecure, to say the least. Nothing in their self-created life

---

*The exceptional cases of brilliant artists are no counterargument, for there we are dealing with personalities whose conflict can, if they possess sufficient inner strength, be transmuted into productive energy through the safety-valve of artistic creation. But how seldom even they are completely successful! Jakob Wassermann's book *Mein Weg als Deutscher und Jude* (1921; *My Way as German and Jew*, 1928) is the confession of a German-Jewish writer about this conflict.

and activity seemed to them intrinsically justified any longer, nothing seemed self-evident by virtue of their own rights and tradition.

This inner insecurity had various consequences. For one thing, it did not make the Jews any more likable in the eyes of the surrounding world; if anything, they became even stranger and almost more suspect. Surely the Jew must have something to hide if he acts so insecure and strange! But if this insecurity and a feeling of inner dependence made a Jew submissive and all too compliant, if he tried to adapt to the customs of the surrounding world all too eagerly, he aroused contempt and revulsion for that very reason: The Jew is a slave by nature after all, and our fathers were right in treating him as one. Give the slave a kick and make sure that the man who seems so humble doesn't attack you from behind! But if a Jew became presumptuous as he tried to conceal his weakness and insecurity, and also out of a feeling of superiority fed by instinct and an old tradition, a feeling that he often did not understand himself, this was simply the Jewish insolence (*chutzpa*), the ingratitude of the "guest" to his "host nation,"* and even worse. People do not examine the reason for phenomena or explore their roots; they accept them and interpret them in line with their emotional world, their experiences and those of their forefathers. A person does not stop to think that his own behavior or that of his fathers might have evoked these phenomena or at least contributed to them. Even if more thoughtful persons occasionally become aware of such a connection, this insight has only very little effect on the spontaneous emotional reactions of the people. Thus the unfriendly attitude of the surrounding world produced a chain of intensifying effects and countereffects, of reactions and counterreactions.

The Baptism of Jews

The Jews' inner dependence on the surrounding world produced various attitudes and tendencies on their part. The logical consequence for many Jews was Christian baptism. At all times there have been conversions by individual Jews to the dominant religion, including forcible mass conversions. Now the baptism of Jews became a volunatry mass phenomenon, or at least it appeared that way. There were many different reasons for converting to Christianity. For some it was a way out of despair over the *condition juive* that did not seem to offer them enough religiously, nationally, or socially to make it worth their while to accept the adversities associated with loyalty. For others baptism was the price they paid not to be excluded from the cultural community of the nations. It was, as it were, the "ticket of admission to European culture," to quote Heinrich Heine, who despite his baptism never severed his

*Concerning the concept "host nation", see p. 142 above and the references in the index.

inner connection with Judaism and unabashedly uttered what many others were thinking, feeling, and suspecting but did not dare to express or even to admit to themselves, and hence frequently rejected Heine's utterance as "shameless."*

As we have seen, this conversion to Christianity as the cultural foundation of the European past and present was demanded precisely by many who were favorably disposed toward the Jews, from Lavater to Mommsen, as a prerequisite for complete integration into the national or European cultural community. Frequently it became a virtual condition for appointment to higher government positions or teaching posts at universities as well as advancement in many other occupations, even artistic ones. Thus it is not surprising that many Jews availed themselves of the opportunity for economic, professional, and social advancement by taking a step that seemed to involve no inner obligation.

Often this opportunity meant even more. Closer contact with the surrounding world, the loosening of the old shackles, and the free entry into the highly developed world of European culture had awakened new artistic energies (or released pent-up ones) in the Jews for which there was no outlet within the Jewish realm. Was it surprising or reprehensible if Jewish artists took the route that was bound to seem the only practicable one to them and that often took them to the heights of artistic achievement? Think of composers and conductors like Felix Mendelssohn-Bartholdy, Gustav Mahler, or Bruno Walter, to name only a few of the great ones!

Many of the Jews who converted to Christianity did so with a heavy heart and then, in an effort to prove themselves not unworthy in their own eyes, tried to demonstrate that they had become Christians out of conviction. Others adopted the Christian faith together with the European Christian culture out of real conviction, or they came to it out of desperate longing for the religious satisfaction that the Jewish religious law, which was or seemed rigidified, did not give them. Out of such motives a man like Friedrich Julius Stahl (1802–61) became a theoretician of the Christian state and the leader of the Conservative Party in Prussia. Others, and perhaps the majority of the baptized Jews, took their conversion more lightly; having become indifferent to religion, they regarded their conversion as a mere formality and took the (quite often erroneous) view that the surrounding world also regarded it as no more than that. For them Judaism was, to quote Heine again, "not a religion but a misfortune." They pushed this misfortune away, or if they still had compunctions about converting, they had at least their children

*Concerning Heine and his attitude toward Judaism, see the excursus "Heinrich Heine, the Man Without Shame" in Part 2.

baptized in order to make it possible for them without pangs of conscience to have a easier life.

Jewish "Self-Hatred"

Still others, and often the most gifted and sensitive Jews, developed feelings of self-hatred as they viewed and evaluated themselves by the standards of a hostile environment. This Jewish self-hatred, which was not a completely new phenomenon but was far more widely disseminated after the emancipation, often assumed virtually pathological forms. It drove many beyond flight from Judaism and made them oppose everything Jewish, and it led a considerable number of people to end their own lives that seemed so worthless and ugly to them. These Jews, as it were, accepted the hatred of their surroundings as justified and transferred it to themselves with guilt feelings that they expiated by taking hostile action against the Jews or themselves.*

Nevertheless, only a minority of the Jews went so far as to sever their last connection with Judaism through conversion (or at least endeavored to do so). Often this was only a step taken in consequence of natural relationships with the surrounding world. Mixed marriages between Jews and Christians may not always have removed the Jewish partner from the fold, but in most cases the children were estranged from Judaism.** That there were an ever-increasing number of mixed marriages was a natural process and a normal consequence of the closer contract with the environment and the weakening of the Jewish tradition and religious ties. Beyond that, however, mixed marriage was propagated as a desirable goal by the consistent champions of the Jews' complete absorption by their environment. Gabriel Riesser, the outstanding Jewish fighter for equal rights in Germany, expressly demanded this in his famous address before the Frankfurt National Assembly on 29 August 1848.*** The complete assimilation of the Jews to the surrounding world, from clothing to thinking, was now the declared goal of the leading circles of Jewry, even if they did not desire to give up their Jewish religion. The more bitter the hostility became, the more vigorously did the Jews asseverate that they did not differ from non-Jews in anything but certain religious precepts and practices.

---

*See the excursus in Part 2.
**Only since the founding of the State of Israel has there been a change in this. In addition to the many who leave the Jewish fold with or without conversion to Christianity there are a considerable number of people who convert to Judaism. In cases where one parent retains the Christian faith, a Christian education for the children is no longer such a foregone conclusion.
***See the quotations in Part 2.

Emancipation—an Assimilation Contract?

Whether explicitly or implicitly, the Jews now adopted the strange theory of leading circles of their environment according to which the granting of equal rights constituted, as it were, a contract made between the Jews and the Christian peoples. "Our state never viewed the Jews as anything but a religious community," wrote Treitschke in his polemic with Graetz,* so to speak as a continuation of the debate about emancipation in the French National Assembly (see pp. 210 and 215ff. above), "and it granted them equal civil rights only in the expectation that they would strive to be like their fellow citizens. . . . If, however, Judaism demands that it be acknowledged as a nationality, the legal foundation on which emancipation rests will collapse. . . ." As we have noted,** the representatives of French Jewry had already declared at Napoleon's conference of notables that the Jews would henceforth not claim to be a separate people. Now the Jews were unable to understand why this demand was made again and again.

Assimilation as an Ideology and Conscious Endeavor

For decades the Jews had striven to assimilate to the nations in everything and to differ from them as little as possible. Never before in the history of the Jewish Diaspora had the leading circles tried as hard as the western Jews did in the nineteenth century not only to learn from the surroundings what was appropriate for them and what they needed for coexistence (which is entirely natural for human groups living together), but to be absorbed by the world around them, to think and evaluate like it and to adopt its ideals and even its hatreds. To them, assimilation was not only a practice and purposive action, but they also developed it into an ideology and raised it to the status of an ideal.*** Thus they were all the more hurt by the rejection of the surrounding world and by the hatred that lashed out at them. Before the emancipation the hatred of the nations had been accepted as normal, almost as something God-given. The Jews had their own values, and these were not affected by it. Now rejection, unfriendly criticism, discrimination, accusations, and hatred stung to the quick a generation of Jews who had become more sensitive and—at least unconsciously—were making the same valuations as their attackers. These Jews were hardest hit precisely when the struggle for equality before the law had already been decided. As long as it was a matter of fighting for equal rights there was a clear

*Cf. p. 252 above as well as the notes and excursuses in Part 2.
**See pp. 210f. above and the excursus in Part 2.
***Cf. pp. 211f. above and chap. 5.

goal and, as it were, an address to which the defenders and the complainants could turn. The attacks made now were much harder to deal with; there was no unmistakable direction, the front was everywhere, and these were feelings and currents that formed around the Jews and were hard to seize hold of. As Hannah Arendt put it, the Jews were "socially speaking, in the void." Berthold Auerbach, a writer widely read at the time to whose Germanness even a Jacob Grimm had attested, concluded in late 1880 that he had lived and worked in vain.

Efforts at Religious Reform: Judaism as a Creed

Assimilation to the surroundings and viewing one's own life with the eyes of one's environment were probably among the principal impetuses for religious reform movements within Judaism. There can be no doubt that much about the outward form of Jewish religious services was in need of improvement* and that the form of these services needed to be brought into line with a new aesthetic sense derived from the outside world. It was also understandable and legitimate that people impelled by an inner need and true faith sought a way to have a religious service without strict observance of all commandments and prohibitions that were hallowed by tradition but appeared to many as unimportant externals. These factors, however, were unduly obscured and colored by political tendencies. In this connection it was revealing that here and there the places in the liturgy that referred to "Zion" as the topical goal of Messianic longing began to be removed from the prayer books because they conflicted with the conviction that continued striving for a return to Palestine was incompatible with the granting of political rights of residence. The Messianic idea was reduced to a universally human idea of redemption, and "Zion" became its watered-down symbol. In line with this, religious reform was fatefully fused with a striving for political emancipation, and at the Frankfurt rabbinical assembly of 1845 the demand was made that the Hebrew language be abolished as the sole or leading liturgical language and that it be replaced with the vernacular, which was more comprehensible to all worshippers. Abraham Geiger, the learned leader of the Reform movement, motivated this proposal by saying that if the Hebrew language "were declared an essential element of Judaism," the latter would be presented as a national religion, "since a special language is the characteristic factor of a

*To outsiders the babel of voices of individuals saying prayers at their own speed in many synagogues (*Judenschulen*)—because God was addressed directly by each worshipper, though in an established liturgical order—seemed like uncultured disorder (and of course it was that, among other things). There was a popular saying about "noise like in a *Judenschul*."

separate national existence." But those Jews thought they should definitely deny that even after the emancipation the Jews were leading the life of a distinct people, and, if possible, keep them from doing so. It was their intention not to jeopardize the liberation from ghetto life that had been achieved. They also acted out of a feeling of honesty: People who had their home here did not seriously desire to return to Palestine, and so they should not pray for it.

In this view of their countries of domicile as their fatherland the Orthodox Jews of Western Europe did not basically differ from those who officially favored the Reform movement. Even Samson Raphael Hirsch's neo-Orthodoxy eliminated Palestine as the *real* land of Messianic longing, though his adherents did stick to the strict observance of all traditional precepts and practices, and it was replaced with a theological reinterpretation of the concept *Zion*. This was now viewed as an ideal realm and goal that no longer had any connection with reality and thus did not prevent people from regarding in real life their country of domicile as their homeland, with all the consequences for participation in the political and cultural life of this homeland. The spirit of assimilation and reform, even the aesthetic organization of the religious services—though here without the introduction of the organ, of which observers of the Jewish law still disapproved as a symbol of Christianity—also entered Orthodox Judaism. People wanted to integrate themselves and use any means to remove the curse of homelessness. Depending on their religious preference, people expressed this desire by no longer mentioning Zion or, when it was retained, making it a symbol for exalted human goals.* The return to Palestine seemed superfluous or such a distant goal that it no longer had anything to do with the work of man. Whether Jews kept simplifying religious practices and attached little importance to them or whether they preserved and practiced every commandment, prohibition, and the smallest custom with minute care, they thought they were not and did not wish to be anything but a religious community, a community of faith, a *Konfession* (creed or denomination, using a Christian term that is not properly applicable to Judaism). That is how even those Jews defined their connection with Judaism, and often with particular emphasis, who had actually long ago ceased to participate in any way in Jewish religious services and Jewish practices.**

---

*Fifty years later, in 1897, Herzl wrote these mocking words in his well-known essay "Protest Rabbis," part of his polemic with rabbis who were offering determined opposition to his national Jewish endeavors: "When they speak of Zion, it means everything but—God forbid!—Zion."
**I can give only a brief outline here. Concerning the attempts at reform and Samson Raphael Hirsch's views, see as supplement and motivation the excursuses in Part 2.

The Jews as Champions of Political Libertarian Movements

No human being can live without faith, and a Jew least of all. If religion no longer has the power to assuage the longing for faith, other ideals with quasi-religious pretensions take its place. Many Jews no longer found satisfaction in the Jewish realm, but out of a feeling of loyalty and piety they were loath to detach themselves from the Jewish community, too honest and upright to convert without conviction and only for the sake of profit to a Christianity that did not attract them any more than Judaism. For these Jews, and for many members of the Jewish intelligentsia who had entered political life or had been drawn into it, in the struggle for their own freedom the political libertarian movements—at first liberalism and then to an ever-increasing degree socialism—assumed a quasi-religious character. This is one reason why the Jews managed to gain leading positions in those movements so quickly. They entered them as believers, and their faith swept others along. In their demands they were usually more radical than the majority of the non-Jewish adherents. Their belief was often a kind of secularized Messianic faith, and their will to realization (this, too, in many ways a typically Jewish inheritance) was more unconditional and absolute. Among the native population, which had a closer connection with the land and the people in nature and history, even the most radical movement still had a national-conservative touch; its purpose was to change and improve actual conditions in the homeland. People generally knew that this could not be done overnight; they took the facts of life into account and had a more natural view of things. The Jews, whose recognized connection with the country was briefer and whose historical ties to it were weaker, saw the general, ideal goal more clearly; their eyes were less deflected by the conditions that had once existed, and their will propelled them straight to the goal. They were predestined to become the theoreticians of the movements. Often they were their most radical spokesmen, and in general they could be found more on the left wing than on the right. Their demands were more directly and unrestrainedly oriented toward the ideal. Their great historic achievement was that they propelled the movements forward and upheld the ideal in the face of reality. Politics, however, reckons with reality, compromises, and slow progress. Thus, after the first excitement is over, the leader who is firmly grounded in realities usually is more effective than the pure idealist, who forgets the reality of the present for the sake of the future. The love for what exists and is familiar wins out over the will to destroy what has developed and to replace it with something new and unknown.

Thus it came about that frequently even the most libertarian movements disassociated themselves from their Jewish leaders after a time. Often their members perceived the Jewish elements with their Messianic-radical coloration and their absoluteness as a falsification of their own volition. Added to this were feelings of aloofness, dislike, and distrust toward the Jews. These were adopted from tradition, even educated people never completely lost them, and they always came to the fore when trust had been shaken by some circumstances. Then suddenly anything a Jew might say sounded spurious, the pathos of a Jew seemed exaggerated and his mockery of existing conditions presumptuous and almost offensive. The fact that in his critique and in his aspirations a Jew often unconsciously proceeded from the injustices done him as a Jew by society and then projected them onto a universal plane was perceived as a flaw, whereas in others such motivations born of personal or social resentment were accepted as almost natural.

The opponents of the new currents went even further than that: As in earlier epochs, they combined the Satanic-mythical image of the Jew with his appearance as a deliberate destroyer of what existed. According to them, the Jew used these revolutionary movements to undermine the nations from within with his criticism, the corrosive acid of his mockery, and the dominating influence of the press, with which he poisoned the minds just as in the Middle Ages he had poisoned the wells. In the face of such accusations the fellow members of the party generally considered it prudent not to compromise themselves by giving the Jews too much visibility. Through this welter of action and interaction the purest projects were rendered suspect and the most honest endeavors often came to naught. No wonder that this turned many a believer among the Jews into a desperate nihilist, a seemingly carefree snob, or a power-hungry parvenue who sought to buy with money what was denied him for services of greater value.

The Supersensitivity of the Jews

This confusion was exacerbated by the supersensitivity with which the Jews reacted to any criticism of them, even in cases where this criticism was justified and definitely had no malicious intent. The constant attacks by their antagonists, and a highly developed sense of honor on the part of the Jews, which was oriented toward the standards of their surroundings, produced inner insecurity and feelings of inferiority in them. This in turn created a tension that made it very difficult for all parties to engage in an objective discussion or to test objective arguments that concerned the Jews without prejudice. The Jews were all too ready to suspect reproaches behind everything; they always felt attacked and forced into a defensive position. Hence it was understandable that they found it hard to admit the true facts cited in the accusations, especially because their opponents were all too eager to use these confessions against them. The non-Jews regarded this hypersensitivity, the causes of which they usually did not clearly understand, as additional evidence of the Jews' rottenness. We have already cited some of their arguments, which ran like this: The Jews are not asking for equal rights but for a privileged position; it is all right to cricize all people and groups except the Jews; even if one criticizes real defects, one is accused of being illiberal, of acting on the basis of medieval prejudices, and of being an anti-Semite. The reproach made by each side that the other side was full of prejudice actually contained more truth than either side realized. There really were massive prejudgments, especially on the part of the non-Jews but on that of the Jews as well—judgments that, as we have seen, had existed before there was any rational thought, that had been formed over the centuries, had developed in a long tradition, and now guided people's thoughts and feelings. Thus there never was a real dialogue between Jews and non-Jews (though it is currently fashionable to think otherwise), neither a German-Jewish nor a Christian-Jewish dialogue in the true sense of the word. It was always more a matter of attack and defense; at best more or less sincere monologues were spoken, often by both sides, and observations were made with reservations and asides really not meant to be heard, like those in old plays that are intended for the audience rather than other actors. A true conversation requires inner freedom, open-mindedness in speech and response, a chance to persuade as well as a readiness to be convinced by arguments and not to exploit the partner's rhetorical weaknesses unfairly. As soon as a Jew analyzed and presented himself and others, both friends and foes, freely and unconcernedly, mockingly or admiringly, positively or negatively, the non-Jews were all too apt to regard this as shameless or destructive. The outstanding example of this is, as we have already remarked (pp. 267f.), the controversial figure of Heinrich Heine,* who is possibly the best reflection of the inner life of the Jews and the world around them in the first half of the nineteenth century.

Jewish Apologetic Writings

The Jews completely misjudged this situation. Hostility toward them was not primarily a reaction to their actions but to their very existence among the nations. All arguments against the Jews were only rationalizations of this fact, intended to prove something that at bottom had already been established. The Jews, however, reacted—somehow in tune with the official pre-Freudian psychology—as if everything were occurring in the sphere of reason and consciousness: they *reasoned*. To every argu-

*See the excursus on Heine in Part 2.

ment they responded with a counterargument, and they defended themselves against every attack. An apologetic literature came into being in newspapers and periodicals, pamphlets and books that were written and disseminated by the hundreds of thousands but were usually read only by those who did not need them. If others read them, the arguments generally bounced off the wall of traditional prejudgments.

This is not to say that every defense against attacks was or is unnecessary. For practical reasons of daily communal living and for the sake of one's own inner self-esteem one must ward off attacks, unmask lies as lies, clear up misunderstandings, and expose forgeries. The Jewish opponents of Jewish apologetic literature, especially in Zionist ranks, often went too far with their criticism if under the impression of a misguided defense movement they rejected apologetic activities altogether. Their point that a defense must be truthful if it is not to boomerang is well taken. Despite the possibility that it will be unfairly or maliciously interpreted it must admit whatever may be true in the opponent's assertion; above all, it must derive any justification from the inner nature and intrinsic value of what is defended. Judaism could be justified properly only if its apologist had a sense of self and a positive attitude toward himself—that is, if he did not separate Judaism from Jewry—and if he regarded the present as a continuation of the past instead of wanting to lead the life of a present without a past (which in the final analysis is cultureless) or with a past derived and adopted from the surrounding world. It was not right to adopt the viewpoint of the opponents of the Jews and attempt to justify everything on that basis, often in the manner of those clever lawyers in court who do not exactly increase respect for jurisprudence.* Instead of constantly averring— contritely, plaintively, and humbly, or indignantly and arrogantly—that they were no different from the others and wanted to improve further and become even more colorless and similar, the Jews had to search their souls, be true to themselves, and seek to perform the tasks and eliminate the deficiencies that were the inevitable consequence of their entry into the modern world. If there was no other way and the adversaries insisted on their theory of the pact according to which emancipation could be attained only by giving up the Jewish character, the Jews had to be ready to make certain sacrifices if they wished not to abandon themselves and to be at peace with themselves.

Soul-Searching and Re-formation

In point of fact, the encounter between the Jews and the world around them brought forth such reactions as well. That world had a dual effect

*For an example of good apologetic writing, see the remarks about Joseph Popper-Lynkeus's *Bismarck und die Juden* in Part 2.

on the Jews: it rebuffed them and attracted them; it was hostile toward them and was a culturally stimulating force beyond compare: Like every enemy, it aroused energies of resistance and it released Judaism from the rigidity of long centuries. How much could be learned from this nineteenth century that revolutionized all branches of human cultural life and that we recognize today as a prelude to the even more revolutionary twentieth century! If the Jews had a chance to utilize the new opportunities for human social life created by science and technology to regenerate the life of the Jewish community and to reform the life of the larger community, if they applied the methods of the new Germany and European historiography, philology, and sociology to the study of Judaism, this could lead to decisive transformations in the Jewish realm. This development actually took place within Judaism in connection with the defense movement, by way of supplementing and supporting it or as a reaction to it.

Every community that is attacked closes ranks, and this is what the Jews did. The will to be completely scattered and to be individually absorbed by the world was seriously present only in a relatively small number of upper-class Jews, especially in the big cities. In the middle and lower classes, in the country and in small towns, there was always greater cohesion and less mingling with the surroundings. Assimilation was slower there, and its full effect was felt only after one or two generations. The need to defend themselves and to feel less constrained and more at home now led many members of the leading classes to establish closer and more conscious connections with Judaism. Dangers to the Jews of certain countries, such as the blood libel of Damascus (1840) and in particular the persecutions in Russia (from 1881 on) strengthened a feeling of solidarity among the Jews and inspired active endeavors. The Jewish communities, which had since the emancipation been officially limited to the organization of religious life, actually assumed the function of centers of Jewish social life, thus continuing old traditions of Jewish life in modern forms, even though they called themselves Israelitische Kultusgemeinden and officially appeared under this or similar names.

In 1860 the Alliance Israélite Universelle was founded in Paris—a first great attempt to reorganize the entire Jewish community, which was no longer united in its religious activities, and now on a nonreligious basis: for mutual support, to defend the rights of imperiled Jewish populations, and to raise the cultural level of Jews on a lower cultural plane. The Alliance Israélite did very meritorious work in warding off threats and improving the Jewish educational system, particularly in the communities of the Orient. It did not, however, create a comprehensive organization of world Jewry. The opponents of the Jews became particularly aware of the Alliance's political and diplomatic intervention in behalf of hard-pressed Jews in distant countries, and in line with their anti-Jewish ideology they believed it had been created by world Jewry for the combating and domination of non-Jews and was a Jewish nationalistic or secret political organization of "international Jewry." In point of fact, it was precisely the fear of such accusations that led Jewish leaders to create in various countries special organizations with similar goals so that they would not have to belong to an all-Jewish or comprehensive international organization and thus sin against their patriotic feelings toward their fatherlands. To arrive at a fair judgment, one must consider the overwrought patriotism of the European nation-states in the nineteenth century, as well as their fear of international political organizations that were suspected of revolutionary, communistic, or anarchistic schemes to overthrow the existing social order.

Thus the Anglo-Jewish Association was founded in London in 1871, two years later the Israelitische Allianz in Vienna, and in 1901 the Hilfsverein der deutschen Juden in Berlin—organizations that exerted a certain influence on the consolidation of the Jewish populations in the countries concerned and also collaborated on necessary larger actions. The B'nai B'rith lodges that spread over Europe beginning with the 1880s had a similar function, the mother organization having been founded in the United States in the 1840s.

Beginning with the early 1890s, special organizations for defense against anti-Semitism came into being in various countries. The first ones were founded in 1891 by non-Jews in Berlin and Vienna. In particular they opposed the vulgar denigration of the Jews and attempted to cut the ground from under anti-Semitism by providing objective information and issuing appeals to reason. In 1893 leading Jews founded the Centralverein deutscher Staatsbürger jüdischen Glaubens, generally known as C.V., in Berlin. Its aim was "to rally the German citizens of the Jewish faith regardless of their religious and political persuasion." The Centralverein opposed any manifestation of Jewish national ideas and missed no opportunity to emphasize the Germanness of the Jews it represented. However, it owed its existence in large measure to the reawakening of Jewish pride. This is evidenced by a booklet by Dr. Raphael Löwenfeld (1854–1910), which appeared anonymously under the title Schutzjuden oder Staatsbürger (Protected Jews or citizens) and urged the founding of the Centralverein as an act of self-help. It is doubtful how many antagonists of the Jews the C.V. disabused of their enmity, but by spreading enlightenment internally and externally and disseminating information about Judaism it and similar organizations in other countries made great contributions by providing people of good will with informative literature and especially by strengthening the self-confidence of Jews who had become alienated from Judaism so that they did not leave the fold without dignity for lack of knowledge and faith.

The *Wissenschaft des Judentums* and the Regeneration of Jewish Historiography

To be sure, the Judaism of those Jews who were kept from leaving the Jewish fold only by a feeling of solidarity with their fellow sufferers from attacks was only a kind of *dafke* Judaism, and they contributed no values of their own. The task of rediscovering such values for Judaism and to make the Jews aware of them was assumed by the creators of the new "Science of Judaism," the program of which was formulated in 1822 by Leopold Zunz. They introduced the methods of modern scholarship and particularly modern historiography into the study of the Jewish past, which seemed to have been completed, as it were, with the entry of the Jews into the life of the modern nations as citizens and their relinquishment of the conscious continuation of a national life of their own. This view was, of course, reflected in the historical works and led initially to an overemphasis on literary creations and the intellectual-cultural development vis-à-vis the realities of daily life. Not infrequently the apologetic tendency with which the Wissenschaft des Judentums had been established determined the direction and the valuations of the research to an inordinate degree. At the same time, however, historical works like the monumental eleven-volume *Geschichte der Juden* (History of the Jews) by Heinrich Graetz, which was published between 1853 and 1875 and quickly became very popular, had an influence on the consciousness of the Jews that can hardly be overestimated; this was particularly true of the abridged three-volume "popular" edition that appeared between 1888 and 1891. As long as the Jews remained devoutly in the chain of tradition and adopted Jewish values as teachings and commandments, no matter how rigid the forms of this tradition might have become, it could happen that there was really no important Jewish historiography after the days of Josephus Flavius. In the traditional books and the traditions of daily life the past was nevertheless preserved as a living cultural possession. With the breakdown of this tradition caused by emancipation and assimilation for ever-increasing numbers of Jews there arose a danger that Jewry as such would disintegrate into an amorphous, cultureless mass. The new Jewish historiography gave the Jews who were organizing against the attacks of the world around them a new picture of their own past and thus the foundation for a new cultural consciousness. Graetz was the first to present the history of the Jews, from the beginnings to his time, as the history of a united people, and he did so with a critical love and a national pride against which, as already mentioned, Treitschke polemicized in 1879. The historical works, of course, reached only a relatively small readership at first, but their ideas and results received ever wider dissemination through the lectures and pamphlets of the newly created associations for Jewish history, literature, and the like.

Modern Jewish historiography laid the foundation for a return of the Jews to their own selves. As the Jews dared to take their own past as a standard again, the way was paved for a new view of their own present and future as well. The lost historical consciousness that had emphasized shared elements and disregarded the special nature of events in the particular countries was replaced by a view of history formed under the influence of modern historicism. At first this view was still frequently colored rather strongly by the rationalistic tendencies of the Enlightenment and the period of emancipation, and its goal was in large measure apologetic in nature. In the face of ignorance in both the Jewish and non-Jewish spheres and of anti-Jewish distortions, the past was to be shown in its true light. The historians strove particularly to emphasize the achievements of Jews for the benefit of mankind and arouse sympathy for their undeserved sufferings, thereby demonstrating their right to complete equality and a normal life as citizens of the states. However, study of their own history constantly made the Jewish historians aware of the past as their own national past and prelude to the present, and it aroused in them a desire to continue this past in worthy fashion. Their tendency to demonstrate that the figures of the Jewish past were at least of equal rank with those of the European nations led them to emphasize their heroic nature and to depict the Jews as flesh-and-blood people who led strong and proud lives despite all hostilities. It was only natural that this pride in the common national past also affected the Jews' feeling of solidarity in the present and their desire to shape the future.

The New Feeling of Solidarity

This feeling of solidarity was constantly strengthened by the hostile attitude of the surrounding world—even among those Jews who had been close to severing their last religious and organizational ties to Judaism. The community of fate was impressed upon these Jews, and the Jews in general, with particular intensity when somewhere in the world there were anti-Jewish occurrences that attracted attention beyond the sphere of the Jewish population involved. The Damascus Affair of 1840 in what was then Turkish Syria, the ritual-murder trials in other countries decades afterwards, the Jew-baiting in Germany, Austria, and Galicia, the persecution of the Jews in Rumania, and especially the pogroms in Russia beginning in the early 1880s aroused even among those Jews not directly affected a sympathy that went far beyond the normal empathy with anyone who is persecuted, and led to large-scale relief actions.

The Westward and Overseas Migrations and Their Consequences

Catastrophes like the pogroms in Russia had even more profound consequences. Since the Cossack massacre of 1648–49 the migration of Jews from Eastern Europe to the more western countries had never ceased. It was only logical that it should have increased in proportion to the obvious easement of the lot of the Jews in the western countries as compared to the eastern states. A fall was created, as it were, in preparation for a stream of migrants. It was natural for Jews with a strong will to live to leave their paltry homes in the eastern Pale and attempt to secure a livelihood and a chance to study or get occupational training in Germany, Austria, or other western states. Even prior to the pogroms of 1881 Treitschke had made his abovementioned, not exactly tasteful remarks about a group of ambitious young pants salesmen who were year after year streaming across Germany's eastern border "from the inexhaustible Polish cradle" and whose children and grandchildren would, so he feared, dominate German stock exchanges and newspapers. Such fears determined reactions in Germany, the country that was closest to Eastern Europe and was linguistically closest to the emigrating Jews. Similar voices were also raised in other countries, even though usually not in such crude fashion, and they became louder as immigration increased. In consequence of the pogroms that started in 1881, this migration assumed proportions that were unheard of by contemporary standards. What happened after 1881 was from time to time not a migration but a flight. Jews left their homes aimlessly and out of fear that they might be destroyed by their persecutors tomorrow even if these had not managed to take their lives or their existence today. This westward stream of fleeing migrants that flooded the adjoining countries but increasingly also surged into new settlement areas overseas brought about a completely new distribution of world Jewry. The number of Jews in the countries of Central and Western Europe increased. The Jewish population of the United States of America, which around 1825 had amounted to barely 10,000 and around 1880 to about 250,000, increased by the turn of the century to about 1,175,000 and by our time to around 6 million. The Jewish population of Palestine grew from about 24,000 in 1880 to about 85,000 in 1914 and over 3 million in our days. Jewry was on the move again, outwardly and inwardly. There were protest rallies in the countries not directly involved, as well as attempts to induce the governments of the western countries to exert some political influence on the Russian government in behalf of the Jews. At the same time it organized the greatest possible systematic aid for the destitute Jews of Russia, for those who were migrating without means, and for the inex-

perienced immigrants in their new countries of domicile. In these ways
Jewry reacted spontaneously and impressively to the plight of the eastern Jews. Again and again the catastrophes and the migrations caused by
them made people consider what was behind those catastrophes, what
had caused them, and what conclusions must be drawn from them—
especially because the mass immigrations stopped and disrupted the
assimilative movement of the Jews living in those countries, some of
which were already considering legal measures against the mounting
stream of immigrants.

Synopsis: The Reactions of a Threatened National Community

If one summarizes the reaction of the Jews to the hostility of their
surroundings since the beginning of the emancipation, it can perhaps
best be characterized as the reaction of an endangered people. The Jews
acted instinctively, as any threatened creature does: accommodating
themselves, pretending to be blind to the danger, defending their
rights, banding together with like-minded people, and searching their
souls. Basically, the Jews of the nineteenth century were for the second
time decisively confronted with the question and demand that they had
faced after the defeat of 1870: Were they ready to play according to the
rules of the life of nations, give up their own identity as members of an
inwardly shaken people scattered over the entire world, and be completely absorbed by the nations controlling the states? Every people
must make sacrifices if it wants to gain a real homeland—this is what
Mommsen had clearly said in his 1880 pamphlet in defense of the Jews.
The Jews were confronted with the decision whether they wanted to
continue leading a greatly improved ghetto existence or completely lose
their identity in the life of the nations.

To formulate the question in this way is to simplify it unhistorically.
Was there really such a choice? Had the Jews had this choice after the
catastrophe of the year 1870? They certainly had not, and they had it
even less in the post-1789 reality. As we have tried to show, seventeen
hundred years of Diaspora history with its implications for the Jewish
question could not be canceled—neither for the Jews nor for the nations. On both sides the men of good will (the least historical thinkers)
tried to solve the problem radically, but the harsh reality brought them a
rude awakening from their dreams. There began a drama between the
Jews and their surroundings that has still not been presented adequately
in its entanglement of goodwill, guilt, and self-assertion.

Even in the countries of emancipation the Jews reacted as members of
the Jewish people, for a long time without realizing it. When their
adversaries, who as outsiders saw things more clearly, discerned a
Jewish collective action and called it national, they denied this with

subjectively honest indignation. These divergent ways of looking at things only exacerbated the differences. The non-Jews really found it incomprehensible that the Jews interpreted their own conduct so differently. To them the Jews were and remained a people—despite all the politely periphrastic terminology. In the apologias of the Jews that disputed these obvious facts they saw a kind of stratagem in the struggle for power and domination. All this fitted so well into the traditional picture of the Jew that always received topical colors and embellishments from the present.

This was the atmosphere in which a new political movement was organized among the Jews toward the end of the century under the name *Zionism*. It claimed to have a correct view of the Jewish question as a world problem and to have the solution, provided its proposals were followed. The appearance of Herzl's pamphlet *Der Judenstaat (The Jewish State)* in 1896 was the beginning of a new chapter in the history of the Jewish question.

8

Zionism and the Jewish Question

"Zionism," the Word and the Concept

The word *Zionismus* was coined in early 1890 by the Viennese Jewish writer Nathan Birnbaum.* It was first used as a translation of the Hebrew concept *hibbat Zion* (love of Zion), but by virtue of its linguistic form *(-ism)* and its usage it increasingly took on the meaning of a political concept. As an out-and-out political concept—in contrast to philanthropic or unpolitical efforts to found Jewish settlements in Palestine—the word was introduced to political reality by the Zionist movement, organized by Theodor Herzl in 1896, which created a worldwide organization with a political program for itself at the First Zionist Congress held at Basel in August 1897. The following year the German Kaiser already used the word as a recognized political term.

A scant two years after his first use of the word, on 1 February 1892, Birnbaum gave the following definition and interpretation of it:

> Zionism is derived from the word Zion. Zion, the name of a hill in Jerusalem, has since olden times been the poetic designation for Jerusalem. Since that city was regarded as the focal point of the Jewish land, it became by extension the poetic name of this land and of the Jewish nation insofar as it was rooted in the soil of Palestine and had become one with it. When the Roman legions dissolved this unity, the word Zion acquired the flavor of longing; the hope of a national rebirth was embodied in it . . . Zion became the ideal of the Jewish tribe and accompanied it on its road of life and sorrow for two thousand years. This ideal is the foundation of Zionism, but it did not build on it until an unconscious emotion had become thinking consciousness, sorrowful yearning had turned into an active will, and an unfruitful ideal had become a saving idea.**

Birnbaum published this definition in the biweekly newspaper founded and edited by him, which bore the revealing name *Selbstemancipation*. This name had been inspired by the epoch-making pamphlet *Autoeman-*

---

*The adjective *zionistisch* seems to have been used a few years earlier in the Zionist students' circle Kadimah, founded in 1882 by Nathan Birnbaum and others.
**Cf. the notes in Part 2.

cipation by the Jewish physician Leon Pinsker from Odessa, itself published in 1882 as a soul-searching reaction to the Russian pogroms of 1881. With this "Exhortation to his Fellow Jews" Pinsker accomplished a reversal of the struggle for the implementation of individual emancipation and the striving for complete assimilation of the Jews to their surroundings and issued a call for national awareness and self-help. By giving these few facts about the origin, development, and reception of the term *Zionism* we have already mentioned the important factors that led to the origin and development of Zionism as a philosophy and political movement.

The Foundations

Three decisive influences can easily be identified. The foundation was the religious-Messianic-national tradition with its belief in the eternal existence of the Jewish people, its religious mission and chosenness, and its eventual release from exile through the return to its own land. The second decisive influence came from the European national movements since the end of the eighteenth, and especially in the nineteenth, century, as well as the modern political and social libertarian movements in general. All of them shared the desire to produce a collective awareness of the yearnings, wishful thinking, and inner distress of individuals in a bourgeois world increasingly liberating itself from the domination of the churches and feudal powers by means of conceptual coinages; to help put these ideas into practice by systematically organizing their adherents and their dissemination; and thereby to release individuals from the isolation threatening them. Added to this as an important third element was the complicated situation of modern Jewry—the dissolution of the ghetto with its attendant problems and the clash of the emancipated Jews struggling for a new inner support or those fighting for emancipation with the defensive efforts of the non-Jews. This happened at a time when the development of international communications and politics made Palestine more real again.

All these elements have almost always been present in the endeavors of the Zionist movement and its adherents. However, the share of the individual elements and their emphasis in the total picture have varied according to countries and periods, background, social class, and personal destinies and experiences.

The Messianic Belief in Redemption and the Problem of Practical Realization

The preceding chapters contain a detailed discussion of the basic element, the connectedness of the Jewish people in the course of history with Palestine as the land belonging to it, the national-religious tradition of the Jews, and their Messianic belief in redemption. The confusion of feelings and concepts caused by Jewish fate in the Diaspora was evidenced in the downright paradoxical situation that many Christians accepted the idea of the Jews' return to their land as an almost obvious consequence of their historical existence, that for the most part the assimilated Jews sharply rejected it for that very reason, and that the most devout Jews, who prayed for a return to "Zion", frequently offered the most determined opposition to Zionist endeavors to facilitate this return. We have seen (on pp. 60f.) how after the collapse of all hope for a forcible reconquest of Palestine the Messianic faith transformed itself into resigned renunciation of all earthly help and into mystic hope of redemption through a divine miracle. To these rigid believers any attempt to bring about the return through self-help appeared as an interference in God's decree. One must not precipitate the end by force; it would come when the time was ripe. Impatience and self-help were tantamount to deficient faith in God's goodness and insufficent readiness to subject oneself to the divine will.

Precursors of the Zionist Movement

It took great courage and independence of thought as well as perservance for pious men like Judah Hai Alkalai, Tzevi Hirsch Kalischer, and others to endeavor to demonstrate on the basis of the Scriptures and the commentaries on them that it was permitted, and indeed commanded, to take practical steps toward the resettlement of the Holy Land, and for them to attempt to take the first steps on that road themselves.

MOSES HESS

These precursors of the Zionist movement, who paved the way from the traditional religious view to a more modern one, were already influenced by the national movements of the nineteenth century. But the spokesmen who came from the ranks of the emancipated Jews were even more strongly imbued with the ideas of the new liberal nationalism. The early socialist and early Zionist Moses Hess (1812–75) most clearly shows the connection with the ideas of nationalism as well as the efforts for a renewal of society, the strength of tradition, and the effect of anti-Semitism upon proud Jews. His work *Rome and Jerusalem*, which appeared in 1862, has a revealing subtitle: "The Last Nationality Question." In Hess's view, the French Revolution ushered in a new era, a springtime of the nations. One people after the other awakened to a new life, and the last one (in 1859) was the Italian people (*Rome*). Now it is the turn of the Jewish people (*Jerusalem*). In the foreword we read: "Among the peoples once thought to be dead which in the awareness of their historical task are entitled to claim their national rights there indubitably is the Jewish people, which has not braved the storm of world history for two thousand years in vain and, no matter where the flood of events may have carried it, has always kept, and is still keeping, its eyes on Jerusalem from all the ends of the world."

This work was written *before* the final granting of equal rights to the Jews in Germany. Hess regards the road taken by the Jews of the emancipation period, namely to demand these equal rights as individuals on the basis of their individual achievements, as false: "What brother was not able to get from brother or one man from another, a people will get from a people and a nation from a nation. It cannot be a matter of indifference to any people whether it will have another people as a friend or as an enemy in the last European war of liberation" (Foreword). Hess says that all attempts to bring the Jewish people out of its ossification and to breathe new life into it were doomed to fail in the Diaspora. "Among the Jews, even more than with nations who are oppressed on their own soil, national independence must precede any political-social progress" (12th letter). For the Jews a "common homeland" has been the prerequisite for healthier working conditions. "In exile the Jews cannot be regenerated, and reforms and philanthropic endeavors can at most lead it to apostasy" (12th letter). Hence the solution of the problem lies in the resuscitation of their own language and culture. The European nations that serve progress, headed by France, must and will help the Jewish people in this endeavor. Hess hoped, as Herzl did later, that the young generation of Jews, "which is receptive to everything exalted and sacred, will enthusiastically support the national endeavors."

It was a vain hope. Hess's book attracted some attention and for the most part determined resistance in the contemporary Jewish press, but it met with little response from the public and was forgotten for decades until the Zionist movement rediscovered it in the late 1890s. After all, political movements are not born of the will of individuals, no matter how profound their insights may be. Only when their personal leadership abilities are joined by external circumstances that make larger numbers of people realize the need for change do the words turn into seeds that bring forth blossoms and fruit. It is not merely the truth and depth of his insight that usually distinguishes a so-called precursor from the inspirer of a political movement. The decisive thing is whether the time is "ripe" for his ideas.

THE HOVEVEI ZION (FRIENDS OF ZION) MOVEMENT

The decisive turning point in this regard was the pogroms in southern Russia in 1881 which, as we have already seen, marked the beginning of similar excesses against the Jews in the following years and decades (see pp. 257ff. above). These pogroms brought about an inner transformation among the Jewish intelligentsia, for which these persecutions were totally unexpected.* Many of the most ardent champions of radical assimilation to other nations now recognized that the complete adaptation of the Jews to the surrounding world might be possible for individuals but not for Jewry as a whole, and they returned to Judaism, for which they began to have a new understanding and appreciation as a nationality and whose national existence they endeavored to invigorate. These intellectuals strove to redirect to Palestine the aimless, precipitous overseas emigration that began after the pogroms and assumed ever greater dimensions, in an effort to breathe new life into the country that was to become the homeland of the dispersed people again. To many plain Jews who were living in the Jewish religious traditions this striving for a return to the "Holy Land" appeared to be the only natural thing, especially since a spontaneous agricultural settlement movement had begun toward the late 1870s in Palestine as well. Consequently, beginning in the winter of 1881–82 associations of the *Hovevei Zion*, the Friends of Zion, were formed under different names in numerous Russian and Rumanian towns with the intention of gathering men and means for the new settlement of Palestine. Practical work was started right away.

As early as the summer of 1882 the first members of the Bilu society set out for Palestine; they were students who wished to exchange their books for plows and establish communal settlements as pioneers and role models. The first Jewish agricultural settlements came into being: Rishon le-Zion and Gedera in Judea, Rosh Pinnah and Yesud Hama'alah in the Galilee, and Zihkron Ya'akov in Samaria. Petah Tikvah, which had been founded by Jerusalem Jews north of Jaffa as early as 1878, was now restored.

LEON PINSKER'S "AUTOEMANCIPATION"

In the midst of this excitement, first movements, and activities, there appeared in September 1882 an anonymous German pamphlet, printed in Berlin, under the title *Autoemancipation: An Exhortation to His Fellow Jews by a Russian Jew*. Its author, Dr. Leon Pinsker (1821–91), a sixty-year-old physician in Odessa and adherent of the Enlightenment and assimilation, had hitherto not been a supporter of national endeavors, believing that Russianization and the dissemination of modern culture would at the least lead to tolerance and peaceful coexistence. *His* eyes, too, had been fully opened only by the pogroms of 1881, and it was under their impression that he analyzed the Jewish question. Pinsker's

*Concerning these unexpected pogroms, see the notes in Part 2.

psychological point of departure, as Herzl's would be later on, was hurt pride: "To be plundered as a Jew or to have to be protected as a Jew is equally humiliating and equally painful for the Jews' sense of themselves as human beings."* From this point of departure he fearlessly proceeds to the crux of the problem: the abnormal situation of the Jews among the nations. He makes this diagnosis as a doctor and attains to profound insights and formulations.

What is the cause—so he asks—of the foreignness of the Jews and the hatred of the surrounding world, where the Jews are everywhere perceived as a "heterogeneous element"? He believes it is because after the destruction of their state and country the Jews lived on intellectually as a nation but no longer in the visible reality and political formation of "normal" peoples; on the one hand, they were detached from their country, and on the other, they remained inwardly bound to it and maintained a national attachment to it in all sorts of disguises. That is why the world sees in the Jewish people "the uncanny figure of a dead man who walks among the living." This "ghostlike apparition of a walking dead man" which Pinsker almost surrealistically perceives as standing before the world has inspired fear, a kind of fear of ghosts that Pinsker calls "Judophobia". He feels that all the arguments adduced against the Jews by anti-Semites—arguments whose often hair-raising contradictoriness really ought to be obvious to any insightful person—are only attempts to give a rational motivation for this instinctive dislike of the sinister, Ahasuerus-like stranger, and that this dislike is really based on that fear of ghosts which has been handed down over the generations. Pinsker makes this diagnosis: "Judophobia is a psychosis; as such it is hereditary, and as a sickness transmitted for 2000 years it is incurable."** Hence it can be tackled only by removing its real cause, the abnormal situation of the Jews among the nations. The Jews without a state and homeland are no longer equal to the other nations: "Only when the equality of the Jews to the other nations has become reality can the problem of the Jewish question be considered as solved."

Hence the real solution can be effected only by the Jews themselves. The solution is not the liberation of the Jews by the other nations, but their liberation by themselves—autoemancipation! The isolated Jews without a national sense of themselves must again form a self-assured, self-sustaining nation living on its own soil and leading the natural life of an normal people. Wherever the number of Jews among the nations has exceeded the saturation point, the Jews should emigrate—not, as hitherto, to form a new Diaspora but to settle in a self-contained territory

*On "hurt pride" as the point of departure for Pinsker, Herzl, and many others, see the excursus in Part 2.
**Concerning this diagnosis, see the excursus in Part 2.

where they can establish a polity of their own with the approval of the Powers. That, to be sure, is work for generations, but the first steps should be taken immediately. Pinsker prefaces his pamphlet with words spoken two thousand years earlier by the religious teacher Hillel: "If I am not for myself, who is for me? And if not now, when?"

At first Pinsker did not care about the location of the country in which the Jewish commonwealth was established, whether in the East (Palestine) or in the West (North America). "The goal of our endeavors now should not be the 'holy' land but our own land." Thus his plan was initially a Jewish state on a certain territory rather than a "Zionist" one centered on Palestine. However, as Pinsker joined the Friends of Zion (Hovevei Zion) and became one of their leaders, he also adopted their goal, the settlement of Palestine, and this also meant a constriction of his original view.

The first attempts at practical settlement in Palestine with heroic but agriculturally inexperienced settlers from the beginning met with unexpected internal and external difficulties that threatened to wreck the project. Hence it was only natural that the work of the Zion associations concentrated primarily on the collection of funds intended to support the young settlers in their struggle with nature and the population surrounding them. Thus the great national goal of a political and cultural regeneration was increasingly replaced with the daily spadework of relief actions. The movement foundered, particularly because the new settlements were soon supported with very considerable funds by the great Paris philanthropist Edmond Rothschild (1845–1934) and placed under his protection and administrative oversight. The action by Edmond Rothschild did save the new settlements from threatening collapse, but it also determined their nature as a philanthropic relief action. It did not become the basis of a national rescue project until new ideas and new people freed the movement of the Friends of Zion from its narrowness and transformed it into a modern national movement.

AHAD HA-AM: JEWS AND JUDAISM

This liberation was first attempted with a view toward an intellectual and cultural revival. The situation of the settlement project, its settlers working under well-meaning tutelage, and the movement of the Friends of Zion with its adherents and leaders who were disappointed and often doubted the rightness of their ideas and goals, among them the aging and ailing Pinsker, evoked sharp criticism from a man who under the Hebrew pseudonym Ahad Ha-Am (One of the people) had a great influence on the Jewish national and Zionist movement for generations.*

*Concerning Ahad Ha-Am and the cultural problem in Zionism, see the excursus in Part 2.

In 1889 the Hebrew periodical *Ha-Melitz* published under that pseudonym (which soon supplanted the real name of the author) the first essay of the hitherto unknown writer Asher Ginsberg (1856–1927), *"Lo Zeh Ha-Derekh"* (This is not the way). What attracted attention about this essay as well as the following one, both of which henceforth accompanied all developments of Zionist history, was not only the style, which in its simplicity and conceptual formulations constituted an innovation in Hebrew and became a model for the author's contemporaries and successors. It was also the author's views, presented with untiring consistency and uncompromising courage to tell the truth, that attracted attention and aroused both dissent and consent. Ahad Ha-Am rejected as mistaken not only the methods of settlement and their philanthropic financing but also their national-political foundations and objectives.

Ahad Ha-Am declares that the entire national and Palestine movement has been based on false assumptions. It endeavors to free the Jews from their distressful situation; that it cannot do, and it is not its task. The question of the physical existence of the Jews is not the most urgent problem for Ahad Ha-Am nor, in his view, for the Jewish national movement. Attending to the cultural crisis, the distressful situation of Judaism, is more important than doing something about the physical plight of the Jews. This Judaism has become rigidified in the Diaspora and alienated from its original essence, a national feeling of community; the emphasis has been shifted from the totality to the individual. Hence the revival of national feeling, a feeling of attachment to Palestine, is the most important task; before this task has been accomplished, any other work has no foundation. The settlement of Palestine should also serve that goal. What counts is not the number and size of the settlements— the present aim—but their quality. Palestine's significance is not as an end in itself and as a place for assembling masses of people; rather, an intellectual and cultural center should be established there—on the basis of a sound economy, of course—which all Jews should help to build and which would brighten their lives. Grasping and regenerating the "spirit of Judaism"—which Ahad Ha-Am actually conceives of as abstractly as the reformers did, though with different premises—through a deepening of true love of Zion: that is the goal that Ahad Ha-Am tried to drum into his generation as a critic, exhorter, and teacher.

Ahad Ha-Am brought a new element into the Palestine movement. It was due to his efforts that henceforth the cultural question and the struggle for the revival of the Hebrew language and the spiritual possessions of the Jewish people (in place of religious faith and practices as a unifying force) gradually occupied an important place in Zionist ideology and activities. The teachings of Ahad Ha-Am were, however, at first formulated in overwrought form, and by reversing causes and effects and attempting to eliminate the material plight of the Jews as a motivating factor they got into a vicious circle. Above all, Ahad Ha-Am underestimated the dangers to the physical existence of the Jews. Thus, until his teachings had been understood by part of the movement and built into it as one of its goals, they led to vehement polemics with the proponents of work in Palestine in the spirit of the Hovevei Zion and later with Herzlian political Zionism. In any case, they were not designed to shake the Hovevei Zion movement out of its stagnation. Even though this movement, all things considered, made fundamental contributions in Palestine, we may assume that it would have gradually foundered if it had not been shown new directions.

Nathan Birnbaum: Zionism, the Word and the Concept

An important stage in this process was the appearance of Nathan Birnbaum (1864–1937),* whose periodical *Selbstemancipation* has already been mentioned at the beginning of this chapter. In it he used the word *Zionismus* for the first time and introduced it as a concept into the movement for a Jewish national renaissance. The work in which he set forth his Zionist program is much clearer in its objectives than those of his forerunners and many of his successors. Its very title indicates it: *Die nationale Wiedergeburt des jüdischen Volkes in seinem Lande als Mittel zur Lösung der Judenfrage* (The national rebirth of the Jewish people in its country as a means of solving the Jewish question) (Vienna, 1893). Here the Jewish question is for the first time clearly and organically connected with the Jewish national movement and with Palestine as its goal. This work appeared at a time when the Jews already enjoyed formal equal rights in the western states, but Birnbaum felt that this did not solve the Jewish question: "Even if individual Jews have a fatherland, the Jewish people has none, and that is its misfortune."

In his pamphlets and essays Birnbaum attempted to establish a synthesis between the views of Pinsker and Ahad Ha-Am, both of whom he regarded as his teachers, and modern trends in Central and Western Europe. He thought it probably was not necessary for *all* Jews to be gathered in one country, but Jewry as a whole ought to have a national center where the Jews could emigrate from all the countries in which their numbers had passed the saturation point. This would considerably decrease the tension between them and the nations. The awareness of belonging to a living people, of having a home and a cultural center as well as a refuge in times of need, would restore the Jewish people to health. Politically, too, a land of their own could come to the aid of the Jews. "The smallest political community has a seat and a voice in the concert of the nations. It can protest if the rights of its citizens or the fellow nationals of its citizens are violated or if their lives are threatened

*See the excursus about him in Part 2.

anywhere, and it can demand satisfaction for any such infringements. A people without standing under international law is fair game" (p. 13).

The last sentence is emphasized in the original, and this leads to the following conclusion: "Land, land—so this is the secret of the solution to the Jewish question. But where shall this land that is to shelter the two-thousand-year-old wanderer be sought? It need not be looked for; everyone knows it, and there is no other that could be considered. And that is why the national Jewish party, which also calls itself the Zionist party, has really decided in favor of this land, Palestine" (p. 13).

The Zionist solution, says Birnbaum, does not conflict with the Jews' duties as patriotic citizens of the states in which they live or with the efforts for universal peace and inner harmony among the nations. On the contrary; a purified nationalism can only promote these endeavors. Hence Birnbaum appeals to the "good and noble-minded people of all nations" to aid the Jewish people in the great work of national rebirth.*

In Nathan Birnbaum we already find all elements of the Zionist view of the Jewish question and its solution. He did more than create the word *Zionismus* as a political concept and thus introduce the new current into the political conceptual world of the nineteenth century; he also recognized the central importance of the land and the language, of Palestine and Hebrew, for the regeneration of the Jewish people.

Theodor Herzl and Political Zionism

From this vantage point the first appearance of Herzl almost marked a step back. The Viennese journalist Theodor Herzl (1860–1904), a charismatic leader such as the Jewish Diaspora had never known, actually initiated a new epoch in the history of the Jewish people and in that of the Jewish question with the publication of his pamphlet *Der Judenstaat (The Jewish State)* in 1896 and with his political activities aimed at the implementation of his ideas until his untimely death eight years later. At least at the beginning of his activities, however, he had no clear idea of the significance of Palestine and the Hebrew language for the preservation and regeneration of Judaism. In other words, he underestimated the fundamental factor of historical continuity and remembrance that was expressed and continued to be active in the relationship of the Jews with their country and their language, even when there no longer were any religious bonds uniting the Jews of all countries and classes. Herzl had experienced some of this at first hand. His parental home in Budapest, and from 1878 on in Vienna, still had a rather close connection with Jewish tradition. However, in his consciousness he had increasingly removed himself from it in the years of his development—as a

*His pamphlet is subtitled "An Appeal to the Good and Noble-Minded People of All Nations."

law student, as a freelance writer with moderate success on the stage, and as a recognized writer of essays and Paris correspondent of the great Viennese newspaper *Neue Freie Presse* (1891–95). The undignified way in which liberal Jewish circles of the emancipation period often pursued their assimilation repelled him. But what then fully drove him back to Judaism with elemental force and taught him to see it and value it in a new way was the hurt pride that had initially alienated him from Judaism and led him into a world of liberal and aesthetic wishful thinking. This development was inspired and triggered by the mounting anti-Semitism by which he was surrounded and that led in 1894–95 to the sentencing and degrading of the innocent Jewish captain Dreyfus, but this was not the real cause, as has often been erroneously assumed. To be sure, over the course of a decade and a half the increasing hostility gradually brought the man who constantly strove for self-knowledge closer to a recognition of the Jewish question and aroused in him a desire to solve it with the exertion of his entire personality.*

This, however, marks only the psychological point of departure.

HERZL'S UNROMANTIC VIEW OF THE JEWISH QUESTION

The decisive innovation of Herzl was that this point of departure did not lead him to a romantic transfiguration or defiant excess but to an altogether realistic, unromantic view of the Jewish question, one that might almost be called an antiromantic one.**

Herzl analyzed the forces that he saw at work in the Jewish question and fearlessly acted on the basis of this analysis with the straightforward logic and the unpretentious simplicity with which children and geniuses view the world. As someone who had almost gone to the end of the road of emancipation and assimilation, and without knowing anything about earlier Zionist writings, proposals, and attempts at realization, he independently attained to a fresh view of the Jewish question and its solution, one that combined the energies of destruction and construction almost in accordance with the law of nature.

According to Herzl, the Jewish question has not been solved by emancipation but, if anything, exacerbated. Hatred of Jews continues to exist and manifests itself in a variety of forms. It is deeply rooted in the people, and to become convinced of it one only has to listen to the voice of the plain people, to legends and jokes. Hence it will not disappear in the foreseeable future; in fact, it will continue to grow because of the constantly intensifying nationalism and mounting economic competi-

---

*Concerning Herzl's road to Zionism, a special case that, as it were, mirrors the development of Jewry in the nineteenth century, see the excursus in Part 2.

**Concerning this and the following remarks, see the supplementary notes in Part 2.

tion, particularly in the professions and in the middle class, to which for historical reasons the majority of the Jews belong. This Jew-hatred, which has found its modern, racial-nationalistic form in the anti-Semitic movement, no longer finds the modern Jews as a united body, as in the days of the ghetto; they were emancipated as individuals and have to bear the enmity of their surroundings as individuals. Socially isolated, economically feared and fought, they are "homeless" (because not recognized by the world around them as belonging) even in places where they have resided for many centuries.* This has placed them economically and spiritually in a special predicament, the *Judennot* (Jewish distress). With the increase in anti-Semitism this distress is bound to become more severe. It is a situation that is bound to lead to a catastrophe for the Jews if a radical remedy is not created in time.

This remedial action cannot be taken on a philanthropic basis or through well-intentioned relief actions, no matter how great in style and scope, for the Jewish question is neither a social nor a religious question, "even though it may assume these and other guises." It is a national question: "We are a people, one people." As a national question it can be solved only with the means of politics. Only by banding together as a people again and rebuilding their existence on a sound territorial basis can the Jews free themselves from the difficult situation in which they are living. The pressure to which the Jews are exposed can lead to their destruction.** However, if the right road is taken, the "Jewish distress" resulting from this pressure can also become a tremendous force for self-liberation.*** It is the task of the Zionist movement to transform the forces of misfortune and malediction into forces of construction and blessing by organizing the people and pursuing a purposeful policy.

Herzl clearly names as his goal the establishment of a Jewish state. The solution of the Jewish question cannot be achieved by establishing individual areas of settlement but only by concentrating in a territory at least a significant part of Jewry, all those "who are unable or unwilling to assimilate."

---

*Cf. this formulation (among many others) in Herzl's essay "The Hunt in Bohemia" (5 November 1897; in Herzl, *Zionist Writings, Essays and Addresses*, vol. 1, p. 171: "For home is not merely a locality . . . Home must be more than a connection with something lifeless. Home is the acknowledged connection with the thought and feeling of a national community. The emphasis is on 'acknowledged'; without this acknowledgment there can be no home."

**In the first notes for *The Jewish State* (7 June 1895) Herzl writes (*Complete Diaries*, vol. 1, p. 38): "Things cannot improve, but are bound to get worse—to the point of massacres."

***Herzl likens "Jewish distress" to the steam power that is generated by boiling water and leads to an explosion in a closed kettle, but can be transformed into a tremendous driving force of productive machines by channeling this power into pipes and constructing well-designed mechanical devices.

NEW CANDOR IN THE TREATMENT OF THE JEWISH QUESTION

What distinguished Herzl from his predecessors and almost all his contemporaries and made him a revolutionary in the treatment of the Jewish question was the openness and straightforwardness of his appearance. As we know, public discussion of the Jewish question had hitherto been frowned upon by the Jewish circles of the West; in fact, the very existence of such a problem was denied, and even the term "Jewish question" was rejected as an anti-Jewish fabrication.* It was said that the Jewish question had been solved in western countries through the granting of equal rights. Of course, the backward East still had to fight for what had already been won in the West. Here, however, in enlightened Europe, the only fight was for the protection and full implementation of the rights that often were only on paper while in practice the government and society went their own ways. The anti-Semites were almost the only ones who openly claimed that despite all assurances to the contrary there still was a Jewish question. Any non-Jews who recognized or suspected the existence of such a problem usually refrained from saying so publicly so as not to be accused of anti-Semitism by his Jewish friends. On the one hand, people did not wish to be on the same level as the anti-Semites, and on the other, it seemed illiberal and intolerant to emphasize in public the differences between the Jewish and non-Jewish citizens. Among the Jews of the West there were only a few who clearly realized the untruthfulness and unworthiness of this situation: seemingly eccentric individualists and numerically insignificant groups of Friends of Zion and students. Even these were usually cautious in their remarks so as not to give offense and through imprudent speech do harm to the Jews in the Diaspora or in the new settlements in Palestine.

With his characteristic honesty, pride, and dignity Herzl smashed this narrowness and dishonesty that were in keeping with the spirit of hypocrisy and outward moralizing so typical of the Victorian age. In him, the emancipated Jew, the libertarian feeling of modern man struggled against the stifling atmosphere that surrounded him and did not permit him to breathe freely. Honesty and frankness were the first demands for the treatment of the Jewish question. It should not be whispered about, and the threats and dangers should not be discussed in secret conventicles; they should be talked about openly and with the freedom appropriate to sons of old nobility. Hence the first demand made by Herzl was to have an open discussion of the Jewish question. This is what he intended when he wrote his drama *The New Ghetto* in

---

*Concerning the concept "Jewish question," see pp. 18ff. above, as well as the notes and excursuses in part 2.

late 1894, this is what he did by publishing his book *The Jewish State* in February 1896, and this was one of his goals when he convened the First Zionist Congress in August 1897. "The Jewish question exists," he wrote in the introduction to *The Jewish State*. "It would be foolish to deny it. It is an atavistic bit of medievalism which the civilized nations have not been able to shake off to this day."* Herzl was convinced that such a discussion of the Jewish question, conducted openly and fearlessly all over the world, would already be an important step toward its solution and that this was the only method of finding a way out of the blind alley in which the Jewish question was stuck. Being convinced of the correctness of the solution he was proposing, he was certain that the international discussion would "transform the Jewish question into a Zion question," i.e., demonstrate the Zionist solution as the only feasible one.

His demand of a free and fearless discussion of the problem was in keeping with his view of the Jews as a people among the nations. In so doing he anticipated, as it were, his goal—namely, the recognition of the Jews as a people—as a fact, as though this recognition had already been achieved. If the Jews were recognized as a people among the peoples despite the special nature of their existence, it should be possible to discuss and deliberate on the vital questions of the Jewish people with the same freedom as on the problems of other peoples. Being himself honest in his endeavors, he assumed (and unfortunately often erroneously) that the others, even his Jewish and non-Jewish opponents, would also deal with this question honestly and rationally. He believed that it was precisely the insincerity of mutual dealings that caused much bitterness to enter the discussions. Anti-Semitism was not born of mere hatred and ill will either. "I believe I understand anti-Semitism, a highly complex movement," wrote Herzl with a freedom of analysis unaccustomed among Jews at the time. "I view this movement from the standpoint of a Jew, but without hatred or fear. I think I can discern in it the elements of vulgar sport, of common rivalry, of inherited prejudice, of religious intolerance—but also of a supposed need for self-defense."**

ASSIMILATION: THEORY AND REALITY

According to Herzl, the ideology of assimilation that was connected with the struggle for emancipation and its implementation have confused the Jews about their position as a nation among nations. Actually, the non-Jews have never regarded the Jews as anything but a people.

*See Part 2 for the full quotation. Herzl already emphasized this point in the subtitle of *The Jewish State*: "An Attempt at a Modern Solution of the Jewish Question."
**See Part 2 for Herzl's conclusions (the continuation of his theoretical prefatory remarks in *The Jewish State*) as well as the sources for these quotations.

Lack of clarity about the Jews' position in the modern world has brought dishonesty into the relationships between Jews and non-Jews. Dislike of the Jews is closely bound up with the thinking and feeling of the nations with their history and tradition. Added to this is the social status of the Jews as a "bourgeois people par excellence"; historical circumstances have made it one. This status is driving the Jews to extreme positions; they are in the vanguard in both the capitalistic and the socialistic camps. "On the lower level we are proletarianized and become revolutionaries, the petty officers of all revolutionary parties, and at the same time our terrifying financial power grows on the upper level." Hence the social battle in modern society will be fought on the backs of the Jews. All these elements and factors—religious tradition, inherited prejudice, national dislike, fear of undue alien infiltration and vengeance by those freed, professional jealousy, and social tensions in general—add up to dreadful dynamite. There is bound to be a catastrophe unless the explosives are quickly diminished and gradually eliminated by some remedy on a national basis, unless they are transformed into positive energies for reconstruction and into driving forces for the solution of the Jewish question.

Under these circumstances, assimilation cannot be a solution even if the totality or majority of the Jews sincerely desired to accomplish it. True assimilation, becoming completely equal in mentality and manner, in the conscious as well as the unconscious, could only be accomplished by systematic interbreeding. This, however, could be a successful solution in only a certain number of individual cases. On a large scale, however, for the totality or majority of the Jewish people mixed marriages could be accomplished only if the Jews had previously attained to so much economic power that social prejudice were eliminated. "Such a first step toward absorption cannot be taken, for it would mean the subjugation of the majority by a minority that was but recently despised, a minority that would not possess any military or administrative power." Besides, the outward condition for this would be the cessation of persecution, the Jews' permanent social and political well-being for at least two generations. But there will not be such a period of peace, becuse after brief periods of tolerance the powerful old prejudices always give rise to hostility toward the Jews, as though the welfare of people despised for centuries constituted an incitement. Dislike of the Jews is so deeply rooted that even well-disposed governments can hardly do anything effective about it.

REVALUATION OF EMANICIPATION

If emancipation was intended to dissolve the Jews and have them absorbed by the nations, it came too late. Because of their long history in the ghetto it was no longer possible to emancipate the Jews in this sense. Now Herzl revalues the historical meaning of emancipation by saying that it really was not the historical task of emancipation to dissolve the Jews as a people and that hitherto everyone, the nations as well as the Jews, has misunderstood this. If emancipation is understood as the liberation of individuals from legal and social restrictions, it cannot be the final goal but only a developmental stage. It created the Jewish question in its modern form with all its emotional confusion, but also set the stage for the constructive solution of the problem. By freeing the Jews from the confinement of the ghetto and integrating them into the modern world it gave the Jews a new attitude toward life as well as *Staatsmut*, the will and the ability to take political action. Emancipation has also taught the Jews to use all the modern world's wonderful achievements in science and technology for their own redemption as a people.

DEFINITION OF THE TERM "PEOPLE"

Pressure and persecution have not destroyed the Jews. On the contrary, precisely the best have been brought back to the fold. "Thus, whether we desire it or not, we are and shall remain a historical group of people that clearly belong together. We are a people—our enemies make us one without our volition, as has always happened in history." This is Herzl's definition of his idea of a people, and it is one that may have general validity: a historical group of people that clearly belong together and are kept together by an external enemy. To Herzl, the real constitutive elements are not race, which is not uniform in any people (and thus not in the Jews either), or religion, though this may strengthen the feeling of cohesiveness and become a sign of communality. In the final analysis, the decisive thing is the national will to live that is manifested in uniform reaction to an external foe. Herzl makes these apodictic statements in his Introduction to *The Jewish State:* "Whoever can, will, and must perish, let him perish. But the distinctive nationality of the Jews cannot, will not, and need not perish. It cannot, because external foes hold it together. That it does not want to perish it has proved through two thousand years of enormous suffering. It need not perish; this is what I am trying to demonstrate in this pamphlet, following many other Jews who did not abandon hope. Whole branches of Jewry may wither and fall off, but the tree remains alive."

Thus the Jewish people must be led to an awareness of itself and organized for the foundation of its state. At the same time the political stage for the foundation of a Jewish state must be set by negotiating with the powerful of the earth. The liberation of the Jews as a people from the unhappy and profoundly untruthful and unworthy situation in which it has been placed by history, its own and that of the other nations, through the establishment of its own state will be a redemption even for those nations that, in Herzl's view, are suffering because the Jewish question has not been solved. This will bring about reconciliation between the Jews and the nations: "Prayers will be offered up in the temples for the success of our undertaking. But in the churches as well! It will relieve an old pressure, one under which all have suffered" (*The Jewish State*, Conclusion).

FROM TERRITORIALISM TO ZIONISM

As it had been for Pinsker, sovereignty over a territory suitable for founding a state was of decisive importance for Herzl. Where this territory was located initially seemed to him a question of secondary importance, one that should be decided by scientific experts and political conditions. He had primarily two countries in mind: Argentina, "a country with some of the greatest natural resources in the world [that] extends over a vast area, is sparsely populated, and has a temperate climate," and Palestine, "our unforgettable historic homeland. The very name would be a powerful rallying cry for our people." In contrast to earlier drafts, the emphasis in *The Jewish State* is already on Palestine. It eventually became the only goal as Herzl established ever closer contact with the existing Zionist groups and encountered the Jewish masses with their still unbroken religious-national tradition. Herzl clung to his conviction that Palestine had to be the only final destination even when he was negotiating with England about territorial interim solutions for the Jewish masses in Europe whose lives were threatened by persecutions and pogroms. In April 1904 the mortally ill Herzl said in the debate on the so-called Uganda Plan at the last Zionist conference he was able to attend: "It was as a Jewish Statist that I presented myself to you. I gave you my card, and on it was printed 'Herzl, Jewish Statist.' In the course of time I learned a great deal. . . . Above all, I learned to see that the solution for us may be found only in Palestine. . . . I have become a Zionist and remained one, and all my efforts are directed toward Palestine."*

THE JEWISH STATE AND THE DIASPORA

Herzl frequently said and described how he imagined the Jewish state—in the work by that title, in addresses and essays, as well as in his programmatic fictional utopia *Old-Newland* (1902): a flourishing country governed in freedom, a social model state based on cooperation, utilizing all accomplishments of science and technology, unencumbered by

*See the notes in Part 2.

national chauvinism (in *Old-Newland* it is not called a "state" but "the new society"!), full of tolerance and living in peace with its neighbors and the world, and having its peace palace in Jerusalem serving as a center for relief actions in the entire world—a true home for all those living in it. By virtue of the freedom prevailing in it and through its beneficial institutions and the feeling of security and home that it offers the Jews as Jews, the Jewish state will attract Jews from all over the world. The strength or weakness of the immigration from the countries of the Diaspora will be determined by the strength of this attraction and by the degree of the repelling forces in the Jews' places of domicile— thus by the natural physical and psychological forces that induce people to change their localities and cause, intensify, or reduce the migration of a people. "The solution of the Jewish question," said Herzl in his testimony before the Royal Commission on Alien Immigration in London in 1901, "is that the Jews should be recognized as a people and that they should find a legally recognized home to which Jews in those parts of the world in which they are oppressed would naturally migrate, for they would arrive there as citizens just because they are Jews, and not as aliens."

As we have said, the new element in Herzl's view of the Jewish question is the close connection between diagnosis and therapy.* To him the Jewish question in the Diaspora as it had developed by the end of the nineteenth century—and by Diaspora we mean primarily Europe, where the overwhelming majority of the Jews were living—seemed insoluble in the Jews' countries of residence without radical surgery. The Gordian knot would have to be cut; only an exodus organized in timely fashion could bring about a solution. While he was writing *The Jewish State,* Herzl probably had in mind a more or less complete emigration of European Jewry (and perhaps also of American Jewry, which was by comparison not of great numerical significance)—a giant transportation and settlement project organized in almost military fashion. However, he very soon revised this view. As early as 18 February 1896, days after the appearance of his basic pamphlet, he wrote to the Austrian Prime Minister Badeni: "What I am proposing is actually no more than the regulation of the Jewish question and certainly not the emigration of all Jews."** He later wrote to many others in a similar vein.

Pinsker and Birnbaum had already assumed that the countries and nations could absorb only a certain number of Jews and that an efflux for the Jews would have to be provided where the saturation point had been

---

*Sometimes this closeness seems like a physical necessity, like a "stychic process," to use a later formulation of the Zionist socialist Ber Borochov. "The Jewish State is something the world needs," wrote Herzl in the Introduction to *The Jewish State,* "and consequently it will come into being."

**For a selection from Herzl's statements on this problem, see Part 2.

reached or passed. For this process Herzl used the image of U-tubes. Repulsion and attraction, increase of the Jewish population in the Jewish state and decline in the countries of the Diaspora, are related, as are physical forces. All those elements will emigrate "that are unable or unwilling to assimilate"—that is, those whom the environment refuses to admit or in whom the awareness of their separate existence strengthens that will to self-preservation that is natural in every healthy person and without which a human personality cannot develop. As these elements that are unable or unwilling to be absorbed by their surroundings found their own state, they make it possible for the other Jews, those whose Jewish consciousness is weaker and who usually have a better social position, to be completely integrated into the nations or to establish more normal relationships with the surrounding world even if they continue their separate existence. On the whole, Herzl does not make it clear what the fate of these Jews remaining in the Diaspora will be, whether they will permanently preserve their existence as a special group or completely blend with their surroundings through intermarriage (which would probably often lead to conversion to the established religion). Herzl did not reject the phenomenon of the Diaspora in national life as a matter of principle, though he has often been erroneously interpreted that way. He must have noticed that every nation lives in a partial Diaspora nowadays. However, he regarded the Jewish Diaspora, which had no way out, no mother state to which Jews could return or which they could leave, as an anomaly. One could overstate this and say that he did not negate the Diaspora of the Jews but was of the opinion that this Diaspora negated the existence of the Jews—in any case, their existence with dignity.

How did Herzl imagine the final fate of the Jews continuing to live in the Diaspora after the foundation of the Jewish state? There are no clear statements about this, for whatever Herzl said on the subject was prompted by certain circumstances and influenced by them. He was convinced of one thing, however: The building of a country of their own would very rapidly improve the Jews' situation in the Diaspora morally and materially, particularly in countries in which there had been especially great tension and hostility toward the Jews. Material improvement would be effected primarily by creating new employment for Jews and thus reducing the pressure from Jewish job-seekers in the Diaspora. The emigration of Jewish competitors of the non-Jewish bourgeoisie would reduce the tension between Jews and non-Jews that had been created by economic competition, and this decrease in tension would have a salutary effect on other spheres of coexistence as well. This would also improve the moral standing of the Jews.

These effects of the Jewish state on Jewry are, however, predicated on an important factor: After legal guarantees have been secured and immigration and development have utilized all the resources of science, technology, sociology, etcetera, the new state must be organized in such a way that it has a natural attraction for the Jews of the Diaspora, thus making the choice between emigrating and staying put at least one between equal values.

It is for this reason, and also to demonstrate that his plan is feasible, that Herzl gives pride of place—in *The Jewish State* and the programmatic novel *Old-Newland*—to descriptions of the economic, social, and cultural institutions of the new state. A model state is to come into being, a cooperatively organized economy and society that will fully develop all energies of the land and its inhabitants in a harmonious balance of freedom and restraint, humanitarianism and utmost mechanization, becoming a true home for its inhabitants. Through tolerance toward inhabitants of all races and classes the Jews will demonstrate in this state that they are serious about the demands they have made for themselves in their struggle for equal rights in the Diaspora. This will then benefit the Jews remaining in the Diaspora as well.

JEWISH CULTURE

These viewpoints determined Herzl's attitude in the question of future "Jewish culture" as well. Here he was misunderstood and attacked even by many adherents of the Zionist movement. He was reproached with not being close to Jewish tradition and its values (including the Hebrew language), never having found the proper access to it, and deriving his vision of the old-new Jewish state almost exclusively from western European notions. Much of this criticism surely is well taken, although in his striving for social justice in the Jewish state Herzl probably received an important impetus from the sense of justice that is a traditional Jewish inheritance. In this respect, however, Herzl's critics, past and present, have disregarded an important point that mattered to him. For hundreds of years the Jews had lived under duress and both external and internal restrictions. If the mummylike national body was to be resuscitated, Herzl believed the most important thing was not to prescribe narrow confines for the future development of this life again. The prerequisites for a healthy cultural life and a national Jewish renascence that Herzl strove for were independence of the opinion of an environment that was critical of or malevolent toward the Jews and the Jews' ability to lead a free life and shape the life of individuals and of the totality on the basis of their own needs. Culture cannot be created deliberately; it must grow out of the natural processes of life. Hence Herzl resisted any detailed definition of the concept "Jewish culture." To him any culture created by the Jews in freedom was the culture appropriate to them, Jewish culture. "The Promised Land," wrote Herzl in his diary notes for *The Jewish State*, "where it is all right for us to have hooked noses, black or red beards, and bandy legs without being despised for these things alone. Where at last we can live as free men on our own soil and die in peace in our own homeland; where we, too, can expect honor as a reward for great deeds . . . so that the derisive cry 'Jew!' may become an honorable appellation, like 'German,' 'Englishman,' 'Frenchman,' etc., like the members of all civilized peoples, so that by means of our state we can educate our people for tasks which still lie beyond our horizon." Herzl closes these remarks in the believing tone of an anti-Hegelian: "For God would not have preserved our people so long if we did not have another role to play in the history of mankind."

ORGANIZATION AND POLITICS

In his abovementioned basic Zionist work Nathan Birnbaum had addressed the "good and noble-minded" of all nations. Herzl, too, was of the opinion that the benevolence of public opinion was an important factor in the solution of the Jewish question through the proposed foundation of the Jewish state. This benevolence, however, could not be attained through appeals to humanitarianism or the intercession of influential personalities. On the contrary: such a course of action would debase the Jews in the eyes of the nations. If the Jews were a people and desired a state, the means to achieve it were the normal ones of international life: politics and organization.

According to Herzl, politics is based on giving and taking, on the principle of *do ut des,* negotiations between equal powers. To conduct a Jewish policy in this spirit thus meant primarily to gain recognition for the Jews as a people rightfully striving for the state-form to which all nations are entitled, a people that has a claim to an appropriate territory—*its* territory, its ancient homeland—and that has to offer an appropriate quid pro quo to the Powers for their consent and aid in the realization of this goal of their national life. To Turkey, which controlled Palestine at that time, he offered as a quid pro quo the regulation of the country's disarrayed finances by means of loans and annuities that would free Turkey from its dependence on the Great Powers. The establishment of the Jewish state would quickly benefit the other powers because the emigration of some of the Jews would decrease inner tensions. At the same time, Palestine, the holy land of many nations and a transit area from Africa to Asia, would be prevented from becoming the sole possession of a major power. The small Jewish people, which surely could not have the plans of a world power, would be the best administrator and developer of a country valuable to all in many respects. The holy places would be extraterritorialized, belonging to no country and accessible to all nations; the Jews would only have to provide order and security, and this Jewish guard of honor at the places sacred to so many religions would be a symbol of the reconciliation of the people of Israel with the other nations that had been attained through the solution of the Jewish question.

The First Zionist Congress: Foundation and Program of the Zionist Organization

To set the stage for the conduct of such a policy, for negotiations with the Powers about the recognition of the Jews as a people, and for the implementation of the plan for a Jewish state by means of ordered immigration, systematic development of the land, and a sensible organization of the political organs, it was a matter of arousing the will of the Jews to a new existence as a people and state and to organize them for their tasks in politics and development. With a self-confidence that could never be shaken for long and with unparalleled consistency and organization Herzl himself tackled this task after it had turned out that no one else was ready and able to do so. At his initiative and under his direction the First Zionist Congress met in Basel from 29 to 31 August 1897, earlier attempts to convene such a national congress having failed. The Congress, composed of representatives from all nations, regarded itself as the national assembly of the Jewish people and was deliberately directed as such by Herzl.

The two hundred participants assembled in Basel declared, so to speak as a response to the synhedrion convened by Napoleon in 1807, that the Jewish people continued to exist and that it was taking its fate in its own hands. For the implementation of its endeavors the Congress created a state-like organization consisting of the Congress as a parliament, an executive, an electoral system, and a division into local and regional organizations. The goal, the means, and the methods were embodied in the so-called Basel Program. Its main tenet read as follows: "Zionism strives to create for the Jewish people a home in Palestine secured by public law." This program has since then been the official program of the Zionist movement which in the ensuing years and decades—until 1904 under Herzl's almost magic leadership—extended all over the world and eventually became the greatest national movement in Jewish history. All differentiations according to views and philosophies that developed and organized in the course of time, from devout Orthodoxy to radical socialism, added to this common program of Zionism only elements that were in keeping with their special endeavors and gave programmatic expression to these.

In this program and in the incipient organization of Zionism as a political movement, part of the Jewish people proclaimed its will to the continuation and regeneration of national life beyond all differences of countries, periods, social stratification, and ideological aims. At first, and for decades to come, this part remained a minority within the Jewish people; however, all movements for a national renascence have been led by minorities who regarded themselves as the vanguard and representatives of the entire people and deemed the expression of their will to be the expression of the national will. In this spirit Herzl was able to register the result of the First Zionist Congress three days after its conclusion in these words: "Were I to sum up the Basel Congress in a few words—which I shall guard against pronouncing publicly—it would be this: At Basel I founded the Jewish state. If I said this out loud today, I would be answered by universal laughter. Perhaps in five years, and certainly in fifty, everyone will realize it." "The foundation of a state," he continued by way of elucidation, "lies in the will of the people for a state, and even in the will of one sufficiently powerful individual (*l'État c'est moi*—Louis XIV). Territory is only the material basis; the state, even when it possesses territory, is always something abstract. . . . At Basel, then, I created this abstraction which, as such, is invisible to the vast majority of people. And actually with infinitesimal means. I gradually worked the people into the mood for a state and made them feel that they were its national assembly." (*Complete Diaries*, 3 September 1897). History has confirmed this judgment. From the First Zionist Congress there is a direct line via the Balfour Declaration of 1917 to the November 1947 decision of the United Nations to establish a Jewish state and the founding of the State of Israel in May 1948.

"Expiation of Money"

The organization of the Jewish people that Herzl had in mind also had to include the organization of the means of power at the disposal of the Jewish people, primarily its money. Just as Herzl wished to transform, in the process of solving the Jewish question, forces of misfortune into forces of salvation, the Zionist solution was to bring about an "expiation" of Jewish money, as it were. (One can see how anti-Jewish arguments are reflected even in the thinking of so self-confident a Jew as Herzl.) In Herzl's view, Jewish financial power, which had come into being under the compulsion of historical circumstances, was one of the main reasons for modern anti-Semitism. Herzl thought that the anti-Semites imagined Jewish financial power to be as great as it could be if, in contrast to reality, it united for common action to solve the Jewish question. Properly organized, it was now to facilitate the acquisition and settlement of Palestine and thus the return of the Jews to their land. Here, too, new methods were to be employed. Supplication and mere charity, which were humanly degrading to the beneficiary, were to be replaced in the building of the land by economic financing through investment and credit from banks and settlement societies. Next to its importance for the work of settlement this was the purpose of the Jewish Colonial Trust (1899) and the Anglo-Palestine Company (1899, today Bank Le'umi l'Yisrael), the foundation of which was misunderstood by most people in Herzl's time, as financial institutions of the Zionist World Organization, as well as of the Jewish National Fund as an instrumentality for the purchase of soil in Palestine as the common property of the Jewish people.

Idea and Reality

In Herzl's lifetime his ideas about the Jewish question and its solution were grasped and approved of in their full significance by only a small minority of the Jewish people. The entire Jewish "establishment" was opposed to them, regarded the new ideas as dangerous, and fought against them. To be sure, Herzl had a certain success in his diplomatic-political negotiations with the European Great Powers (Austria, Germany, Russia, England) and with the Turks, and in them the Jewish people was recognized as a political factor. Since, however, Herzl did not manage to interest Jewish financiers in Zionism and organize them as a supporting force, there was no decisive result by Herzl's untimely death in July 1904.

That his ideas and proposals were not more rapidly accepted by the Jews and in the political world may be called tragic and calamitous. If it had been possible to implement the Zionist solution earlier than the founding of the State of Israel in May 1948, the Jews and the world might have been spared the horrendous misfortune that Hitler brought upon them. On the other hand, it is understandable that the new ideas did not immediately caputre people's hearts and wills. They were too much in conflict with the theory and practice of a century that had become accustomed to seeing and solving the Jewish question from other vantage points—in the spirit of a liberalistic belief in a world becoming more and more humane.

The idea of founding a Jewish state did not fit the political framework of the time either. That was, after all, the heyday of European imperialism and colonialism. Even states that had not managed to gain their national unity and independence until the latter part of the nineteenth century were influenced by these trends. Statesmen had little appreciation of the nascent national movements within their empires. Thus Zionism started its struggle as a political movement of a Jewish people reentering history actively and responsibly at a time when the older national movements had gone to nationalistic and chauvinistic extremes and the *raison d'être* of the newer ones had not yet been recognized. From the outside Zionism might have resembled the imperialistic and colonial movements (and to our days it has often been equated with them), though in its nature and goal it was diametrically opposed to them. After all, Zionism, a movement in which age-old longings and endeavors were organized in modern political forms, did not strive for the conquest of a foreign country and the subjugation of an alien population; it was its aim to settle its own people in a country traditionally (and now with renewed awareness) regarded as a homeland, and to do so with the protection of legal and political guarantees that would safeguard its national existence. It was a movement that was backed by no political power and whose adherents were scattered all over the world. How was it to prevail in the political game of the Powers?

Effects of Zionism: Revitalization of the Jewish People

Viewed against the background of this world opinion and political situation, it is nothing short of astonishing how quickly the new ideas made their way and how soon they united with old tradition and frequently dissmilar endeavors both within the Zionist movement and without. Political and cultural trends of the surrounding world were caught hold of by the Zionist movement and fruitfully integrated into it. Reversing their earlier methods, people began to adapt alien elements to themselves instead of surrendering to these uncritically. A new pride came into being, a new awareness of one's own worth, a new will to live and to lead a responsible life in that free restraint which is the sole home of culture. Fresh forces awakened, lovingly immersed themselves in the past, and devotedly worked in the present for a happier future as Jews and human beings. It was the atmosphere of a renaissance.

This effect of the Zionist movement was not restricted to the limited, only gradually growing circle of registered adherents but spread farther and farther. What happened appeared as a miracle to many: The Jewish people, which had been believed to be dead and almost to have been given an honorable burial, began to rise and enter history again actively and consciously. The waves of the new movement touched some of the youth in the West, the Jewish masses in eastern Europe, and many plain people as well as disillusioned intellectuals. Some desired the new life with heart and soul; others were less enthusiastic about it. Many opposed the new ideas, but even this opposition roused them from their lethargy. There are historic events, ideas, and actualities that one cannot escape, whether one embraces them or opposes them. Their appearance changes the entire situation, and what happens afterward is part of a new epoch no matter how close its connection with the old one. Zionism was such an event in the life of the Jews and in the history of the Jewish question.

This made itself felt in all aspects of Jewish life. The principle of organization became part of it. In the course of the ensuing decades many local Jewish communities in central Europe assumed a different, more comprehensive character, and regional associations of communities were formed. To an increasing extent the Jewish associations for the combating of anti-Semitism began to do positive cultural work as well, fighting not only outside threats but also endeavoring to strengthen Jewish self-awareness even if they indignantly rejected the ominous term "Jewish people" and still more indignantly "Zionism." Jewish sports clubs came into being, and it was not just accidental if they chose names like Makkabi as their symbol.* Jewish students organized themselves and Jewish youth movements were founded—Zionist, anti-Zionist, "Jewishly neutral" ones—that attracted more and more young members. Cultural organizations were created; relief organizations were expanded and increasingly assumed an interterritorial character. World War I, in which a greatly augmented American Jewry appeared on the scene for the first time, led to the foundation of the largest Jewish relief organization (Joint Distribution Committee) ever known to Jewry. No matter whether Jews called themselves the Jewish people, a tribe, or a community, the solidarity of the Jews and their assumption of mutual responsibility were given ever greater and more organized expression.

The Balfour Declaration

This Jewish people, which in the meantime had had certain successes in the practical settlement work in Palestine under the direction of the Zionist Palestine Office in Jaffa, received through the Balfour Declaration of 2 November 1917 and the decisions of the San Remo Conference in April 1920 the international recognition and solemn assurance of the Powers that "a national home for the Jewish people" would be created in accordance with the demands first made by the First Zionist Congress of 1897.

The Balfour Declaration and the British mandate for Palestine were the result of political work in the Diaspora, especially in England, and of "practical" settlement work in Palestine. The political work was continued after Herzl's death by his friend and successor David Wolffsohn as the head of the Zionist Organization, and the Zionists were able to exploit a situation arisen after the outbreak of World War I through the expected disintegration of the Turkish Empire. Under the leadership of Chaim Weizmann and with support from Nahum Sokolov, Louis D.

---

*This memorialized the uprising of the Maccabees (165 B.C.E.), which led to the founding of the second Jewish state.

Brandeis, and others, they were able to convince the British government that the Zionist endeavors in Palestine were justified and that it would probably be in the British interest to support them.

Politics and Settlement Work

This policy was the result of a political faction that had taken charge after Herzl's death, the so-called "synthetic Zionism" which called for work "from below and from above," on the soil of Palestine and on the political-diplomatic plane. The settlement work of the Zionist Organization, accomplished from 1908 on under the direction of the jurist and sociologist Arthur Ruppin (1876–1943), sought to preserve the enthusiasm of the new wave of self-sacrificing immigrants from Eastern Europe that started in 1904–5, the so-called "second aliyah." It attempted to do so by trying out new methods of settlement and forms of colonization of a cooperative and collective nature (the first of which, Kvutza Degania, was founded in 1909), giving parity to the settlers and the settlement agencies as partners in planning and construction. This enthusiasm was to be channeled into creative directions and at the same time lay the foundations for a time when a legal basis would make it possible to work more systematically and on a larger scale.

That time seemed to have come in 1920, when England was given the mandate for Palestine and charged with promoting the establishment of a Jewish "national home" in Palestine without abridging the civil and religious rights and political status of the Jews in other countries.* The cautious formulation, particularly in its restrictive clause in favor of the resident population, left the door wide open for interpretations of all kinds. At first, however, the new status for Jewish immigration and settlement work was regarded and hailed by many almost as carte blanche for the foundation of a Jewish state. Leading British politicians also regarded the promise in this light and accepted or opposed it for this very reason. In connection with the Balfour Declaration and the mandate for Palestine there actually began a new immigration and an expansion of settlement work in urban and rural regions. The Jewish population in Palestine grew from 85,000 in 1914 (and only 57,000 at the end of World War I in 1918) to 175,000 in late 1931. Large, unsettled or thinly settled, partly swampy and malaria-infested areas like the Jezreel Valley (Emek Yezre'el) and the Hefer Valley (Emek Hefer) were cultivated and decontaminated, the coastal plain was settled and reforestation of the calcified mountains was begun on an ever larger scale. New agricultural settlements and experiment stations for scientific research came into being, the cities expanded, commercial and industrial enter-

*See the documents in Part 2.

prises were founded, water power was developed, electrification was accomplished, and a comprehensive educational and cultural system was established in Hebrew, a language that had been completely revitalized and systematically developed. A new Jewish type, the Jewish settler and pioneer, began to take shape and affect the Jews in the Diaspora. To be sure, at the same time new problems and crises arose, and these also had an effect on the Diaspora.

The Tragedy of the Time

It was the tragedy of Zionism and hence the tragedy of the Jewish question that it began in a period between the decay of the old national movements and the as yet scarcely visible inception of the new ones— that is, one or two generations too late as compared with the great national movements of the nineteenth century. Zionism was given an opportunity to do legitimate, more extensive work in Palestine at the same time that the Jews of Eastern Europe, on whose active participation and material support the construction program was largely based, finally received the desired equal rights and sometimes even national minority rights in the eastern states that had gained their independence after the collapse of the Czarist Russian empire (Poland, Lithuania, Latvia, Estonia), which means that their need for emigration and settlement was noticeably diminished. In the Soviet Union, which had just come into being, Jewish property was expropriated by the communist system, the Jewish population in the new closed state was increasingly cut off from the outside world, and its emigration was legally impeded. American Jewry, which had made its first conspicuous appearance in World War I, had not yet sufficiently developed to play a role as the leading force, at least financially, in Judaism and Zionism. Thus it was tragic that the Zionist movement as the vanguard of world Jewry was not able to utilize the political conditions (which in this regard—and probably in others as well—had also been created one or two generations too late) as quickly and extensively for the work of construction as would have been necessary. As compared to the magnitude of the task the available funds were minuscule, and thus opportunities for land purchase and systematic settlement were missed that never arose again. Time, however, is irreplaceable; once it passes unused, it is irrevocably gone. Tragedy arises when historical conditions coincide that impede the utilization of the favorable moment and when at the same time the people who might have helped do not do so because of a misreading of the situation or out of egotistical considerations.

The consequences of these conditions were multifarious. In addition to economic crises in the Jewish sector of Palestine there was growing resistance from the Arab population. This resistance began in rudimentary form before World War I and then took organized shape as a national movement. In 1920–21 and 1929 it gave rise to violent eruptions and from 1936 on developed into armed resistance against Jewish settlement and the British mandatary regime.* Another consequence was that under the pressure of these circumstances the British government, disappointed at the insufficient flow of money and independent Jewish settlers, retreated farther and farther from its obligation to help with the creation of a national home for the Jewish people. It increasingly interpreted the restrictive provisions as equal to the main objective and limited the immigration to Palestine of impecunious Jews to an ever greater extent. This was the situation in 1933 when Hitler came to power in Germany and the plan of a final solution of the Jewish question through the expulsion and extermination of European Jewry, with the gruesome consequences of its implementation, first took shape.

*We shall deal with the Arab problem in greater detail in the following chapters, particularly chap. 10.

9

The Attempt at a Radical "Final Solution" of the Jewish Question in Accordance with the Anti-Semitic Racial Doctrine (1933–1945)

If one wants to understand this chapter in the history of the Jewish question, one that is beyond all comprehension in its frightfulness, one does well to start with a brief recapitulation of the bare facts, for they speak a more forceful language than any artful description. The next questions will have to be these: How did this development come about, how was it possible? On what basis and under what conditions—physical, intellectual, and spiritual—did it take place? What were its effects and its immediate and long-range consequences?

The Facts

In early 1933 the so-called National Socialist Workers' Party (known as the National Socialists or, in common parlance, the Nazis) came to power in Germany under the leadership of the Austrian-born German Adolf Hitler, the anti-Semitic *Führer* and a brilliant paranoid personality. It put a sudden stop to the era of emancipation and equality for the Jews in Germany. Liberalism and representative democracy, which had increasingly prevailed in political life since the French Revolution and on whose principle of legal equality of all people and citizens the formal equality of the Jews had been based, was now replaced by a totalitarian political system with its hierarchy of leaders and led, of superior and inferior people. The formation of opinion and decision through free discussion and elections by majority vote were replaced with the authoritarian principle of command and obedience, as well as organized mass propaganda directed from the highest level and involving terror, mass arrests, detainment in concentration camps, murders, and unlimited propaganda in the spirit of party ideology. The anti-Jewish racial idea occupied a central place in this ideology and thus became the foundation of the laws in force.* It was on this basis that the National Socialist rulers undertook the final solution of the Jewish question—in Germany, Europe, and if possible the entire world.

FOURTH PHASE: DEPRIVATION OF CIVIL RIGHTS, GHETTOIZATION,

This attempt to solve the Jewish question was made in stages. The first phase began on 1 April 1933, with a one-day organized boycott of Jewish stores. Its declared aim was the defamation of the Jews as "non-Aryans" and parasites, their elimination from government service and the cultural life of the German people as well as the curtailment of their economic influence. By means of the so-called *Gleichschaltung* (bringing into line, or coordination) of the regional governments of the German federal state all the measures ordered by the Reich's government always had validity for all of Germany. The so-called Nuremberg Laws concluded this phase and formed the basis of the following stages.

SECOND PHASE: LEGAL "DIS-INTEGRATION" AND "DISASSIMILATION"

The "Reich Citizenship Law" and the "Law for the Protection of German Blood and German Honor," both promulgated on 15 September 1933 at the convention of the National Socialist Party in Nuremberg, as well as the regulations for their implementation declared that the racial principle was the legal foundation of citizenship. Henceforth only those could be citizens of the Reich who were "subjects [*Staatsangehörige*] of German or kindred blood"; only they could be "holders of full political rights." Jews were excluded from Reich citizenship, participation in public life, and holding public office. Marrying a Jew and extramarital intercourse with one were punishable by a prison term and in some cases even the death sentence. More and more laws and hundreds of decrees for their enforcement extended the *Arierparagraph* to almost all areas of professional and social life. If the "assimilation" of the Jews to their surroundings had been the aim of policies toward Jews in the era of emancipation and liberalism, the exact opposite, their "disassimilation," was now striven for. By means of law and a defamatory propaganda the Jews were "eliminated from the German people" as enemies of the state and isolated from the non-Jewish population in every respect. Only within the ghetto created in this way—not a spatial but a legal, social, and spiritual one—were the Jews permitted Jewish cultural activities. Its only connection with the outside world was through their position in the economy, which was constricted but left

---

*About points 4 to 7 of the party platform, which concerned the legal status of the Jews, see Part 2.

essentially intact in order not to disarray the total economy by precipitous intervention.

THIRD PHASE: DESTRUCTION OF THE RELIGIOUS AND ECONOMIC BASIS
OF JEWISH EXISTENCE (1938–1939)

The third phase began *schlagartig* (a favorite word of the Nazis: at one blow) as a "spontaneous reaction" to the shooting of the German embassy counselor Ernst vom Rath by the young Polish Jew Grynszpan. A pogrom, the so-called *Kristallnacht* (night of broken glass), was organized throughout Germany on 9 and 10 November 1938, exactly twenty years after the collapse of imperial Germany and the proclamation of the Weimar Republic, and fifteen years after Hitler's abortive *Putsch* in Munich.

On that night synagogues all over Germany were set on fire, and their ritual objects were desecrated and destroyed. Organized gangs of Nazi thugs under the leadership of the SS broke into Jewish shops and apartments through smashed windows and doors, destroyed Jewish movable property, and arrested about 30,000 Jews, sometimes amid horrendous verbal and physical abuse. This well-organized "spontaneous" action was the prelude to new legal measures. The Jews were now systematically expelled from the economy in which they had hitherto still occupied a certain position, and at the same time they were forced to pay a billion Reich marks (250 million dollars) by way of atonement, an amount that was soon raised by 25 percent. This essentially completed the elimination of the Jews from the life of the German people and state, as well as their degradation as pariahs outside the legal order of the state. The forcible *Anschluss* of Austria in March 1938 and the occupation of Czechoslovakia by Germany in March 1939 extended the sphere of validity of all these anti-Jewish laws, decrees, and regulations to the areas incorporated into or "attached" to the German Reich.

FOURTH PHASE: DEPRIVATION OF CIVIL RIGHTS, GHETTOIZATION,
DEPORTATION (1939–1942)

The next phase started shortly after the outbreak of World War II, which began on 1 September 1939 with the Hitler-ordained invasion of Poland by German troops. Up to that time the powers that be had worked with all the means at their disposal to isolate the Jews as non-Aryans, inferior people, and parasites and to pressure as many of them as possible to emigrate. Now the leading circles began to find these aims inadequate. Emigration had been limited all along by the legal restrictions in force in all states and their unwillingness to change these laws in the Jews' favor, but as more and more countries entered the war, this immigration gradually came to a stop. At the same time, the German conquests in the East, North, and West brought the Jewish population of almost all of continental Europe under the control of the Nazi state and its laws and regulations concerning the Jews. The "new order of Europe" in the spirit of the National Socialist claim to domination and the solution of the Jewish question in accordance with racial ideology now entered the realm of possibility and feasibility.

FIFTH PHASE: "LIQUIDATION"—THE MASS MURDER OF THE "FINAL SOLUTION" (1941–1945)

Hitler and his henchmen did not hesitate to make use of these opportunities. The code words "final solution of the Jewish question" were increasingly used for their plans.

As early as November 1938 Hermann Göring had announced that there would be "a great reckoning with the Jews" if there was a war. In the summer of 1939 Hitler had repeated the threat he had made fifteen years earlier in his programmatic book *Mein Kampf:* a coming war would not bring the destruction of Germany but that of the European Jews—and from the outset to his testament, written shortly before his suicide, he blamed the Jews for provoking it. Now the time seemed to have come to translate these threats and plans into reality. After some vacillation and hesitation they were implemented with an organization and a scientific technique that seem incredible and ghastly to this day, even though we know that they were a gruesome reality.

Even during the one-month campaign in Poland (1 September to 1 October 1939) numerous pogroms (called "actions") had taken place in more or less organized fashion. After the completion of the campaign Poland became the central area for testing new decrees against the Jews and for the implementation of a "final solution" of the Jewish question. In early October 1939 there began the first deportations of Jews from Vienna and Bohemia to Poland. In the course of the years these assumed even greater dimensions and were extended ever more systematically to the entire territory under Nazi domination. The property of the deported Jews was "confiscated for the benefit of the German Reich." In late October forced labor was decreed for "all Jews residing in the *Generalgouvernement* [Poland]," and in late November 1939 the Jews were required to wear the Yellow Badge—measures that were extended to the entire Reich two years later."* In April 1940 the first demarcated, enclosed, and closely guarded ghetto was established in Lodz, and six months later the blocked-off Warsaw ghetto was set up. Ghettos in other

*Police regulations concerning the identification of Jews dated 1 September 1941 (after Hofer, *Nationalsozialismus*, p. 297): "Jews . . . past the age of six are forbidden to appear in public without a Yellow Badge. . . . The Yellow Badge is a palm-size, black-bordered hexagram of yellow cloth with the black inscription *Jude*. It is to be worn on the left side of the chest, firmly sewn on the garment."

places in Eastern Europe followed. The plans of Reinhard Heydrich, who was responsible for the "final solution" of the Jewish question, called for the removal of the Jews from the rural settlements and their concentration in the larger urban ones. For the Jews deported to Poland a Jewish reservation was to be established in the Lublin area. The ghettos may have been planned only as a transitional measure for the systematic murder of the Jews, and it is probable that the powers that be already intended their extermination at least through the "natural" factors of overwork, hunger, disease, and so forth.

The next phase on the way to the "final solution" began with the Hitler-ordained attack on Soviet Russia. *Einsatzgruppen* (special-duty groups) of the SS—the Nazi "protective troops" which, trained for unquestioning obedience, were a willing tool, one impeded by no moral scruples, in the hands of an unscrupulous government—were now given orders to "liquidate" Jews, gypsies, and political leaders, as well as intellectuals known to be hostile to the Germans in the occupied areas of the East. They killed about a million people, mostly Jews, through mass shootings and organized pogroms. Since these methods still seemed too slow in producing the desired results and placed too great a strain on the nerves of the executioners, the powers that be began, in the summer of 1941 at Auschwitz, to accomplish the mass murder by gassing. This method was technically more efficient, attracted less attention, and had already been tested on a smaller scale in what had been called "euthanasia" (mercy killing)—the extermination of deformed children, mental patients, and other human lives that were "unworthy" from the viewpoint of an "Aryan" racial policy.

A decisive step on the road to this "final solution" of the Jewish question by means of systematic mass murder was the Wannsee Conference, a discussion of the final solution held on 20 January 1942 (Am Grossen Wannsee No. 56–58, Berlin). In contrast to most other deliberations on the Jewish question, an official protocol prepared by Adolf Eichmann, that ambitious bureaucrat of extermination, has been preserved. At the beginning of the conference Heydrich, the "Chief of the Security Police and the Security Service," announced that he had been appointed by Reich Marshal Göring as "Plenipotentiary for the Preparation of the Final Solution of the European Jewish Question." According to the minutes, Heydrich went on to say: "The Reich Marshal's request to have a draft sent to him about the organizational, substantive, and economic matters with a view to the final solution of the Jewish question necessitates prior joint consideration by all central agencies directly concerned with this question, with a view to keeping policy lines parallel." Thus the task of the conference was the coordination and systematization of the measures to be taken by the various governmental and administrative agencies.

Heydrich gave an overview of the stages in the implementation of the

National Socialist policy toward the Jews. Forced emigration, for which a special Reich central office under his direction had been created in January 1939, had caused 537,000 Jews to leave by 30 October 1941.* However, since then it had been necessary to halt this emigration, for in wartime it involved risks. "Emigration has now been replaced by evacuation of the Jews to the East. However, these actions are to be regarded as alternative options, though practical experience is being gathered that will be of major importance in view of the coming final solution of the Jewish question."

This "final solution" would involve eleven million *Glaubensjuden* (people of the Jewish faith), among them five million in the Soviet Union, plus the Jews by race not included in this definition. Heydrich described the planned implementation as follows:

> In the course of the final solution the Jews shall, under appropriate direction, be suitably assigned to labor duty in the East. In big labor gangs, with the sexes separated, Jews capable of work will build roads as they are brought to these areas. In the process a large part of them will undoubtedly disappear through natural diminution—that is, overwork, illness, malnutrition, etc. The remnant that will eventually remain, being undoubtedly the part most capable of resistance, will have to be dealt with accordingly, since it represents a natural selection and in the event of release must be regarded as the germ cell of a Jewish renewal. (Witness the experience of history.) In the course of the practical implementation of the final solution, Europe will be combed through from West to East. The Reich area, including the Protectorate of Bohemia and Moravia, will have to be dealt with first, if only because of the housing problem and other sociopolitical necessities.
>
> The evacuated Jews will first be taken, group by group, to so-called transit ghettoes, to be transported from there farther East. . . .
>
> The intent is not to evacuate Jews over 65 years of age, but to assign them to a ghetto for the aged; Theresienstadt is earmarked for this.

Mischlinge ("hybrids," persons of mixed blood) married to "Aryans" were to be exempted from this treatment under certain circumstances, provided that they consented to be sterilized.

When this conference took place, the mass extermination of Jews in the gas chambers of Auschwitz (where it had begun on 23 September 1941) and other extermination camps (such as Belzec, Treblinka, and Majdanek) was long past the experimental stage and had been developed into a system of murder worked out to the last detail. The area of the Reich and the occupied countries in eastern, southern, and western Europe were "combed through" and Jews were transported to

*360,000 from the *Altreich* (Germany before March 1938), 147,000 from the *Ostmark* (Austria), and 30,000 from the "Protectorate Bohemia and Moravia."

these centers of mass murder in closed cattle cars by the thousands, hundreds of thousands, and millions. Between 1933 and 1945 more than six million Jews, over a third of the Jewish people and two-thirds of European Jewry, were killed in these death factories by shooting, starvation, slave labor, torture, gassing, medical experiments on living persons, and other kinds of murder.

The Uniqueness of Hitler's Murder of the Jews

These are the bare facts, soberly marshaled. It is not easy to arrive at a balanced judgement. The dimensions of the killings, the systematic and reckless way in which they were carried out, their justification by theories, assertions, and accusations (which stand up to no scientific scrutiny and even run counter to sheer common sense), the bureaucratic cruelty in the implementation of the measures, the relatively slight resistance of those persecuted, the lethargy of the surrounding world, and the deficient readiness of the Powers to intervene in behalf of the Jews*—all these phenomena render the complex of events incomprehensible. Any attempt at an explanation immediately raises more questions and deepens the feeling that we are here dealing with something that had never before existed in this form and to this extent. Hence we must try to strike out in new directions in grasping these events.

If we ask what so radically distinguishes them from the events of earlier periods in the history of the Jewish question, we shall find that it is not primarily the number of victims, or rather, the percentage of those killed in relation to the total number of the Jewish people. The victorious Roman armies in the second half of the first century and the first decades of the second also claimed hundreds of thousands of Jewish lives—a not inconsiderable part of the Jewish people at that time. But in those days these were victims of acts of war or died in connection with fights started and carried on actively by Jews as political and military opponents of the Romans, which means that they were treated in accordance with the cruel rules of war then in force and with the practices of the Roman Empire. Substantial parts of the Jewish people lost their lives in the persecutions of the Middle Ages under the aegis of Christianity, and often under rather cruel circumstances. But there it was, at least officially, a fight against infidels (and, by the legal standards of the time, a legitimate one) for the sake of the true faith and eternal salvation, and those threatened always had an opportunity to save their earthly life and their eternal salvation by adopting this one and only redeeming faith. It was similar with the mass murders of adherents of

---

*Further details on the behavior of the surrounding world, the Powers, and the Jews may be found on p. 379ff. below.

Christian sects, from the Albigenses and the Hussites to the Huguenots. The extermination of alien populations by barbarian conquerors like the Mongols are most comparable to the mass murders of Hitler's hordes. But those involved people who had grown up with different, more primitive cultural, religious, and moral notions and were able to regard what they did as normal actions for the safeguarding of their conquests and their existence as conquerors.

None of these premises apply to the systematic mass murder of the Jews by the machinery of the National Socialist state. By all standards valid up to that time it could not be regarded as an act of war, let alone a martial action admissible in accordance with the prevailing military law. No war against infidels was waged here; it was not a matter of a struggle for the purity and acceptance of a religious faith by fanatic adherents of this faith, at least not according to existing ideas of the nature of religious belief. Added to this was the fact that the persecutions and mass murders did not take place in an era of primitive notions of human culture and human nature. They happened, rather, in a period of highly advanced cultural life with a very widely disseminated general education and a development of science and technology such as no earlier period had known. At the peak of this development one of the most advanced peoples of Europe was commanded to commit the mass murder of the Jews. This order was given with a cold-bloodedness and carried out with a recklessness and organization that are unexampled in world history.*

In seeking an explanation for these deeds we shall do well to ask first what the *ideological motivations* of the perpetrators were. If one looks at the writings of the time with this question in mind, one can find a variety of rational motivations and behind them, supporting them or fabricated to justify them, nonrational and irrational arguments of the strangest kind. Let us examine both the overt assertions and the covert dogmas on which they are based.

Motivations such as are presented in typical and exemplary form in Hitler's programmatic autobiography *Mein Kampf* have as their point of departure Germany's military defeat in World War I (1914–18), the political collapse at its end, and the founding of the Weimar Republic and the dictated peace of Versailles that followed this collapse.

The Trauma of the Lost War

No people likes to admit failure in a fight. It is always more natural for it to blame a defeat on the machinations of unworthy adversaries, on betrayal by evil elements in its own ranks, and on the devilish actions of pernicious powers to which the selfless and brave fighters had to suc-

*Cf. the note in Part 2.

cumb. To view oneself and one's actions critically in order to recognize the reasons for one's own failure takes the kind of courage and strength that people and their leaders only seldom muster in defeat. It is more comfortable, and even to informed persons often seems more salutary, for the "wounded soul of the people" and for the preservation of a healthy self-confidence to shift the blame for failure onto others, at least until one has recovered from the shock of the collapse. The shift of social forces that becomes apparent in political upheavals, the transfer of spheres of power and influence, and the rise and fall of population strata in the economic, social, and political realm (frequently perceived as the "end of the world") facilitate this transference of guilt feelings to certain people and groups of people who appear to be the real beneficiaries of such upheavals and hence—this conclusion seems logical—their causes as well. After the end of the lost world war the Jews all too easily presented themselves as such a group, one that did not fit into the picture of what was easy to understand and integrate.

The Jews in the Upheavals

As we have seen, the Jews of Germany had for decades, and particularly since the founding of the Reich and the turn of the century, become increasingly visible in the economy, the professions, journalism, art, and literature. On all levels of national life they frequently occupied such leading positions that this situation aroused concern, criticism, and displeasure even among Germans not anti-Semitically inclined (and among many Jews as well). Then came the military and political collapse, the decline of the economy, and the inflation—first undesired, then deliberately fostered by the government, and exceeding in dimensions anything hitherto known. As a consequence large parts of the population lost their possessions and savings of many long years. The working class, hitherto underprivileged, and the socialist parties began their rise to a dominant position in the Weimar Republic, which had replaced the Wilhelmian monarchy, and in more radical form in Soviet Russia. On the ruins of the old economic forces, which had been shaken by war, revolution, inflation, and economic crises, there developed new economic forms which also favored the rise of new economic enterprises. In all these transformations Jews occupied leading positions. They were in the leadership of the socialist movements and parties, and they were skillful (and often also unscrupulous) in exploiting the new economic conditions and opportunities. As already mentioned, Herzl had seen the danger as early as 1896, when he wrote in *The Jewish State* that the social battle would be fought on the backs of the Jews because they were "at the most exposed positions in both the capitalist and the socialist camps." Moreover, those whose economic, social, and spiritual balance had been upset by these upheavals were all too prone to regard this omnipresence of the Jews at the head of opposing, contending powers, coupled with an unclear notion of the inner cohesion of the Jews, as a demonically planned conspiracy of corruption. This, at any rate, is how it was perceived and impressed upon the masses by the man without whom the National Socialist movement with its frightful consequences would probably never have turned out the way it did: Adolf Hitler.

Hitler's Notions of the Jews and the Jewish Question

Hitler and his adherents, thralls, and henchmen viewed the collapse of Germany (in one of those "terrible simplifications" that Jacob Burckhardt termed characteristic of such dictators)* as follows. In volume 1, chapter 10 of *Mein Kampf* Hitler says that it took "truly Jewish insolence" to blame Germany's collapse on its military defeat and more than that, "the whole unbounded mendacity of the Jews and their Marxist fighting organization" who know that in reality *they* are to blame for this misfortune. The Jews have systematically worked on the destruction of Germany and the establishment of their world domination. Through the liberal, Marxist press, the "so-called intellectual press" (like the *Frankfurter Zeitung* and the *Berliner Tageblatt*) "they pour poison into the hearts of their readers" with the aim of "breaking the national backbone of the people." Since the principle of freedom of the press prevented the state from taking serious measures against it, "this poison was able to enter the bloodstream of our people unimpeded."**

THEOLOGY OF RACE

In general, Hitler considered insufficient attention to racial hygiene as the primary reason for decay, even among the aristocracy. This leads

---

*In his writings and conversations Hitler, one of Burckhardt's *"terribles simplificateurs,"* repeatedly stressed his ability to simplify problems that appeared complicated. Note this excerpt from a conversation with Hermann Rauschning: "I have the gift of simplification, and then suddenly everything works." This simplifying speaking style evidently fascinated many partners in conversation and especially the masses. Sensitive ears found them cliché-like, flat, ordinary, and totally unoriginal—and this is how it strikes any objective person in writing. In his *History of the Weimar Republic* ([Cambridge, Mass., 1963], 2:217) the historian Erich Eyck writes: "The miserably low intellectual and literary value of the book explains also why Hitler's political opponents failed to pay it much attention. For they simply could not imagine that such shoddy scribbling could make an impression on any reasonable man. . . ."

**Hitler states threateningly: "I believe that today's generation, if properly guided, will bring this danger under control more easily." Those screams about violating the freedom of the press will "bother us younger people less than our fathers. A thirty-centimeter grenade has always done more hissing than a thousand Jewish newspaper vipers."

to a poisoning of the blood, "because any Jewish shopgirl is regarded as suitable for completing the offspring of His Highness." Here the author remarks with pathos and assurance: "Sinning against blood and race is the cardinal sin of this world and the end of a humanity that surrenders to it." The chapter entitled "People and Race" in *Mein Kampf* (1:11) is devoted to this question. There Hitler says that the crossing of two people not on the same racial level is in conflict with nature's will to breed selectively: "The stronger must rule." Historical development has shown that any mingling of Aryan with lesser blood produces "the end of those who embody culture." Hence any crossbreeding is "a sin against the will of the eternal Creator" (!) The Aryan is the only creative, culture-creating human type, the sole founder of a higher type of humanity; he represents "the prototype of what we mean by the word *Mensch*."

THE JEW AS A "PARASITE AMONG THE NATIONS"

According to Hitler, the Jew represents the greatest contrast to the Aryan. Caring about nothing but his self-preservation, the Jew is devoid of any idealistic feelings; his sacrifical spirit is only pretense. "Jews are united only when compelled by a common danger and attracted by a common loot. . . . If the Jews were alone in the world, they would choke on their dirt and garbage and also try to outsmart and eliminate one another in hate-filled struggles." By his whole nature and disposition a Jew is devoid of culture and creativity. He is not even a nomad, as has been thought, for even a nomad has a certain attitude toward labor. "In a Jew this attitude is missing; thus he has been no nomad but always nothing but a parasite in the body of other peoples." Unlike a nomad, he did not wander freely, but from time to time the peoples he has abused have forced him to leave his place of residence. "But the fact that he continues to spread is a phenomenon typical of all parasites, he is always looking for new breeding grounds for his race." A nomad roams from country to country; a Jew is settled until he has to leave his country and finds suitable conditions for his existence in another country. "He is and remains an eternal parasite who keeps spreading like a horrible bacillus as soon as a favorable culture medium beckons. The effect of his existence is also like that of parasites; wherever he appears, the host nation sooner or later dies."

LYING AS THE BASIS OF JEWISH EXISTENCE

His "existence as a parasite among the nations" forces the Jew to lie constantly and thus makes lying the basis of Jewish existence generally. The Jew so cleverly disguises his national life as religious life that "large parts of the host nation will wind up seriously believing that the Jew really is a Frenchman or Englishman, a German or an Italian, though of a special faith." This first and greatest lie—that Judaism is not a race but a religion—was then bound to become the foundation of more and more other lies.*

HITLER'S BIOLOGICAL PICTURE OF JEWISH HISTORY

In order to show the Jews' devastating influence on the "nations devoured by them," an influence that was and is the same everywhere, Hitler gives a historical survey of the Jewish influence on Germany in the course of history, their function as "middlemen" in the medieval economy, as usurers whose "blood-sucking tyranny" over land as well stirred up general hatred of them. The masses, who perceive "the Jew's very existence as a misery equal to the plague," resort to self-help against him "in order to defend themselves against the scourge of God." By means of his fawning and his finances the Jew, the "eternal blood-sucker," manages to throw his weight around with the government and regain admittance to places from which he has just been expelled: "No persecution can keep him from exploiting people after his fashion." In the era when the power of the nobility was in the ascendant, he received privileges in return for loans to the princes that he always collected with interest and compound interest—"a true bloodsucker who attached himself to the body of the unfortunate people and could not be removed until the princes themselves needed money again and personally drained the sucked-out blood from him again." That the German potentates played this gruesome game and took the Jews under their protection instead of freeing the German nation from them is their great guilt and led to their perdition: "They allied themselves with the devil and landed with him." While the people "instinctively see the Jews as a foreign body among them," the princes even allowed their Court Jews to rise to the hereditary nobility and thus helped "not only to expose this institution, too, to ridicule but also to poison it."

In the meantime the Jews had achieved some facility in speaking and writing the German language. They saw that the influence of the princes was declining and knew that their own "financial domination of the entire economy had already progressed to the point where they could no longer support the entire enormous edifice without possessing all 'civil' rights and that, in any case, their influence could not increase any further. But they desire both things: for the higher they climb, the more enticingly does their old, once-promised goal rise from the mists of the

---

*As striking proof for his assertions Hitler refers to the so-called *Protocols of the Elders of Zion*, concerning which see pp. 337ff. below.

past, and with feverish greed the brightest among them see their dream of world domination move within reach again. . . . This is the basis for emancipation from the ghetto."

The Jews now played up to the people, pretended to be benefactors of mankind, and shouted their accomplishments from the rooftops in hopes of making the world forget their evil deeds again. They became liberal, appointed themselves the mouthpieces of the new age, and attempted, with the aid of the press and the Freemasons, to strengthen their political security by tearing down "the racial and civic barriers" of the host nations while themselves practicing "the strictest segregation of their race." In mixed marriages the bastards usually turn out to have Jewish traits, and prarticularly some of the higher nobility has degenerated completely in this way. "The Jews knew this very well, and therefore they systematically pursued this way of intellectually disarming their racial opponents. To mask their activity and lull their victims, however, they kept talking about the equality of all people without reference to race and color." At that stage the Jews' goal was the victory of parliamentary democracy with its replacement of personality by "the majority of the stupid, incompetent, and—last but not least—the cowardly. The final result will be the downfall of the monarchy, something that is bound to happen sooner or later."

Added to this was the industrial development, which brought about changes in the social stratification of the people. The new working class "had, by and large, not yet been infected with the poison of pacifistic weakness, but was robust and, if necessary, brutal as well." While the bourgeoisie faced the new question without really understanding it, "the Jews grasped the incalculable opportunities for the future offered here, and by single-mindedly organizing the capitalistic methods of exploiting people, they laid hold of the victims of their spirit and their activities and in a short time became the leaders of these people's struggle against themselves. . . . From that point on the only task of workingmen was to fight for the future of the Jewish people. A worker was unwittingly placed in the service of the power that he thought he was fighting. . . . People always attacked international capital and in reality meant the national economy. The latter was to be demolished so that the international money market could triumph on its graveyard."

For this purpose the Jews created the Marxist doctrine, but "under this cloak of purely social ideas truly devilish intentions lie hidden." The goal of Jewish marxism is the disintegration of everything national and racially pure and healthy as well as the destruction of the human personality and the foundations of human culture. "The destruction of personality and race removes the main obstacle to the rule of the inferior—and this is what the Jews are." Their methods to reach this goal "are not honest fight but lies and slander. Here the Jew shrinks from nothing and becomes such a giant in his meanness that no one need be surprised if among our people the personification of the devil as a symbol of all evil assumes the bodily figure of the Jew."

THE ROLE OF ZIONISM

After the rule of the Jews in the state already seemed secure, some of the Jews, according to Hitler, "ruthlessly admitted their national and political ideas" and openly avowed that they were an alien people. But there, too, the Jews were lying, for the Jews were not really striving for the resettlement of Palestine and the establishment of a Jewish state, as the crafty Zionists tried to tell the world in order to outwit the "dumb goyim." "They do not plan to build a Jewish state to live in it; all they want is an organizational center of their international cheating that has sovereign rights and that other states cannot touch."

Once a Jew has destroyed the basis of his host nation's independent existence through Rassenschande* (racial defilement—i.e., sexual intercourse with "Aryans") and by undermining it politically and culturally, he drops his mask and openly becomes "Jew by blood and tyrant of the nations." The most horrendous example of this tyranny is Russia, "where the Jews killed or starved to death about 30 million people in truly satanic savagery, sometimes amidst inhuman tortures, in order to make sure that a great people was dominated by a bunch of Jewish scribblers and stock-exchange bandits."

After this survey of world history in Mein Kampf Hitler comes to the conclusion that the destruction of the peoples in general and that of imperial Germany in particular is primarily the work of the Jews, of their systematic bastardization of all peoples of the white race, particularly the Aryans with German blood, and of their craving to subjugate the peoples and to establish their world domination over them. "The end, however," prophesies the author, "will not only be the end of freedom of the peoples oppressed by the Jews but also the end of these national parasites. After the death of its victim, sooner or later the vampire dies as well."

Looking back on the German collapse, Hitler thinks that in August 1914, when the German workers had discovered their peoplehood again, Germany could have freed itself from the "plague and pestilence" of Jewish Marxism, "whose goal is and remains the destruction of all non-Jewish nation-states." At that time it would have been the duty of

---

*In the style of trashy novels loaded with demonism and sex as well as of pornographic-sadistic anti-Semitic caricatures Hitler writes: "For hours on end and with satanic glee on his face, the black-haired Jewish youth lies in wait for the unsuspecting girl that he defiles with his blood and thus removes her from the bosom of her own people." Compare similar formulations by Dinter, whom Hitler surely read, on pp. 346ff. below.

the government to "mercilessly root out the inciters of the German people. . . . It should have ruthlessly used all its military power to eradicate this pestilence. "This eradication should have been carried out with force and perseverance. "At a time when the best were falling at the front, the people at home should at least have exterminated the vermin." At the end, looking back on the recent past and pointing to the immediate future, Hitler expresses himself about the missed settling of accounts with Marxism: "If at the beginning of the war and during it twelve or fifteen thousand of these Hebrew despoilers of the people had been exposed to poison gas such as hundreds of thousands of our very best German workers from all classes and occupations had to endure, then the millions of victims at the front would not have been in vain."

The Correspondence Between the Time and the Personality: The Pathological Nature of Hitler and His Age

It would be superfluous to refute in this presentation the individual accusations and those of the Jews in general; today their lunacy is evident to every insightful person. They all too clearly reflect Hitler's own wishful thinking, and the philosophy of brazen lying attributed to the Jews already anticipated the methods of his later propaganda and reign of terror.* But how did it come about that such a distorted picture could be painted and that it could be passed off and accepted as the truth? Attempts have been made to explain Hitler's anti-Semitism and his paranoid chimeras on the basis of his pathological disposition and also of his personal experiences in the decisive years of his youth and development. If one wishes to accept this as a point of departure, one must keep in mind that Hitler's contemporaries had had similar experiences and that this correspondence between trends of the time and the man who had risen to the unique role of *Führer* in it created the conditions for the trustful acceptance of the National Socialist teachings about the Jew as an international pest as well as for the readiness to take extreme action in line with this belief.** Let us take a look at the period from the First World War to Hitler in this light.

*Cf. also Alan Bullock, *Hitler: A Study in Tyranny* (New York, 1964), 40): "Hitler's anti-Semitism bore no relation to facts, it was pure fantasy: to read these pages is to enter the world of the insane, a world peopled by hideous and distorted shadows. The Jew is no longer a human being, he has become a mythical figure, a grimacing, leering devil invested with infernal powers, the incarnation of evil, into which Hitler projects all that he hates and fears—and desires. Like all obsessions, the Jew is not a partial, but a total explanation. The Jew is everywhere, responsible for everything. . . ." Cf. also the remarks on works about Hitler in part 2.
**Cf. Hermann Rauschning in his foreword to his *Gespräche mit Hitler* (Zurich, 1940), 7: "Hitler is not only the expression of Pan-Germanism but of an entire deluded age. Here a person of limited intelligence who is profoundly slavish in his instincts takes literally what others have experienced only as an intellectual temptation."

"OUR NEUROTIC AGE"

In 1932, on the eve of the Nazi revolution, there appeared in America a collection of essays under the title *Our Neurotic Age* (Farrar & Rinehart). In his Introduction (p. ix) the editor, Samuel D. Schmalhausen, writes: "That the times are strangely and desperately perturbed even congenital optimists now know. All the economists have taken to writing of contemporary civilization as if they were specialists in psychiatry and psychopathology. The social system is admitted to be in the last stages of a wasting disease. The atmosphere of modern life smells like a sickroom. . . . Is our age peculiarly neurotic? There can be no doubt of it." The editor goes on to say that man had never before felt so insecure and full of contradictions. There was a wide gulf between belief, thought, and reality. Cynicism and disillusionment were the prevailing moods. Man had lost control over his life, was fascinated with death, and our poets were knee-deep in pathology. Science from Copernicus and Galileo to Freud and Einstein had caused progressive disillusionment. In this transitional period from traditional notions to new insights and life-styles man had lost his security and faith in life without having been able to put this situation to creative use as yet. The deep, unsolved problem of this neurotic age was whether it was simply a case of a social order making way for another, better one or whether our entire civilization was plunging into a dark abyss.

THE CRISIS OF THE BOURGEOIS-LIBERAL WORLD

This characterization of the age on the eve of Hitler's ascent to power is typical of the atmosphere that prevailed in large parts of the West and especially in Germany. It was similar in various strata of the population—from the intellectuals, who were struggling with the philosophical problems of their "existence" without finding the way leading from them to life and their fellow men, to the armies of the four million unemployed, who had been pushed from the labor process by an economic system put out of joint by war, inflation, and political and economic unreason. Starting particularly with the German and worldwide economic crisis of 1929–30, these unemployed people had been reduced to idleness and receiving alms from the hands of a state machinery that they perceived as senseless and cruel. Between these strata there was the petty bourgeoisie that felt threatened from above and from below, was no longer able to maintain its position as an independent stratum and class in the face of the economic organization of the big capitalists, and was afraid of plunging into the ranks of the proletariat.

The crisis of the age was perceived and diagnosed as a spiritual malaise in other countries as well, but this was particularly the case in

Germany, where it was exacerbated by political impotence, political and economic dependence on the victor states in the West, and the spiritually never completely overcome disgrace of a lost war. The Germans were living in a republic that owed its existence to a lost war. Anyone who had been hurt by the war, the inflation, the economic crisis, and the passing of political and economic power into the hands of hitherto powerless people was able to blame the parliamentary-democratic republic, a political form new to Germany, for general and personal misfortune—even though this Weimar Republic had succeeded in lifting Germany out of the impotence and opprobrium of the first postwar years and gaining for it a respected place among the nations. The most visible sign of this was the country's admittance, in 1926, to the League of Nations, which had been founded in 1917. Under these circumstances, the political Right, the petty bourgeoisie, and the army of the unemployed were only too ready to listen to the apostles of radical movements of every kind. What all these movements had in common was opposition to the bourgeois-liberal world.

This bourgeois-liberal world, as developed in the nineteenth and early twentieth centuries, was attacked not only by the political opponents on the Left but also by those on the Right who wished to replace it with authoritarian and totalitarian systems of domination. But despite economic and socio-psychological conditions that were favorable to them, the new political teachings would not have been so well received if the ideological and spiritual foundations of society and its pillars had not been shaken for decades.*

BIOLOGICAL IRRATIONALISM

Every radical change in the power relationships of human society is determined by upheavals in the prevailing tenets of faith, and it leads to new upheavals in turn. The century that began with the French Revolution of 1789 had been dominated by liberalism—with fluctuations and in all sorts of gradations—and its more or less universally recognized foundation was faith in constant progress by means of a systematic scientific application of the human intellectual faculties. By contrast, at the end of the nineteenth century people began to doubt the importance of human reason for a meaningful life, and in the first decades of the twentieth century, and particularly after the end of World War I, this doubt became ever more deeply and widely rooted. People began to

*Cf. A. Bullock, *op. cit.*, 806: "Hitler, indeed, was a European, no less than a German phenomenon. The conditions and the state of mind which he exploited, the *malaise* of which he was the symptom, were not confined to one country, although they were more strongly marked in Germany than anywhere else. Hitler's idiom was German, but the thoughts and emotions to which he gave expression have a more universal currency."

believe in irrational forces that affected the fate of mankind more decisively than any rational considerations and calculations. True, the Romantic movement in the early nineteenth century had been under the sign of irrationalism; its influence on a variety of spheres of life never completely ceased, and if anything it intensified in various trends. The new irrationalism, however, differed from Romanticism in important points. It was not oriented toward the past but toward the present and the future; unlike Romanticism, it did not transfigure the object under consideration but tried to see it as realistically as the disillusioned could see it; it devalued all traditional standards and replaced them with new ones that had not been derived from the past or an intellectual-ethical sphere; it generalized facts and insights of a biological nature and origin and used them to formulate laws for the regulation of human social life whose realization was viewed as the duty of the present.

THE UNLEASHING OF INSTINCT-DIRECTED LIFE

The new valuation of instinct-directed life was symptomatic of this new view of the laws of life. It was expressed in Nietzsche's psychology and philosophy as well as in Freud's psychoanalysis and passed over into the consciousness of the time. To an unrealistic ethics and the attitude, often perceived as hypocrisy, that its champions adopted toward a very unethical reality Nietzsche opposed his "revaluation of all values," derived from a biological view and based on a world without God. He called for a "detachment from all moral values," an "affirmation of and confidence in everything that has hitherto been forbidden, despised, and cursed." In his psychoanalysis, which strove for absolute truth, Sigmund Freud, personally a moralist with rather ascetic inclinations, freed human emotional and sensual life from God and sin and analyzed the mechanics of the forces active in it with the methods of empathy and logic. The world of the conscious, ruled by reason, was stripped of its sole dominance as the stratum of the so-called unconscious underneath it was lifted from the mystery of darkness into the light of examination and treatment. Freud's teachings underwent further development by him and his disciples and were transferred from the plane of individual psychology to that of social life. Beginning with the 1920s they became, in all sorts of interpretations, reinterpretations, and misinterpretations, the popular reading material and conversational fodder of the time. From Freud's fearless analysis of instinctual life many of his readers (though not Freud himself) came to the conclusion that the time for controlling the senses was past and that modern man must give free rein to his drives. Many regarded this view as true not only for sex life but also for related primitive instincts like cruelty and violence. Everything became a subject of free discussion, and there developed an atmosphere free from moralizing hypocrisy in the spirit of a misunderstood Nietzsche—homosexuality, free love, sadism ("Not the Murderer but the Murdered is Guilty," to quote the title of a much-read novel by Franz Werfel, published in 1919)—a value-free atmosphere not based on a real understanding of Freud but regarded by many as the logical consequence of his doctrine: What right does one have to evaluate and condemn crimes if they can be explained as consequences of natural dispositions and psychic experiences and developments?

"THE DECLINE OF THE WEST"

Oswald Spengler's historical vision of "the decline of the West" was perhaps the most characteristic expression of the period between 1918 and 1933. The first volume of the work thus titled appeared in 1918 and the second volume in 1922. Basing himself on Nietzsche, Spengler painted in outline and frequently in dazzling colors a picture of world history that he called a morphology, using a term derived from the natural sciences. What is decisive about this view is not the individual nature of historical happenings but the typical elements. Cultures are conceived of as organisms subject to their laws of growth, rising, falling, fading, rigidification, and decline. In this there is no general progress. Every civilization leads its own life that is determined by the natural realities of landscape, race, and destiny. The title of this book and much of its contents gave sustenance to the profound cultural pessimism of a generation disillusioned by inflation and shaken in its sense of values. However, a generation ready for action was also able to base itself on many of Spengler's views if in its search for new goals and paths it drifted into crudely nationalistic channels—surely often contrary to the author's intentions. Did Spengler not speak of the transition of the West from the stage of "culture" to the period of "civilization," at the beginning of which democracy succumbs to the power of Caesarism, and of the replacement of the parliamentary system by the enormous will to power of one individual? Did he not include in his philosophy of history as a central idea the old doctrine of struggle and war as the source of all human events, and as a consequence thereof the cult of power, the glorification of force, the right of the stronger, the victory of the better blood? It is true that Spengler—like Nietzsche a despiser of the masses and an opponent of the cheap, plebeian cult of race—rejected the National Socialist *Weltanschauung* and was in turn rejected by the National Socialist leaders, who were rather akin to his Caesarean dictatorial type. But his hatred of Marxism, parliamentary democracy, and the Weimar constitution, his antitheses of soulful culture and sober materialistic civilization, of the rule of blood and the rule of money, and his abandonment of carefully weighing research in favor of an intuitively

perceiving (and hence hardly controllable) "view" *(Schau)* with its mythologization of cultural events—all this was certainly in keeping with
the thinking and feeling of the time, guiding and shaping it.*

SPENGLER'S IMAGE OF THE JEWS

Spengler's book also made an important contribution to the popularization and mythologization of the Jewish image of his time. We may
compare its influence in this regard to that of Treitschke forty years
earlier, though Spengler, unlike Treitschke, did not express himself on
the Jewish question in separate writings. But through his book the
contemporary stereotypes about the Jew reached a readership that
resisted the influence of the crude falsifications of history by National
Socialist authors as recognized scientific truths, views of a respected
cultural philosopher, and results of a profound survey of world-historical
events.

As we have said, it is true that Spengler dissociated himself from the
National Socialist concept of race. To him race had less to do with
measurable and definable physical attributes than with gestures, mo-
tions, and every expression of something spiritual—and this spiritual
element is rooted in the landscape: "A race does not wander." It is
similar with Spengler's concept of a people: "For me *Volk* is a unity of
soul." But even these definitions exclude the Jews from European
human coexistence. Spengler declares that the Jews have never had a
real fatherland or a real connection with a soil. The cohesion of the Jews
is a consensus on a magic-religious basis. The chapter that contains his
views on Judaism—significantly enough, part of the big chapter "Problems of Arab Culture"**—is a strange mixture of antitheses and comparisons formulated in the semidarkness of biologic-mythic concepts.
Their linguistic brilliance cannot hide the fact that in addition to many

---

*Cf. L. Bentin's remarks ("Die Massengesellschaft im 19. Jahrhundert. Eine termi-
nologische Besinnung," *Die Welt als Geschichte*, no. 2 [1957]: 69): *"Ducunt fata vol-
entem, nolentem trahunt* [Fate leads him who is willing and drags him who resists—
Seneca]—this is how Spengler concluded his book. And many a reader concluded from
this that it was now a matter of affirming the predicted ineluctable fate of Caesarism and
declining culture, to help bring about an age of merciless toughness, of the work-soldier,
of the totalitarian state."
**Cf. "On Judaism," vol. 2, chap. 3. Spengler regards his concept of an "Arab culture"
(for which the history of Israel is only a prehistory) as a great discovery. "Late Arabs had
an inkling of its unity, but Western historians completely missed it, so that not even a
good designation for it is to be found." From this there is a direct path to Arnold
Toynbee's view of Judaism as a fossil of "Syriac Culture" and probably also to make
present-day Arabic nationalistic distortions of history. The makings of this may already
be found in anti-Jewish Arabists like Paul de Lagarde and Adolf Wahrmund. Concerning
Spengler's view of Judaism, cf. especially Max Grunwald, *Das Judentum bei Oswald
Spengler* (Berlin, 1924).

intuitively grasped truths about the nature of Jewish existence among the European nations many stereotypical opinions have been included and are disseminated. Spengler speaks of the "abysmal metaphysical hatred . . . in which the divergent tempo of two existential strains appears like an unbearable dissonance, a hatred that can become tragic for both sides," of the inner alienation with which the Jews participate in the life of the "host nation," even if they regard themselves as members of it. That is why Jewry has a devastating effect wherever it intervenes. The fate of the Jews is nothing out of the ordinary or incomparable. "The Jews are a unique phenomenon in world history only as long as one regards them as such from the outset." Stripped thus of their special nature they are given the usual attributes: "corrosive element," bearers of a "poisoning cynicism"—"enlightenment to the point of cynicism and the harshest atheism toward the other religion, while the fellah-like practices of their own religion are completely untouched by it." And even though Spengler does not expressly refer to the Jews, surely his readers were all too inclined to think of the Jews when Spengler at the conclusion of his basic work (and in many later essays on politics and contemporary issues) speaks of the last struggle "in which civilization receives its final form," the struggle between money and blood. "Money is overpowered and neutralized only by blood. . . . What matters in history is life, always only life, race, the triumph of the will to power, and not the victory of truths, inventions, and money."

Among the particularly effective, impressive, and widely disseminated distortions of history and historical mythologies produced by leading figures in politics and the border region between politics, philosophy, history, and religion there were a number of writings that brought similar ideas to various groups of the population—from Julius Streicher's pornographic anti-Semitic weekly *Der Stürmer*, an up-to-date version of all instincts and traditions of Jew-hatred, to the writings of Hans Blüher, Wilhelm Stapel, and Alfred Rosenberg, *The Protocols of the Elders of Zion*—published in huge editions with authoritative introductions—and novels like Arthur Dinter's *Die Sünde wider das Blut.*

Let us take a closer look at some of these writings.

BLÜHER'S "SECESSIO JUDAICA"

Hans Blüher, mainly known for his books about the "Wandervogel" and the German youth movement in general,* of whose outlook he is typical in many ways, concerned himself with the Jewish question in various writings between 1919 and 1934, the most important of which is

---

*Blüher's view of the modern youth movement as a homoerotic movement aroused spirited discussion at the time.

the pamphlet *Secessio Judaica*, published in 1922. As its subtitle indicates, Blüher intended to give a "philosophical foundation of the historical situation of Judaism and the anti-Semitic movement." Blüher asks: What is this historical situation? His answer is: "The Jews are the only people that engages in mimicry, mimicry of blood, of name, and of form." Its self-concealment differs from that of other nations, being more deeply rooted in its substance. In mythical exaggeration of the Christian tradition from St. Augustine to Hegel, Blüher claims that this is owing to its historical failure; its chosenness refers solely to the birth of Christ. By rejecting him the Jewish people and every individual Jew became sick to the core. "They gave birth to Christ and killed the man for whose sake they became active. This guilt won't let go of them."

According to Blüher, the one great historical event in this situation was the development of the Zionist movement. In Zionism the Jews have from within created a cast of thought that roots out the mimicry of substance. Blüher regards the Zionists as a special tribe among the Jews, like the Levites of old.* "They do the most terrible thing that can happen to a Jew today: they shout out the name 'Jew' and add 'I am . . .' They are the greatest embarrassment that Jewry has ever had to endure. And yet they will prevail, for the situation of the other Jews will become more and more unbearable in the course of the decades."

The second great historic event taking place is, according to Blüher, the detachment of Jewry from the host nations. Blüher evidently felt that in a "philosophical foundation" he had to give this a Latin name, *Secessio Judaica*. "The Jews have attempted to graft themselves on Germany in such a way that the place of coalescence is no longer visible," but this attempt has failed. The growing anti-Semitic movement is the empirical expression of the ongoing historical process of the Jews' segregation from the nations.

While Zionism receives the "Chandal masses of Judaism that are streaming back"** and makes the exemplary attempt to transform them from a race into a state-forming people again, "all the non-Zionist Jews are in the service of a destructive historical effect" vis-à-vis the nations among whom they live. This effect becomes noticeable when the Jews enter the historically sensitive strata of a people, and in Germany they have deeply penetrated such strata. "Their task is to impede the Reich. Every Jew, be he high or low, participates in it." The methods used by

---

*Zionism, he writes elsewhere, "is derived from the Jewish nobility. . . . Today it is a power that protects the Jews who are streaming back."
**"Chandal masses," derived from Nietzsche, became a favorite term of antiliberal writers, from Spengler to Hitler. They evidently used it to place themselves in the small upper class of aristocrats in contrast to the underdeveloped masses, to whom they transfer the name and concept of a despised Hindu caste.

Jewry are "the corruptive ideas" that the people are always fed and that are drummed into them like spells in order to confuse their "historical basic instincts." The most important corruptive and destructive idea of Judaism is Marxist socialism. "Judaism is the bearer and propagator of the materialistic view of history that is expressed inconsistently in liberalism and consistently in socialism." No matter how sincerely individual Jews may exert themselves in behalf of their "host nations," they cannot escape the historical pressure of their race, and this always makes them pernicious. "Any people that listens to the voice of the Jews is lost."

"YEHUDA PATET"

The present historical situation is characterized by the failure of the Jews' mimicry. The Jews have been laid bare to the nations: "*Yehuda patet!*" And as a result, "they face a threatening world pogrom." Anyone who recognizes this detachment of the Jews as a historical law and works toward its implementation is an anti-Semite—*sine ira et studio*. This segregation of Jews and non-Jews (particularly Germans) is evident to sensitive people in a variety of spheres of life. Blüher declares in his 1922 work that "without people being willing to admit it fully, anti-Semitism has become a basic reaction of a German." Wherever one turns, one hears anti-Semitic words, and no refutation of the "stab-in-the-back legend" after World War I can change this. Every German feels in his blood that "Prussianism and heroism go hand in hand, and so do Judaism and defeatism. . . . Germans will soon realize that the Jewish question is at the core of all political questions."

Blüher regards as evidence of this the ever-increasing dissemination of the "German symbol," the swastika, which "has already moved from its mythological situation into the historical situation." In consequence of the *secessio Judaica* the physiognomic difference between the Jewish type and the German type will become obvious to everyone, and the Jew and Jewish features will everywhere be discerned with such sure instinct that he and they will no longer be able to conceal themselves. The result will be that the latent ghetto of the Jews will become a real one. "Since public recognition of Judaism will not center on subtle intellectual characteristics but on the cruder economic and political ones, there is danger for the Jews that their reghettoization will be rapid and immediately turn into a pogrom. . . . There is no doubt that the world pogrom will come." In his quasi-prophecy Blüher believes that the only country shrinking back from murder will be Germany. "It is ignoble to torture a disarmed enemy. A German is not a Frenchman." We have quoted from this work so extensively because it is typical of the thinking of young German intellectuals who were sincerely striving for an understanding of the Jewish question, greatly admired certain Jewish personalities or movements,* and both then and later distanced themselves from the brutality and barbarity of the National Socialists, though they shared many elements with the latter in their basic views: opposition to liberalism and socialism, mythologization of history and its bearers, high regard for the instincts in contrast to a "destructive Jewish intellectualism," and—though perhaps less in Blüher than in many others—use of biological concepts to explain historical phenomena.

WILHELM STAPEL

We find similar tendencies in another younger political writer, Wilhelm Stapel, who was also a product of the German youth movement and became the editor of the periodical *Deutsches Volkstum*. The very title of a small collection of his essays on the Jewish question is revealing: *Anti-Semitism and Anti-Germanism*. It is subtitled "On the Spiritual Problem of Symbiosis between the German and the Jewish Peoples" (Hamburg, 1928).** To Stapel (as to Spengler) race is not a dogmatic concept, and he speaks more of the peoplehood of the Germans and the Jews; the latter are in a form of symbiosis with which the Germans are not comfortable. On the basis of their biological, historical, and spiritual backgrounds the two peoples are alien to each other, and hence the Germans have a right to resist the foreign infiltration to which the growing influence of the Jews on German cultural life exposess them. In his analysis of the nature of this influence the author views and criticizes from a German point of view many things that the German Zionists viewed and criticized from a Jewish viewpoint,*** and he comes to the conclusion that the situation is untenable. How it can be solved is another matter. Stapel hints ominously that "it is possible to imagine political radical cures, but how could they be effected in practical terms? . . . The problem simply is not yet ripe for a solution."

What disquiets people of the type and rank of this author is the unfathomable and uncanny element about Judaism which, for all kinds of historical, biological, and spiritual reasons, forms a common front

---

*Blüher, for example, admired Spinoza and Martin Buber, and he called the murder of Gustav Landauer a monstrous deed that would be a heavier burden on Germany than the Versailles peace treaty. In addition to Zionism Blüher respectfully refers to Hasidism, as made known and elucidated in Western Europe by Martin Buber. Other writers voiced similar sentiments regarding Buber and his version of Hasidism.

**The word *symbiosis* to designate the way in which Jews and Germans lived together is generally used only by Jews and very seldom by non-Jews. Concerning the use of the biological concept of symbiosis to characterize the relationships between the Jews and the peoples in whose midst they live (a usage that is, in my opinion, impermissible), see the excursus in Part 2.

***See the excursus about the 1912 debate in *Der Kunstwart* in part 2, pp. 703f.

across the nations despite and above all inward and outward differences. Stapel does not go beyond stating this and refuses to be lured away from demonstrable facts in favor of "crime stories" about a Jewish world conspiracy, etcetera, but he does consider it appropriate to point out that in the face of this common Jewish front many people are convinced of the existence of a joint Jewish supreme command. "They believe in some high council that directs the Jewish front according to some unified plan and that appreciates the multifariousness of this front because it needs it for the purposes [of penetrating everywhere] as a military leader needs different types of arms."*

THE PROTOCOLS OF THE ELDERS OF ZION

This is the title of a work to which Stapel alludes; it reached a wide readership in many countries, especially Germany, in the decisive years between 1919 and 1933 and was accepted by large numbers of people in some form—as truth or myth, as a possibility or as an allegory with a true background.**

If one gives this pseudo-historical monstrosity an unprejudiced reading, one faces an enigma. How could such a crude collection of contradictions, absurdities, and apocryphal "confessions" by Jewish leaders of their plans for world domination have been evaluated and believed as a historical document (as it is in certain circles even today), how could it have been disseminated, accepted, and seriously discussed among educated people even when the literary sources and the techniques of forgery had been irrefutably exposed? As early as 1924, B. Segel rightly remarked: "With these *Protocols* history made an experiment, as it were, to see how much can be palmed off in an enlightened age and in enlightened countries on classes that boast of being the representatives of 'culture and property.'" Let us try to pursue this question a bit further.

The so-called *Protocols of the Elders of Zion* first became known in Western Europe in 1919, when they were issued by the anti-Semitic publishing house "Auf Vorposten" in Berlin-Charlottenburg under the title *Die Geheimnisse der Weisen von Zion* (The secrets of the sages of Zion). The book was edited by Gottfried zur Beek, a pseudonym of Müller von Hasen, a retired army captain. Within one year there were five editions, and the succeeding years brought new ones. In 1923 the

---

*Baron Ernst von Reventlow, a National Socialist with a Pan-German background, formulated this view as follows: "The Jewish people . . . regards it as both its right and its divine mission to dominate the nations, to corrupt them and exploit them" (*Die Judenfrage*, special issue of the *Süddeutsche Monatshefte*, September 1930, p. 851).

**Concerning the literature on this, see the remarks in Part 2. Here only the authors' names are given for quotations.

Baltic German Alfred Rosenberg, who was to become known seven years later for his book *Der Mythus des 20. Jahrhunderts* (The myth of the twentieth century), a Nazi mythology of history, published excerpts from the *Protocols* as well as interpretations of their contents and meaning under the title *Die Protokolle der Weisen von Zion und die Weltpolitik*. The following year the doyen of anti-Semitic literature and propaganda, Theodor Fritsch, issued in his Hammer-Verlag (Leipzig) a new edition, written in more readable German and entitled *Die zionistischen Protokolle. Das Programm der internationalen Geheimregierung* (The Zionist protocols. The program of the international secret government). At the same time translations appeared in almost all European countries and in America, usually with extensive forewords and afterwords.* Of the commentaries in the spirit of the *Protocols* (generally with extensive excerpts from them) two attracted particular attention: the collection of essays issued in 1920 by the British *Morning Post* under the revealing title *The Cause of World Unrest* and the two-volume collection *The International Jew: A World Problem*, published by the auto magnate Henry Ford in 1922 and consisting of essays that had appeared in Ford's weekly *The Dearborn Independent*. Hundreds of thousands of copies of the latter were disseminated in the original and translations (the German edition appeared in 1922 in Fritsch's Hammer-Verlag) even after Ford had officially disowned it in 1927.

All these publications were based on an edition of the Protocols which the Russian professor S. A. Nilus started disseminating in 1905. In 1901 he published a confused mystical-political book entitled *The Great in the Small, or Antichrist Is Approaching*. According to one of the stories told in it, in 929 B.C.E. King Solomon together with other Jewish sages devised a scheme on Zion Castle in Jerusalem for the bloodless conquest of the world for Judaism. In the second edition of that book, published in 1905, and in the suceeding editions of 1911 and 1917 the ominous "Protocols" of those "Elders of Zion" or "Zionist Sages" appear for the first time as an appendix to chapter 10. These subsequently appeared as an appendix to other books and finally in separate editions.

The editors and disseminators tell all kinds of stories about the origin of the *Protocols*. Most of them agree that the *Protocols* were authored in 1897 at the First Zionist Congress in Basel or in a parallel secret meeting of Jewish sages** and that these secret documents fell into the hands of

---

*The British edition appeared under the title *The Jewish Peril: Protocols of the Learned Elders of Zion*, and the first American one as *The Protocols of World Revolution*. These titles are, of course, indicative of the nature of people's thoughts and fears.

**We need not emphasize how absurd this assertion is. As we have said in chapter 8, Herzl's intention in convening the First Zionist Congress was the very opposite: to remove the Jewish question from the fearful and secretive constriction of small conventicles and to turn it into an openly discussed political problem. In his opening

Nilus, the first editor, through theft, the systematic work of the Russian secret police, or in some other way. In 1923 Alfred Rosenberg wrote: "As things stand today, there is no legally conclusive evidence for either absolute genuineness or forgery. Some of the leaders of the 1897 Congress are dead, and others will take good care not to tell the truth. And the Russians who made a copy 25 years ago are probably long dead too."

This half-admission of spuriousness was the result of sensational discoveries. One year after the appearance of the first German edition the political writer Otto Friedrich published a book entitled *Die Weisen von Zion—das Buch der Fälschungen* (The sages of Zion—the book of forgeries) in which he points out astonishing parallels between the *Protocols* and a chapter in the trashy novel *Biarritz*, which the conservative German writer Goedsche had published under the pseudonym Sir John Retcliffe in 1868. In that chapter, "Auf dem Judenfriedhof in Prag" (At the Jewish cemetery in Prague), which was published separately in 1919,* the author has the representatives of the twelve tribes of Israel report at a nocturnal session at the Prague Jewish cemetery about the progress and the future prospects of the plans for Jewish world domination. In August 1921 the British journalist Philip Graves, at that time the Constantinople correspondent of the *Times*, demonstrated in three articles that substantial portions of the *Protocols* had been copied, with slight changes, from a work by the French writer Maurice Joly (1821–78), an anti-Napoleon III tract that had appeared anonymously in Brussels in 1864 under the title *Dialogue aux enfers entre Machiavel et Montesquieu ou la politique de Machiavel au XIXe siècle* (Dialogue in hell between Machiavelli and Montesquieu, or Machiavelli's politics in the nineteenth century).**

The inner contradictions, the conflicting statements about the origin, and finally the proof of plagiarism really were bound to convince any insightful person that the *Protocols* were a crude forgery that had evidently been fabricated in Russia in connection with the persecutions of the Jews and the struggle against the liberal and revolutionary elements. As we have said, however, these exposures did not curtail the dissemina-

---

address at the First Zionist Congress in 1897 he declared: "For the solution of the Jewish question we Zionists desire not an international association but international discussion. . . . In our movement there cannot be intrigues, secret interventions, and devious methods, but only frank discussion under the constant and complete control of public opinion."

Das Geheimnis der jüdischen Weltherrschaft. Aus einem Werk des vorigen Jahrhunderts, das von den Juden aufgekauft wurde und aus dem Buchhandel verschwand (The secret of Jewish world domination. From a work of the last century that was bought up by the Jews and disappeared from the bookstores) (Berlin: Verlag Deutsches Wochenblatt, 1919).

**"The Truth About the Protocols. Literary Forgery," *The Times* (London), 16–18 August 1921.

tion of the *Protocols* in all countries, especially in Germany. "The question as to their genuinenes or spuriousness is really not important," wrote Theodor Fritsch in his *Handbuch der Judenfrage*, which was repeatedly reprinted in expanded editions; the only decisive thing is "the intelligible contents of the *Protocols*, and that is Jewish." And this is what Adolf Hitler wrote in *Mein Kampf:* "The extent to which the entire existence of this people [i.e., the Jews] is based on an ongoing lie is shown in incomparable fashion in the *Protocols of the Elders of Zion*, a work that is so immensely hated by the Jews. They are said to be based on a forgery, according to the moaning of the *Frankfurter Zeitung*, but this is the best proof that they are genuine. What many Jews may be doing unconsciously is set out consciously here. And that is the important thing. It does not matter what Jewish head these disclosures come from; the decisive thing is that they expose the nature and the activity of the Jewish people with downright horrifying assurance and present these in their inner connections and ultimate aims."*

THE "UNVEILING" OF JUDAISM

What is it that appeared so revealing to the non-Jewish readers of the *Protocols?* First of all, that once again an attempt was made to strip this mysterious phenomenon called Judaism of its secret, or rather, to get to the bottom of the presumed mystery of the existence of the strange community that the Jewish people constituted for the nations in its dispersion and unity, its multifariousness and its enigmatic typology. As we have tried to show repeatedly in this book, the Jews had since time immemorial had a mysterious character in the eyes of the nations, and every generation and era had added new features to this mysterious picture. More and more fresh veils seemed to surround what was already shrouded in mystery, and only now and then did these veils permit glimpses of the plain truth. An endeavor to lift these veils may be sensed in many treatises on Judaism and presentations of its practices and its history—from Apion to Tacitus, from the church fathers to Luther, in Eisenmenger's *Entdecktes Judentum* (Judaism unmasked), to which G. zur Beek expressly refers, and in Blüher's cry *Yehuda patet* (Judaism laid

---

*In a similar vein Gottfried zur Beek wrote at the beginning of his Introduction to his edition of the *Protocols:* "The Jews may dispute the authenticity of our description of the way in which the protocols of the sages of Zion were made public, but non-Jewish readers will easily recognize that every word of these reports exudes the Jewish spirit, every idea in it is in keeping with the Jewish *Weltanschauung*, and all the stated aims have been pursued by the Jews since their entry into world history." Hitler avowed in a conversation with Rauschning that he had learned a great deal from the *Protocols* and utilized it for his own tactics: "the political intrigue, the technique, the conspiracy, the revolutionary corruption, the camouflage and deception, the organization."

bare). It is revealing that Gottfried zur Beek titled his introduction to his edition of the Protocols *Das entschleierte Judentum* (Judaism unveiled).

THE CONTENTS OF THE "PROTOCOLS"

What did the "unveiling" reveal? The so-called Protocols reproduce a (24-hour!) speech of an (unnamed) Jewish leader who discusses before a Jewish assembly, and frequently as in a monologue, the principle of Jewish world politics and the tactics for the attainment of the Jews' ultimate goal that have been employed in the past and should be employed in the future. This final goal is, of course, the achievement of world domination by the Jews.

The speaker begins with general principles, virtually all of them taken, with certain modifications, from Joly's book—ideas that Machiavelli expresses as the representative of a policy of unrestrained domination or that Montesquieu, the representative of constitutional democracy, interprets in his response as Machiavelli's principles.* According to these, human beings are beasts of prey by nature, and they can be dominated only by power, in which law resides. Public law has nothing to do with moral law: "Our law resides in strength." The end justifies the means. The masses are blind, and they can be led only by autocratic rulers.

These principles, however, are better suited to all other communities than they are to the Jews. Hence they are immediately adapted to the image of the Jews that large parts of the population had and still have. A section that introduces a terrifyingly mysterious element, the Freemasons and the lodges, in connection with the Jews presents "Principles of the Jewish Freemasons' lodge": "Our watchwords are power and trickery . . . . Hence we must not shrink back from bribery, fraud, or treason whenever these can help us realize our plans." The dissemination of the ideas of liberalism, liberty, and equality has also been only a means to this end. Among the non-Jewish peoples these destroyed the aristocracy, the only means of defense against the Jews. "On the ruins of the old nobility of blood and lineage we have put up the nobility of our educated men, and at its head our aristocracy of wealth."

In the second session the Zionist chief sage philosophizes that wars must become economic wars, for then both parties will be in Jewish

---

*It surely was no accident that in the 1920s Machiavelli as a historical figure had a great comeback in the scientific and political literature as well as in fiction. Gobineau's brilliant scenes on the Renaissance, with their glorification of the figure of Machiavelli, also experienced a number of new editions. In 1924 appeared Friedrich Meinecke's *Idee der Staatsräson* which took Machiavelli as its point of departure. The figure of the leader inhibited by no moral laws that Machiavelli painted in his *Principe* was part of the wishful thinking of many intellectuals disappointed by their age.

hands. "It is the task of the press, the lodges, and intellectualization to paralyze the resistance of public opinion by means of a corrosive criticism of all events and to wean people away from thinking for themselves, for otherwise they might turn against us." In the following sessions it is revealed that this purpose is served by the parliaments, the entire liberalistic state machinery, the incitement of the workers, and talk of freedom. In the final analysis, the goal of all this is the opposite: "the degeneration of the non-Jews."

Once the Jews have power, they will make all these sham goals disappear and establish their despotic world dominatiion. "*Per me reges regnant*—the kings reign through me," it is said in the fifth session. "The prophets have taught us that God himself has chosen us to rule over the entire world. God himself gave us the talent to prove fully equal to this great task."* Resistance against this Jewish endeavor to attain world domination must be broken at all costs—through money, public opinion, the instigation and exploitation of internal conflicts and crises, and even through wars. "As soon as a non-Jewish state dares to offer resistance to us, we must be able to induce its neighbors to go to war against it. But if the neighbors side with that state and march against us, then we must start a world war." In point of fact, however, and often without knowing it, all are serving the Jewish world power, no matter how antagonistic the camps may seem to be. "In our service," it is said in the ninth session, "are people of all views and persuasions—monarchists, liberals, democrats, socialists, communists, and utopians of various kinds. We have harnessed them all for our purposes. Every one of them undermines in his place the last props of governmental authority and seeks to overthrow the existing legal order. This plunges all states into confusion; everyone yearns for peace and is ready to sacrifice everything for its sake. We, however, shall not leave them in peace until they have unconditionally recognized our world domination." Then a king from the house of David will assume world supremacy and will be hailed as a savior from chaos; in fact, he will combat all sensuality and all natural animal forces and lead his life in such a way that he will appear as a moral model to all.

From this brief summary, which has omitted the numerous repetitions and absurdities in an attempt to extract the basic ideas (to the extent that one can speak of "ideas" without doing violence to the word and the concept), one can discern many things that evidently impressed the readers of this monstrosity. This work seemed to predict all phenomena of political and social life of the modern world in the crisis-ridden transitional years between the two world wars.** However, these

---

*In the section headed "Who Serves the Jewish Lodges?" (p. 92).
**In 1923 Alfred Rosenberg wrote in the preface to his book about the *Protocols:* "When

are not predicted as the consequences of a natural development but as deliberately produced phenomena, as the actions of a group of international conspirators who have made it their task to corrupt the world in order to subjugate it to their control all the more easily. This group of international conspirators is the one that people have always known about from religious and secular tradition: the Antichrist, the world daemon, the poisoner of wells and spreader of the plague—the Jew. The adversaries of the Jews had always maintained that they were striving for world supremacy, and in making this claim they had based themselves on the Bible, the Jews' belief that they were the chosen people, and also on many imprudent, tactless, and arrogant statements by the Jews themselves. Their numerical growth as well as their mounting influence in the economy, the press, and cultural life was striking and aroused resentment, fear, and frustration. Now there seemed to be documentary evidence for all fears: confessions by the Jews themselves about their depraved aims and methods. If prejudice against the Jews, popular opinion regarding their devilish plans, and fear of their superiority and their presumed resolve to take revenge for the injustice done them had not been deeply anchored in the conscious and subconscious of the non-Jews, such an abstruse fabrication could never have had any credibility. Now many people regarded it as a confirmation of facts they had long "known" deep down inside and as a prophecy of the events and phenomena of the present. The mythic-demonic figure of the Jew stood, as it were, unveiled in its devilish nakedness before the eyes of an endangered world. In the titles we have cited, in the formulations of the various editions and translations, and in the commentaries—everywhere a cry of fear may be heard: "Watch out, soon the world spider of the Jews will ensnare you in its web! Take care and fight back so you won't fall prey to eternal bondage!" Such words were uttered by many with the ring of conviction; others converted them into effective slogans, often with less naive faith in their truth but with an all the more realistic assessment of the credulity of the masses, which essentially extended far into the ranks of educated people. These watchwords combined with notions and traditions of all kinds. *Judaeus ante portas!* Stick together in the struggle against the Jewish conquest of the world!*

---

the *Protocols* appeared in German in late 1919, they immediately created an enormous stir. Suddenly millions found in them an explanation for many otherwise inexplicable phenomena of the present."

*In 1920, when the *Protocols* appeared in the *Dearborn Independent* of the auto king Henry Ford, even a critic and philologist of the rank and reputation of an H. L. Mencken (1880–1956) could bring himself to write: "The case against the Jews is long and damning; it would justify ten thousand times as many pogroms as now go on in the world" (*EJJ* 15:71).

ALFRED ROSENBERG'S "MYTH OF THE 20TH CENTURY"

The mythologization of these anxiety feelings found its most typical expression in a book first published in 1930 that sought to reinforce the National Socialist ideology with a racial-mythical philosophy. Despite, or because of, the often incomprehensible bombast of the author's mystic view of history, Alfred Rosenberg's *Mythus des 20. Jahrhunderts* became one of the most widely disseminated National Socialist books.*

To Rosenberg, race was the "exterior of a soul . . . the intangible combination of all aspects of the self, of the people, and of a community in general"—its myth. According to Rosenberg, the myth of a people is its productive and preserving power. Applying this theory to the Jewish question, he writes (459ff.): "Such an enormous power is exerted not only by a creative dream vision; enormous power, albeit the destructive kind, was engendered also by the Jews' parasitic dream of world domination." For almost three thousand years this mythical faith has propelled "black magicians of politics and the economy." In the figure of Mephistopheles Goethe drew an inimitable picture of this force, which in the present is embodied by the "masters of today's grain and diamond exchanges, the 'world press,' and the League of Nations diplomacy." In the bombastic imagery characteristic of him, Rosenberg philosophizes: "Whenever the strength of a Nordic flight of the imagination begins to wane anywhere, the earthbound creature Ahasuerus attaches himself to the slackening muscles; where a wound is opened on the body of a nation, the Jewish daemon always burrows into the sore spot and as a parasite utilizes the weak hours of the great of this world. His intention is not to fight for domination as a hero: rather, the parasite possessed of dreamlike strength is guided by a desire to make the world his 'tributary.' Not to fight but win by stealth; not to serve values but exploit devaluation—this is the law by which the Jew has always lived and that he can never escape for as long as he lives."

---

*Its full title is *Der Mythus des 20. Jahrhunderts: Eine Wertung der seelisch-geistigen Gestaltungskämpfe unserer Zeit* (The myth of the twentieth century. An assessment of the spiritual-intellectual struggles for form of our time) (Munich: Hoheneichen Verlag, 1931). By the end of 1936 half a million copies were in print and by 1942 more than a million. The *Protocols*, about which Rosenberg had published an extensive commentary in 1923, are not expressly mentioned in this book, but their philosophy is embodied in it. Rosenberg stuck to his views even as a defendant in the Nuremberg trials. Cf. G. M. Gilbert, *Nuremberg Diary* (New York, 1961), 71, 245, 325. See p. 248 concerning his influence on Nazi ideology (propagandist Hans Fritsch: "Rosenberg became the high priest of the Nazi ideology."). Of course, this book fared much like many "deep" books of this kind: Many people contented themselves with leafing through it or using certain ideas that had become popular. According to Gilbert (*op. cit.*, p. 321), when he asked the defendants at the Nuremberg trial about it, it turned out that hardly any of them had really read Rosenberg's book.

His nature is *Schmarotzertum* (parasitism). The author says that this concept should not be regarded as a moral judgment but as the "characterization of a (biological) fact of life-history . . . just as we speak of parasitic phenomena in plant and animal life. If a crab bores its way into the anus of another crab and gradually grows into it, sucking away its last vital energy, this is the same process as when the Jew penetrates society through the people's open wounds and feeds on its racial and creative strength until it is destroyed." The Jew possesses no organic psychic form. What is involved in Judaism is not real race but what Rosenberg terms "counterrace,"* a group of people held together by a certain blood selection which in its "parasitic activities constitutes the opposite of the constructive work of the Nordic race." Lying is the element of Judaism—or, in paradoxical terms, "constant lying is the 'organic truth' of the Jewish counterrace."

But even this "parasitic revaluation of creative life" has its myth—the myth of chosenness. To be sure, it sounds like mockery if one says a god has chosen "this counternation" as its favorite, but "the Jewish parasitism is actually derived from the Jewish myth of world supremacy that the god Yahve has promised to the righteous." Zionism has not produced a significant change in this either: it is not a national political movement ("as incorrigible European dreamers suppose"), but its sole purpose is to create a strategic center for the parasitic plans for world domination. "For this world-hope of chosenness must consist in living attached to all nations like bloodsuckers and in restoring Jerusalem only as a temporary conference center."**

In his book Rosenberg did not openly discuss the consequences of his teachings, and later he claimed that mass murder had been alien to him, though as Reich minister for the occupied eastern territories he surely took a leading part in the implementation of eastern policy, from the oppression of all non-Germans to the extermination of the Jews. He does hint at this in his *Mythus* when he characterizes the ideology of collaboration and mixing of the races after the Austrian pattern as "racial

---

*Rosenberg was "modest" enough not to claim authorship of this deleterious term. He took it from an abstruse work entitled *Sozialparasitismus im Völkerleben* (Leipzig, 1928) and credited its author, Arno Schickedanz, with having furnished the "strictly scholarly proof of the true laws of the Jewish parasite's life." Concerning this book, see my essay "The Jewish Parasite: Notes on the Semantics of the Jewish Problem, with Special Reference to Germany," *LBYB* 9 (1964), 3–40.

**In the early 1920s Rosenberg had already opposed Zionism in a special treatise (*Der staatsfeindliche Zionismus* [Hamburg, 1922]). In it he wrote: "Part of the swarm of locusts that has been eating away at Europe's marrow is returning to the Promised Land in order to look for fresh rich meadows." And he underlined this passage: "Zionism is at best an impotent attempt at productive achievement by an incompetent people, but most of the time it is a means for ambitious speculators to create for themselves a staging area for world usury."

plague and psychic murder" and formulates the goal of the National Socialist revival movement as follows: "Mythic grasping and conscious perception for once are not in conflict today in the spirit of the German idea of renewal: the most ardent nationalism is no longer oriented toward tribes, dynasties, and creeds but toward the primal substance, the species-specific peoplehood itself; that is the message which one day will melt all slags in order to pick out the precious elements and eliminate the dross" (p. 84).

ARTHUR DINTER'S "DIE SÜNDE WIDER DAS BLUT" (THE SIN AGAINST THE BLOOD)

Rosenberg's book was aimed at intellectual circles, but there were other books that disseminated the same teachings in primitive, catchy images among other groups of people. The books of the anti-Semitic writer Arthur Dinter (1876–1948) were probably the most characteristic of this literature and the most widely read, particularly his novel *Die Sünde wider das Blut,* which was published in 1917 and had already sold more than 100,000 copies in 1920 and more than 250,000 in 1934. With its mixture of petty bourgeois, nationalistic romanticism,* cheap dime-novel techniques, racist mythology coupled with Christian theosophic mysticism,** and pseudo-scientific notes and commentary,*** this anti-Semitic bestseller appealed to instincts, fears, and interests of many kinds.

The hero of the book, an "Aryan" natural scientist, marries a Jewish and then a non-Jewish woman; the latter was impregnated in her youth by a Jewish officer, which—in the author's view—corrupted her genotype forever. This makes the hero understand the natural and psychic laws of the racial doctrine, and he recognizes that it is his life's task to disseminate these.

It is the foundation of these teachings that any contact with the bad Jewish blood sullies and spoils the good Germanic blood for generations to come. If a German girl has sexual relations with a Jew, Jewish

---

*The novel concludes with these words: "Thus he was granted his wish to die for his sacred fatherland after all."

**From the Afterword, p. 431: "Next to my religion, race is the highest and holiest of my possessions. In fact, I possess my religion only through my race. . . . Race and religion are one! And the knowledge that I stem from the noblest race that has ever walked the earth and is destined to lead all peoples of the globe to their highest and ultimate destiny [Aryan world domination in contrast to the Semitic kind?] imposes upon me the exalted obligation to make every effort to keep this race pure and holy and untouched by alien blood."

***From the Afterword, p. 430: "The fact that he [Houston Stewart Chamberlain, whom Dinter regarded as his inspirer and intellectual leader], like me, stood on the solid foundation of natural science increased my confidence in him immensely."

hereditary characteristics will be apparent in all her later births, even if the birth is the fruit of a liaison between two pure Aryans.* The hero, who suffers this dreadful fate, discovers that the Jews systematically exploit this fact to corrupt the Aryans. A Jewish businessman, the father of his first wife, had systematically made mothers out of "blonde virgins"; this is brought out by some correspondence that has come to light after his death. "It must be assumed that the rich Jewish businessman did not do this racial poisoning of the German people only to indulge his lust, but that he methodically pursued almost devilish goals. . . . The German people was methodically contaminated and poisoned" (p. 294). The revealing correspondence found after the businessman's death corresponds in many details to the *Protocols of the Elders of Zion*, which were first disseminated in Germany at that time. The "counsellor of commerce" acted on a worldwide basis and, apart from his demonic-pornographic affairs, limited himself to the role of a middleman. "From every activity carried on by industrious people the counsellor of commerce managed to derive his profit. Hundreds of thousands and even millions of people working by the sweat of their brow dangled from the wires that he pulled. He sat in his Berlin office like a spider, sucking the marrow from their bodies and souls through these wire canals. . . . He was the big, pitiless heart that soaked up human blood in order to turn it into cash, whether it came from the veins of white or black, yellow or red people, Christians or pagans. He smilingly walked over the dead bodies of individuals and families if he could make money from them. But he would never have hurt a hair on the head of any member of his race"—for he needed those to help him with his manipulations and machinations. "After all, the destinies of the world are guided only by a few hundred people, and all of them belong to his race."** They have an army of Jewish middlemen at their disposal, and above all the press of the whole world that is dominated by them.

---

*From the 13th printing, 1920, p. 238: "A dark-skinned something covered with pitch-black, curly hair screamed at him [the "Aryan" father!]. . . . A flat nose gave the head an apelike appearance." This is how the "Jewishly infected" infant is characterized, and the scientific explanation of the fact is given in these words (p. 350): "It is a significant law, and one well known in animal breeding, that a purebred female is rendered permanently unfit for pure breeding if it is fertilized even once by a male of an inferior breed. Such a motherhood that derives from impure male blood poisons the entire organism of the pure female creature. . . . Now you can gauge the damage that is done year after year to the German race by the Jew boys who every year seduce thousands upon thousands of German girls." This argumentation reappears in very similar form in Hitler's *Mein Kampf,* and in *Der Stürmer* of the Franconian Gauleiter Streicher it is elaborated upon *ad nauseam* pornographically and in yellow-press fashion with illustrations, woodcuts, and tales of rape and ritual murder. Cf. also Gilbert, *Nuremberg Diary*, 111f.

**P. 276. In a note on this passage (p. 401) Dinter, like many of his contemporaries

Day after day millions and millions of copies of these sheets flutter down upon people and drum those mendacious ideals into their brains and hearts. By destroying the working middle class, by building department stores and palatial whorehouses, and by means of the most shameless, dirtiest advertising they manage to foment unnatural and perverse desires among the masses of the people, feeding, spreading, and preserving them to make money and more money. Healthy people who enjoy life are systematically transformed into miserable creatures who are sick in body and spirit, discontented with God and the world, and easy to incite against the existing order. Wherever masses are incited under the mendacious catchword "freedom and progress," it is members of this race who engage in this subversive activity. . . . For only in chaos can this chaotic race be in clover; where law and order prevail, it cannot thrive.

Accordingly, the liberation of the German people from Judaism is a sine qua non for its progress. After the "Aryan" hero of Dinter's book has shot the Jewish seducer of his second wife (*before* marrying her!), he says this to the jury in the courtroom: "If the German people does not manage to shake off and render harmless the Jewish vampire whom it is unwittingly nursing with its heart's blood—and this can be done through simple legal measures—it will be ruined in the foreseeable future."

THE "UNTERMENSCH"

In all these forms of literature—from the scientific, pseudo-scientific, nationalistic, political, and mythological kinds to polemics, lampoons, and sexual-erotic dime novels—the image of the Jew was presented to the eyes and senses of people in ever new hues, but as a stereotypical and uniform creature: as the archenemy and embodiment of the "counterrace," as a new transformation of the ancient image of the Antichrist. He is not a human being in the true sense of the term but something far below one—an "*Untermensch*," a subhuman being. A later National Socialist primer gave this definition:

"The *Untermensch*, that creation of nature which seems to be biologically the same—with hands and feet, a kind of brain, eyes and a mouth—is neverthe-

---

obsessed with the *Protocols*, refers to a quotation from an article by Walter Rathenau that had appeared in the Vienna *Neue Freie Presse* on 25 December 1909: "Three hundred men [Dinter interprets this to mean "Jewish big bankers"], who are acquainted with one another, dominate the economic life of Europe." In point of fact, Rathenau's article, which took the form of a letter to the editor responding to the paper's inquiry about the "nature and worth of our new generation of businessmen," had nothing to do with the Jewish question. The quoted sentence reads as follows: "Three hundred men, who are acquainted with one another, are guiding the economic destinies of the continent and look for their successors in their own circles."

less an entirely different and terrible creature, only a rough draft of a human being, with manlike facial features, but intellectually and spiritually lower than any animal. Inside this being there is a frightful chaos of wild, uncontrolled qualities: an unspeakable destructive impulse, the most primitive appetites, the most undisguised baseness. An *Untermensch*, nothing else. . . . He hated the work of the others [i.e., of real human beings]. He raged against it—secretly as a thief, openly as a blasphemer and murderer. . . . Never did the *Untermensch* leave others in peace. . . . For his self-preservation he needed the swamps and hell, but not the sun. And this underworld of the *Untermensch* found its leader: the Wandering Jew!*

Here we have the devil, the Antichrist, and the Wandering Jew interwoven into a biological myth. In this form and similarly in the pornographic-sadistic caricatures à la Streicher's *Stürmer*, in songs and slogans the teachings of hatred were disseminated among the people—from Treitschke's repeatedly quoted formulation "The Jews are our misfortune!" to the frightful battle song of the Nazi hordes training for the near future: "When Jewish blood spurts from our knives, all things go twice as well."

MYTHOLOGIZATION AND DEMONIZATION OF THE IMAGE OF THE JEW

A critical examination of the foundations, arguments, and presentations of this entire literature, of which we have given only a few concise examples, leads one to the conclusion that nothing essentially new is added to the anti-Semitic literature of the 1880s and 1890s, that "classical" literature of modern anti-Semitism. Everything was already present, at least in embryonic form, in the writings of Dühring, Lagarde, H. S. Chamberlain, and like-minded people. But what differentiated the image of the Jew that we encounter in the literature of the early twentieth century, and particularly since the end of World War I, from that of its predecessors in the 1880s? And above all, what had changed in the attitude of the intelligentsia and the masses under the influence of this image?

On more than one occasion we have mentioned one of the most striking characteristics of the new epoch: the mythologization and demonization of the image of the Jew. Presumably it was already present in rudimentary form in the 1880s, but more as a remnant of notions from ancient times, the Christian Middle Ages, and the tradition shaped by them. In general, however, and despite many incipient changes, the

---

*Quoted after Leon Poliakov and Josef Wulf, *Das Dritte Reich und die Juden* (Berlin, 1961), 120. Concerning the concept *Untermensch*, see the notes in Part 2.

generation of the 1880s still leved in the atmosphere of Naturalism and its successors: a positivistic Realism in art and literature, and liberalism in politics and social life. In the intervening decades the world and people's attitude toward it had fundamentally changed. In a world rendered incomprehensible by war, revolutions, displaced persons, economic booms and crises, technical progress and social problems, an explanation and liberation from a responsibility that had become unbearable seemed to be offered by myth—that intermediary layer between fantasy and reality in which dream images are given credence as reality and amalgamate with the experience of the present in such a way that fear, belief, and reality seem to be identical. In its picturesque way, myth explains reality and lends it a fateful-symbolic meaning, whereupon every event of the present is designed to confirm the myth anew. In this atmosphere the racial idea of the waning nineteenth century became a racial mythology and the Jew was transformed from a biological-scientific lower racial type into the demonic embodiment of everything negative and destructive, the personification of evil per se.

The Changed Reality

There had been a decisive change not only in the intellectual and spiritual atmosphere but also in the realities of people's existence in general and of the Jews' existence in particular. In line with the new ideologies and mythologies these changes could be understood and interpreted as confirmation that the demonized image of the Jew was correct.

CHANGES IN THE JEWISH WORLD: THE EAST-WEST MIGRATION AND THE "OSTJUDENFRAGE"

As compared with the Jewry of the twentieth century, the Jewish world of 1880 was still amorphous and static, though it had been reforming and transforming itself for a hundred years. In the 1880s the migration from Eastern Europe to Central and Western Europe and overseas had only just begun—and yet it had already alarmed the nationalistic circles in Germany and caused them to adopt a defensive posture. In those days Treitschke had spoken of the "pants-selling Jewish youths" who were crossing the eastern border into Germany in order to become its rulers tomorrow. In the western countries of immigration, England and America, countermovements had come into being, especially among workingmen who felt that their economic and social achievements were being threatened by a hungry mass of new immigrants working for low wages. In the meantime this migratory movement had turned into a mighty stream. For these emigrants Germany was primarily a transit country on their way to Western Europe and America. Only a small portion of the migrants remained in Germany for a long period or permanently—and yet the number of the foreign Jews rose steadily.* In addition to this actual increase there was a seeming one— the many people in transit. It was assumed that despite all legal and police decrees many of these would remain in Germany.

The First World War created a new situation. In the eastern areas ocupied by German troops the German high command tried to get the Yiddish-speaking Jews who were suffering under the Czarist regime to support German power politics. In this endeavor they were supported by influential Jewish circles in Germany who believed that a community of interests between Germany and the Polish Jews would be of mutual advantage and who founded for this purpose the so-called Committee for the East. This was a great experience for many Jews from Germany who came to Eastern Europe as German soldiers and saw for the first time Jewish ethnic life with an unbroken tradition and vitality, as Heinrich Heine had almost a hundred years earlier (cf. Part 2, pp. 642ff.). The German high command took tens of thousands of eastern Jews to Germany to work in factories essential to the war effort. Their working conditions were contractually specified, but this approximated forced labor.

The retreat of the Germans from the eastern territories at the end of the world war, the rise of the independent border states, and the Bolshevik revolution in Russia made it difficult or impossible for the Jews working in Germany to return, but they also forced many Jews in the eastern states whom the upheavals had deprived of their livelihood to emigrate. This marked the beginning of a new stream of migrants, and again Germany was the main country of transit. To be sure, the number of the foreign Jews residing in Germany between 1910 and 1925 increased by only about thirty thousand, but for many Jews Germany was a briefer or longer way station. In any case, the Jews attracted attention as aliens, and fear of "foreign infiltration" thus was given ever fresh sustenance in a Germany shaken by economic and political crises, even though Jewish organizations took care of needy Jews passing through. After all, in general the public heard only about the immigrants who were unscrupulously exploiting the economic boom. In reality these were only a very small minority, but now they were regarded as typical representatives of Jewry as a whole, and ignorant people or those with an axe to grind presented them as such. Despite all efforts by insightful Jews and non-Jews, "profiteers" and "eastern Jews" became almost

*In 1900 there already were 41,000 foreign Jews in the German Reich and in 1910, 79,000. Between 1880 and 1900, 1,097,857 Jewish immigrants came to the United States, and between 1901 and 1910 there were 976,263. Cf. the notes and the bibliography in Part 2.

identical concepts in Germany. The image of the Jew as a demonic destroyer of indigenous life and the traditional domestic economy was given topical features and new nuances.

The fact that many of the immigrants very quickly assimilated to everything German, acted like Germans, and thought they felt as Germans certainly did not effect any improvement. This neo-patriotism aroused suspicion and struck many as a new form of mimicry, which was regarded as typical of the Jews in any case. Contact with the Jewish migratory movement deepened mutual understanding among a well-intentioned minority in both camps, but on the whole it tended to lead to greater alienation. The image of the "Wandering Jew" and the "Eternal Jew" was revived. It is surely no accident that it appears again and again in the literature of the time, psychologically interpreted, raised to a mythic realm, or crudely popularized in trashy novels and cartoons.

THE ORGANIZATION OF JEWRY

A second decisive change had come about since the 1880s through the large-scale organization of the Jews. As we have said, the First Zionist Congress and the founding of the World Zionist Organization (1897) marked the beginning of a great movement to organize. The Jews of individual countries as well as Jewry as a whole, at first splintered by the centrifugal effects of the emancipative movement, banded together in organizations for all kinds of purposes: defense movements against anti-Semitism, organizations to help with the regulation of global migration, welfare organizations for those harmed by the upheavals, national-political organizations, and associations for cultural education and understanding. There came into being a confusing profusion of organizations that supported, influenced, or opposed one another, or collaborated with one another, but despite all differences agreed on their desire to preserve Judaism and defend it against attacks from without. The non-Jews, and especially those opposed to the Jews, saw in these endeavors especially the common features, the common stand against attacks, and the organization of Jewry as a whole for the protection of each of its members. In the eyes of that anxiety-ridden generation the multiplicity of these organizations and their working at cross-purposes—something that insightful Jews often bemoaned—might have appeared as a stratagem,* as a secret conspiracy aiming at that world domination that those

---

*Cf. pp. 336f. above. An example may also be found in Alfred Rosenberg's *Der staats-feindliche Zionismus* (1922), 58: "When Jewish world policy, and in special instances Zionist policy, is attacked, the 'religious' and 'assimilatory' associations usually appear and emphasize their 'basic opposition' to the Jewish national assault troop. This ruse of the separately marching armies of Israel has been effective thus far, and therefore it is appropriate to demonstrate briefly that all these various associations are of course in basic agreement on the goals of the political fighting forces of Judaism."

defeated in the First World War had not achieved and that the crisis of imperialism caused increasingly to slip out of the hands of the victors as well. Traditional fear of the Jews as well as hidden longings and frustrations (like the former pagan gods, which under the rule of Christianity were transformed into demons) now became delusions about the demonic desires of the Jews. The rationally incomprehensible multiplicity of the organized and organizing Jewish groups all over the world thus contributed to the creation of an atmosphere in which the *Protocols of the Elders of Zion* could be regarded as documents and their absurd contents believed as demonic reality.

ZIONISM

Added to this as a new factor was Zionism and its beginning realization in Palestine.

What was new and surprising for many people (see chap. 8 above) was the Zionists' proud avowal of Jewish peoplehood, something that the majority of the Jews had denied in their struggle for emancipation and legal, social, and professional equality. True, Zionism was and always remained a minority movement, and within the Zionist movement it was a small minority that was active, really took the aims of the organization seriously, and emigrated to Palestine. The majority of the Jews in the western countries as well as an ever-growing portion of the assimilating Jewish bourgeoisie in the eastern countries still wished to be regarded only as a religious community and to belong to the peoples among which they lived. Zionism, however, had generally strengthened Jewish self-awareness and aroused a will to organization and self-defense. During and after World War I it had become a world-political movement recognized by the nations. The Balfour Declaration of 2 November 1917 and the Palestine mandate for its implementation which the League of Nations had given to England in 1920 had laid the foundation for the realization of the Zionist goals. At the same time the Jews in the eastern European states (with the exception of Soviet Russia) were recognized as a Jewish-national minority.

But Zionism, too, was one reason why the Jewish image of that era became even more complicated and confusing. In general, the avowal of Jewish peoplehood appeared to the non-Jews as normal and natural; basically, they had always regarded the Jews as members of the Jewish people. Consequently it seemed all the more astonishing to them that only a minority of the Jews avowed this principle and that only an infinitesimal part of them took radical action in accordance with it and emigrated to Palestine as soon as the legal conditions for this existed. Anyone who wished to do so could easily add all this to the image of the Jew who strives for world supremacy. Avowal and nonavowal of Jewish peoplehood, Jewish settlement and assimilation, even baptism—all this could be interpreted as a tactic fabricated and used to confound and disconcert the non-Jews. This, at any rate, was how what happened was reflected in the anti-Semitic literature and under its influence in the general literature as well.

The developments in Palestine itself appeared in the same light. The unprecedented phenomenon of members of a people returning voluntarily to a country that despite centuries of separation it regarded as its homeland, the cultivation and settlement of desolate soil under unfavorable conditions by immigrants that had grown up under other climates, in urban occupations, and in different linguistic and cultural atmospheres—all this did arouse the admiration of many well-disposed people. Many others saw only the negative sides: the economic crises that this naturally involved and caused many immigrants to return; the political resistance of the Arabs, who felt threatened, and of the British, who were worried about their hegemony in the Middle East. To the opponents of the Jews, the economic reverses, the political impediments, and the remigrants only seemed to confirm what they had always known: that the Jews were incapable of leading a truly productive life, that their existence was parasitic in nature, that they were really not serious about their Jewish-national goals, and that consequently all those who were dealing with them in Palestine were right to oppose them.*

THE JEWS IN THE UNITED STATES OF AMERICA

If the Zionist settlements in Palestine constituted beginnings that could be interpreted by one side as promising seeds of a Jewish regeneration and by the other as proof of the Jewish incapacity for settlement and their disinclination to return to responsible, productive labor, the new Jewish center in the United States of America was highly visible as an accumulation of Jewish-capitalistic power and influence. From an

---

*An early example of such a negative assessment may be found in *Menschliche Betrachtungen zur Politik* (1916) by the poet and essayist Gottfried Benn (1886–1956): "Zionism, on the other hand, declares that it is settling the Poles in Turkey with the aid of these funds donated by German Jews—in Turkey because this economically, i.e. capitalistically, backward empire needs the good Polish traders most. Probably only a few ideologues enamored of King David will deny that Zionism is an agent of capitalism; such people do not know or do not care to admit that in Palestine a flourishing speculation in landed property has long been carried on by Jewish colonists who gave up the cultivation of the land long ago and are living in Jerusalem on beggary, trading, or speculation. . . ." For a time Benn championed the idea of biological breeding and the Nazi racial doctrine. Concerning this cf. Ernst Loewy, *Literatur unter dem Hakenkreuz* (Frankfurt, 1969), 286f. As an example of a more positive view of Zionism by an anti-Semitic intellectual, cf. Blüher's remarks on pp. 333ff. above.

insignificant Jewish settlement, which in 1820 numbered only 5,000, in 1850 about 50,000, and in 1880 275,000, it had developed into the most important Jewish community in the western world. And its numerical growth went hand in hand with its socioeconomic rise and its influence on the economy and politics of the United States. To be sure, it was never as great as anti-Semites claimed, but in elections and certain economic decisions Jewish opinion sometimes made an important and visible difference.

THE JEWS OF RUSSIA

Equally decisive changes for the Jews had taken place in Russia. Before 1917 they had been an oppressed minority restricted to certain settlement areas, and for this reason they had been viewed with suspicion before and especially during the World War. The Bolshevik revolution, like Kerenski's before that, did give them equal rights but it also deprived them of the foundation of their economic existence. The world was blind to the misfortune that had befallen large numbers of Russian Jews and did not recognize the difficulties of their economic restructuring or the insecurities and risks involved in their national-cultural uprooting. The world read about the Jewish communists who were able to rise to leading positions in the Bolshevik party and state structure in the first two decades of the revolution because there was for a time a dearth of people for the new tasks of a planned direction of the government and the economy. People reflected on such press reports with mistrust and in the light of the prevailing mythologies of the *Zeitgeist* and of history, and at the same time they learned from this very press how the Jews in the Germany of the Weimar Republic entered all areas of economic, political, social, and cultural life and often rose to positions of leadership in them. How were they supposed to make sense of this profusion of contradictions and these purely outwardly related phenomena? After all, even most Jews could not understand this Jewish participation in the most divergent revolutionary changes. Those, however, who experienced these developments as non-Jews, that is, from without, and assessed them with reference to their hopes and fears, ideals and interests found the simplest and most plausible explanation in the new myths about the Satanic Jew and his delight in the corruption and domination of the world—myths that were based on centuries-old tradition.

The fashionable tendency to biologize all historical happenings fitted very well into this mythological image of the Jew. Under its influence the anti-Jewish racial doctrine experienced an undreamt-of rise—until it became the foundation of National Socialist ideology and the ammunition for its policies.

The Further Development of the Racial Doctrine

In chapter 6 we gave a detailed report about the origin of the modern racial doctrine and its extension to the Jewish question. In the early 1880s it had led to the development of the theory of modern anti-Semitism. As we have pointed out, this theory of racial anti-Semitism already contained all later developments in latent form, as germ cells and possibilities. New developments had to be added to produce a world florescence from these seeds and to allow the possibility to become realities.

The theoreticians of race from Gobineau to Dühring still based their teachings on relatively primitive biological knowledge. Eight years after Gobineau's racial theory there appeared Charles Darwin's (1809–82) epoch-making book *The Origin of Species by Natural Selection, or The Preservation of Favoured Races in the Struggle for Life*. His basic idea of the descent of all the diverse creatures from a common root was not new. References to this may already be found in Greek philosophers, from Anaximander to Aristotle, and then, after the influence of the biblical conception of the divine creation of every species and living being had waned, from the eighteenth century on in philosophers (Kant), poets (Goethe), and naturalists (especially Jean Baptiste Lamarck).* But only Darwin's attempt to explain this evolution on the basis of a few fundamental biological considerations made it the foundation of extensive branches of the natural sciences and also enabled it to enter philosophy and the social sciences (which, to be sure, were only too receptive to it). After all, in biological terms this theory was in keeping with the period's general optimistic belief in steady progress and the views prevalent in politics (liberalism with its free play of forces) and in economics (the Manchester School and its successor, the theory of laissez-faire). For the sphere of social life Spencer had already formulated the basic principle of "survival of the fittest" prior to Darwin. In Darwin's *Origin of Species*, chapter 4, "Natural Selection or the Survival of the Fittest," this principle played such a fundamental role and became the point of departure for such significant developments in the racial theory that we shall have to discuss it separately. At first the racial theory took little cognizance of Darwin and Darwinsim. After all, the new theory of evolution about the constant changing of species through adaptation and selection really contradicted the theory that the races were the permanent and unchangeable element in the history of mankind.** Nietzsche, whose phi-

*Darwin himself prefaced his work with a historical survey of the views on "the origin of species." Concerning this, cf. also Arthur Ruppin, *Darwinismus und Sozialwissenschaft* (Jena, 1903), 162ff., and Jacques Barzun, *Darwin, Marx, Wagner: Critique of a Heritage* (New York, 1958).

**That is why Ludwig Schemann, the historian of the study of race who translated

losophy and psychology are permeated with biological and Darwinist ideas, therefore quite logically did not aim at a pure European race but one mixed from the best hereditary element, conceding an important share to the Jewish element. Only by simplifying, reinterpreting, and vulgarizing his multifariously iridescent ideas was it possible to turn his image of the superman into a model for the champions of the breeding of a pure Aryan race and into a barbaric Hitlerian ideal. Nietzsche had utterly despised their precursors.

Nevertheless, Darwinism played a disastrous role in the development of racial theory, and in a dual respect. First of all, the racial theory, which had really not been taken seriously as a science, was, as it were, legitimized as a recognized doctrine by the reception of Darwinism since the end of the nineteenth century. It now entered all fields of culture, including literature and art history, and everyone recognized it in some fashion, be it by acceptance, rejection, or dissociation.

"SOCIAL DARWINISM"

Even more significant was the attempt to apply the principles of Darwinism to societal life. In this way there came into being a school that was called Social Darwinism.* If the same laws apply to human society that Darwinism thought it had demonstrated for the development of the species and the evolution of man from animals—struggle for existence with victory of the strongest and most competent, natural selection and "weeding out" of the incompetent—then all interventions in social life in favor of the weak, the care and preservation of the physically or mentally ill, and help for members of population groups not strong enough to win the struggle for existence are an offense against the hallowed laws of nature. That would only promote the degeneration against which all theoreticians of race since Gobineau had warned. When the big industrialist Friedrich Alfred Krupp financed a contest in 1900 under the title "What do we learn from the principles of the theory of evolution in regard to the domestic development and the legislation of the states?", the book *Vererbung und Auslese im Lebenslauf der Völker*

Gobineau into German in 1898, criticized H. S. Chamberlain for trying to "deny all permanence to race, exaggerating Darwin's teachings or giving them an extreme interpretation, and stamping it as a merely fluctuating entity." Cf. Ludwig Schemann, *Die Rassenfrage im Schrifttum der Neuzeit* (Munich, 1931), 230. This is the last volume of a three-volume work titled *Die Rasse in den Geisteswissenschaften* (Munich, 1928–31).

*The main source for the following presentation is Hedwig Conrad-Martinius's important book *Utopien der Menschenzüchtung. Der Sozialdarwinismus und seine Folgen* (Munich, 1955). Cf. also Karl Saller, *Die Rassenlehre des Nationalsozialismus* (Darmstadt, 1961); Harry Pross, *Die Zerstörung der deutschen Politik—Dokumente 1871–1933* (Frankfurt a.M., 1959).

(Heredity and selection in the life of the peoples) by the Bavarian physician and scholar Wilhelm Schallmeyer won first prize.*

The choice of subject is typical of a number of other writings scarcely worth mentioning today that appeared around the same time. The question asked was whether the development that had led from lower forms of life to man was automatically continuing or whether new conditions had come into being that were leading to a physical degeneration, and if that was so, how such an undesirable development should be dealt with. Schallmeyer observed that one organ in man had undergone excessive development, his brain, and that "the moral sense of the people had become deformed in favor of the individual," which is why "up to now any sacrifice in favor of race has been rejected as an unfair presumption." Many other writers came to the same conclusion and adopted a radical course of action. Those who took this critique of mankind's development toward the intellectual and the individual's responsibility seriously and viewed it as an undesirable degeneration drew the further conclusion that the principles of automatic selection that had led to a higher development of living creatures under primitive natural conditions were no longer operative under the complex conditions of modern society with its humanitarian interference in the natural process. Thus it was necessary to help it along with *deliberate*, systematic selection—that is, to apply to man the principles and practices of artificial breeding that had long been successfully applied to pets and cultivated plants—principles and experiences that had also led Darwin to make his observations and formulate his theories. If nature did not by itself promote what deserved to live and destroy what was undeserving, then *homo sapiens* had to come to its aid by promoting what was valuable and "weeding out" what was harmful.

In the circles of the "racial hygienists" and "eugenicists" (as the champions of these views now called themselves) there were all kinds of schools that differed in their humanitarian, political, philosophical, or religious views as well as in their readiness to accept the rational-biological consequences without reservation. All of them shared the conviction that in civilized modern society man could no longer rely on the unrestrained workings of nature. Just as in economics people increasingly abandoned the free play of forces in favor of a policy of national control, they wished to bring about desirable developments or prevent undesirable ones through purposeful intervention. There were discussions from various points of view about how far one could go,

---

*The second prize was given to Arthur Ruppin's book *Darwinismus und Sozialwissenschaft*. The ophthalmologist and race researcher Woltmann also received a prize for his book *Die politische Anthropologie*.

under what conditions and for what cases the "weeding out of the harmful," the prevention of propagation, and so forth, were permitted and indicated, and how legislation should be brought in line with the new insights and requirements of racial hygienics and eugenics. Thus proposals that a generation earlier had been considered unthinkable or mere utopias and unrealistic, fantastic dreams now became the subjects of serious debates, and people had fewer and fewer scruples about the practical implementation of these proposals.

If these proposals and demands involving the deliberate breeding of the racially pure and the rooting out of what was harmful to race were transferred from individual racial hygiene to racial politics and the struggle between races or national groups, and if the ruling race was given the right to apply them to dominated races and racial minorities, the consequences were apt to be frightful. Everything that was or seemed alien to the real or presumed characteristics of one's own race could be stamped "racially harmful" and thus "unworthy of living" and condemned to destruction. Then woe to all that would be regarded as humanly and racially inferior!

STRUGGLE AGAINST "HUMANITARIAN" INHIBITIONS

If these possibilities were to become actualities and such an unimaginably logical and cold reality that people did not shrink back even from the most horrible consequences, as happened under Nazi rule, first all inhibitions of a religious and humanitarian nature had to be removed and replaced with principles of a new biology based on racial politics or a racially embellished theory of national utility. In point of fact, the rise of racial ideology did go hand in hand with a struggle against the influence of religion (particularly the Christian religion, which in line with Nietzsche's interpretation was viewed as a Judeo-Christian uprising of slaves' morality against the natural masters' morality of the strong) and against the idea of humanitarianism that had developed particularly since the eighteenth century. If the humanitarian idea had placed man above the animal world as a higher being and emphasized the special nature of human reason, the obligations of human understanding, and the elements unifying all people striving for a higher morality, toward the end of the nineteenth century an ever more narrow-minded nationalism and the biologization of intellectual life caused more and more people to place the special existence of the individual, the nation, and finally the race above the universally human, and in fact to regard the cultivation of the latter as degenerate.

As early as 1861 Treitschke had spoken of the "merciless racial struggle of history" and contemptuously dismissed religion as a subjective need of weak human hearts.* "We must break with humanitarianism," Lagarde had written in 1884.** The poisonously deprecatory word *Gefühlsduselei* (humanitarian twaddle)*** gained currency; under its influence the vital energies and instincts of man were said to be stunted. In 1895 the radical Social Darwinist Alexander Tille wrote in his book about Darwin and Nietzsche, which he intended as a "developmental ethics": "We pitiful little humans have brewed ourselves a minimorality out of all sorts of weaknesses. You, great Nature, have a different morality, and that is why according to our minimorality you are immoral. . . . You let the fittest survive, and we let the unfit survive too. We have special institutions in which we coddle cripples, paralytics, blind, insane, tubercular, and syphilitic people and then occasionally set them free so they can procreate and pass their illnesses on." To a "shortsighted neighbor-morality" Tille (and his successors) oppose the species-morality of the theory of evolution with the right of the stronger race to destroy the weaker and lower race. "What cannot hold its own must submit to being ruined."

The biological view from the vantage point of the animal world as the standard for human beings as well, combined with the new teachings about the nature of instinct-directed life and the illnesses that its suppression might cause, led to a devaluation of morality as the force controlling the instincts and directing instinctual life into civilized channels. In the view of the philosopher Ludwig Klages, formulated in his *Brief über Ethik* (Letter on ethics) in 1918, dependence on a moral conscience constitutes "the stigma of those . . . whom Nietzsche called 'slave men.'. . . A philosopher of life sees only one thing in he phenomenon of morality: the intellectual expression of bad blood. . . . The principle of all crime against life is called categorical imperative. Anyone

*George G. Iggers, *Deutsche Geschichtswissenschaft* (Munich, 1971), 160. Iggers points out that around this time "nationalistic views of power . . . supplanted the idealistic view of power as a moral force." In 1853 A. L. von Rochau had created the concept of *Realpolitik*, and it increasingly (and in vulgarized form) became part of the consciousness of the time.
**Three years later, Herzl, in an ironic article about the declined project of a Heine memorial, has Heine ask the students who despise him: "You've gone very far in science, as far as I can see. . . . But what about that which we, in our old-fashioned way, used to call humaneness?" (Cf. A. Bein, *Theodor Herzl* [Vienna, 1934, 1974], 90f.)
***In an article published on 14 July 1892 the Vienna *Neue Freie Presse* deplored this word. In 1898 H. S. Chamberlain already used it in his *Grundlagen des 19. Jahrhunderts* as a common expression. Concerning the further course of this simultaneous development toward anti-humanism in art at the end of the nineteenth century and especially in the twentieth, see Hans Sedlmayer, *Verlust der Mitte. Die bildende Kunst des 19. und 20. Jahrhunderts als Symptom und Symbol der Zeit* (Berlin, 1955), especially pp. 95ff., 103ff., 121ff.; Richard Biedrzynski, ed., *Das verlorene Menschenbild* (Zurich, 1961).

who teaches 'morality' unwittingly commits a systematic crime against life."

In *Partenau,* a novel by Max René Hesse published in 1929, the Junker Kniebald appreciately says to the hero of the novel, Captain Partenau: "You were the first person whom I felt free to ask what conscience, remorse, and morality mean in relation to people and country, and we both shook our heads in profoundest incomprehension."* It was ever more generally argued that "nature" knows no inhibitions, and this was the disastrous conclusion that people drew more and more openly from it: Man should not raise himself above nature in rationalistic presumptuousness; he must subject himself to nature's laws. The liberation of the libido from the fetters of religious and bourgeois tradition; the Marxist devaluation of the intellect as an artificial superstructure over the real forces of the economy and society and over the struggle of the social classes for bread and power; Social Darwinism and nationalistic fanaticism—they all seem to point in the same direction: Do not repress the natural law that has been recognized as correct but systematically work toward its unimpeded effectiveness!

Thus the inner inhibitions are removed step by step, inhibitions that had in the 1880s, the time of emerging racial anti-Semitism, kept even its most radical champions from drawing the ultimate logical conclusions from their premises.

By blurring the dividing line between man and animal and including man in the animal sphere, the stage was set for the disastrous consequence: the sanctioning of every cruelty as given by nature and hence justified. Adolf Hitler often said, and so did his henchmen, that "if nature is cruel, it is all right for us to be cruel too."**

On this road to the abyss, which opened up in our days, an important and still insufficiently appreciated role was played by semantics, the change in meaning of words and concepts, particularly the entry of biological ideas into language and the dissemination of these biological-

---

*This quotation is drawn from Victor Klemperer's book *LTI. Aus dem Notizbuch eines Philologen* (Berlin, 1949), to be cited in greater detail below. The author remarks on p. 34: "The lansquenet Partenau, not a creature of the imagination but a classically stylized portrait of many contemporaries and colleagues, is a learned man who is well versed not only in the works of the German general staff; he has also read his Chamberlain and his Nietzsche and Burckhardt's *Civilization of the Renaissance in Italy* etc. etc."

**Golo Mann writes in *Der Antisemitismus—Wurzeln, Wirkung und Überwindung* (Munich, 1960), 7: "Once, in his 'Table Talks,' Hitler likened his anti-Semitism to the reaction of apes that trample an intruding stranger to death because he is not part of their nature-given family." In a conversation with Rauschning (*Gespräche*, 22) Hitler remarked: "We must regain our good conscience for cruelty." Or (p. 78): "Yes! We are barbarians and want to be. It is an honorary . . . title. We are the ones who will rejuvenate the world. This world is through."

mythical words and incantations, as well as the notions underlying them, with all the means of mass propaganda.

The Semantics of the Jewish Question

Those who ask how the persecutions of the Jews in the Hitler period, so unfathomable in their systematic and cruel nature, were possible, may not have sufficiently considered the problem of semantics in the Jewish question. If we examine the notions which the persecutors and their contemporaries had of the Jews, it is logical to analyze the *language* in addition to considering pictorial depictions in caricature. Language reflects our conceptions and ideas, and more than that: it is the element without which our thoughts would not be possible; it directs our images and notions and gives them their decisive expression. Hence investigations of changes in the meaning of linguistic notions in the last few decades have properly occupied an increasingly important place in historiography. This semantic approach has particular importance for our problem.

In the earlier chapters of this book we have repeatedly pointed out that there is a close connection between the surrounding world's image of the Jews and the behavior of this world toward them. In our discussion of the Middle Ages we have shown that the Christian world's notion of the Jew and his comparison to or equation with the devil may have been a decisive factor in the cruelty of that age's persecutions of the Jews. It would probably be possible to establish a connection between the image of the Jewish usurer, who was repeatedly said to "suck the blood" from the people, and the accusation that Jews use Christian blood for ritual purposes. To reach a definite conclusion here, detailed investigations would of course have to be made of the people's language and notions about the Jews. However, we gain a somewhat clearer picture if we turn to modern and recent times, for we have a large number of literary documents for these.

VICTOR KLEMPERER ON NAZI LANGUAGE

Victor Klemperer was a German philologist of Jewish descent who was able to survive the Nazi period in Berlin—though under the most degrading conditions, as a slave laborer without rights and honor—because he was married to an "Aryan" woman. Making notes on Nazi language helped him get through difficult times, and after the war (1949) he collected them in an extraordinarily revealing book.* In his introduc-

---

LTI: Aus dem Notizbuch eines Philologen (Berlin, 1949). LTI is the abbreviation of *Lingua Tertii Imperii*, the language of the Third Reich, and in his notes it served the

tory chapter Klemperer asks what the strongest means of Hitlerian propaganda was. He answers that the most powerful effect was not made by the *Führer's* individual speeches, "nor by articles, leaflets, posters, or flags; it was not made by anything that could be absorbed by conscious thought or feeling. Rather, Nazism became part of the masses' flesh and blood through individual words, phrases, and sentences which it forced upon the crowd in millions of repetitions and which were absorbed mechanically and unconsciously." According to Klemperer, Schiller's words about the "cultivated langauge that writes and thinks for you" may have been interpreted too aesthetically and innocuously. For "language not only writes and thinks for me; it also guides my feelings and my entire spiritual being, and the more unconsciously I surrender to it, the more naturally does it do so. And what if the cultivated language has been cultivated from poisonous elements or has been made the carrier of poisonous substances? Words can be like tiny doses of arsenic: they are swallowed unnoticed and seem to have no effect, but after some time the toxic effect is there after all."* Klemperer prefaced his book with a motto from Franz Rosenzweig: "Language is more than blood."

Klemperer discerns two characteristic features of the Nazi language, and their development can easily be noticed in the literature of the nineteenth and early twentieth centuries that led up to the Nazis. One characteristic is the exclusive appeal of this language to faith, to its magical effect.** In a similar vein, Ernst Cassirer points to this change in the function of language in his book *The Myth of the State* (New Haven, 1946). According to him, words have performed two entirely different functions in the history of civilization, functions that can be briefly defined as the semantic and the magical. He says that the significant thing about the developments in the decades preceding Nazi rule was that the magical word gained supremacy over the semantic word. "New words have been coined, and even the old ones are used in a new sense; they have undergone a deep change of meaning. This change

---

author as a code word that was incomprehensible to outsiders and thus did not arouse suspicion. However, Klemperer's deprecatory remarks about Zionism are quite wrong-headed and out of place. The author's assimilatory complex as a baptized Jew let him see in Zionism only the same perverted Romanticism that was responsible for National Socialism. In the third edition (Munich, 1969) he even pointed out similarities in the linguistic usage of Herzl and—Hitler.

*Victor Klemperer, *LTI*, 21. Cf. also Heinrich Böll in *Die Kiepe* (Cologne, 1959), no. 1: "The saying 'If words could kill . . .' has long since been changed from subjunctive to the indicative. Words *can* kill, and it only a question of conscience whether one allows language to skip into realms where it becomes murderous."

**Klemperer, *LTI*, 29: "Any language that is permitted to work freely serves all human needs; it serves reason as well as the emotions, it is communication, conversation, soliloquy, prayer, command, incantation. The LTI serves only incantation."

of meaning depends on the fact that those words which formerly were used in a descriptive, logical, or semantic sense are now used as magic words that are destined to produce certain effects and to stir up certain emotions. Our ordinary words are charged with meanings, but these new-fangled words are charged with feelings and violent passions" (paperback edition [New York, 1955], 356).

The second characteristic discerned by Klemperer is the coupling of the mechanical with the organic. "While it [the Nazi language] everywhere emphasizes the organic, the naturally grown, it is at the same time flooded with mechanical expressions and devoid of any sense of the stylistic incongruity and lack of dignity inherent in such combinations as "*eine aufgezogene Organisation* [a drawn-up organization]."*

The change in language might also be characterized another way. In the late nineteenth century and the early twentieth three developments took place in language: its biologization, mechanization, and mythologization.

THE BIOLOGIZATION OF LANGUAGE

The beginnings of what may be called the "biologization" of language go back to the late eighteenth century. If first became apparent in the Romantic movement with its emphasis on the "organic" and what has "grown." Modern nationalism is hardly imaginable without this biological concept of what has "grown organically"; it is all too easy to blend with it mythical notions of "blood and soil" as the foundations of true national life. At first the concepts derived from the natural sciences were used mainly as similes, and as long as they essentially served for the illustration of abstract ideas, this usage was not objectionable. Language, however, has its own laws, and an image locked into a word has the tendency to free itself from the restrictions of the comparison and the allusion and to be taken seriously in its natural meaning.

Thus, for example, the image of a *Volkskörper* (body politic/national) that was used for decades by the conservative parties in Germany could increasingly assume a real biological meaning when it was said that the poisons of Bolshevism, capitalism, and intellectualism were seeking to enter this body and destroy it. This image was carried *ad absurdum* when people bemoaned "the ruin of the living body of the German language by Jewish infection" and said that "the Jewish element had eaten its way" into that body.**

---

*Klemperer, *LTI*, p. 53. Some examples are words like *Betriebszellen* (cells of operation) and combinations like *Menschen gleichschalten* (to switch people on equal current, or bring people into line) or *eine Organisation aufziehen* (to mount an organization).
**Die Juden in Deutschland, published by the Institute for the Study of the Jewish Question (Munich, 1939), 184.

THE JEWS AS "NATIONAL PESTS" AND "PARASITES"

The words and images derived from biology were at first used more as similes in the discussions about the Jews and the Jewish question. A case in point is Mommsen's aforementioned, neutrally or positively meant statement about the Jews who in the Roman empire and later constituted an "element (or ferment) of decomposition of the peoples and tribes" for the benefit of greater human entities. In anti-Semitic literature this statement was combined with the notion of the "disintegrating" influence of the Jews, was given wide dissemination in this negative sense and increasingly interpreted in the sense of its scientific-biological root. It was similar with the image of the "cancerous growth of usury"* that Wilhelm Marr had used in 1879 in his work *Der Sieg des Judentums über das Germanentum,* or with the comparison between the stock exchanges and a poison tree that was first used by Lagarde and became a standard quotation among the anti-Semites. If the Jews were called *Schädlinge* (noxious or harmful persons) and *Volksschädlinge* (national pests), this expression does sound like an accusation, but it is *linguistically neutral.* But if one remembers that in general usage the word *Schädling,* according to the definition in the big Brockhaus encyclopedia, designates "animals and plants that curtail human interests in agriculture, forestry, gardening, provisions, raw materials, products, pets, game, breeding stock, and even the human body and which are therefore more or less systematically combated and destroyed," the word *Volksschädling,* used to refer to Jews even in legal circles, assumes a different character (as "national pest"). It comes perilously close to the ominous words *Schmarotzer* or *Parasit,* which in this context are perhaps the most deleterious words that were transferred from biology to social and political life and were and are applied particularly to the Jews. It is therefore appropriate to trace the history of the word *Parasit,* its use and practical effect in relation to the Jewish question, in somewhat greater detail.

HISTORY OF THE WORD *"PARASIT"*

The Greek word *parasitos* ("one who eats at another's table"), originally applied in a good sense to priests or municipal employees who were fed at the expense of the state, conferred from the fourth century B.C.E. on "poor wretches who at dinnertime show up uninvited at the homes of the rich and high-born and in return for a noonday meal put up with the most degrading treatment and the meanest practical jokes from the host and his guests. The parasites were stock figures in the Greek

---

*Concerning "usury", see the notes in Part 2.

comedy of the middle and modern periods." (From the *Grosser Brockhaus* encyclopedia, vol. 14 [Leipzig, 1933], p. 66.) With the reception and regeneration of the Greek and Latin languages and literatures by Humanism the word became part of European linguistic usage in the sixteenth century as a contemptuous term for people who live at the cost of others, wheedle benefits out of the rich and mighty through flattery and servility without doing any real work in return, and are hard to shake off again. In German *Parasit* is used synonymously with the word *Schmarotzer,* a word of uncertain origin that also came into use in the sixteenth century. In the eighteenth century *Parasit* entered the natural sciences; it seems to have initially been used only in botany, but in the nineteenth century it was applied also to animals as a general *biological concept.**

In his basic book *Le Parasitisme et la Symbiose* M. Caullery gives the following definition of the concept (2d edition [Paris, 1950], p. 21):

> Parasitism may be defined as the normal and necessary condition of the life of an organism that feeds at the expense of another, called host, without destroying it. . . . To be able to live regularly off its host, a parasite generally is in constant contact with it, either on its surface or inside it. Thus parasitism constitutes a generally lasting connection between two different organisms, one of which lives at the expense of the other. This connection is essentially one-sided in nature; it is necessary for the parasite, because it dies if it is separated from the host, being unable to provide for itself, but it is by no means necessary for the host. The organization of the parasite is specialized in accordance with the living conditions of the host; adaptation is the hallmark of parasitism.

Similar definitions and formulations may be found in other scientific works, dictionaries, and general encyclopedias.****

As the natural sciences entered the social sciences, the concepts

---

*In 1802 the German naturalist G. R. Treviranus (1776–1837) coined *Biologie,* the word and the concept for phenomena encompassing all living creatures, in his work *Biologie oder Philosophie der lebendigen Natur* (6 vols., 1802–22).

**The *Fischer-Lexikon* (Frankfurt a. M., 1962, 1:208, s.v. "Biologie") defines parasites as "those organisms which live at the expense of other, host organisms which they befall, damage, and often kill. . . . Among the lower plants they appear as many forms of bacteria which find their most favorable living conditions as pathogens in humans, animals, and plants." The definition of the biological concept of *Parasit* in the latest edition of the Brockhaus encyclopedia (vol. 8, p. 743) reads as follows: "An organism that lives at the expense of a host (parasitism) without killing it immediately, but which can damage it by depriving it of food and by its excretions etc. and can thereby cause parasitic diseases (cf. *Schmarotzer*). Parasitology is the study of parasites, and the interrelationship between the parasites and the environment." *Schmarotzer* is defined similarly. The common feature of all definitions is that the parasite exists at the expense of another organism that is called host. By existing in this way it damages its host, often to the point of destruction.

"parasite" and "parasitism" were adopted by the humanities and particularly the social sciences in their new biological definition. We encounter them especially in socialistic, anticapitalistic literature. The urban class of merchants and manufacturers that the physiocrats call *classe stérile* (or *classe stipendiée*)—in contrast to the only productive class, those who stay on the soil and cultivate it—now became the parasitic class of exploitative capitalists in commerce and industry. In linguistic usage, "unproductive" in the sense of Marxist doctrine and "parasitic" became almost identical concepts, as did "exploiter" and "parasite," words that were often combined: "parasitic exploiters!"*

APPLICATION TO THE JEWS AND THE JEWISH QUESTION

Since the Middle Ages the Jew had been decried as a bloodsucker and exploiter of his "host nation." Later, he was included in the odium of capitalism as its representative, and everywhere he was regarded as an alien, and, according to the racial theory of anti-Semitism, a member of an inferior, uncreative race. Since the biological definition of a parasite seemed to fit him as though created expressly for him, was there anyone to whom the image of the parasite could be transferred more easily?

In point of fact, the word began to be applied to the Jews as soon as it was used in this new biological sense. As we have seen, even Johann Gottfried Herder, surely no anti-Semite in the modern sense, used it in that way, and so did many others later, as his disciples or independently.** In the further course of the development, two schools of thought liked to use the word "parasite" in their anti-Jewish statements. *Racial anti-Semitism*, whose origin and teachings we have dealt with in some detail in chapter 6, presented the Jews as an uncreative race that could live only on the exploitation of other peoples and races. As we repeatedly see, the Jewish-Semitic race is depicted as a parasitic race; its members are parasites who can live only at the expense of their "hosts." The image of the "host nations"*** among which the Jews live increasingly came under the spell of these naturalistic notions of the parasite and the host on which it lives and on whose blood and vital juices it feeds, thus harming and often destroying it. The image of the "parasite" is frequently found not only in this ethnogenic thinking but also in the *anticapitalistic theories* of many socialists, which are often based on physiocratic ideas, and of numerous other opponents of the Jews.**** In 1858 P. J. Proudhon attributed the dispersion of the Jews to their innate

*Cf. the documentation and notes in Part 2, as well as the references in the index.
**See "Parasites" in the index.
***Concerning the concepts of "host nation" and "guest nation," see the notes, as well as the index in Part 2.
****See the note on this in Part 2.

"mercantile and usurious parasitism," in which even the freedoms granted them by the French Revolution had produced no change. In 1890 the socialist Albert Regnard established a parallel between Jew versus Aryan and capitalist versus proletarian. The anarchist Bakunin, an opponent of both capitalism and Marxism, wrote in 1871 that the entire Jewish world constituted "an exploitative sect, a people of bloodsuckers, one voracious parasite" that simultaneously served Marx and the Rothschilds.

Thus the word *parasite* in its two versions, the racial–anti-Semitic and the anticapitalistic kind, became intertwined in all kinds of locutions and increasingly served as the designation of the Jew as an individual, a member of the Jewish or Semitic race, and a representative of an economic stratum. As stated on pp. 236ff. above, Eugen Dühring said about the Jew in this spirit that as a parasite he felt most comfortable in a society already somewhat corrupted. In 1887 Paul de Lagarde, the well-known Orientalist and cultural politician whom we have already discussed (pp. 250f. above), compared the Jews in this connection with bacilli and trichinae. He said that any foreign body produced in another living body discomfort, illness, and often even suppuration and death.

We can see how the image of the parasite, at first used more as a simile, was increasingly identified with natural reality. This could be demonstrated by the details of formulation in many examples. In 1893, for instance, the Florentine physiologist Paolo Mantegazza wrote in a critical essay about contemporary anti-Semitism published in the Vienna *Neue Freie Presse* (23–24 September) that the Jews were being reproached with "not being limbs of our European body, not being sinews of our flesh or veins of our blood but nodes, excrescences, and tumors that are widely scattered and impede the free circulation of our juices and energies. In short, they are being accused of being the rash and brash parasites of European life."*

In his essay "The Hunt in Bohemia" Theodor Herzl wrote in late 1897 that the Germans had suddenly started to shake off the Bohemian Jews who had identified with them: "Suddenly they were called parasites who were sucking the host dry." As an example of this term's great currency in politics we shall mention a remark by the British commissioner for Uganda, Lord Delamere, who wrote in *The Grant of Land to the Zionist Congress and Land Settlement in British East Africa* (London, 1903), which dealt with the projected assignment of a settlement area to Jewish settlers ("Uganda Project"): "Jews in a free country are never agricultural, they are purely parasitic, and require a large population for the

---

*From his diagnosis he draws this Zionist conclusion: "And if we could give free rein to our hatred, we would gladly give them Jerusalem and restore a Reich Israel if this were in our power." This essay has been reprinted in Hermann Bahr, *Der Antisemitismus. Ein internationales Interview*, ed. Hermann Greive (Königstein, 1979), 126ff.

exercise of their various trades," George Saint-Bonnet's book *Le Juif, ou l'International du Parasitisme,* published in 1932, may serve as an example of the use of this word in France. Language became so deeply anchored in the consciousness and thought of the time that the words *parasite* and *parasitism* were almost frivolously adopted by Jews themselves. Zionists, and particularly Zionist socialists, used it primarily to characterize the "unhealthy," abnormal occupational structure of the Jews in the Diaspora and to motivate the necessity for them to return to Palestine, to a life in their own state, and to "primary production," agriculture.

As already stated, such comparisons became even more frequent after the end of the First World War, and the nature of the comparison became increasingly subordinate to the scientific identification. At the same time the biological elements were often raised to the sphere of mythology—something that, as we have seen, was in keeping with the *Zeitgeist.*

On page 323 above we have already quoted formulations of Hitler and his forerunners in which the word "parasite" in its strictly biological sense was applied to the Jews. Earlier, after the pattern of A. Wahrmund (see pp. 240f. above), the nomadic nature of the Jew had been emphasized and people had spoken of the parasitic nature of a nomad more figuratively than in the biological sense.* Now, however, Hitler wrote that even a nomad had a certain attitude toward labor, but not the Jew: "Thus he has not been a nomad but at all times only a parasite in the body of other peoples." Like all true parasites, a Jew is always looking for "fresh culture mediums" for his race. Unlike the nomad, he does not roam. On the contrary; as an "eternal parasite" and *Schmarotzer* he keeps expanding like a "horrible bacillus" wherever "a favorable medium" beckons. His effect, too, is that of a parasite; wherever he appears, the host nation sooner or later dies.

Alfred Rosenberg uses the concept "parasite" even more deliberately in its biological sense and, as stated above (pp. 334ff.), gives it an organismic-mythological interpretation that he can easily interweave with similar traditional notions still present in people's consciousness. The insufferable bombast of Rosenberg's formulations is revealed by an analysis of his concepts. "The earthbound creature Ahasuerus attaches himself to the slackening muscles" of the tiring Aryan; "the Jewish demon" (the term is used as a synonym for "parasite") "burrows into the diseased place and as a parasite exploits the weak hours of the great. . . ."

---

*Cf. Adolf Wahrmund, *Das Gesetz des Nomadentums und die heutige Judenherrschaft* (1882); 3d ed., Munich, 1919), 67: "If the Arabs . . . are parasites to this day and have been in all periods, because as nomads they have to be parasites, and if, on the other hand, the Jews are called parasites by today's non-Jews, there is no reason to assume that they did not live as parasites in Palestine, too."

Parasitism is here quite deliberately conceived of as a biological process that the parasite himself cannot escape because of the inner, nature-given law of his life.

As in Rosenberg, so in other National Socialist authors the concepts of devil, demon, Antichrist, plague and pestilence,* locusts and leeches, spiders and vampires—terms that had always been used in reference to the Jews—also mingle with the notion of parasites and the idea of bacteria and bacilli, the tiny, invisible creatures that are inconceivably great in their effects, producing putrefaction and destroying the organisms beset by them.

In 1938, in a speech about "The Truth in Spain" delivered at the Nuremberg convention of the Nazi party, Joseph Goebbels combined the various overlapping images and notions of the Jew in the following words: "Look, this is the enemy of the world, the destroyer of cultures, the parasite among the peoples, the son of chaos, the incarceration of evil, the concrete demon of the ruin of mankind."

"A JEW IS NOT A HUMAN BEING"

This biology-oriented image of the "parasite among the peoples" was now drummed into the people with all the resources of modern National Socialist "enlightenment" and propaganda. As an advertisement of the Institute for the Study of the Jewish Question said in 1939 in announcing a book about "The Jewish World Pest," "The meaning and purpose of this book is to disseminate information about the danger of the Jewish world pest among the widest possible readership."** A syllabus for the ideological training of the SS and the police, evidently from the 1930s, teaches the following about the "corrosive influence of racial mingling with the Jews": "These parasites of mankind have managed to avoid to this day complete interbreeding with their host nations. . . . Beyond this there was a special danger in the fact that Judaism had begun to systematically undermine the species-conscious actions and thoughts of the peoples. . . . The Jews disparaged any genuine feeling, and their entire propaganda work was deliberately aimed at the inner undermining and disintegration of the *Volkskörper* [body politic]. The aftereffects of these decades of infection and corrosion before 1933 may be felt among the peoples to this day. It will take hard work to eliminate even

---

*Concerning these similes, cf. the notes in Part 2.
**In a similar vein Rosenberg writes at the conclusion of his book about *The Protocols of the Elders of Zion* (4th ed., 1933), 132: "One of the most profound statements about the Jew was made by Richard Wagner. He called him the concrete demon of the decay of mankind. . . . The recognition of the nature of the demon of our present decay is one of the portents of this coming struggle for a new world order."

the last traces of this pestilence and bring Europe back to the natural and only proper course of life."*

An educational pamphlet issued in 1941 and distributed by the office of Rosenberg, "the *Führer's* commissioner for the supervision of the intellectual and ideological training and education of the NSDAP," teaches the biology of the Jewish question as follows:

> The old methods of historiography no longer suffice for the consideration of such racial matters. Here different perspectives, derived from biological thought, emerge. Just as the creative and the parasitic principles are represented in nature, this is also true of the life of a people. These principles, the creative and the parasitic, have been valid in all parts of Creation from the very beginning, and races and peoples must be regarded as a part of Creation. . . .
>
> A good example for a discussion of this type is offered by the human body. It constitutes a highly developed cell-stage permeated by parasites (e.g., bacteria) which are themselves not in a position to form a state. They can live in a body, multiply there, and settle in certain places. There they secrete their poisons and thus bring about reactions in the body that can very well be compared with internal processes in the life of nations which take place for similar reasons. A body thus befallen must overcome the penetrated parasites or it will be overcome by them. Once it has overcome them, it must be interested in clearing them from its environment as well in order to prevent future infection. . . .
>
> In such discussions and processes humanitarian principles can no more be applied than they can be when a body or a contaminated room is disinfected. A complete new thinking must take hold here. Only such thinking can truly lead to the ultimate decision that must be made in our age in order to safeguard the continued existence of the great creative race and its great task in the world. (Quoted after Hofer, *Der Nationalsozialismus,* 279f.)

There can be no doubt that accusations against the Jews were here not presented merely with satanic malevolence and cloaked in biological similes. Those who wrote and taught this *believed* in their teachings—if not at the beginning of their career, then in its further course. The language of their images and similes gained such power over them that image and reality became one for them—and to an even greater extent for those taught and led by them. For the masses of the people a Jew was not a human being but a subordinate member of the animal world, frightful and incomprehensible in its destructive power—like worms and insects,** bacteria, the parasitic, pathogenic organisms that were invis-

---

*Quoted after Hofer, *Der Nationalsozialismus,* p. 281. Note how "host nations" is here used in analogy to the biological concept of "host" in parasitology.
**Cf. the notes in Part 2.

ible to the human eye and that were heard and read about every day. As we have seen, the inflammatory cry *"Hepp-Hepp, Jude verreck"* of 1819 already embodied the notion of the animal nature of the Jews, for the verb *verrecken* (croak) is in general used only for animals. It was revived by the Nazis in the battle cry *"Deutschland erwache, Juda verrecke"* (Germany awake, Judah croak) which contrasted the human German with the Jewish animal. The words of Walter Buch, the supreme judge of the NSDAP, were only a cynical summing up when he made this precise declaration with the authority of a jurist: "The National Socialists have recognized that a Jew is not a human being but a phenomenon of putrefaction."

The Conclusions: Translation of Images and Similes into Reality

If we recall what we have said about the change of the general atmosphere in the direction of the antiliberal and antihuman and about the recognition of the right to "exterminate" and eradicate" what was racially and socially harmful, it becomes clear where the imaginative, linguistic, and conceptual worlds of the Nazis in relation to the Jews and the Jewish question were bound to lead.

In this atmosphere of the biologization of the humanities and social sciences and the mythologization of biological facts, of an upheaval of all material, intellectual, and moral values in the wake of World War I and its aftereffects, and in the de-individualization and totalization of every aspect of life—from motorized traffic to politics and the regulation of traffic and advertising with its technique of suggestive dissemination of catchy words, pictures, and slogans—language and the images and notions embodied in it played an ever more penetrating and fateful role. Nietzsche's misunderstood longing for the natural barbarian with strength of will and instincts, as well as Richard Wagner's theatrically revived mythology of Germanic gods that reached the people with the magic strength of the pathos-filled musical settings of Wagner's alliterative language, formed the substratum for this enlivening of semantics, in which the word was increasingly taken by its natural root, in which similes and allusions were taken as reality, and nightmares and wishful thinking were magically transformed into images of hatred and commands to destroy.

If in the nineteenth century a demand for the "downfall of Judaism" was made, this was generally understood to mean that if the Jews laid claim to complete equality, they should dissolve as a national body and mix with the peoples in whose midst they lived. It was said that "no state within a state" was wanted. People were ready to concede to the Jews separate religious practices, though often hesitantly and with inner repugnance, but they denied them anything that looked like national singularity. On this most friends and enemies of the Jews were agreed, and differences of opinion revolved mainly around the means by which this goal could best be reached. Thus, for example, Mommsen demanded as something logical that the Jew give up their special national existence and consciousness, and on the other side conservative opponents of the Jews like Treitschke and even Lagarde were ready to accept the Jews living in Germany fully if they unreservedly intermingled with the German people. Even Richard Wagner's demand for the downfall of the Jews at the end of his famous-infamous essay *Das Judentum in der Musik* was made in this spirit. He presented Ludwig Börne as a model for the Jews, a man who sought redemption by attaching himself fully to the German people and seeking to be absorbed by it. "However," said Wagner, "to become a human being in association with us means for a Jew, first of all, to cease to be a Jew." In this spirit Wagner demanded the end of Jewry by ruthless self-destruction of the Jews as Jews; "Redemption from the curse on you . . . the redemption of Ahasuerus."* There were only few people who took such a serious and radical view of the racial idea that they rejected this complete assimilation of the Jews to their "host nations" as deleterious for the "host."

In the new atmosphere of the 1920s and the 1930s the moral inhibitions of the liberalistic epoch were swept away and people came to radical conclusions on the basis of biologistic views. A striking example of the effect on the anti-Jewish literature of this change in the general atmosphere is furnished by a comparison of the various editions in which Eugen Dühring's book on the Jewish question appeared.** In the first edition of 1881 Dühring only hints at the consequences of the anti-Semitic racial doctrine. He says that in the long run the impossibility of coexistence between the Jews and other peoples will increase in proportion to the growth of the Jews' national consciousness. What will happen then, where the Jews will have to move, is *their* problem. Only in special cases could one consider "the deportation of entire groups of the Jews involved." For the time being, people will have to content themselves with depriving them of all public influence and to proscribe marriage with them. For the future, to be sure, there must be a more long-range goal, "and the way to it cannot be cleared without the most forceful methods." The Jews are "an inner Carthage the power of which will have to be broken by the modern nations." In the expanded sixth edition of the book, completed in 1920 and published in 1930 after the author's death, Dühring writes: "In the first four editions of this book secondary and half-way measures were recommended and discussed because of seeming impossibilities, but on the basis of the varied experi-

*See pp. 234f. above and particularly the excursus in Part 2, pp. 636ff.
**Concerning this "classic" book of modern anti-Semitism, see pp. 236ff. above.

ences to date this is no longer indicated. The world must settle accounts with the Hebrew people in drastic fashion." The drawback of any gentle way is that it prolongs the adversity. After all, terror and violence have been appropriate for the Jews since Sinai. "One must also consider that the laws of war, especially a war against the anti-Aryan and even anti-human attacks of alien parasites, must be different from the laws of peace." In the face of the ongoing Judaization of the civilized world the author's original statement about the "inner Carthage" no longer suffices. In the present age, "in which even tyrannicide has almost been turned into a system, we face a more physical task."* Now Dühring's statement about the duty of Nordic man to eradicate the parasitic races "as one must simply exterminate dangerous poisonous snakes and wild beasts of prey"** must be taken seriously.

Lagarde had spoken of the "mass of decay" that had accumulated in "Israel Europe" and whose pus could be removed only by a surgical procedure. He had turned against the weak-willed, "who—out of humaneness!—are too cowardly to crush this vermin." As he had written in 1887, there was no negotiating with trichinae and bacilli, nor could they be educated; "they are destroyed as quickly and thoroughly as possible."*** What Lagarde had principally meant by his so very dangerous images and similes was that the Jews ought to be deprived of the money on which their power was based. Now those images of putrefaction and suppuration, bacilli and vermin, parasites and the pest represented by the Jews were taken literally and made people decide to take action.

THE ERADICATION OF THE JEWS AS PARASITES

In a Reichstag speech of 30 January 1937 Hitler explained National Socialist Germany's policy toward the Jews in these words: "Efforts are being made to immunize the German people against this infection as much as possible. As part of this we are avoiding any closer contact with the carriers of this poisonous bacillus." A poster distributed in France in the early 1940s has this inscription on the back of a picture illustrating the fight against parasites and insects: *Tuberculose, Syphilis, Cancer sont guérissables. . . . Il faut en finir avec le plus grand des fléaux: Le Juif!***** (Tuberculosis, syphilis, and cancer are curable. . . . They must

---

*Eugen Dühring, *Die Judenfrage als Frage des Rassencharakters und seiner Schädlichkeit für die Existenz und Kulture der Völker. Mit einer gemeinverständlichen und denkerisch freiheitlichen Antwort, Sechste, vermehrte Auflage, in Frau Beta Dührings Auftrage herausgegeben von H. Reinhard* (Leipzig, 1930), 134, 136, 140.
**Quoted after Theodor Lessing, *Der jüdische Selbsthass* (Berlin, 1930), 112 (from an essay about the Jewish anti-Semite Arthur Trebitsch).
***Cf. chap. 6, p. 230 above and Part 2, p. 616.
****Jacques Polonsky, *La Presse, la propagande et l'opinion publique sous l'Occupation*, Paris 1946, p. 108.

be finished off together with the greatest of scourges: the Jews!). In 1943, when the gassing was already in full swing, Hitler told the Hungarian regent Horthy that the Jews "must be treated like the tubercle bacilli that might infect a healthy body. This would not be cruel if one considers that even innocent creatures like rabbits and deer must be killed to prevent damage."* What objection could there be, he remarked in 1942 in one of his "table talks in the headquarters of the *Führer*" (p. 310) in reference to the Jewish transports to the East, "to the state's rendering a downright *Volksschädling* [national pest] harmless?" And a book of instruction issued in 1944 by the National Socialist Leadership Staff of the German Army motivates the systematic murder of the Jews with these words: "To this day there are among our people persons who in their hearts are not quite certain when we speak of the extermination of the Jews in our living space. In our midst it took the strength of character and drive of the greatest man of our people in a thousand years to clear the Jewish delusion from our eyes : The Jew wishes to force us into a life of slavery so that he may live among us as a parasite and squeeze us dry."** The sound life-style of the German people is opposed to the parasitic life-style of the Jew. In this struggle, who can still speak of mercy, love of one's neighbor, and so on? In an obvious allusion to Lagarde's abovementioned statement the author goes on: "Who believes in the possibility of improving the parasite (for instance, the louse)? Who believes that there is a way of compromising with a parasite?*** We have only the choice of being devoured by the parasite or of destroying him. The Jew must be annihilated wherever we meet him! By this we do not commit a crime against life but serve its law of struggle, a law which always stands up against everything that is hostile to healthy life. Thus our struggle serves for the preservation of life."

THE DEMONIC NATURE OF LANGUAGE

At the beginning of this chapter we asked how it was possible for the Nazis to organize the murder of the Jews systematically and with the

*Hitler's words are quoted after R. Schaefer, "Zur Geschichte des Wortes 'zersetzen,'" p. 73.
**Quoted after Max Weinreich, *Hitler's Professors* (New York, 1946), 212, 258 (translation altered).
***Similar statements may be found in a collection edited by Robert Körber and Theodor Pugel in 1935 and entitled *Antisemitismus der Welt in Wort und Bild* (Dresden: Verlag M. O. Groh, 300): "Thus, anyone who sings us a song of 'symbiosis' has the wrong tune. . . . For us Judaism is and remains what Andreas Suter said almost 200 years ago (in 1740) [in "Der 100-äugige blinde Argos und zweygesichtige Janus," p. 375]: 'The Jews are as useful to a country as the mice in a granary and the moths in a dress.' As upright German men we reject a 'peaceful coexistence' with human mice and moths." Concerning the word *symbiosis*, see the excursus in Part 2, pp. 715ff.

resources of the latest technology. It will probably not be possible to find a fully satisfactory explanation for this. Every human action arises from the concurrence of complex factors, and thus only a thorough analysis of all of them and their effect on one another can lead to real insight and full understanding. It seems, however, that a semantic approach brings us quite a bit closer to such an understanding. People thougt that the Nazis were driven to commit their horrendous deeds, almost against their will, by the demons they had unleashed.* Is not one of these demons, and perhaps especially so, the demon of language with the images and notions embodied in it? If a demented person possessed by some delusion kills another person, he often commits his deed in the belief that he is freeing himself and the world from a dangerous monster that is embodied in the human being standing before him.** The question arises whether the paranoid person that headed the Nazi state did not act on the basis of such delusions. This would not be ruled out by the fact that in conversations with confidants Hitler occasionally spoke cynically about his views and actions as though he, devoid of any belief in them, was far above them and was using theories like the anti-Semitic racial doctrine only in order to facilitate his plans for political domination. Even the possessed have their lucid moments in which they can speak very sensibly and rationalize their chimeras. At any rate, Rauschning, who recorded such conversations, came to the conclusion that Hitler believed in the corrupt nature of the Jew and his pernicious effect on the world. "To Hitler," writes Rauschning (*Gespräche mit Hitler*, p. 221), "the Jew is evil incarnate. He has raised him to the position of lord of his counterworld. He views him with a mythical eye. . . . The durability of his anti-Semitism becomes comprehensible only in terms of the mythic enlargement of the Jew into an eternal human prototype." Hitler excitedly explained to his partners in conversation that two worlds were confronting each other: "The man of God and the man of Satan! The Jew is counter-man, anti-man." Jews and Aryans are "as far apart as animals and humans."*** As our linguistic analysis has shown, such mythical-demonic notions blend with the images of parasites, bacilli, and vermin, of national pests that eat their way into the body politic, poisoning and disintegrating it. In the world of mythical notions there are no

---

*Leon Poliakow, *Breviaire de la haine* (Paris, 1951), 3f.

**Cf. Robert Gaupp, *Der Fall Wagner* [a serial killer]. *Ein ärztliches Gutachten, zugleich eine kriminalpsychologische Studie*, in *Verbrechertypen*, ed. Hans W. Gruhle and Albrecht Wetzel (1914), 1:3, especially pp. 182 (368 ff.). Cf. also Klaus Mann's comparison of Hitler's physiognomy with that of the serial killer Haarmann in Part 2, p. 697.

***Rauschning, *Gespräche mit Hitler*, 227f. On another occasion Hitler said that the discovery of the Jewish virus was one of the greatest discoveries, comparable to those of Pasteur and Koch. (*Hitler's Secret Conversations* [New York: Signet Books, 1961], 320.)

constants; small things become enormous and giant ones are reduced to ordinary size.

Surely not all of those people were possessed or driven by chimeras. As regards a person like Alfred Rosenberg, it is safe to assume that he believed in his biological-mythical racial world and the image of the Jew in it.* In the case of a virtuosic demagogue with the intellectual pliancy of a Goebbels this assumption cannot be made in the same way. In his forgery workship, theories and biological-mythological chimera were turned into cheap slogans. Between these extremes there were men in middle leadership positions, staff-sergeant types, schoolmasters, and officers, who either faithfully accepted the teachings of the *Führer* or, being trained to obey, regarded the disciplined execution of orders from the high command as the supreme law and the greatest manly virtue.** From them the theories, orders, and instructions filtered down to the masses of the thousands and tens of thousands who were charged with the implementation of the work of destruction as broken down into partial actions. Among these, fear of the possible consequences of doubt and disobedience was probably added to the "morality" of unconditional obedience to an even greater extent than among the higher-ups.

Normally, however, the question of obedience or disobedience was not even raised, and here language played a decisive role. The stereotypical presentation of the Jews as parasites, vermin, bacteria, and bacilli that work their way in everywhere, disintegrating and poisoning, and with demonic power seek to destroy the German body politic and every individual German largely eliminated the inner doubt and resistance of the masses to the multifarious forms of hatred and persecution of the Jews***—and who is not part of the masses, at least in a certain

---

*As mentioned above, he clung to them even while imprisoned prior to his sentencing in the Nuremberg trial. Cf. what the psychologist G. M. Gilbert said after a conversation with Rosenberg (*Nuremberg Diary* [New York: Signet Books, 1961], 72): "And so it goes, like the perseveration in an obsessive-compulsive neurosis or an organic psychosis. There is neither sadism nor shame in his attitude; just a cool, apathetic obsessive quality." Cf. also ibid., p. 325.

**Adolf Eichmann probably belongs to this type (cf. the notes in Part 2, p. 699). That he, too, regarded the biological notions as self-evident is shown by occasional remarks in his memoirs. Cf. the international edition of *Life* dated 1 January 1961: "Eager to strike against these parasites, the Roumanians . . . liquidated thousands and thousands of their own Jews." "I am no anti-Semite. I was just politically opposed to Jews, because they were stealing the breath of life from us." It was similar with Rudolf Höss, the commandant of the Auschwitz death camp. Cf. his "autobiographical memoirs" edited and provided with a very perceptive introduction by Martin Broszat (R. Höss, *Kommandant in Auschwitz* [Stuttgart, 1963]; American edition: *Commandant at Auschwitz*).

***Benno Cohn, the last chairman of the German Zionist Federation, reports the following incident from the Germany of September 1938. In passing he overheard a child ask his mother: "What kind of people are these?" Whereupon the mother straight-

stratum of his being?* Lagarde's words, still meant metaphorically, about the bacilli with which one did not negotiate but which one destroyed could now, in an atmosphere of anti-humanism and bio-mythology, become frightful reality. These biological linguistic images and notions weakened the last moral inhibitions. They also weakened the inner resistance against injustice and crime of millions who did not actively participate in the persecution and destruction of the Jews but who knew about them or could have known if they had not preferred to ask no questions that could have been interpreted as rebellion and deficient readiness to believe and obey.

Beyond this, the image of the Jews helped in large measure to determine the methods of the destruction of the Jews. Just as in the Middle Ages Antichrist and Satan were slain and turned in them, the method of gassing in Hitler's murder camps was the logical consequence once the notion of the Jews as parasites had been widely accepted. If the Jews really were parasites, bacilli, and vermin, it was not only necessary to eradicate them,** but also logical to use for this extermination the means by which bacilli and vermin are exterminated: poison gas. In *Mein Kampf* Hitler had already intimated that poison gas was a possible weapon against the Jews; at that time he was remembering the poison-gas battles in World War I during which he himself had been wounded. Experiences, delusions, and biologizing semantics translated into reality now combined with an untrammeled demagoguery and systematic obedience training as the highest value in the totalitarian state to turn these intimations into a system of gassing Jewish parasites and Jewish vermin that was implemented with all the methods of science and technology.

Of course, showing these inner connections and interpreting them has nothing to do with a justification or an extenuation of the responsibility that must be borne by those who participated in these historical events in any form. Psychology and historiography are deceptive if they lead anyone to believe that an effort to understand and explain is tantamount to justification and forgiveness. Injustice and crime remain injustice and crime even if their psychological foundations are exposed. But the revelation of inner motives is designed to give us warnings about how one must not act if one does not wish to find oneself in similar situations as a victim or as a perpetrator. Nothing is unavoidable in historical happenings if it is recognized betimes as injustice and the will

---

ened him out: "These aren't people; they're Jews." (Cf. B. Cohn, "Das letzte Jahr," *MB* [Tel Aviv], 18 October 1963, p. 26).

*Cf. Thomas Mann in *Doctor Faustus* about the "archaic and alarming element" in the concept of the people: "I speak of the people, but this archaic folk layer exists in all of us."

**Cf. the notes in Part 2.

to prevention is aroused. We cannot prevent lunatics from striving for leadership, but we can educate ourselves and others not to succumb to their criminal quest for power.*

The Behavior of the Germans

THEIR ATTITUDE TOWARD THE HITLER REGIME

From this point of view we must now concern ourselves with a question that has been persistently asked to this day: How could the German people as a whole and the Germans as individuals permit all this without offering serious resistance? Any attempt at an answer must deal with two separate, almost independent series of events and modes of reaction. One is life under the bondage of the authoritarian *Führer* state, the criminal, totalitarian SS state; the other is the attitude (active or at least passive) toward the Jewish program in all its stages from denigration, isolation, disenfranchisement, despoliation, and deportation to systematic murder.

The first cluster of problems interests us only as background for the more specific second one. In its nature it is a many-sided problem of German history, sociology, the psychology of peoples and the masses, the nature of force and domination, demagoguery, elitism, dictatorship, ideology, obedience, criminality, and many related questions of public and private life. Some comments on these have already been made in the preceding sections, which indicated that the whole atmosphere— economic, social, cultural, and political—in the fourteen years of the Weimar Republic promoted, if not demanded, the rise of authoritarian rule. Thus Hitler's pathologically fascinating personality, which embodied the neurosis of the time in gigantic fashion, could be elevated to a religious, Messianic, and demonic sphere by his National Socialist adherents and propaganda virtuosos like Joseph Goebbels: Hitler was the godsent savior. This mixture of fanatical faith in his vocation and an extremely skillful propaganda that grasped and exploited the longings of the masses with a sure instinct won over the middle classes, which were threatened from above and from below, considerable portions of the younger intellectuals, who were vainly looking for work appropriate to their education and social standing, and large numbers of workers, especially the unemployed but increasingly also those who had hitherto been Communists and Social Democrats. It was certainly a smart move

---

*One of the conclusions ought to be caution in the use and adoption of language and the images and comparisons embodied in it. One would like to apply Abtalion's words in the Talmud tractate *Pirkei Avot* ("Chapters of the Fathers," 1:11) in this sense: "You sages, be careful with your words," for as we read in Proverbs 18:21, "Death and life are in the power of the tongue."

to elevate the first of May, which the Social Democratic governments of the Weimar Republic had not dared to make an official holiday, to the status of a "Day of German Labor" as early as 1933 and to celebrate it as a state holiday with all the theatrical pomp at which the new rulers excelled, satisfying the curiosity and the pride of the people. Then came the domestic and the foreign successes: Unemployment was eliminated—first primarily through the Hilfsdienst für öffentliche Arbeiten (Auxiliary service for public works), later by means of the newly organized or expanded large-scale arms industry, which, in violation of the provisions of the Treaty of Versailles, equipped a large army with all the weapons of modern warfare.

The Versailles treaty, the universally hated dictate of bondage, was declared invalid and scrapped, whereupon German troops moved into the Rhineland and the Saar region. The boundaries of the state, which had for years been considered too narrow for the "people without space" (*Volk ohne Raum*, the title of a novel by the nationalistic writer Hans Grimm, first published in 1920 and soon become a watchword) were pushed far to the East; Austria was incorporated into the new "Greater Germany," as was Czechoslovakia—and all this under the eyes of the former victor states in the West which looked on passively and at best protested with paper notes—before World War II was officially started on 1 September 1939 by the German invasion of Poland. Success seemed to vindicate the new rulers; it disarmed whatever opposition there was to their system of government. Besides, everything was done legally on the basis of authorizations, laws, and decrees to which a people trained for many centuries to obey in general submitted willingly. Public resistance was really possible only before the new regime had firmly established itself. After that, well-organized terrorism mercilessly suppressed all opinions that conflicted with the official ideology of the state, and fear kept people from expressing any opinion that ideological indoctrination had not yet managed to channel into the mainstream. The leading intellectuals of the country who might still have raised objections with impunity, at least in the beginning, kept silent—for lack of political insight and courage. The courage of their convictions was not among the virtues of the members of the German intelligentsia; that was left up to the Jewish intelligentsia, which was then decried as "corrosive" and devoid of a sense of governmental order and authority. True, there were small groups of doubters and those offering inner resistance. However, they did not tightly organize and make serious attempts to eliminate the system—the most important of which, and the only convincingly organized one, was the abortive attempt on Hitler's life on 20 July 1944—until the war situation had changed so much in Germany's disfavor that larger groups were able to see the last salvation in revolution. In this attempt the Jewish question played practically no role.

THE ATTITUDE OF THE GERMANS TOWARD HITLER'S JEWISH POLICY

If it was astonishing that most Germans let Hitler and his regime have their way, their attitude toward everything that happened to the Jews was even more shameful. Here Hitler, Goebbels, and all those responsible in the Nazi regime from the outset counted on the indifference, antipathy, and even enmity toward the Jews that were at least latently present in Germany and the world. These feelings derived from all the motives on which modern anti-Semitism was based, from misguided idealism and patriotism to envy and cheap rapacity. One way in which the *Führer* demonstrated his leadership qualities was that his measures against the Jews were at first not prominent. After the boycott of April 1933, which had created a great stir abroad, for a time the next steps were taken at fairly long intervals. Every intensification was legally sustained and thus seemed hardly contestable—until the beacon of November 1938 with the burning synagogues, which were visible far and wide, started a new phase of the policy toward the Jews and the war in the East gave it room (and resources) for an unrestricted implementation.

Anyone who read the literature (analyzed above) that led to Nazism, all those who read Hitler's *Mein Kampf* and took it seriously, must have realized what goal all this was heading for. But how many did read this literature and really take it seriously? Who could bring himself really to absorb the "philosophy of history" and political teachings of *Mein Kampf* in all their crude vulgarity? In his first programmatic speeches after his ascent to power Hitler deliberately spoke much less about the Jewish question than about the "dictate of Versailles," about unemployment and labor, new pride and new honor. The Jews were mentioned only as the causes of those evils, as impediments to the elimination of those troubles and to the establishment of the new Third Reich that was to endure for a thousand years and surpass in splendor everything that had preceded it. There were, to be sure, many individuals who helped their Jewish friends wherever they could, perhaps secretly squeezing their hands and silently empathizing with them.

ARMIN T. WEGNER

Only few people, however, openly stood up for Jewry as a whole. Only in rare instances did people raise their voices, thus attempting to save Germany's honor. One of the first among these—and possibly the first and only one of this kind—was the writer Armin T. Wegner, a man of integrity who on 11 April 1933 fearlessly opposed the degradation of the Jews in a letter of protest to Hitler which culminated in these words: "I implore you to preserve the dignity of the German people." He paid for his courage with confinement in prisons and concentration camps in which he was beaten half to death. The general reaction was silence, even when former friends were deported and disappeared, "address unknown."

COMPLICITY THROUGH SILENCE AND ACQUIESCENCE

People later cited as an excuse that the Nazis had managed to conceal their systematic murder of Jews from the public, completely or at least for a long time, by using code words that disguised their activities. Thus they claimed they had known nothing about the shootings and gassings, the pillaging, medical experiments, rapes, and sadistic cruelties visited upon the Jews, and that therefore they bore no blame. This may be true of the first murderous deeds but hardly of the later ones. Anyone who wanted to know was able to know—unless he deliberately closed his eyes and ears. Above all, what preceded the mass murder was open for anyone to see. Everyone saw the boycott of 1 April 1933; the stores and apartments destroyed in November 1938 were there for everyone to see; the deportations were visible, or at least they were confirmed by the disappearance of Jewish neighbors, empty apartments, and the transfer of Jewish businesses, shops, and property to "Aryan"-Christian hands. Anyone who wants to share in the luster of a people's achievements, even if he did not produce them himself, cannot escape responsibility for the misdeeds of a people that he did not prevent and did not even publicly disapprove of, even when it was still possible to do so without heroically endangering his life (something that no one has the right to require). "A country is not only what it *does*," wrote Kurt Tucholsky to Arnold Zweig in 1935, "it is also what it tolerates."

"DISPLACEMENT" OF STRATA OF CONSCIOUSNESS

In addition to the all-too-human fear and cowardice, the psychic substrata played an important role in the syndrome of the persecutors and the inactive onlookers—the layers of the Jewish question that were anchored in the historical conscious and subconscious. From ancient times to modern anti-Semitism with all its outgrowths they had developed in an atmosphere of cultural pessimism, antirational philosophy of life, mythological biology, and incantatory magic. As in a volcanic displacement of geological strata, elements believed dead and gone and regarded as archaic and obsolete came to the fore in a confused age,

supported the new ideologies of force in the strangest intermingle-
ments, paralyzed inner resistance, and despite pitiful human weakness
even helped those guilty of moral failure to have a good conscience.

The Attitude of the World

A similar answer may be given to the question why the world did not
react more sensitively to the establishment and the actions of the violent
totalitarian regime in Germany and even acquiesced in the persecution
and systematic extermination of the Jews in Germany and in the European countries under German rule without taking forceful action.

THE POLITICS OF APPEASEMENT

That the open breach of the Treaty of Versailles with which Hitler
early on confronted the world was passively accepted might seem to
make some sense. After all, this treaty, which had not brought the world
the hoped-for peace but had created a source of strife and tension had
come in for ever more vocal critique in the western countries as well.
The Russians had never recognized it; rather, like Germany, they were
interested in a revision that would again give them possession of the
areas they had lost between 1917 and 1919. Europe and America were in
the grip of a large-scale economic crisis that had put many millions of
blue-collar and white-collar workers on the rolls of the unemployed and
welfare recipients. Having disarmed, these countries were completely
unprepared for war. In England, conscription had been abolished, and
ground forces had again been limited to a relatively small army of
professional soldiers. The United States of America had almost completely withdrawn from European politics after 1919. Few people recognized the danger facing the world and warned against it; foremost among
these was Winston Churchill. People refused to see it and hoped to save
the peace by meeting Hitler half-way and making political and territorial
concessions to him—at least until they themselves were better prepared
for war. This is how the famous or notorious policy of appeasement came
into being, under England's direction, which allowed Hitler to incorporate Austria and conquer Czechoslovakia without a struggle. When the
British prime minister Neville Chamberlain in late September 1938
returned from the Munich conference at which he had given Hitler his
consent to the occupation of the Czech Sudetenland, the British people—and, in fact, popular opinion in Western Europe and America—
enthusiastically hailed him as the bringer of "peace for our time." The
umbrella that he used to carry ("my gamp") was regarded as so typical of
his demeanor that no cartoon of the time could do without it. The British
prime minister took Hitler's professions of peace seriously and evidently

believed that he could, in the face of the imminent total deluge, use the old-fashioned fair diplomacy and the compromises of a bourgeois-conservative democracy, which had traditionally been deemed successful, as an umbrella. Chamberlain had to realize too late that in a new period of unrestrained Machiavellian plans and actions of totalitarian states and in the face of new types of leaders of Hitler's and Stalin's ilk the Victorian ideas of diplomatic decency and decorum or the democratic self-determination of nations were wide of the mark. A year later he himself had to declare war on Hitler's Germany following the German invasion of Poland.

THE NAZIS' EXPLOITATION OF THE ANTI-JEWISH ATMOSPHERE

In his actions Hitler had also taken account of the latent anti-Jewish atmosphere in the western countries and exploited it in his propaganda. Chamberlain and the British people were against being pushed into war with Germany for the sake of a "distant country" like Czechoslovakia or a distant city like Danzig, but the idea of intervening in behalf of the endangered Jews was even less popular. Goebbels remarked about this in his diary that he was going to intensify the anti-Semitic note of his propaganda to such an extent that no statesman would dare to come out openly in favor of the Jews without being discredited among his own people as a figurehead for the Jews. Added to this was the fact that according to the prevailing opinion the Jewish question was a problem of the position of emancipated citizens of the Jewish faith in their country of residence and that therefore the treatment of the Jews in Germany could logically be regarded as a domestic matter in which no foreign state had a right to interfere. Besides, the reports about the measures against the German Jews that appeared in the world press were played down by the Germans and called enemy *Greuelpropaganda* (a word coined in World War I to ward off accusations of German atrocities in illegally occupied neutral Belgium), whereupon the German Jews as the alleged initiators of this "atrocity propaganda" were threatened with more severe measures.

CLOSED GATES

The states and peoples struggling with the economic crisis and the oppressive employment also resisted an intensified immigration of refugees from Germany, at first out of genuine fear and a concern about a further exacerbation of unemployment. This concern, however, was immediately skillfully exploited by Nazi propaganda and the anti-Semites in all countries and directed into generally anti-Jewish channels. In the face of these fears and influences the existing immigration laws in the European countries and in the United States, whose annual immigration quotas had already been determined by ethnic considerations, were not eased anywhere; if anything, they were enforced even more strictly. Even neutral Switzerland resolutely closed itself off from the stream of undesired Jewish immigrants from Germany. It was at Switzerland's suggestion that German passports for Jews were stamped with a big *J* as an easily visible identifying mark (and under the prevailing circumstances almost a warrant for arrest).

There were also gratifying endeavors, to be sure. An effort was made to transform the unregulated flight of Jews (and politically endangered Germans) into an orderly emigration based on the size and absorptive capacity of certain countries. This, for example, was the aim of the conference of the League of Nations in October 1933 at which the helpful American politician James G. MacDonald was elected high commissioner for fugitives from Germany—without, however, placing the necessary funds at his disposal.* Like a number of other actions, the conferences at Evian in July 1938, three months after the occupation of Austria by the Germans, and in Bermuda, whose opening on 19 April 1943 coincided with the "liquidation" and uprising of the Warsaw ghetto, documented the good will of well-meaning persons and organizations but also the helplessness of almost all countries and their lack of readiness really to see the problem and take decisive action to solve it. With the exception of the Dominican Republic, whose dictator Trujillo agreed to admit 100,000 agricultural settlers to his undeveloped country, not one of the 32 countries represented at Evian was ready to accept any refugees from Germany over and above the normal immigration quota.

In this rejection the statesmen were of one mind with the representatives of professional organizations and trade unions. All of them feared competition from immigrating job-seekers, rising unemployment, decreased wages, and lower morality; the "Jewish bacillus" was viewed as a danger outside Germany as well. The arguments of humanitarian or even philo-Semitic spokesmen like Norman Angell and Dorothy Frances Buxton, who emphasized in addition to the moral obligation the economic and demographic benefits of a more liberal immigration policy, were not accepted and their words of admonishment and warning went unheard. It redounds to the honor of mankind that humanitarianism was evidenced in many individual cases through helpfulness and personal efforts to the point of self-abnegation and true self-sacrifice in the rescue of imperiled people. As a total phenomenon and group quality, however, humaneness had reached a nadir in the life of the

---

*After a little over two years, on 1 January 1936, James G. MacDonald resigned under public protest.

nations that both a contemporary who lived through this period and a historian who looks back on it can register only with shame and revulsion.

COMPLICITY THROUGH PASSIVITY

In the face of the ever more gruesome reality of the murder of the Jews, the world—the nations, states, and, on the whole, even the churches*—remained passive. As must always be pointed out qualifyingly and appreciatively, in many individual cases they helped, saved, and assuaged suffering, but in the face of the total problem they failed utterly. Thus they share in a great guilt of which no one can acquit them, though—as one must always explain to the Nazis and their defenders—this complicity is not comparable to the guilt of those who advocated, motivated, planned, organized, ordered, and implemented the mass murder. Anyone who does not come to the rescue of an endangered person, who does not by word and deed keep or try to keep a murderer from murdering, shares in the guilt—morally and often also actually if he could have prevented the murder by his intervention. But only the murderer himself and his instigators are clearly guilty—morally, factually, and legally.

If one attempts to gauge the degree of the complicity of others, one will arrive at different results depending on one's evaluation of facts and circumstances. Here the questions are more easily raised than clearly answered. If the ruling powers, both secular and spiritual (the latter headed by the Pope), had issued clear condemnations of the injustice as well as unambiguous rejections of its ideological foundations, if they had condemned the murder of the Jews unmistakably and without political, economic, and personal considerations, could the misfortune have been averted or reduced? This is a question that must be asked even today. After all, no human power is independent of the criticism of the other powers, provided that it is expressed forcefully and definitely enough. Hitler groped his way forward step by step, and when there was no decisive and harsh reaction, he became more and more radical. True, his intentions were in essence established early on and had even been formulated in writing, but they did not crystallize as concrete plans until it was clear which real power factors he had to reckon with and which he could ignore.

THE INFLUENCE OF THE WORLD ON THE IMPLEMENTATION OF THE "FINAL SOLUTION"

This was true to a greater extent of the problem of emigration and the readiness of various countries to accept refugees. In the early years,

*See the excursus in Part 2.

even in radical National Socialist circles (and not only the misguided believing "idealists," who certainly existed) the talk was only of the legal and spatial separation of the Jews and the Germans, of domestic *Ausgliederung*, of emigration or deportation to other countries (principally Madagascar). Surely there were from the beginning radical people, uncontrolled in their thoughts and actions to the point of pathology and sadism, to whom such words were only linguistic veils behind which they could conceal plans for mass destruction, which in those days would have seemed unreal and unfeasible even to large numbers of their own adherents. But certainly the barbaric plan to murder the Jews systematically at first existed only among a small minority. If an organized mass emigration of the German Jews, and later of the Austrian and Czech Jews, in the first years of Hitler's rule and then especially between 1938* and the outbreak of the world war in September 1939 had managed to solve the problem of these Jews by transplanting the majority of them to other countries, the dimensions of the subsequent catastrophe could at least have been reduced. Perhaps then the road would have been open to a similar solution for the Jewish mass settlements of Eastern Europe from which many hundreds of thousands had emigrated overseas in the fifty years preceding the Hitler regime. Even after the beginning of the mass pogrom in its modern, technically organized form, would there not have been chances for rescue if help for the threatened had been regarded as the paramount aim and all possibilities of negotiation, exchange of men and merchandise, the threat and the application of force from bombing to the employment of paratroopers in collaboration with local partisan groups had been utilized?

In point of fact, no urgent task was recognized here—at first because people did not believe the seriousness and the extent of the danger, regarded the reports of the anti-Jewish measures in line with the denying and soothing Nazi propaganda as at least greatly exaggerated, and because they did not want to admit large numbers of undesirable elements to their own countries as refugees. With undisguised mockery Hitler, Goebbels, and their henchmen repeatedly referred to this attitude of the western countries, which they had foreseen and systematically fostered by means of their anti-Semitic agitation: These countries were giving Germany good advice about the treatment of the Jews but were not prepared to admit the so warmly recommended Jews themselves! Even after August 1942, when increasingly clear and authentic reports about the systematic mass murder reached the West, people at

*This theory is buttressed by the fact that in August 1938, a few months after the occupation of Austria (13 March), Adolf Eichmann was appointed as head of the Zentralstelle für jüdische Auswanderung (central office for Jewish emigration), promoted the emigration of Jews from Austria with all sorts of pressure and coercion, and the following year was transferred to Berlin in the same capacity. A similar central office for the emigration of Jews was established in Prague in June 1939.

first could not imagine such criminal actions by the Germans, which flew in the face of all traditional concepts of combat and war in the modern world.

Even when the facts could no longer be denied and became more and more generally known, people did not immediately consider taking practical measures, saying that only victory over the Germans could remedy the situation. No intervention by Jews in the Diaspora and in Palestine was able to induce the Powers to abandon this viewpoint. Even the "national homeland for the Jewish people in Palestine," which between 1933 and 1936 had absorbed more than a third of the Jewish emigrants, was impeded by a British government that yielded to Arab resistance and could offer refuge to only decreasing numbers of people.

THE ATTITUDE OF WORLD JEWRY

World Jewry cannot be exculpated in this regard either. The propagandists of the Third Reich, more or less expressing the opinion of the world, presented it as all-powerful, but it did not act as quickly and effectively as the need required it. Above all, differences of opinion and interests prevented it from taking concerted action in time. One reason for this was the Nazi propaganda about the pernicious Jewish omnipotence which exploited its international position only for its own benefit. Unjustified though this accusation was, it hit a sore spot on both sides: among the nations it intensified the fears that were at least latent, stemmed from Christian and secular tradition, and were allegedly confirmed by "experiences" of their own; among many Jews it aroused or heightened fears of being accused of "dual loyalty," a divided patriotism for the states and nations in whose midst they were living and working as citizens with equal rights. This weakened opposition against the hardened hearts of narrow-minded officials that resisted the numerous demands for a liberalization of the immigration laws, and it also reduced public intervention in parliaments and with high authorities for generous relief and rescue actions. It is true that Jews all over the world were generally ready to intervene with authorities for their relatives and friends by making donations and giving guarantees to facilitate or accelerate their admittance as immigrants, and committees were organized for the support of refugees in the countries of immigration. However, the systematic organization of aid to an extent that might have corresponded to the unexampled dimensions of the catastrophe in progress was set in motion only slowly, too slowly—for one thing, because of the unprecedented dimensions of the persecution and destruction of the Jews, which the Jews of the world, no longer as familiar with persecutions as their ancestors, could not grasp, believe as authenticated truth and real danger, and resolutely accept as a demand for immediate, vigorous, concentrated action. Arthur Ruppin may be cited as an example of the innocence and naiveté with which even the most insightful Jewish leaders viewed the situation as late as 1934, even if they had spent a lifetime concerning themselves with the theory and practice of the Jewish question and had attained to a clear understanding of its nature. In his diary entry of 27 September 1934, a year and a half after Hitler's ascent to power, Ruppin, one of the greatest experts on the problem and one of the most active fighters for its solution in the Diaspora and in Palestine, reported a conversation in Geneva with James G. Mac-Donald, the League of Nations' high commissioner for refugee affairs: "I explained that the solution of the German Jewish question lay in the emigration of 20,000 Jews a year from Germany. Of these, 10,000 would settle in Palestine; for the other 10,000 he, the High Commissioner, should find shelter in the United States and the ICA [Jewish Colonization Association] settlements in South America."

Recognition of the magnitude of the danger and of the systematic nature of the monstrous deeds always lagged behind the brutality of the latest anti-Jewish decisions and measures, and thus at any given time the projected relief actions no longer matched the need. Above all, the most influential circles were reluctant to engage in open political activity and to mobilize economic powers. On the one hand, they worried that this might, as it were, confirm the arguments and accusations of their adversaries, and on the other, they were as a matter of principle averse to interfering in the politics of the Powers. In keeping with the conception of the Jewish question as one of civil rights they were accustomed to handling critical situations through charitable action—on a small scale through the merciful help of one human being for another, on a large scale through organized collections and as systematic a use of funds as possible. People attempted to solve in this way even semipolitical problems like the release of emigrants or groups (e.g. children) to certain countries. This was, after all, in keeping with an old tradition; prisoners had always been ransomed and entire communities preserved from threatening explusion by payments of money. None of the Jewish leaders foresaw the full extent of the imminent danger. At best occasional flashes of presentiment were expressed in conversations or speeches; today these seem prophetic, but at the time they were not taken quite seriously even by the warners themselves. Since people did not recognize the ultimate aims of the National Socialist policy toward the Jews, perhaps did not want to recognize them (out of a kind of inner self-protection), they responded to individual actions with tactical means, but the strategy of the destruction of the Jews was not answered with a comprehensive counterstrategy intended to prevent it. It is, of course, impossible to say whether such a counterstrategy would have been possible and successful. As with all *ex post facto* "ifs" of history, we can only pose the question here, not answer it, especially because no serious attempt to do so has ever been made.

The Attitude of the Jewish Victims

Under the circumstances described above—the contempt, hatred, bureaucratic efficiency, and sadistic criminality of the persecutors; the hostility or indifference of the surrounding world; the silence and inactivity of the people and states; the lack of insight and leadership, the well-meaning interest but little active help of world Jewry—what was the behavior of the victims, the persecuted Jews, first of all the German Jews, then the Jews in the other central, eastern, and western European countries under the heel of Hitler Germany, and finally the Jews in the concentration camps, the Polish forced ghettos, the death camps, at the mass shootings, on their way to the gas chambers camouflaged as showers, during the selection of victims by the SS, the medical experiments on living human beings and all the other degrading, sadistic torments which they had to endure, which are beyond the wildest imagination and the strength of a half-way normal person to enumerate and imagine, and for which there is no comparison with other historical events known to us? One has to ask this question, which is lengthy and anxious not only in its formulations, in this way if one wants to make a hesitant attempt to answer it. Then one will be careful not to make hasty judgments, as has happened all too often. Perhaps we shall not arrive at a clear judgment at all, because in the final analysis we are here dealing with an industrially operated mass murder that all too easily obscures the millions of individual cases with their individual destinies and their individual sufferings.

We know very little about what went on inside these millions of individuals. The dead left few notes, and as for the living, if they do not keep silent and silently seek to forget or come to terms with their horrible experiences, they generally reveal only experiences that are especially deeply engrained in them and say nothing about their daily life, the long days from morning to night with their daily cares, conflicts, fears, torments, and small joys, with their hopes and despairs, prayers and imprecations and mute submissiveness—with most of them retaining their will to live in the seemingly endless suffering.

Of course, the behavior of the Jews under Nazi rule differed according to time and place, the countries and their traditions. The Jews of Germany were the first to be affected, while the Jews of the adjoining countries were still feeling safe—just as the German Jews had felt safe when the most brutal pogroms were occurring in Eastern Europe. People told themselves that something like that could happen only in the barbaric countries of the East even when there were warning signals in their own country. One is reminded of the Rhenish Jews' deceptive feeling of safety at the beginning of the first Crusade, when the French Jews told them about the anti-Jewish excesses in France (see p. 95 above). The German Jews simply could not imagine—any more than the Russo-Jewish intelligentsia could at the outbreak of the progroms of 1881 (cf. Part 2, pp. 621f., 672)—that the emancipation could be rescinded and that they would be exposed to violence, to say nothing of a murderous machinery constructed and set in motion by the state. At first they could not imagine the fecklessness and passivity of the world, though similar things had been experienced (but evidently repressed) during earlier persecutions, and not only of Jews. Had the world not remained just as silent and inactive when the Turks were systematically exterminating the Armenians before and during the First World War, and had it not left it to individual outsiders, writers like Armin T. Wegner and Franz Werfel (*The Forty Days of Musa Dagh*) to save the honor of humanity and humaneness at least through words of accusation and historical remembrance? Now people were at first thunderstruck in the face of these events, repeatedly deceived by temporary mitigations for economic or propagandistic reasons, until the new violent regime was firmly enough in the saddle and the economy and the production of arms were in full swing. Now the powers that be needed to have less and less regard for world opinion and world powers reacting more and more compliantly.

GERMAN JEWRY

At the beginning of this chapter we have briefly outlined the course of events and the reaction of the threatened Jewries. The German Jews recognized the situation facing them only gradually. The Zionists were the first to grasp the seriousness of the situation; after all, they had always warned against the imminent catastrophe of which Herzl had already spoken, though they had not expected it to come as it did. They appealed to the sense of justice and decency of their adversaries, but particularly to the sense of honor and the pride of the Jews themselves: "Wear the Yellow Badge with Pride!"—that was the boldly printed heading of Robert Weltsch's editorial with which the *Jüdische Rundschau*, the organ of the German Zionist Organization, reacted to the boycott of 1 April 1933. This appeal to avow their existence as Jews was gradually heeded even in anti-Zionist circles, though these kept affirming their Germanness for a while. The new bearing that Zionism had brought into modern Judaism increasingly prevailed among the Jews of Germany and in the further course of events among world Jewry as well. This was true of the countries attacked and occupied by Germany, but in the "free" world, too, the Jewish population moved closer together in the face of National Socialist violence. In this process the tone was increasingly set by the expanding Jewish settlement in Palestine and by the Jews of the United States.

The work of Jewish organizations in Germany—tolerated if not authorized and promoted by the government, until a forcible stop was put to it in late 1938—concentrated on the political representation of the interests of German Jewry, the best possible defense against the attacks on the Jews, the organization of the emigration of those willing or forced to emigrate, and the strengthening of inner resistance, self-confidence, and productive power under the ever more threatening conditions by educating the young people and establishing cultural institutions for adults. The center was the Reichsvertretung der deutschen Juden (Representative body of German Jewry in the Reich), the founding of which on 17 September 1933 "as an organic amalgamation of the entire Jewish population of a country" has been deemed to constitute a "unique event,"* a goal for which German Jewry had striven for decades but which was not attained until seven years before its downfall. The principles of the Reichsvertretung's work were then transferred to the work of Jewries in other countries insofar as the prevailing conditions permitted it. With the aggravation of the situation in Europe and the deficient receptivity of possible countries of immigration as well as the increasing curbs on Palestine, which had in the early years absorbed more than a third of the Jewish emigrants from Germany, the emigration movement, which was pushed forward simultaneously by the Germans and by the Jews themselves, became a more and more complex and often also a dangerous matter. The so-called illegal immigration to Palestine was attempted with barely seaworthy refugee vessels. Ships crammed with refugees far beyond their capacity roamed the high seas and were stranded or intercepted by British guard ships, whereupon their passengers were deported to refugee camps on the isle of Mauritius in the Indian Ocean.

THE JEWS DOOMED TO DIE IN THE GERMAN FORTRESS EUROPE

Between the outbreak of the world war on 1 September 1939 and its end in early May 1945 emigration came to an almost complete standstill. With the exception of England, the neutral states Switzerland and Sweden, and fascist Spain, Europe became an armed camp, ruled by the most evil tyrants and regimented brutes, in which the Jews were confined under sentence of death. The only variables were the form of confinement and the kind of execution that these Jews faced.

---

*Friedrich S. Brodnitz, "Die Reichsvertretung der deutschen Juden," in *Zwei Welten* (Tel Aviv, 1962), 106ff. Concerning earlier attempts and aspects of the activities of the Reichsvertretung and the organization associated with it, see the note in Part 2.

In this enormous prison camp, which Hitler called the Europe of the "new order," the Jews behaved as people behave in predicaments of this kind. Only in exceptional cases did they sink below the level that may still be expected in such a situation, and in many instances they rose far above it. One cannot expect every ordinary person to act heroically, whatever may be meant by that word. In general, people in distress and engaged in a daily fearful struggle for their lives that are threatened by brutal despots do not improve morally. How can they maintain their faith in God and love of their fellow men if violence, hunger, disease, and death threaten them at every turn, if no helping hand may be seen anywhere, neither from heaven nor from earth, if daily reality gives the lie to conceptions of divine justice, human freedom, and human rectitude, if admired models prove disappointing, and if daily living in excessively close quarters brings the painful experience of the human, all too human?

It is miraculous and reveals human inner strength and the intensity of positive historical group traditions if under such circumstances the evil in man does not assume immeasurable dimensions, if traditions and customs of faith, mutual aid, and the cohesiveness of families are preserved, if the bonds of maternal love, interpersonal affection, friendship and helpfulness are not completely severed but often even cemented (sometimes too much so for the utilization of opportunities for escape), if the will to live does not completely flag and give way to resignation and apathy. That despite everything the Jews maintained humane association with one another is attested by all reports that are not maliciously distorted or informed by human and sociological incomprehension. One must also consider that the situation of the Jews was now even more insecure or desperate than in any comparable earlier period. All that had been prefigured in the anti-Semitic theory (and has been discussed in detail above) was now translated into reality by the ideology-obsessed rulers and their thralls.

The New Conception of "Kiddush Hashem"

All earlier persecutions of the Jews, including the most cruel and disorganized ones, had been based on religious faith. In principle, and usually in actuality as well, anyone in the Christian countries could save himself from death by converting to Christianity and through the act of baptism.* From the Jewish standpoint, to be sure, such a person sacrificed his soul by adopting the Christian faith. That is why physical martyrdom unto death was demanded of the Jews—for the "sanctification of the [divine] name," or *"kiddush hashem,"* to use the Hebrew

*It was similar in countries in which Islam was the official faith.

term. Many Jews, both individuals and entire communities, steadfastly endured it from the days of the Maccabees to the Crusades, from the plague in the fourteenth century to the Spanish persecutions and expulsions of the Jews and the Chmielnicki rebellion in the Ukraine in the seventeenth century, to recall only a few of the most striking events that have already been discussed. Those who died in that fashion had moral satisfaction despite all suffering; they were fulfilling a divine command in a chain of generations, continuing a sacred tradition and keeping faith with it. Their memory was therefore honored by their succesors. They could also hope, and were in fact sure in their faithful belief and conviction, that God would give them credit in a future world for this unbendingness "for the sake of his name" and his honor.

All this was lacking now. Respected less and treated worse in their daily lives than animals, these Jews had no consolation for their souls. Who cared about their souls? It was no longer their faith, their spirit, their intellect, and their thought that made them sinners; these were in any case not the primary reason for their sin but at most an additional crime that stemmed from original sin and was its consequence. What was now being reviled, threatened, and eradicated was their very life, their existence. This existence of theirs as a pernicious parasitic race— that is, their life itself—was their sin, and it was punished by death.

This deprived the old traditional concept of *kiddush hashem*, the sanctification of the divine name, of its real meaning, though it too was revived again; after all, traditions continue to be effective even if their vitality is preserved or renewed only by new interpretations and extensions. Hence a maxim found increasing acceptance that first bore the name of the Warsaw Zionist rabbi Yitzhak Nissenbaum (1868–1942) but was probably taught by others as well and was increasingly accepted and disseminated by people's instincts. It became a watchword: Survive! Stay alive and outlive the persecutors! If the enemy wants your soul—so the teaching went—you must sacrifice your body for the sake of your soul. If the enemy's persecution and bloodthirstiness are aimed at your body, your God-given body and the seat of your soul, the important thing is to keep the body alive as long as possible despite all persecutions. Sooner or later the enemy *must* be vanquished; such a crime cannot go unavenged and the fight between a criminal state, no matter how powerful, and the great powers of the world cannot end with that state's victory. Hold out, then, till the turning point comes, live for as long as you can under the circumstances. "Survive!"—that is the commandment, the explicit or implicit demand for a strengthening of this will to live that also incorporates the spiritual and profoundly religious elements of the ancient concept of *kiddush hashem*. The new enemy, after all, denied both: the teachings of the Jews and their lives, their intellectual and physical existence. It was thus a matter of preserving both as far as possible—life per se and a life with dignity to the extent that this was possible, as well as a dignified way of surrendering to death or of resisting it. Never become an animal or the kind of brute that your enemy is! Sanctification of life is a basic substance of the Jewish commandments and the Jewish way of life. Here it was given a new meaning.

THE ORGANIZATION OF THE WILL TO LIVE

All efforts of the Jewries and their leadership, of individuals and their families now were aimed in some form at strengthening this will to live. These endeavors included the organization of emigration while it was still possible, and later the attempts to overcome the growing resistance of states and bureaucracies; cultural activities with educational institutions for children and institutes of adult education, theatrical performances and concerts, festivals and celebrations, all of which were organized by top experts and frequently by those voluntarily staying in Germany, but later also in all other countries under Nazi rule, in concentration camps and in the Polish ghettos; social work and the expansion of mutual aid in continuation of a tradition that had always existed in every Jewish settlement; and the collection and concealment of archival material about what was going on so that the survivors and coming generation might learn what was done to human beings behind walls and barbed wire, what was suffered by human beings, and how the persecuted and the persecutors conducted themselves—in remembrance of the past, in the sense of an old Jewish tradition and for the instruction and warning of the future.

THE JUDENRÄTE AND THEIR LEADERSHIP

All these were spontaneous reactions or actions directed from high up with the toleration and at first the near-cooperation of the Nazi authorities. These independently developed administrative, social, and cultural institutions, supervisory boards, and councils were increasingly transformed into compulsory organizations that were at least approved and authorized by the powers that be and frequently even formed by them with or without the consent of those to be served by these organizations. At the time opinions differed greatly about these agencies and leaders, which functioned under the name *Judenräte* (Jewish councils) or similar designations, and judgments on them have been highly contradictory. It is not surprising that their human, cultural, and moral level and sense of responsibility were quite variable. We are not writing a history of the Jewish people but examining the problematic nature of its existence; hence we can, as before, forgo a presentation and characterization of historical details and also refrain from making partial and comprehensive judgments on the *Judenräte*. Here we must deal only with the much-discussed problematic nature of their activities, which have often been presented emotionally and in biased fashion and more rarely with knowledge of the facts and human insight.

We must start by excluding from this cluster of problems the self-evident fact that as in any human community, and particularly in communities under dictatorial duress, there were in these closed-off or outwardly not delimited ghetto communities people with little moral inhibition who shamelessly exploited the predicament for their own benefit—to the point of closest collaboration with the enemy and the treacherous abandonment of the Jews under their care or rule. These were a minority. All that may be said in their defense—if one is possible at all—is that many of them had been worn down by long suffering and that in many instances they hoped, though generally in vain, to save themselves and their immediate family. By contrast, there were many who were devoted to their work, identified with the Jews entrusted to their care, and did everything humanly possible to make life in the ghetto more endurable and more worthy of human beings. They, too, often faced a dilemma when they had to make decisions about the life and death of human beings; at such times there was almost no dividing line between solicitude about life and blame for the death of people, and the intention and the consequences of a decision might do so diametrically opposed that afterwards it was possible to pose the questions but not to answer them, at least not adequately.

Without the Jews involved being aware of it and reflecting about it, the entire system was built into Hitler's power structure, which operated with unrestrained terror and violence from the beginning, and after 1941 was with increasing consistency expanded into a death machinery that employed the latest technology. Hence the Jewish leadership's freedom of decision was mostly illusory. Basically, the *Judenräte* were but a cog in the enemy machinery that promoted its smooth operation. This is why sometimes a scathing judgment has been rashly pronounced on the leaders of the Jewish communities and ghettos, and even the best and most reputable among them have been accused of collaboration with the enemy, making them, so to speak, accomplices in the criminal machinery of murder. If they had offered open resistance and—so goes the argument—called upon the Jews under their care to resist and organized them for that purpose, or if they had at least refused to collaborate with the enemy in any way, his measures would at least have been carried out more slowly and with greater difficulty, thus saving many lives. According to these critics, the enemy found it easier to reach his goals with the aid of organized Jews than if he had faced masses of unorganized individuals.

At first blush this argument, like many logical-ingenious conclusions, seems to make sense, but in reality it is only a mental exercise that unduly simplifies the facts, mental acrobatics like every retrospective *if* and *but* of history, and like those it is admissible only as a question leading to the illumination of the tragic situation in which the Jews found themselves. The Jews have faced truly tragic situations on frequent occasions in their history. It is virtually a characteristic of the Jewish question, with whose nature and history we are concerned here, that the coincidence of forces of all kinds, the concurrence of traditions, ideologies, economic conditions, human actualities, and isolated phenomena, often placed the Jews in positions in which guilt and real or apparent justification or even virtue were closely, almost inextricably, interwoven, making a subsequent judgment entirely dependent on the standpoint of the judge. Let us try to find a few clues for the disentanglement of this problem.

THE TRADITIONAL SELF-GOVERNMENT AND COOPERATION OF THE JEWS

Whenever people find themselves in the land, or hand, of the enemy, there are basically two possible modes of conduct: active or passive resistance and negotiation, which in its nature always constitutes some degree of cooperation. Which way out is more promising, or seems so, depends on the local and human factors: whether there is a real choice and what combinations of elements of both modes of conduct are realistically possible and feasible. And another question is closely connected with it: To what extent were the actors, those responsible, aware of their situation, how comprehensive was their knowledge of the machinery in which they were one of the cogs, of the scheme according to which it worked, and of the purposes for which it had been put in operation?

The answer to this question must be considered separately in each case and will differ in accordance with circumstances, provided there can be a clear answer on the basis of the existing sources and the different situations. A general consideration of the problems facing those responsible must start with the insight that the Jewish leaders and committees at first regarded their work as the continuation of the centuries-old tradition of Jewish self-government that had existed everywhere in the Middle Ages and continued to exist in many of the mass settlements of Eastern Europe and, despite all emancipative legislation, also in Western Europe in the forms and dimensions dictated by local conditions and needs. This organization of self-government, which was coordinated with the authorities of the surrounding world and often was embodied in the law or approved and regulated by it, with its tax system and its institutions, from the administration of synagogues via cultural institutions and social services to hospital care and burial, called for constant cooperation with the authorities.

This cooperation of the Jewish leadership, which was generally supported by more or less democratically elected parliamentary bodies, was particularly important in times of political conflict, social upheaval, economic hardship, and concomitant threats from popular leaders and groups. At such times the governments usually cared as much as the Jews did about a peaceful settlement of conflicts, because any unrest among the people entailed the risk that it would not stop at the limits of the Jewish corporation but encroach on the general institutions of the states. Hence a certain measure of cooperation between the Jewish administrative organs and the non-Jewish government offices was generally in the mutual interest, and in this the state's organs were guided by the existing legislation, the implementation of which the Jewish institutions could, if necessary, enforce by court action. The civil service might be unfeeling and bureaucratic and individual officials might be anti-Jewish, but in general this affected the behavior of the administrative machinery only slightly, for it was given its impetus and direction by the legal regulations.

THE FUNDAMENTAL CHANGE IN THE NAZI SYSTEM

That the Nazi regime had fundamentally changed and that this change was not, as was at first assumed, only a quickly passing surge but an upheaval affecting all areas of life and decision-making with a "revaluation of all values" (a horrible, inhumane reinterpretation of Nietzsche) according to which the Jews no longer had human rank and were in the most literal sense of the words equated with parasites, bacteria, and insects—all this was utterly unfathomable and manifested itself in reality only very gradually. Only very slowly did the responsible Jewish leaders and executive committees become aware of this completely new, traditionless situation, and in many cases they did not fully realize it until the last moment. Therefore a feeling of responsibility toward the Jewish community and every individual member caused them—in the face of an enemy who was breaking with all tradition, a mortal enemy in the truest sense of the word—to cling to the traditional practice of collaboration in an effort to protect and save what could, actually or presumably, still be protected and saved. In the face of the untrammeled cruelty and barbarity of the new rulers who, obsessed with their mission as purgers of the world of *Untermenschen* (with the Slavic peoples and the gypsies numbered among them) and of vermin in human form, sneered at any traditional appreciation and conception of a state's legal system and human action, the *Judenräte* and Jewish leaders of all kinds acted in accordance with views and traditional wisdom that often strike a later observer as absurd. The persecutors and the persecuted lived anachronistically, as it were, in different temporal and cultural worlds. The racial-mythological destructive world of the SS was, as was later observed, like a new, unknown planet on which the victims, ruled, enslaved, and murdered by sadistic nihilism and an insensitive bureaucracy, simply could not get their bearings and saw no pole for orientation.*

LISTS OF DEATH AND LIFE

Among the principal tasks given the responsible Jewish organizations by the German Nazi powers were the preparation and submission of lists of Jews, their assignment to forced labor, and the production of weapons and other war material (uniforms, shoes, etc.) Many responsible members of the Jewish committees hoped to demonstrate by this mobilization of workers the value of the Jewish population, to provide gainful employment for it, and to avert the worst from it. (In point of fact, there was a dispute among and within military and administrative bodies, the SS and especially those responsible for the murder machinery, headed by Eichmann, whether Jews should be regarded as workers or only as parasites to be gassed; even in the face of the growing shortage of transportation the ideology and the stolid machinery of officials won out over considerations of utility.)

When things went downhill step by step, it was hoped that by the partial abandonment of victims others could be saved—and in such reflections it was of course only natural and human that in the selection special consideration was given to family members, friends, and helpers. Can anyone who never was in such a predicament fully appreciate the difficulty of such decisions and feel so free from blame and fault that he can cast the first stone? Who can say how he himself would have acted in the case of such decisions? We know about some of those who had to perform this superhuman task that they became aware of hopelessly slithering into a stinking swamp of human entanglement and then realized that the only way to escape responsibility for making wrong decisions and the reproach of complicity in murder was to take their own lives. Others responded to the first indications of such misfortune by refusing to accept positions of leadership or by resigning from them. The consequence of this was that the Nazis installed elements acceptable to them in leadership positions, getting even more compliant helpers who sometimes vied with the rulers in unscrupulousness, in the (usually illusory) hope that they were thereby saving their lives and those of their family.

"LIKE A SHEEP LED TO THE SLAUGHTER"

Why—so people ask even today—did the leaders of the Jews not decide on resistance? Why was there no call to fight, to offer passive

---

*Cf. the notes in Part 2, pp. 723f. ("The Planet Auschwitz").

resistance, to commit sabotage, or even to try to escape? Why did they permit a Jew to be "like a sheep led to the slaughter" or even to go voluntarily? Astonishingly enough, these questions have been asked even by some of those who did not believe the fact of systematic mass murder until they saw, at the end of the war and thereafter, the survivors and the murder instruments with their own eyes, having previously allowed things to happen incredulously, often uninterestedly, and almost always inactively. These questions have been raised by Israelis, particularly young people, who cannot imagine any Jewry before the founding of the State of Israel and who have experienced the victorious battles of the Israeli army. From their point of view it is logical to assume cowardice on the part of Diaspora Jewry and to contrast it with the bravery of the Israelis who have grown up in their own country.

Let us first look at the biblical simile "like a lamb [or sheep] led to the slaughter." When the prophet Jeremiah (Jer. 11:18), complaining before and about God, said that his fellow Jews and fellow citizens in his hometown Anathot intended to lead him "like a docile lamb . . . to the slaughter," he added: "I did not realize that it was against me they fashioned their plots: 'Let us destroy the tree with its fruit, let us cut him off from the land of the living. That his name be remembered no more!'"* Not the words taken out of context, but the quotation as a whole characterizes the situation correctly; the patient walk to the slaughterhouse becomes explainable when one adds the words "I did not realize . . ." The Nazis' victims often did not realize the extent of their danger and often went to their doom without suspecting anything. Those involved usually did not fully realize it, at least in the first phases of the murderous policy, until it was too late to take any effective action against it even if they had decided to do so. The tactic of obfuscation that was employed with virtuosic unscrupulousness, often till the last moment; the situation of terror in which the Jewish population in the ghettos and camps found itself; the belief of the leaders and the led in release and speedy liberation; the retaliatory measures that were taken by the Nazis against the slightest resistance, with public hangings, tortures, shootings, and starvation—all this hardly permitted any armed resistance, let alone the organized kind.

JEWISH RESISTANCE

This is how things were not only for the Jews but in all areas affected by the German reign of terror, including the occupied countries where

---

*There are similar images in Isaiah 53:7 and Psalm 44:23. The former speaks of the tormented prophet who endures his tortures silently, "like a sheep being led to slaughter." This was later applied to Jesus as a distinction (John 1:29; Acts of the Apostles 8:32). In Psalm 44 God is addressed reproachfully: "It is for Your sake that we are slain

non-Jewish resistance groups could count on the support of a resident population in sympathy with them. Partisan movements of appreciable dimensions did not come into being anywhere until the situation for those involved had become so desperate that no risk seemed too great any more, or until things began to go badly for the enemy and reverses in the fortunes of war became apparent. This was particularly the case after the defeat in the battle of Stalingrad where in February 1943 the encircled German Sixth Army under General Paulus surrendered to the Russians with 90,000 survivors—barely 40 percent of the original army of 220,000 men. This impressively demonstrated to everyone the possibilities and prospects of partisan-like fighting factics. Under these circumstances, and when the goals of the "final solution" became ever more clearly discernible to the Jews, armed resistance movements arose among them as well, and frequently they even preceded the general ones.

The extent and effectiveness of armed partisan resistance, both the general and the Jewish kinds, should not be overestimated. The military value of all enterprises of the resistance in the European countries and of the armed resistance on the part of the Jews was slight. It increased when in connection with the retreat of Hitler's armies it had the advancing Russian and western troops as a support—like the *résistance* and the *armée juive* in France. That this help came so late, that it did not come until the "final solution" had already been carried out on a large part of European Jewry without serious obstruction by non-Jewish powers and forces, is part of the tragedy of the Jewish question in this period and of the Jewish attempts at resistance. Only those who were there and acted differently have a right to accuse the Jewish leaders, the executive committees, and those murdered in the ghettos and death camps. The members of the other peoples do not have this right; *they* deserve the *"J'accuse!"* of the Jews, not the other way around.

There were good reasons for it if the leaders officially responsible for the fate of the Jews, and especially those who took their responsibility seriously,* usually decided against armed resistance; none of us knows whether he would not have made a similar decision in their predica-

---

all day long, that we are regarded as sheep to be slaughtered. Rouse Yourself: why do You sleep, O Lord! Awaken, do not reject us forever! Why do You hide Your face, ignoring our affliction and distress?" (*The Writings* [Philadelphia: Jewish Publication Society of America, 1982], p. 58).

*It is almost self-evident that, as we have already pointed out, there were also many inferior elements, weaklings who could not resist temptation, cowards, egotists, informers, and collaborators with the enemy. These types have always existed among human beings. Their legal or moral condemnation has nothing to do with judging Jewry as a whole. The Jews have a right to have their share of evil and weak individuals measured in the same way as that of any other people.

ment. They saw that ten or a hundred Jews or entire Jewish communities were held responsible for the killing of one German soldier, and that meant not a trial or imprisonment but death without a sentence—and it was merciful if the victims were spared additional tortures. It was known that Jewish rebels could generally not count on the aid of the populace; on the contrary, it often collaborated with the Germans or at least sympathized with them where the Jews were concerned. In their hostility toward the Jews even the national partisan groups in the East were hardly different from the general population. The only exception were certain groups of the radical Left in Poland and Russia; these, however, demanded the integration of the Jews into the general partisan troops and prohibited separate Jewish actions or permitted them only reluctantly. The reason was that for them the Jewish problem as such theoretically did not exist or existed only as a special aspect of the general social problem; this standpoint was similar to that of the western powers. One can gauge the measure of the courage, the despair, and the almost Messianic faith and hope if despite all these (and many additional) difficulties resistance groups and partisan camps of all types were formed in forests and fortified bunkers starting in October 1941 (in the ghettos of Tatarsk and Starodubsk in the Smolensk districts), from July 1942 after the "liquidations" of individual ghettos in various places, and in increasing measure after 1943. Now there were forcible outbreaks from ghettos and destructions of Jewish settlements—in some instances under the leadership and with the participation of *Judenräte*, in others with their approval and silent acquiescence, but occasionally also against the violent protest of responsible Jewish authorities. The zenith (and prelude to resistance in other places) was the armed uprising of the Warsaw ghetto from April to May 1943, which illuminated the whole situation like a beacon. All forms, manifestations, and shades of the conduct of the persecutors and the persecuted that are known in the Jewish people's struggle for existence are contained in the history of this uprising. Hence it is worthwhile to give it at least in outline form here.

The Uprising of the Warsaw Ghetto

LIVING CONDITIONS IN THE WARSAW GHETTO

Warsaw was the largest Jewish community in Europe. Until the outbreak of World War II its approximately 400,000 Jews constituted about a third of the city's total population. (Only 500,000 Jews lived in all of Germany in 1933!) Among the Jews of Warsaw there were rich people and prosperous ones but a much larger number of poor people. In 1933 the income of half of them was so low that they did not have to pay any municipal taxes. Between October 1939 (after the capture of Warsaw) and January 1940 the Nazis put into effect a number of anti-Jewish measures which were more or less equivalent to those in force in the Reich: Jewish badges (not a yellow Star of David with the inscription *Jude* on a black background, as in the Reich, but a white armband with a blue Star of David), the marking of Jewish shops and enterprises, the confiscation of Jewish land and other immovable property, the prohibition of the use of public transportation, and conscription for forced labor. The establishment of the ghetto began in April 1940 with the erection of a wall, and in early October of that year the regulations governing it went into effect. All non-Jews ("Aryans") had to leave the fenced-in area, and the Jews were strictly prohibited from living and working outside the ghetto walls unless they had special work permits for firms outside the ghetto. Its area was initially rather extensive, but new walls that established narrower limits gradually brought about progressive reductions. In the fall of 1941 the spatially reduced ghetto was divided into two parts that were connected by a bridge. The outside walls and gates were guarded by German and Polish police, the inside by a kind of Jewish militia, the *Ordnungsdienst*. From April 1941 on, supreme authority was vested in a German high commissioner.

During the siege of Warsaw (13 September 1939) the engineer Adam Czerniakow was installed as head of the Jewish community by the then mayor; a few days later (on September 28) Hans Frank, the Nazi governor of the newly created *Generalgouvernement* Poland, appointed a *Judenrat* consisting of twenty-four members and headed by Czerniakow. The latter did what he could to improve the situation, supported social and cultural institutions, and negotiated with the German authorities, always endeavoring to prevent worse things from happening by cooperating, supplying workers, and so forth.

The constriction of the settlement area and the additional Jews (ca. 72,000) brought into the ghetto by the Germans from the adjoining towns and districts caused an unbearable housing shortage. In July 1941 an average of thirteen persons lived in one room and many Jews were without shelter. Expropriations and confiscations assumed ever greater dimensions. Added to this was the official apportionment of foodstuffs to the Jews which can only be described as starvation rations. The official daily ration for Jews amounted to 184 (!) calories as compared to 634 calories for the Poles, who were also regarded as *Untermenschen* but enjoyed a somewhat higher status, and 2,310 calories for the Germans. A Jew officially received 2 kilograms (about 2.41 pounds) of bread per month (!) that was made of sawdust and potato skins. The prices that had to be paid for this were in inverse ratio to the quality and quantity; for their few calories Jews paid more than the Germans did for their far greater rations. Unemployment assumed immeasurable dimensions; in June of 1941, 60 percent of the Jewish population were without work.

The skilled workers employed by the Germans received starvation wages about 0.5 to 1.0 zloty for ten to fifteen hours of hard work. Fuel was extremely scarce; in the winter of 1941/42 about 90 percent of the dwellings had no heat. Many died of hunger and disease, and there were epidemics, particularly of typhus—another excuse for the Germans to seal the ghetto off as tightly as possible. Despite the death sentence threatening those who passed over into the "Aryan" area without authorization it was possible to smuggle into the ghetto additional food amounting to many times the official ration by means of barter (for the products of illegal small workshops), purchase, and bribes. Children played a great role in transporting these over the border walls. Under these starvation conditions about 100,000 Jews lost their lives in "natural" fashion by the summer of 1942—far fewer than the Nazi scheme called for. In a conference held on 20 August 1942 the German governor Hans Frank told the assembled Nazi officials to bear in mind that two million Polish Jews were under sentence of death by starvation and the fact that they were not dying to the extent envisioned would have to cause them to accelerate other measures in keeping with that goal.

This famine was one of the reasons the Jews regarded any alternative that offered itself as an improvement of their situation. Hunger was used by the Germans with calculating deception to get the Jews to volunteer for deportation to death camps. They were promised work and given a big bread ration as earnest money or a handsel, as it were—and with diehard optimism desperate, jobless starvelings accepted it as the price for supposed work with lodging and food.

THE "ACTIONS" AND "TRANSPORTS" FOR THE LIQUIDATION OF THE WARSAW GHETTO

The summer of 1942 marked the beginning of the accelerated "actions" of the "final solution" which went beyond starving and working the Jews to death. They began with murders in the streets and the taking of hostages. At the same time increasingly dependable information came through about the real goal of the projected transports for which the *Judenrat* was required to provide lists of candidates. Adam Czerniakow, its chairman, requested an explanation from Nazi officials and SS officers of various ranks. According to Czerniakow's diary entry of 20 July 1942, all declared that they knew nothing, that it was all *"Unsinn und Quatsch"* (stuff and nonsense), and that he should see to it that the rumors were denied.

On 21 July 1942 the members of the *Judenrat* were arrested. Czerniakow, who wanted to go along, was instructed to stay in his office. Some of those arrested were soon released, and the chairman was promised that the others were going to be. The next morning the SS officer responsible for the "action" appeared at the office of the Jewish community and said that all inhabitants of the ghetto, with the exception of some special cases, would be transported "to the East" and that 6,000 were to be ready by 4:00 P.M. That afternoon Czerniakow received a warning: For the time being his wife, who had been taken hostage, would be released, but she would be the first to be shot if the deportation failed. When Czerniakow inquired on the morning of 23 July how long the action would continue, he received this cynical-laconic answer: seven days a week. People were still hoping. Czerniakow noted in his diary: "In the city, strenuous efforts to set up workshops. A sewing machine can save a person's life." At 3:00 P.M. he made this entry in his diary: "Right now 4000 are ready for deportation. My orders are that there must be 9000 by 4 p.m." Shortly thereafter Czerniakow took poison and died. He had always carried on him a lethal tablet in case the worst happened. The day before he had refused to sign the deportation order. The Nazis' refusal to exempt children from deportation may have been the last straw. After all, it was logical that in their extermination of the Jews as the final solution the Nazis should have paid special attention to the new generation. In a farewell letter Czerniakow wrote that he could not be expected to send helpless children to their doom. Here life-protecting human compassion clashed with the ideological, merciless logic of death. "I am powerless," he went on to say in his farewell letter, "my heart trembles with pain and compassion. I cannot endure all this any more. May my action show everyone what the right way is."

Czerniakow's suicide produced no change, and surely no change for the better, in the course of the evacuation action. His successor, like him an engineer, was more obedient and cooperated with the Nazis. Every day 5,000 to 7,000 Jews of every age and sex were deported. Between 22 July and 13 September 1942 approximately 300,000 of the 370,000 Jewish inhabitants of the ghetto were deported. The number of Jews who were to remain permanently was fixed at 35,000, mostly workers in the factories located in the ghetto or nearby and their families. As many as 20,000 to 30,000 other Jews stayed in the ghetto "illegally." In addition there were a few thousand Jews from abandoned work camps in the vicinity.

THE ORGANIZATION OF ACTIVE RESISTANCE

At that time and in that situation the resistance movement began to assume more concrete shape and to make serious preparation for armed resistance by procuring weapons. In the meantime some members of the underground movements who had managed to escape from the Treblinka death camp and to return to the ghetto had supplied reliable information about the aim of the transports: physical destruction and extermination—"liquidation" in the technicalized Nazi language. There had always been resistance of some kind—in the form of organized help, cheering up, care for children and the sick, exchange of information, and whatever else might serve to preserve oneself and others from physical and spiritual ruin. That made sense for as long as there was some prospect or vague hope of survival, aid, and rescue from the worst. Now the naked truth was plain for everyone to see: certain death. All traditional slogans in opposition to it had lost their meaning. *Kiddush hashem*, the sanctification of the divine name, might have retained some significance for those unshaken in their belief in God and helped them go to their death in upright fashion. "Survive," the newer watchword, was appropriate for the transitional period, when there still was hope of rescue; to the hour of death it remained for many an inner commandment based on human nature and in the spirit of Jewish experience. The young generation of members of youth organizations and Zionist or socialist political parties who had grown up with a modern secular *Weltanschauung* had also adopted the ideals of heroism, human honor, and the noble, manly defense of these by force of arms. These ideals had undergone transformations at various times since the Middle Ages, but they had endured, and the young people had combined them in their outlook on life with older ideas and models from the Jews' own heroic history—from King David via the Maccabees to Bar Kochba. The 24-year-old Mordechai Anielewicz, an activist from the Left Zionist youth movement *Hashomer Hatzair* (The young guardsman) who was to become the leader of the Warsaw uprising, said to Emanuel Ringelblum, the historian, social worker, and organizer of the collections of documents about the contemporary fate of Polish Jewry (and a man twenty years his senior), that he regretted having wasted three years on educational and cultural work. He said that the only choice now was to die "like sheep led to slaughter or like honorable men." Like sheep led to slaughter—here we first encounter this phrase, spoken passionately, and, detached from its meaning in the biblical writings, it now became an invective used against those unwilling to fight.

THE TRADITION OF JEWISH SELF-DEFENSE

It was a continuation of the spirit of resistance that had been aroused by the Kishinev pogrom of 1903 and was fed equally by Jewish-national and socialist sources. Chaim Nachman Bialik, the Hebrew poet of the awakening Jewish nation, had at that time hurled his verses of uncontrollable rage, revenge, and contempt for cowardly, inactive acquiescence against the world, the slaughterers, the Jews, and God: "And if there is justice—let it show itself at once! But if justice show itself after I have been blotted out from beneath the skies—let its throne be hurled down forever! Let heaven rot with eternal evil! . . . And cursed be the man who says: Avenge! No such revenge—revenge for the blood of a little child—has yet been devised by Satan."* His call was heeded. The pogroms of 1904 and 1905 were already confronted with Jewish self-defense troops organized by Zionists and Jewish socialists. From then on self-defense was a tradition—in the Diaspora and even more in a Palestine being built by Zionists. From there the impulses came back to the pioneer movements of the Diaspora; a new sense of life and honor arose among those young people, a new feeling of respect for the human body and for one's obligation to protect it from defilement and murder. That was the background against which the desperate recognition of reality was transformed into the will to action: Take revenge on the enemy, do not submit to his bidding! If you have to die, then die honorably, and if there is still a chance at rescue in a God-forsaken and man-forsaken world, then only rescue by your own hand. Do not allow it to happen, but act! It was the spirit of Massada, the last great struggle against the Romans, combined with the modern conceptions of heroic fight and death.

ARMED UPRISING

The uprising in the Warsaw ghetto began when the Germans attempted to deport and liquidate in the customary way the last remnants of the Jews living there. It had been carefully prepared by the erection of protective bunkers, etc., and it was accomplished with few weapons and no significant support from the outside but with organization and an unparalleled fighting spirit. This uprising has frequently been described in reports of the few survivors, in historical presentations, and in poetic accounts. From a military point of view it was ineffective. After an initial astonished retreat from the unexpected armed resistance of the Jews—the "Jewish bandits," as they are called in the reports of the Nazi leaders—General Jürgen Stroop, who was charged with putting down the uprising, used the heaviest war materials and with German thoroughness and the mercilessness of Nazi ideology systematically mowed down, shot down, and burned down the Warsaw ghetto block by block, including fighters ready to surrender. He had every stage carefully captured by photographers as a glorious deed, down to the piles of rubble and human bodies. When it was all over, he proudly sent this pithy victory message to Hitler: "The Warsaw Jewish quarter is no more!" This area, too, had become *judenrein*, in the tasteful Nazi

*From "On the Slaughter." Unrhymed translation by T. Carmi, *The Penguin Book of Hebrew Verse* (Philadelphia, 1981), 512–13.

parlance, even though with somewhat greater military expenditure and losses than most other areas.

According to Stroop's report, 56,000 Jews were killed in battle or forcibly deported to death camps. On 8 May 1943 the Germans managed to destroy the headquarters of the resistance. Four days later, on 12 May, Arthur Zygelbaum committed suicide in London. This leading Bundist had been able to flee from Warsaw in late 1939 and had become a member of the Polish National Council in London, representing Jewry together with the Zionist Ignaz Schwarzbart. In his farewell letter Zygelbaum wrote: "I cannot keep silent. I cannot go on living while the last remnant of Polish Jewry, which I represent, perishes. My friends in the Warsaw ghetto fell in the last heroic struggle, weapon in hand. It was not given to me to die together with them, but I belong with them in their mass graves. Through my death I wish to make a final protest against the passivity with which the world is looking on and permitting the extermination of the Jewish people."

THE CONTINUED HISTORICAL EFFECTS OF THE UPRISING

As we have indicated, the Warsaw uprising was of no military significance. It was undertaken under conditions that precluded a military success from the outset. Historical effectiveness, however, is not tantamount to momentary success or failure. There are events whose immediate effect is slight but which transcend space and time in their effects in breadth and depth and in this continued effectiveness achieve historical greatness and become epochal events of paramount importance. In this sense the Warsaw ghetto uprising is a great historical event. Almost immediately afterwards it was so perceived by both Jewish and non-Jewish contemporaries, and this is how it appears ever more graphically to posterity. It really marked a new chapter in Jewish history and in the Jewish question. It was the expression and became the symbol of a new attitude of the Jews toward the world. It was the result and the widely visible embodiment of a variety of forces, the point of intersection and culmination of numerous lines of development that led from the beginning of the European stateless Jewish Diaspora, the *galut*, to it. The destruction of European Jewry and its culture of many centuries which here became visible to the world carried *ad absurdum* the theory of individual emancipation with its demand for or will to assimilation and the frictionless integration of the Jews as individuals, and it demonstrated the unreality of this theory. The mass murder of the Jews by one of the culturally most advanced peoples, a murder tolerated by the world and even supported by silence and deficient readiness to help, was the end of the epoch of emancipation that had started with the French Revolution. It was the logical consequence of the biologically founded racial ideology that had been elevated to the status of a racial mythology and was executed as a judgment in mass factories of death by obedient henchmen of all ranks and classes who had been induced to do so by ideology, mythology, and terror and acted at the behest of a power-crazed, hate-obsessed, and deluded horde chieftain.

In this era of emancipation and race mania, however, beginning with the end of the nineteenth century new energies were released in Judaism which found their most concrete positive expression in the building of the Jewish national home in Palestine that was struggling for its existence and expansion. These energies also affected the life of large groups in the Diaspora by bringing about a national and social transformation and regeneration. This development represented a continuation of ancient Jewish hopes and endeavors and also reflected the absorption of modern ideas of national rebirth and social transformation in accordance with democratic principles. Without this new posture, which became increasingly prevalent in certain circles, particularly among young people, the reaction to the desperate situation of the Jews by an armed rebellion against a much stronger adversary who was crushing any opposition and any Jewish existence with unrestrained brutality would be inconceivable. For years the Jews had endured inhuman pressure and coercion. The Warsaw uprising was the signal and the widely heard and understood proclamation that this was now a thing of the past. The growing power of national regeneration gained the upper hand over the waning strength of patient, obedient accommodation and endurance. From this impulse, which was revolutionary in the truest sense, a line runs from the organization of illegal immigration to Palestine of the remnants of European Jewry, which were vegetating in refugee camps after the collapse of the Hitler state, to the founding of the State of Israel and the transformation of world Jewry. A new chapter in the history of the Jewish question began. The attempt at a radical solution of the problem through destruction and mass murder was followed by an attempt at a positive solution through rebuilding on the basis of a Jewish state and reorganization of the Diaspora and its goals.

10

The State of Israel, the Jewish Diaspora and the Jewish Question

The Founding of the State of Israel

On Friday, the fifth of Iyyar 5708 according to the traditional Jewish calendar, 14 May 1948 in terms of the European-Christian calendar, an event occurred for which many generations of Jews had been waiting anxiously and hopefully and for which they had worked and fought with mounting intensity for two generations: the foundation of a Jewish State. In the hastily prepared auditorium of the small Tel Aviv Museum, originally the residence of the first mayor of the first Jewish city of "Old-Newland," the chairman of the Zionist World Organization, David Ben Gurion, read the Declaration of Independence of the new state in the early afternoon, before the Sabbath rest. With the official expiration at midnight of the British mandate for Palestine, the "State of Israel" was to assume legally the administration of the country. On the following morning the State was accorded *de facto* recognition by the United States of America, and three days later it was recognized *de jure* by the Union of Soviet Socialist Republics and by Guatemala. Within the first month of its existence it was recognized by nine other states (five communist ones, three in South America, and South Africa), and others soon followed. With the foundation and recognition of the State of Israel, the third Jewish state in the Land of Israel, there began not only a new chapter in the history of the Jews but a decisive turning point in the history of the Jewish question. The period of homelessness of the Jewish people was at an end.

The Declaration of Independence of the State of Israel

The first ten sections of the Declaration of Independence* which Ben-Gurion read aloud at the festive session at which the State was founded (after he had given it its final formulation the night before and it had

*An English translation of the (Hebrew) Declaration of Independence may be found in Part 2, pp. 730f.

been unanimously approved by the Jewish National Council in the morning) contain a resumé of the history of the Jewish question as a motivation of the claim to the renewal of Jewish existence in the form of a state in Eretz Yisrael. They speak of the importance of the land in giving rise to the Jewish people and developing its character, of the development of its national and universal culture, the creation of the Bible, the Jewish people's clinging to its homeland even after its expulsion from the land, and its efforts to return, which had in recent decades intensified despite all obstacles and led to a Jewish settlement that was constantly expanding and defending itself against all attacks. In addition, the Declaration speaks of the convening in 1897 of the First Zionist Congress by Theodor Herzl and its proclamation of the right of the Jewish people to national rebirth in its country: "This right was recognized in the Balfour Declaration of the 2nd of November, 1917, and reaffirmed in the Mandate of the League of Nations which, in particular, gave international sanction to the historic connection between the Jewish people and Eretz Israel and to the right of the Jewish people to rebuild its National Home." It goes on to say that the massacre of millions of Jews in our time had irrefutably demonstrated that the problem of the Jewish people's homelessness and lack of independence could be solved only by the reestablishment of the Jewish State in Eretz Yisrael, a state that would keep the gates of the homeland open to every Jew and confer upon the Jewish people the status of a fully privileged member of the family of nations. The document mentions the efforts made by survivors of the Nazi massacres in the face of all obstacles and dangers to reach the country and to "assert their right to a life of dignity, freedom, and honest toil in their national homeland." By virtue of their active participation in the struggle against the Nazi forces the Jews of Palestine have gained the right to become members of the United Nations—a right that was actually not granted them at the founding of the new organization three years earlier (1945), in contrast to the Arab states, which did not earn this right in the war and some of which collaborated with Germany, not declaring war on it until its defeat was imminent.

"On the 29th November, 1947, the United Nations General Assembly passed a resolution calling for the establishment of a Jewish State in Eretz Israel; the General Assembly required the inhabitants of Eretz Israel to take such steps as were necessary on their part for the implementation of that resolution. This recognition by the United Nations of the right of the Jewish people to establish their State is irrevocable." (This fact is emphasized in the face of attempts to dilute, delay, or rescind the decision.) "This right is the natural right of the Jewish people to be masters of their own fate, like all other nations, in their own sovereign State." The Declaration appeals to the United Nations, the Arabs in the country, the neighboring Arab states, and the Jewish people to help with the establishment of the State of Israel, which will strive for a peaceful development of the country in the spirit of the prophets, grant all citizens equal rights in every respect, guard the "Holy Places" of the land, respect the Charter of the United Nations, and be open to Jewish immigration.*

This Declaration and the decrees and regulations subsequently promulgated for its implementation placed the Jewish question on an entirely new footing.

The Remnants of European Jewry as Refugees

It was high time that this happened. Despite what one might have expected, the Second World War had not ended with an attempt at a positive solution of the Jewish question. True, the National Socialist hegemony over Europe had collapsed under the combined onslaught from the East and the West, and in 1945–46 some of those chiefly responsible for the crimes had been sentenced by the international military tribunal in Nuremberg. But most of the remnants of European Jewry that had been saved from dying in the death camps could not have returned to their old domiciles even if they had wanted to. Cities and countries had been destroyed, new boundary lines had been drawn, the eastern states included in Russia's sphere of power had turned communist between 1945 and 1948, the populations were not free from the influence of the anti-Jewish propaganda of the Third Reich, and as the beneficiaries of stolen Jewish property they were not at all interested in having the Jews return. The main obstacle, however, concerned the western states, the only possible countries of immigration. Their immigration laws, which had already prevented many rescue-seekers from immigrating during the Nazi period, had not been rescinded or liberalized, and the same was true of the laws of Palestine as controlled by the British mandatory government. The Jewish refugees, whose physical and spiritual health was badly impaired and many of whom, disappointed by the attitude of the nations, tried their utmost to settle in the "national homeland of the Jewish people," were for years detained in refugee camps in Germany and Austria. After their bitter experiences in

---

*The right to free immigration was stipulated on the same day in a decree by the provisional Council of State that was published simultaneously with the Declaration of Independence in the first issue of the official legal gazette and rescinded the restrictions on immigration embodied in the mandatory laws. Two years later, on the 20th of Tamuz of the Jewish year 5710 (3 July 1950)—the anniversary of Theodor Herzl's death, commemorated as an official memorial day—the Law of Return (hok hash'vut) was promulgated, which assures the right of free immigration to the State of Israel to every Jew who does not jeopardize the health of the country or has not actively transgressed against the Jewish people.

the concentration camps they had begun to have doubts about the morality of the so-called civilized world, and now they were further demoralized by the lack of integration into the economy and society of the surrounding world.

Under these circumstances it is not surprising that as a consequence of these experiences, as well as the physical and spiritual injuries, and in the face of the indifference and even hostility of the world some anti-social elements came into being whose activity was immediately decried by that world with hypocritical self-righteousness (and is decried even today). What is truly astonishing and almost incomprehensible is the amount of utterly unshakable faith, moral courage, preparedness, and unfaltering determination that was manifested in these Jews' quest to start a new life in the old homeland. To the extent that circumstances permitted it, this determination had been revived and strengthened during the war by the youth movements, most of them Zionist.* It was directed into orderly channels by the soldiers of the Jewish Brigade who, after a long struggle with the mandatory government, came to Italy with the British army in late 1944, were able to participate in the battles against the Germans in northern Italy in the spring of 1945, and then, until the disbanding of the brigade in the summer of 1946, systemati-cally organized the immigration of the Jewish refugees to Palestine, particularly from the camps in Germany and Austria. These camps kept receiving an influx of refugees from Eastern Europe who had since the end of the war taken various routes to Italy and Central Europe under the guidance of leaders and fighters of the Jewish partisan movements and uprisings in the eastern European ghettos and death camps. This influx increased significantly after the return of 175,000 Polish-Jewish fugitives from Soviet Russia to Poland, beginning in late February 1946. It became a flight after the pogrom in the Polish town Kielce in early July 1946—the climax of a number of smaller pogroms in Poland since the end of the war—in wich forty one Jews and four Poles lost their lives, a larger number of victims being prevented only by the quick action of the Polish army.

This pogrom took place almost simultaneously with the arrest by the British of those members of the Jewish Agency in Palestine whom they could get hold of as well as of other leading personalities whom they confined for five weeks in a concentration camp in Lod (the "Black Sabbath" of 29 June 1946). In August 1946 the British began to deport "illegal" immigrants, whose ships they seized, to Cyprus.

---

*These youth movements had supplied most of the leadership of the uprisings as well as activating and keeping in motion, though with scant success, the rescue attempts made by the Zionist Organization, the Jewish population of Palestine, the big Jewish institu-tions (like the World Jewish Congress in Geneva), and the Jewish relief organizations (such as the Joint Distribution Committee in the United States).

"Legal" and "Illegal" Immigration

The legal limitation of Jewish immigration at the time of the greatest Jewish need had always caused a better organization of an officially "illegal" immigration, which the Jews in the country called *Aliya Bet*, the second immigration movement. This immigration without permission and against the will of the state's rulers has a long history. It began in the 1880s, when the modern immigration and settlement projects under Zionist auspices had their start. In those days, under Turkish rule, all Jewish immigration and settlement were actually accomplished with the consent of the authorities—at best without official permission and frequently with the methods of circumvention and bribery that were customary in the territories of the Ottoman empire at the time. Herzl had opposed this so-called policy of infiltration, saying that only legal immigration and settlement on the basis of a state treaty with the government could guarantee the safety of the settlers and their work and lead to the development of the new, upright type of Jew that he and the Zionist movement created by him were striving for. Only in this way could the Jewish question be brought closer to a solution.

The Question of the Absorptive Capacity of the Land

The new epoch beginning with the end of World War I was initiated by the Balfour Declaration and the assignment of the mandate for Palestine to England with instructions to establish a national homeland for the Jewish people in Palestine (by which the eventual foundation of a Jewish State was undoubtedly meant at that ime). This seemed to offer guarantees for a legal immigration, and after some hesitation the capacity of the land to absorb new Jewish immigrants was specified as the sole criterion. As to how great this receptivity was to be and how it was to be measured there often was substantial disagreement between the Zionist offices applying for permission to immigrate and the competent British authorities. It was only natural for the Jews to use every loophole in the laws to expand immigration as much as possible, and all the more so the greater this discrepancy between the Jewish demands and the British interpretation became. The increasingly rigid attitude of the British combined a desire to avoid Arab pressure and terrorism (which are to be discussed later) with an antipathy to the recalcitrant Jewish immigrants on a high intellectual and social level of European Jewish culture, and the narrow, almost provincial economic views of the colonial officials on the scene and their superiors in London. The Jews opposed to this a belief strengthened by the history of the settlements that the absorptive capacity of a country in general and their own homeland in particular was less dependent on static conditions than on the dynamic elements that influenced them. In this concrete case these were the profound inner connection between the Jewish immigrants and the soil of the homeland, which was hallowed by religious and national tradition—a connection that is closely akin to the usual love of one's homeland but often surpassed this in intensity because the tension caused by the long spatial and temporal separation was now being reduced; the optimal utilization of science and technology by an intelligentsia bred by the process of selection of grave historical experiences; and the growing predicament of European Jewry, which had since 1933 exceeded all hitherto known dimensions.

Organized Illegality: Immigration and Armed Resistance

The sporadic attempts by individuals to circumvent the immigration laws, which, following some years of extensive legal immigration, were enforced with increasing severity after 1937 and eventually were for all practical purposes tantamount to a ban on immigration, turned into an increasingly organized movement to bring refugees from Europe to Palestine illegally—most of the time by sea with the aid of more or less seaworthy old ships and small vessels. This *aliya* (immigration) was first raised to the status of a program by the Zionist opposition parties, which aimed at rebellion against the British mandatory government because it had mishandled the task assigned to it and thus was an enemy of the Jews. After 1938, when the distress of the European Jews rose steeply and the progressive restrictions on immigration, which could have saved the lives of at least tens of thousands (or, as the immigration after the foundation of the Jewish State was to demonstrate, hundreds of thousands), the organization was promoted, at least unofficially, by the recognized representatives of the Zionist movement and the Jewish population of the country, above all by the labor organization *Histadrut* and the *Haganah*, the defense force of the Jews in the country, which was also officially "illegal." There came into being a formally independent institution, which was actually supported and financed by the official Jewish authorities, for the systematic organization of the illegal *aliya*, *Ha-mosad L'Aliya Bet*, which transferred its official headquarters to Paris in 1946. Between 1934 and 1948 a total of about 120,000 Jews reached the country by "illegal" routes—or, rather, reached its coasts, for more than half of these were intercepted by the British before they could enter the country, deported to Mauritius or (after August 1946) to Cyprus, where more than 50,000 Jews were detained in camps, or interned in Palestine itself. Some small boats that were denied permission to land sank and hundreds of immigrants drowned. A particularly glaring case was the sinking of the refugee ship *Struma* in February 1942, crammed with 769 passengers who had been barred from landing in Turkey because they lacked the British permission to immigrate. The climax of exasperation and indignation came with the forcible impound ment, return to Europe, and compulsory landing, in early September 1947 at the German port of Bremen, of more than 4,500 refugees from German camps and ghettos who had two months earlier set out for the long voyage from the French port of Port-de-Bouc on the *Exodus 1947,* the provocative new name of the *President Warfield,* a boat chartered and operated by the Haganah. This shameless action had been taken upon express instructions from the British foreign minister Ernest Bevin while UNSCOP, the United Nations Special Committee on Palestine, was meeting to discuss a proposal for the partition of the land and the founding of a Jewish and an Arab state which were to be closely connected economically. In a dramatic vote on 29 November, this proposal became a decision of the general assembly of the United Nations and cleared the way for the foundation of the State of Israel.

The Legal Immigration after the Foundation of the State

As already mentioned, all restrictions on immigration were removed by the founding of the State of Israel. There began a mass immigration which within four years more than doubled the Jewish population of the country before the State came into being—a sign of the great need that was met by the opening of the country's gates to Jewish immigration.

It was only natural that the immigration was not able to sustain this level; there were periods of stoppage, remigration, rise and fall. Not even the most highly developed country can absorb over a prolonged period an influx of the magnitude of the immigration in the first years after the foundation of the State of Israel.* In its further course the immigration took place in accordance with the physical and psychological laws of any immigration movement, being governed by the repelling forces in the country of emigration and the attracting forces in the country of immigration. The ebb and flow of the immigration or emigration movement is in proportion to these two factors. Hence the size of the immigration to Israel from a given Jewish settlement in the Diaspora always reveals something about the situation of the Jews in the country of emigration and about the strength of the attraction and the immigrants' ability to integrate themselves in the State of Israel. The immigration movement is, of course, only one of the elements in the cluster of relationships between the Diaspora and the State of Israel. There are

---

*In terms of large countries and their resident population, this would have corresponded to an immigration of about 150 million to the United States and 60 million to Germany. To be sure, this does not include the Arabs living in Israel, hundreds of thousands of whom fled. This certainly did not benefit the economy of the country. For statistics of immigration and emigration see Part 2.

many others in Israel and in the Diaspora. One of the most important of these is the struggle for the preservation of the State.

The Military Struggles for the Existence of the State of Israel

The State of Israel, after all, did not come into being as the founder of the Zionist movement had envisaged it and his successors and adherents had always desired it: as a great act of peace between the Jews and the nations. The founding of the Jewish State was supposed to lay the groundwork for the solution of the Jewish question for the benefit of the Jews as well as the peoples in whose countries Jews were living. This included the Arabs; the cultivation of the underdeveloped land by modern science and technology would also benefit them as fully privileged citizens and, beyond that, promote the development of the neighboring countries with which the new state would collaborate to produce a renascence of the Near East. To be sure, this hope had been dampened again and again by the experience of a half-century since the founding of the Zionist Organization and a quarter-century of the existence of the British mandate for Palestine, and the problem of peaceful coexistence with the Arabs and the nascent Arab national movement had become more and more acute.* After all, the decision of the United Nations to divide the country into a Jewish and an Arab state had been made as a compromise between the antithetical views of the problem by the Jews and the Arabs. But this decision, too, had been based on the hope that the two sides would abide by the decision of the highest authority of the international community of nations and states which at that time had not yet sustained the grave loss of authority that the following decades would bring. Both parties had to give up important aspects of their claims. This hope was still expressed in the Declaration of Independence of the State of Israel, even though it had already been preceded by hard fights.

Against all desires and hopes of the nations, which had elevated the proposal to the status of a majority decision, and the Jews, who agreed to it despite numerous doubts and inner resistance, this decision was immediately rejected by the Arab states. These had been included by England in the deliberations for the solution of the Palestinian problem, previously still viewed as a local affair, as England's partner against the Jews; this had been done for the first time in the fall of 1936 and then steadily from 1939 on, and now these states were the official representatives of the Palestinian Arabs as members of the international organization of states. The Arabs immediately expressed their rejection through armed attacks that soon spread through the entire country as an armed uprising supported by the neighboring countries with money and volun-

*See pp. 437ff. below.

teer troops. When the Jewish defense force Haganah defeated the rebels on a number of occasions, the foundation of the State was immediately followed by an invasion of well-armed military units of the neighboring countries of Egypt, Jordan, Syria, and Lebanon that were supported by military contingents from Iraq and Saudi Arabia.

The newly founded State of Israel thus was forced from its very first hour to defend by force of arms its land, its people, and its political structure against the threatening enemy armies, even as it was building its administration and working on the peaceful development of the land for the reception of the imminent stream of immigrants. The events of the days of the first return from exile were now, as it were, repeated on a larger scale. As in the vision of the prophet Ezekiel the death-like bones of the remnants of the Jewish people were freshly covered with skin, sinews, and muscles and rose to life, and as in the days of Ezra and Nehemiah they had to combine labor with constant readiness to fight, "doing work with one hand while the other held a weapon," as Nehemiah formulated it in his well-known narrative (Nehemiah 4:11).* This proved how correctly Herzl had assessed the effect of a life in freedom on the soil of the homeland when at the conclusion of *The Jewish State* he spoke of his belief that "a wonderful breed of Jews will spring up from the earth. The Maccabees will rise again." This was the first and the most enduring impression that the Jews in the Diaspora and also the world received from what was happening in the newly founded State of Israel.

The Jew as Fighter

The fighting Jew was a new phenomenon. True, as we have already seen, since the beginning of the century (and in isolated instances even earlier) Jews had shown their mettle in self-defense in the Diaspora and especially in Eretz Yisrael, and in the wars of the nations, since the beginning of the emancipation and particularly in the two great world wars, thousands and tens of thousands of Jews had fought as soldiers as bravely as any other citizen and had frequently excelled in an effort to

---

*The following account of an incident may serve to illustrate the great extent to which the minds of the defenders were on building rather than fighting. It was published by Naomi Shemer, the author of the words and music of the popular song "*Yerushalayim shel zahav*" (Jerusalem the golden), almost thirty years later (*Davar*, 3 June 1977). In 1948 Naomi was a young girl standing with her mother next to Stoller, one of the first cultivators of the date palm, in a dugout of the Jewish kibbutz Kinneret: "When there was quiet for a moment, Stoller said to my mother in his deep voice: 'Today was a great day for me.' My mother kept silent in astonishment. Perhaps he had heard some important news that would console and help them. But Stoller went on: 'Today was a great day for me. I managed to pollinate date palms artificially.'"

demonstrate their (often-doubted) patriotism and refute the malicious legend of the Jews' cowardice and unfitness for military service by displaying particular courage and bravery. This had sometimes been noticed and registered, but more frequently it had been disputed through a false interpretation of statistics, and usually it had been presented at best as the self-evident fulfillment of the duties of citizens. However, with the founding of the State and the fight of the defensive forces of the State of Israel,* which had just been formed out of the hitherto more or less illegal military units, against the armies of the neighboring states, which were far superior to them in numbers, training, and equipment, and the Jews' victory over them against all predictions of the "experts," the Jew as victorious fighter became highly visible to the world for the first time. Peoples are not fully recognized until they form a state; that was the insight gained from the bitter experiences of Jewish history in the Diaspora, which constituted the point of departure of the Zionist teachings and goals. If a people does not have a state, and especially if it lives scattered among other nations like the Jews, its existence is perceived as unreal and frequently as ghostlike (see p. 289 above). Now the Jew made his first appearance as a member of his own state and his own army, as a fully privileged person and fully recognized fighter, as a victor in a life-and-death struggle for his human and national existence. As such he aroused astonishment and admiring recognition.

That is how it was in the War of Independence of 1947–1949, which ended with the armistice agreements of February to July 1949 and claimed the largest number of victims—6,000 dead, at that time almost 1 percent of the Jewish population of the country. This was repeated seven years later (1956) in the victorious Sinai Campaign (four days, 200 dead) and eleven years later in the "Six-Day War" of 1967 (800 dead), the quickest and most momentous conflict, the subsequent war of attrition at the Suez Canal (1968–70, 400 dead), and finally the "Yom Kippur War" in the fall of 1973, which caught Israel by surprise and unprepared on the most solemn fast day of the Jewish year. All this was accomplished amid great disappointments and with great losses—2,522 dead, almost one-thousandth of the Jewish population, which had greatly increased in the meantime. The climax of this surprised and admiring recognition probably came in 1976 with the unexampled Entebbe project which

---

*The official name of the army of Israel is *"Tzvah Haganah l'Yisrael"* (abbreviated as *"Tzahal"*), defense army for Israel. On the one hand, this name contains the name of the pre-State military defense organization *Haganah*, which was legalized thereby. On the other, it expressed the character and the goal given to the army; it was to be an instrument of defense rather than attack, even though the defense of the country, small as it is, sometimes required and still requires attack on strategic and tactical grounds. Analogously, the ministry responsible for it is not the Ministry of War, as in many states, but the Ministry of Security *("Mizrad ha-bitahon")*.

involved the 7,000-kilometer flight of an Israeli troop of commandos to Uganda and the liberation and return to Israel of the Jewish passengers kidnapped on a French airplane by Arab (and German) terrorists. In between there were numerous smaller border fights as well as the struggle against Arab terrorists who were constantly threatening the development and the very existence of the State of Israel and its Jewish population through kidnappings, threats, bombings, and all other types of terroristic activity, mainly aimed at innocent civilians. These warlike acts since the beginning of the systematic Jewish work of settlement have been regarded, not without justification, as one long-drawn-out struggle for the existence of the State of Israel and its Jewish population.*

This struggle for the preservation of Israel as a country and as a people, as a project and state, as the foundation and creative expression of the Jews living and immigrating there, and as a center, source of strength, and visible embodiment of the Jewish people as a whole can, of course, be evaluated from two aspects, the Jewish and the Arab. Let us try to do justice to both and pose this question: What were the consequences of the struggles for the Jews in Israel and in the Diaspora, and what did they mean and symbolize for the Arabs? The first viewpoint leads us to the problem of the relations between the State of Israel and the Diaspora, one of the central problems of the Jewish question, and the second aspect is the problem of the opposition to the realization of the Zionist attempt to solve the Jewish question. For years this was discussed as the "Arab question," but now it tends to be termed the question of the "Palestinians" (in contrast to the "Israelis").

The New Type of Jew

As already stated, the Jewish fighter as "Jewish fighter"—that is, a fighter for the interests of Israel and Jewry and not for other ideas or nationalities—was a new phenomenon, one that became visible only now. He was an expression of the statehood of the Jews living in the country, for the newly gained corporeality of the idea of Judaism. To what extent this new corporeality actually was and is in keeping with the idea of Judaism was open to discussion, like everything that concerns the relations between the country and the Diaspora and between the past, with its expressions and interpretations differing according to time and substance, and the present with its equally different manifestations and goals. We can refrain from discussing this here, for beyond all antithetical conceptions of the nature and the mission of Judaism one thing is certain: Here a new type of Jew appeared before the world and before

*Nataniel Lorch, *One Long War: Arab versus Jew since 1920* (Jerusalem, 1976).

Jewry, one that did not harmonize with the stereotype of the Jew as developed in the course of many centuries.

What was new about this changed image of the Jew, the image of the typical Jew of the State of Israel? What first struck the attention of both non-Jews and Jews was, as already indicated, the fighting spirit, the determination not simply to accept threatening misfortune and to endure it without striking back, without an attempt to blaze the trail regarded as right—if necessary by force of arms. What was manifested here was a new pride and a new sense of honor. We saw the first manifestations of this manly pride in the uprisings of the Polish ghettos (see pp. 402ff. above). There it was a desperate struggle without prospect of military success or even personal survival. The few who came out of these fights alive felt that they had been saved by a miracle. They had all prepared for a Massada, for a last heroic fight to the death. Their watchword, goal, and prospect was to die as men and not like "lambs led to slaughter."

Now, too, the fighters were prepared to die, and this readiness was demanded beyond the usual measure. As we have pointed out, the 6,000 who fell in the War of Independence, twice as many as in all the ensuing wars combined, represented almost a full one-hundreth of the country's Jewish population at the time, among them a considerable number of new arrivals from the European DP camps. All of them had been ready to give their lives for the community if need be, but this sacrifice was not their goal or in the forefront of their consciousness. Their aim was victory against the enemies and in most cases also the inner certainty that this goal would be attained, though in view of the enemy's preponderance with great sacrifices of men and armaments.

Here as on numerous subsequent occasions, the Jewish fighters had two weighty elements to pit against this preponderance. One was that if the Arabs' threats were taken seriously and appropriate conclusions from individual events were drawn, a defeat in war would mean the downfall of the newly created state, the work of construction, and of the Jewish population, as well as their own death and that of their wives and children. Jews did not fight to make conquests but with their backs against the wall; there could be no retreat. Any conquests and territorial expansions of the boundaries too narrowly drawn by the original partition plan that victory brought was not intended but only a consequence- and not always only a salutary one—of the struggle forced upon the Jews.* This awareness that defeat is tantamount to doom was—and is!— one of the strongest pillars of the vaunted bravery of the Israeli fighters.

---

*When the members of the People's Council who were debating the formulation of the Declaration of Independence demanded that the boundaries be fixed in it, Ben-Gurion told them that if the Arabs peacefully accepted the partition plan, he would be ready to

The Israeli as fighter is at the same time the Israeli as creator, the builder of a country and a state that are being fought for and with which the Jews of the Diaspora identify to an ever greater extent, just as the world identifies them with Israel. The process is, of course, more complex than it seems to be in this formulation. There are many gradations, fluctuations, and demarcations as well as a great many internal and external problems that are determined by basic considerations and by temporal and local conditions and influence.

Initially the enthusiasm predominated. The Jew as heroic fighter, the Jew as farmer and cultivator of land who used and developed new methods of scientific technology in his work and in the organization of social living—all this had evolved and been tested in two generations of activity in the country and in Zionist socialist education. Also, the Jewish question and Jewish life in the Diaspora with its problems, its drama, and tragic catastrophe in Europe had occupied public attention. However, it took the struggle for the foundation and existence of the State of Israel to impress the world most profoundly and confront it with the facts. It produced a change in the physical, political, and even psychological landscape. The entry of Jews into history and politics as active factors, something that Zionism had striven for and initiated with the appearance of Herzl, had now become a political reality, with all the good and evil, the risks and promises that this entails.

"Komemiut" as a Symbolic Word

A second pillar of the Israelis' bravery was the new pride, the new sense of honor, the newly gained erect bearing. It is no accident that the Hebrew word denoting this, *komemiut,* was one of the basic words of Ben-Gurion, the real founder of the state, its prime minister for many years, and virtually its symbol.

The history of this word and its use is of some interest in this connection. It occurs once in the Bible (Lev. 26:13). There God admonishes his people Israel to fulfill the Commandments and reminds them that he has freed them from Egyptian bondage, broken the bars of their yoke, and led them out of Egypt walking "erect." Later, shortly after the destruction of the state, the word was included in one of the basic prayers:* "And bring us to the peace from the four ends of the earth and

---

accept and respect the boundaries specified in the United Nations decision even though they were inadequate, but that if the Arabs chose to fight, the outcome of the battle should decide the boundaries, as happened in every war.

*In the introduction to the prayer containing the profession of faith at every religious service: "Hear, O Israel, the Eternal is our God, the Eternal is One."

lead us upright into our country!" Somewhat later a complete reference to God's words in the Bible was included in the grace as a supplication: "May the merciful one break the yoke around our necks and lead as upright into our land!" Life outside the land, and even life in the country without statehood or independence of joint action and feeling, both religious and secular, is here perceived not only as exile and banishment but as bondage (like the first bondage in Egypt), as a yoke under which one is harnessed like an animal, and the supplication, which is repeated several times a day in the liturgical ritual and accompanied with (audible or inaudible) sighs is for the Jews to be freed from their depressed bearing in exile and to be led back to the homeland as free persons with erect bearing.

The adherents of the movement for a national regeneration, which joined up with Zionism and organized under its banner, people with a new self-awareness, now demonstrated that even the life of the emancipated Jews, the western Jews with formal and legal equal rights, was free only in appearance. There is an essay by the aforementioned Ahad Ha-Am, the writer on cultural Zionism and teacher of teachers and leaders, that has been repeatedly cited to this day. In it he expressly excoriates the "inner bondage" in the "external freedom" of these emancipated Jews, a bondage in which even those on a high intellectual and human plane and even the intellectual and religious leaders are living. In late 1902 the leading poet of the national regeneration, Hayyim Nahman Bialik, reverted to the traditional word in an enthusiastic ode to Ahad Ha-Am: "And heeding his courageous voice we all straighten up, and in upright fashion [*komemiut*] and with raised hands we point the way forward and eastward for those scattered in the Diaspora." In this way (and in a similar fashion in others) the word denoting erect bearing, *komemiut*, came into use as a symbolic word for the life of the new Jew connected to the soil of his land among the settlers of the so-called "Second Aliya," the immigration movement, starting around 1905, of Russian and Polish Jewish workers whose goal was to do all work with their hands and not be, like their predecessors, supervisors of Jewish or Arab serfs. Basing themselves on this principle, they (and even more consistently their successors in the third wave of immigration after World War I) wanted to organize their settlements in such a way that they could till their soil themselves, and for this reason and for the sake of the justice that was to prevail they created new forms of settlements, the collective kind called *kvutza* or *kibbutz* and the cooperative settlement of small farmers, the *moshav ovdim*. Any work not done with their own hands appeared to them, and especially to their teacher of this lifestyle, the Tolstoian A. D. Gordon, like a parasitic way to act and life. From this viewpoint the life of the Jews in the Diaspora appeared as an inferior activity, as the role of middlemen rather than truly productive work, and the bearing of the people seemed cowed and cringing rather than upright.

Thus the word denoting liberation from bondage and the attainment of freedom, as well as the change from a life depressed by a yoke imposed on one's neck to a life with erect bearing on one's own soil in one's own land, became the watchword for the achievement of liberation through labor and, if necessary, struggle. For Ben-Gurion and the generation led by him the War of Independence became the *milhemet komemiut*, the struggle for uprightness, and the decoration that the state bestowed upon the participants in this struggle for independence and the existence of the newly founded state was given the name *ot hakomemiut*, the badge of uprightness. Political independence, national rebirth, and upright bearing *(komemiut)* became nearly identical concepts. The fundamental experience in the Jews' historical consciousness, the exodus from an alien land (Egypt) to their own land, from bondage to freedom, from humble submission to erect independence was now fully reexperienced, relived, and renewed as a deed and as an everyday action.

Uprightness, the new bearing of the Jew on his own soil and in his own state, thus became the emblem in contrast to the Jew in the Diaspora, who had to adapt his life to the majority opinion and the majority practices of his surroundings, who could in any case not act without reference to these or consideration for them, even if only in his own feelings or consciousness. Hence such a Jew often appears to an Israeli as unfree and cringing despite all his external freedom. By contrast, the Israeli appears as a new type of Jew and as such becomes the model for many Jews and helps many others who identify with him to a new pride. In imagination, however, he is often exaggerated and turned into an ideal type to such an extent that encounters with real-life Jews in Israel not infrequently prove to be disappointing and evoke disillusioned criticism that then easily exceeds the justified dimensions and purposes.

In this way the Diaspora and Israel become poles that attract each other but run the constant risk of repelling each other as well.

Identity, Truthfulness, and Responsibility

Certain questions about which it had earlier been possible to hold different opinions were now decided. The founding and existence of the State of Israel had decided the definition of the nature of Jewish existence that had been discussed for six generations—whether the Jews are a people, whether their existence as a people was finished long ago and they constitute only a religious community, a tribal group, or (as a neutral historical concept) a "community of fate," and what conclusions are to be drawn from the various views by the Jews themselves and by the surrounding world. The Jews were recognized as a people entitled to exist in its own state; this was not doubted even by most Arabs, even if they disputed the Jews' claim to existence with statehood in Palestine and rejected the United Nations decision made in that spirit. After all, the brutal persecution of the Jews under Nazi rule had already made the world "Jew-conscious"—if not under the influence of the racial doctrine, then under that of the massacres, the most horrible and indubitable evidence of which could be read and seen in photos and films after the end of the war. Besides, the remnants of European Jewry that had survived the ghettos and death camps had created a burning refugee problem which had also substantially contributed to the decision of the United Nations. Unlike what had been possible in the era of emancipation, which had come to an abrupt and catastrophical end with the Nazi rule, the Jews of the Diaspora could no longer hide behind seemingly harmless code words like "Israelites" or "citizens of the Jewish faith" (or lack thereof). The founding of the State of Israel and the political, economic, and military struggle for its existence had torn all such masks from people's faces. Without the Jews of the Diaspora realizing it right away, this had confronted them with decisions about the nature of their own existence. "Jewish identity," hitherto a rarely used concept, meaning the search for the wellsprings of one's own being, for a feeling of agreement and oneness with Jewry as a whole, a sense of responsibility toward it, with the State of Israel as its most visible expression if not its representative, became intellectual vogue words that appear again and again in innumerable articles, speeches, and books as an urgent question.

Dual Loyalty?

As the history of the Jewish question shows, the question of whether the Jews were a people had really never seriously arisen for the non-Jewish world. Of course they were a people; that they had denied being one since the French Revolution (not since Moses Mendelssohn, as has often been supposed) seemed to the non-Jews like a suspicious escape from reality. Here may be found the roots of their catchphrase that the Jews formed "a state within a state" and their demand that they unequivocally give up their separate existence as a people and even their religiously decreed segregation if they wanted to be fully accepted by the nations of their states of residence. Now the question had been decided by the public recognition of the State of Israel. If the Jews formed a state and Hebrew, having been renewed as a living language over a period of two generations, became the language of that state, the existence of a Jewish people could not very well be denied any longer. It was possible for Jews to dissociate themselves from it, declare that they had nothing to do with the State of Israel and even as a people considered themselves only as part of the nation in whose state they were living as fully privileged citizens. "We have no dual patriotism or dual loyalty"—this was said by small groups of Jews and thought and said by Jewish individuals as well, out of conviction of timidity, particularly if the political interests of the State of Israel did not coincide with those of their countries of domicile. On some occasions governments also exploited this insecurity, inner conflict, and dilemma by pressuring such Jews and Jewish groups into influencing the government of the State of Israel in the direction they desired. On the whole, however, the argument of dual patriotism and divided (that is, not complete) loyalty that was always feared at the beginning of the Zionist movement and used to weaken its influence on the Jews has never posed a serious danger to the rights of the Jews, least of all after the foundation of the State of Israel.

The Uniqueness of the Historical Situation

On the contrary; if anything, the founding of the State strengthened the situation of the Jews even in the countries of the Diaspora. Like the decision of the United Nations, it had been accomplished in a unique constellation and was a historic event of the greatest magnitude in this sense alone. It happened at the threshold of an epoch in which the peoples of Africa and Asia achieved their independence and were able to form a majority front with the Arab states. The conscience of the world was still shaken by the events of the Hitler period and their aftereffects, and thus the homelessness of the Jews as a people struck everyone's attention like a reproach. One decade earlier or later it would hardly have been possible to obtain the consent of the nations to this act of founding a state, and its effect would have been much less profound and far-reaching. The degree of an event's historical effect, however, is the surest measure of what might be called its historical legitimacy, its reasonableness and necessity in the Hegelian sense.

This, at any rate, was how the event was perceived by a large number of contemporaries. The Jew came into the consciousness of the nations as more of a person of quality whom they regarded as more similar to them, more comprehensible, and more equal to them. Suddenly many elements of mystery that had surrounded and veiled the image of the Jew and caused it to appear vaguely distorted and blurred had disappeared. The ghostlike or supernaturally caricatured image of the Jew by which the real-life Jewish neighbors and the personally more distant Jewish figures of the present or recent past had been measured and evaluated was more and more palpably replaced by the Israeli Jew of the present as reflected in the mass media. In these he was often heroically exaggerated, and frequently he was judged hypercritically under the influence of tradition and present-day polemics pertaining to ideologies, local politics, and international strategy. On the whole, however, the new figure of a living person and a living people prevailed. The rebellion against the unreality and ghostliness of the Jews and the ahistorical, extrahistorical, and contrahistorical nature of Jewish existence that had been initiated by Zionism was successfully accomplished.

Problems and Successes in the Relations between the Diaspora and Israel

This concerned not only the citizens of the State of Israel, although there were and are many attempts—by the Christian peoples, the Jews in the Diaspora, and even by many natives of Israel—to differentiate the Israelis as types from the Jews of the Diaspora and even to create an antithesis between them. This happened especially in the early years of the new statehood and was repeated in some periods of crisis when the Jews of the Diaspora disappointed the Jews of Israel, or when the policies and the domestic conditions of the State of Israel appeared to the Jews in the Diaspora as problematic or a danger to their own position. To many of the most important Jews of the State of Israel it was one of the deepest disappointments that while after the founding of the state the Jews from refugee camps and the eastern Arabic countries had immigrated, the latter in their great majority, the Jews of the West came only hesitantly, a mere trickle in the stream of immigrants. It was a particular disappointment that the declared Zionists who in America, England, and other countries had bravely fought with the powers that be for recognition of the Jewish national and political rights behaved no differently from the other Jews; this was true even of the Zionist leadership. A leader like Ben-Gurion, who always demanded absolute consistency and oneness of word and deed, was so disillusioned by this that the henceforth refused to call himself a Zionist. He, and Israeli youth along with him, viewed the gulf that opened up between the life of the Jews in the Diaspora and in Erétz Yisrael with alarm and apprehension. Was there not a risk of a break between the Diaspora and the State of Israel if the pulses of the Jews in the two places beat at such different rhythms? And, on the other hand, could the Jews of the United States identify with Israel if in the Sinai Campaign of 1956 their government was in open opposition to the Israeli policies? The same situation was faced by the Jews of France when in the Six-Day War de Gaulle and his government, which had for a decade been the declared friends and allies of Israel, radically changed course and supported the other side. There were similar inner conflicts in a number of other countries, to say nothing of the Jews who had remained in Arab countries and the large Jewry in the Soviet Union that had for decades been condemned to the silence of a Marrano-like existence.

In all these inner conflicts the Jews of the Diaspora, especially the United States, stood the test beyond all expectations. They did not shirk their responsibility, with the exception of some individual cases did not take refuge behind a monistic patriotism for their countries of domicile, and refrained from public disapproval of those views and actions of the Israeli government that deviated from the opinions of their governments. This is what the Jews of the era of emancipation frequently did when Jewish interests were being discussed and were not accepted by public opinion or the policies of a majority of the government. On the contrary; in such situations of conflict the inner connectedness of the Jews with the State of Israel was repeatedly manifested, and with and through it a new pride, a new self-awareness, and an open avowal of affiliation with the Jewish people transcending all particular opinions and local patriotism despite any risk that might be associated with this.

Self-Avowal

This avowal by the Jews of themselves and their profession of loyalty to the Jewish people and to the State of Israel, which from the beginning regarded itself as the representative and purest expression of the Jewish people and was increasingly so viewed by the world and the majority of Jewry, is a sign of the transformation that took place, and is still taking place, after the end of World War II and particularly after the foundation of the State, which influenced this transformation. Because we are still in the midst of this new process of development and of this new epoch, it is difficult to give a clear description and evaluation of it. It behooves us to make only a hesitant and cautious assessment and refrain from hasty generalizations—a problem that faces anyone who writes contemporary history.

Despite all caution in judgment, one thing can already be stated: There can be no doubt that the ongoing development represents a process of recuperation, a progression to greater truthfulness and inward honesty as well as to greater integrity and clarity in the relation of the Jews to other nations, no matter whether these are closer or more distant in space and ideology. It may sound like a paradox, but it reflects a profound inner truth and truthfulness if a highly respected American Jew who had accepted high positions in state and municipal government and still held such positions told his Zionist-Israeli relatives in May 1948 that on the day of the founding of the State of Israel he felt for the first time that he was a full American.

The New Equality

What was happening here? Because the Jewish people had formed a state and had been recognized as the equal of other nations, the American who said this evidently felt recognized as a full human being for the first time and thus as a fully privileged American—precisely because by virtue of the recognized formation of a state his Jewishness no longer constituted a flaw that at best was disregarded with forgiving tolerance. As Herzl had foreseen, the Jew of the Diaspora now had a chance to reject his affiliation with the Jewish people precisely because this no longer meant a disgrace or a taint and sometimes even brought him greater respect—particularly after military victories and unparalleled actions that involved courage and exact planning, like the liberation of the kidnapped Jews from Uganda. The general public does not evaluate peoples and persons by the achievement or exemplary morality of individuals but by the actions and attitudes of the corporate totality whose expression in the communal life of the nations is the state. The more a nation embodied in its state distinguishes itself through actions that have traditionally been regarded, whether rightly or wrongly, as signs of strength, courage, human ability, manly honor, and equality, the higher its rank in the judgment of the nations will be. Victorious wars, particularly wars of small countries against numerically superior enemies that threaten their existence, may rank highest in this regard. Perseverance under difficult conditions, the systematic development and expansion of underdeveloped countries by means of labor, organization, and well-thought-out and systematically applied science and technology also have a high value in the esteem of the nations.

Prejudice against the Jews and the New Reality

The State of Israel now distinguished itself in both kinds of highly rated achievements of nations—to the admiration and joy of some, the astonishment and disappointment of others, and against the expectations of almost everyone. Had it not been only yesterday that people had read about, and at least half-heartedly believed, the cowardice and unfitness for war peculiar to the Jews by virtue of their disposition and education? Had the anti-Semitic literature disseminated throughout the civilized world and in somewhat less shrill tones the general literature as well not said so? And now people saw on television and at the movies pictures of the victorious fights of the Israeli troops and read in newspapers, magazines, and books or heard on the radio about the courage of Israeli soldiers, the ability and resourcefulness of their officers even in unexpected situations, and the organizational ability and superior planning of the military leadership. Even the manufacture of their own weapons, begun in the period of pre-State "illegality," made unexpectedly rapid progress to the point where highly sophisticated weaponry (tanks, ships, airplanes, and electronically remote-controlled rockets) was manufactured in the country. The government stepped up the production of weapons in an effort to be less and less dependent on the readiness of other states to supply arms and on the political pressure from these states that was often connected with it. The respect thereby attained by the State of Israel also benefited the Jews of the Diaspora—directly by heightening their self-awareness and pride, indirectly by the increasing recognition extended by the surrounding world to them.

And it was the same way with the work of development in the country. It seemed like only yesterday that both anti-Semitic and Nazi propaganda and sophisticated arguments in books about the most diverse fields of knowledge, from history to sociology, had spoken about the parasitic nature of Jewish existence, the Jews' inability to develop an economy of their own, their reluctance to engage in physical activity, and their unfitness for agricultural pursuits. On the basis of centuries-old stereotypes and also of the middle-class Jew from the neighborhood with whom one had daily intercourse, a non-Jew might believe in some of these deprecatory generalizations despite all logical counterarguments. Now the Israeli-Zionist work of reconstruction that had been in process for decades and had been more or less ignored became evident for all to see. Who had imagined that Jewish agronomists from Israel would go to Africa, Asia, Central and South America as instructors of undeveloped nations and economies and would there fruitfully share their experiences for the benefit of other nations—the experiences acquired through hard work, experiments, failures, and successes in the exploitation of the soil, in the opening of sources of water and their economic utilization, in the social development of the settlements and the appropriate education of the settlers? The reputation thus gained by the Jews did not, of course, remain without effect on the Jews of the Diaspora, their position in the surrounding world, and their relationship with the State of Israel.

The Auschwitz Trauma

In addition to these influences emanating directly from Israel there were other elements that had only a loose and indistinct connection with the new Jewish State. The most important of these probably is what might be called the Auschwitz trauma. In the Diaspora as in Israel, Jews have not forgotten what happened to European Jewry in the Nazi period—directly through the perpetrators and indirectly through the inactive onlookers of the drama that was performed before their eyes. If people were really about to forget those events, the Eichmann trial of 1960–62 in Jerusalem, which placed the bureaucratic executor of the "final solution" of the Jewish question before the bar of justice and before the eyes of the world, made them common knowledge and recalled them to everyone's mind. Was it only a coincidence that the excavation and reconstruction projects on the desert hill Masada by the Dead Sea that were carried on in the succeeding years (1963–65) under the direction of Yigal Yadin, the archeologist and former chief of staff of the Israeli army, were enormously popular and attracted thousands of volunteers, Jews and non-Jews, not only from Israel but from some twenty other countries?* Did this perhaps bespeak a recognition of the community of Jewish fate that was perceived as an admonishment?

This, at any rate, is how world Jewry seems to have understood the message of danger and heroism. When two years later, in 1967, three Arab states—Egypt, Syria, and Jordan—banded together to do battle with the State of Israel, and the United Nations border guard, stationed there since 1957, responded to Egyptian pressure by leaving the Sinai region without resistance, emotional and active solidarity with the State of Israel was manifested in the Diaspora with unprecedented unanimity and fervor. The Diaspora felt, as it were, the threat to Israel as if its own life had been threatened. An almost incomprehensible excitement took hold of it, and a readiness to help was manifested—a readiness to help not only with money and by exerting political and personal influence but also to perform personal service in the country and even to volunteer for military action (an offer that Israel did not accept). The Jews of Israel and the Jews of the Diaspora felt more strongly than ever before as a united people with a shared fate. And in this spirit—joy and pride as well as sadness about the fatalities—they also perceived the quick victory won by the Israeli troops in this three-front war, the release from the threat of destruction, and the falling of the border ramparts in Jerusalem, a divided city since 1948. It was similar with the excitement and solidarity of the Jews in the Diaspora during the Yom Kippur War of 1973, when Egyptian and Syrian armies mounted a well-prepared attack on the unprepared Israeli defenses and breached these, putting the state in great danger for a few days until the Israeli troops were able to organize for a counteroffensive. They managed to beat the enemy back to such an extent that only a quick armistice arranged under American pressure was able to save the Egyptian army from complete destruction. (To be

*In his book about Masada, published in 1966, Yigal Yadin writes: "Here we had one of the greatest and most pleasant surprises. A brief announcement in the Israeli press and in the London *Observer* caused thousands of volunteers, Jews and non-Jews from twenty-eight countries, to come forward."

sure, America had earlier saved Israel from a threatening arms shortage after the losses caused by the first enemy attack, by means of an airlift organized after some hesitation.)

Community of Danger and Destiny

This attack in particular but also the wars and earlier and later threats from terrorism, economic boycott, the use of the Arab countries' oil power, and the political and economic influences founded on it showed the Jews in Israel and in the Diaspora that the existence of Israel can be safeguarded only if they are aware of the constant danger and ready to exert jointly all forces to stave off these threats. These events and situations have increasingly impressed upon the minds and hearts of Jewry as a whole how closely the destinies of both parts of world Jewry, the State of Israel and the Jewish Diaspora, are connected. As for the Israelis, a considerable number of them, and particularly many young people, had felt entitled to look down upon the "*galut* Jews" with a kind of arrogant pride, if not downright contempt, and to regard their generous donations of money for the financing of the immigration and the concomitant tasks as an obligation, a kind of compensation for their own failure to immigrate and for continuing to lead their more comfortable lives in the Diaspora undisturbed. Now it also dawned on those Israelis that their own destiny was more closely connected with that of the Jews in the other countries, particularly American Jewry, after the Eichmann trial and the widely disseminated facts about what had happened in the Hitler period had awakened or revived and intensified among the young generation of Israelis a feeling of solidarity with the lives of their fathers and forefathers.

As for the Jews in the Diaspora, the ever-renewed threats to the State of Israel and the excitement and concern that took hold of them on such occasions and that at first seemed inexplicable even to them made them realize over and over again and with increasing intensity how closely connected their own existence was with that of the State of Israel. They sensed a kind of functional connection between their reputation and that of the Israeli State and realized that even their lives might be no more assured than those of the Israelis if the latter did not prove a match for the forces threatening them. The assurance with which as late as the 1930s Jews and Jewries long resident in the countries of Central and Western Europe had responded to warnings against threatening danger that such crass anti-Semitism could exist only in Hitler's Germany and not in their country and with which American Jews argued twenty years later ("It can't happen here") had been increasingly shaken by the events of the postwar years. How many mass murders and mass expulsions there had meanwhile been in the world without any state or federation of states taking any serious action against them! What seemed to be threatening Israel and what happened in Europe could under certain conditions happen in any other country too. Any danger to the State of Israel could become a danger to the people of Israel, including those Jewries in the Diaspora that felt secure. It may be assumed that something like this is the vague fear in many Jewish hearts. Their support of Israel is also a bit of self-protection.

Changes in the Way the Jews View Themselves as a Nation

This open avowal of the Jews that they belong to the Jewish people, including the State of Israel, was facilitated in the western democracies, particularly the United States, by the altered view of the nature of a nation and of nationalism that had increasingly prevailed there during recent decades. To an increasing extent Americans had abandoned the so-called melting-pot theory according to which the ethnic and traditional differences and peculiarities of the very different groups of immigrants would be eliminated or homogenized in the "melting pot" of American life in favor of a more uniform "Americanism." This was basically an American version of Central European nationalism, with the ideas of the Puritan Mayflower element as the dominant note and its descendants as the socially and political leading stratum. Assimilation— or acculturation, as it was now called—meant essentially the expected assimilation to the life-style and *Weltanschauung* of this ruling class. Under the influence of anticolonialism, the movements for independence, and their successes everywhere, particularly in Africa and Asia, since the Second World War, the sense of self of those who had immigrated from foreign countries and their descendants became stronger. Their third generations again began to value what the second generations had striven to forget for the sake of adapting to the prevailing life-styles. This process was so general that one could almost derive an emigrants' law of life from it. The ethnicism that manifested itself to an ever-increasing extent—that is, the tendency to combine identification with American patriotism (however that was defined) with loyalty to one's own special history, its traditions and hopes for the future—surely facilitated the process of inner transformation of American Jewry (and in similar fashion of the Jews in other western democratic countries) and legitimated it, as it were.

Remigration and Emigration

As already pointed out, this again affected the attitude of the Jews in the State of Israel toward the Jews in the Diaspora, and the effects were by no means only positive. The closer contact between these Jewries resolved conflicts and blurred differences. In this process important roles were played by the steadily growing tourism—visits to Eretz Yisrael by an increasing number of Jews from the Diaspora, many of whom had close relatives in the country—as well as trips abroad by an ever-increasing number of Israelis—out of interest, for rest, relaxation, and artistic enjoyment, to attend international conferences, for study and practical training. To an increasing extent former immigrants returned to countries of the Diaspora, and some Israelis, even native ones, who had long resided there also emigrated to these countries. This often began with supposedly temporary stays for study or faurther training and then became subject to the laws of convenience and the attraction of better living conditions, and on many occasions it was all too apt to lead to the emigration of others. In this process all sorts of motivations were involved: the encouragement of earlier emigrants, envy, and the lure of a better life. Should one see in this signs of a deterioration in the atmosphere of the State of Israel, a symptom of an internal malaise of the new—no longer so new—State, or perhaps a natural phenomenon of a healthy people in the process of normalizing itself, with an opportunity for every citizen freely to choose his place of residence in accordance with his needs and materialistic or idealistic endeavors?

There can be no doubt that in the case of Israel an important factor in these remigrations and emigrations, normal as they are up to a certain extent, was the need for peace and quiet, for an escape from an atmosphere of constant danger and preparedness for war, with the concomitant inconveniences even in the years of an armed peace: call-ups for annual reserve duty in the army; uncommonly high taxation; and nervous tension even in relatively calm periods. The root, the background, and substratum of these conditions is the unsolved problem of Israel's relations with the Arab neighboring states and the closely related problem of coexistence with the Arabs in the country itself—what usually is briefly referred to as the "Arab question" and thus is contrasted with the Jewish question and the attempts at its solution.

The Arab Question and the Jewish Question—Myths and Realities

To emphasize it again, the subject of this book is not the history of the Jewish people, Zionism, or the State of Israel, and of course not of the Arabs or the Middle East, but the history of the Jewish question. Thus it cannot here be a matter of giving a detailed presentation of the history of the relationship between the Jews and the Arabs in the country or to weigh the ins and outs of questions of guilt or right and wrong in the relationship between the Zionist and the Arab national movements, and within the latter of the Palestinian movement. On these matters there are an enormous literature and even more extensive source material of every kind—historical, sociological, political, and moral works that are brief and comprehensive, profound and superficial, benevolent and malevolent, passionate and dispassionate, exculpatory and self-accusatory.

Since the earliest attempts at new settlement in the land and the beginnings of the organized Zionist movement Jews have been confronted with the problem of the Arabs in the country and since the start of an Arab and Arab-Palestinian movement with their aspirations as well. It is a legend created in part by the Zionists themselves because of a later ideological dilemma that the founders and early leaders of Zionism were not aware of the Arab presence in the country. According to another legend, one cultivated by the Arabs, Jews and Arabs coexisted peacefully in the country until political Zionism, and especially its recognition by the Balfour Declaration of 1917, destroyed this idyllic relationship. This legend resembles one discussed in an earlier context about the ideal coexistence between Jews and Muslims in the countries of imperial Islamic rule in the Middle Ages and the "golden age" of Islamic Spain. The realities are more complex—and simpler. Let us attempt to summarize them briefly and show their problematic nature.

The Jewish colonization of Palestine did not take place in a vacuum or in a deserted country. An appreciable Arab population lived in Palestine, and this population grew especially fast precisely because the Jewish work of reconstruction cleared large territories, improved health conditions in general, and developed economic life to such an extent that births exceeded deaths by an increasing margin and many Arabs came from neighboring countries as immigrants. It was not only the Jewish settlers who were aware of this fact from the outset. After all, they always confronted it in daily life, whether they were buying land or products from their Arab neighbors, employing them as workers, learning from their experience, or being obliged to defend themselves against their thefts and robberies. The Zionist Organization did not overlook this state of affairs either. Herzl already realized that the Jews would have to reckon with a considerable resident population. This was one reason why he always opposed small-scale immigration without guaranteed sovereign rights, because there invariably comes a moment "when the government, under pressure of the native population, which feels threatened, bars any further influx of Jews" (*The Jewish State*, 1896). Once he was in possession of sovereignty Herzl wanted to win over the resident population by means of systematic care, and he was convinced that the great economic and cultural benefits it would receive from the Jewish immigration and systematic development of the country would turn them into friends of the Jews and induce them to collaborate peacefully with them for the benefit of the general welfare. A few years before his death he had given vivid expression to this idea in his programmatic novel *Old-Newland* (1902).

Since that time Zionists have repeatedly tried to reach an understanding with the Arabs: Arthur Ruppin, from 1908 on as the representative of the Zionist World Organization in Palestine and director of its settlement project during his long activity in the country; Leon Motzkin, Nahum Sokolow, and other representatives of the Zionist Executive in the summer of 1914—to mention only a few such attempts. A particularly magnanimous step was taken in 1919 by Chaim Weizmann, the president of the Zionist Organization. Through the good offices of T. E. Lawrence, the strange, adventurous British leader of the Arab uprising against the Turks, he made an agreement with Emir Feisal, the recognized head of this Arab national movement, in accordance with which the Zioinist Organization pledged itself to support the Arabs' demands for their national independence in the forthcoming peace negotiations (which was done) and offered its assistance in developing the Arab countries, in return for which Feisal recognized Palestine as the site of the Jewish homeland.*

This and similar attempts that were repeatedly made by responsible Jewish representatives both before and after the foundation of the State, from the earliest days to the present, produced no lasting results and in only very few instances even a temporary one. Between neighboring Jewish and Arab settlements there often prevailed, and prevail, very good, peaceful relations, and some of these even survived times of the greatest crisis. Not infrequently there have been public discussions between Arabs and Jews and a free exchange of views between them. At no time, however, have such dialogues developed into real negotiations between responsible representatives or even led to recognition by the Arabs of the legitimate existence of the Jewish settlements in the country and later of the Jewish State as a point of departure and basis for negotiations. The sole exception may have been the armistice agreements of 1949, but these were not followed by the envisioned peace negotiations because the Arab states were not ready for them.

The Jews have frequently been blamed for the failure of these endeavors to achieve a peaceful compromise; in fact, strangely enough, many Jews both in Israel and in the Diaspora have done so—with their by now traditional inclination (which frequently degenerates into amost perverse self-accusation and self-hatred) to regard misfortune befalling them as a result, punishment, and disaster stemming from their own moral failure. A Jew has never recognized objective facts as such but has always looked for a hidden meaning behind them and always asked first about his own guilt. Not infrequently he has given his opponents arguments

*See some documentation of this in Part 2.

against him in this way—that he has been arrogant and not obliging enough; that he has looked down on the Arabs from his vantage point of evidently superior European civilization or from the heights of his own cultural consciousness and thereby hurt their natural pride; that he has forgotten that as residents they have at least equal and perhaps prior claims to the country; that his efforts to be friends with them have been at best sporadic and never systematic and enduring; and more accusations and self-accusations of this type.

There is, of course, always some truth in such accusations. When have people, as individuals and groups, ever been free of such human weaknesses, presumptions, inconsistencies, and inadequacies in their behavior toward one another? These should not be denied or justified, but where such mistakes have been made, their effect should not be exaggerated. In individual cases as well as in the aggregate they may have contributed to many an aggravation, embitterment, and overreaction, and they may have supplied arguments for the rationalization of the problem. But they are not at the root of the problem, and in the final analysis they are not even decisive for its historical development.

The Historical Development of the Jewish and the Arab National Movements

Let us begin with the historical development. As we have seen in chapter 8, the modern Jewish national movement developed on a centuries-old basis in the second half of the nineteenth century and received its political program and organization in the last years of that century from Zionism. The Arab national movement is younger, and the organization of an Arab-Palestinian movement is of even more recent date. The Arab national movement, too, is based on historical memories, particularly of the imperial rule of Islam, Arab dynasties, and the Arab language and script in wide areas of Asia and Africa since the seventh century. The abovementioned elements and components of this rule differed in different areas and at different times. In the aggregate they created a tradition of Arab culture and life-style that was preserved even in times of political independence and under the influence of modern nationalism. As a proud dream of a glorious past they constituted the emotional and spiritual background for the creation of a Pan-Arab national movement, including a Pan-Islamic one that could be identical with it to a certain extent but could also differ from it. There was, after all, an appreciable Christian Arabic minority, and within it a stratum of intellectuals with a European culture who were particularly receptive to the influences of modern European nationalism. Anti-Jewish Christian influences, including French anti-Semitic ones à la Edouard Drumont, were discerned by observers as early as the turn of the century.

An organized, self-confident Arab national movement, however, did not yet exist when Zionism came into being. Its beginnings could be noticed after the rebellion of the Young Turks in 1908, especially in the elections to the Turkish parliament in Constantinople, but the Near East did not awaken to political life in the real sense of the term until World War I. Having existed only in rudimentary form before the war, the Arab movement for independence now was supported by England as an ally in its struggle against Turkey and became a political factor. It had originally been conceived as a Pan-Arab movement that was to fulfill the dream of a great state from Syria in the North to the Hejaz on the Arab peninsula. Of course, the interests of the dominant political powers—France, England, Russia—were immediately involved, and under their influence there were delimitations (like the Sykes-Picot Agreements) and assurances (as in the correspondence between Sir Henry McMahon and Sherif Hussein of Mecca) that did not always seem to be in full agreement with one another and with such other promises as the Balfour Declaration and were deliberately (and sometimes perhaps inadvertently) given unclear formulation. The negotiators and signatories or recipients of such agreements and declarations knew nothing or only some details of the assurances that were given to others at the same time or shortly afterward. In the postwar period this led to conflicting interpretations, distrust, rashness, and delays, as well as to quick actions, both violent and peaceful, with the aim of fundamentally influencing political decisions and boundaries by creating *faits accomplis*. In this context the Palestinian question also received its political form and significance.

If the point of departure was a Greater Arabian conception, it was possible to make concessions like those made by Emir Feisal in his 1919 agreement with Weizmann. In his holograph postscript to the agreement Feisal expressly committed himself only if his total Arabian program was approved and implemented by the Peace Conference. Since this did not happen (and certainly not through the fault of the Jews and Zionists) and the Arab national movement became fragmented—partly through the intervention of the Powers (particularly France, which removed Feisal from the Syrian throne by force of arms), partly through internal and dynastic tensions, as so often in Arab history—the national movement of the Palestinian Arabs assumed new importance.

THE ARAB-PALESTINIAN NATIONAL MOVEMENT

As we have already mentioned in a number of places, from the beginning of the Jewish settlement projects there had been differences of all kinds with the resident Arab population, and these were always voiced as fears when there was an increase in the Jewish immigration.

But there could be no real Arab-Palestinian national movement prior to World War I because then Palestine was not on the map as a separate country or even a particular territorial entity.* In the Arabian or Islamic empire down to the Turkish Ottoman empire individual parts of the country with shifting boundaries were separate administrative districts, but they were not combined under the name Palestine or any other name as a separate territory. Until it was conquered by the British the northern part of the territory west of the Jordan was part of the province (*vilayet*) of Beirut as *sanjak* (district) Nablus and *sanjak* Acre; the southern part formed as the "independent *sanjak* Jerusalem" a separate administrative unit, and the area east of the Jordan belonged to the *vilayet* Damascus. Only the British mandatory government called the entire country Palestine again, in Hebrew with the addition of "E.I." in parentheses—the abbreviation of the Hebrew name Eretz Yisrael, the Land of Israel.

Thus no Palestinian patriotism or nationalism could have existed earlier. This, of course, does not mean that there was no attachment to the native soil, for there certainly was. But it crystallized into a conscious patriotism for the land as a whole and into something that can be called Palestinian nationalism only gradually under the influence of the new realities—the administration of the British mandatory government and the increasing immigration of the Jews with their ever thicker rural and urban settlement of the country. The elements out of which an Arab-Palestinian nationalism developed were the new political and administrative framework and the clash of European ways of thinking and Jewish-Zionist nationalism with the Arab tradition, and the fear, exploited by interested politicians for their purposes, that these new immigrants and modes of thought would deprive the Arabs of their property and their accustomed life-style. This development initially took the form of a fighting stance against these new factors, and there really was nothing unusual about this. After all, peoples and states are generally formed in the struggle against a common foe, against a real or supposed threat. In his *Jewish State* Herzl had observed, almost as an axiom for the existence of a people generally, that the common foe was keeping the Jews together as a people.

Added to this was the fact that the defense of a country which appeared threatened was able to serve as a unifying factor for the more or less independent Arab neighbor states that had been created after World War I. It was possible to shift the blame for the nonexistence of a unified Pan-Arab state from the internal and dynastic disputes, which shared the blame with the imperial interests of the Great Powers, to the "unredeemed" Palestine. From such viewpoints the Jewish national

*Concerning the name of the country in ancient times, see p. 48 above.

home that was coming into being was, as it were, a foreign body and a thorn in the flesh of the Arab nation. The joint efforts for the liberation of Palestine were a unifying factor and often almost the only one, of Pan-Arabian nationalism and a common goal, in contrast to the many divisive interests that actually prevailed, despite the dreams and speeches about a great past and a great common future to be attained.

Fighting Situations and Hostilities

In this situation it would have been necessary not only to make well-meaning declarations but for the Jews as well as the British to promulgate a clear, far-sighted program and to develop the land systematically in such a way that it would have been possible for both people to thrive and advance. This might at least have allayed the fears of the Arabs that it was intended to force them from their soil and their country. In point of fact, very few important steps were taken to that end. What Jewish offers of collaboration were made fell on deaf ears or bounded off the traditional overweening pride of the Arabs. At that time the Zionist Organization lacked the financial means for systematic work beyond the expansion of Jewish settlement projects. Even the latter were always short of funds; the Jews of Europe and especially America were not yet ready to make the financial sacrifices they made after the experiences of the Second World War and the founding of the State of Israel.

British policy was variable. Wide circles were uninterested in Palestine or interested only insofar as the mandatory rule seemed designed to further Britain's imperial interests in the Near East. In the important transitional period after the end of the First World War the Balfour Declaration was more or less ignored by the military administration of the time, nor was its implementation ever made a central administrative task of the civilian mandatory government (after 1920). The Arab big landowners, who had hitherto held unrestricted sway over the impoverished Arab masses that were submissive to them as laborers and tenant farmers and had often sold their immovable property to the Jews at ever higher prices without consideration for their leaseholders (with the Jews often voluntarily compensating the leaseholders by paying them money or giving them other plots of land), now were bound to see a threat to their own power in the influence on the Arab masses of the modern ideas and work methods brought in by the Jewish immigrants. They were encouraged in their resistance to the Zionist work of reconstruction by the irresolute and all too obliging attitude of the British administration, which they interpreted as weakness or approval of their own aims.

Thus, as soon as the opportunity arose, they used religious pretexts and the tension that always exists between nations to incite the Arab population against the Jews and thereby strengthen their own position vis-à-vis the populace and the British government. This gave rise to the violence of 1920 and 1921, the riots of the last week of August 1929, the armed uprisings against the Jews and the British government from 1936 to 1939, and the wars of the Arab states against the State of Israel since its foundation. Each time the attacks were more powerful and better organized and armed, and the Jewish resistance and defense were also improved, from the tactical-defensive to the strategic-offensive kind.

By and large, the official occasions for each outbreak of hostilities were of secondary importance; they were only the triggering elements that exacerbated existing tensions. The real reason behind them was always the same: the refusal of the Arabs to recognize the legitimacy of the Jews' return to the country and its systematic settlement by them. Whenever the claim of the Jews to the territory they regarded as their historic and current homeland was given greater political and legal recognition, whenever this claim was coming closer to being honored by virtue of increased immigration and a more intensified settlement, the resistance of the Arabs stiffened. Any increased dynamism on one side triggered an intensified dynamism on the other. One claim fought—and is still fighting—another claim. Let us take a closer look at these claims.

Claims and Entitlements of the Arabs and the Jews

THE ARAB CLAIM

The Arab claim is based on two fundamental facts—or if you will, on two modes of conduct that are normal in the life of nations. One is the long-sanctioned right of conquest and nationalization of a certain territory that is therefore regarded by a people as legally belonging to it and is so recognized by the other nations as well. The other is the resistance, regarded as equally normal and natural, of a resident population to new immigrants with a life-style and economic system that are different from its own tradition and by which the resident population feels disturbed and threatened in its accustomed life. The area conquered by Arab-Islamic armies in the seventh century (638), called Palestine by the Romans and Byzantines, was at the time of its conquest settled mainly by descendants of the Jews who had not left the country even after the downfall of their state and some of whom had converted to Christianity under pressure from the ruling Christians. There was also an admixture of (Christian) Greeks and Romans who had come to the country with their conquering armies and the subsequent administrations and had settled there. During the next centuries this resident population adopted the Islamic religion and the Arabic language. At that time there was no appreciable stream of immigrants of Arab provenance. On the other hand, immigrants, of the most diverse ethnic backgrounds came to the country with the conquering armies of the succeeding centuries—the Seljuks (1071), the Crusaders (1099), the Egyptian-Syrian dynasty of the Ajubids (1187), the Mamelukes (former Turkish slaves who had risen to rule in Egypt), and finally the Turkish Ottomans—and mingled with the resident population that had been decimated by Mongolian invasions in the thirteenth and fourteenth centuries. We are thus dealing here with a population that was not ethnically uniform, and genetically only the Bedouins, who lived nomadically in the border and desert region and from there often moved to the farmland and sometimes settled there, were of purely Arab descent.*

This population received its Arab consciousness primarily from the dual tradition of Islam and the Arabic language that had developed with it and had been hallowed by it. The presence of the historical factor of an Arab consciousness is, of course, not altered or diminished by this clarification of the historical facts and strata. Nowhere is the emotional content of a national consciousness curtailed by being broken down into its constituent elements, but such a breakdown can affect the sole claim to the legitimacy of a property and of the national affiliation of a territory. It is the same way with the normal and therefore justified opposition of the people living there who feel that they are the original population, are regarded as such by other nations, and are evaluated in accordance with their "normal" attitude toward "intruders."

THE JEWISH CLAIM

We are here facing a striking contrast between the "normality" of the "Arab question" and the "abnormality" of the Jewish question. Measured by the normal standards of the life of nations and history, many aspects of the Jewish question are hard to understand; this is something we have repeatedly pointed out. From this point of view, what about the claim of the Jews—"abnormal" and thus often regarded as "unjustified"—to return to the country that they consider their national home and that has therefore been called, since time immemorial, the Land of Israel, Eretz Yisrael?

The objection made to this claim by the opponents, but frequently also by friends, of the Jews and by people who are neutral on the subject

---

*As already mentioned, this population experienced a special increase precisely in connection with the development of the country by the Jewish immigrants—through a much greater number of births than of deaths and through immigration from the less developed neighboring Arab countries.

is that it is unjustifiably based on the fact that in olden times, about two thousand years ago, the land was under Jewish control and populated by Jews. By this reasoning, even if the question whether the Romans and the later conquerors had been justified in their military and administrative actions against the Jews is left open, such historical actions cannot be erased. After all, the states existing today came into being in similar fashion, through conquest and settlement. By the same reasoning any number of peoples and tribes could claim their old domiciles as belonging to them. Where would we be if we tried to revise the political map accordingly?

At first blush these "clever" arguments of the *Realpolitiker* against the "historical" claim of the Jews which seem designed to carry it *ad absurdum* appear to make a lot of sense. However, like many other arguments of the *Realpolitiker,* their analogy and the conclusions drawn from it allow them to see only the surface of the phenomena. This reasoning does not grasp and consider the historical depth and the essentially different nature of the problem posed by the Jewish question, and especially in this instance. Here we are, after all, dealing with the basic question and the real root of the problem, the close connection between the people and the land in the life and history of Judaism. We have discussed it in detail in an earlier chapter (p. 51 above) and can recapitulate only some of the elements here.

The Jewish argumentation, the Jewish claim, is not based primarily on an ancient right of possession or on the wrongful, forcible expropriation of their country but on the attitude of the Jewish people, unique in world history, to this historic event, the relationship of the Jews to this land, and perhaps also the relation of this land to the Jewish people. There is no other example in known history of a people refusing, as the Jews have, to exchange the country in which it developed its existence as a people and produced its most original creations as a people for another country as its homeland. In the many centuries of its stateless existence in the Diaspora the Jewish people did not accept the verdict of history but fought it—appealing to God and to humans, including itself, with its faith, its Messianic hope, its customs and practical endeavors. It did not celebrate its festivals in accordance with the seasons of the nations in whose midst its groups of settlers lived but according to the times of sowing and harvesting in the agricultural life of their ancestral country and the historic events of its early period—from the exodus from Egypt, "the house of bondmen," the desert wanderings, and the reception of the Ten Commandments at the act of divine revelation on Mount Sinai to the settlement in the land and the building of the Temple in Jerusalem. Whenever circumstances permitted it, and particularly in times of especial need, Jews, both individuals and larger groups, set out to translate the hopeful cry of a Passover evening, "Next year in Jerusalem!" into action and prepare the return of the Jewish people—until these endeavors were given their modern, concrete form in the Zionist movement and its work of settlement that led to the foundation of the State of Israel.

And as for the soil of this land, which is sacred to the people and with which it is closely bound up—is it not as if this soil had waited for the return of the Jews to awaken from decay and lethargy to new florescence and luxuriant growth? In any case, it may be stated as a fact that the full flowering of the land came in periods of Jewish settlement and control, both in ancient times and in our day. The intervening eras of foreign rule were times of decay and cultural decline. The country was never without inhabitants, but the density of the population, which is always a measure of the degree of its development, decreased. Land that had once been fertile—and whose high cultural level, known from literary tradition, is now being confirmed by the excavations of the archeologists—became swampy or deteriorated into barren desert again. The Jewish work of settlement awakened it, and is still awakening it, to new life and intensive fruitfulness.

The earth is becoming smaller and smaller for the number of inhabitants that is assuming immeasurable dimensions. From this point of view a future morality of settlement will perhaps be able to grant possession of a territory only to those who develop it for the sustenance of the greatest possible number of inhabitants. But even today it is reasonable to measure the inner bonds of a people to its land and its right to it by the physical, intellectual, and spiritual energies it has invested in it. There can be no doubt that, if such a criterion is applied, the Jewish people has won the greatest claim to its homeland.

To its homeland . . . That is the basis and impetus for all these efforts—the settlement work and the military action for the foundation, the preservation, and consolidation of the State of Israel. There is no other country to which every Jew who is persecuted or rejected because of his Jewishness can immigrate and be active in all branches of human activity as a person and citizen. The Arab people—in its totality and all individuals belonging to it—has enormous territories open to it whose soil is waiting for people who will lovingly bring it to fruition. The Jewish people has many domiciles that have become homelands to many individuals—at least subjectively, on the basis of a personal sense of belonging, but objectively only as long as it suits the majority of the population or its ruling class. As a national homeland the Jewish people has only the narrow strip of land between the Mediterranean and the desert that the world has grown accustomed to calling, after the pattern of the Roman Empire, Palestine, but which has never ceased to live in the consciousness of the Jewish people as Eretz Yisrael, the Land of Israel.

THE SPECIAL PLACE OF JERUSALEM

It is similar with the position of Jerusalem. The two world religions to which Judaism gave birth, Christianity and Islam, have a number of holy and most sacred places. Among these holy places Jerusalem ranks high, but for neither of these religions does it occupy the unique central position in life and consciousness that it does for the Jews. Since King David around 1100 B.C.E. set out from Hebron, conquered the Jebusite fortress Zion, and made it the City of David, the city has become the political, religious, and national center of the Jewish people, its only center. Over the centuries, over the three thousand years since it became the capital of the Land of Israel, the inner connection with the city of Jerusalem became so deeply engraved on the consciousness of the Jews, and later also on the consciousness of the nations, that the nearly synonymous concept Jerusalem-Zion also became virtually synonymous with the Land of Israel and the People of Israel. This synonymy of Zion-Jerusalem and Israel, the land and the people, passed over from the poetic equation to prosaic everyday usage, from use by the prophets and psalmists to the liturgies; it was used both in the most sacred contexts and for anti-Semitic abuse. It is an identification of a city with a land and a people that is virtually unprecedented in such oneness and interconnectedness.

The Jewish Question as a Singular International Problem

From the viewpoint of contemporary history, in the final analysis the Jewish question again appears as an unparalleled special problem that transcends every accustomed framework. And again the special nature of this claim and existence conflicts with demands and phenomena of life that are more normal and unexceptional in nature, more familiar on the basis of experience, which means that the world is more accustomed to them and finds them more comprehensible. Is it a tragic conflict of clashing claims and entitlements, an insoluble conflict? There are no insoluble conflicts. At all times conflicts were somehow resolved or resolved themselves—by the habituation of coexistence; by the wisdom of great conceptions in which room was found for things that seemed mutually exclusive; by the prudence of compromise and mutual accommodation in discussions and patient negotiations; and often, much too often, by bloody fights whose outcome was often regarded as divine judgment in the life of nations. Is it due to the Jewish people's long remoteness from history that, despite all readiness to defend by every means its right to national existence in its country, it has never abandoned the hope of bringing conflicts closer to a resolution in peaceful fashion—through discussions, negotiations, and compromises?

People laughed at Herzl's program for the founding of a Jewish State or regarded it as a utopia with no greater prospect of realization than other utopias. Contrary to all arrogant, deprecatory, or pusillanimous predictions the State of Israel has come into being, stood its ground, and exerted a radical influence on the life of the Jewish people as a whole, both in Eretz Yisrael and in the Diaspora. The dream has become reality—or, putting it more cautiously, has begun to be reality. In his programmatic novel *Old-Newland*, which he prefaced with the much-quoted "If you will it, it is no fairy tale," Herzl described his vision of the new state in great detail. It was not to be a state in the old, narrowly nationalistic sense but a community, which he called "The New Society" and in which peace was to reign among all parts of the population and between it and the neighboring countries. In the heart of Jerusalem a peace palace was to rise from which relief actions were to be organized for oppressed people all over the world.

Does one have too high an opinion of mankind if one expresses the hope that despite everything these dreams will some day prove to have been something of a prophecy and that the world will learn from the history of the Jewish problem, that international problem which—as an example, a symptom, and a seismograph—comprises many of the existential problems of the human world?

11

Retrospect and Prospect

History and Historical Consciousness

We do not know how peoples came into being. Our reliable information starts with the time of their visible appearance and effect on the surrounding world, provided that verifiable documentation of this has been preserved. Such information is not always identical with what is entrenched in the consciousness of a people as its history. This consciousness of its past, however, often determines the life of a people more enduringly than the facts of chronologically documented historical events, and it guides the decision which the people has to make in the face of changing circumstances. To know what memories of the early past have been engraved on a people's memory is therefore just as important as such knowledge has proved to be for the psychology and characterology of an individual. For the knowledge of Jewish history and Jewish historical consciousness that has continued to shape the people we have richer sources in the books of the Bible and the national-religious traditional literature that supplement them exegetically than in the literature of any other people.

Fundamental Experiences of the Jewish Historical Consciousness

If one examines the literature of the Jews in this spirit, one will find in it several events or traditions from the early period as fundamental experiences: the submission to God's will of the patriarch Abraham, who had immigrated to Canaan from the old cultural region of Mesopotamia, to the point of readiness to offer his dearest possession, his son Isaac, as a sacrifice, and God's refusal to accept this human sacrifice—in its dichotomy between loyalty to God and human cruelty a constantly reinterpreted motif from the border region between didactic legend and actual happening; the desert wanderings of Abraham's descendants, the ten tribes of Israel, from bondage in the highly developed Nile region to the divine revelation on Mount Sinai and chosenness for God's service; the conquest of Canaan as taking possession of the land promised and

447

allotted to the people by God; and on the way the strange curse-blessing of Balaam. "A people that dwells apart, not reckoned among the nations" (Num. 23:9)*—words that combined with the imposition of chosenness for the fulfillment of God's commandments and with being cursed and banished when the people sins. Added to these deeply engraved memory images from the early period of historical existence are, as later historical experiences, the warnings about the future, both curses and blessings, of the prophets and then the executions: banishments and returns, new destruction and exile as well as the never-waning hope, elevated to the Messianic level, of a new and definitive return to the land and to peace. These are the fundamental notions of the people of Israel about the fate imposed upon it; in its symbolic images it experiences its history. In parables and typical comments these also reflect the nature and the history of the Jewish question.

The Historical Layers of the Jewish Question

The ten chapters of this book have attempted to outline and interpret the historical development and layers of the Jewish question. Let us briefly recapitulate the result.

The basis is the consciousness of being singled out for the fulfillment of the imposed and accepted obligation to lead an exemplary life, an obligation that is in language and substance equated with the concept and commandment of "holiness." The Jewish question in its layers is based on it in a chain of fateful reactions and counteractions. Every new historical layer is rooted in the preceding one and has derived from it elements, often deleterious seeds, as traditions, customs, and stereotypes and added its own versions in accordance with its total view of the world and the needs and problems of its period. Thus the ancient pagan, Greco-Roman stratum was overlaid by what may have been the most disastrous and enduring one, the Christian stratum with its divine curse on the Jews as deicides and Satanic countertypes of everything good and God-ordained. With the development and expansion in accordance with the Christian view of God and the world of the civilization of the Mediterranean countries, of Europe and the areas dominated by it politically or culturally this image of the Jews was generally adopted by the "civilized" Christian world. Accordingly, this world provided for the Jew only the place of an outsider who was existing illegally, though he was also filling important gaps. Beginning with the Renaissance these strata were overlaid by the modern strata of the scientific and enlightened rationalizations of the Jewish image. This image was now deepened and individualized in inward, religious terms and by a toler-

*Cf. also Part 2, p. 489.

ance which accepted Jewishness with more or less well-intentioned, forgiving longanimity as not actually justified but as an evil existing in the world that had been brought into being by historical circumstances and the culpable involvement of many forces.

The Stereotype of the Jews and its Effects

What all these periods of the Jewish question had in common was that in them a stereotype of the Jews was created and new features and hues were added to the traditional image. Alongside these renewed and progressively elaborated Jewish types the older ones persisted in the populace untouched, just as all periods of history do not simply succeed one another but live on in some form. One must take care not to assume that there always was basic hatred of the Jews. Initially the relationship was always that of strangeness, a dislike of something alien that, as we have repeatedly pointed out, appeared as uncanny and aroused feelings of fear and resistance. This fear and the reaction to it appear in various gradations that are determined by the time, the place, and numerous coincidental circumstances. They can grow into hatred, lead to eruptions of violence against the Jews, or be deliberately shifted onto the Jews by those really deserving of hatred. The common feature of all these phenomena is that they are generally not directed against specific Jews. On the contrary; the individual Jew, the Jew known as a neighbor, often is exempted from them. One can maintain a friendship with him even in bad times; the more familiar he is, the more of an exception he is to the thrice-familiar stereotype of the Jew. The latter, the anonymous Jew of the typical image of the Jew, is actually the target of the hatred and the resistance through contempt and violence. In general, the Jew, and particularly the Jews as a society and mass, are met with hostility and persecuted because they are identified with the phantom of the Jew, both in their totality and as individuals.

The Failed Attempt at a Legal Solution of the Jewish Question

Basically, the persistence of this stereotypical image of the Jew in religious and secular tradition, art and literature, legends and fairy tales, jokes and curses and bawdy stories, in proverbs and linguistic usage, the survival of this figure of the "Eternal Jew" beyond all changes in space and time was responsible for the failure of the attempts of legislators, well-intentioned philanthropists, and progressive politicians since the French Revolution to solve the Jewish question by granting the Jews formal and legal equality. Laws do not change popular opinion even if they are enforced with pedantic punctilio. Even for their full implementation they require approval and not merely the formal consent of a thin stratum of the population—even if this stratum is elitist and formally represents the numerical majority of the people. People perceive and fully accept laws as true rights only if they are in line with their thoughts and feelings. Therefore the experienced local and national politicians of the nineteenth century were not really wrong if they warned against prematurely granting Jews full legal rights in the face of the anti-Jewish atmosphere prevailing among the rural population and the urban middle class.

The Tragedy of the Jewish Question

Of course, this anti-Jewish atmosphere received ever fresh sustenance and rational motivation from the actual position of the Jews in the economy and society, and this was so even where the religious prejudices or those transferred from the religious to the philosophical sphere were less important.

And here we face tragic situations again and again, tragic in the true original sense of the Greek dramatists. "Fate" confronted the Jews with forces against which they had to fight hopeless battles that pitted entitlements against entitlements or, to put it more cautiously, prior claims and supposed rights against prior claims and supposed rights. Events assess as fate or divine dispensation occurred and decisions were made in which right and wrong, sin and guilt were intertwined and hence were viewed and evaluated by those affected, the actors and the sufferers, in diametrically opposed fashion.

Exile *(Galut)* as Exclusion from the Prevailing World Order

The Jews, a nation of farmers residing on their soil with a Diaspora that surely had a different structure, were condemned to statelessness in their clash with the Roman Empire, which derived from its *Pax Romana* the right to ruthless conquest. From then on the existence of the Jews became an "exile" even before the dispersion over all parts of the inhabited earth was complete, while an appreciable number of Jews were still living in their own land. This actually gave rise to the concept of exile in this sense of statelessness and homelessness—of the Jewish people and of each individual Jew. With its divine curse Christianity gave this existence the stamp of sacred damnation. Hence Jewry, no matter where it lived in the civilized world ruled by Christian doctrine, was excluded from the life of "legitimate" society, the only legally existing kind. This is something we must always bear in mind. This exclusion was primarily from the economy and society of the new feudal world of the Middle Ages, which had not been created by Christianity but was approved, confirmed, and permeated by it, as well as being enveloped with the luster of holiness and the God-ordained as the only justified order. Thus, no matter what the Jews did, even if they acted on the basis of specially granted rights and solemnly sealed legal actions and certified privileges, they were, as far as the popular consciousness was concerned, transgressors against the universally valid Christian-divine world order. From that time to the period of the struggle for equality, attested, formally guaranteed rights were in basic conflict, or at least not in harmonious agreement, with what "people" regard as "right and proper."

"Illegal" Occupations as a "Legal" Function of the Jews

No one who respects objective data will overlook the fact that the Jews performed important functions in the economy (and to a certain extent also in the cultural life) of the states and nations. They filled gaps which according to the dogmatic-Christian views of right and wrong the non-Jewish native population was not able or allowed to fill. Without these occupations and lines of business, the only ones to which the Jews were admitted, the economy could hardly have functioned and certainly could not have developed. The Jews were thereby violating the world of the accustomed, and yet they were tolerated, admitted, and called in by the rulers for that very purpose. They were used for activities in the economy and administration of the states that the rulers deemed important, useful, profitable, and promising. The Jews became accustomed to this life and often regarded it as a merciful act of divine providence. Since their Messianic hopes for the future made them regard this existence among the nations as only temporary, they were able to counter the contempt shown them, despite their outward humility, with arrogant, supercilious disdain for the surrounding world.

Tragedy and Guilt

In reality the Jews always found themselves in a tragic confrontation of powers each of which was bound to regard itself as right. The existence of the Jews, as well as the economic activities and social situation into which they were maneuvered by the nations and for which they did not bear any moral blame, was regarded by the surrounding world as guilt and an offense against an accustomed world order that was hallowed by tradition. To preserve what one is accustomed to is a natural impulse; it is a preservation of one's own nature, and thus one regards any deviation from tradition as disloyalty to oneself. The Jews lived in different traditions; those of the surrounding world usually were not theirs, at least not of the same long standing and strength. Hence a Jew found it easier to abandon them, turn to newer methods, branches of the economy, or modes of organization, and still keep faith with himself. This conduct, however, was apt to be regarded by large parts of the surrounding population as disloyalty attributable to the bad character of the Jews. That the Jews clung to their own religious-national tradition appeared to them as obstinacy; that they did not uphold the traditions of the surrounding world but often fought them with entirely sound rationalistic arguments meant to that world a menacing alienation of its own nature that seemed to need combating. If in an effort to do justice to the "nobler" motives one disregards the often very real economic and social interests (which of course also have their *raison d'être* within certain bounds), one can regard this as the social-psychological background and substratum of the modern anti-Semitic movements.

Modern Anti-Semitism and the "Final Solution"

In chapter 6 we gave a detailed presentation of the origin of modern anti-Semitism, its teachings, and its significance in the history of the Jewish question, and in chapter 9 we discussed the development and radical implementation of its conclusions down to the systematic mass murders in the Hitler period. It was the consequence of the failed assimilation theory of the period of emancipation. At that time people wanted to give the Jew as a human being a chance to live legally in the modern economy and society on the assumption, or at least in the hope, that his existence as a Jew would come to an end and that he would no longer have a history of his own. He was to adopt fully the history, lifestyle, and tradition of the surrounding world despite the fact that this was bound to involve disloyalty to himself and the abandonment of a large part of his own nature. Under the decisive influence of modern nationalism, particularly the biologically based racial theory, the actual (not the theoretical) refusal of the Jews to abandon themselves, as well as everything that had been charged to them over the centuries as defects and guilt, was now regarded as a racial heritage rotten to the core. But if the Jews' character was completely corrupt and incorrigibly inferior by nature, if nature had made them harmful to the European "Aryan" races that had been more favored by fortune and thus were more worthy of living, there was logically only one means of warding off the danger posed by them: their physical extermination. The supposedly scientific nature of the theoretical foundations and the argumentations stilled the voice of conscience and eliminated any inhibitions that may still have existed in those giving the orders for the massacres of individuals and for the genocide, as well as in those who obediently carried them out.

In the attempt at a "final solution" of the Jewish question by means of the physical destruction of the Jews all motifs of the anti-Semitism of past epochs were combined under a common denominator, and the history of the Jewish question with all its historical layers was brought to a horrendously consistent conclusion—and carried *ad absurdum*, though it did not come to an end.

The World's Lack of Readiness to Help as a Manifestation of the Jewish Question

That it did not come to an end is to only a minor degree to the credit of the states and groups of states that fought against the Nazis. Their victory, which came three years too late for six million European Jews, did keep the number of the Jewish victims of Nazi madness, which assumed the guise of logic, from being higher by millions. But this was only an incidental result of the struggles of these states and nations for their own physical and cultural existence. The Jewish question and the rescue of European Jewry from complete extermination played no part in this, neither in the goals nor in the spatial and temporal strategy or tactics of war; it was more of an inhibiting than a stimulating factor. The powers that be refused to admit Jewish refugees or Jews ready to emigrate with the speed and to the extent that would have been necessary. Such actions might have prevented the systematic massacres of Jews and at the least would have delayed them and significantly reduced the number of the victims. Precisely this lack of readiness was a function and a consequence of the Jewish question. The leaders were concerned—and Hitler's propaganda did its best to aggravate this concern and gloat over it—that greater aid for the Jews and mention of the rescue of the Jews as a war aim would make the fight against Germany unpopular among their own population as a "Jewish war" and hence have a negative effect on its conduct. It was precisely this attitude of the eastern and western Powers fighting against Hitler that clearly demonstrated to everyone who was willing to see that the Jewish question existed in those countries, too.

The Founding of the State of Israel as a Prelude to a Positive Solution

As we have seen, the abyss of inhumane actions that opened up before the world in those days was one of the points of departure for the attempt at a positive solution. The process of its realization, with its problems, successes, struggles, and tensions, has not been completed to this day. The founding of the State of Israel, the United Nations decision of November 29, 1947 which created the legal basis for it, and the international recognition of the new State are surely owing in large part to the bad conscience of the Powers that had failed to help the Jews in mortal danger when many of them could still have been saved and to the feeling of complicity in murder through acquiescence and passivity. In the difficult years of transition from a war economy to a peace economy that also had to absorb the soldiers returning from the armed forces, the governments were afraid of being swamped with a stream of Jewish refugees from the death camps. Added to this were, of course, political considerations in the struggle of the Great Powers for influence in the Near East. How could it be different with political decisions? But the conscience of the world did have a substantial share in the decisions made at that time. From this viewpoint there is some truth in the reproachful arguments of the Arabs that the world had shifted onto them atonement for the injustices committed under the Hitler regime (of which, incidentally, they were not quite as blameless as they pretended to be, considering their direct support of their recognized leader, the Mufti of Jerusalem, as well as their pressure on England against Jewish immigration to Palestine).

The Founding of the State as a Consequence of the Zionist Conception of the Jewish Question

Despite all appreciation of this help from the Powers, whatever their motives may have been, there would never have been a decision in favor of a Jewish State, let alone its foundation and preservation in the struggle against every kind of opposition, if the Jews had not taken their fate into their own hands. Only in this way could the catastrophic events of the Hitler period become the prelude to new and promising developments.

The founding of the State of Israel was the direct consequence of the Zionist conception of the Jewish question and its solution as formulated by Herzl and accepted as a program and a goal. To be sure, for tactical reasons this goal had not always been clearly enunciated, but clothed in formulations that sounded more conciliatory. There were also a considerable number of people, at times even among the official leadership of the Zionist Organization, who hoped to be able to achieve a peaceful and amicable solution to the Jewish-Arab conflict by means of compromise programs like the construction of a "binational" Jewish-Arab state ("without rulers and ruled" and with no regard for population ratios). No program of this kind, which may be fair in theory but disregards the realities of the life of peoples, has ever been able to convince the adversaries, and probably rightly so. Hence, when conditions become more and more critical and the need of those seeking a home grew in the same proportion as the resistance of the Arabs and the British to their immigration, Jews returned with increased energy to Herzl's goal, the founding of a Jewish state. From 1942 on (Biltmore Program) it was ever more openly proclaimed as the goal of the Zionist struggle.

The State of Israel and the Jewish Question

The decisions, the founding of the State, and the defense of its existence were, of course, not enough, no matter how much these taxed the energies of the Jewish population of the country, often to the outer limit. Nor did the admittance of the immigrants, particularly the mass immigration in the early years of the State, do the trick. Despite the deficiencies that have repeatedly been pointed out, particularly within the country, with the often excessively sharp self-criticism characteristic of the Jews, what has been accomplished here is hardly matched by anything anywhere in the world: In the three decades since the founding of the State, 550 new settlements have been established and a highly developed civilian and military industry has been built up; education and research have been developed in universities and specialized research centers; all fields of culture, music, and the graphic arts have been allowed to flourish; desert areas have been opened up to human activity; and a land still underdeveloped despite all the labor invested in it for two generations has been transformed by an influx of immigrants from even less developed Asian and African countries into a country and community that has increasingly equaled the industrial countries in the level of its civilization and culture. As has been said over and over again, no modern national movement or modern "utopia" has approached its goal as closely as the Zionist movement did with the building of the State of Israel. However, every step forward created new problems and made the fundamental questions of Jewish existence a matter for discussion again. Let us therefore conclude our traversal of the history of the Jewish question with these questions: How does this problem appear today? What was the actual effect on the Jewish question of the foundation of the Jewish State, which according to Herzl's goals was supposed to lead to the solution of the question, and how did the State of Israel affect it? Does the Jewish question still exist or has it been solved, and if not, is it closer to a solution and are we on the way to one?

The Jewish Question—a Theoretical Question or a World Problem?

As we attempt to answer these questions, it will be best if we return to the preliminary definitions and questions in chapter 1. After attempting to shed some historical light on present-day problems and endeavoring to identify within the confines of our problem the temporally and spatially ever-changing combinations of basic elements and motives, can we say more about the Jewish question in our time than we could at the beginning of our investigation? Is it possible to make more definite statements about its status and the prospects of its solution and perhaps also about its nature as a world problem within the framework of the international problems of our time? And here is a preliminary question: Are we dealing with a problem that can be solved, and if so, is it a world problem or more of a series of separate local problems that are so different that they can be solved only locally? Or is our question a purely theoretical one? These preliminary questions are not meaningless, for the synonymous use of "problem" and "question" has repeatedly been questioned from a linguistic point of view, and certainly with some justification. It has been pointed out that one can solve, or strive to solve, problems, but that one can only answer questions and not really solve them, that frequently it is more important to pose a question than to answer it.

Today there can no longer be any doubt that the Jewish question is not merely a theoretical question about the formulation and answer of which it is possible to have a noncommittal discussion—despite all the efforts of isolated Jewish intellectuals, who base themselves on all kinds of philosophical and theological systems and use a highly sophisticated language, often borrowed from Hegel's vocabulary, to keep the Jewish question theoretical. Anyone who does not live in isolation is bound to come to the conclusion that a real problem is involved, a living problem on whose solution, or degree of solution, depend not only the psychic well-being of a significant number of people (what today is often called awareness of identity) but also their physical, economic, and social existence in the simplest sense of the word. No matter how much linguists may regret this, the words *question* and *problem* were and are really used synonymously for the Jewish question. If one wishes to stay within the limits of linguistic imagery, one might say: It is a question that does not demand theoretical responses but answers that reach into reality and shape it, the full reality of human existence from the physical-material to the intellectual-spiritual kind, from individual reality to group reality. No combination of words, no matter how euphonious, no finely crafted sentences, no matter how artfully chased, can obscure that fact. Demands for virtues and modes of behavior for Jews in general cannot simply be derived in this way from predicaments of isolated individuals, even if these are on a particularly high moral and intellectual level.

Is Theodor Herzl's Conception of the Jewish Question Still Valid?

Theodor Herzl, whose appearance marked a new epoch in the history of the Jewish question, an epoch in which we are still living and working, in his work *The Jewish State: Attempt at a Modern Solution of the Jewish Question* (cf. pp. 293ff. above and part 2, p. 681) characterized the Jewish question as existing everywhere as "an atavistic bit of medievalism which the civilized nations have not been able to shake off to this day." According to him, the majority in a country decides, *nolens volens*, who is to be regarded as a person who fully belongs and who as a stranger. Full absorption by the surrounding world is unlikely, even under the best external conditions, because after a certain time of apparent peace the populace rebels against it. The Jewish question is neither a social nor a religious one, even though it may contain elements of these and other kinds and "even though it may assume these and other guises." It is a political question and can therefore be solved only in a political way. "We are a people, one people." Hence the way out proposed by Herzl was the creation of a Jewish State and the recognition of the Jews as a nation among other nations. Legal equality for the Jews as individuals must be matched by equal status for the Jews as a people.

In Herzl's view, the creation of the Jewish State will bring about a "regulation of the Jewish question." All Jews who cannot or will not assimilate in their countries of domicile—that is, those who are denied their wish to cancel their membership in the Jewish people and be completely absorbed by another people or, conversely, those who want to express their Jewishness in complete freedom and without concessions to a differently constituted surrounding world—will thereby be given the chance to immigrate to a Jewish State conceived as "national homeland for the Jewish people." Regardless of the reason for their immigration they will be able to lead a life of creative freedom in their State. On the other hand, those Jews remaining in the Diaspora who grow tired of their Jewishness and are fully accepted by the surrounding world will be free to abandon Judaism in favor of another nationality without having this interpreted as a moral defect. To be sure, Herzl's reasoning here was based on what was to him a self-evident premise— that the new Jewish State would certainly not be inferior to the old states in all branches of culture and civilization but would, if anything, be superior to them, because it would not need to continue and slowly transform any old traditions but would be able to build everything systematically in accordance with the most modern principles and methods of science and technology.

Is this analysis of the Jewish question and the possibilities of solving it still valid or have the living conditions of the world and the Jews changed so radically that Herzl's ideas must be rejected as obsolete as far as the present is concerned and replaced with more modern and more relevant definitions and practical proposals? There is no doubt that Herzl's words derived from the linguistic usage and the atmosphere of his time. Thus much about them may sound strange to our ears, which are accustomed to the diction of our time. But if one disregards the fact that Herzl's style reflects his period, which is something one must do with all authors of past times, one will be able to recognize that his insights have lost little of their timeliness and validity.

"The Jewish Question Exists Everywhere" (Herzl)

Let us begin with Herzl's point of departure: "The Jewish question exists wherever Jews live in appreciable numbers." This statement is valid even today. In fact, on the basis of the experiences of our time, one might perhaps add that it exists where only a small number of Jews live and sometimes even in places where there are no Jews any more or Jews have hardly ever existed in appreciable numbers. After all, as our detailed historical presentation in the preceding chapters and the summary at the beginning of this one have shown, dislike of Jews, which can turn into hatred and all that flows from it, is not primarily based on the actual existence of a Jew whom one meets as a person earning a living or as a neighbor, but on the image of the "typical Jew" that has evolved in the course of history, a figure that was created and developed under the influence of religious dogmas and ideologies of all kinds. This stereotypical notion of the Jew and his bad and threatening characteristics is present even prior to any encounter with a real person, a really existing Jew, and it is tantamount to a prejudgment that often impedes or prevents a fair evaluation of an individual Jew as a person existing in the flesh.

The elements out of which this dogmatically founded notion of the Jew and the prejudgments based on it were formed exist today as much as they ever have. They are the foundations of European culture and the non-European civilizations, primarily the Christian countries, that have been decisively influenced by them or their emanations. However, since, as we have seen, the process of rationalization and enlightenment extended these notions in secularized form to nonreligious literature, tradition, and linguistic usage, they also spread to non-Christian countries along with European civilization.

The Worldwide Dissemination of the Stereotypes and Caricatures

Above all, the stereotypes that assumed graphic and plastic form under the influence of the racial theory—the caricature of the Jew with a large hooked nose, a bent back, and deceitful, shifty eyes—also circulated in the countries and among the nations who have no connection with Christianity or reject and fight it and who are, if anything, related to the Jews ethnically and linguistically. Wherever there is any kind of clash with Jews and —since its foundation—the State of Israel, or wherever it seems to serve the interests of states and nations, this caricature and the literature conforming to it, such as the monstrous *Protocols of the Elders of Zion*, present themselves as an eminently effective weapon. Arab countries and Soviet Russia use it, as do interested circles in Europe and America, and where these images are not employed for a specific purpose, they haunt people's minds and hearts.

"It Can't Happen Here"

From this vantage point it cannot be ruled out that under certain circumstances—in times of upheaval and crisis and under the influence of demonically fascinating personalities—catastrophic events may occur. A warning proverb says, with some justification, that one should not speak of the devil. But neither should one lull oneself, in the face of reality and its possibilities of misfortune, with worn-out catchwords like "It can't happen here,"* thus salving one's conscience with this ingenuous formula: This can never happen here, in our civilization, in our democracy with its safeguards. Who would have believed Germany capable of what happened at the time of Hitler's rule? In those days, how many people missed the time for action and rescue because they believed only savages could perform such massacres, savages who would actually never have been capable of the kind of systematically and precisely organized mass murder that was staged by one of the most highly developed civilized nations. One can only hope that mankind has learned more from the experiences of our generation than it has from those of bygone ages. When the threatening elements continue to exist, there can be no guarantee of this. No matter how well explosives are secured, they can be ignited and explode if under the unforeseen influence of accidentally converging forces safeguards and restraints that have been deemed foolproof are removed.

The Normalized Diaspora

If there is anything that has decisively changed in the diagnosis of the Jewish question since Herzl's days it is the existence of the State of Israel, which came into being as the result of Herzl's initiative. In the preceding chapter we discussed the influence of the founding of this State, surely one of the most memorable and most momentous events of our century, on the attitude of the Jews in the Diaspora. Since the foundation of the State of Israel, Diaspora Jewry has been fundamentally different from the Jews of the prestate period, a Jewry that the generation born since then cannot even imagine. It has become healthier and more self-assured and no longer doubts that it is part of the Jewish

*Cf. also p. 432 above.

people. One may assume and expect that it will also confront dangers more actively than the preceding generations did. No one can foresee where and how future emergencies will arise for the Jewish people and its members, but one thing may be regarded as certain: They will no longer find the Jews as helpless and perplexed as the pogroms of Kishinev did in Herzl's time and the Hitler massacres in ours.

The Diaspora of Other Nations

Beyond this, the foundation and existence of the State of Israel have produced a fundamental change in the nature of the Jewish Diaspora. As we have stated above (pp. 28f.), there has been a Jewish Diaspora since ancient times, even when the people of Israel lived in their own land and had a state. Every people has members living outside the boundaries of its state, and the greater the population becomes and the smaller the available territory is, the more the surplus will be pushed out. In the case of warlike nations there are then violent movements to expand beyond the existing boundaries and conquer neighboring territories, and these violent breakouts from the original settlement area often entail migrations of peoples and military campaigns extending over wide and remote areas. If a people is less bellicose or if natural barriers or superior human resistance impede the territorial expansion, the surplus population emigrates to more distant countries. Such dispersions are promoted by problems and wartime predicaments in one's own country and by the attraction of flourishing cities and countries; Alexandria in Greek antiquity and New York in modern times are cases in point. There is nothing abnormal about such a Diaspora, even if the number of those living outside the country exceeds those in their own country. Such outside settlements are not perceived as unusual and therefore abnormal until the physical or political existence of the mother settlement is destroyed. Then the scattered settlements generally lose their independent character. For a few generations memories of a distant past of the fathers may live on, but even they will gradually fade, and the natural factors of coexistence and especially intermarriage with the population of the country and the adoption of the country's language will do their part to make the immigrants feel like natives, at least within a few generations.

The Special Character of the Jewish Diaspora as Exile *(Galut)*

The concurrence of religious-national circumstances on the part of the Jews and the world surrounding them (which was discussed in some detail in chapter 2) was responsible for the fact that even after the destruction of Israel's political existence—and even after the extinction, centuries later, of a numerically significant physical existence of the Jews in their land—the identity of the Jews and groups of Jews scattered over ever greater areas of the world was not lost. The voluntary dispersion and the dispersion forced upon them by lost wars combined both in reality and in the consciousness of the Jews. Both were now regarded as exile and banishment from the homeland, the work of accursed barbarians—although in the strangely paradoxical view of the Jews these must have acted on divine orders, for otherwise their work of destruction could not have succeeded. Thus the Diaspora increasingly assumed for these Jews the character of an exile, a punitive banishment for committed sins and for disloyalty to God. It became a constant warning and admonition to cling to the faith and the life-style required by it, the details of which were increasingly specified in the course of the centuries and which was ever more clearly differentiated from the life-style of the outside world. This also preserved the Messianic belief in a return to the homeland that belonged to Israel according to this same divine decision and promise.

The Unifying Force of Shared History

This view of history anchored in faith was able to comprise everything that happened to the Jews in the various countries and domiciles as events that were unimportant in detail but in their basic substance served to solidify and confirm the common and typical elements. In their memory and their consciousness the Jews retained less their individual destinies than what was the same for all Jews, and this typical historical consciousness of the Jews created and strengthened the feeling of a common past and the hope for a common future in their own country. This consciousness of a shared, typical past was one of the strongest unifying forces when the return to the homeland became an actuality and reality that many Jews had hardly hoped for. Yemenite, African, Iraqui, and European Jews were able to find a common language. The regenerated Hebrew language not only was used for daily communication but harbored also the history of the common past in the land and made people conscious of it again. All these past events were Jewish fate and now became a common present and future.

Exile *(Galut)* or Diaspora?

This, of course, applies particularly to the Jewries from countries in which a majority of them had still continued to lead traditional lives tied to religion and least of all to the Jews in western countries. In the countries of Western and Central Europe and in America, and since the end of World War I also in Russia and the newly independent eastern border states in which the Jews achieved formal equality as the emancipative movement progressed, the countries of domicile were to an increasing extent regarded as homelands in the full sense of the word. Logically, for these Jews the Diaspora, living dispersed among the nations, was no longer "exile" (*galut* in Hebrew, or *golus* in the Ashkenazic pronunciation customary there); they rejected this term as a characterization of their existence. More radical reformers consistently eliminated from the prayerbooks the supplication for return to "Zion," the poetic name of the ancient homeland, which was derived from the idea of exile. This often really burdensome inner conflict was in essence eliminated with the establishment of the State of Israel. If, as happened now, every Jew was entitled to immigrate to the State of Israel and through the act of immigration immediately received the right to become an Israeli citizen, being not only admitted but privileged as a Jew, the existence of the Jews—at least in the states that did not impede their emigration—could no longer be regarded as compulsory exile, as *galut*, except from the theological viewpoint of a radical orthodoxy that rejected the foundation of a secular State of Israel because this was in conflict with the Messianic belief in a miraculous return under the guidance of a redeemer sent by God.

For all others the Diaspora now assumed the character that it had had before the destruction of the Second Temple and the state: that of voluntary residence in other countries. Surely the first impetus for the dispersion of a large number of these settlements had in the final analysis been the forcible conquest of the land by the Romans. The freedom of return that was now granted had removed the compulsory situation and restored a motherland to which one could move. However, it was and is possible for an individual to reject such a return, and for all sorts of reasons: because one feels comfortable and, despite some social discrimination, at home in one's place of residence; because one shrinks from the arduous resettlement in a country with strange and unfamiliar living conditions as well as from the risks and inconveniences involved; because it is a natural process for larger population movements to take place only under the pressure of emergencies; and for other entirely legitimate reasons. Only true believers and especially resolute persons leave their countries of residence out of idealism.

But no matter how people decided and decide, it is the very opportunity to decide between remaining in one's place of residence and immigrating to Israel that normalizes the Diaspora. In the consciousness of the Jews and the nations the freedom of choice and the existence of the State of Israel as the homeland of the Jewish people increasingly obliterates the character of the dispersion as *galut*. The preferred word now is the Hebrew *tfutzot*, which means "Diaspora" without the theological and political overtone of "exile" and "banishment." It is left to the discretion of every Jew to feel completely at home in the countries of the Diaspora, to have a homeland in the full sense of the word beyond the self-evident obligation to fulfill all the duties of a citizen. But if outward or inner difficulties cause him to leave his country of residence, the homeland of the Jewish people as a whole is open to him as a personal, individual home as well.

The New "World Jewry"

This also changes the character of the relations between the Diaspora and the Land of Israel and the Land of Israel and world Jewry. Actually, the concept "world Jewry" received its true meaning only after the foundation of the State of Israel. Up to then it had generally been used more by the anti-Semites, most recently especially by the National Socialists, with a somehow unsavory connotation. "World Jewry" or "international Jewry"—that was the destructive demon of Jewish world domination which threatened the peaceful, creative world of European civilization (or of the "Aryans" and the "Nordics"); it was something mysterious and unfathomable that could be connected with the secret conspiracy of the "sages of Zion." This *"Weltjudenheit"* reacted to the troubles of the Jewish people the way an organism reacts to stimuli and threats and without becoming apparent as a political entity by means of some visible representation. The founding of the State of Israel turned this specter into a reality without ghostlike character: the Jewry of the world with the State of Israel as the center of gravity.

Eretz Yisrael as the Center of Gravity of World Jewry

We have deliberately chosen the term *center of gravity* rather than any of the other verbal or conceptual formations that are frequently used to describe the actual or desired relationships. Under the influence of Ahad Ha-am and in his spirit people said for a long time that a "cultural center" would or should be established in the Land of Israel that would have a preserving and profoundly regenerative effect on the Jewries of the Diaspora. Let us hope that this will come about some day. It has been regarded as one of the tasks of the Jewish State to give political aid to the Jews of the world in times of need. It would be desirable for the State of Israel to become stabilized and its influence on the political world to grow to such an extent that its intervention in behalf of Jews oppressed anywhere will carry more weight than has been possible up to now. If we speak of the present, it is better to avoid such overly sweeping concepts, which at the same time limit reality too much. However, it is safe to say about the present situation that world Jewry is gravitating toward Israel and that active interest in the State and the Land of Israel is the strongest factor uniting world Jewry today.

Prior to the period of emancipation this function was performed by the religious law which bound all to a uniform life-style and in which Eretz Yisrael as the land of the past and the future occupied an important place in memories and hopes. As this influence decreased among the majority of Jews, Jewry became fragmented by countries and environments. Whether in the long run cohesion could have been preserved by religiously founded ethical teachings, as the liberal Jewish circles hoped when they reduced the walls of the law to different heights, is open to doubt. Herzl was not really wrong when he diagnosed the enemies and the anti-Semitic movements that prevented the complete absorption of the Jews by their surroundings as the forces that kept the Jews together. These negative bonds have now been replaced or supplemented by the positive force of Jewry's relationship with Israel. Increasing numbers of Jews regard it as their task to support Israel, the State and the people, in every way they can, and the State of Israel will need this help for itself and its work for as long as it must struggle for its security and its economic and social stabilization—prerequisites for a natural growth of immigration from the Diaspora.

The Jews of the State of Israel and World Jewry

In the same way the Jewish population of the country, including the young people, is increasingly convinced that world Jewry is its best ally and its only completely reliable one. Only it has an inner connection with the Land of Israel that transcends interests and (usually temporary) friendships, because it is based on the consciousness of an inner unity and on the feeling of the inseparability of fate among all parts of Jewry.

This feeling toward the Diaspora was not always present to the same degree in a certain part of Israeli Jewry. At first a number of circumstances militated against it. After all, Zionism is a complex movement, and its impulses and tendencies often seem to conflict. On the other hand, it is a revolution against the inwardly unfree existence of the Jews in the Diaspora, a rebellion against the very existence of the Diaspora, no matter what one calls it. Zionism wants to eliminate this condition of bondage and dependence on opinions, prejudices, and the phenomena based on these—precisely through the establishment of a polity in which Jewishness is not a defect. Everything among the Jews of the Diaspora that was reminiscent of this condition aroused the contempt of many Israelis raised in this spirit.

On the other hand, Zionism is a movement of continuity, and in this sense it is conservative in nature, desiring to continue the history of the Jewish people. It is not only concerned with making life secure for as many individual Jews as possible, but also with developing collective life and the continuing and reforming Jewish history as the history of the Jewish people. Continuing what history? Logically the answer to this question had to be: the entire history from the oldest times to the present. However, many elements in the emotional life and creative drive of the Zionist revolutionaries (many of whom were also rebelling as socialists against the bourgeoisie and the anomalous occupational structure of the Jews) and the younger generation born or raised in the country resisted this. To them the life-style of the Jewish middle class in the western countries was alien. Since they were influenced both by the bearing of the ghetto fighters and the depiction of the Jews in world literature, they found it unworthy and even despicable. On the basis of this emotional attitude they endeavored to eliminate the history of the stateless Diaspora, the *galut*, as "unhistory," as it were, as something almost shameful, not to take full cognizance of it, and, skipping over it, to connect the new present in the State of Israel with the time of the ancient state and the national life in Eretz Yisrael. Archaeology, whose excavations to a large extent corroborated and illustrated the historical texts of the Bible as well as the historical reports of Flavius Josephus, became the most popular branch of history and almost a national hobby and sport. Smaller groups went even beyond this and strove to establish a connection, through literature and lore, with the pre-Mosaic-mono-theistic period of a life even closer to nature—in a certain way with the life of the Canaanites, which is what they were called, first by their opponents, then generally. All these movements and trends faded away in the course of the years if they went beyond the goal of stimulating research in early history and increasing awareness of it. They gave way to a sounder picture of history intended to explore the past as a whole in the full context of historical life and make it conscious.

This also promoted a fairer assessment of the past and the present of the Diaspora and its Jewries in historiography and life. In the course of the past decades the times of war and need in the country, the attendant political isolation of the State of Israel, and the spontaneous and organized help of world Jewry have strengthened this bond and made it ever tighter.

The Complexity of the Jewish Question and Its Solution

We have reached the end of our examination, which started with the present, took us through thousands of years of general and Jewish history, and brought us back to the present. We have sought to expose the roots of the world problem and to show what grew from them. Often the trouble with oversimple proposals for a solution, which at first even seem consistent and elegant, is that the complex ramifications of a problematic situation are overlooked. It is precisely such impermissible simplifications that this book has striven to avoid by adding to a presentation of the main lines and the particularly important events numerous sidelights and excursuses in an effort to present a more differentiated total picture. We have traced the complex relationships between the Jews and the nations—that is, the problem that we usually call the Jewish question—from the origins to the present situation. This did not yield the history of a unilateral hatred or guilt that simplifying treatises—well-intentioned, malevolent, or neutral, "objective" ones—sometimes present. It could not be our purpose to examine sociological or psychological theses or theories and perhaps present them in modified form. We have been concerned with more than that: with the existential problem of a human group that is unexampled in history in its dispositions, destiny, achievements, sufferings, and deeds.

This problem of Jewish life has become a world problem, and not only because the Jews live scattered over the civilized world and their existence and everything they do or don't do are bound up with the activities of many nations and individuals and have had a greater qualitative influence on them than the quantitative ratio would have warranted. From the very beginning this problem has harbored many fatefully determinative elements for the history of numerous nations and individuals as well as many symbolic and paradigmatic features for the past and present of mankind as a whole. Viewed in this way, the "biography" of this world problem becomes part of the life history of our entire world. Hence the solution of this problem, too, concerns not only the Jews but also many other nations and states. It touches on the fundamental problems of human coexistence on earth.

Having traversed the historical space, we ask these questions: Is there a solution for this problem called the Jewish question? Are we on the road to a solution? And if the answer is yes, are there not such tremendous obstacles on this road that the supposed way out will in the end prove to be but a blind alley or a wrong track leading to an abyss? Unfortunately we must admit that these are not just theoretical questions that must logically be asked; they are questions posed to us daily and hourly by the present. Hence no one can escape giving answers to them, least of all a historian, for at bottom he examines the history of the problem for the sake of such answers.

The Founding of the State of Israel—a Way of Solving the Problem?

But perhaps we have posed the question too theoretically after all, for the presentation of the historical development that we have given in this book, especially in its last chapters, tends toward a definite answer and seeks to buttress it with the present life of our generation, the history of the last fifty years: namely, that the foundation of the State of Israel and the effects this has had and is still having have opened up the road to the solution of the Jewish question. We have heard about the normalization of the life of the Jews that was initiated by the founding of the State, about the freer discussion of it, about the regained pride and the new, more upright bearing of the Jews, the Israelis, and the Jewry of the Diaspora that is closely bound up with them. In the judgment of the world a new type of Jew has come into being, at least in Israel, one that serves as a model to many in the Diaspora. It has entered the literature of the world with many nuances, often with the usual simplifications and exaggerations—be it the heroic pose or the shrewdness and flair for uncovering all enemy plans—as often happens with figures that have hardened into a stereotype.

The less theoretical questions derived from this state of affairs can perhaps be formulated thus: How strong are the counterforces? Is the power of the dogmas and traditions not so full of the old notions about the Jew and his typical image based on them that the new image of the Jew cannot prevail against it? Is it not evident, on the contrary, that the old stereotype of the Jew has recently spread to countries that have not known it before and where it is not supported by traditions but is deliberately disseminated in connection with the struggle of the Arabs against the State of Israel?

The Continued Existence of the State of Israel

This brings us to the last and most important question with which all the others are connected in view of the ever closer intertwinement of the problems of the State of Israel with the destinies of world Jewry: Can the State of Israel maintain itself and can it last in the face of the military, political, and economic hostility surrounding it on all sides?

No one, not even the new brotherhood of "futurologists," can predict the future with certainty, because it contains ever new, unforeseeable and therefore incalculable elements. Therefore, if a historian tries (in Goethe's sense) to "give an accounting to himself of three thousand years," he will always weigh the historical experience of the distant past (far more remote than in Goethe's day) against the recent past up to the present and venture only a hesitant look into the future. He must not evade this risk, however, if his subject requires it. The more deeply he has delved into the subject of his investigation, the more categorically he will reject the pessimistic evaluations and devaluations of the so-called *Realpolitiker,* who in general regard as "reality" only the obvious, evident, and palpable factors and do not see the true realities underneath or behind them. Nothing is easier than being a pessimist, for one foresees every misfortune and is pleasantly surprised if something good happens. It is just as easy to overlook the world of hard facts in a superficial optimism and to follow a sort of ostrich policy by sticking one's head in the sand in the face of danger. In contrast to such actions, a contemporary who is convinced of the justness of his cause, or who at least is interested in the peaceful solution of world problems will display a vigorous, realistic optimism and consider the current real balance of power, but at the same time he will not forget the power of the true forces that affect the life of individuals and nations.

The True Reality

That was the attitude of the Jewish prophets. Their characteristic was not that they foretold the future; the soothsayers of all nations and primitive religions did that, and the figures who have become part of Holy Writ and gone down in history as prophets have contemptuously denounced those augurs as "false prophets." The statements and actions of the true prophets were permeated by the belief that goodness, righteousness, and truthfulness are the real, fundamental forces of existence. Hence man's destiny will change for the better as soon as, and to the extent that, he helps these immanent forces of existence to prevail in reality. In other words what happens is not anonymous, not a disaster or a Greek drama being enacted as a fateful, inescapable tragedy, but action imposed upon us. To a great extent, the way things develop depends on what we do.

Like our legendary image of the "Eternal Jew," we have passed through many human ages and have traversed many epochs, changing constellations of power, cultural transformations, and revolutions from the remotest ancient times to the present. None of the nations and cultures that started out in life together with us are around any more, though all of them still have long-distance effects in all the forms of historical survival. We, however, are the only ones who have preserved our physical and spiritual identity as a people, as a religion, and as bearers of historical traditions, and consequently we have been able to build up a new existence as a state in our ancient homeland—despite all the vicissitudes of the past and the present.

The New World Constellation

We are now in a new constellation of nations, states, and powers, of ideas and perspectives, of fears and hopes, of hatred and love—at a watershed of time similar to the downfall of ancient civilization and the evolution of the modern period, with the constant new discoveries and inventions since the Renaissance. Someone who is not on the victoriously rising side is apt to interpret such times of revolutionary change as the end of a world, at least until he has found his bearings under the new conditions. It may be assumed and hoped that the Jews, being historically experienced in such upheavals and revaluations, will face the constantly changing situations with greater flexibility than many other people. They have survived the worst constellations and the most threatening dangers—from their struggle against the Great Powers of antiquity to the period of Hitler's genocide and the wars fought to date for the existence of the State of Israel.

In fighting the Jews people have always used all instruments of power. In this respect the oil boycott of the Arab states in our day constitutes only a change of means, not of principles and methods. Energy sources and weapons change from time to time, and in our era of revolutionary change they do so faster than ever before. While we are using one instrument, for construction or destruction, others are already at hand, and no one knows how quickly they will be employed. Things can happen any day, like the coming of the Messianic liberator in the Jewish religion, and what yesterday was still an urgent need and an obscure threat can tomorrow deteriorate into a superfluous product. The new means of defense and attack make possible long-distance rescue and counterthreats; this was demonstrated by the totally unexpected liberation of kidnapped Jews from Entebbe in Uganda by the Israeli air force and high command. Their success was due to a conviction of the justness of their actions and of their necessity and to a combination of clear goals, consideration of all circumstances and possibilities, courage, and self-confidence. This can be confirmed in other emergencies, when the *Realpolitiker* can only counsel submission to the "realities."

If, as seems from our examination, the road to the solution of the Jewish question, to the extent that it can be solved, is via the existence of the State of Israel, the Jews have no choice in their decision. They must continue on that road with their "elastic obstinacy," as one could perhaps call the way they react to the threats to their life and life-style. The idea that during the last three generations the Jews should have concentrated in Israel with their greatest constructive strength, only to be destroyed there in a last, powerful attack by their enemies, and with them world Jewry's greatest hopes for the future and the prospects of solving or at least relieving the international problem of the Jewish question—that, as it were, after a long odyssey through space and time Ahasuerus should have reached his homeland, only to die there—such a notion would really be tantamount to embracing the Christian legend of the Jewish "reprobate" from which even Christianity is beginning to detach itself in our days. Anyone who believes there is sense in history, at least to the extent of not regarding everything as merely accidental, will not be able to accept such an idea.

Pluralism of Values and Valuations

People like to speak, with fear and a strange delight in disparaging and execrating, of the anarchy of values prevailing in our time—that is, an all too tolerant acceptance of the equality of different values, which they call basically a lack of values. Such people overlook the positive elements behind it. In the face of the tolerance of "enlightened" former times that at bottom was only an inactive disregard and an indulgent, tolerant acceptance of what was considered as false and inferior, progress in scientific thinking is facilitating an understanding of a true pluralism of values and valuations. If such a pluralism prevails, it will also mean recognition of the equality of different types of people, ethnic realities, nations, and states regardless of their size and special features. In a world that revises its fundamental conceptions in this fashion there will also be a more legitimate and less disputed place for the Jews.

The Cardinal Sin of the Jews: Their Continued Existence as a People

Despite what the Christian dogma says and the secularized modern European philosophy of history teaches, the cardinal sin of the Jews was not that they failed in their historical mission by not recognizing the son of God or by killing him. It was something else: The Jews broke the basic law of world history as interpreted by mankind. In violation of all known rules governing the lives of nations they did not become extinct when defeat and expulsion condemned them to extinction—not at the time of the Assyrians and Babylonians, not after the judgment of the Roman world empire, and not after the many death sentences that were pronounced and that people tried to execute. This caused them enormous losses of life and property, greater losses than any other people has sustained. Without these huge losses they, as one of the oldest nations in history, would have to be a people of the greatest dimensions. As eternal nonconformists the Jews have bowed to no view of life that was alien to them—not as a people and many among them not as individuals either. Their existence has thus appeared as uncanny and disquieting to the nations and has often had a revolutionary effect on all branches of life. Usually the nations took less cognizance of the fruitful elements of this effect than of what seemed threatening to them. Perhaps a change in valuations will assign to the Jews a juster place in the world, and surely a more legitimate one—as a people that no longer has the character of a sinister specter but has assumed the visible, corporeal form of a state— because of the struggles for its existence often more prominently and painfully than it would like.

The New Will to Live of the Jewish People

In these struggles the new will to live of the Jewish people has been documented. With astonishment and admiration the world has registered it, increasingly also with detached neutrality to the point of decided rejection when it was not in tune with their interests and their consequent sympathies for the Arab adversaries. To a chronicler of the Jewish question who is experiencing current events sympathetically and critically it seems as though the world does not sufficiently realize the transformation produced in the Jewish question by the founding of the State of Israel and the struggle of the Jews for their existence and their life as Jews, both in Israel and in the Diaspora. The Jews' will to live no longer permits them merely to endure attacks and simply to bear suffering as destiny or the consequence of guilt. It has become a fighting will to live and not a submissive one, no matter what the circumstances may be.

At the end of a book about the Jewish question it may not be appropriate to admonish the world to try to understand the consequences of this new bearing of the Jews. Anyone who today involves the State of Israel in a decisive battle for its existence must know that such a struggle for the existence of the State and the life of the Jews will pull many nations and states, both neighboring and more distant ones, into the vortex of destruction. Given the close interconnection of events in our world of shrinking distances, no nation and no state can be certain that the struggle for the world problem of the Jewish question will not involve it too.

Appeal to Reason and for Peace

These words of a nonpolitical but not unconcerned observer are not intended as a threat, for as such they would be absurd from a powerless person. They are intended as an appeal to reason. Just as the enormous instruments of destruction accumulating in the armories of the Great Powers—and not only theirs!—admonish all responsible leaders to let reason speak and allow the nations' desire for peace to prevail, one must hope and wish that those directly involved and those who are by virtue of their power and influence decision-makers will put a permanent stop to armed conflict and destruction in the Jewish question in general and the concomitant struggle between Jews and Arabs in particular. Enough blood has flowed and enough lives have been snuffed out! The sanctification of life is one of the great principles of Judaism and one of the great postulates of our time.

No problem is insoluble if there is a will to solve it, no differences are irreconcilable if there is a will to settle the conflict. The greatest sin of mankind is the lack of such a will, which is manifested in fights and also in inactive aloofness if active intervention could prevent combat. No progress toward peace and cooperative coexistence comes by itself, it requires the timely intervention of doers who act before it is too late. Let us close with an epigram by Goethe as words of warning (and hope):

> Die rechte Zeit zum Handeln stets verpassen,
> Nennt ihr: die Dinge sich entwickeln lassen.
> Was hat sich denn entwickelt, sagt mir an,
> Das ihr nicht selbst zur rechten Zeit getan?
> (The proper time of action to postpone
> You call: let things develop on their own.
> What has developed, may I ask, that *you*,
> When it was time for action, did not do?)*

*English version by Max Knight.

PART 2
Notes and Excursuses

Prefatory Note

In keeping with the nature of this book, it is not my purpose to document every fact, statement, and opinion. That would produce thousands of notes that nobody would read. Wherever possible, I have based my views on sources and presentations that are accessible to everyone. Where it was necessary and possible, sources were included in the text of the first part. Over a number of decades, while I was concerning myself with the problem of the Jewish question, which I always kept in mind even when I was working on other books and essays, as well as the publication of source material, I read or skimmed many hundreds of books and articles on the subject—primary materials and numerous archival sources which I came across in my work as an archivist at the German Reichsarchiv, as director of the Central Zionist Archives, and as the first State Archivist of Israel (1956–71). Except for the documentation of quotations, I am reproducing of all this only what seemed particularly helpful to me and what may be especially useful to readers in their own further work. This, of course, gives short shrift to the basic works on Jewish or general history and to the general and Jewish encyclopedias that are in constant use as sources of knowledge and information. These are mentioned only if major articles contained in them serve as special sources of information.

On the other hand, the presentation in Part 1 is to be freed of ballast by excursus-like comments and, wherever necessary, amplified and illustrated by the details provided here. The page numbers in the margin refer to the corresponding sections in Part 1.

Abbreviations: In the following notes the commonly used reference and historical works are often cited in abbreviated form. The most important abbreviations are:

EJ	*Encyclopaedia Judaica.* 10 vols. Berlin, 1928–34 (A–K only; the publication of the other letters was stopped).
EJJ	*Encyclopaedia Judaica.* 16 vols. Jerusalem, 1971–72.

HE   *Hebrew Encyclopedia (Encyclopaedia Ivrit)*. 31 vols. to date, 1949–79.

JE   *Jewish Encyclopedia*. 12 vols. New York and London, 1901–6.

JL   *Jüdisches Lexikon*, edited by G. Herlitz and B. Kirschner. 5 vols. Berlin, 127–30.

LBI, LBYB *Year Book of the Leo Baeck Institute*. Vols. 1–24. London, 1956–79.

MB   *Wochenzeitung des Irgun Oleg Merkas Europa*. Tel Aviv.

MGWJ   *Monatsschrift für Geschichte und Wissenschaft des Judentums*.

Baron   Salo W. Baron, A *Social and Religious History of the Jews*. 3 vols. New York, 1937; revised and expanded second edition, 16 vols. Philadelphia, 1952–76.

Dubnow Simon Dubnow, *Weltgeschichte des jüdischen Volkes*. 10 vols. Berlin, 1925–29.

Graetz   Heinrich Graetz, *Geschichte der Juden von den ältesten Anfängen bis zur Gegenwart*. 11 vols. Berlin and Leipzig, 1854–70.

Preface

The assumption of historical strata presented here must not be confused with the theory of psychic or biological layers that is current in psychology and with which it shares only the image. The strata assumed by psychology for human psychic life are part of a theory (or physiological demonstration) of remote developmental stages that are biological, ontogenetic, or phylogenetic in nature. The stratification meant here involves essentially perceptual factors from *historical* times in the narrower sense—that is, contents passed on by tradition through historical epochs down to the the present. Past eras live on, both in societal strata and groups and in ourselves. Cf. Friedrich Nietzsche, *Thoughts out of Season:* "Exact reflection leads to the insight that we are a multiplication of numerous past times. . . ." J. Wellhausen, *Israelische und jüdische Geschichte* (Berlin, 1921), p. 371: "The stages of religion, like the stages of history generally, remain juxtaposed."

We say this by way of clarification and to eliminate misunderstandings from the outset. I hope that in the course of my presentation things will fall into place and be clarified. Cf. also Benedetto Croce, *La Storia* (English edition: *History as the Story of Liberty* [London, 1941], pp. 43f): "We are products of the past and we live immersed in the past which encompasses us. How can we move towards the new life, how create new activities without getting out of the past and without placing ourselves above it? And how can we place ourselves above the past if we are in it and it is in us? There is no other way out except through thought, which does not break off relations with the past but rises ideally above it and converts it into knowledge. The past must be faced or, not to speak in metaphors, it must be reduced to a mental problem which can find its solution in a proposition of truth, the ideal promise for our new activity and our new life."

1
Introduction

18   "THE JEWISH QUESTION": THE TERM AND THE CONCEPT: The quotation from Martin Buber is from his *Drei Reden über das Judentum* (Frankfurt, 1911) (2d ed., 1919), 27. Cf. also Hans Kohn, *Martin Buber: Sein Werk und seine Zeit* (Cologne, 1961), 92ff. The problem is defined similarly by P. Horowitz in *The Jewish Question and Zionism* (London, 1927), 27: "The Jewish Question, then, is the problem that arises out of the conflict between the heredity and the environment of the Jewish people. Or, in more specific terms: the Jewish Question is the problem that arises out of the conflict between the 'Palestine' within the Jew, which is the source of his spiritual life, and the 'America,' the 'England,' the 'Russia' or the 'Germany' that constitutes the sphere of his physical existence."

18   MORITZ GÜDEMANN: The quotation is from a review by Güdemann which appeared in the *Monatsschrift für Geschichte und Wissenschaft des Judentums* 62:61ff. Concerning the encounter between Herzl and Güdemann, cf. A. Bein, *Theodore Herzl* (Philadelphia, 1941), and Joseph Fraenkel, "Moritz Güdemann and Theodor Herzl," Leo Baeck Institute, *Year Book 11* (1966), 67–82.

18   JEAN-PAUL SARTRE: From his essay "Réflexions sur la Question Juive." Quoted here from the American edition, *Anti-Semite and Jew*, trans. George J. Becker (New York: Schocken Books, 1948), 145, 147. Chapters 2 and 3 contain a detailed discussion of the Jews in the mind of antiquity and the Middle Ages.

18ff.   THE HISTORY OF THE CONCEPT "JEWISH QUESTION": Cf. Jacob Toury, "The Jewish Question—A Semantic Approach," Leo Baeck Institute, *Year Book 11* (1966), 85–106; Volkmar Eichstaedt, *Bibliographie zur Geschichte der Judenfrage*, vol. 1: 1750–1848 (Hamburg, 1938). Toury indicates the elements that combined to produce this concept. (We shall return to this in chap. 5.) He rightly emphasizes the fact that the decisive thing is not the occasional, quasi-accidental and unconscious use of a new concept but its general acceptance as the characterization of a problem. Hence it is immaterial (and can hardly be established with certainty) who first used the term *Judenfrage* as the title of a separate publication. Toury attempts (p. 93) to establish a chronology of the first writings, though without claiming certainty and significance for it. It is more important to bear in mind that the discussion was actually stimulated by the appearance of Bruno Bauer's essay "Die Juden-Frage" [*sic*] in *Deutsche Jahrbücher für Wissenschaft und Kunst* 5 (1842). Shortly thereafter this essay was published as a pamphlet titled *Die Judenfrage* (now one word, without a hyphen. [Braunschweig, 1843], 115 pp.). No earlier writer had put the Jewish question up for discussion as a problem of the integration of the Jews into the Christian states of Europe so incisively and comprehensively as Bauer. Many of the independent writings that appeared in print at the time for and against Bauer or as a continuation of the discussion he had stimulated have the concept "Jewish question" in their title or subtitle. All used it as the customary term for the problems connected with the question of the emancipation of the Jews. For the titles, some of them with concise summaries of the contents, cf. Eichstaedt's bibliography, no. 1259ff. Cf. also Nathan Rotenstreich, "For and against Emancipation: The Bruno Bauer Controversy," *LBYB* 4 (1959), 3–336 as well as part 1, chap. 5 of this book. Eichstaedt writes in the foreword to his bibliography (p. 5): "The major part of the first volume is devoted to a discussion of the political questions of 'toleration,' 'civic amelioration,' 'equal rights,' and the 'emancipation' of the Jews and the 'Jewish question'—the various catchwords of the period between 1750 and 1848."

The word *Judensache* is also used in this connection; cf., e.g., the letter from Moses Moser to Immanuel Wohlwill (both members of the Verein für Cultur und Wissenschaft der Juden) of 23 May 1823, quoted by H. G. Reissner in his book about Eduard Gans (Tübingen, 1965), 102: "To me there is nothing more tedious than talking about the *Judensache*." Herzl also used this term at the beginning of his work for a "solution of the Jewish question," heading his Zionist diary "Die Judensache" (the Jewish Cause, 1895). Among the writings that appeared in 1840 we should perhaps give particular attention to Constantin Frantz's pamphlet *Ahasverus oder die Judenfrage* (Berlin, 1844). This title combines the legend of the "Eternal Jew" (discussed in chap. 4) with the new concept of the Jewish question. "*The Jewish people is itself the Eternal Jew* [emphasis in the original]. It has cast out the Savior and thus it has been scattered over the whole earth and finds peace nowhere; it wants to mingle with the nations and thus destroy its peoplehood, but it is unable to do so . . ." (p. 47). To my knowledge, there still is no comprehensive examination of the dissemination of the term *Judenfrage* (significantly enough, in English "Jewish question" and not "question of the Jews," and in French usually "La question juive" rather than "La question des Juifs").

For the most important works on the Jewish question since the 1880s, cf. *Germany: Its History, Life and Culture*, Catalogue Series no. 3 of the Wiener Library (London, 1958), pp. 205ff.

DISCUSSION AMONG THE JEWS: S. Feuchtwanger, *Die Judenfrage als wissenschaftliches Problem* (Berlin, 1916); Lucien Wolf, *Notes on the Diplomatic History of the Jewish Question* (London, 1919). 20

NATIONAL SOCIALISTS: In 1935 Wilhelm Grau published in Hamburg a programmatic work, *Die Judenfrage als Aufgabe der neuen Geschichtsforschung*, and from 1936 on he edited a section entitled *Geschichte der Judenfrage* in the *Historische Zeitschrift*, the leading periodical of the German historians (which had a National Socialist orientation at the time). By Jewish question he meant "all those problems . . . that manifested themselves in every period in the encounter of the nations with the Jewish people." According to him, the Jews always viewed these problems from the standpoint of Jewish history rather than from that of the "host nations." In his programmatic work Grau aimed at a "natural solution of the Jewish question in accordance with the principle of a clean break." Concerning the further development of the problem in the Nazi period, see chap. 9. Regarding the National Socialist tendencies and institutes for the so-called "investigation of the Jewish question," see Werner Schochow, *Deutsch-jüdische Geschichtswissenschaft* (Berlin, 1969), 149–95; M. Weinreich, *Hitler's Professors* (New York, 1946); Walter Frank, "Die Erforschung der Judenfrage: Rückblick und Ausblick," *Forschungen zur Judenfrage* 5 (1941): 7–21. 20

In the great encyclopedias the term *Judenfrage* is often equated with other concepts (e.g., *EJ* 9:542 refers to the articles "Anti-Semitism," "Emancipation," and

"Zionism") or not treated as a separate concept at all (e.g., in the new *EJJ*, 1971), Cf. also the following notes.

21 NATURE OF THE JEWISH QUESTION: Friedrich Nietzsche is here quoted after A. Mitscherlich, "Zur Analyse der Massen," *Du. Schweizerische Monatsschrift*, March 1952, 20.

21ff. DEFINITION AS POINT OF DEPARTURE: Cf. Benedetto Croce, *History as the Story of Liberty* (London, 1941), 23: "The unity of an historical work lies in the problem formulated by an historical judgement and in the solution of the problem through the act of formulation. This is therefore a unity of a thoroughly logical kind."

22 PROBLEM OF THE EXISTENCE OF JEWS AMONG THE NATIONS: *JL* 3:422 defines *Judenfrage* as the "totality of the problems created by the Jews' coexistence with other peoples." This article, written by Robert Weltsch and Hans Kohn, goes on to say that "the Jewish question is, in the final analysis, a product of the 'enigma' of Jewry itself—its existence, its will to live, and its intellectuality that has lasted for millenia." In the *Universal Jewish Encyclopedia*, which is based in part on *JL*, Isaak Landmann polemicizes against this formulation: "The term 'Jewish Question,' while often employed to designate the totality of problems that confront the Jews particularly in matters of adjustment to their environment, is actually a misnomer. In the first place, there is no single Jewish question anywhere. . . . The Jews . . . never, at any time or any place, considered themselves a problem to themselves or to the people among whom they lived. . . ." As already mentioned, *Encyclopaedia Judaica* (Berlin) and *Encyclopaedia Judaica* (Jerusalem) have no article on the Jewish question.

We shall have more to say below (see the index) about the problem of the Jewish enigma and what non-Jews have often regarded as the "mysterious" nature of the Jews' existence—a problem raised in the abovementioned article of the *Jüdisches Lexikon*. The title of Ernest van den Haag's eminently serious and perceptive book *The Jewish Mystique* (New York, 1969; paperback edition, 1971) is characteristic of this feeling, which has survived to this day. In 1947 Rotenstreich characterized the relation between the Jews and the nations as "magical tension" (*Ha-aretz*, 19 December 1947).

22 OUTWARD CHARACTERISTICS: Cf. chap. 6, on modern anti-Semitism, for further details. Cf. a book that is still worth reading, *Zur Volkskunde der Juden* by the German geographer and ethnologist Richard Andree (1835–1912) (Bielefeld and Leipzig, 1881), p. 22: "We are all familiar with the 'Jewish type'; we can immediately tell a Jew by his face and his entire bearing. . . . But if we are asked to define this type and devise some general formula for it, we are perplexed."

22f. "FOREIGN BODY": We shall discuss this in detail below. What may be the best characterization of the modern Jew as an "alien" was given by Georg Simmel, a German sociologist of Jewish descent, in his "Excursus on the Foreigner" (*Soziologie* [1908]; pp. 509–12 in the 1922 edition): "Here we mean stranger not in the sense of the wanderer who is here today and gone tomorrow, but as someone who comes today and stays tomorrow—so to speak, the potential wanderer who has not moved on but has not fully overcome the flexibility of coming and going." Cf. also René König, "Judentum und Sociologie," *Der Monat*, August 1961, 70ff., esp. 75; Hans Liebeschütz, *Von Georg Simmel zu Franz Rosenzweig* (Tübingen, 1970), 103ff.; Margarete Susman, *Die geistige Gestalt Georg Simmels* (Tübingen, 1959).

UNIQUENESS OF THE PROBLEM: Objections to this assumption have frequently been   23
raised. Even though many of these appear in scholarly guise, they are motivated by
an endeavor to free Judaism from the halo or the stigma of uniqueness, depending on
the standpoint of the observer, and to adapt it to the general norm. (We shall concern
ourselves with this in the succeeding chapters of Part 1.) The concept of the
uniqueness of Judaism's path through history is often confused or jumbled with the
concept of chosenness, which can be affirmed, rejected, or registered as an existing
tenet with an indisputable historical effect, a tenet that may be evaluated positively or
negatively. The recognition of the uniqueness of the problem that we call the Jewish
question is wholly independent of one's attitude to the concept of, or belief in,
chosenness. The vehemence with which this is frequently attacked shows that here,
too, more than a scholarly debate is involved. It is a kind of theological dispute on a
secularized basis. Toynbee mounts a particularly sharp attack on the concept of
"uniqueness," but his analogies are totally inadequate—e.g., the fate of the Parsees,
an ethnic group of around one hundred thousand inhabitants who clung to the
religion of Zoroaster and hence fled from Persia in the early eighth century to escape
the "conversionary zeal of Mohammed's adherents" (Helmolt, *Weltgeschichte* [1929],
359) and settled in India. Oswald Spengler also used them as comparisons on some
occasions. Surely this is one of the instances where there might be some interesting
parallels to partial phenomena, but the analogy would be carried *ad absurdum*
because here, as in the natural sciences, quantity turns into quality. What gives
phenomena their historical quality is their historical effect, not the mere fact of their
existence. Many things that happen are not history. And what a difference there is in
the fate, the extent of the dispersal, the tragic clashes with the surrounding world,
and the fruitful reforging of the Diaspora destiny of a despised majority into values of
epochal human validity and the will and the strength to bring about a radical change
in its situation. Cf. especially Arnold J. Toynbee, *A Study of History,* vols. 8 and 12,
477 ff. and 620ff., as well as James Parkes, "Toynbee and the Uniqueness of Jewry,"
Jewish Journal of Sociology 4, no. 1 (June 1962): 3–13. We shall have more to say
about Toynbee's theory of Judaism as a fossilized branch of Syrian culture.

J. BURCKHARDT, "TERRIBLES SIMPLIFICATEURS": Burckhardt used this term (in the   23f.
definitive French form, which had been preceded by some similar formulations) in a
letter to his friend Friedrich von Preen dated 24 July 1889. It seems that he had used
it somewhat earlier in conversations with friends. Cf. *Jacob Burckhardts Briefe an
seinen Freund Friedrich von Preen 1864–1903* (Stuttgart and Berlin, 1922), 248. (I
owe this information to the kindness of Dr. Rudolf Marx, Leipzig, and particularly
Professor Werner Kaegi, Basel, Jacob Burckhardt's biographer.)

THE METHODS OF SOCIOLOGY: Cf. Peter L. Berger, *Invitation to Sociology* (1963,   24
1970), 191: "While most sociologists, by temperament perhaps or by professional
specialization, will be concerned mainly with contemporary events, disregard of the
historical dimension is an offense not only against the classic Western ideal of the
civilized man but against sociological reasoning itself—namely that part of it that
deals with the central phenomenon of predefinition. A humanistic understanding of
society leads to an almost symbiotic relationship with history, if not to a self-
conception of sociology as being itself a historical discipline. . . . . ." Concerning the
problem of communal psychology, with which we are largely dealing here, Leonard
Woolf's remarks seem very noteworthy to me (*After the Deluge: A Study of Communal Psychology* [Pelican Books, 1937], 29f.):

> The strangest and the most important fact about communal psychology is that its content is
> largely the ideas, beliefs, and aims of the dead. There used to be, and still is in some

countries, a law of mortmain or the dead hand under which it is not the living but the dead who determine the use and ownership of property. The dead man's hand was always being stretched out of the grave to control the holding of land, the sowing of fields, the building of houses. It requires but little knowledge of history to recognize that there is also a psychological law of the dead hand. A great deal of the complexity in such ideas as freedom and democracy, much of the difficulty of understanding what they mean, comes from their history . . . there can be no understanding of history, of politics, or of the effects of communal psychology which does not take into consideration the tremendous influence of this psychological dead hand, the dead mind. At every particular moment it is the dead rather than the living who are making history, for politically individuals think dead men's thoughts and pursue dead men's ideals.

People have attempted to understand the Jewish question particularly as a special case of the problem of "prejudice." Gordon W. Allport's *The Nature of Prejudice* (1953) influenced such views, and in particular the research sponsored by the Anti-Defamation League. Such investigations promote an understanding of part of the problem but not of the problem as a whole, because they do not pay sufficient attention to the special nature of the Jewish question, particularly the dimension of its historical depth. Concerning the criticism of these investigations, cf. Isaak Frank's dissertation "The Concept of Human Nature: A Philosophical Analysis of the Concept of Human Nature in the Writings of G. W. Allport, S. E. Asch, Erich Fromm, A. H. Maslow, and C. R. Rogers": "The image of man propounded by the group of writers under discussion . . . is shown to be less a product of descriptive, empirical research, and more a result of their normative preconceptions, and related to the ethical and social doctrines exposed by them in their role as disguised moralists and social philosophers" (*Dissertation Abstracts* 27:4, 1966).

Cf. also Ruth Benedict, *Patterns of Culture* (Pelican Books, 1946), 13f.): "We must accept all the implications of our human inheritance, one of the most important of which is the small scope of biologically transmitted behavior and the enormous role of the cultural process of the transmission of tradition." Note also p. 217: "Cultural interpretations of behavior need never deny that a physiological element is also involved."

24 HISTORY: Cf. Herbert Schade, "Der Mensch vor dem Geheimnis: Zum Menschenbild der modernen Malerei," *Stimmen der Zeit*, December 1966, 438: "Anyone who shrinks from the arduous road through history runs the risk of piling up word shells without penetrating to reality. Man is a historical being; therefore his works and man himself are incomprehensible without history."

25ff. NUMBER AND DISSEMINATION OF THE JEWS: "History without demography"— Salo W. Baron quotes this formulation by the Spanish sociologist Xavier Ruiz Almanza at the beginning of his comprehensive article "Population" (*EJJ* 13:866–903) in which he sums up the results of his own research and that of others on Jewish population movements in the course of history. For recent times see the articles by U. O. Schmelz, "Demography" (*EJJ* 5:1493–1521), "Vital Statistics" (*EJJ* 16:177–90), and "Migrations" (*EJJ* 16:1518–29). The standard works on the problems of Jewish demography and statistics are still those of Arthur Ruppin (1876–1943): his book *Juden der Gegenwart*, first published in 1904, which actually established Jewish demography and statistics as a subject of research, particularly his two-volume *Soziologie der Juden* (Berlin 1931–32), and *Jewish Fate and Future* (London, 1940). Concerning him see the introduction to my edition of his *Memoirs, Diaries, Letters* (Jerusalem, 1971) and my essay in *LBYB* 17 (1972). Regarding current research on Jewish demography and statistics, cf. U. O. Schmelz and P. Glikson, eds., *Jewish Population Studies 1961–1968* (Jerusalem and London, 1970) and the critical "Selected Bibliography 1961–1968" contained therein. Concerning the historical development, cf. Bruno Blau, "Sociology and Statistics of the Jews," *Historia Judaica* 11 (1949): 145–62. A comprehensive survey of the Diaspora of the present may be found in the books of Jacob Lestschinsky (1876–1966), the pioneer of Jewish sociology, particularly *European Jewry Ten Years after the War* (New York, 1956) and *Ha-pesura ha-yehudit* (The Jewish Diaspora, Jerusalem, 1961) as well as in Jehuda Tubin's Hebrew study of the Jewish question in the 1960s (Merhavia, 1968) and Moché Catane's *Les Juifs dans le monde* (Paris, 1962). Concerning the influence of World War II on the demography of the Jewish people, cf. the Hebrew dissertation of C. S. Halevi (Jerusalem, 1963, with an English summary on pp. 4–32). The most comprehensive book about Jewish demography, past and present, dealing especially with Israel but also with the Diaspora, is Roberto Bachi's *The Population of Israel* (Jerusalem, 1977).

The latest data about the number and dissemination of the Jews, based on official statistics, inquiries, and estimates, may be found in the *American Jewish Year Book*. Slightly different data are contained in *The Jewish Communities of the World: Demography, Political and Organizational Status, Religious Institutions, Education, Press*, 3d rev. ed. (London: World Jewish Congress, 1971). The best survey of the situation of the Jews in the mid-1930s may be found in Mark Wischnitzer, *Die Juden in der Welt: Gegenwart und Geschichte des Judentums in allen Ländern* (Berlin, 1935). Cf also Ernest Levy's informative essay about present-day Jewry in *L'Arche* (Paris), 25 February 1971, 46–49, and Moshe Davis, *The Jewish People in Metamorphosis* (Syracuse, 1963). Concerning the situation of the Jews before the beginning of the great overseas migrations, cf. Richard Andree, *Zur Volkskunde der Juden* (Leipzig, 1881).

THE MIGRATIONS OF THE JEWS: W. W. Kaplun-Kogan's *Die Wanderungen der Juden*   29ff.
(Bonn, 1913) is a pioneer study of this problem. Concerning migrations in general, their nature and their significance, see Alexander and Eugen Kulischer, *Kriegs- und Wanderzüge: Weltgeschichte als Völkerbewegung* (Berlin, 1932). On p. 36 Kulischer quotes from Franz Oppenheimer's *Soziologie* 1 (1923), 769: "The entire history of the world is basically the history of migrations." Also cf. Aryeh Tartakower, *Ha'adam ha-noded* (Migrating man) (Tel Aviv, 1954). Concerning the Jewish migratory movement, see B. Kirschner and J. Traub, "Wanderungen der Juden," *JL* 5: 1295–1322; Jacob Lestschinsky, *Nedudei Yisrael* (Jewish migrations) (Jerusalem, 1945); Zvi Rudi, *Soziologie des jüdischen Volkes* (Hamburg, 1965), 31–54; Eugene M. Kulischer, *Jewish Migrations: Past Experiences and Postwar Prospects* (New York, 1943); and Mark Wischnitzer's comprehensive study *To Dwell in Safety: The Story of Jewish Migration since 1800* (Philadelphia, 1948). Maps of the migration may be found especially in Martin Gilbert, *Jewish History Atlas* (London, 1969).

2
Foundations and Conditions: Jews and Environment in Ancient Times

The literature on the Jewish question in general and this period in particular is so extensive and multilayered that only a small selection can be given—especially what was particularly useful to the author and might aid the reader's further investigation and reflection. In some instances, what has been said in the text will be supplemented or nuanced, but we shall not go into details of the views expressed in the literature, which is often based only on suppositions. In most instances there is no special mention of the big, generally known historical works and encyclopedias, though they have of course been constantly consulted.

32ff. DIASPORA, THE WORD AND THE CONCEPT: Cf. *EJ* 5:1088ff., *EJJ* 6:7ff. In the glossary of *The Legacy of Israel* (Oxford, 1927), 525 and also in Greek dictionaries, e.g., the *Greek-English Lexicon* by H. G. Liddell and R. Scott, new rev. ed. (Oxford, 1940), 1:412, it is pointed out that the Greek word Diaspora in the sense of "dispersion of the Jews among the nations" was first used in the Septuagint, the Greek Bible translation that was prepared in the third century before the Common Era, probably for the use and under the influence of the great Jewish settlement in Alexandria. In this first translation of the Bible into a European language the Hebrew word *sa'ava* (from a stem meaning "move," "shake," and "scare off") in Moses' threat of curses for nonobservance of the biblical commandments (Deut. 28:25) was translated as "Diaspora," i.e., dispersal among the nations, which harmonized with the preceding words about flight from enemies as well as the succeeding verses about dispersal. This meaning in the Greek version of the Bible, which later became the official one for the Christians, was taken over by the Vulgate, the Latin translation of the Bible prepared by St. Jerome around 400 (*"et dispergaris per omnia regni terrae"*) and passed from these two official Christian versions of the Old Testament into almost all later Christian Bible translations, such as Luther's into German and the King James version in English. Strangely enough, the Jewish-Hebrew tradition here differs from the (Judeo-)Greek one, interpreting the word to mean something like "horror." What Luther translates as *"und wirst zerstreut werden unter alle Reiche auf Erden"* Moses Mendelssohn renders as *"und wirst allen Reichen auf Erden zum Entsetzen werden"* (and you shall become a horror to all the kingdoms on earth—the wording of the new Torah translation of the Jewish Publication Society of America, 1962). Martin Buber uses the word *Popanz* (bugaboo). The most important Jewish Bible commentator, R. Shlomo Yitzhaki (called Rashi, 1040–1105), whom Mendelssohn cites approvingly in his commentary, explains the Hebrew word as follows: "(You will become) a fright and a shock, so that all who hear about your blows will be aghast at you and say, May nothing befall us that has come over them." The two very dissimilar traditions of this word later somehow coalesced in the Hebrew word that is actually used in the Judeo-Hebrew tradition for the word Diaspora, which has become part of common linguistic usage: *galut* in the sense of exile or *golah*. Concerning the origin and meaning of this word and concept, cf. Meyer Waxmann, *Galut ugeulah besifrut Yisrael* (Exile and redemption in Jewish literature, New York, 1952) as well as the detailed review of this book in the Hebrew monthly *Bitzaron* (New York) 27:(1952):124–128, and the pertinent articles (with bibliographies) in the Jewish encyclopedias, esp. *HE* 10:812ff. and *EJJ* 7:275ff.

BEGINNING OF THE DIASPORA: Though the Jewish tradition took cognizance of the   32
existence of Jewish communities outside Palestine even before the downfall of the State, it regards the destruction of the Temple of Jerusalem and the state of Judea by Titus as the real beginning of the Diaspora, which it calls *golah* or *galut* (banishment, exile). On the other hand, in the popular consciousness this first destruction and banishment, which fifty years later was succeeded by a return, assumed more the character of a temporary misfortune and a historical episode. Later the two destructions of the Temple somehow coalesced in the people's consciousness: they were given the same date and annually observed on the ninth day of Av as a day of mourning and fasting. Particularly in recent generations there has been no dearth of severe self-criticism among the Jews, according to which the exile was blamed on the Jews' readiness to leave their devastated country and disperse themselves over the world. Cf. M. J. bin Gorion (Berdyczewski), *Vom östlichen Judentum* (Berlin, 1918), 72 and Hugo Bergman, *Jawne und Jerusalem* (Berlin, 1919), 34ff., "Das zionistische Problem bei Berdyczewski"). Cf. also chap. 11 in Part 1.

NUMBERS OF DEPORTEES AND REMIGRANTS FROM BABYLONIA: Like all statistics from   33
ancient times and the Middle Ages, the statements about this in the Bible and in victory steles must always be subjected to critical examination. Hence their interpretation in modern literature fluctuates. In contrast to various other estimates, I essentially base myself on the conclusions in the chapters "Das Ende des Reiches Israel" and "Exil und Rückkehr" of Elias Auerbach's fine pioneering study *Wüste und Gelobtes Land* (Berlin, 1936), vol. 2, pp. 90ff. and 223ff. On p. 24 he writes: "If we assume that the Judean *golah* of initially 45,000 souls had in the meantime doubled and the Israelite one of around 35,000 had tripled, about a third of the Judeans and around one-tenth of the Israelites participated in the return. The number of the returnees was about 42,000 (or 50,000, if one counts the slaves)."
We have only very little direct information about the Jewish settlement in Babylonia. After all, even Flavius Josephus was only a historian who lived five hundred years later—that is, as far removed from that period as we are from the Middle Ages, but without the systematic collection and examination of contemporaneous sources that we have at our disposal for that age.

NUMBER OF JEWS IN THE DIASPORA: Concerning the sources for the statistical   34ff.
estimates and their evaluation, cf. Salo W. Baron, *A Social and Religious History of the Jews*, 3:33f. (2d ed., 1:370ff.) and *EJJ* 13:864–72. Cf. also the more conservative estimates in A. Ruppin, *Soziologie der Juden*, 1:67ff., "Palästina und Diaspora." A good survey may be found in Meir Waxmann's Hebrew essay on Eretz Yisrael and the Diaspora in the epoch of the Second Temple in *Ausgewählte Schriften* 1 (New York, 1943), pp. 215–45, including sources, the best-known of which are the writings of Flavius Josephus and the reports of Philo. A new edition of the latter is Philo of Alexandria, *Von den Machterweisen Gottes: Eine zeitgenössische Darstellung der Judenverfolgungen unter dem Kaiser Caligula*, trans., ed., and with an introd. by Hans Jochanan Lewy (Berlin: Schocken Bücherei, 1935). Our quotation is from that edition. The most comprehensive presentation of this entire epoch is Emil Schuerer,

Geschichte des Volkes Israel im Zeitalter Jesu Christi (Leipzig, 1886–90). The most extensive source material is contained in *Textes d'auteurs grecs et romains relatifs au Judaisme*, gathered, translated, and annotated by Theodore Reinach (Paris, 1895). An expanded collection of the Greek and Latin sources in English translation and with English commentary is being sponsored by the Israel Academy of Sciences and Humanistics, under the title *Greek and Latin Authors on Jews and Judaism*. Volume 1, *From Herodotus to Plutarch*, ed. Menahem Stern, appeared in Jerusalem in 1974. Cf. also I. Elbogen, *Die Feier der Wallfahrtsfeste im zweiten Tempel*, 46. Bericht der Hochschule für die Wissenschaft des Judentums (Berlin, 1929), 27–46. More recent literature is contained in the second edition of the study by Baron, whose stupendous erudition cannot be surpassed, even though some readers will not always agree with his conclusions. Cf. also S. Appelbaum's collection of Hebrew lectures on the Mediterranean in the history of Israel and the world, Jerusalem, 1930, pp. 49–56.

35   NAME OF THE COUNTRY (JUDEA, ERETZ YISRAEL, PALESTINE): *HE* 6:25–222228; *EJJ* 9:107–12. First use of the word Palestine to designate the country in 139: Baron (2d ed., 2:380), after A. Shalit, *Hamishtar Haromai B'Etetz Yisrael* (Roman rule in the Land of Israel) (1937), 12ff.

36   DATE OF THE DESTRUCTION OF THE TEMPLE AND FAST DAY: Best modern summary in *EJJ* 3:936–40.

36ff.   EVALUATION OF THE DESTRUCTION OF THE TEMPLE FOR JEWISH HISTORY: Franz Rosenzweig, *Kleinere Schriften* (Berlin, 1937), 12–15 (quotation on p. 23). Theodor Mommsen's presentation in vol. 4 of his *Römische Geschichte* is still of fundamental importance. For its evaluation and correction of a number of concepts and the like, the afterword by Eugen Täubler, an expert on both Roman and Jewish history, is worth reading. It appeared in the reprint of the chapter "Judäa und die Juden" (Berlin: Schocken-Bücherei, 1936). Cf. also Max Dienemann, "Galut," in *Der Morgen* 4 (1928): 325–34.

36   THE DISCUSSION ABOUT THE BEGINNING OF THE DIASPORA: In my text I summarize the opinions of various authors. Fundamental for the discussion: Benzion Dinur, *Yisrael Ba-Golah* (Israel in exile) (Tel Aviv, 1926, 1958), Introduction; Yitzhak F. Baer, *Yisrael Ba-amin* (Israel among the nations) (Jerusalem, 1955). Cf. also Baer's Hebrew essay on "Jerusalem in the Time of the Great Revolt: Based on the Source Criticism of Josephus and Talmudic-Midrashic Legends of the Temple Destruction," in *Zion* 36, nos. 3/4:1270140 (Eng. synopsis, p. 1). Cf. also this radically deprecatory remark of Cecil Roth in *A Short History of the Jewish People*, ill. ed. (London, 1948), 110: "Contrary to what is generally imagined, the fall of Jerusalem was an episode in the history of the Jewish people, rather than the close of an epoch." By contrast, we have the evaluation of Titus himself, who, according to Flavius Josephus (*The Jewish Way*, 7:5, 2), responded to the request by the citizens of Antiochia for his approval to expel the Jews from the city by saying that was impossible because the destruction of their metropolis had rendered them homeless. Cf. also the remarks made by Theodor Herzl, the founder of political Zionism, in an address to Viennese Jews in 1896, the year in which his *Jewish State* appeared ("Judaism," in Herzl's *Zionist Writings: Essays and Addresses*, vol. 1 [New York, 1973], 45): "You know that our history, the history of the Diaspora, began in the year 70 after the birth of Christ. The military campaign of Titus, which Mommsen describes as the cause of the spread of Christianity and which ended with the Jews being carried off as captive slaves, is the actual beginning of that part of Jewish history which concerns us closely, for we are still

suffering frm the consequences of those events. . . . The effects of this captivity have
been felt for sixty generations. . . ."

THE JEWS AND THE SURROUNDING WORLD BEFORE THE DESTRUCTION OF THE 40ff.
JEWISH STATE: In addition to the abovementioned sources and accounts of Jewish
history and the Jewish Diaspora in antiquity: J. Heinemann's *Antisemitismus* [*im
Altertum*] is still a standard reference (reprinted from Pauly-Wissowa, *Real-En-
cyclopädie der classischen Altertumswissenschaft*, Supplement 6, col. 3–43), though
the use of the concept "Antisemitismus" seems anachronistic to me. A concise
summary of the basic ideas in this essay may be found in Heinemann's article
"Ursprung und Wesen des Antisemitismus im Altertum," *Festgabe zum zehnjährigen
Bestehen der Akademie für die Wissenschaft des Judentums 1919–1929* (Berlin,
1929), 76–91. Other basic works: Ralph Marcus, "Antisemitism in the Hellenistic-
Roman World," in Koppel S. Pinson, ed., *Essays on Antisemitism* (New York, 1946),
61–78; Johann Maier, "Die religiös motivierte Judenfeindschaft 1. Aus Missdeutung
des jüdischen Selbstverständnisses," in Karl Thieme, ed., *Judenfeindschaft* (1963),
22–47; J. Bernfeld, "Griechische und römische Schriftsteller über Juden und Judentum," in *EJ* 7:662–80; Michael Guttmann, *Das Judentum und seine Umwelt: Eine
Darstellung der religiösen und rechtlichen Beziehunger zwischen Juden und Nicht-
juden mit besonderer Berücksichtigung der talmudisch-rabbinischen Quellen*
(Berlin, 1927). For the Hellenistic period, particularly in Egypt, see Avigdor
Tcherikover, *Ha-yehudim batekufa ha-hellenistit* (Jerusalem, 1931); "Ha-Antishemiut
ba-Olam ha-atik," in *Molad* (1958): 361; and *Hellenistic Civilization and the Jews*
(1959). A. Tcherikover and A. Fuks, eds., *Corpus Papyrorum Judaicarum*, 1–3
(1960–64) contains a documentation of the situation of the Jews in Hellenistic Egypt
as well as excellent introductions and notes by the editors. Cf. also Angelo Segré,
"The Status of the Jews in Roman Egypt: New Light from the Papyri," in *Jewish
Social Studies*, October 1944, 375–99.

PERIOD OF THE MACCABEES AND THE UPRISING AGAINST HELLENISM: A basic work is 41
Elias Bickermann, *The Maccabees* (New York, 1947). The rebellion of the Maccabees
against Hellenism and, as Bickermann shows, their subsequent adoption of many
elements from it when they assumed control was, as Y. F. Baer has pointed out,
something completely new and thus a world-historical event despite the small size of
the territory involved. Whether one evaluates it positively or negatively, this was the
beginning of the struggle for ways of faith, of self-sacrifice and martyrdom for the sake
of a faith. Without the victorious fight of the Maccabees there might be no monotheistic faith today.

"*UNHEIMLICH*": The connection between the "uncanny" and the "alien" may be 41
discerned in many other languages as well. For European languages, cf. Sigmund
Freud's essay on "The Uncanny" (originally published as "Das Unheimliche" in
Imago 5 [1919]). This connection exists in Hebrew, too *(Sar-Musar)*. Cf. also the
instructive remarks about "Das Unheimliche" and "Das Besondere" in Wilhelm
Lange-Eichbaum and Wolfram Hurth, *Genie, Irrsinn und Ruhm* (1967), 110–25 and
about "Mischungen und Gefühlsakkorde" (mixtures of positive and negative feelings)
and "Das Numinose" (the numinous) on pp. 125–36 of the same work, which also
contains an informative bibliography.

ORIGIN OF THE JEWS; APION, MANETHO, ETC.: Heinemann, "Antisemitismus," 26f. 41f.
and 33ff.; *EJJ* 2:959ff. The most important source is Josephus's *Contra Apionem*
(Against Apion); other sources may be found in Reinach. A basic work for the Roman

viewpoint is Jean Juster, *Les juifs dans l'empire romain*, 2 vols. (Paris, 1914). The German-Jewish scholar Hans Jochanan Lewy, who died young, produced an important comprehensive investigation, "Ha-yehudim le-or ha-Safrut ha-Romit" (The Jews in the light of Roman literature), in *Zion* 7–8 (1943), reprinted in the Hebrew collection of Lewy's essays on the position of the Jews in the Greco-Roman world, which appeared posthumously under the title *Olamot Nifgashim* (The encounter between worlds) (Jerusalem, 1960); pp. 79–203 deal with Cicero's and Tacitus's views of the Jews. Other important works: J. Heinemann, "Hayehudiam be-einay ha-olam ha-atik" (The Jews in the eyes of the ancient world), in *Zion* 4:269–93; E. Bickermann, "Ritualmord und Eselskult," in *Monatsschrift für Geschichte und Wissenschaft des Judentums* (1927): 173ff. The biblical Book of Esther (which probably came into being at the time of the Maccabees), with its apocryphal supplements, has Haman, the enemy of the Jews, present some of the accusations that the gifted Jewish author of the book had derived from the Greek world around him.

41 RITUAL ACTIONS: In general, people disregard the extent to which public life in the ancient world was pervaded by cultic actions—from the sacrifices to the oracles and the interpretation of signs by the augurs before every important official action in war and peacetime—and to what extent anyone who shunned such actions and the attendant meals was bound to inspire mistrust and repugnance. Cf. Ludwig Friedländer, *Sittengeschichte Roms* (Phaidon edition), 854ff, and especially N. D. Fustel de Coulanges, *The Ancient City: A Study on the Religion, Laws and Institutions of Greece and Rome* (New York, 1956), chap. 12, "The Citizen and the Stranger": "The citizen was recognized by the fact that he had a part in the religion of the city, and it was from this participation that he derived all his civil and political rights. . . . The stranger . . . is one who has no access to the worship, one whom the gods of the city do not protect. . . ." (pp. 193f.) Despite the skepticism of the intellectuals the religious foundation was always preserved among the people and in the civil service. Even a Tacitus regards it as a self-evident premise and as the basis for his evaluation of the Jews.

42 CHOSENNESS OF THE JEWS: The Jews' belief in their "chosenness" by God has given rise to numerous misunderstandings. From ancient times to recent days non-Jews have often interpreted it as unfounded arrogance and even as a claim to world dominion. In their best human representatives and in the authoritative literature—Deut. 7:6ff. and 14:2 are of fundamental importance—the Jews have understood this belief as a boon and as an obligation to lead a pure life, to "sanctify" life in the spirit of a divine mission, to love and be just to their neighbors; God's covenant *(brith)* with the Jewish people was interpreted in this spirit. Of course, since the Jews were as human as anyone else, some of them interpreted this "chosenness" in an almost superstitious way, regarding it as an absolute safeguard against any danger. The prophets already opposed such popular interpretations, as did all responsible spiritual and secular leaders over the ages. On the other hand, this popular belief in chosenness "became the strongest support in times of need" (*EJ* 3:701).

Concerning this problematic concept and the variegated literature on this question, cf. *JL* 1:575ff. and *EJJ* 5:498–502. *EJJ* defines the concept as follows: "Chosen People, a common designation for the people of Israel, expressing the idea that the people of Israel stands in a special and unique relationship to the universal deity. This idea has been a central one throughout the history of Jewish thought: it is deeply rooted in biblical concepts, and has been developed in Talmudic, philosophic, mystical and contemporary Judaism." Cf. also Leo Baeck's books *Das Wesen des Judentums* (Frankfurt a.M., 1922) and *Dieses Volk: Jüdische Existenz* (Frankfurt a.M., 1955); Isidore Epstein, *The Faith of Judaism: An Interpretation for Our Times* (London,

1954), chap. 14; and the writings of Franz Rosenzweig, which contain an interpretation free from apologetic tendencies. Concerning the position of Jewish theology since Moses Mendelssohn on the problem of chosenness, cf. Arthur Hertzberg, "The Secularity of Israel's Election," *Judaism* 13:4, 387, 392. Cf. also David Baumgardt's fine remarks on the Jewish "Grace after Meals" in *Commentary*, July 1946, 15–19. It may be pertinent to state here that any consecration and separation are ambivalent by nature. Among persons of a higher level their substance and significance are understood as an obligation and humility, but among the masses this is all too apt to turn into nothing but undue self-confidence, presumptuousness, and arrogance. Since the latter usually have more daily contact with the surrounding world, this cruder view then becomes the point of depature for equally crude reactions.

It has rightly been pointed out that every people regards itself as chosen (concerning primitive cultures, cf. Ruth Benedict, *Patterns of Culture* [1946], 7), and philosophers of history since Voltaire, Herder, and Hegel have attempted to present the history of this chosenness and unique world-historical mission. In general, the philosophers of history have clung to this view of the singularity of the mission and chosenness: Once the world-historical task has been completed, the people has finished its role. The Jewish idea of chosenness, however, transcends these historical traditions; the sanctification of life demanded by it is interpreted as an eternal assignment and includes segregation; in Hebrew, being holy also means being set apart. It is in this sense that the word is understood by God and by the Jews as human beings (cf., e.g., Lev. 19:2). The much-discussed curse-blessing of Balaam, the son of Beor, must be viewed in light of this commandment of loneliness (Num. 23:9): "There is a people that dwells apart, not reckoned among the nations" (*The Torah* [Jewish Publication Society of America, 1962]. The *Jerusalem Bible* has a similar wording. Kautzsch, Luther, and Mendelssohn used the word *Heiden*, i.e., heathens). A public discussion about "Israel among the Nations" which took place in Jerusalem in recent years used Balaam's words as one of its points of departure. Among the participants were David Ben-Gurion, Prof. Ernst A. Simon, E. S. Rimalt, Prof. A. Rubinstein, and Rabbi J. Rabinowitz, and the Proceedings appeared in *Dispersion and Unity* 15–16, Jerusalem, 1982.

Of course, the commandments of segregation were always based on the fear that the Jews might adopt heathen customs and be alienated from their monotheistic faith. Cf. *JL* 1:1402–1404 (*Hukkot Hagoyim*, the precepts or customs of the nations). Concerning the influence of the idea of singularity and chosenness among the Greeks and the Jews, cf. Hans Kohn, *Nationalism: Its Meaning and History* (Princeton, 1955), 11ff.:

> The roots of modern nationalism spring from the same soil as Western civilization: from the ancient Hebrews and the ancient Greeks. Both peoples had a clearly defined consciousness of being different from all other peoples: the Hebrews from the Gentiles, the Greeks from the Barbarians. The bearer of group consciousness was with them not king or priesthood but the people as a whole, every Hebrew or every Greek. . . . Three essential traits of modern nationalism originated with the Hebrews: the idea of the chosen people, the emphasis on a common stock of memory of the past and of hopes for the future, and finally national messianism. . . . The Greeks shared with the Hebrews the feeling of cultural and spiritual superiority over all other peoples. . . . In addition the Greeks developed the concept of supreme loyalty to the political community. . . . Sparta in ancient Greece and Plato in his *Republic* postulated the absolute precedence of the state over the individual. . . .

TACITUS: Here we shall reprint what Tacitus says about the Jews in his *History* before he describes Titus's campaign against them and the destruction of Jerusalem (*The Complete Works of Tacitus*, trans. A. J. Church and W. J. Brodribb, [New York: Modern Library, 1942], 657–60):   42f.

2. As I am about to relate the last days of a famous city it seems appropriate to throw some light on its origin.

Some say that the Jews were fugitives from the island of Crete, who settled on the nearest coast of Africa about the time when Saturn was driven from his throne by the power of Jupiter. Evidence of this is sought in the name. There is a famous mountain in Crete called Ida; the neighbouring tribe, the Idaei, came to be called Judaei by a barbarous lengthening of the national name. Others assert that in the reign of Isis the overflowing population of Egypt, led by Hierosolymus and Judas, discharged itself into the neighbouring countries. Many, again, say that they were a race of Ethiopian origin, who in the time of king Cepheus were driven by fear and hatred of their neighbours to seek a new dwelling-place. Others describe them as an Assyrian horde who, not having sufficient territory, took possession of part of Egypt, and founded cities of their own in what is called the Hebrew country, lying on the borders of Syria. Others, again, assign a very distinguished origin to the Jews, alleging that they were the Solymi, a nation celebrated in the poems of Homer, who called the city which they founded Hierosolyma after their own name.

3. Most writers, however, agree in stating that once a disease, which horribly disfigured the body, broke out over Egypt; that king Bocchoris, seeking a remedy, consulted the oracle of Hammon, and was bidden to cleanse his realm, and to convey into some foreign land this race detested by the gods. The people, who had been collected after diligent search, finding themselves left in a desert, sat for the most part in a stupor of grief, till one of the exiles, Moyses by name, warned them not to look for any relief from God or man, forsaken as they were of both, but to trust to themselves, taking for their heaven-sent leader that man who should first help them to be quit of their present misery. They agreed, and in utter ignorance began to advance at random. Nothing, however, distressed them so much as the scarcity of water, and they had sunk ready to perish in all directions over the plain, when a herd of wild asses was seen to retire from their pasture to a rock shaded by trees. Moyses followed them, and, guided by the appearance of a grassy spot, discovered an abundant spring of water. This furnished relief. After a continuous journey for six days, on the seventh they possessed themselves of a country, from which they expelled the inhabitants, and in which they founded a city and a temple.

4. Moyses, wishing to secure for the future his authority over the nation, gave them a novel form of worship, opposed to all that is practised by other men. Things sacred with us, with them have no sanctity, while they allow what with us is forbidden. In their holy place they have consecrated an image of the animal by whose guidance they found deliverance from their long and thirsty wanderings. They slay the ram, seemingly in derision of Hammon, and they sacrifice the ox, because the Egyptians worship it as Apis. They abstain from swine's flesh, in consideration of what they suffered when they were infected by the leprosy to which this animal is liable. By their frequent fasts they still bear witness to the long hunger of former days, and the Jewish bread, made without leaven, is retained as a memorial of their hurried seizure of corn. We are told that the rest of the seventh day was adopted, because this day brought with it a termination of their toils; after a while the charm of indolence beguiled them into giving up the seventh year also to inaction. But others say that it is an observance in honour of Saturn, either from the primitive elements of their faith having been transmitted from the Idaei, who are said to have shared the flight of that God, and to have found the race, or from the circumstance that of the seven stars which rule the destinies of men Saturn moves in the highest orbit and with the mightiest power, and that many of the heavenly bodies complete their revolutions and courses in multiples of seven.

5. This worship, however introduced, is upheld by its antiquity; all their other customs, which are at once perverse and disgusting, owe their strength to their very badness. The most degraded out of other races, scorning their national beliefs, brought to them their contributions and presents. This augmented the wealth of the Jews, as also did the fact, that among themselves they are inflexibly honest and ever ready to shew compassion, though they regard the rest of mankind with all the hatred of enemies. They sit apart at meals, they sleep apart, and though, as a nation, they are singularly prone to lust, they abstain from intercourse with foreign women; among themselves nothing is unlawful. Circumcision was adopted by them as a mark of difference from other men. Those who come over to their religion adopt the practice, and have this lesson first instilled into them, to despise all gods, to disown their country, and set at nought parents, children, and brethren. Still they provide for the increase

of their numbers. It is a crime among them to kill any newly-born infant. They hold that the souls of all who perish in battle or by the hands of the executioner are immortal. Hence a passion for propagating their race and a contempt for death. They are wont to bury rather than to burn their dead, following in this the Egyptian custom; they bestow the same care on the dead and they hold the same belief about the lower world. Quite different is their faith about things divine. The Egyptians worship many animals and images of monstrous form; the Jews have purely mental conceptions of Deity, as one in essence. They call those profane who make representations of God in human shape out of perishable materials. They believe that Being to be supreme and eternal, neither capable of representation, nor of decay. They therefore do not allow any images to stand in their cities, much less in their temples. This flattery is not paid to their kings, nor this honour to our Emperors. From the fact, however, that their priests used to chant to the music of flutes and cymbals, and to wear garlands of ivy, and that a golden vine was found in the temple, some have thought that they worshipped Father Liber, the conqueror of the East, though their institutions do not by any means harmonize with the theory; for Liber established a festive and cheerful worship, while the Jewish religion is tasteless and mean.

The great influence of Tacitus on the historiography of the Enlightenment is demonstrated, *inter alia*, by Gibbon's *Decline and Fall of the Roman Empire*, vol. 1, chap. 15.

THE NATIONAL BREAKDOWN IN THE EYES OF THE SURROUNDING WORLD: For the   43ff.
general view of the ancient world "that the political defeat . . . was evidence of the inferiority of the people and the impotence of its god" (*EJ* 2:969) cf. Cicero in his defense of the Roman proconsul Flaccus, who had been accused of enriching himself by stealing temple funds: "*Quam cara illa gens dies immortalibus esset, docuit, quod victa, quod elocata, quod serra facta*" ("the value placed on that people by the immortal gods is indicated by the fact that it was vanquished, obliged to pay tribute, and enslaved") (following Pompey's conquest of Jerusalem).

VICTORY COINS "JUDAEA CAPTA": For depictions of all the abovementioned victory   44f.
coins in honor of Vespasian and Titus, see *EJJ* 5:713f.; some may be found in Adolf Reifenberg, *Denkmäler der jüdischen Antike* (Berlin, 1927), plate 24. A good illustration of the coin with the captured, bound warrior sitting under a fig tree is included in *Geography*, Israel Pocket Library, (Jerusalem: Keter, 1973), 6. Concerning the concepts *triumphus* and *triumphator*, cf. Hans Lamer, *Wörterbuch der Antike* (1959), 811f.; H. S. Versnel, *Triumphus: An Inquiry into the Origin, Development, and Meaning of the Roman Triumph* (London, 1970).

FISCUS JUDAICUS (TAX ON JEWS): For literature on the subject, see *EJJ* 6:1325;   45
Baron, 2d ed., 2:105ff., 373f.; Guido Kisch, *The Jews in Medieval Germany* (Chicago, 1949), 154ff., 165. The *Fiscus Judaicus* differed from taxes levied on other subjugated peoples in that this tax was collected not only from the Jews of Palestine but also from Jews living in any part of the Roman Empire. Cf. S. Zeitlin's review of Tcherikover's (Hebrew) book on the Jews of Egypt in the Hellenistic-Roman period in the light of papyrology (1945) in *Jewish Quarterly Review* 37:91: "Vespasian levied this tax on the Jews not to rebuild the temple of Jupiter, but to demonstrate the triumph of Jupiter over the God of Israel. We know that when a people was conquered, the god was taken into captivity. Since Vespasian could not take the God of Israel into captivity, he ordered that the Jews, regardless of where they lived and no matter what their ethnic descent, should pay two drachmas to Jupiter as they used to pay to the God of Israel." A documentation for Egypt and an analysis of the Documents may be found in Tcherikover and Fuks, *Corpus*, 2:110–36.

46   ON THE EXPELLEES OF THE ISRAELITE NORTHERN EMPIRE: (Cf. *EJJ* 6:1134ff. ("Exile, Assyrian") and the literature given there. Concerning the legend of the "ten lost tribes" and the search for them, cf. *EJJ* 15:1003–6 ("Ten Lost Tribes"). Claims have been made that they, or some of them, have been spotted in all countries from Asia to America. To the Jews who maintained their identity (and to many Christians) it was simply inconceivable that they, like many other peoples or tribes, might have been largely absorbed by their countries of exile and migration.

46f.   NONMINGLING WITH THE NATIONS AS A FOUNDATION OF THE JEWISH QUESTION: This was pointed out by the geographer and ethnologist Richard Andree as early as 1884. Cf. his *Volkskunde der Juden*, 60f.: "In my view, the essence of all that used to be called Jew-hatred and is now called the Jewish question resides in the attitude of the Jews toward intermingling. Intermarriage between peoples living together is the rule; minorities that settled among larger different peoples were usually absorbed by them, amalgamated with them physically and hence spiritually as well. Not so the tribe of the Jews, which maintained itself among the nations at all times and in all places and segregated itself—because of its religion and possibly also out of a kind of inner reluctance—although since the dispersion it has proved incapable of forming an independent nation in the political sense [i.e., a state]."

47   JEWS IN WORLD HISTORIOGRAPHY: Cf. the series of (Hebrew) lectures about the history of Israel in the framework of world historiography ("Mekomam shel toldot Yisrael bemisgeret toldot ha-ammim") in the collection *Hartzaot bekinussei ha-ium ba-historia* (Lectures at the historical congress, Jerusalem 1933) as well as Hans Liebeschütz, *Das Judentum im deutschen Geschichtsbild von Hegel bis Max Weber* (Tübingen, 1967).

47f.   CONSEQUENCES OF THE BAR KOCHBA UPRISING: For a recent discussion of the prohibition for Jews to enter Jerusalem, cf. Mordechai Peron, "Issur ha-aliya l'yerushalayim bitekufat Romi" (Prohibition of a pilgrimage to Jerusalem in Roman times), *Ha'aretz*, 27 July 1973, 19. The prohibition is not mentioned in Talmudic sources. The most important source is the ecclesiastical history of Eusebius, who was born approximately 150 years after the Bar Kochba rebellion, when the prohibition was still in effect. General treatments may be found in the Jewish histories of Graetz, Dubnow, Baron, etc.

50   *"VIS INERTIAE"* (Meinecke): See my Hebrew essay "Pegisha im he'avar" (Encounter with the past) in *Raphael Mahler Jubilee Volume* (Merhavia, 1974), 211–18.

51   RELIGION, NATION, AND HOMELAND. HISTORICAL DEVELOPMENT OF THE PROBLEM: See the basic works of Yeheskel Kaufmann, especially *Gola venechar* (Exile and foreign lands) (Tel Aviv, 1929–30, new ed., 1954); Martin Buber, *Israel und Palästina. Zur Geschichte einer Idee*) (Zurich, 1950; new ed. Munich, 1968); *The Historical Connection of the Jewish People with Palestine: Memorandum Submitted to the Palestine Royal Commission on Behalf of the Jewish Agency for Palestine* (Jerusalem, 1936, 1938).

53   PROPHECY AS A NATIONALITY-PRESERVING ELEMENT: On page 25 of his book *Weltgechichte und Heilsgeschehen: Die theologischen Voraussetzungen der Geschichtsphilosophie* Karl Löwith voices agreement with Hermann Cohen's *Die Religion der Vernunft aus den Quellen des Judentums* (Leipzig, 1919):

The concept of history is a creation of prophetism. . . . It managed to do what Greek intellectualism had not been able to produce. In the Greek consciousness, "history" is tantamount to knowledge in general. For the Greeks, therefore, history always remained directed toward the past. A prophet, however, is a seer. . . . His vision produced the concept of history as the existence of the future. . . . The eschatological future replaced a golden age in a mythological past with the true historical existence on earth.

Cf. also p. 178:

The eternal law which the Greeks saw embodied in the regular movement of the visible sky was revealed for the Jews in the vicissitudes of their history, which deals with divine interventions. . . . When the Assyrian world power conquered the Near East, the prophets saw in the material downfall of Israel a direct manifestation of God's omnipotence rather than evidence of God's impotence. As far as Isaiah was concerned, Yahve rather than Baal triumphed when Juda fell. Assyria itself was only a tool in the hand of the God of Israel that he dropped as soon as his purpose had been attained. Precisely the catastrophes in the Jews' national history strengthened and spread their faith in the sovereignty of the divine will. God, who sets world empires in motion in order to execute his judgment, will equally be able to use them for liberation.

ON THE NATURE OF JEWISH MONOTHEISM, the antimythical view of God and its nonassimilation to the mythological world of the adjacent Near Eastern cultures, cf. H. and H. A. Frankfort et al. *Before Philosophy* (Penguin Books, 1949), 241ff.   53f.

ON THE NATURE AND INFLUENCE OF PROPHECY: Elias Auerbach, *Wüste und Gelobtes Land*, 2 vols. (Berlin, 1932–36); J. Wellhausen, *Israelitische und jüdische Geschichte* (Berlin, 1921).   53

DEMOCRATIZATION OF THE DOCTRINE OF GOD: Wellhausen, chap. 15.   54f.

PHARISEES: Cf. the beautiful and profound remarks in Leo Baeck's *Die Pharisäer: Ein Kapitel jüdischer Geschichte* (Berlin, 1934). For further literature on this subject see *EJJ* 13:366.   55

SAGES: E. E. Urbach, *The Sages, Their Concepts and Beliefs* (Jerusalem, 1969), and "Sages," *EJJ* 14:636–55.   55

THE COMMUNITY AND ITS NATIONAL-RELIGIOUS FUNCTION: S. Baron, *The Jewish Community, Its History and Structure* vol. 1 (Philadelphia, 1948), 62: "This was a truly epochal revolution, Building upon precedents . . . the exilic community shifted the emphasis from the place of worship, the sanctuary, to the gathering of worshippers, the congregation, assembled at any time and any place in God's wide world." S. Baron, *A Social and Religious History of the Jews* 2d ed., 1:134ff. ("Rethinking Fundamentals") Ismar Elbogen, *Der jüdische Gottesdienst in seiner geschichtlichen Entwicklung*, (1931), chap. 3 (on the reading and interpretation of the Bible).   55ff.

NONPARTICIPATION IN THE COMMON (RITUAL) MEALS: Cf. Fustel de Coulanges, *The Ancient City* (New York, 1956), 158: "Human association was a religion; its symbol was a meal, of which they partook together. . . . Neither interest, nor agreement, nor habit creates the social bond; it is the holy communion piously accomplished in the presence of the gods of the city."   56

TALMUD AND MESSIANISM: Of the extensive literature on the Talmud I shall mention only a few readily accessible items: Hermann Strack, *Einleitung in Talmud und*   57f.

Midrasch, 5th rev. ed. of *Einleitung in den Talmud* (Munich, 1931); S. Bernfeld, *Der Talmud, sein Wesen, seine Bedeutung und seine Geschichte* (Berlin, 1900); N. N. Glatzer, *Geschichte der talmudischen Zeit* (Berlin: Schocken Bücherei, 1937); Judah Goldin, "The Period of the Talmud," in *The Jews, Their History, Culture and Religion*, ed. Louis Finkelstein) (New York, 1949), 1:115–215.

Concerning the Messianic foundation, cf. particularly the essays of Yitzhak Baer in *Zion* (bibliography in *Yitzhak Baer Jubilee Volume* [in Hebrew, with English synopses] (Jerusalem, 1960) and Baer's Hebrew work *Israel among the Nations: An Essay on the History of the Period of the Second Temple and the Mishna and on the Foundations of the Halacha and Jewish Religion* (Jerusalem, 1955).

M. A. Tennenbaum, *Perakim Hadashim le-toldot Eretz Yisrael uvavel bitekufat ha-talmud* (new chapters on the history of Palestine and Babylonia in the Talmud epoch) (Tel Aviv, 1966), takes the view that the Babylonian center worked against the hegemony of the Palestinian center. Cf. the detailed review of this work in *Ha'aretz*, 19 May 1967.

60f. NATURE OF JEWISH MESSIANISM: Moritz Zobel, *Gottes Gesalbter: Der Messias und die Messianische Zeit in Talmud und Midrasch* (Berlin: Schocken Bücherei, 1938); Schuerer, 3d ed., 2:522ff.

It is remarkable that to the Talmudic teachers the present and its occurrences appeared so insignificant as compared to the doctrine and its interpretation for a life pleasing in the eyes of God that the events of their own time were not recorded and are hardly mentioned in the discussions. The discussions about the details of the ritual customs, sacrifices, synagogue functions, etc. become comprehensible if one considers the high valuation placed upon consecrated rituals in the ancient world. Concerning this, cf. Fustel de Coulanges, *The Ancient City* (New York, 1956), 157: "To deviate in the least from the usage followed in primitive times, to present a new dish or alter the rhythm of the sacred hymns was a grave impiety, for which the whole city was responsible to the gods."

61f. THE CONTINUATION OF THE JEWISH SETTLEMENT IN PALESTINE AND ITS GRADUAL DECAY: *Sefer Hayishov* (Book of settlement), 2 vols. (Jerusalem, 1939–44); General Council (Vaad Leumi) of the Jewish Community of Palestine: Three Historical Memoranda (*Number and Density of the Population of Ancient Palestine; The Jewish Population in Palestine from the Fall of the Jewish State to the Beginning of Zionist Pioneering; The Waves of Jewish Immigration into Palestine (640–1882—Submitted to the United Nations Special Committee on Palestine* (Jerusalem, 1947); Avi-Yona, *Geschichte der Juden im Zeitalter des Talmud* (Berlin, 1962).

62f. JUDAISM AND CHRISTIANITY: In addition to Schuerer, James Parkes's *The Conflict of the Church and the Synagogue: A Study in the Origins of Antisemitism* (London, 1934) is still a basic work. Cf. also the author's short study *A Reappraisal of the Christian Attitude to Judaism* (1962). Another important work is Marcel Simon's *Verus Israel: Etude sur les relations entre chrétiens et juifs dans l'empire romain* (Paris, 1948). For a good survey of the problems as well as bibliographic information, see *Kirche und Synagoge: Handbuch zur Geschichte von Christen und Juden. Darstellung mit Quellen*, ed. Karl Heinrich Rengstorf and Siegfried von Korkfleisch, vol. 1 (Stuttgart, 1968); and Karl Thieme, "Die religiös motivierte Judenfeindschaft," part 2, "Aus christlicher und mohammedanischer Sicht," in *Judenfeindschaft*, ed. Karl Thieme (Frankfurt, 1965), 48–79. A brief survey may be found in A. Cohen, *The Parting of the Ways: Judaism and the Rise of Christianity* (London, 1954). Cf. also the pertinent detailed articles in *JL, JE, EJ,* and *EJJ.* For the viewpoint of a "non-Christian" with a Christian upbringing, cf. the work of the well-known educator

Gustav Wyneken, *Abschied vom Christentum: Ein Nichtchrist befragt die Religionswissenschaft* (Munich, 1963; paperback ed., Reinbek bei Hamburg 1970).

REASONS FOR THE REJECTION OF CHRISTIANITY: A basic work in Yeheskel Kaufmann,   63ff.
Gola Venekhar (Exile and foreign lands) (Tel Aviv, 1920), vol. 1, book 2. A concise summary of the historical and above all the basic differences between Judaism and Christianity may be found in Trude Weiss-Rosmarin, *Judaism and Christianity: The Differences* (New York, 1943, 1965).

PRAYER AGAINST HERETICS AND CHRISTIANS: I. Elbogen, *Der jüdische Gottesdienst*   65
(1931), 36ff., 51f., 252ff., 518.

CRUCIFIXION OF JESUS: Not even a fraction of the enormous literature can be given   66f.
here. Instead, the reader is referred to the standard histories and the presentations and bibliographies of the encyclopedias (for the Jewish point of view, particularly *JL*, *EJ*, and *EJJ*). A work of the Jerusalem chief justice Haim Cohen may be mentioned as an important recent attempt to approach a solution of the problem by examining the sources from legal points of view: *The Trial and Death of Jesus* (London, 1972). This work also contains a discussion of recent literature on this question. A brief summary of the problems may be found in Fritz Bauer, "Der Prozess Jesu," *Tribüne. Zeitschrift zum Verständnis des Judentums* 4 (1965): 1710–22.

ON THE NATURE OF THE BIBLICAL TRADITION (OLD TESTAMENT) AND THE GOSPELS: 66
Regarding the reflection and shifting of the focal points in the events and their eventual recasting by the narrators setting them down in writing, see the revealing and perceptive investigation by Leo Baeck, *Das Evangelium als Urkunde der jüdischen Glaubensgeschichte* (Berlin: Schocken Bücherei, 1938).

PILATE: The contemporaneous quotation about Pilate is from Philo of Alexandria, *Von*   67
den Machterweisen Gottes: Eine zeitgenössische Darstellung der Judenverfolgungen unter dem Kaiser Caligula, ed., trans. and with an introd. by Hans Lewy. Berlin: Schocken Bücherei, 1935), 69f. The process of exculpation of the Romans and incrimination of the Jews was continued in the Middle Ages. Cf. Heinrich Loewe, *Die Juden in der Marienlegende* (Berlin, 1912), 63f., where a German church hymn from the thirteenth century is cited in which the piercing of the sides of the crucified Jesus by a Roman soldier (John 19:34) is transferred to a Jew.
     The extent to which belief in the innocence of Pilate and the guilt of the Jews is disseminated even today is indicated by the responses to an inquiry made by the University of California at Berkeley at the request of the Anti-Defamation League; cf. Charles Y. Glick and Rodney Stark, *Christian Beliefs and Anti-Semitism* (New York: Harper Torchbooks, 1969), 43ff.
     It is interesting, to say the least, how this sanitized image of Pilate in the Gospels is reflected in as critical an "anti-Christian" as Nietzsche. In Book 1 of his *Revaluation of All Values* ("The Antichrist") Pilate becomes "the only figure" in the New Testament "that must be honored," because he refuses "with the elegant mockery of a Roman . . . to take a Jewish deal seriously"; he had "enriched the New Testament with the early words of value—that are its own critique and destruction: 'What is truth?'" In his posthumously published aphorisms Nietzsche calls this skeptical statement "the greatest civility of all times."

THE BIBLE AS A WEAPON AGAINST THE JEWS: Above all, James Parkes's *The Conflict*   67f.
of the Church and the Synagogue (London, 1934). The quoted passage is on p. 106. Cf. Marcel Simon, *Verus Israel* (Paris, 1948).

68f.   THE JEW AS A SPAWN OF THE DEVIL AND ANTICHRIST: The chief source is J. Tra-
       chtenberg, *The Devil and the Jews* (Oxford, 1943; paperback ed., 1961). Cf. also
       Norman Cohn, *The Pursuit of the Millenium* (1957, paperback ed., 1962), 60f. On pp.
       394ff., James Parkes includes the text of confessions of Jews converting to Christianity
       in which they had to expressly renounce belief in the Antichrist, "whom all Jews
       expect in the shape and form of Christ." I shall have more to say about the signifi-
       cance of the Devil in the Christian picture of the world.

68f.   JUDAS: Concerning the further development of the figure of Judas into the mythical
       figure of the Jew in the Middle Ages, see Ludwig Feuchtwanger, "Die Gestalt des
       'Verworfenen Juden': Ein Versuch über Mythenbildung," in *Der Morgen* 11 (1933):
       310–16, a chapter of a larger work planned by Feuchtwanger that was to bear the title
       Judas: Die Verfemung eines Volkes. Cf. Max Gruenwald's essay about Ludwig Feucht-
       wanger in Leo Baeck Institute, *Year Book* 17 (1972), 75ff., esp. 90. Two examples may
       suffice to illustrate the continued effect of this figure as a symbol of the Jew and traitor
       down to our days. Theodor Herzl, the Paris correspondent of the Vienna *Neue Freie
       Presse* (and later the founder of political Zionism), reported that at the public
       degradation of the Jew Captain Dreyfus, who had been (wrongfully) accused of
       betraying his fatherland, a group of French officers shouted at him: "Judas! Traitor!"
       (cf. Alex Bein, *Theodore Herzl* [Philadelphia, 1962], 113). At a mass demonstration in
       Moscow in January 1937 the later Russian prime minister Nikita Khrushchev said:
       "Judas-Trotzky and his gang wanted to sell out the Ukraine as well as the Pacific and
       Amur regions to the German and Japanese imperialists." Cf. L. Pistrak, *Chrustschow
       und die Trotzkisten* (Stuttgart, 1972) (here quoted after *Ausfahrt*, house organ of the
       Deutsche Verlags-Anstalt, Stuttgart, [Fall 1962], 10).

69   "A CONTINUED CRUCIFIXION OF CHRIST": The quotation is from a lecture on the
       "Parable of the Three Rings" by the German historian Bernhard Erdmannsdörfer
       (1833–1901), and I noted it down when I put his papers in order at the Deutsches
       Reichsarchiv in Potsdam in the early 1930s. I do not know whether this lecture has
       appeared in print or whether the manuscript survived the fire at the Reichsarchiv.
       Here is the complete sentence: "In the strict view of the Church and in the popular
       mind as shaped by the Church, post-Christian Judaism is not really a religion but a
       crime, like a continued crucifixion of Christ."
           Cf. also Dominic Crossan, "Antisemitism in the Gospel," in *Theological Studies*
       (June 1965); Jeffrey G. Jobosan, "The Trial of Jesus," in *Christian Attitudes on Jews
       and Judaism* 28 (June 1973), 13–18. The Greek Orthodox Church goes even further
       in its condemnation of the Jews than the Roman Catholic one; here even the
       identification of Jesus and his Christian adherents with all the good that God has done
       for Israel is carried *ad absurdum*. Cf. Charlotte L. Klein, "The Image of the Jew in
       Oriental Liturgies," in *Christian Attitudes on Jews and Judaism* 28 (February 1973):
       12–16.

69ff. THE SIGNIFICANCE OF THE CHRISTIAN IMAGE OF THE JEWS FOR THE DEVELOPMENT
       OF THE JEWISH QUESTION: In addition to the literature already mentioned, there are
       especially the writings of the French Jewish historian Jules Isaac (1877–1963). The
       traumatic experience of the Nazis' systematic murder of the Jews, which claimed his
       wife and daughter as victims, caused him to undertake the task of investigating the
       foundations of Jew-hatred, especially the Christian ones, and he worked toward a
       revision of the Christian teachings that aimed at the degradation and defamation of
       the Jews. His most important writings on this question are *Jésus et Israël* (1948;
       English translation, 1971); *Genèse de l'antisémitisme* (1956); and *L'enseignement du*

mépris (1962; in English: *The Teaching of Contempt*, 1964). In 1960 he gave a brief synopsis of his views in the booklet *The Christian Roots of Antisemitism*. Cf. also Arthur A. Cohen's review essay about him in *Commentary*, September 1971, 92–95.

As examples of modern books on this thesis written by devout Christians, I shall name, in addition to the Protestant James Parkes, the Catholic Malcolm Hay (*The Foot of Pride: The Pressure of Christendom on the People of Israel for 1900 Years* [Boston, 1951]) and the Catholic clergyman Edward H. Flannery (*The Anguish of the Jews: Twenty-Three Centuries of Anti-Semitism* [New York, 1965]). Cf. also Solomon Grayzel, "Christian-Jewish Relations in the First Millenium," in Koppel S. Pinson, ed., *Essays on Antisemitism* (New York, 1946), 799–92; *Christlicher Antisemitismus*, in *Germania Judaica: Schriftenreihe 4* (Cologne, 1962).

In this context a statement by Nietzsche (from his posthumously published aphorisms) may be worth noting: "Once Christianity has been destroyed, there will be a juster assessment of the Jews—as originators of Christianity and of the highest moral pathos to date."

FATUM AND FORTUNA: Cf. the article "Fortuna" in *Der kleine Pauly. Lexikon der* 70
Antike (1967) 2:596–600; Fustel de Coulanges, *The Ancient City*, 145; J. G. Droysen, *Geschichte Alexanders des Grossen* (Kröners Taschenausgabe), 511: "The king sacrificed . . . to the gods . . . in the customary way; he sacrificed to good fortune." St. Augustine's *City of God* contains a detailed discussion of these notions of gods; cf. 4:17ff. Cf. also Josephus, *The War of the Jews* 6. 8. 4: "Now God's power over the depraved was really revealed, as was the good fortune of the Romans." In his *Secret History of Emperor Justinian and Empress Theodora* (chap. 10), written around the middle of the sixth century, the Byzantine historian Procopius, a native of Caesarea, says that Fortune controls all human affairs and, not caring whether an action is just or sensible, magnifies and debases people as it sees fit.

PREJUDGMENT: Concerning the nature of the concept "prejudice" in modern social 70f.
psychology, cf. R. M. MacIver and Charles H. Page, *Society: An Introductory Analysis* (New York, 1949), 407ff. ("Group Prejudice and Discrimination"); Gordon W. Allport, *The Nature of Prejudice* (New York: Anchor Books, 1954); Myre Sim, "The Paranoia of Prejudice," in *Patterns of Prejudice* 4 (1970): 19ff.; "How to Understand Prejudice: An Exchange," *Commentary*, November 1959, 436ff. It is, of course, generally known that all of us have prejudices and that there is no life, and surely no social life or life as a member of a group, without prejudices. How could one lead a fruitful, active life if one had to judge everything anew every day and could not rely on a judgment made a day, a year, or ten years ago or adopted from others along with one's education and tradition? All thought and scientific systematization proceed from the investigation of such prejudgments and the examination of their truth content. Whether we include them in our conscious judgments, modify them, or reject them depends on the result of this examination. This, however, is rendered impossible if a prejudice is viewed as a judgment made by God and thus not subject to our examination. In that case the prejudice becomes an unshakable axiom on which all further thinking is based. If such a prejudgment is directed against some group, it becomes disastrous for it. Viewed in this way, the prejudgment that the Jews are deicides and therefore condemned and damned by God is placed outside the customary concept of prejudice and assumes a menacing character.

TYPES AND STEREOTYPES: In his book *Public Opinion* (Pelican Books, 1946), 73, 70f.
Walter Lippmann has this to say about the modern sociological concept of the stereotype (which he was the first to use, in 1922): "Its hallmark is that it precedes the

use of reason. . . . There is nothing so obdurate to education or to criticism as the stereotype. It stamps itself upon the evidence in the very act of securing the evidence" (cited here after Adolf Leschnitzer, *The Magic Background of Modern Antisemitism* [New York, 1956], 220). Cf. also "Psychologie," *Fischer-Lexikon* 6:207f. This is why a defense against a stereotypical image is doomed to failure from the start, for it is immune to logic, evidence to the contrary, and appeals to reason and reality. These cannot be considered or absorbed because basically everything is already set. The view of anything individual is blocked or deflected to the region of exception or demonic fantasy.

71f.   ST. AUGUSTINE: Marcel Simon, *Verus Israel*, 93–95, 119ff.; Adolf Leschnitzer, *Das Judentum im Weltbild des Mittelalters* (Berlin, 1935), esp. 9; J. Klatzkin, "Augustin," *EJ* 3:690ff.; Eduard Strauss, "Augustinus der Bekehrte," *Der Jude* 7 (1923): 355–76; Bernhard Blumenkranz, *Die Judenpredigt des Augustinus: Ein Beitrag zur Geschichte der christlich-jüdischen Beziehungen in den ersten Jahrhunderten* (Basel, 1946), esp. 178ff.; Henri Marrou, *Augustinus in Selbstzeugnissen und Bilddokumenten* (Hamburg, 1958). In his preface to Marcus Dods's English translation of *Civitas Dei (The City of God)* (New York: Modern Library, 1950), xi, Thomas Merton writes: "Just as truly as the *Confessions* are the autobiography of St. Augustine, *The City of God* is the autobiography of the Church written by the most catholic of her great saints." Cf. also Dubnow, *Weltgeschichte des jüdischen Volkes*, 3:243; on p. 241 Dubnow quotes the Church Father Jerome on the Jews: ". . . an unfortunate people which, however, does not deserve pity." Cf. also William G. Braude, "The Church Fathers and the Synagogue," *Judaism* (1960): 112–19.

76ff.   DEFAMATORY LAWS: Dubnow, *Weltgeschichte*, vol. 3; George Caro, *Sozial- und Wirtschaftsgeschichte der Juden im Mittelalter und der Neuzeit*, vol. 1 (1924), 19–43; Solomon Grayzel, "The Jews and Roman Law," *Jewish Quarterly Review* 59 (1968): 93–117; Grayzel, "The Beginnings of Exclusion," *Jewish Quarterly Review* 61 (1970): 15–26. A list of all anti-Jewish laws from the time of Constantine to the eighth century may be found in James Parkes, *The Conflict of the Church and the Synagogue*, 379–91. In his book *The Jew in the Medieval Community* (London, 1938) Parkes comments: "Few of the laws passed against the Jews before the fall of the Western Empire were the result of any political or constitutional necessity. The law of the pagan second century had dealt with the menace of a rebel nation: those of the Christian fourth and fifth were designed to crush a hated religious sect."

Cf. also P. N. Ure, *Justinian and His Age* (Penguin Books, 1951), 112f., 130f., 151, 153f., 168f.

79f.   PROSELYTISM: Concerning the nature of Jewish proselytism, see, in addition to the general literature and the articles in *JL* and *EJJ*, especially Michael Guttmann. *Das Judentum und seine Umwelt* (Berlin, 1927), chaps. 1–5.

80f.   JUDAISM AND ISLAM: The most comprehensive book, which weighs and presents the relationships expertly and prudently, is S. D. Goitein's *Jews and Arabs: Their Contacts Through the Ages* (1955; paperback ed., New York, 1964). A popular presentation of the mutual cultural relationships and influences may be found in Erwin I. J. Rosenthal's *Judaism and Islam* (London and New York, 1961). Cf. also Cecil Roth's essay "The Jews in the Arab World," *Jewish Forum* (London), October 1946, 28–33; Leon Poliakov, *Histoire de l'Antisémitisme: De Mahomet aux marranes* (Paris, 1961). In the Koran, the basic book for all believers in Islam, there are many anti-Jewish and anti-Christian passages as well as a continuing discussion of the teachings of Judaism and Christianity. Cf., e.g., Sura 5, 52ff.: "O ye believers, do not make friends with Jews or Christians, for they are friends only to one another. . . . O believers, do not make friends with those who had the scriptures before you did, nor with the unbelievers, who mock and ridicule your faith."

Concerning Islam's tolerance toward the Jewish Bible and its interpretation (in contrast to Christianity), cf. James Parkes's *Jews in the Christian Tradition* (1963), 17: "Muslims did not claim the Old Testament as theirs. For them the Quran completely replaced the Old and the New Testament. It was a new and complete revelation of the nature and will of God. So Muslims could allow Jews and Christians to possess their scriptures in peace and to interpret them as they liked.—This was just what Jews and Christians could not allow each other to do."

A good introduction and selection of documents is given by Philip K. Hitti in his *Islam and the West: A Historical Survey* (Princeton, 1962). Concerning Islam's present-day attitude toward Judaism, see *Arab Theologians on Jews and Israel* (Geneva, 1971) (Proceedings of a convention of Islamic religious leaders at Al Azhar University, Cairo). On this subject, cf. Yvonne Glickson's essay "Islamic Prejudice," in *World Jewry* (London), June 1973, 24–28. The author shows how part of the Christian image of the Jews was adopted by Islam, having been introduced by Christians who converted to Islam in the period of its dissemination.

DEVELOPMENT OF THE JEWISH "RACIAL TYPE": Arthur Ruppin, *Soziologie der Juden* 82
1 (Berlin, 1930), chaps. 1–3, esp. pp. 28f. ("Die drei Engzuchtgebiete Babylonien, Spanien, Polen"). Cf. also Harry J. Shapiro, *The Jewish People: A Biological History* (Paris: UNESCO, 1960).

3

The Development of the Jewish Question
in the Christian-European Middle Ages

84ff. MIDDLE AGES: There is a variegated literature about the Middle Ages, the term and the concept, and especially about the delimitation of the epoch it is supposed to designate. In recent decades the discussion of the subject has been renewed and intensified to the point of rejecting the concept altogether. We know that it originated during the Renaissance and Humanism, ages that deemed themselves to be renewers of antiquity and regarded the eras between them and the age of the Greeks and Romans as an intermediate period of barbarism. It is assumed that it prevailed as an established concept of historiography in the seventeenth century under the influence of the compendiums of a schoolmaster, Rector Christoph Keller (1638–1717), a man better known by his Latinized name Cellarius (following the usage of the humanists). He divided world history into three great epochs, *Historia antiqua, Historia medii aevi,* and *Historia moderna.* Of course, any division into epochs is only a device for helping us grasp the uninterrupted course of historical life. This is similar to the so-called ages of man and developmental stages in the life of an individual. It is always difficult to define their beginning and end exactly; they appear different to an outsider and to the person experiencing them, and their temporal delimitation depends on the way in which the actor and the observer experience them. The Romantic period in the late nineteenth century placed a far higher value on the Middle Ages than the sixteenth, seventeenth, and eighteenth centuries did, and it often overvalued them as a way of life united in its faith and founded on a hierarchy of allegiances, in contrast to the modern period with its negation of old traditions and dissolution of established, "organic" social orders. The debate about the upper and lower limits has repeatedly been renewed in recent decades as specialized research made any boundary line appear as artificial and the transition as far more complex. The contemporaries, the people of the Middle Ages themselves, had mixed feelings about their time. On the one hand, it always represented to them a direct continuation of the preceding period; and on the other, the predominant religious doctrines caused them to regard their age as a transitional period to the Messianic end of days—thus again as a kind of "middle age," an actually unhistorical time. On this the Jewish, Christian, and Mohammedan views of history were in basic agreement, no matter how different their views about the delimitation and evaluation of the points of departure and terminal points might have been.

The delimitation of the epoch became a particular problem for modern *Jewish* historians. Were they to adopt the division into epochs and definitions of the surroundings in whose spatial and cultural sphere Jewish Diaspora history took place, or were they to choose their own division into epochs, one more in keeping with the inner and outer course of Jewish history as the total history of the Jewish people, letting the Middle Ages begin with the victory of Christianity or Islam and dating them from the seventeenth century (Sabbatai Zevi) or the eighteenth (Enlightenment, emancipation)? (In recent years a good case has been made for the latter course in universal history as well.) Any such damming of the flow of history has its justification and its defects. Despite all reservations about divisions into epochs generally, we have here retained the traditional, academic division since no other one is as universally recognized and the history of the Jewish question is by its nature closely connected with developments in the world and is in fact largely determined by them. In specific instances, however, I have not slavishly followed these definitions, since they are by nature not precisely ascertainable.

Concerning writings about this question, cf., in addition to the pertinent sections in the encyclopedias and standard introductions to historiography, Herbert Grundmann, "Über die Welt des Mittelalters," *Propyläen-Weltgeschichte*, 12, "Summa Historia" (Berlin, 1965), 363ff.; Ben-Zion Dinur, *Yisrael ba-Golah* (Israel in exile) vol. 1 (Jerusalem, 1926, 1958), Introduction; Jacob R. Marcus, *The Jew in the Medieval World: A Source Book, 315–1791* (New York: Meridian Books, 1960); Chaim Ben Sasson, *Toldot Yisrael bimei habeinayim* (History of Israel in the Middle Ages) (Tel Aviv, 1969), Introduction; Cecil Roth, ed., *The Dark Ages: Jews in Christian Europe 711–1096*, (The World History of the Jewish People, 2d Series, vol. 2) (Tel Aviv, 1966), Introduction.

Some basic sources (in addition to those already mentioned): I. Aronius, *Regesten zur Geschichte der Juden im fränkischen und deutschen Reich bis zum Jahre 1273* (Berlin, 1887–1902); J. R. Marcus, *The Jew in the Medieval World: A Source Book* (Cincinnati, 1938; paperback ed., New York, 1961); Julius Höxter, *Quellenlesebuch zur jüdischen Geschichte und Literatur* vols. 2, 3 (Frankfurt a.M., 1927–28); James Parkes, *The Jew in the Medieval Community* (London, 1938); Bernhard Blumenkranz, *Juifs et Chrétiens dans le monde occidental, 430–1096* (Paris and The Hague, 1960). Cf. also the pertinent volumes and chapters in the more comprehensive presentations of Jewish history.

Hans Liebeschütz's stimulating essay "The Relevance of the Middle Ages for the Understanding of Contemporary Jewish History" (Leo Baeck Institute, *Year Book* 18 [1973], 3–25) appeared after the completion of this chapter.

SHIFTING OF THE CENTER OF JEWISH SETTLEMENT FROM THE EAST TO EUROPE: 84
Cecil Roth, *Dark Ages*, 64ff.; Baron, *EJJ* 13:875ff.

IMMIGRATION OF THE JEWS: This is the assumption of virtually all researchers and   85f.
historians of general Jewish history as well as the history of Jewry in various countries (Germany, France, etc.). A different view was recently presented by Irving A. Agus in his book *Urban Civilization in Pre-Crusade Europe*, vol. 1 (New York 1965), 14ff., which utilizes in particular the Jewish Responsa literature. According to Agus, Western Jewry is descended from the Jews who lived in the Western Roman Empire in the early centuries of the Common Era—from the physically and morally strongest elements that stood their ground against the persecutions and conversions of the Christian Church and the depredations of the new barbarian peoples. Having passed through this cruel process of selection, they were an elite that also preserved the cultural traditions of the Roman Empire and passed them on to the peoples of northern Europe. Hence they made, in Agus's view, an important contribution to the creation of the foundations of European urban civilization. By virtue of an uncommonly strong propagation on the basis of hereditary qualities acquired through this selection they gave rise to European Ashkenazic Jewry. For our problem—the origin and development of the complex that we call the Jewish question—it is immaterial whence the Jews of Christian Europe came. No matter where they came from and irrespective of the details of their settlement and dissemination, their religious and cultural tradition was different and regarded as alien by the world around them. They

clung to this historical heritage, refined it further, and remained an ethnic entity that refused to assimilate to the surrounding world and be absorbed by it.

We must surely add proselytism as a factor in their numerical increase, though we have only little documentation and no statistical material concerning this. But without this assumption there is no explanation for the ever-recurring defensive warnings and Council decisions of the Church.

86ff.   MODES OF JEWISH SETTLEMENT: Concerning this, and particularly the concept of "ghetto colonization," see Yeheskel Kaufmann's *Golah ve-Nehar* (Exile and alien lands), a fundamental study on the history of Jewish religion and the sociology of the Jews that unfortunately exists only in Hebrew (4 books in 2 vols. [Tel Aviv 1930–32; reprinted in Tel Aviv, 1954], particularly vol. 1, chap. 10, pp. 456ff.). For specific details see the histories of Jews in various countries—e.g., I. Elbogen for Germany, Cecil Roth for Italy, Blumenkranz and Robert Anchel for France, Hyamson and Cecil Roth, as well as H. G. Richardson, *The English Jewry under Angevin Kings* (London, 1960) for England. See in addition to the general encyclopedias the specialized ones for various countries (*Germania Judaica, Gallia Judaica*) as well as the numerous and very diverse books about the history of the Jews in provinces and cities. References to these may be found in the pertinent articles in *JL, EJ, HE, EJJ*, etc.

88ff.   THE JEWS IN THE ECONOMY OF THE MIDDLE AGES (DISPLACEMENT OF THE JEWS FROM RURAL AREAS: JEWS AND TRADE, ETC.): A critical treatment of the literature on the role of Jews in economic history, particularly in the Middle Ages, may be found in Toni Oelsner's essay "The Place of the Jews in the Economic History as Viewed by German Scholars: A Critical Comparative Analysis," Leo Baeck Institute, *Year Book* 7 (1962) 183–212, with an extensive bibliography that includes specialized studies. The author rightly warns against hasty generalizations and critically examines in particular the theses of Wilhelm Roscher, Max Weber, and Werner Sombart. To be sure, we must bear in mind that no theory can encompass all details of reality; a model never completely corresponds to reality. A historical line is no more accurate to the last detail than the geographical design of a map. Cf. also Hans Liebeschütz, *Das Judentum im deutschen Geschichtsbild von Hegel bis Max Weber* (Tübingen, 1967), particularly 220ff. (about Jacob Burckhardt) and 308ff. (about Max Weber and his argument with Werner Sombart) as well as the English version of this chapter in Leo Baeck Institute, *Year Book* 9 (1964), 41ff. It is difficult to determine the share of the Jews in the development of medieval trade and the money economy because we have too little continuous primary material and the Jewish sources, especially the Responsa literature, have not been investigated systematically enough. Basic references on this material are Moses Hoffmann, *Der Geldhandel der Juden während des Mittelalters bis 1350* (Leipzig, 1910); Jacob Katz, *Jewish-Gentile Relations in Medieval and Modern Times* (New York, 1962), and Irvin Agus, *Urban Civilization in Pre-Crusade Europe . . . Based on the Responsa Literature*, 2 vols. (1965). Then, too, among both Jews and non-Jews discussion of this problem has been to an uncommon extent influenced by extra-scholarly arguments of sympathy and antipathy and the evaluation of developments in the economy, society, religion, and culture. For our posing of the problem the decision about this is less important than the question how the economic activity of the Jews was reflected in the surrounding world's image of the Jews, what effect it had on the social position of the Jews in the Christian world, and how it affected social life in the Jewish world and the Jews' self-image. Cf. also Part 2, pp. 536ff.

90f.   MEDITERRANEAN TRADE IN THE MIDDLE AGES: The basic references in addition to the general and abovementioned literature: Henri Pirenne's books *Histoire économi-*

que et sociale du moyen âge (English translation: *Economic and Social History of Europe* [London 1937]) and *Mahomet et Charlemagne* (German translation: *Mahomet und Karl der Grosse: Untergang der Antike am Mittelmeer und Aufstieg des germanischen Mittelalters* [Frankfurt a.M., 1963]); Karl Bosl, "Staat, Gesellschaft, Wirtschaft im deutschen Mittelalter," in Gebhardt, *Handbuch der deutschen Geschichte*, vol. 7 (Stuttgart, 1970).

THE ROLE OF THE JEWS IN THE MEDIEVAL ECONOMY: Cf. Ignaz Schipper, "Der   90f.
Anteil der Juden am europäischen Grosshandel mit dem Orient," in *Heimkehr: Essays jüdischer Denker*, ed. by the Jewish national association Emunah of Czernowitz (Berlin, 1912), 138–72, esp. 143f.; idem, *Toldot hakalkalah ha-yehudit* (History of the Jewish economy), 2 vols. (Tel Aviv, 1935–36); George Caro, *Sozial- und Wirtschaftsgeschichte der Juden im Mittelalter und der Neuzeit* (Frankfurt, 1908–20, 1924) (the author's early death prevented him from going beyond the late Middle Ages); James Parkes, *The Jew in the Medieval Community: A Study of His Political and Economic Situation* (London, 1930; henceforth cited as Parkes 2); Raphael Strauss, "The Jews in the Economic Evolution of Central Europe," *Jewish Social Studies* 3:15–40; idem, *Die Juden in Wirtschaft und Gesellschaft: Untersuchungen zur Geschichte einer Minorität* (Frankfurt a.M., 1964).

RADANITES: L. Rabinowitz, *Jewish Merchant Adventurers: A Study of the Radanites*   91
(London, 1948).

CRUSADES: Steven Runciman, *A History of the Crusades*, 3 vols. (Cambridge,   93ff.
1952–54); Joshua Prawer, *Toldot Mamlehet Hazalbanim be-Eretz Yisrael* (History of the crusaders' state in Eretz Yisrael), 2 vols. (Jerusalem, 1963); idem, *The Latin Kingdom of Jerusalem: European Colonialism in the Middle Ages* (London, 1972).

In the literature on the period of the Crusades the persecutions of the Jews occupy only an insignificant place, as do almost all events of the history of the Jewish Diaspora in general historical literature. They are usually treated as an aberration of incited masses. They are, however, logically connected with the entire ideology of the Crusades that the sword could and should obtain dominance for the Christian Church and that everyone who deviated from the orthodox faith was to be regarded as a foe of the Roman Church. The ingenious official doctrine of the Church that the Jews should be suppressed and preserved at the same time could not stand up to this ideology—barely in times of peace and certainly not in periods of crisis and unrest. In his article on problems of modern research on the Crusades (*Vierteljahrsschrift für Sozial- und Wirtschaftsgeschichte* 50, no. 4 [January 1964]: 4 507) Hans Eberhard Mayer rightly points out that around 1095 most knights and peasants were equally illiterate and listened to the same preachers. Thus their faith and actions could hardly have been basically different. There the primitive view always manifested itself that has been formulated as follows in the case of the Normans in Sicily (in the volume *Bilder und Dokumente* of the *Propyläen-Weltgeschichte* [1965], 327): "Unlike Leo IX, Roger I was not concerned with liberating Christianity; rather (as related by Gaufried Malaterra), he regarded the heathens as rebels against God . . . and the Normans as 'avengers of injustice.'" Mayer's general verdict on the Crusades is noteworthy as well (p. 509): "Success is its own justification, failure needs to be justified. No historian denies that the Crusades were a failure."

On the other hand, Runciman's world-historical evaluation of the Crusades (in the preface to the first volume of his *History*) is also justified: "Whether we regard them as the most tremendous and most romantic of Christian adventures or as the last of barbarian invasions, the Crusades form a central fact in medieval history. Before their inception the centre of our civilization was placed in Byzantium and in the lands of the Arab Caliphate. Before they faded out the hegemony in civilization had passed to Western Europe. Out of this transference modern history was born. . . ."

The importance of the Crusades for the fate and the historical consciousness of the Jews is also documented by the fact that they brought about the reawakening of Jewish historiography—befitting the style of the period, in the form of chronicles and martyrologies. Cf. *Hebräische Berichte über die Judenverfolgungen während der Kreuzzüge*, ed. A. Neubauer and M. Stern, trans. into German by S. Baer (Berlin, 1892). A critique of this edition was published by I. Elbogen ("Zu den hebräischen Berichten über die Judenverfolgungen im Jahre 1096," reprint from the *Festschrift zum 70. Geburtstage Martin Philippsons* [Breslau, 1916]). A more recent Hebrew collection of all reports with a selection of lamentations from the time of the Crusades was published by A. M. Habermann (*Sefer Gezerot Ashkenaz ve'Zarfat* [Jerusalem, 1945]). Other important works are R. Joseph haCohen, *Emek habakha*, trans. and provided with music by M. Wiener (Leipzig, 1858); R. Ephraim ben Yaakov, *Sefer Sekhira* (Book of remembrance), ed. A. M. Habermann (Jerusalem, 1970). Cf. also my presentation of the events at Mainz in late May 1096 in *Germania Judaica* 1 (1934): 178–81, and the general account of the events in I. Elbogen, *Geschichte der Juden in Deutschland* (Berlin, 1935), 28ff. (I prefer Elbogen's earthy language in the first edition to Eleonore Sterling's revision as issued in Stuttgart in 1966.)

97f.   BLOOD LIBEL AND ACCUSATION OF DESECRATION OF THE HOST: The accusation that the Jews were—out of vengefulness and hatred, to repeat the crucifixion, or for ritual reasons—torturing and murdering Christian children and using their blood for curative purposes and particularly for the baking of Passover *matzot* is generally known. What is less known is the foundation of this accusation, and it is hard to understand that it kept emerging and was believed down to our days. It is, of course, based on the popular belief (which exists among the Jews as well) that the blood contains the soul and vital energy, a belief that originated and was preserved through the observation that life expires when a person "bleeds to death." Hence miraculous powers have been ascribed to blood from ancient times, including the power of transmitting characteristics ("blood relationship"), though we know today that it has nothing to do with it. Blood has always been regarded as "a very special juice" (Goethe, *Faust I*) with which, among other things, friendships or pacts with the devil were sealed. As already mentioned, a kind of blood accusation already appeared in the Hellenistic period (Part 1, p. 41), and in the early centuries of Christianity, before Christianity was recognized as the state religion, it was leveled against the Christians, who were often persecuted on that account. The first blood accusation against the Jews known to us was made in England in 1144 (William of Norwich). From then on it spread over almost all Christian countries, though the Popes repeatedly condemned it as an untruth. It surely was an expression of the fact that the Jew was regarded as uncanny, a foe of the Christians, in league with hellish forces, and a practitioner of magical acts. At the same time it was—sometimes naively and often with deliberate intent—used and misused for all kinds of purposes: for the creation of sainted martyrs whose veneration at certain places secured for both ecclesiastic and secular institutions a steady stream of believers and clients; for the extortion of money; for vengeance, nonpayment of debts, or confiscation of the property of executed Jews; and in modern times also for the political purposes of organized anti-Semitic parties. In the 1880s and later by the Nazis in the 1920s and 1930s (particularly by Julius Streicher in Nuremberg, who added pornographic-sadistic elements) the accusation was renewed and believed, and by no means only by people of ill will. In the early 1930s a colleague in the Reich Archives in Potsdam—a former officer, a man from a family of Protestant pastors, and in World War II a general in Paulus's army—told me that in the Lower Saxonian village in which he grew up his parents gave this as the reason for forbidding the children to buy rolls from the Jewish baker. When the boy did make a purchase one day out of curiosity, he remembered having an uncanny feeling: Was there or wasn't there Christian blood in the bread he just ate? Around the same time I was asked this question by a Christian scene painter of the Communist persuasion whose children played with ours and whom we housed and fed for free when he had lost his job and was destitute: "Dr. Bein, tell me the truth as a friend: Do the Jews use the blood of Christian children for their *matzot* or don't they?" In one of his essays the well-known Zionist writer Asher Ginzberg (known by his Hebrew pseudonym Ahad Ha-am, one of the people) presented the general belief in the blood libel to his Jewish contemporaries as a typical example of the phenomenon that a "conventional opinion" can be false. According to him, every Jew knew that the blood accusation was nonsense, and yet it was generally believed; the Jews should learn from this not to believe other malicious assertions about them and not to accuse themselves of bad qualities just because people in general were doing so. (Cf. the essay "Ein halber Trost" in Ahad Ha-Am, *Am Scheidewege*, trans. Israel Friedländer I, [Berlin, 1913], 162ff., esp. 168.)

"The Prioress's Tale" in Geoffrey Chaucer's *Canterbury Tales* (1386–87) may be regarded as the first great example of the blood accusation in world literature. Five hundred years later, in Dostoievski's *The Brothers Karamazov* (1879–80), Alyosha the Pure answered to the question whether the Jews consumed Christian blood: "I do not know."

Similar accusations were leveled in Europe against Gypsies and in Asia against Europeans. In the Boxer Rebellion of 1900, for example, Tu Tung Chen, the leader of the rebels, accused the Western Powers and in particular Germany of having "consumed our children like food" (J. M. D. Pringle, *China Struggles with Unity* [Penguin Books, 1939], 24).

As far as the accusation of the desecration of the host is concerned, the abovementioned foundations and motives of the blood libel were, of course, joined by the belief in transubstantiation, Christ's assumption of bodily form in the mystery of the Holy Communion. It is interesting to note that in ancient times even some Jews seem to have occasionally believed that a sacred object can bleed. The Talmud (*Gittin*, fol. 56b), tells of Titus that he and a whore had broken into the holy of holies in the Temple in Jerusalem, desecrated the Torah scroll, and pierced the curtain with his sword. "Then a miracle happened and blood came out so that he thought he had killed himself [a euphemism for God]."

Concerning the literature on the blood accusations, cf. in addition to the well-known historical works the articles and bibliographies in *JL*, 1082ff.; *HE* 12, 722ff.; *EJJ* 4, 115ff. (on p. 1125 there is a map with the places in which blood accusations were made in the twelfth, thirteenth, nineteenth, and twentieth centuries); Strack, *Das Blut im Glauben und Aberglauben des Menschen* (Munich, 1900); D. Chwolson, *Die Blutanklage und sonstige mittelalterliche Beschuldigungen der Juden* (Frankfurt, 1901–10); J. Trachtenberg, *The Devil and the Jews* (1961 ed.), 109–55; Malcolm Hay, *The Root of Pride* (Boston, 1951), 110–39 ("The Murderous Lie").

MONEY-LENDING AND USURY. THE JEW AS "USURER": In all pertinent historical works 98ff. there are sections of varying length on money-lending, interest, and usury in the Middle Ages—in general, as well as about the role of the Jews and the problems arising from this for the position of the Jews in Christian society. For a summary of the problems and bibliographical information, cf. especially the pertinent articles (financial and monetary system, interest, usury, etc.) in *JL*, *EJ*, *EJJ*. The Jews have been criticized because a dual morality is expressed in the biblical prohibition to take interest from Jews and the permission to take it from strangers. (It should be noted that some of the passages cited were often translated incorrectly or inaccurately and were not accessible to researchers in the Hebrew original but only in dubious versions.) Such a dubious morality, however, prevailed everywhere in antiquity, and to a large extent it still prevails among nations, societies, and groups. Since Gumplowicz and Durkheim all sociologists have assumed its presence (in-group, out-group). Cf., e.g., "Soziologie," *Fischer-Lexikon* (Frankfurt a.M., 1958), 106; MacIver and Page, *Society* (1949), 217ff. Frequently a stranger is perceived as an enemy, or he is at least suspected of being hostile. The universal person who is to be evaluated purely as a human being is a demand of the modern "Enlightenment" that has not been realized anywhere. On the dual evaluation of the "believer" and "unbeliever" almost all religions and doctrines are agreed, no matter how they may differ on everything else.

The "dual morality" in the conception of interest is probably explainable by the attitude of the Jewish farmers, most of whom were unaccustomed to trading and hostile to it, toward the dealers, who usually were not Jewish. The coastal towns that were important for the Mediterranean trade were in the hands of the Philistines and Phoenicians. The Prophets inveighed against the taking of interest, and the teachers of the Talmud and many of the later interpreters of the Biblical-Talmudic laws also emphatically declared their opposition to the taking of interest in general and overcharging in particular, including lending at interest to non-Jews. With the curtailment of gainful employment for Jews in the Christian economy of Europe, however, they had to make basic concessions relating to the preservation of the existence of Jews among non-Jews. As always happens in practice they often went far beyond that, whether under compulsion or voluntarily.

There is a wealth of literature on the subject, including Matthias Mieses, *Der Ursprung des Judenhasses* (1923), chap. 13, pp. 288ff.; "Der jüdische Wucher und der Judenhass"; Mieses's article with the same title is similar (in *Der Jude*, ed. Martin Buber, 6, no. 7 [April 1922]: 416ff.; there all pertinent passages from the Talmud are utilized and documented). Concerning economic morality and the prohibition to take interest in the Talmudic period, see Nahum N. Glatzer, *Geschichte der talmudischen Zeit* (Berlin, 1937), 53; Yitzhak Baer, *Yisrael ba-Ammim* (Israel among the nations) (Jerusalem 1955), 50 and in *Zion* 17 (in Hebrew). That despite all prohibitions Jews were already charging Jews interest in the Hellenistic period is shown by papyruses from Egypt (cf. V. A. Tcherikover and A. Fuks, *Corpus Papyrorum Judaicarum*, 1 [1957], 35). Concerning the problems and the dissemination of lending at interest (and usury) in the Middle Ages, cf. F. Funk, *Geschichte des kirchlichen Zinsverbots* (Tübingen, 1876); R. H. Tawney, *Religion and the Rise of Capitalism* (1926; Pelican Books, 1938), chap. 1, sec. 2, "The Sin of Avarice," 49ff.; Parkes 2, 269ff. and 395ff.; Hermann Sinsheimer, *Shylock: Die Geschichte einer Figur* (Munich, 1960), 173–80 ("Der Wucher"); Abraham A. Neumann, *The Jews in Spain: Their Social, Political, and Cultural Life During the Middle Ages*, vol. 1 (Philadelphia, 1948), 192ff.; Marvin Lowenthal, *The Jews of Germany: A Story of Sixteen Centuries* (Philadelphia, 1944), 53ff.

99f.   ON THE CONCEPT OF "USURY": The Hebrew word for "interest" (or "usury") is *neshekh*, literally "bite." In addition, the Bible uses *tarbit* or *marbit;* in later, post-Mishna literature (and to this day) we find *ribbit*. All these terms are derived from the stem *RBH* and mean "increase" or "augmentation." The Vulgate (Deut. 23:20–21) translates *neshekh* as *usura*, and thus the word entered the Western European languages (*usure, usurier,* usurer, etc.) Cf. also H. Loewe, *Starrs and Jewish Charters in the British Museum* 2 (London, 1922), xcv. According to Kluge, 887, the German word *Wucher* originally meant "yield," "fruit," "profit" and did not assume the pejorative meaning of excessive main, exploitation, etc., until later. Luther used it as a translation of *usura* (or *neshekh*). The word subsequently assumed the meaning of profuse, weedlike, or pathological growth, giving rise to a *Wucherung* or excrescence. This image later gave the word its biological coloration. The word *judaizare* for the practice of usury, which then entered many European languages in similar form and meaning (e.g., "to jew" in English), was first used in 1146 by the French monk and preacher Bernard of Clairvaux (1090–1153) in an appeal (*Epistola*, 363) opposing the persecutions and murders of Jews to which his fellow friar Radulf had incited in Lorraine, the Rhineland, and Bavaria. Bernard, to be sure, was accusing the Christians of usury even more than he was the Jews (cf. *EJ* 4:294).

HEIGHT OF THE INTEREST RATES: Cf. the remarks and statistical information by 101
H. W. Gerhard, "Die wirtschaftlich argumentierende Judenfeindschaft" in *Judenfeindschaft: Darstellungen und Analysen*, ed. Karl Thieme (Frankfurt: Fischer Bücherei, 1963), 96ff.

DEGRADATION AND DEFAMATION BY THE CHURCH: A fundamental collection of 104f.
source material (Part 2) and presentation (Part 1) is Solomon Grayzel's *The Church and the Jews in the 13th Century: A Study of their Relations during the Years 1198–1254, Based on the Papal Letters and the Conciliar Decrees of the Period* (Philadelphia, 1933; reprint: New York, 1966). Cf. also Grayzel, "The Avignon Popes and the Jews," in *Historia Judaica* 2 (1940): 1–12; Hans Kühner-Wolfskehl, "Die Juden Roms unter der Herrschaft der Päpste," *Zeitschrift für die Geschichte der Juden* 6 (1969): 65–73; for the fifteenth century, Max Simonsohn's dissertation *Die kirchliche Judengesetzgebung im Zeitalter der Reformkonzilien von Konstanz und Basel* (Breslau, 1912); *EJJ*, articles "Church" and "Popes" and bibliographies; and the abovementioned literature about the Jews in the Middle Ages.

The high-mindedness of the great Italian poet Dante Alighieri as well as his independent position in his era are indicated by the fact that in his *Divina Commedia* the Inferno depicted by him with all its torments (here he is altogether a child of his time) is peopled with evildoers and sinners of all kinds but not with Jews. On the other hand, it is symptomatic of the low estimate placed on Jews by devout Christians if a pure and noble person like Francis of Assisi refused to pronounce the word *Jew* for fear of soiling himself with it. Concerning this, cf. Yitzhak Baer in *Zion* 3 (Jerusalem, 1938).

THE FOURTH LATERAN COUNCIL: The text of the anti-Jewish decisions (11 November 105ff.
1215) may be found in the Latin original and in English translation in S. Grayzel, *The Church and the Jews*, 306ff.

THE YELLOW BADGE: Here is the section of paragraph 68 that deals with the 107f.
distinction between the clothing of the Jews and Saracens on the one hand and that of the Christians on the other: "Whereas in certain provinces of the Church the differences in their clothes sets the Jews and Saracens apart from the Christians, in certain other lands there has arisen such confusion that no differences are noticeable. Thus it sometimes happens that by mistake Christians have intercourse with Jewish or Saracen women, and Jews or Saracens with Christian women. Therefore, lest these people, under the cover of an error, find an excuse for the grave sin of such intercourse, we decree that these people (Jews and Saracens) of either sex, and in all Christian lands, and at all times, shall easily be distinguishable from the rest of the population by the quality of their clothes; especially since such legislation is imposed on them also by Moses." Literature: Cf. the articles and bibliographies in *JL* 3:411f. ("Judenabzeichen"); *EJ* 9:545ff. ("Judenzeichen"); *HE* 2:335ff. ("Ot-Kalon," badges of shame); *EJJ* 4:62ff. ("Badge, Jewish"). These articles also mention the pointed Jew's hat which was compulsory in some countries, particularly Germany, in a

number of countries but has been "documented since the middle of the 12th century in writings on art" (B. Blumenkranz, *Juden und Judentum in der mittelalterlichen Kunst* (Stuttgart, 1965), 82, n. 17). Cf. also Raphael Straus, "The Jewish Hat as an Aspect of Social History," *Jewish Social Studies* 4 (1942): 59ff. A more detailed and thoroughly researched presentation of the history of the Yellow Badge may be found in Guido Kisch, "The Yellow Badge in History," in *Historia Judaica* 4 (1942): 95–144. Concerning Jewish garb in countries under Islamic rule, cf. E. Ashtor (Strauss), *Toldot hayehudim bimitzrayim vesuria takhat shilton hamamelukim* (History of the Jews in Egypt and Syria under the rule of the Mamelukes) (Jerusalem, 1944–70). According to this work, the Yellow Badge was introduced as early as 489–50 by Caliph Mutavakkil. Cf. also the same author's *Korot hayehudim besefarad hamuslemit* (History of the Jews in Islamic Spain) (Jerusalem, 1966), 231f., and Salo Baron, *Social and Religious History* 3:139ff. Cf. also Alfred Rubens, *A History of Jewish Costume* (London, 1967).

Regarding the evaluation of the Jewish badges, there can hardly be any doubt that a strict interpretation of biblical precepts or the continuation of ancient tradition frequently caused Jews to distinguish themselves voluntarily from the fashion of the surrounding world in their clothing, hairstyle (Jewish beard, earlocks—Hebrew *peyot*—and Jewish hat), just as they often settled in separate streets or districts (*Judengassen*, etc.) of their own accord. As long as this difference in garb is voluntary, there is nothing shameful about it, but it becomes the point of departure for oppression if it is mandated by law and especially if this segregation involves defamatory intent. That Pope Innocent III had such an intent is evidenced by his letters (reprinted in Grayzel), especially one dated 1205 and addressed to the Count of Nevers in which Innocent expressly compared the Jews with Cain—an analogy that had already been used on other occasions. In any case, in the course of time the badge increasingly became not merely a distinguishing mark, as mandated by the Council decision, but a "badge of shame," and this is how the Jews perceived and characterized it. Seven hundred years later the German National Socialists revived it in this spirit (cf. Part 1, chap. 9). The derivation of the color yellow, which increasingly prevailed, is not clear. There is an occasional reference to this color as having been designated for Jewish garb in Islamic countries and also as defamatory clothing in general (Kisch, 115), like yellow hatbands for prostitutes. Kisch cites, and probably with justification, Goethe's remarks on the color yellow (paragraphs 770–71 in his *Farbenlehre* [Theory of Colors]): "770. In its purity and brightness this color is pleasant and gratifying and there is something cheerful and noble in its full strength, but it is extremely sensitive and thus has a very unpleasant effect if it is soiled or is used somewhat negatively. Thus there is something unpleasant about the color of sulphur, which tends towards green. 771. If the color yellow is imparted to unclean and ignoble surfaces—such as common cloth, felt, and the like—on which it does not appear in its full strength, such an unpleasant effect arises. Through a slight and imperceptible movement the fine impression of fire and gold is transformed into a perception of something dirty and the color of honor and joy is converted into a color of shame, disgust, and displeasure. This is how the yellow hats of bankrupt persons and the yellow rings on the cloaks of the Jews may have originated; in fact, the so-called cuckold's color is actually only a dirty yellow."

109f. PROTECTED JEWS: I. Elbogen (*Geschichte der Juden in Deutschland*, 35) has the following to say on this subject: "For the first time the Jews were numbered among those who did not bear arms and were unable to protect themselves, and their need for protection was emphasized." Eleonore Sterling, the editor of the second edition of this book, puts it in more accurate and precise terms (p. 31): "Here the Jews were numbered for the first time among those who did not bear arms and were unable to protect themselves. For the first time the special need for protection of the Jews in general and not as particular individuals or groups was emphasized."

Cf. Caro 1:130ff.; Parkes 2:158ff.; G. Kisch, *The Jews in Medieval Germany: A Study of their Legal and Social Status* (Chicago, 1949), 135ff. and 424, n. 20. Regarding the general situation, Kisch (p. 140) quotes from the chronicle of Provost Burchard of Ursberg (ca. 1177–1231) as *"mos Teutonicorum,"* Teutonic custom: *"Sine lege et ratione voluntatem suam pro jure statuunt . . . et omnem justitiam destantantur et odio habent"* (They exert their will as a right without any law and reason; they detest and hate any justice). Thus privileges that guaranteed protection against sheer despotism were to a great extent necessary not only for Jews as such, but for them in particular as strangers, people of different or no faith, and as individuals living by their own traditions. At first there was nothing degrading about that. The degradation did not come about until Christianity was radicalized under the influence of the ideology and propaganda of the Crusades, and it led to the institution of *Kammerknechtschaft*, with increasing emphasis on the second part of the word (i.e., servitude) in which the Church doctrine and secular laws combined.

KAMMERKNECHTSCHAFT: For a discussion of the problems, a presentation, and   110ff. bibliographies, see Fritz Baer in *EJ* 1:257ff.; H. Fischer in *EJ* 9:8611; Cecil Roth in *EJJ* 14:1188 (including an account of conditions in England); Guido Kisch, "The Jews in Medieval Law," in *Essays on Antisemitism*, ed. Koppel S. Pinson (1946), 130ff.; idem, *The Jews in Medieval Germany* (Chicago, 1949); idem, *Forschungen zur Rechts- und Sozialgeschichte der Juden des Mittelalters* (Stuttgart, 1955); idem, *Jewry Law in Medieval Germany* (New York: American Academy for Jewish Research, 1949). On pp. vii–vii of the last-named work Pinson defines the concept "Jewish Law" ("formed after and equivalent to the expression *Judenrecht*, a compound found—characteristically—only in the German language") and comments: "The status in law assigned to the Jew by the world around him and described by the norms of Jewry law exerted a determining influence on his entire intellectual, economic, social and cultural life." Cf. also Chap. XI and the bibliography in Baron, *A Social and Religious History of the Jews*, 9 (1965), 135ff. and 308ff. Of the older (but not outdated) literature I shall mention O. Stobbe, *Die Juden in Deutschland während des Mittelalters* (1866; reprinted 1902); Scherer, *Die Rechtsverhältnisse der deutschen Juden in den deutsch-österreichischen Ländern* (1901) (a critique in J. Kauffmann, *Golah ve-Nekkar* 1:473). Concerning the relationship between the Jews, the state, and the church in England, see the clear presentation by F. A. Linoln in *Starrs and Jewish Charters*, 2 (London, 1932), lvii ff. Cf. also the summary by M. Lieberich in Mitteis-Lieberich, *Deutsche Rechtsgeschichte* (Munich, 1969), 148: "The Church's conviction that there could be *'nulla salus extra ecclesiasm'* [no welfare outside the Church] prepared the ground for the belief in the God-ordained *servitus Judaeorum'* which gave rise to the *Kammerknechtschaft (servi camerae imperialis)* in the 13th century." E. Täubler published documents relating to the development of this institution and idea in *Mitteilungen des Gesamtarchivs der deutschen Juden*, 4 (1913), 44–622.

THE JEWS IN THE DOCTRINE OF THOMAS AQUINAS: Cf. Aronius, *Regesten*, 11–113,   112f. 324–27; G. Caro 1:308–13; *The Legacy of Israel* (Oxford, 1927), 265f.; H. Liebeschütz, "Judaism and Jewry in the Social Doctrine of Thomas Aquinas," *Journal of Jewish Studies* 13 (1962):57–82; Willehad P. Eckert, "Thomas von Aquino: Seine Stellung zu Juden und zum Judentum," *Freiburger Rundbrief* 20, nos. 73–76 (December 1968): 30–38. On p. 37 Eckert points out that in contrast to some teachers of early Scholasticism, who saw in the sentencing of Christ out of ignorance only a venial sin *(peccatum veniale)* or (like Peter Abelard) no sin at all, Thomas imputes to the Jews full responsibility for this crucifixion: "Even making allowance for unavoidable ignorance, according to Thomas the crucifixion of Christ remains a grave sin, since this very ignorance is culpable. . . . Many Catholic theologians have shared Thomas's view down to our time." By way of summing up, he remarks: "Anyone who surveys the various statements about the Jews in the writings of Thomas Aquinas will come to the conclusion that his remarks show little originality. They are worth mentioning, however, because they are a faithful reflection of the way in which the Christian Middle Ages viewed the Jews."

113f. THE JEWS IN COMPARISON WITH OTHER OPPRESSED GROUPS: Cf. Cecil Roth, "The Most Persecuted People?" *Menorah Journal* 20 (1932): 136–47.

114ff. PERSECUTIONS AND EXPULSIONS OF JEWS IN THE WANING MIDDLE AGES. THE "BLACK DEATH": There are detailed accounts of the medieval persecutions of the Jews in the pertinent sections of the great histories of the Jews (Graetz, Dubnow, Baron, etc.) and the books about the Jews in the Middle Ages (Parkes, Caro, etc.). In general histories written by non-Jews they are mentioned only briefly, if at all.

Regarding the bubonic plague—so called because of the swelling of the lymphatic vessels, especially in the armpit and the inguinal lymph node (*bubo*, Greek *boubon*), and called Black Death because of the black spots appearing on the skin)—and its history, see H. W. Haggard, *Devils, Drugs and Doctors: The Story of Healing* (New York, 1929; paperback, 1946), 184ff. It was not learned until the late nineteenth century that it is transmitted by fleas from infected rats; the bacillus was discovered in 1894. To this day the disease is combated chiefly through hygienic prophylaxis. In his novel *The Plague* (New York, 1952), set in the Algerian city of Oran, Albert Camus described how terrifying the appearance of this disease can be even in our days. At the end of the novel the physician Rieux is hardly able to rejoice with the people about the cessation of the plague: "He knew what those jubilant crowds did not know but could have learned from books: that the plague bacillus never dies or disappears for good; that it can lie dormant for years and years in furniture and linen-chests, that it bides its time in bedrooms, cellars, trunks, and bookshelves and that perhaps the day would come when, for the bane and the enlightening of men, it would rouse its rats again and send them forth to die in a happy city" (p. 278).

There is, of course, an extensive literature about the impression and influence on the people of the time, which Boccaccio, a contemporary in Florence, described in a flashback portion of his *Decameron*. Of more recent studies I shall mention Egon Friedell, *A Cultural History of the Modern Age: The Crisis of the European Soul from the Black Death to the World War*, 1 (New York, 1930), chap. 3, "The Incubation Period" (i.e., for the Renaissance and the modern period); Paul Frischauer, *Sittengeschichte der Welt*, 2 (Zurich, 1969), 268ff.; Millard Meiss, *Painting in Florence and Siena after the Black Death*, (New York, 1951), esp. 59–93. The Christian world's fear of death (and the Last Judgment thereafter!) resounds to this day in the anxious words and the traditional melody of *Dies irae, dies illa,* which was evidently composed in the thirteenth century by Celano, the friend and biographer of Francis of Assisi, has been sung since the fourteenth century in the second part of the requiem mass, and became an official part of the liturgy in the middle of the sixteenth century (Council of Trent). To this day Giuseppe Verdi's musical setting makes even nonbelievers shudder. The terrible plague was now added to the general fear of death, and it was all the more gruesome because people had no idea whence it came, how it spread, why it appeared in one place but not another, disappeared and returned, claiming victims in numbers that frightened even the people of the Middle Ages who were used to mortal illnesses and early mortality. That it was hardly possible to escape it was due to the indescribably primitive hygienic conditions of the time. The fact that certain people and regions were spared led people to regard the plague as a punishment of God or the action of Satanic-demonic forces. This is the background of the accusation that the Jews, who were always seen in a mystic-real connection with God and the Devil, had caused the plague by poisoning the wells. That any kind of confession can be extracted through torture has been shown in our days by the modern, "more humane" (that is, less obvious) methods of torture by totalitarian forces. In the Middle Ages there was not only systematic sadistic cruelty but also the widespread belief that the results of certain tortures were divine judgments (just like chivalric duels) and that they were legal methods of jurisprudence. As late as 1763 the *Constitutio Criminalis* of the German empress Maria Theresa was published together with seventeen copperplate engravings depicting the proper execution of judicial torture for the guidance of court officers who did not know how to read (H. W. Haggard, *Devils, Drugs* [1946], 210ff.). Hence it is astonishing, and evidences the moral strength of the tortured Jews, how few forcible "confessions" have been documented. If such confessions could be obtained (as in Chillon, Savoy—today in Switzerland), they were very quickly disseminated and ready to serve as "evidence" even before the plague had reached a certain area. Regarding the cruelty of the tortures, it should perhaps be noted that persons doing penance inflicted similar injuries on themselves at times of religious mass penance; cases in point are the flagellants at the time of the "Black Death" who flogged themselves until they bled and for that reason may have felt no moral repugnance in the face of cruelty toward Jews and heretics. This is, of course, not the place for a discussion of the psychiatric background of such actions.

Concerning the influence of the "Black Death" on the Jews, see the good summaries in *JL* 5:298ff.; *HE* 11:866ff. (general), 874ff. (on the Jews); C. H. Ben-Sasson in *EJJ* 4:1063ff. (includes a chart detailing the dissemination of the plague throughout Europe and the Jewish communities involved). Also, I. Elbogen, *Geschichte der Juden in Deutschland* (1935), 67ff. (also pertinent to the following sections); J. Trachtenberg, *The Devil and the Jews*, chap. 7 ("The Poisoners"); Georg Liebe, *Das Judentum in der deutschen Vergangenheit* (Leipzig, 1903), 18f. The temper of the times and its effect on the Jews are well captured in Selma Stern, *Ihr seid meine Zeugen: Ein Novellenkranz aus der Zeit des Schwarzen Todes 1348–1349* (Munich, 1972).

THE DESTRUCTION OF THE STRASSBURG JEWISH COMMUNITY: Friedrich Closener's 118f. report about the destruction of the Jewish community of Strassburg is here cited after J. Höxter, *Quellenbuch zur jüdischen Geschichte und Literatur*, 3 (1927), 28ff.

SHORT-TERM SETTLEMENT: Ellen Littmann, *"Studien zur Wiederaufnahme der Ju-* 119f. *den durch die deutschen Städte nach dem Schwarzen Tode"* (dissertation; Breslau, 1928).

THE JEW—A UTILITARIAN OBJECT: A general treatment in I. Elbogen, *Geschichte* 120 *der Juden in Deutschland* (1935).

"GOLDEN BULL": The edition used here is *Die Goldene Bulle Kaiser Karls IV., 1356,* 121 Latin text with German translation (Bern, 1958), 48–51.

THE IMAGE OF THE JEW AT THE END OF THE MIDDLE AGES: In this connection an 121f. important chapter is the *representation of the Jew in the Christian art of the Middle Ages:* cf. Part 1, pp. 153f., and Part 2, pp. 529f. Here I should like to refer only to the importance of these representations—in stone and wood sculptures, frescoes, oil paintings, and woodcuts—for the popularization of the image of the Jew. Medieval art in general at first depicted not the individual but the typical, and it played an important part in the typification of this image. It did so particularly by graphically modernizing the Passion of Christ, often including an anachronistic representation of the Jews with the Jewish hat and other marks (not Jewish noses!) that characterized them for their contemporaries. In this development, too, the first Crusade is the decisive turning point. Often all infidels and heretics were depicted as Jews. On this point, cf. especially Bernhard Blumenkranz, *Juden und Judentum in der mittelalterlichen Kunst* (Stuttgart, 1965) and Wolfgang Seifert, *Synagoge und Kirche im Mittelalter* (Munich, 1964). Even though we find, from the thirteenth century on, here and there individualized or caricaturing portraits of Jews as marginal drawings in documents or book illustrations (and later in paintings), the depiction of the Jews remained stylized until the end of the fourteenth century—that is, until the transition from the High Gothic period to the Renaissance. The Jews were characterized less by physiognomic peculiarities, etc., than through their clothing, hats, beards, etc. In numerous sculptures, e.g., the particularly beautiful and humanly noble ones of the Strassburg cathedral, the victorious Church was symbolized by a proud woman with a wreath and the vanquished Synagogue by a humbly bowed woman with a broken staff and a law tablet or book falling out of her hand—one of the most frequent allegorical depictions of the struggle. Many other depictions centered around the narration of the holy stories of the Old and New Testaments, and they were especially impressive because most people did not know how to read. Besides, the impression of a picture is often more lasting than that of a word because it persists in silence, as though coming from silent eternity, constantly plaintive in its gestures and, in contrast to words and writing, not open to contradiction. As the accusations became more severe, the images became more and more brutal. The increasingly realistic, often cruel and downright sadistic depiction of Christ's Passion and the sufferings of the Christian martyrs was, of course, bound to intensify the hatred of the Jews and call for vengeance against those really to blame for his condemnation and even for his crucifixion and the attendant cruelties—a development that had started with the Gospels. Next to the struggle against the demonic-devilish elements discerned in the Jews, this was the psychological background for numerous cruelties, sadistic tortures, and murders of Jews. In the conscience of the executors of such cruelties, the real interests—competition, envy, and avarice—were thereby given a religious-metaphysical justification, as it were. The murder of children, the desecration of the Host, and the like were depicted in the most horrible details. The defamation of the Jews gave rise to the abstruse image of the "Jews' sow" (cf. part 1, p. 154).

In the face of this, it is strange that sometimes the crucified Jesus should have been given a markedly Jewish face. Cf. Frederick Buechner and Leo Boltin, *The Faces of Jesus* (New York, 1974), 106 and 127. Concerning the earliest known caricature of a Jew, cf. Joseph Jacobs, "Aaron, Son of Devil" in his book *Jewish Ideals and Other Essays* (London, 1896), 225–33. Of the other literature about the Jews in the Christian art of the Middle Ages I shall mention the essays of Joseph Reider in *Essays on Antisemitism*, ed. K. S. Pinson (New York, 1946), 93–102; H. Barash in *Eretz-Yisrael: Archaeological, Historical, and Geographical Studies* 6 (*Dedicated to the Memory of Mordecai Narkiss*) (Jerusalem, 1960), 179–88 (in Hebrew) and 39f. (English synopsis); W. P. Eckert in *Freiburger Rundbrief*, nos. 77–80 (December 1969): 57ff.

The two-volume catalogue of the exhibit *Monumenta Judaica* (Cologne, 1963) contains a great deal of pictorial material.

Concerning the problem of the demonization of the image of the Jew, cf. J. Trachtenberg's *The Devil and the Jews* and the same author's *Jewish Magic and*

Superstition: A Study in Folk Religion (New York, Meridian Books, 1961); and Norman Cohn, *The Pursuit of the Millennium: Revolutionary Messianism in Medieval and Reformation Europe and its Bearing on Modern Totalitarian Movements* (London, 1962). See also the basic remarks in my essay "Der jüdische Parasit: Bemerkungen zur Semantik der Judenfrage," *Vierteljahrshefte für Zeitgeschichte* 13, no. 2 (April 1965): 122–49.

THE "ETERNAL JEW": Cf. the bibliography for the next chapter. Regarding the origin   121f. of the *Shylock figure*, see Graetz, *Geschichte* 3, 3d ed., p. 2 and the bibliography given for the next chapter.

REACTION OF THE JEWS: About this problem a Jew, and certainly a Zionist and citizen   122ff. of the State of Israel, can express himself more freely today than the Jews of the Diaspora could when they were fighting for legal and social equality. In his basic book *Der Judenstaat* (1896) Theodor Herzl wrote: "The pressure exerted on us does not make us any better. We are no different from other people. It is quite true that we do not love our enemies. But only he who is capable of conquering himself is entitled to reproach us with that. Naturally, the pressure inspires in us hostility against our oppressors—and our hostility in turn increased the pressure. It is impossible to escape this vicious circle." (*The Jewish State,* trans. H. Zohn [New York, 1970], 48). Note that this characterization was written for the situation at the end of the nineteenth century and that in the Introduction to his book Herzl described the Jewish question of his time as "an atavistic bit of medievalism which the civilized nations have not been able to shake off to this day, try as they might" (ibid., 33).

THE NON-JEW ("GOY") IN THE EYES OF THE JEWS: Unfortunately there still is no   124 concentrated scholarly treatment of this problem. The anti-Jewish literature in antiquity, in the Middle Ages, and in the modern period (Eisenmenger, etc.) as well as the anti-Semitic writings of the nineteenth and twentieth centuries are full of accusations of every kind about the arrogant, blasphemous, and cynical Jewish judgments on non-Jews when they are among themselves and often also when they associate with non-Jews. It is understandable that in the face of such accusations the Jews have generally limited themselves to apologetic writings, among which the book *Ha-Kuzari* by the poet-philosopher Judah Halevi occupies a central place in the Middle Ages. The Jews defended themselves against the accusations of the non-Jews, emphasized the exalted precepts of Jewish morality toward the non-Jews as well, and sought to prove that deprecatory expressions like "idolaters" (Hebrew *akum*, star worshippers) did not refer to Christians (or Mohammedans). By changing expressions that appeared offensive to them (*goy, nokhri* = stranger) Christian censors of Talmudic books only increased the confusion. Only in the freer atmosphere created by Zionism and the founding of the State of Israel did people begin to shed the anxiety in the treatment of the problem felt by well-meaning individuals on both sides. It is only natural that even today this anxiety should persist to a certain degree, because a person never knows how frank talk from one side will be understood by the other or exploited by malevolent people (or simply those fettered by tradition). These problems, of course, exist not just in the relation of the Jewish minority to the Christian majority. Cf., e.g., Peter R. Hofstätter's remark in his article "Minoritätsproblem" in the *Fischer-Lexikon* 6 ("Psychologie"), 209: "Least known is the image of the majority in the eyes of the minority, e.g., the image of the *goyim* from the viewpoint of the Jewish minority." This "unknownness" to the non-Jews and the unclarity and frequently lacking self-awareness or the deficient will to frankness with themselves not infrequently weave a kind of mysterious spell around the Jews which arouses fresh suspicion in the non-Jews and makes them endeavor to lift the veil from the secret. Often the attitude of the Jews is ambivalent. The Christian neighbor is usually the privileged one, and he frequently is in command. He has business dealings with the Jews, and thus one must act toward him in a way that inspires confidence and must not abuse his trust. Such a breach of trust is repeatedly warned against, as are the consequences that bad behavior toward non-Jews might have for Jewry as a whole. In this spirit immoral acts toward non-Jews are almost designated as a desecration of the name of God *(hillul ha-Shem)*. On the other hand, the Talmudic-rabbinical precepts forbid close contact with people of different faith (the eating or drinking of a stranger's meat or wine, etc.) to preserve the purity of the Jewish faith and religious service. In large measure the non-Jews of the Middle Ages could neither read nor write, and hence the Jews, who needed to be able to read Hebrew for their religious services, often felt culturally superior to them. In this way the *goy* (originally meaning "people" and in the Bible applied to the Jews in this sense) often received the deprecatory connotation of "simple-minded," "uneducated," or "barbarian."

Some attention should be paid to the evaluation of the comprehensive *Jewish ethical literature of the Middle Ages.* The most important of the specialized writings is the *Sefer Ha-hasidim* (Book of the pious), which is attributed to *Judah He-hasid* (Judah the Pious). The most important author of the many-sided literature of the Bible and Talmud commentators and exegetes was R. Shlomo Yitzhaki (1040–1105), called Rashi. This includes the Responsa literature, which gave decisions about current practical, legal, and moral problems the character of juridical or ethical precedents. Any ethical literature is based on two presuppositions: (1) that there were conditions which the moralist deemed necessary to improve and therefore painted only in black colors, and (2) that the admonisher distanced himself from these conditions, rejected them, and in general belonged to an elite group that shared his goals. In the scholarly utilization of this literature there are corresponding dangers: that the importance of the negative elements pilloried by the sensitive, pure moralists will be exaggerated (as Christian criticism—down to the modern, "scientific" kind—has often done with the Jewish prophets), that these criticized negative conditions will be identified with the generally prevailing ones, and that conversely the moralists will be identified with the community with apologetic intent—which, of course, can be done only if their writings were regarded by their contemporaries and later generations as standards and models for which the best people were striving. It does say something about the ethical standards of the Jews in the Middle Ages that an ascetic but open-minded moralist like Judah He-hasid, a contemporary of Francis of Assisi and a Jewish parallel to him, was regarded as a popular model and his teachings were widely disseminated in various literary versions (that is, transmitted and often elaborated) on the basis of hearsay. Thus many Jews evidently identified with him even though they may have been too weak always to live by his precepts. Basically, every moralist takes a dim view of his time, for it never corresponds to the ethical standards that he applies to it.

Literature on these questions may be found in the pertinent articles and bibliographies in the comprehensive Jewish histories and encyclopedias as well as in the following: Jacob Katz, *Exclusiveness and Tolerance: Studies in Jewish-Gentile Relations in Medieval and Modern Times,* paperback ed. (New York, 1962); M. Guttmann, *Das Judentum und seine Umwelt* (Berlin, 1927); M. Güdemann, *Geschichte des Erziehungswesens und der Kultur der abendländischen Juden,* 3 vols. (Vienna, 1880–88); F. J. Baer, "The Religious-Social Tendency of *Sefer Hasidim*" (Hebrew with English synopsis), *Zion* 3 (1938): i–50, i–ii; Ephraim E. Urbach, *Baalei Ha-Tossafot (The Tosaphists: Their History, Writings and Methods* (Jerusalem, 1955), index, esp. pp. 50, 58, 78, 204, 388; Israel Abrahams, *Jewish Life in the Middle Ages,* new ed. (London, 1938); Cecil Roth, "The Ordinary Jew in the Middle Ages," in *Studies and Essays in Honor of Abraham A. Neumann* (Philadelphia, 1962), 424–36.

THE COMMUNITY AS A SUBSTITUTE FOR A HOMELAND: Louis Finkelstein, *Jewish Self-* 124ff.
Government in the Middle Ages (New York, 1924); Kurt Wilhelm, *Von jüdischer Gemeinde und Gemeinschaft* (Berlin, 1938); S. W. Baron, *The Jewish Community: Its History and Structure to the American Revolution*, 3 vols. (Philadelphia, 1942) (vol. 3 contains extensive bibliographies). Concerning the beginnings and traditions of the Jewish community from ancient times, see Fritz Baer (Hebr. with Eng. synopsis) in *Zion* 15 (1950), esp. 2. C. H. Ben-Sasson, *Mekoma shel Hakehilla Vehair Betoldot Yisrael* (Community and city in the history of Israel) in the collection of the Historical Society, Jerusalem (1967), 161f. Cf. also Fritz Baer in *EJ* 7:191ff. about the West European Jewish community in the Middle Ages and the modern period. On p. 191: "The Jewish community performs all functions of the medieval city government with the exception of the military ones." Concerning a parallel phenomenon to the preserving function of the Jewish religion and communal constitution, see *Der Grosse Brockhaus* 7 (1930): 630 about Greece: "It was two institutions that preserved the Greek national feeling during the centuries of bondage: the church, bearer of the national idea to this day, and the communal constitution under the archons or Kodia Bashi which the Greeks had been conceded by the Turks, who were incapable of administrative innovations." The communities often practiced strict authority and used expulsion as a coercive measure against any deviation from the established norm. The statutes of the community of Crete from the thirteenth century oppose expulsion for insignificant offenses and decree "that from now on and henceforth no member of our community shall be permitted to lie to a non-Jew or to deceive him, whether a Jew buys from him or whether he sells to him. Anyone who cheats and deceives non-Jews blasphemes His name among the nations. . . ." (Kurt Wilhelm, *Von jüdischer Gemeinde* 15).

SANCTIFICATION OF PRACTICES *("MINHAG")* AND EQUATION WITH THE COMMAND- 127f.
MENT *("MITZVAH"):* Cf. I. Elbogen, *Der jüdische Gottesdienst*, 356f., 368ff.; Ephraim E. Urbach, *Baalei Ha-Tossafot*, 71. The local *minhagim* were carefully collected and recorded. Given our rational viewpoints and standards, we often lack proper understanding for an evaluation of rigid adherence to ritual precepts and practices among both Jews and non-Jews. However, in the view of antiquity which still prevailed in the Middle Ages (and in certain areas has prevailed to this day), the precise observance of religious practices is redemptive in nature, and lapses from their painstaking observance are regarded as an offense to the deity, which explains the frequently cruel punishments and expiations from Greek drama to medieval torture, from excommunication to expulsion from the synagogue. Malicious intent has always been discerned in the evildoer, something that may endanger the totality and expose it to divine wrath. Cf. also Rudolf Ihering's remarks about the people's love for its own jurisdiction in his well-known book *Der Kampf ums Recht* (first published in 1872; new ed., Rudolf Huch, 1925), 31.

The Jews later established their customs in such a way that they took their old practices, clothes, and linguistic usage along when circumstances forced them to flee or emigrate to other towns and countries.

THE MEANING OF LIFE IN THE DIASPORA: Yitzhak Fritz Baer, *Galut* (Berlin, 1936), 127f.
16ff.

THE THIRTEEN ARTICLES OF FAITH OF MAIMONIDES: These articles, which Maimoni- 127
des formulated in his commentary on the Mishnah, were one of many attempts since the time of the Mishnah to set down the Judaic faith in binding form. They were never given the universally valid character of dogmas, though they became very popular in their original form, their abridgment, or their poetic formulation in song. With the possible exception of belief in God's indivisible unity, Judaism does not have

dogmas in the strict sense of the term—bidding and salvation-giving doctrines and truths, as in Christianity. Judaism places the emphasis on action rather than on creed and faith. Of the comprehensive literature I shall mention *EJ* 5:1167ff. ("Dogmen"); *EJJ* 3 ("Articles of Faith"), esp. 355ff. ("Maimonides"); Leo Baeck, *Das Wesen des Judentums* (1922), 4ff.; Isidore Epstein, *Judaism* (Penguin, 1959), 215ff.

128   "KIDDUSH HASHEM" (Voluntary death for the sanctification of God's name): The word *shem* (name) takes the place of God's name, which is too holy to utter. The concept and the reality in the sense of martyrology for the Jewish-monotheistic religion (and for an idea in general) date from the time of the Maccabees. Cf. Yitzhak F. Baer, *Yisrael bein Ha-ammim* (Israel among the nations) (Jerusalem, 1935), as well as the summary in the newspaper *Ha-aretz*, 19 December 1958. Concerning the history of the concept and literature about it, see C. H. Ben-Sasson in *EJJ* 10:977ff. Cf. also *Holy War and Martyrology: Lectures Delivered at the Eleventh Convention of the Historical Society of Israel* (in Hebrew) (Jerusalem, 1967). *Kiddush Hashem* was the Jewish counterpole to the Christian "Holy War" since the time of the Crusades. *EJJ* 10:983: "Thus, through the curious workings of irony of history, the Christian crusading venture and Jewish martyrdom by *kiddush ha-Shem* each became in its own particular way expressions of a holy war waged for the glory of God." The readiness for self-sacrifice, for which Abraham's readiness to sacrifice Isaac often served as an example and comparison, by no means excluded armed self-defense. Such defense was practiced in various places (e.g., Mainz) during the Crusades and on numerous subsequent occasions; it may, in fact, have made a significant contribution to the bravery and sacrificial spirit of the soldiers in the fights for the defense of the work of construction in Palestine before and after the foundation of the State of Israel, for any readiness for self-sacrifice has always been transcended by the highest commandment of Judaism, the sanctification of life. The question as to when this highest precept of Judaism should take precedence over the other precept of letting oneself be killed, or even killing oneself, for the "sanctification of God's name" *(kiddush hashem)* was always posed anew at various times by authoritative personalities within Jewry and answered in various ways according to the circumstances and the personal convictions. Because such questions were asked, a martyr was never venerated (even though he was given the Hebrew name *kadosh*, holy man) like the martyrs of Christianity, and he was never eager to obtain this honor. Wherever people were able to save their lives and the life of the Jewish community through emigration, flight, intercession, donations of money, and services, often even through a sham conversion to another faith (on this problem, cf. Part 1, p. 132f.) they did so— out of a natural vital instinct, but also because Judaism has always regarded the preservation of life per se as the supreme duty. Not infrequently Leopold Ranke's words about the French Huguenots who left their country for the sake of their religious conviction could be applied to the Jews who fled from their enemies' demand that they convert: "This time the heroism of creed is evidenced not in resistance but, if one may use a paradoxical term, in flight" (L. Ranke, *Französische Geschichte* 3 [1852–61], 396). As reported by Emanuel Rackmann (*American Zionist*, March 1971, 35), it was in this spirit that in the Hitler period the religious Zionist leader Rabbi Yitzhak Nissenbaum admonished his fellow inhabitants of the ghetto that it was now every Jew's duty to do his utmost to save his own life, for the commandment of *kiddush hashem* had different meanings at different times: "During the Middle Ages it required martyrdom. Why? The enemy wanted to conquer the souls of the Jews. He had no design to massacre—only to convert to Christianity. . . . When the Jews committed suicide, or allowed themselves to be slaughtered, they thereby made it impossible for the enemy to capture the souls. However, Hitler and his cohorts wanted to destroy the Jewish body—to annihilate us physically. The

Mitzvah of *Kiddush ha-Shem* therefore required that he be frustrated by our survival. Jews should do everything—by flight or bravery—to live."

PILGRIMAGES: Cf. Abraham Jaari's *Massa'ot Eretz-Yisrael* (Journeys to Palestine from   129
the Middle Ages to the beginning of the return to Zion) (Tel Aviv, 1936).

JEWISH MYSTICISM: Cf. the fundamental works of Gershom Scholem, primarily   130f.
Major Trends in Jewish Mysticism (Jerusalem 1941) and the essay "Zum Verständnis
der messianischen Idee im Judentum," in his collection *Judaica*, 1 (1963), 7–74.

HISTORICAL CONSCIOUSNESS OF THE JEWS: As we know, the application of the term   130f.
"pariah people" to the Jews as a scientific idea, as distinct from its emotional use in
the popular discussion of the Jewish question since the eighteenth century, was
originated by Max Weber (*Religionssoziologie* 1:181f., 3:388ff.) In Weber's
Wirtschaftsgeschichte (1958), 175, his view is summarized as follows: "Prophecy and
the aftereffects of exile changed the long-settled Jewish people into a guest nation,
and its rituals exclude any rootedness in the future. Anyone who clung to the Jewish
ritual could not be a farmer. Thus the Jews became a pariah people." Cf. also pp.
305ff. For a discussion and critique of this theory, cf. Hans Liebeschütz, *Das Judentum im deutschen Geschichtsbild* (1967), 314ff.; Toni Oelsner, Leo Baeck Institute
Year Book 7 (1962), 194ff.; Hannah Arendt, "The Jew as a Pariah," *Jewish Social
Studies* 6:99ff.; S. W. Baron, *A Social and Religious History of the Jews*, 1, 2d ed.,
297.

VALUATION OF WEALTH: By way of qualifying my remarks, it should be noted that a   131f.
rule of the rich developed in the surrounding urban economy as well, a rule that was
even more powerful than it was among the Jews (according to Y. F. Baer in *EJ*
7:202ff.), just as Jewish life was by no means as isolated from the surrounding world as
it might appear. However, in the Jewish urban community there was hardly anything
comparable to the bitter struggles of the lower classes of urban artisans against the
dominant wealthy patrician class.

The philosophy of the Jews in the Middle Ages (and to a certain extent to our day)
is perhaps best reflected in the daily grace after meals. Its essence—the four
benedictions—derives from ancient times. In a number of countries and places
different supplications were frequently added that tell us about the needs and desires
of those who said those prayers. There still is no·exact presentation of this development of the prayer. Up to now research has had what may be called an essentially
archaeological orientation—that is, it has attempted to establish the text of the
earliest core prayers, but insufficient systematic attention has been paid to the
evolution of the prayer in accordance with the needs of an age and its living
conditions. This, however, is important for the history of the plain people, which has
unjustifiably been investigated far less than that of the intelligentsia. The history of
the latter has often been virtually identified with the history of the entire Jewish
people. Cf. David Baumgardt's fine article "Grace after Bread: The Jewish World
View as Reflected in a Prayer," *Commentary*, July 1946, 15–19; concerning the
personality of the author, see his memoir "Looking Back on a German University
Career," *Year Book 10* of the Leo Baeck Institute (1965), 239ff. The ancient part is the
expression of thanks for the food, the Land of Israel (for the possession of which
thanks were always given, even when it was no longer really possessed), and for the
rebuilding of Jerusalem, which was confidently expected. But consider all the other
things this prayer contained: thanks for having been led out of Egypt, the "house of
bondage," at the beginning of known national history, something that is to be kept so
vivid that in the Passover haggadah every Jew is requested to be aware of it as if he

himself had participated in the exodus from Egypt; thanks for "thy convenant which thou hast sealed in our flesh" (that is, in the act of circumcision which makes it impossible for a Jew to forget his existence as a Jew even when he is performing the most intimate act of his life. And then the supplication that God may have mercy upon his people, Israel, and his city, Jerusalem, and free them from all their troubles, is followed by what seems like a deep, heartfelt sigh: "O Lord our God, let us not be in need either of the gifts of mortals or of their loans, but only of thy helping hand, which is full, open, holy, and ample, so that we may never be put to shame or humiliated," by an expression of unshakable faith in the kindness of God—"thou hast dealt kindly, dost deal kindly, and wilt deal kindly with us"—and by a number of supplications which begin with *"Harachman,"* the All-merciful One. We shall mention this particularly characteristic one: "May the All-merciful break the yoke from off our neck and lead us upright to our land." The prayer ends with a dual supplication for peace: "He who maketh peace in his high places, may he make peace for us and for all Israel. . . . May he grant his people strength and bless it with peace." (The English wording is based on the *Authorized Daily Prayer Book,* edited by Joseph H. Hertz.)

133ff.   THE PROBLEM OF THE MARRANOS: Cecil Roth, *A History of the Marranos* (Philadelphia, 1947); concerning the word and the concept, cf. p. 27. Attempts have been made to trace the word to fragments of Hebrew words. Roth remarks, and probably rightly so, that "all this linguistic speculation is needless. The word Marrano is an old Spanish term dating back to the early Middle Ages and meaning swine. Applied to the recent converts in the first place perhaps ironically, with reference to their aversion from the flesh of the animal in question, it ultimately became a general term of execration, which spread during the sixteenth century to most languages of Western Europe. The word expresses succinctly and unmistakably all the depth of hatred and contempt which the ordinary Spaniard felt for the unsincere neophytes by whom he was surrounded. It is the constancy shown by them and their descendants that has redeemed the term from its former insulting connotation, and endowed it with its enduring power of romance."

133f.   THE BAPTIZED JEWS' ATTACHMENT TO JUDAISM: Naturally, detachment involved the abandonment of many economic interests. Internal and external conditions had made the Jews in the medieval cities develop into what the sociologists call an "interest group"—that is, they were not just a religious community, though later they may have appeared as one from a modern, liberal point of view; of course, the religious elements always remained the foundation. A presentation of the events and problems may be found in Graetz, vol. 5; Dubnow, vol. 5; and especially in Yitzhak F. Baer, the greatest expert on this period and its problems. Cf. in particular his comprehensive books *Die Juden im christlichen Spanien* (2 vols. of archival documents) (Berlin, 1929–36) and *History of the Jews in Christian Spain,* a detailed history in 2 vols. (1961–66). E. Rivkin (*Jewish Quarterly Review* 48 [1957]: 190ff.) emphasizes and overemphasizes the political and social background of the persecutions of the Marranos.

Concerning the problem of the baptized Jews, cf. Baer's article about the apostate Abner of Burgos in *Korrespondenzblatt des Vereins zur Gründung und Erhaltung einer Akademie für die Wissenschaft des Judentums* 10 (1929): 20–37 as well as his *Galut,* 54ff. A vivid presentation based on a trip to Spain may be found in M. Ehrenpreis, *Das Land zwischen Orient und Okzident* (1927), and there is a detailed account of the life and thought of the Marranos and the viewpoint and methods of the Inquisition, based on its documents, in Haim Beinart, *Conversos on*

Trial by Inquisition (Hebr.) (Tel Aviv, 1965). The standard work on the Inquisition is H. C. Lea, *History of the Inquisition of Spain*, 4 vols. (1922).

Among the shorter studies is A. S. Turbeville, *The Spanish Inquisition* (London, 1932). Good overviews may be found in most general encyclopedias (e.g., *Der Grosse Brockhaus* 9 (1930): 137ff.) and the Jewish encyclopedias, particularly *EJ* 8:431–460 (Yitzhak F. Baer and Cecil Roth) and *EJJ* 8:1380–1470 (Cecil Roth). The institution of the Inquisition *(Inquisitio haereticae pravitatis)* was officially introduced at the Councils of Verona (1183) and the Fourth Lateran Council (1215) to fight the heretics. It differed from other court procedures principally in that the ecclesiastic committee of inquiry—at first the bishops, later central investigative (inquisitorial) bodies—were able to undertake the investigation, indictment, and sentencing of any Christian suspected of heresy without giving any notice of charges against him. It was not necessary to furnish the accused person with exact information about the charges against him. Whenever possible, "confessions" were exacted through cruel torture. Those who were "obdurate" and refused to confess or repent were sentenced to death. The passing of sentence was turned into a festive public "act of faith" (Spanish *Auto de Fé*, Portuguese—after its introduction to Portugal in 1540—*Auto da Fé*). Participation in it and its sadistic elaborations was regarded as a pious act. The Jews were treated as heretics by the Inquisition if they had (voluntarily or forcibly) converted to Christianity, but not if they remained loyal to Judaism. The property of sentenced persons was confiscated, and of course this was apt to produce accusations and sentences for the sake of such confiscations. This procedure encouraged informers. When a death sentence was pronounced, the sentenced man was turned over to the "secular arm," the authorities of the state, and the punishment was "mitigated" through a recommendation that it be executed "without bloodshed"—that is, by means of burning. This legal fiction of the Catholic Church was based on this passage in John 15:6: "If any man abide not in me, he is cast forth as a branch and is withered, and men gather them and cast them into the fire, and they are burned." In point of fact, killing by fire had been performed by various peoples as a cruel punishment since ancient times, particularly by the Romans during the persecutions of Christians.

PURITY OF BLOOD: In addition to the works already mentioned, see Albert A. Sicroff, 135 *Les controverses des statuts de 'Pureté de Sang' en Espagne du XVᵉ au XVIIᵉ siècle* (Paris, 1960), as well as the review of that book in *Jewish Journal of Sociology* 2:383f.

At the conclusion of this chapter I shall reprint excerpts from the characterization of the Jews in the Middle Ages given by Leopold Zunz in his book *Über Geschichte und Literatur* (1845): "Tractable as individuals, inexorable in their totality . . . suffering with conviction for the sake of a dreadful future and unsure of what the next day would bring . . . this tragic situation produced that contrast between unalterable steadfastness and ceaseless change. People who, if there is a conflagration at their place, are not rescued but thrown into the fire. . . . To be a pious Jew in order to be purified by suffering for the time of the Messiah and a happy life—that was the task of existence and determined the substance of life. . . ."

4

The Development of the Jewish Question in the Modern Age up to the French Revolution

137 THE MODERN AGE: THE IDEA AND DELIMITATION OF THE EPOCH: Cf. the basic remarks on the concept of the Middle Ages in Part 2, pp. 500f. For the idea of the modern age the discussion is closely connected with the debate about the concept, the nature, and the beginning of the Renaissance in Italy and Europe. Since Jacob Burckhardt's famous book *The Civilization of the Renaissance in Italy*, which first appeared in 1860 and made the concept of the Renaissance part of the European cultural tradition, a great deal has been written about the beginning, the nature, and the existence of the Renaissance and its significance as the beginning of the modern age and a transition to it—especially after Konrad Burdach had, in his academic treatise *Sinn und Ursprung des Wortes Renaissance und Reformation*, emphasized the uninterrupted continuity between this turn of an era and the Middle Ages, at least since Dante (who already plays a big role in the writings of Burckhardt). Despite all animadversions and specialized studies about the connection with the Middle Ages—a connection that the analysis of every historical event makes almost self-evident for any knowledgeable student of history—it would be a methodological mistake to deny the idea of the Renaissance as a specific period, as Arnold Hauser did in his excellent *Sozialgeschichte der Kunst und Literatur* (Munich, 1953, 1973), or to place its beginning too far back in the Middle Ages. When it is a matter of making divisions into periods, the self-awareness of an age is not always the decisive thing, but if such a self-awareness exists, it surely has determinative force. There has hardly been another period that perceived itself as new—first in Italy and then also in more northern parts of Europe—as a "renaissance," a resuscitation not only of antiquity but also of original creative powers, particularly in art and the sciences, to the extent that this period of the fifteenth and sixteenth centuries did. The fact that this consciousness was not present in all population groups and all psychic strata of leading personalities does not militate against this. As we have already emphasized on a number of occasions, past times continue to live in every age, and it is the mixture of the old with the new, its juxtaposition and superimposition, that determine the character of an age and its personalities. The secular elements, scientific curiosity, the new notions of a wider earthly world, and skepticism about traditional dogmas and teachings about supernatural powers gradually capture the minds not only of a select minority but the minds and hearts of wider circles of the population as well. It has rightly been pointed out that new continents have been discovered amidst medieval notions in almost paradoxical fashion. The discovery of America by Columbus is a case in point. The age was to a great extent anticlerical, but it was by no means anti-Church or unbelieving. The authority of the Church was replaced by a

new authority, that of Latin and Greek antiquity, and often the old mingled with the new. This can be seen especially graphically in the new portrayals of events from the Old and New Testaments, such as Michelangelo's painting "The Holy Family" of 1504–6. With the influence of Roman and Greek literature the ancient image of the Jews, as formulated by Tacitus and others, was revived as well. As we have shown, it already served as the basis for the Christian image of the Jew (cf. Part 1, pp. 40ff. 68f.). Now this image newly and independently entered the consciousness of educated persons and could be absorbed by them as an additional confirmation of the Christian dogmatic and economic-social stereotype of the Jew.

As for the literature on these questions, I refer to G. Barraclough, *History in a Changing World* (1955), 59ff.; W. Ferguson, *The Renaissance in Historical Thought* (Cambridge, Mass., 1948); William J. Bouwsma, *The Interpretation of Renaissance Humanism* (New York, 1959); Egon Friedell, *A Cultural History of the Modern Age*, vol. 1 (1930); Denis Hay, *The Italian Renaissance in Its Historical Background* (Cambridge, 1970); J. Huizinga, *Men and Ideas* (1959–70), 243ff.; *Propyläen-Weltgeschichte* 6 (1964); 431ff., 10 (1965); 612ff.

THE JEWISH QUESTION AT THE BEGINNING OF THE MODERN AGE GENERAL CHARAC-   137f.
TERISTICS: As emphasized earlier, I regard it as inappropriate to make a different division for Jewish history than for general history. Basically, any history of a people has a division of its own, but at the same time it is so closely bound up with the history of the inhabitants of the realm in which it takes place that it is impossible to isolate it from that history. The dichotomy, the ever-increasing gap between the inner and the outer world of Jewry, is characteristic of this transitional period of Jewish history from the Middle Ages to the Age of Emancipation beginning with the late eighteenth century. The expectations and disappointments of Jews and Christians that were produced by the concurrence of the Renaissance, schisms, economic transformations, etc., among Jews and Christians were important elements in the development of the complex called Jewish question in that period. Of the literature on this, cf. especially Salo W. Baron's notes in his *Social and Religious History of the Jews* 13 (1969), 389ff.

LUTHER'S ATTITUDE TOWARD JUDAISM AND THE JEWISH QUESTION: Here, of course,   138ff.
we can consider Luther's personality in its brilliance and numerous contradictions only to the extent that it concerns our problem. But even in Luther's attitude toward the Jewish question his personality is evidenced in this mixture of apparent or real contradictions and its inner consistency. Luther's influence upon his age, and even more beyond it and down to our time, can hardly be overestimated. He was the central personality of the Reformation and the Protestantism that emerged from it. His Bible translation became the family reading of the German people; its language and that of his writings laid the foundation for the modern German language and literature and thus became the basis of German thought and feeling.

As regards his attitude toward Judaism and the Jewish question, the antithesis between the supposed philo-Semitism of his work *Dass Jesus ein geborener Jude sei* (1523) and the crudely anti-Semitic statements twenty years later *(Von den Juden und ihren Lügen, Vom Schem Hamphoras)*, which had been preceded in 1538, five years earlier, by the equally anti-Jewish *Brief wider die Sabbater*, has been interpreted to mean that disappointing encounters with Jews as well as the nonfulfillment of his hopes for their conversion had caused a radical change in his thinking. By contrast, Reinhold Lewin pointed out in his book *Luther's Stellung zu den Juden: Ein Beitrag zur Geschichte der Juden während des Reformationszeitalters* (published in Berlin in 1911, but still a standard reference) that those who quote the philo-Semitic statements in the Introduction and conclusion out of context and on that basis praise the "unprejudiced tolerance of the Reformer" mistake the nature of the first-named work. "Anyone who does this," he writes, "who sees the main value of the work in the rejection of the papal policy toward the Jews completely misinterprets Luther and imputes to him intentions that he never thought of. He was interested in the Jews only as objects for conversion. . . . It was from this vantage point that he viewed the Jewish question. With his remarks and proposals he wanted to gain the confidence of the Jews in order to convert them to Christianity, which was for him, too—and especially for him!—the one and only redeeming faith. Luther's book is no more and no less than a missionary tract and does not pretend to be anything else." (In 1943 Reinhold Lewin was deported by the Nazis to Poland from Breslau, where he had been active as a liberal rabbi since 1938. Cf. *EJJ* 4 : 1355). The view that Luther had a uniform conception that was "applied differently in accordance with the events of the time but never changed" is espoused from a theological point of view by one of the most recent writers on that subject. In chapter 5 of his book *Kirche und Synagogue: Handbuch zur Geschichte von Christen und Juden*, vol. 1 (Stuttgart, 1968) ("Die Zeit der Reformation," 363–452) Wilhelm Maurer writes on page 375: "There is no fundamental change in Luther's attitude toward postbiblical Judaism. Thus it won't do to play the young Luther off against the old one and to correct or replace whatever one finds intolerable about the later Reformer with statements of the younger one. In all basic questions of Luther's theology and in ours, any Lutheran apologias for Luther are inappropriate. . . ." Luther's work of 1523, which has often been given a philo-Semitic interpretation, could "best be characterized as a Christological study of the human nature of Jesus, though an apologetic-missionary attitude toward Judaism is inherent in it." The greater emphasis on the negative sides of this theological view is closely connected with the progress of Luther's Bible translation in which he clashes with the rabbinic exegesis in hostile fashion and consequently bases himself more on the Christian-scholastic interpretation of the Middle Ages. On the other hand, the political alliance between the Reformation as headed by him and the territorial sovereigns also played a part here. This gave greater dogmatic and pragmatic importance to sociopolitical questions like interest and usury, the legal position of the Jews as *Kammerknechte* or serfs of the Christian authorities, the toleration or expulsion of the Jews from the territories that had adopted the Reformation, etc. Added to this was the religious appeal of Judaism that manifested itself in radical religious movements and seemed dangerous to Luther. After all, after the Peasants' War he opposed with increasing severity all movements that questioned the existing political and social powers, and he advocated a merciless struggle against these as well as the radical religious reform movements (Sabbater, Anabaptists, etc.), a struggle for which he created the concept "severe mercy."

In this religiously, politically, and socially supercharged atmosphere the notions of the Christian Middle Ages, which Luther embraced to a far greater extent, at least emotionally, than is often assumed, gained ever greater power over him. He, the profoundly pious man who knew that he and others were freed from the constant threat and burden of sin only by unconditional faith in Jesus the redeemer, everywhere saw demons and devils who sought to thwart his work. The image of the Jew that had developed in the Middle Ages as a stereotype increasingly coalesced with that of the devil who threatens a Christian at every turn. Against the devil no word is too harsh and no measure too severe. The unrestraint of his temperament and his absolute belief that he, Luther, was called to rid the world of devilish demons (among which he included the popes and their Catholic adherents) were additional factors. This is the foundation of his anti-Jewish formulations, which in crudity, cruelty, and the directness of their consequences surpass anything that had previously been written against the Jews and any practical suggestions that had been made concerning them as well as most writings and suggestions of later times.

MOCKERY OF CHRISTIANITY BY JEWS: Regarding Luther's (and numerous later Jew-   141
haters') accusation that when among themselves the Jews orally and in a number of writings derided Jesus and Mary or called them names, it should be pointed out that despite the denials of Jewish apologetes of yesteryear and today, this accusation is basically correct. Considering the antithetical nature of the views and the inhumane treatment meted out to the Jews by "Christian charity," how could it be otherwise? As we see things today, in their writings, which were accessible only to them—in general, for linguistic reasons alone—and in their intercourse with one another, the Jews had every right to say and write what they thought and felt and what they defended themselves against. It was, of course, different by the standards of that time, for which the Christian world was the only valid one and which regarded any expression that conflicted with its dogmas as blasphemy, sacrilege, and heresy.

In addition to the literature already mentioned, we shall refer to the following: H. Graetz, *Geschichte der Juden* 9; Dubnow, *Weltgeschichte des jüdischen Volkes* 6; S. W. Baron, *A Social and Religious History of the Jews*, 2d ed., vol. 13, including detailed information about sources and literature down to the present time; Ismar Elbogen, *Geschichte der Juden in Deutschland* (1935), 103ff. In the revised edition of the last-named book (Frankfurt, 1966) Eleonore Sterling analyzes "the psychological and theological transformation" that took place in Luther after 1523 and writes (p. 92): "While Luther had in his youthful work spoken of a brotherhood of truly believing Christians and Jews against the popes and misrepresenters of the Bible, he now [1543] only spoke to Christians, and in particular to the authorities—princes, clergymen, and communities. The Jews he now only regarded as lost and damned . . . children of the devil who did not share in the annunciation and grace of God." On page 93 she writes that he had "burdened the victims with the curse of God that was feared. The faith of the Jews was demonized and his own wickedness was projected onto them." In this way the Jews become "a brood of vipers and children of the devil."

Cf. also Ludwig Geiger, *Die deutsche Literatur und die Juden* (Berlin, 1910), 25–45 ("Johann Reuchlin und der Kampf um die Bücher der Juden"); Samuel Kraus, "Luther und die Juden," in *Der Jude*, ed. Martin Buber, 2:544–47, reprinted in Kurt Wilhelm, ed., *Wissenschaft des Judentums im deutschen Sprachbereich* (Tübingen, 1967), 1:309–14; Selma Stern-Täubler, "Die Vorstellung vom Juden und vom Judentum in der Ideologie der Reformationszeit," in *Essays Presented to Leo Baeck* (London, 1954), 194–211; Selma Stern, *Josel of Rosheim* (Philadelphia, 1965); Carl Cohen, "Martin Luther and His Jewish Contemporaries," *Jewish Social Studies* 25 (1963): 195–204; Salo W. Baron, "John Calvin and the Jews," in *Harry A. Wolffsohn Jubilee Volume I* (Jerusalem, 1965), 141–63; Carl Cohen, "Martin Buber and His Influence on the Jewish Situation," Leo Baeck Institute, *Year Book 13* (1968), 93–101; Arnold Agus, "Luther and the Rabbis," *Jewish Quarterly Review*, July 1967, 63–698; H. H. Ben-Sasson, *The Reformation in Contemporary Jewish Eyes* (Jerusalem: Jewish Academy, 1970).

To my knowledge, there is no study on the continued influence of Luther's image of the Jews that is based on thorough research and weighs all factors. Cf. J. Neeb, *Luthers und Herders Stimmen über die Juden* (Lübeck, 1817); Ludwig Fischer, *Martin Luther: Von den Juden und ihren Lügen—Ein crystallisierter Auszug aus dessen Schriften über der Juden Verblendung, Jammer, Bekehrung und Zukunft. Ein Beitrag zur Charakteristik dieses Volkes* (Leipzig, 1838) (with a preface attacking the Jewish "Jung-Deutschland" movement); Walther Linden, ed., *Luthers Kampf-*

schriften gegen das Judentum (Berlin, 1936); Peter F. Wiener, "Martin Luther: Hitler's Spiritual Ancestor," in *The Peace Pamphlet No. 3* (London, ca. 1945); Winfried Schiffner, "Luther, Hitler und die Juden: Eine Blütenlese aus dem Jubiläumsjahr der 450. Wiederkehr des Geburtstages Luthers im Jahre 1933," *Tribüne. Zeitschrift zum Verständnis des Judentums* 3, no. 10 (1964): 1064–71.

At the Nuremberg Trial of the chief war criminals, Julius Streicher testified that it was actually Luther who ought to be in the dock, for he said and wrote all the things against the Jews with which he, Streicher, was now being charged, and often in even more drastic formulations. Cf. the official proceedings of the international military tribunal (Nuremberg, 1947–49), 12:346ff., 364, and *Wiener Library Bulletin* 15, no. 3(1961): 45. Concerning Luther's influence on Kant's view of Judaism, cf. Nathan Rotenstreich, *The Recurrent Pattern: Studies in Anti-Judaism in Modern Thought* (London, 1963), 44. It may be appropriate to point out that in the general works on the Reformation, from Ranke to the *Propyläen-Weltgeschichte*, the attitude of Protestantism toward Judaism and the Jewish question is usually not mentioned. To Heinrich Heine, Luther was "not merely the greatest but also the most German man in our history"; in his character "all virtues and defects of the Germans are most magnificently combined" (Elster ed., 4:190; Insel ed., 7:227). Nietzsche struggled with Luther's personality all his life; as his biographer Walter Kaufmann points out (*Nietzsche* [New York, 1968], 348), his fight against Christianity is essentially a coming to terms with Luther's view of Christianity. The numerous pertinent passages in Nietzsche's writings are listed in Richard Oehler's *Nietzsche-Register* (Kröner Taschenausgabe, no. 170), 275–77. An unconventional but perceptive evaluation of Luther's personality, one that is probably fair in its positive and negative judgments, of Luther's position between the Middle Ages and the modern age, and of the nature of the Protestantism created by him may be found in *A Cultural History of the Modern Age* by the writer, actor, and cultural historian Egon Friedell, vol. 1 (New York, 1930; new ed., 1964). In chapter 6, "The German Religion," Friedell does not mention Luther's stand on the Jewish question, but he possibly contributes to its illumination by presenting Luther's struggle with God at a period of personal crisis as a struggle with the Jewish God Jehovah. With typical self-hatred Friedell, a Viennese Jew, characterizes the Jewish God as one "imagined as a purely national figure, concerned only with the interests of his own people, a hard autocrat and a pitiless persecutor of all rivals" (241) and Christianity as "the purest doctrine that has ever been or ever will be put before the world" (242). In light of this it is paradoxical and tragic that in March 1938, a few days after German troops had marched into Vienna, Friedell hurled himself to his death from the window of his fourth-floor apartment when Nazis rang his bell—presumably as part of their program to translate Luther's recipes for the solution of the Jewish question into action.

145f. INTENSIFICATION OF ANTI-JEWISH SENTIMENT IN THE CATHOLIC WORLD: Concerning the Reform movements in the Catholic Church and the Counter Reformation, cf., in addition to specialized studies (e.g., Gustav Droysen, *Geschichte der Gegenreformation* [Berlin, 1893]; Reinhold Schneider, *Philipp der Zweite oder Religion und Macht* [Frankfurt: Fischer-Bücherei, 1953]) and the pertinent sections in the well-known histories of the world, Leopold Ranke's *Geschichte der römischen Päpste in den letzten vier Jahrhunderten* (first published in 1834 and later in numerous editions; chapters 5–7 are still very informative and worth reading); chapters 5–10 in Lord Acton's *Lectures on Modern History* (1906; Fontana Library, 1960); and chap. 7 in Friedell, *Cultural History.* ("The Night of St. Bartholomew"). Concerning Jewish history in that period, see Graetz, vol. 9; Dubnow, vol. 6; Baron, vol. 14

("Catholic Restoration and Wars of Religion" [1969], with very extensive bibliographies); Cecil Roth, *The History of the Jews of Italy* (Philadelphia, 1946), chaps. 5–8.

THE GHETTO: The literature on the ghetto, its origin, its nature, its history, the effect 146ff. of ghetto life on the Jews, and the ghetto as a general socioeconomic and anthropological phenomenon is so extensive—who has never made at least a few significant or banal and sterotypical, biased or melodramatic remarks on the subject?—that we can here mention only what the author found particularly revealing or what may serve the reader as documentation and supplementation of the information given in the text and the excursuses. Despite this varied literature there still is no presentation that sums up the results of specialized research from a semantic and historical-sociological point of view and pays due attention to the specifically Jewish aspects of the problem. (In recent years similar yet basically different phenomena have frequently—and dubiously—been subsumed under the same name.) The most comprehensive attempt was made in 1928 by the German-Jewish American sociologist Louis Wirth (1897–1952) in his book *The Ghetto* (originally written as a dissertation; reissued in 1956 by Phoenix Books, Chicago). Naturally, this book does not take account of the literature that has appeared since then or the transformations through the events of the Nazi period of the concept and the reality designated by it, not to mention the present-day transference and occasional falsification.

For information about the word and the concept, cf. especially S. Kahn in *JE* 5 (1903): 625–55; A. Kober in *JL* 3 (1929): 457–60; Umberto Cassuto in *EJ* (1931): 390–93; Joshua Starr in *Universal Jewish Encyclopedia* 4 (1948): 597–603; Cecil (Bezalel) Roth in *HE* 10 (1955): 595–601; and in *EJJ* 10 (1971): 81–84; Cecil Roth, *History of the Jews in Italy* (New York, 1946), chap. 8 ("The Age of the Ghetto"); idem, "Origin of Ghetto," in *Romania* 60 (1934): 67–76, reprinted in *Personalities and Events in Jewish History* (Philadelphia, 1953), 226–36; I. B. Sermoneta, "Regarding the Origin of the Word 'Ghetto'" (Hebr. with Eng. synopsis), *Tarbiz* 8–9 (January 1963): 1925; C. Schmeruk in *Scritti in Memoria di Umberto Nachon* (Jerusalem, 1978), 235ff.; Ferdinand Gregorovius, *The Ghetto and the Jews of Rome* (New York: Schocken Library, 1948); Hermann Vogelstein, *Rome* (Philadelphia, 1940); Travers Herford in *The Legacy of Israel* (Oxford, 1927), 127ff.; Israel Abrahams, *Jewish Life in the Middle Ages*, (London, 1932), 78ff.; David Philippson, *Old European Jewries* (Philadelphia, 1894); Moritz Stern, *Urkundliche Beiträge über die Stellung der Päpste zu den Juden* (1894); Oswald Spengler, *The Decline of the West*; Franz Oppenheimer, *Soziologische Streifzüge* 2 (Jena, 1927), 242ff. Concerning the connection between the ghetto and the oriental "millet" system, see Toynbee, *A Study of History* 8:272ff. (abridged ed., 2:171ff.) Regarding Heinrich Heine's use of the concept, see the index for the quotations, in English and German, in Israel Tabak, *Judaic Lore in Heine* (Baltimore, 1948). Concerning the concept of a "psychological ghetto" in Theodor Herzl, see Alex Bein, *Theodore Herzl* (Philadelphia, 1941), index.

The origin of the word and the stages in which it was adopted as a general Jewish and international concept have still not been fully elucidated, and there is no modern, comprehensive semantic investigation. Such an investigation would have to show how the word entered linguistic usage, official documents, and literature, and how it came to be commonly employed. Possible derivations include the Greek word *geiton* (neighbor), the German words *Gatter* (fence) and *Gitter* (lattice), the Hebrew *get* (document; specifically: writ of divorcement—a word occasionally used in that sense in Italy and elsewhere), the Italian *guidecca* (Jewish quarter), *borghetto* (small suburb), *ghetto* or *getto* (words that Spanish-Jewish exiles used around 1492 for the quay of Genoa [I. B. Sermonetta], and *getto nuovo* (new foundry, near which the walled-in settlement of the Jews readmitted to Venice after long banishment was erected in 1516). Cecil Roth, one of the greatest experts on the history of Italian Jewry, regarded the last-named derivation as the only correct one. According to his account, the Jews were admitted in 1516 under the condition that they settle in the *getto nuovo quarter,* an isolated island surrounded by canals, which could easily be completely cut off from its surroundings by a wall, gates, and drawbridges. In 1541 the *getto vecchio* (old foundry) suburb was added to receive Jews from eastern countries, and henceforth the entire area became known by the name *ghetto.* In 1555 a bull of Pope Paul IV relegated the Jews of Rome to a new quarter on the left bank of the Tiber, which was immediately surrounded with a wall. Other cities in the papal states soon followed suit. In 1562 the word *ghetto* appeared for the first time in a papal bull as the designation for this walled-in coercive settlement, and afterwards its official use became more general in Italy.

None of the above explanations is completely conclusive, and it may well be that the name of the Venetian Jewish quarter was adopted because of its similarity to words from other languages that could be identified with the concept. There are no systematic investigations and documentations for the adoption of the concept by other states (in England and Germany after the early seventeenth century). The term, at any rate, seems to have been used predominantly for the Jewish quarters in Italy, particularly Rome, while the Jewish districts of other countries were well into the nineteenth century called by local names, such as *Judengasse, Juiverie, Carrière.* The ghetto concept seems to have attained more general significance only in the struggle for emancipation and under the influence of Romanticism and the new valuation of the Middle Ages and the historiography influenced by this movement, particularly in Germany. Thus it appears in Heine in 1834 (*Zur Geschichte der Religion und Philosophie in Deutschland,* Elster edition 4, 197) and on a number of later occasions. However, Webster's *Dictionary of the English Language* (Springfield, 1867) still gives this brief definition of the word: "The Jews' quarter in Rome." In his famous essay of 1855, three hundred years after the establishment of the ghetto in Rome, Ferdinand Gregorovius uses the word as a masculine noun (*Der Ghetto und die Juden in Rom*). Kluge's *Etymologisches Wörterbuch der deutschen Sprache* (1963) states that "among us the word began to be used in 1627 as a description of Italian conditions" and suggests that it was derived from *Ägypter (Egitto).* It should be pointed out that the English word "gypsy" is generally traced back to "Egyptian" as well.

The application of the word *ghetto* to immigrants' settlements of all kinds, slums, settlements of natives in colonial areas and of people of different colors and races is an extension of the concept in our century, which materially differs from the substance of the original concept of the ghetto as an isolated coercive settlement of Jews.

In diary entries of 1882 as well as his play *The New Ghetto* (1894) Theodor Herzl speaks of an inner ghetto that the Jews carry around with them and of invisible ghetto walls built by the surrounding world of prejudices against them. This idea of a "psychological ghetto" was adopted by modern social psychology. Cf., e.g., P. R. Hofstätter, *Gruppendynamik* (Reinbek bei Hamburg, 1957), 154f.: "Now we are in a position to define the concept 'psychological ghetto': it describes the situation of a subgroup that is far removed from the main group and whose inner distance is kept small. This definition is not adequate, however, for then we would have to attribute a ghetto existence to an elite, such as the aristocracy, as well. The difference lies in the fact that the ghetto dwellers were distanced by the majority more than they distanced themselves from it, while the elite distances itself from the majority to a greater extent than it is distanced by it. In other words, the ghetto is an involuntary isolation, and hence people strive to leave it, while the elite is a voluntary and desirable isolation, and therefore people strive to enter it."

THE BULL "CUM NIMIS ABSURDUM" OF 1555: Gregorovius (*The Ghetto*, 68) gives this 148
freer and elegant version: "It is absurd and improper that the Jews who have fallen
into eternal servitude by their own guilt should presume, under the pretext that
Christian charity has taken them up, to make so bold as to live intermingled with
Christians, to wear no distinguishing mark, to employ Christian servants, even to
purchase houses."

Both general and Jewish historical works have frequently pointed out that often
reality was not so bad and circumstances, interests, carelessness, and even the
compassion of individuals frequently caused a moderation or even nonobservance of
the severe regulations. This is of interest to a chronicler but not to a historian of a
cluster of problems. The principles that were set down continued to be effective even
if not every detail was absorbed in all places and at all times. In the face of all
mitigations the judgment of an honorable Christian and historian of the rank of a
Travers Herford (1860–1950) retains its validity even today. In 1927 Herford wrote (in
Legacy of Israel, 123): "Perhaps no more deadly injury has ever been inflicted upon
any considerable number of human beings than that by the ghetto, or rather by those
who devised it. . . . Being an unnatural life it worked ill both to those who enforced it
and to those who suffered under it. Both Christians and Jews were made to accept, as
one of the settled factors in social and national life, that there should be a permanent
barrier between them, not to be surmounted or removed. To the Christian the ghetto
was a cage where certain dangerous and repulsive animals were confined. To the Jew
it was the prison in which he was shut up from the free world outside, where as a man
he ought to take his part." To be sure, the ghetto continued to afford a certain
protection from the attacks of the mob in times of unrest, and it is possible that the
losses of human life during the religious wars, including the Thirty Years' War (1618–
48), would have been even more devastating without the protection of the ghetto
walls. But on the other hand, down to our day the deleterious effects of the ghetto
principle are well-nigh incalculable not only for the further development of the
Jewish question but also for the legal, forcible exclusion of ethnic or ideological
minorities from the ruling society.

FEAR IN TRANSITIONAL PERIODS: Concerning the problem of fear, which we keep 149
encountering in the history of the Jewish question, cf. *Die politische und
gesellschaftliche Rolle der Angst*, ed. and with an introd. by H. Wiesbrock (Stuttgart,
1967) and the bibliography there.

FEAR OF THE DEVIL AND WITCHES: H. R. Trevor-Roper, *The European Witch Craze* 149f.
of the 16th and 17th Centuries (Penguin Books, 1969), gives a comprehensive, well-
documented account of the phenomenon that the author describes as a "new diabolical religion." Emphasizing the societal basis and the transition from a feudal to a
capitalistic economic and social structure, he regards both Jews and Marranos as
nonconformists par excellence: "Both witches and converted Jews were first subjected to the Inquisition as heretics; but before long both were being burnt without
reference to ideas, the former as witches, the latter as Jews. . . . The witch and the
Jew—both represent social nonconformity. . . . In the sixteenth century the witch
gradually replaces the Jew, and in the seventeenth the reversal is complete. If the
universal scapegoat of the Black Death in Germany had been the Jew, the universal
scapegoat of the Wars of Religion will be the witch. . . . And really good Germans
(like Luther) would contrive to hate both together: At the close of the sixteenth
century the Catholic Elector of Trier and the Protestant Duke of Brunswick would set
out to exterminate both. But in general the emphasis fell either on one or the other.
In our own days it has fallen back upon the Jews" (pp. 33, 35). As examples of the
similarity and interchangeability of the victims Trevor-Roper mentions that in medie-

val Hungary witches against whom there was one complaint were sentenced to stand in a pillory in a public place for an entire day and to wear a Jew's hat. On the other hand, the Jews were frequently accused of practicing witchcraft. In reports about successes in the persecution of witches the Jews are not forgotten; by turns the share of Jews and witches is given pride of place in both theory and practice. Belief in witches and in the diabolical influence of the Jews was so widespread that even "enlightened" people were not free of it. To deny it would have been tantamount to denying the entire religious, philosophical, and social thought-structure, the entire *Weltanschauung* and cosmology of the period—and who was capable of doing that? Basically, the belief in witches was bound up with belief in the saints of the Church. If deceased people were able to help as saints, why could scoundrels not do harm as devils? Cf. also chap. 3 (26ff.) in Wilhelm Koch's monograph about Friedrich Spee (Mönchen-Gladbach, 1914), the Catholic poet (1591–1635), one of the few who fought against the witchcraft trials. Cf. also Hartmut Lehmann, "Hexenverfolgungen und Hexenprozesse im Alten Reich," in *Jahrbuch des Instituts für Deutsche Geschichte* 8 (Tel Aviv, 1978), 13–70.

About witchcraft in general, cf. Geoffrey Parrinder, *Witchcraft, European and African* (London, 1958, 1963). Concerning the continued belief in diabolical forces and witchcraft, cf. Brad Steiger, *Sex and Satanism* (New York, 1960); Montagu Summers, *The Vampire: His Kith and Kin* (New York, 1960); Alois Winklhofer, *Traktat über den Teufel* (Frankfurt, 1962); Emil Kremer, *Geöffnete Augen—über die List Satans und die Erlösung am Kreuz* (Leinfelden, 1974); "Der Teufel kommt wieder," photo essay by U. Schippke, in *Der Stern* 16 (10 April 1974). Concerning the devil in art, cf. Roland Villeneuve, *Le diable dans l'art—essai d'iconographie comparée à propos des rapports entre l'art et le satanisme* (Paris, 1957); E. and J. Lehner, *Devils, Demons, Death and Damnation* (a collection of woodcuts from the fifteenth to the eighteenth century) (New York, 1971).

Concerning the connection with the Jews, cf. the abovementioned books by Joshua Trachtenberg, *The Devil and the Jews* (New Haven, 1943; New York, 1961) and *Jewish Magic and Superstition: A Study in Folk Religion* (New York, 1939; paperback, 1961).

151f.   PROBLEMS OF BUREAUCRACY: See the presentation and detailed bibliography in Martin Albrow, *Bureaucracy* (London, 1970).

153   LEIBZOLL: See the article so headed in *EJJ* 10:1588f. and the bibliography there. The name varied in different places: *Judengeleit, Leibmauth, Judenzoll, Péage corporel,* etc. As in the case of the institution of *Kammerknechtschaft,* presumably its point of departure was a tax for safe conduct in times of unrest that frequently posed a particular threat to the Jews. However, as so often with laws and taxes, only the toll was maintained; it was a source of revenue for the governments and frequently served to keep the influx of Jews within bounds. For the Jews it was a heavy economic burden as well as a more and more socially degrading special tax. The Edict of Toleration issued by Joseph II in 1782 rescinded it, but ten years later Emperor Francis II (I) reintroduced it under the name *Judenbolleten.* It was not definitively abolished until 1848. In Prussia the *Leibzoll* was eliminated in 1787, in Bavaria in 1799, and in the other German states in the first decade of the nineteenth century as a direct or indirect effect of the French Revolution. In Russia the "Safe-conduct toll" (for crossing the Polish-Russian border) was in effect until 1862.

153f.   FURTHER TYPIFICATION OF THE IMAGE OF THE JEW: Cf. also the section on the image of the Jew at the end of the Middle Ages (Part 1, p. 121f.) and the notes on it in Part 2, pp. 511ff.

CARICATURES: Eduard Fuchs, *Die Juden in der Karikatur: Ein Beitrag zur Kulturgeschichte,* Munich 1921 (with numerous illustrations); the quotation may be found on p. 4, and the broadside appears in facsimile between pages 16 and 17. The latter deals with the usury of the "accursed Jews," uses Latin on the upper and German on the lower part, shows in the text and the pictures the dangers of the Jews' money-lending, which was practiced in all circles, and ends with this advice: *"Demnach was du tust das tu weisslich/ Bedenck das ende das rate ich"* (Accordingly, whatever you do, do it wisely. Consider the outcome; that is my advice). 153f.

DEPICTIONS OF DESECRATIONS OF THE HOST: These may be found in pictures of all kinds, but now they were given far greater dissemination through the inexpensive printing of woodcuts. They were no longer restricted to a definite locality but could easily come into any house and serve as an inexpensive wall decoration. Examples in Fuchs; *EJJ* 4:1122; G. Liebe, *Das Judentum in der deutschen Vergangenheit,* (1903), 17–20, 26f.; and numerous historical works. Fuchs (18–19) reproduces a satirical pictorial sequence from the seventeenth century on the very common subject *"Der Juden Badstub"* (The Jews' bath). The duplicity and deceitfulness of the Jews are depicted in their various forms, and at the end the murder of a child in Trent is shown with this caption: *"So lang Trient und dies Kind wird gnant/ Der Juden Schelmstück bleibt bekant"* (As long as Trent and this child are talked about, the Jews' knavery will be remembered). 153f.

Concerning the caricatures on churches and town halls and the *Judensau* in sculptures and woodcuts, cf Fuchs, 111ff. and 144ff. Municipal records indicate that the sculpture of the Jews' sow on the Salzburg town hall was made in 1487; a reputable sculptor was given that commission. In the sixteenth century the sculpture was affixed to the town hall at Kehlheim and the stone bridge in Frankfurt, though the original has not been preserved. This depiction was found also in other German towns and on Flemish and French churches. For the sculptures on the Regensburg Cathedral (thirteenth century) and the town church at Wittenberg (1440), cf. *JL*:598; others may be found in Fuchs 2 (choirstall carvings in the Notre Dame church of Aerschot, fifteenth century). The various figures differ in detail, but all of them show a close connection between the Jews and pigs (the flesh of which, as everyone knew, the Jews had always been strictly forbidden to eat) and are obscene in nature. With the wider dissemination in the form of woodcuts the obscenity seems to have increased, for now more and more details could easily be added. Jews were depicted riding backwards on a pig, licking and sucking it everywhere. Sometimes the figure of the devil was added, e.g., in the abovementioned copperplate engraving from the early seventeenth century, *"Der Juden Badstub."* There the seventeenth century picture, the one depicting the *Judensau* and immediately preceding the Trent blood libel, is provided with this verse: *"Saug du die Milch fris du den treck/ Das ist doch euer best geschleck"* (You suck the milk, you eat the shit; why, that's your greatest delicacy). A copperplate from the early eighteenth century, printed in Frankfurt with German and French captions, evidently attempted to include Amschel Rothschild as well; it also features a woman and a billy goat, with this caption: *"Au weih Rabbi Anschl!, au, au! Mausch, au weih au au!/ Sauff mauschi sauff de Milch! friss du Rabbi den Dreck/ es ist doch alle Zeit euer bestes Geschleck!"* (Oy vey, rabbi, Anschel! oy, oy! Moyshe, oy vey, oy, oy! Swill, Moyshe, drink the milk! Rabbi, eat the shit. Why, it's always your greatest delicacy!) The devil, who is depicted with a Jew riding a pig backwards and lifting the pig's tail for another Jew, has horns, a Jew's badge, eyeglasses (like the two Jews), and (in contrast to the straight-nosed Jews) a crooked nose. The inscription next to him reads "This is the Jews' devil." A similar earlier version (seventeenth century) depicts a woman riding on a billy goat; cf. Liebe, *Das Judentum,* 35. According to Fuchs (118), a chronicler commenting on the

Jews' sow affixed to the stone bridge in Frankfurt wrote that the picture indicated "that Jews and pigs are forbidden to enter the city." Fuchs (122f.) sums up his presentation of this lampoon by saying that "the obscene nature of almost all depictions of the *Judensau* (as well as other anti-Jewish caricatures) is an expression and demonstration of a truly boundless contempt for the Jews." In this way, he says, that period in general expressed the acme of its scorn, and the longevity of that caricature demonstrates that this contempt lasted for centuries: "It is a fact that no other caricature in the world, whether of Jews or others, has attracted such enduring attention. No other one was seen by so many in the course of time." Concerning the riding or backward riding on the pig, cf. *Der Grosse Brockhaus* 17 (1934), 139: "According to old popular belief, the witches rode on pigs"—perhaps in reversal of the nature symbol that was originally held sacred. Cf. F. W. Dought, *Taschenlexikon der Sexualsymbole* (Munich, 1971), 123: "Excavations of early clay figures show Isis, the goddess of nature, sitting on a pig with her legs astride." On the other hand, a pig is everywhere used as an epithet for inward or outward uncleanliness. The Spaniards, incidentally, used *marrano*—meaning "pig"—as an abusive word for the forcibly baptized Jews who did not entirely abandon their Judaism—at first probably by way of mocking the Jews for spurning the good pork. It is possible that the German epithet *Saujude*, which was later translated and gained currency in other languages, was suggested both by the image of the *Judensau* and that of the pig as a term of abuse.

154ff.   THE "ETERNAL JEW": Concerning the origin of the figure, cf. part 1, p. 121f. On the history of the Eternal Jew" or the "Wandering Jew" ("Juif Errant, "L'Ebreo Errante") there is extensive literature in many languages—from Leonhard Neubaur's pioneering study *Die Sage vom Ewigen Juden* (1884, 1893) and his *Bibliographie der Sage vom Ewigen Juden* (*Centralblatt für Bibliothekswesen* 10 (1893) and 18 (1914) to George K. Andersen's *The Legend of the Wandering Jew* (Providence, 1965). Good summaries of the current state of research (with basic bibliographies) may be found in *EJJ* 16:259–263 and in Baron, 11 (1967), 177–82. The summaries (often with original commentaries) in earlier works on the history of the Jews and the encyclopedias are still of value; cf., e.g., *JE* 12 (1905–25), 461ff. (Joseph Jacobs), *JL* 1 (1927), 159ff. (Samuel Rappaport), *EJ* 1 (1928), 1147–56 (B. Heller, "Ahasver, der ewige Jude"), and *Der Grosse Brockhaus* 5 (1930), 761. For the appearance of the figure in world literature, cf. Theodor Kappstein, *Ahasver in der Weltpoesie* (Berlin, 1905), including on pp. 146–55 an interesting appendix on "Judas der Verräter in Dichtung und Kunst"); Adolf Leschnitzer, *Saul und David* (Heidelberg, 1954), 111–13 and the same author's article "Der Gestaltwandel Ahasvers" in *Zwischen zwei Welten* (Festschrift for Siegfried Moses [Tel Aviv, 1962], 470–505); Hyam Maccoby, "The Legend of the 'Wandering Jew': A New Interpretation," *Jewish Quarterly* 20, no. 1 (1972): 3–8. Despite this extensive literature, many essential features have gone unclarified to this day.

There seem to be a number of facts. Evidently the point of departure was Matthew 16:28 (some of those present will not die "till they see the Son of man coming in his kingdom"—a similar formulation in Luke 9:27), a statement by Jesus cited in the first known edition of the chapbook (1602). Added to this was the story (in John 18:22) about a servant of the high priest Caiaphas who had struck Jesus on the cheek. In the chronicle *Historia major* by the French monk Matthew Paris (written in 1250 and printed in London in 1571 and in Zurich in 1586) there is a story, based on older accounts from England, about a doorkeeper of the Roman procurator Pilate who is said to have struck Jesus, whom his master had just sentenced to be crucified, with his fist and to have shouted to him that he should not tarry but walk faster, whereupon Jesus is said to have replied: "I am going, but you shall wait until I return." In the chronicle the sinful doorkeeper bears the strange name Cartaphilus, but after the crucifixion he had himself baptized, received the name Joseph, and henceforth lived as a poor penitent awaiting the return of the Savior. According to a later version of the legend, Cartaphilus-Joseph was condemned by Jesus to constant wandering and was rejuvenated every hundred years in order to go on living. In the Italian version of the legend (also from the thirteenth century) the wanderer is called Juan Espero en Dios (John who is waiting for God). In the *Festschrift zum 75jährigen Bestehen des Jüdischen Theologischen Seminars* ([Breslau 1929], 2:370f.) the Copenhagen rabbi and learned bibliophile David Simonsen explained the name Cartaphilus as "Cartophylax," a word that meant "archivist" in late antiquity and in the Middle Ages and was used in this sense against the Jews by the Church Father Asterius because they had received and preserved the Bible only as archivists without understanding it properly in a Christian sense. In succeeding centuries a number of similar stories were told, and these were embellished and even dramatized.

However, the real history of the legend and its identification with the Jew as wanderer began only with the printed chapbook of 1602. Its unknown author may have been acquainted with the Matthew Paris chronicle, of which a number of editions appeared in the late sixteenth century, and expanded its substance in fictional form. Whether he used actual statements or employed the poetic license of a storyteller, he based himself on a report by the bishop of Schleswig, Paul von Eitzen, who claimed to have seen the Wandering Jew in Hamburg in 1542. Here he is called Ahasver, though it is not clear why he chose the name of the Persian king in the Book of Esther. Perhaps he took it from Jewish Purim plays. The Israeli folklorist Yomtov Levinsky has attempted to establish a connection with Luther's hostility toward the Jews and his hatred of the Book of Esther (*Omer* [Tel Aviv], 23 March 1940, 3). Referring to E. König's book *Ahasver, der ewige Jude* (1907) he writes that Luther never forgave King Ahasuerus for not following Haman's advice to destroy the Jews; the story developed from there, and Ahasuerus, the stupid royal friend of the Jews, turned into Ahasuerus, the Wandering Jew. There were Jewish shoemakers in Germany at that time; they came into the villages as more or less disreputable cobblers, and so the Wandering Jew Ahasuerus became a shoemaker in the story. So much for the more or less dubious or logical theories about the origin of the legend before its appearance in print.

From that time on there were reports that the "Wandering Jew" had been seen in various places and at various times—as H. Maccoby points out, just as in our days there have repeatedly been reports about the sighting of flying saucers from distant planets. According to such reports, he was seen in Spain in 1575, in Vienna in 1599, in Lübeck in 1601 and 1603, in Prague in 1602, in Bavaria in 1604, in Ypres in 1623, in Brussels in 1640, in Leipzig in 1642, in Paris in 1644, in Stanford in 1658, in Astrakhan in 1672, in Frankenstein in 1676, in Munich in 1721, in 1766 in Altbach, in 1774 in Brussels again, and in 1790 in Newcastle. This list is based on *Je* 12:461ff., and there we read: "The last reported appearance seems to have been in America in 1868, where *Desert News* reported on Sept. 23, 1868 that he had visited a Mormon named O'Grady."

In the spirit of Christian theology the chapbook stated that God had preserved the Jew Ahasuerus, who had been an eyewitness to Christ's crucifixion and a hundred years later to the destruction of Jerusalem, as a "living witness of Christ's passion to convince the Godless and the unbelievers." In his book *Ahasver, der ewige Jude* ([1907], 5ff.) Eduard König characterizes the story as a myth. In German publications and other editions influenced by them, the "Wandering Jew" is also called the "Eternal Jew"—first in 1694 and on repeated subsequent occasions. The figure is shrouded in legend, but it has remained a peculiar figure with which everything of contemporary interest can be combined: fear of death or the wish for a "blessed death" in the spirit of Protestant theology; curiosity about foreign countries and phenomena that can be satisfied through frequent travels; and the mingled feelings of disdain and awe with which one encounters a frequently shabby and seedy Jewish peddler.

A change in the conception of this figure began with the interpretation given by the Lutheran theologian and orientalist Johann Jakob Schudt of Frankfurt am Main (1664–1722) in his four-volume work *Jüdische Merckwürdigkeiten* (1714–17). In Book 5, chap. 14 we read: "This itinerant Jew is not a single person, but the entire Jewish people which has been dispersed throughout the world after Christ's crucifixion and will, in accordance with Christ's testimony, continue to roam the world to the Day of Judgment." Here, then, Ahasuerus, the "Eternal Jew," seems to be identified fully with the fate of the entire Jewish people for the first time.

This opened the way to the mythicization that the Romanticists loved and enabled Heine to speak in a letter from the year 1826 (*Briefe*, ed. F. Hirth, vol. 1 [1950], 284) of the "myth of the Eternal Jew" that had been thus created. Under the influence of modern nationalism this identification of the Jew who is unable to die with the Jewish people as a whole became more and more widespread. As Adolf Leschnitzer has pointed out, in his novella *Das Fähnlein der sieben Aufrechten* (1860) the Swiss writer Gottfried Keller contrasts the evanescence of earthy, natural nations with the dragged-out existence of the "eternal Jew, who cannot die, subservient to all newly awakened peoples, he who has buried the Egyptians, the Greeks, and the Romans." Accordingly, the earth belongs to the mortal nations; they have the right to dominate it, not the immortal people of the "Eternal Jew," who continues to exist in an uncanny and meaningless way.

This viewpoint then gave rise to all kinds of interpretive possibilities in which the Eternal Jew became a symbol for everything unsettled, brilliant, or degenerate, down to the nationalistic, anti-Semitic invocations of the concept in the jargon of the Third Reich. Jews also adopted the term—as an accusation, in defense, and, in a positive reversal in a Zionist sense, as an invitation to put an end to the life of wandering and its stereotypical image, the "Eternal Jew," by becoming rooted in the soil of Israel. (Concerning its connection with the Jewish question in Constantin Frantz, cf. p. 479 above.)

156   DEPICTIONS OF THE "ETERNAL JEW": Cf. the pertinent articles in the encyclopedias, in Fuchs, *Die Juden in der Karikatur*, and other works. Gustave Doré's pictures have become especially well known. See also Kubin's drawing "Ahasver" in his *Abendrot* (Munich, 1952). To my knowledge, there is no comprehensive treatment of the "Eternal Jew" in art.

156ff. SHYLOCK: The literature about Shakespeare's *Merchant of Venice* and the figure of Shylock is enormous. Here I shall mention only the books that I found particularly useful. An extensive bibliography is included in a comprehensive study by the theater critic and writer Hermann Sinsheimer (1883–1950), *Shylock, die Geschichte einer Figur* (Munich, 1960); an abridged English version, *Shylock; The History of a Character*, appeared in London in 1947 and was reprinted in New York in 1963. Cf. also Bernard Grebanier, *The Truth about Shylock* (New York, 1962). Additional bibliographical information is contained in Hans Lamm's essay "Juden und Shylock" and the interview with the Cologne theater critic Karl Richter on the occasion of the West German Radio Network's presentation of *The Merchant of Venice* (with Fritz Kortner as Shylock), both in *Emuna* 4 (1969): 85ff. On p. 96 Arnold Zweig's proud epilogue to Shakespeare's play (1936) is reprinted. Cf. also Hyam Maccoby, "The Figure of Shylock," *Midstream* 16, no. 2 (February 1970): 56–69, an attempt to assign the figure its place in the history of the Christian image of the Jew. For the historical background and situation, cf. Clemens Klöpper, *Shakespeare-Realien: Alt-Englands Kulturleben im Spiegel von Shakespeares Dichtungen* (Dresden, 1912), esp. 12ff.; Cecil Roth, "The Background of Shylock," in his collection *Personalities and Events in Jewish History* (Philadelphia, 1953), 237–47; P. Quennell and H. Johnson, *Who's Who in Shakespeare* (London, 1975), 254ff.; Montagu Frank Modder, *The Jew in the Literature of England* (Philadelphia, 1939, 1960), 19ff.; Edgar Rosenberg, *From Shylock to Svengali: Jewish Stereotypes in English Fiction* (London, 1961), 21ff.; Harold Fish, *The Dual Image: A Study of the Jew in English Literature* (London, 1959, 1971). For interpretations and later literary treatments of this material, cf. the last chapter in B. Grebanier ("Other Men's Shylock") and Ludwig Lewisohn's novella *The Last Days of Shylock* (New York, 1939).

IHERING'S JUDGMENT: Cf. Rudolf Ihering, *der Kampf ums Recht*, ed. Rudolf Huch   160 (Reclams Universalbibliothek, 6552–53), 80ff. In his preface Ihering discusses the arguments of his adversaries, particularly Joseph Kohler. Heine's statement may be found in his collection *Shakespeare's Mädchen und Frauen*, Elster ed., 5:448ff.: "Truly, next to Portia, Shylock is the most respectable person in the whole play. He loves money, he does not conceal this love but loudly proclaims it in the public market. . . . Yet there is something that he esteems more highly than money: satisfaction for his hurt heart, fair restitution for unspeakable revilement." Similar formulations may be found in "Shylock's Plädoyer" by the Austrian-Jewish writer Alfred Polgar, written ninety years later and quoted by Hans Lamm in his abovementioned essay. Polgar has Shylock ask his unjust judges: "I am permitted to take this action—except for what is included in it naturally, legally, and by the law of nature? Why do you use this trick involving blood? . . . Are you simply trying to kick all the Jews out of Venice? The law states that we have a right to stay here, but it does not say that we are permitted to breathe, eat, and sleep—there you have a handy means of getting rid of us." Cf. the pertinent discussion in Gustav Landauer, *Shakespeare*, vol. 1 (1922) and in the abovementioned book by Grebanier. Cf. also this remark by Ernst Simon (cited by Lamm), with which I fully agree: "In his England Shakespeare could not see a Jew or have a Jewish friend; he may have visited the Venetian ghetto, but in any case he had a grand poetic conception of the enormous dark figure of the ghetto Jew who distorts the prophetic struggle for rights in the form of a capitalist's struggle for *his* right, but carries it on in Jewish fashion. Today we ought to acknowledge this tragic brother Shylock instead of warding him off apologetically" (*Jüdische Rundschau*, 22 January 1929; reprinted in *Brücken: Gesammelte Essays* [Heidelberg, 1965], 218).

Hence we should stop carrying on banal or timid discussions about whether it is appropriate to have new productions of Shakespeare's *Merchant of Venice* and whether this would cause or encourage anti-Semitic tendencies. Using such arguments, one could subject many works of art to censorship. The play and the figure of Shylock ought to be presented as truthfully, as profoundly, and as conflict-laden as they are and as is in keeping with the reality in which we live and must stand the test. In this spirit Arnold Zweig wrote in 1936 (in the abovementioned Epilogue): "Grüss Dich, Venezia, schüttel mir die Hand!/ Denn antritt zum Gefecht mit Deinen Ständen/ Der hingeschlagne, wieder auferstandene,/ Mit Zukunftsmut bewehrte Jude Shylock" (Greetings, Venezia, shake my hand! For preparing to do battle with your estates is the Jew Shylock—beaten down, resurrected, and armed with courage for the future). Cf. also Proteus, "Olivier's Shylock," *Midstream* 20, no. 3 (March 1974): 68–71.

ON THE NAME SHYLOCK: Its derivation has been much-discussed but remains un-   156ff. clear. It is compounded of "shy" and "lock." There are two entirely different meanings of the latter word, deriving from Anglo-Saxon and Middle English. Referring to something that closes or locks, it is related to the German word *Loch*; hence Gustav Landauer translates Shylock as *Scheuloch* (*Shakespeare* 1 [1922]: 51). The second meaning relates to hair. In this connection it may be noteworthy that in the first and second printings (1600) the name appears as Shylocke (*The excellent History of the Merchant of Venice. With the extreme cruelty of Shylocke the Jew towards the saide Merchant, in cutting a iust pound of his flesh. And the obtaining of Portia, by the choyse of three Caskets. Written by W. Shakespeare. Printed by J. Roberts, 1600*). If one accepts the second meaning, it might be a reference to the sidelocks or earlocks (Hebrew *peot*, Yiddish *payess*) which Lev. 19:27 commands the Jews to grow. To this day they are worn by many orthodox Jews, and it is likely that in one form or another they were worn by everyone in those days (e.g., in combination with sideburns). If Shakespeare was not acquainted with any Jew who wore them, he might have known them from pictures and caricatures. The word also sounds like "look" (in Middle English, i.e., until about one hundred years before Shakespeare, *loken*, related to German *lugen*), and then the meaning might be "shy look" or "sly look." Of course, the name might have been derived from an actual name that sounded similar, or it might contain an allusion to a known person that was comprehensible to the audience of the time and is incomprehensible to us today.

In the biography of the philo-Semitic Pope Sixtus V (1585–90), which the Milan historian Gregorio Leti published in 1669 (*Vita di Sisto Quinto*), we read about a wager between a Jewish merchant in Rome (Shimshon Cendi) and a Christian businessman (Paolo Sacchi), the former asserting that the British admiral Francis Drake captured the city of Santo Domingo on the island Hispaniola. The Jew bet a pound of flesh from his body against 100 scudi and lost the bet. The Pope decided that the wager was legitimate, but he forbade the Christian on pain of death to cut even the least amount above the stipulated weight from the Jew's body. Thereupon the two were officially sentenced to death and thrown into prison, but the sentence was commuted to a fine of 2,000 scudi, and the men were set free.

The Shylock theme was poetically refashioned by the Austrian-Jewish writer Richard Beer-Hofmann (1866–1945), who is undeservedly all but forgotten today. The figure of the Jew Itzig appears in his tragedy *Der Graf von Charolais*, published in 1904 and reprinted in Beer-Hofmann's *Gesammelte Werke* in 1963.

161f.   INTERNAL INFLUENCE. THE GHETTO WALLS AS PROTECTION: In a number of places, such as Vernona and Mantua, the legal institution of the ghetto was annually commemorated in a special prayer every year. Cf. Roth in *EJJ* 10:84.

In wartime, particularly during the Thirty Years' War in Germany (1618–48), as well as in the social struggles between the craftsmen of the guilds and the patricians in the cities, the ghetto walls frequently did provide protection during the uprisings and excesses of the mob.

162ff.   "SHULHAN ARUKH": Cf. the articles on *Shulhan Arukh*, Joseph Caro (Karo), Isserles in *JL*, *EJ*, and *EJJ* as well as the bibliographies there; R. J. Z. Werblowsky, *Joseph Karo: Lawyer and Mystic* (Oxford, 1962; paperback ed., Philadelphia, 1977). The Shulhan Arukh is described as a kind of written constitution for the dispersed Jewish people by Shimon Bernfeld in his (Hebrew) essay "Joseph Caro, the Dreamer of the Israeli Constitution"; it may be found in his collection *Shomrei Homot* (Guardians of the walls) (Tel Aviv, 5698 [1938]), 71ff. Cf. also the presentation and evaluations in Meir Waxman, *A History of Jewish Literature* 2 (1943), 44f.; Graetz 9; Dubnow 6. In the last-named work we read (p. 55 of the German edition): "The Shulhan Arukh constitutes the acme of the rabbinic legislative art. . . . The most striking thing is the complete elimination of the section devoted to the basic laws of Judaism which heads the code of Maimonides [written four hundred years earlier] and examines these basic dogmas in a philosophical light. In contrast to [Maimonides'] Mishne Torah, the Shulhan Arukh appears only as a product of rigidified rabbinic Judaism of a late period, as a compendium of religious customs and the prevailing norms of family law and civil law. . . . Living in accordance with the Shulhan Arukh henceforth became a watchword of orthodox Jews, who were attracted rather than repelled by the petty, categorical religious-ritual prescriptions of the new code."

Despite what Jewish apologists have believed, the Jew-haters from the seventeenth century on, particularly after Eisenmenger, were justified in identifying the Jews of their time with the Shulhan Arukh in their attacks. To be sure, they cannot escape the reproach that they were taking statements out of context and misinterpreting certain words in translating them into German (or other languages), whether deliberately or out of ignorance of Hebrew and the tradition of Hebrew literature, and also that they gave pride of place to some superstitious notions contained in this work, as in so many other contemporary Jewish and non-Jewish writings. Has there ever been a period that did not have superstitious notions that it regarded as truth? Luther and Calvin, for example, were under the spell of abstruse views and anxieties, and as we have already pointed out, incipient modern science was a mixture of insights and "religious truths" that seem ludicrous to us today. Despite its apologetic tendency, *Der Schulchan Aruch und die Rabbinen über das Verhältnis der Juden zu Andersgläubigen* (Berlin, 1894), a book by D. Hoffmann, a rabbi and university lecturer, is a basic study that deals with certain accusations in characteristic fashion.

LURIANIC KABBALAH: The most recent presentations of the Kabbalah, its history,   164ff. nature, and effects are Gershom Scholem's comprehensive article "Kabbala" in *EJJ* 10:490–649 and a number of his supplementary articles in *EJJ* that are referred to in the main article. An extensive bibliography may be found on pp. 649–53. Scholem's book *Major Trends in Jewish Mysticism* (Jerusalem, 1941) has been of fundamental importance for research on the subject, and shortly after its publication Yitzhak F. Baer wrote a detailed appreciation of its significance for Jewish historiography in *Zion* 7 (1942): 55–64. Examples of more recent (and sometimes more critical) appreciations of Scholem's work and of the Kabbalah as a living force in Judaism are Robert Alter's article in *Commentary* 54, no. 4 (April 1973); Harold Bloom's in *Commentary* 59, no. 3 (March 1975): 57–65; and Herbert Wiener, *9½ Mystics: The Kabbala Today* (New York, 1971), chap. 3 ("The Accountant," based on Baruch Kurzweil, Scholem's main critic from a religious viewpoint). Scholem's German writings about the Kabbalah and its problems include *Die Geheimnisse der Schöpfung: Ein Kapitel aus dem Sohar*, (Berlin: Schocken-Bücherei, 1935): *Über einige Grundbegriffe des Judentums*, Edition Suhrkamp 414 (1970); *Zur Kabbalah und ihrer Symbolik*, Suhrkamp-Taschenbuch (Zurich, 1960); *Judaica* 1 and 3, Bibliothek Suhrkamp 106 (1963) and 333 (1973). Among earlier historical works, cf. Dubnow 6 (1927), 59–75.

CHANGES IN THE RELATIONS BETWEEN THE JEWS AND THE SURROUNDING WORLD: 168f. For general literature on the history of the period and the Jews, see the pertinent volumes in the general historical works, e.g., the new *Propyläen-Weltgeschichte* 7 (1964) and 11 ("Summa Historia"), 477ff., or the old one, edited by Wilhelm Mommsen; B. Erdmannsdörffer, *Deutsche Geschichte vom westfälischen Frieden bis zum Regierungsantritt Friedrichs des Grossen, 1648–1740*, 2 vols. (1892–93); Martin Philippson, *Das Zeitalter Ludwig des Vierzehnten* (1970); Ludwig Oncken, *Das Zeitalter Friedrichs des Grossen*, 2 vols. (1881–82). Cf. also Friedrich Meinecke, *Die Idee der Staatsraison* (Munich, 1924); Ernst Cassirer, *Vom Mythus des Staates* (Zurich, 1949); August Oncken, *Geschichte der Nationalökonomie*, vol. 1 ("Die Zeit vor Adam Smith") (Leipzig, 1923); Charles Gide and Charles Rist, *Histoire des* doctrines économiques (Paris, 1922); O. Spann, Die Haupttheorien der Volks-wirtschaftslehre (Leipzig, 1923); Henri Sée, Les Origines du capitalisme moderne (German ed., Vienna, 1948); Arnold Hauser, Sozialgeschichte der Kunst und Literatur (Munich, 1953, 1973); Egon Friedell, A Cultural History of the Modern Age, vol. 2 (a brilliant survey despite some abstruse evaluations—e.g., of Spinoza—and occasional remarks about Judaism that are redolent of anti-Semitism). For the Jewish aspect in general, cf. Graetz, Geschichte der Juden 9, 10; Dubnow, Weltgeschichte des jüdischen Volkes 6, 7; Baron, A Social and Religious History of the Jews 13, 16, important for its use of the latest research and its comprehensive bibliographies.

169 SOMBART: Cf. the remarks in Part 1, p. 90 and Part 2, p. 502 about Werner Sombart's book Die Juden und das Wirtschaftsleben, first published in 1911 and subsequently in numerous editions and translations. (I have used the edition of 1922.) Even in its time more attention was aroused by reports about this work or quotations from it than by a reading of the book itself—which is the case with numerous books of this kind. As Sombart himself states in his preface, Die Juden und das Wirtschaftsleben was inspired by "Max Weber's investigations of the connections between puritanism and capitalism" (first published in 1905) at a time when Sombart was extensively revising his comprehensive work Der moderne Kapitalismus (first issued in two volumes in 1902 and in three from 1919 on). "A thorough examination of Weber's arguments showed," writes Sombart (p. v), "that all those components of Puritan dogma that seemed to be of real importance for the development of the capitalistic spirit were borrowings from the ideas of the Jewish religion." Then, too,, in the course of Sombart's studies he "gained the conviction . . . that the share of the Jews in the building of the modern economy is far greater than has hitherto been suspected." He compared the shifts in the economic focuses from the fifteenth to the late seventeenth century with the direction of the great Jewish migration in Europe during that period and realized that "once again the Jews experienced an almost complete restructuring of their location. Upon closer examination I became absolutely certain that it was really the Jews who in important points promoted the economic upswing wherever they appeared and produced a decline wherever they left" (vi). On p. 15 he reiterates this in a rhetorical and lyrical style: "We are astonished that up to now not even the outward parallelism between the spatial movements of the Jewish people and the economic destinies of the various nations and cities has been perceived. Israel passes over Europe like the sun; where it appears, new life blooms; where it leaves, everything that has hitherto bloomed withers."

"The Shifting of the Economic Center since the Sixteenth Century" (chap. 2); "The Stimulation of the International Trade in Goods" (chap. 3); "The Foundation of the Modern Colonial Economy" (chap. 4); "The Founding of the Modern State" (chap. 5); "The Commercialization of Modern Economic Life" with the development of securities and the stock exchange and their influence on all economic life, including industry (chap. 6); "the development of a capitalistic economic mentality" with the "idea of free competition," free trade—all this the Jews are said to have brought about, or at least they are said to have been an important, often decisive factor in the development of all these things. In the succeeding sections of his book Sombart investigates this "capacity of the Jews for capitalism," the historical-social causes, "the importance of the Jewish religion for economic life" (chap. 9), and the "Jewish special character" (chap. 12). In the third section the author asks "how the Jewish character originated" and examines "the racial problem" (chap. 13) as well as "the destiny of the Jewish people" from this viewpoint. He comes to this conclusion: "As the special nature of the Jewish character, in which we found all other characteristics embedded as seeds are embedded in a seed capsule, we have identified the outstanding intellectuality of this people. This may be explained by the fact that from the ancient times of their bucolic existence they have never had to perform heavy physical labor, or even predominantly physical labor. In all periods the Jews were little affected by the curse with which Adam and Eve were expelled from paradise, that man would have to earn his bread by the sweat of his brow—if we interpret this to mean physical sweat rather than worry and reflection, which cause only 'intellectual' labor for an ordinary mind" (420f.). The Jews have always remained nomads, and this basic characteristic of the nomads in the desert, the lack of a farmer's closeness to the soil, has qualified them for life in the city, which is always remote from the organic growth of nature. "The forest that is cleared and the marsh that is transformed into fertile soil that is plowed gave rise to the characteristic economic mode which prevailed in Europe for thousands of years before the rise of capitalism and which we have called the mode of the peasant and feudal craftsman. . . . From the unending desert, from the herd economy there developed the opposite of the old, indigenous economic order: capitalism" (425). Similar formulations recur frequently in other writings of this author. In his analysis of the Jewish national character Sombart leans heavily on Karl Marx, whose work about the Jewish question (1844) he quotes approvingly in his book *Die deutsche Volkswirtschaft im neunzehnten Jahrhundert* (first published in 1903 and later reprinted numerous times).

Sombart's book is typical of many similar works about the Jews and the Jewish question. In the Preface and numerous other places he states that it is his intention to give only an objective and very scientific presentation without making value judgments or taking a personal stand. However, the mixture of factual research with unproven theories and anything but value-free conclusions, as well as the absolute assurance with which Sombart constructs connections and makes rash judgments have made this book a source for the motivation of very antithetical views. Like all books containing ingenious half-truths, this one had the merit of stimulating thought, but it also ran the risk of leading to false conclusions. In the course of the years Sombart's evaluation of capitalism changed, as did his political and sociopolitical attitude, beginning with a positive (albeit not uncritical) evaluation of Marxist socialism and ending with a positive attitude toward National Socialism. Sombart was fortunate enough to die in 1941, before the worst anti-Jewish horrors and the collapse of the Hitler regime.

Sombart's book about the Jews and economic life became truly important for the development of the Jewish question by virtue of the debate about it that started immediately and continued for years and decades. The author himself actively and zestfully participated in this debate, primarily through his statement in the symposium about the baptism of Jews (which he edited in 1912 together with A. Landsberger) and in the more detailed work *Die Zukunft der Juden*, which he published in the same year. In the latter he advocated formal equality of rights, but he counseled the Jews not to make any extensive use of it. During his National Socialist period he was able to point out, and not without justification, that rudiments of his later views had already been contained in his earlier statements. He had always opposed the mixing of Jews with Germans, though he unstintingly expressed his admiration for the Jewish people, "whose fate surpasses that of all other nations in grandeur and profundity." However, to these remarks in his essay on "Judentaufen" he adds (p. 20): "But I would not want to be accused of being in the least mealy-mouthed, and so I will tell you that I am not particularly fond of Judaism in its objective cultural life; I much prefer German culture." Cf., in addition to the literature cited on p. 502. Eliezer Livneh in *HE* 16:712ff.; Marcus Arkin. *Jewish Affairs*, July 1969, 18–21; Fritz Friedländer, "From Marx to Hitler," *EJR Information*, January 1963, 6 and the bibliography there. Concerning the discussion about Sombart, see also Kurt Blumenfeld, *Erlebte Judenfrage* (Stuttgart, 1962), 58.

All these subjective and objective developments and effects should not make us forget Sombart's merit in bringing the Jewish question and its economic aspects up for discussion and inviting people to reflect about it.

Here are the most important writings published shortly after the first appearance of his book that discuss, reject, or correct his theses: Felix Rachfahl in *Preussische Jahrbücher*, vol. 147; G. Below in *Historische Zeitschrift*, vol. 108; H. Wätjen, "Das Judentum und die Anfänge der modernen Kolonisation," *Vierteljahrsschrift für Sozial- und Wirtschaftsgeschichte* 11 (1913); Lujo Brentano, *Die Anfänge des modernen Kapitalismus* (1916). Cf. Brentano's remark in rebuttal of Sombart's assumption that the Jews think in capitalistic terms (p. 170): "Mosaic law regarded alms as a means of restoring the normal order that had been disturbed by the distribution of the common property among the temporary usufructuaries."

169f.   MARRANOS AS PIONEERS: Concerning the Marranos, their nature, the problems of their existence, and their effects, cf. the remarks in Part 1, p. 133ff. and the bibliography in Part 2, p. 518. Cf. also the pertinent chapters in the larger Jewish histories and in Sombart.

170   NEW SETTLEMENT OF JEWS IN ENGLAND, ETC.: Cf. the monographs in the Jewish encyclopedias and the bibliographies there. Concerning the role of the Spanish Jews, especially in Hamburg but also in the economy of other northern countries, cf. the detailed documentation in Hermann Kellenbenz, *Sephardim an der unteren Elbe, ihre wirtschaftliche und politische Bedeutung vom Ende des 16. bis zum Beginn des 18. Jahrhunderts* (Wiesbaden, 1958). In contrast to Sombart's thesis it demonstrates that the Jews did not create the new early capitalistic economic forms but used them and promoted their development and dissemination through their connections with Jews all over the world.

170ff.   THE JEWS IN THE MERCENTILE SYSTEM: The most comprehensive and most balanced presentation of this problem and the influence of the new conditions on the Jewish question is still Felix Priebatsch, "Die Judenpolitik des fürstlichen Absolutismus im 17. und 18. Jahrhundert," in *Festschrift für Dietrich Schäfer* (1915), 564–651. Cf. also J. Strieder, "Staatliche Finanznot und Genesis des modernen Grossunternehmertums," *Schmollers Jahrbücher* 49 (1920), 432ff.; R. Ehrenberg, *Grosse Vermögen, ihre Entstehung und ihre Bedeutung* 1 (1925).

The most detailed and most thorough of the monographs about individual countries is Selma Stern, *Der preussische Staat und die Juden*, 6 vols. (1925–1971). This work goes far beyond the problems of the Prussian state, particularly in the factual first volumes, and presents the origin of the modern political and economic system, as well as the special problems posed by the Jewish role in these developments, giving numerous details that illuminate the period and its conditions. Our presentation can, of course, only show the elements that were important for the development as a whole.

171   THE "JUDENSPIESS": The humanist and writer Sebastian Brant used the expression "mit dem Judenspiess rennen" in his *Narrenschiff* (1494; *The Ship of Fools*, 1944); cf. M. Güdemann, *Geschichte des Erziehungswesens*, 3:276; James Parkes 2:338; A. Kohut, *Geschichte der deutschen Juden*, 419 and note 648. Thomas Murner also used it later (Kohut, 422). A Strassburg caricature from the year 1541 shows the activity of a Jewish money-lender and money-changer with these verses: "Der Judenspiess bin ich genant/ Ich fahr daher durch alle Landt,/Von grossen Juden ich sagen wil,/ Die schad dem Land thun in der still" (I am called the Jews' spear and travel through all the lands. I want to tell about big Jews who secretly harm the country) (Liebe. 43). A woodcut caricature, "Der Geltnarr," in Jost Amman's *Ständebuch*, with text by Hans

Sachs (1568; *The Book of Trades* [New York 1973]) has the "Money Fool" say: "Mit dem Judenspiess thu ich lauffn/ Mit Wucher aufsätzen und verkaufn" (I run with the Jews' spear, I practice usury in making contracts and selling). The woodcut headed "Der Jud" depicts a number of bearded Jews with crooked noses (in contrast to most other presentations) together with the usual satiric verses (Liebe, 24f.) A broadside with lampoons printed around 1620 is called *Engellaendischer Bickelhaering, welcher jetzt und als ein vornemer Händler und Jubilirer mit Allerley Judenspiessen nach Frankfurt in die Messe zeucht* (Judaica catalogue, S. Gewinde [Basel, 1963]). In his novel about the Thirty Years' War, *Simplicius Simplicissimus* (1668), Grimmelshausen writes about Christians who reflect in church "how the Jews' spear should be carried" and about someone "able to fight well with the Jews' spear."

As an example of the identity between the concepts "Jew" and "money-lender" (or, according to the ban on interest that was officially still in force, "usurer") I refer to the formulation in an Alsatian law of 1714 that was directed against Christians practising "usury": "Chrétiens de cette province exerçaient le judaisme envers leurs frères" (S. Szajkowski, *The Economic Status of the Jews in Alsace, Metz, and Lorraine 1648–1789* [New York, 1954], 77).

COURT JEWS, COURT FACTORS (and similar titles, which those involved regarded as honors and which did not have today's negative connotation): In historical works the phenomenon of the Court Jew in Central Europe (and sometimes in Eastern Europe—Poland—as well) in the seventeenth and eighteenth centuries is generally treated in temporal and societal isolation. At least since the Middle Ages there were in many countries financially, economically, and thus also politically influential Jews at the courts of the potentates—in the Moslem countries, particularly in Spain (before and after the *reconquista*), in France and England, in all areas of the Holy Roman Empire, and in the Italian states—wherever rulers endeavored to extend their sphere of power beyond the boundaries set by traditional factors and sought to satisfy their need for luxuries and the like. Apart from the burgeoning Jewish trade of the *sephardim* in Holland, England, etc., the existence of such influential Jews (for example, in the Ottoman Empire) not infrequently enabled the Court Jews of Central Europe to expand their economic connections.

There was also another factor. To a much too great extent the Court Jews in the big capital cities have been regarded as a phenomenon isolated from the rest of Jewry. They were that only in respect to some special rights, such as their domicile outside the ghetto and frequently also by virtue of their official-like position (generally reserved for Christians) with titles and social honors. Historians have attempted to view this as a bit of "emancipation" or a pioneering precursor of the Emancipation. Here it does not matter whether this is justified or not; we shall deal with it in another context. But it is all too easy to forget that these are only peaks in a landscape in which they belong—with mountains, valleys, gorges, and abysses. Put in more prosaic terms, the big Court Jew was not an isolated phenomenon; there were Jewish "Court Factors" at almost every residence of a potentate, including those whose property consisted only of a court with a frequently rather modest ruler's residence and a few estates. From these little "Court Factors" to the big royal ones there were a number of intermediate stages of all kinds. The big ones often developed from the medium, small, and tiny ones—through ability, luck, and political changes as well as the rise and expanded territory of their masters. The small territories in particular, but also the big ones, were closely connected with the farm economy that provided part of their income, in products or in cash. In this farm economy the Jews played a very significant role as financiers and mediators between the city and the country. On the bases of the rural and urban products that they received through this pawnbrokerage the Jewish traders acquired ownership of cattle, wine, grain, wood, and farmland. As peddlers, traveling salesmen, and later also as proprietors of country stores, they brought from the city foodstuffs, clothes, and household items that the villagers needed. The village Jew and the little Court Factor often coalesced, and so did the little Court Factor and the Court Jews at larger courts. There were mutual dependencies as well. The big Court Jew used the smaller one for everything from peddling merchandise and coins, as well as delivering letters to acting as a middleman in negotiations of all kinds. The "little" Jew who wanted to settle in larger towns hired himself out as a servant and helper to privileged "big" Jews and thereby received permission to stay in places in which other Jews were legally barred from settling. If one wishes to draw the line still farther, one must bear in mind that often it is impossible to make an exact distinction between the little traders and peddlers on the one hand and the beggars and gangs of thieves on the other. People bought goods plundered by soldiers and bought and sold stolen merchandise, and thus it was logical to begin supporting enterprises that supplied such goods. Then, too, the increase in the Jewish population and the limitations on the legal opportunities for settling and earning a living often left beggary as the only way out, and then it was all too easy to descend even lower. In the seventeenth and eithteenth centuries Jewish gangsterism seems to have occupied a not insignificant place among the gangs of thieves and bands of robbers of a depraved society, and probably this place is greater than has been recorded in Jewish and philo-Semitic historiography, which for reasons of apologetics has refrained from detailed research on these seamy sides of Jewish life and has thus failed to illuminate this field or else abandoned it to anti-Semites as an uncontrolled poaching area. Until recent years, the investigation of these criminal "underworlds," which had their own social and legal codes, has generally been neglected. "Underworlds" always come into being when economic and social orders offer no legal scope for activity to certain elements. Having no sound legal basis of existence, these elements then use loopholes and the negative sides of the existing order to create an "illegal" order in which they can thrive. Since the Jews were regarded and evaluated as an alien element that was morally outside (Christian) society, it is, if anything, astonishing that despite their impoverishment and the squalor of the time their share in the criminal element was not even greater. Concerning the last-named problem, cf. Friedrich Christian Benedict Ave-Lallement, *Das deutsche Gaunertum in seiner social-politischen, literarischen und linguistischen Ausbildung zu seinem heutigen Bestande,* 3 parts in 2 vols. (Leipzig, 1858–1962); Rudolf Glanz, *Geschichte des niederen jüdischen Volkes* (New York, 1968).

For literature on the Court Jews, in addition to what has already been cited, see Selma Stern, *The Court Jew* (Philadelphia, 1950); Heinrich Schnee, *Die Hoffinanz und der moderne Staat,* 6 vols. (1953–67) (a good summary may be found in chap. 1 of his monograph *Rothschild: Geschichte einer Finanzdynastie,* [Göttingen, 1961], 9–26); F. K. Carsten, "The Court Jews: A Prelude to Emancipation," *LBYB* 3 (1958), 140–56; *JL* 2:1642–46; *EJJ* 5:1006–11; Julius H. Schoeps, "Ephraim Veitel Ephraim—ein Vorkämpfer der Judenemanzipation," in *Mendelssohn-Studien* 2 (Berlin, 1975), 51–70.

Concerning the Court Jews in Spain, see C. Beinart in *Elites and Leading Groups* (Hebr.) (Jerusalem [Historical Society], 1966), 55–71. Concerning the relationship to the rural Jews, see Bernhard D. Weinryb in *LBYB* 1 (1956), 298ff.; Jacob Katz, *Exclusiveness and Tolerance,* chap. 13; Werner J. Cahnmann, "Village and Small Town Jews in Germany," *LBYB* 19 (1974), 107–30 and the addenda by E. Schorsch, 131–33. Details may be found in monographs on countries and towns, the most important of which are cited by Cahnmann.

Regarding the status of rural Jews as "little Court Jews," a statement made by Luther's adversary, Dr. Johann Eck, is revealing: "There are noblemen who, if asked why they tolerate Jews in their village, reply, 'Yes, I have three or four Jews in my village, and they make more for me in a year than all my peasants!'. . . . Yes, many lords treat the Jews better and more honorably than the Christians, get angrier and punish more severely when a Jew is beaten and insulted than if a Christian is insulted" (J. Eck, *Ains Juden buechlin verlegung*, chap. 24, here quoted after T. Fritsch, *Handbuch der Judenfrage* [1937], 438).

FRANKFURT "JUDENSTÄTTIGKEIT": Cited after Höxter, *Quellenbuch* 4 (1928), 89. 173

FREDERICK THE GREAT: From the revised *General-Privilegium und Reglement für die* 174
Juden in den Preussischen Landen vom 17. April 1750 (printed on 18 July 1756), here cited after Höxter, *Quellenbuch* 4 (1928), 135f. A revealing part of this privilege is the enumeration of the occupations and activities that are permitted or prohibited to the Jews. It is decreed "that no Jew may carry on a civil trade except for signet-making, painting, grinding optical lenses, cutting diamonds, polishing stones, embroidering in gold and silver, sewing white goods, cleaning metal scrapings, and similar occupations of that kind in which there are no [Christian] practitioners and privileged guilds, nor should they presume to brew beer or make brandy, though they are allowed to distill spirits for noblemen, officials, and others. . . . However, without a special concession our protected Jews in Berlin should not manufacture or sell woolens, raw wool, or wool yarn. . . . Jews are not permitted to buy or own landed estates anywhere."

DEFENSE OF THE RIGHT NOT TO ADMIT JEWS: Concerning the struggle of Polish cities 176
for the privileges "de non tolerandis Judaeis" in the sixteenth to the eighteenth centuries, cf. Jacob Goldberg, "De non tolerandis Judaeis: On the Introduction of the Anti-Jewish Laws into Polish Towns and the struggle against Them," in the Festschrift *Sefer Raphael Mahler* (Tel Aviv, 1974), 39–52. On occasion even immigrants who themselves constituted a religious or national minority procured such rights. Thus French Huguenot immigrants who were admitted to the middle Franconian university town Erlangen (north of Nuremberg) toward the end of the seventeenth century "had their charters include the stipulation that no Jew should ever be allowed to settle in Erlangen and environs" (*EJ* 6:718). The Berlin merchants who had not been able to get Jewish shops closed included, by way of vengeance and protection, the following section in their commercial code: "Whereas the merchants' guild consists of honest, upright people, no Jew, culpable killer, blasphemer, thief, adulterer, perjurer, or other person afflicted and stained with public vices shall be admitted to our guild, but shall be and remain excluded from it" (Ludwig Geiger, *Geschichte der Juden in Berlin* [Berlin, 1871], 34).

CURRENCY DEVALUATION: Concerning the systematic and unsystematic currency 176
devaluation since the sixteenth century and in particular since the Thirty Years' War, cf. the pertinent general literature and works on economic history. The reason why the "coinage privilege" was a much-desired right that was often subleased or sold, even to Jews, was that it was a quick way of solving financial problems. In the sixteenth and seventeenth centuries the German derisive terms and epithets for debasers of currency and counterfeiters was "Kipper und Wipper" (from *kippen*, to cut off, and *wippen*, to bob; cf. *Der Grosse Brockhaus*, 15th ed., 10:152). A vivid presentation of the customs based on contemporary sources may be found in Gustav Freytag, *Bilder aus der deutschen Vergangenheit*, 1925 reprint, 2:642ff.: "Die Kipper und die Wipper und die öffentliche Meinung" (about Jewish merchants as helpers), 651. Caricatures of Jews as "Kipper und Aufwechsler" in E. Fuchs, *Die Juden in der Karikatur*, 27, and G. Liebe, *Das Judentum in der deutschen Ver-*

gangenheit, 68f.; the caricature on p. 60 shows in the foreground the devil in the shape of a Jew with a Jewish badge and hawk's nose. The quotation from the age of Frederick the Great is from Otto Hintze, *Die Hohenzollern und ihr Werk* (Berlin, 1915), 377.

It is, of course, difficult to estimate the share of the Jews in this and other business deals of that period, for no systematic statistics were kept. This makes all data subjective, and surely the Jewish share is often exaggerated, especially when the contemporary sources speak of the negative sides. We must always bear in mind that in those days there were so many kinds of coins that money-changers had an important role in commerce and everyday activities and that it was all but impossible to control every coin's weight and gold or silver content on which its value was based. It is safe to assume that by virtue of their international connections the Jews played an important role in all related business transactions and manipulations, but their share cannot be determined with certainty.

176   JEW SÜSS (OPPENHEIMER): About him there is an extensive literature (broadsides, caricatures, etc.), but it reproduces the popular sentiment more than it does objective facts. This ambiguous figure has repeatedly inspired biographies and works of fiction. The best biography is Selma Stern's *Jud Süss: Ein Beitrag zur deutschen und zur jüdischen Geschichte* (Berlin, 1929); cf. also her article in *Korrespondenzblatt der Akademie für die Wissenschaft des Judentums* (1926), 23–40. The best-known historical novel about Jud Süss is by Lion Feuchtwanger, first published in 1925 and translated as *Power* and *Jew Süss*. Jud Süss was charged with "high treason and lese majesty, squeezing the country dry through mad machinations, founding new ministries and offices, robbing the state's coffers, buying jobs and selling offices, bribery of justice, establishing monopolies [?] on tobacco, salt, leather, and wine, debasing the currency, and offending the religion established in the dukedom" (Selma Stern, 164). Many of the practices Jud Süss was charged with were customary commercial practices at the time, especially the buying of offices and bribery; cf. Golo Mann (in *Propyläen-Weltgeschichte* 7:222) on the negotiations leading to the Peace of Westphalia, 1648: "Almost everyone was venal, which gave rise to a nice term, *Realdankbarkeit.*" What was behind many other things—that is, the extent to which the struggle of an absolutistic potentate (after whose death Jew Süss was immediately arrested) with the estates and old privileges is reflected here—is revealed by the rescript of 18 May 1737 to the Court of Appeals which says that the infamous villain "sought to drag in the dust our most loyal and faithful district and most grievously impaired its hard-won privileges, rights, and liberties by quietly instituting more than 50 taxes of various kinds" (Selma Stern, *Jud Süss*, 338f.).

177   GOTTHOLD EPHRAIM LESSING'S "DIE JUDEN": This is a youthful work (1749), today rather unknown, by the writer known for his tolerance and later friendship with Moses Mendelssohn, and it is a precursor of *Nathan the Wise*, the well-known play that appeared thirty years later. The noble-minded and worldly wise Jew in this play is a model of humaneness, but the aristocrat whose life he has saved and who is grateful to him regards him as an almost incomprehensible exception: "Oh, how estimable the Jews would be if they were all like you!" To which the Jew responds: "And how lovable the Christians if they all possessed your qualities!" The preceding words, which Lessing has the Jew (who at first appears as an anonymous "Traveler") speak, are characteristic of the period of the Englightenment and Lessing as one of its main representatives: "All I ask by way of recompense is that in future you judge my people a bit less harshly and less generally. I did not conceal myself from you [as a Jew] because I am ashamed of my religion. No! I see, however, that you liked me and disliked my nation. And a person's friendship, no matter who he is, has always been priceless to me."

The reaction of the Göttingen theologian and orientalist Johann David Michaelis (1717–91) was typical of the time. Reviewing Lessing's play in the *Göttingen Gelehrter Anzeiger* he said it was not impossible but highly improbable that "in a people with the principles, life-style, and education" of the Jews "such a noble disposition could develop by itself. . . . Even average virtue and honesty is found among this people so seldom that even the few exemplars of them cannot reduce the hatred of the Jews as much as one would wish." Cf. Lessing, *Gesammelte Werke*, ed. P. Rilla, 3:653.

PHYSIOCRATIC ECONOMICS: Concerning the deleterious effect of the theories of the 177ff. "organic" in historical life and in the evaluation of the Jew as a "Parasite" on the body of the nations—from the origin of the modern biological concept in the 18th century to our days and particularly during the Nazi period—cf. Part 1, chap. 9, as well as my essay "The Jewish Parasite: Notes on the Semantics of the Jewish Problem, with Special Reference to Germany" in *LBYB* 9 (1964), 3–40).

JOHANN GOTTFRIED HERDER (1744–1803): With his writings and collections of folk 178 poetry *(Stimmen der Völker in Liedern)* as well as his studies of ancient Jewish literature *(Vom Geiste der ebräischen Poesie, etc.)* the theologian, writer, and philosopher of history, who is barely known to present-day readers, profoundly influenced not only Goethe but German classical and romantic literature in general. His unfinished *Ideen zur Philosophie der Geschichte der Menschheit*, published after a great deal of preliminary work in Riga in 1784–91 (4 sections divided into 20 "books") have exerted an influence far beyond Herder's time (Hegel, Ranke, Spengler, Toynbee). Herder was the first to breathe true historical life into Voltaire's concept of a "philosophy of history." In going far beyond the rationalism of the "classical" philosophy and historiography of the Enlightenment, he was impeded by the lack of real factual research and often more dependent on his sensitive empathy and intuition than on true knowledge of countries and nations. Here we cannot detail his general, often brilliant insights into the nature of historical processes and connections which make him one of the most important precursors of modern historicism. Friedrich Meinecke has traced and expressed them with his customary sensitivity; cf. *Die Entstehung des Historismus* 2 (1936), 383–479.

This far-reaching effect justifies a few remarks about the chapter "Hebräer" (part 3, book 12, section 3) whose (almost fateful) concluding sentences are quoted in part 1 above (Cf. also my abovementioned article on the Jewish parasite.) It is an attempt to view the history of the Jewish people as objectively and untheologically as was possible for a man of Herder's background, his comprehensive literary education, and his vocation as a theologian. In fairness to him, we must note that he bases himself primarily on the Bible as "written annals of its events" and not on "the calumnies of other despisers and enemies of the Jews" (such as Manetho), but he still wishes that "the tales of their adversaries should not be simply scorned but utilized." All laws given by Moses are "wonderfully thought through," but they have been executed only incompletely: "people divided and rested too soon." The badly situated and ruled country was thereby involved in constant unrest, and at length it was laid waste and his people led to "disgraceful bondage" in Babylon. "Viewed as a state, there is hardly a people that cuts a more miserable figure than this one." Small numbers of them returned from Babylon, but they had learned little politically, and "their religiosity now became pharisaism, their scholarship a ruminant hairsplitting that chewed on only one book, their patriotism a servile dependency on a misunderstood ancient law—all of which made them despicable or ludicrous to all neighboring nations."

Herder uncomprehendingly regards Jewish Messianism as a hope based on ancient, misunderstood prophecies, a hope that was supposed to "assure them of the sheerest world domination." Thus it happened that "through an embitterment that is hardly equaled in history" the land and its capital were destroyed and the Jews were scattered over all lands of the Roman world. But this very dispersal "initiated an influence by the Jews upon the human race that could hardly have been conceivable from their own country." Through Christianity, which had come into being shortly before the fall of the state, "the books of the Jews came into the hands of all nations that embraced the teachings of Christianity." Depending on how they were interpreted and used, these books have had "a good or evil effect on all Christian ages." Through them monotheism became the "basis of all religion and philosophy," and the one God was spoken of "in so many songs and teachings of these writings with a dignity and exaltation, a devotion and gratitude that is matched by little else in human writings." If one compares them with other earlier and later religious writings, "the superiority of the Hebrew writings to all ancient religious books of the nations" is unmistakable—among other things, by virtue of "the pure moral teachings in several books of this collection."

On the other hand, "the misinterpretation and the misuse of these writings," as if everything in them were the indisputable truth, has retarded or impeded the free development of the natural sciences. The "intolerance of the Jewish religious spirit" has served as a model for the intolerance of other religions, including Christianity, and the opinion that the laws of Moses must be emulated "in every clime" has often had a deleterious effect on the independent legislation of the nations.

"Since its dispersal the Jewish nation has benefited and harmed the nations of the earth depending on how it has been used." In Christian Europe it managed "by means of its enterprising spirit to control domestic trade, in particular money-trade, almost everywhere, and this made the cruder nations of Europe voluntary slaves of their usury." To be sure, the Jews did not invent trading in securities, but they perfected it for their purposes. "Undeniably, then, so widespread a republic of clever usurers for a long time kept many a European nation from their own initiatives and utilization of trade because such a nation regarded itself as too great for a Jewish pursuit." If one were to collect all facts about the history of the Jewish people in all countries, "one would see a showpiece of humanity that would be equally remarkable as an event of nature and politics, for no people on earth has spread as this one, no people on earth has maintained its identity and vigor in all climates as this one."

This, however, should not lead one to the "superstitious conclusion" that the Jews have been preserved for epochal events: It is probable that they have already performed their task, "and neither in the people itself nor in the analogy of history does there appear the slightest disposition for any other. For the preservation of the Jews there is just as natural an explanation as for that of the Brahmins, Parsees, and Gypsies." (One can hear these words echoing down to Spengler and Toynbee!)

Then again, there is no denying the great talents, the zeal, and the martial courage in ancient times of the Jewish people, "which became such an effective driving force in the hands of fate." To be sure, the Jews have not been creative in the graphic arts, and they were never a seafaring people. "Like the Egyptians, they feared the sea, and hence they have always preferred to live among other nations—a trait of their national character that Moses already vigorously opposed. In short, the Jews are a people that was spoiled in education because it never attained the maturity of a political culture on its own soil and hence did not gain a true sense of honor and freedom. The studies carried on by their best minds always revealed more of a faithfulness to law and order than a fruitful freedom of the spirit, and their condition has always deprived them of the virtues of a patriot." This mixture of appreciation and deprecation—remarks that lend themselves to a variety of interpretations—is followed by the damning conclusion cited above. It is clear that Herder's personality combined the inwardness of Protestant piety, Spinozan Bible criticism, and pantheistic thought with traditional doctrines and·a new, intuitive, empathic appreciation of the poetry of the biblical books, creating a new image that harbored both a curse and a blessing. In this respect Herder is representative of many similar, smaller-scaled attempts.

Concerning Herder's attitude toward Judaism, see especially Ludwig Geiger's (one-sided) lecture "Herder und das Judentum," delivered on the occasion of the one hundredth anniversary of Herder's death in 1903 and printed in Geiger's *Die deutsche Literatur und die Juden* (Berlin 1910), 63–80; F. M. Barnard, "The Hebrews and Herder's Political Creed," *Modern Language Review* 54 (1959): 533–46; idem, "Herder and Israel," *Jewish Social Studies* 28 (1966): 25–33 (according to the author, Herder was a precursor of Zionism); Hans Liebeschütz, *Das Judentum im deutschen Geschichtsbild* (1967), 23f.; Herder, *Ideen*, chap. "Hebräer," in *Werke*, ed. Suphan, 14: 58–63. The edition of the Goldene Klassiker-Bibliothek (parts 3–6) has an introduction by Ernst Naumann.

OCCUPATIONAL RESTRUCTURING: Sucher B. Weinryb, *Der Kampf um die* 179 *Berufsumschichtung: Ein Ausschnitt aus der Geschichte der Juden in Deutschland* (Berlin, 1936). The author, a well-known Jewish economic historian, rightly points out something that we have repeatedly emphasized—namely, that in the course of their history the Jews frequently had to change their occupations for the sake of their subsistence in a changing economy. The economic basis of the efforts to integrate the Jews into German agriculture was the need for interior colonization. There was a desire to make the land productive and to build up industries, but labor was scarce, while there were an enormous number of people, both Jews and non-Jews, who had not been integrated into the economic labor process. "In the ecclesiastic territories of 18th-century Germany there were 260 beggars for every 1000 inhabitants; in 1790 the ratio is said to have been 20,000 to 50,000 in Cologne. The princes and potentates of that time thus faced the problem of bridging the gulf between shortage of labor on the one hand and unemployed masses on the other. . . . This made it logical to apply the principle of putting the poor to 'productive' work—occupational restructuring and greater productivity—to the Jews as well" (Weinryb, 12). According to Weinryb (8), the occupational structure in the Germany of the late eighteenth century was such that about three-fourths of the non-Jewish population lived off the land, while the same percentage of Jews were tradesmen or innkeepers. In J. Lestschinsky, *Das wirtschaftliche Schicksal des deutschen Judentums* (Berlin, 1932), 15ff., we read that 1 or 2 percent of the Jewish tradesmen belonged to the small upper class of the Court Jews, rich money-changers, and suppliers, 8 percent were on the so-called middle level of traders, 40 percent in the retail trade, and 20–25 percent were peddlers.

In addition, there were a large number of Jewish beggars who were not integrated into the normal economic structure. From the 18th century on they were known as *schnorrer*, a Judeo-German expression derived from the German word *schnurren* (to beg with a *Schnurrpfeife*, a sort of jews'-harp). Lestschinsky writes (17): "If we bear in mind ·that in virtually all larger Jewish communities there were shelters for the so-called *Betteljuden*—a real scourge for the Jews, but in view of German Jewry's lack of rights until their full emancipation an unavoidable phenomenon—we get a cheerless picture of Jewish life in Germany in the late 18th and early 19th century—more gloomy and alarming than later generations were able to imagine. . . . It is entirely possible that among this large number of beggars there were also some impoverished peddlers who had no *Schutzbrief* and therefore were obliged secretly to wander from place to place. . . . As late as 1849 Dr. Dieterici, the director of the Prussian Statistical Office, responded to the anti-Semitic objections to equal rights for the Jews by saying that going from village to village with a heavy load of merchandise on one's back was by no means an easy occupation."

Concerning the situation of the Jews, cf. also Graetz 10, chap. 10, pp. 289ff.

179ff.   ENLIGHTENMENT: It stands to reason that here we were able to give only a brief outline of this movement by way of background for the problems of interest to us. Present-day observers often do this movement an injustice by evaluating it as a purely rationalistic endeavor that recognized only reason. This is how it was deprecated by Romanticism and other subsequent irrational currents. In reality it was far more complex and antithetical in its tendencies, modes of thought, and emotional atmosphere. It was different at different times (e.g., the beginning and end of the eighteenth century are quite different), in different countries (England, France, and Germany had different modes of thought and belief and different literary forms), and with different personalities whose individuality was able to unfold in that particular age, which continued the tendencies of the Renaissance, and gain increased recognition. Rationalism was almost always allied with a profound religiosity. The almost universal struggle of the enlighteners against ecclesiastical dominance and coercion in matters of faith should not be confused with lack of faith. The very detachment from the orthodoxy of the Church enabled the Christian faith to achieve pietistic profundity; its excesses involved a theology and poetry of suffering and blood. The most exalted expression of this pietism may be found in Bach's Passions, and the deistic faith (sometimes with a Freemasonic tinge) was expressed in the music of Mozart (*The Magic Flute*), Beethoven, and Haydn (*The Creation*, 1798). The Enlightenment began with a critique, based on the natural sciences, of what could not be proved rationally, and from this vantage point it attacked the authority of the Bible as the foundation not only of faith but of thought as well. To be sure, it often replaced the authority of the Bible with that of the Greek or Roman "classics." It ended with Kant's clear differentiation between thought and belief and with the currents of incipient Romanticism (Storm and Stress), the Classicism of the late eighteenth century, and Romanticism, as well as the rationalistic liberalism of the nineteenth century. This manysidedness and equivocality also shaped the Enlightenment's problematic attitude toward the Jewish question.

The literature on the Enlightenment is so extensive that I can mention only some books and articles that were particularly useful to me and that supplement the most important sources and the pertinent chapters in the general histories of world events, politics, literature, art, philosophy, the economy, technology, etc. It was a century of decisive achievements (and transitions) in all fields, and it has been characterized as "that change in the air at the start of the eighteenth century" (Denis May, *The Italian Renaissance in Its Historical Background* [1970], 202) and the "crisis of the European conscience" (Paul Hazard, 1939). Concerning the complicated nature of the times and the rational and emotional elements that held sway in the second half of the century, cf. the colorful account in Friedell's *Cultural History of the Modern Age*, 2 (1931), book 3, p. 249: "This period in which soberest rationalism and crassest superstition, audacious charlatanry, and true prophecy moved side by side." (But cf. also Friedell's attitude toward Moses Mendelssohn—that of a Jewish apostate, pp. 233ff.) Of the older literature, the following works are still worth reading: Wilhelm Mommsen, *Das Zeitalter Friedrichs des Grossen*, 2 vols. (1881–82); H. Hettner, *Literaturgeschichte des 18. Jahrhunderts*, 6 vols. (1:895); W. Scherer, *Geschichte der deutschen Literatur* (1886; new ed., 1931). Of the newer presentations, I found useful Veit Valentin, *Weltgeschichte: Völker, Männer, Ideen*, vol. 2 (Amsterdam, 1939), chap. 3 ("Die Aufklärung"), 131–209; Golo Mann, "Der europäische Geist im späten 17. Jahrhundert," in *Propyläen-Weltgeschichte* 7 (1964), 349–84; and Fritz Schalk, "Die europäische Aufklärung," ibid., 469–512. Concerning the ideas of the Enlightenment and their influence on the modern libertarian movements, cf. also the introductory chapters in my book *Die Staatsidee Alexander Hamiltons in ihrer Entstehung und*

Entwicklung (Munich, 1927). About the connection between the "disenchantment of the world" by the Enlightenment and the origin of new myths like those of the National Socialists, cf. Theodor Adorno and Max Horkheimer, *Dialektik der Aufklärung* (Amsterdam, 1947). (Concerning the latter, cf. Martin Jay in *Midstream* 15, no. 10 [December 1969]: 68.)

Shortly before finishing this book I was able to read—with profit and gratitude, which, as so often, unfortunately comes too late—Hugo Bergmann's history of modern philosophy from Nikolaus Cusanus to Immanuel Kant (Hebr.) (Jerusalem, 1973–74), the warm, insightful, and instructive work of a man who always strove for purity, perfection, and justice, a wise philosopher and kindly teacher and guide in whom Jewish and general education and piety were combined.

ENLIGHTENMENT AND JUDAISM: (Cf. also Part 1, p. 202 on the attitude of the Jews   179ff. toward the Enlightenment.) Isaac Barzilay, "The Jew in the Literature of the Enlightenment," *Jewish Social Studies* 18 (1956): 243–61; S. Ettinger, "The Beginnings of the Change in the Attitude of European Society towards the Jews," *Scripta Hierosolymitana* 7:193–219; idem, "Jews and Judaism as Seen by the English Deists of the 18th Century" (Hebr.), *Zion* 29 (1964): 182–207; Arthur Hertzberg, *The French Enlightenment and the Jews* (New York, 1968) (with an extensive bibliography); Jacob Katz, "The Term 'Jewish emancipation': Its Origin and Historical Impact," in *Studies and Texts*, vol. 2, ed. Alexander Altmann (Cambridge, Mass., 1964), 1–25; Jacob Katz, "Die Anfänge der Judenemanzipation," *Bulletin des Leo Baeck Instituts* 13, no. 50 (1974): 12–31; Jacob Toury, Julius M. Schoeps, L. Borinski, et al., "Judentum im Zeitalter der Aufklärung," in *Wolfenbütteler Studien zur Aufklärung*, vol. 4 (1977).

"THE EDUCATION OF THE HUMAN RACE": The one hundred paragraphs that Lessing   179 published in 1780 under the title *Die Erziehung des Menschengeschlechts*, half of which had already appeared in 1777, were an attempt to reconcile the historical religious systems with the deistic rational religion. Judaism with its revelation of monotheism as formulated in the Old Testament and Christianity, with Christ as "the first reliable, practical teacher of the soul's immortality" as well as the New Testament as the crystallization of this doctrine, are regarded as historical and philosophical, conceptual stages. Divine providence used them, and is still using them, to educate mankind to reach the third and highest developmental stage, "complete enlightenment," which "is to produce that purity of heart that makes us capable of loving virtue for its own sake." Concerning this, W. Windelband (*Geschichte der neueren Philosophie*, 1:552) remarks: "Just as Germany's political enlightenment expected salvation from the reforms of a benevolent government, Lessing attributes the perfection of religious life to the progressively clearer revelation of the godhead. He was not yet acquainted with the concept of self-development, just as the political enlightenment did not know the idea of the people educating itself for libertarian institutions." One must bear this attitude of the leading champion of the Enlightenment in mind if one wants to understand the attitude of the surrounding world toward the Jews and that of the Jews to their surroundings in the eighteenth century. Even personalities of the stature of a Lessing who were fighting for a tolerant attitude toward the Jews on the part of the Christian world by no means regarded Judaism as the equal of Christianity; rather, they espoused a purified form of Christian dogmas and regarded Judaism as a preliminary stage of Christianity, which in turn was for them a preliminary stage of something higher. Tolerance was a toleration rather than a recognition of differences as something of equal value. Even the most outstanding champions of tolerance evaluated Judaism as a lower stage of development.

180   SPINOZA: The personality of Baruch (Benedictus) Spinoza in the history of the
      Enlightenment in general and his attitude toward Judaism in particular deserves a
      separate chapter. To speak about his life, his philosophy, his stature, and his signifi-
      cance in general is not within our task and competence. The most important facts of
      his short life (1632–77) and his importance in the history of philosophy, based mainly
      on his two basic writings *Theologico-Political Treatise* (1670) and *Ethics* (1677), are
      generally known, though these writings, like those of many other great men through
      the ages, were and are more praised or damned than read. Here we can only attempt
      to determine his place in the history of the Jewish question. There can be no doubt
      that he must in many regards have a place in it—first of all, as an important Jew,
      perhaps one of the most important ones. No Jew who had a great impact has
      remained without influence on the complex of the relations between Jews and non-
      Jews, and the more important he was and the greater the effects, good or bad, that he
      had on his time within and without Judaism, the more weighty were the con-
      sequences of his life, his teachings, and his activities in the history of our problem. In
      the case of Spinoza, there is the additional factor that he was a lively and controversial
      personality in his time and continues to be one in ours. We can perhaps even say that
      he was the first personality in the history of the Jewish Diaspora that came from the
      Jewish world, transcended it, entered the European Christian cultural world and was
      fully accepted by it—in love and in hate—without converting to Christianity. Other
      Jewish personalities—physicians, Hebraists, theologians, philosophers, Court Jews,
      spokesmen for the Jews, kabbalists, and Messianic figures like Spinoza's contempo-
      rary Sabbatai Tzevi—had an impact on certain esoteric circles or for a short time on
      wider circles, but none has had as profound an effect, or one extending over space
      and time down to the present, as Spinoza. In this sense he probably was the first truly
      emancipated Jew more than a century before the beginning of the epoch of the Jewish
      Emancipation.

          In the European intellectual movement that reached its first zenith in the En-
      lightenment of the eighteenth century the Dutch Jew Spinoza—outwardly mellow,
      dispassionate, opposing any influence of the emotions, and fighting for the domi-
      nance of reason—ranked as one of the great revolutionaries of mankind, even though
      in accordance with his watchword *Caute!* (which was engraved on his signet ring) he
      was generally cautious in his life-style and mode of expression. He was not a popular
      leader; like the Dutch aristocracy, to which he was close, he despised the masses, for
      they could not understand him—any mass of people, even the so-called educated
      who were in the grip of, and guided by, superstitions and prejudices. He did battle
      with whatever he regarded as prejudice and superstition—because it could not stand
      up to the critique of a reason that analyzed, defined, and judged by mathematically
      clear standards. He fought in the name of a social and political order based on
      freedom of thought and belief (an order that was, from a sociological viewpoint,
      aristocratic and authoritarian) and in the name of a concept of the divinity that
      equated God with nature and the "this-worldly miracle" (Max Brod) of its mathe-
      matical-physical lawfulness and the love of God with the recognition and joyously
      faithful acceptance of this fate decreed by the world and its effect on the life of an
      individual.

          At a time and in a country in which "the Bible had become the absolute master of
      life" (Karl Gebhardt in the introduction to his German version of the *Tractatus
      Theologico-Politicus* [1921], xxvi—because of Luther's religious Reformation in Ger-
      many and Calvin's in the western countries, including Holland—it was only natural
      that Spinoza's struggle for freedom of thought from the authoritarian tutelage of the
      Church should turn against the authority of the Bible as the universally valid
      foundation of human belief, thought, and life-style. That was the point of departure

and the goal of Spinoza's critique of the Bible in his *Theologico-Political Treatise*, a work that made him the real founder of modern systematic biblical criticism. He had precursors, of course—from Ibn Ezra and Maimonides to Luther and Hobbes, to name only a few of those with whom he was acquainted. Despite their critique of inconsistencies in individual writings and of the question of their authorship, all of them treated the Bible as believers. To them it was the sacred book that was revealed or inspired by God, the foundation of the faith that they faced with the awe of veneration and fear of punishment, death, and an afterlife in heaven or hell. Spinoza had no faith in these things and no fear of the nonearthly consequences of his thinking. That is why most of his contemporaries regarded him as a denier of God, an atheist, and thus an underminer of the moral foundations of communal living. Only after the middle of the eighteenth century—through Jacoby, Lessing, Mendelssohn, Herder, and particularly Goethe, later through Schelling, Schleiermacher, and Fichte—did his reputation grow and did he achieve the stature of one of the great philosophical spokesmen of mankind with whom one has to come to terms if one wishes to clarify one's own thinking.

In the Jewish realm Spinoza's position is even more complicated. What isolated him from the Jewry of his time and place was that the barely twenty-four-year-old Spinoza, who at the age of eight had experienced the religious tragedy of the chivalrous and heroic Portuguese Jew Uriel Acosta—excommunication, expiation, and suicide in Amsterdam—after warnings and futile spiritual and material attempts to induce him to abandon his "wrong way" was excommunicated on 27 July 1656 and thus was barred from associating with Jews and influencing them orally and in writing. Hence this direct influence on Judaism did not begin until almost a century later—with Moses Mendelssohn, who was also regarded by his surroundings as an unusual "exceptional Jew" and accepted as such (cf. the remarks in the excursus about Mendelssohn, Part 2, pp. 566ff.). That the Amsterdam Jewish community expelled Spinoza from its ranks after he had evinced no interest in any manifestations of Jewish life was entirely in the style of the time. The excommunication of members of the community with heretical views was standard procedure also in the Calvinist communities of Holland, as well as in the Catholic communities of other countries. Spinoza presumably regarded this as a normal consequence of his struggle against religious constraint and the encroachment of theology into free, philosophical thought. It cannot be established with certainty how much inner pain the hostile attitude of his community caused him and whether in his arguments against the authority of the Bible in his *Theologico-Political Treatise* it occasioned his sharp remarks that are almost expressive of an aversion to Judaism or even hostility toward it, while he often found far more friendly words for Pauline Christianity—whether out of conviction or for tactical reasons. A sensitive reader will "occasionally perceive this aversion and the harshness of language, which often goes beyond a sober judgment, as ill feeling" (Max Wiener, "Spinoza," in *Gemeindeblatt der Jüdischen Gemeinde zu Berlin* 12, no. 11, November 1932, 265). Perhaps the epigram "An Spinoza" by Nietzsche, who admired Spinoza as his own precursor and who may be regarded as the real discoverer of the effects of *ressentiment* as a psychological force, is not wide of the mark:

Dem "Eins in Allem" liebend zugewandt,
amore dei, selig aus Verstand—
Die Schuhe aus! Welch dreimal heilig Land!—
—Doch unter dieser Liebe frass
ein heimlich glimmender Rachebrand:
am Judengott frass Judenhass. . .
Einsiedler! hab' ich dich erkannt?

(Lovingly inclined toward "one in all," amore dei, blissful from understanding—
Shoes off! What a thrice holy land!— —Yet underneath this love a secretly glimmer-
ing fire of vengeance was devouring things. Jewish hatred gnawed away at the Jewish
god. . . Hermit! Have I recognized you?)

In any case, Spinoza's Bible criticism, which was founded on his good knowledge of
the Hebrew language and turned primarily against Maimonides as a representative of
Jewish authoritarian interpretation and against the Christian Calvinist view, being
based on his own rational judgment as the only valid authority, was designed to strip
Judaism of the aura of uniqueness and its religious teachings and laws of the character
of universality and even of the "religious" in a higher sense. In the Preface to his
Tractatus Spinoza said he "determined to examine the Bible afresh in a careful,
impartial, and unfettered spirit, making no assumptions concerning it, and attribut-
ing to it no doctrines which I do not find clearly therein set down." With the aid of
this method he comes to the conclusion "that the authority of the prophets has weight
only in matters of morality and that their speculative doctrines affect us little. Next I
inquired why the Hebrews were called God's chosen people, and discovering that it
was only because God has chosen for them a certain strip of territory where they
might live peaceably and at rest, I learned that the law revealed by God to Moses was
merely the law of the individual Hebrew state, therefore that it was binding on none
but Hebrews, and not even Hebrews after the downfall of their nation." (Translation
of R. H. M. Elwes [New York, 1951], 8.)

This is, of course, not the place to give details of Spinoza's investigation and the
conclusions he drew from it, so we shall add only a few remarks that concern our
problem. "Pharisees," the word and the concept, is used as deprecatingly as was the
custom in the gospels and the Christian literature dependent on them; often the
Pauline view is adduced as documentation of Spinoza's own view. Like Tacitus, whom
he quotes more than once, Spinoza declared that the Jews were xenophobes and that
this hatred of all other nations was profoundly connected with their religious faith.
"After they had transferred their right to God," he writes in the seventeenth chapter
of the *Tractatus*, "they thought that their kingdom belonged to God and that they
themselves were God's children. Other nations they looked upon as God's enemies
and regarded with intense hatred which they took to be piety (see Psalm 139:21–
22):* nothing would have been more abhorrent to them than swearing allegiance to a
foreigner. . . Thus the love of the Hebrews for their country was not only patriotism,
but also piety, and was cherished and nurtured by daily rites till, like their hatred of
other nations, it must have passed into their nature. . . . Such daily reprobation
naturally gave rise to a lasting hatred, deeply implanted in the heart: for of all hatreds
none is more deep and tenacious than that which springs from extreme devoutness or
piety, and is itself cherished as pious" (*Tractatus*, 229). This hatred was exacerbated
by the fact that it evoked the bitterest hatred of the nations for the Jews and their
peculiar customs; Spinoza names circumcision in particular. It is primarily owing to
this hatred of the nations for the Jews and not to a special providence or chosenness
that the Jews have maintained themselves despite their dispersion.

Concerning the influence on posterity of "what is clearly expressed or indicated in
the *Tractatus*, or may be found in it in disguised form" a religious philosopher and
historian of the rank of Max Wiener writes in the abovementioned essay, p. 265:
"Christian thinkers up to Kant and beyond have seen Judaism substantially as
depicted here; and if this son of our own people lacked love for his mother, we surely
cannot expect it of strangers. Moses Mendelssohn, who bore the pantheist such ill

*It is hard to understand how Spinoza could adduce these verses, which refer to hatred of
blasphemers who hate God.

will, is completely in the shadow of Spinoza with his view of the exclusive legal character of Judaism." If it led him to different conclusions, this was due primarily to the "difference in feeling, the solidarity which they display to their traditional community." According to Wiener, Spinoza marked "an interruption in the tradition of feeling, though not in the intellectual tradition."

These remarks are not intended to diminish Spinoza's epochal significance. They do, however, place him in a tragic context of Jewish history that enmeshed the Jews, both as individuals and as a totality, in situations in which even the best intentions and aims could have a deleterious effect. At the same time, the human entanglements that have been indicated here make Spinoza's figure more comprehensible than if he had been depicted only as a modest lens-grinder and "divinely" harmonious philosopher who was above his time and its realities.

The posthumously published *Ethics* did not have a positive effect until much later. At first this work, too, was regarded as that of a godless person—and from the standpoint of the church justifiably so. If the superworldly and supernatural existence of God was denied and his existence was equated with the inner nature of the world and its natural laws, there was no room for any churchly-institutional religious service based on prayer and ritual, or even for the personal prayers of individuals or a pious dialogue with God.

Hermann Cohen was a passionate monotheist and anti-Zionist Jew, and it may be particularly instructive to refer to his attempt to come to terms with Spinoza in 1910. Ernst Simon discusses this in a fine essay entitled "Zu Hermann Cohens Spinoza-Auffassung," *Monatsschrift für Geschichte und Wissenschaft des Judentums* ([Berlin, 1935], 181–94; reprinted in Simon's collection of essays *Brücken* [Heidelberg, 1965], 205–19). Cohen actually reproaches Spinoza with lovelessness. In contrast to Kant, Cohen's particular intellectual mentor who never entirely rid himself of "the intimate obsessions" of his Christian-religious matrix and hence was cautious rather than uninhibited in his religious critique, Spinoza was "bolder and sharper" in carrying on his struggle "for the liberation of man from the power of religion." Yet one cannot help reflecting "how much more illuminating and purer the historical effect of this work of Spinoza would have been if it had contained any sense of gratitude and loyalty, any joyous sense of mission, any modesty and its attendant theoretical self-criticism. . . ." According to Cohen, Spinoza left the Jews even before they left him. Together with the personality of God, pantheism destroys the human personality. If God equals nature, might becomes right—a doctrine that is bound to lead to the idolization of the total state. Spinoza's affectless man cannot love, because if he did, he would also have to hate. It is only natural that the anti-Zionist should have vehemently opposed Spinoza's view, as occasionally expressed in the third chapter of the *Tractatus* (and to be discussed at a later point), that a restoration of the Jewish state might come about. Spinoza's remark was made in connection with his emphasis on circumcision, which maintained the Jews as a group, and it sounds like a cool, unconcerned response to a question (which was actually directed at Spinoza); after all, it was the time of the sensational appearance of Sabbatai Tzevi as Messiah; cf. Part 1, pp. 196ff.): "I would go so far as to believe that if the foundations have emasculated their minds, they may even, if occasion offers, so changeable are human affairs, raise up their empire afresh, and that God may a second time elect them" (*Tractatus*, 56). He compares the Jews with the Chinese: "they, too, have some distinctive mark on their head which they most scrupulously observe" (ibid.). They have maintained themselves in this isolation, and have lost and then regained their independence. Surely one factor in Spinoza's independence of Jewish tradition and his lack of reverence for it (which Hermann Cohen criticized) was his Marranic descent, a point that may have been neglected in assessments of Spinoza. His German biographer, translator, and editor Karl Gebhardt particularly emphasizes this point in his Introduction to his translation of the *Theologico-Political Treatise*, and Hugo Bergmann agrees with him in his abovementioned Hebrew history of modern philosophy. In Gebhardt's view, the *Tractatus* is a political polemic in favor of a friend named Jan de Witt, the leader of the corporative Republican party and a retired councilor, but it probably originated from Spinoza's rebuttal of the charges that had led to his expulsion from the Jewish community and hence included his critique of Judaism. This background explains Spinoza's rejection of eternal vocation and his denial of the validity of Jewish ceremonial law for the Jews of his time, who "have only a very loose connection with his real purpose, the defense of the rights of philosophy and freedom of thought. . . . This fighting stance also explains Spinoza's harsh and even hostile judgments on the people from which he came; fairness is not the virtue of a fight." If one wishes to make a fair judgment, one should consider that "he was not a Jew in the real sense, but a Marrano"—that is, a member of that part of Sephardic Jewry "which had professed the Catholic faith for over a century, meaning three generations. Even though this profession was in many cases only an external one, even the outward adherence to the Catholic religion meant a disruption of every Jewish tradition." It was hard for the Marranos to reestablish contact with the Jews of their surroundings, and this was exacerbated by the fact that these Jews had a different Jewish tradition, that of Ashkenazic Polish Jewry. "What historians have hitherto regarded as apostasy from the faith of the fathers was really an inability to recapture what was no longer a living past. And those whom their time excluded as heretics and apostates only made a choice of religion that differed from that of the majority of their people. While men like Abraham Herrera [a Catholic religious philosopher] or Manasse ben Israel [an Amsterdam rabbi and scholar who worked for the readmittance of the Jews to England] established contact with the kabbalistic tradition of the Ashkenazim, Da Costa and after him Spinoza took different routes." Gebhardt points out that Da Costa, who was a generation older, had "dared to doubt the biblical tradition" and "saw human work with very earthly intentions where a very rigid inspired belief had hitherto worshiped divinity." From this Spinoza derived his polemical attitude toward traditional believers "whom he called 'Pharisees' from the earliest periods to his time."

Gebhardt characterizes the intellectual situation of the Marranos (cf. Part 1, p. 133ff.) as "schizophrenia" ("eine Spaltung des Bewusstseins"): "They had been shaped by a Catholic education, but since these were outward influences, they were bound to lack inner unity. In their heart of hearts the religion they professed remained idolatry, and yet that is all they had. While every European was born into certain categories of thought, be it the category of law and justice or that of original sin and redemption, there were for the first time people without compelling categories of their own and with a split consciousness. This split gave rise to modern consciousness. A people sought the coast of its ancient homeland, and Spinoza found a new world."

We shall encounter similar phenomena in a considerable number of Jews since the middle of the eighteenth century, in their endeavor to get their bearings in the modern world, whose culture they regarded as a universally human one but which was to a great extent really determined by the Christian tradition. The criticism of these Jews will be similar to the one that was, rightly or wrongly, leveled at Spinoza.

Compare the perceptive remarks by H. J. Schoeps in his little book *Barocke Juden, Christen, Judenchristen* (Bern, 1965) about the intellectual history of the seventeenth century, when "very untraditional thinking was brought to bear on traditional themes" (p. 7) as well as this characterization of Marranism in his essay on Isaak de la Peyrere, a precursor of Zionism (and probably a Marrano): "Typical of Marranism is doubt of tradition and a critical attitude toward it, be it Christian and

Jewish, as well as the split personality of a Marrano, who can be a Christian in his belief and a Jew in feeling" (p. 22). There is also the characterization in a letter from the poet Rainer Maria Rilke, dated 22 April 1925 (and quoted in *MB*, 12 December 1975), who says that the Jew driven from his native soil has "transformed his instability into a superiority," which had both good and bad effects. Wherever "the same process, the same survival wrested from fate was accomplished in an entity with great resolve, the same inexorableness gave rise to the humaneness for which Spinoza would be a famous example. . . . The mobility and transferability of the inner center, its independence (but also rootlessness if contemplation does not extend to its roots in God), its really transportable spirit were brought into the world by the fate of the Jews—an unparalleled danger and an unparalleled freedom of movement."

As for literature on Spinoza, cf. the summary and bibliography in *EJJ* 15:2275–84. In addition to the abovementioned essays and the pertinent chapters in histories of the Jews and of philosophy, see Leo Strauss, "Zur Bibelwissenschaft Spinozas und seiner Anhänger," in *Korrespondenzblatt des Vereins zur Gründung und Erhaltung einer Akademie für die Wissenschaft des Judentums*, vol. 7 (1926), 1–22; idem, *Die Religionskritik Spinozas als Grundlage seiner Bibelwissenschaft* (Berlin, 1930); Alfred Klaar, *Spinoza: Sein Leben und seine Lehre* (Berlin, 1926); Ernst Kohn, "Spinoza und der Staat" (diss., Berlin, 1926); Julius Gutmann, *Die Philosophie des Judentums* (Munich, 1933), 278–300; C. Wirszubski, "Spinoza and Tacitus" (Hebrew, with brief English summary), *Iyun* 6 (1955): 18–24, 63.

If one wishes to get an idea of what a Catholic intellectual thought of the Jews, Judaism, and the Jewish question at that time, the best example may be Blaise Pascal (1623–62), the brilliant mathematician and religious thinker, a man who awakened to profoundest faith and was incorruptible in his love of the truth. In his book *Pensées*, a collection of fragments and intellectual sketches for an apologia for Christianity that by virtue of its incisive critique and self-criticism as well as its linguistic precision is even today regarded as a classical work of world literature and widely read not only by believers, Pascal repeatedly writes about Judaism. He is completely free from hate of the Jewish contemporaries of Jesus, the Jews of his time (who really are not the subject of his reflections), or Judaism as a religion and a people. On the contrary, he is full of astonished admiration for them. For him they are the oldest existing people and have the oldest and best political laws. Pascal is full of praise for their stubborn loyalty to their tradition, their inner cohesion and their solidarity with one another, their unlimited love of the Bible and their unshakable adherence to it even though it contains the chastisement of their leaders—especially Moses and Isaiah—for the Jews' ingratitude to God and their leaders' prophecies of misfortune and dispersion among the nations. At the same time, however, the *Pensées*, a work that has been assessed as a basic book of world literature and intellectual-religious experience, repeats as self-evident all the dogmatic views and teachings about Judaism that were established by Pauline-Augustine Christianity and confirms them for world literature: the crucifixion of Christ by the Jews and their nonrecognition of him as a sin and missed vocation; the assessment of the Jewish religion as an important preliminary stage of Christianity, but no more than that; the preservation of the Jews despite all failings and persecutions as witnesses to the truth of Christianity—all this because it was thus foreseen and determined by God. "It is a thing amazing and worthy of special attention," writes Pascal at one of the most striking places, "to see this Jewish people existing for so long, and always in misery: it being necessary to prove the truth of Jesus Christ, both that they should continue and always in misery, since they crucified Him; and, although misery and continued existence are contrary states, this people nevertheless continues to exist despite its misery" (*Pensées* 454, trans. H. F. Stewart [London, 1950], 241).

180   JOHN TOLAND: It is revealing that the English title uses for the acquisition of
      citizenship in the sense of "natural right" the word "naturalising"—that is, granting
      the rights of a citizen that are a human being's natural due. In this sense the word has
      entered British and European jurisprudence. As a motto Toland uses Malachi 2:10:
      "Have we not all one father? Did not one God create us? Why do we break faith with
      one another, profaning the covenant of our fathers?" (*The Prophets* [Philadelphia:
      Jewish Publication Society, 1978], 895).

      Concerning the polemics about Toland's work, which appeared anonymously, and
      the author's personality and his anti-Church deist publications (of which *Christianity
      Not Mysterious*, 1696, was the most widely disseminated and the most bitterly
      fought), see the editor's introduction and the bibliography given there. The polemic
      repeated the abusive arguments against the Jews that were common in the sermons
      and even demanded a strict enforcement of the still valid medieval law according to
      which Jews staying in England illegally were subject to the death sentence. After all,
      even Cromwell had not managed to act favorably on the application of the Amsterdam
      rabbi and politician Manasse ben Israel that the Jews be admitted to England, though
      to a certain extent there was tacit nonenforcement of the law. Toland showed that he
      was astonishingly well-read and acquainted with the situation of the Jews. He
      demanded their admittance to England for humanitarian as well as economic reasons
      in the spirit of mercantilism. His defense of the Jews, one of the first and most
      thorough, was far ahead of his time. Even a writer of the rank of Jonathan Swift, the
      author of *Gulliver's Travels*, wrote around that time in opposition to the British
      freethinkers that the time had come when they would evidently convert to Judaism
      and the sultan would receive the foreskin of Toland and Collins in a golden cassette.
      The prematurity of Toland's plea is indicated by the fact that the law sanctioning the
      admittance of Jews under certain conditions which was adopted by the British
      parliament in May 1753, about forty years after the publication of Toland's book and
      thirty years after the author's death, aroused such outrage among the population that
      it was repealed in December of that year. To be sure, in the meantime numerous
      defenders had come forward who did not approve of the government's retraction.
      There, too, universally humane, libertarian, and mercantilist arguments were ad-
      vanced in favor of admittance; the opponents cited arguments from Chrstian the-
      ology ("deicides," "traitors," etc.). Some polemical writings for and against the "Jew
      Bill" were reissued in a photo-offset reprint by the Hebrew University in Jerusalem
      (*Kuntressim mi-Polmoss ha-Jew Bill*).

180ff. PRO-JEWISH CURRENTS IN THE SEVENTEENTH CENTURY: To speak of "philo-Semitic"
        currents, as is often done, seems terminologically inappropriate to me. After all, the
        word "anti-Semitism" and the antithetical concept "philo-Semitism" were not created
        until two hundred years later, toward the end of the nineteenth century (cf. part 1,
        chap. 6), and one should be careful about what I regard as an anachronistic application
        of modern concepts to phenomena of distant and different times. Apart from that,
        however, an appreciation of the Old Testament is not *eo ipso* to be equated with an
        appreciation of contemporaneous Jewry. On the contrary; the Jews living on the next
        street were frequently regarded as the opposite of the idealized Jews of the heroic
        past, people who still had not atoned for the crime against Jesus. The composition of
        and reverent listening to Handel oratorios about heroic figures of the Jewish past
        (Esther, Deborah, Joseph and his brethren, Joshua, Judah Maccabee, Solomon, etc.)
        from the 1730s and 1740s on is, if we may say so, more classicistic than tolerant or
        altruistic in nature. After all, people also glorified and idealized the figures of Roman
        antiquity as "classical" models without identifying them with the living, contempo-
        rary Italians. The latter, on the contrary, were viewed all the more critically as the

antithesis of this background painted in ideal colors and forms, and thus the judgment on them was all the more derogatory.

PIETISM AND JUDAISM: We have already briefly mentioned pietism on p. 546 above, 181
and so we shall add only a few remarks about its position on and in the Jewish question. As far as I can determine, there are hardly any monographs on this problem, and it is barely mentioned in the general Jewish histories. Yet the Protestant religious movement of renewal in the seventeenth and eighteenth centuries that was, at first mockingly, called pietism, was effective far beyond its heyday and the circle of its adherents, who, with the exception of the Herrnhuter or Moravian Brethren, never formed a comprehensive organization. Under its founder Jacob Spener (1635–1705, a contemporary of Sabbatai Tzevi and Baruch Spinoza) pietism had a quietistic, wholly internalized character. In this respect it was a continuation of the ideas of young Luther coupled with the idea of individuality of the personality that had increasingly prevailed since the Renaissance. Under August Hermann Francke (1663–1727) it took a more active direction, and with Zinzendorf (1700–1760, a contemporary of Israel Baal Shem Tov, 1698–1760, the renewer of Hasidism in Poland) and his community of "brethren" the Lutheran theology of the cross was developed into a theology of blood and wounds. The concept of inner conversion, with prayer as the most important element of redemption and self-liberation, occupied a central position—first as personal conversion, then, with an outward direction, as a mission to convert those of different beliefs within and without Christianity. Connected with this are seemingly contradictory trends: the study of other religious teachings (in particular Judaism) and the beginnings of tolerance toward them as a means of converting them through love, like the active mission. The latter was in contrast to the aggressively damning attitude of orthodox Protestantism. The Protestant mission to the Jews and heathens had its point of departure here. Through the theology of blood and wounds, in which a believer primarily identifies with Christ's sufferings and strives to relive them, and through the introduction of analogies from married life this religious inwardness led to a flood of emotions in religious writings and lapses from good taste that are hard to endure today, even if they appear in the musical perfection of Bach's settings. And this identification with the pain and death of the human-divine redeemer was apt to keep reviving and deepening the hatred of the Jews, who were, after all, regarded as the causes of this pain and death. The new pious people did desire to understand Judaism, and many of them occupied themselves in a subjectively honest endeavor with Jewish literature, the learned Hebrew literature as well as the Hebrew and Judeo-German popular literature, which in the nature of things was anything but pro-Christian and decidedly condemned and derided Christianity, its dogmas, its tales of miracles, and its anti-Jewishness. In their blissful belief and their profoundly inward identification with Jesus the Pietists regarded everything that deviated from their own convictions, even within contemporaneous Christianity, as an error, as godlessness and sin, and hence deemed it to be the duty and the mission of the "true Christians" to redeem all those who did not share their beliefs from this pernicious devilish delusion through conversion. This was to be accomplished through humane measures and not through curses and compulsions; in this spirit people have tried to find the seeds of religious tolerance in their writings and activities. But this toleration was only sufferance and not acceptance of something different, more of a tactical means on the road to the necessary conversion to the true faith. The opposing mentality retained its preponderance over hearts and minds precisely because, unlike what was the case among the orthodox Lutherans and Calvinists, the liturgical-legal observance was not regarded as the decisive thing.

Thus the occupation with the history and literature of the Jews and familiarity with their lifestyle and religious customs in the distant past and the immediate present were able to produce books in which attacks on false accusations and hostile aggression against the Jews were combined with the most poisonous attacks on their teachings and customs, their relationship to the Christian religion, and their obdurate adherence to their reprobate, Satan-inspired faith. Learned works like those of Wagenseil and Eisenmenger (cf. Part 1, pp. 184ff.) were shaped by these basic tendencies and later became arsenals of that renewed hatred of the Jews even if they were not written with this intention.

Herder and others who were strongly influenced by Pietism thus infected modern literature with anti-Jewish elements to a not inconsiderable degree. The Christian theology and philosophy of the nineteenth century also received from Pietism positive and negative impulses in their attitude toward the Jewish question.

It seems to me that people have generally disregarded the negative effect that the musical "Passions" written in the spirit of Pietism have had on the listeners. True, Johann Sebastian Bach was an orthodox Lutheran and adopted a "severely negative attitude" toward Pietism as a sect. Yet Albert Schweitzer says in his monumental biography of Bach that his works "bear visible traces of Pietism; the texts of his cantatas and passions were strongly influenced by it, as was the entire religious poetry of the early eighteenth century. One can see this from the reflections and the sentimental attitude with which Bach's librettists were familiar. Thus the opponent of Pietism provided pietistically tinged poetry with his music and thus preserved it for all time."

These wonderful musical settings brought the Christian-Protestant image of the Jews via concert halls, choral societies, and present-day records and tapes to people far from the influence of the Church. I myself have been an admirer of Bach since my youth and particularly love the St. Matthew Passion. For as long as I could I listened to it every year and studied the piano score beforehand and afterward. Naturally, as a Jew and Zionist I have often had ambivalent feelings and shuddered when I heard the choral fugue with the words "Let him be crucified!" which, as it were, the people of Israel has called out to Pilate to this day. It is similar with the narrative of the Evangelist, with dramatic interruptions and pietistic observations about the betrayal of Judas, like these stormily dramatic words of the double chorus: "Have lightning and thunder vanished in clouds? Open the fiery abyss, o hell, destroy, devour with sudden rage the false betrayer, the murderous blood." Or this recitative of Pilate: "I am innocent of the blood of this righteous man; take care." Then the entire people answered him and spoke [here the two choruses swell into a *unisono*]: "Let his blood come over us and our children." The last phrase is repeated seven times! Thus the present repeatedly is called upon to bear witness to the Jews' continuing crime, crucifixion, and the teachings about the Jews as deicides and traitors that people absorbed in their youth and may then have almost forgotten are renewed in this fashion and newly (and perhaps more securely) anchored in their minds and hearts.

On the other hand, pietistic impulses also gave rise to the Württemberg movement of the *Tempelgesellschaft* and its founding, since 1866, of rural and municipal settlements in Palestine. Its leader, the theologian Christoph Hoffmann (1815–85) was raised in the pietistic community Korntal that was directed by his father. In 1866 he emigrated to Palestine in order to gather the true Christians there in expectation of the imminent end of the world. The Jewish settlements founded after 1882 later learned from the German ones, particularly the agricultural settlement Wilhelma, near Ben-Shemen. (Cf. my book *The Return to the Soil* [Jerusalem, 1952]). On the other hand, the rise of Hitler and his hordes in Germany also caused a blossoming of the anti-Jewish and patriotic-nationalistic seeds present in this sect and its beliefs. The majority of the Palestinian German Templars became nationalistic and anti-

Semitic in the spirit of the National Socialists and also joined them organizationally, and thus their settlements were liquidated by the British and the settlers deported from the country. After the foundation of the State of Israel the former German settlement Sarona, north of Jaffa-Tel Aviv, served for some years as the seat of the Israeli government, and even today numerous government offices, among them the Ministry of Security, are located there.

As for literature (in addition to the abovementioned works and reference works like *Christliche Religion*, Fischer-Lexikon), cf. J. Martin Schmidt, "Judentum und Christentum im Pietismus des 17. und 18. Jahrhunderts," in *Kirche und Synagoge* 2 (1970): 87–128; Gerhard Kaiser, *Pietismus und Patriotismus im literarischen Deutschland* (Wiesbaden, 1961), particularly the introductory chapter; Gustav Freytag, *Bilder aus der deutschen Vergangenheit* 3 (1862), chap. "Die Stillen im Lande"; Christoph Hoffmann, *Mein Weg nach Jerusalem*, 2 vols. (1882–84).

REMBRANDT AND THE JEWS: Cf. Franz Landsberger's fine book *Rembrandt, the Jews   181
and the Bible* (Philadelphia, 1946, 1972) and M. Barash's incisive study "Rembrandt's Representation of Jews" in *Eretz-Yisrael* 6 (1960): 179–88 (in Hebrew, with an English synopsis, 39f.) Barash contrasts Rembrandt's image of the Jews with the iconography of the "typical" Jew (as the criminal traitor) in the Middle Ages and with the Renaissance's image of repentant Judas. To this Rembrandt opposes his drawings and paintings of Jews with a profound understanding of their outer and inner reality. A particularly revealing aspect of this study is its pictorial and textual demonstration that portraits of contemporary Jews served as the model for Rembrandt's highly humanized figure of Jesus.

THE IMPRESSION OF THE JEWS ON CONTEMPORARY OBSERVERS: The most com-   182ff.
prehensive book on this subject is the collection *Jüdische Merckwürdigkeiten* by the scholastic, Lutheran theologian, and orientalist Johann Jakob Schudt (Frankfurt 1714–17). Concerning him, cf. Efraim Frisch's Afterword in his small selection from this work, *Von der Franckfurter Juden Vergangenheit (Sitten und Bräuchen)*, Schocken-Bücherei 12 (Berlin, 1934). The remark made by the Methodist leader John Wesley (1703–91) after attending a religious service (cited by H. Mainusch in his introduction to the abovementioned work by John Toland) is typical of the general incomprehension: "My spirit was moved within me, at that horrid, senseless pageantry, that mockery of God, which they called public worship."

LESSING'S *NATHAN THE WISE:* Regarding Lessing's attitude toward Judaism and the   182
influence of this attitude on the Enlightenment, cf. the remarks in this volume on his early play *Die Juden* and his prose work *Die Erziehung des Menschengeschlechts* (Part 2, pp. 542, 547). By contrast with the cliché generally disseminated by Jewish historiography and literature about the ideal Enlightenment figure of Lessing's Jew Nathan, Ernst Simon has properly pointed out (*Jüdische Rundschau*, 22 January 1929; reprinted in *Brücken* [1965], 215–19) that like most Christians favorably disposed to the Jews, from the Enlightenment to the present, Lessing regards as the ideal Jew the type who is so completely assimilated to his surroundings that "one notices nothing about him"—that is, who makes one forget that he is a Jew. The influence exerted by Lessing's image of the Jew in general and his Nathan in particular was extraordinary. After all, Lessing was one of the most influential spokesmen of the Enlightenment period; in his *Geschichte der neueren Philosophie* 1:550, Windelband calls him "the greatest philosopher of the Enlightenment." Especially in the nineteenth century his writings achieved general recognition and were read as "classics" by all circles, particularly the liberal bourgeoisie. Until the 1920s his plays were widely performed, especially in German-speaking countries,

first and foremost *Nathan der Weise*, a play in which Lessing adapted a narrative of Boccaccio for his parable of the three rings. There the three leading religions—Judaism, Christianity, and Islam—are presented as being of equal moral value, and its adherents are called upon (the new turn in Lessing) to demonstrate the high value (and perhaps the superiority) of their creed by means of a morally exemplary life. Ernst Simon has summarized the historical position of the Jew Nathan as follows: "He did not shape an adequate past and present but he helped to effect a future that emulated him. The well-nigh canonical respect that Lessing's *Nathan the Wise* enjoyed among the assimilated German Jews made his emancipatory picture of the future a pedagogical model. . . . In combination with the social, political, and intellectual development Nathan fashioned hundreds of thousands of pseudo-Jews in his image." Thus, alongside its positive effects, Lessing's "brave humanitarianism" (Simon) helped produce those dangerous illusions from which many Jews did not awaken until the 1930s, when it was already too late to save their lives from the inhuman intolerance of the Nazis . . .

182ff.   DOHM: Here I have used, in addition to the original writings, the presentations in the well-known historical works, and the literature on Mendelssohn (cf. Part 2, p. 569), the essay by E. G[ottgetreu], "Zwischen Dohm und Homberg," in *MB*, 13 June 1975.

184   EISENMENGER: The sub-title of this work, which is prolix in the style of the Baroque Age, boasts that "everything is powerfully demonstrated from their own numerous works, which have been read with great effort and undaunted zeal, with Hebrew extracts and their faithful translation into the German language." Concerning the struggle for the publication and early dissemination of this book, cf. G. Wolf, "Der Prozess Eisenmenger," in *Monatsschrift für Geschichte und Wissenschaft des Judentums* 18 (1869). For literature about Eisenmenger see *EJ* 6:358ff. For the use of the *Shulhan Arukh* see my remarks in Part 1, pp. 162ff., and Part 2, pp. 534f. About the continued effectiveness of this work Leopold Zunz, the founder of the modern Science of Judaism, was able to say in his Preface to his book *Die gottesdienstlichen Vorträge der Juden* (1832; 1892 ed., viii): "The actual (alleged) knowledge of Judaism is still where Eisenmenger put it 135 years ago. . . ." Quotations may be found in all anti-Jewish works in the German language up to Rohling, Fritsch, and Nazi literature.

186ff.   VOLTAIRE'S ATTITUDE TOWARD JUDAISM: For Voltaire's significance in general, see the more comprehensive works on the period, which has been called both the "epoch of Frederick the Great" (in the political respect) and "the epoch of Voltaire" (in the intellectual-ideological respect). For a selective bibliography, see the appendix to the picture biography by Georg Holmsten (Hamburg, 1971), 169–79; on pp. 164–67 there are some judgments on him that are characteristic of their periods—from Lessing and Goethe to the present. Hanna Emmrich's detailed study *Das Judentum bei Voltaire* (Breslau, 1930) is still a basic reference for Voltaire's attitude toward Judaism; unless otherwise noted, the quotations in this book are drawn from it. The various editions of Voltaire's *Dictionnaire philosophique* contain substantially different compilations of articles; e.g., the new edition of 1961 (Garnier Frères) contains no article about the Bible. Concerning the influence of the English Deists on Voltaire's hostility toward the Jews, cf. S. Ettinger in *Zion* 29 (1964): 183ff. For supplements and a general evaluation, see also Arthur Hertzberg, *The French Enlightenment and the Jews* (New York and London, 1968) and Leon Poliakov, *De Voltaire à Wagner* (*Histoire de l'Antisémitisme* 3) (Paris, 1968). Regarding Voltaire's position in the history of historiography and the history of ideas generally, Friedrich

Meinecke has an informative chapter in *Die Entstehung des Historismus,* vol. 1 (Munich, 1936), 78–124. Concerning his influence on modern anti-Semitism, see also the remarks (with quotations) of H. S. Chamberlain in his well-known book *Die Grundlagen des Neunzehnten Jahrhunderts,* popular edition (1907), 398–401—a book that was widely read at the turn of the century and even after World War I as a work of "general education" like Spengler's *The Decline of the West* since 1918 and Toynbee's *A Study of History* after the 1930s and 1940s.

THE JEWS AS JUNK DEALERS: For Voltaire the Jews were that intellectually as well. Cf.   187
the article "Abraham" in *Dict. philosophique,* 5: "Les Juifs firent donc de l'histoire et de la fable ancienne ce que leur fripiers font de leur vieux habits; ils les retournent et les vendent comme neufs le plus chèrement qu'ils peuvent." Here is his remark on the purity laws (cited after *Oeuvres complètes,* 31 [Paris, 1878], 1189): "Le peuple juif était si grossier, et de nos jours même la populace de cette nation est si malpropre et si puante, que ses legislateurs furent obligés de descendre dans les plus petits et les plus vils détails." In similar vein he wrote about 2 Sam. 11:4: "C'était un grand acte de religion de se laver; la négligence et la saleté étaient si particulières a ce peuple, que la loi l'obligeait à se laver souvent, et cela s'appelait se sanctifier" (30:191). In *Oeuvres* 19:521, he calls the Jews "an ignorant and barbaric people: "Vous ne trouverez en eux qu'un peuple ignorant et barbare qui joint depuis longtemps la plus sordide avarice à la plus détestable superstition, et à la plus invincible haine pour tous les peuples qui les tolèrent et qui les enrichent. Il ne faut pourtant pas les brûler."

RETURN TO JERUSALEM: *Oeuvres* 19:538: "Ne me reprochez pas de ne vous point   188f.
aimer: je vous aime tant que je voudrais que vous fussiez tous dans Hershalaim au lieu des Turcs qui dévastent tout votre pays. . . ." *Oeuvres* 19:540: "Retournez en Judée le plus tôt que vous pouvez. Je vous demande seulement deux ou trois familles hébraiques pour établir en mon Krapak, où je demeure, un petit commerce néces-saire." On the next page he writes even more harshly: "Vous fûtes des monstres de cruauté et de fanatisme en Palestine, vous l'avez été dans notre Europe; vous êtes des animaux calculants; tâchez d'être des animaux pensants."

KANT AND JUDAISM: Kant's attitude toward Judaism already concerned his Jewish   189f.
contemporaries, some of whom were among the first champions of his doctrines, which revolutionized philosophical thought. Of the contemporaneous writings against Kant's attitude toward Judaism we should mention especially the book by Schaul Ascher that appeared in 1793 under the title *Eisenmenger der Zweite.* It is primarily directed against J. G. Fichte and criticizes the sharply anti-Jewish remarks in Fichte's book *Beitrag zur Berichtigung des Urtheils des Publikums über die französische Revolution* (published that same year and to be discussed in our next chapter). The author includes a detailed discussion of Kant, Fichte's teacher, to whose influence he ascribes Fichte's hostility toward the Jews (which was often differently motivated and was much more sharply expressed). Recently Jacob Katz emphatically called attention to Schaul Asher's book in his comprehensive (Hebrew) article on Kant and Judaism (in *Tarbiz* 41 [1971–72]: 219–37) which also contains a discussion of the main earlier literature. The most important of the latter are Julius Gutmann, "Kant und das Judentum," *Schriften, herausgegeben von der Gesellschaft zur För-derung der Wissenschaft des Judentums* (Leipzig, 1918), 42–62; Hermann Cohen, "Innere Beziehungen der Kantischen Philosophie zum Judentum" (1910), reprinted in Cohen's *Jüdische Schriften* (Berlin, 1924), 1:284–305; Nathan Rotenstreich, *The Recurrent Pattern. Studies in Anti-Judaism in Modern Thought* (London, 1963), 23–47; H. M. Graupe, "Kant und das Judentum," *Zeitschrift für Religions- und*

Geistesgeschichte 13 (1961): 308–33; Emil Fackenheim, "Kant and Judaism," *Commentary* 36 (1963): 406–67; S. Axinn, "Kant on Judaism," *Jewish Quarterly Review* (July 1968): 1–23. The problem is, of course, also dealt with in the well-known histories of the Jews, of Jewish philosophy, etc., as well as in the biographies of Kant, e.g., Ernst Cassirer's *Kants Leben und Lehre* (Berlin, 1921).

Kant's views on Judaism are contained mainly in two works, and we shall discuss them here as a summary of his views although they appeared after the outbreak of the French Revolution, with which we shall begin our next chapter. They are *Die Religion innerhalb der Grenzen der blossen Vernunft* (Königsberg, 1793) (*Kants Werke*, ed. Ernst Cassirer, 6 [1923], 139–353) and *Der Streit der Fakultäten* (1798) (*Werke* 7 [1922], 311–431). Some remarks in other writings will serve as supplements.

The most important and most frequently cited statement about Judaism may be found in the first-named work (*Werke* 6 : 171f.) There Kant denies that the Jewish faith is a religion in the real sense of the word: "The Jewish faith is in its original form an embodiment of merely statutory laws on which the constitution of a state was based." Here, of course, one immediately senses the influence of a view widely disseminated at the time that was based on Spinoza's *Tractatus* and in modified form had also shaped Mendelssohn's view of the Jewish question as formulated ten years earlier in his book *Jerusalem* (cf. Part 2, pp. 550 and 567). Kant's further remarks and his conclusions, however, were new and wholly negative in their evaluations. His judgment was not affected by what developed on this statutory legal basis, for "whatever moral additions were *attached* [Kant's emphasis] to it then or later are not really part of Judaism as such." And this arbitrarily apodictic explanation is followed by this conclusion: "The latter [i.e., Judaism] is actually not a religion but merely an association of a number of people who, because they belonged to a special tribe, formed a community under merely political laws and thus not a church; rather, it *was* [emphasis in the original] to be a merely secular state, so that even if it was torn asunder by untoward accidents it would still have the political faith (which was an essential part of it) that it could be restored some day (upon the arrival of the Messiah)."

It can be seen that Kant here essentially follows the arguments of Spinoza (cf. Part 2, p. 549), which influenced him directly or indirectly. But now the Christian-pietistic influences were added, and, as Cassirer shows (in *Kants Leben*, 13ff.), in dual form: as modest, inward Christian religiosity in his parental home and as a strict, intolerantly orthodox religious coercion and ritualism in his school, the Fridericianum at Königsberg. These determined emotionally his view of religious faith on the one hand and his opposition to religious coercion and all ritualism on the other. According to him, Jewish law (of which he only knew or recognized the Bible) made no moral demands, since it was conceived merely as secular, political legislation, but punished only nonobservance of the law and expressed no belief in a future life. "Since no religion is conceivable without belief in a future life, in its purity Judaism as such contains no religious faith at all" (*Werke*, 6:273). To be sure, subsequently every Jew surely fashioned "a certain religious faith" for himself, but this faith "never constituted part of the laws of Judaism." Hence, contrary to what is frequently asserted, it is not a preliminary stage of a universal church or of the Christian Church—a notion that Mendelssohn utilized "very cleverly . . . to reject any suggestion that a son of Israel convert. For if, as even the Christians admit, the Jewish faith is the lowest floor on which Christianity as the upper floor rests, it is as if someone were expected to demolish the ground floor in order to move into the second floor" (vol. 6, note on p. 315). In reality Judaism regarded itself so little as a universal church "that it excluded the entire human race from its community as a special people chosen by Jehovah for himself which displayed hostility toward all other nations and was therefore treated with hostility by all of them" (6:273). On the basis of these premises Kant also deprecates the Jewish monotheism that he had greatly praised five years earlier in his *Critique of Judgment*. In his analytics of the exalted (*Werke*, 5:347) he writes: "There may be no more exalted passage in the legal code of the Jews than this commandment: Thou shalt not make for thyself a graven image, or any likeness of what is in the heavens above, or on the earth below, etc. This commandment alone can explain the enthusiasm that the Jewish people felt for its religion in its civilized epoch when it compared itself to other nations, or the pride that Mohammedanism instills." Now, in his book *Die Religion in den Grenzen der blossen Vernunft* (*Werke*, 6:273) Kant writes: "Here it should not be valued too highly that this people installed for itself as a universal ruler of the world one god who cannot be represented by a visible image." Something similar may be found among most other nations, even though "their *veneration* [emphasis in the original] of certain powerful subordinate deities made them suspect of polytheism." A God who demanded only the observance of commandments or an improvement of morality—as Kant believes is the case with Judaism—"is really not the moral being whose idea we need for a moral religion. It is more likely that such a religion would materialize if there were a belief in many such powerful invisible beings [here Kant continues his anti-Jewish remarks with seemingly objective logic], if a people imagined these as agreeing, despite their different competences, to bestow their favor only on those who were wholeheartedly dedicated to virtue, as if faith were devoted to only a single being—one, however, that makes a mechanical cult the main thing." Suddenly, though not without preparation, Christianity arose from Judaism, which had in the meantime mingled with moral teachings of other nations. The teacher of the gospel proclaimed himself as having been sent from heaven by simultaneously declaring, as being worthy of such a mission, that compulsory belief (in days with religious services, confessions of faith, and rituals) was null and void. On the other hand, he declares that moral faith, the only one that hallows human beings "and proves its genuineness through the leading of a good life, is the only redeeming kind. He made that declaration after he had, through teachings and sufferings and to the point of an undeserved and at the same time meritorious death, served as an example that was appropriate for the prototype of the only humanity that found favor in the eyes of God." A note is appended to the word *death*: "with which his public history ends. What has been added as an appendix—the more secret history of his resurrection and ascension which transpired merely before the eyes of his confidants— . . . cannot, despite its historical appreciation, be used as a religion within the boundaries of mere reason." Kant explains that the long preservation of the Jewish people is due to its possession of written sacred books. Like Voltaire before him and Spengler and Toynbee after him, Kant says that the Parsees, the remnants of believers in the religion of Zoroaster, have fared like the Jews; they, too, preserved a written religious book (6:284). For the rest, the continued existence of the Jewish people could be regarded as a blessing, as the Jews do, or, in the Christian view, "as warning ruins of a destroyed state that resists the coming heavenly kingdom." Thus the Jewish religion, as Kant views it, is finally declared a form of pseudo-service rather than a real religious service—unless, as many of the "enlightened" Jews close to Kant did, it abandoned the empty formulas, the "burden of the law," in favor of a purified religion based on morality.

In reading Kant's remarks about Judaism and Christianity one is immediately struck by his forced argumentation. In point of fact, Kant did not even convince the Christian authorities of his time, and after the appearance of his book his king gave him a serious warning (which Kant did not really protest). In a seminar on Kant's *Critique of Pure Reason* almost sixty years ago, my teacher Eduard Spranger (1882–1963) pointed out, on the occasion of an obscure passage that we struggled to understand, that such obscure passages often were a key to psychological insight into a personality. He said that in such passages logical thinking clashed with emotions and ideas that came from other spheres and for which the philosopher thus vainly strove to give a logical explanation. There is no doubt that in Kant's judgments on Judaism (and, of course, his presentation of Christianity is not subject to criticism here) the great philosopher repeatedly gave way to the far less great citizen of Königsberg and the Christian raised in the spirit of Pietism. His philosphical biographer Ernst Cassirer formulates this with great reserve in his *Kants Leben und Lehre*, p. 415: "Toward Judaism . . . and the Old Testament Kant displays from the very beginning such subjective bias that he is unable to see in the religion of the prophets and psalms anything but a collection of 'statutory' laws and customs. Soon a peculiar *methodological* circle develops. . . . The ethical standard is applied to the religious forms as a universally valid and objective criterion, but it is unmistakable that subjective feelings and experiences help to determine the manner of its application. . . . Rational analysis was only supposed to confirm in detail what he already knew to be the total result." What was done in this way was, however, a dangerous innovation. Even though it was possible to regard prejudgments of the Church and the people as traditions to be rejected or opposed in the name of the Enlightenment and tolerance, these prejudgments were now presented by the leading philosopher of the late eighteenth and early nineteenth centuries, one of the most important thinkers in the entire history of philosophy, with what seemed to be philosophical substantiation and thus, as it were, presented as irrefutable truths to "intellectuals" and independent thinkers who felt free from the old prejudices. The traditional stereotype became a philosophical *a priori*, so to speak. This is one of the dangerous processes that we shall repeatedly encounter in the course of our presentation. Traditions and half-truths about Judaism are adopted by important persons without a real examination and, provided by their authority with the stamp of truth, disseminated among people who would never have accepted them from less recognized writers or thinkers. Such judgments had a profound effect on many Jews as well, and they strengthened tendencies pointing away from Judaism, aroused a will to reform, or created a self-hatred whose roots those affected did not clearly understand. We shall revert to this in a later context.

When Lessing's *Nathan the Wise* appeared, Kant made deprecating remarks about it. The mystical thinker J. G. Hamann (1730–88) reported this to Herder and remarked that Kant "cannot bear a hero from this people. . . . This is how divinely severe our philosophy is in its prejudices despite all its tolerance and impartiality" (quoted here after Kuno Fischer from the abovementioned article by J. Katz, p. 222, note 10).

The great extent to which Kant's judgment was based upon, or influenced by, the Jews of his time and the general opinion of them is shown by a note in one of his last writings, *Anthropologie in pragmatischer Hinsicht*, a book published in 1798. Cassirer writes that it was only a compendium of "the rich material on human history and anthropology that Kant had collected during a long life on the basis of his own observation and from other sources." It contains, among other things, peculiar generalizations about nations and people that one might make in a conversation but would not like to see in a scientific work. We are here interested in the note about the Jews included by Kant at the end of paragraph 46 (*Werke*, 8:94f.), which is about swindlers.

Their usurious spirit since their exile [he writes] has gained the Palestinians living among us, even the greatest number of them, the not unfounded reputation of deceivers. It does seem strange to imagine a nation of cheats, but it is just as strange to imagine a nation of merchants, most of whom, bound together by an ancient superstition recognized by the state in which they live, seek no civil honor but desire to compensate for this lack by the benefits gained from outwitting the people among whom they have found protection and even their own kind. This cannot be otherwise with an entire nation of merchants as nonproductive members of society (e.g., the Jews in Poland); hence their constitution, which we, among whom they are living, recognize by means of ancient statutes, cannot be rescinded without inconsistency even though they make the saying "Buyer, beware!" the foremost principle of their morality in associating with us. Instead of pointless plans to make this people moral in regard to deceit and honesty I shall state my conjecture about the origin of this peculiar constitution (namely, that of a people consisting entirely of merchants). In ancient times, trade with India brought wealth overland to the west coasts of the Mediterranean and the ports of Phoenicia (of which Palestine is part). It was able to make its way via many other places, e.g. Palmyra, in older times Tyre, Sidon, or at some distance overseas Eziongeber and Eilat, also from the Arabian coast to Greater Thebes and thus via Egypt to the Syrian coast; but Palestine, of which Jerusalem was the capital, also was very favorably located for caravan trade. Presumably the phenomenon of the former Solomonian wealth was the result of this, and the surrounding land was full of merchants up to Roman times. After the destruction of this city these merchants, who had previously had extensive contacts with other merchants of this language and faith, gradually spread out over distant (European) countries, remained in touch with them, and owing to the benefits of their trade were able to find protection in the states to which they moved. Thus their dispersion all over the world with their common religion and language cannot be deemed to be due to a curse on this people, but must rather be regarded as a blessing—especially because its wealth, estimated on an individual basis, now probably exceeds that of any other nation with the same number of people.

This note about the "Palestinians living among us" is a good example of the way in which, as far as the Jewish question (which is only a model for similar emotionally charged problems) is concerned, superficial knowledge and alehouse opinions can irresponsibly combine in usually responsible scholars and, in the guise of learned theories, can be presented as truth in academic lectures and disseminated in books. Later anti-Jewish literature did not, of course, overlook such pearls of authoritatively strutting professorial wisdom. We can find them quoted down to the Hitler period; cf., for instance, Fritsch's *Handbuch der Judenfrage* (1937), 445.

GIBBON: The British historian Gibbon, a contemporary of Kant, may serve as another   190
example of the way in which traditional opinions entered works of the Enlightenment and through them were disseminated as authoritative truths.

Edward Gibbon (1737–94) wrote his *History of the Decline and Fall of the Roman Empire* (1776–88), a work regarded as a classic to this day, translated into all civilized languages, and repeatedly reissued, in the anti-Christian spirit of Deist Enlightenment. As Meinecke remarks (in *Historismus*, 1:248), it is a grandiose survey of nations "from the height of the Capitol on which Gibbon, moved by the remnants of the mightiest of all empires, had conceived the idea of his undertaking in 1764." From this vantage point he also views the history of Judaism and the Jewish people almost through the eyes of a Tacitus, and in the well-known chapters 15 and 16 of the first volume he makes his frequently quoted judgments on the stubbornness and the misanthropy of the Jews, whose intolerance and religious fanaticism the Christians have adopted. The Jews interest him only as the disrupters of the Roman polytheistic, imperial tolerance and as the founders of Christianity, to which he assigns the main blame for the decline and fall of the Roman empire. His presentation does not reflect Kant's Christian-pietistic prejudice against the Jews but, rather, a condescending, deprecatory, somewhat derisive attitude of an independent citizen of the British empire who as such feels akin to the citizen of the Roman empire. To be sure, he quotes approvingly the Christian view of the destruction of the Temple as a consequence of divine wrath, emphasizes the Israelites' cruelty toward the original inhabitants when they conquered the land of Canaan, and in the name of humanity expresses indignation at the savagery of the Jewish uprisings at the time of Trajan and

Hadrian: "Humanity is shocked at the recital of the horrid cruelties which they [the Jews] committed in the cities of Egypt, of Cyprus, or Cyrene, where they dwelt in treacherous friendship with the unsuspecting natives [in a note details are given from the account of the historian Dion Cassius], and we are tempted to applaud the severe retaliation which was exercised by the arms of the legions against a race of fanatics whose dire and credulous superstition seemed to render them implacable enemies not only of the Roman government, but of human kind" (chap. 16). In his discussion of the doctrine of incarnation and the development of Christian sects (chap. 47) Gibbon once more writes about the Jews and the further development of their originally strictly secular belief in the Messiah through the adoption of Greek or Chaldaic philosophical ideas about the immortality of the soul.

The extent to which actual conditions and traditions affected the Christians' image of the Jews and their evaluation of them, and the way in which they affected it, are eloquently demonstrated by Goethe's remarks about Frankfurt Jewry in his memoirs. They reflect both the impressions of the young Goethe and of the mature man who thinks about them. "Among the things which excited the misgivings of the boy, and even of the youth," he writes in *Dichtung und Wahrheit* (vol. 1, bk. 4),

> "was especially the state of the Jewish quarter of the city *(Judenstadt)*, properly called the Jew Street *(Judengasse)*, as it consisted of little more than a single street, which in early times may have been hemmed in between the walls and trenches of the town, as in a prison. The closeness, the filth, the crowd, the accent of an unpleasant language, altogether made a most disagreeable impression, even if one only looked in as one passed the gate. It was long before I ventured in alone; and I did not return there readily, when I had once escaped the importunities of so many men unwearied in demanding and offering to traffic. At the same time, the old legends of the cruelty of the Jews toward Christian children, which we had seen hideously illustrated in Gottfried's *Chronicle*, hovered gloomily before my young mind. And although they were thought better of in modern times, the large caricature, still to be seen, to their disgrace, on an arched wall under the bridgetower, bore extraordinary witness against them; for it had been made, not through private ill-will, but by public order. [The reference is to the picture of the so-called *Judensau*; cf. Part 2, pp. 529f.) However, they still remained the chosen people of God, and passed, no matter how it came about, as a memorial of the most ancient times. Besides, they also were men, active and obliging; and, even to the tenacity with which they clung to their peculiar customs one could not refuse one's respect. The girls, moreover, were pretty, and were far from displeased when a Christian lad, meeting them on the Sabbath in the Fischerfeld, showed himself kindly and attentive. I was consequently extremely curious to become acquainted with their ceremonies. I did not desist until I had frequently visited their school, had attended a circumcision and a wedding, and formed a notion of the Feast of the Tabernacles. Everywhere I was well received, pleasantly entertained, and invited to come again; for it was by persons of influence that I had been either taken there or recommended. *(The Autobiography of Johann Wolfgang von Goethe*, trans. John Oxenford [Chicago, 1974])

191ff.   JEWS IN POLAND: In addition to the well-known Jewish histories (especially Dubnow 7), see M. Balaban, *Zur Geschichte der Juden in Polen* (Vienna, 1915); M. Wischnitzer, *Die Juden in der Welt* (Berlin, 1935), 197ff.; J. Heilprin, ed., *Bet Yisrael be-Polin* (The House of Israel in Poland), 2 vols. (Jerusalem, 1948–54); and the comprehensive articles in *JL*, *EJ*. and *EJJ* 13:709ff.

192ff.   CHMIELNICKI AND THE CATASTROPHE OF 1648–1649: In addition to the abovementioned literature, cf. Hans Kohn, ed., *Die Welt der Slawen*, Fischer-Bücherei (Frankfurt a.M., 1960–62), 1:70ff., 2:240ff.; Philip Longworth, *The Cossacks* (London, 1971), 97ff.; Nathan Neta Hanover, *Yevein Mezula* (Hebr.), introd. by I. Fichmann, notes and map of the places affected by the catastrophe by J. Heilprin (Tel Aviv, 1945) (cf. the note on this work in Part 1); *EJJ* 5:479–84, including a photo of the

Chmielnicki memorial and a bibliography; S. Ettinger in *Zion* 20 (1955) and 21 (1956); J. Halpern in *Zion* 25 (1960) and Y. F. Baer Jubilee Volume (Hebr.), 1960; J. Katz, "Martyrdom in the Middle Ages and in 1648–1649," ibid.

SABBATAI TZEVI AND SABBATEANISM: Gershom Scholem's research and writings are 196ff. today basic for the facts as well as the psychological and historiosophical interpretation, particularly his biography of Sabbatai Tzevi (and contemporaneous Sabbateanism) (Tel Aviv, 1957), his abovementioned books, and his comprehensive summary of the present state of research and literature in *EJJ* 14 : 1219–54, which also includes a discussion of Sabbateanism after Sabbatai Tzevi's death down to the eighteenth century (on Jakob Frank, cf. *EJJ* 7 : 55ff.) as well as the authentic pictures and those painted by popular imagination. Josef Kastein's well-illustrated biography *Sabbatai Zwi: Der Messias von Ismir* (Berlin, 1930) is based mainly on (mostly non-Jewish) published material and is still worth reading as a presentation of the atmosphere of the time.

GLÜCKEL VON HAMELN: The autobiography of the prosperous Hamburg Jewess 199f. Glückel (1645–1724) constitutes something entirely new in Jewish literature. At the age of barely fourteen she married the merchant Chajim from the little town of Hameln (of Pied Piper fame—on the Weser River, south of Hanover) and lived happily with him in Hamburg for almost thirty years. A woman, an upper-class Jewish woman, writes her autobiography! It was the first autobiography of that kind, a forerunner of the literature from the time of the Enlightenment and the Emancipation. After the early death (in 1689) of her husband, whom she counseled in business matters and whose businesses she later carried on with skill, Frau Glückel, the mother of thirteen children, put down her memoirs in "seven little books"—primarily to keep the memory of the past alive for her children and to comfort and divert herself in sad, sleepless nights. She wrote the last two books later, between 1715 and 1719, in Metz, after an unhappy second marriage to the banker Cerf Levy, who went bankrupt two years after the wedding.

Being devoid of any literary ambitions, Mother Glückel wrote with no thought of publication. Proud and yet modest, firmly rooted in her Jewish faith and her family tradition, and an interested participant in everything that happened around her, she wrote a chronicle of contemporary Jewish life in Germany with glimpses of the cultural life of her surroundings. The well-known Jewish scholar David Kaufmann (1852–99) was responsible for the first publication of the book in the original Judeo-German (1899). B. Pappenheim's translation into High German was privately printed in 1910, and a somewhat abridged version by A. Feilchenfeld appeared in 1913 and 1923. Cf. also the English translation by Beth-Zion Abrahams (London, 1962; New York, 1963).

NEUTRAL OR SEMINEUTRAL SPHERE of the encounter of Jews and Christians: I have 202 derived these concepts from the studies of Jacob Katz, "Die Entstehung der Juden-assimilation in Deutschland und deren Ideologie" (diss., Frankfurt, 1935); "Die Anfänge der Judenemanzipation," *Bulletin des Leo Baeck Instituts* 13, no. 50 (1970): 12–31. A. Altmann greatly narrowed down the idea of "neutral society" in his biography *Moses Mendelssohn* (University of Alabama Press, 1973), 194. The national and religious differences are always kept in mind. We have already detailed the extent to which the atmosphere was removed from true neutrality and usually also from real tolerance of what was different. Neutrality was often more wishful thinking on the part of the Jews than reality.

202   ACADEMICIANS: Cf. the detailed study of Monika Richarz, *Der Eintritt der Juden in die akademischen Berufe: Jüdische Studenten und Akademiker in Deutschland 1678–1848* (Tübingen, 1974), as well as Jacob Toury's documentation *Der Eintritt der Juden ins deutsche Bürgertum* (Tel Aviv, 1972), chaps. 1–2. See also Azriel Schochat's (Hebr.) book *Im Chilufei ha-Tekufot* (In changing epochs: The beginnings of Enlightenment in German Jewry) (Jerusalem, 1960).

204f.   MOSES MENDELSSOHN: At one time the figure of Moses Mendelssohn (1729–86) was so well known in the educated Jewish world (and in much of the non-Jewish world as well) that the mere mention of his name evoked definite knowledge of the facts of his life, his effectiveness, his general and Jewish views, and his influence on the development of Jewry and the Jewish question since the second half of the eighteenth century. The evaluation of these data varied according to the religious or political position of the observer. In accordance with these shifting positions Mendelssohn's image has fluctuated in Jewish polemics and historiography between overestimation, underestimation, and attempts at a balanced view. Today it may be necessary to look at this in some detail.

The phenomenon of Mendelssohn was something completely new and almost incredible for his contemporaries, Jews and non-Jews alike, and there is no doubt that even from this viewpoint alone his influence on the Jewish question was tremendous and almost revolutionary. When Lessing's play *Die Juden* was published and the theologian Michaelis wrote a review in which he doubted the possibility or probability that such a noble Jew as the hero of the play could exist, Lessing published a letter from his friend Mendelssohn (whom he did not name) as proof that such a Jew was not only conceivable but actually existed as a contemporary. Those who became acquainted with Mendelssohn were profoundly impressed by the intellectual vigor, superior humanity, and Jewish pride of this man with an almost repulsive appearance. Friedrich Munter, a young Dane of German descent, wrote about him in his diary of 1782, four years before Mendelssohn's death: "A small, homely, hunchbacked man in shabby clothes. . . . His intellect does not show. He looks very Jewish and also wears a hat on his head" (quoted after Jacob Katz, *Zion* 39 [1964]: 117). Mendelssohn's philosophical writings, some of them in the style of Platonic dialogues, were widely disseminated; educated people of all classes regarded it as an honor to communicate with him in writing and in person, or they sought his counsel in questions of conscience. At the same time it was known that he was a bookkeeper by profession, later a partner in a silk factory, and strictly observed the laws and precepts of traditional Judaism. When one of his admirers, the clergyman, philosopher, and physiognomist J. K. Lavater (1741–1801), a friend of Goethe, publicly called upon him to refute the truth of Christianity or to espouse it openly as a truth-loving philosopher, this conversionary importunateness aroused the displeasure even of Lavater's friends. This challenge, as well as a similar one, thirteen years later, by an anonymous person (who, as J. Katz showed in *Zion* 36 [1971]: 116f., was actually the writer A. F. Cranz) caused Mendelssohn to take a clear stand and to give a philosophical motivation of his conception of Judaism. His response to Lavater already brought about a decisive turning point in Mendelssohn's life. Until then he had lived his Judaism as something self-evident. He had apparently assumed or hoped that his personal example and that of other Jews who lived in similar fashion would be sufficient evidence that the world of the Enlightenment and the world of Judaism did not constitute an antithesis but could be combined for an exemplary life, that humanity and Judaism were one, and that a Jew could therefore claim to be evaluated on the same level as a Christian and to receive equal legal recognition as a citizen. After 1769 he became an increasingly conscious champion of Judaism as well as a guide of the Jews to the modern cultural world. By translating the Pentateuch and the

Psalms into German and having his rendition first printed in Hebrew letters in order to make it accessible to his Jewish contemporaries, as well as by appending a commentary *(Biur)*, he sought to make the basic writings of their religion comprehensible to German Jews. For many this translation did become a bridge to an understanding of the German language and thereby of modern scholarship and literature. Mendelssohn inspired Kriegsrat (Military Councilor) Dohm to write his epoch-making book in defense of the Jews and for the promotion of equal civil rights. Finally, he publicly defended Judaism in a number of writings and attempted to demonstrate its compatibility and even identity with reason and a religion based on reason. The most comprehensive and most important of these writings is his book *Jerusalem oder über religiöse Macht und Judentum,* which appeared in May 1783.

We have already characterized the basic theses of this book: Judaism is not a dogmatic religion with rigid tenets but a religion of deeds: "To put it briefly, I believe that Judaism knows no revealed religion in the sense in which Christians understand it. The Israelites have God-given laws, commandments, commands, practical precepts, and instruction about God's will that tell them how they must conduct themselves in order to achieve temporal and eternal bliss. Such tenets and precepts were revealed to them by Moses in a wonderful and supernatural way, but there were no doctrines, no truths of salvation, no general rational tenets. These the Eternal One constantly reveals to us, as he does to all other human beings, through nature and objects, never through words and writing."

Mendelssohn does not believe in perpetual progress in which a certain religion or the life of a people constitutes only one step: "I for my part have no idea of the education of the human race which my sainted friend Lessing derived from I do not know what historian of mankind. [Cf. Part 2, p. 547.] People imagine this collective thing, humankind, as a single person and believe that providence has, as it were, sent this person to school here to be raised from a child to a man. At bottom, the human race is in almost all centuries a child, a man, and an old man at the same time, though in different places and regions of the world." Thus Mendelssohn is opposed to a romantic, organismic, simplifying, Christian, Europe-centered view of events which in the history of Christianity has led via Lessing and Herder to Hegel (and Marx). "Everyone goes his own way all his life . . . all make progress on the journey. . . . But that the totality, mankind here below, should over the ages constantly move ahead and perfect itself does not seem to me to have been the purpose of providence." In any case, such an assumption is not necessary to save the idea of divine providence. "You are trying to guess," he writes with his natural piousness, "what intentions providence has for mankind? Do not fashion any hypotheses, but simply look around at what is really happening and, if you are able to survey the history of all times, what has happened since ancient times. . . . Providence never fails of its ultimate purpose." With a formulation that almost anticipates Hegel but is perhaps simpler and more believing, he continues: "What actually happens must always have been its intention or have been part of it."

To be sure, Israel's revealed legal code also "includes an unfathomable treasure of rational truths and religious doctrines that are so closely bound up with the laws that they are one with them. All laws relate to, or are founded on, eternal rational truths, or they are reminiscent of them and invite reflection about them; thus our rabbis have rightly said that the laws and teaching are as related to one another as the body is related to the soul." Nowhere, however, is *belief* in these truths demanded in any form: "Not a single one of all the precepts and ordinances says 'Thou shalt believe!'— but all of them say 'Thou shalt or shalt not do!' " For faith cannot be commanded; it can come only through conviction. Mendelssohn points out that the Hebrew word that is generally rendered as "belief" *(emunah)* really means trust, confidence, a definite pledge and promise. "Where eternal rational truths are concerned, it is a matter of knowledge rather than faith. 'Know therefore this day and keep in mind that the Lord alone is God in heaven above and on earth below; there is no other' [Deut. 4:39]. . . . Hear, o Israel, the Eternal, our God, is one eternal being!"

Mendelssohn is consistent, then, in not translating the beginning of each of Maimonides' Thirteen Principles of Faith ("*Ani ma'amin* . . .") as "I believe with perfect faith" but, in a free paraphrase deviating from the usual rendition, as "I acknowledge as true and certain" ("Ich erkenne für wahr und gewiss," *Lesebuch für Jüdische Kinder* [Berlin, 1779], 9–13).

All commandments are fundamental. If one wanted to find a common denominator for them, one could limit them to the response given by Hillel the Elder to a heathen who wished to hear the entire Law while standing on one foot: "Son, love thy neighbor as thyself. This is the text of the Law; the rest is commentary. Now go forth and study!"

According to Mendelssohn, the divine law was given to the Jews and only to the Jews. It is binding only on Jews and proscribes the proselytization of others. But it is valid for them until "the supreme law-giver deigns to reveal to us his will in this matter, to reveal it to us as clearly, publicly, and beyond all doubts and scruples as he has given us the law itself. As long as this is not done, as long as we cannot demonstrate an authentic dispensation from the Law, our sophistry cannot release us from the strict obedience that we owe the Law, and the reverence for God draws a line between speculation and practice that no conscientious person is permitted to cross." The state has no claim—and here Mendelssohn goes far beyond the view of most of his contemporaries—to demand of its citizens a recognition of articles of faith as a prerequiste for the granting of human and civil rights; anyone who fulfills the obligations of a citizen is entitled to these rights. Religion and public law are completely distinct spheres. A state can force its citizens to perform their duties; religion can appeal to a citizen's conscience only by admonishing, instructing, and challenging him, and it cannot be granted any penal powers. Hence Mendelssohn is consistent in rejecting the preservation of separate Jewish jurisdiction and privileges.

The Jews should be given civil rights without being required to give up the fulfillment of their religious commandments. Here Mendelssohn holds firm against any other claims; toward the end of his book he writes: "If civil union can be preserved only if we deviate from the Law that we still consider binding upon us, we are truly sorry to declare that we would rather give up this civil union. Then the humanitarian Dohm has written in vain and everything will remain in its present tolerable condition, or the condition in which your humanitarianism cares to put it. . . . We cannot, in all conscience, deviate from the laws, and what do fellow citizens without a conscience avail you?" Mendelssohn appeals to the "regents of the earth" not to heed the advice of those who wish to suppress freedom of thought in the name of religious union. "For the sake of your and our happiness, religious union is not tolerance; it is the very opposite of true toleration!"

Whoever reads these words today is bound to be impressed with the courage of the man who was trying to promote freedom of conscience and human rights. His contemporaries, too, were moved by his language and his proud loyalty to the Jewish tradition. To be sure, the logical reasoning, the human warmth, and the smooth language could not mask the inner contradictions that people sensed in them from different points of view. The reason we quoted Mendelssohn at length is that in the years to come people espousing all kinds of views, both Jews and non-Jews, were able to base themselves on Mendelssohn, draw diametrically opposed conclusions from his assumptions, or adopt only some of his arguments and conclusions, interpreting and elaborating them in their own spirit. All trends in nineteenth-century Judaism were in some way derived from Mendelssohn—neo-orthodoxy as well as liberalism and reform Judaism, antinationalistic and nationalistic tendencies, rational and irrational, conservative, Enlightenment-oriented, and revolutionary ones. Similarly, those holding any of these points of view were able to disagree with him and oppose him. Non-Jewish thinkers and theologians who rejected Judaism were also able to base themselves on his arguments, particularly his thesis (as anticipated by Spinoza) of Judaism as divine law-giving. Thus Mendelssohn really was an epochal figure in the full sense of the word, one that stood at the border between the eighteenth century and the nineteenth, the century in which the ideas of the preceding one appeared in new constellations as they entered political reality via the French Revolution. Down to the present we feel the continuation of the development that Mendelssohn initiated or raised to consciousness. We shall have more to say about this in the succeeding chapters.

The literature about Mendelssohn is so extensive that we can give only a few references here. The most comprehensive scholarly biography is Alexander Altmann's *Moses Mendelssohn: A Biographical Study* (University of Alabama Press, 1973); it contains an extensive *apparatus criticus*. Cf. also I. Barzilay's review of this book in *Jewish Social Studies* 36 (1974): 330–35. The older biography by M. Kayserling is still worth reading (*Moses Mendelssohn, sein Leben und Wirken* [Leipzig, 1888]), as is Bertha Badt-Strauss's collection *Moses Mendelssohn, der Mensch und das Werk* (Berlin, 1929). The article by A. Jospe and Leni Yahil in *EJJ* 11 : 1328–42 offers a good summary of Mendelssohn's life, work, and continued relevance. A good critical bibliography is Hermann M. Z. Meyer's *Moses Mendelssohn-Bibliographie* (Berlin, 1965). Of the essays and appraisals that I found useful I shall mention, in addition to those already cited, Julius Gutmann, *Die Philosophie des Judentums* (Munich, 1933), 303–17 (on p. 313 there is a discussion of the two contiguous worlds in which Mendelssohn lived); Fritz Bamberger, "Die geistige Gestalt Moses Mendelssohns," *MGWJ* 73 (1929): 84–92; idem, "Mendelssohns Begriff vom Judentum," in *Korrespondenzblatt des Vereins zur Gründung und Erhaltung einer Akademie des Judentums* (1929), 4–19; Ludwig Feuchtwanger, "Das Bild Mendelssohns bei seinen Gegnern bis zum Tode Hegels: Ein Beitrag zum Neuaufbau der geistigen Gestalt Moses Mendelssohns," *Zeitschrift für die Geschichte der Juden in Deutschland* 1 (1929): 213–32; Max Wiener, "Moses Mendelssohn und die religiösen Gestaltungen im 19. Jahrhundert," ibid., 201–12; Isaac Eisenstein-Barzilay, "Moses Mendelssohn: A Study in Ideas and Attitudes," *Jewish Quarterly Review* 52 (1961): 69–93, 175–86; H. Lewy, "Moses Mendelssohn und die Zeit der Berliner Salons," in *Allgemeine Zeitung des Judentums* (Düsseldorf) 29, no. 9 (1 March 1974): 33–37. Concerning the Mendelssohn family, cf. Sebastian Hensel, *Die Familie Mendelssohn 1727–1847*, 2 vols. (Leipzig, 1924); Josef Körner, "Mendelssohns Töchter," in *Preussische Jahrbücher* 214 (November 1928), 167ff.; Alex Bein, "Arnold Mendelssohn und Joseph Mendelssohn: Ein Briefwechsel," in *Jahrbuch für jüdische Geschichte und Literatur* (1931), 56–98; Felix Gilbert, *Bankiers, Künstler und Gelehrte: Unveröffentlichte Briefe der Familie Mendelssohn aus dem 19. Jahrhundert* (Tübingen, 1975).

THE JEWISH QUESTION AT THE END OF THE EIGHTEENTH CENTURY: A few documents from the time may serve as illustrations. **206**

1. On 13 February 1745 the *Haude-Spenersche Zeitung* (Berlin) carried the following report from Prague: "Tomorrow a *Te Deum* will be sung in all churches in honor of the birth of the second archduke. Only the Jews, whose interests and principles distinguish them from the rest of the human race, do not participate in this general celebration, nor are they able to do so. The pleas of those courts which have striven for the good of the Jews have been in vain, and the Jews themselves have not prevailed at the court with their supplications. It remains definite that they have to leave here at the end of this month, and therefore they are now seriously beginning to

sell their furniture and securities. Their places will soon be taken by a colony of *Rascier* [Serbs settled in Hungary], a nation that is exceedingly thrifty, industrious, and vigorous, in addition to professing the Christian religion." (E. Buchner, *Das Neueste von Gestern* 2 (1912), 415f.)

2. Ibid., 420. Vienna, 12 August [1745]: "Now that the queen has rescinded the decree banning the Jews from her lands, that nation is carrying on its trade in the royal lands in the same way as before." (*Vossische Zeitung*, Berlin, 1745, no. 103.)

3. In 1788, shortly before the French Revolution, Adolph Freiherr von Knigge wrote *Über den Umgang mit Menschen*, a book which, though not widely read, has (unjustly) become synonymous with rules of etiquette. On p. 244 of an undated new edition published by the Bibliographisches Institut, Leipzig, we read the following statements that are still relevant today. (It is significant that they follow a discussion of horse dealers, who have "the ominous name *Rosstäuscher*" [literally, "horse cheats"] though it was originally *-tauscher*, one who barters):

> Despite all the advances of modern times, and the altered political and civil position of the Jews in the state and society, despite the wealth at their command and the education one finds among them, there are still a great many prejudices against them and associating with them that are not justified. Since I am not minded to promote that sort of thing, I cannot present the Jews as a separate class of people and can only suggest that they be treated like other people whose human or commercial qualities determine the worth of an individual, be he a junk dealer or the head of a high court of law, a banker or a professor. And since throughout my book I have intended to derive rules of social intercourse from the qualities of people, their class, occupation, and trade, the general statements I have made also apply to the Jews. My remarks about behaving toward those who profess another religion or creed are also valid for the Jews and their faith, which cannot offer any reason to disparage, oppress, or persecute them. If you have any fault to find with a Jew, this will usually be due to his personal qualities and not to his faith.

5

Emancipation and the Jewish Question (1789–1880)

THE FRENCH REVOLUTION AS THE BEGINNING OF A NEW EPOCH: Like the leading 208ff. figures of the Renaissance (cf. Part 2, p. 520), the chief representatives of the French Revolution of 1789 regarded their period as a new beginning, the start of a new historical epoch that was destined to put to practical use (in a legal, social, and economic sense) the intellectual and social developments of the eighteenth century, the century of the Enlightenment. Everything that had preceded the Revolution seemed like a precursor to them.

Historians would be well advised to go along with this temper of the times and to let the nineteenth century begin with this event rather than, as has sometimes been the case, with the conclusion of this turbulent transitional period, the Congress of Vienna of 1815.

This also applies to the division of Jewish history into epochs. In my opinion, attempts to use other events in individual countries (the Edict of Toleration of Joseph II in Austria, the ascent to the throne of Frederick the Great in Prussia, the appearance of Moses Mendelssohn, the Declaration of Independence or the Constitution of the United States of America, or—as proposed by Benzion Dinur—the organized immigration to Palestine by Judah Hasid and a thousand of his followers in 1700) as an orientation are methodologically untenable because they blur the difference between preparatory phenomena (characterized by personalities that we call "precursors") and triggering events that translate these developments into far-reaching occurrences of political, economic, and social reality. As far as the history of the Jewish question is concerned, there can be no doubt that the French Revolution marked the beginning of a decisive new era.

It is more difficult to determine the end of the epoch. This depends to a great degree on the historical standpoint, the views, and the valuations of the observer. The definitive conclusion surely is the year 1948, the foundation of the State of Israel, the consequences of which have given a new character to Jewry and the Jewish question. However, other important turning points were the origin of the anti-Semitic movement, the outbreak of the Russian pogroms in the early 1880s, the founding and organization of the Zionist movement, the Russian revolution (which gave the Jews equal civil rights), and Hitler's assumption of power with its consequences. All these were decisive developments and hence must be evaluated, at the very least, as periodlike milestones in history. Our presentation will evaluate them as such.

This epoch is so close to our time that I believed I could do without a detailed presentation of the generally known events. Instead of giving such a presentation, I have mentioned them only briefly, in an attempt to recall them to mind, and the emphasis has been on their analysis and utilization for the history of the Jewish question.

Literature on this epoch: The debate about the emancipation of the Jews, the beginnings of which were discussed in the preceding chapter, began in western countries, primarily in England and France. With its concomitants, striking events, and sociopolitical movements since Mendelssohn and especially since the early nineteenth century it has increasingly concentrated on German-speaking countries and those influenced by them. This was its primary sphere of action—from the Romantic period to the development of modern anti-Semitism, the currents within Judaism, and finally National Socialism. Hence this area must be given pride of place in the history of the Jewish question. During the past twenty or thirty years the Leo Baeck Institute (Jerusalem, London, New York) has published a number of valuable books. It has also printed numerous essays on the subject in its periodicals, particularly in its *Year Book* (London, 1956ff.; 32 volumes to date) and its *Bulletin* (Tel Aviv, 195–7). No. 49 of the *Bulletin* contains an index of volumes 1–12; a comprehensive index of the *Year Book* is in preparation. Some important essays from these publications have already been cited at pertinent places; others will be.

For the rest, the literature about this period and its problems is so extensive that no attempt can be made to list it in anything approaching complete form. Hence we shall cite here only some fundamental works as well as those books and essays that appear particularly serviceable for our synoptic presentation as a basis for expansion. In addition to the general histories (which will occasionally be referred to for specific problems) and the well-known presentations of Jewish history (from various Jewish points of view), we shall mention, first of all, Graetz 11 and its continuation (from 1848 on), Ismar Elbogen, *A Century of Jewish Life* (Philadelphia, 1946); Dubnow, 8–10; S. W. Baron, *A Social and Religious History of the Jews*, vol. 2 (1937), 164ff.; S. Bernfeld, *Juden und Judentum im 19. Jahrhundert* (Berlin, 1898); Martin Philippson, *Neueste Geschichte des jüdischen Volkes*, 3 vols. (Frankfurt a.M., 1907–11, 1922–30); Raphael Mahler, *History of the Jewish People in Modern Times*, vol. 1 (1780–1814), books 1–4 (Hebr.) (Merhavya, 1952–56), vol. 2 (1815–48), book 1 (Merhavya, 1970); Howard M. Sachar, *The Course of Modern Jewish History* (New York, 1958). After I had written the sections of this book that deal with the problems of emancipation, assimilation, etc., the following works appeared or came to my attention, some of which I was able to utilize during the printing of the German edition of this book: Jacob Katz, *Emancipation and Assimilation: Studies in Modern Jewish History* (Westmead, 1972); idem, *Out of the Ghetto: The Social Background of Jewish Emancipation, 1770–1880* (Cambridge, Mass., 1973); Reinhard Rürup, *Emanzipation und Antisemitismus: Studien zur "Judenfrage" der bürgerlichen Gesellschaft* (Göttingen, 1975) (with an extensive bibliography); Hans Liebeschütz and Arnold Paucker, *Das Judentum in der deutschen Umwelt 1800–1850* (Tübingen, 1977).

Good summaries with bibliographies may be found in the well-known Jewish encyclopedias, most recently in *EJJ*. Information about specific countries is contained in histories of countries and cities.

208ff.　THE EMANCIPATION OF THE JEWS—THE WORD AND THE CONCEPT: Emancipation— *e-man-cipatio*—meant in Roman law the freeing of a son and later also of another member of the family, of a natural son as well as one acquired through adoption or purchase (slave), from the unlimited domination of the paterfamilias. This compound word still reflects the old custom of sealing the belongingness by a laying on of hands (*manu capere*, a verb meaning "to seize with one's hand"; the noun is *mancipium*), and the man involved was freed from it by the *e-mancipatio*. Since Roman law did not know the legal majority that nowadays is attained at a certain age, it required the act of voluntary release from the dominance of the head of the family through the act of emancipation to give a family member legal freedom of action. Just as the word *mancipium* denoted the acquisition of property, particularly slaves, the word *e-mancipatio* was given the meaning of liberation from a ruling power, a guardianship, or a forcible special status of individuals or groups (women, slaves, etc.).

In its original sense the word "emancipation" survived in French law. In the legal code of the French Revolution, first published as *Code Civil* 1803 and later known as the *Code Napoléon*, the concept "majority" was called *"émancipation"* (Titre IX, *De la puissance paternelle*, paragraph 365: "L'enfant, à tout age, doit honneur et respect à ses père et mère." Paragraph 366: "Il reste sous leur autorité jusqu'à sa majorité ou son émancipation"). In politics the term appears to have been used first in 1792 in France in connection with the emancipation of the black rebels in Haiti. The *Shorter Oxford Dictionary* states that the term was first used in this sense in 1797.

As far as I can tell, the word was not used in the legal documents relating to equal civil rights for the Jews either in France or in other countries in the age of the French Revolution. In those days as well as in later developments the laws generally decreed the abolition of special rights or legal limitations that had been in force owing to membership in a religious community, a class, etcetera, with or without expressly naming the Jews. (Cf. the examples to be given later.) On the other hand, it became a political catchword in the second quarter of the nineteenth century.

The nineteenth century was very creative in inventing and popularizing political slogans. While the eighteenth century was noted for its creation of philosophical tenets, the French Revolution and its political consequences brought philosophical principles into political reality—through legislation and the public discussion that preceded and followed it. The principle of universal human and civil rights that the French Revolution adopted from the American Declaration of Independence was expanded into a general philosophic-political principle, resounded through the world, and changed human consciousness. In the light of these universally human and philosophical-political principles, compromises relating to the legal position of population groups that had earlier been accepted as acts of tolerance and tolerable coexistence now appeared inequitable as the consequence of an authoritarian sovereignty unjustly exercised by a majority, as an impermissible act of violence, and as an improper tutelage and curtailment of the legal equality and freedom of action that are every free person's and citizen's due. In this way the idea of emancipation from this condition of human and civil nonage, a state that was perceived as unjust and unbearable, became a political catchword. It appears to have gained currency first in the Catholics' struggle for civil equality in Protestant England; such equality became law in 1829. (In the law itself the word *emancipation* does not appear; its official title is An Act for the Relief of His Majesty's Roman Catholic Subjects.) In connection with this the word was used occasionally (e.g., in 1821) in proposals that this legislation be extended to the Jews as well.

In the debates on the Jewish question in other countries the first appearance of the word seems to have been in a memorandum addressed by the British missionary Lewis Way to the Russian Czar Alexander I on the occasion of the Aachen congress of 1819. With a somewhat different ending (*Emanzipierung* rather than *Emanzipation*) the word occurred three years earlier (1816), in a broadside attributed to the German-Jewish journalist Ludwig Börne concerning the much-discussed rights of the Frank-furt Jews that had been abridged by the actions of the Congress of Vienna a year earlier (*Aktenmässige Darstellung des Bürgerrechts der Israeliten in Frankfurt/Main* [1816], xliv). To be sure, R. Rürup (*Emanzipation und Antisemitismus* [Göttingen, 1975], 126ff.) and Jacob Katz (personal communication) recently discovered the words *Emanzipation* and *Emanzipierung* in some earlier writings. The word seems to have come into use as a generally used catchword after the post-Kantian philosopher and politician Wilhelm Traugott Krug had employed it in an essay entitled "Über das

Verhältniss verschiedener Religionsparteien zum Staate und über die Emancipation der Juden" (first published in the historical and political periodical *Minerva* and then issued as a pamphlet at Jena in 1828). This word, which Krug derived from the British debate about the emancipation of the Catholics and its possible extension and applied to the Jews, was immediately adopted by both friends and foes and came into increasing use in the ensuing years. That same year Heinrich Heine used it in the third part of his *Reisebilder* (Italian journey from Munich to Genoa), chap. 29 (Insel edition [Leipzig, 1912], 4:298ff.; Elster edition, 3:275f.), generalizing it and raising it to a catchword expressive of the temper of the times. Using Napoleon's martial fame as a point of departure during a visit to the battlefield of Marengo, Heine believes that the time of military glory and the narrow nationalistic interests of princes is past; now tremendous partisan struggles that transcend political and linguistic boundaries are being carried on for the great political principles and the great philosophical and political tasks of the times: "But what is the task of our time? It is emancipation—not just the emancipation of the Irish, the Greek, the Frankfurt Jews, the East Indian Blacks and similarly oppressed peoples, but the emancipation of the entire world, particularly of Europe, which has come of age and is now breaking loose from the iron leading strings of the privileged, the aristocracy. . . . It will, to be sure, be some time before . . . the emancipation takes hold; but that time will eventually come. . . . Every age believes that its struggle is the most important of all; this is the real faith of this age, the faith with which it lives and dies, and we too want to live and die with this religion of freedom that may deserve the name religion more than the hollow, fossilized psychic specter that we are still in the habit of calling thus. . . ."

I have quoted the young Heine at some length, because his words show to what a great extent the newly applied word "emancipation" was in keeping with the mood of the age. In continuation of the Kantian definition of the Enlightenment, as cited above, and the original meaning of the word—release from caprice and immaturity—people now understood emancipation to mean also liberation from slavery in general, and to the Jews it meant liberation from the slavery inherent in the Christian view of the position of the Jews and in the medieval idea of *Kammerknechtschaft*. In the discussion of Bruno Bauer's 1843 work about the Jewish question (see Part 1, p. 19) Ludwig Philippson wrote in *Die Judenfrage von Ludwig Bauer näher beleuchtet*) (Dessau, 1843), p. 39: "We have once more become convinced that Israel has not yet been released from its slavery."

The generation nurtured on the ideas of the French Revolution was bitterly disappointed at the fact that reactionary political and intellectual movements were impeding the realization of the ideas of liberty and equality to such a great extent. This generation regarded the legal position of the Jews, which for the most part constituted a fundamental improvement over earlier times, as being closer to slavery than their much less free position had seemed to earlier generations, which had lived in the autonomous world of the ghetto. Thus the word "emancipation" was endowed with the emotions of the time. Gabriel Riesser, the Jewish champion of emancipation, declared in 1831 that he had made the fight for emancipation his mission in life, and Bruno Bauer, an opponent of emancipation, wrote in 1843 in a transvaluation of Heine's formulation: "If the cause of the Jews has become popular, this is not to the credit of their defenders; the only explanation can be that people surmise the connection between the emancipation of the Jews and the development of our conditions generally." The debate about Zionism fifty years later was also fueled by the evaluation of this development and the meaning and substance of a true "emancipation." (Concerning this, cf. Part 1, chap. 8.)

Literature on the history of the Jews in the French Revolution and its consequences: In addition to the well-known histories and encyclopedias, cf. especially the comments and bibliographies in *Histoire des Juifs en France*, ed.

B. Blumenkranz (Toulouse, 1972), sec. 3, chaps. 1 and 2, pp. 265ff. The major documents may be found in Achille-Edmond Halphen's collection *Recueil des lois . . . concernant les Israélites depuis la Révolution de 1789, suivi d'un Appendice, contenant la discussion dans les Assemblées Législatives . . .* (Paris, 1851). Selections from the most important documents are contained in S. Ettinger, ed., *Ma'amadam hachuki shel ha-Yehudim be-Europa* (Jerusalem, 1969) (documents about the legal position of European Jews from the mid-eighteenth century to the 1970s in the original and in Hebrew translation); Raphael Mahler, ed., *Jewish Emancipation: A Selection of Documents* (New York, 1944); J. Höxter, *Quellenbuch zur jüdischen Geschichte*, vol. 5 (Frankfurt, 1930).

DECLARATION OF HUMAN AND CIVIL RIGHTS: To understand the reactions one must   209
always bear in mind the wording of these declarations of the equality and equal rights of all human beings, which is what the contemporaries and the following generation did. Jefferson's formulation in the Declaration of Independence of the United States (4 July 1776) reads as follows: "We hold these truths to be self-evident, that all men are created equal, that they are endowed by their Creator with certain inalienable rights, that among these are life, liberty, and the pursuit of happiness. . . . That to secure these rights, governments are instituted among men. . . ." In the preamble to the French "Déclaration des droits de l'homme et du citoyen," proclaimed by the National Assembly on 26 August 1789 and then included in the constitution of 3 September 1791, we read that ignorance, forgetfulness, or disregard of the :natural, inalienable, and sacred human rights" are the only causes of public evils and political corruption. These rights are formulated in the first two sections: "I. Les hommes naissent et demeurent libres et égaux en droits. Les distinctions sociales ne peuvent être fondées que sur l'utilité commune. II. Le but de toute association politique est la conservation des droits naturels et imprescriptible de l'homme. Ces droits sont la liberté, la propriété, la sûreté et la résistance à l'oppression." Section X: "Nul ne doit être inquiété pour ses opinions, mêmes religieuses, pourvu que leur manifestation ne trouble pas l'ordre public établi par la loi."

Similar formulations may be found at the beginning of the constitutions of 1793 and 1795. These declarations, which were met with enthusiasm by the liberal world, were the basis for the Jews' hopes and demands of legal equality and also for their disappointment at the fact that they did not automatically apply to the Jews.

MAX NORDAU'S STATEMENT AT THE FIRST ZIONIST CONGRESS: In the *Protokoll des 1.*   209
Zionistenkongresses in Basel vom 29.–31. August 1897 (Vienna, 1897; Prague, 1911], 24f.; reprinted in Max Nordau, *Zionistische Schriften* [Berlin, 1923], 45) we read:

The history of the emancipation of the Jews is one of the most memorable chapters in the history of European thought. This emancipation is not a consequence of the insight that a grave injustice has been done to a people, that horrible things have been done to it, and that it is time to atone for a thousand years of injustice. It is solely the consequence of the linear geometric mode of thinking of French rationalism in the 18th century. . . . The philosophy of Rousseau and the encyclopedists had brought about the Declaration of the Rights of Man, and from this the rigid logic of the men of the great revolution derived the emancipation of the Jews. They formulated a veritable equation: Every human being has certain rights by nature; the Jews are human beings; consequently the Jews have human rights by nature. And thus the equality of the Jews was proclaimed in France—not out of a feeling of brotherhood, but because logic required it. Popular feeling even resisted it, but the philosophy of the revolution demanded that principles take precedence over feelings. If you will pardon the expression, which does not reflect ingratitude: the men of 1792 [he meant 1791] emancipated us because of a pedantic adherence to principles.

Nordau says that subsequently the other nations of Western Europe adopted the emancipation of the Jews not out of conviction but because it was, as it were, the fashion of the time. Just as they adopted the metrical system created by the French Revolution, as well as some of its other achievements, they adopted the emancipation of the Jews: "Now the emancipation of the Jews was one of those indispensable furnishings of a high-minded political household. . . ."

210   THE FRENCH REVOLUTION AS THE CONTINUATOR OF AN ABSOLUTISTIC TENDENCY TOWARD CENTRALIZATION: The French historian (and statesman) Alexis de Tocqueville (1805–69) was the first to demonstrate and describe this in his famous book *L'ancien régime et la révolution* (1856). To a certain extent this applies to the Jewish question as well. However, all these connections between the prerevolutionary, the revolutionary, and the postrevolutionary period should not make one lose sight of the fact that the revolution was the decisive event which made dormant or gradually prevailing tendencies manifest, thus accelerating them and systematically putting them into practice.

210f.   NO "STATE WITHIN THE STATE": Concerning the history of this concept and its application in the history of the Jewish question, cf. J. Katz, *A State within a State: History of an Anti-Semitic Slogan*, Israel Academy of Science and Humanities (Jerusalem, 1969).

210   CLERMONT-TONNERRE: Here is the original wording of the quotation: "Il faut refuser tout aux Juifs comme nation et tout leur accorder comme individus; il faut qu'ils ne fassent dans l'Etat ni un corps politique ni un ordre; il faut qu'ils soient individuellement citoyens. On prétend qu'ils ne veulent pas l'être; qu'ils le disent et qu'on les bannisse; il ne peut y avoir une nation dans une nation."

210f.   THE LAW EMANCIPATING THE JEWS IN FRANCE: The resolution of the National Assembly *(Constituante)*, proposed on 27 September 1791, adopted on 28 September and signed and issued by King Louis XVI on 13 November (significantly enough, simultaneously with a resolution concerning the regulation of debts owed to Jews in the Alsace), reads as follows in the original: "L'Assemblée Nationale, considérant que les conditions nécessaires pour être citoyen français et pour devenir citoyen actif sont fixéees par la Constitution; et que tout homme qui, réunissant les dites conditions, prête le serment civique et s'engage a remplir tous les devoirs que la Constitution impose, a droit à tous les avantages qu'elle assure; révoque tous les ajournements, réserves et exceptions insérés dans les précédents décrets relativement aux individus juifs que prêteront le serment civique, qui sera regardé comme une renonciation à tous privilèges et exceptions produits précédemment en leur faveur." The statement clearly formulated here for the first time that everyone who undertook to perform his constitutional duties also had a right to the benefits promised by the constitution was important for the further development. That was the formal principle on the basis of which Jews and non-Jewish liberals in all countries henceforth fought for equal rights for the Jews and against their disadvantaging, doing so in the face of counterarguments formulated by historical tradition.

211   DECLARATION OF THE ASSEMBLY OF NOTABLES: This declaration was made as a response to the fifth question (regarding the relations between Jews and non-Jews) which had been asked of the Jewish notables. Here is its full text: "Aujourd'hui que les Juifs ne forment plus une nation, et qu'ils ont l'avantage d'être incorporés dans la Grande Nation, ce qu'ils regardent comme une redemption politique, il n'est pas

possible qu'un Juif traite un Français qui n'est pas de sa religion qu'il ne traite un des coreligionnaires."

Behind these words one immediately senses the refutation of the accusation that the Jews were permitted to treat non-Jews differently from their coreligionists (especially in the question of charging interest and usury).

NAPOLEON AND THE JEWS: Scholarship and the popular imagination have greatly concerned themselves with Napoleon's attitude toward the Jews and the problem of their integration into the modern world. In his case, and in the cases of other personalities, it has often been forgotten that the Jewish question surely was not a central problem for him. For the most important literature on the subject see *EJJ* 12:825. In addition to Graetz 11 (particularly the excursus on pp. 620ff.), Dubnow 8, and the above-cited literature on the history of the emancipation and the French Revolution I shall mention Robert Anchel, *Napoléon et les Juifs* (Paris, 1928). Researchers have particularly concerned themselves with the proclamation to the Jews concerning the reestablishment of their state that Napoleon issued in 1799, on the occasion of his Egyptian expedition and his campaign from Egypt through Palestine to Acre, the unsuccessful siege of which doomed this campaign. There seems to be a conflict between this declaration and the declarations that Napoleon demanded in 1806–7 from the Assembly of Notables and the Synhedrion, and even more so the decree of 17 March 1808 (which the Jews regarded as "infamous") about temporary legal limitations on the Alsatian Jews accused of usury. There is a balanced summary of the discussion of this question in *Napoleon and the Jews* (New York and Jerusalem, 1975) by Franz Kobler, who discovered and published a German translation of Napoleon's 1799 proclamation. This removed any doubt about the existence of this proclamation, which had previously been known only from a contemporary account in the French government's *Gazette Nationale*. In light of this decision Kobler also assesses Napoleon's other actions toward a solution of the Jewish question, points to hitherto largely ignored formulations by Napoleon, and attempts to find a key to what appears to be a duality in Napoleon's attitude, a duality that has always been noted and emphasized. Napoleon was certainly affected by different traditions and influences. First of all, it was the French Revolution and the constitution propagated by it which said that there must be "no state within the state" or, in the French formulation of the time, "no nation within the nation," and expressly stipulated that citizenship was to be given to an individual and not to a corporation. On the other hand, Napoleon's imagination was stirred by the heroic figures of the Bible, particularly in connection with his Egyptian-Palestinian campaign. After this enterprise had failed and he had to deal with the practical tasks of reorganizing the French state, Napoleon, who had in the meantime become the emperor of the French state and empire, also faced the complaints of the Alsatian population that had always been part of the discussion of the Jewish question in France. These revived the notion of the Jew as a usurer from ancient times and on the basis of the Mosaic laws, a notion that Napoleon himself had adopted from tradition. Even though the Jews complied with the official desire that was brought to their attention and tried very hard to deny any membership in a separate nation, Napoleon does not appear to have placed much credence in these declarations, possibly because they seemed too subservient to him. His measures appeared to be intended to reorganize the Jews, who to a realistic observer of the conditions did appear as a national group as well, to reeducate them through pertinent laws, civilize them by means of the consistorial constitution introduced by him, and thus integrate them into French political and social life. Later, on St. Helena, he went so far as to explain to Dr. O'Meara, his Irish physician, that by virtue of his measures the Jews ought to regard him as their ruler, like King Solomon or Herod, and treat the French as though they were members of the tribe of

210f.

Judah, from whom the taking of usurious interest was forbidden by the biblical laws. This is in keeping with Napoleon's self-image, for he always viewed himself in the light of his great predecessors Alexander, Caesar, and Augustus; thus King Solomon could also fit into this picture. Napoleon's entire attitude toward the Jews shows once more how complex the image of the Jews was in the minds of even the most important personalities, how ideas, traditions, doctrines, and considerations of a practical nature intermingled, and how even a brilliant man of action like Napoleon remained entangled in these contrarieties. Another problem is this: What effect did the figure of Napoleon, his campaigns and the attendant dissemination of revolutionary ideas, the creation of a European community of states, and the arousal of national counter-movements in the countries dominated by Napoleon have on the Jewish question? It is hard to overestimate the degree of this influence in the complex of countries called Europe, which, despite all dissimilarities, were awakened to a new consciousness of their unity—in the Jewish question and many other clusters of problems. Cf. also P. Girard, "Napoleon contre les Juifs?" in *L'Arche*, February 1976, 53–59; S. Z. Pipe, "Napoleon in Jewish Folklore," *YIVO Annual* 1 (1946); B. Mevorack, *Napoleon and His Epoch in Contemporary Hebrew Accounts* (Hebr.) (Jerusalem, 1968).

211 THE EMANCIPATION AS MESSIAH: As a typical example of this approach more than a hundred years later, cf. the essay "La Société juive en France depuis la Révolution" (in *Revue des Études Juives* 48 [1904]) by the Franco-Jewish historian Maurice Bloch. In his view, the Messianic period began with the French Revolution, and the New Jerusalem will exist wherever the ideas of 1789 prevail. There is a reference to this in M. R. Marcus, *The Politics of Assimilation: A Study of the French Jewish Community at the Time of the Dreyfus Affair* (Oxford, 1971), 280f.

Similar formulations may also be found in the literature, especially the religious-liberal and Reform kind, in other countries. For the United States, cf. as one example among many an 1898 statement by the Reform Union of American Hebrew Congregations: "America is our Zion, the fruition of the beginning laid in the old." Such assurances are often repeated: "America is our Zion and Washington our Jerusalem." Cf. Naomi W. Cohen, *American Jews and the Zionist Idea* (New York, 1975), here quoted from S. P. Lachmann's review in *Present Tense* 2, no. 2, p. 77. There is quite a distance between that position and the membership of the Union of Reform Congregations in the Zionist Organization in 1976.

211ff. COOPERATION IN THE CULTURAL DEVELOPMENT OF THE NATIONS: Cf. Part 1, p. 246 and Part 2, pp. 625ff., as well as the summaries and extensive bibliographies in books like Cecil Roth, *The Jewish Contribution to Civilization* (1938, 1943); Louis Finkelstein, ed., *The Jews: Their History, Culture and Religion*, vol. 2 (New York, 1949); Siegmund Kaznelson, ed., *Juden im deutschen Kulturbereich* (Berlin, 1959).

212 RUSSIANIZATION OF EASTERN EUROPEAN JEWRY: Cf., among others, Yehuda Slutsky, *The Russian Jewish Press in the Nineteenth Century* (Hebr.) (Jerusalem, 1970).

THE TERM "JEWISH QUESTION": Cf. the introductory chapter in Part 1, pp. 18ff. and Part 2, p. 478.

214f. THE JEWISH QUESTION AT EUROPEAN PEACE CONFERENCES: Cf. Lucien Wolf, *Notes on the Diplomatic History of the Jewish Question: With Texts of Protocols, Treaty Stipulations and Other Public Acts and Official Documents* (London, 1919); Salo W. Baron, *Die Judenfrage auf dem Wiener Kongress* (Vienna, 1920); Nathan Feinberg, "The Jewish Question at the Congress of Aix-la-Chapelle, 1818," in *Israel Yearbook of Human Rights* 2 (1972), 176–93; N. M. Gelber, "The Jewish Question Before the

Berlin Congress of 1878" (Hebr.), *Zion* 8 : 35–50; idem, "The Intervention of German Jews at the Berlin Congress 1878," in Leo Baeck Institute, *Year Book* 5 (1960), 221–47; A. M. K. Rabinowicz, "Classical International Law and the Jewish Question," *Netherlands International Law Review* 24 (1977), Special Issue 1–2, 205–31.

REWBELL: in *The French Enlightenment and the Jews* (353ff.) Arthur Hertzberg   216
rightly emphasizes the beginnings of an anti-Jewish ideology of the political Left: "The most anti-Jewish views of all occurred among some of the members of the extreme left." The most systematic and tireless fighter among these was Rewbell. He expressly emphasized that he was not opposing any religion; no one could be excluded from equality before the law on account of his creed. But in their petition of 31 August 1789 the Jews of eastern France expressly requested the preservation of their communal autonomy, including internal Jewish jurisdiction, and this, he said, was incompatible with French citizenship. He himself did not wish to bar the Jews from civil equality; the Jews were excluding themselves by clinging to their tradition and the organizational forms based on it. Added to this were the arguments against the Jews, derived from tradition and reality, as incorrigible usurers. On a later occasion Rewbell said that the Jews were a counterrevolutionary element and an impediment to the regeneration of revolutionary France. He also pointed to their different racial quality ("Africans"). "What Voltaire and d'Holbach had said or hinted at in theory had become a political program," writes Hertzberg (p. 357), and he may be overstating his case a bit when he continues: "The new secular anti-Semitism of the left had taken its first step toward 'solving' the Jewish problem by isolation or pogroms."

NEGATIVE REPORTS OF LOCAL AUTHORITIES ABOUT THE JEWS: There are numerous   216f.
published sources and a great deal of unpublished archival material about this. Less known material from the middle of the nineteenth century may be found in a number of articles and surveys in the twelve-volume collection *Die Gegenwart: Eine enzyklopädische Darstellung der neuesten Zeitgeschichte für alle Stände* (Leipzig: F. A. Brockhaus, 1848–56). Cf., e.g., vol. 1 (1848), 353–407: "Die bürgerlichen Verhältnisse der Juden in Deutschland"—an overview with quotations from official reports about the economic, social, and political situation of the Jews, the accusations against the Jews (some of which are regarded as justified), and the remedies proposed: rejection of emancipation, gradual granting of full rights in accordance with the moral improvement of the Jews, rescission of the laws against mixed marriages, etc. The (unnamed) author concludes (p. 406): "The mixing of races is a far-reaching consequence of the complete emancipation of the Jews." It can be achieved by permitting mixed marriages. "Such a mingling is bound to end even the specifically Jewish traditions, customs, and notions in the circle of the families and thus completely allay the fear that the emancipation might promote the continued proliferation of an alien, hostile nationality in the bosom of the Germanic society."

THE STOCK EXCHANGE AND THE JEWS: Cf. the articles in the encyclopedias and the   217ff.
bibliographies there, e.g., *EJJ* 4 : 166ff. and 15 : 405f. For a lively picture of life at the stock exchange and its effects on nineteenth-century society Sombart always recommended to his students Zola's novel *L'Argent*, from which, according to him, one could learn more than from many textbooks on economics.

AVOIDANCE OF THE WORD "JEW": Here people sometimes resorted to words that had   221f.
been in use prior to this word: "Hebrews" (esp. in Russia: *Evrei*) in official documents from the late eighteenth century (in place of *zhid, Jüd*; cf. Dubnow 8 : 351); "Hebrew" (*ivri*) was, after all, the oldest name of the people. After the conquest of the land it

was replaced by "children of Israel," and after the return from exile (Josephus, *Antiquities* 11, 5, p. 7) the word "Jews" *(Yehudim, Yudaei)* came into use. *Israeliten*, a translation of the idea "children of Israel," was demanded and considered in Prussia from the late eighteenth century on (Dubnow 8:196); its first official use seems to have been in France in 1806. Berr Isaac-Berr, the representative of Alsatian Jewry and secretary of the Assembly of Notables of 1806 and of the Synhedrion of 1807, demanded in his work about the reform of the living conditions of Jews (*Réflexions sur la régénération complète des juifs en France*, p. 12) that the word *juif*, which had been used as a term of abuse, be replaced with *Israélite* or *Hébreu*. He pointed out that the word *juif* was connected with the land of Judah and hence lost its justification as soon as the French Jews regarded France as their only fatherland, whereas the name *Israel* ("wrestler with God") had been bestowed on the patriarch Jacob by God himself. Around that time these designations first appeared in official documents, as did formulations like "Français professant la religion juive" or "la religion hébraïque." In the course of the nineteenth century *Israélite* and similar terms were increasingly used in official documents and in associations between non-Jews and Jews. However, at the same time these retained much of the pejorative character of the old word *juif*, frequently with a touch of mockery as well, for when among themselves non-Jews continued to use the word *juif* with all its overtones almost exclusively. Hence proud champions of emancipation among the Jews, such as Gabriel Riesser (1806–63), rejected the hide-and-seek game with the words *juif* or *Jude*, a pursuit that seemed useless, senseless, and degrading to them. Riesser named his periodical, which appeared between 1832 and 1837 and was devoted to the struggle for emancipation, *Der Jude*. The word *Jude* was increasingly used and respected when Jewish nationalistic tendencies came to the fore and the Zionist movement became stronger. Theodor Herzl wrote in the foreword to the first issue of the official Zionist organ *Die Welt*: "Our weekly is a 'Jewish sheet.' We are adopting this term, which has been intended as one of opprobrium, and intend to turn it into something honorable." On the other hand, to this day champions of Jewish honor have seen fit to oppose, with quixotic zeal, the continued inclusion in the *Oxford Dictionary* and other reference works of all semantic nuances of the word *Jew* (such as "usurer," "to practice usury," etc.), even if it is stated that these are historical in nature.

The State of Israel, founded in May 1948, uses the word "Israelis" (not "Israelites") to designate the citizens of the country in distinction to "Jews" as the designation of the members of the Jewish people who live in Israel and in the Diaspora.

223   INCREASING URBANIZATION, ETC.: Statistics (which became more reliable only after the introduction of official statistics, having previously been based largely on estimates) may be found especially in A. Ruppin, *Soziologie der Juden* 1 (1930), and very detailed statistics for Germany in Jakob Lestschinsky, *Das wirtschaftliche Schicksal des deutschen Judentums* (Berlin, 1933) (with a foreword by M. Kreutzberger dated December 1932, on the eve of Hitler's assumption of power). Cf. also my remarks in Part 1, chap. 1 (p. 25) and bibliographies in the notes. For the Jewish population of Germany around the middle of the 19th century, see also the brief section in the abovementioned Brockhaus encyclopedia, *Die Gegenwart* 3 (1849), 14f. The section on the Jews in its comprehensive article on "Deutschlands Bevölkerungsverhältnisse" (p. 5) bears the revealing title "Semiten," a word that had but recently been adopted from philology for general use. This section begins as follows: "Even though the Jews as a rule use the language of their home town, their adherence to the faith and the customs of their fathers does oblige us to differentiate them clearly as an ethnic group from the Germans or Slaves among whom they live and to regard them as scattered members of the Semitic tribe."

MODERN NATIONALISM: Of the enormous literature on this subject I shall mention a basic work of intellectual history, Friedrich Meinecke's *Weltbürgertum und Nationalstaat: Studien zur Genesis des deutschen Nationalstaates*, as well as H. L. Featherstone, *A Century of Nationalism* (1939); Benjamin Akzin, *State and Nation* (London, 1964); George L. Mosse, *The Culture of Western Europe: The Nineteenth and Twentieth Centuries* (Chicago, 1961); and Eli Kadouri, *Nationalism* (London, 1961).

The characteristic feature of all political movements since the nineteenth century (liberalism, socialism, conservatism, etc.) is that they raise unconscious or semi-conscious feelings into consciousness and turn them into a political philosophy. This is linguistically expressed by the suffix *-ism*, which is derived from philosophy. I shall have more to say about this phenomenon in the next chapter.

Beginning with Hume, Jefferson, and Alexander Hamilton in the eighteenth century, political thinkers and writers have drawn attention to the dangers inherent in the proclamation of the people as declared sovereigns. Later developments, from Robespierre and the Jacobins to Hitler's National Socialist and Stalin's Bolshevist regimes, have confirmed the predictions that the "sovereign" people and the leaders they elevate to absolute power can be the worst tyrants. Of the variegated literature on this phenomenon I shall mention J. L. Talmon, *The Origins of Totalitarian Democracy* (London, 1961) and the literature about mass psychology, collective sociology, and group dynamics since Le Bon's *Psychologie des foules* (1895). I shall revert to these problems and developments in a later context (especially chaps. 6 and 9), when the effects on the Jewish question that have been indicated here become apparent and concrete.

THE IMAGE OF THE JEW IN GERMAN HISTORIOGRAPHY OF THE NINETEENTH CEN- 224f. TURY: Nineteenth-century German historiography exerted a tremendous influence on the historiography of the other European nations. A knowledgeable and balanced biographical presentation, one that is sensitive to intellectual history, is given by Hans Liebeschütz in his book *Das Judentum im Geschichtsbild von Hegel bis Max Weber* (Tübingen, 1967).

HEGEL AND JUDAISM: Hegel's influence on historiography and philosophical thought 226 in the nineteenth century can hardly be overestimated, and hence his view of Judaism and his attitude toward the Jews is of extraordinary significance. He was an opponent of ancient, historic Judaism to the extent that he was acquainted with it, but in the struggle for emancipation he advocated legal equality for the Jews as a human right. As has repeatedly been pointed out, his views on Judaism are at bottom the Christian dogmatic teachings in secularized form. Here is a selection from the enormous literature about Hegel, his idea of the state, and his attitude toward Judaism: Frederick Copleston, *A History of Philosophy*, vol. 7, part 1, (New York, 1963), Chaps. 9–11 (with a detailed bibliography); R. V. Delius, *Hegel: Eine Einführung in seine Philosophie* (Leipzig, 1928), esp. pp. 36f., 51; Karl Löwith, *Weltgeschehen und Heilsgeschichte* (Stuttgart, 1953), 55ff.; Gerd-Klaus Kaltenbrunner, ed., *Hegel und die Folgen* (Frieberg, 1970); Ernst Cassirer, *Vom Mythus des Staates* (Zurich, 1949), 322–359; Ernst Simon, *Ranke und Hegel* (Munich, 1928); idem, "Hegel und das Judentum," *Jüdische Rundschau*, 11 November 1931; E. L. Frankenstein, "Hegel," *EJJ* 8:245ff.; Levinger, in *HE* 13:388ff.; Rotenstreich, "Hegel's Image of Judaism, *Jewish Social Studies* 15 (1953): 33ff.; idem, *The Recurrent Pattern* (London, 1963), chap. 3: "Man and the Estranged God" [Hegel], 48–75; idem, "For and against Emancipation: The Bruno Bauer Controversy," *LBYB* 4 (1959), 3ff.; Shlomo Avineri, "Hegel and Nationalism," *Review of Politics* 24 (1962);

461–84; idem, "A Note on Hegel's View on Jewish Emancipation," *Jewish Social Studies* 25 (1963): 145–51. For an example of Hegel's influence on Jews who strayed from Judaism, see Lassalle's confessional letter to his mother (who in all likelihood did not understand its contents and consequence) of 30 July 1944 (in Gustav Mayer, ed., *Ferdinand Lassalles nachgelassene Briefe und Schriften* 1 (1921), esp. p. 109; "One is fully justified in stating that the world of the Jewish people presents, if you will, an image of utter ugliness, of man's outward dejection before God, of inner strife and instability. . . . As Hegel so aptly put it, the Jewish world is 'the world of the pitiful personality.' . . . In its spirit and consciousness as well as its outward fate, the whole Jewish world—religious, political, etc.—is best epitomized as the world of misfortune." Cf. my article "Herzl und Lassalle" in the Jewish journal *Die Stimme* (Vienna), 8 (3–12 July, 1935) and S. Na'aman, *Ferdinald Lassalle: Deutscher und Jude* (Hanover, 1968). Heine concerned himself with Hegel for a while in an effort to make him comprehensible to the French, but he said that he had burned the manuscript of his essay instead of having it printed. In his "Geständnisse" (Confessions), written in 1854, two years before his death, Heine characterizes Hegel's style as follows (*Werke*, Insel ed., 10:171), "To be honest, I seldom understood him, and only later reflection permitted me to grasp his words. I believe he did not wish to be understood, and that is the reason for the intricacy of his style. . . ." (Such a statement could be made about many a philosopher and sociologist down to our days!)

Here are some quotations from Hegel's writings that document what has been said in this book (including the notes) and served as the foundation for later developments. From *Philosophy of History*, Introduction, iii: "The only thought which philosophy brings with it to the contemplation of history is the simple conception of *reason;* that reason is the sovereign of the world; that the history of the world therefore presents us with a rational process" (trans. J. Sibree, *Encyclopedia Britannica Great Books of the Western World*, vol. 46 [Chicago, 1952], 157). Actually, this is close to the Jewish view that God has created everything in wisdom. Introduction, 171: "In the history of the world, only those peoples can come under our notice which form a state. For it must be understood that this latter is the realization of freedom, i.e., of the absolute final aim, and that it exists for its own sake. It must further be understood that all the worth which the human being possesses, all spiritual reality, he possesses only through the state."

From *Philosophy of Right*, section 257 (*op. cit.*, trans. T. M. Knox, p. 80): "The state is the actuality of the ethical Idea. It is ethical mind *qua* the substantial will manifest and revealed to itself, knowing and thinking itself, accomplishing what it knows and in so far as it knows it. . . ." Section 258 (p. 80): "The state is absolutely rational inasmuch as it is the actuality of the substantial will which it possesses in the particular self-consciousness once that consciousness has been raised to consciousness of its universality." Section 345 (p. 111): "Justice and virtue, wrongdoing, power and vice, talents and their achievements, passions strong and weak, guilt and innocence, grandeur in individual and national life, autonomy, fortune and misfortune of states and individuals, all these have their specific significance and worth in the field of known actuality; therein they are judged and therein they have their partial, though only partial justification. World-history, however, is above the point of view from which these things matter. Each of its stages is the presence of a necessary moment in the Idea of the world mind, and that moment attains its absolute right in that stage. The nation whose life embodies this moment secures its good fortune and fame, and its deeds are brought to fruition." Section 347 (p. 111): "The nation to which is ascribed a moment of the Idea in the form of a natural principle is entrusted with giving complete effect to it in the advance of the self-developing self-consciousness of the world mind. This nation is dominant in world history during this one epoch, and it is only once that it can make its hour strike. In contrast with this its absolute right of being the vehicle of this present stage in the world mind's development, the minds of the other nations are without rights, and they, along with those whose hour has struck already, count no longer in world history."

Today one is tempted to ask whether it is not really an inadmissible presumption, an arrogant hubris, and cruelty of thought and judgment on the life of human groups if, following and secularizing the Christian dogmatic view of history, one ascribes to a people only a single task, whereupon world history mercilessly sends it to its death, as the Eskimos do with old people, in order to make room for a younger people that the world mind has now destined for sovereign dominance. After all, life does go on— as life, with a legitimacy of its own and with multifarious effects, even below the point that a certain outlook may regard as the apex and even though those effects cannot be so easily discerned and documented from an individually or philosophically exalted viewpoint. Concerning the conclusions that people were able to draw from such premises in the twentieth century and utilize for the justification of totalitarian systems, cf. E. Cassirer, *Vom Mythus des Staates* (1948), 356ff.

About Judaism Hegel writes in his *Philosophy of History*, part 1, sec. 3, chap. 3 ("Judaea," *op. cit.*, pp. 246–47): "We observe among this people a severe religious ceremonial, expressing a relation to pure thought. . . . It is true that subjective feeling is manifest—the pure heart, repentance, devotion; but . . . it remains closely bound to the observance of ceremonies and of the law. . . . The Jews possess that which makes them what they are, through the *One:* consequently the individual has no freedom for itself. Spinoza regards the code of Moses as having been given by God to the Jews for a punishment—a rod of correction. The individual never comes to the consciousness of independence; on that account we do not find among the Jews any belief in the immortality of the soul. . . . But though in Judaism the *individual* is not respected, the *family* has inherent value; for the worship of Jehovah is attached to the family. . . . But the state is an institution not consonant with the Judaistic principle, and it is alien to the legislation of Moses. . . . We see in this history the transition from the patriarchal nomad condition to agriculture. On the whole the Jewish history exhibits grand features of character; but it is disfigured by an exclusive bearing (sanctioned in its religion) towards the genius of other nations (the destruction of the inhabitants of Canaan being even commanded), by want of culture generally, and by the superstition arising from the idea of the high value of their peculiar nationality. . . ."

In his *Phenomenology of Spirit* Hegel writes that the Jewish people is and has been the most depraved precisely because it stands before the gate of salvation. It is plain to see that Hegel, like Kant and others, made apodictic judgments on the basis of altogether inadequate knowledge of the material and that next to intuitively correct insights the most ordinary prejudices, half-truths, and misjudgments were pressed into a philosophical system that was regarded as irrefutable and was embraced by others as the unquestionable truth.

Concerning Hegel's positive attitude toward the question of emancipation, cf. *Philosophy of Right*, section 270 (*op. cit.*, p. 84) which deals with the "relation of the state to religion." In connection with the principle of tolerance that a strong state might apply to religions even if their principles do not permit the fulfillment of certain duties to the state (e.g., the Quakers' refusal to take oaths and perform military service), Hegel discusses the Jews in a rather long note and writes (*op. cit.*, p. 87): "Technically it may have been right to refuse a grant of even civil rights to the Jews on the ground that they should be regarded as belonging not merely to a religious sect but to a foreign race. But the fierce outcry raised against the Jews, from that point of view and others, ignores the fact that they are, above all, *men;* and manhood, so far from being a mere superficial, abstract quality, is on the contrary itself the basis of the fact that what civil rights rouse in their possessors is the feeling of oneself as counting in civil society as a person with rights, and this feeling of selfhood, infinite and free from all restrictions, is the root from which the desired similarity in disposition and ways of thinking comes into being. To exclude the Jews from civil rights, on the other hand, would rather be to confirm the isolation with which they have been reproached—a result for which the state refusing them rights would be blamable and reproachable, because by so refusing, it would have misunderstood its own basic principle, its nature as an objective and powerful institution. The exclusion of the Jews from civil rights may be supposed to be a right of the highest kind and may be demanded on that ground; but experience has shown that so to exclude them is the silliest folly, and the way in which governments now treat them has proved itself to be both prudent and dignified."

226f.   THE IMAGE OF THE JEW IN THE LITERATURE OF THE PERIOD OF EMANCIPATION: While Hegel and many of those influenced by him (and who was not?) evaluated the classical period of Judaism negatively but at the same time advocated emancipation for the Jews of their time (something in which some of Hegel's disciples, such as Bruno Bauer and Karl Marx, parted company with him), we often encounter an entirely different image of the Jews in literature. True, as pointed out in the preceding chapter, many of the stereotypical judgments adopted from theology and tradition may be found in fiction and the drama as well. At the same time, in that period and later in the 19th century tendencies that had since the seventeenth and eighteenth centuries found expression in music, especially in the biblical oratorios of Carissimi, Handel, and their successors, were continued in literature to an increasing extent: Figures and events of ancient Judaism, from the biblical figures to the time of the Second Temple, were glorified, psychologically interpreted, and made comprehensible. The dramas of Friedrich Hebbel are cases in point. Actual or fictional figures of bygone ages were idealized and made mouthpieces of the author (e.g., in Scott's novel *Ivanhoe* or Karl Gutzkow's play *Uriel Acosta*). On the other hand, contemporary Jews appearing in novels remained encumbered by traditional stereotypes and usually were a sinister contrast to the more radiant Christian figures (e.g., the novels *Soll und Haben* by Gustav Freytag, *Der Hungerpastor* by Wilhelm Raabe, *Oliver Twist* by Dickens, or *Ein Kampf um Rom* by Felix Dahn). The Jewish usurer, careerist, and heartless exploiter continued to be familiar figures in fiction, and the revolutionary who negates all existing things was added. Only rarely do we find depictions of warmly sympathetic Jews with a humanly attractive character; stories like Annette Droste-Hülshoff's *Die Judenbuche* or Adalbert Stifter's *Abdias* are exceptions. In general, the Jewish figures, including those presented as good people, are abstractions, black or white stereotypes with exaggerated good or bad qualities, rather than reflections of reality. This may be expressive of an adherence to tradition or of a desire not to commit an injustice and to promote a greater appreciation, but it always remains evidence of unfamiliarity with the real life of the Jews of the time. In 1816, after decades of personally associating with Jews and visiting Jewish salons, Wilhelm von Humboldt, a true humanist and democrat, one of the most important champions of the Prussian emancipation of the Jews (1812) and one of the most influential spokesmen for Jewish rights at the Congress of Vienna, brought himself to write these strange words in a letter to his wife: "I love the Jews really only *en masse; en détail* I rather avoid them" (*Wilhelm und Caroline von Humboldt in ihren Briefen* [Berlin, 1900], 5:236; here cited after Hannah Arendt, *The Origins of Totalitarianism* [New York, 1951], 30). In other words, it was possible to be a friend of the Jews, fight for their equal rights, esteem them as a totality, and regard oneself as a liberal—and yet try to have as little contact with them as possible in daily life.

Thus it was in the period of "classical" literature in the eighteenth and early nineteenth centuries, and so it remained in the nineteenth century. It was possible to be attracted to the figures and strange customs of the Jews with curiosity and a secret thrill and at the same to feel revulsion, as Goethe did; it was possible for someone (as Goethe wrote on 19 May 1812 to his friend, the composer Zelter, rejecting the latter's proposal to write a libretto for an opera to be called *Samson*) to view the mythical figures of the Old Testament as "truly great . . . respectable from an earnest distance. But when these heroes enter the present, it occurs to us that they were Jews, and we feel a contrast between the ancestors and their descendants that causes us confusion" (Teweles, *Goethe und die Juden*, p. 29). It was also possible, as in the case of Goethe, to oppose injustices to the Jews and at the same time shrink back from too close contact with them and from their complete integration into a Christian society that people wanted to have preserved as the foundation and backbone of a sound state and which alien elements might place in jeopardy. It would not be fair to deny any society the right to accept or exclude anyone it wants, provided that this does not amount to a general value judgment or run counter to principles that are regarded as binding. Yet informed observers cannot have any doubt that this is what happened in large measure and found expression in literature and through it in the educational system and cultural life of the European nation-states. In the final analysis, this spelled the doom of the emancipative movement in the form given it by the French Revolution.

An added factor in the nineteenth century was the increasing typological expression of the unpleasant elements and bad character of Jewish figures in physical terms. The "bad" Jews are homely, repulsive, foul-smelling, and instantly recognizable as Jews by their noses. We shall have more to say about this aspect in the next chapter.

Here is some of the literature on the "Jewish image in literature" that I have used: "Jüdische Gestalten in der Weltliteratur," *JL* 5:1382–1404; Sol Liptzin, "The Image of the Jew in German Literature," *EJJ* 7:442–46; Heinrich Teweles, *Goethe und die Juden* (Hamburg, 1925); Montagu Frank Modder, *The Jew in the Literature of England* (New York, 1939, 1960); Harold Fish, *The Dual Image: A Study of the Jew in English Literature* (London, 1959); Edgar Rosenberg, *From Shylock to Svengali: Jewish Stereotypes in English Fiction* (London, 1960); Isaac Barzilay, "The Jew in the Literature of the Enlightenment," *Jewish Social Studies* 18 (1950); George L. Mosse, "The Image of the Jew in German Popular Culture: Felix Dahn and Gustav Freytag," *LBYB* 2 (1957): 218–27; Sol Liptzin, *The Jew in American Literature* (New York 1966.

Concerning Jews as writers in European literature, in particular Heinrich Heine, cf. Part 1, chap. 7 and the notes and excursuses in Part 2.

THE IMAGE OF THE JEW IN THE EARLY SOCIALIST LITERATURE OF THE PERIOD OF   227
EMANCIPATION: In his book *Sozialisten zur Judenfrage: Ein Beitrag zur Geschichte des Sozialismus von Anfang des 19. Jahrhunderts bis 1914* (Berlin, 1962) Edmund Silberner has presented all the important material on this problem, making full use of all sources with exemplary scholarship. An appendix to the Hebrew edition (Jerusalem, 1955) includes even more extensive quotations from some of these sources. Both editions contain very full bibliographies. All data may be found in this fundamental book, though it is possible to raise certain objections to the terminology and an occasional overconfident evaluation of the personalities and their motives and to miss a clear division into periods. All the facts and quotations in the following commentary have been derived from Silberner's book.

Although Silberner does not do so, one has to draw a methodological distinction between the period before the origin of modern anti-Semitism as an organized political movement based on racist ideology in the late 1870s and the preceding ninety years after the French Revolution, the period under discussion here. (Concerning the new epoch in the Jewish question, which designated itself with the new concept "anti-Semitism," see chap. 6.) Naturally, any social movement, its leaders, its faithful adherents, and its fellow travelers are influenced by the atmosphere of their time with its notions, prejudgments, evaluations, and the catchwords that give currency to the formulations of leading thinkers, poets, and writers in simplified (and thus falsified) form. If the old image of the Jew persisted in leading thinkers and writers, if ancient doctrines and Christological traditions were disseminated in secularized form in basic writings of the time by recognized philosophers (from Kant to Hegel and Schopenhauer, and by the last-named in particularly contemptuous and hateful formulations) and thus became part of the "culture" of the century, one should not be surprised that these were also adopted by noted representatives of the movements to reform bourgeois society that in the 1830s were given the new name "socialism." In one of his major works Pierre Leroux (1797–1871), one of the leading anti-Jewish early socialists, characterized the Jews as "rois de l'époque"; he did this in 1846, one year later than his contemporary Alphonse Toussenel (1813–85), and gave the *Dictionnaire de l'Académie française* as the source for his derogatory use of the word *juif*. There, he said, the word appeared not as the name of a nation but as the designation for a person who takes usurious interest on loans or sells things at inflated prices, who is avaricious and mercenary: "We speak about the Jews as the Academy does." Hence he means by *juif* "the Jewish mind wherever it appears (even among non-Jews)—the spirit of profit, acquisitiveness, self-interest, trade and speculation; in other words, the spirit of banking."

Thus Judaism is equated with the new spirit of the capitalistic economy, which makes the struggle against capitalism the struggle against Judaism. On occasion the biblical history of Judaism is glorified and Moses is viewed as the lawgiver of justice. By contrast, the Jewish people was bad from the beginning, for did not the Prophets say so? This was derived from Christian dogma, and frequently the stories about the provenance of the Jews, and especially the charge of misanthropy, were adopted with or without reference to Tacitus (depending on the level of the author's education). In early socialist literature the specter of the Jew that haunts general literature is identified with the symbolic figure of Ahasuerus as the Wandering Jew. (That is how he appears in Schopenhauer as well). The uncanny, incomprehensible aspect of the anonymous financial power that was organized in the new form of credit banks and joint-stock companies and by way of stock exchanges encouraged many people to participate in the new striving for profit, enriching them or disappointing them with financial misfortune, was now connected with the traditional image of the Jews. Thus people regarded the Jew as an uncanny demon of world domination (Toussenel, *Les Juifs: Rois de l'époque* [1845]; Pierre Leroux, 1846) or interpreted him, following Hegel, antithetically-dialectically, depending on the writer's general mode of thinking. To Ludwig Feuerbach (*Wesen des Christentums*, 1843) "utilitarianism . . . [was] the basic orientation of Judaism" and the God of the Jews was "the practical principle of the world—egotism, egotism in the form of a religion." According to Bruno Bauer (*Die Judenfrage* [1843]) the Jews are characterized by their "egotistic stubbornness"; they are not a real people but "a sum of atomistic individuals, a chimerical nationality, a caste." Only when they free themselves from their religion and via the higher stage of Christianity (which Bauer also rejects) become people of modern culture can they be emancipated and accepted by the existing bourgeois society as citizens with equal rights.

In his polemical review of Bauer's work, which appeared in 1844 in the *Deutsch-Französische Jahrbücher* (edited by him and Arnold Ruge) as "Zur Judenfrage," Karl Marx adopted concepts of his predecessors Feuerbach and Bauer. However, here these concepts are transposed to the economic-material plane with a resolute single-mindedness that foreshadows its later development into the theory of historical materialism, thus authoritatively sanctioning it, as it were, for the developing modern socialist movement. Marx, who was descended from rabbis on his father's and mother's side but had at his father's behest been baptized at the age of six, here and elsewhere uses a particularly mordant style that betrays an apostate's defense against actual or presumed accusations. Near the beginning of his article he writes: "Let us consider the real Jew, not the *Sabbath Jew*, whom Bauer considers, but the *everyday Jews*. Let us not seek the secret of the Jew in his religion, but let us seek the secret of the religion in the real Jew" (K. Marx, *Early Writings*, trans. and ed. T. B. Bottomore [New York, 1964], 34).

This is the point of departure for his questions, and his answers are sharper than those of most declared Jew-haters. "What is the profane basis of Judaism? *Practical* need, *Self-interest*. What is the worldly cult of the Jew? Huckstering. What is his worldly god? *Money*. Very well; then in emancipating itself from *huckstering* and *money*, and thus from real and practical Judaism, our age would emancipate itself" (ibid.). Thus Judaism and the money economy, Judaism and commerce are equated here as well. Society must free itself from the bondage of the capitalistic economy, and then the existence of the Jews as Jews will automatically come to an end; as society emancipates itself in this way, the Jewish question will be solved at the same time. Or, in Marx's formulation, "The *social* emancipation of the Jew is the *emancipation of society from Judaism*" (ibid., 40).

It cannot be our task here to deal with the absurdity of these formulations, which for the most part Marxist literature adopted without any modifications and indeed frequently with a sense that these were brilliant insights. By way of illustrating the dangerous associations that Marx's formulations were capable of arousing we shall reproduce a few more of his statements:

> We discern in Judaism, therefore, a universal *antisocial* element. . . . The Jew has emancipated himself in a Jewish manner, not only by acquiring the power of money, but also because *money* had become, through him and also apart from him, a world power, while the practical Jewish spirit has become the practical spirit of the Christian nations. The Jews have emancipated themselves in so far as the Christians have become Jews. . . . Money is the jealous God of Israel, beside which no other god may exist. . . . The bill of exchange is the real god of the Jew. His god is only an illusory bill of exchange. . . . The *chimerical* nationality of the Jew is the nationality of the trader, and above all of the financier. The law, without basis or reason, of the Jew is only the religious caricature of morality and right in general, without basis or reason; the purely *formal* rites with which the world of self-interest encircles itself. . . . From the beginning, the Christian was the theorizing Jew; consequently, the Jew is the practical Christian. And the practical Christian has become a Jew again. . . . The tenacity of the Jew is to be explained, not by his religion, but rather by the human basis of his religion—practical need and egoism. (Ibid., 34–39)

By way of excusing this one may point out that these are the formulations of a twenty-six-year-old and thus perhaps those of an immature young man. However, these statements were repeatedly reprinted and Marx never disowned them but repeated them in private and public statements—though not in his major works, where he takes only an occasional passing shot at the Jews.

As Silberner has remarked (p. 133), Marx says of the trading nations of the ancient world that they lived only in its intermundane space, like the god of Epicurus "or like the Jews in the pores of Polish society."

Here he conjures up the image of the Jews as parasites that recurs repeatedly in the early socialist literature. We shall have more to say about this in a later context (chap. 9). The argument of the Jews' bad racial character also appears in the literature with increasing frequency. The ambivalent attitude of other Jewish socialists, such as Lassalle, and the attitude of the later socialist movements and organizations of Jewish leaders will be discussed at a later point as well.

Concerning Karl Marx's attitude toward Judaism, cf. also (about Mehring, Vorländer, and others) Werner Blumenberg's balanced judgment in his book *Karl Marx in Selbstzeugnissen und Bilddokumenten* (Hamburg, 1962), 57ff. as well as Hans Lamm, *Karl Marx und das Judentum* (Munich, 1969) and R. S. Wistrich, "Karl Marx and the Jewish Question," *Soviet Jewish Affairs* 4, no. 1 (1974): 53–60.

An exceptional case is the later Moses Hess, who published the book *Rom und Jerusalem* in 1862, when he was fifty. By virtue of this book Hess became the most far-reaching forerunner of political Zionism and socialistic Zionism. We shall have more to say about him in chap. 8. On the other hand, the younger Hess had an ambivalent attitude toward Judaism, and at the time of his close collaboration with Marx he disparaged it and was hostile to it. E. Silberner, whose comprehensive biography of Hess (*Moses Hess: Geschichte seines Lebens* [Leiden, 1966]) is my main source, rightly points out that Marx's views in his essay "Über das Geldwesen" (written shortly before the abovementioned review of Bauer's remarks but not published until somewhat later) were influenced by Hess, his co-worker (1843–44) in the editorial office of the *Deutsch-Französische Jahrbücher*. For Hess the capitalistic social order of his time turns into a social animal world in which humans appear as out-and-out egotists, beasts of prey, and bloodsuckers. As for Feuerbach, so for Hess, Judaism and Christianity contributed a great deal to this condition. Here money is equated with "social *blood*" (what a dangerous equation!), and this leads Hess to formulations compared with which Marx's sound almost gentle. "Money," writes Hess,

> is the *social* blood, but the shed, the *spilled* blood. The *Jews*, who in the natural history of the social animal world had the *world-historical* assignment to bring out the *beast of prey* in mankind, have now finally completed their *professional duty*. The mystery of Judaism and Christianity has been revealed in the modern *Judeo-Christian shopkeepers' world*. The mystery of the *blood of Christ* as well as that of the *ancient Jewish worship of blood* appear here completely unveiled as the mystery of the *beast of prey*. In ancient Judaism the blood cult was only *prototypical;* in *medieval Christianity* it was realized *theoretically, idealistically, logically,* i.e., people really consumed the shed, *spilled blood of mankind,* but only in *imagination the blood of the God-man.* In the modern Judeo-Christian world of shopkeepers this penchant and proneness finally no longer appear *symbolically or mystically* but quite *prosaically.* (Quoted after Silberner, *Hess,* 189)

In the age of materialism, when people no longer content themselves with the celestial food, "the sacred sleight of hand [becomes] profane and the heavenly deception an earthly one." The social animal world of capitalism is coming to an end and will be succeeded, peacefully or violently, by a new era of human community.

What a tangled path through philosophies, mystical speculations, dangerous equations of images and realities, rejection and recognition, a Jew had to take before he attained to self-knowledge and recognized his integration into the past and the future of his people!

Cf. also Martin Buber in *Israel und Palästina* ([Munich, 1968], 118ff.) and his introduction to the Hebrew edition of Hess's Jewish and Zionist writings ([Jerusalem, 1954], 16ff.). In Hess's early writings we already find the designation of the Jews as a "ferment" (a word frequently encountered in the later literature with an antithetical valuation) as well as the image of the "Jewish specter" which was later creatively revalued by Pinsker. Cf. also Zeev Levy (Hebr.) in *Yalkut Moreshet* 1:95ff., esp. 102ff., and R. S. Wistrich, *Revolutionary Jews from Marx to Trotzki* (New York, 1976).

SCHOPENHAUER: Concerning his negative attitude toward Judaism, cf. I. Unna's article "Schopenhauers Stellung zum Judentum" in the Josef Wohlgemuth Festschrift (Frankfurt, 1928), 103–19.

ANTI-JEWISH MOVEMENTS AND RIOTS: We shall discuss the ideological background of   228f.
these movements and events in chaps. 6 and 9 and the reaction of the Jews to these
phenomena in chaps. 7 and 8. A detailed discussion of events before 1850 may be
found in Eleonore Sterling's book *Er ist wie Du: Aus der Frühgeschichte des Antisemitismus in Deutschland (1815–1850)* (Munich, 1956). The second revised edition
of this book, which I have used, published under the title *Judenhass: Die Anfänge des
politischen Antisemitismus in Deutschland (1815–1850)* (Frankfurt, 1969), contains
on pp. 171–74 a chronological list of the "violent acts committed against Jews
between 1800 and 1850."

The *"Hepp-Hepp Riots"* of 1819 merit separate investigation because they furnish
particularly graphic evidence of the interweaving of local occasions and general
sociopolitical conditions with historical traditions and had radical and far-reaching
consequences for Jews and Christians.

The latest presentation, one that is based on detailed research in archives and
libraries and takes cognizance of earlier literature on the subject, is Jacob Katz's "The
Hep-Hep Riots in Germany of 1819" (Hebr., with English synopsis), in *Zion* 38
(1973): 62–115 and ii–v. I am in agreement with all the essential points in this article.
Other particularly revealing presentations are by Eleonore Sterling—in the abovementioned book and in her article "Anti-Jewish Riots in Germany in 1819: A Displacement of Social Protest," *Historia Judaica* 12 (1950): 105–42. I believe, as does
Jacob Katz, that the explanation indicated in the subtitle is too one-sided and
exaggerated. Detailed accounts, quotations, and well-considered conclusions may be
found in Utz Jeggle, *Judendörfer in Württemberg* (Tübingen, 1969), 90–98. There
are, of course, more or less detailed accounts in Graetz (11:354–62) and Dubnow
(9:22–26), and in *Neueste Geschichte des jüdischen Volkes* (Berlin, 1920), 2:15–19.
Cf. also M. Philippson, *Neueste Geschichte des jüdischen Volkes* 16 (Frankfurt, 1922),
106ff.; regional histories like Stephan Schwarz, *Die Juden in Bayern im Wandel der
Zeiten* (Munich, 1963), 216–19; and B. Rosenthal, *Heimatgeschichte der badischen
Juden* (Bühl, 1927), 249ff. Cf. also the well-known Jewish encyclopedias (*JL* 2:1954;
EJJ 8:330ff., including a map of the most important places affected by the riots). Of
the general historians, only H. Treitschke deals with the subject, in *Deutsche
Geschichte im Neunzehnten Jahrhundert*, new ed. (Leipzig, 1927), 2:417–29,
528–31.

All presentations and the contemporary accounts (published in the original German by Katz, 115–19) reveal that the riots began in Würzburg on 3 August 1819 and
during the next two months spread all over Germany, with offshoots as far as Prague,
Graz, Vienna, and Cracow in the East and Copenhagen and Helsinki in the North. In
the West they did not spread beyond the Rhine. As already mentioned, these riots
often started with some local clash but immediately assumed a more general
character. The riots were especially severe in the cities and villages of Bavaria and
Baden with their relatively large Jewish rural populations, but they also occur in the
free cities of Frankfurt and Hamburg. Jewish houses were broken into, merchandise
was thrown into the street, and synagogues were set on fire. In general the perpetrators belonged to the lower levels of society—indebted peasants (there were crop
failures in 1816 and 1817), journeymen, unemployed persons, rabble. But behind
these there stood—at least with "understanding" approval, if not with intellectual or
alcohol-providing encouragement—large parts of the population. They saw to it that
in the reports of the authorities and the press the life-style and conduct of the Jews as
usurious financiers, unfair competitors, etc., were given as the real reasons and that
in official investigations hardly anyone was willing to appear as a witness and give
evidence against the culprits. The police often watched without taking any action,
and thus the military frequently had to be called in. The rulers did so because it was
in their interest to suppress riots, which might also turn against other adversaries,

undermining the authority of the state and its rulers. In addition to the interests that often bound the rulers to the Jews, their intervention was surely also based on fear that the social tension might discharge against them, as actually happened in 1830 and 1848. It was, after all, the era of the struggle of libertarian liberal and national endeavors against the old, restored and restoring forces that had found their expression in the Metternich system.

Nevertheless, E. Sterling goes too far (and here I agree with J. Katz) when she interprets these riots as a transfer of general social discontent to the Jews. (Similarly, at a later date Eva Reichmann interpreted anti-Semitism as a "flight into hatred".)

Putting it more precisely, it is not *only* a displacement. Any disgruntlement, be it the personal or the social kind, turns first against the closest persons who are weaker, unprotected, or less protected. Parents take it out on children, employers on subordinates, discontented social groups on easily attackable groups. In this spirit Heine (whose soul reflected and whose writings expressed everything that stirred his times; we shall discuss this in detail later) wrote after the Hamburg Jewish riots of 1830: "One Jew said to another: I was too weak. This statement suggests itself as a motto for a history of the Jews" (*Werke*, Insel ed., 10:242f.). But the Jews were, in point of fact, the visible exponents of the new liberal-capitalistic system of which many people took a dim view and which they opposed because it impaired their interests as they saw them. But in the case of the Jews there was always added the old image with its religious coloration as well as the age-old attendant demonic notions and pent-up feelings of hatred that were apt to be constantly rekindled and fanned into rebellion by envy of the economic position of the Jews. According to the author of the first detailed newspaper report about the Würzburg riots (*Frankfurter Journal*, 7 August 1819), they were caused by the fact that there had long been "an obscure discontent with the significant increase in local Jewry" and that "it finally turned into a full uprising against them, like the eruption of a volcano." He regrets the incidents, "which fill the heart of any humanitarian with grief," but he finds that "on the other hand, it is only too true that the Jews in Germany are in every respect better off than the Christians. They do not work and do not want to work, get hold of all trade, and since they disregard any abuse and degradation, they do manage to sell their merchandise dirt cheap, while the honorable Christian merchant sits in his shop without sustenance" (Katz, 113). On the other hand, a proclamation (which E. Sterling publishes as an appendix to her book, p. 171, after an "official copy") admonishes the "brothers in Christ" to arm themselves with courage and strength against the "foes of our faith." According to this proclamation, it is time to suppress the race of Christ-Killers so they will not become "rulers over you and your descendants." The power still is in Christian hands; "therefore let us now execute the judgment which they have passed on themselves and in accordance with which they have cried 'Let His blood come over us and our children!'" Baptized Jews are not to be exempted from the vengeance: "These Jews who are living among us and spreading like rapacious locusts . . . they are the children of those who once cried 'Crucify, crucify! Now for vengeance! Hepp, hepp, hepp shall be our battlecry!!! Death and destruction to all Jews. You must flee or die."

228   THE "HEPP HEPP" CRY (THE WORD AND THE MEANING): All the riots and the reports about them have in common the cry "Hepp-Hepp!" ("Hep-Hep!"; "Heb-Heb!" in the dialect of Bavaria and Baden Württemberg). The cry rhymes with "Jude verreck!" (Croak, Jew!) and was also used with other additions, such as the one cited above or this one: "Jud, Jud, Jud! Hepp, hepp, hepp! Steck die Nas in die Wasserschlepp!" (after Hanns Heinz Ewers in W. Sombart, *Judentaufen* [Munich, 1912], 36).

Various explanations have been given of "Hepp, Hepp" (*JL* 2:1546): (1) An abbreviation of *Hebräer*, with reference to a similar form in Southern Germany and Italy (according to Kluge). (2) Formed from the first letters of *Hierosolyma est perdita* (Jerusalem is lost); this explanation already appears in early reports and has been adopted by many historians and writers. (3) A call to billy goats in Franconia that was derogatorily applied to Jews on account of their goatees; this explanation may be found in Grimm. Other explanations in early reports make little sense (J. Katz, p. 74, A 58). It may be regarded as certain that the third explanation is the right one; it was already adopted by Philippson (1:117). In his address to the fifth general assembly of the World Jewish Congress in 1966 (published in Rolf Vogel, ed., *Deutschlands Weg nach Israel* [Stuttgart, 1967], 253) Salo Baron rightly remarks that this goat call was applied to the Jews "because of their connection with goats, which resemble the devil." We have already mentioned this connection (Part 2, pp. 529f.) in our discussion of the caricature of the *Judensau*. Cf. also Max Grünewald in *JL* 1:739: "In some parts of Southern Germany where, as in England, every profession had its specific form of beard, the so-called goatee was the sign of a rabbi or a teacher ("Gaisrebbele"—the origin, according to Grimm, of Hep Hep!)." (For a similar goat call with which the menacing addition "Jude verreck!" rhymes even better, cf. Wilhelm Busch's cartoon story *Max und Moritz:* "He, heraus! du Ziegen-Böck! Schneider, Schneider, meck, meck, meck!") It is etymologically absurd to assume that a popular term of abuse could have been an abreviation of a Latin sentence that was completely unknown in such a context. At the very least a similar term would have had to be known earlier, perhaps in the Age of Humanism. Why this explanation nevertheless was disseminated by the press and in the literature almost instantly and was even adopted by historians bears investigating. Katz (p. 103) is probably justified in seeing an explanation in the endeavor to integrate the locally or socially conditioned riots against the Jews into the historical tradition. Thus they were related to earlier events in Jewish history that seemed similar—the persecutions during the Crusades and at the time of the destruction of the Second Temple—and so the explanation involving *Hierosolyma est perdita* arose two weeks after the Würzburg tumults. Since it met a need and lent a deeper meaning to the vulgar outrages, it was evidently adopted by public opinion. In his *Judendörfer in Württemberg*, Utz Jeggle gives other interesting details on the basis of contemporary printed and archival sources. In one village, Jagstberg, a Jew was pursued with the words "Heave the Jew!" He fled to the mayor, but the latter was afraid and left him in the lurch, whereupon the persecutors beat the Jew with their fists. Then the mayor's mother, who obviously had more courage than her son, helped the Jew escape. As Katz has pointed out, the term "Hepp-Hepp" was evidently not used for the first time on that occasion but only applied in a particularly hostile manner and disseminated beyond Southern Germany. This is evidenced by the reports; they mention that term as a well-known bit of raillery and speak of the "tense Zeitgeist" against the Jews that had now led to violence (Jeggle, pp. 90f., after the newspaper *Schwäbische Kronik*).

In my opinion, the added rhymed curse "Jude verreck!" has received insufficient attention in the literature. For one thing, this is in keeping with the derivation of the word from a little-respected animal that was associated or identified with the devil, and for another, it gives brutal expression to hatred and shifts the Jews, as an image and in actuality, from the human sphere to that of a subhuman animal, as the Nazis did to a gruesome extent a hundred years later. The verb *verrecken*, to croak, was used as a threat beyond the abusive jingle as well. In the Württemberg village Berlichingen, for example (Jeggle, p. 91), "Hepp Seligmann" was yelled at Isaac Seligmann's son, and this was followed by the threat, "Tomorrow several of us will get together and then we'll beat you till you croak!" In Ingelfingen, a village with no Jews, a sheet of paper with this threat was found in early September 1819: "Nächsten Samstag als den 11. dieses Monats wird geliefert werden/ Eine grosse Judenschlacht/ wornach sich jeder Hepp richten kann/ Jud Hepp Hepp/ Am Samstag musst verreck"

(Next Sunday, the 11th of this month, a big battle will be fought against the Jews, and every Hepp can be guided by this. Jew hepp hepp, on Saturday you've got to croak.) A Jew with a beard and knapsack is depicted under this text, and the caption reads "Die Himmelfahrt eines Hepp" (The Ascension of a Hepp).

The riots of 1819 manifested the distance between Jews and Christians as well as the desire of the surrounding world to maintain this distance and make it impossible for the Jews to rise from the sphere of contempt. They left a profound impression on many Jews and probably affected those Jews most strongly who were advanced in their assimilation to the world around them and thus were particularly sensitive about attacks on their honor. The riots impelled some young intellectuals to form in November 1819 an association "for the improvement of the situation of the Jews" which a year and a half later gave rise to the "Verein für Cultur und Wissenschaft der Juden" (cf. Adolf Strodtmann, *H. Heine's Leben und Werke* [Berlin, 1867], 245; Hanns Günther Reissner, *Eduard Gans* [Tübingen, 1965], 49ff.). According to his own account, the interpretation *Hierosolyma est perdita* impelled the (half-Jewish) historian of religion Joseph Salvador (1796–1873) to embrace Judaism fully and occupy himself with its history. His books inspired contemporaries like Moses Hess and H. Graetz. Concerning this, cf. H. Reinhold, "Joseph Salvador: His Life and Views" (Hebr. with Eng. synopsis), in *Zion* 9 (1944): 109ff., esp. 117.

6

Modern Anti-Semitism and Its Place in the History of the Jewish Question

Prefatory Note: I published the first part of this chapter in October 1958 under the title "Der moderne Antisemitismus und seine Bedeutung für die Judenfrage" in *Vierteljahrshefte für Zeitgeschichte* 6:340–60 (but not including the rest, which was already finished in draft form). An English version entitled "Modern Anti-Semitism and Its Place in the History of the Jewish Question" appeared in *Between East and West: Essays Dedicated to the Memory of Bela Horovitz*, ed. A. Altmann (London, 1958), 164–93. I spoke on the same subject in July 1957 at the Second World Congress for the Science of Judaism, and my talk was published in Hebrew and English in *Yad Vashem Studies on the European Jewish Catastrophe and Resistance*, vol. 3 (Jerusalem, 1959). These publications were widely quoted in the subsequent literature, and their research results, presentations, and theses were generally accepted. In the revised version of my remarks that is published here I have, wherever I deemed it necessary, made use of the recent literature to the extent that it came to my attention (nowadays no one can claim to be acquainted with everything that is published), particularly in my notes. I also found oral and written statements made in conversations and at symposia useful. In all essential respects, however, I have retained the original text of my earlier publications.

"ANTI-SEMITISM," THE WORD AND THE CONCEPT: Concerning the origin of such political concepts, cf. the introduction to my article (referred to in the notes to chap. 8, Part 2, p. 669) on "Zionism," as well as R. Köbner, "Zur Begriffsbildung der Kulturgeschichte," *Historische Zeitschrift* 149 (see the remarks about the coining of the word *Sozialismus* on p. 160, n. 2). As far as the names of political movements are concerned, in general three stages may be noted: (a) the creation of the concept; the authorship and the first use are often difficult to determine and thus debatable; (b) the gradual adoption of the concept, often initially by opponents (e.g., the names *Les Gueux* for the rebels in the Dutch war of independence or *Marranos* for the Spanish crypto-Jews, and the use of the word *capitalism* by the socialists); (c) the recognition as an official name of a movement that eventually is known only by that name. Afterward the name is often transferred to precursors or similar movements in earlier times—a process that, in my opinion, ought to be rejected as anachronistic. One should therefore not speak of anti-Semitism in antiquity, in the Middle Ages, etc., but of hatred of the Jews, anti-Jewish movements, etc., and use "anti-Semitism" only for the movement that called itself by that name—certainly not for movements that were active *before* the creation of the concept. Cf. also Eduard König, *Das antisemitische Hauptdogma* (Bonn, 1914).

One must differentiate among these three stages in the history of the word *anti-Semitism* as well: (a) the coining of the word; (b) its first use as a political concept; (c) its general adoption and extension beyond its original meaning. I (and many others

230f.

before and after me) regard Wilhelm Marr (born in 1819 at Magdeburg, died in 1904 in Hamburg) as the originator of the concept. After the publication of my articles the Hebrew writer and Nobel laureate Shmuel Yosef Agnon (1888–1970) drew my attention, in one of our numerous conversations, to an earlier use of the word, one that has to my knowledge not been mentioned anywhere. He referred me to the article about anti-Semitism in the Hebrew encyclopedia *Ozar Yisrael*, edited by Jehuda Eisenstadt, (London, 5684/1924), 2:130ff. There we read, after a brief survey of the origin and use of the word *Semites* (which we shall discuss later): "The compound anti-Semitism appears to have been used first by Steinschneider, who challenged Renan on account of his 'anti-Semitic prejudices' [i.e., his derogation of the "Semites" as a race]. But Steinschneider, too, did not use the word as a special concept but only in a general way, as one expresses many other concepts, such as 'anti-capitalistic' to designate those who fight against the rich. As an independent concept, however, the word is not encountered until the end of 1879, when the Antisemites' League was founded (according to a correspondent's report in the *Allgemeine Zeitung des Judentums*, October 19, 1879)."

The abovementioned quotation as the first known use of the word is found in the periodical *Hamaskir: Hebräische Bibliographie. Blätter für neuere und ältere Literatur des Judentums* 3 (Berlin, 1860), 16, of Moritz Steinschneider (1816–1907), the famous Jewish scholar and bibliographer. There Steinschneider notes and discusses an article by the philologist and philosopher Heymann Steinthal (1823–1900) in the *Zeitschrift für Völkerpsychologie und Sprachwissenschaft* 1:328, which Steinthal edited together with his brother-in-law, the philosopher and ethnopsychologist Moritz Lazarus (1824–1903). In this essay, which was reprinted by G. Karpeles in his collection of Steinthal's addresses and essays, *Über Juden und Judentum* ([Berlin, 1918], 91ff.), Steinthal sharply and ironically polemicizes against E. Renan's article "Nouvelles considérations sur le caractère général des peuples sémitiques, et en particulier sur leur tendance au monothéisme" (published in the *Journal Asiatique*, 1859, and as a pamphlet). Steinthal regards Renan's theses about the inferiority of the Semitic peoples and their monotheistic religion (cf. Part 1, pp. 233f. and Part 2, pp. 598f.) as superficial, misleading generations despite his seemingly great erudition and his always "captivating *esprit*." Part of Steinthal's essay takes the form of a Socratic dialogue between him and a philosopher: "Hm, I said; you yourself seem to be infected by sterile Semitism. But I have two things to tell you in Renan's name. First, monotheism was really not a boon for mankind for which we ought to be grateful to the Semites. . . . It is true that the Jews have made extraordinary contributions to the progress of mankind, but they impeded political progress in that a people spread over the earth without having any fatherland" (p. 92).

With his special skill in making bibliographically pregnant condensations Steinschneider summarizes Steinthal's extensive polemic in the following two sentences: "With his characteristic incisiveness the critic demonstrates the contradictions in Renan's basic views and their unfruitfulness for scholarship and research. The more Renan's brilliant dialectic and stylistic talent captivates the readers, the more necessary it is to expose the consequences—or, more accurately, inconsequences—of his *anti-Semitic prejudices,* which finally could not remain without a specific addition." It is not quite clear what is meant by "specific addition"; apparently it is the characterization of the Jewish people that Steinthal presents as an advocate of Renan: "Here, among this crudely sensual, intensely lustful, vulgarly voluptuous people, this egotistic, violent, perfidious tribe, among these people without any sensitivity who have never separated self-interest from morality, among these Arabs, these Jews, the holiest man among whom 'ne se fait scrupule de commettre des crimes atroces pour arriver à ses fins'—here a doctrine is supposed to have been achieved in late antiquity, centuries before philosophy had any inkling of it, which mankind, in adopting it, recognized as 'la plus avancée.'" It is possible that the reference was to Renan's strange admonition that "critics should guard well against the temptation to apply laws to the development of the Semitic race that apply to other, entirely different families."

These passages reveal that the words *Semitism* and *anti-Semitic* did not yet have an outright political character. They do, however, designate the negative qualities and dispositions that are ascribed to an entire race. In Renan's view, the "instinct" of the Semitic peoples, and not a moral will, gave rise to a kind of monotheism. His attitude toward "Semitism" is a decidedly negative one and his characterization is sharply derogatory; he is an opponent of "Semitism." That is why Steinschneider calls Renan's outlook "anti-Semitic." He senses, and indicates in his designation, that Renan's judgments are not rooted in objective, scientific research and insights, but that they are in reality only traditional prejudgments in scientific guise, that everything negative is emphasized and the positive elements are admitted grudgingly and immediately devalued with qualifications of all kinds. Thus Renan's remarks contain all the elements that may be found in the later political, militant version of the word.

Thus far it has not been possible to establish when the word passed from occasional scholarly and literary usage into the general political vocabulary, for there is no thorough research based on contemporary sources, particularly journal articles. The word is not yet contained in Wilhelm Marr's pamphlet *Der Sieg des Judenthums über das Germanenthum, vom nicht konfessionellen Standpunkt aus betrachtet,* the first edition of which appeared in mid-March 1879 and which went through twelve more printings that same year. Marr speaks of "Semites," "The Semitic people," and "Semitism," as well as of the ethnic and racial contrast to the Germanic people; but *anti-Semitic* and *anti-Semitism,* words that would be logical in such a context, do not appear. As far as I know, Marr never claimed to have coined the word or used it for the first time—either in the published booklets that have come to my attention or in Marr's unpublished memoirs in the State Archives in Hamburg, which I have examined in microfilm. However, the word seems to have come into use without being registered as a new word in connection with the broadsides and press reports pro and contra Marr that his agitation inspired, and of course also in connection with the polemics concerning Treitschke's *Ein Wort über unser Judentum* (from November 1879 on) and the speaking campaign of the court preacher Adolf Stoecker against Judaism (from September 1879) and for his Christian-Social party. The first official use that I was able to establish was the founding of the "Antisemitenliga" by Wilhelm Marr (or with his active participation) in late 1879. The *Allgemeine Zeitung des Judentums* (43, no. 46, 11 November 1879, p. 724) printed this "private report" from Berlin dated 28 October 1879: "The 'Antisemites' League' began an activity of sorts by hiring a number of thugs who handed out leaflets at busy streetcorners and then quickly disappeared. . . . The whole thing is so ridiculous that its existence will probably soon vanish from the scene." Treitschke also used the word in his first article on the Jewish question ("Unsere Ansichten," dated 15 November 1879) in the November issue of the monthly *Preussische Jahrbücher,* of which he was the editor. (Its most important part later formed the beginning of his pamphlet *Ein Wort über unser Judentum;* the preface is dated 15 January 1880.) On page 1 of this booklet we read: "Anti-Semitic associations are being formed. The 'Jewish question' is being discussed at heated meetings, and a host of anti-Jewish polemics are flooding the book market. There are too much dirt and brutality in these goings-on, and one cannot help but feel disgusted when one notices that many of those incendiary writings evidently are from the pens of Jews. . . ." This seems to be an allusion to Wilhelm Marr, whom contemporaries as well as historians down to recent times regarded as a baptized Jew or descendant of Jews, probably without justification. Marr's memoirs as well as archival genealogical research (published by Fritz Zschaek in the anti-Semitic periodical *Weltkampf*, no. 2 [1944], 94ff. under the title "War Wilhelm Marr ein Jude?") reveal that while Marr was twice unhappily married to half-Jewish women, once "too happily" (in his own words) to a Jewish woman, and finally to a non-Jew, he had no Jewish ancestors. What he knew about Jews, the good and bad things he had learned about them, came from his marriages, his experiences as a writer who could not really get established in journalism, and perhaps also his membership in the Young German movement in Switzerland about which he published a "boastful anti-liberal exposé" ([Leipzig, 1846], 364 pp.) after his deportation (cf. Barnikol in *Religion in Geschichte und Gegenwart* 3:2023f.). He had already concerned himself with the Jewish question in a booklet self-published in Hamburg in 1862, but this work did not attract much attention. In 1880 he published at Chemnitz (as a sequel to his Bern broadside of 1879 and as no. 1 of a projected series of *Antisemitische Hefte*) a pamphlet entitled *Der Judenkrieg, seine Fehler und wie er zu organisieren ist. Zweiter Teil von: Der Sieg des Judenthums über das Germanenthum.** In this polemic, which views the Jewish question even more drastically as a question of race, the terms "Semitism," "anti-Semites," "anti-Semitic party," "anti-Semitic movement," "anti-Semitic writings," and "Antisemites' League" are used as a matter of course, though not the more abstract word "anti-Semitism." In 1880 the secondary-school teacher Bernhard Förster (the brother-in-law of Friedrich Nietzsche, who despised him) and the first lieutenant Max Liebermann circulated the so-called "Antisemites' Petition," which bore 225,000 signatures and was debated in the Prussian House of Deputies on 20 and 22 November 1898 on the basis of an interpellation by the Progressive Party under Eugen Richter. (In March 1880 this petition was submitted to Chancellor Bismarck, but he made no response.) Thus this word increasingly became a term and a concept commonly used for political actions against the Jews.

As Dühring had done, Hitler's Rassenpolitisches Amt later rejected the use of this word to avoid giving offense to the Nazis' Arabic allies. In a "Stellungnahme des Rassenpolitischen Amts zur Araberfrage" dated Jan. 15, 1943, which achieved (limited) publication as "confidential information" from the Parteikanzlei (II B 4, Beitrag 7), the Jews are described as "an inharmonious racial mixture that should be clearly differentiated from the Near Eastern and Eastern nations, including the peoples of the Near East who speak a Semitic language." Accordingly, "the expression 'anti-Semitism,' which has been used in Europe for decades, is incorrect, since that movement is exclusively directed against the Jews, a corrosive influence on nations, but not against the other peoples with a Semitic language, who have also had an anti-Jewish orientation since olden times. . . ." Cf., in addition to the abovementioned writings, Kurt Wawrzinek, *Die Entstehung der deutschen Antisemitenpartei 1873–1890* (Berlin, 1927); Paul Massing, *Rehearsal for Destruction* (New York, 1949); Theodor Fritsch, *Handbuch der Judenfrage* (Leipzig, 1937); A. Valentin, *Antisemitism, Historically and Critically Examined* (New York, 1936); "Antisemitism" in *JL* 1, *EJ* 2, *EJJ* 3; James Parkes and W. Gurian, "Antisemitism in Modern Germany," in *Essays on Antisemitism*, ed. K. S. Pinson (New York, 1946), 218ff.; Peter G. J. Pulzer, *The Rise of Political Antisemitism in Germany and Austria* (New York, 1964); Stephan Lehr, *Antisemitismus—religiöse Motive im sozialen Vorurteil* (Munich, 1974). The most important polemics surrounding Treitschke's articles in the *Preussische Jahrbücher* are now readily available in the good collection *Der Berliner Antisemitismusstreit*, ed. Walter Boehlich (Frankfurt, 1965) (henceforth cited as Boehlich); cf. also Boehlich's balanced afterword and his bibliography of the polemics

---

*This pamphlet does not seem to have sold very well. On the title page of part of the first printing the words "Chemnitz 1880, Verlag Ernst Schmeitzner" are blotted out by a sticker that reads "Leipzig, Verlag von Theodor Fritsch, 1885."

that appeared at that time. (Further literature on this subject will be listed in pertinent places.)

RACIAL THEORY: The word *Rasse* (Spanish *raza*, Italian *razza*, French *race*) entered   231ff. the English language, via the Italian (fourteenth century) and the French (fifteenth century), in the sixteenth, and the German language in the seventeenth century. The root of this word has not been established with certainty. In English the word "race" is often used synonymously with "people" and "nation." In German it remained a foreign word and retained its French spelling *(Race)* until the late nineteenth century, although in some instances it appeared as *Rasse* before that time, e.g., in the writings of Friedrich Schiller. At first it was applied only to groups of plants and animals. Johann Gottfried Herder still refused to apply this "ignoble word" to humans. Cf. Wilhelm Schmidt, *Rassen und Völker in Vorgeschichte und Geschichte des Abendlandes* (Lucerne, 1946). Concerning the etymology, cf., in addition to the Oxford and Webster dictionaries, Kluge and Goetze, *Etymologisches Wörterbuch der deutschen Sprache.* Cf. also *HE* 10:563. In modern Hebrew the word *geza* ("tribe") is used. Biblical and Talmudic Hebrew has no word for it, but speaks only of peoples *(am, goi, umah)* or generations *(dor).*

GOBINEAU: In addition to the work itself, I have drawn on E. Cassirer's presentation   231f. and evaluation in his book *The Myth of the State* (New Haven, 1946). Gobineau's work was translated into German by L. Schemann *(Versuch über die Ungleichheit der Menschenrassen,* 4 vols. [Munich, 1898–1901, 1922]). Cf. also Otto Hintze, "Rasse und Nationalität und ihre Bedeutung für die Geschichte," in *Historische und politische Aufsätze* (1918), 4:160ff.; Ludwig Schemann, *Die Rasse in den Geisteswissenschaften* (3 vols. [Munich, 1928–31], as well as his biography and other writings about Gobineau). Here we must draw a basic distinction between anthropological and ethnological investigations of the nature, the history, and the special characteristics of ethnic communal formations on the one hand and the history of philosophical-political theories that sail under the name *Rassenkunde* (racial theory) and the like on the other. The anthropological questions can be given only cursory treatment here. For the history of the Jewish question the racial theories interest us as an expression of the image of the Jew in the mind of the surrounding world and in their effects on the behavior of that world toward the Jews.

Gobineau had forerunners, of course. The idea of race had entered the discussions of the Jewish question in one form or another as an additional element, viewed emotionally or rationally. It had done so since the problem of the Marranos in Spain (cf. Part 1, p. 136) and since the Romantic movement at the end of the eighteenth century. Gobineau, however, marked the beginning of modes of thinking and belief that made "race" the only, or most important, driving force in human events. With his theory Gobineau influenced virtually all theoreticians of race, and it is relatively unimportant whether or not they read and cited his books. Theories that are fundamental in nature influence even people who do not read books; how many of those who call themselves Marxists have read a major work of Marx?

Concerning the way in which the theory of race entered historiography from Voltaire to Taine and Renan as a constant, cf. Eduard Fueter, *Geschichte der neueren Historiographie,* Munich 1925, pp. 362, 584, 591. Regarding Gobineau's amicable relationship with Alexis de Tocqueville, who rejected his racial theory, cf. Melville Richter, "Der Begriff der Rasse: Aus dem Briefwechsel zwischen Tocqueville und Gobineau," in *Der Monat* 11, no. 121 (October 1958): 33–49. Concerning his alleged influence on Nietzsche, cf. Walter Kaufmann, *Nietzsche,* (New York, 1968), 296f. and the literature cited there. Kaufmann justifies Schemann's and Westernhagen's view *(Nietzsche, Juden, Antijuden* [Weimar, 1936]) that in their conception of the racial principle Nietzsche and Gobineau were actually antipodes. (For any sources of my quotations not given in the text, see my abovementioned article on modern anti-Semitism.)

In one's concern with the critical evaluation of Gobineau's racial theory and its generally deleterious influence on the humanities, politics, and the Jewish question one should not disregard Gobineau's literary writings, particularly his magnificent, lively series of dramatic scenes *The Renaissance*, first published in 1877 and since then frequently reprinted in many languages.

232f.   SOLE AUTHORITY OF RACE: The quotation is from Gobineau's *Essai sur l'inégalité des races humaines* 2, 548. Cf. also the dedication of the first edition (1853) to George V, King of Hanover (German translation 1898), xii: "That is when one conclusion after another filled me with the absolute certainty that the question of race dominates all other problems of history and provides the key to them, and that the inequality of the races whose consolidation forms a nation can serve as an explanation for the entire chain of national destinies." In the abovementioned article about Tocqueville and Gobineau, M. Richter remarks that this theory constitutes "a radical abandonment of the ethical ideas and political achievements of the 18th century. . . . His [Gobineau's] sorrow at the decline of his class may have caused him to view the European society of the 19th century as sterile and decadent. . . . In his search for the one moving force of history he embraced the way of thinking characteristic of the despised 18th century; causal monism." It was not his aim to have a direct influence on politics, but to have an educative effect by presenting the decline of peoples as the consequence of bad racial mixtures. "It did not behoove me," he wrote in the abovementioned dedication, "and I did not intend to leave the pure regions of scientific discussion to descend to the level of contemporary polemics. . . . My calculations involve only a succession of centuries. In short, I practice intellectual geology."

233f.   ANTHROPOLOGY AND LINGUISTICS: Concerning the status and development of early anthropology and linguistics and their position on the racial question, particularly since the eighteenth century and in the British colonies and the United States of America, cf. Thomas F. Gossett, *Race: The History of an Idea in America* (New York, 1970), esp. chaps. 1–8.

233   FRIEDRICH MAX MÜLLER AND ARYAN RACIAL THEORY: In later life F. M. Müller abandoned his identification of languages and races, evidently under the impression of the deleterious racist, anti-Semitic exploitation of the Aryan theory. He said that "Aryan" was to him only a linguistic concept and had nothing to do with natural race. To him an ethnologist who spoke of an Aryan race, Aryan blood, Aryan eyes and hair was as great a sinner as a linguist who spoke of a dolichocephalic lexicon or a brachycephalic grammar. He had created his terminology for the classification of languages, and the ethnologists ought to create one of their own for the classification of skulls, hair, and blood (T. F. Gossett, *Race*, 125f.; Fritz Kahn, *Die Juden als Rasse und Kulturvolk* [Berlin, 1922], 25). In a similar vein, and even more trenchantly, the well-known anthropologist Felix von Luschan wrote in *Völker, Rassen, Sprachen* ([Berlin, 1922], 53f): "It is rather dubious to speak of an Aryan language . . . but it is totally inadmissible to speak of an Aryan race." He goes on to say that there has never been an Indo-European people, though it is possible to speak of an Indo-European language family.

233f.   RENAN'S EARLY WORK: In his *Histoire générale et système comparé des langues sémitiques. Ouvrage couronné par l'Institut* (Paris, 1855) and in other works Renan appears to have been directly influenced by his reading of Gobineau's work on race.

Cf. Ludwig Schemann, *Gobineaus Rassenwerk* (Stuttgart, 1910), 42ff. See also the quotation in my excursus about anti-Semitism, the word and the concept, in Part 2, pp. 593ff.

RENAN'S WARNING AGAINST PARALLELS WITH JEWISH CONTEMPORARIES: *Histoire*   233f. *générale*, p. vii: "Combien d'Israélites de nos jours, qui descendent en droite ligne des anciens habitants de la Palestine, n'ont rien du caractère sémitique, et ne sont plus que des hommes modernes, entraînés et assimilés par cette grande force supérieure aux races et destructive des originalités locales, qu'on appelle la civilisation!" He says that all his judgments refer to "Sémites purs" like the Arabs and Armenians. At the same time, however, like many other scholars before and after him, he transfers to the ancestors those qualities of his Jewish contemporaries that strike his attention, e.g., their alleged military incompetence: "L'infériorité militaire des Sémites tient a cette incapacité de tout discipline et de toute subordination. Pour se créer des armes régulières, ils furent obligés de recourir à des mercenaires: ainsi firent David, les Phéniciens, les Carthaginois, les Khalifes" (p. 14). How absurd these judgments, presented with the assurance of a scholar, sound in the light of subsequent experiences and particularly the reality of the State of Israel!

INFERIORITY OF THE SEMITIC RACE: *Histoire générale*, p. 4: "Ce serait pousser outre   233f. mesure le panthéisme en histoire que de mettre toutes les races sur un pied d'égalité. . . . Je suis donc le premier de reconnaître que la race sémitique comparée à la race indo-européenne, représente réellement une combinaison inférieure de la nature humaine."

RELIGION: *Histoire générale*, p. 15: "La religion . . . est pour le sémite une sorte de   233f. devoir spécial, qu n'a qu'un lien fort éloigné avec la morale de tous les jours."

PRE-"SCIENTIFIC" RACIAL IDEOLOGIES: Concerning attempts in the first half of the   234 19th century to exploit a primitive racial theory in an anti-Jewish spirit, cf. the abovementioned book by Eleonore Sterling, *Er ist wie Du. Aus der Frühgeschichte des Antisemitismus in Deutschland (1815–1850)* (Munich, 1956); new edition titled *Judenhass. Die Anfänge des politischen Antisemitismus in Deutschland (1815–1850)* (Stuttgart, 1969), esp. chap. 7 ("Die Germanomanie und der Früh-Antisemitismus"). There we read (1st ed., 140; new ed., 156): "In the writings of the physiognomists of the 18th and 19th centuries the Jews are either not mentioned at all or designated as members of the Caucasian race. The specific 'Asiatic, Oriental, South Syrian' racial difference of the 'Jewish race,' which is said to be basically different from the 'German or Germanic' one, is not a discovery of the physiologists but an invention of a large number of politicians, historians, theologians, and others. Specific notions of a 'Semitic' and 'Germanic' race may already be found in the historian Georg Kriegh (1848), the philologist and historian Heinrich Leo (1843), the psychologist Theodor Rohmer, one E. C. v. T. (who wrote in the *Neue Jahrbücher für Politik und Geschichte*, 1847), and the diplomat Friedrich Kölle. About the last-named Heine wrote in 1840 (Börne 4, *Werke*, Insel ed., 8:475), that "he was the most inveterate carper about race, and every third word of his is Germanic, Romance, and Semitic race!" In 1841 the Young German writer Karl Gutzkow (1811–78) spoke of the "national antipathy and attraction" between Jews and Christians and describes the aversion to the Jews as a "physical-moral idiosyncracy which is as hard to combat as the antipathy that people have to blood or insects." Thus that writer already came close to doubting, like the Nazis after him, that the Jews are human beings. In 1839 the Hegelian Arnold Ruge was able to liken the Jews to "maggots in the cheese of Christianity." Cf. also "Race" in the index.

A special chapter in this context is Richard Wagner's attitude toward Judaism and the Jewish question.

234   EXCURSUS ABOUT RICHARD WAGNER AND THE JEWISH QUESTION: A great deal has been written about Richard Wagner's attitude toward Judaism and the Jewish question. Any biography of Wagner must of necessity deal with this question and take a stand on it. Nor can books about the Jewish question pass it by, least of all in connection with the later development of the problem, which led to the catastrophe of European Jewry. "Hitler did not recognize any forerunners," wrote Hermann Rauschning in his *Conversations with Hitler*, "with one exception: Richard Wagner." Hitler's biographer Joachim C. Fest reports that seeing *Siegfried* at the Linz opera house transported young Hitler into ecstasy. He writes (in *Der Stern* 26, no. 28, 6 July 1973, 40): "Wagner's heroes and his mythology of blood, his pomp and pathos as well as the powerful direction influenced Hitler's ideas about life and politics." Kubizek, a friend of young Hitler, reports that Wagner's opera *Rienzi* made a profound impression on Hitler in 1906; he was overwhelmed by the spectacular dramatic musicality of the work and stirred by the fate of the late medieval rebel and tribune of the people Cola di Rienzi, a man "alienated from his fellow men and destroyed by their incomprehension. . . . When these boyhood friends met again thirty years later in Bayreuth, Hitler remarked: 'It began at that hour!'" (Joachim Fest, *Hitler*, trans. Richard and Clara Winston, [New York, 1974], 22). Other National Socialist leaders, too, have acknowledged the profound influence that Wagner's music, his mythology and mystique, and his prose writings had upon them. (Cf. also Part 1, chap. 9). We are thus dealing with an effect that extended over a full century—and possibly even into the present.

Let us for the moment disregard the problem of the influence of the figures in Wagner's music dramas and their *Weltanschauung*; we shall deal with this in a later context. Here we shall limit ourselves to the more important writings of the musical theoretician and polemical writer. Occasional expressions of his opinions may be found in numerous essays, and fundamental ones particularly in two, *Das Judentum in der Musik* (1850) and *Erkenne dich selbst* (1881). The former was written at the time of the debates about the emancipation of the Jews following the abortive revolution of 1848, in which Wagner had participated at Dresden, the latter at the time of the polemics about the Jews when modern anti-Semitism was in its infancy as a political movement. We shall, therefore, consider primarily these two essays.

In early September of 1850 Wagner published an article in the *Neue Zeitschrift für Musik*, which had been founded by Robert Schumann and was edited by Franz Brendel. It appeared in no. 19, pp. 101–7 and no. 20, 109–12 under the pseudonym K. Freidank, and the editor was held officially responsible for it. However, friends and foes who had read Wagner's other writings immediately recognized his authorship by his style, and Wagner did not deny it when inquiries were made. "You ask me about *Das Judentum*," he wrote on 18 April 1851 to his friend (and later father-in-law) Franz Liszt; "surely you know that the article is by me, so why do you ask me? I appeared pseudonymously not out of fear, but to prevent the Jews from dragging the question into a purely personal sphere. I harbored a long-repressed resentment against this Jewish mess [*Judenwirtschaft*], and this resentment is as necessary to my nature as gall is to blood." He thereby wished to draw a clear line of demarcation between himself and the Jew Giacomo Meyerbeer, at that time the most celebrated opera composer and (since 1842) the all-powerful music director of the Berlin Opera. Wagner said that he did not hate him, "but he is infinitely repugnant to me. This eternally amiable, obliging person once led people to believe that I was his protégé, and so he reminds me of the most confused—I am tempted to say, the most profligate—period of my life, the period of connections and back stairs when the patrons to whom we are inwardly anything but devoted make fools out of us. . . . This is a necessary act of the full birth of my mature personality—and, God willing, I intend to be of service to many in taking this action with such zeal!" (Cited here after Tibor Kneif's commentary in his new edition of Wagner's works *Die Kunst und die Revolution*, 1849; *Das Judentum in der Musik*, 1850; and *Was ist deutsch?*, 1865, 1878.)

This passage, in which Wagner goes on to say that despite all deceptions and disappointments he really had no external occasion for this attack on Meyerbeer, already contains some basic elements that determine Wagner's attitude toward the Jews and Judaism. A personal need for inward liberation causes him to take a fundamental stand, and in so doing he does not stop to think that he is thereby severely denigrating and hurting a group of people that he dislikes. His rancor against the Jews becomes the point of departure for a general negative judgment on them. They are regarded as a menacing power that is persecuting and wronging him as well as many like him. His personal act of liberation is declared to be a beneficent act for many others—and it was so perceived by many, at least later. Wagner's identification of himself with the German people or its ruling classes later led to his glorification as a symbol of that people.

Personal rancor as a point of departure need not, of course, invalidate an essay. Many of our actions and writings are prompted or triggered by personal motives as well as feelings of envy and vengefulness, which have since Nietzsche and Scheler customarily been called *ressentiment* if they go beyond the unique and purely personal and are constantly relived, accompanied by impotence, and thus turn into "existential envy." (Cf. H. Schoeck, *Der Neid und die Gesellschaft* [Freiburg, 1873], 186ff.) If deeds progress to positive action and if our personally motivated thinking is expanded into a more objective recognition of a general plight that injured us first (possibly because we were more thin-skinned and sensitive than the others), we can simply ignore the psychological point of departure as insignificant and forget about it. Wagner was convinced that this applied to him. In 1869 he printed his essay, this time under his own name, as a separate publication and introduced it with an open letter to one of his aristocratic friends, Marie Kalergis-Muchanoff, which contained ruthless attacks on Jewish adversaries, particularly the half-Jewish Viennese critic Eduard Hanslick. When he expressed himself on the Jewish question again in 1881, in a publication devoted primarily to that subject (*Erkenne dich selbst*), he remembered his 1850 essay almost as a heroic feat. In the latter essay, too, the argumentation appears as an act of self-knowledge and self-liberation; there, too, the personal is identified with the universal. Thus Wagner's writings reflect the development of the Jewish question in Germany and in many other countries with a Jewish population— from the preemancipative to the postemancipative period. This makes his attitude toward the Jewish question exemplary for the position of numerous other intellectuals, artists, and educated persons. In Wagner's case there is added the aura of his artistic and fascinating charismatic personality as well as the systematic and unrestrained mobilization of all that emanates from him and has through his words, music, and theatrical organizational talent affected his adoring devotees.

As already mentioned, the essay on the Jews in music was not a time-bound bit of occasional writing, no matter what earlier polemics or personal occasions had led him to write it. Wagner rightly included it in his *Gesammelte Schriften und Dichtungen* (vol. 5 of the ten-volume collection that appeared from 1871 to 1883; the later essay is contained in vol. 10). *Das Judentum in der Musik* is one of the four fundamental essays in which Wagner, coming to terms with contemporary currents, formulated his artistic philosophy—the realization of the Romantic ideal of the *Gesamtkunstwerk* in the music drama—as well as his philosophy of life. (Cf. Robert Gutmann, *Richard Wagner: Der Mensch, sein Werk, seine Zeit* [Munich, 1961], 168.)

Wagner's essay about Judaism and music presents, first of all, the Jewish question as a non-Jewish free-thinker was able to see it around 1850—that is, during the period of the struggle for emancipation. Even though Wagner says that he does not intend to give a general characterization of the Jewish question, let alone discuss the Jewish question in politics, he does cover it in some detail in his introduction. Wagner claims that he is not bent on saying something new but only intends to explain "the unconscious feeling that is revealed in the people as a profound antipathy to the nature of the Jews, thus giving clear expression to something that really exists but certainly not trying to give artificial life to something unreal through the power of the imagination."

Wagner says that he need not discuss religion. In that sphere the Jews have "long since ceased to be odious enemies—thanks to all those who have incurred popular hatred within the Christian religion." In pure politics, too, modern man "has never had a real conflict with the Jews. We do not even begrudge them the establishment of a Kingdom in Jerusalem, and in this regard we really regretted the fact that Herr von Rothschild was too intelligent to make himself the King of the Jews; as we know, he preferred to remain "the Jew of the kings." To be sure, people have gone too far in the administration of justice. "When he fought for the emancipation of the Jews we were . . . actually fighters for an abstract principle rather than for concrete cases." As with liberalistic endeavors in general, "our zeal for equality for the Jews stemmed far more from the stimulation of a universal idea than from a real sympathy; for despite all the talk and writing in favor of the emancipation of the Jews, we always felt *instinctive revulsion* at actual contact with Jews."

Here Wagner comes to a point that seems very important to him, and he expresses what many of his contemporaries felt, speaking of the "instinctive repulsiveness which the personality and nature of the Jews have for us." He desires to explain and justify this instinctive revulsion, which is "stronger and weightier than our conscious zeal to rid ourselves of this revulsion." As a remark apparently made *en passant* he repeats the ideas that Marx and his school expressed long ago. The emancipation of the Jews has long since been accomplished, and more than that: the Jews have already risen to dominance. "Quite imperceptibly the creditor of the kings became the king of the creditors, and now we cannot help but regard the request of this king for emancipation as extremely naive, since now *we* find ourselves in the position of fighting for emancipation from the Jews. The way things stand in the world today, the Jew really is more than emancipated; he is in control, and he will dominate for as long as money remains the power that deprives all our doings and activities of their energy."

Wagner admits that "the historical misery of the Jews and the predatory brutality of the Christian-Germanic rulers themselves have given this power to the sons of Israel." Now, however, with the aid of money the Jews have also brought the artistic taste of the public and the trade in works of art under their control [Felix Mendelssohn-Bartholdy and Giacomo Meyerbeer were the sons of wealthy bankers], and this must be opposed with all the power at our disposal. The way to do this is to gain a clear insight into the foundations of this "instinctive repugnance at the nature of the Jews" and of the hatred of the Jews. "Through the mere exposure of this we can hope to rout the demon [!] from the field in which he is able to maintain himself only under the protection of semidarkness, a darkness with which we good-natured humanists surround him in order to make his sight less repugnant to us." One can see how traditional materials are here combined with more modern stereotypic images and demonized. Even humanism is already depreciated as good-natured frivolousness.

In his consideration of the Jews' relationship to music, the real subject of the essay, Wagner takes the problem of language as his point of departure. According to him, the Jew, whose outward appearance contains something repulsively alien for all other nationalities, does speak the language of the nation in which he lives from generation to generation, but he always speaks it as a foreigner. He never uses it fully, the way someone inwardly, culturally, and ethnically bound to the language does. In the spirit of Jacob Grimm and with his customarily exaggerated interpretation and evaluation of correctly seen phenomena, Wagner writes: "A language with its expression and development is not the work of individuals but of a historical community. Only someone who has unconsciously grown up in this community also participates in its creations. The Jew, however, has stood outside such a community, solitary with his Jehovah in a fragmented, landless ethnic group that was bound to be denied any development of its own, just as even the language peculiar to this group (Hebrew) has only been preserved as a dead language." Thus he cannot participate in its development with artistic creativity. Even if he masters the language, so to speak, there always remains something singular in its sound, something inherent in the "Semitic pronunciation": "Our ears immediately notice as something utterly alien and unpleasant the hissing, shrill, buzzing, and halting inflection of Jewish diction. A usage and capricious distortion of words and phraseology that are totally uncharacteristic of our national language really give this speech the nature of an unbearably confused babbling, and as we listen to it our attention is instinctively drawn to this repulsive manner more than to the content of Jewish speech."

Wagner goes on to say that the Jew is incapable of any true passionate excitement. If he exchanges feelings with a non-Jew, his excitement actually "finds expression only in the altogether singular egotistic interest of his vanity or his advantage," and then "such excitement, coupled with the distorting expression of his diction generally, always becomes ludicrous in nature" and hence arouses no sympathy. Perhaps one Jew speaks to another Jew with purer human emotions, but in his associations with non-Jews a Jew does not arouse this feeling, least of all in art. "If the nature of his diction outlined here makes a Jew virtually incapable of the artistic expression of his feelings and views through *speech*, his ability to express them in *song* must be even far less," for singing is "speech stirred to the highest passion, and music is the language of passion." If a Jew heightens his diction with a passion that is alien to him and thus appears ludicrous, and if he bursts into song, this renders him "downright insufferable to us."

Wagner rightly remarks that true art arises from an artist's inward connection with the people, but the Jew has no real connection of this sort. If he detaches himself from his people, the Jewish people, he is all the more lonely, for if the person thus isolated has any ethnic connection, it is only with his own people. That is why the cadences of Jewish chanting in religious services have become part of his musical feeling, and to the extent that Wagner became acquainted with them these cadences appeared ludicrous to him, though they might once have been as expressive and exalted as anyone could imagine.

When he visited a synagogue, its singsong and disorder seemed to Wagner like a naive caricature of real music. He felt that this missing connection of the Jews with real ethnic and artistic tradition caused them to jumble up words and constructions from all sorts of ages and styles in curious inexpressiveness, as they did in Yiddish. "There we find the formal pecularities of all schools crowded together in colorful chaos." As a typical example Wagner names Felix Mendelssohn-Bartholdy, Moses Mendelssohn's grandson. He does not question his sense of honor and his seriousness as an artist, but Mendelssohn has not been able to go beyond preliminaries and could only write empty music without giving a true expression of an artistic nature. As a warning example Wagner refers to Giacomo Meyerbeer, though he does not actually name him. In the abovementioned letter to Liszt we encountered Meyerbeer, a man by whom Wagner felt slighted and persecuted, as the real target of Wagner's polemic.

In conclusion Wagner also mentions Heinrich Heine, with whom he was personally acquainted and whose novella *Memoiren des Herrn von Schabelewopski* gave him, in 1838, the idea for the libretto of his opera *Der fliegende Holländer* (C. Westernhagen, *Richard Wagners Dresdener Bibliothek* [Wiesbaden, 1966], 56).

> I said above that the Jews have not produced a true poet. At this point we must mention Heinrich Heine. At the time when Goethe and Schiller wrote there was, as far as we know, no Jewish poet in Germany. but when writing literature became a lie among us and everything but a true poet grew on the totally unpoetic soil of our life, it was the task of a very talented Jewish writer to expose with entrancing mockery this lie, this abysmal emptiness and Jesuitic hypocrisy of our scribblers and poetasters who were still behaving as if they were poets. He also mercilessly excoriated his famous musical fellow Jews for their insistence that they were artists. He would no longer countenance any deception. He was ceaselessly driven by the inexorable demon [another demon!] of rejection of everything that appeared worth rejecting past all illusions of modern self-deception to the point where he made himself a poet again by lying, and as a reward he had his poetic lies set to music by our composers. He was the conscience of the Jews, just as the Jews are the bad conscience of our modern civilization.

(We shall discuss this remark in a later context; cf. the excursus about Heine, Part 2, pp. 642ff.)

At the end of his essay Wagner discusses Ludwig Börne.

> We must mention another Jew who appeared among us as a writer. From his special position as a Jew he came to us as a seeker of salvation [a favorite motif of Wagner!]; he did not find it and had to realize that he would be able to find it only *together with our salvation, which would make us true human beings* [emphasis in the original]. However, for a Jew, becoming a human being together with us means to cease to be a Jew. Börne grasped this. He teaches us that this redemption cannot be achieved in comfort and casual, cold ease but that it costs, as it cost us, sweat, deprivation, anxiety, and a full measure of pain and suffering. Jews, participate heedlessly in this work of redemption, which will bring rebirth through self-destruction, and we shall be one, without distinctions! But consider that only one thing can be your release from the curse hanging over you: the redemption of Ahasuerus—destruction [*der Untergang*].

If one attempts to give a fair judgment on Wagner's essay *Das Judentum in der Musik*, one has to admit, first of all, that in his sensitivity to everything that endangered, or appeared to endanger, his own development and productivity Wagner correctly grasped many aspects of the situation of contemporary Jewry. In his characterization (not cited here) of those Jews from the prosperous upper class who sought to break away from everything Jewish and absorb the other culture as quickly as possible, often without plumbing its depths, he concurs with Heine—the difference being that the latter makes it the target of his (basically affectionate) mockery (e.g., in *Die Bäder von Lucca*), whereas Wagner's venomous, hate-filled style makes it hard for those concerned to acknowledge even the correct elements in his critique. Wagner is also basically right in his presentation of the problems of the Jewish artist in an environment that inwardly does not accept him and does not regard him as belonging in it even if he identifies with it, thus isolating him even more than an artist already is and making him essentially homeless even where he feels at home. But in his loveless analysis of the situation Wagner comes to conclusions that block any way out of it. He mentions the Jewish nationalistic solution, a return to Palestine, only with a mocking gesture similar to Voltaire's. After all, no matter how much people might desire it, this way out seemed absurd to most of them in view of the Jews' attitude toward it and of the negative physical and emotional capacity the Jews were thought to have. The only other solution Wagner sees for the Jews is self-abandonment, complete intermingling with the nations among which they live, and thus the death of the Jews as Jews. Wagner's essay contains as yet no deliberate reference to the racial idea, but the basis of his argumentation is the Jews' unalterable physical and emotional endowment and their "Semitic" nature.

Added to this are formulations that in their trenchancy and demonic-mythological allusions constitute the point of departure for sinister developments in thought and action and which in an antiliberal atmosphere lent themselves to unmythological, realistic interpretations. When Wagner concluded his essay by saying that "only one thing can be your release from the curse hanging over you: the redemption of Ahasuerus—destruction," he did not, of course, have the murder of the Jews in mind. With its combination of curse, repentance, expiation, and destruction this formulation is typical of Wagner's sense of life and philosophy of life. With no reference, or no direct reference, to the Jews, it repeatedly recurs in his writings and operas, from *The Flying Dutchman* and *Tannhäuser* to *The Ring of the Nibelung* and *Parsifal*, where "amidst the pealing of bells and reminiscences of the Mass and the Passion a religion of race is presented in the guise of a Christian legend" (R. Gutmann, *Richard Wagner*, 483). In that opera Kundry, the female transposition of the figure of Ahasuerus, is burdened with the monstrous deed of mocking Jesus as well as her disaster-producing and redemptive femininity (something that recurs in almost all Wagner dramas), and she is actually released from the curse through her expiatory death. There would come a time when people would take this work of redemption into their own rough hands.

In 1850 Wagner's essay appears to have exerted no great influence beyond narrow artistic circles. It was different in 1869, when it appeared as a separate polemic, now bearing the name of Wagner, who had in the meantime become widely known. The fact that he had it reprinted under his own name indicates that he still subscribed to the contents and formulations of his work and that he believed the time was ripe for, or in need of, wider dissemination of his thoughts on the Jewish question. In 1869 the work did attract some attention and inspired both agreement and opposition. A modern biographer (Robert Gutmann, *Richard Wagner*, 341) writes: "To many the reprint appeared to be the deed of a fanatic asking for trouble. He simply had not been able to resist the urge. The Jewish problem captivated him more and more and occupied him constantly until his death. It would not leave him in peace and stubbornly entered all his conversations, letters, and articles. Prejudice hardened into a groundless hatred and finally became a morbid leitmotif. In all seriousness he regarded his attitude toward the Jews as 'eminently objective,' and this consciousness gave him, in his own words, the strength to stand up to the barbs of the outraged Jews." The Jew-hatred of Cosima Liszt-Bülow, his lover (from 1864) and second wife (from 1870), may have intensified this antipathy. For him—and through him for his admirers—the Jews increasingly became the symbol of modern materialism and the antipodes of the idealistic Aryans.

In 1876 Wagner made the personal acquaintance of Gobineau, with whose racial theory he must have become familiar earlier, for he absorbed everything that was part of the thought world of his time. In May and June 1881 the two men became friends in Venice, and a year later, in June 1882, Gobineau (who died three months later) visited Wagner in Bayreuth for a week. In late 1880 or early 1881 Wagner published (in the *Bayreuther Blätter*) an introduction to a work of Count Gobineau (*Ein Urteil über die jetzige Weltlage*) in which he explicitly endorsed Gobineau's racial theses as the teachings of "a most perspicacious ethnologist": "Anyone who is acquainted with Count Gobineau's great work about the inequality of the human races must have become convinced that it contains no errors such as are made every day by the investigators of the daily progress of mankind" (*Schriften und Dichtungen* 10:34).

And in the last essay of his *Schriften* ("Heidentum und Christentum," 10:283) he refers to Gobineau as he warns against "the enormity of the assumption . . . that the human species is destined to achieve full equality," calling it a "deterrent image."

In his essay "Erkenne dich selbst" of 1881 (*Schriften* 10:263–74) Wagner sums up his views on the Jewish question more than thirty years after the appearance of his first essay. It was the time of the birth of modern anti-Semitism, the polemics concerning Marr and Dühring, and the Berlin *Antisemiten-Debatte* triggered by Treitschke's *Ein Wort über unser Judentum*. Wagner now looks back on his first publication about the Jewish question, which as late as 1869 had aroused "the greatest indignation among Jews and Germans." The renewed and now open debate on the subject, Wagner believes, "reveals the late reawakening of an instinct that seemed to have been completely extinguished in us." He sees as the reason for the change in atmosphere the "authorization given to the Jews in the meantime to regard themselves as Germans in every conceivable respect—roughly the way the blacks in Mexico received blanket authorization to consider themselves white." He characterizes this occurrence as astonishing, frivolous, ludicrous, and thoughtless, a "frivolity of our national authorities" under the formula of "equal rights for all German citizens without regard to religious differences." How could "everything that makes the tribe of the Jews extremely remote from us" ever have been regarded as a religion? After all, the Jews have "always remained a totality." There follow the conclusions of a pathological anti-Jewish persecution complex that are reminiscent of the later *Protocols*. As the result of present-day culture and civilization, which are in glaring contrast to Christian teachings, "the Jew drawing up the final balance sheet sees the necessity to wage war and the even greater necessity to have money for it." He leaves it to others to fight wars, something for which he is not qualified, but he does undertake the raising of funds. A lot of clever things have been said about the invention of money, "but as one sings its praises, one should not disregard the curse to which it has always been exposed in legend and literature"—most recently, as every reader will remember, in Wagner's own *Ring of the Nibelung*. "If in that work gold appears as the demon [!] of mankind that strangles innocence, our greatest poet [an allusion to a well-known scene in Goethe's *Faust, Part Two*] presents the invention of paper money as the devil's work. The fateful ring of the Nibelung as a financial portfolio [here the reference to the Jews is made even clearer] was able to complete the horrible picture of the ghastly lord of the world." If the Jews bear the blame for this, it is only "because our entire civilization is a barbaric-Judaistic mixture and by no means a Christian creation." The "salvation of mankind" consists only "in the production of great characters," and these appear "especially, and almost exclusively, among races that are kept pure." At present there still is something left of the old racial and generational pride "in the genuine noble families of Germanic provenance"; for the rest, there has been a "decline of the German people, which is now defenseless against the encroachments of the Jews." What is needed is "the rebirth of a true sense of race that expresses itself particularly in a sure instinct."

By contrast with the German, who displays no power of resistance when "the mindless journalist or political pettifogger insolently harasses him with mendacious talk" or when "the Jew with his paper stock-exchange bell" rings for him, the Jew is "the most astounding example of racial consistency in world history. . . ." Even intermingling does him no harm; "no matter whether a male or a female mixes with the races most alien to the Jews, it is always a Jew that is produced." A Jew has and needs no real religion, and it is hardly necessary for him to learn how to do figures, for everything, even the most difficult calculation, "surely is already there in flawless form in his instinct, which is closed to any idealism." And now comes the ominous sentence which in the future no work of anti-Semitic "philosophy" failed to notice: "A wonderful, incomparable phenomenon: the plastic demon of the degeneration of mankind in triumphant safety and as a German citizen of the Mosaic faith into the bargain, the darling of our princes and the guarantor of the unity of our Reich!" The only way for Germans to oppose this would be to gain a greater sense of their own race and dignity and to overcome a false reluctance to face reality. With oracular vagueness Wagner makes this prophetic declaration: "Only when the demon . . . is no longer able to find among us any Where and When to give him shelter will there be no Jews among us any more."

These formulations of a paranoid, demonic Jew-hatred contain everything that National Socialist theoreticians later needed to justify their brutal practices. In this spirit all mythological figures and their pompous dramatizations and musical settings in Wagner's *Gesamtkunstwerke* could be interpreted as embodiments of these basic teachings. In any case, they were able to lead to a blurring of the boundary lines between figments of the imagination and reality and give all doctrines and insights a disastrously demonic and threatening character. Wagner's believers and adherents served to intensify this effect; after all, monarchists are usually more dangerous to free thought and actions than monarchs, no matter how complacent and egotistical these may be, and, as the saying goes, papists are "more papal than the Pope." Here we are, of course, not discussing the brilliant musician whose paramount importance in musical history is beyond question. What interests us here is not the greatness and problematical nature of Wagner's music, and if it interests us at all, it is only because it greatly magnified the effects of Wagner's extra-musical pronouncements. Wagner kept his distance from plebeian anti-Semitism and refused to sign the anti-Semites' petition of 1880. However, up to the Russian pogroms of 1881 he never condemned any manifestation of anti-Semitism, and his mythically nebulous intimations lent themselves to all kinds of unmythically clear interpretations. It cannot be determined to what extent Wagner himself rejected them or tacitly approved of them. In light of this, the fact that he accepted Jews as collaborators in his artistic activities—the conductor Hermann Levi, impresarios, business managers (Angelo Neumann), self-less supporters, or mesmerized followers (e.g., Joseph Rubinstein, who took his own life shortly after Wagner's death)—is of no consequence. Most Jew-baiters have tolerated "Jewish exceptions," at least to a certain degree. However, Wagner's judgment on the Jews' incapacity for artistic creativity in general and for music in particular was adopted, consciously or unconsciously, by historians of music and music critics. In one form or another it appears in many statements, no matter how greatly the facts disprove it.

As regards literature, in addition to the books and articles already mentioned in this discursus cf. Friedrich Nietzsche's essays "Richard Wagner in Bayreuth," *Sämtliche Werke* (Kröners Taschenausgabe 71), and "Nietzsche contra Wagner" (Kröners Taschenausgabe 77) as well as Nietzsche's remarks in other works (cf. Richard Oehler, *Nietzsche-Register*, 481–85); Leon Stein, *The Racial Thinking of Richard Wagner* (New York, 1950); Dov Kulka, "Richard Wagner und die Anfänge des modernen Antisemitismus," *Bulletin LBI* 4:281–300; Robert Edwin Herzstein, "Richard Wagner at the Crossroads of German Antisemitism, 1848–1933: A Reinterpretation," *Zeitschrift für die Geschichte der Juden* 4 (1967): 119–40; Max Nordau, *Entartung* (Berlin), vol. 1 chap. 5, "Der Richard Wagner-Dienst" (306–80) and Meir Ben-Horin, *Max Nordau: Philosopher of Human Solidarity* (London, 1956); Oskar Walzel, *Richard Wagner in seiner Zeit und nach seiner Zeit: Eine Jahrhundertbetrachtung* (Munich, 1913); H. E. Jacob, *Felix Mendelssohn und seine Zeit: Bildnis und Schicksal eines Meisters* (Frankfurt, 1951); Jacques Barzun, *Darwin, Marx, Wagner* (New York, 1941, 1958); Jacob Katz, *The Dark Side of Genius* (New Hampshire, 1986). The profound influence exerted by the magical enchantment of Wagner's music (in combination with his writings and the cult around him) on his contemporaries and later generations is perhaps best illustrated by Thomas Mann's struggle with him which is reflected in an enthusiastic critical essay of 1933 ("Leiden und Grösse Richard Wagners") down to a review dated 1951 in which Mann finds in Wagner "too much 'Hitler,' really too much latent and soon enough also manifest Nazism" (*Altes und Neues*, 623).

235   D. H. NAUDH: "DIE JUDEN UND DER DEUTSCHE STAAT": This work went through several printings that same year. Its author never revealed his pseudonym, at least in public. In his abovementioned work *Der Judenkrieg* . . . (1880), p. 3, Wilhelm Marr praises the booklet effusively: "A masterpiece in style and content. It is as if a plastically perfect marble sculpture had been given breath, spirit, language, and motion. Whatever has been written about the Jewish question since then is no match for this pronunciamento of the anti-Jewish genius." At the same time Marr accuses the author of being a coward and afraid of the Jews because he did not use his name, though in his new work, *Professoren über Israel*, he himself inveighed against the anonymity of writers and demanded that they give their full names. Marr identifies him as "Herr Nordmann, former owner of a manor in Posen or Silesia" and says that Naudh had insisted on becoming a contributor to Marr's periodical *Deutsche Wacht* (the organ of the Antisemites' League), but had refused to sign his articles with his own name. Others thought the author behind the pseudonym was Lothar Bucher (1817–92), the radical writer and Prussian deputy during the revolutionary period 1848–49, who lived as an emigrant and journalist in London until the amnesty of 1861 enabled him to return to Germany. After he had modified his political views, he was (from 1864 to 1892) the closest associate of Bismarck in the Foreign Office. After its eleventh printing, in 1883, Naudh's little book was issued by the distinctly anti-Semitic publishing house of Theodor Fritsch in Leipzig. In his foreword to the thirteenth printing (1920) the editor, Theodor Fritsch, writes (p. 3):

> To this day the author remains obscure. The name Naudh stands for the Nordic rune "N" and also for "Nobody." What I have been able to find out about the author is this: When the twelfth printing appeared in 1890 and the question of the copyright holder arose, the Berlin writer Johannes Nordmann came forward and identified himself as the author. In a correspondence with him I expressed my surprise at the fact that a man of no particular literary prominence had created such an excellent work and told him that the presentation reminded me of a master of style like Lothar Bucher. Thereupon Nordmann admitted that he had written the work together with Lothar Bucher and the Prussian Privy Councilor E. Wagener. He (Nordmann) had provided the bulk of the material in a form based on the methods of the natural sciences, Wagener had added political and legal viewpoints, and Bucher had made a stylistic revision of the entire material.

As a motto for the first section the booklet uses an extensive quotation from Tacitus and as the motto for the fourth section one from Mommsen's *Römische Geschichte*, (vol. 5), which was later widely quoted—the by no means negatively intended statement that the Jews are "an effective ferment of cosmopolitanism and national decomposition." As a motto for the tenth section the author chose Ludwig Feuerbach's statement "Theology is anthropology."

236ff.   EUGEN DÜHRING: The full title of the original is Dr. E. Dühring, *Die Judenfrage als Racen-, Sitten- und Culturfrage. Mit einer weltgeschichtlichen Antwort* (Karlsruhe and Leipzig: Verlag von H. Reuther, 1881). In later printings Dühring brought out the basic ideas of this work more and more trenchantly and consistently, and he also expressed this in the title. The fifth, revised edition (Nowawes, 1901) appeared under the title *Die Judenfrage als Frage des Rassencharakters und seiner Schädlichkeit für Völkerexistenz, Sitte und Cultur*. Similarly, the "sixth, augmented edition" which E. Dühring completed in 1920 and provided with a new foreword but which was not published until 1930 (edited by H. Reinhardt "at the behest of Frau Beta Dühring") bore the title *Die Judenfrage als Frage des Rassencharakters und seiner Schädlichkeit für Existenz und Kultur der Völker.* Regarding these title changes and their significance for the development and reception of Dühring's ideas and demands, cf. Part 1, p. 373. Regarding the systematic and novel nature of his presentation, Dühring (who never suffered from modesty) wrote in his foreword to the new edition of 1920: "When I published the first edition of my work on the Jewish question in November 1880, I had already begun to identify, in various scholarly works of a systematic and historical nature published since the 1860s, the Hebrew racial character in its deleterious effect on literature. . . . My work was the first presentation of the racial standpoint in the Jewish question in contrast to the religionism that was the sole authority at that time."

The single-mindedness with which Dühring systematized and formulated his views and disseminated a socialistic doctrine that deviated from Marxist theory exerted a great influence on German social democracy in the 1870s. As August Bebel later wrote in his memoirs, Dühring had managed "to win over for his theories almost the entire leadership of the Berlin movement."

This caused Friedrich Engels to oppose Dühring in a series of articles. These appeared in book form (first in 1878, in new editions dated 1885 and 1894, and finally in numerous reprints down to the present) under the ironic title *Herrn Eugen Dührings Umwälzung der Wissenschaft,* generally known as "Anti-Dühring." According to Engels ([Berlin, 1948], p. 33), Dühring is convinced that his philosophy is the only true one. "Many people before Dühring *thought* of themselves that way, but with the exception of Richard Wagner he is probably the first man who calmly said it about himself." Even then (and thus before the appearance of *Die Judenfrage*) Engels noticed "the Jew-hatred exaggerated to the point of ludicrousness" that Dühring displayed at every turn. Dühring, the "philosopher of reality" who looks down on all prejudices from on high, is himself so deeply mired "in personal crotchets that he calls the personal prejudice against the Jews that was adopted from the bigotry of the Middle Ages a 'judgment of nature' based on 'natural grounds.'"

The one-sided clarity and trenchancy of the questions asked as well as the argumentation also made an indelible impression on the young Herzl, then barely twenty-one, who read Dühring's work on the Jewish question shortly after its appearance. He reacted to it at length and with uncommon mordancy in his youth diary. (His remarks were first published in Leon Kellner's *Theodor Herzls Lehrjahre* [Vienna, 1920]). In his Zionist Diary Herzl acknowledged that his inner change that had led to Zionism had begun with his reading of that book. In *The Jewish State* we find remarks by Herzl that sound like an echo of Dühring and an answer to him. Cf. A. Bein's biography *Theodor Herzl* (Vienna, 1934)—new edition, with a foreword by Golda Meir (Vienna: Österreichisch-Israelische Gesellschaft, 1974)—the places indicated in the index, esp. 61ff.

In *Dührings Hass* (Hanover, 1922) the Jewish writer and philosopher of history Theodor Lessing (who, by way of thanks, was murdered by the Nazis in 1933) wrote a kind of obituary of Dühring, who is seen as a tragic figure. Concerning his influence on the social theories of Theodor Hertzka and Franz Oppenheimer, cf. Gerhard Albrecht, *Eugen Dühring: Ein Beitrag zur Geschichte der Sozialwissenschaften* (Jena, 1927). Cf. also Gerd-Klaus Kaltenbrunner, "Vom Konkurrenten des Karl Marx zum Vorläufer Hitlers: Eugen Dühring," in Karl Schwedhelm, ed., *Propheten des Nationalismus* (Munich, 1969), 36ff.

DRUMONT: Cf. I. Schapira, *Der Antisemitismus in der französischen Literatur: Edouard Drumont und seine Quellen* (Berlin, 1927); R. F. Byrnes, "Edouard Drumont and *La France Juive*," *Jewish Social Studies* 10 (1948): 165–84; W. Rabi, "Drum-   239f.

ont, l'apôtre myope," *L'Arche*, June 1961, 36ff.; idem, "L'antisémitisme en France de 1886–1914," *Cahiers Paul Claudel* 7 (1968): 46ff. The role that Drumont played in the later Dreyfus affair through his inflammatory reports and articles in the newspaper *La Libre Parole*, of which he was the editor, is well known. Auguste Burdeau, the vice-president of the French Chamber of Deputies, sued Drumont for defamation of character; in the trial Drumont handled his own defense and was sentenced to three months in jail for slander. Theodor Herzl reported about this trial on 15 June 1892 as the Paris correspondent of his newspaper, the Vienna *Neue Freie Presse*. Cf. *Theodor Herzl, From Boulanger to Dreyfus: Reports and Political Articles from Paris* (Hebr.), ed. A. Bein and M. Schaerf (Jerusalem, 1974), 1–109ff., and Bein, *Theodor Herzl*, 134ff. In one of his preparatory notes for *The Jewish State* Herzl wrote on 12 June 1895: "I owe to Drumont a great deal of the present freedom of my concepts, because he is an artist" (*The Complete Diaries of Theodor Herzl*, ed. R. Patai, trans. H. Zohn [New York, 1960], 1:99). Herzl may be referring here to a remark made by Drumont in court, where he admitted to all kinds of "inaccuracies" in his incriminated article and said, by way of excusing himself, that his "artistic imagination" might have run away with him. With this monomaniacal "artistic imagination" Drumont turns any person he dislikes into a Jew whenever a name, foreign origin, a facial expression, or a gesture provides him with a handle. If none exists, scoundrelly conduct can serve as evidence, for surely only a Jew could act that way. In his speech of defense he even turned Paris, the Trojan prince who, according to Homer's *Iliad*, caused the Trojan War, into a Jew. Yet one gains the impression that Drumont believed his assertions, that he did not maliciously lie or falsify but had faith in his mission to free the Aryan race, and in particular the French, from the hegemony of the Semitic race—that is, especially the Jews.

In a conversation with the Austrian Foreign Minister Goluchowski in May 1904 Herzl attributed the growth and influence of anti-Semitism in France up to the Dreyfus affair to "Drumont's talent and the hatred aroused by the Rothschilds" (*Complete Diaries* 4:1624). At that time Drumont's influence and fear of him had mounted to such an extent that in July 1902 Herzl wrote to Lord Rothschild in London that his cousins in Paris were being "governed indirectly by Drumont" (ibid., 1309). On the other hand, in January 1897 Drumont wrote a very favorable editorial in his newspaper about Herzl's *Jewish State*, which had recently appeared in French translation (ibid., 2:509). In chap. 8 we shall have more to say about these and similar mutual appreciations of anti-Semites and Zionists (which usually were harmful to both sides).

241ff.   HOUSTON STEWART CHAMBERLAIN: I have used and quoted from the popular edition of *Grundlagen des 19. Jahrhunderts*, 8th ed. (Munich, 1907). On the margin it gives the pagination of the standard edition, because the very detailed index of persons and subjects refers to it; with the aid of this one can easily inform oneself about Chamberlain's attitude toward problems and personalities. Few German books of that time have such a detailed index, which has facilitated the use and quotation of pertinent passages for many readers.

Chamberlain was born in England and lived in Vienna for twenty years. In 1908 he visited Wagner's Bayreuth for the festival, and after he took Eva Wagner, the youngest daughter of Richard and Cosima Wagner, as his second wife, he settled there. Cf. Gerd-Klaus Kaltenbrunner, "Wahnfried und die *Grundlagen*," in K. Schwedhelm, ed., *Propheten des Nationalismus* (Munich, 1969), 36–55; idem, "The Most Germanic of Germans," *Wiener Library Bulletin*, Winter 1967/68, 6–12. A selection from contemporary reviews of *Grundlagen* was issued as a booklet by F. Bruckmann, Munich, in 1902.

Writing in the Zionist weekly *Die Welt* (Vienna, no. 35–37, 1899) shortly after the appearance of the book, the Austrian-Jewish writer Felix Salten gives an incisive characterization of the engaging aspects and the weaknesses of this book. He says that the book is basically a feuilleton stretched to cover two volumes, as easy to read as an essay but also strikingly careless about accuracy, and that despite the numerous quotations and references it gives (deliberately or inadvertently) false interpretations of important facts.

Chamberlain's book, which devotes comprehensive chapters to Hellenic Art, Roman Law, The Chaos of Peoples, religion, and the state, also contains an important section that discusses The Entry of the Jews into Occidental History. Chamberlain assures his readers that he is not an anti-Semite, at least not in the usual sense of the term. This section, however, and a hundred other passages in the work indicate that he is a convinced and, it seems to me, a virulent adversary of the Jews—not of Jewish individuals or of certain Jewish groups (he is too civilized for that), but of Jewry in general, an opponent of the people, an opponent of its mission, a condemner of its role in history. However, of all adversaries that are raising their voices today Houston Stewart Chamberlain is the most significant, the one with the greatest intelligence and talent. That is why he is not only the most important one; he is virtually the only one with whom one would care to have a discussion, the only one whom hatred has not made blind but seeing. It is really not hate but an antipathy, that deep-rooted, inherited, and inculcated aversion to the Jews which with one-sided acuity seeks motives for its ready-made judgment. Houston Stewart Chamberlain derives all these motives from various fields of knowledge, and he goes so far as to praise the Inquisition as the rescuer of civilization from the Jews. Of all the writings against the Jews in these times of Jew-hatred none is so armed with cold facts and all weapons of modern thought, none as logical and as carefully documented as this one. Hence it is worthwhile to settle accounts especially with Chamberlain—to engage him, who really gives the impression that he is speaking from honest conviction, in discussion and to show how dishonest this honest conviction is in its methods, how speculatively he has plundered an army of books in order to prove to himself and to others that he is really and truly in the right . . . to show how the facts may be correct but their meaning falsified. . . . Neither open abuse nor crude rancor or shameless slander can be as noxious in their effects as a talented man who manages to balance science and his personal opinion and by whom the crowd feels convinced though he has simply cajoled and outwitted it. Thus one should react less to abuse and calumny than to such earnestly presented objectivity.

Concerning the influence of this book and the problems raised by it, cf. Otto Hintze, "Rasse und Nationalität und ihre Bedeutung in der Geschichte," in *Historische und politische Aufsätze* (1919), 160ff.; Heinrich Ritter von Srbik, *Geist und Geschichte vom deutschen Humanismus bis zur Gegenwart* (Salzburg, 1951), 2:355ff.; Georg Lukács, *Von Nietzsche bis Hitler oder Der Irrationalismus in der deutschen Politik* (Frankfurt, 1966), seq. 3, pp. 217–31: "H. S. Chamberlain als Begründer der modernen Rassentheorie."

Chamberlain's influence on the thought of the time can hardly be overestimated. An example is provided by the letter of appreciation which Kaiser Wilhelm II wrote him on 31 December 1901 after reading the *Grundlagen:* "And now all the pure Aryan-Germanic elements that were lying dormant in me in mighty stratification gradually had to be brought out in a great struggle. . . . Then you came, and as with a magic wand you brought order into the chaos and light into the darkness—goals that must be striven and worked for, explanations for things dimly surmised, paths that are to be taken for the good of the Germans and thus for the good of humanity! . . . Forsooth, let us give thanks to Him up above for still being so kindly disposed to us Germans, for it is my unshakable, firm belief that it was God who sent your book to the German people and you personally to me." Like the Kaiser, many now were able to regard themselves as belonging to an elite and as chosen if they simply had an intuitive feeling that they were part of the Germanic-Aryan race.

During World War I the English-born Chamberlain wrote chauvinistic pamphlets for Germany. On 7 October 1923, when he was already completely paralyzed, he sent an appreciative letter to Hitler which in many respects resembled the one he had once received from Wilhelm II. Chamberlain wrote that Hitler was not a fanatic, as he had been erroneously described, for he wanted to convince, not persuade. Chamberlain wished to have him numbered among the constructive rather than the destructive people. "My faith in *Deutschtum* [the German national character, the German spirit, the German people, things German, etc.] never wavered for a moment; however, I confess that my hopes were at low ebb. With one stroke you have changed the state of my soul. That Germany gives birth to a Hitler in the hour of its greatest need is evidence that it is alive." (Letters quoted from the abovementioned essay by Kaltenbrunner, 110f., 122f.)

241 BENJAMIN DISRAELI: It seems paradoxical that Chamberlain, along with many other ideologues of race before and after him, was able to refer, with some justification, to the famous Jewish-born British statesman (and author of political novels) Benjamin Disraeli (Earl of Beaconsfield, 1804–81) and cite some fundamental statements by him in support of his own theses. Disraeli repeatedly (and especially in his political novels) wrote that race was everything, the only key to an understanding of world history, that blood was more important than all other bonds. He (and, as we have seen, many others) said these things before Gobineau, who met Disraeli as a young attaché and may even have received some ideas from him. This, at any rate, was the opinion expressed by the German professor of law and history Carl Koehne in an essay (published in vol. 18 of the *Archiv für Rassenbiologie*) that was briefly discussed in the *Vossische Zeitung* of 10 August 1932: "To be sure, the form that Gobineau gave to the ideas he had derived from Disraeli amused the latter too much for him to take them seriously. In *Lothar*, one of his last novels, Disraeli gives an unmistakable portrait of the French count, but he has the hero of his novel fall asleep while reading Gobineau's work on race."

Disraeli's evaluation of the races is diametrically opposed to that of Gobineau and his successors down to Chamberlain and Hitler. To him the noblest and purest race is the Jewish race, a holy race to which European culture owes all its important features. Christianity is completed Judaism. The Jewish race is the oldest civilized race and the Jews are the oldest nobility of mankind. By virtue of their physical and intellectual merits they dominate economic life, and beyond that they have a significant influence on the politics of the nations—an influence to which their racial qualities clearly entitle them. This theme recurs in various formulations in Disraeli's writings—in appropriate places and frequently also where one would not expect it. However, the best psychological key may be that it always reappears as an argument and is given pride of place. At the age of thirteen Disraeli had been baptized by his father, who was at once a Voltairean rationalist and a conservative royalist, and he needed—for himself and the surrounding world—proof that he was not inferior in rank to any British nobleman. Thus it came about that the man who rose to be the leader of the British Tories and became Prime Minister and the confidant of Queen Victoria as a champion of a social nationalism and imperialism never denied his Jewish origin even as a politician, and in fact repeatedly emphasized it as a patent of nobility. Yet, in contrast to Gobineau and his successors, race was not a scientific concept to him, and he firmly rejected the encroachment of the natural sciences on social life as well as Darwinism and the progressive ideas deriving from it. His conception of race fluctuated and defies clear comprehension and definition. It was Romantic and mystical in nature, a God-given disposition, something that was fatefully active in the past and would affect the future. In emphasizing the psychic, intuitive content his racial fantasy was at times somewhat related to the idea of race used by Chamberlain. Even the high value he placed on pure blood and ancestral soil as the foundations of civilization was a far cry from the scientific (biological) argumentation and mechanistic, martial orientation that later came to the fore in the nationalistic and National Socialist movements. In Disraeli's conception of race there was nothing aggressive or hostile toward other races and peoples; at most there was an occasional arrogant depreciation of other races as compared to the Jewish race, which the others despised. Still, in their aphoristic catchiness his formulations about the crucial importance of race for human events were dangerous statements that could only too easily be employed, and were indeed used, to corroborate anti-Jewish racial doctrines, thus making them a weapon against the Jews.* Here—so one could argue—a courageous Jew has revealed the secret and admitted the truth that other Jews have always denied out of cowardice and fear. That this insecurity of the isolated Jew was behind this theory as well (something that will also concern us in the next chapter) is of relatively little importance. After all, the need for a new stability in an unstable age and society played an important role in the development of the anti-Semitic racial theory and its reception by the foes of the Jews. Psychology makes historical processes more comprehensible, but it cannot justify them. Disraeli died in April 1881. One wonders how he would have reacted to the pogroms in Russia that erupted scarcely a month later.

As for literature about Disraeli, Judaism, and his theory of race, the monumental biography by W. F. Monypenny and G. E. Buckle is still a standard work (new ed. in 2 vols. [London, 1929], especially 1:871ff.). (Cf. also the extensive review, which discusses our problem as well, of the first edition of this book, by E. Daniels in *Preussische Jahrbücher*, vol. 193, pp. 129ff.) The semifictional biography by André Maurois, first published in 1927 and later in many editions and languages, is revealing. Of the monographs that also deal with Disraeli's pre-Zionist statements and figures I shall mention Cecil Roth, *The Jew Disraeli* (I used the Hebrew translation, Tel Aviv, 1955); Leon Kellner, "The Earl of Beaconsfield," *Die Welt* (Vienna) 1:1; Joseph Caro, "Benjamin Disraeli, Juden und Judentum," *Monatsschrift für Geschichte und Wissenschaft des Judentums* 76 (1932): 152ff., 217ff.; Benjamin Jaffe, *Benjamin Disraeli* (Hebr.) (Tel Aviv, 1960); Isaiah Berlin, "Benjamin Disraeli, Karl Marx and the Search for Identity," *Midstream* 16, no. 7 (1970): 29–49.

BIBLE CRITICISM AND THE JEWISH QUESTION: The problem to which we have 245ff. repeatedly referred, particularly in the excursus about Spinoza, can of course only be sketched here. To go into it in detail would involve an investigation of a number of literary, historical, and theological aspects for which there is no space here and the author lacks the requisite expert knowledge. Here we shall point out only that such investigations have been carried on, down to recent times, chiefly by Protestant theologians or scholars with such an education. Only in the last forty to fifty years have Jewish scholars dealt with it independently. See the literature in *EJJ* 4:913ff.; Yeheskel Kaufmann, *The Religion of Israel from Its Beginnings to the Babylonian Exile*, trans. and abridged by Moshe Greenberg (Chicago, 1960, New York, 1972). An

---

*Cf., e.g., H. S. Chamberlain, p. 273 (322): "Now that so much nonsense is being talked about this question, people should let Disraeli teach them that the whole importance of the Jews lies in the purity of their race and that it alone gives them strength and permanence. Just as the Jews have outlived the peoples of antiquity, they will, thanks to their knowledge of this natural law, outlive the constantly intermingling peoples of the present." Chamberlain refers to the novels *Tancred* and *Coningsby*: "In the latter Sidonia says that all is race and that there is no other truth; any race is bound to be ruined that carelessly gives up its blood." Forty years later the Nazis' Institute for the Study of the Jewish Question (Berlin) described its program as follows: "Through rational research the Institute wants to serve the living insight which a Jew, and one of the most significant of all times, Benjamin Disraeli, expressed in the formula 'All is race'" (W. Ziegler on the cover of K. Schickert's *Die Judenfrage in Ungarn*, 1937).

important work for the cluster of problems dealt with in this book is Hans Liebeschütz's *Das Judentum im deutschen Geschichtsbild von Hegel bis Max Weber* (Tübingen, 1967), chap. 8 ("Das Geschichtsbild der Bibelkritik: Julius Wellhausen"), chap. 9 ("Das Judentum in der Weltgeschichte des Altertums: Eduard Meyer"), as well as parts of chap. 10 ("Soziologische Weltgeschichte: Max Weber").

247　THE "JEWISH NOSE": The problem of the "Jewish nose" in caricature and in the history of the Jewish question deserves separate treatment in view of the fact that it did not appear as a decisive characteristic until late. In point of fact, only a minority of Jews have so-called Jewish noses. Anyone who spends even a short time watching Jewish passers-by in Jerusalem or other major cities of the State of Israel can easily see for himself or herself. Cf. particularly Eduard Fuchs, *Die Juden in der Karikatur* (Munich, 1921); Karl Schwarz in *EJ* 9:963–70; *JE* 9:338f. ("Nose"); Maurice Fishberg, *Die Rassenmerkmale der Juden*, (Munich, 1913), 51–59; A. Ruppin, *Soziologie der Juden* (Berlin, 1930), 1, section 1 and the illustrations at the end of the volume; Salo Baron, *A Social and Religious History of the Jews* (New York, 1937), 2:287. Concerning transference of the devil's face, cf. the English caricatures from the thirteenth century in Cecil Roth's *A Short History of the Jewish People*, illustrated edition (London, 1948), after p. 209, and Israel Abrahams, *Jewish Life in the Middle Ages*, ed. Cecil Roth (London, 1932), after p. 400. Cf. especially Joshua Trachtenberg, *The Devil and the Jews: The Medieval Conception of the Jews and Its Relation to Modern Antisemitism* (New Haven, 1943).

247　WILHELM BUSCH: For the dissemination of the stereotype of the physically unattractive, degenerate Jew no one has perhaps done more in words and cartoons, at least in German-speaking countries, than the German artist and poet Wilhelm Busch (1832–1908). His books are among the most widely disseminated in all classes of the people. As an example here are two descriptions in verse: "Und der Jud mit krummer Ferse/ Krummer Nas' und krummer Hos'/ Schlängelt sich zur hohen Börse/ Tief verderbt und seelenlos."—From *Die fromme Helene*, 1872. (And the Jew with a crooked instep, crooked nose, and crooked pants slinks along to the great stock-exchange, completely corrupt and soulless). "Kurz die Hose, lang der Rock/ Krumm die Nase und der Stock,/ Augen schwarz und Seele grau,/ Hut nach hinten, Miene schlau—/ So ist Schmulchen Schiefelbeiner./ (Schöner ist doch unsereiner)."—From *Plisch und Plum*, 1882. (Short pants, long cloak, crooked nose and stick, black eyes, grey soul, hat far back, sly face—that's Sammy Skewbones. Our kind sure is better-looking!) Busch certainly was not an "anti-Semite" in the literal sense of the word; he simply shared the antipathies and prejudices of the majority of his fellow citizens. However, with his respectable artistic typification of the image of the Jew he paved the way into all circles for the anti-Semitic agitators, just as Treitschke's *Deutsche Geschichte* and other works of historiography and literature had done among the "intellectuals." Cf. Joseph Kraus, *Wilhelm Busch in Selbstzeugnissen und Bilddokumenten* (Hamburg, 1970), 84ff. (the source of our quotations); *The Genius of Wilhelm Busch: Comedy of Frustration*, ed. and trans. Walter Arndt (California, 1982); *Wilhelm Busch and Others: German Satirical Writings*, ed. Dieter O. Lotze and Volkmar Sander (New York, 1984).

248　NEO-DARWINIAN THEORY: Concerning the influence of Darwinism and neo-Darwinism on the social sciences ("Social Darwinism"), the further development of the racial doctrine, and its application to the Jewish question, cf. Part 1, chap. 9, pp. 357ff.

248f.　JOHANN GOTTLIEB FICHTE: Here we are not discussing Fichte's general philosophy or the significance of his *Reden an die deutsche Nation* for the awakening of the

German people as a prerequisite for the struggle against Napoleon I. These addresses really had an enduring effect on the heightening of the idea of nationalism as a self-avowal and self-realization of a people and also on the Jewish national idea, which at the end of the century found its expression in Zionism. (Cf. S. H. Bergman in *EJJ* 6:126ff.) To be sure, Fichte's words about the importance of the Germans lent themselves to subsequent exploitation in the spirit of pan-Germanism and anti-Semitism. Fichte's high esteem for the Jewish philosopher Solomon Maimon (1754–1800) is well known, as is his support of a disparaged Jewish student at the time of Fichte's rectorate at the University of Berlin. Many Jews in his lifetime and later were his adherents and champions, e.g., Ferdinand Lassalle (cf. J. Levy, *Fichte und die Juden* [Berlin, ca. 1925]). The fact remains, however, that Fichte profoundly despised Judaism as a religion and the Jews as a people and expressed this contempt in a work that appeared anonymously in 1793 and was reprinted fifty years later, after his death, under his name. This work was occasioned, in connection with the defense of the right to make a revolution, by the discussion of the objection that this could give rise to a state within the state. Fichte points out that there already are a number of states within the state: the Jews, the military caste, the nobility, etc. Fichte uses sharp words against the military and the nobility as well, but they are not as caustic as those against the Jews. Understandably enough, the anti-Semites have not missed these passages; they have been cited again and again. Of course, they really are only extreme formulations of remarks that may be found in similar form in Kant, Hegel, and other philosophers.

Here is a major portion of the quotation in context, taken from *J. G. Fichtes Beitrag zur Berichtigung der Urteile des Publikums über die Französische Revolution—zur Beurteilung ihrer Rechtmässigkeit*, reprint of the edition that appeared in 1793 without name and place (Zurich and Winterthur, 1844), 132–35:

Through almost all European countries spreads a powerful, hostile state that is engaged in constant warfare with all others and in many respects has a terribly oppressive effect on the citizens; it is Judaism. I do not believe that it is so fearsome because it constitutes a separate and solidified state, but because this state is based on hatred for the entire human race. A people whose lowliest member exalts his ancestors more than others exalt their entire history and regards as its progenitor an emir who is older than that history—a legend that we ourselves have adopted as one of our articles of faith; a people that sees in all nations the descendants of those who have expelled it from its passionately loved fatherland; a people that has condemned itself, and is condemned by others, to petty trading which exhausts the body and deadens the mind to every noble feeling; a people that its religion excludes from our meals, our cups of joy, and the sweet exchange of merriment from their hearts to ours; a people that in its duties and rights and down to the soul of the Father of us all isolates itself from all others—such a people might be expected to be different from what we see it is. As things stand, in a state in which the absolute king is not permitted to take my father's hut away from me and I am given my rights against an all-powerful minister, any Jew who pleases can rob me with impunity. You are watching all this and cannot deny it; you speak honeyed words about tolerance, human rights, and civil rights even as you violate our elementary human rights. You cannot deny enough to express your loving toleration of those who do not believe in Jesus Christ by giving them titles, dignities, and honorary offices, and yet you publicly abuse those who believe in him, as you do, and deprive them of their civil honor and their honestly earned livelihood. Have you forgotten about the state within the state? Does not the logical idea occur to you that if you give the Jews, who without you are citizens of a state that is more solid and more powerful than all your other states, civil rights in these states, they will completely trample your citizens underfoot? Far be from these pages the poisonous breath of intolerance, which is far from my heart! Any Jew who breaks through the solid—one is tempted to say, insurmountable—barriers before him and attains to the universal love of justice, mankind, and truth, is a hero and a saint. I do not know if there is or ever was such a Jew. I shall believe it as soon as I see one; in the meantime, let no one sell me a beautiful illusion as reality; let the Jews not believe in Jesus Christ, let them believe in no god at all, as long as they do not believe in two different moral laws and a misanthropic god. They must be given human rights even if they do not grant *us* such rights, for they *are* human beings, and their unfairness does not entitle us to become like them. Do not force a Jew against his will, and do not allow it to happen when you are nearby to prevent it, for you simply owe it to him. If you ate food yesterday and are hungry again but have only enough food for today, you will do well to give it to the starving Jew next to you if he did not eat yesterday. But I see only one way to give them civil rights: to cut off all their heads in one night and put others on them in which there is not a single Jewish idea. To protect ourselves against them I see no other way but to conquer their Promised Land for them and send them all there. . . .

249f.   HUNDT-RADOWSKY: The quotation is from his book *Der Judenspiegel* (Würzburg, 1819) (cited here after Graetz, *Geschichte* 11 (1870), 361. Cf. also Eleonore Sterling, *Judenhass* (1969), 113f. Around the same time the historian Friedrich Rühs demanded (in *Über die Ansprüche der Juden* [Berlin, 1815], 35) that the Jews be encouraged to "convert to Christianity through leniency so as to bring about in time the end [*Untergang*] of the Jewish people." If, however, the Jews cannot be induced to accept baptism, according to the "proposal of a pious Prussian Senior Financial Councilor" there is only one remedy: "to exterminate them by force." For similar proposals (in addition to those already mentioned), cf. E. Sterling, *Judenhass*, 101f., 128.

250f.   LAGARDE: "Transplantation to Palestine": The quotation is from Lagarde, *Deutsche Schriften*, new ed. with extensive index of persons and subjects (Munich, 1924), 42. Cf. also *Die Wiedergeburt durch Lagarde. Eine Auswahl und Würdigung von Mario Kramer* (Gotha and Stuttgart, 1925), 92 and the introduction to this selection, esp. 69ff. Concerning Lagarde, cf. also Alfred Prugel's essay "Träumereien am grossdeutschen Kamin: Paul de Lagarde," in Schwedhelm, ed., *Propheten des Nationalismus* (1969), 56–71.

250   CARRIERS OF PUTREFACTION: "Any foreign body inside another living body produces discomfort, illness, often even suppuration and death. The foreign body may even be a gem; the effect would be the same if it were a little piece of rotting wood. The Jews are as Jews aliens in every European state, and as aliens they are nothing but carriers of putrefaction. If they wish to be members of a non-Jewish state, they must wholeheartedly and with all their strength repudiate the law of Moses, the intention of which is to make them aliens everywhere but in Judea, and they will have to turn their backs on all views related to this law with all their zeal and hatred. For it is this law and the exasperating arrogance stemming from it that preserve them as an alien race; but we simply cannot tolerate a nation within the nation."—From "Die Stellung der Religionsgemeinschaften im Staate," 1881 (*Deutsche Schriften*, definitive complete edition, 1924, 295f.)

250   TRICHINAE, BACILLI, PUTREFACTION: Paul de Lagarde, *Juden und Indogermanen. Eine Studie nach dem Leben* (Göttingen, 1887), 339, 347. The anti-Semitic literature did, of course, not state the context. Theodor Fritsch, the author of the *Handbuch der Judenfrage* (first published in 1887 as *Antisemiten-Catechismus*), reproduces only the abovementioned statements as well as a few other, similar ones by Lagarde and leaves it to the reader to draw the logical conclusions. (In my edition, the 41st printing, 1937, pp. 478–81.) Concerning terms like trichinae and bacilli, derived from biology, as well as the (insufficiently considered) significance of semantics for the history of the Jewish question, see my essay "Der jüdische Parasit: Bemerkungen zur Semantik der Judenfrage," in *Vierteljahrshefte für Zeitgeschichte* 12 (1965): 121–49, as well as chap. 9 of this book (Part 1, pp. 364ff.)

In his position on the Jewish question Lagarde at first rejected the quasi-anthropological racial theory; in "Die gegenwärtigen Aufgaben der deutschen Politik," 1853 (*Deutsche Schriften*, 30) he wrote: "*Deutschtum* is not in one's blood [*Geblüte*] but in one's heart [*Gemüte*]. Of our great men, Leibniz and Lessing were surely Slavs; Händel, as a native of Halle, was a Celt; Kant's father was a Scotsman. And yet, who will call these un-German?. . . The fact that these Jews came from Palestine is in itself no reason not to throw them into the big melting-pot. But if the Jews' nationality is tied to their religion, we can eliminate their nationality only by taking their religion from them, and we have no right to do that." However, accepting them without this decisive transformation would mean "the preservation of their alien nature, making them in this respect, too, only carriers of putrefaction [here is that term again!]. . . . A foreign body in one's body causes suppuration."

At a later time Lagarde adopted many anti-Semitic formulations and ideas. In 1887 he wrote in "Juden und Indogermanen," p. 330:

> We Germans know that we are of Indo-European, Aryan descent. However, we feel not as Indo-Europeans or Aryans but as Germans, different from the Romanians and Slavs, who also belong to the Indo-European stock, and different even from the non-German Germanic peoples. If all of us, with the exception of the dyed-in-the-wool progressives, reject the Jews not as Jews but as Semites, or more rarely as Phoenicians, this term also states the reason why we do so: the instinct of the people has coined this word without knowing what it has managed to do, and that is why the view underlying this word is correct, for it was brought forth by the psyche of the nation. . . . We are anti-Semites because in 19th-century Germany the Jews living among us represent views, customs, and demands that go back to the times of the division into peoples shortly after the Flood, which makes them look as strange among us as flint knives or arrowheads made of nephrite. We are anti-Semites, not enemies of the Jews, because in the midst of a Christian world the Jews are Asiatic heathens. The circumcision and the dietary laws of the Jews are atavisms. The Jews' monotheism is on the same level as a sergeant called to the quartermaster's office who reports the availability of only one object: one god, two tables of the law, three fathers, four mothers, and the rest of the items in the Passover song to be found in Bodenschatz, No. 2307. The Jews' belief in their chosenness or, as the phrase now goes, "the world-historical mission of Israel," is the very acme of absurdity. A people that has contributed nothing to history over thousands of years—I dare anyone to name one contribution—has the impudence to scream in the face of the Indo-Europeans, who have toiled for nearly everything we are living on, that it is the Creator's favorite people. The first prerequisite for making peace with the Jews and benefiting them as well as us is to return to the situation before the unfortunate emancipation. The Jews will become Germans only if we keep telling them that they are not Germans yet and that as Jews they are nothing but a burden that is repugnant to us and useless to history, a load we are dragging along with energies that would be better employed elsewhere. After the emancipation the Jews are even worse than they were before. We told them they were as good as we were and had the same rights that we had; by way of thanks the Jews are telling us that they are better than we are and that we could learn from them. . . .

Lagarde's polemic was triggered by very unfavorable reviews of his pamphlet against Zunz, whose translations of Jewish poetry he had called garbage. The well-known Jewish scholars Dr. A. Berliner, M. Güdemann, David Kaufmann, A. Ziemlich, and others protested. Lagarde dealt with their objections and discussed the general questions which, he said, underlay his assertions and the critiques of his opponents.

THE TREITSCHKE POLEMIC: The articles and pamphlets published after the appearance of Treitschke's first essay and his booklet *Ein Wort über unser Judentum* (cf. Part 1, pp. 215f.) provide a good cross section of public opinion, especially in the academic and "educated" circles of Germany. The most important of these are now readily accessible in *Der Berliner Antisemitismusstreit* (Frankfurt, 1965), a book with

251f.

a rather misleading title that was edited and supplied with a revealing afterword by Walter Boehlich. The problem was actually not the new concept "anti-Semitism" (which rarely appeared as an abstract idea; only the words *anti-Semites* and *anti-Semitic* were used), but what was behind it: the Jewish question, especially in Germany toward the end of the nineteenth century, a decade after the Jews received full legal equal rights and almost a century after the beginnings, the first emancipative law of the French Revolution. Here we shall only deal with Treitschke's and Mommsen's basic points of view; we shall cover the Jewish reactions in the next chapter. Cf. also Hans Liebeschütz, "Treitschke and Mommsen on Jewry and Judaism," *LBYB* 8 (1962): 153–78; idem, *Das Judentum im Geschichtsbild von Hegel bis Max Weber,* chap. 5 ("Das Judentum in der Politik des Bismarckreichs: Heinrich von Treitschke"), chap. 6 ("Das Streitgespräch um Treitschke"), chap. 7 ("Das Judentum und die Kontinuität der abendländischen Kultur: Jacob Burckhardt"), including an extensive bibliography; Stanley Zucker, "Theodor Mommsen and Antisemitism," *LBYB* 17 (1972), 237–41. My statement in the abovementioned article (which I repeated in Part 1 of this book) that a great, widely read historical work like Treitschke's *Deutsche Geschichte im 19. Jahrhundert* may have contributed more to the spread of anti-Jewish tendencies than many radical tracts by rabid anti-Semites, was used by Sigurd Graf von Pfeil as the point of departure for a polemical article published in 1961 ("Heinrich von Treitschke und das Judentum," in *Die Welt als Geschichte* 21:49–62). However, like an author quoted by him (W. Bussmann, "Treitschke als Politiker" *Historische Zeitschrift* 177 [1954]) Pfeil winds up agreeing with me that "from a political point of view, Treitschke's work had, in the final analysis, a deleterious effect" (p. 62). The author says that in Treitschke's case one cannot speak of "anti-Semitism" (which I did not do, because I use this word with great caution; cf. Part 2, pp. 593ff.) but at the most of "a-Semitism." Concerning that concept, cf. C. Schatzker, "The Term 'Asemitism' in the German Youth Movement," in *Studies in the History of the Jewish People . . . in Memory of Zvi Avneri* (Hebr. with Eng. synopsis) (Haifa, 1930), 267–86. Boehlich and others have associated themselves with my point of view. A similar evaluation was given earlier by Hans Kohn in his comprehensive essay about Treitschke in his book *Propheten ihrer Völker: Studien zum Nationalismus des 19. Jahrhunderts* (Bern, 1948), which contains biographical essays about John Stuart Mill, Michelet, Mazzini, Treitschke, and Dostoievski as representatives of their nations. In this essay, which did not come to my attention until later, Kohn writes (p. 144): "Treitschke saw in the Jews a danger that threatened the innermost nature of *Deutschtum*. He demanded the complete assimilation of German Jewry and a ban on Jewish immigration from the countries on Germany's eastern border. His outstanding importance as a national scholar and popular prophet helped make anti-Semitism respectable in Germany, and perhaps in even greater measure than Richard Wagner's racial tirades against the Jews. Treitschke's statement 'The Jews are our misfortune' served German anti-Semitism as a battlecry for the next sixty years." Cf. also Liebeschütz's very (perhaps overly) balanced presentation of Treitschke's attitude toward the Jews. Liebeschütz does come to this conclusion (p. 191): "But it remains true that Treitschke is most responsible for introducing into the world of German *culture* an outlook according to which Judaism is alien in nature to everything positive and valuable." In one's evaluation one should consider not only the negative value judgments on the Jews' activity and influence on the economy, the press, and society, as well as the frequent use of stereotypes like "Jewish usurers," etc., which are unworthy of a scholar and university professor, but also the whole tenor of the presentation with its overvaluation of everything German and its deprecation of phenomena that are different in nature and repugnant to him (such as British character traits). On the other hand, one must not lose sight of the fact that in his critique of the Jews (in his historical works as well as his polemical articles) Treitschke actually expressed what many of his contemporaries felt and thought even if they did not openly voice it. This is why his words met with such a great response; many of his contemporaries felt as though these words lifted a pressure from them. This brings us to the same conclusion that Mommsen formulated: The shame was removed from Jew-baiting and it became respectable. Cf. also Alfred Prugel's essay "Ein grosser Verführer: Heinrich von Treitschke," in Schwedhelm, *Propheten des Nationalismus* (1969), 72–87. As an example of an appreciation of Treitschke from the National Socialist point of view, cf. Wilhelm Baher, "Treitschke und die Juden," in *Weltkampf* (1944), 68–77.

ADOLF STOECKER: Cf. Walter Frank, *Hofprediger Adolf Stoecker und die christlich-soziale Bewegung* (Berlin, 1928, 1924). About this book and its author, the well-known National Socialist, Hans Liebeschütz writes (*Das Judentum im deutschen Geschichtsbild*, 183f.) that Frank had started his book as a student after Hitler's beerhall *Putsch* of 1923 "and became the dictator of the historians under the Nazi regime, which he resolved not to survive. What interested him was Stoecker's plan to create and control a mass movement, and thus he was not tempted to idealize the conservative demagogue."   252f.

MOMMSEN'S DEMAND OF COMPLETE ASSIMILATION OF THE JEWS: Mommsen favored the dissolution of the small separate ethnic groups in favor of the big nations or national territories. In this spirit he wrote in his *Römische Geschichte* in very positive terms about the role of the Jews in the ancient world, with obvious reference to the present. The Jews, he wrote, were just right for Caesar's state that was to be "built on the ruins of a hundred living polities. . . . In the ancient world, too, the Jews were an effective ferment of cosmopolitanism and national decomposition, and in that respect they were privileged members of the Caesarian state, whose polity was basically nothing but world citizenship and whose popularity was essentially nothing but humanitarianism" (*Römische Geschichte* 3 [1856], 550; new ed., *Das Weltreich der Caesaren* [Vienna, 1933], 23). Treitschke had picked up the phrase in his response to a polemic against him by Mommsen; both were dated 14 November 1880 and appeared in the *Nationalzeitung* (now in Boehlich, 210ff.). Treitschke wrote that he did not share the pessimistic view of his colleague Mommsen "that all over the world Judaism is an effective ferment of cosmopolitanism and national decomposition, but I harbor the hope that in the course of the years the existing emancipation will be followed by inner amalgamation and reconciliation." In his reply, "Auch ein Wort über unser Judentum," Mommsen endorsed this characterization, which he had written almost twenty-five years earlier, and openly applied it to the present: "Without doubt the Jews are a decomposing element, as they once were in the Roman state, and in Germany they are an element of decomposition of the ethnic groups. . . . Processes of decomposition are often necessary but never pleasant, and they inevitably bring a long series of ills in their train. . . . Conditions definitely require a certain mutual abrasion and polishing as well as the creation of a German nationality that does not conform with a definite regional group. . . . I certainly do not regard it as a misfortune that the Jews have for generations effectively worked toward that end . . ." (cited after Boehlich, 219f.). Treitschke, on the other hand, believed that the influence of the Jews, far from furthering, as an "element of decomposition," the dissolution of the German ethnic groups in favor of a uniform German nationality, was promoting "only a homeless cosmopolitanism" and destroying "our national pride, the enjoyment of our fatherland." Since that time the terms "ferment" or "element of national decomposition" have been a staple of anti-Jewish vocabulary, and in Nazi ideology they combined with synonyms like "corrosive element" and worse. (Cf. Part 2, pp. 713f.) However, this identification of *Dekomposi-*   255f.

tion with *Zersetzung* (corrosion, corruption) is already found in Treitschke. In his lectures on *Politik*, later given wide dissemination in book form, he said in reference to Mommsen: "The Jews have always been 'an element of national decomposition'— in plain German, of national *Zersetzung*" (Boehlich, 263).

256   GENERAL DEMAND OF COMPLETE ASSIMILATION: As already stated, the opponents agreed in calling upon the Jews to give up their separate existence and to be completely absorbed by German society and culture (with or without formal conversion to Christianity). The question remains which of the two men was more radical in this demand, and it was asked by Ludwig Philippson in his *Allgemeine Zeitung des Judentums* right after the appearance of Mommsen's work (reprinted in Philippson's *Gesammelte Abhandlungen* 2:339): "Treitschke says that the Jews can remain Jews but must become Germans. Mommsen says that the Jews are Germans but must, for the sake of *Deutschtum*, become Christians. The question is who is the more liberal in his conclusions. . . . But what kind of community is it that is supposed to be able to exist only if an individual sacrifices everything that is peculiar to him and becomes a mere stereotype?" This touches on a problem that was to occupy both Jews and non-Jews a great deal.

256   EDUARD VON HARTMANN: A typical example of the attitude of German intellectuals to the Jewish question in the early period of modern anti-Semitism is Eduard von Hartmann's book *Das Judentum in Gegenwart und Zukunft*, which appeared in 1885 (Leipzig and Berlin) and created a certain stir, especially because of its author. Eduard von Hartmann (1842–1906), hardly known to the present generation, was in his day a very respected and even famous philosopher and writer, having published a book about the philosophy of the unconscious at the age of twenty-six (1868). Like Treitschke and Mommsen, Hartmann distanced himself from anti-Semitism and anti-Jewish tendencies and endeavored to view the problem as philosophically and objectively as was possible for a man who was also very critical of Christianity. He rightly regards "the systematic denial of the existence of the Jewish question in the Jewish-influenced press [a typical formulation of the time] as a very imprudent strategy, for its inconsistency with the facts contributed to the anti-Semitic reaction." Thus Hartmann tries to do justice to the problem and guards against making sharp attacks, but this is precisely what brings out his prejudices and his radical conclusions. His chief complaint is the one also made by Treitschke and Mommsen: Thus far the Jews have only very inadequately kept the pact made with them when they were granted emancipation. Their "host nations"—I will discuss this expression in several later contexts—have taken them in as guests and granted them equality under the condition, explicit or implicit as self-evident, that they give up their separate existence as a national corporation and without reservation become integrated into, and absorbed by, the nations among which they lived. In contrast to thoroughgoing anti-Semites, Hartmann praises the qualities of the Jews and regards mixing with them as anything but harmful to the other nations, and possibly even beneficial. Nor does he mistake the psychological difficulties on the part of the Jews, and he opposes the exertion of any pressure and coercion to get the Jews to convert to Christianity, even though he regards the real differences between the two religions as insignificant. He is aware that complete integration or intermingling is a process that takes several generations, but the Jews are not sufficiently promoting this process, which has now been impeded by anti-Semitism. At the same time Herr Hartmann believes—and this is astonishing in a thinker of his stature—that the Jews are striving for world domination. For him this is manifested by their adherence to the Messianic faith, in the persistence and continued effectiveness of the pan-Jewish feeling of

solidarity beyond the boundaries of countries, and in the organizational endeavors of Jewry that have found their focus in the Alliance Israélite Universelle in Paris.

> Thus Judaism constitutes an international freemasonry [also an ever-recurring reproach] which possesses in religion its ideal substance, in the ethnological type its visible distinctive mark, and in the Alliance Israélite Universelle and its financial power the crystallization center of an international organization. . . . Even though the anti-Semites are greatly over-estimating the present importance of the Alliance, it cannot be denied that in the eyes of the Jewish patriots it represents the first embryonic center of the future Jewish world government and that its existence is a tonic not to be underestimated for the Jewish dreams of the future and a regrettable obstacle to the rapid de-Judaization of the Jews. . . . If, however, the present conditions remain, the German people will have been *cheated* by the Jews through their demand and acceptance of emancipation.

Cf. Hugo Bergmann's fine article "Eduard von Hartmann und die Judenfrage in Deutschland," *LBYB* 5 (1960), 177–97.

In the succeeding chapters we shall have more to say about the responses to these accusations, and the views, fears, and apprehensions behind them, that were made by the Jews in more or less dignified form and with more or less open-mindedness and inner freedom. Here I shall mention only what may be the best (and proudest) rejoinder. It appeared anonymously in Vienna in 1886 under the title *Fürst Bismarck und der Antisemitismus*, and its author was the brilliant Jewish scientist, inventor, and social philosopher Joseph Popper (Popper-Lynkeus), 1838–1921. Popper uses as his point of departure Bismarck's message of 17 November 1881, which declared in the spirit of state socialism that social welfare for the working class was one of the foremost tasks of any polity "that is established on the moral foundations of Christian national life." Popper points out that Bismarck, whose policies have usually been based on the secular views that have increasingly prevailed since the Renaissance, here emphasizes, in place of the principles of humanitarianism and love of mankind, Christianity as the foundation of modern political and social life. He then concerns himself with anti-Semitism ("In earlier centuries such people were called *Judenfeinde* [enemies of the Jews]; because of the anthropological cloak that they wear, the *Judenfeinde* are today called *Antisemiten*"), discussing primarily Dühring, Carlyle, and Eduard von Hartmann (pp. 74ff.). His analysis of the foundations of Jew-hatred is probably among the most incisive made then or later. In its approach it comes close to the Zionist orientation (and, appropriately enough, Popper willed his literary estate to the Jewish National Library in Jerusalem). He sharply opposes the idea of "host nations" who have as an act of mercy and under certain conditions granted human and civil rights to the Jews as their "guests." "The attainment of human rights is and was not a *business deal* or a contract between Jews and non-Jews. . . . Human rights, equality for all and thus also the emancipation of the Jews, were advances in the area of social ethics, and so there can be no stipulation of a quid pro quo" (91). "People dare to call them [the Jews] ungrateful 'because they have made bad use of the freedoms they were given,' but in the exuberance of majority feeling they do not consider that no one has a right to schoolmaster another person and that it certainly cannot be called a gift when, after forcibly denying human rights, people finally stop acting like robber barons and release these rights like civilized human beings" (124).

THE RUSSIAN POGROMS: Concerning the situation of the Jews in Russia, cf. Dubnow 257ff. 10; *EJ*; *EJJ*; Mark Wischnitzer, *Die Juden in der Welt: Gegenwart und Geschichte der Juden in allen Ländern* (Berlin, 1935), 194–230; Bernhard D. Weinryb, *Neueste Wirtschaftsgeschichte der Juden in Russland und Polen* (Hildesheim, 1969); Hans Rogger, "The Jewish Policy of late Tsarism: A Reappraisal," *Wiener Library Bulletin*

25, nos. 1–2:42–51; Yehuda Slutsky, *The Russian-Jewish Press in the Nineteenth Century* (Hebr.) (Jerusalem, 1970).

Concerning the cultural life, cf. Mark Zborowski and Elizabeth Herzog, *Life Is with People: The Culture of the Shtetl*, foreword by Margaret Mead (New York, 1962, 1967).

Regarding the pogroms themselves, cf. especially *Die Judenpogrome in Russland*, edited anonymously by Leo Motzkin and largely written by him, published for the Zionist Aid Fund (London) by a committee to investigate the pogroms, 2 vols. (Cologne, 1919). The quotation is from Motzkin's article "Prototyp des Pogroms in den achtziger Jahren," 1:18–20. Cf. also my biography of Leo Motzkin in *Sefer Motzkin* (Hebr.), ed. Alex Bein (Jerusalem, 1939); Committee of the Jewish delegations, *The Pogroms in the Ukraine under the Ukrainian Governments (1917–1920)* (London, 1927).

7

The Reaction of the Jews to the Renewed Jew-Baiting and Anti-Semitism

Prefatory Note: In this chapter we can, of course, only give the basic outlines rather than—with a few typical exceptions—the individual phenomena in their myriad guises. That would be the concern of comprehensive presentations of recent modern history as well as specialized studies of certain aspects, such as have been made in the past few decades, and of biographical studies, all too sparse thus far, which could show the complexity of the problems as well as the constantly varying interplay of different, often antithetical impulses and influences in human life. For us it is a matter of pursuing the basic questions that were involved as the Jews entered modern (Christian) civilization. The hostile reaction of this world, discussed in detail in chapters 5 and 6, was one of the most important of these problems and certainly the most visible one. The way in which the Jews reacted to hostile acts cannot, of course, be sundered from the general problematic nature of their existence under the new conditions created by the emancipation, but it is closely bound up with the question of their identity as Jews and citizens. Thus many things stated in the preceding chapters had to be repeated and sometimes supplemented in this new context. Details about the events of the time may be found in the well-known historical works and in the bibliographies for chapters 5 and 6. As a general supplement I shall mention the following: Ismar Elbogen, *A Century of Jewish Life* (Philadelphia, 1941); Howard M. Sachar, *The Course of Modern Jewish History* (New York, 1958); H. M. Graupe, *Die Entstehung des modernen Judentums: Geistesgeschichte der deutschen Juden, 1650–1942* (Hamburg, 1969). In his foreword (p. 9) Graupe writes, by way of motivating his subtitle (and in a certain sense also our presentation, with its emphasis on conditions in German-speaking countries or those influenced by German civilization): "Since the middle of the 17th century we notice more and more distinctly a separate development of the small German branch of Ashkenazic Jewry, which became the decisive factor in the development of modern Judaism. In the 19th century it influenced the much larger Eastern European branch, which had been preeminent for a long time. . . . Present-day Jewry—particulary in the new centers in Israel, America, and a few European countries—was shaped by these two currents, long since largely confluent, of European development. Until around 1890, however, German Jewry was the leading force in the modern development." Albert Lewkowitz, *Das Judentum und die geistigen Strömungen des 19. Jahrhunderts* (Breslau, 1935); N. N. Glatzer, ed., *The Dynamics of Emancipation* (Boston, 1965); Michael A. Meyer, *The Origins of the Modern Jew: Jewish Identity and European Culture in Germany, 1789–1824* (Detroit, 1968); Isaiah Berlin, *Jewish Slavery and Emancipation* (New York, 1961); Joachim Prinz, *The Dilemma of the Modern Jew* (Boston, 1962); Franz Kobler, ed., *Jüdische Geschichte in Briefen aus Ost und West: Das Zeitalter der Emanzipation* (Vienna, 1938); Ismar Schorsch, *Jewish Reactions to German Anti-Semitism 1870–1914* (New York and Philadelphia, 1972); Abraham G.

Duker and Meir Ben-Horin, eds., *Emancipation and Counter-Emancipation: Se-lected Essays from "Jewish Social Studies"* (New York, 1974); Jacob Katz, *Out of the Ghetto: The Social Background of Jewish Emancipation, 1770–1870* (Cambridge, Mass., 1973); Jacob Toury, *Die politischen Orientierungen der Juden in Deutschland von Jena bis Weimar* (Tübingen, 1966); Ernest Hamburger, *Juden im öffentlichen Leben Deutschlands* (Tübingen, 1968); Uriel Tal, *Christians and Jews in the "Second Reich" (1870–1914): A Study in the Rise of German Totalitarianism* (Hebr.) (Jerusa-lem, 1969); Monika Richarz, *Der Eintritt der Juden in die akademischen Berufe in Deutschland, 1678–1848* (Tübingen, 1974); idem, ed., *Jüdisches Leben in Deutsch-land: Selbstzeugnisse zur Sozialgeschichte*, vol. 1, 1780–1871 (Stuttgart, 1976), vol. 2, *Im Kaiserreich* (Stuttgart, 1979); Hans Liebeschütz and Arnold Paucker, *Das Judentum in der deutschen Umwelt 1800–1850* (Tübingen, 1977); Werner E. Mosse, ed., *Juden im Wilhelminischen Deutschland 1890–1914* (Tübingen, 1976); Felix Gilbert, *Bankiers, Künstler und Gelehrte: Unveröffentlichte Briefe der Familie Men-delssohn aus dem 19. Jahrhundert* (Tübingen, 1975); Robert Weltsch, ed., *Deutsches Judentum, Aufstieg und Krise: Gestalten, Ideen, Werke* (Stuttgart, 1963); idem, *An der Wende des modernen Judentums: Betrachtungen aus fünf Jahrzehnten* (Tübingen, 1972); Jehuda Reinharz, *Fatherland or Promised Land: The Dilemma of the German Jew, 1893–1914* (Ann Arbor, 1975); Eva G. Reichmann, *Grösse und Verhängnis deutsch-jüdischer Existenz: Zeugnisse einer tragischen Begegnung* (Heidelberg, 1974).

262f.   AGRICULTURE: The demand always made of the Jews, at least since Luther, was that they become farmers and earn their bread by the sweat of their brow rather than taking up occupations which required (though often only seemingly) less effort—effort being equated with physical labor. This demand was made not only by foes of the Jews, and it was not merely one of the constant catchwords in anti-Semitic literature. Since the time of the Enlightenment this change of occupation was demanded also by well-meaning persons who were favorably disposed toward the Jews, for they expected that this would improve the moral level of the Jews and bring them greater respect from their Christian fellow citizens. For a great variety of reasons all these demands and endeavors met with little success in Europe. Following an old tradition, the peasants opposed the sale of landed property to Jews and even the employment of Jews as farm workers. Of course, those Jews who decided to work on the land were not interested in remaining farmhands. The switch from urban to rural occupations (which usually were far less respected and remunerative) ran counter to the general economic and social trend; it was, after all, the time when many people were fleeing from the country and the farm population was flocking to the cities, where the development of industry and commerce was creating better sources of income. For that reason the settlement of Jews in rural regions was successful only outside Europe—in the United States, in Argentina, and especially in Palestine, where they were able to work in autonomous settlements that were independent of the native farmers. Concerning the premises, the goals, the living conditions, and the achievements of these settlements, cf. chaps. 8–10. Cf. also the remarks in Part 2, p. 545.

262f.   HEAVY INDUSTRY: It was similar with trades in Western and Central Europe; until the nineteenth century the guild system barred Jews from these almost everywhere. A considerable number of industries grew out of the ranks of the craftsmen, and thus the Jews had no important share in them. However, substantial numbers of Jews did participate in industries that had developed from trading, particularly in the clothing industry. They came to it from dealing in old clothes, an occupation that had for a long time been forced upon them, and they introduced a revolutionary innovation, the manufacture of ready-to-wear clothes. Some Jews also took a leading part in industries that manufactured new products, such as the electrical industry. Being less tradition-bound than the artisans, they were quicker to grasp and utilize new things. Thus electric current as a source of illumination and energy was introduced in Germany by Emil Rathenau (the founder of the AEG—the German equivalent of General Electric—and the father of Walther Rathenau) and in Austria by the Russian-Jewish engineer Johann Kremenezky. Similarly, Jews quickly took a leading part in railroad construction, and there they were aided by their sense of what would be important in the future, their adaptability, and especially their experience in long-term financing. The situation was different in Eastern Europe, where a considerable number of Jews were craftsmen and the economy was less developed. Since, however, the discussions of the Jewish question were carried on largely in Central Europe and particularly in Germany, the different conditions in Eastern Europe were largely disregarded.

Specific information about the occupational distribution of the Jews in the nineteenth century may be found in the bibliographies on the sociology and statistics given for chap. 1 (Part 2, p. 482f.) Cf. also Jacob Segall, *Die beruflichen und sozialen Verhältnisse der Juden in Deutschland* (Berlin, 1912); R. Rürup, "Jewish Emancipation and Bourgeois Society," *LBYB* 14 (1969): 67ff.

ACHIEVEMENTS OF THE JEWS: Within the framework of this book it is not possible to 263 discuss the accomplishments of Jews in all fields of their activity, in the natural sciences, the social sciences, and the humanities. There is an extensive literature on this subject, and some of these works will be mentioned here. It is probably safe to say that the number of Jews with special accomplishments generally is far greater than their percentage in a given sphere or activity or occupation. The reason why this hardly shows up in any official statistics is that valuable achievements were credited to the various nations as a whole rather than to certain population groups. (Cf. also my remarks in the introductory chapter, Part 1, p. 22.) To gain a clear picture one must examine biographical details and look at names and backgrounds, remembering that people frequently changed their names in the course of assimilation. This often leads to errors, not to mention the difficulty of definition: Jewish or part Jewish? By origin or religion? etc. If one uses the number of Jewish Nobel Prize winners as a yardstick, this amounts to ten times their share in the world population. To arrive at a general judgment on that basis would, of course, amount to one of those customary statistical fallacies, for a number of other social factors would have to be considered as a basis for comparison. It is more revealing if one states that approximately half of all Nobel laureates in medicine were Jews and that of thirty-eight German laureates before 1933 eleven were of Jewish or partly Jewish descent, as were half of the six Austrian ones. But even if all factors are considered, one can point to above-average and frequently fundamental and revolutionary achievements of many Jews in a great number of fields; suffice it to mention men like Einstein or Freud. It is, of course, possible to qualify this by pointing out that the top achievements of individuals do not say anything about the average achievements of the other members of the group and that the positive achievements of some must be balanced by the negative behavior of other members of the group. There is another important factor: the problem of evaluating certain works and accomplishments. What seems to be a great creative achievement to some is often given a negative evaluation by others. Artistic and scientific achievements can be interpreted in a variety of ways and classified accordingly. In point of fact, persons who were anything but demagogic or radically anti-Jewish have frequently denied the Jews any creative ability, especially in the fields of art (painting, sculpture), music (despite Felix Mendelssohn, Gustav Mahler, and Arnold Schönberg), and the theater (despite Max Reinhardt, Arthur Schnitzler, and others). Undeniable achievements were then simply called not truly "creative." In such judgments the observer's general scale of values plays a decisive role.

In general, it is safe to say that in mnay fields of endeavor that had been closed to them prior to the emancipation the Jews had to achieve particular distinction to be able to work in them at all. Those with average or below-average achievements had no chance to be considered. Then, too, they always felt that the observing, critical eyes of the surrounding world were on them, and hence they had to exert all their strength in order to overcome the prejudices (actual or simply suspected and feared) of public opinion. This was, of course, at the expense of naturalness and was apt to bring uneasiness, strain, and tension into works and activities. To be sure, inbreeding and selection as the result of centuries of persecution and forced segregation as well as the Jewish commandment of procreation did their share in developing adaptable and intellectually superior Jews. In *The Jewish Mystique* (New York, 1971), p. 14, Ernest van den Haag points out that among the Jews it was especially the descendants of rabbis, and therefore the intellectually superior, who had prospects of getting married and being successful, while the most intelligent group of the Middle Ages, the Catholic clergymen, were not permitted to marry and thus did not propagate. The feeling of superiority that occasionally arose among the Jews for all these reasons (and others that have repeatedly been mentioned) and aroused in their non-Jewish fellow citizens feelings of insecurity and even inferiority often exacerbated the tension and produced in the non-Jews an anxiety that expressed itself in Jew-hatred as a defensive reaction and supposed protective measure.

In addition to the pertinent articles in the Jewish encyclopedias, factual material may be found, sometimes with a critical commentary, in books like Cecil Roth, *The Jewish Contribution to Civilization* (London, 1938 and numerous later editions); Siegmund Kaznelson, ed., *Juden im Deutschen Kulturbereich* (greatly expanded second edition, 1959; the first edition of this copious compendium [1934] was confiscated by the Gestapo before its publication and distribution, ostensibly because it gave readers "an altogether erroneous picture of the true activities, especially those of a destructive nature, of the Jews in German culture"); Annedore Leber, ed., *Doch das Zeugnis lebt fort: Der jüdische Beitrag zu unserem Leben* (Frankfurt a.M., 1965); Arthur Eloesser, *Vom Ghetto nach Europa: Das Judentum im geistigen Leben des 19. Jahrhunderts* (Berlin, 1936); Jacob Marcus, *The Rise and Destiny of the German Jew* (Cincinnati, 1934); Jacob Lestschinsky, *Das wirtschaftliche Schicksal des deutschen Judentums* (Berlin, 1933); Paul Emden, *Money Powers of Europe in the 19th and 20th Centuries* (New York, 1938); Richard Ehrenburg, *Die Fugger, Rothschild, Krupp* (Jena, 1925); Stephen Aris, *The Jews in Business* (London, 1970, 1973); Kurt Zielenziger, *Juden in der deutschen Wirtschaft* (Berlin, 1930); Rudolf Schay, *Juden in der deutschen Politik* (Berlin, 1929); Ernest Hamburger, *Juden im öffentlichen Leben Deutschlands: Regierungsmitglieder, Beamte und Parlamentarier in der monarchischen Zeit, 1848–1918* (Tübingen, 1968); Gustav Krojanker, ed., *Juden in der deutschen Literatur* (Berlin, 1922); Arthur Sakheim, *Das jüdische Element in der Weltliteratur* (Hamburg, 1924); Siegmund Kaznelson, ed., *Jüdisches Schicksal in deutschen Gedichten: Eine abschliessende Anthologie* (Berlin, 1959); Solomon Liptzin, *Germany's Stepchildren* (Philadelphia, 1948); Peter Gay, "Encounter with Modernism: German Jews in German Culture, 1888–1914," *Midstream* 21, no. 2 (February 1975): 23–65. A unique publication appeared at the beginning of the period of emancipation: M. P. Yung, *Alphabetische Liste aller Juden und Jüdinnen, Patriarchen, Propheten und berühmten Rabbinen vom Anfange der Welt bis auf unsere Zeit, nebst einer kurzen Beschreibung ihres Lebens und ihrer Werke* (Leipzig, 1817)—probably the first Jewish biographical encyclopedia. It was the purpose of this well-intentioned book to show that the Jews deserved to be on an equal footing with the other citizens and "at the same time to familiarize young Jews with the wise and

important men of their nation and instill in them greater respect for these men"
(foreword, 13).

THE INFLUENCE OF THE JEWS AS WRITERS AND JOURNALISTS: The share of the Jews   263
in the cultural life of the nations in the narrower sense—that is, Jews as writers and
journalists, in particular the Jewish influence on the press—is a story in itself.

This influence has been significant since the eighteenth century—first, in that
century, through outstanding individuals, particularly Moses Mendelssohn as philosopher, German writer, and exemplary human being and Jew; equally through the
salons of Jewish women, whose beauty, empathy, and ability to gather around
themselves people of the most varied backgrounds and characters for social intercourse and refined conversation and to discover, encourage, and promote young
talents contributed a great deal to the tempering of class distinctions and the free,
creative exchange of ideas both orally and in letters. As the best-known among these
we shall mention only Henriette Herz (1764–1847), Moses Mendelssohn's oldest
daughter Dorothea Veit-Schlegel (1764–1839), and especially Rahel Levin-Varnhagen
(1771–1833).

Here we shall only refer to the well-known fact that the Jews assumed increasing
importance in medicine, a branch of knowledge familiar to them since olden times,
and all branches of jurisprudence, including legal commentary.

In the nineteenth century Jews increasingly achieved prominence as writers,
poets, and especially journalists, and from the middle of the century in all areas of the
liberal arts—from philosophy and psychology to sociology, which has been characterized as a social science particularly suited to the Jews (cf. René König, "Die
Freiheit der Distanz: Der Beitrag des Judentums zur Soziologie," in *Der Monat*,
August 1961, 70–76).

There is almost universal agreement that since the beginning of the struggle for
emancipation and its ever more widespread implementation the Jews increasingly
participated in journalism and exerted an obvious influence on the daily press (as
they often do to this day), though there are great differences in the (positive or
negative) evaluation of this influence. Daily newspapers (and with them journalism as
a profession) came into being at the same time as the emancipation of the Jews and
the emancipative, political, and social libertarian movements generally. These dailies
have evolved from specialized learned journals and "intelligencers," amid a rapid
transformation of the information system (from carrier pigeons to the electrical
telegraph and telephone, photography, and phototelegraphy), to modern political
journals with political positions, financial reports, book and art reviews, the advance
printings of literary works, and especially feuilletons or similar essays which at their
best are little works of art that combine clarity and readability with a well-shaped
style. In all stages of this development and in all fields of activity Jews have played a
leading and often a trailblazing role. The development of the daily press and the fight
for its freedom were part of the struggle for freedom of expression and political
activity generally, and they were closely connected with the participation of the
bourgeoisie and later of the working class in political and social life.* Thus it was only

---

*Cf. Karl Schottenloher, *Flugblatt und Zeitung: Ein Wegweiser durch das gedruckte Schrifttum*
Berlin, 1922), 378f.: "Together with the new appreciation of the masses in political and economic
life, political writings, especially in newspapers, assumed an enormously increased importance
as well. Almost overnight the newspaper turned from a private financial enterprise into a
political power, an effective vehicle and promoter of public opinion, and an indispensable
propaganda medium for the political parties. It is safe to say that 1848 was the year in which the
political press was born [in Germany]. . . . The new state of affairs of the modern age was that
the newspaper, which earlier had largely limited itself to providing information, now became

natural for the Jews to make increasing use of the press in their struggle for freedom and a liberalization of living conditions generally as well as their specific fight to enjoy freedom and equality before the law and practice their Judaism. This goes rather far in explaining their interest in this occupation and the verve with which they carried it on. Their struggle for freedom and influence was rendered more absolute and intense by the fact that the spheres of influence open to other citizens—primarily higher government positions, the military, and many professions—were closed to them as long as they clung to their Judaism. Even the normal exertion of influence—through high social standing, honorary positions, and the like—was difficult for them; nothing was as easy for them as it was for non-Jews of equal or even lesser ability. The bourgeoisie and later the working class also used the so-called public opinion as a "way of exerting pressure on the upper classes and the press as one of the most important means of forming and visibly recording public opinion." For the Jews, literature and the press were almost the only way, the most logical and most easily accessible means of exerting a legitimate influence on the state and society by producing and influencing "public opinion." "The deer sees the hunter before the hunter sees the deer. The Jewish heritage in high-level journalism was a sense of tact, a sensitivity to nuances, a fine ear for subtle differences, and a nose for things to come . . . A keen ear is one of the things that distinguish a journalist from a reporter" (Paul Mayer and Maximilian Harden, in Krojanker, ed., *Juden in der deutschen Literatur* [Berlin, 1922], 107f.).

Yet the typical Jewish journalist, and surely the important, visible kind, is in general anything but Schmock, the unprincipled scribbler in Gustav Freytag's comedy *Die Journalisten*, who says this about himself: "I can write on the right and I can write on the left. . . ." Of course, there have also been such destitute and humiliated figures among both Jews and non-Jews who cannot afford to have an opinion that differs from the one prescribed by their employers. However, the characteristic type of Jewish journalist, and the one that has aroused the surrounding world, is the writer and critic who fights for just causes (or at least causes that seem just to him) more unequivocally than many of his non-Jewish colleagues, the champion of truth and justice who sides with the oppressed against their oppressors, the fighter for humanity in opposition to a narrowly conceived ultranationalism. Representative Jewish journalists were Ludwig Börne, Maximilian Harden, Georg Brandes, André Spire, Alfred Kerr, Karl Kraus, and Kurt Tucholsky. Heinrich Heine was, of course, the most important Jewish poet, writer, and journalist in a German-speaking country and culture (cf. the excursus about Heine in Part 2, pp. 642ff., as well as the index). It is against these Jewish writers and journalists that the wrath of their adversaries is directed—and not always entirely without reason when in the fight for justice the former consider no constraints, historical situations, or legitimate interests and when their corrosive criticism burns painful wounds into living flesh. However, the critique of the anti-Semites and many who are not outright foes of the Jews is directed generally against the excessive influence of the Jews on the press as the organ of public opinion. If the Jews controlled a major portion of the big dailies financially and through the influential editors, the surrounding world regarded this as the domination of an ethnic minority that had always been despised and was working from a different historical-cultural tradition, and it indignantly rejected it as an undue alien

---

the vehicle of public opinion." The evaluation of this institution in the conservative and reactionary circles of Germany was usually negative. On the other hand, in the countries of Western Europe and in North America (by contrast to any kind of totalitarian state) freedom of the press is regarded as one of the most valuable prerequisites for, and guarantees of, civic and human freedom in the state.

influence. Paranoid anti-Semites have even discerned behind it a plan to poison and enslave the healthy native population. Yet the influence of the Jews through the press was largely limited to the intellectuals and certain strata or circles of the population in the big cities. Only few of their writings were read by the petty bourgeois; they were not carried by the provincial press and had no effect on the small-town and rural population. Despite all their reputation in the world, the big newspapers that were called "Jewish sheets" (newspapers of the stature of the *Frankfurter Zeitung* in Frankfurt am Main, the *Vossische Zeitung* and the *Berliner Tageblatt* in Berlin, and the *Neue Freie Presse* in Vienna) had only very little influence on political decisions and almost none on parliamentary elections. If astute observers need any proof of this, the years 1932 and 1933 supplied it for Germany.

THE BAPTISM OF JEWS: Concerning this problem, cf. the articles and bibliographies   265f.
under this and similar headings in the Jewish encyclopedias—articles on "apostasy," "mixed marriages," and on well-known personalities who had themselves baptized (*JL, JE, EJJ*). *EJ* 2:129ff. also provides detailed statistics on conversions, although it should be kept in mind that there have been several critiques of the unreliability of demographic statements about the Jews (cf. Part 1, p. 25ff), *Judentaufen*, ed. by W. Sombart and A. Landsberger (Munich, 1912), contains the responses of well-known Jews and non-Jews to an inquiry about their position on the problem of baptism. A good, balanced presentation of basic statistical material may be found in A. Ruppin, *Soziologie der Juden;* for a comparison with substantially different figures (with variations up to ten times) see Carl Cohen, "The Road to Conversion," *LBYB* 6 (1961), an attempt to illuminate the conversionary movement historically and psychologically from the viewpoint of the present and to deal with the most important literature on the subject. Cf. also Guido Kisch, *Judentaufen*, (Berlin, 1973), a historical, biographical, psychological, and sociological study with special emphasis on Berlin and Königsberg. In *Der Untergang der deutschen Juden* (Berlin, 1911, 1921) Felix A. Teilhaber attempted to demonstrate with the aid of statistical material, in sadness and by way of a warning, that mixed marriages, conversions, birth control, and superannuation—concomitants of the free life in the big cities—had caused a steady decline in the Jewish population of Germany and threatened to put an end to German Jewry. Concerning the problem of mixed marriages (and the conversion frequently associated with them) in the twentieth century, cf. Werner J. Cahnmann, ed., *Intermarriage and Jewish Life: A Symposium* (New York, 1963); Moshe Davis, "Mixed Marriage in Western Jewry," *Jewish Journal of Sociology* 10, no. 2 (December 1968), 177ff. Concerning the psychology of the converted Jew, cf. Erich Kahler, *Israel unter den Völkern* (Zurich, 1936), 74ff.; Peter Gay, "Begegnung mit der Moderne," in *Juden im Wilhelminischen Deutschland* (1976), esp. 244ff.

Of course, a great deal could be said about the baptism of Jews, a problem of which there is as yet no comprehensive treatment, from historical, psychological, religious, ethnic, racial, nationalistic, utilitarian, and moral points of view. These aspects cannot be treated here, but I shall add a few remarks by way of a general and a Jewish appraisal.

At a time when there is a Jewish State with free immigration and Jews need not change their religion to have freedom of action (at least in the West, but to a considerable extent in Eastern Europe as well, though in most countries this freedom is not as great as is generally assumed), it is easy to make a deprecatory judgment on the converts of the nineteenth century and the first half of the twentieth, with a moral indignation that often comes close to an immoral arrogance. In order to arrive at a fairer judgment it may be best to follow Carl Cohen's abovementioned, very valuable investigation of the "road to conversion." The very term "conversion" is food for thought. After all, in a great many cases it was not a turning around (the literal meaning of the word) but an external adoption of certain forms and customs of the Church. In this process the dogmas, the acceptance of which would have meant a true "conversion," were hardly given serious consideration. It is astonishing that this was ignored by the Christians, who converted the Jews with great missionary zeal. What is even more astonishing is that the Christians, who often were on a high level not only in rank but intellectually and ethically as well and openly demanded the conversion of the Jews as a mere formality or prerequisite for the attainment of certain academic or political offices, did not see, or refused to realize, even if honorable Jews drew their attention to it, that this "conversion" actually meant a nihilistic depravement of Christianity and encouraged the baptized Jew to live a lie, feign a profession of faith, and act like a hypocrite. In this connection Hermann Cohen spoke of a *Glaubensmeineid* (religious perjury). Hence, in writing about the problem of conversion, it is impermissible to ignore the conversions for "selfish reasons," as Cohen does in his article (though surely with noble intentions). After all, even selfishness is justified if it stays within "normal" bounds—that is, if it serves for the preservation of a life without an unjust oppression of another life. Why should a Jew who takes his Christian fellow citizen as a model expose himself—and his children and grandchildren—to discrimination if he hears daily preachments and teachings in school, in public life, in friendly intercourse, and in the warnings of well-intentioned people that conversion to Christianity is only a formality and will bring him great benefits, that it is hardly more than false piety that ties him to the Jewish religion, a pride that may be estimable but is really unfounded and may tempt him to be imprudently stubborn? A historian of the rank of Leopold von Ranke told outstanding students (such as Harry Bresslau) who rejected baptism with astonished incomprehension that to him they were really "historical Christians" (F. Meinecke, *Erinnerungen 1901–1919* [Stuttgart, 1949], 27f., and "Rankes Tagebuchdiktat," in *Historische Zeitschrift* 151). These arguments were involved in almost all conversions, and the desire to lead an untrammeled life played a part, though it may not have been the major reason. Only the aims varied; they might be on a higher plane and correspond to more differentiated needs—perhaps the desire to do research and teach without constraints, or to develop and work in the arts. (To be sure, such "higher selfishness" was frequently bound up with the "lower" kind.) If one wants to raise the question of blame for the conversions of the period of emancipation, the main and greatest fault lies with the Christian world, which, in keeping with its view of the "emancipative contract," was seductive and threatening as it induced the Jews to convert.

In light of all these inducements it is really astonishing and speaks for the power that Judaism—as a faith and as a historical, religious, national tradition, though often reduced to mere "piety"—still exerted despite everything that the majority of the Jews did not abandon their Judaism.* As already mentioned in Part 1, the conversionary movement was at first essentially limited to the upper classes of the Jewish population—the city dwellers, the intellectuals, or those who had advanced socially through wealth. The lower classes, the petty bourgeois, the Jews in the villages and country towns, the paupers, the peddlers, and the beggars—not an inconsiderable part of the Jewish population—were subject to far less harassment and continued to lead their traditional lives, at least for one or two generations and not infrequently even longer. Among these the Jewish customs had been preserved in more natural form and had not been diluted into challengeable "articles of faith" that hardly shaped anyone's activity or inactivity. Unlike those who were really remote from Judaism, there was as yet no need for these Jews to claim that they were proud of their

---

*The number of Jewish converts in nineteenth-century Germany has been estimated at only 22,000.

Jewishness or that they despised it; they were living it. (I myself, born in a Franconian village in the early years of the twentieth century, still witnessed this as a child, and also the temptations that came with our move to a medium-sized city.) In most cases the Jews, particularly in the big cities, did not have enough counterforces and attractions to counteract the instructions and temptations of the Christian surrounding world, too little knowledge of Judaism and too little true faith, connection with the past, and genuine, natural pride.

Thus the Jewish communal institutions are also to blame, especially the Jewish schools or the so-called *Religionsstunden* (religious instruction) in the public schools (for many the only place for a Jewish education) and the heads of Jewish community councils, rabbis, and teachers. The writer Max Brod, Franz Kafka's closest friend and the preserver and editor of his writings, a Zionist who was always true to himself and kept faith with Judaism, wrote an "Elegy to the Apostates" in 1920, at the beginning of a new era in the rebuilding of Palestine under the protection of the mandate given to England by the League of Nations. In this poem, which has been reprinted in *Jüdisches Schicksal in deutschen Gedichten* (ed. S. Kaznelson [Berlin, 1959], 454–56), he blames the Jewish Establishment for their apostasy. The baptized Jews appear like a living cemetery to him: "Lebendiger Friedhof meines Volkes! Ich durchwandre still/ Dein dämmerndes Geviert, das nichts als Ruhe will/ Das nur zerbröckeln will, das nur verfallen will . . ." (Living cemetery of my people! I quietly walk through your dim area which wants nothing but quiet, wants only to crumble and decay . . .). The poet asks his countless sisters and brothers why they look at him so coldly and accusingly and wonders what he has done to them: "O Frage weich, auf die es eine harte Antwort gibt:/ Du hast uns nicht genug geliebt!" (O gentle question to which there is a harsh answer: You did not love us enough!) ". . . Und nun erkenn' ich manchen, der mir wert . . . O Knabe dort, von bleichen Rätseln ausgezehrt,/ Du bist im Recht—man hat Dich nichts gelehrt./ Ach wo sind Deine Lehrer, Israel?/ Zwar schläft und schlummert nicht der Hüter Israels,/ Doch seine Lehren dösen, dick vermummt,/ Der grosse Mund der Tugend ist verstummt/ . . . Dem Bösen und dem Kind, das nicht zu fragen wagt, Unwissenden und Klugen—keinem ward das Wort gesagt,/ Das Berge öffnet, das in Finsternisse tagt . . ." (And now I recognize many who were dear to me . . . You boy there, consumed by pale riddles! You are right— you have not been taught anything. Oh, where are your teachers, Israel? True, the guardian of Israel is not sleeping or slumbering, but his teachers, thickly swathed, are dozing. The great mouth of virtue has become mute. The evil man and the child who does not dare to ask, the ignorant and the wise—none has been told the word that opens mountains and brings light into the darkness). And now that there is a new hope flashing in the East, a brighter light—"euch strahlt es nicht./ Verdrossen dreht ihr euch. Und wir, gequält/ Am schönsten Tage, merken, dass ihr fehlt,/ Und dass auf ewig uns verlorner Chor umgibt/ Wie Geisterstimmen: Wehe, nicht genug geliebt!" (—it does not shine for you. Dispiritedly you turn away. And we, tormented on the finest day, notice that you are absent and that we are eternally surrounded by a chorus of the lost, ghostly voices saying: Woe, not enough love!)

This strikes the chords whose echo resounds in our ears to this day: the inexpiable sin of having failed, for lack of love, to free questioning human beings from their ignorance and to impart to them the knowledge, the courage, and the pride of upright Jews. The main problem that is raised here is this: The Jewish leaders of the period of emancipation had themselves become unsure of what Judaism really was. They had lost love for themselves, their history, and the values of their Jewishness and thus could not educate others to identify with Judaism (which, in the final analysis, is tantamount to "loving" and "keeping faith"). Part 1 contains some comments about the attempts to remedy the lamentable lack of Jewish knowledge and the ossification of the teachers of Judaism. Here I shall point out that out of ignorance even many Jews adopted the basic Christian pattern of Judaism—if only through language and literature with their deprecation and misinterpretation of numerous Jewish words, concepts, and historical phenomena. A case in point is the completely erroneous view of the Pharisees as hypocrites or of Judas as a traitor, which was given currency by the New Testament. Martin Buber said about Henri Bergson* and Simone Weil that they had turned away from a Judaism that they did not know: ". . . In actual fact they turned aside from a conventional conception of Judaism, created by Christianity" (M. Buber, "The Silent Question," in *At the Turning* [New York, 1952], 40). Given such premises—an attractive Christian-Germanic culture and an unattractive, even repulsive contemporary Jewish life—there are many instances of the best and the brightest among the Jews coming very close to conversion before they regained their faith in Judaism and found the road to regeneration for themselves and others. That even Leopold Zunz, the founder of the Wissenschaft des Judentums (Science of Judaism) for a short time thought of converting has recently been documented by his biographer Nahum N. Glatzer (*Leopold Zunz: Jude, Deutscher, Europäer* [Tübingen, 1964], 20; *Leopold and Adelheid Zunz: An Account in Letters* [London 1958], xvi and 13). Concerning the inward despair of I. M. Jost, the first Jewish historiographer of the nineteenth century and a man who rejected baptism for himself but thought it was at least understandable if the young generation converted, cf. the two letters edited by N. N. Glatzer in the Siegfried Moses Festschrift *In zwei Welten*, (Tel Aviv, 1962), 404 and 411. Franz Rosenzweig, too, was close to converting to Christianity when he made a sharp turn and found the way to a regeneration of Judaism through a new understanding of himself. Cf. his *Briefe*, ed. by Edith Rosenzweig (Berlin, 1935), 45ff., 71ff., 162f., and Hans Liebeschütz, *Von Simmel zu Rosenzweig* (1970), 146ff. In his articles in *LBYB* 2 (1957), 178ff. and *In zwei Welten*, (p. 449), Ernst Simon has shown that Sigmund Freud also flirted with the idea of converting to Christianity. Many have fared similarly, whether or not they spoke of it, down to our days. Perhaps the best-known case is that of Theodor Herzl, who devised a scheme for baptism about two years before he transformed himself into a Zionist (cf. Part 2, p. 680). He did not propose to bring the adult generation into the Christian fold, for their pride would forbid this, but planned to lead all of their children there in order to free them from the senseless burden of Judaism while they were not yet of age and thus still blameless, thereby eliminating the Jewish question once and for all.

Little is known about what went on inside the converts—because most of them kept silent even when they wrote autobiographies (like the art historian Bernard Berenson). Much can be learned from the correspondence of contemporaries close to them (e.g., about Gustav Mahler from the memoirs of his wife Alma). There is as yet no extensive investigation and presentation of the subject, though there is some important material in the abovementioned book by Guido Kisch. It was an unbelieving time, a time of no faith in destiny, in which the Jews assumed or hoped that they would be able to escape the Jewish fate, which, like Heine at a certain period, they regarded only as a misfortune. In general, keeping silent about the past did not cause them to be greatly honored by their new coreligionists and fellow nationals. Somehow their vociferous "We Germans," "We Frenchmen," etc., did not ring true to all those with sensitive ears unless they themselves somehow provided it with conscious or unconscious question marks—through self-irony, as in Heine, or through shrill sequences and dissonances, as in Gustav Mahler. There were, of course, others, such

*Actually, Bergson never officially left the Jewish fold. When France surrendered to the Nazis, he refused to let the French government make an exception and exempt him from the anti-Jewish laws—because, as he wrote in his will of 1937, "J'ai voulé rester parmi ceux qui seront demain les persecutés" (cited after Carl Cohen, *LBYB*, (1961): 270).

as the classical philologist Jacob Bernays (1824–81), the son of the conservative *hakham* (rabbi) Isaac Bernays (1792–1849). He kept the promise he had given his father and refused to convert to Christianity even when the influential German diplomat, theologian, and philologist Christian von Bunsen, who was very kindly disposed toward him, told him that he could expect to have a great career. Cf. his correspondence with Bunsen in Hans I. Bach, *Jacob Bernays* (Tübingen, 1974), 112ff.

Whether or not the Jewish people was to blame, how much it has lost through its sons and daughters that became alienated from it! How much other peoples often gained when they received credit for the positive achievements of the converts, while the Jews were charged with the harmful ones, or those regarded as harmful! Today the Jews in the Diaspora and in the State of Israel face the problem of putting in the proper perspective the life of those Jews who have officially "left" the Jewish fold as Jews, as citizens of their adopted fatherlands, and as human beings, without consideration of emotions and preconceived judgments. What Jewish heritage may or may not be discerned in those Jews by origin who no longer wanted to be Jews but were nevertheless somehow regarded as Jews by the world around them or by the Jews, without operating with rash generalizations and dubious theories about race and blood, as Jews have often done? How does one avoid the "double bookkeeping" that claims for a people those that belong to it by birth if it enhances its own glory and disowns them if it does not? After all, saints and sinners, heroes and cowards, loyal and perfidious persons are equally members of a people, disagreeable though this may be in certain cases, and if one removes the barriers of religion as merely formal boundaries, one has to say that they are members for the glory, the shame, and everything between these extremes. These are some of the problems that must at least be raised here, no matter how far from a generally recognized solution they may still be.

JEWISH SELF-HATRED: Concerning the roots and ramifications of Jewish self-hatred, 269 cf. also the remarks in Part 1, pp. 269ff.

It appears that the idea of "Jewish self-hatred" was originated by the Jewish writer and philosopher of history Theodor Lessing (1872–1933), the author of *Die Geschichte als Sinngebung des Sinnlosen* (1919), who was murdered by the Nazis in 1933. In any case, he introduced the term into the literature on the Jewish question by means of his book *Der jüdische Selbsthass* (1930).* Before he wrote the book, he had experienced Jew-hatred, the problem of the emancipation of the Jews, and self-hatred in his family, his surroundings, and especially in himself, and it was presumably intended for his inner salvation. In the theoretical introductory chapter, "Vorhalle," he writes: "In his youth the author, too, went through a period of exclusive devotion to *Deutschtum* and preclusive resistance to *Judentum*. Has there ever been a noble-minded young truth-seeker, born in the twilight and placed in the predicament of having to choose between two peoples, who did not have to grapple with the same uncertainty? There is no person with Jewish blood in whom we would not find at least the makings of 'Jewish self-hatred.'" Cf. also Lessing's memoirs *Einmal und nicht wieder,* which appeared after his murder and World War II; Erich Gottgetreu's knowledgeable and perceptive article "Zum Thema des jüdischen Selbsthasses" (*MB,* Tel Aviv, 18 September 1963); and Baruch Kurzweil's Hebrew essay on the roots of Jewish self-hatred in *Ha'aretz,* 4 June 1957.

In accordance with his philosophy of life, which is indebted to Nietzsche and

---

*The phenomenon itself probably was noted earlier. For example, in his book *Der Antisemitismus als Gruppenerscheinung* (Berlin, 1926), 47, F. Bernstein calls the inclination of many Jews to endorse the hatefully distorted Jewish image of the non-Jews "a perverted phenomenon of enslavement."

Klages, Lessing regards self-hatred as a universal human phenomenon that originated from the "I and Thou split" between the spirit and the natural facts of life. "However, this universal human phenomenon of self-hatred can be illuminated particularly brightly through the psychopathology of the history of the Jewish people" (p. 27). According to T. Lessing, man seeks to give every historical event and every misfortune befalling him an *ex post facto* morally meaningful interpretation, asking what or who is to blame. "This act of endowing even all senseless and meaningless suffering with meaning can be accomplished in two ways—either by laying the blame on the 'other' or by seeking the fault within oneself. It is one of the most profound and most certain insights of ethnopsychology that among all nations the Jewish people was the first, and perhaps the only one, that sought the blame for what was happening in the world only *within itself*" (13). The readiness to shoulder the blame for every misfortune befalling it with profound faith in God's justice "put the Jews at a disadvantage in the competition among the nations. . . . On the other hand, this self-judgment turned the Jewish people into the real ethical people." The confession of guilt of Christianity, particularly Protestantism, is an individual one *("mea culpa, mea maxima culpa")*, "while the Jewish self-judgment is based on collective responsibility." Every Jew is responsible, incurs guilt for all other Jews, and bears personal blame for the actions of the totality (228f.). The logical response to the questions "Why don't they love us? Why do they hate us?" is "Because we are guilty"—unless there is the counterpoise of faith in the mission, the chosenness, and the superiority of the Jewish teachings and way of life. That was the case in the life of the ghettos prior to the period of emancipation. The realm of human values probably derives from suffering and the blame for this suffering, the "negative aspect of life": "Self-hatred is only the unavoidable shadow of this insight into the negative." At bottom the self-hating Jews are suffering from "an unrequited love for their enemies" (40). As T. Lessing and others have pointed out, the same root frequently gives rise to an extreme self-assurance to the point of arrogance, as well as irony and mockery of others and oneself—a kind of rebellion of the vanquished and subdued against the victor, whom one would really like to serve and by whom one would like to be accepted among the people he respects.

In all countries and areas of life there are symptoms of this modern Jewish self-hatred, which began in the eighteenth century (cf. Yeheskel Kaufmann, *Behevlei Hasman* [Hebr.] [Tel Aviv, 1936], 259) and steadily increased in the course of the nineteenth and twentieth centuries. Cf. Barkai's article "The Austrian Social Democrats and the Jews: An Investigation into the Self of the Progressive Jew at the Turn of the Century," *Wiener Library Bulletin* 24, no. 1 (1970): 32–40, or I. Gotthelf's cautionary article in the Hebrew daily *Davar* (Tel Aviv, 18 Nov. 1955) about manifestations of self-hatred even in the State of Israel—for example, when Western Jewish intellectuals regard everything Western European as culturally far superior to things Israeli. Only on the basis of a healthy amour propre (which is not to be confused with narcissism) can one be productive and do justice to oneself and others with love or at least tolerant understanding.

The relatively brief theoretical remarks in Theodor Lessing's book about Jewish self-hatred are followed by biographical essays—understanding and affectionate thanks to the author's own experience—about six Jewish personalities as types of Jewish self-hatred: Paul Ree (Nietzsche's friend), Otto Weininger *(Sex and Character)*, Arthur Trebitsch (a Jewish anti-Semite), Max Steiner (a very gifted student who was weary of modern life and equated it with his Jewishness), Walter Calé (a gifted poet who worked in isolation), and Maximilian Harden (a journalist who was at times a powerful, almost too powerful, seeker of justice and hater, or at least despiser, of the Jews, finally himself a victim of ostracism). Many others could be added, and Lessing mentioned some of them in his essays: Karl Kraus, Egon

Friedell, Kurt Tucholsky, Walter Rathenau (at least for a certain period), to name only a few from the first third of the twentieth century.

The tragic situations in which self-hating Jews could wind up are evidenced by Harden's closing speech at the trial of the nationalistic thugs who had in 1922 knocked him down with an iron bar and to their (and many others') regret had failed to kill him. As most Jewish assimilationists have always done (and are doing today), he spoke of "we" and "us" in the name of the Germans and said that the acquittal of the cutthroats would "prove that all those who have a low opinion of us are in the right." Then he suddenly interrupted himself and said: "No, I made a mistake. I did not mean to say 'of *us*,' I meant 'of *you*,' those who say bad things about *you!* If you reject me because I came into the world as a Jewish boy, all right! I often told Rathenau: Why do you always write and say 'We Germans'? After all, they don't want to number the Jews among the Germans. I love the Germans, but I won't force myself on them." (Cited after T. Lessing, *Jüdischer Selbsthass*, 203f.)

In one of his remarks on human psychology that anticipate so many later developments Nietzsche writes (in *Human, All Too Human*): "Luke 18:14 improved: He that humbleth himself wants to be [instead of: shall be] exalted." Applying this to our problem, this sentence might be varied, with reference to Max Brod's abovementioned Elegy, to read: He who despises himself wants to be respected; he who hates himself, wants to be loved . . .

MIXED MARRIAGES: For literature on this subject, see the beginning of the excursus on "Baptism of Jews" (Part 2, pp. 629f.). Mixed marriages have, of course, always existed when Jews had closer contact with non-Jews, but since the period of emancipation the tendency toward such marriages has grown steadily. After all, people lived in the same residential areas, attended the same schools and universities, and met socially, in theaters and concerts, and in recreation and amusement centers. This increased the inducements and temptations. The introduction of civil marriages in many countries created a nonreligious legal basis. Romantic relationships transcend and surmount boundaries of all kinds if no excessive barriers are put in their path. Mixed marriages were often based on material considerations as well; the money of marriageable Jewish girls gilded a considerable number of aristocratic coats of arms, and the prospect of being fully accepted by Christian society frequently induced young Jews to take Christian wives. But the real innovation was that non-Jewish and Jewish fighters for emancipation proclaimed intermarriage as a desirable goal and proof that the Jews were sincere in their desire for complete integration. It was, so to speak, the "biological assimilation" (Ludwig Lewisohn) that was to render the intellectual and spiritual kind permanent. In Part 1 I already mentioned Gabriel Riesser's speech in the Frankfurt National Assembly on 29 August 1848. After condemning the existing laws, which had prohibited mixed marriages or required that the children from such marriages be baptized, Riesser continued, with the optimism that was characteristic of that stage of the German revolution (which later failed miserably): "It will be a consequence of our new legal code that there will be mixed marriages and that religion will no longer be a lasting and insurmountable barrier to ethnic union, whereupon ethnic divisions will cease" (cited after the Minutes, p. 1755; also contained in Dubnow's *Neueste Geschichte des jüdischen Volkes* 2 [Berlin, 1920]; 312; Höxter's *Quellenbuch* 5 omits the sentences about the desirability of mixed marriages, and so does Dubnow's *Weltgeschichte* 9:323). Almost fifty years later, in his speech in defense of the Jews during the great debate on the Jews in the French Chamber of Deputies (25 to 27 May 1895), the Franco-Jewish deputy Alfred Naquet championed this principle in similar and even more drastic terms. He declared that he was undertaking the defense of the Jews only to avoid being branded as a coward and that he had long ago demonstrated his "endeavor to intermingle the races" by

269

marrying a Catholic woman. Cf. Alex Bein, *Theodor Herzl* (Vienna, 1934 and 1974), p. 201, after the *Annales de la Chambre des Députés* (1895), 2:100ff. and Herzl's report in the *Neue Freie Presse*. Numerous similar examples could be adduced.

270   EMANCIPATION: AN ASSIMILATION CONTRACT? in addition to the literature given in the preceding chapters, cf. Michael R. Marrus, *The Politics of Assimilation: A Study of the French Jewish Community at the Time of the Dreyfus Affair* (Oxford, 1971), chap. 5 ("The Political Theory of Assimilation"); Zevi Sahavi, *Tnuat ha-hitbolelut be-Yisrael* (Hebr.) (Tel Aviv, 5703/1933); H[arry] Sacher, *Jewish Emancipation: The Contract Myth* (London, 1917). A work typical of its time is Samuel Back's *Das Synhedrion unter Napoleon und die ersten Emanzipationsbestrebungen: Vortrag zum hundertjährigen Jubiläum des Lessingschen "Nathan"* (Prague, 1879). Many writers before and after Treitschke voiced opinions similar to his. Cf. also the above remarks about Eduard von Hartmann and Popper-Lynkeus (Part 2, pp. 620f.).

270f.   ASSIMILATION AS AN IDEOLOGY AND CONSCIOUS ENDEAVOR: Concerning the beginnings of this endeavor in the eighteenth century, cf. Part 1, pp. 179ff. and for the period since the French Revolution, p. 208ff. Here I shall add some general remarks by way of summing up.

The word "assimilation" (from Latin *similis*, giving the idea of similarity, likeness, or resemblance) was, like many other concepts, borrowed by sociology from biology. In the latter, "to assimilate" means "to absorb and incorporate . . . to transform food into living tissue" *(American Heritage Dictionary of the English Language)*. The word seems to have been first used by the social sciences in the late eighteenth or early nineteenth century, when in the wake of the Enlightenment and Romanticism a number of terms from the natural sciences (e.g., the idea of "race"; cf. Part 1, p. 318) were adopted by the humanities and social sciences. (We shall have more to say about this process in subsequent chapters; cf. Part 1, pp. 362f.). The first use of *Assimilation* in connection with the Jewish question that is known to me is from an essay about civil education published in 1808. There we read about the Jews: "Education, and especially the physical kind, is the only way to assimilate these unfortunate remnants of that old nation to the Europeans" (N. Vogt, *Europäische Staatsrelationen* [Frankfurt a.M., 1808], 11:161, here cited after H. D. Schmidt "The Terms of Emancipation 1781–1812," *LBYB* 1 [1956], 37, n. 1; the use of the preposition *mit* with *assimilieren* still betrays its origin in biology). The ideology of assimilation—at first to "humanity" and "mankind"—had originated among the Jews in the second half of the eighteenth century (cf. Part 1, p. 202 and J. Katz, *Die Entstehung der Judenassimilation in Deutschland* [Frankfurt a.M., 1935]). With the beginning of legal equality, the further struggle for full equality, and in the polemic regarding the implementation of emancipation—its justification, premises, conditions, successes, and failures—it was expanded and more and more generally associated with the idea of "assimilation."

Social, cultural, and political assimilation is a process in the life of nations that always occurs, in one form or another, among population groups that live in the same locality but are ethnically different. The process may be voluntary (as an imitation, adaptation, adjustment, or acculturation) or forcible, as the subjugation of an entire people or part of it by another, numerically stronger or more powerful one. There are all kinds of assimilation. For example, the victorious Romans "assimilated" from the Greek world of ideas whatever seemed suitable for them and incorporated it into their own cultural life. (Cf. R. H. Barrow, *The Romans* [Pelican Books, 1949], 59f.) In their entire history the Jews, too, have repeatedly adopted ideas from the world around them and assimilated them, that is, creatively integrated them into their world, just as the world has adopted a great deal from the Jewish world of culture. Similarly, again and again the Jews assimilated to the surrounding world in their clothing and their customs. That was a natural process. Such adoption and adaptation—an active and passive assimilation—is a sine qua non for normal coexistence with other peoples. Locking the Jews into fortified ghettos, which reduced mutual influences and assimilation to a minimum, to what was absolutely necessary, and the Jews' support of this exclusion through a "fence around the Law," in order to keep their lives pure in the sense of their sanctification, constituted an abnormal process in national life. The assimilation movement that accompanied the emancipation was the consequence of the endeavor, on the part of Jews and the world around them, to normalize the life of the Jews and make their countries of domicile their homelands.

Thus the demand of complete assimilation in and since the period of emancipation was a consequence of the modern idea of the national state, in accordance with which the ethnic minorities had to amalgamate with the dominant nation. To all intents and purposes the minorities were not given the right to have a different life-style. The development in the past two generations has shown that the demanded and expected amalgamation did not succeed in most cases in which it was implemented by force. The states of Central Europe can serve as an example, not to mention the "imperialism"—a heightened nationalism—that aimed at bringing distant peoples of Africa and Asia under its national and often also cultural sway and keeping them there permanently.

These connections shed some light on many aspects of the Jewish assimilation movement. Yet we are still astonished at the Jews' naive faith in the success of assimilation. After all, it was no longer an assimilation to an abstractly viewed mankind and a rationally conceived natural right, as it had been in the eighteenth century, but an assimilation to very concrete states and nations with their own cultural world of ideas and their very real economic and political endeavors and interests. On the part of the Jews this gave rise to the strangest theories about the profound congruence between the German (or the French) spirit and the Jewish spirit, and these may be found even in personalities of the intellectual and moral stature of a Hermann Cohen.

If we take another look at the original meaning of the word *assimilation*, as adopted by the social sciences from biology, we can say that the assimilation of the Jews was successful only in relatively few cases—practically speaking, only in families that converted to Christianity, and even among those it succeeded fully only in the second or third generation. Even in these exceptional cases it was always a matter of the lives of individuals or those of families or family groups, usually of the upper classes. Cases in point are the Mendelssohn family and other families from the enlightened elite of their generation and that of their children and grandchildren, some of whom completely severed their connection with Judaism, while others—especially members of the Mendelssohn family—maintained their interest in their Jewish ancestors and sometimes even in Judaism generally. The assimilation of larger groups of people tends to be slow, and usually it fails because of the inner resistance of the minority group, whose historical traditions profoundly influence people's outlook on life, down to everyday matters, and because of the resistance of the majority, to whom the intrusion of a population regarded as alien into all branches of economic, political, and cultural life meant competition in all professions and spheres of influence as well as threatening alien elements in cultural life. Then countermovements arise which, if one may use a parallel from biology, are comparable to the "antibodies" produced by an organism against foreign proteins (antigens). This is what happened with all efforts to accomplish the assimilation of the Jews from the beginning of the emancipation down to our days. Concerning the critique of assimilation by the Jewish nationalist movements, particularly Zionism, cf. chap. 8; regarding the related concept "symbiosis," cf. Part 2, pp. 715ff.).

Despite all the lessons taught by the past, assimilation is still regarded as a chance to solve the Jewish question, even by personalities of the stature of a Toynbee, and it is propagated by all sorts of political orientations, especially those of a totalitarian, Marxist-Leninist, or cosmopolitan nature.

Having already discussed the misfortune that failed assimilation brought upon many individuals, I will speak in this chapter and the following ones about the lessons derived from the idea of assimilation, the belief in it, and the reaction to the outward and inward resistance that it encountered. It is, after all, the central phenomenon in the Jewish question since the period of emancipation.

To provide a more rounded picture, I will here say at least a few words about the positive effects of assimilation on the life of the Jews. Close contact with the surrounding world had a profound effect on their lives; they were freed from stagnation and encouraged or obliged to reflect or transform. Since that time no movement among the Jewry of Europe and the world has failed to be influenced by it. This is what will be discussed in the succeeding sections and chapters of this book.

In addition to the references already given, I will list the following: the synoptic articles in *HE* 18:793–97; *JL* 1:517–23; *EJJ* 3:770–83; Arthur Ruppin, *Soziologie der Juden* (1931), 103ff.; Zvi Rudi, *Soziologie des jüdischen Volkes* (Hamburg, 1965), chap. 5; Peter L. Berger, *Invitation to Sociology* (Penguin Books, 1963), chap. 4 ("Society in Man"), esp. 120ff.; Albert Massiczek, *Antisemitismus: Die permanente Herausforderung* (Vienna, 1968), 95ff.; Isaac B. Berkson, *Theories of Americanization: A Critical Study, with Special Reference to the Jewish Group* (New York, 1920); Yeheskel Kaufmann, *Gola ve-Nekhar* (Hebr., "Diaspora and Foreigners") 2 (Tel Aviv, 1932).

JEWS GROWN MORE SENSITIVE: I shall quote from Theodor Herzl's and Max Nordau's remarks in their addresses at the First Zionist Congress of 1897. Herzl: "Our adversaries may be quite unaware of how deeply they have wounded the sensibilities of the very people among us who perhaps were not even the primary targets of their attack. That part of Jewry which is modern and cultured, which has outgrown the ghetto and weaned itself from petty trading, was hurt to the quick" (Herzl, *Zionist Writings: Essays and Addresses*, trans. H. Zohn, vol. 1 [New York, 1973], 132–33). Max Nordau: "This is the moral distress of the Jews, which is more bitter than the physical distress because it afflicts more sophisticated, prouder, more sensitive human beings. The emancipated Jew is unstable, insecure in his relationship with his neighbors, timorous in contacts with the unknown, suspicious of the secret feelings even of his friends."

270   HANNAH ARENDT: The quotation is from her book *The Origins of Totalitarianism* (New York, 1951), 14.

270   BERTHOLD AUERBACH (1812–1882): Cf. S. Liptzin, *Germany's Stepchildren*, chap. 5. In a letter to Karl Emil Franzos (1879, cited in Höxter's *Quellenbuch* 5, 146f.) Auerbach writes: "This breaks my heart! I, whom Jacob Grimm once told 'Your writings are so quintessentially German that they could have come directly from Hermann the Cheruscian [Arminius]—I, a man who has felt, suffered, and fought for Germany all his life, am now supposed to be an 'alien'?" And in the fall of 1881, a few months before his death, he wrote: "What I suffer cannot be expressed in words. It was a fall from an ideal tower; I am crushed."

271f.   EFFORTS AT RELIGIOUS REFORM: Here, as in earlier chapters, we are not concerned with the history of the Jews and Judaism but with the history and nature of the Jewish question. Historical events belong in this context only to the extent that they influenced our problem, and thus we must limit ourselves to the essentials. The fact themselves are either familiar and perhaps need only to be recalled to mind here, or they may easily be found in the well-known historical works that have repeatedly been cited. As for the Jewish encyclopedias, the articles in *EJJ* reflect the latest research and list the most important literature; cf. particularly those about "Reform Judaism" (14:23ff.), "Orthodoxy" (12:1486ff.), "Neo-Orthodoxy" (12:956ff.), and "Conservative Judaism" (5:901–6). Of the works that I found useful I shall name Albert Lewkowitz, *Das Judentum und die geistigen Strömungen des 19. Jahrhunderts* (Breslau, 1935); Joseph L. Blau, *Modern Varieties of Judaism* (New York, 1966); Max Wiener, *Jüdische Religion im Zeitalter der Emancipation* (Berlin, 1933) (cf. also Yehoshua Amir's introduction to the Hebrew translation [Jerusalem, 1974], 7–32); Caesar Seligmann, *Geschichte der jüdischen Reformbewegungen von Mendelssohn bis zur Gegenwart* (Frankfurt, a.M., 1933); Moshe Davis, *The Shaping of American Judaism* (New York, 1951) (Hebr. ed., *Yahadut Amerika B'hitpatkhutah*); idem, *The Emergence of Conservative Judaism* (Philadelphia, 1963); Max Dienemann, *Liberales Judentum* (Berlin, 1935); Max Wiener, *Abraham Geiger and Liberal Judaism: The Challenge of the Nineteenth Century* (Philadelphia, 1962); idem, "The Conception of Mission in Traditional and Modern Judaism," *Yivo Annual of Jewish Social Science* 2–3 (New York, 1947/48), 9–24; Franz Kobler, *Jüdische Geschichte in Briefen aus Ost und West: Das Zeitalter der Emanzipation* (Vienna, 1931), part 2, "Die Reformer," 55–108; Yeshayahu Wolfsberg, "Popular Orthodoxy," *LBYB* 1 (1956), 237–54.

The following remarks are intended to supplement those in Part 1. In examining and evaluating the religious reform movements in nineteenth- and twentieth-century Jewry one must bear in mind that these were efforts to regenerate Judaism with the aim of integrating the Jews into the European cultural world and making Judaism comprehensible to the surrounding world and attractive or at least acceptable to the Jews in view of the lure of the dominant Christian religion. The champions of radical religious reform probably were not ready to go as far as David Friedländer, a friend and pupil of Mendelssohn, had done in 1799 in his well-known pamphlet for the Protestant pastor Wilhelm Abraham Teller in Berlin, which accepted a dogma-free, theistic-Protestant Christianity that actually existed only in the minds of Jewish rationalists.* In practical terms, however, these men wished to free Judaism from the ballast of what could not be grasped by reason, from everything that people generally (including these rationalists) took to mean "Talmudic Judaism." They believed they were in agreement with the spirit of the Jewish prophets, who valued a morally pure life above anything liturgical or ceremonial. In point of fact, German prayerbooks like those of the radical Reform congregation of Berlin almost read like the libretti of freemasonic operas, their style being like Sarastro's speeches and declarations in Mozart's (or Schikaneder's) *The Magic Flute*. Many of those ready for reform were not willing to go that far, at least not in most European congregations. Being free from any communal tradition, the Jews of the United States went much further in a radical direction. In the larger communities of Central and Western Europe, which regarded themselves as adherents of a "liberal" Judaism, a more moderate reform prevailed. In general it followed the old liturgy, enhanced it with organ playing and choral singing, retained many Hebrew prayers but added some German ones or gave Hebrew prayers in a free German translation, gave pride of place to German sermons by way

---

*However, as a young man the philosopher Hermann Cohen (1842–1918) still identified enlightened Christianity with prophetic Judaism. In his essay about Hermann Cohen (*Between East and West* [London, 1958], 22f.) Hugo Bergmann recalls a conversation between Hermann Cohen and the much younger philosopher Albert Lange (1828–75), the well-known author of *Geschichte des Materialismus*, who had obtained an appointment at the University of Marburg for Cohen. "Lange said to him: 'Our views on Christianity probably differ.' To this Cohen replied: 'No, what you call Christianity, I call prophetic Judaism.'"

of admonishment and edification, and eliminated from the text of the prayers everything that seemed incompatible with the conviction of the worshipers, their teachers,
and their leaders. Here one has to bear in mind that this represented not merely a
concession to the surrounding world in the spirit of the emancipation contract, at
least not a deliberate one; it was also an act of honesty. The Jews' adversaries regarded
it as an act of submissiveness, and so do we, because we do not consider that the
thoughts and feelings of the surrounding world had been transferred to the Jews and
that they now expressed these, almost proudly, as their own convictions. In the
program of the champions of reform of the Jewish community of Worms, dated 23
June 1848 (Kobler, 79f.) we read: "We must strive for truth and dignity in religious
services as well as congruence between faith and life; we must remove empty forms
and create new institutions for the spirit of Judaism. We must no longer pray for
return to Palestine with our mouths while our hearts are chained to our German
fatherland with the strongest bonds. . . . We must not mourn the destruction of the
Temple in sackcloth and ashes when we have long possessed another fatherland, one
that has become so dear to us. . . . A new temple on the old foundation must be built
for the genuine spirit of our faith. . . ." (The word *Tempel* in this sense was increasingly used in the liberal and Reform communities, replacing the traditional—
and hence somehow devalued—word *Synagoge.*) A similar formulation may be found
in Abraham Geiger's "Plan zu einem neuen Gebetbuch nebst Begründungen" (in
Jüdische Zeitschrift für Wissenschaft und Leben 8:246f., quoted after G. Kressel,
David Gordon [Hebr.] [Tel Aviv, 1942]): "The belief in the restoration of a Jewish
state in Palestine and thus also in the building of a temple in Jerusalem as a place of
unification for Israel, in the ingathering of the exiles and everything connected with
such a restoration of vanished conditions, has been completely extinguished in our
consciousness. The expression of such a hope in prayer and the supplication for its
fulfillment would be a bare-faced lie."

The too radical reform was opposed by the so-called positivist-historical school. Its
initiator, Zacharias Frankel (1801–75), from 1854 the director of the new Jewish
Theological Seminary in Breslau, advocated a reform that would be moderate in time,
form, and substance as well as being in harmony with the historical development of
Judaism and the central importance of the Hebrew language. This outlook later gave
rise to the so-called Conservative Judaism in America, with the Jewish Theological
Seminary, founded in New York in 1887, as the central educational institution. For a
comparison of characteristic prayers current in the various Reform movements (which
often differed according to the congregation and its rabbi), from radical reformers to
"conservatives," cf. the tables in Moshe Davis's abovementioned book *Yahadut
America* (New York 1951, 307–17; cf. also the same author's *The Emergence of
Conservative Judaism: The Historical School in 19th Century America* (Philadelphia,
1963). All these schools arose in close connection with the "Science of Judaism,"
which originated at the same time and was, among other purposes, intended to
motivate and support them. (We shall discuss the *Wissenschaft des Judentums* in
another context; cf. Part 2, pp. 661ff.) See chaps. 8, 9, and 10 for an account of these
schools' change in outlook on the idea of Jewish nationalism under the influence of
the Zionist movement and especially in light of the establishment of the State of
Israel.

Samson Raphael Hirsch's view of Judaism, which has been termed "Orthodoxy" or
"neo-Orthodoxy," seems to be in crassest contrast to these schools. His *Neunzehn
Briefe über das Judentum*, first published in 1838 under the pseudonym Ben Uzziel,
rejects both radical reform and the "historical" view of Judaism (including the new
Science of Judaism). But in his rejection of the thoughtless fulfillment of all commandments Hirsch parts company with the traditional Orthodox Judaism that had
been practiced in the ghetto and was still being practiced in Eastern Europe. Hirsch

does not want a Judaism that centuries of pressure and misery caused to turn away from the creative influence of the surrounding world and mummified. He opposed empty ritualism, mysticism, and any kind of superstition: "The exercises that were supposed to educate the intellect and produce life were not understood and often debased to the status of amulets." He, too, desires a regeneration of Judaism, and in this sense he is part of the history of the Jewish reform endeavors of the nineteenth century. However, as far as he is concerned, this regeneration cannot be accomplished through the renunciation or abandonment of ancient laws and religious customs but only through a new understanding of Judaism on the basis of the words and spirit of Jewish teachings—everything that he designates with the word "Torah" (in the Ashkenazic pronunciation that was natural for him, "Touroh"), and that includes for him not only the Bible but also the Talmud, the Midrash, and the religious literature based on these. He does not want Jews to isolate themselves from the culture of the surrounding world that he himself has absorbed. Herder, German classical literature, and the polemical writings concerning the emancipation influenced Hirsch, too. However, in the historical world, whose origin and course he (somewhat like Herder) explains on the basis of the Bible, Israel occupies a special place as a people whose only task it is to bear witness to God's existence in its teachings and its life. Hence the Torah must remain the point of departure and the focus, and its study as well as life in its spirit and in accordance with its precepts must remain the foundation of Jewish life. Jews should not close themselves off from the world, nor should there be an arbitrary philosophical construction of its nature. The thinking demanded by him "accepts nature, man, and history as facts and attempts to derive insights from them," but "Judaism adds Torah to them; it is as much of a reality as heaven and earth" (Letter 15). Thus Judaism is removed from the stream of history (as Rosenzweig removed it later) and becomes "a system of revealed truths" (Lewkowitz, 333). What is to be renewed is understanding; what is to remain, with strict consistency, is everything that relates to a way of life based on the Torah. Hirsch formulates this as "Torah in the *derekh eretz.*"

From this viewpoint Hirsch regards the teachings and lives of the religious reformers of every kind, both the radical and the more moderate ones, as disloyalty to true Judaism. He rejects collaboration with them like a sin, and thus he does not even shrink from the founding of special congregations, managing to obtain a legal basis for them in Germany in 1876 (with the help of liberal Jewish politicians like Eduard Lasker). Up to that time there had generally been unified congregations in European towns with a Jewish population—in accordance with their own desire or the interest and decree of the ruler. Now the adherents of Hirschian "Orthodoxy," hitherto an unknown concept in Judaism, left the unified congregations and as Orthodox believers formed special congregations (*Austrittsgemeinden*, or secessionist congregations) with names like *Adat Yisrael* (in Ashkenazic Hebrew, *Adass Yisroel*) which did not recognize the authority of the majority congregations. (The organization of the congregations in the United States was different from the outset.) Since there was an official separation between church and state and the Christians were and are organized in many sects and communities, the Jewish community, too, formed around synagogues and rabbis. Instead of forming unified congregations, it organized according to beliefs (Orthodox, Conservative, Reform, etcetera).

Despite all their differences in religious faith and activities, however, the Orthodox Jews and the liberal, Reform Jews of the nineteenth century had two principles in common: the recognition of modern political and social life (including the patriotism demanded of a citizen) and the renunciation of the ultimate aim of a return and ingathering of exiles (*Kibbutz Galuyot*) in the fatherland Palestine. We have already discussed the missionary idea of the reformers and their interpretation of the Messianic idea; in this respect the new Orthodoxy differed only in nuances and style.

Hirsch bases himself on Jeremiah's advice (Jer. 29:5–7) to the Judeans who had been
deported to Babylon shortly before the destruction of the First Temple (597 B.C.E.):
"Build houses and live in them. . . . And seek the welfare of the city to which I have
exiled you. . . ." Thus it is all right to participate in the life of the surrounding world
provided that one does not violate any of the revealed commandments and prohibitions, for, as Hirsch writes in Letter 16, "that earlier, independent life in the State
was not the *essence* or the *purpose* of Israel's peoplehood, nor was it only a *means* for
the fulfillment of its spiritual mission. The bond that united it was never land or soil
but the shared task of the Torah." This is why it has been possible to preserve a unity
outside the land. Even if God "some day unites the people outwardly too, in one
country, and the teachings of the Torah are again the principle of a state . . . a future
which, as a goal of the *galut*, has been promised but cannot be promoted actively by
us, can only be hoped for," this will happen only to enable Israel to be a better model
in the fulfillment of its world mission. Cf. Pinchas E. Rosenblüth, "Samson Raphael
Hirsch: Sein Denken und Wirken," in H. Liebeschütz and A. Paucker, eds., *Das
Judentum in der deutschen Umwelt 1800–1850* (Tübingen, 1977), 293–324.

Two points must be added to the outline of the various views of a religious
regeneration of Judaism. First, these were movements in the big cities. It must be
emphasized that in the rural and small-town communities of Central and Western
Europe there were Jews who were naturally rooted in tradition and continued the
Jewish life inherited from their fathers in the accustomed way. These Jews had never
lived in a walled-off compulsory ghetto, and thus emancipation did not have the
revolutionary significance for them that it did for the urban Jews. In many respects
life in those small communities was more like that in the *shtetls* of the Eastern Jews
than in the big cities of the Western Jews. Secondly, we must draw attention to the
altogether different mystical-ecstatic regenerative movement of Hasidism, which
originated in eighteenth-century Eastern Europe and spread over wide areas, as well
as to the countermovement of the more rationalistic *mitnagdim* (opponents), which
emanated from Vilna (Lithuania) and had its center there. I did not mention them in
Part 1 and can only refer to them in passing here, because they had hardly any
influence on the fight for emancipation that was carried on in Central Europe and
thus played no part in the struggle for a solution of the Jewish question. To the extent
that it was known (mostly from its excesses rather than its sources), Hasidism was
rejected as superstition in the more rationalistic spirit of Western European Jewry. It
did not begin to have a regenerative effect on Western Europe until the twentieth
century, when the Jewish national "renaissance" of Martin Buber and others effectively presented it to the Jews raised in European culture in modern versions and
interpretations.

274f.   GERMAN-JEWISH DIALOGUE: I fully agree with the views of Gershom Scholem,
        expressed in his letter "Wider den Mythos vom deutsch-jüdischen Gespräch" (1964)
        and his address "Juden und Deutsche" (1966) with his characteristic critical in-
        cisiveness and clarity and beauty of formulation as well as with a profound sadness
        about the underlying tragic events. (Now included in G. Scholem, *Judaica* 2 [Frank-
        furt a.M., 1970], 7ff.)

275   HEINRICH HEINE, "THE MAN WITHOUT SHAME": A great deal has been written about
        Heine in general and about his attitude toward Judaism and his position among the
        Jews as a representative of Jewry in the first half of the nineteenth century and
        beyond. It is hardly possible to have a comprehensive view of the literature in all
        languages (already in the year of Heine's death someone wrote "Heine und kein
        Ende"; cf. *JL* 2:1556), let alone to make full use of it. Much of it, to be sure, is merely
        a variation and a repetition in new formulations of the older literature. Of the latter,

Adolf Strodtmann's biography (*Heinrich Heines Leben und Werke* [Berlin, 1867]) has not been superseded by subsequent research. Among the more recent biographies, those by Max Brod (Amsterdam, 1935) and Ludwig Marcuse (Hamburg, 1960) are particularly useful for our problem. There have been many studies, by non-Jews and Jews alike, of Heine and Judaism; these writers are positive and negative, often of two minds, more rarely making a clear endorsement of his message or displaying a full human understanding of his life. Certainly, Heine did not make it easy for his interpreters. There is something uncanny about his life—from his youth to the difficult years in the "mattress grave" which made him a legend (one promoted by him) in his lifetime.

Of the writings that are important for our problem and almost invariably contain more or less extensive bibliographies or quotations from the earlier literature, I shall mention the following: Max Jungmann, *Heinrich Heine, ein Nationaljude: Eine kritische Synthese* (Berlin, 1896); Mathias Acher (Nathan Birnbaum), "Heine der Jude," in *Die Welt* (Cologne) 10, no. 9 (2 Mar. 1906), 14f.; Georg Plotke, *Heinrich Heine als Dichter des Judentums* (Dresden, 1913); Israel Tabak, *Judaic Lore in Heine* (Baltimore, 1948); Hans Kohn, *Heinrich Heine: The Man and the Myth* (New York, 1959); Erich Lüth, *Hamburger Juden in der Heine-Zeit* (Hamburg, 1961); Abraham Landesberg, "Last Traces of Heinrich Heine in Hamburg," *LBYB* 1 (1956), 360–69 (with a deeply moving continuation of Heine's poem about the new Jewish hospital in Hamburg, dated a hundred years later, 10 June 1941, from the pen of Hamburg's last chief rabbi, Dr. J. Carlebach, and Landesberg's concluding sentence, which sounds like *finis* written under an epoch: "In December of that year, Chief Rabbi Dr. Carlebach was deported with his wife and four children to Riga, where they were all murdered"); Cuno C. Lehrmann, "Heinrich Heine, ein deutscher, französischer oder jüdischer Dichter?" in *Bulletin LBI* 11, no. 43–44 (1968): 225–47; Ernst Simon, "Heine und die Romantik" and "Arthur Schopenhauer über Heinrich Heine" (both essays may now be found in his collection *Brücken* [Heidelberg, 1965], 135–60); Alex Bein, "Heine wäre verblüfft . . . Theodor Herzl über den Streit um das Heine-Denkmal," *Allgemeine Wochenzeitung der Juden in Deutschland* 7 no. 17 (1 August 1952); Theodor Herzl, "Heine und die Liebe," *Neue Freie Presse*, 12 December 1897, reprinted in *Feuilletons* (Berlin, 1911), 243–53; Dolf Sternberger, *Heinrich Heine und die Abschaffung der Sünde* [Hamburg, 1972]; Pepita Haezrahi, "Heine, Poet of Inconsistency," *Jerusalem Post*, 24 February 1950; Walther Victor, *Marx und Heine* (East Berlin, 1953); Shlomo Na'aman, "Heine und Lassalle: Ihre Beziehungen im Zeichen des Dämons des Geldes," in *Archiv für Sozialgeschichte* 4 (Hanover, 1964), 45–86; S. Liptzin, *The English Legend of Heine*, (New York, 1954), esp. chap. 5 ("The Wandering Jew"); Wolfgang Bühl, "'Der Poet ist bloss ein Teil von mir': Materialien zum Thema Heine und der Journalismus," in *Tribüne* 11, no. 43 (Frankfurt a.M., 1972), 4852ff. (includes a discussion of Karl Kraus); Werner Kraft, "Die Lüge als Motiv bei Heine," in *MB* (Tel Aviv), 26 September 1975, p. 9. With three recent books—Ludwig Rosenthal, *Heinrich Heine als Jude* (Frankfurt and Berlin, 1973); Hartmut Kircher, *Heinrich Heine und das Judentum* (Bonn, 1973); and Siegbert S. Prawer, *Heine's Jewish Comedy* (Oxford, 1983)—I am acquainted only from reviews (e.g., in the *Heine-Jahrbuch* 1975, 197ff. and in *Tribüne*, 1974, 5650–5654). Cf. also Richard Wagner's remarks (Part 2, pp. 600ff.) and the references in the index of this book. The following comments first appeared in the *Heine-Jahrbuch* 1978, 152–74.

Most of Heine's comments on the Jews, Judaism, and the Jewish question, as well as many things connected with these subjects, are now readily available in the (unfortunately inadequately edited) selection from his poetry, prose, and letters that Hugo Bieber published as *Heinrich Heine: Confessio Judaica* (Berlin, 1925). The second edition, *Heinrich Heines jüdisches Manifest* (New York, 1946), was supplemented with a selection from the "Gespräche mit Heine," collected and edited in exemplary fashion by H. H. Houben (Frankfurt a.M., 1926). An English-language edition of Bieber's book appeared in Philadelphia in 1956 under the title *Heinrich Heine: A Biographical Anthology*. Cf. also the introduction by Ernst Elster to the critical edition of Heine's *Werke* (7 vols. [Leipzig, 1890]); to the 10-volume Insel edition by Oskar Walzel (Leipzig, 1911–15; after 1920 with an extensive index volume, here referred to as Insel); by Veit Valentin to vols. 12–15 of the edition in Bongs Goldene Klassiker-Bibliothek; by Felix Stössinger from the comprehensive and excellently edited selection from Heine's writings (*Mein wertvollstes Vermächtnis: Religion, Leben, Dichtung* [Zurich, 1950]—unfortunately out of print), an edition that takes Heine especially seriously and displays a profound understanding of him; by Walther Victor in the East German collection *Heine: Ein Lesebuch für unsere Zeit* (Weimar, 1956); and by Alfred Kerr to the illustrated new edition of Heine's *Romanzero*, issued by Heine's original publisher, Hoffmann & Campe (Hamburg, 1933). For the letters I have used the six-volume complete edition by Friedrich Hirth, 3 vols. of text, 3 of commentary (Mainz, 1950–51) with an introductory essay entitled "Heinrich Heine im brieflichen Verkehr."

Heine's figure in the mind of his contemporaries and later generations in all its duality (one would have to coin a word like "multility" to describe him) deserves a thorough study in itself. Such a work would reveal not only a great deal about Heine but also about those who observed and evaluated him; about their understanding, lack of understanding, and misunderstanding; about their variously accentuated interest in life—political, social, private, and intimate; about the individual impression that his various writings made on them; and about their widely varying agreement with his views or their more or less radical rejection of his outlook on life. As we have already indicated, the assessments of Heine were almost diametrically opposed to one another from the very beginning, even those of the same readers and critics. A historian like Treitschke who, as it were, walked and judged in the toga of a moralistic, patriotic Prussian by choice, was regarded by many as a model for the assessment of Heine. At bottom Treitschke hated Heine and despised him as "shameless," but in his striving for historic justice (almost against his will—like Balaam, the son of Beor) Treitschke did accept Heine as a poet—and sometimes even as a "German". (Cf. the statements in his indictments of the Jews and in his subsequent *Deutsche Geschichte*, esp. vol 3, 1927 ed., 703ff.; "Einbruch des Judentums.") Nietzsche repeatedly concerned himself with Heine (cf. the *Nietzsche-Register* published by Kröner), and in 1873 he sharply rejected him as a destroyer of German style and a *farceur*: "Who will believe in the genuineness of feeling in someone like Heine?" This is almost like Karl Kraus's famous (or notorious) essay *Heine und die Folgen*, first published in 1910 in *Die Fackel*, the journal of a man who was far more of a *farceur* and *poseur* than Heine and may have been influenced by Nietzsche. But Nietzsche later praised Heine effusively, writing that Germany had "produced only one poet in addition to Goethe—and that is Heinrich Heine, a Jew." Elsewhere Nietzsche expresses reservations: "almost genuine"; "imitation as a talent of the Jews, adaptation to forms, hence actors, hence poets like Heine. . . ." In his late writings Nietzsche mentions Heine in the same breath with Napoleon, Goethe, Beethoven, Stendhal, and Schopenhauer and numbers him among the "deeper and more wide-ranging persons" who have experimentally anticipated the European of the future (*Beyond Good and Evil*, 1885) or ranks him together with Goethe, Hegel, and Schopenhauer as one of the few spirits of importance for Europe (*Twilight of the Idols*, 1888). In Nietzsche's confessional work *Ecce Homo*, written in 1888 shortly before his nervous breakdown, we read: "The highest conception of the poet was given to me by Heinrich Heine. I have looked in vain in all the realms of thousands of years for an equally sweet and passionate music. He possessed that divine malice without which I cannot imagine perfection . . . The god not separated from the satyr. And how he handles German!" With the exaltation bordering on megalomania that is characteristic of the last period of his creativity Nietzsche writes that "Heine and I have been by far the best artists of the German language—at an incalculable distance from everything that mere Germans have done with it." With Heine and the composer Jacques Offenbach the Jews have "touched genius"; with Offenbach, Heine, and brilliant buffoonery "European culture has truly been raised to a new level" (in one of the later, posthumously published notes). In this context Nietzsche's biographer Walter Kaufmann (*Nietzsche: Philosopher, Psychologist, Antichrist* [New York, 1956], 323f.) points out that it was Heine's irony and not that of the German Romanticists which served Nietzsche as a model and that Heine's antithesis Judaism-Hellenism (Heine speaks of "Nazarenes") as basic conceptions of the world and civilization provided one of the most important inspirations for Nietzsche's contrast between (ancient) paganism and Christianity and for his psychology of *ressentiment*. On this point Thomas Mann agrees. In his "Notiz über Heine" (1908), to which Kaufmann rightly refers and which Thomas Mann included in his Collected Works, Mann writes: "Of his works I have long loved the book about Börne most. . . . His psychology of the Nazarene type anticipates Nietzsche. . . . And incidentally, this book contains the most brilliant German prose prior to Nietzsche. Incidentally? Oh, only those who understand the blissfully abstracted smile with which he replied to friends who warned him about the human, personal, political offensivenes of the book, 'But isn't it beautifully expressed?'—only those will comprehend what a memorable figure this artistic Jew was among the Germans!"

Next to this effusive praise by literary giants there are deprecatory judgments by less important commentators, including Jews, who have felt uneasy about Heine, to say the least, and often rejected him quite sharply and vehemently. (One senses an occasional underlying unease in the abovementioned giants as well, but they overcame this, at least for a time). Those commentators censure Heine for his sharp criticism as well as his mockery of everything, particularly Prussians, Germans, Jews, and Christians; for his personal confessions about love and love affairs; for his cutting attacks on adversaries like the homosexual poet Count August von Platen, who had irritated him with personal, anti-Jewish abuse, and on the dead and therefore defenseless Börne, whom he regarded as a typical narrow-minded radical and ascetic "Nazarene"; and for his changing views of the age, his contemporaries, and current events, which he always expressed openly and drenched in mockery and irony. All this appears in the criticism of Heine under the rubrics "lack of character" and especially "shamelessness." The opponents of the Jews and other non-Jews connected or equated the latter with "Jewish insolence" and "*chutzpah*," that lack of *verecundia* (Schopenhauer) and true reverence for God or divine powers that was said to be peculiar to Judaism. To be sure, in general the Jews publicly rejected such attacks if these affected them personally, but their relationship to Heine remained dichotomous. They gladly accepted praise of the poet, but they pointed out that what he said in his critical remarks (which they, too, disliked) had nothing to do with Judaism, which he had officially abandoned with his baptism, and that he could and should certainly not be regarded as representative of Judaism and the Jews. One might say that the Jews were motivated by the feelings that one not infrequently has about a relative or friend who seems to be cast in a different mould—a cross between an instinctive feeling of kinship and dissociation. However, in my opinion the analysis of Heine's writings reveals that Heine's so-called shamelessness was really the unconstrained, almost childlike expression of the truths which he discovered for himself; that his changing views were due to the integrity of his insight into himself and others; that he did not find freeing himself from traditional opinions as easy as he tried to make it seem; and that the so-called shamelessness of his style, his mockery and wit, his irony and his sarcasm, and his caustic criticism, which occasionally bordered on cynicism, obscenity, and nihilism, were really indications that he found it difficult to surmount his bashfulness and shyness and tried to overcome (and cover up) these inhibitions by resorting to an uninhibited style. Many of his readers perceived it as "shamelessness" (or pretended to do so) that he unconstrainedly uttered, or blurted out, what they felt in their hearts but did not dare to express and often probably did not even dare to admit to themselves. The vehemence with which many Jews rejected Heine was basically a confirmation that he was in reality the representative of their emotional and intellectual world. Anyone who wishes to understand the Jews of the age of emancipation, and beyond, in the complexity of their lives, desires, thoughts, and feelings can do no better than to read Heine's writings. They express everything that went through the Jewish soul—the conscious and the unconscious, the positive and the negative and everything in between, or in a paradoxical union of all antitheses. Thus a person's attitude to Heine is often identical with his attitude to the Jews in general—in love and hate and all ambivalence of feeling.

It is impossible to demonstrate this in detail; it would exceed the scope of an excursus and must therefore be reserved for a separate study. Here I shall give only a few key ideas, though even those threaten to be too extensive.

First, about Heine's style. The leap from the serious, lyrical, frequently dreamlike to the ironic, sarcastic, or soberly realistic is an expression of bashfulness and is made especially when feelings have become too exposed or have been raised to the point of pathos. At such times his style frequently becomes mannered, but even such affectation often is only the mask of a shy, all too bashful person. Abrupt transitions of this sort appeared two generations later in the music of Gustav Mahler who, like Heine, was criticized for what was regarded as shameless and uncivilized—a sudden change of mood from seriousness and solemnity to informality, crudity, vulgarity, irony, and shrillness. When I began to read and listen to these two artists and strove to understand them, I had to grapple with the same objections and inhibitions as other people, but this relationship grew into a love which, like every true love, incorporates all weaknesses into its understanding. Everything that each of these artists says is a bit of autobiography, even if he speaks, or pretends to speak, about other people and emotional worlds, and this is so to a greater extent than is the case with every artist. An additional factor that is still present here is a Jew's penchant for an open confession before the world and himself, a confession heightened to the point of ecstasy in the Prophets and expressed as well in the liturgy of the synagogue, in the prayers, and in the self-accusations, particularly on Rosh Hashanah and Yom Kippur. In Heine and Jewish figures akin to him everything remains within the framework of a great faith— not in a definite God but in a hidden divine harmony. In Mahler this faith manifests itself in his clinging to the fiction of a traditional harmony and tonality which is not abandoned even though the dissonances really break it, though tricks of modulation, harmonic shifts, the endings of movements, etc., always restore the existing tonality. (This striving for a fictive harmony was first disrupted by Arnold Schönberg through his twelve-tone system in which every note and step of the scale were given a value of their own. There faith manifests itself in this confidence in individuality.)

Closely connected with this is Heine's mode of expression, which seems to be amorphous and casual. (I do not wish to pursue the comparison with Gustav Mahler any further, though it does suggest itself.) Here, too, many things that at first were natural later often became mannered. An examination of Heine's manuscripts, his letters, and conversations shows that the ease and seeming randomness of language was often achieved after a great deal of effort and polishing. But truthfulness toward himself is again in back of it. All his life Heine was a confessor who had the courage to confess. He frequently presented himself as worse than he was—and this, too, may be a reflection of the Jewish sense of sin, the "Nazarene spirit" against which his mind sharply rebelled from time to time. As Rahel Varnhagen, whom he admired (and who was his admiring and occasionally angry educator), noted, he could neither keep silent nor lie. Börne, the republican who did not understand Heine and regarded the playfully brilliant, sparkling, constantly changing man who was so full of *joie de vivre* as a "bad character," had to admit, almost against his will, that Heine was incapable of lying, keeping silent, and dissimulating; if he tried to do these things, everyone immediately noticed it: "If ever there was a man whom nature had destined to be honest, Heine is that man" (Börne, quoted in Brod's *Heine*, p. 196). In his second testament, dated September 1846, ten years before his death, Heine wrote that he was dying without funds, positions, and honors: "My heart wanted it that way, for I have always loved truth and detested lies" (Insel ed., 10:371). And as early as 1839 a two-stanza love poem has "O, lüge nicht!" as its title and refrain. In his article "Die Lüge als Motiv bei Heine" (*MB*, 26 September 1975) Werner Kraft comments on this poem: "The fear of lying is a new motif that did not exist in German poetry before Heine." What is involved in this conception of lies is not an untruthful statement about a fact but a life-lie, truthfulness in the closest interpersonal relationships and in love, which proceeds from shyness to a kind of naked shamelessness as its climax but must always preserve a kernel of modesty to keep it from degenerating into something commonplace. What is behind all important statements of Heine is this fear of the life-lie and a desire to destroy illusions and life-lies with all the resources of language, to proceed from seriousness and solemnity to frequently crude mockery, to the truth behind appearances, and to express this truth without conditions and constraints, "shamelessly." Hence the frequently human, all-too-human motives which demand expression are insignificant. The decisive thing is the truth of what Heine writes; the psychological factors diminish in importance and almost are of merely historical or scholarly interest. But precisely this expression of the deepest layers of our existence and actions always has to struggle against the traditional, against what is morally valid and is anchored for us in the form of shame. In Heine's last poem, the most beautiful love and farewell poem written for the woman he called the "Mouche" shortly before his death, we find these lines: "The word that is spoken is devoid of shame. . . . Silence is the chaste blossom of love."

It should be noted that Heine, who treated friends and supplicants with kindness, made personal attacks in his polemics (as did his opponents, though with less sure aim), but in his love poems he exposed only universally human elements and almost never anything too personal. We know next to nothing about the lives of the numerous lovers that appear in his poems and nothing about their intimate remarks. Heine's grateful loyalty to his wife and his care beyond the grave for that woman, who surely never understood him intellectually (but whose concern is that?), are revealing and touching; Ludwig Marcuse regarded that union as "a marriage between two children."

I have mentioned the seeming formlessness of Heine's writings, particularly his prose. To the extent that they are not deliberately used as a shocking stylistic device, the leaps from one subject to another (as in Mahler the shifts from one motif to the next) derive from his mode of thinking, which is associative rather than systematic. It has been related, and probably with justification, to the world of the Talmud, where logical argumentation is for large stretches interrupted by an associative series of arguments and examples that may be expanded into narratives. Anyone who ever conversed with the great Hebrew storyteller Agnon, who jumped from one story to another that was for him somehow connected with the first through some association, only to interrupt himself to insert a third or fourth anecdote, will never fail to understand this kind of linkage of seemingly incongruent elements in speech, argumentation, and narrative: This associative linking of elements of thought and feeling is in some form always present in speech and writing but is frequently directed into logical channels by an urge to systematize. In Heine it is preserved in unadulterated or at least clearly recognizable form and reflects his experiential world. It, too, can give the outward expression of unruliness and shamelessness, but it is in reality an expression of his fear of mendacity and his desire to make truthful statements about himself and his world.

One is tempted to say that Heine carried on a constant conversation with everything that surrounded him and gave himself the "fool's privilege" of telling everyone what he was thinking. It was not just by chance that he compared himself with Kunz von der Rosen, the court jester of Emperor Maximilian I, in the Afterword to his *Englische Fragmente* (29 November 1830). He spoke to people and spoke of them and out of them—or they spoke out of him—because he knew them, because he shared their experiences and sufferings by constantly observing himself and others, by always being on guard. Thus he acquired the ability to say what he and they were suffering, what passed through their souls at every moment of their existence. He spoke to and about the Germans, among whom he unhesitatingly included himself all his life (even in his most private letters he wrote "We Germans"), to and about the French, whom he loved as the people of freedom and *esprit* (his wife was a French-woman). He regarded it as his mission, to which he devoted a number of his prose writings, to deepen mutual understanding between the French and the Germans. And behind everything is his dialogue with Judaism, with the Jew in himself, his critique of Jews and Judaism, his mockery of many features of the Jews in the process of emancipating themselves that he deemed worth satirizing, his ever-increasing understanding of the history and destiny of the Jews. He never completely identified with them and Judaism; he did not say "We Jews" the way he said "We Germans." However, nothing that happened in Jewish life in his lifetime failed to leave its mark on him or to evoke some reaction in his writings, just as nothing that happened in contemporary history failed to be reflected in his words.

Just as he talked with human beings, he communicated with the gods—the Greek gods who loved joy and sensuality, and with the one God of the Judeo-Christian tradition. Misjudging the extensive differences between Judaism and Christianity, for a long time he regarded that God as an embodiment of the ascetic Nazarene spirit and contrasted him with the life-affirming and art-loving Greek gods, until he strove for a synthesis between the two types of deities and came close to achieving one. When Heine, in keeping with the needs of an ailing, bedridden man who was very consciously facing death, abandoned his pantheistic or atheistic view of God and returned to a deistic, personal view, his mockery stayed with him. Even as he was saying and writing very profound things, he told his wife Mathilde, a devout Catholic who was praying for forgiveness for her husband: "Dieu me pardonnera. C'est son métier" (God will forgive me; that's his job).

In all this he was a typical representative of the Jewry of his time and of many Jews down to ours—in identification and detachment, in his love for his adopted nation and homeland, and in his disappointed awareness that this love remained basically unrequited. He called France and his beloved Paris his exile as compared to his real homeland, Germany. This Germany, however, was a Germany of his memories and dreams, above all the land of his language as an artist, a thinker, and a human being. It seems to me that the German language is the only thing he never derided but always venerated as something sacred; in this, too, he was typical of modern Jewry, particularly the German Jews. Of Jewish matters he spoke with the greatest freedom, a freedom made possible for him by his *Distanzliebe* for Judaism, which would probably have been more appropriate for things German. (This word, which was coined by Max Brod, indicates a dispassionate love, or one characterized by detachment). This freedom, which also released his wildest mockery, biting irony, and sarcastic criticism, may have made Heine the first modern Jew (after Spinoza) who had completely left the ghetto and "emancipated" himself, no longer living in an "inner ghetto" in constant fear that his mockery and his censure could be exploited by adversaries against him and the Jews. Outsiders were all too prone to interpret all this as a confirmation of their own antipathies. His derision of the people that he had sprung from and grown out of (and outgrown) was branded as "shamelessness," and since the non-Jews regarded him as the most pronounced Jewish type, this stigmatization was transferred to the Jewish people, which was said to have been "shameless" since olden times. In this spirit the non-Jews interpreted, exploited, and adduced as evidence the holy books containing the legends of Creation and Jewish history, the Prophets' blazing world of metaphors, and the didactic conversations of the Talmudic scholars, which contained unconstrained discussions of every detail of daily life and the right way.

Heine climbed all steps of modern Judaism and took all its paths, reporting about them and commenting on them. In his acceptance and rejection, in his seriousness and his derision he usually went more deeply into the problems than most of his contemporaries and frequently anticipated the judgments of later generations. We would go too far if we attempted to claim him for the Jewish nationalism and Zionism that did not begin to take shape until a generation after his death (and will be discussed in the next chapter). However, in his last years, which brought him great suffering, he sometimes came very close to the insights of these movements. If Heine had lived a generation later, he might have hailed them, but who can be at all certain in making such an *ex post facto* prophecy in the case of such a complicated man and artist? As with all such historical "What ifs," such a question can only serve as a vantage point for what can actually be grasped.

In this connection I should mention as perhaps the most astonishing product of Heine's early period the essay on Poland which the twenty-five-year-old wrote in the fall of 1822 on the basis of a journey to the Prussian part of the country and published in January 1832 (Insel ed., 5:282ff.). What he says about the Jews there anticipates many things that were not recognized again until the end of the century.

Heine's intial feeling—this was typical of him as well as of most Western Jews at their first encounter with Polish Jews—was one of revulsion. This revulsion is complex in nature; it was the antipathy of Western man to Eastern man, of those advanced in civilization or culture to those who had newly entered European civilization. This feeling was so intense among Western Jews because they, too, had but recently acquired this European culture, now felt the contrast with primitive conditions all the more keenly, and, to keep from being identified with their Eastern brethren, expressed this difference in eloquent and often exaggerated ways. "The external appearance of the Polish Jew is terrible," writes Heine. "A shudder runs down my spine when I remember my first experience (just beyond Meseritz it was) of a Polish village inhabited mainly by Jews. Not even W's weekly [Franz Daniel Friedrich Wadzeck's *Berliner Wochenblatt*], if boiled to mush, could have nauseated me as much as the sight of those filthy and ragged apparitions. Not even the high-minded oration of a high-school pupil waxing enthusiastic about physical education and patriotism could have hurt my ears as excruciatingly as the jargon spoken by Polish Jews."*

Soon enough, however, he feels differently and writes: "But disgust soon gave way to compassion when I took a closer look at the way these people lived; when I saw the pigsty-like hovels which they inhabit and in which they jabber [*mauscheln*], pray,

---

*Yiddish was not recognized as an independent language, and not merely a mixture without a character of its own (called a "jargon"), until the early twentieth century. This must be kept in mind when one encounters judgments from earlier periods.

haggle, and are miserable. The language they speak is a kind of German shot through with Hebrew and decked out with Polish." And now Heine begins to investigate the historical conditions that shaped the life of the Polish Jews. In Poland the Jews, who number almost one-fourth of the population, stand between the peasantry and the nobility; in reality, he says, they are the *tiers état*, the third estate of Poland (which is generally said not to exist).

> They immigrated into Poland in very early times because of religious persecution in Germany—in such cases the Poles have always been distinguished by their tolerance. . . . It was the Jews who first brought industry and trade to Poland, and King Casimir rewarded them with important privileges. They seem to have been much closer to the nobility than to the peasantry. . . . In those early days the Jews must surely have stood far above the noblemen in intellectual and spiritual cultivation, for the nobility then practiced only the rough arts of war and still lacked the French polish of later times. At the very least, however, the Jews always pored over their Hebrew scientific and religious books, for the sake of which they had left their fatherland and their creature comforts behind. However, they evidently failed to keep pace with European civilization, and their spiritual world sank into a morass of unedifying superstition squeezed into a thousand grotesque shapes by a sophistic scholasticism.

Here Heine reverts to the critique of a modern Western European who sees the world of Eastern European Jewry through the eyes of Western culture. At the same time, however, he notices that these Jews have a wholeness that Western Jews lack. He stands in admiration before this type of a Jew, who is far more self-contained than the Western Jew of his time (and of later times as well). "And yet, and yet," he writes,

> despite the barbarous fur cap that covers his head and the even more barbarous ideas that fill it, I value the Polish Jew much higher than the German Jew. . . . In rigid seclusion the Polish Jew's character became a homogeneous whole; by breathing a more tolerant air it took on the stamp of freedom. The inner man did not become a composite medley of heterogeneous emotions, nor did it atrophy through being constrained within the walls of the Frankfurt ghetto, by ordinances decreed by the city fathers in their great wisdom, and by loving legal limitations. I still prefer the Polish Jew with his filthy fur, his populated beard, his smell of garlic, and his jabbering jargon [Gemauschel] to many another who stands in all the glory of his gilt-edged securities.

Since the end of the century quite a number of Central and Western European Jews received a similar impression of the Eastern European Jews' wholeness. After the First Zionist Congress a pleasantly surprised Herzl eloquently expressed this. In Heine's day such an independent positive judgment was a great exception and, like many other observations and remarks in his essay, was not understood by his contemporaries. On the basis of this appreciation of the wholeness, self-sufficiency, and inner strength that he observed in the Polish Jews and that he also praised in the great men of the past, he wrote critically and with good-natured to sarcastic mockery about the activities of the Jewish religious reformers, who were, in his estimation, just fiddling around with endeavors that seemed superficial and deleterious to him. By contrast, he had a high opinion of a man who seemed strange to his contemporaries and was not recognized in his full stature until our time: Leopold Zunz, the real founder of the new Science of Judaism (cf. Part 2, pp. 661ff.) "I like him very much," wrote Heine on 1 April 1823 to Immanuel Wohlwill, his friend and associate in the Society for the Culture and Science of the Jews,

> and it greatly pains me to see this wonderful man so misunderstood because of his rough, repellent exterior. I expect a great deal from his sermons, which are soon to appear in print— not edification and soothing plasters for the soul, but something much better; something that will arouse dormant strength. That is precisely what is lacking in Israel. A few corn-cutters

(Friedländer & Co.) tried to heal the horrible boil on the body of Judaism through phlebotomy, and because of their maladroitness and gossamer rational bandages Israel has to bleed to death.* May there be a speedy end to the delusion that the most magnificent thing is impotence, the relinquishment of all power, and one-sided negation. We no longer have the strength to wear a beard, to fast, to hate, and to endure out of hatred. That is the motive of our reformation.**

At the end of the letter, however, he reverts to these judgments with self-irony: "Everything is not meant that seriously; nor do I have the strength to wear a beard, to let them call me *Judenmauschel* [jabbering Jew], to fast, etc. I don't even have the strength to eat *matzot* properly. You see, I am now living at a Jew's apartment (across the street from Moser and Gans), get *matzot* instead of bread, and am cracking my teeth. But I console myself by reflecting that we are in the *goles* [*galut* or exile]!"

In his letters from those years he broached all the subjects that he would express in strange antitheses in his later writings—e.g., his sharp rejection of Christianity. In a letter to his brother-in-law Moritz Embden (3 May 1823) he wrote (Bieber, 14): "What you say about the Jews is my view as well. I am also an indifferentist, and my devotion to Judaism is rooted only in a deep antipathy to Christianity. Yes, I, a despiser of all positive religions, may one day embrace the crassest rabbinism because I regard it as a proven antidote."

In other letters he expresses a contempt for the Jews that borders on Jewish self-hatred: "The Jews here as everywhere are insufferable hucksters and slobs" (to Moses Moser, 18 June 1823; Bieber, 15): "The Jews there are a miserable bunch; if one wants to take an interest in them, one must not look at them, and I find it more beneficial to stay away from them" (to Moser, 23 August 1823; Bieber, 17). But in the abovementioned letter of 18 June 1823 Heine also describes the Christian middle class as unedifying, "with an unusual amount of *rishes* [Hebr. *rishut*, nastiness or anti-Jewish attitude], and the higher social classes have it to a higher degree. . . . I feel a great urge to express the great *Judenschmerz* (as Börne calls it) in an article for our Journal [*Wissenschaft des Judentums*]. . . ." Heine never wrote such an article, but he increasingly occupied himself with Jewish history and problems of Jewish life, and he did express this concern in letters, the poems "Donna Clara" (1823), "An Edom," and "Brich aus in lauten Klagen/ Du düstres Marterlied" (1824), and in the fragmentary opening chapters of a projected novel, *Der Rabbi von Bacharach*. There are various reasons why this depiction of Jewish life and suffering, Jewish pride and Jewish persecution, Jewish preservation and Jewish assimilation and apostasy (which was probably intended to present contemporary problems through the historical depiction of the Middle Ages) remained a fragment. One is a formal reason: Heine was not a great story-teller and lacked the endurance, patience, and staying power of a novelist. He was too volatile and too bent upon quick effects to write a successful historical novel. There were, however, many other factors, first and foremost his baptism. On 23 June 1825 Heine was converted to Protestantism by a pastor in Heiligenstadt.

---

*In the well-known chapter 9 of *The Baths of Lucca* Heine has the corn-cutter and lottery collector Hirsch-Hyacinth make good-natured, guileless fun of all religions. About the Jewish religion he says that it is not a religion but a misfortune, and for the time being he makes do "with the new Israelite temple . . . I mean the pure Mosaic service with orthographical German chants and moving sermons and a few little sentimentalities that a religion simply can't do without."

**The emphasis on inner strength as a standard of value is a frequently recurring motif. We may perhaps group it with the aphorism, already cited in another context, which Heine wrote after the Hamburg riot of 1830 (*Gedanken und Einfälle*, Insel ed., 10:242): "One Jew said to another: 'I was too weak.' This suggests itself as a motto for a history of the Jews."

A great deal has been written about this baptism and what it meant—and did not mean—for Heine as well as about his motives. All this is part of his personal history and at the same time is a reflection of the educated Jewry of the period of emancipation. There is no doubt that it was not a genuine conversion, just as Heine's subsequent return to belief in a personal God was not a "return to the synagogue." "Je suis *baptisé*, mais je ne suis pas *converti*," he said to his friend Alexander Weill twenty-five years later (Bieber, 291). For him as for many of his contemporaries and their descendants, baptism was an external act. Two years earlier he had still had inhibitions about it. "As you can imagine," he wrote from his home to his close friend Moses Moser on 27 September 1823 (Bieber, 18), "baptism is being discussed here. No one in my family is against it, but *I* am. This *I* is something very willful. From my way of thinking you can probably deduce that baptism is an indifferent act to me, that I do not even attach any symbolic importance to it, and that under the conditions and in the manner in which it would be accomplished in my case it would have no significance for others either. Its importance for me might lie in the fact that I would consecrate myself all the more to the struggle for the rights of my unfortunate fellow Jews. Nevertheless, I would regard it as beneath my dignity and as a stain on my honor if I had myself baptized in order to accept a position in Prussia. . . . I really don't know what to do in my bad situation. In chagrin I may yet become a Catholic and hang myself. . . . We are truly living in sad times. Rogues get to be the best people, and the best people have to become rogues. I understand very well the words of the Psalmist: Lord, give me my daily bread, lest I blaspheme Thy name." This is a collection of almost all arguments pro and con. While Heine was continuing work on *The Rabbi of Bacharach*, asking Zunz for information about the Jews of Spain and reading old chronicles as well as more recent literature about Jewish history, he wrote to Moritz Embden (11 May 1825) that only "the gods who create hunger" knew what he was going to do and whether he would settle in Hamburg. As for him, he would in any case "do everything; baptized and as a Doctor of Laws . . . I shall come to Hamburg in the near future." A month after his conversion (31 July 1825) he wrote to his sister Charlotte Embden: "Give my best regards to Moritz [her husband], and if you are certain that he is not a gossipmonger, tell him that now I am not only a Dr. juris but also." (He was evidently too embarrassed to add the word "baptized"). In early September (Bieber, 63) he advised his friend Moser to read a travel book about Japan, for he had been astonished to learn "how people there hate and loathe nothing as much as Christianity. They hate the cross more than anything. I want to become a Japanese." He despised Eduard Gans, one of the leaders of the Society for the Culture and Science of the Jews, for having been the first to leave the sinking ship of Judaism in order to receive a professorship at the University of Berlin, did not want his friend Moser to view "my own baptism in a favorable light," and wrote (as an attack on Gans—and on himself!) the poem "Einem Abtrünnigen" (To a Renegade), which includes these verses: "Und du bist zu Kreuz gekrochen/ Zu dem Kreuz, das du verachtest,/ Das du noch vor wenig Wochen/ In den Staub zu treten dachtest!/ O das tut das viele Lesen/Jener Schlegel, Haller, Burke./ Gestern noch ein Held gewesen,/ Ist man heute schon ein Schurke" (And you crawled to the cross, the cross that you despised, that only a few weeks ago you sought to trample into the dust! That's what comes from all that reading of people like Schlegel, Haller, and Burke. Yesterday still a hero and today already a knave).

In his work *Die Romantische Schule* (1835) Heine wrote that his membership in the Protestant church meant only that his name was inscribed in a Lutheran church register. In his book on Börne (1840) he discusses conversations that he had had in Frankfurt in 1827, two years after his conversion, with Ludwig Börne, eleven years his senior and also a baptized Jew. He has Börne pour ridicule on baptism as an act of conversion: "Baptism is now the order of the day among the rich Jews, and the gospel that was preached in vain to the poor in Judea is now flourishing among the wealthy. But since its acceptance is only self-deception and perhaps even a lie, and because unhypocritical Christianity occasionally contrasts rather glaringly with the old Adam, these people expose themselves quite horrendously to ridicule and mockery. Or do you believe that a person's inner nature is completely changed by baptism? Do you believe that one can turn lice into fleas by pouring water on them?" In his 1844 memorial essay on Ludwig Marcus, his old friend from the Society for the Culture and Science of the Jews, Heine discusses the Society as well as the emancipation of the Jews, saying that it would have to be granted sooner or later "out of a sense of justice, out of prudence, out of necessity." He goes on to say that among the upper classes antipathy to the Jews is no longer rooted in religion, and among the lower classes it is being increasingly transformed "into social resentment of the proliferating power of capital and the exploitation of the poor by the rich." In the organic state that governments are striving for, none of its parts, not even the smallest, can be left in an unhealthy condition. In the feud between knowledge and faith the governments actually ought to be glad that there still are Jews in the world, "that the Swiss Guard of deism . . . still is on its feet, that God's people still exists. . . . Beware of promoting the baptism of Jews! It is nothing but water and dries easily. Promote circumcision instead. It is faith carved into the flesh; it can no longer be carved into the spirit. . . ." Among the undated aphorisms first published posthumously by Strodtmann under the title *Gedanken und Einfälle* we find this frequently quoted sentence (though we do not know when Heine wrote it down): "The certificate of baptism is the ticket of admission to European culture." Heine probably intended this statement to be far more profound than it has generally been supposed to be. After all, the European culture into which Jews strove to integrate themselves was a culture permeated and formed by Christianity. In the same collection we also find what seems to be a more casual remark, motivation of his conversion: the rescission of many laws relating to emancipation in Germany after the fall of Napoleon: "That I became a Christian is the fault of those Saxons who suddenly changed horses at Leipzig [left Napoleon and joined his enemies], or of Napoleon, who surely did not need to go to Russia, or of his geography teacher at Brienne, who failed to tell him that in winter it is very cold in Moscow."

When Heine acknowledged his renewed faith in God more and more openly and people spoke of his reconversion to Judaism, whispering about illuminations that he must have had, he repeatedly rejected such explanations. In conversations (e.g., with Ludwig Kalisch in January 1850) he would say that he had not returned to Judaism because he had never left it, not even when he had been baptized. He said that if he officially remained a member of the Protestant faith, this was only "because it does not bother me too much now, just as it did not bother me too much earlier." "No, my religious convictions have remained free of any ecclesiasticism," he wrote in 1851 in his Afterword to *Romanzero*, a collection of his most mature poems (which Alfred Kerr later praised as "a Jewish book"). "I have not forsworn anything, not even my old pagan deities. From these I have turned away, but I parted from them in love and friendship." In point of fact, Heine stipulated in his will that there were to be no religious ceremonies at his funeral. He had regained his faith, though he still conversed with his God quizzically and with good-natured mockery, but he did not completely feel part of any organized religion, just as he never committed himself to any clearly defined political position.

In reality, however, Heine did have far closer ties to Judaism than to Christianity, which he hated from the bottom of his heart; in this respect, too, he was a typical representative of the Jews who were emancipated or were struggling for emancipation. He was serious only in his avowal of *Deutschtum*, no matter how much he criticized it. Like so many Jews after him, including the best ones, he occasionally claimed to see a *Wahlverwandtschaft* (elective affinity) between *Deutschtum* and *Judentum*, the German spirit and the Jewish spirit, repeatedly calling the Jews and the Germans "the two peoples of morality" (cf. Insel ed., 8:260f., 10:189ff., 242). Heine never ceased to concern himself with Judaism and always regarded the Bible as one of the greatest books—and finally the greatest. To it he attributed a great share in his "return," and about this special book and the Jewish people he found formulations that anticipated the insights of later generations. In his *Geständnisse* (Confessions), written near the end of his life, he said that he used to appreciate Protestantism for its merits, but now he particularly treasured it "because of the great services it has rendered by finding and disseminating the sacred book. I say 'finding,' for the Jews who snatched the Bible from the great conflagration of the Second Temple and throughout the Middle Ages dragged it around with them in exile like a portable fatherland kept this treasure well hidden in their ghetto, whither German scholars, the precursors and initiators of the Reformation, crept secretly in order to learn Hebrew and thus find the key to the shrine that housed the treasure."* In a similar vein Heine wrote in the second part of his book on Börne: "If I am not mistaken, it was Mahomet who called the Jews 'the people of the Book,' a name they have retained in the Orient to the present day and that is profoundly revealing. A book is their fatherland, their property, their ruler, their good fortune and misfortune." In the *Memoiren des Herrn von Schnabelewopski* (chap. 14) the Bible is called "the written fatherland of the children of God." Anticipating Leon Pinsker's diagnosis in his *Autoemancipation* (cf. Part 1, pp. 20 and 288ff.) Heine regards the Jews as a "ghost of a people." In his *Reisebilder* (3, *Die Stadt Lucca*, Insel ed., 5:55), written in 1831, at the time of his sharpest critique of religious institutions, he views the Jews as "a mummified people that roams the earth wrapped in its age-old lettered swaddling clothes, an indurated bit of world history, a ghost that earns its living by dealing in bills of exchange and old pants." And in discussing Luther's Bible translation in *Religion und Philosophie in Deutschland* (1835) Heine uses formulations quite similar to those in his *Geständnisse* twenty years later (though he evidently had no memory of that): "Like a ghost guarding a treasure that had once been entrusted to it—that is how this murdered people, this ghost of a people, sat in its dark ghettos guarding the Hebrew Bible. . . ."

It would lead too far to cite even a substantial part of what Heine wrote in the course of the years about his times and his contemporaries, about the Jews and Judaism, and about historical figures and mythical characters that occasionally coalesce in his writings, as in the memory of the people. Nothing that happened failed to be reflected in his writings, whether seriously or mockingly (with seriousness always underlying his mockery), in verse and in the lively prose that was so characteristic of him: the reform of Judaism (for which he worked and whose externals he derided like no one else); the revolutions and emancipative movements of his time (the positive aspects of which he desired and demanded, though he feared their seemingly unavoidable mob rule); the Damascus Affair (which he discussed and judged in his newspaper reports from Paris); the reactionary movements in politics, theology, and philosophy; and the social movements from Saint-Simonism to Marxism (with whose leaders Kark Marx and Ferdinand Lassalle he had close, occasionally amicable contact and whom he may have influenced with some of his formulations, which sound like an anticipation of their later statements). Did he not frequently use (and this is again an integral part of our problem, the Jewish question) Jews and trading as near-synonymous concepts, as did many early socialists and young Marx

---

*The undated *Gedanken und Einfälle* includes a note that probably constitutes the first version of this idea: "The Jews—this ghost of a people that ineluctably stood guard over its treasure, the Bible! The exorcism was in vain—Germans gained it."

(cf. Part 2, pp. 584f.)? Did he not speak of money as "the god of our age"—e.g., in the letter from Paris dated July 1840 (*Lutetia*, part 1, xxxii; Bieber, 157) in which he writes about Rothschild's power: "Here we may see the littleness of man and the greatness of God. For money is the god of our time, and Rothschild is his prophet"?* In *Die Stadt Lucca* Heine had earlier spoken of the perfidy of business people and added this pithy—and dangerous—sentence: "Every rich man is a Judas Iscariot." Heine meant this only as an image, as a kind of typological, mythological comparison. Unlike Christian dogmatics, he certainly did not intend to identify Judas with the Jews. In a conversation of late 1850 (Bieber, 298) he expressly stated: "From my knowledge of the Jews, the personality of this disciple of the Savior has always remained incomprehensible to me. What he did is no more part of the Jewish nature than murder, arson, or highway robbery."

In his *History of Religion and Philosophy in Germany* Heine already predicted the death of God in Nietzsche's sense: "Do you hear the tinkling of the bell? Kneel down—they are administering the last rites to a dying god."** A statement that may be interpreted as a premonition of the catastrophic events of our time is Heine's warning against the barbaric, destructive German revolution that would come when Christianity ceased to keep the Germanic fighting spirit in check (*Religion und Philosophie in Deutschland*, 3; Insel ed., 7:351ff.). And in his discussion of Shakespeare's *The Merchant of Venice* (from which we have already quoted in connection with the figure of Shylock, Part 1, p. 156ff. and Part 2, pp. 532f.) he writes: "But if one day Satan, the sinful pantheism, is victorious . . . a tempest of persecution will gather over the heads of the poor Jews that will far surpass anything they have had to endure before. . . ."

In Heine's mind the figure of Moses crystallized more and more powerfully as the creator and law-giver of the Jewish people and even of its God: "What a giant figure! . . . How small Sinai appears when Moses stands on it! This mountain is only the pediment for the feet of the man whose head reaches to the heavens as he speaks with God. May God forgive me this sin, but it sometimes seems to me as though this Mosaic God were only a reflection of the refulgence of Moses himself, whom he resembles so much in anger and in love." In his *Geständnisse* Heine writes that he was "not particularly fond" of Moses earlier, probably because of his opposition to graven images which had appeared incomprehensible and hostile to culture to Heine, the admirer of the Greeks and a man who had escaped from the ghetto to a new land of beauty.

> I failed to see that Moses, for all his hostility to art, was nevertheless a great artist and possessed the true artistic spirit. However, in his case, as in that of his fellow Egyptians, this artistic spirit was oriented solely toward the colossal and the indestructible. Unlike the Egyptians, however, he did not fashion his works of art from baked bricks and granite but built human pyramids; he carved out human obelisks; he took a tribe of poor shepherds and

---

*In one of his earliest known letters (to Christian Sethe, 27 October 1816) the nineteen-year-old Heine calls Hamburg a "huckster city" in which there is a tension between baptized and unbaptized Jews and gives this parenthetical explanation: "I call all Hamburgers Jews, and those whom I call baptized Jews, in order to distinguish them from the circumcised ones, are commonly known as 'Christians.'" Six years later he wrote in the second letter of his *Briefe aus Berlin* (16 March 1822, Insel ed., 5:240): "But—to speak like a Frankfurter once more—have the Rothschilds and the Bethmanns [the name of a Christian banker] not been at par for a long time? A businessman's religion is the same all over the world. His counting house is his church . . . his gold is his god, and credit is his faith." There is an abundance of similar remarks in virtually all of Heine's prose writings.

**In *Gedanken und Einfälle* we find this pertinent aphorism: "In church. A doleful organ sound, the dying gasp of Christianity."

from it created a people that was also to defy the centuries, a great, eternal, holy people, a poeple of God that could serve as a prototype for all other peoples, all of mankind—he created Israel! This artist, the son of Amram and of Jochebed the midwife, has more of a claim than the Roman poet to have erected a monument that will outlast all structures of bronze!

As about the foreman, I have never spoken about his people, the Jews, with sufficient reverence—and this is surely once again due to my Hellenic nature to which Judaic asceticism was repugnant. My predilection for Hellas has since decreased. I now see that the Greeks were only beautiful youths, while the Jews were always men, powerful, unyielding men—not just in ancient times but to this day, despite eighteen centuries of persecution and misery. I have since learned to appreciate them more, and if any pride of birth were not a foolish contradiction in a champion of the [French] Revolution and its democratic principles, the writer of these pages would take pride in the fact that his ancestors belong to the noble house of Israel and that he is a descendant of those martyrs who have given the world a God and a morality and who have fought and suffered on every battlefield of thought.

The real nature of the Jews is not known to the world any more than their deeds are. People think they know them because they have seen their beards, but this is all that has ever been revealed of them, and the Jews are a walking mystery in the modern age, just as they were in the Middle Ages. (Insel ed., 10:182ff.)

In his *Englische Fragmente* 11 (Insel ed., 5:164) Heine wrote: "Seriousness emerges all the more powerfully when it is introduced by jests." Behind all of Heine's jests there really is seriousness, the seriousness of the confessor, the fighter against illusion who, like all great confessors, was "shameless" and therefore became a reflection of his time, a spokesman who gave voice to everything he saw, sensed, and surmised with the sensibility of a Jew, an artist, and an invalid. It is possible that some opponents of the Jews have had a clearer view of him than many Jews and people favorably disposed to the Jews. Richard Wagner wrote about him in *Das Judentum in der Musik* (1850): "He was the conscience of Judaism." And Schopenhauer, who was anything but a friend of the Jews, remarked in 1859: "Heinrich Heine appears as a true humorist. In his *Romanzero* we notice, behind all his jests and tomfoolery, a profound seriousness that is too bashful to come forth unveiled" (cited after Ernst Simon, *Brücken* [Heidelberg, 1965], 159).

275f. JEWISH APOLOGETIC WRITINGS: Concerning the history, nature, and aims of Jewish apologetic writings, cf. *EJJ* 3:188–201 and the literature cited there.

As was only natural, in the nineteenth century such writings were triggered especially when there was a sharp attack. Cases in point in the first half of that century was the Hepp-Hepp movement of 1819, the debates and unrest during the revolutionary movements of 1830 and 1848, and Bauer's 1842 work about the Jewish question. We have discussed this earlier, and much of it is reflected in Heine's writings. Cf. E. Sterling, "Jewish Reaction to Jew-Hatred in the First Half of the Nineteenth Century," *LBYB* 3 (1958), 103–21 and the references given in chaps. 6 and 7.

The reaction of the Jews to the agitation of Marr and Stoecker is typical of the period after the acquisition of official equality, and this is especially true of the debate surrounding Treitschke's polemics of 1879–80, which were gathered in his pamphlet *Ein Wort über unser Judentum* (January 1880). In the last chapter (Part 1, p. 251) I discussed in detail the substance of the attacks as well as the views of the attackers and of the few—disappointingly few!—Christian defenders, whose views were not substantially different. My task here is to characterize the stand of the Jews. In addition to the sources, the most important of which (though of course by no means all) have been reprinted in Walter Boehlich's *Der Berliner Antisemitismusstreit* (Frankfurt, 1965), we are basing ourselves especially on Michael A. Meyer, "Great Debate on Antisemitism: Jewish Reaction to New Hostility in Germany 1879–1881,"

LBYB 11 (1966), 136–70; Michael Reuben, "Graetz contra Treitschke," *Bulletin LBI* 4, no. 16 (1961): 301–21, as well as on the literature on Heinrich Graetz in Part 2, pp. 661f.; Ingrid Belke's introduction to her exemplary edition of *Moritz Lazarus und Heymann Steinthal: Die Begründer der Völkerpsychologie in ihren Briefen* (Tübingen, 1971), esp. lxi ff. and cxxvi ff.; Hugo Bergmann, "Eduard von Hartmann und die Judenfrage in Deutschland," *LBYB* 5, (1960), 177–97 (a study in which the Jerusalem philosopher discusses the abovementioned anti-Jewish book by the philosopher Eduard von Hartmann [Part 2, pp. 620f.] and a counterpamphlet by a Jew issued by the *Israelitische Wochenschrift* in Leipzig, though unfortunately not the abovementioned [Part 2, p. 621] work by Popper-Lynkeus); W. W. Mosse, ed., *Juden im Wilhelminischen Deutschland* (Tübingen, 1976), 155–61.

THE JEWISH RESPONSES TO TREITSCHKE'S POLEMIC: In the preceding chapter we noted that Treitschke and his only important non-Jewish adversary, who did not come forward until the end of the newspaper and pamphlet debate that had started with Treitschke's first remarks in the *Preussische Jahrbücher*, were by no means as far apart in their basic views on the Jewish question as their sharp polemics might indicate. If one now subjects the numerous responses by Jews to a critical examination, one has to note with astonishment that the Jewish defenders essentially attacked Treitschke's anti-Jewish tone and his antipathetic and even hostile attitude toward the Jews. They also sought to correct or refute facts, statistical foundations, and evaluations, but in his basic assumptions they agreed with the attacker. (Heinrich Graetz, an exception, will be discussed later).

The Jews offered no, or only weak, objections to the basic assumption that the Christian peoples (or in the special case under discussion, the Germans, with the Prussians as the leading force among them) had as the masters and "host nations" given equal civil rights to the Jews as guests or "guest nations" under the condition that there would be only one legitimate nationality in the country, that of the German *Herrenvolk* (master race). Hence the Jews kept asseverating that nationally they felt only as Germans, and more than that, that they were Germans, just like the Christian Germans, and were distinguished from them only by certain differences in their religious beliefs. They did not express disappointment or offense at the fact that their emotions and thinking were condemned as not being up to the "Germanic standard"; rather, they repeatedly denied that such differences existed. If any did still exist, then the Jews ought to make every effort to eliminate such obstacles to amalgamation. On this point they certainly did not disagree with Treitschke, and this was the position of virtually all Jewish participants in the debate. These were Jews of high rank and great repute: Manuel Joel, the learned rabbi of the Breslau community; Harry Bresslau, a recognized expert on medieval documents; Hermann Cohen, the philosopher and later author of basic works on Jewish ethics; the ethnopsychologists Moritz Lazarus and Heymann Steinthal; Ludwig Bamberger, the respected liberal economist and politician; Ludwig Philippson, the editor of the *Allgemeine Zeitung des Judentums;* and others. Harry Bresslau wrote to Treitschke: "I fully subscribe to the demands that you are making," and in semi-ironic, semi-serious fashion he added: "If you also informed us of the means by which this process of transforming Jews into Teutons might be accelerated, every open-minded and unprejudiced Jew could be indebted to you." And Hermann Cohen brought himself to write at that time what he would not have written later and what was reminiscent of "Höre Israel," Walther Rathenau's ominous article of 1897: "All of us wish we simply had the German, the Germanic appearance of which we now display only the climatic side effects." If there was any mention of Judaism having any validity in its own right, this was limited to religious views. These Jews went even further and tried to demonstrate (as Heine had already insinuated) that the Jews and the Germans had especially distinguished themselves

275f.

as champions of humanitarianism and as peoples of the intellect and morality, and that by virtue of these dispositions and endeavors they were related. Ludwig Bamberger's pamphlet is entitled *Deutschtum und Judentum*. Hermann Cohen's *Ein Bekenntnis zum Judentum* (which marked the beginning of his occupation with Judaism) contains this thesis perhaps even more explicitly, and the booklet he published during World War I with the same title as Bamberger's (Giessen, 1915, with a number of later editions) is only a continuation and corollary of it. In rejecting Treitschke's accusations these defenders believed they were acting in the name of the *Deutschtum* that Treitschke and the anti-Semites were damaging and degrading in the eyes of other nations. With all their indignation and display of pride these apologetic writings were bound to appear to many non-Jews—and not only enemies of the Jews—as statements that deliberately skirted the real questions and were at bottom undignified attempts at ingratiation; in many respects we must view them in this light today. We can arrive at a more lenient judgment only if we consider the situation of the Jews at that time, their faith in progress and reason that would surely prevail—a faith that they shared with the bourgeois liberalism of that age. Steinthal was the only one who toward the end of his life seems to have been convinced of the futility of debating with the enemies of the Jews—as evidenced by his foreword to his posthumously published work *Über Juden und Judentum*—because those anti-Jewish persons "do not really mean what they say out loud but reveal what they have in mind only inadvertently."

276   HEINRICH GRAETZ'S RESPONSE: The only laudable exception in this debate was Heinrich Graetz, the primary target of Treitschke's attack. The German historian's main point of departure had been the unfavorable impression he had gained from reading volume 11 of Graetz's great History (though he surely did not read the other volumes). This volume, which had been completed and published before the founding of Bismarck's German Reich, was essentially a piece of recent history. With a temperament and a personal involvement which, as Philippson noted in the debate, were closely related to Treitschke's own style of historical presentation, Graetz told the story of the Jews from Mendelssohn's time to the middle of the nineteenth century, the period immediately preceding his own. It is understandable that the champion of a free and equal life for the Jews should have included overly caustic value judgments on adversaries of the Jews and of their emancipation as well as on the fragmentation of the German people into many petty principalities, even though these judgments were not to the taste of all readers. Graetz frequently was even less discriminating in his condemnatory language than Treitschke, whose command of a very personally styled German was superior to the language of the man born at Xion, a small Polish border town in the province of Posen. In his second response ("Mein letztes Wort an Professor von Treitschke") Graetz withdrew the judgments that the developments of the succeeding years showed to have been distorted, and he changed the passages in question for the English translation, which was in press at the time. Graetz proudly rejected all other accusations and stuck to his judgments on recognized German personalities who were wronging the Jews. He measured all of them, often too one-sidedly, by their attitude toward the Jews, and in this too he was somewhat similar to Treitschke, whose value judgments were based on *Deutschtum*. Graetz responded dispassionately only to historiographic objections, seeking to demonstrate Treitschke's ignorance of facts and connections in the field of Jewish history as well as his distorted interpretations and quotations torn out of context. His sharpest language was reserved for Treitschke the politician and enemy of the Jews, whom he accused of demagoguery. Unlike most Jews, who were trying to prove that they were good Germans, Graetz stood his ground on what Treitschke regarded as his most important charges. Treitschke had in particular accused Graetz of two transgres-

sions: one was that he hated Christianity and regarded it as the *"Erbfeind"* (hereditary or traditional enemy; Treitschke misquoted the word *"Erzfeind,"* archenemy, which Graetz had occasionally used). In the face of this accusation Graetz rightly reiterated that Christianity and many Christians had behaved as such an enemy, and that it was his duty as a historian to report how things had happened. Treitschke's second major charge was directed at Graetz's central view of Judaism. The Jewish historian had concluded his book with these words: "The recognition of the Jews as citizens with full rights has been more or less accomplished; the recognition of Judaism [*Judentum*], however, still requires hard fights." Treitschke interpreted this to mean a demand for the recognition of the Jews as a nation, and with all his patriotic-moral rage he opposed this demand, as it were, for a "state within the state." Those who desired a nationality of their own, he wrote, ought to emigrate and found their own state: "On German soil there is no room for a dual nationality." To this Graetz made no clear response. He rejected Treitschke's interpretation of his words, which equated *Judentum* with Jewish nationality: "Is Judaism identical with nationality?" However, he evaded an unambiguous answer. In point of fact, Graetz surely did not demand or even desire that the Jews be recognized as a national minority. However, his history of the Jews was a history of the Jewish people, even after the destruction of the Temple and the State, and, as we shall show in another context, this was the foundation of his extensive and profound influence in his time and far beyond. But did Graetz himself have a clear notion of what he had meant by that demand at the conclusion of his work and what he now really meant by his unanswered rhetorical question? He was, after all, living in a transitional period, and this excuses many things in the other apologetic champions of Judaism as well. It was one year before the pogroms in Russia that startled the Jews and the world and revealed consequences of anti-Semitism that had been deemed impossible in a modern European state. As we shall show in the following chapter, a movement for the rebuilding of Palestine began to be organized in Eastern Europe under the name *Hibbat Zion* (love of Zion) which extended to the West and developed into the Zionist Organization there fifteen years later. Graetz was in sympathy with the new movement, which really was in keeping with his innermost endeavor, but he declined active participation in it. Was it possible or permissible for Jews to commit themselves to what seemed like an unpromising movement and thus possibly jeopardize the goal of complete emancipation for which they had fought all their lives? Stronger personalities and forces were needed to dispel such scruples even among those Jews who were about to proceed from defensiveness to new thoughts and actions.

Added to this was the fact that Graetz was almost completely alone in this debate; none of the Jewish fighters against Treitschke also came to the defense of Graetz, the main target of the professor's attack. Virtually all clearly distanced themselves from him, saying that his way of thinking and his judgments were not theirs. (It is questionable how many of Graetz's works some of the Jewish fighters against Treitschke had read and to what extent they merely followed the lead of Treitschke, whose distorted quotations from Graetz's History really ran counter to their views.) To Graetz this was a deep disappointment that surely affected the tone and the substance of his response. He viewed himself as repudiated, isolated and rejected, in embarrassment or with professorial arrogance, by representative personalities of the Jewish people, representatives of that assimilation that he (and in the final analysis this was the crux of the matter) had sharply condemned in the controversial last volume of his History.

There were, to be sure, other people who were not directly involved in the debate and had a far more positive attitude toward him. This will be discussed at a later point. Concerning Graetz, cf. also the bibliographies and remarks in Part 2, pp. 661f.; regarding his History, cf. Part 2, pp. 667f.

276ff.   NEW EFFORTS TO ORGANIZE: Cf. the pertinent articles and sections in the Jewish
          encyclopedias and histories and the bibliographies given there. Here we cannot go
          into detail on this and must limit ourselves to a few references and quotations
          concerning those organizations that were of special importance for our problem.
          Regarding the organization and significance of life in the Jewish communities, cf.
          Kurt Wilhelm's article "The Jewish Community in the Post-Emancipation Period,"
          LBYB 2 (1957), 47–75. Concerning the Alliance Israélite Universelle, cf. André
          Chouraqui, *Cent ans d'histoire—L'Alliance Israélite Universelle et la renaissance
          juive contemporaine, 1860–1960* (Paris, 1965); Zosa Szaykowski, "Jewish Diplomacy:
          Notes on the Occasion of the Centenary of the Alliance Israélite Universelle," *Jewish
          Social Studies* 22 (1960): 131–58. Concerning the B'nai B'rith, cf. B. Maretzki,
          Geschichte des Ordens Bnei Briss [the Ashkenazic pronunciation of the word] *in
          Deutschland, 1881–1907* (Berlin, n.d.). On p. 2 we read about the motives for its
          foundation: "Our association sprang from the struggle for the greatest possessions of
          mankind. We had the courage to respond to the loss of equality by establishing our
          order, to seek a substitute for the curtailed emancipation in the development of the
          intellectual and moral powers of our people, and to bestir ourselves for the restora-
          tion of our dignity and our honor. Our order stands as a shining memorial to our faith
          in our goodness." Concerning the Centralverein deutscher Staatsbürger jüdischen
          Glaubens, cf. District Rabbi Dr. Rieger-Braunschweig, *Ein Vierteljahrhundert im
          Kampf um das Recht und die Zukunft der deutschen Juden* (Berlin, 1918) (pp. 18ff.:
          the story of its founding; p. 56: its negative attitude toward Zionism in 1913); M.
          Mendelssohn (its first chairman), *Die Pflicht der Selbstverteidigung . . . Jah-
          resbericht des Vorsitzenden in der ersten öffentlichen Generalversammlung des
          Centralvereins . . .* (Berlin, 1894). On p. 7 of this book there is a reference to the
          Verein zur Abwehr des Antisemitismus: "But can it be permissible for us and in
          keeping with our self-esteem and dignity to let ourselves be defended only by others
          without acting ourselves?" What differentiated the new association from the Verein
          zur Abwehr des Antisemitismus, whose leaders were motivated "primarily by right-
          eous indignation at the ignominy being visited upon our dear fatherland," was "the
          principle of self-help, that it is every decent person's duty to defend himself and not
          simply let others champion his cause." R. Löwenfeld's theses, the foundation of the
          association and, as it were, its philosophy, are reprinted on pp. 13f.: "We are not
          German Jews, but German citizens of the Jewish faith. As citizens we need and
          demand no protection other than the constitutional rights. As Jews we do not belong
          to any political party. Political views, like religious beliefs, are the concern of an
          individual. We stand on the firm foundation of German nationality. The only common
          interests we have with Jews in other countries are those that the Catholics and
          Protestants of Germany have with the Catholics and Protestants of other countries.
          We have no morality that differs from that of our fellow citizens of different faiths. We
          condemn immoral actions of individuals, no matter what their faith may be; we reject
          any responsibility for actions of individual Jews and protest against the generaliza-
          tions that lead negligent or malicious observers to hold all Jewish citizens responsible
          for the actions of individual Jews."
                 Cohesion was, of course, also promoted by the Jewish press, which began to
          develop in the middle of the nineteenth century. In almost all countries there were
          Jewish weeklies, after the pattern of Ludwig Philippson's *Allgemeine Zeitung des
          Judentums* (Berlin, 1837–1922) and *The Jewish Chronicle* (London, 1841 to date) as
          well as monthlies. In Eastern Europe *Hazefirah* was founded in 1862, and dailies in
          Hebrew and Yiddish developed in America at a later date. As Dinaburg rightly
          remarks (*Bemifnei Hadorot* [Hebr.] [Jerusalem, 1955], p. 37, n. 49), the significance
          of the Jewish press that presented news and articles about Judaism and Jews in all
          countries and periods is still not sufficiently appreciated. Between 1837 and 1881—

that is, until the beginning of the Russian pogroms—about fifteen hundred Jewish newspapers and periodicals of all kinds appeared in twenty countries, many of which, to be sure, were short-lived. Since then this development has continued and intensified. Information about this Jewish press, which should be distinguished from the participation of Jewish journalists, writers, and scholars in general journals and magazines, may be found in the articles and lists in the Jewish encyclopedias, especially in *JL* 4:1162ff., which includes an extensive list of Jewish newspapers and periodicals, even those published for only a short time (pp. i–xxxv) and *EJJ* 13:1923ff. Concerning the beginnings of the Jewish press, cf. B. Poll, ed., *Jüdische Presse im 19. Jahrhundert*, catalogue of the Tel Aviv exhibit of the international newspaper museum of the city of Aachen (Aachen, 1967).

THE "SCIENCE OF JUDAISM" AND THE REGENERATION OF JEWISH HISTORIOGRAPHY: 279f. Here is some literature on the subject, in addition to Graetz, Dubnow, etc., and the encyclopedias: The most detailed and most authentic presentation on the basis of documents about its origin, and especially the founding of the Verein für Cultur und Wissenschaft der Juden in 1819 (mentioned in Part 2, p. 592), may be found in Nahum N. Glatzer's book *Leopold Zunz, Jude, Deutscher, Europäer: Ein jüdisches Gelehrtenschicksal des 19. Jahrhunderts in Briefen an seine Freunde* (Tübingen, 1964). Cf. especially Hanns Günther Reissner's book *Eduard Gans: Ein Leben im' Vormärz* (Tübingen, 1965) (on pp. 174ff. there is a list of all known members of the association and the biographical data relevant to the history). Of the contemporaries and members, Heinrich Heine (who was one of the founders) gave the most important presentation of the period, the outstanding personalities, the orientation, and the intellectual and spiritual atmosphere in his memorial essay *(Denkworte)* about Ludwig Marcus (22 April 1844; Insel ed., 9:458–76). The presentation in Adolf Strodtmann's Heine biography (Vienna, 1867) is still worth reading (chap. 8, "Das junge Palästina"). Cf. also Zalman Rubashoff (Zalman Shazar, later the president of the State of Israel), "Erstlinge der Entjudung: Einleitung zu den drei Reden von Eduard Gans im Kulturverein," in the journal *Der Jüdische Wille* 1, no. 1 (Berlin, April 1918, 3042; the addresses may be found in nos. 2 and 3). Concerning the Wissenschaft des Judentums (more accurately, Wissenschaft vom Judentum), cf. Kurt Wilhelm's introduction and selection from the sources *Wissenschaft des Judentums im deutschen Sprachbereich: Ein Querschnitt*, 2 vols. (Tübingen, 1967) and the literature cited there. A critical appreciation may be found in Gershom Scholem's lecture "Wissenschaft vom Judentum einst und jetzt," *Bulletin LBI* 19 (1960): 9–12 (reprinted in G. Scholem, *Judaica* 1 (Frankfurt, 1963), 147–60). For a critique from a neo-traditional standpoint, cf. Baruch Kurzweil, *Bama'avak al Erkhei Hayahadut* (Hebr., Struggling for the values of Judaism) (Jerusalem, 1970), 184ff. Cf. also Robert Gordis, *Jewish Learning and Jewish Existence*, Leo Baeck Memorial Lecture 6 (New York, 1963).

Concerning the evaluation of the Wissenschaft des Judentums and its place in history, cf. Ephraim Urbach, Gershom Scholem, Hans Liebeschütz, and Alexander Bein, colloquium on the Science of Judaism in Germany and its influence on modern research, in Leo Baeck Institute (Jerusalem), *Zur Geschichte der Juden in Deutschland im 19. and 20. Jahrhundert* (1971), 43–52.

Regarding Abraham Geiger, cf. the introduction and selection by Max Wiener, *Abraham Geiger and Liberal Judaism* (Philadelphia, 1962) and H. Liebeschütz' essay "Wissenschaft des Judentums und Historismus bei Abraham Geiger," in *Essays Presented to Leo Baeck* (London 1954), 75–93.

Concerning Heinrich Graetz, cf. the special issue of *MGWJ* on the one hundredth birthday of Heinrich Graetz (vol. 61, nos. 9–12, Breslau, 1917) with essays by H. Brann, M. Güdemann, Hermann Cohen, et al.; Joseph Meisl, *Heinrich Graetz*

(Berlin, 1917); Salo Baron, *History and Jewish Historians* (Philadelphia, 1964), including essays about the great bibliographer I. M. Jost, Moritz Steinschneider, and Levi Herzfeld, "The first Jewish economic historian"); Georg Herlitz, "Three Jewish Historians: Isaak Marcus Jost, Heinrich Graetz, Eugen Täubler—A Comparative Study," *LBYB* 9 (1964), 69–90; S. Ettinger, "Heinrich Graetz," in *EJJ* 7:845–50; S. Ettinger and Reuben Michael in the introductions to the Hebrew edition of Graetz's shorter writings (Jerusalem, 1969); Ludwig Feuchtwanger, "Zur Geschichtsschreibung des jungen Graetz von 1846," afterword to the new edition of *Heinrich Graetz, die Konstruktion der jüdischen Geschichte—eine Skizze* (Berlin, 1936); Reuben Michael, "The Unknown Heinrich Graetz: From His Diaries and Letters," *LBYB* 13 (1968), 34–56; E. Silberner's edition of Graetz's letters to Moses Hess (Milan, 1961). For Graetz's impression and influence on the first generation of Zionists, cf. Spectator, "Erinnerung an H. Graetz," in Herzl's *Die Welt* 1:26 (Vienna, 26 November 1897) and L. Motzkin and H. Loewe in Nathan Birnbaum's *Selbst-Emancipation* 4:18 (Vienna, September 1891). M. Brann's essay "Aus H. Graetzens Lehr-und Wanderjahren" (*MGWJ* 62 [1918] to 64 [1920]) is very informative about Graetz's development, as well as his generation's relationship to the Hebrew and German languages. German was not the mother tongue of most of those Jews, and almost all of them were self-taught. Only the following generation had a more natural and more organized access to the vernacular and to European culture. Graetz frequently gives one the impression that he translated locutions from the Hebrew, a language with which he was conversant from his earliest youth. This is evidenced by the early diaries which M. Brann used and quoted from in his article. Michael Reuben recently published them on the basis of the manuscript in the National and University Library in Jerusalem (*Heinrich Graetz: Tagebuch und Briefe* [Tübingen, 1977]).

In assessing the Science of Judaism in connection with our problem, the Jewish question, we must distinguish three phases: (a) the history of its establishment, which reflects the atmosphere and the orientations of the period of its founding and of the founders, (b) the achievements of the first generation, and (c) the further development in the twentieth century. What all these stages have in common is the basic problem of the way in which modern Jewry dealt with its history within the framework of world history and with its own continuity and nature under the new conditions created by the Jews' entry into the modern world in the wake of the emancipation movement.

The point of departure was the emancipation and the new situation it had created for the Jews in the mutual relationships between the Jewries and their surroundings—in particular the disappointment at the fact that the Jews, including those of high intellectual rank and farthest removed from tradition, were not received with open arms by their Christian (and especially German Christian) neighbors as equal fellow nationals and fighters for human freedom.* A small group (twenty-three) of such young intellectuals, mostly students, who found themselves outwardly and inwardly rejected by their fellow students, formed a "scholarly circle" that met weekly or semimonthly from November 1816 to July 1817 but did not primarily concern itself with questions of Judaism. The friendships thus made between members of this circle survived the temporary separation caused by study at different universities. In the meantime the Hepp-Hepp riots of 1819 had produced a profound disillusionment among these young men and many other German Jews. This atmosphere gave rise, on 7 November 1819, to the Verein zur Verbesserung des

---

*Eduard Gans, later a teacher of law, wrote to the Prussian Minister of Culture, Altenstein: "I belong to the unfortunate class of people that is hated because it is uneducated and persecuted because it is educating itself."

Zustandes der Juden im Deutschen Bundesstaate, which was founded by seven men. The best-known of these, and those who were most important for its further development, were Isaak Marcus Jost, Leopold Zunz, Eduard Gans, and Moses Moser. "The nucleus formed at that time gave rise to the Verein für Cultur und Wissenschaft der Juden a year and half later" (H. G. Reissner, *Eduard Gans*, 51). The historian Jost resigned from the Society in May 1820, and deliberations about the formulation of its program went on until August 1821, whereupon one was submitted to the government for its approval. In March 1821 Eduard Gans had been elected president. The two years between March 1821 and April 1823 were the period of the Verein's greatest activity. Occasional meetings took place until early January 1824, but after that the members dispersed, though the Verein was not formally dissolved. In its heyday the Society, which Heinrich Heine had joined, had twenty-five regular members in Berlin, and there were also twenty-three members in the Hamburg branch and eleven in other places, plus twenty associate members. However, only the Berlin members were of real importance in the activities of the Society.

Of the Society's instrumentalities, two were of lasting significance, the so-called Wissenschaftliches Institut, which regularly sponsored scholarly lectures, and the *Zeitschrift für die Wissenschaft des Judentums*, edited by Leopold Zunz, of which four numbers appeared in 1822 and 1823. The first number of volume 2 was announced in the last issue (May 1823) for that fall, but it was not published for lack of support. However, this first and only volume contained a number of fundamental contributions, some of them originally lectures given at the Wissenschaftliches Institut. The *Zeitschrift für die Wissenschaft des Judentums* was the first of the scholarly publications about the Science of Judaism that were edited by Jews. It first publicized the Science of Judaism, the term and the concept.

What Heine wrote in his *Denkworte* about one of the members, Ludwig Marcus, probably applied in some measure to him and most other members of the Berlin Society as well. Heine writes: "To him . . . the period in which he devoted himself to the endeavors and illusions of that Society may have appeared as the sunniest blossom time of his paltry life." About these "endeavors and illusions" Heine says that "the esoteric purpose of that Society was to establish a connection between historic Judaism and modern science, of which it was assumed that it would in the course of time achieve world domination." The Society had pursued "a lofty but unfeasible idea. . . . Men with great intellectual gifts and generous hearts attempted to salvage a long-lost cause, but at most they managed to find the bones of some older fighters on the battlefields of the past. The total yield of that Society consists of some historical writings and historical research, of which Dr. Zunz's monographs on the Spanish Jews in the Middle Ages must be numbered among the remarkable achievements of higher criticism." And now Heine, who, disappointed at the Society and the conditions in Germany and within Jewry, had like Gans accepted baptism in 1825, effusively praises "the excellent Zunz . . . who in an unstable period of transition always manifested the most unshakable steadiness and despite his acuity, his skepticism, and his erudition remained faithful to the promise he had made himself and to the magnanimous caprice of his soul. A man of words and a man of action, he worked and created when others dreamed and fell by the wayside bereft of courage."

This says everything essential about the aims of the Society for the Culture and the Science of the Jews, even though in retrospect the writer changed the emphases and evaluations in accordance with his disappointments and new experiences. The founders and leading members of the Society had really set themselves a task that has not been accomplished to this day: to produce a harmonious union between perseverance and progress; faith and science; the past, the present, and the future of Judaism; and the Jews and the world around them—and all this under the banner of emancipation, the struggle for freedom and equal rights for all, including the Jews. They were convinced that it was impossible to continue Jewish life in the old, traditional, pious way, and with similar words as the Christian world and under the influence of the new European culture and Hegelian philosophy they opposed what they called rabbinism or Talmudism and regarded as an impediment to any vibrant development of Judaism. On the other hand, they wished to get to the "essence of Judaism," recapture its real substance as revealed in literature and history, and in attractive form bring it to the attention of the public—informing the Jews in order to strengthen their shaken self-confidence, and the surrounding world in order to prove the equal human worth of the Jews, as a weapon in the struggle for legal and social equality. Only the methods of modern science could be employed for this—the systematic investigation of the past with a self-chosen detachment and deliberate alienation. This frequently accorded with a real estrangement but often only isolated the inner warmth with a thin insulating layer that occasionally was pierced by the flame of enthusiasm or revulsion. "The Jews must once again stand the test as stalwart collaborators on the common work of mankind," said Immanuel Wolf at the end of his programmatic address; "they must elevate themselves and their principle to the standpoint of science, for that is the standpoint of *European life*. On this standpoint the alienation that has hitherto characterized the relationship of Jews and Judaism to the outside world must *disappear*. And if one bond is ever to bind the entire human race together, it is the bond of science, the bond of pure reason, the bond of truth . . ." (*Zeitschrift für die Wissenschaft des Judentums*, 1:24). According to Wolf, the Science of Judaism embraced two main areas: (1) "The study of Judaism in its historical-literary documentation," that is, the history of Judaism; (2) "Statistical Jewish studies in relation to present-day Jewry in all countries of the earth"—what we would today call the demography and sociology of the Jews.

As Heine rightly remarked, Zunz was the only member of the Society who began to perform this wide-ranking task and through fundamental books and articles erected the pillars for the construction of a "Science of Judaism." It was he who, in Sinai Ucko's formulation (K. Wilhelm, *Die Wissenschaft*, 321), "rescued science itself from the ruins of the Society that originated the concept Science of Judaism."

If one reads the volume of the periodical, it is fascinating to see how the members of the Society searched and groped as they tried to perform their task. There are three essays (a few of them chapters of later books) by the versatile and precocious jurist Dr. Eduard Gans, the enthusiastic disciple of Hegel, whose work on the history of the law of inheritance (a subject he may have chosen because of that problem in his own family) was to lay the groundwork for comparative jurisprudence in contrast to the romantic-historical orientation of the dominant school of Savigny. The titles of Gans's essays are "Legislation Governing the Jews in Rome," "Lectures on the History of the Jews in Northern Europe and the Slavic Countries," and "The Basic Features of the Mosaic-Talmudic Law of Inheritance." The Berlin city councilor David Friedländer, one of the few members of the older generation that had still been directly inspired by Mendelssohn, wrote *Brief über das Lesen der heiligen Schriften* for the young generation, which had already grown up with modern culture and to which most members belonged. These essays about reading the Scriptures combine Jewish deistic piety with a desire to take an unprejudiced approach, and they are supplemented by a "Translation of Micah 6 and 7" which is almost a dramatization. The Kantian Lazarus Bendavid—he, too, thirty years older than the others and director of the secular Jewish Freischule in Berlin—set forth his views on the changing "belief of the Jews in a future Messiah." In his radical conclusions he arrived at a formulation that seems strange to us (as it did to many of his contemporaries): no one could blame a Jew "if he finds his Messiah in the fact that good potentates have granted him equality with their citizens and given him hope of obtaining full civil rights when he fulfills all his civic duties." At the beginning of a second piece of Bible criticism, "Über geschriebenes und mündliches Gesetz," Bendavid writes: "The blows of the critical ax must be struck vigorously and in rapid succession if one wants to rid the magnificent tree called religion of the parasitic plants that ignorance, inordinate ambition, avarice, and lust for power have gradually caused to grow on its bark."

As we have indicated, the truly progressive contributions are those of Leopold Zunz, the editor. The periodical contains three essays by him, each of which is programmatic. The last one, "Grundlinien zu einer künftigen Statistik der Juden," defines statistics (as Immanuel Wolf had done in his programmatic essay) much as the coiner of the word, the Göttingen professor Gottfried Achenwall (1719–72) had defined it: a comprehensive description of the demographic, social, and political situation of a people—what Herbert Spencer called "destructive sociology" in his book *Social Statics* (1850). In this last article of his periodical Zunz outlines a gigantic program for a description of the life of the Jewish people in cross sections of periods, countries, and places. He proposes to examine this life in all its manifestations and utilize every imaginable source, which he specifies with astonishing insight—from relics and traditions to archival sources and literary creations that are to be systematically utilized philosophically and with regard to form and content, from laws to administrative documents of Jewish and non-Jewish provenance. This adds up to a more extensive and comprehensive program than has ever been executed for any people and country, and certainly for the Jewish people. "What is needed for the present, which is to be the capstone of the great statistical structure, is a perspective that surveys and explores the creations of the past and of science and that is able to derive from the Jews' mentality, their laws, and their conduct a complete picture of both the passive and active condition of present-day Jewry." It was thus to be an enormous inventory of the past and the present, but there is no reference to a future. A second essay, about "Salomon ben Isaac, genannt Raschi" is the first, and still not outdated, attempt at a biography of the great Franco-Jewish commentator on the Bible and the Talmud—the first modern attempt to write a systematic biography of any Jewish personality of the Middle Ages. The first of Zunz's articles in the *Zeitschrift* was pioneering and characteristic of Zunz's method of investigating and presenting the past. It bears the unpretentious title "Über die in den hebräisch-jüdischen Schriften vorkommenden hispanischen Ortsnamen," and in order to justify his choice of subject Zunz gives (pp. 114ff.) a survey of the nature and course of Jewish history and the methods to be used in investigating it (including an outline of the "Statistics of the Jews"). He emphasizes the significance of areas and localities for the history of the Jews and motivates his choice of Spain as the first in his series by pointing to the importance of the Judeo-Spanish period as a golden age in the history of the Jewish Diaspora. Since then Jewish historians have viewed this period in this light, though surely not altogether rightly so, and this is how it lives on in the historical consciousness of the Jews that was created by this historiography. "Of all endeavors of the Jewish people since its political decline," writes Zunz, "none equals the Hispanic period, when the Jews were on the same plane as Europe and frequently on an even higher one. Some men who lived there deserved every recognition; there was not merely a dead language and an honored legacy of the ancestors but also a living, understood, and developed one. Poetry and science vied with the Moors and found their admirers. Even external history was more significant, more vigorous, and, after the barbaric Visigothic period, more attractive there than anywhere else." That area and that period, he wrote, were too important "for me to undertake my first excursion to other steppes of Jewish history. For the wanderer looks from the German-Polish barbarism to the Hesperian land as to a friendly oasis and is transported from the present to a more important past. Disconsolate about what has perished, he would be even more disheartened by the misery at home—

unless his wanderings could give him an insight into the causes of the aridity and the bounty, unless he did not see justice and human dignity rise, at long last, from their severe maltreatment and did not observe them wrecking the Inquisition there and planting seeds for future fruits here, among Germany's Jews." To take the completed past, which is to be investigated, and to hold it up to the unpleasant past like a mirror—Zunz had formulated something like this, and in even more pessimistic terms, four years earlier (1818) in his first fundamental essay "Etwas über die rabbinische Literatur":

> Precisely because in our time the Jews—and we shall limit ourselves to the German Jews—are reaching more earnestly for the German language and German culture and thus—often perhaps without desiring or realizing it—are witnessing the interment of modern Hebrew literature, scholarship appears and demands an accounting from the Hebrew culture of the *past*. Now that no new significant phenomenon could easily disturb our overview and that we have a larger ancillary apparatus at our disposal than the scholars of the sixteenth and seventeenth centuries did, now that greater culture makes one expect a more enlightened treatment and the Hebrew books are more easily obtainable than they might be in 1919—now, we believe, carrying on our research on a large scale becomes a duty and an all the more weighty one because it appears to enable us to answer the complex question about the fate of the Jews in a few paragraphs. The price to be paid for every heedless so-called improvement is the skewed result; overhasty innovations give a higher value to the *old*, and worst of all, to the *antiquated*. Therefore, in order to recognize and distinguish among the old and usable, the antiquated and harmful, and the new and desirable we must circumspectly set out to study the people and its political as well as moral history. But this has a serious drawback—namely, that the cause of the Jews is treated like their literature. Both have been tackled with self-conscious passion and either undervalued or overvalued.

A not inconsiderable portion of the investigations was prompted by practical considerations, but then far transcended these. Cases in point are Zunz's treatise about Jewish names, which was intended to prove that in all periods the Jews used not only biblical names but adopted some from the surrounding world, or his great work on homiletics, *Die gottesdienstlichen Vorträge der Juden*, which aimed at demonstrating that even in earlier ages didactic and hortatory sermons in the vernacular were common in Jewish religious services. Similarly, in his historical writings Geiger wanted to show that Jewish writings and customs had had a historical development and undergone transformations. From this it was possible to derive contemporary Jewry's right to reform whatever turned out to need reforming.

There was a certain ambivalence about the Science of Judaism in its early period and about many of its champions and researchers for a long time thereafter. In his abovementioned essay, which despite its brevity may be the most comprehensive, Gershom Scholem was perceptive and sensitive enough to discern "a funeral breath in the atmosphere of this Science."* Scholem writes: "There is occasionally some-

---

*As a matter of fact, one of its most renowned representatives, Moritz Steinschneider (1816–1907), who as a student belonged for a short time to a pre-Zionist group, in his old age contemptuously told one of his last students, Gotthold Weil, that the "rebuilding of Judaism in the spirit of national regeneration is nonsense." Pointing to his library, he said: "Our only task now is to give the remnants of Judaism an honorable burial." Shmarya Levin, a Jew (and Zionist) from Eastern Europe who went to Berlin in 1891 to study at the university and the Hochschule für die Wissenschaft des Judentums, made this judgment in his memoirs (*Jugend im Aufruhr*, Berlin, 1933): "The Jewish scholars of the Zunz-Geiger era (around the middle of the nineteenth century), who accomplished truly great things in Jewish scholarship, had made it their task to reveal to the world the intellectual and cultural treasures of the Jews of the past. Zunz himself made it clear that the road to emancipation led only through Jewish scholarship; as soon as the big world found out about the noble ancestry of the Jews, it would recognize them as its equal. The difference between a Jewish scholar and his Christian colleague was only a quantitatively

thing uncanny about these writings. At the same time, however, the positive aspects prevail contrary to their intentions, and in many of these scholars romantic enthusiasm overwhelms their original intent to liquidate, spiritualize, and dematerialize Judaism and produced positive insights far removed from their original ideas."

From Germany the Science of Judaism spread through all countries in which Jews lived, which proves that it had arisen in response to a deeply felt need. There was no later work on Judaism, of whatever orientation, that was not influenced by the new method of scholarly access in place of the pious interpretation of sacred traditions. This was an enormous achievement, one whose importance for Judaism can hardly be overestimated, even though in the first hundred years the areas alien to rational thought, especially Jewish mysticism and Jewish popular life below the intellectual or prosperous upper class, were consciously or unconsciously excluded. Institutions like the Lehranstalt (later Hochschule) für die Wissenschaft des Judentums were founded in that spirit, and all other teaching and research institutions at least had to concern themselves with the questions raised by the Science of Judaism and its scholarship.

HEINRICH GRAETZ AND HIS "HISTORY OF THE JEWS": A major part of the products of 279f. the Science of Judaism remained limited to the narrow circle of scholars and intellectuals who bought and read such publications—scholars always complain of the weak response, and publishers of the small sales of their publications—but Heinrich Graetz's *Geschichte der Juden* found its way into the heart of the Jews. What was new about it was precisely what its Jewish and non-Jewish critics generally censured about it, though they did acknowledge the enormous erudition of its author. Graetz viewed even Jewish history in the Diaspora as the history of the Jewish people, affirming it rather than distancing himself from it. Unlike what may be noted in many other representatives of the Science of Judaism, in Graetz the methodological detachment of the scholar is not perceived as detachment from the human and national history of the Jewish people. As a complete Jew he is part of history; he experiences it warmheartedly and conveys this experience with the zest of a born story-teller as a person who believes in the future—qualities that were lacking in most of the other researchers and writers on Jewish history, such as his predecessor Jost. Graetz influenced people of all ages and social strata and created a new consciousness of the continuity and promise of Jewish history, Jewish thought, and Jewish action. His work represented the transition from a defensive, apologetic attitude in the Jewish question to a new, positive position which later manifested itself in Zionism, the Jewish movement of national regeneration. When Graetz died in 1891, one of the early Zionists, the Russian-Jewish student Leo Motzkin,* wrote in his obituary of him (published as an editorial in Nathan Birnbaum's *Selbst-Emancipation. Organ der Jüdisch-Nationalen* [Vienna], 18 September 1891) that Graetz, "the representative of the past, of positive, historical national Judaism," had exerted a profound influence on young people fighting for a Jewish regeneration by instilling in them pride in the Jewish past. "Just open the volumes of his grandiose History; every page bears witness to the greatness, the worth, and the capability of the Jewish nation. However, we also learn from every page how shamefully we got on the wrong track during our

---

temporal one; for both the Jewish values lay buried in a big cemetery. For the Christian scholar this cemetery was completed with Nazareth, for the Jewish scholar with the modern period. A deep feeling of piety impelled the Jewish researchers to erect the most magnificent memorials to our past and to adorn them richly with flowers: 'Here a glorious period existed once; may it rest in peace forever!' And the inevitable happened. If the past is dead for the modern Jew, the modern Jew is dead for his past."

*Later chairman of the Zionist Actions Committee and the long-time head of the Comité des délégations juives, which gave rise to the World Jewish Congress.

bondage, when we frequently created colossal things but seldom anything unified, how low we sank during each of our periods of assimilation, because we abandoned *our* ideals and were not able to adopt others, though we thought we did, and therefore created only by halves." And another collaborator, the Magdeburg student Heinrich Loewe (later director of the university library in Berlin and the municipal library in Tel Aviv), added in his biographical appreciation: "For the history of the Jews is of as tremendous an importance for Jewish national consciousness as a Graetz is for the history of the Jews."

8

Zionism and the Jewish Question

Prefatory Note: This chapter does not deal with Zionism—its history, ideology, and organization—as such, but only insofar as these concern our problem, the Jewish question. I shall limit myself essentially to the personalities and events that were of decisive historical, ideological, and practical importance for this problem—the nature of the Jewish question and the attempts at its solution. Other aspects will occasionally be included for the sake of clarification.

BIBLIOGRAPHY: Israel Klausner, *History of Zionism. Bibliography of Jewish History* 3 (Jerusalem, 1975).

HISTORY: Adolf Böhm, *Die Zionistische Bewegung*, 2 vols. (Tel Aviv, 1935–37); Alex Bein, *Der Zionismus und sein Werk* (Prague, 5699/1931) (translated into numerous languages; in French, 3d expanded ed., *Introduction au Sionisme* [Jerusalem, 1946]); Rufus Learsi, *Fulfillment: The Epic Story of Zionism*, (Cleveland and New York, 1951); Walter Laqueur, *A History of Zionism* (London and New York, 1972); Ben Halpern, *The Idea of the Jewish State* (Cambridge, Mass., 1961); David Vital, *The Origins of Zionism* (Oxford, 1975); Arthur Hertzberg, ed., *The Zionist Idea: A Historical Analysis and Reader* (New York, 1959); Zvi Barmer, ed., *Zionist Thought: Essays and Basic Writings* (Hebr.) (Jerusalem, 1967); Julius H. Schoeps, ed., *Zionismus: Vierunddreissig Aufsätze* (Munich, 1973); Conor Cruise O'Brien, *The Siege: The Saga of Israel and Zionism* (New York, 1986). Cf. also the general and specific articles in the Jewish encyclopedias, esp. *EJJ* and Raphael Patai, ed., *Encyclopedia of Zionism and Israel*, 2 vols. (New York, 1971) as well as the references given below for the various sections.

ZIONISM, THE WORD AND THE CONCEPT: A detailed investigation of this may be found in my essay "The Origin of the Term and Concept 'Zionism,'" *Herzl Year Book* 2 (New York, 1951), 1–27; a German version appeared as "Von der Zionssehnsucht zum politischen Zionismus: Zur Geschichte des Wortes und Begriffes 'Zionismus,'" in *Robert Weltsch zum 70, Geburtstag von seinen Freunden* (Tel Aviv, 1961), 33–63, XXVI–XXVII (Hebr. with Eng. synopsis in *Yitzhak Baer Jubilee Volume* [Jerusalem, 5721/1960], 454–73; a brief resumé in *Zeitschrift für deutsche Wortforschung* 19 [1963]: 178f.). Supplementary information about the use of the word in Hebrew *(Zionut)* is given by G. Kressel in the newspaper *Yediot Akhronot*, 28 November 1975, 2.

The adjective *zionistisch* was first used by Nathan Birnbaum in his journal *Selbst-Emancipation* on 1 April 1890 and the noun *Zionismus* in the edition of 16 May 1890. The suffix *-ism* integrated the concept into the political and philosophical intellectual world of the late nineteenth century (like socialism, nationalism, anti-Semitism, etc.) This made people aware of its aims and opened debate on them. Originally the word *Zionism* was also directed against the efforts to create a Jewish mass settlement in

284f.

Argentina (in place of Palestine) that had been propagated and initiated since 1890 by the Jewish financier and philanthropist Moritz von Hirsch (Baron Maurice de Hirsch, 1831–96), and in the face of this enterprise it was intended to emphasize the Palestine-centered nature of the national movement of the Jewish people. Theodor Herzl (see below) adopted the term, but in the discussions about the convening of the First Zionist Congress (beginning in March 1897) he gave it a distinctly political, antiphilanthropic slant (see further details below). The conclusion of Herzl's letter to W. Bambus of 7 May 1897 is revealing in this regard: "The Congress will definitely take place—and as a Zionist Congress." Here this word denoted a fundamental distinction between the earlier efforts at a Jewish resettlement of Palestine, as undertaken from 1882 on primarily by the Hovevei Zion (Friends of Zion) in Russia, Rumania, and other countries, and the new movement of political Zionism under Herzl's leadership. The First Zionist Congress of 1897 and the subsequent actions introduced the word into the general press and literature and made it a diplomatic concept. On the occasion of his audience with Kaiser Wilhelm II in Constantinople Herzl made this entry in his diary on 19 October 1898: "I was a little inattentive, since I had to make a mental note of the effectiveness of my three years' work in making the obscure word "Zionism" a *terme reçu* [household word], one that the German Kaiser used readily in talking to me" (*Complete Diaries of Theodor Herzl*, trans. H. Zohn, 2 [New York, 1960], 728). Regarding the importance that, in my estimation, should be attached to the creation and adoption of such concepts as an epochal phenomenon, cf. Part 1, pp. 230f.

284   NATHAN BIRNBAUM'S DEFINITION: The beginning of Birnbaum's lecture "Die Prinzipien des Zionismus," given on 23 January 1892 before the Jewish nationalist association Admat Yeshurun (Soil of Israel), uses the somewhat pompous language of many writers of the time, including political writers. The biweekly *Selbst-Emancipation*, the first Zionist journal in the German language, was published in Vienna from 1885 to 1886 and then from 1 April 1890 to late December 1893. It bore the subtitle *Organ der Jüdisch-Nationalen* and later *Organ der Zionisten*. Its "publisher and editor-in-chief" Nathan Birnbaum (1864–1937) was probably the intellectually most outstanding personality in Jewish nationalist circles of Austria and Germany in the decade before Herzl's appearance.

285f.   MESSIANIC BELIEF IN REDEMPTION AND PRACTICAL REALIZATION: Cf. the conclusion of G. Scholem's essay "Zum Verständnis der messianischen Idee im Judentum" (*Judaica* 1 [1963], 73f.) about "the price which the Jewish people had to pay from its substance for the idea that it gave to the world. The greatness of the Messianic idea corresponds to the infinite weakness of Jewish history, which in exile was not ready for action on a historical plane." Pinsker had already remarked in his *Autoemancipation* (cf. Part 1, pp. 288ff.): "Besides, the Messianic faith, the belief in the intervention of a higher power in favor of our political resurrection, and the religious assumption that we must patiently bear a punishment inflicted on us by God have freed us from any worry about our national liberation, our unity and independence."

286ff. PRECURSORS OF ZIONISM: We cannot deal with these precursors here, though some of their projects were interesting and the lives of some of their planners and initiators were adventurous. Some of these aspects have been mentioned in this book in a different context (see the index). For our problem the appearance of these figures is more of a symptom. In the history of the Jewish question they did not play an active role, though one can of course never be certain whether they did not influence later generations in one way or another. Herzl's grandfather, for example, surely knew about Alkalay's ideas and endeavors; Kalischer influenced Hess; the Christian movement for the "restoration of the Jews" had an influence upon politicians in England and probably upon Jews as well; and so on. For the history of these ideas I shall refer, in addition to the literature given at the beginning of this section, to N. M. Gelber, *Zur Vorgeschichte des Zionismus: Judenstaatsprojekte in den Jahren 1695–1845* (Vienna, 1927); Franz Kobler, *The Vision Was There: A History of the British Movement for the Restoration of the Jews to Palestine* (London, 1956); M. Verete, "The Restoration of the Jews in English Protestant Thought, 1790–1840," *Middle East Studies* 8, no. 1 (January 1972): 3–50.

MORDECAI MANUEL NOAH: In this connection the project of a Jewish state of the   286
American Jew Mordecai Manuel Noah (1785–1851) is of importance as a symptom of this situation. It was probably his personal experiences as an American consul in Tunis, a position from which President Monroe recalled him in 1815 because of his Jewish faith, that he began to concern himself seriously with the Jewish question, gaining the conviction that it could be solved only territorially through the foundation of a Jewish state. In a ceremony held in 1825 at Buffalo he inaugurated the Jewish city of Ararat on Grand Island in the Niagara River (New York State), a community that was intended to become the center of a Jewish state. He envisaged it as a refuge for persecuted Jews and issued an appeal to Jewish communities all over the world to immigrate to his state. The project was generally derided or indignantly rejected. The leaders of the Verein für Cultur und Wissenschaft der Juden (see above) probably took it most seriously, for in 1822 the Society named Mordecai Manuel Noah an associate member, and some of its members, disappointed at the anti-Jewish German reaction, seemed to have contemplated emigration at that time. The mockery of Heine, who addressed Zunz in a letter as "designated judge in Israel" and, as he wrote his friend Moser on 23 April 1826, dreamt of a meeting between Noah and Gans, had, as always, a serious background. At a later date Noah again pleaded for a restoration of the Jewish state, but this time in Palestine. Cf. also H. G. Reissner in his abovementioned biography of Gans and his essay "Ganstown, U.S.A.: The First Migration Plan of Jews from Germany," in *American Jewish Archives* 14 (Cincinnati, 1962). Regarding the problem of the "precursors" of Zionism, in contrast to its creators and implementers, cf. also J. Katz's fundamental Hebrew essay on the clarification of the concept "precursors of Zionism" (now in his book *Jewish Nationalism: Essays and Studies* [Hebr.] [Jerusalem, 1979], 263ff.) In 1840, at the time of the Damascus Affair, the young Lassalle (as evidenced by his diary) dreamt of leading the Jews, sword in hand, in the conquest of Palestine; cf. my article "Herzl und Lassalle" in *Allgemeine Wochenzeitung der Juden* 7 (1952): 12–14. We have already discussed Benjamin Disraeli. Here we shall refer to the Zionist utopian novel *Daniel Deronda* by the British writer George Eliot (pseudonym of Mary Ann Evans, 1819–80), which appeared in 1876 and made an impression on many Jews and non-Jews.

MOSES HESS: Concerning the socialist Moses Hess and his position on the Jewish   286f.
question, cf. part 2, p. 588 (with bibliographical information). For decades Hess was all but forgotten as a forerunner of Zionism, but then the leading German Zionist Isidor Bodenheimer (1865–1940) arranged for a new edition of *Rom und Jerusalem*, a book that had long been out of print. (Its title was to have been *Wiedergeburt Israels*, but Heinrich Graetz, whom Hess admired, prevailed upon him to change it.) It has since appeared in numerous editions and languages. The first biography of Hess was written by the Zionist physician Theodor Zlocisti; it appeared in Berlin in 1921 and is still worth reading. Theodor Herzl began to read *Rom und Jerusalem* in 1898 in Jerusalem, but he did not finish and study it until late April 1901, six years after his conception of the Jewish state and shortly before his audience with the Sultan. On 10

May of that year he wrote in his diary: "Now I was enraptured and uplifted by him. What an exalted, noble spirit! Everything that we have tried is already in this book. The only bothersome thing is his Hegelian terminology. Wonderful the Spinozistic-Jewish and nationalist elements. Since Spinoza Jewry has brought forth no greater spirit than this forgotten, faded Moses Hess!" (*Complete Diaries* 3 : 1090). Hess's very wealth of ideas may have been an impediment to the dissemination of his book. It is in the form of a collection of letters, which was not unusual at that time, but with its excursuses and notes it certainly did not make for easy reading. His treatment of historical and contemporary Jewry is as comprehensive and perceptive as any previous or subsequent presentation. Hess anticipated many later insights, such as the importance of Hasidism. All these insights are embedded in a cosmological, religious, social, and national view of history and permeated by a faith in a world harmony in which all peoples (he often uses *Völker* synonymously with *Rassen* and *Nationen*, as in English) will have their definite place and be able to develop freely in accordance with their particular qualities, without the stronger nations being entitled to conquer the weaker nations and make them submit to their will to power and their culture. Arnold Ruge, "a good-natured anti-Semite, as all these Prussian democrats probably were" (T. Zlocisti), was the first to call Moses Hess "the rabbi of the communists." This appellation was intended to be derisive and deprecatory, but if viewed in positive terms, there is much truth in it. What mattered to Hess was the deliverance of mankind from social evils, but his personal focus was his Jewish, religious-national piety, and his thoughts, emotions, and desires revolved around it. This lent his life, thought, and activity something mystical, profound, and indefinite; it made him a great inspirer and helper but denied him the role of a leader and implementer. His proposals for practical colonization (note 9) are quite vague. As with Heine, reading Hess brings the currents and influences that affected Jewish life around the middle of the nineteenth century to life for us. Hess attempted to grapple with these on a deeper level than Heine, though he lacked the latter's directness and linguistic power. One of the speakers at the First Zionist Congress, David Farbstein, celebrated Hess as the proclaimer of socialist Zionism. In October 1961 his remains were transported to Israel and interred in the cemetery of Kvutza Kinneret. Of the numerous appreciations and articles published in the last few decades we shall mention Martin Buber's "Der erste der Letzten," in *Israel und Palästina: Zur Geschichte einer Idee* (Zurich, 1950) and Helmut Hirsch's well-illustrated centennial volume *Moses Hess: Vorkämpfer der Freiheit* (Cologne, 1975). Hess's *Jüdische Schriften* were edited in 1905 by T. Zlocisti; the Hebrew edition, with an introduction by Martin Buber, was issued by Sifriah Zionit (Jerusalem) in 1954.

287f. THE UNEXPECTED NATURE OF THE RUSSIAN POGROMS OF 1881: The Russo-Jewish Zionist and initiator of the World Jewish Congress, Leo Motzkin (1867–1933), experienced the Kiev pogrom as a boy and fifty years later reported in his speech at the international Jewish conference in Geneva (1932) that he still remembered "with what biting irony the pillars of Jewish society disposed of all those who spoke of signs of threatening attacks and riots. I remember listening as a little boy to the thoughtful conversations of serious-minded men. . . . 'What?', they said, 'it is ridiculous to imagine that in a state with a real police, army, and cultural institutions a whole horde of people might suddenly attack others; it is quite out of the question that the authorities would permit innocent people to be robbed, beaten, and manhandled.' A few days later, in April 1881, the first terrible pogroms of modern times broke out. . . ." (Quoted from the German manuscript, a Hebrew version of which may be found in my edition of *Sefer Motzkin* [1939]).

THE FIRST IMMIGRATION AND SETTLEMENT MOVEMENT IN PALESTINE: It is generally   287f.
called the First Aliyah (in Hebr. *aliyah* means "ascent"; the term derives from the
pilgrimages to 800-meter-high Mt. Zion, to Jerusalem, and to the Palestinian mountain region generally, and it denotes immigration to Palestine). One should always
bear in mind, however, that for many years immigration to Palestine and Eretz
Yisrael was impeded by the Turks and was only a trickle compared to the stream of
the great migration movement to England, America, and other countries. But even
among the emigrants whose main destination was America there were groups that
aimed at settlements on a nationalist, socialist, or communist basis. In those days
there were heated discussions between those who favored a national settlement in
America and the Hovevei Zion. Concerning this Jewish national movement for
America, which called itself Am Olam (world people—in the Ashkenazic pronunciation, Am Oylom) and failed after a few attempts at colonization, cf. Abraham Menes,
"The Am Oylom Movement," in *Yivo Annual of Jewish Social Science* 4 (New York,
1949), 9–33; Joel Geffin, "Whither, to Palestine or to America?" in "The Pages of the
Russian Hebrew Press Ha-Melitz and Ha-Yom (1880–1890: Annotated Docu-
mentary," in *American Jewish History Quarterly* 59 (December 1969): 179–200.

PINSKER'S "AUTOEMANCIPATION": There is as yet no adequate biography of Leon   288ff.
(Yehuda Leib) Pinsker. Alter Druyanow, the greatest expert on the history of the
Hovevei Zion and the collector and editor of a comprehensive selection from their
documents, wrote a Hebrew biography of Pinsker, but the only parts that have been
preserved go only up to the writing of *Autoemancipation*. Still, it is the most
important source for an appreciation of Pinsker's personality and development
(*Pinsker u-smano*), Jerusalem 5713/1953). There are also Hebrew introductions and
articles by Joseph Klausner and Ahad Ha-Am in *Sefer Pinsker* (Jerusalem, 5681/1921)
and by Mordechai Yoeli in *J. L. Pinsker, the Proclaimer of National Rebirth* (Hebr.)
(Tel Aviv, 5720/1960). The most comprehensive presentation and appreciation of his
life in English is B. Netanyahu's introduction to *Leon Pinsker: Road to Freedom* (New
York, 1944), 7–73.

Pinsker (1821–91), the son of the Jewish scholar Simcha Pinsker (whose pious
father already sympathized with the Haskalah [Enlightenment]), was raised in
Odessa, a center of the Haskalah, attended a Russian secondary school, and studied
law as well as medicine. As a doctor he served with courage and dedication in the
Crimean War. As a leading member of the Society for the Promotion of Enlightenment and coeditor of Russian-Jewish periodicals he believed that the dissemination of
secular culture and the Russian language among the Jews would produce a more
harmonious relationship between them and the Russians. In 1871 this belief was
shaken for the first time by local pogroms in Odessa, in which even the Russian
intelligentsia participated, and definitively by the great wave of pogroms that swept
Russia in 1881. Now Pinsker abruptly resigned from the Society for the Promotion of
Enlightenment, calling its aims and activities meaningless if the very life of the
Jewish people was in danger. He failed in his attempts to convince leaders of western
and central European Jewry in personal discussions that only a national solution
could save the Jews from a catastrophe. The famous Vienna scholar and rabbi Adolf
Jellinek (1821–93) advised him to take a pleasure trip and cure his nervous strain.
Pinsker was by nature a slow, ponderous thinker and writer, but in the summer of
1882, utterly disappointed at the failure of Jewish leaders and institutions, in despair
over the situation of the Jews, and deeply hurt in his pride as a Jew and a human
being, he wrote his *Mahnruf* (Warning) in Berlin, apparently in a very short time,
and it appeared there that fall. In the brief "Author's Preface," dated September 1982,

he wrote, full of bitter irony, words that are generally not quoted but afford a deep insight into his motives, visions, and goals:

> The misery of bloody violence had been succeeded by a moment of peace, and both the persecutors and the persecuted can catch their breath for a while. In the meantime the Jewish refugees are being *"repatriated"* with the very funds that were raised for the purpose of emigration. But the Jews in the West have learned to endure the cries of "Hepp, Hepp" again, as their fathers did in bygone days. The blazing outbreak of indignation at the mortification that we have suffered has turned into a shower of ashes that are gradually covering the fiery ground. Just close your eyes and bury your heads in the sand like ostriches; you will not be vouchsafed a *lasting peace* unless you utilize the fleeting moment of quiet and devise more radical remedies than those palliatives that have messed up our unfortunate people for thousands of years!

At first Pinsker's *Autoemancipation* did not enjoy wide circulation, and the reviews in the German-Jewish press were generally negative. Regarding the new editions and translations into other languages, cf. the (Hebr.) bibliographies by B. Schochetmann (Jerusalem, 5694/1934) and Hella Abrahami in the collection (which is dedicated to me) *Zionut* 3 of the Institute for Zionist Research of Tel Aviv University (1973), 548–557 and 598. These indicate that the first German reprint did not appear until 1903 and the second ten years later. The first translation into Hebrew, which was delayed by censorship, appeared in the Hebrew daily *Hamagid* (nos. 43–48, 1882 and no. 3, 1883); the first complete translation was issued as a pamphlet in Vilna in late 1883 and the second one in 1889. The first English-language edition appeared (still anonymously) in 1891, the year of Pinsker's death. The following episode indicates how little known Pinsker was at that time among the foreign groups of the Hovevei Zion, even though he had been recognized as the leader of the movement in Russia since the Kattowitz Conference of 1884. On 22 December 1891 H. N. Adler, the Chief Rabbi of London, wrote the president of the British group of Hovevei Zion, Elim Henry D'Avigdor, that he had just received a telegram from Russia informing him of the death of Dr. Pinsker, the president of the Russian Hovevei Zion. D'Avigdor forwarded the letter to the secretary of the British Hovevei Zion with this note: "I was not aware of the name of the gentleman whose death he [the Chief Rabbi] announces. An appropriate telegram of condolence should immediately be sent in the name of the association." What a contrast to what was to happen thirteen years later with the personality of Theodor Herzl!

289   WOUNDED PRIDE AS A MOTIVE: It seems to me that motives like wounded pride and striving for the same honor as the other citizens of a state or for the vindication of one's honor have not been sufficiently appreciated. Such motives have played an important part in all modern libertarian movements, and these can only be briefly indicated here—particularly since the American struggle for independence and the French Revolution of 1789, as well as the emancipative movements of all minorities and the national movements of oppressed peoples. The concept *Ehre* (honor) in its two senses, recognition and equal or greater value of a person in the judgment of society (outward honor) and the recognition of his person and his conduct by himself (inward honor), entered the consciousness of modern man through medieval philosophy and natural right as well as through the declaration of the rights of man and civil rights. In Montesquieu (*De l'esprit des lois;* Kurt Sternberg, *Staatsphilosophie* [Berlin, 1923], 156ff.) it is as "the preconceived judgment of every person and every position" the enlivening and preserving principle of the monarchy. Among the Jews the concept of honor in the modern sense of the word—that is, recognition by the surrounding world—has played little or no role for as long as they had a home in their

own ghettos and separate districts. The concept of honor in these districts was oriented toward the religiosity of the individual and what he did for the Jewish community under the guidance of his piousness. Since he has been created in God's image, man deserves honor (Hebr. *kavod,* derived from the idea of weight) to the extent that he is like God in his deeds and his relation to his fellow men, those on a higher as well as a lower level than he (cf. the articles in *JL, HE* and *EJJ,* as well as the one about "Ehrentitel" in *EJ*). As the Jews entered non-Jewish society as individuals (human beings), they adopted its conceptual and value system (which we have discussed in some detail in Part 1, p. 265f.) and hence also its conception of honor. The little bit of honor that the world conceded to the Jews affected their self-esteem and produced a frequently exaggerated striving for honor as an external recognition and an overwrought inner sense of honor or feeling of dishonor. The striving for equality of rights, assimilation, and outside confirmation of recognition through honorary posts and honorific titles is rooted in this, and so is the pursuit of prosperity and distinction through outstanding achievements, display of courage, and so forth, in place of the "normal" honors gained by "normal" Christian citizens. (We shall return to this point in the section on Herzl). The lack of honor and the sense of honor that rebelled against it in many Jews of the transitional period alienated important Jews of the nineteenth and twentieth centuries from Judaism. (An example is Ferdinand Lassalle; cf. my abovementioned article "Herzl und Lassalle".) Others realized that it was futile to acquire honor in the surrounding world by giving up their own special characteristics, and this prompted them to intensify their efforts in behalf of Judaism in order to restore the honor of the Jews as a whole. This gave an important impetus to the new Science of Judaism and the Jewish historiography, especially that of Graetz; the proper perception and presentation of the past were to contribute to the restitution of the external and the consolidation of the internal honor. The world around him made Pinsker, whom his biographer Druyanow compared in this regard to Gabriel Riesser, the pioneer of emancipation, keenly aware of the lack of equal rights and honor—at least after he had completed his legal studies and found himself excluded from public office. His protest, which, in accordance with his nature, had been restrained for many years, erupted after the pogroms of 1881 and what he regarded as the dishonorable attitude of the Jewish Establishment toward these events. He came to the conclusion that the Jews enjoyed no honor as a people because they did not feel as a nation but were a disorganized flock. To restore their honor they would therefore have to organize themselves as a nation on their own territory and thereby give their ghostlike intellect a body again. Only in this way could a Jew be respected as an equal.

JEW-HATRED AS A FEAR OF GHOSTS (JUDOPHOBIA): The Jews as ghosts—as we have 289 seen, Heine sometimes viewed the Jews in this way (see the excursus about Heine, Part 2, pp. 642ff.); others also likened them to ghosts on occasion. Pinsker was basically correct in sensing that this notion has somehow always been present among Christians. It is behind the image of the Antichrist, of the Jew as devil, and of the Eternal or Wandering Jew who is unable to die. This is what makes the Jewish image as imagined by non-Jews in the past (and, let us face it, often in the present as well) so sinister. What was completely new, however, was Doctor Pinsker's diagnosis that antipathy to the Jews was a kind of anxiety neurosis, a fear of ghosts, and a phobia— Judophobia. Pinsker regarded it as hereditary and, since it had been transmitted for many generations, incurable.

The psychoanalyst Rudolph M. Loewenstein writes about this diagnosis from a present-day psychiatric point of view (*Psychoanalyse des Antisemitismus* [Frankfurt a.M., 1968], 12f.):

Let us not fasten on Pinsker's error about the direct hereditary transmission of psychosis; it may be attributed to the psychiatric theory of his time. He is also wrong from a psychiatric standpoint when he calls Judophobia a psychosis; a phobia is not a psychosis. Nevertheless, despite these inaccuracies in Pinsker's diagnosis present-day psychiatrists agree with him up to a certain point. In the opinion of Richard M. Brickner [*Is Germany Incurable?* (Philadelphia, 1943)] anti-Semitism is related to paranoid states. . . . A phobia is a neurosis marked by irrational states of anxiety which can, for example, be produced by empty or closed spaces. . . . People under the spell of a phobia may be suffering from a disturbance, but they are quite harmless. . . . It is completely different with paranoiacs; they are not neurotics but patients afflicted with psychoses and expressing delusions. . . . By exchanging roles a paranoiac frequently becomes a persecuted persecutor—that is, he brings himself to attack and kill the person he regards as the author of the conspiracy.

As regards Pinsker's perceived transmission of the psychosis he called Judophobia, it seems to me that we must not merely take him literally as a natural scientist. The hereditary transmission of qualities, customs, and ideas is accomplished not only in a purely genetic, physical way but also through tradition, habituation, and education over many generations, through verbal images, legends, fairy tales, and other traditional materials. Whether a fear of ghosts is physically transmitted through genes of psychically instilled in a person in early childhood through such traditional materials is of little importance compared to the fact that it has been present in the human psyche for many generations and has affected people's actions. If viewed in this way, Pinsker's diagnosis contains more truth than a purely medical judgment may be able to admit.

Incidentally, Pinsker's little book was not the only one of its kind. Around the same time and in the succeeding years a number of writings with similar ideas appeared, but none of such affective power and graphic memorability.

290ff.   AHAD HA-AM AND CULTURAL ZIONISM: About Ahad Ha-Am there is an enormous literature, though most of it is scattered in journals, articles, and chapters of general Zionist literature. Every writer about Zionism has had to take cognizance of him, especially since his polemic with Herzl and Herzlian political Zionism. Only rarely have Ahad Ha-Am's personality and views been examined and evaluated as a whole; usually certain aspects have been dealt with in accordance with an author's personal views. Sometimes Herzl and Ahad Ha-Am were juxtaposed as two personalities of equal value, like Goethe and Schiller in the history of German literature. One is reminded of this well-known verse of Nietzsche: "Darwin neben Goethe setzen/ heisst die Majestät verletzen—/ majestatem genii" (To place Darwin next to Goethe is lese majesty—an offense to the majesty of genius). Such comparisons and elevations are unfair to Ahad Ha-Am, and so is the underestimation of his achievements and his wide-ranging educational influence. His forte was criticism, and it is no accident that a major part of his essays was prompted by polemics with people holding different views. His essays were (and some of them still are) of great importance as correctives and exposures of theoretical and human weaknesses. He wished to destroy secular Messianic hopes that were all too easily aroused by the settlement work in Palestine or political-diplomatic activities for the establishment of a Jewish state. He believed that the nonfulfillment of such hopes, which he regarded as pipe dreams, could only lead to despair. Ahad Ha-Am's first essay, "This Is Not the Way," already contains in a nutshell almost everything that he presented in ever new formulations and comparisons over a period of three decades. It came into being during a crisis in the Palestine movement and was intended as a consolation and support in the face of threatening despair and abandonment of the work in and for Palestine. On the other hand, it produced new dangerous illusions: that a secular Jewish nationalist culture, in which religion had a place only as an expression of the Jewish people's life and will to live and not as an intrinsic value and guiding star, could be created on the narrow territorial basis of a "cultural center" in Palestine; that the cultural life of the Jews in the Diaspora and their inner cohesion could be revived and strengthened even without a Zionist territorial solution; and above all, that while the life of the Jews in the Diaspora—and at that time this meant mainly Europe and especially Eastern Europe—was subject to attacks and threats of all kinds, it was possible to continue it, as in the past, with various ways of accommodation and expediency. Ahad Ha-Am saw no danger of a real catastrophe and, like most of his contemporaries, severely underestimated the time factor in the Jewish question, something to which Herzl then gave special emphasis. He warned against overhasty action, projects without sufficient preparation, and the like. His critical insights may have been correct, but they were all based on the assumption that there was time, that it was possible to make accommodations in the Diaspora and wait until the educational work had reached the point where systematic reconstruction work could be done in Palestine. The political worlds of the Diaspora and Palestine were for him basically static factors; only the intellectual life of the Jews was dynamic, and that was the only thing that really interested him. This was the basic flaw in all the cultural aspirations that became part of the Zionist movement under the influence of Ahad Ha-Am's ideas and contributed a great deal to its inner enlivenment but also produced the illusion that an authentic Jewish culture was possible in the Diaspora and that a Jew could therefore go on living his accustomed life and at the same time be a *Volljude*, a complete Jew. From the vantage point of the catastrophic years 1933 to 1945 it is tempting to ask whether these ideas and other endeavors that affirmed and strengthened the Diaspora (such as the national minorities movement after World War I) did not induce many Jews who might have emigrated to Palestine to remain in Europe, where they finally perished. (We shall return to this problem in the following chapter.) Herzl's letter of May 1903 to Martin Buber, the young leader of the "cultural Zionists," must be viewed in this light. He wrote Buber that the "democratic faction" led by him was on the wrong track: "My advice is that you try to find your way back to the [political] movement." And in a debate at the Sixth Zionist Congress Max Nordau gave this mordantly ironic reply to a leading Russian Zionist propagator of Ahad Ha-Am's views (Meir Dizengoff, later the mayor of Tel Aviv): "One of the speakers . . . made a statement that is quite familiar to me: 'We are not concerned with the Jews but with Judaism.' Judaism without Jews! Oh yes, we know you, fair mask! Go and tell this to a conference of spiritualists. You won't have much luck with it among living people, who want to have life around them and before them." On the other hand, Ahad Ha-Am's critical exposés of the "assimilated" Jews and their inner insecurity despite external equality and apparent freedom had a profound educative effect; for many he was *the* teacher and educator for a dignified Jewish life without the constraints of the religious laws.

Ahad Ha-Am's writings have appeared in four volumes in Hebrew (in numerous editions) as well as in German translation (2 vols. [Berlin: Jüdischer Verlag, 1913–16, 1923]), and his letters have been published in Hebrew (6 vols. [Tel Aviv, 1923–25]). The most detailed biography is Leon Simon, *Ahad Ha-Am—Asher Ginsberg: A Biography* (Philadelphia, 5721/1961). Concerning his debate with Herzl and political Zionism, cf. A. Bein, *Theodor Herzl* (Vienna, 1934, 1974). Cf. also M. Bileski, *Achad Haam: Darstellung und Kritik seiner Lehre* (Berlin, 1916) as well as H. Tuchman's fine edition of essays about him that differ in their evaluations, published on the occasion of the fortieth anniversary of his death: *Evaluations: Ahad Haam, the Philosopher of Cultural Zionism* (New York, 1967).

NATHAN BIRNBAUM: Unfortunately Birnbaum has not yet found a biographer who can   292f. give an adequate presentation of his development, which is interesting individually and typologically. In addition to my abovementioned (Part 2, p. 669) essay about the history of the word Zionism, the literature mentioned in it, and the discussion of Birnbaum's booklet in Part 1, cf. especially *Vom Sinn des Judentums*, a collection edited in his honor by A. E. Kaplan and Max Landau (Frankfurt, 1925); Leo Herrmann, *Nathan Birnbaum, sein Werk und seine Wandlung;* G. Kressel's Hebrew essay on *Selbst-Emancipation* in *Shivat Zion* 4:5715/16 (195/56). Birnbaum's writings on Zionism and Jewish nationalism appeared in 1910 at Czernowitz in two volumes under the title *Ausgewählte Schriften zur jüdischen Frage.* This does not contain his early writings (which in 1910 he did not regard as mature enough to be included in a collection of his literary works, or the 1882 pamphlet *Die Assimilationssucht: Ein Wort an die sogenannten Deutsche . . . mosaischer Konfession*, or the articles, most of them published in *Selbst-Emancipation*, in which he took a stand on all questions of his time and anticipated many ideas that were more widely discussed after Herzl's appearance. Birnbaum was a pioneer in many things, not only in the introduction of the word *Zionismus*. He was the founder (or cofounder) of the first Jewish nationalist student association, which was established in Vienna as *Kadimah* (Hebr. for "forward" or "eastward"), a name suggested by the Hebrew writer Peretz Smolenskin. As already mentioned, he was the founder, editor, and chief contributor of *Selbst-Emancipation*, the first Jewish nationalist and later Zionist newspaper. He was probably the first to use the words *Ostjuden* (instead of the terms customary before him, *russische Juden* or *osteuropäische Juden*) and *Westjuden* (since 1903 or earlier; cf. *Ausgewählte Schriften* 1:202); he also seems to have introduced, at least in Central and Western Europe and in 1902 or earlier, the designation *jüdische Sprache* (later *Jiddisch*) for the vernacular of the Eastern European Jews (customarily called *Jargon*). Cf. the article "Hebräisch und Jüdisch" in the monthly *Ost und West* 2, no. 7 (July 1902); *Ausgewählte Schriften* 1:301ff. He was one of the first fighters for Jewish national autonomy even in the Diaspora and organized and opened on 30 August 1908 the first "Jewish language conference" in Czernowitz. With such endeavors he strayed farther and farther from the Zionist movement. As early as September 1902 he wrote in an essay about the "Jewish renaissance" movement (*Ost und West; Ausgewählte Schriften* 1:162): "I wish to God I were as innocent of introducing the word *Zionismus* some years ago as I am now of the expression *Jüdische Renaissance!* In any case, I accept it." That expression had been used by Herzl and then was popularized by the young Martin Buber in the service of cultural Zionism. At that time Birnbaum had evidently forgotten that he had used, in a pamphlet published in 1893, the equivalent expression "the national rebirth of the Jewish people." His increasingly intensive and extensive occupation with the nature and the problems of the Jewish people led him to concern himself anew with the Jewish religion and tradition, particularly as one of the important expressions of the Jewish people's life. An eternal seeker and a man who for many years did not achieve peace, security, and stability, Birnbaum finally became an avowed Jew who professed and lived by the Orthodox tradition. Concerning his transformation and inner "conversion," cf. his booklets *Gottes Volk* (Vienna and Berlin, 1918 (and *Vom Freigeist zum Gläubigen* (Zurich, 5679/1919).

Despite all his pioneering occupation with new Jewish politics, Birnbaum was a basically apolitical person. His political and cultural standpoints at any given time were developmental stages on his way to a new devoutness. Even though his writings and speeches pointed the way to self-knowledge for many Jews of his generation, he was not a charismatic leader who could permanently bind people to himself and unite them for joint action. When Herzl appeared on the scene, Birnbaum felt misunderstood (as did Ahad Ha-Am for a time) as the Jewish masses and adherents of the Zionist idea gathered around Herzl although he, Birnbaum, had already expressed virtually all the ideas propagated by Herzl.

A harmonious collaboration between Birnbaum and Herzl was rendered impossible, despite many efforts on both sides, by the former's disappointment and occasional bitterness as well as by the contrast in their personal appearance, their social position, and their appeal to the Zionist youth, intellectuals, and the Jewish masses in Eastern Europe that were won over by Herzl almost overnight. Each of the men felt superior to the other and viewed him with mistrust. These psychological factors combined with Birnbaum's years of destitution and his easily hurt pride that clashed with an equal pride, feeling of superiority, and lust for power on the part of Herzl, and they may have contributed to Birnbaum's ever more critical attitude toward the Zionist movement led by Herzl and promoted and accelerated his estrangement from it.

THEODOR HERZL: In my biography of Theodor Herzl I have attempted to show the development of Herzl the Zionist, his progress within the Zionist movement, and his significance in the history of the Jewish people and the Jewish question as well as his importance for the foundation of the State of Israel. This book was first published in German in Vienna (Fiba Verlag, 1934); an expanded edition was issued in 1974 by the Österreichisch-Israelische Gesellschaft, Vienna, with an introduction by Golda Meir. A Hebrew edition first appeared in 1934 and was reprinted many times (most recently as a paperback, Jerusalem, 1976), as was the English translation (first published in 1940; Philadelphia and London, 1957; paperback ed., 1962, 1970). All later editions contain extensive listings of the important literature, much of which is based on my book. Most of the unpublished sources that I used are readily accessible in the Central Zionist Archives in Jerusalem (which I directed until 1971). On the basis of these sources I was able to demonstrate that the once widely held view that until the trial of Dreyfus (late 1894) and his degradation (January 1895) Herzl was unconcerned with the Jewish question, having evaded it as an assimilationist, and that the Dreyfus Affair suddenly caused him to become a convert to Zionism, was factually and psychologically untenable. As with most human transformations that seem to be sudden, Herzl's insight came as the result of the developments of many years, and there were a number of precipitating events, the most impressive and best-known of which was the Dreyfus trial. In the summer of 1895, at the beginning of his activities in the field of political Zionism, Herzl began to keep a diary in order to record, as in the logbook of a ship, all the events and stages of his adventurous political journey. As he began by reflecting how he had recognized the nature of the Jewish question and found a way to solve it, he did not even mention the Dreyfus trial. Not until three years later, when the case had turned into the "affair" that occupied not only France but the entire civilized world (oh, how civilized the civilized world was in those days as compared to the same world thirty-five years later!) and the case was reopened, did Herzl realize the importance of the Dreyfus trial for his development. But even then he clearly stated what had shaken him in those days. It was not really the fact that Dreyfus had been unjustly sentenced; at the time of his degradation no one knew this, though Herzl had certain doubts about his guilt, because he could not find a psychological motive for the high treason of an ambitious, wealthy, assimilated Jew who had risen to the rank of an officer on the general staff. Besides, given the nature of human judgment, miscarriages of justice can never be completely avoided. What profoundly agitated Herzl was really the behavior of the masses at the public act of the officer's degradation. They demanded not only the death sentence for the "traitor," which would have been understandable, but cried "Death to the Jews!" This made Herzl realize that the equality given the Jews by the acts of emancipation did not accord with the feelings of the people, that "the Jew" was viewed as an alien, suspected, and condemned—not because of anything he did but because of his existence as an alien among the nations—and that

293f.

there was no hope of a change in this attitude of the people in the foreseeable future despite all the fine speeches about equality and tolerance, something in which he still had somehow believed despite many disappointments.

He had already encountered the Jewish question since his childhood. Was there any Jewish child that did not have any unpleasant experiences in school and in associating with non-Jewish fellow pupils and their parents? The decisive thing was Herzl's later encounter with Eugen Dühring's "classical" foundation of racial anti-Semitism in his book *Die Judenfrage als Racen-, Sitten- und Culturfrage* (cf. Part 1, p. 236ff.), which he read as a law student in 1882, a year after its appearance. In a diary that he kept at that time Herzl reacted with anger and indignation to Dühring's hate-filled conclusions and demands in the Jewish question, but it was characteristic of the young Herzl that at the same time he praised the author's good style and regarded some of his critical analyses of assimilated Jewry as instructive and worthwhile reading for every Jew. From then on, the Jewish question really never let go of Herzl, even though from time to time he attempted to repress it and drown it out by bustling activity and striving for literary success. By 1883 he had already resigned from a student fraternity because it had failed to disavow the anti-Semitic tendencies that had surfaced at a memorial meeting for Richard Wagner. Toward the late 1880's he already planned to write a Jewish novel. In those days he regarded the Jewish question as essentially a social question.

During the years of his activity as a newspaper correspondent in Paris (October 1891 to July 1895) the reading of anti-Semitic literature like Drumont's *La France juive* (cf. Part 2, pp. 609f.), his reporting about trials, scandals, anarchistic assassinations, duels between Jews and anti-Semites, the Panama scandal, and the debates in the French Chamber of Deputies brought him into ever closer contact with questions of society and politics and with the Jewish question within this framework. He always sought a radical solution of the problem and personally went through all the stages of Jewish development in the nineteenth century. As already mentioned (Part 2, p. 632), he also envisaged a solution by means of an organized mass baptism of the young generation as a public action toward a solution of the problem with the approval of the Pope; the parents were to be the terminal generation and remain Jews so as to escape the suspicion of deriving disrespectable personal benefits from the act that was to free their children from the burden of the past. He contemplated an organized conversion of the Jews to socialism for the solution of the Jewish question as a social problem and as a counterpoise to the threat from the reactionaries. This led him to the realization that while the Jewish question had religious and social aspects, it was not identical with these. Between late October and early November 1894, a few weeks *before* the beginning of the first Dreyfus trial, he wrote, as in a state of intoxication, the Jewish drama *Das Ghetto* (later called *Das neue Ghetto*) with which he intended to put the Jewish problem on his familiar theatrical stage and throw it open for public discussion. In this drama, which has many autobiographical features, all types of Jews appear and are analyzed, as are all attempts at a solution and all non-Jewish attitudes toward the Jews. This is actually the beginning of a new Jewish politics; the Jewish problem was to be freely and openly discussed rather than being whispered about or evaded through mockery or apologetics, with anxious threats or dishonorable self-abandonment on the part of the Jews. Behind this there still was some hope on Herzl's part that by courageously tackling this problem a solution could be found through mutual understanding and toleration without giving up what was everyone's due by virtue of his origin and capability. This hope was dashed by the act of Dreyfus's degradation amid the howling of an enraged mob. During the ensuing months Herzl drew the proper conclusions from this. After unsuccessful attempts to initiate a solution "from above" with the aid of the rich Jewish philanthropist Maurice de Hirsch (called "Türkenhirsch" because of his building of Eastern railroads) or of the

Rothschild banks, Dreyfus's degradation led Herzl to publish a plan for a "Jewish State" and to organize Zionism as a modern popular movement with a political program.

HERZL'S UNROMANTIC VIEW OF THE JEWISH QUESTION: Numerous critics of Herzl's views of the Jewish question and its solution, including political scientists and historians, err in reading only Herzl's *The Jewish State*. In many cases they give even that work no more than a cursory reading, doing so with a bias found even in many Zionists—namely, that it was written quickly by an imaginative essayist. Herzl sought to prevent or refute such a misconception by expressly putting his academic degree, Doctor of Laws, after his name on the title page—the only work in which he did this. As regards his formulations and proposals in this work, right after its publication and in numerous subsequent conversations, letters, and articles he pointed out that his work, while well thought out, was only an initial proposal that could serve as a basis for discussion but would, in these discussions and in its implementation, be changed in accordance with actualities.

294f.

NEW CANDOR IN THE TREATMENT OF THE JEWISH QUESTION: There were, of course, individual efforts, some of them antedating Herzl, to break the polite silence about the Jewish question or its public circumvention by issuing (nonbinding) declarations. For example, the writer Hermann Bahr, who in his student years had inclined toward a Pan-German anti-Semitism and in this spirit had made a speech at a student meeting in honor of the recently deceased Richard Wagner (which caused Herzl to resign from the student fraternity Albia in 1883; cf. Part 2, p. 680), in 1893–94 conducted a survey that appeared first in the *Presse*, then as a 215-page book entitled *Der Antisemitismus, ein internationales Interview*, described as a "curious document" of the trend of the times.* He carried on conversations with respected persons of widely varying professions, orientations, and views. Many spoke their minds, but this did not lead to any conclusions. At about the same time as Herzl, Dr. Bernhard Cohn, a physician who knew nothing about the Zionist movement, published a booklet in Berlin with the title *Vor dem Sturm: Ernste Mahnworte an die deutschen Juden*. In it he issued a warning against a threatening catastrophe, and in view of the degrading and dangerous situation he urged the Jews to emigrate: "We must, as it were, produce an emigration fever in German-Jewish youth" (p. 36; cf. Hans Tramer, "Bernhard und Emil Cohn [the latter was the author's son, a rabbi who in 1907 was dismissed by the head of the Berlin Jewish Community Council because of his open championship of Zionism], zwei Streiter für den zionistischen Gedanken," in *Bulletin LBI* 8:326–45; it includes Cohn's correspondence with Herzl, to whom he wrote shortly after the appearance of *Der Judenstaat*). These, however, were isolated voices that were barely heard.

296f.

"THE JEWISH QUESTION EXISTS": Here is the full text:

297

The Jewish question exists. It would be foolish to deny it. It is an atavistic bit of medievalism which the civilized nations have not been able to shake off to this day, try as they might. They did show a magnanimous desire to do so when they emancipated us. The Jewish question exists wherever Jews live in appreciable numbers. Where it does not exist, it is brought in together with Jewish immigrants. Naturally, we move where we are not persecuted; our appearance then gives rise to persecution. This is a fact and is bound to remain a fact everywhere, even in highly developed countries—France is a case in point—as long as the

*A new edition of this book by Hermann Greive was published by Jüdischer Verlag (Königstein/Taunus) in 1979.

Jewish question is not solved politically. The unfortunate Jews are not importing anti-Semitism into England; they have already introduced it into America. (Herzl, *The Jewish State*, trans. H. Zohn [New York, 1970], 33)

294f.   FEARLESS ANALYSIS OF ANTI-SEMITISM: Herzl continues as follows:

> I believe I understand anti-Semitism, a highly complex movement. I view it from the standpoint of a Jew, but without hatred or fear. I think I can discern in it the elements of vulgar sport, of common economic rivalry, or inherited prejudice, of religious intolerance—but also of a supposed need for self-defense. To my mind, the Jewish question is neither a social nor a religious one, even though it may assume these and other guises. It is a national question, and to solve it we must first of all establish it as an international political problem which will have to be settled by the civilized nations of the world in council.
>
> We are a people, one people.
>
> Everywhere we have sincerely endeavored to merge with the national communities surrounding us and to preserve only the faith of our fathers. We are not permitted to do so. In vain are we loyal patriots, in some places even extravagantly so; in vain do we make the same sacrifices of life and property as our fellow citizens; in vain do we strive to enhance the fame of our native countries in the arts and sciences, or their wealth through trade and commerce. In our native lands where, after all, we too have lived for centuries, we are decried as aliens, often by people whose ancestors had not yet come to the country when our fathers' sighs were already heard in the land. The majority can decide who the strangers are; like everything else in relations between peoples, this is a matter of power. I do not waive any part of our prescriptive right when I make this statement as an individual, one with no particular authority. In the world as it is now constituted and will probably continue to be for an indefinite period, might precedes right. (Ibid., 33–34)

297f.   ASSIMILATION OF THE JEWS: Cf. *The Jewish State*, General Part, "Effects of Anti-Semitism":

> I have already referred to our "assimilation." I am not saying for a moment that I desire it. Our national character is too famous in history and, despite all degradations, too noble to make its decline desirable. But we might be able to merge with the peoples surrounding us everywhere without leaving a trace if only we were left in peace for two generations. But they will not leave us in peace. After brief periods of toleration their hostility toward us erupts anew time and again. There seems to be something provocative about our prosperity, because for many centuries the world has been accustomed to regarding us as the most contemptible among the poor. Yet out of ignorance or narrow-mindedness people fail to observe that our prosperity weakens us as Jews and eliminates our peculiarities. (Ibid., 48–49)

Elsewhere (p. 44) Herzl writes: "Every single one of the nations in whose midst Jews live are shamefacedly or brazenly anti-Semitic."

297f.   ACHIEVEMENTS OF TECHNOLOGY: Cf. also the remarks on the section "Jewish State and Diaspora." Herzl writes in *The Jewish State* (p. 32):

> This century has brought us a splendid renaissance through its technical achievements; but this fabulous progress has not yet been utilized for the benefit of humanity. The distances of the surface of the earth have been overcome, and yet we are beset by problems of congestion. Swiftly and safely our great steamships now rush us over hitherto unknown areas. We build safe railroads in a mountain world which people once scaled on foot and with trepidation. Events occurring in countries which were not even discovered when Europe confined the Jews in ghettos are known to us within an hour. This is why the distress of the Jews is an anachronism—and not because there was the Age of Enlightenment a hundred years ago, something that actually existed only for the noblest spirits.

300   FROM TERRITORIALISM TO ZIONISM. THE "UGANDA PLAN": Herzl's true transformation from a "Jewish Statist" who regarded the question of the country as a minor

matter into a Zionist for whom only the old homeland as the fulfillment of Jewish longings could be a solution was always suspect to his adversaries within the Zionist movement and to many Eastern European Zionists. When Herzl's negotiations with Turkey regarding a sovereign settlement in Palestine had failed and he brought before the Sixth Zionist Congress (August 1903) a declaration by Lord Lansdowne, the British Secretary of State for Foreign Affairs, according to which the British government was prepared to place at the disposal of the Zionist Organization (which was thereby recognized as a national negotiating partner) a territory in East Africa for the establishment of an autonomous Jewish settlement under British sovereignty, this proposal, which was erroneously called the Uganda Plan, aroused the fiercest opposition of the Russian Zionists, the representatives of those Jews for whose benefit Herzl was contemplating such a settlement as an interim solution. The steadily increasing emigration of masses of Jews that was caused by a wave of new pogroms (from the Kishinev pogroms at Eastertime 1903 to the October pogroms of 1905, which were intended to sidetrack an attempted Russian revolution by smothering it with Jewish blood), was to be transformed from a disorganized flight to the West and overseas into an organized emigration and systematic settlement on a suitable territory. This was to be a reserve of strength for the time after the breakup of the Ottoman Empire, which was expected in the near future ("with watch in hand") when the Great Powers would give Palestine to the Jews as their national homeland. Despite their enthusiasm for Herzl, the Eastern Jews, who lived in close proximity to one another with their own culture in the Pale of Settlement and thus had stronger ties to Palestine, had never quite ceased to suspect that the "transformation" of this Western Jew, who had emerged from assimilation and found his way to the Zionist movement and to the hitherto completely unknown Jews of Eastern Europe, was more of a tactical move than the result of profound conviction. They now regarded the negotiations about the new settlement project, which Herzl had conceived mainly as a tactical maneuver with which he wished to tie England to the Zionist movement and finally induce it to support its claims to Palestine (fourteen years later these contacts actually contributed to the issuance of the Balfour Declaration), as a deviation from the official program of the Zionist movement and Herzl's return to his original, purely territorialistic conception of the Jewish State. The heated debates at the Congress and the almost rebellious opposition (under the leadership of Menahem Ussishkin, Chaim Weizmann, and others) to the decision of the Congress to send a study commission to East Africa threatened to lead to a split in the young movement. Herzl was able to avert this danger by having a frank discussion in a big conference in April 1904. At that time he also made certain concessions in the question of settlement work in Palestine, which he had hitherto made dependent on the granting of legal guarantees (cf. Part 2, p. 687). The Seventh Zionist Congress, which met in Basel in the summer of 1905, one year after Herzl's death, made unambiguous decisions that pledged the Zionist Organization not to occupy itself with settlement projects outside "Palestine and its contiguous countries . . . both as an end and as a means." By "contiguous countries" the Congress meant particularly the border region around El Arish about which Herzl had negotiated with England. These negotiations had failed because of the opposition of the Egyptian government and of the British high commissioner, Lord Cromer.

THE JEWISH STATE AND THE DIASPORA: At this point we shall cite a number of 300ff. remarks by Herzl on this problem in addition to those quoted in the text. If no reference is given, the source may be found in the Central Zionist Archives, Jerusalem. 6 February 1896. *Complete Diaries* 1:295 (From a conversation with a journalist before the appearance of *The Jewish State*): "I used the simile of a U-tube. Relief for all Jews begins with an outward flow. In the arm marked 'Jewish State,' the level gradually rises, while it sinks in the arm representing the places where Jews now reside. No one is ruined; on the contrary, the foundations for new wealth are laid. And through the progressive improvement of the standing of the Jews who emigrate, the situation of those who remain behind improves." *The Jewish State*, 50–51: "The departure of the Jews must not be imagined as a sudden one. It will be gradual, taking decades. The poorest will go first and make the land arable. . . . The emigrants standing lowest in the economic scale will gradually be followed by those of the next grade. Those who are now in desperate straits will go first. They will be led by the average intellects whom we overproduce and who are persecuted everywhere." Elsewhere (39) Herzl writes: "Only those will depart who are certain of improving their lot thereby: first those who are desperate, then the poor, after them the well-to-do, and finally the wealthy. Those who go first will have raised themselves to a higher level by the time the members of the higher class follow. Thus the migration will be an ascent in class at the same time." *To Badeni*, 18 February 1896, *Complete Diaries* 1:303: "What I am proposing is actually no more than the regulation of the Jewish question, and certainly not the emigration of all the Jews."

23 April 1896. *Complete Diaries* 1:334: "I explained to him [the Grand Duke of Baden] that only those Jews shall go who want to. Since the Jews of Baden are happy under his liberal reign, they will not emigrate, and rightly so."

To the Grand Duke of Baden, 26 April 1896. *Complete Diaries* 1:343–44. "There is, incidentally, no thought of a complete evacuation. Those Jews who have been, or still can be, assimilated will remain. The emigration will be voluntary."

To Georg Brandes, 10 December 1896 (*Herzl-Jahrbuch*, ed. Tulo Nussenblatt) [Vienna, 1937], 168): "I do not believe for a moment that the Jewish State will come into being the way I outlined it in the booklet presented to you. Living things develop independently of the one who planted or engendered them. I believe, however, that it will come into being and that part of the Diaspora will continue to exist, for all peoples are now living in such a Diaspora."

To Maximilian Harden, 24 February 1897: "The crux of the matter is this: Initiation of a *self-regulating* efflux. If anti-Semitism declines in a country, the outflow will be weaker. The canalization will serve to fructify a desolate corner."

To Max Nordau, 29 November 1897 (Instruction for a possible conversation with the German Kaiser): "Zionism wants to free the states from an internal danger by diverting the Jews whom despair has pushed into the revolutionary parties, but certainly not by taking all the Jews out of a country. Those who can and want to assimilate will stay."

"*Leroy-Beaulieu on Anti-Semitism*" (*Die Welt*, 9 July 1897; Herzl, *Zionist Writings: Essays and Addresses* 1, trans. H. Zohn [New York, 1973], 114–15): "It would not even be in the interest of the anti-Semitic countries to lose all their Jews. A healthy emigration would begin, and it would continue for as long as anti-Semitism continued. From the day . . . that the atmosphere of a country changed in favor of the Jews, no one would want to move any more, certainly no one who is well-do-do. Zionism supplies the nations with a means of regulating the number of their Jews according to their need. This, this is the solution of the Jewish question."

Address at the Second Zionist Congress, August 1898: "We probably cannot contemplate a complete Jewish exodus from any country. Those who can and want to assimilate will remain and will be absorbed."

To Philipp Eulenburg, 21 September 1898. *Complete Diaries* 2:670: "In the natural course of things each country would relinquish only as many Jews as it can spare. In each country the drainage would come to a standstill along with anti-Semitism itself, for the stimulus to emigrate, which, as it is, is lacking or only slight in the upper economic strata, would then be eliminated."

To Bertha von Suttner (regarding her intercession in Russia), 16 January 1899. *Complete Diaries* 2:783: "By no means all Jews would emigrate from Russia—no more than they would from other countries—but only a surplus of proletarians and desperate ones who, supported by their wealthy fellow Jews, would be able to establish a new, permanent home for themselves and at the same time substantially increase the cultural resources of civilization in the Orient. Furthermore, the weakening of the revolutionary parties would go hand in hand with this augmentation of culture and order. . . . All of the desperate Jews would have to become anarchists if Zionism did not draw them into its sphere of influence."

To the German Kaiser, 1 March 1899. *Complete Diaries* 2:794: "Our endeavor has many aspects. One of them is the absorption of the Jewish elements that will remain in every country. . . . The way to complete assimilation can probably lead only through the established church. Only those are to go along who are not able or willing to assimilate at their present places of residence. This is our principle. Those who remain behind will of necessity be even better citizens."

To Bülow, 10 March 1899. *Complete Diaries* 2:798: "A solution of the Jewish question which promises such an absorption [of the wealthy and their property in their countries of domicile] as well as the draining off of the socially and economically frustrated and nearly despairing elements should perhaps not be rejected out of hand."

Draft of a memorandum for the Russian Czar, 22 November 1899 (*Gesammelte Zionistische Werke* 5:498): "However, we certainly do not want to bring about an exodus of all Jews. That is only asserted by our opponents in their caricatures of Zionism. We know that the well-to-do do not wish to and will not go with us. Our rich people, however, are ready to help the poor, and there is no need to investigate whether they are motivated by kindness or egotism. For Zionism will solve the Jewish question—on the one hand, by draining off the elements that cannot be absorbed and on the other, by means of the complete assimilation of those who stay behind. The latter will join the majority of the people in everything, probably including religion, and mingle with it through intermarriage. They will have disappeared within one generation, and with them will go everything that has been a torment for Christians and Jews."

Altneuland (Old-Newland), 1902 (an account of the effects in the Diaspora twenty years after the founding of the Jewish state "The New Society" and the beginning of organized mass immigration and systematic urban and rural settlement work): "For the tremendous settlement projects also required a large staff of engineers and legal and commercial officials with modern training. Suddenly there was employment for the large numbers of educated young people who in the earlier, anti-Semitic periods had not been able to succeed anywhere. While the Jews graduating from the universities, technical institutes, and business schools had formerly found themselves helpless and hopeless, in Palestine they now found employment in both public and private concerns. The result was that the Gentiles were no longer bothered by them. The Jews stopped being burdensome competitors, and of course this caused the gradual disappearance of economic hatred and envy. More than that, the useful qualities of the Jews began to be appreciated when a sellers' market developed. The less you offer your services, the more valuable they become. Everyone knows that. Why should this not have been true of the Jewish services in commerce? And so there was an all-around improvement in conditions. In countries that did not want any more Jews to emigrate, public opinion changed in favor of the Jews. Jews were given full equality—not only on paper and in the letter of the law, but in actual practice, in daily life, in manners and customs as well. . . . Only when the hounded Jews found peace in their own land was the grandly conceived emancipation implemented in every state. Those who were capable or desirous of assimilating to another national body were now permitted to do so in an open way that was neither craven nor mendacious. There were some who wished to adopt the faith of the national majority around them; now they could do so without being suspected of careerism or push-iness. Those Jews who felt at one with their fellow citizens in everything but religion enjoyed their undiminished esteem even as adherents of a minority religion. For tolerance can and will always be based only on reciprocity, and only when the Jews proved tolerant here in Palestine, where they constitute the majority, did moral reciprocity let them enjoy the same tolerance everywhere." Elsewhere Herzl writes: "Warshavski had a secondary assignment, too. He was to initiate the return of the Eastern European Jews who had emigrated to America."

It may be appropriate to point out here that such statements were largely intended to allay the fears of governments that the founding of a Jewish state would cause such a mass emigration of the Jews, including the prosperous and wealthy ones, that the economy of their countries would be adversely affected.

305f.   CONVENING OF THE FIRST ZIONIST CONGRESS: Concerning the history of the idea of a congress, which was adopted by the modern national and libertarian movements (beginning with the founding of the United States) and applied to the national libertarian movement of Zionism, cf. my (Hebr.) address at the First World Congress for Jewish Studies, Summer 1947 (Jerusalem, 1952), 469–76), as well as my article "How the Basle Congress Was Convened," in *The Jubilee of the First Zionist Congress, 1897–1947*, (Jerusalem, 1947), 47–50. The Proceedings of the first congress, as well as those of all succeeding ones (which at first were held annually, then biennially, and with two long interruptions during the two world wars and early postwar years have since 1946 met at three-year or four-year intervals), have appeared in print—until 1933 (Eighteenth Congress) in German and since then in Hebrew. The change of language is not only an expression of the changed political situation after 1933 but also indicates the importance the German language had for the Jews as a lingua franca since the Enlightenment in the eighteenth century. It has been replaced by Yiddish, by Hebrew, which has steadily gained in vitality and dissemina-tion, and to an increasing extent that reflects the influence of British and especially American Jewry, by English. An informative account of the atmosphere at and around the First Zionist Congress may be found in *Warum gingen wir zum ersten Zionistenkongress?*, a collection of contributions by its participants (Berlin, 1922).

305f.   BASEL PROGRAM OF THE ZIONIST ORGANIZATION: The first, basic sentence of the Basel Program, "Zionism strives to create for the Jewish people a home in Palestine secured by public law," has already been quoted in Part 1. The program continues: "For the attainment of this aim the Congress envisages the following means:

"1. The promotion, on suitable lines, of the settlement of Palestine by Jewish agriculturists, artisans, and tradesmen.
"2. The organization and unification of the whole of Jewry by means of appropriate local and general institutions in accordance with the laws of each country.
"3. The strengthening of Jewish national sentiment and national consciousness.
"4. Preparatory steps toward securing the consent of governments, which is neces-

sary to attain the aim of Zionism." (*Encyclopedia of Zionism and Israel*, vol. 1, ed. Raphael Patai [New York, 1971], 114.)

Like most political programs, the Basel Program came into being as a compromise among various orientations, views, and ideas of the roads to be taken and the priorities of the work. It was based on Herzl's formulations in *The Jewish State*, in his essays for the preparation of the Congress in *Die Welt*, the weekly founded by him, and in his opening address at the Congress. In strict contrast to the existing movement of the Hovevei Zion (Friends of Zion) Herzl had opposed the establishment of new Jewish settlements in Palestine (in addition to the eighteen agricultural settlements founded between 1881 and 1896 and then called "colonies") as long as there was no legal basis for them. In the despotic state of Sultan Abdul Hamid II (1842–1918) such settlements were, in Herzl's estimation, nothing but pawns in the hands of the ruler and thus tended to impede the political negotiations. He therefore believed that it was the primary task of the Zionist movement to work toward the attainment of the political goal, the consent to the foundation of the Jewish State—with or without this express designation, but in any case an autonomous settlement on a broad territorial basis and with autonomy in all internal matters, immigration, construction, and armed self-protection. For the attainment of this goal, Herzl said, the Jewish people must be organized in such a way as to carry a great deal of weight in the negotiations with the Sultan and the other interested states. On the one hand there was the desire of the "Friends of Zion" to continue the settlement work (called "practical work" in the style of the time) in Palestine peacefully, without creating a great stir, and without making politically risky declarations about ultimate goals; and on the other, there was the impetuous demand by young people, who were disappointed at the "practical" spadework, that the political aim be spelled out as clearly as Herzl had formulated it, thus winning the hearts of these young people and all those impatiently hoping for relief. The debate at the Congress was particularly fanned by the formulation *rechtlich gesicherte Heimstätte* (legally secured home) which Nordau had proposed on behalf of the program committee. The hope was that this would express the goal without using the ominous word *Judenstaat*, which, so it was feared, would preclude negotiations with the Sultan. The young followers of Leo Motzkin wanted to replace the word *rechtlich* (which could also be taken to mean *privatrechtlich*, referring to private or civil law) with the more explicit word *völkerrechtlich* (by international law). By way of a compromise Herzl proposed the word *öffentlich-rechtlich* (opposed to *privatrechtlich*), a term which he had already used earlier and which with its deliberate vagueness was more in keeping with their aims. This was accepted by all. As a concession to the "practical" Zionists, their demand was put first among the "means," but it was modified by adding the adjective *zweckdienlich* (suitable) to "promotion of the settlement." For years Herzl and the elected leaders were able to interpret this word to mean "to the extent that the settlement work furthers the political aims." In point of fact, the Zionist Organization did not begin its systematic settlement work in Palestine until 1908.

The dignified frankness of Herzl's appearance had an illuminating and moving effect on the participants in the Congress, particularly on the hurt pride of the young people. It is exemplified by the programmatic statements in the periodical *Die Welt*, the first German-language Zionist journal edited along modern lines and until World War I the official organ of the World Zionist Organization. Its cover was yellow like the Jews' badge of shame in the Middle Ages; yellow was to become the color of the Jews' honor. Its programmatic statement began with these words: "Our weekly is a 'Judenblatt' [Jewish sheet]. We are taking this, which is meant to be a term of abuse, and intend to turn it into an honorable word." *Die Welt* was to be an open journal and not shrink back from reporting anything; it was to be equally free in self-criticism, in its presentation of the past and its wishes for the future. "And between memory and hope stands action. . . . *Die Welt* will be the organ of the men who will lead the Jews out of this time and upward to better times."

306f.   THE EXPIATION OF MONEY—THE ADOPTION OF ANTI-JEWISH ARGUMENTS AND CON-
CEPTS: As already mentioned in Part 1, the influence of anti-Semitic (including socialistic) arguments may frequently be noticed in Herzl's attitude toward rich Jews. He speaks of "money Jews" and of the dangerous *haute banque* (big bankers), and he calls the type of Jew who derides Judaism and Zionism and values money more highly than pride and honor *Mauschel* (in an article by that title in *Die Welt* of 15 October 1897; *Ges. Zion. Werke* 1:209-15; *Zionist Writings: Essays and Addresses* 1:163–168). In Herzl and other Zionists this influence can easily be demonstrated in their rejection of Jewish characteristics and customs and of the ghetto Jew in general, a rejection that borders on self-hatred. The negative evaluation of the Jews in the economy of the surrounding world is also frequently adopted, and the desire to settle the Jews in Palestine primarily as agriculturists stems not only from a determination to lay the foundations for a sound economy, in which every kind of work is done by Jews, but also from the overvaluation of this branch of the economy as productiveness par excellence *(Urproduktion)*, compared to which all others are less prized and are often described as virtually "parasitic." (I will have more to say about this in the next chapter; cf. Part 1, pp. 368ff.) Cf. Yeheskel Kaufmann's (Hebr.) essay "Hurban Ha-Nefesh" (Destruction of the Soul) in the monthly *Moznayim* (Scale) (Tevet, 5694/1934), reprinted in Kaufmann's collection *Behevlei Ha-Zeman* (Tel Aviv, 5696/1936), 257–74; an English synopsis appeared under the title "Antisemitic Stereotypes in Zionism" in *Commentary* (1949). This Jewish and Zionist anti-Semitism that began with the period of the Enlightenment is, as Kaufmann rightly remarks, an insufficiently recognized result of the tragic situation in which the historical circumstances placed many Jews, one in which all manifestations of life that were not intrinsically bad appeared bad from certain viewpoints. The thinking and the vocabulary of an age are bound to affect everyone—unless a person clearly realizes this influence and its origin, thereby stripping the stereotypes of their universal character and exposing the unscientific and untrue elements that masquerade as scholarship. Herzl was quite aware of this problem, even though he (one man among others) did not always escape the seduction of the word. In his introduction to *The Jewish State*, for example, he discusses *Wirtsvolk* (host nation), a concept and term that had been used in anti-Jewish literature (the seeds going back at least to Luther), later appeared in the "scientific" anti-Semitic literature, and eventually became part of the common usage (where it was used by Jews as well; cf. Part 1, p. 142 and chap. 9, pp. 177ff). Herzl begins his introduction as follows: "Men of affairs who are in the mainstream of life often have an astonishingly slight knowledge of economics. This is the only explanation for the fact that even Jews faithfully parrot the catchword of the anti-Semites: We are supposed to be living off the 'host nations,' and if we had no 'host nation' surrounding us, we would have to starve. This is one of the points at which the undermining of our self-respect through unjust accusations manifests itself. What is the truth about this 'host nation' theory? To the extent that it is not based on old, narrow, physiocratic views, it reflects the childish misconception that in the life of commodities the same things keep going around" (*The Jewish State*, 31).

Herzl also opposes the romanticization of the peasantry. Under the heading "Previous Attempts at a Solution" he writes in the General Part of his book: "But anyone who wishes to turn Jews into peasants labors under a strange misconception." Peasants of the old type will give way to the machines. "The agrarian question, too, is merely a question of machinery. America must conquer Europe. . . . Will anyone, then, expect Jews, who are intelligent people, to agree to become peasants of the old type? That would be like saying to a Jew: 'Here's a crossbow for you; now go off to war!'" (ibid., 45–46). Similarly, in essays that appeared shortly after the "Mauschel" article Herzl perceptively discusses the "Stock-Exchange Woes" of the Jews as well as the tragic situations of the Jewish "money dealers" who have been excluded from soil and honor. "The derivation of soil on the lower levels," he writes in his article "Der ewige Jude," "and of honor on the higher ones makes the Jew what he is."

SUMMING UP HERZL'S STATURE: By way of a summary, we may say the following about Herzl and his influence on the Jewish question: He was a charismatic leader of the first rank and translated many people's dreams of and schemes for a national rebirth of the Jewish people into reality, thus beginning a new chapter in the history of the Jews. Even his adversaries are agreed on that, and the ordinary people, the masses in the East and many young people in the West, recognized this immediately. Considering this achievement, his theoretical statements are often underestimated if one says that at bottom they do not contain anything that others had not said before him and that many details are utopian in nature. This latter point is inconsequential. Herzl himself admitted that he provided such details in order to demonstrate how his scheme could be carried out and to capture the imagination of the people, but he did not regard these details as relevant. The first objection is weightier, though it proceeds from false premises and comes to false conclusions. Almost every idea has already been expressed by others; Herzl says so at the very beginning of *The Jewish State:* "The idea which I develop in this pamphlet is an age-old one: the establishment of a Jewish State. The world resounds with outcries against the Jews, and this is what awakens the dormant idea" (p. 27). Herzl called his plan a new "combination" of existing, well-known elements.

306ff.

In point of fact, Herzl's theory created a *framework ideology* unlike any other before and after him. This framework contained all the basic elements of the Zionist solution of the Jewish question (which made it a suitable basis for the Basel Program of Zionism) and could accommodate all additional ideologies—such as that of the socialist Zionists. Nachman Syrkin (1867–1924) was able to develop his program of a cooperative socialism and Ber Borochov his of a Marxist socialism. The Labor Zionist movement and the Jewish Palestinian movement were able to organize on the basis of these programs without going beyond the scope of this framework. Currents in cultural Zionism in the spirit of Ahad Ha-Am, Martin Buber, and others, which had sprung up in opposition to Herzl could be integrated without ideological difficulties as long as they did not reject the political framework.

The synthesis of practical settlement work and political activity for the creation of legal foundations for this work that was produced by the dispute about an immature and unduly doctrinaire conception of Herzl's ideology was promoted by this ideology. It provided a new foundation for the direction of the political activities of Chaim Weizmann (1874–1952)—who opposed this ideology and yet carried on negotiations in its spirit that were based on its premises and substance and led to the Balfour Declaration and its implementation in Palestine—as well as for the settlement work in the country.

Arthur Ruppin (1876–1943), who directed this settlement work from 1908 on and regarded himself as an opponent of Herzlian Zionism because he was influenced by the ideologies of Herzl's successors, who often carried the political elements of unfruitful extremes (as monarchists often do with the views of monarchs), and thus misinterpreted its basic character, essentially acted in the spirit of Herzl's views: that all individual activities should be placed in the framework of a comprehensive plan or vision; that settlers should be encouraged to take their own initiative and responsibility; that the settlements should be built on an economic rather than a philanthropic foundation; that the towns and their economy should be developed as well, and that all projects should make maximal use of the achievements of science and technology with due regard for all human factors. It was also to Ruppin's credit that he introduced statistics and sociology into the debates about the solution of the Jewish question through his book *Die Juden der Gegenwart*, which appeared in 1904 and in connection with the author's experiences during the settlement work and his systematic research was expanded into a *Soziologie der Juden* (Berlin, 1930/1); cf. my essay about him in *LBYB* 17 (1972).

Jacob Klatzkin: A radical analysis of Judaism was also able to base itself on Herzl, such as that of the philosopher and Hebraist Jacob Klatzkin (1882–1948), who saw no place in the Diaspora for the continuation of Jewish life and demanded that the Jews act accordingly. In his book *Krisis und Entscheidung im Judentum* (the second, expanded edition of *Probleme des modernen Judentums* [Berlin, 1921]) he demanded that the Jews of the Diaspora deliberately detach themselves from their involvement with the culture of the national majority despite the fruitful results that such involvement might have produced in some places. In the summary at the end of his book (p. 207) Klatzkin writes: "In the *galut* we are in a bad position culturally as well. The alien culture in exile becomes a national threat to us." "If our own culture is rooted in the soil of our homeland," he continues in the spirit of Herzl and with near-Herzlian formulations, "all the foreign elements that we bring along will be a blessing for us. We shall be enriched as we emigrate and immigrate. . . . In the final analysis, if our *national* liberation is not to degenerate into chauvinism, it can only mean freedom to become complete human beings and incarnations of the blossoming of our culture." With the threat of Hitler before his eyes, Klatzkin wrote in his pamphlet *Die Judenfrage der Gegenwart* (as "a proud Jew and profound thinker"—Albert Einstein in his foreword), 34f.: "In the face of this exceptional situation the Jewish people demands a home in the land of its fathers. Only its national normalization, which is to release it from the necessity made virtue of a heroic mode of existence, can solve the Jewish question for Israel and all other nations. This demand, however, is conditioned by this sincere declaration by the Jews: *Galut* means to us disrespect and lack of rights, torment and torture, hatred and persecution. *Galut* means to us exile from our homeland, dispersion in foreign countries, national homelessness—and no equality of rights, no benevolence, and no welfare can eliminate the *galut* nature of our existence, the character of alien climes." Klatzkin therefore demanded equal rights (for the fulfillment of equal duties), Jewish minority rights in the lands of Jewish mass settlement in Eastern Europe, and a Jewish home in Palestine. The minority rights he advocated soon turned out to be illusory in the new nationalistic Eastern states, an illusion that could not stand up to the political realities.

Herzl's Zionism was a secular movement—a seeming reversal but, in Herzl's view, actually a continuation of the Jewish emancipation movement, which, after all, had also started as a secular movement.

306   PLURALISM (H.M. KALLEN): This movement was continued in radical terms within American Zionism and gave rise to theories of cultural pluralism like that of the philosopher Horace Meyer Kallen (1882–1974). These were later adopted by the Supreme Court Justice Louis Dembitz Brandeis (1856–1941), who headed the American Zionist movement for some years. In contrast to the prevailing melting-pot theory, which in an America developing into a nation (and like the European theory of assimilation) demanded that immigrants give up their traditional ethnic background in favor of an American nationalism (which in reality approached an adjustment to the ideas of the leading Puritan circles of the first immigrants and their descendants), pluralism demanded the equal coexistence and cooperation of the ethnic groups without an abandonment of their traditions, way of thinking, and religious beliefs.

According to the latter view, which has prevailed in our time, it is precisely this variety that constitutes an enrichment of cultural life and productive creativity in all fields. Cf. Sara Schmidt, "Horace M. Kallen and the Progressive Reform of American Zionism," *Midstream* (New York), December 1976, 14–23 and S. Schmidt, "Messianic Pragmatism: The Zionism of Horace M. Kallen," *Judaism* 25, no. 2 (Spring 1976): 217–26.

Zionism with a religious orientation was also able to fit into the framework of Herzlian Zionism as it began to organize in 1902 under the name *Mizrahi* (an abbreviation of *Merkaz Ruhani*, "spiritual center"). In contrast to many Orthodox Jews it approved of the political framework of the Zionist movement but felt impelled to give it the proper substance by including the values and life-style of the religious tradition. This was also true of a religious movement of regeneration like Hasidism that spread in Eastern Europe (Poland, Galicia, the Ukraine, Rumania) since the middle of the eighteenth century. In the early twentieth century its positive emanations began to have a spiritual effect, as religious mysticism, on Central European intellectuals, particularly in the romantic, poetic interpretations and presentations of Martin Buber. The Zionist movement developed much as Herzl had envisaged and expressed it. Zionism was not a party in the real sense of the word; it was possible to approach it from all partisan orientations. "Zionism is the Jewish people on the march—on the way to its homeland."

IDEA AND REALITY: A good presentation of the problems within the Zionist movement and the position of some of the non-Zionist and anti-Zionist Jews shortly after Herzl's death may be found in the collection *Die Stimme der Wahrheit: Jahrbuch für Wissenschaftlichen Zionismus*, edited by Lazar Schön ("with the participation of authorities of all creeds"), volume 1 (the only one ever published), Würzburg, 1905. The editor set himself the not inconsiderable task of contributing, through the "power of truth" to be generated by free discussion, to the accomplishment of two tasks: "to create a united Jewry and bring about a new era in Zionism, the era of the realization of the Zionist ideals." Even the advertising section (pp. 407–80) is interesting; it lists the Zionist literature of the time, including periodicals. The best expression of the profound transformation produced by Herzl's appearance among a Jewish intelligentsia gaining self-knowledge is *Vom Judentum*, a collection issued by the Verein jüdischer Hochschüler Bar-Kochba in Prague (Leipzig, 1913). A profound discussion of the problems with which young Zionists striving for regeneration were struggling in those years may be found in the essays written at that time by the educator Moses Calvary; they were republished in 1936 by the Schocken Bücherei, Berlin, under the title *Das Neue Judentum*.   307f.

EFFECTS OF ZIONISM: Cf. the references given at the beginning of this section and the literature about Herzl, as well as the general works on recent Jewish history.   308f.

BALFOUR DECLARATION: Concerning its history, cf. Leonard Stein, *The Balfour Declaration* (London, 1961). Cf. also Isaiah Friedmann, *The Question of Palestine 1914–1918: British-Jewish-Arab Relations* (London, 1973), as well as Renée Neher-Bernheim's popular book *La Déclaration Balfour* (Paris, 1969). Regarding the settlement work in Palestine and its ideological and human background, cf. my book *The Return of the Soil: A History of Jewish Settlement in Israel* (Jerusalem, 1952; Hebr. ed., 1977) and the bibliography given there. Cf. also A. Ruppin, *Memoirs, Diaries, Letters*, ed. and with an introd. by Alex Bein (London, 1971). The Balfour Declaration, which is quoted verbatim in the decision of the San Remo Conference about the British Mandate for Palestine, was formulated as the following letter to Lord Rothschild, dated 2 November 1917:   309f.

Dear Lord Rothschild,

I have much pleasure in conveying to you, on behalf of His Majesty's Government, the following declaration of sympathy with Jewish Zionist aspirations which has been submitted to, and approved by, the Cabinet: "His Majesty's Government view with favour the establishment in Palestine of a national home for the Jewish people, and will use their best endeavours to facilitate the achievement of this object, it being clearly understood that nothing shall be done which may prejudice the civil and religious rights of existing non-Jewish communities in Palestine, or the rights and political status enjoyed by Jews in any other country."

I should be grateful if you would bring this declaration to the knowledge of the Zionist Federation.

Yours,
Arthur Balfour

The Declaration was the result of a compromise following lengthy negotiations and various proposals; hence every word was well thought out. The reference to the non-Jewish population thus was limited to the protection of its civil and religious rights, not of national and political ones. A Palestinian national movement was regarded as nonexistent—whether justly or unjustly will be discussed in the appropriate context (cf. Part 1, pp. 434ff). On the other hand, the nonimpairment of the "political status" of the Jews in the countries of the Diaspora is expressly assured in order to allay the fears of the Jewish opponents of Zionism and to prevent, as far as possible, the exploitation of the Declaration by anti-Jewish governments. In the preamble to the Mandate for Palestine, which received final approval from the Council of the League of Nations on 24 July 1922 and thus was given the force of a decision, the substance of the Declaration is reiterated in the following words: "Whereas the Principal Allied Powers have also agreed that the Mandatory should be responsible for putting into effect the declaration originally made on the 2nd November 1917, by the Government of His Britannic Majesty, and adopted by the said Powers, in favour of the establishment in Palestine of a national home for the Jewish people, it being clearly understood. . . ." In line with the Zionist demands and proposals the following words were added by way of strengthening the promise and the Jewish position: "Whereas recognition has thereby been given to the historical connection of the Jewish people with Palestine and to the grounds for reconstituting their national home in the country"—which means that the right to establish a national home was motivated by the recognition of the "historical connection of the Jewish people with Palestine" and the reasons of the Jews "for reconstituting their national home in that country."

The profound impression which the Balfour Declaration made on many people within and without Jewry who had previously been indifferent or even hostile to the Zionist movement is exemplified by Maximilian Harden's article "Neu Jerusalem" in his journal *Die Zukunft* (12 January 1918, 167–84), which hails the regeneration of Judaism in the Zionist spirit with something close to enthusiasm.

The Attempt at a Radical "Final Solution" of the Jewish Question in Accordance with the Anti-Semitic Racial Doctrine (1933–1945)

Prefatory Note: So much has been written abut the catastrophic Hitler era in the history of Europe and of mankind in general and the history of the Jews and the Jewish question in particular that no one can know and consider all of this literature, frequently not even what has appeared about subsections of this subject. The same applies to the enormous amount of source material, both published and unpublished. Despite this plethora of sources and literature some basic questions and details of certain actions and events have yet to be clarified, because important sources and frequently also our understanding of sources are lacking. This is closely connected, on the one hand, with the monstrous nature of the events, which exceeds what had previously been known about historical occurrences, and on the other with the tactics of the "elite" leadership that registered many things with bureaucratic exactitude but made no written record of others, among them what was decisive for the history of the Jewish question, or else recorded them under pseudonyms, in code, or as instructions and orders formulated in the style of telegrams. The memoirs of later dates also leave some questions unclarified, as all memoirs do—because memory grows dimmer in the course of time and on account of the conscious or unconscious selective technique of memory and of the writer, who also has personal intentions and interests of all kinds to consider. Added to this is the fact that the enormity of the events and the related problems of guilt, behavior in sorrow, resistance, and rescue, responsibility for oneself and others, and the legal consequences of public confessions, etcetera, endanger the objectivity of any testimony.

Obviously, I cannot say that I am completely free from the subjectivity of a person who remembers what he experienced and is still experiencing. I lived through this period, until September 1933 in Germany and thereafter in Jerusalem, always as an attentive observer with a personal interest in the fate of those who were persecuted, which included myself and all those close to me by virtue of their extraction, kinship, or friendship. At the same time I attempted to view the events at the time and afterward through the eyes of a historian, and for this purpose I preserved and collected many important documents. Later, as an archivist in important offices I actively participated in the collection of documentary materials for the Israeli archives and research institutes, of which I was a cofounder. In addition, as a historian I participated in scholarly discussions with some articles that have influenced the course of research and have been frequently cited. These publications were always intended as sections of this book, and I have used them for this chapter—some almost verbatim, others in their substance. (The most important of these are cited in the pertinent places). Much of the literature published since the Hitler period came to my attention shortly after its appearance—but with the abovementioned limitations. On the following pages I shall list only some works that seem fundamental to me or give a good recapitulation of earlier writings. Some others I cite as notes to the text, but of necessity all these constitute only a selection from the numerous essays and statements that I have read, which have helped shape my views in recent decades, and to which I am indebted even if I was not able to name them in every instance or could no longer recall them to mind when I wrote this book.

313ff.   "HOLOCAUST": For the past twenty years or so the word *Holocaust* has been used in the literature, particularly writings in English, to designate this epoch in the history of the Jewish question. At first this word was used only occasionally in this sense for this historical period in general and the fate of the Jews in particular, but between 1957 and 1959 its ever-increasing currency as a collective term for the systematic murder of the Jews by the Nazis led the Library of Congress in Washington to start registering the specialized literature on these events in 1968 under the title "Holocaust, Jewish, 1939–1945." (Cf. Gerd Korman, "The Holocaust in American Historical Writing," in the special issue of *Societas: A Review of Social History* devoted to this subject (2, no. 3 [Summer 1972]: 251–70, esp. 259–62). Yet most people were and are hardly aware of the basic meaning of this word. As a matter of fact, I have frequently been asked, usually by nonexperts, what kind of word that was and what it meant. The Greek word *holocauston* is used in the Septuagint as a translation of the biblical Hebrew word *olah*, meaning burnt offering, and the corresponding Latin word, *holocaustum*, is used in the Vulgate. Only relatively late was it used in English for "a great and complete devastation or destruction, esp. by fire" (*Random House Dictionary of the English Language*) and for "any widespread destruction" (*American Heritage Dictionary of the English Language*). The second edition of *Webster's New Universal Unabridged Dictionary* (1983) defines Holocaust as "the systematic destruction of over six million European Jews by the Nazis before and during World War II." In Hebrew the word *shoah* (catastrophe, ruin) has come into use; the word was used in a similar sense in Isaiah 10:3 and has been variously rendered as "calamity," "destruction," etc. Initially *hurban* (destruction) enjoyed greater currency in Hebrew and in Yiddish, a term generally used for the destruction of the First and Second Temple in Jerusalem and the Jewish State in Palestine. The question arises whether in applying these words to the epoch one does not in a certain sense continue the policy of the Nazis, hiding their cruel actions and barbaric deeds behind anonymous, harmless-sounding words instead of calling them by their less poetic real names. Here we are, after all, dealing with the actions of criminals that were carried out brutally and not with sacred sacrificial acts, a catastrophe that erupted by chance, or an expiation of crimes committed in the past—unless one wants to call the misjudgment of the real situation of the Jews by the majority of their responsible leaders such a crime. We are dealing with nothing less than the systematic destruction and annihilation of the Jews, a mass murder carried out with all methods of killing, from the usual, traditional kinds to the new method of gassing, and with a previously unknown systematization and mechanization—that is, an unparalleled crime that was committed with such "perfection" only against the Jews.

We shall have more to say about the significance of semantics for the Jewish question in general, which has already been discussed, and for the Nazi period in particular (cf. Part 1, p. 362), but it is appropriate to issue a warning against obfuscating words and terms at this point. Apart from the modern tendency to employ scientific or quasi-scientific terminology in sociology and psychology and the trend toward abstraction that predominates in life and art, the use of the term

Holocaust was probably promoted by a reluctance to utter the hated name of Hitler and his National Socialist fellow criminals—in accordance with the ancient Hebrew and Yiddish curse "Let his name and his memory be expunged" *(yimmakh sh'mo v'sikhro)*, a curse and a wish which, as Freud has shown, continue to be at the root of our forgetfulness in daily life. Cf. also Heine's well-known angry poem "Nicht gedacht soll seiner werden" (Elster ed., 2:1097ff.; Insel ed. 3:401f.), 2d stanza: "Ausgelöscht sein aus der Menschen/ Angedenken hier auf Erden,/ Ist die Blume der Verwünschung—/ Nicht gedacht soll seiner werden!" (To be blotted out from human memory here on earth, that is the flower of all imprecations: Let him not be remembered!) With its "scientific" character and its conceptuality rooted in Greek and Latin the word *genocide*, too, tends to mask the simple, horrible extermination of a people rather than branding the crime as shameful in the international world. Viewed in human terms, the raising of an occurrence to a conceptual and objective sphere is always a means of freeing us, as far as possible, from its immediate effects through abstraction, integration, and equation with similar occurrences. Cf. also the notes in Part 2, pp. 700f.

Concerning the history of the concept "The Third Reich" from the Middle Ages via Spengler and Moeller van der Bruck to Hitler, cf. S. D. Stirk in *The German Mind and Outlook*, ed. G. P. Gooch (London, 1945), esp. 137ff.; Fritz Stern, *Kulturpessimismus als politische Gefahr* (Bonn and Stuttgart, 1963), 302f.; Ruth Kestenberg-Gladstein, "Das Dritte Reich: Prolegomena zur Geschichte eines Begriffes," *LBJ Bulletin* 5, (1962): 267ff.

LITERATURE ABOUT THE HITLER PERIOD AND THE MURDERS OF THE JEWS: The 313ff. works published before 1960 and the published and unpublished sources of all kinds that had come to light then as well as the institutes, etc. devoted to research on this period are listed in *Guide to Jewish History under Nazi Impact*, edited in exemplary fashion by Jacob Robinson and Philip Friedman (New York, 1960), issued jointly by Yad Vashem, Martyrs' and Heroes' Memorial Authority (Jerusalem) and Yivo Institute for Jewish Research (New York) as the first volume of a Bibliographical Series. To date eleven additional volumes have appeared in this series—five about works in Hebrew, four about writings in Yiddish, and one about the catastrophe of Hungarian Jewry. The latest volume, edited by Jacob Robinson with the participation of Mrs. Philip Friedman, appeared under the title *The Holocaust and After: Sources and Literature in English* (New York, 1973).

Cf. also the selective bibliographies in the latest comprehensive presentations—by Jacob Robinson et al., *EJJ* 7:828–905 (the article about this era in *EJJ* appeared in 1974 in book form under the title *Holocaust* in the Israel Pocket Library of the Keter publishing house in Jerusalem); Lucy S. Dawidowicz, *The War against the Jews 1933–1945* (London, 1975). Cf. Yisrael Gutmann's review of the last-named work, including a number of corrections on the basis of Hebrew sources and writings not used by the author, in *Yad Vashem Studies* 11 (1976).

Of the earlier general presentations I shall mention the following: William L. Shirer, *The Rise and Fall of the Third Reich: A History of Nazi Germany* (New York, 1960; Greenwich, Conn., 1962); Moshe Prager, *Hurban Yisrael b'Europa* (Hebr.) (En Charod, 1948); *Nazi Germany's War against the Jews* (New York: American Jewish Committee, 1947); Leon Poliakov, *Breviaire de la Haine: Le IIIe Reich et les Juifs* (Paris, 1951) (*Harvest of Hate: The Nazi Program for the Destruction of the Jews of Europe* [New York, 1954; London, 1956]); Anatole Goldstein, *From Discrimination to Annihilation* (New York: World Jewish Congress, 1952) (a brief characterization of the stages); Gerald Reitlinger, *The Final Solution: An Attempt to Exterminate the Jews of Europe 1939–1945* (London and New York, 1953; rev. ed., 1968); Joseph Tennenbaum, *Race and Reich: The History of an Epoch* (New York, 1956); Raoul

Hilberg, *The Destruction of the European Jews* (Chicago, 1961; paperback ed., 1967); Nora Levin, *The Holocaust: The Destruction of European Jewry 1933–1945* (New York, 1968, 1973); Mark Dworetzky, *Europe Without Children: The Plan for Biolog ical Extermination* (Hebr.) (Jerusalem, 1958); Walther Hofer, *Der Na- tionalisozialismus: Dokumente 1933–1945* (Frankfurt a.M.: Fischer Bücherei, 1957); Leon Poliakov and Joseph Wulf, *Das Dritte Reich und die Juden: Dokumente und Aufsätze* (Berlin, 1961); Wolfgang Scheffler, *Judenverfolgung im Dritten Reich, 1933–1945* (Frankfurt a.M., 1961); H. G. Adler, *Die verheimlichte Wahrheit: There- sienstädter Dokumente* (Tübingen, 1958); *Medizin ohne Menschlichkeit: Dokumente des Nürnberger Ärzteprozesses,* ed. and with a commentary by Alexander Mitscherlich and Fred Mielke (Frankfurt, 1960); cf. especially Mitscherlich's intro- duction; Robert M. W. Kempner, *SS im Kreuzverhör* (Munich, 1964); Rudolf Höss, *Kommandant in Auschwitz: Autobiographische Aufzeichnung,* with an introduction and commentary by M. Broszat (Stuttgart, 1958; paperback ed., 1963, 1979); *Com- mandant of Auschwitz* (Cleveland and New York, 1960; in Hebr., ed. and with an introd. by Zvi Schner, Tel Aviv, 5725/1965).

A comprehensive selection of fundamental essays about the background, the history, and the effects of the National Socialist war of extermination against the Jews is offered in Yisrael Gutmann and Livia Rothkirchen, eds., *The Catastrophe of European Jewry: Antecedents, History, Reflections, Selected Papers* (Jerusalem, 1976) (henceforth cited as Gutmann-Rothkirchen). In the last part there are impor- tant remarks about the period as a subject of research, problems of evaluation, and the attitude of the world and the Jews to the Nazi schemes for extermination and their actions.

The latest attempt to come to grips with problems of the epoch is an essay by one of the greatest experts in the field: Saul Friedländer, "Some Aspects of the Historical Significance of the Holocaust," *Jerusalem Quarterly* 1, no. 1 (1976): 36–59. I agree with his conclusion in large measure, both in his formulation of the questions and in his attempts at answering them with the realization that definite answers are harder to give here than with many other problems of historiography, for it is a matter of "trying to explain in a rational context events which cannot be encompassed in rational categories alone, or described solely in the usual style of historical analysis" (p. 36).

My presentation cannot compete in completeness with any of the abovementioned works or be a substitute for them, nor is it intended to. It must limit itself to placing the events (the course of which is barely outlined here) in the context of the history of the Jewish question and from this vantage point giving a more detailed discussion of some problems or illuminating them somewhat differently than has previously been done.

313   HITLER THE FÜHRER, A BRILLIANT PARANOIAC: Cf., in addition to the abovemen- tioned presentations and the biographies mentioned below, the pathography, with a detailed bibliography in W. Lange-Eichbaum and W. Kurth, *Genie, Irrsinn und Ruhm: Genie-Mythus und Pathographie des Genies* (Munich, 1967), 381–88; Wal- ter C. Langer, *The Mind of Adolf Hitler* (London, 1974) and Robert G. H. Waite's afterword, 291–92. As early as spring 1934 an elderly Munich neurologist, the chairman of Eufrat (the parents' and friends' committee) of the local group of the German-Jewish youth organization Schwarzes Fähnlein, spoke these words of warn- ing to the "Jewish-Prussian" young scholar and youth leader Hans Joachim Schoeps, who, as he reports on p. 14 of his book *Ja—Nein und Trotzdem* (Mainz, 1974), had the strange idea of calling on Hitler with some members of his German-Jewish youth group and asking him what he had against these young Jewish Germans: "The so- called Führer is a paranoiac—that is, he suffers from delusions. Patients with delu-

sions display compulsive symptoms, but they live in a logically contained, hermetically sealed world, and their delusional image of the world cannot be invalidated by any objections or counterarguments. Part of Hitler's pathological delusion is the devilish role of the Jews, who are at work everywhere in the world as the bearers of evil. How are you going to deal with this full-blown delusion of reference of an . . . obsessive-compulsive neurotic?" Concerning these delusional ideas about Jews, cf. Part 1, pp. 322ff.

In his autobiographical book *The Turning Point*, Klaus Mann, the eldest son of Thomas Mann, tells about watching Hitler gorging himself on strawberry tarts with whipped cream at the Carlton Tea Room in Munich in 1932. Klaus was repelled by Hitler's homeliness and vulgarity, and he wondered what familiar face Hitler's reminded him of.

It was not Charlie Chaplin. Chaplin is engagingly attractive. No, the great comedian does not have Hitler's fleshy, nasty nose. Chaplin looks like an artist, whereas that gluttonous rat over there looked—like a gluttonous rat. . . . While I called the waitress to pay for my cup of coffee, I suddenly remembered whom Mr. Hitler resembled. It was that sex-murderer in Hanover, whose case had made huge headlines several years before. His name was Haarmann. He was in the habit of killing young boys whom he lured to his flat. Forty or fifty disappeared in his hospitable bedroom. . . . A sort of homosexual Bluebeard, on an impressive scale. . . . The likeness between him and Hitler was striking. The sightless eyes, the mustache, the brutal and nervous mouth, even the unspeakable vulgarity of the fleshy nose: it was, indeed, precisely the same physiognomy. "You won't rule Germany, Schicklgruber," I thought, while rising from my chair. (K. Mann, *The Turning Point* [New York, 1942], 236–37).

There is a reference to this incident in Otto Friedrich's book *Before the Deluge: A Portrait of Berlin in the 1920's* [New York, 1972], 350–51; the chapter following the quotation from Mann's book is entitled "What Germany Needs Is a Strong Man, 1932." One is reminded that in 1939–40 Chaplin made a Hitler film, *The Great Dictator*. While he was working on it, it seemed doubtful whether the British government would permit an anti-Hitler film to be released, but in the middle of the filming World War II broke out. How naive people were in those days! Chaplin thought he was exposing Hitler to ridicule and thus finishing him off. "Had I known of the actual horrors of the German concentration camps," he later wrote in *My Autobiography* ([New York, 1964], 392), "I could not have made *The Great Dictator;* I could not have made fun of the homicidal insanity of the Nazis. . . ." In this respect the film documents the atmosphere of the time.

"NAZIS": The abbreviation, reflecting the pronunciation of the first two syllables of *Nationalsozialisten*, evidently was patterned after "Sozis" for *Sozialdemokraten*, a word widely used for many years.   313

NULLIFICATION OF THE EMANCIPATION: The program of the NSDAP (Nazi party),   313ff. which was made public on 25 February 1920 in a huge mass meeting in the banquet hall of the Hofbräuhaus in Munich and declared to be "unalterable" in paragraph 2 of the party's statutes, has this to say on the subject: "4. Only a person with German blood, regardless of religion, can be a citizen. Hence no Jew can be a *Volksgenosse* [fellow German]. 5. Anyone who is not a citizen will only be able to live in Germany as a guest and be subject to the laws governing aliens." Point 6 states that all functions in the state can be performed only by "citizens" in that sense. Point 7 declares that it is the primary obligation of the state "to promote the livelihood and subsistence of its citizens. If it is not possible to provide sustenance for the entire population of the state, the members of other nations (noncitizens) shall be deported from the Reich" (cited after Nationalsozialistische Bibliothek, No. 1: *Das Programm der N.S.D.A.P. und seine weltanschaulichen Grundlagen* by Gottfried Feder [Munich, 1932], 19f.)

313ff. IDEOLOGY AND TERROR: Concerning ideology and terror as a new political form, cf. chap. 13 of Hannah Arendt's book *The Origins of Totalitarianism*, New York 1951.

314 BURNING OF THE BOOKS: A clear signal for the suppression of all thought that was not in keeping with the party line was the public burning of books, so-called "corrosive" literature, on 10 May 1933 in Berlin by students who had been incited by Joseph Goebbels, the Reich's Minister of Propaganda. This brought to mind (less then than later) Heine's verses in his tragedy *Almansor* (1820): "Das war ein Vorspiel nur, dort, wo man Bücher/ Verbrennt, verbrennt man auch am Ende Menschen" (That was only a prelude. Where books are burned, people will be burned some day). (Insel ed. 1:314.) For a presentation of the book burnings on the basis of contemporary accounts, cf. Leon Poliakov and Joseph Wulf, *Das Dritte Reich und seine Denker* (Berlin, 1959), 120f.; Ernst Loewy, *Literatur unterm Hakenkreuz: Das Dritte Reich und seine Dichter* (Frankfurt a.M., 1969), 11ff.

315 KRISTALLNACHT: This was the Nazis' derisive term for the pogrom, derived from glass (crystal) broken in the windows of Jewish shops and in Jewish homes by the Nazi mob led by the SS. Later the term was, rather unthinkingly, adopted for general use. Eva Reichmann rightly opposes this expression, which evokes "visions of boyish pranks or perhaps dirty tricks": "What happened in those days was the crime of sacrilege. The spirit imposes a duty upon us. We must not trivialize things—not even with words, and especially not with words." (*Die Reichskristallnacht: Der Antisemitismus in der deutschen Geschichte* [Bonn: Friedrich-Ebert-Stiftung, 1959], 19; on 9ff. there is a moving eyewitness account by Erich Lüth). Cf. also Haim Shamir, "Die Kristallnacht: Die Notlage der deutschen Juden und die Haltung Englands," *Jahrbuch für deutsche Geschichte* 1 (Tel Aviv, 1972), 171–214. The pogrom actually lasted until 11 November. In October Hershel Grynszpan's parents had been deported from Germany to the no man's land on the Polish border, and with his outrageous act their son wanted to avenge his parents. The instructions for the organization of the pogroms were issued by telephone. As with other actions, as little as possible was put in writing so as to maintain the fiction of spontaneity in the eyes of the world. Though that world did not believe in this spontaneity, it watched these actions as passively as the Germans. Cf. *EJJ* 10:1263f. and the bibliography there; H. Rosenkranz, *Reichskristallnacht: 9. November 1938 in Österreich* (Vienna, 1968).

Shortly before and during the actions as well as in the ensuing weeks orders were issued by telephone and in writing to spare the Jewish archival material, for it was intended to be used against the Jews. Regarding the storage of the documentary material a dispute arose between the Nazi offices and the civilian archival authorities, with the latter usually prevailing. Cf. "Dokumente über die Rettung jüdischer Gemeindearchive in Deutschland nach der 'Kristallnacht,'" presented by Alexander Bein in the collection *Michael* of the Diaspora Research Institute 2 (Tel Aviv, 1973), 247–65. At my initiative and with my participation, and in cooperation with the German archival authorities, a major portion of the surviving archival material of the Jewish communities has been transferred to Jerusalem, beginning in 1951.

316ff. FINAL SOLUTION: The term *endgültige Lösung* or *Endlösung* did not at first mean *Vernichtung* (annihilation or destruction). In 1940 it was used for the implementation of the projected deportation of European Jewry to Madagascar. The decision to destroy the Jewish people completely seems to have been made in late 1940 in connection with the decision to attack the Soviet Union, or soon thereafter. The order was evidently issued orally (not in writing) by Hitler to Himmler in mid-March of 1941, and from that time on the word *Endlösung* meant annihilation. Cf. Y. Bauer in Gutmann-Rothkirchen, 611ff.; the author's presentation is based on H. Krausnik, M. Broszat, and H. Buchheim, *Die Anatomie des SS-Staates* (Olten and Freiburg, 1965). Of course, the decision and the order came as a consequence of the delusional ideas and ideological developments that are described in Part 1, pp. 322ff. The destruction was the consequence of the totalitarian ideology of racist hatred of the Jews and was implemented when the time was ripe. Concerning the much-discussed question whether this decision could have been stopped by a timely reaction of the world to the persecution of the Jews, cf. the section "The Attitude of the World" (Part 1, pp. 383ff., and Part 2, p. 719).

WANNSEE CONFERENCE: It should be emphasized that it was not the beginning of the destruction but an important step toward its better systematization. The minutes that Eichmann kept of this conference are one of the few written documents about the organization of the systematic mass murder (cited in Part 1 after Poliakov-Wulf [1961], 70ff.)   317ff.

ADOLF EICHMANN: Eichmann was a mediocre bureaucrat and accordingly performed the task, which was imposed upon him or which he desired, of systematically implementing the "final solution" by destroying the Jews with the ambition and sense of duty of a middle-level German official. At his trial, which the Israeli government conducted from June to December 1961 in Jerusalem, one year after the Israeli Secret Police had arrested him in Argentina (May 1960) and taken him to Israel, Eichmann was almost able to base himself on Kant's categorical imperative, which, according to him, had served him as a guiding principle in carrying out Hitler's and Himmler's order to destroy the Jews. There was about him nothing of the demonic that one generally imagines in criminals of this dimension; rather, he displayed the psychology, raised to an absurdly enormous dimension, of a German sergeant or middle-level official who is eager to distinguish himself by carrying out his orders obediently and superefficiently. In this sense Hannah Arendt presented him as a virtual prototype of her theory about the "banality of evil" in her report about the Jerusalem trial (which was rightly attacked because of other aspects, which will be discussed later, and her ironic, scornful tone). Cf. Hannah Arendt, *Eichmann in Jerusalem: A Report on the Banality of Evil* (New York, 1963). In her exchange of letters with Gershom Scholem after the publication of her book (printed in *MB* [Tel Aviv], 16 August 1963) she explained the intention of this expression as follows: "It is indeed my opinion now that evil is never 'radical,' that it is only extreme, and that it possesses neither depth nor any demonic dimension. It can overgrow and lay waste the whole world precisely because it spreads like a fungus on the surface. Only the good has depth and can be radical" (*Encounter* 22, no.1 [January 1964]: 56). Cf. Part 2, p. 724.   317

THE NUMBER OF THE VICTIMS: This cannot be established precisely because the statistical starting point (the Jewish population before the Holocaust) and the end point (the number of Jews after the collapse of the Third Reich and the end of World War II) are to a large extent based on divergent estimates. Then, too, there is the question of what can be regarded as "normal" deaths during this period (and also in the ensuing years among the survivors of the concentration camps and the other Jews vegetating in Europe) and what must be considered the results of the system of extermination in all its manifestations and effects, including starvation, illnesses caused by hunger, forced labor, etc. In judging what was done it hardly matters whether there were half a million more or half a million fewer victims of the system.   318f.

Such great numbers boggle our imagination, and the human tragedies and the incomparable, unique nature of each individual case disappear behind anonymous mathematical calculations. The decisive point here is the purposiveness and mechanical organization with which the destruction of the Jews was carried out. Only the breakdown of the Nazis' military power and supremacy was able to stop the machinery of death at a certain point, and it is solely due to this collapse that the "final solution" ended with the murder of a greater or lesser part of the Jewish population of Europe instead of including all of Jewry in the execution of the death sentence. In the postwar period, and particularly in recent decades, hopelessly uneducable people, accomplices in the atrocities or new converts to the Nazi doctrines, attempted in publications of all kinds to continue the tactics of the leaders and drumbeaters of the Third Reich by devaluating the statements about the mass murder of the Jews as "horror stories" and forgeries of anti-German "international Jewry"—to the point of complete denial, even in trials like those of the murderers of Treblinka. To go into this would mean debating with deluded or malevolent people, which is always hopeless, though it is often necessary to preserve innocent bystanders from false information and beliefs. Cf. Ino Arndt and Wolfgang Scheffler, "Organisierter Massenmord an Juden in nationalsozialistischen Vernichtungslagern: Ein Beitrag zur Richtigstellung apologetischer Literatur," *Vierteljahrshefte für Zeitgeschichte* 24 (1976): 105–35. In a prefatory note, an English version of which appeared in *Patterns of Prejudice* 10:5, 11ff., Martin Broszat, the director of the Institut für Zeitgeschichte in Munich, states that in view of the facts that have been published and investigated or have come to light in the Eichmann trial and other legal proceedings, "the denial of the mass destruction of the Jews must seem almost ghastly."

319ff. THE UNIQUENESS OF HITLER'S MURDER OF THE JEWS: My remarks are based, sometimes verbatim, on two of my essays: "Die Judenfrage in der Literatur des modernen Antisemitismus als Vorbereitung der 'Endlösung,'" *Bulletin LBI* 6, no.21 (1963): 4–51 (published in numerous translations) and "Der Jüdische Parasit: Bemerkungen zur Semantik der Judenfrage," *Vierteljahrshefte für Zeitgeschichte* 13 (1965): 121, 149 (English version in *LBYB* 9 [1964], 3–37 with an additional excursus that appeared in German as "Das Wort von der 'deutsch-jüdischen Symbiose'" in *MB* [Tel Aviv], 5 June 1964; this excursus has been used with slight changes, in Part 2, pp. 715ff.). In these two articles the references are sometimes given more fully than in this book; on the other hand, here I have included and cited those newly published writings that have come to my attention and appeared important to me.

The uniqueness of the systematic murders of Jews was noted by the American prosecutor Robert H. Jackson in his opening address at the international war crimes trial in Nuremberg on 22 November 1945: "History does not record a crime ever perpetrated against so many victims or one carried out with such calculated cruelty. . . . Determination to destroy the Jews was a binding force which at all times cemented the elements of this conspiracy" (quoted after Max Weinreich, *Hitler's Professors* [New York, 1946], 6). Cf. also R. W. Cooper, *The Nuremberg Trial*, (Penguin Books, 1946), 113: "Genocide in theory is one thing; but how human beings belonging to one of the most advanced countries of Europe could be found to annihilate people in their millions not in the heat of battle, but in cold blood, and by the most diabolical devices, defies logical analysis!" What happened was so new that in 1944 Raphael Lemkin (1901–59), a Polish-Jewish jurist and political adviser to the War Department in Washington, coined the word "genocide" for it (from the Greek word *genos*, race or kind, and the Latin *cida*, from *caedere*, to fell, beat to death, or kill). On p. 695 of Part 2 and in my remarks about semantics (Part 1, pp. 362ff.) I have already stated my critical objections to such expressions, which may have their justification as technical terms but tend to obscure the cruel personal fate of those involved by turning it into something anonymous and abstract. R. W. Cooper, a British war correspondent of the London *Times* who also covered the Nuremberg trial, remarked ironically (110): "It is a commentary on the failure of so many people to grasp the dire significance of these happenings that the word 'genocide' was greeted by the purists less as a crime against humanity than a crime against the English language" (as a Greco-Latin hybrid). The repeated attempts at a sociological typification also produce only a blurring of the objective and moral facts.

Concerning the machinery of mass destruction (macroviolence) and the integration of the murders of the Jews into the history of mass murders in the twentieth century, cf. Gil Elliot's *Twentieth Century Book of the Dead* (Penguin Books, 1973), a book profoundly moving with its sarcastic scholarship. Cf. also an earlier publication, Lord Russell of Liverpool, *The Scourge of the Swastika* (New York, 1954).

THE TRAUMA OF THE LOST WAR: Anyone who wishes to gain a proper understanding   320f.
of the disillusionment (in the truest sense of the word) of the Germans at the end of World War I must bear in mind the hopes and emotions with which they had gone to war and what ideas they had had about the role that Germany had to play in the imperialistic system of world powers as a cultural pioneer in the broadest sense by virtue of its material, intellectual, and artistic position. Regarding Germany's ideas about global politics, cf. Ludwig Dehio, *Deutschland und die Weltpolitik im 20. Jahrhundert* (Munich, 1955; Frankfurt a.M.: Fischer Bücherei, 1961). One of the profoundest experiences of the Germans (and the overwhelming majority of German Jews) was the feeling of unity, the leap from the isolation of the individual to the experience of community as expressed by "We," the willingness to make sacrifices for the totality that manifested itself like a revelation at the outbreak of the war in August 1914. People believed in the justice of their own cause and in the victory of this just cause—and ironically not only in Germany but in the enemy countries as well. Only few people discerned the very real, materialistic, and Machiavellian aims, interests, and strategies that were behind it. They kept silent, or their voices were drowned out by the idealistic enthusiasm for the war. Even the Social Democrats, who had long been persecuted and defamed as traitors, were carried away by this excitement and voted in the Reichstag for the authorization of war credits. In his memoirs, written as late as 1949, the famous historian Friedrich Meinecke described 3 August 1914, the date on which this vote was taken, as "one of the most beautiful moments of my life, one that suddenly infused into my soul the deepest trust in our people and the greatest joy" (p. 137). Thirty years after the event he affirmed the emotions that had stirred him at that time: "Even though in those days we may have overestimated the degree of our internal national cohesion, even today there is no doubting the fact that it happened with unexpected strength." Many intellectuals experience it the way Meinecke did, not to mention the uncritical enthusiasm of the masses. A cross section of the thoughts and feelings of the intellectuals, among them Germans of all political persuasions as well as Jews, may be found in the collection *Das grosse Jahr 1914–1915* (Berlin: Fischer Verlag, 1915). It is astonishing how unanimous these intellectuals—from Alfred Weber, Thomas Mann, and Ernst Troeltsch to Moritz Heimann, Jakob Wassermann, Alfred Kerr, Max Scheler, and Emil Ludwig—were in their conviction of the justness of the war and its prospects for Germany.

STAB-IN-THE-BACK LEGEND: Faith in a victory was kept alive with all means of   320f.
propaganda when, particularly after America's entry into the war, perceptive people realized more and more clearly that Germany had overestimated herself and that the war had really been lost long ago. Even when Ludendorff, on 29 September 1918, pressed for an immediate armistice in order to prevent the complete disintegration of the German army, this came to the attention of only a very small circle. For all others

the military and political collapse came as a complete surprise despite the waning of the enthusiasm for the war and the restrictions on consumer goods that had increasingly produced conditions close to starvation. A man as well informed about the general situation as the German-Jewish industrialist and writer Walther Rathenau, who had marshaled Germany's raw materials in die-hard fashion despite the enemy blockade, as late as 7 October 1918 issued a passionate appeal in the *Vossische Zeitung* for a *"levée en masse,"* a new armed people's fight against the Allied troops. When an armistice was signed in early November at the urgent request of the army's command, this was done by the politician Erzberger (who was assassinated three years later) and not by Field Marshal Hindenburg, whose responsibility this would have been and who, by shirking it, was able to live on in the popular imagination as the "victor of Tannenberg" rather than the man who had been defeated at Compiègne. This was the atmosphere for the reception of the legend that the victorious army had been stabbed in the back by the profiteering, unpatriotic beneficiaries of the war economy—and, of course, first and foremost by the numerous Jews among them. This watchword was disseminated among the people by those who bore the major blame. This was first done in public by Hindenburg in his testimony of November 1919 before the parliamentary committee investigating the causes of the war and and the defeat. Cf. the collections edited by Werner E. Mosse for the Leo Baeck Institute, *Entscheidungsjahr 1932: Zur Judenfrage in der Endphase der Weimarer Republik* (Tübingen, 1965) and *Deutsches Judentum in Krieg und Revolution 1916–1923* (Tübingen, 1971), in the latter particularly Saul Friedländer's essay "Die politischen Veränderungen der Kriegszeit und ihre Auswirkungen auf die Judenfrage," 27–66. Concerning the origin of the stab-in-the-back legend, cf. Erich Eyck, *A History of the Weimar Republic* 1 (Cambridge, Mass., 1967), 137ff.

320f.   THE "DIKTAT" OF VERSAILLES AND THE WAR-GUILT QUESTION: Another problem that was much discussed in public from 1919 on was Germany's forced recognition of its exclusive blame for the outbreak of World War I, a stipulation of the Treaty of Versailles (articles 231) and the accompanying memoranda. In accordance with Wilson's declarations the Germans had counted on a peace treaty that, while severe, would be dignified, strive to be just, and be based on the principle of self-determination for all nations. The Treaty of Versailles, however, was in all essential points a unilateral treaty drafted by the victorious powers, which Germany was forced to sign on a peremptory basis. In Germany it was immediately called the *Friedensdiktat*, the dictated peace. The Germans were not alone in believing that the outbreak of the war had been caused by a complex interaction of interests and circumstances. The "guilt" was not only on the side of Germany and its allies but, as soon enough shown by the publication of documents and memoirs of the statesmen involved, also on the side of the Western powers and Russia. The treaty and the demands of indeterminate sums of fantastic dimensions that were based on it profoundly affected the interests and offended the sense of honor of large numbers of people in Germany. The debate about the so-called war-guilt question, which seemed to be a problem for the historians (who did most zealously concern themselves with it and produced an enormous literature about it), became a problem for the entire nation. It was no accident that opposition against the "Versailles *Diktat*" became one of Hitler's most successful propaganda themes, one with which he gained many adherents and weakened the opposition of his adversaries. I will have more to say about this later.

321f.   THE JEWS IN THE UPHEAVALS: Cf. the abovementioned collection issued by the Leo Baeck Institute, *Deutsches Judentum in Krieg und Revolution 1916–1923.*

PARTICIPATION OF THE JEWS IN POLITICAL AND CULTURAL LIFE: THE "KUNSTWART"   321f.
DEBATE OF 1912: We are familiar with the position of Zionist leaders that greater
reserve on the part of the Jews in their participation in politics and cultural life was
indicated. Cf. especially Kurt Blumenfeld, *Erlebte Judenfrage: Ein Vierteljahrhun-
dert deutscher Zionismus*, a publication of the Leo Baeck Institute (Stuttgart, 1962).
Perhaps the most characteristic document for the position of the most sincere Jews,
those averse to any self-deception, is "Deutsch-jüdischer Parnass," an essay by the
Zionist journalist and writer Moritz Goldstein. It appeared in the semimonthly *Der
Kunstwart* (subtitled *Halbmonatsschau für Ausdruckskultur auf allen
Lebensgebieten*), edited by Ferdinand Avenarius, a nationalistic writer who was not
officially an anti-Semite but shared the usual antipathy to the Jews that was clothed in
civil forms. (The literary critic of this journal was the literary historian Adolf Bartels, a
radical anti-Semite.) Goldstein had first submitted his article to the liberal *Berliner
Tageblatt* and other journals, but only the *Kunstwart* opened its columns to this
confession of an upright Jew who endeavored to see and show an undisguished and
undistorted reality. His esssay initiated a spirited debate in the *Kunstwart* and in the
press generally. In three issues of the periodical (25, nos. 11, 13, and 22, from March
to August 1912) Jews on both sides of the issue, a declared anti-Semite with all the
delusions and arguments familiar from the literature, and the editor himself, who on
the whole inclined toward the anti-Jewish point of view, commented on it. Goldstein's profound and impassioned article noted the growing influence of the Jews in all
areas of German cultural life and said that it increasingly appeared as though
"German cultural life were passing into Jewish hands. This, however, the Christians
had neither expected nor desired when they granted the Pariahs in their midst a
share in European civilization. They began to resist, they began to call us aliens
again, they began to consider us a danger in the temple of their culture. And thus we
are now confronted with this problem: We Jews are administering the intellectual and
spiritual property of a nation that denies our right and our abilty to do so." The author
showed how unjustly the Christians, even the most important among them (such as
Schopenhauer and Wagner), reacted to the Jews' desire to integrate themselves
completely into the European national cultures of the world around them and to
achieve something. The Jews pretended to be blind to this resistance; according to
Goldstein, all their arguments against the false accusations were pointless: "We can
easily lead our adversaries *ad absurdum* and show them that their hostility is
unfounded. What would we prove by that? That their hatred is genuine. Even when
all calumnies have been refuted, all distortions have been rectified, all false judgments about us have been corrected, their antipathy itself will remain as irrefutable.
Anyone who does not realize this is beyond help." The author points out that this is
why the Jews are measured by entirely different standards from those applied to the
non-Jews and why their words really meet with no response: "Heinrich Heine, who is
still the only Jewish poet of European stature, is a symptom. Anyone who knows how
to interpret it will have no desire to compete with the oh so much more fortunate
German poets; he will pack his bag and be on his way." But the author immediately
asks: "Be on his way—but which is our way?" Actually, the only consistent, truly
productive way out would be "a leap into neo-Hebrew literature. The only salvation
and at the same time the absolutely safe one. . .". Yet this path cannot be taken by
those already raised in another language and culture: "For we German Jews, those
living today, cannot become Hebrew poets any more than we can emigrate to Zion."
(That is how it looked two years before World War I and twenty years before Hitler
and the great immigration of German Jews to Palestine.) The only thing left, according to Goldstein, is continued coexistence with the clear realization and awareness of

the difference. "What differentiates us need not lead to differences between us. Once we Jews have all reached the point where do we not wish to be anything but Jews, Europe, too, may get to the point where it will not take us for anything but Jews. Then it will admit to itself that it needs us—as Jews."

At the time of its appearance Goldstein's essay, which is still impressive in its fearless analysis and its incisive, sometimes probably too sharp, formulations (as the author himself thought forty-five years later), surely made many people think, though it probably induced only few of them to change their opinion. As Goldstein pointed out, that was determined by other factors, more by emotions than by clear thinking. The anti-Semites, of course, did not fail to notice this self-criticism of a Jew, tore quotations suitable for their purposes from the context and repeatedly used them down to the Hitler period and beyond. In this article and the public debate about it historians find a reflection of the image of the Jewish question in the minds and hearts of some of the intelligentsia—Jews and Christian Germans—shortly before World War I. Cf. Moritz Goldstein's essay "German Jewry's Dilemma: The Story of a Provocative Essay," *LBYB* 2 (1957), 236–54; and also Yehuda Eloni, "Die umkäampfte nationaljüdische Idee," in the Leo Baeck Institute's collection *Juden im Wilhelminischen Deutschland 1890–1914*, ed. Werner E. Mosse (Tübingen, 1976), 673–76.

321f.   JAKOB WASSERMANN: *Mein Weg als Deutscher und Jude* (Berlin, 1921), the rather desperate autobiography of Jakob Wassermann, at that time a widely read novelist, is perhaps the most eloquent expression of the dichotomous position of Jewish writers in postwar Germany. As early as 1921 he came to this conclusion: "Unfortunately the Jew is an outlaw today—if not in the legal sense, then in the emotions of the people." To a Dane who had asked him about the Germans' hatred of the Jews, he replied: "A non-German cannot possibly imagine the heartbreaking situation in which a German Jew finds himself. German Jew—mark these words well and regard them as the last stage of a long course of evolution. With his dual love and his fight on two fronts the German Jew has been pushed to the brink of despair." Wassermann was fortunate enough to be spared the worst. He died on New Year's Day 1934. That year, thirteen years after the appearance of Jakob Wassermann's book, the writer Arnold Zweig, who emigrated to Palestine and returned to East Berlin after the war, published in Amsterdam his *Bilanz der deutschen Judenheit 1933: Ein Versuch* (English edition: *Insulted and Exiled: The Truth about the German Jews* [London, 1937]). Concerning Wassermann, cf. the remark in Part 2, p. 725.

322ff.   HITLER'S NOTIONS OF THE JEWS AND THE JEWISH QUESTION: In addition to *Mein Kampf* Hitler summarized his conception of the Jewish question in 1928; cf. *Hitlers zweites Buch: Ein Dokument aus dem Jahre 1928*, with an introduction and commentary by Gerhard L. Weinberg and a foreword by Hans Rothfels (Stuttgart, 1961), 220–23. Like all of Hitler's delusional ideas, the Jewish question recurs in many of his speeches and writings down to his last will and testament—and as is characteristic of delusional ideas, even where it is not relevant.

For literature about Hitler, in addition to the books already mentioned, cf. the bibliography in Joachim Fest, *Hitler: Eine Biographie* (Berlin, 1973) (*Hitler: A Biography* [New York, 1974]); Werner Maser, *Adolf Hitler: Legende, Mythos, Wirklichkeit* (Munich, 1971) (*Hitler: Legend, Myth and Reality* [New York, 1973]). *Hitlers Briefe und Notizen: Sein Weltbild in handschriftlichen Dokumenten*, ed. W. Maser (Düsseldorf) (*Hitler's Letters and Notes* [New York, 1974]) is revealing for the psychology of Hitler, as is H. Picker, *Hitlers Tischgespräche im Führerhaupt-quartier 1941–1942*, with an introduction by Gerhard Ritter (Bonn, 1951) (the English edition, *Hitler's Secret Conversations*, is more complete and has an introductory essay on the mind of A.H. by H. R. Trevor-Roper [New York, 1953; paperback, 1961]). A good characterization of Hitler's image of the Jews may be found in J. R. von Salis, *Weltgeschichte der Neuesten Zeit* 3 (Zurich, 1960), 469ff.; the author calls it "a ghastly and obscene vision of the Jew" and points out that "its sexual, pornographic note was characteristic of Viennese anti-Semitism." It has been rightly remarked that Hitler's first speech in 1919 and the last words in his will bear the stamp of his hatred of the Jews.

"OUR NEUROTIC AGE": Concerning the death motif in the literature of the period,   328
particularly the "Young Vienna" circle (Schnitzler, Hofmannsthal, Beer-Hofmann) and also in Kafka and Broch, cf. Martin Buber's fine introduction to Richard Beer-Hofmann, *Gesammelte Werke* (Frankfurt a.M., 1963), 5ff. Freud's memorable conception of a death instinct in humans also dates from that period.

SIGMUND FREUD: Freud the man was a moralist with rather ascetic leanings. Cf.   328
Ernst Simon, "Sigmund Freud, the Jew," *LBYB* 2 (1957), esp. 292–95.

"THE DECLINE OF THE WEST": In his Preface to the revised edition of his work *Der*   329f.
Untergang des Abendlandes Spengler wrote: "A thinker is a person whose part it is to symbolize time according to his vision and understanding. He has no choice; he thinks as he has to think. Truth in the long run is to him the picture of the world which was born at his birth. It is that which he does not invent but rather discovers within himself. . . . Those who make definitions do not know destiny." (*The Decline of the West* 1, trans. C. F. Atkinson (New York, 1929), xiii–xiv).

"CULTURAL PESSIMISM": Cf. Fritz Stern, *The Politics of Cultural Despair: A Study in*   331
the Rise of the Germanic Ideology (Berkeley, 1961), 1: "This is a study in the pathology of cultural criticism." Cf. also George E. Mosse, *The Crisis of German Ideology: Intellectual Origins of the Third Reich* (New York, 1964); idem, *Germans and Jews: The Right, the Left, and the Search for a "Third Force" in Pre-Nazi Germany* (New York, 1971).

"KULTUR" AND "ZIVILISATION": This is a typically German conceptual distinction,   331
probably deriving from Romanticism, which is alien and barely comprehensible to the Western European and American conceptual worlds.

HANS BLÜHER: Cf. the critical essay by Günter Schloz, "Wandervotel, Volk und   333ff.
Führer: Männergesellschaft und Antisemitismus bei Hans Blüher," in K. Schwedhelm, *Propheten des Nationalismus* (1969), 211–27. In 1919 and 1920 Blüher published "Deutsches Reich, Judentum und Sozialismus," a speech made before the Free German Youth that consisted of affirmations and negations, a mixture of strange mythological, abstruse formulations and attempts at attaining insight. In it he spoke of a fate similar to that of the Germans, of Jewish elitist figures on the one hand and an "overproduction of Chandals" on the other. "That is, it [the Jewish race] constantly produces a very great number of inferior and unstable human refuse [*Ausschussgeschöpfe*]. Among the Jews these have a very special philosophy that, of course, has the secret purpose of concealing the inferior nature [a spooky foreshadowing of the *Untermensch*, the subhuman creature of the Nazis] of its representatives. This includes eudemonism, liberalism, progressivism, enlightenment, scientific superstition, rationalism, and others. . . . We Germans are encircled by this Jewish spirit. Like all evil things, it is, of course, the most numerous by far, and though naturally there is no point in eradicating it, it would make even less sense for us to ally ourselves with it. . . . Political socialism is a predominantly Jewish intellectual

product" (2d ed., 1920, 21f. In that edition Blüher declared that the 1st ed. of 1919 was "invalid"). In 1931 he published an even more sharply anti-Jewish book, *Die Erhebung Israels gegen die christlichen Güter.* There he goes so far as to characterize a forged document in the spirit of the *Protocols of the Elders of Zion* as "definitely written . . . on the plane of pure history" even if it were proved spurious by "empiric historiography with its mountains of documents and its endless back and forth as to whether something happened or not." This argumentation is similar to the later reasoning of Hitler, Rosenberg, some editors of the *Protocols,* and many others. Even after the Hitler period Blüher adhered to this peculiar conception of truth and history, a view that with charlatanic mythological twaddle and a megalomaniacal gesture pushes aside everything that is inconvenient or twists it into its opposite. Blüher rejected the actions and the vulgarity of the Nazis, though he took pride in the fact that Hitler sent for the abovementioned work when he was imprisoned at Landsberg and started working on *Mein Kampf.* In a peculiar exchange of letters in 1953 with Martin Buber, who rightly reproached him with his false quotations and his use of forged documents, Blüher with a true "Germanic" berserker's rage inveighed against the "God of vengeance" and Buber as his representative and expressly affirmed his theory of "pure" and "empirical" history as well as the right to utilize even such forged documents if they were in keeping with inner reality and made history comprehensible. Buber answered him with Hillel-like patience (which is incomprehensible to me and which Blüher surely did not deserve) and with an occasional ironic rebuke. Cf. Martin Buber, *Briefwechsel aus sieben Jahrzehnten,* ed. and with an introd. by Grete Schaeder, 3 (1975), letters no. 271, 275, 307, 308, 323, 325. The impression made by Blüher, the "youth leader," in the early twenties may be documented by a personal experience. Around the middle of June 1921, as an eighteen-year-old leader of the Zionist youth association Blau-Weiss in Nuremberg, I attended a lecture by Blüher on *Secessio Judaica* shortly before the publication of his book (1922). His motto evidently was *"Yehuda patet,"* for among my private papers I found a poem scribbled in great excitement and dated 14 June 1921 which I evidently wrote the night after the lecture and in which I warned against the bloodiest pogroms. If I print a few verses here it is not because of a poetic importance that they do not have but as a first-hand testimony to the impression made by Blüher's speech: "Heute ist's *ein* Rufer noch, doch wartet, morgen/ Da kommt euch Angst bereits, da bangen Sorgen/ Und dann aus Drohn und Rufen kommt die Tat/ Und Schrei und Mord reift grauenhaft die Saat./ Ich höre euch, ihr Mütter, stöhnen/ Ich sehe, Schwestern, wie euch Leiber höhnen/ Ich fühle, Brüder, euch zertreten/ Und zitternd seh ich euch, ihr Kleinsten, beten./ Dann ist's zu spät, und euer Krampfen/ wird eitel mit dem Blut zum Himmel dampfen./ Ich sehe zuckend schon in euren Leibern wühlen/ Und sehe euch: zerstampft verkühlen . . ." (Today it's still one voice, but wait—tomorrow there will be fear and sorrow. And then threats and shouts will turn into actions, and screams and murders will ripen the seed horrendously. You mothers, I can hear you moaning; sisters, I can see bodies mocking you. Brothers, I can feel you ground into the dust; and I can see you, little children, praying. Then it will be too late, and your convulsions and your blood will futilely evaporate heavenward. I can already see them burrowing through your twitching bodies and visualize your crushed bodies getting cold . . .).

In 1933 Blüher published a new (third) edition of his *Secessio Judaica* and wrote in his foreword: "This book was written in 1921, at a time when the Jews in Germany were at the height of their power and generally were not bothered by anyone. At around the same time the popular forces that are victorious in Germany today were preparing their propaganda strike against the Jews. Whether this was influenced by *Secessio Judaica* is hard to say, but the events of today are happening exactly as if they were the literal effect of this work. . . . As regards the swastika, it will have to be admitted that in my book it shines in its full brilliance and victorious significance independently of the popular forces which have today brought about its victory and that I would therefore be fully entitled to wear it, though I am not a National Socialist—albeit *under* the cross, not next to it."

PROTOCOLS OF THE ELDERS OF ZION: The remarks in Part 1 are based, in addition to 337ff. the editions of the *Protocols* mentioned there, on Benjamin Segel, *Die "Protokolle der Weisen von Zion" kritisch beleuchtet* (Berlin, 1924); Otto Friedrich, *Die Weisen von Zion: Das Buch der Fälschungen* (Lübeck, 1930); "The Truth about the Protocols: A Literary Forgery," London *Times*, 16, 17, and 18 August 1921; *Confrontation der "Geheimnisse der Weisen von Zion ("Die zionistische Protokolle") mit ihrer Quelle "Dialogue aux Enfers entre Machiavel et Montesquieu" von Maurice Joly: Der Nachweis der Fälschung*, published by the Rechtsschutzabteilung Basel des Schweizerischen Israelitischen Gemeindebundes (Basel, 1933). After the publication of my work, first published as an article in 1963, there appeared the most comprehensive book about the history and effects of the *Protocols:* Norman Cohn, *Warrant for Genocide: The Myth of the Jewish World Conspiracy and the Protocols of the Elders of Zion* (London, 1967; paperback, 1970, including a bibliography of the *Protocols* in European languages, though not in Arabic, and editions in other languages published in Arab countries). Cf. also C. Aronsfeld, "The *Protocols* among Arabs," in *Patterns of Prejudice* (London), 9 (July/August 1975): 4; "The Satanic Plot: Arab Know-your-Protocols Campaign," *Wiener Library Bulletin* (Winter 1967/68), 25ff. I have before me an undated English-language edition issued by the Social Reform Society in Kuwait and entitled *Jewish Conspiracy and the Muslim World*. It includes a map on which a snake encircles a large part of the Arab countries; its heading reads "Dream of Zionism" and its caption "Zionist sages plan to exterminate religion and to dominate the world." In 1958 the Egyptian president Abdel Nasser gave an Indian journalist an English-language edition of the *Protocols* which he approved of and recommended to her (*Jerusalem Post*, 2 October 1958). Concerning the exposure of the forgery by Philip Graves, Constantinople correspondent of the London *Times*, and the source of information, cf. the article by Colin Holmes, which is based on archival material (including the *Times* itself), "New Light on the *Protocols of Zion*," in the London bimonthly *Patterns of Prejudice* 11 (November/December 1977): 13–21 (with comprehensive sources).

A handy German-language edition of Maurice Joly's book appeared as a dtv paperback under the title *Macht contra Vernunft: Gespräche in der Unterwelt zwischen Machiavelli und Montesquieu*. In his foreword, dated June 1948, the translator, Hans Leisegang, writes: "This Foreword was written at a time when Hitler's domination of Germany had reached its zenith. It took him 20 years, from 1918 to 1938, and hence the words uttered by Machiavelli in this book had come true: 'You need not give me more than twenty years to change the most intractable character of a European people completely and make it as submissive to tyranny as the smallest Asiatic nation.'"

Even before the *Protocols* became known, accusations of Jewish secret agreements were disseminated time and again. Thus there was talk of a "Jewish syndicate" in France at the time of the struggle for the legal clarification of the unjust sentence that had condemned the Jewish captain Alfred Dreyfus to life imprisonment on Devil's Island. In 1898 Max Nordau was able to state in his address at the second Zionist Congress (Proceedings [1898], 16): "The legend about a syndicate is believed by the majority of Frenchmen." Theodor Herzl remarked on occasion that the non-Jews described the financial power of the Jews the way it might be if all Jews united and placed their financial resources at the disposal of a common task (Herzl, of course, meant, and wanted it to be, the establishment of the Jewish State). In view of the fragmentation of Jewry, they never even came close to that.

348f. "UNTERMENSCH": Concerning the history of the concept *Untermensch*, cf. Schaul Esch, "Words and Their Meaning: 25 Examples of Nazi Ideas," in *Yad Vashem Studies* 5 (1963); Cornelia Berning, *Vom "Abstammungsnachweis" zum "Zuchtwart": Vokabular des Nationalsozialismus* (Berlin, 1964), 186. Both works give references to Grimm's dictionary, etc.

The word first appeared in the German language in the mid-eighteenth century (just as "subhuman" first appeared in English at the end of that century). It has the biological meaning of animals lower than humans but closely related to them, and it was transferred to lower humans—often in contrast to another old concept (used since the eighteenth century by Goethe and the Romanticists) of the brilliant *Hochmensch* (Jean Paul) or *Übermensch* (e.g., in Grabbe's play *Don Juan und Faust*, 1828; cf. Biese, *Deutsche Literaturgeschichte* 3 [1916], 29f.). In 1898 Herzl spoke of the "subhuman conditions" under which the impoverished Jews of Palestine were living. *Untermenschlich* (subhuman) as a synonym for *unmenschlich* (inhuman) appears in 1918 in Heinrich Mann's novel *Der Untertan* (303). As the antithesis of the highbred *Übermensch* (as renewed by Nietzsche in 1883) the image of the *Untermensch* was given a biological interpretation and applied to politics. In 1925 the word appears in this sense in the title of a book by Theodore Lothrop Stoddard *The Revolt against Civilization: The Menace of the Underman*. The National Socialists initially used it in their struggle against the Bolshevists, and a connection with the Jews arose from the fact that in the eyes of the Nazis Bolshevism was a Jewish weapon, one founded and wielded by Jews. This increasingly turned the Jews into Russian subhumans. In the end Hans Frank applied it to Hitler in his confessions *Im Angesicht des Galgens: Deutung Hitlers und seiner Zeit, auf Grund eigener Erlebnisse und Erkenntnisse* (Neuhaus, 1955), calling him (400) "the most terrible *Untermensch* in world history" and in other places using the term together with *Übermensch*. This confirmed Hermann Cohen's sharp critique of Nietzsche's concept of the *Übermensch*: "Der Übermensch ist ein Unmensch" (The superman is inhuman). Cf. Hugo Bergmann in *HE* 1:534.

350ff. "OSTJUDENFRAGE": Cf. S. Adler-Rudel, *Ostjuden in Deutschland*, (Tübingen, 1959), 20f. and M. Wischnitzer, *To Dwell in Safety*, (Philadelphia, 1949), 289. Concerning the Komitee für den Osten, cf. Adler-Rudel, 34ff. and M. I. Bodenheimer, *So wurde Israel: Erinnerungen* (1958), 183ff. Of contemporary writings about the problem of the Jews from Eastern Europe I shall mention Nathan Birnbaum, *Was sind Ostjuden? Zur ersten Information* (Vienna, 1916) (this well-informed presentation first appeared in August 1914 in the *Mitteilungen des Verbandes der jüdischen Jugendvereine Deutschlands*); idem, *Den Ostjuden ihr Recht* (Vienna, 1915); this disseminated the word *Ostjude*, which had probably been coined by N. Birnbaum around 1903, and the term was adopted by the German public. "Nowhere in politics and economic life," we read in the foreword of the pamphlet *die Einwanderung der Ostjuden*, published by the Arbeiterfürsorgeamt der jüdischen Organisationen Deutschlands (Berlin, 1920), "is there as great a danger that typological myths will develop as where Eastern European conditions are concerned. This has produced a tangled skein of distortions and lies about the numerically weak and insignificant immigration of Eastern Jews. The systematic incitement by certain parties was responsible for this, and as a result even many German men who care about truthfulness, justice, and humaneness have let themselves be led astray." The extent to which the problem occupied the public as early as World War I is shown by the fact that the respected periodical *Süddeutsche Monatshefte* brought out a 170-page special issue on *Ostjuden* as early as February 1916. *Ost und West*, an illustrated Jewish periodical also published a special issue on the subject in 1916, and in its issue of March–April 1920 it already spoke of "the global danger of Jew-baiting in Germany." That long essay, printed as an editorial, is divided into three sections: the new *Ostjudenfrage;* the causes of the migrations of Eastern European Jews (for which the ambivalent behavior of the Germans in the Eastern territories occupied by them, with unkept promises of freedom and increasingly open anti-Semitic tendencies and measures, was in large measure responsible); and the heart of the matter. The last section begins as follows: "Upon closer examination one finds, however, that the opposition to the Eastern Jews is only a diversion, a mock fight, an interlude in the war that has been declared against the German Jews generally by the splendidly organized anti-Semitism. After every global catastrophe, no matter whether it ends with a victory or a defeat for the Germans, they are in the habit of venting their rage on the Jews. A hundred years ago, after the Wars of Liberation and the Congress of Vienna, it was exactly as it is today . . . Anti-Semitism also erupted in the new German Reich as soon as it had consolidated itself after 1870–71. . . ." And the section ends with these words: "In Germany anti-Semitism is being prepared for export. What is produced here is enough to poison whole continents for decades."

An essay entitled "Ostjuden" in Maximilian Harden's periodical *Die Zukunft,* which in general did not exactly plead the cause of the Jews (27, no. 35 [29 May 1920]: 224ff.), points out that the problem "Originated many decades before the war" and that the Jewish immigrants from Eastern Europe have facilitated "commercial and industrial relations between Germany and the Eastern countries, opened up large areas to German imports (eggs, fish, wood, leather, furs) and pointed the way for the export of agricultural machinery and technical products of all kinds to the extensive Eastern markets." The article goes on to say that in the discussion of the subject people "always lose sight of the fact that in wartime the German authorities used any means, particularly brute force, to press indiscriminately a large number of Eastern Jews, including craftsmen and petty tradesmen, who seemed at all fit for any amount of physical labor to work in German war industries, even mines." In the big cities of England and America there are far larger districts that are almost exclusively inhabited by Eastern Jews, "but these domiciles are not decried as a 'boil.'. . . What is shameful is the attempt to fan the flames of this hatred of the Eastern war victims by spreading the lie that the flood of immigrants is going to shake the foundations of the German economy and deprive the German worker of his housing, food, and work."

The German Jews were divided in their attitude toward the *Ostjuden.* Help was organized, but frequently only to the extent of facilitating and accelerating these Jews' departure for other countries, particularly America. There were many Jews who evinced benevolent understanding for, if not open agreement with, the defensive measures that many Germans demanded from the government. Marriage to an Eastern Jew was regarded as a misalliance by many Western Jewish families, and it was opposed or at least regretted. Many Jewish Community Councils were opposed to granting the Eastern Jews equal rights in communal elections. Cf. (in addition to the abovementioned book by Adler-Rudel) Naomi Katzenberger, *Dokumente* [of Dr. Harry Epstein, a fighter for equal rights] *zur Frage des Wahlrechts ausländischer Juden in den preussischen Synagogengemeinden,* offprint from the annual *Michael* of the Diaspora Research Institute, Tel Aviv University, 2 (1973), 191–202.

Concerning the cultural life of Eastern European Jewry, which strongly influenced, via the Youth Movement, West European Jewry and Jewish settlement in Palestine, cf. Mark Zborowski and Elizabeth Herzog, *Life Is with People: The Culture of the Shtetl* (with a Foreword by Margaret Mead) (New York, 1952, 1962).

362ff. THE SEMANTICS OF THE JEWISH QUESTION: The employment of pictures and words in the service of propaganda against the enemy, which had been a general practice since antiquity and the Middle Ages, was turned into an increasingly efficient and effective weapon during World War I. Cf. Hans Thimme's informative book *Weltkrieg ohne Waffen: Die Propaganda der Westmächte gegen Deutschland, ihre Wirkung und ihre Abwehr* (Stuttgart and Bonn, 1923). The author was the democratic archivist at the German Reichsarchiv in Potsdam and lost his life in an air raid. Cf. also Ferdinand Avenarius, *Das Bild als Verleumder: Bemerkungen zur Technik der Völkerverhetzung* (Munich, ca. 1915).

364 THE BIOLOGIZATION OF LANGUAGE: Cf. Renate Schaefer, "Zur Geschichte des Wortes *zersetzen,*" in *Zeitschrift für deutsche Wortforschung* 18 (new ser., 3), 40–80. Nazi language is "full of biologically tinged images, and it is particularly the gloomy, dark, and dirty side of organic life that inspired National Socialist metaphors." In an essay entitled "Über Nationalismus und Judenfrage" and published in 1930 in *Süddeutsche Monatshefte* (27, no. 12, 844) Ernst Jünger writes: "People like notions from popular medicine in which the destruction of swarms of atomistically attacking bacteria and fungi plays a large part."

364 WHAT HAS "ORGANICALLY GROWN": V. Klemperer (*LTI. Aus dem Notizbuch eines Philologen* [Berlin, 1947]) repeatedly emphasizes the close connection between Nazism and German Romanticism, writing on p. 151: "For the seeds of everything that constitutes Nazism are already contained in Romanticism: the dethronement of reason, the animalization of man, the glorification of the idea of power, of the beast of prey, of the blond beast." Similar formulations may be found in E. Friedell, *A Cultural History of the Modern Age*, book 3 ("The Organic"); Ernst Cassirer, *Vom Mythus des Staates* (1949), 236ff.; Schaefer, 42ff. Concerning the vital elements and the temptation of death in German Romanticism and their descent to the level of Hitler's "hysterical barbarity," cf. Thomas Mann's 1945 lecture at the Library of Congress in Washington, *Deutschland und die Deutschen* (Stockholm, 1947), 35ff. (*Germany and the Germans* [Washington, 1945]). From the economic point of view, it was especially Quesnay's physiocratic "Système naturel" that had laid the foundation for the theory of the "organic" (cf. Part 1, p.177ff.) Cf. also the warning of the conservative historian G. Below (*Die deutsche Geschichtsschreibung von den Befreiungskriegen bis zu unseren Tagen* [1924], 80): "The unfortunate thing about using the concept of the organic is that all kinds of things can and have been read into it and that it has been misused by interpreting the 'organic' structure as something strictly in accordance with the law of nature. We must always bear in mind that it is only an image. This limited use of the comparison simile determines the usability of the organic theory."

365 "USURY": The word *Wucher* derives from the Gothic and Old High German and originally denoted the yield or fruit of trees and fields, then that of human labor. The use of the word in the Middle Ages as synonymous with the interest taken for loans of money (which was prohibited to Christians and permitted to Jews, though it was regarded as unjustified and unjust) gave it the pejorative meaning of inordinate profit, no matter how high the interest was. Originally the verb *wuchern* also meant *wachsen, Ertrag bringen* (to grow, yield), but later it assumed the meaning of *übermässig, unkrauthaft wachsen* (inordinate, weedlike growth), until it finally was understood in the biological sense as pathological growth with tumorous formations. Similarly, as the language was biologized, the word *Wucher* came close to the biological and medical term *Wucherung* (excrescence, tumor) and was so interpreted by the people, whether consciously or unconsciously. Cf. Max Neumann, *Geschichte*

des Wuchers in Deutschland (Halle, 1865), 53–56 and the standard dictionaries. We have already mentioned that *judaizare, to Jew,* and similar terms have been used synonymously with "usurious interest" (cf. Part 1, p. 98ff and Part 2, pp. 506f.).

"NATIONAL PESTS": There was a National Socialist decree against national pests   365
(Volksschädlinge); cf. Hofer, 286. In 1933 Heinrich Mann, Arthur Holitscher, Lion Feuchtwanger and others published a collection called *Gegen die Phrase vom jüdischen Schädling.* It was issued in Prague, and among the contributors were such non-Jews as Werner Sombart.

"PARASITE": I can give only part of the documentation here. A more detailed   365
bibliography and documentation may be found in my above-mentioned article "Der jüdische Parasit. Anmerkungen zur Semantik der Judenfrage" (Part 2, p. 700). M. Caullery, *Le Parasitisme et la Symbiose,* defines the concept "parasitism" as follows: "Le parasitisme peut être défini la condition de vie normale et nécessaire d'un organisme qui se nourrit aux dépens d'un autre,—appelé l'hôte,—sans le détruire. Pour vivre regulièrement de l'hôte, le parasite,—sauf des exceptionnels,— vit en contact permanent avec lui, soit sur sa surface extérieure, soit à son intérieur. Le parasitisme se manifeste donc comme une association généralement continuée entre deux organismes différents, dont l'un vit aux dépens de l'autre. L'association a un caractère essentiellement unilatéral; elle est nécessaire au parasite, qui meurt s'il est séparé de son hôte, faute de pouvoir se nourrir; elle ne l'est nullement à l'hôte: l'adaptation est la marque du parasitisme." (2d ed., Paris, 1950, p. 21). Concerning the transfer of the biological concept to the social sciences, note the definition of "parasite" in the *Shorter Oxford Dictionary* (1959, p. 1430): "c.fig. A person whose part or action resembles an animal parasite. 1883."

"PARASITISM" AS A CONCEPT IN SOCIALIST, MARXIST, AND ANTICAPITALIST LITER-   365ff.
ATURE: This is not the place for a more detailed examination of the (still insufficiently investigated) semantics of the social question, socialism, and Marxism. As an example from our time I shall cite an essay by W. Ruge in the (Marxist) periodical *Zeitschrift für Geschichtswissenschaft* 7 (1959), in which imperialism is characterized as "a necessary—and the last—(monopolistic, parasitic) stage . . . of capitalism." The author refers to Lenin, *Ausgewählte Werke in 2 Bänden* (Berlin, 1954), 839ff. I quote from the chapter "Parasitismus und Fäulnis des Kapitalismus," 851: "The pensioners' state is the state of parasitic, decaying capitalism." Concerning the physiocrats and early socialists, cf. Part 2, pp. 585ff., and the literature given there. In the Soviet Republic laws were passed in the 1960s against "parasites," idlers, violent persons, economic malefactors, etc. (*HE* 22:672). In this connection it would be interesting to subject the use of the word *parasite* in the USSR to a more detailed investigation. Proclamations against parasites as nonworking spongers on society, frequently with an express reference toward the Jews in general and Zionists striving to emigrate to Israel in particular, seem to be common practice there. Cf. the article "To the Pillory with Parasites" in the Hebrew daily *Davar* of 21 September 1960 or the anti-Jewish picture reproduced in *Ma'ariv* of 3 February 1962 with the caption "Parasites—out of Moscow!" Khrushchev frequently used this word in his reply to Bertrand Russell, dated 21 February 1963; cf. the official English translation in *Jewish Observer and Middle East Review,* 8 March 1963, 14f.: "Our State . . . protects honest working people from parasites. . . . The capitalist system . . . permits some people . . . to lead a parasitic life. . . ." On 14 May 1964 the Hebrew daily *Ha'aretz* printed a story from the STA News Agency in London under the headline "Soviet Intellectuals Protest the Persecution of a Young Jewish Writer Charged with Being a 'Parasite' and Exiled to Do Forced Labor." The *Jerusalem Post* of 7 May 1976 carried a news item

with the headline "Jewish Activists [for emigration to Israel] Again Harassed on 'Parasitism' Charges by USSR." These, of course, are only a few items that I happened to preserve. For the more general use of the term, cf. Stanislav Andreski's book *Parasitism and Subversion: The Case of Latin America* (New York, 1969); in it parasitism and exploitation of all kinds are used synonymously (cf. index)—e.g., in the section on 12ff., "Poverty as a Stimulant to Parasitism"; 55ff., "Varieties of Parasitism." Cf. also Abba P. Lerner's article "The Myth of the Parasitic Middleman," in the monthly *Commentary* 8, no. 1 (July 1949): 45–50.

367   "HOST NATION": The concepts "host nation" and "guest nation" in their application to the Jewish question merit a systematic examination and clarification. They evidently derive from the laws governing the position of aliens as they developed from the classical tradition in the Middle Ages. In his work *Von den Juden und ihren Lügen* (1543) Luther writes: "We suffer more because of them [the Jews] than the Welsche [Italians] suffer because of the Spaniards! Those take up their hosts' kitchen, cellar, cupboards, and purse, and so do our guests. We are their hosts." Beginning with the 1880s Treitschke, Eduard von Hartmann, Dühring, and others made the term *Wirtsvolk* (host nation) so popular that the Jews themselves wound up using it almost naively without suspecting its implications. The anthropogeographer Friedrich Ratzel applies an image of political geography to the Jews when he writes: "Jews, Armenians, and Gypsies are, as it were, the tenants of other nations" (Friedrich Ratzel, *Erdenmacht und Völkerschicksal: Eine Auswahl aus seinen Werken*, ed. Karl Haushofer [Stuttgart, 1940], 240). In his introduction to *The Jewish State* (1896) Herzl polemicized against the term with remarks prompted by a conversation with Narcisse Leven, the general secretary of the Alliance Israélite. Cf. Theodor Herzl, *Complete Diaries* 1:242, as well as A. Leschnitzer's remarks in his *Saul und David: Die Problematik der deutsch-jüdischen Lebensgemeinschaft* (Heidelberg, 1954), 200f.

368   REGNARD: Cited after E. Silberner, *Sozialisten zur Judenfrage*, Hebr. edition with an extensive documentary appendix (Jerusalem, 1955), 320; about Bakunin, ibid., 354.

368   THEODOR HERZL: "Die Jagd in Böhmen," *Die Welt*, 5 November 1897 ("The Hunt in Bohemia," in *Zionist Writings: Essays and Addresses* [New York, 1973], 170).

368f.   LORD DELAMERE: Cf. his book *The Grant of Land to the Zionist Congress and Land Settlement in British East Africa*, (London, 1903), 1 (here quoted after the copy in the archives of the British Foreign Office): ". . . Jews in a free country are never agricultural, they are purely parasitic, and require a large population for the exercise of their various trades."

369   ADOPTION OF ANTI-JEWISH CONCEPTS BY THE JEWS THEMSELVES: Cf. the remarks in Part 1, chap. 7 about Jewish self-hatred and Yeheskel Kaufmann, *B'Hevlei ha-Zeman* (Hebr.) (Tel Aviv, 1936), 260ff., esp. 262.

369f.   "PEST": This word and terms with a similar meaning as applied to the Jewish question merit a separate investigation. This usage seems to be very old, and it appears that new events and apprehensions increasingly transformed it from a comparison into naturalistic notions, as happened with other abusive and organic expressions. Here we can only give incomplete references and documentations that came to my attention in the preparation of this book and occasionally through chance reading. (By way of supplementation, cf. the quotations in Parts 1 and 2 by using the index.) Manetho already has the Jews expelled from Egypt as lepers (cf. Part 1, p. 41f.), and this version entered the European tradition via the Greeks and Romans. In *Antiquitates*

11. 6. 5 Flavius Josephus puts the word *bubo* for Jews in the mouth of Haman, the enemy of the Jews, who promises the Persian king Artaxerxes 40,000 silver talents if he "frees the empire from this bubo" by destroying the Jews. The early Christians occasionally called merchants "a kind of pest" (M. Neumann, *Geschichte des Wuchers in Deutschland* [Halle, 1865], 3). Later the word appeared in Christian Councils. At the Twelfth Council in Toledo (681) a written proclamation *(tomus)* by the Visigothic king Ervig admonished the people: "Tear the Jewish pest out by the root!" *(Judaeorum pestem radicibus extirpate)*. Such linguistic images may well have induced people at the time of the "Black Death" in the fourteenth century to accuse the Jews of having caused and disseminated the plague and to persecute them cruelly for that reason (cf. Part 1, p. 114ff.) Luther did not fail to use this word, like others of that type, as a term of abuse against the Jews (cf. vol. 1, p. 138ff.).

For Giordano Bruno (1548–1600), the heretical, pantheistic philosopher of the Renaissance who, like many others of his age, adopted and developed the traditions of antiquity in the Jewish question as well, the Jews were "such a pestilential and leprous species, and one so dangerous to the public, that they deserve to be exterminated before birth" (cited after T. Fritsch, *Handbuch der Judenfrage* [1937], 440). As an example of the metaphorical use, cf. Treitschke, *Deutsche Geschichte* 2 (1937), 265, where he half quotes and half paraphrases Vincke's *Übersicht über die Verwaltung Westfalens* of August 1847: "And on top of everything, 'the pest of the land, the usurious Jews in every village.'" The Nazis adopted and disseminated all these anti-Jewish meanings—the antique, the medieval, and the modern ones.

"LOCUSTS," "WORMS": A broadside of 1819 already speaks of the Jews that "spread   370
among us like voracious locusts." Cf. E. Sterling, *Er ist wie Du: Aus der Frühgeschichte des Antisemitismus in Deutschland 1815–1850)* (Munich, 1956), 189. A memorandum issued in Württemberg in the 1840s characterized the Jews as "the noxious worms gnawing away at the law of the land." Cf. the essay about "Die bürgerlichen Verhältnisse der Juden in Deutschland" in *Die Gegenwart: Eine enzyklopädische Darstellung der neuesten Zeitgeschichte* (Leipzig, 1848ff.), 1:362, 390. The Young Hegelian Arnold Ruge said about the Jews that they were "the maggots in the cheese of Christianity" (E. Sterling, *Er ist wie Du*, 114).

"SPIDERS": *Cf.* Part 1, pp. 346ff., about Dinter, also Hitler (who seems to have learned a   370
lot from Dinter's dime-novel imagination), in *Mein Kampf* (1:212) about the Jews in the so-called *Kriegsgesellschaften* of World War I: "The spider slowly began to suck the blood from the people's pores." In 1920 Dietrich Stürmer wrote in a study about Maximilian Harden (p. 17): "Harden is not a lion of the intellect who destroys with a blow of his paw, but a spider that crawls everywhere and is constantly lying in lurch to ensnare its victims with its uncanny arms and to suck the blood from the unfortunates." Walter Frank, from whose book *Höre Israel* ([1942], 195) I am quoting here, adds: "Harden is at home in putrescence; he lives in it and on it as worms live in and on carrion." The National Socialist historian Friedrich Stieve chose the biological image of a sponge; cf. his *Geschichte des deutschen Volkes* (Munich, 1938), 465 about conditions during the Weimar Republic: "The foreign body of Jewry swelled up like a sponge and was constantly augmented by an influx from the East."

"CORROSIVE ELEMENT": Concerning the history of the word *zersetzen* and its use in   370f.
Nazi language, cf. the abovementioned article by Renate Schaefer in *Zeitschrift für deutsche Wortforschung* 18:40–80. One should, however, beware of using the term *jüdisch-zersetzend* today even semi-approvingly, as a quotation, as Golo Mann does in his book *Antisemitismus* (1960), p. 27: "And one should also admit that the expression *jüdisch-zersetzend*, which was current in the Weimar period, was not

entirely without foundation." Or as Friedrich Meinecke does in his overcautious and balanced book *Die deutsche Katastrophe* (Wiesbaden, 1949), where he writes, on p. 29, that the Jews "tend to enjoy economic success that smiles on them unthinkingly" and have contributed a great deal "to the gradual devaluation and discreditation of liberal thought. . . . That alongside this negative and corrosive effect they also did many positive things for the spirit and the economic life of Germany was forgotten by the masses of those who now were combating the damage done by the Jewish character."

370f. "WORLD PEST": The book is by Hermann Esser, and the advertisement appeared in *Die Juden in Deutschland*, a book issued by the Institut zur Bekämpfung der Judenfrage (Munich, 1939).

370f. "INSECTS": Cf. Maurice Maeterlinck's characterization of insects, here cited after the English translation in M. V. C. Jeffreys, *Personal Values in the Modern World* (Penguin Books, 1962), 9: "The insect does not belong to our world. . . . One would be inclined to say that the insect comes from another planet, more monstrous, more energetic, more insane, more atrocious, more infernal than our own. . . . There is, no doubt, in our astonishment and lack of understanding a certain instinctive and profound uneasiness inspired by those existences incomparably better armed, better equipped than our own, by those creatures made up of a sort of compressed energy and activity in whom we suspect our most mysterious adversaries, our ultimate rivals, and perhaps our successors."

372 "VERRECKEN" is the way an animal dies. Cf. the definition in Kluge, *Etymologisches Wörterbuch*, 19th printing (Berlin, 1963), 818: "To die rigidly stretched out—thus still in the literature of the seventeenth century, but since then limited to animals. Hence the crude sound when it is applied to people in modern speech."

372 "NOT A HUMAN BEING BUT A PHENOMENON OF PUTREFACTION": Walter Buch in an article about the honor of a National Socialist in the periodical *Deutsche Justiz* 100, no. 2 (1938): 1660, here cited after Max Weinreich, *Hitler's Professors* (New York, 1946), 89, notes 204 and 249. That man, who headed the supreme court of the Nazi party, said in a New Year's message published on 2 January 1940 in *Der Parteirichter: Amtliches Mitteilungsblatt des Obersten Parteigerichts der NSDAP* (Munich), p. 2 that Hitler's victory would bring Europe a peace that would forever deprive the subhuman Jews of the opportunity to corrode people and nations.

374 VERMIN and similar expressions have been used here and there as a hostile characterization of Jews at least since the sixteenth century. A complaint brought in 1589 at the bishopric of Halberstadt calls the Jews "a peculiar vermin and a people that is insufferable among the Christians" (Liebe, *Das Judentum in der deutschen Vergangenheit* [1903], 37).

For similar linguistic images in modern English literature, e.g., in Ezra Pound, George Eliot, and others, cf. Alfred Eris, "Portrait of the Artist as a Mass Murderer," in *Midstream* (New York), February 1976, 50–60; Richard C. Thurlow, "Ideology of Obsession in the Model of G. K. Chesterton," in *Patterns of Prejudice* 8, no. 6 (November–December 1974), 28f.

374 EXTERMINATION OF THE JEWS AS PARASITES: Cf. Walter Murdoch in his foreword to B. Burgyne Clapman, *The Complete Anti-Semite* (Sidney, 1945): "The kindest thing you can say of the German torturers is that they have been taught to regard their

victims not as human beings, but as noxious animals." In his novel *Eyeless in Gaza* (1936) Aldous Huxley has his Dr. Miller say: "If you call a man a bug, it means that you propose to treat him as a bug" (cited after David Stafford-Clark, *The Psychology of Persecution and Prejudice,* Robert Waley Cohen Memorial Lecture [London, 1960], 3f.). In his *Masse und Macht* (Hamburg, 1960; new ed., Reihe Hanser, ca. 1973), 1:202ff., Elias Canetti compares the process with the runaway inflation in Germany that devalued everything (p. 207). The treatment of the Jews by National Socialism was an exact repetition of this process: "First they were attacked as evil and dangerous enemies, then they were increasingly devalued, and in the end they were literally regarded as vermin that could be destroyed with impunity by the millions. Cf. Kurt Löwenstein, "Juden in der modernen Massenwelt," *Bulletin LBI* 3 (1960): 171ff.

EXCURSUS ABOUT THE "GERMAN-JEWISH SYMBIOSIS": A concept related to parasitism   375 is symbiosis, a term often used to refer to the close coexistence of the Jews with the nations in the Diaspora. Jewish commentators have tended to use it particularly for the close economic and cultural connection between Jews and Germans, *Judentum* and *Deutschtum;* in keeping with the purely linguistic root of the Greek words, they meant by it fruitful, peaceful coexistence for mutual benefit. In a similar sense we occasionally speak of a Spanish-Jewish symbiosis in the Middle Ages and a Greco-Jewish symbiosis in ancient Alexandria, the latter exemplified by the philosophy of Philo.* On the other hand, to my knowledge non-Jews use the word with reference to the Jewish question only rarely and with reservations.**

In order to clarify this and warn against an unbalanced use of this term, it may be useful to take a closer look at it. Symbiosis, the word and the concept, was created in 1879 by the botanist Anton de Bary (born in Munich in 1831, died in Strassburg in 1888) to designate "the lasting intimate union of two organisms whose mutual relationship is beneficial to both partners."*** Thus we are here not dealing with a word

---

*As one of many examples I will cite Martin Buber's essay "Das Ende der deutsch-jüdischen Symbiose" in *Jüdische Weltrundschau* of 10 March 1939: "For the symbiosis of the German and Jewish spirit as I experienced it in the four decades I spent in Germany was the first and only one since the Spanish period that received the highest confirmation that history has imparted—confirmation through *fruitfulness.*" The biological idea clearly remains Buber's point of departure as he continues: "It was not a parasitic existence; their whole humanity was put to the task, and it bore its fruit. But even more deeply than by individual accomplishment the symbiosis is verified by a striking collaboration between the German and the Jewish spirit. ("The End of the German-Jewish Symbiosis," in *Men of Dialogue: Martin Buber and Albrecht Goes,* ed., E. William Rollins and Harry Zohn, [New York, 1969], 233–34). The concept symbiosis is used quite abstractly and unclearly in Adolf Leschnitzer's well-known book *Saul und David: Über die Problematik der deutsch-jüdischen Lebensgemeinschaft,* Heidelberg 1954, 39ff., 100ff., 149ff., and in numerous other places. In *LYBY* 1:312 Eduard Rosenbaum draws attention to the inadequacy of his definitions of symbiosis. In his fine essay "The Rise and Fall of the Jewish-German Symbiosis: The Case of Franz Kafka" (*LBYB* 1:255ff.) Felix Weltsch uses the word without a precise definition. Robert Weltsch, the editor of *LBYB,* told me that he stopped using the expression after the appearance of my remarks in *LBYB* 9 (1964), 38ff. Cf. Y. Ilsar's essay (based in part on my remarks) "Zum Problem der Symbiose: Prolegonema zur deutsch-jüdischen Symbiose," *Bulletin LBI* 14 (1975): 122–65.
**As an example of the (generally negative) use of the term by non-Jews, cf. Wilhelm Stapel's *Antisemitismus und Anti-Germanismus: Über das seelische Problem der Symbiose des deutschen und des jüdischen Volkes* (Hamburg, 1928), 112; cf. Part 1, p. 336f.
***M. Caullery, *Le parasitisme et la symbiose,* 2d ed. (Paris, 1890*, 241: "Le terme a été creé par Anton de Bary, en 1879, pour désigner l'association intime et constante de deux organismes avec des rapports mutuels leur assurant des bénéfices réciproques." The *Shorter Oxford Dictionary* (1959) gives this definition of the biological concept symbiosis: "Association of two different

adopted from antiquity that did not become a biological term until later, like the word parasite; rather, the word and the concept were expressly created to designate a biological phenomenon. Symbiosis is one of the varieties of the close biological connection of different species of organisms, and in this it is so closely related to parasitism that the two forms often coalesce,* which means that it is more a matter of the viewpoint and the definition whether one can speak of symbiosis or parasitism in a given case. Geoffrey Lapage** has defined the similarities and differences between symbiosis and parasitism as follows: "In symbiosis both partners benefit. In parasitism only one partner, the parasite, derives benefit. The other partner, appropriately called the host of the parasite, gets nothing from the partnership. . . . Parasitism, therefore, is a one-sided partnership, a state of conflict that is in striking contrast to the harmony of a symbiotic relationship. Its hallmarks are the resistance made by the host and the injury done by the parasite. The host's resistance, and the injury done by the parasite, may be great or small. . . . It may be difficult, indeed, where we find host and parasite thus living together in a state of what we call tolerance of each other, to decide whether these are instances of parasitism, or even of symbiosis. Parasitism, however, can be infallibly distinguished by one fact. Parasites always injure their hosts. The harm done may be very slight . . . but it does exist and it marks the dividing line between parasitism and all other forms of association between living things."

I have quoted this at some length because it points up the danger of applying this biological concept to social life in general and the relationship of the Jews in the Diaspora to the non-Jewish world around them in particular. Added to this is the fact that in this transfer one very important factor is generally disregarded: the human consciousness. When we observe and define the relations between plants or animals, we as observers are outside the process and consider only reactions that can be physiologically determined by our observation. *Human* phenomena cannot be observed so objectively, because we ourselves are part of these phenomena and because our subjective consciousness with its emotions and values constitutes an integral art of the process itself. Since the process of symbiosis generally involves the social union of unequal quantities, these questions always arise: How does the union look from the viewpoints of the organisms that form this union? Is the viewpoint of the stronger partner the same as that of the weaker? These questions, which probably cannot be answered for the lower organisms, become decisive when one applies the concept of symbiosis to human social life, to the relationship between groups of people that differ in their ethnic context and their historical consciousness. Given the close relationship between parasitism and symbiosis that has been pointed out above, it is logical that the weaker partner should regard the form of coexistence with the stronger group which it has joined and to which it feels attached as a symbiosis, while the stronger partner, convinced that it does not need help from the weaker partner, regards this attachment and closeness of the weaker partner as a parasitism that at best benefits only the weaker partner, which is perceived as a guest and often as an intruder. There can be no doubt that since the emancipation period this mutual

---

organisms (usually, two plants or an animal and a plant) which live attached to each other, or one as a tenant of the other, and contribute to the other's support."

*Caullery, *Le parasitisme:* "Si même l'un vit aux dépens, de l'autre et peut être considéré comme son parasite, son métabolisme fournit au partenaire des éléments plus ou moins essentiels. . . . Comme je le dis ci-dessus, la délimitation de la symbiose et du commensualisme ou même du parasitisme n'est pas toujours aisée. L'analyse des exemples de symbiose . . . montrera, qu'ell n'est pas toujours purement mutualiste et que l'un des deux organismes associés est, en réalité, plus ou moins parasite sur l'autre."

**Geoffrey Lapage, *Animals Parasitic in Man* (Pelican Books, 1957), 17f.

relationship has often been viewed in this antithetical light by both Jews and Germans. What appeared as a symbiosis to the Jews was viewed by the Germans, and not just by declared anti-Semites, as a more or less dangerous form of parasitism practiced by the Jewish parasites on their German "host nation."

Once again the conclusion to be drawn from this ought to be greater caution in the use of biological concepts for human social life. One need not speak of a symbiosis when one means peaceful coexistence for mutual benefit or when one wishes to describe the syntheses of various kinds of currents and endeavors. For the relationship between Jews and non-Jews in particular one should avoid any expression that can be interpreted in the light of notions about the Jewish parasite—notions whose dangerous nature and deleterious effects have been described above.

HITLER'S SUCCESSES: Cf. Hitler's speech before the Reichstag on 28 April 1939, less   379f. than six months before the unleashing of World War II, in which Hitler replies to the American president Franklin D. Roosevelt and gives a proud summary of his achievements: ". . . and I have striven to do all this without shedding blood and thus inflicting the sufferings of war on my people or on others. I have created this, Mr. President, with my own strength as a worker and soldier of my people who was still unknown 21 years ago, and hence I can claim before history to be numbered among these people who have achieved the greatest things that can fairly and reasonably be demanded of an individual." The passive attitude of the Germans was surely promoted by the fact that after the initial unrest everything was bolstered by laws and decrees. This deprived the bad conscience of its legal foundation, as it were: A law is a law! Concerning the real condition of German justice at that time, cf. Hermann Weinkauff, "Die deutsche Justiz und der Nationalsozialismus: Ein Überblick," in *Die deutsche Justiz und der Nationalsozialismus* 1, issued by the Institut für Zeitgeschichte (Stuttgart, 1968), 19–133. Regarding the nature and the impression of Hitler's successes in the first years of his rule, cf. Sebastian Haffner, *Anmerkungen zu Hitler* (Munich, 1968) (*The Meaning of Hitler* [New York, 1979]; "Achievements," 23ff., "Successes," 47ff.).

THE GERMANS' LACK OF THE COURAGE OF THEIR CONVICTIONS: Anyone who has   381 lived among them can testify to that lack. When I was a young research assistant at the Deutsches Reichsarchiv in Potsdam between 1927 and 1933, I repeatedly observed that former high-ranking German officers on the research staff were afraid to raise critical objections to views and decisions of the director, their superior, and were very pleased to have me, the youngest and the only Jew among them, undertake this task.

BELATED AND INADEQUATE OPPOSITION TO HITLER: Cf. Hans Rothfels, *Die deutsche*   381 *Opposition gegen Hitler: Eine Würdigung* (Frankfurt a.M.: Fischer Bücherei, 1958) (*The German Opposition to Hitler: An Appraisal* [Hinsdale, Ill., 1948]); Golo Mann, *Deutsche Geschichte 1919–1945* (Frankfurt a.M.: Fischer Bücherei, 1961), 185ff.

The minor role played by the Jewish question in the initial judgment on Hitler by intellectuals (including Jews) is exemplified by a book published in 1932 that strikes one as strange today, *Die deutschen Parteien: Wesen und Wandel nach dem Krieg* by Sigmund Neumann, a Jewish lecturer at the Deutsche Hochschule für Politik in Berlin. In his detailed and understanding (perhaps overly sympathetic) analysis of the National Socialists, their aims, and their philosophical and sociological background (73–88) the Jewish question is virtually relegated to a footnote. The author completely failed to recognize that it was a focal point of Hitler's world and system.

ARMIN T. WEGNER'S LETTER OF PROTEST: Strangely enough, Wegner's courageous   381f. protest has, to my knowledge, been ignored by scholarship. Yad Vashem, the Jerusalem memorial institute for Jewish history in the Hitler period, publicly thanked him, like many others of the "righteous among the nations," by presenting him with a medal of honor and planting a tree in his name. On that occasion the German Embassy at Tel Aviv published Wegner's letter of 11 April 1933 in a pamphlet entitled *"Ich beschwöre Sie—wahren Sie die Würde des deutschen Volkes."* In his letter Wegner said: "Mr. Chancellor, what is involved is not merely the fate of our Jewish brothers—it is the fate of Germany! In the name of the people for which it is as much my duty to speak as I have a right to do so, like everyone born of its blood, as a German who has not been granted the gift of speech to become an accomplice by keeping silent when his heart is convulsed with indignation, I appeal to you: Put a stop to these goings-on!. . . Even if all remain mute in these days, *I* will no longer keep silent in the face of the dangers that this poses for Germany . . . ." Wegner's *"J'accuse!"* did not come to the attention of the public, because no one dared to print it. But the courageous act of this long-proscribed writer, who had earlier championed the cause of the persecuted Armenians, should not be forgotten, least of all in Germany, a country for whose honor he spoke up and suffered. His "Letter to Hitler" has been reprinted in Armin T. Wegner, *Odyssee der Seele: Ausgewählte Werke,* ed. Ronald Steckel (Wuppertal, 1976), 237–46.

382   COMPLICITY THROUGH SILENCE AND ACQUIESCENCE: The question of what the general public in Germany knew or could have known has been much discussed in speech and writing. Concerning this problem, cf. Romano Guardini, *Verantwortung: Gedanken zur jüdischen Frage* (Munich, 1952); Robert Neumann, *Ausflüchte unseres Gewissens* (Hanover, 1960) (the source of the quotation from Tucholsky's letter, p. 23). Cf. also Ernst Loewy, "Exkurs über die Rechtfertigungsliteratur" in his documentation *Literatur unterm Hakenkreuz* (Frankfurt a.M.: Fischer Bücherei, 1969), 267ff. *Die deutsche Katastrophe: Betrachtungen und Erinnerungen,* written in 1946, shortly after the collapse, by the 84-year-old great German historian Friedrich Meinecke, is quite unsatisfactory in its weighing of the positive and negative elements of the Hitler regime and its many ifs and buts concerning the inhuman occurrences, but it is typical of the attitude of German scholars. Cf. also Eugen Kogon, *Der SS-Staat* (Frankfurt a.M., 1946), 333ff. about the reasons for the Germans' attitude, which he traces particularly to the belief in authority instilled in them by the state and the church. On pp. 335f. he writes: "For the reasons indicated above they relieved themselves of the duty to get to the bottom of the occurrences and quite deliberately closed their eyes to any further knowledge. Such knowledge would have involved an obligation, and hence it was doubly dangerous. Besides, it probably did not seem so certain to them that all those who had been shipped off to concentration camps had been sent there wrongfully. . . ." The Germans' individual sense of justice, in bondage to their loyalty to authority, actually led to the intellectual paradox expressed in Christian Morgenstern's poem "Die unmögliche Tatsache" [The Impossible Fact]—about an automobile accident that its victim, Palmström, logically argues away, "weil, so schliesst er messerscharf,/ nicht sein *kann,* was nicht sein *darf"* [for, he reasons cogently,/ that which *must* not *can* not be]. . . . Their almost unconditional belief in authority gradually made the Germans inclined to regard as criminals those who were arrested rather than those who did the arresting." Kogon goes on (p. 337): "Here the national fault begins to become individual guilt. The German people cannot be blamed morally for what it did not produce over long generations. However, when many individuals did not heed the call of their own conscience, or when they deadened the conscience within themselves, even if only through habituation, they did incur guilt—even in politics, which is not exempt from the demands of morality." For this reason an Israeli court decided, after the unwarranted shooting of Arab inhabitants of the village Kafr Kassem in October 1956 (the

beginning of the Sinai campaign), that soldiers who carry out an order that is militarily unfounded and conflicts with humaneness incur guilt and that their duty to obey does not free them from personal responsibility.

It has often been asserted that the German military distanced itself from Hitler's deeds. Only small numbers did so, and even these became really active only when the fortunes of war were precipitously declining. Cf. Rothfels, *Die deutsche Opposition*, 70ff. and General Otto Korfe's remark in the East German *Zeitschrift für Geschichtswissenschaft* 6 (1958): 497: "It is not true that the German General Staff obeyed Hitler only under duress; rather, as a body it willingly devoted all its ability to the success of the wars of conquest."

"DISPLACEMENT" OF STRATA OF CONSCIOUSNESS: Cf. Jean-Paul Sartre, *Entwurf einer Theorie der Empfindungen* (here cited after Leopold S. Senghor, "Negritude: Zur Psychologie des Negro-Afrikaners," in *Neue Rundschau* (1963): 539ff.—on 549: "In an emotional state conscience descends to an earlier stage and transforms the deterministic world in which we live into a magical one." Hermann Broch writes in his *Massenpsychologie* (*Gesammelte Werke* 9; 191), here cited after *MB* (Tel Aviv), 22 July 1966, 3: "Every people has its atavistic and psychotic periods. But it may be that a people which became Christian as late as the Germanic people did . . . has a particular affinity with atavisms."   382f.

As early as 20 December 1884 the Swiss writer Gottfried Keller remarked in a letter to the ethnopsychologist Moritz Lazarus in which he acknowledged receipt of the latter's book *Das Leben der Seele:* "The foreword, to be sure, reminds me of the thin veneer of culture that barely seems to separate us from the burrowing, howling animals of the abyss and that any shock may shatter" (Franz Kobler, *Jüdische Geschichte in Briefen aus Ost und West* [Vienna, 1938], 436). In an article about the massacre of Italian miners by French miners at Aigues-Mortes the *Neue Freie Presse* (Vienna) wrote on 20 August 1893: "What century are we living in? . . . We are told of the unstoppable progress of human culture, and yet things are happening right before our eyes that are reminiscent of the barbarism of generations long past and painfully remind us of the bestiality of which even modern man is capable." On 11 December 1897 as respected an English weekly as the *Spectator* made this almost prophetic remark in an article entitled "The New Hep-Hep": "The genuine popular feeling is for his [the Jew's] expulsion, and an expulsion could only be effected by terrorism. We are seriously inclined to believe that the 20th century may yet witness a massacre which will recall the days of Peter the Hermit." In his *Knaurs Sittengeschichte der Welt* 3 (Zurich, 1970), 366, Ernst Frischauer makes this remark about the Hitler period: "The countless millions of men and women who lost their lives on the battlefields, in gas chambers, and in air raids were the victims of the 'leader of the masses,' who, in Freud's formulation, had achieved the resuscitation of the *Ur-Horde* [primal horde] as the *Ur-Vater* [first progenitor] and controlled it with unlimited power."

THE ATTITUDE OF THE WORLD: I shall make only a few additional remarks here, for the entire literature on the period gives a general treatment of the problem. It is remarkable that the word *Jew* does not appear in any of the publications of the Allies, including condemnations of Hitler's Germany and threats of punishment. The authors were so afraid that those fighting Hitler might be identified with the Jews and that they might be accused for waging war for their defense and rescue that they spoke only of general crimes against humanity, etc.   383f.

ENTRY IN GOEBBELS'S DIARY: This may be found in C. Aronsfeld, "The Antisemitism of Appeasement," *Jewish Frontier* (New York), March 1972, 34f.   384

384f. CLOSING OF THE GATES AGAINST A GREATER IMMIGRATION OF JEWS: Cf. especially
Arthur D. Morse, *While Six Million Died* (London and New York, 1968). As early as
1945 the well-known Jewish sociologist Jakob Lestschinsky wrote about the Jewish
migrations in his Hebrew book *Nedudei Yisrael* (Tel Aviv, 5705/1945), 70f.: "Closed
gates—some day this may be the title of a chapter in Jewish history, the history of the
past ten years, the most terrible in the long history of our *galut*." He went on to say
that compared to that epoch the expulsion of the Jews from Spain looked like a
Golden Age, for at that time there were countries willing to accept the expellees as
immigrants, foremost among them Ottoman Turkey.

Regarding the attitude of the world to the Jewish question in those days one can
subscribe to what the British politician Lord Vansittart wrote in 1943 in his *Lessons of
My Life:* "Here and in the United States there is a tendency for German atrocities to
become headlines instead of heartaches" (cited after *Jewish Social Studies* 6:191).
Concerning the position of the United States, cf. also Saul S. Friedmann, *No Haven
for the Oppressed: U.S. Policy Toward Jewish Refugees 1933–1945*, Detroit 1973;
Sheldon Spear, "The U.S. and the Persecution of the Jews in Germany 1933–1939,"
Jewish Social Studies 30 (1968). Concerning the conferences at Evian and Bermuda,
cf. Reuben Ainsztein, "How Many More Could Have Been Saved?" *Jewish Quarterly*, Winter 1966/67, 11ff.

386   THE VATICAN AND THE MURDERS OF THE JEWS: The attitude of the Pope toward the
persecutions and murders occupies a special chapter in the literature on the Jewish
question in the Hitler period. Even among his contemporaries opinions were quite
divided on the officially neutral position of Pope Pius XII. The publication and
performance of Rolf Hochhuth's play *Der Stellvertreter* (*The Deputy*, 1963) turned
the discussion of this question into a worldwide debate in which historians and
laymen, Jews and Christians participated. In addition to the very effective and
impassioned dramatization of the problem "Politics or Conscience?" (which the
Vatican faced at that time, deciding in favor of politics and silence), Hochhuth's drama
offers a discussion of this question on the basis of documentary material and takes a
clear stand against the attitude of the Pope. There followed further documents and
documentations (such as Saul Friedländer's *Pie XII et le IIIe Reich* [Geneva, 1963],
from the archives of the German Foreign Office) and presentations (like those by
Günther Lewy, *The Catholic Church and Nazi Germany*, 1964, and Carlo Falconi,
The Silence of Pius XII [Boston and Toronto, 1970]). Since then the release of wartime
files in many countries produced documents and attacks to which the Vatican responded in recent years by publishing selected documents from its own archives. On
the one hand, it is well documented that high-ranking clerics in various countries
(including Germany) denounced certain measures, particularly against Jews who had
converted to Catholicism, and that Pope Pius XI (1922–39) made anti-Hitler statements. On the other hand, the record shows that his successor Pius XII (1939–58)
never made an official declaration condemning the systematic murder of Jews, let
alone threatening to excommunicate and expel from the Church Catholics who were
responsible for it (e.g., Hitler himself) or participated in it. The accusers have argued
that such declarations and threats of punishment might have stopped or at least
delayed the implementation of the "final solution" but that they would, in any case,
have disseminated information about the systematic murder of the Jews throughout
the world, among both Jews and non-Jews, with the authority of the Pope. Then the
world, and in particular the endangered Jews, would have been more quickly
informed about the aim of the deportations as well as the systematic nature and the
scope of the murders, and the Jews might have been able to flee or resist in time. A
clear presentation of the facts and the disapproval of the Pope would also have
encouraged many Christians to be more willing to help the victims.

In defense of the attitude of the Vatican it has been pointed out that many thousands of Jews were saved by Catholic churchmen and institutions, especially convents and monasteries, with the approval of the Pope and perhaps even with his encouragement, particularly when Hitler was beginning to lose the war and the number of Jews being murdered was rising rapidly. This rescue of many threatened individuals, so it has been argued, would have been jeopardized if the Pope had officially abandoned his reserve. Since many Catholics sympathized with Hitler, an official stand against him would have induced these people to leave the Church. It would also have intensified the anti-Christian inclinations of the leading National Socialists and perhaps caused them to take open actions against the Church, its representatives and institutions. On other occasions, too, such considerations have led the Pope to refrain from taking a public stand against political actions. After all, the Vatican has often been confronted with a hard choice between providing spiritual care for Catholics and conducting a realistic policy with secular powers and secular means.

As with all *ex post facto* hypothetical questions regarding historical occurrences, it is difficult to render a definite judgment, for such a judgment depends not only on facts but on principles as well. In connection with the Jewish question we can only point to the problem. In the final analysis, it is once more a special instance of the general problem whether in such emergency situations the decisive factor should be immediate utility or the preservation and avowal of definite moral principles without regard to political and utilitarian considerations. On the other hand, it may be argued that the very adherence to clearcut moral principles in the face of political forces may also increase the practical usefulness; after all, even political affairs are conducted in a world of cultural values and are influenced by the public opinion of the world. In arriving at a judgment one must consider that the attitude of Pope Pius XII may also have been influenced by the anti-Jewish Christian tradition and perhaps by the fact that he was favorably disposed to the Germans by virtue of his work in Munich and Berlin from 1917 to 1929 as Nuncio Pacelli. Cf. Günther Levy's survey in *EJJ* 8:910ff. and the bibliography (in *Holocaust*, Israel Pocket Library, 132ff. and 200). An overview of the debate may be found in *Judaism* 24 (175): 168ff. ("The Vatican and the Jews: Cynicism and Indifference" by Juda L. Graubart) and in *The Jewish Quarterly Review* 63:79ff. (by John J. Hughes). Cf. also A. L. Mordecai Retter in *Beth Yaakov* (Hebr.) 17, no. 6 (March 1976): 4ff.

THE ATTITUDE OF WORLD JEWRY: During and after the war leading personalities in   388f. Europe and America accused themselves and others of failure—not for lack of good intentions but by reason of their insufficient understanding of an unprecedented situation and their underestimation of the ideologies, programs, and persons that threatened the Jews with annihilation. Here as everywhere else the proprietary and jurisdictional interests of the many organizations and the petty ambitions of their representatives played a disastrous role, as did the mistaken belief in obsolete ideologies, traditional apprehensions, reservations about interfering in government policies, and the rigidity of bureaucracies. In all this the Jews of the Diaspora did not differ as much from their surroundings as the time and its sorrows would have required. All eyewitness reports and memoirs of leading personalities indicate that these Jews were assimilated to the world around them in this regard as well. For America cf. *Challenging Years*, the autobiography of Stephen Wise, a Zionist Reform rabbi and an influential speaker and organizer (New York, 1949), chaps. 14–18, and for world Jewry *Staatsmann ohne Staat*, the autobiography of Nahum Goldmann (Cologne, 1970), chaps. 13–18, esp. pp. 188–92), the cofounder and longtime president of the World Jewish Congress, from 1935 to 1939 the representative of the Jewish Agency for Palestine to the League of Nations in Geneva, and after the war the longtime president of the Zionist Organization and the Jewish Agency. Concerning the relief actions and rescue attempts by the Jews of Palestine and their leaders, cf. Part 1, chap. 10, pp. 415f.

389   TRANSFER AGREEMENT BETWEEN THE JEWISH AGENCY AND GERMANY: Among the actions on which Jewish opinion was divided was the boycott of German merchandise that was proposed and in part implemented for some time as well as the negotiations between the Zionist Executive and leading German Jews with representatives of the Hitler government regarding the transfer of Jewish property to Palestine through the export of German merchandise. As so often, the principle of noncooperation with the Nazis was here confronted with the desire to facilitate the immigration of many Jews to Palestine and to finance their productive settlement through the transfer of Jewish property. In point of fact, the so-called Ha'avarah (or Transfer) Agreement of August 1933 accomplished the transfer of Jewish assets in the amount of about $40 million and facilitated the immigration of 60,000 German Jews.

389   RUPPIN: Cited after the German original in the Central Zionist Archives. English translation in Arthur Ruppin, *Memoirs, Diaries, Letters*, ed. Alex Bein (London and Jerusalem, 1971), 268. As Stephen Wise reports in his abovementioned autobiography (p. 237), a level-headed Zionist personality like the American Supreme Court Justice Louis D. Brandeis already believed "categorically and almost too dogmatically, as it then seemed to me" in the early days of the Hitler regime that the emigration of all German Jews would have to be organized immediately as a kind of enormous repetition of the exodus of Spanish Jewry more than four hundred years earlier, but that seemed like an excessive demand even to his closest friends, apart from the fact that the attitude of the world made such an emigration impossible.

390f.   THE ATTITUDE OF THE JEWISH VICTIMS: Making hasty judgments, both negative and positive ones, is, of course, humanly understandable. The passionate nature of the debate down to our time, and probably in the foreseeable future as well, proves that we are not dealing with a bit of history that is complete, basically no longer concerns us, and can therefore be judged with something approaching objectivity. It is an occurrence that continues to have an effect—for one thing, because many contemporaries participated in it as sufferers and sympathizers, planners and helpers, as spiritually involved persons, or as children and grandchildren who learned about it, and for another, because it has affected the emotional life and historical consciousness of entire generations.

390ff.   THE SOURCE MATERIAL: The Nazis feared this effect on contemporaries and their descendants. They tried to prevent it by putting as little as possible in writing, destroying documents as completely as possible, and disguising even verbal commands and their written records with harmless-sounding pseudonyms, linguistic codes, file numbers, and the like. In the face of this many contemporaries set themselves the task of thwarting this offically intended misleading of public opinion, at least for the benefit of posterity, by making notes, preserving incriminating and illustrative documents, and storing these dangerous documentations in secret places as safely as possible. In some places this enterprise was systematically organized by experts. It was a form of inner resistance and opposition to the will of the despots. This work helped those involved to endure the extremely threatening situation in better psychological shape and also frustrated the Nazis' intention of concealing their monstrous deed not only in the present but in the future as well, thus escaping not only judgment in their time but also the devastating judgment of the future. In any case, as a result of the Nazi tactics our historical material is fragmentary; this is especially true of the official documents, though there, too, thanks to the conscientiousness of the bureaucrats, more was preserved than the perpetrators would have liked. But even if the documentary material were complete, it would not tell us much about the inner life, the thoughts and the feelings of the victims. No Nazi concerned himself with that; no one was interested in the emotional life of the "subhumans" and "parasites" whose bodies were being "liquidated." Since the ghettos and concentration camps were sealed off from the outside world and every publication in countries under German domination had to pass through strict censorship, it is only natural that there should be no newspaper articles about the reign of terror and its victims based on eyewitness reports and personal interviews.

JEWISH SOURCE MATERIAL AND RECORDS. THE DIARY OF ANNE FRANK: This fact   390ff.
enhances the importance of the records made and reports preserved by Jews, both individuals and organized groups, particularly the diaries. Among these the diaries kept by young people occupy a special place, and several of them have been preserved despite all the destruction of the war. We still remember the sensation caused by the publication, in Holland in 1947, of the diary of Anne Frank. Her father, the only surviving member of the family, had found it, upon his return from the concentration camp Bergen-Belsen, in the family's old hiding place where Dutch friends had provided them with the necessities of life at great risk to their own lives, a hiding place that had been revealed to the Nazis by informers. Beginning in the 1950s this diary was translated into all languages of the civilized world, dramatized for the stage, and made into a film. This book, written by a precocious child who was very gifted as a writer and as a human being, is still widely read and commented upon. In its unpretentious immediacy it spoke louder than many dithyrambs of accusation and hatred because it described everyday life in plain language. There are a number of other diaries of young people, and some of them have been published by Yad Vashem in Jerusalem and the Kibbutz Lokhamei Ha-getaot (ghetto fighters).

TESTIMONY IN TRIALS OF WAR CRIMINALS: These writings are supplemented by the   390ff.
many statements of witnesses in trials of war criminals—in the Nuremberg trial against the initiators and chief culprits immediately after the end of the war, in the numerous subsequent trials in Germany and other countries (which could all too frequently be misdirected by the lawyers and also by the perpetrators, who barricaded themselves behind their duty to obey commands, readily denied their guilt, or blamed deceased persons), and especially in the Eichmann trial in Jerusalem in 1961, when witnesses from all over the world and all social strata testified in court and had their testimony taken down and extracts from it published in the international press.

"THE PLANET AUSCHWITZ": At that time the testimony of the writer Yehel Di-Nur   390ff.
(originally Feiermann) made the deepest impression on many people. He had already published several books about Auschwitz which described life in the death camps in fictional form. His testimony had to be interrupted because the witness was overwhelmed by the memories that he was trying to express in words, fainted, and had to be taken to a hospital. His books were published under the name Katzetnik (KZ, pronounced "kah tset" in German, was the abbreviation for *Konzentrationslager*). To his legal counsel's question as to why he had chosen this *nom de plume* he replied: "That is not a *nom de plume*. I don't regard myself as a writer of literature. [What I write] is a chronicle of the planet Auschwitz. I was there for about two years. Time there is different from time on the globe; every fraction of a second runs on the wheels of a different time. The inhabitants of that planet had no names, they had no parents, and they had no children. They did not dress the way one dresses here; they were not born and did not procreate; they breathed in accordance with different laws

of nature; they did not live and die in accordance with the laws of the rest of the world; their name was the number Katzetnik." The witness said that he firmly believed in his mission to report about it so that such a misfortune might not happen again. "I deeply believe that just as in astrology stars affect our destiny, the ashen planet Auschwitz confronts our globe and influences it." In a similar vein Alexander Solzhenitsyn called the Russian prison world of terror in which many millions of Russians have lost their lives the "Gulag Archipelago."

390ff.   THE DEBATE ABOUT HANNAH ARENDT'S EICHMANN BOOK: This is the background of the spirited debate about Hannah Arendt's reports about the Eichmann trial which appeared in the well-known periodical *The New Yorker* and were later published in book form as *Eichmann in Jerusalem* (New York, 1963). Concerning her evaluation of Eichmann, cf. Part 2, p. 699. The actual debate did not concern itself with that but with the role of the Jewish leaders, whom she accused of collaborating with the Nazi authorities. She is of the opinion that without these leaders, as unorganized individuals, more people could have saved themselves. According to her, the Nazis would then have had no lists, would have had to search out their victims singly, etc. Cf. also Part 1, p. 395ff and Part 2, p. 727, *Nach dem Eichmann-Prozess: Zu einer Kontroverse über die Haltung der Juden* (Jerusalem, 1963), a booklet issued by the Council of Jews from Germany that discusses the tone and the substance of the accusation; and Aryeh Leon Kubovy, "Criminal State vs. Moral Society: Bettelheim to Arendt's Rescue," in *Yad Vashem Bulletin* 3 (Jerusalem, October 1963): 3–11.

PICTURES: The sources for the life and the reaction of the Jews include, of course, pictures—photos as well as films—that were made by German offices and individual soldiers and officers as well as Jewish photographers. Not even imminent mortal danger deflected the latter from their resolve at least to bring what was happening to the attention of posterity. An example of these is Mendel Grossman's picture book *With a Camera in the Ghetto* (Hebrew text), issued in 1970 by the Ghetto Fighters House and the Kibbutz Hameukhad Publishing House, Tel Aviv. The photographer of the Polish ghetto Lodz, which was even more walled off from the world than most others, made many thousands of photos, hid the negatives, and gave whatever prints he was able to make to his friends and acquaintances. Shortly before the rescue he died of exhaustion at the age of thirty-two. His collection of negatives was taken to Israel and stored in the Kibbutz Nitzanim in the south of the country but then destroyed by the Egyptians, who captured the settlement during the War of Independence and occupied it for a time. The prints in the possession of the photographer's friends have been preserved; they were collected by the archives of the Ghetto Fighters House, and a selection has been published. The origin and fate of this source material reflects in many ways the destiny of Jewish documentation and of its subject in general. The drawings by young artists and all kinds of literary attempts, poems, and songs that have been preserved are another important source, and one that has not been sufficiently exploited.

390f.   THE END OF THE EMANCIPATION: Today it is easy to shake one's head at people's blindness in Germany and the rest of the world to the danger posed during the early years of the Hitler regime by the rescission of the existing laws. The idea of a constitutional state and the ideas of modern liberalism were so firmly anchored in the consciousness of the Western world that people could not imagine a political and economic life without them. Even though Herzl, on the basis of his visions and as the result of his historical and sociological analysis, foresaw a catastrophe threatening the Jews if constructive measures were not taken in time to prevent it, he wrote in 1896 in the Conclusion of *The Jewish State* (108): "The Jews' equal rights before the law cannot be rescinded once they have been granted, for the very first attempts would immediately drive all Jews, rich and poor alike, into the ranks of the revolutionary parties. The very beginnings of official injustice toward the Jews invariably produce economic crises. Thus there is really very little that can effectively be done against us, unless people are prepared to hurt themselves. Yet hatred grows and grows. . . ." Almost forty years had passed since then, and World War I, the Russian Revolution, and other upheavals could have set everyone straight. But it is evidently a psychological law that our emotions are slower to recognize something new than our mind and thus frequently let insights mature into decisions much more slowly than necessity requires.

The night between New Year's Eve 1933 and New Year's Day 1934 brought the death of Jakob Wassermann, who in his life and as a writer has struggled with the conflict between *Deutschtum* and *Judentum* and with an attempt at a synthesis between the two. His death at that time was like a symbol for the end of an era. In his novel *Die Juden von Zirndorf*, published in 1897, the year of the First Zionist Congress, he had given what now seems like a premonitory description of the excitement of the planned return to Palestine under the appearance of Sabbatai Tzevi. Concerning Wassermann, cf. the note in Part 2, p. 704.

EARLIER LARGE-SCALE VIOLENCE AND THE FEEBLE REACTION TO IT: Concerning the   391
extermination of more than a million Armenians by the Turks, beginning in 1915, and the concealment of their fate, cf. Marjory Housepian's article "The Unremembered Genocide," *Commentary*, September 1966, 55–61, which includes the text of the telegraphic order by Talaat Pasha, the Turkish Minister of the Interior, to destroy the Armenians. Basing herself on Louis P. Lochner's book *What About Germany?* (New York, 1942), the author writes about the conclusions that Hitler drew from this (61): "As he announced his own plans for genocide to his Supreme Commanders on August 22, 1939, he noted confidently: Who, after all, speaks today of the annihilation of the Armenians? . . . The world believes in success only." In the case of the pogroms in Russia and the end of World War I in the Ukraine the world generally contented itself with paper protests or vociferous complaints. But in those days there still was free immigration to many countries and particularly to America, where immigration was limited by new legislation in 1924 and based on a quota system according to (racially) desirable and less desirable countries of origin, all of which was intended to facilitate the "adjustment" of the immigrants to their new surroundings and their integration into the American "melting pot." The feeble reaction of the world to the massacres committed by the Italians during their Abyssinian campaign of 1935–36 may be regarded as another precedent. On 18 March, 1937 Arthur Ruppin wrote in his diary: "After the attempted assassination of their Marshal Graziani at Addis Abbeba the Italians seem to have committed a terrible massacre on the Abyssinians and mowed down thousands of people, including women and children. Only England seems to get excited about it; the rest of the world, including the Pope (though those killed were Christians), is silent. We have really attained to a wonderful level of culture."

"WEAR THE YELLOW BADGE WITH PRIDE!": With its courageous and controlled pride   391
this article deeply impressed all contemporaries, including German non-Jews. I became very aware of this when I shared the issue of the *Jüdische Rundschau* in which it appeared (on 4 April, 1933) with my colleagues in the Deutsches Reichsarchiv—high-ranking officials and former officers, including the president, General von Haeften. However, this essay also reflects naiveté about the dimensions and the systematic nature of the threatening misfortune, a naiveté shared even by those who, like the author of this book, were convinced that if there were the expected reverses in the war (which was also to be expected), Germany would try to

stifle people's displeasure with Jewish blood. Here is the quintessence of the article: "The affirmation of our Jewishness—this is the moral significance of what is happening today. The times are too turbulent to use arguments in the discussion. Let us hope that a more tranquil time will come and that a movement that considers it a matter of pride to be recognized as the pacemaker of the national uprising will no longer derive pleasure from degrading others, even though it might feel that it must fight them." (Cited after *The Dynamics of Emancipation*, ed. Nahum N. Glatzer [Boston, 1965], 108.) The author of this article, Robert Weltsch (born in Prague in 1891, died in Jerusalem in 1982), became editor-in-chief of the *Jüdische Rundschau* (Berlin) in 1920. After his immigration to Palestine in 1938 he joined the staff of the independent daily *Ha'aretz* and from 1945 to 1978 served as its correspondent in London, where he became the editor of the *Year Book* of the Leo Baeck Institute (of which 32 volumes have been published since 1956). In later years Weltsch himself realized that his slogan was conditioned by its time and inappropriate in view of a development that he did not foresee. Cf. his articles in *Ha'aretz* ten years later (13 April, 1943) and thirty years later (5 April, 1963), reprinted in German translation in a collection of his essays, *An der Wende des modernen Judentums: Betrachtungen aus fünf Jahrzehnten* (Tübingen, 1972), 29–35. In 1943 he regretted the popularity of the slogan, which, he believed, was "no longer in keeping with the tragic reality of our time. . . . Today I would not dare, and least of all from a safe haven, to urge the Jews in tormented Europe to wear the Yellow Badge 'with pride.' For today this badge, which is intended as a disgrace, is no longer merely an outward sign of belongingness to Judaism but a stigma that marks its bearer as fair game for unbridled murderers." In 1963 Weltsch wrote:

> On that day no one knew of Auschwitz, but one had the feeling that there was an earthquake. One witnessed a spectacle that one would never have thought possible. . . . What went on in Jewish souls? It was that vacillation between despair and hope. . . . Everything seemed unreal, like a bad dream. But strangely and miraculously, what awakened inside the spectators was not only fear and revulsion but an inexplicable feeling of superiority and even triumph. Those who were running riot here [on the day of the boycott of Jewish shops, 1 April, 1933] revealed themselves as an underworld and the persecuted were the moral victors. And it is a fact that the will to moral resistance awakened in the Jews at that time. The response to the editorial in the *Jüdische Rundschau*, "Tragt ihn mit Stolz, den gelben Fleck!," was a sign of the changed attitude.

391f. ORGANIZATIONAL AND CULTURAL WORK IN GERMANY: In addition to what has been said in the text, cf. the essays in *LBYB* and the following monographs edited by Robert Weltsch as publications of the Leo Baeck Institute (Jerusalem): *Deutsches Judentum: Aufstieg und Krise* (Stuttgart, 1963); Ernst Simon, *Aufbau im Untergang: Jüdische Erwachsenenbildung im nationalsozialistischen Deutschland als geistiger Widerstand* (Tübingen, 1959); W. Feilchenfeld, D. Michaelis, and L. Pinner, *Haavara-Transfer nach Palästina und Einwanderung deutscher Juden 1933–1939* (Tübingen, 1972); Adler-Rudel, *Jüdische Selbsthilfe unter dem Naziregime, 1933–1939—Im Spiegel der Berichte der Reichsvertretung der Juden in Deutschland* (Tübingen, 1974). In his foreword to the last-named book Robert Weltsch (xiif.) describes the situation that made it impossible to risk armed resistance in Germany at that time; even the president of Czechoslovakia, Eduard Beneš (who was abandoned by his allies) did not dare to do so in 1938 even though he had a well-equipped army at his disposal: "The problem facing the Jews was therefore not an uprising or active resistance but the question how the Jews could behave in this completely new situation and what they could achieve if they were again expelled from the society around them which they had entered in the course of the emancipation." Regarding

Austria, cf. Herbert Rosenkranz, *Verfolgung und Selbstbehauptung: Die Juden in Österreich 1938–1945* (Vienna and Munich, 1978).

THE NEW CONCEPTION OF "KIDDUSH HASHEM," THE SANCTIFICATION OF THE DI-   393ff.
VINE NAME: Cf. Schaul Esch's fundamental essay "Ha-hayim Betokh Ha-Hurban"
(Hebr., the sanctification of life during the destruction) in the collection of his
Hebrew essays issued after his untimely death (*Studies in the Holocaust and Contem-
porary Jewry* [Jerusalem, 1963], 231–52); an English version ("The Dignity of the
Destroyed: Towards a Definition of the Period of the Holocaust") may be found in
Gutmann and Rothkirchen, *The Catastrophe of European Jewry* (Jerusalem, 1976),
346ff. On Nissenbaum, cf. 355f.

Concerning the problem of active resistance, cf. the Proceedings of the Yad Vashem
conference held in Jerusalem in April 1968, *Jewish Resistance during the Holocaust*
(Jerusalem, 1971), particularly Leni Yahil's preface, in which she says that Churchill's
watchword "Without victory there is no survival" became meaningful for the Jews in
the ghetto Europe in reverse form ("Without survival there is no victory").

THE PROBLEMATICAL NATURE OF THE JUDENRÄTE: This pervades the entire liter-   395ff.
ature about the epoch, and the discussion became especially heated after Hannah
Arendt's charges in her book on the Eichmann trial (cf. Part 2, p. 724). For literature
on this subject, cf. the bibliographies, the comprehensive books about the history
and nature of the epoch, and the pertinent articles in *EJJ*. In early April 1977 Yad
Vashem organized a scholarly conference in Jerusalem on the subject "The Judenrat
and the Patterns of Jewish Leadership in Nazi Europe 1933–1945"; thus far only the
summaries of the papers distributed at the beginning of the conference as a basis for
discussion and the reports in the Israeli press are available. The problems were
illuminated from all points of view by experts on the general subject and researchers
on specific aspects of it, with due attention to their general character as well as to
differences according to places, times, and personalities. Extreme variations in the
behavioral patterns of the Jewish leaders may be noted—from active or passive
support of armed resistance to concealment of the actual situation from the victims
facing deportation (e.g., by Rabbi Leo Baeck, who was widely respected and surely
cannot be accused of immorality, in Berlin and Theresienstadt). The leaders in the
latter category wished to ease for those who were doomed the emotional distress of
their last days and hours, just as most physicians charitably conceal the serious nature
of their illness from patients who cannot be saved from death. Whether they did not
thereby harm some individuals whom full knowledge of the situation might have
given the courage and skill to flee and save themselves is an open question, the
answer to which depends on fundamental ethical and practical attitudes.

THE JEWISH GHETTO POLICE: The judgment of survivors and historians on most   397f.
members of the Jewish ghetto police is uniformly damning. This ghetto police was
subordinate to the German police, and at times its members vied with their Nazi
colleagues in insensitivity, ruthlessness, and cruelty, often in hopes of saving themselves and their family from death. These hopes were usually dashed, because the
Nazis kept Jews alive only as long as they were useful to them and whenever they
could eliminated witnesses to their monstrous deeds as soon as possible. In some
places such scoundrels were sentenced to death by resistance fighters. While they
were alive they had various advantages in addition to their intoxication with power,
such as living accommodations, food, clothes, and the like.

"LIKE SHEEP TO THE SLAUGHTER": Cf. K. Shabbetai, *As Sheep to the Slaughter? The*   399f.
Myth of Cowardice (New York and Tel Aviv, 1963) (World Federation of Bergen-

Belsen Survivors Association); Joseph Tennenbaum, *Underground: The Story of a People* (New York, 1952). For the psychology of those under the reign of terror who surrendered to suffering and death without resisting, cf. Alexander Solzhenitsyn, *The Gulag Archipelago 1918–1956*, 1973ff. with its description of the system of terror in the prisons of Stalin's Russia, where untold millions of political prisoners let themselves be tortured to death.

402 THE ATTITUDE OF THE POLES TO THE JEWS: Cf. Emanuel Ringelblum, *Polish-Jewish Relations During the Second World War*, with an introduction and afterword by Joseph Kermish (Jerusalem, 1974). Concerning the Jewish resistance in France, cf. Anny Latour, *La Résistance juive en France (1940–1944)* (Paris, 1970).

402ff. THE WARSAW GHETTO UPRISING: Cf. the fine survey in *EJJ* 16:341–54 and 13:752–88, including a bibliography, as well as the accounts, sources, and references in the general presentations. Cf. especially Nachman Blumenthal and Joseph Kermish, *Resistance and Revolt in the Warsaw Ghetto: A Documentary History* (Jerusalem, 1965) (Hebr. with Eng. introduction and synopsis).

For the argumentation of the opponents of armed resistance, cf. the statements (quoted in Lucy S. Dawidowicz, *The War Against the Jews 1933–1945* [New York, 1975], 302) made on 21 July, 1942 by the pious Agudist Zisha Friedmann and the eminent historian Ignacy Schipper as representatives of the majority. Friedmann: "I believe in God and in a miracle. God will not let His people Israel be destroyed. We must wait and a miracle will occur. Fighting the Germans is senseless." Schipper: "Defense means destroying the entire Warsaw ghetto. . . . I believe that we can manage to save the core of the Warsaw ghetto. This is war and every people must make sacrifices. . . . Were I convinced that we would not succeed in saving the core of our people, I would have concluded otherwise." Soon thereafter Schipper perished in Treblinka.

403ff. CZERNIAKOW: Cf. Adam Czerniakow, *Warsaw Ghetto Diary* (Jerusalem, 1968) (Heb. with a facsimile of the Polish manuscript and English translation of the introduction). "*Es gibt keinen jüdischen Wohnbezirk in Warschau mehr*" is the illustrated report of the man who suppressed the uprising, General Juergen Stroop; the German edition was published at Darmstadt in 1960 and 1976; an English translation, entitled *The Stroop Report: The Warsaw Jewish Quarter Is No More!* appeared in New York in 1979 and is included in *A Holocaust Reader*, ed. by L. S. Dawidowicz (New York, 1976), 120–30.

In January 1943, at the beginning of the fights in the Warsaw Ghetto, the poet Yitzhak Kaznelson (who a year later, shortly before his death, was to write a "Ballad About the Murdered Jewish People," which was saved for posterity by his companion Miriam Nowicz) said to the fighters: "Let us be glad that we are preparing ourselves to meet the enemy with weapons in our hands and to die. Our armed struggle will be an inspiration to coming generations. Let our brothers in Eretz Yisrael serve as our models! They were not cowardly in danger and fought, few against many, and through their death they educated many generations of Jews. The Germans are killing millions of Jews, but they cannot subdue us. The Jewish people lives and will continue to live" (cited after the Hebr. ed., *Hashir al ha'am ha- yehudi sheneherag*, the song about the murdered Jewish people) (Tel Aviv, 5724/1964), foreword p. 3. Cf. also Yitzhak Kaznelson, *Vittel Diary* (22 May, 1943–16 Sept., 1943) (Tel Aviv, n.d.).

10

The State of Israel, the Jewish Diaspora, and the Jewish Question

Prefatory Note: This chapter and the following one are based less on synoptic literature (some references to which may be found below) than on my reading and my experiences, which I, an eyewitness, have absorbed, noted down, and commented upon daily and hourly during the past few decades. This presentation also includes what I learned from many conversations that I conducted in Israel and on journeys to Europe and America, some of them with leading personalities. I have always made notes about such experiences and conversations, but for obvious reasons the time is not yet ripe to publish them. The literature about the State of Israel, the ramifications of its existence, the problem of coexistence and conflict with the Arabs, the relationship of the Jewish world and the other states to Israel, as well as the literature about questions of politics and economy of the Middle East generally have assumed enormous dimensions. This is one of the most-discussed clusters of problems of our time. As with most contemporary problems, it is impossible to strive for anything approaching completeness in giving sources and bibliographies. One can only limit oneself to making some basic remarks on the subject and cite some fundamental works which contain further bibliographies. Of the specialized studies I shall mention only those that I found particularly useful and that will perhaps also be of use to my readers, as well as works from which I have quoted.

GENERAL LITERATURE: The most comprehensive information about the State of Israel may be found in *EJJ* 11 and individual articles of the other volumes; the most important of these have been issued in the Israel Pocket Library of the Keter Publishing House (fifteen small volumes plus one containing a Register). *HE* 6 and 17 (Register), as well as all other volumes, contain detailed references in Hebrew. Annual reports about Israel appear (in Hebrew) in the *Shnaton* (Year Book) of the State of Israel, and detailed statistical information may be found in the annual Statistical Abstract of Israel issued by the Central Bureau of Statistics in Jerusalem. Every year the Information Department of the Foreign Ministry publishes *Facts about Israel*, a book with maps, tables, and illustrations, and the State Comptroller publishes annual critical reports about administrative defects, along with demands that these be remedied. Since their foundation the World Zionist Organization and the Jewish Agency for Israel (formerly Jewish Agency for Palestine) have published the reports of the WZO to the Zionist congresses about the state of the movement and the settlement work done in the country, as well as the proceedings of the congresses (and sometimes of the meetings of the Actions Committee as well); similarly, the World Jewish Congress issues reports about its meetings. The *American Jewish Year Book* (Philadelphia) and the *Year Book of the Jewish Chronicle* (London) are each year devoted to the Jews of the world, and the *Zionist Year Book* of the Zionist Federation of Great Britain and Ireland (London) reports about Zionist organizations, events, and problems. Detailed information about the Middle East and its problems, organizations, and leading personalities may be found in the *Political Dictionary of the Middle East in the Twentieth Century,* ed. Y. Shimony and E. Levine (Jerusalem, 1972). Cf. further the abovementioned (Part 2, chap. 8) bibliography by Israel Klausner, *History of Zionism,* (Jerusalem, 1975), chaps. J ("Period of British Rule in Eretz Yisrael") and L ("The Zionist Movement after the Establishment of the State").

410   FOUNDING OF THE STATE OF ISRAEL: We are reprinting below the Declaration of Independence of the State of Israel (dated 14 May, 1948) in the English translation published in the *Encyclopedia of Zionism and Israel,* vol. 1.

> Eretz-Israel was the birthplace of the Jewish people. Here their spiritual, religious and political identity was shaped. Here they first attained to statehood, created cultural values of national and universal significance and gave to the world the eternal Book of Books.
>
> After being forcibly exiled from their land, the people kept faith with it throughout their Dispersion and never ceased to pray and hope for their return to it and for the restoration in it of their political freedom.
>
> Impelled by this historic and traditional attachment, Jews strove in every successive generation to re-establish themselves in their ancient homeland. In recent decades they returned in their masses. Pioneers, *ma'apilim* and defenders, they made deserts bloom, revived the Hebrew language, built villages and towns, and created a thriving community, controlling its own economy and culture, loving peace but knowing how to defend itself, bringing the blessings of progress to all the country's inhabitants, and aspiring towards independent nationhood.
>
> In the year 5657 (1897), at the summons of the spiritual father of the Jewish State, Theodor Herzl, the First Zionist Congress convened and proclaimed the right of the Jewish people to national rebirth in its own country.
>
> This right was recognized in the Balfour Declaration of the 2nd November, 1917, and re-affirmed in the Mandate of the League of Nations which, in particular, gave international sanction to the historic connection between the Jewish people and Eretz-Israel and to the right of the Jewish people to rebuild its National Home.
>
> The catastrophe which recently befell the Jewish people—the massacre of millions of Jews in Europe—was another clear demonstration of the urgency of solving the problem of its homelessness by re-establishing in Eretz-Israel the Jewish State, which would open the gates of the homeland wide to every Jew and confer upon the Jewish people the status of a fully-privileged member of the comity of nations.
>
> Survivors of the Nazi holocaust in Europe, as well as Jews from other parts of the world, continued to migrate to Eretz-Israel, undaunted by difficulties, restrictions and dangers, and never ceased to assert their right to a life of dignity, freedom and honest toil in their national homeland.
>
> In the Second World War, the Jewish community of this country contributed its full share to the struggle of the freedom- and peace-loving nations against the force of Nazi wickedness and, by the blood of its soldiers and its war effort, gained the right to be reckoned among the peoples who founded the United Nations.
>
> On the 29th November, 1947, the United Nations General Assembly passed a resolution calling for the establishment of a Jewish State in Eretz-Israel; the General Assembly required the inhabitants of Eretz-Israel to take such steps as were necessary on their part for the implementation of that resolution. This recognition by the United Nations of the right of the Jewish people to establish their State is irrevocable.
>
> This right is the natural right of the Jewish people to be masters of their own fate, like all other nations, in their own sovereign State.
>
> Accordingly we, members of the People's Council, representatives of the Jewish community of Eretz-Israel and of the Zionist movement, are here assembled on the day of the termination of the British Mandate over Eretz-Israel and, by virtue of our natural and historic right and on the strength of the resolution of the United Nations General Assembly, hereby declare the establishment of a Jewish State in Eretz-Israel, to be known as the State of Israel.
>
> We declare that, with effect from the moment of the termination of the Mandate, being

tonight, the eve of Sabbath, the 6th Iyar, 5708 (15th May, 1948), until the establishment of the elected, regular authorities of the State in accordance with the Constitution which shall be adopted by the Elected Constituent Assembly not later than the 1st October, 1948, the People's Council shall act as a Provisional Council of State, and its executive organ, the People's Administration, shall be the Provisional Government of the Jewish State, to be called "Israel."

The State of Israel will be open for Jewish immigration and for the Ingathering of the Exiles; it will foster the development of the country for the benefit of all inhabitants; it will be based on freedom, justice and peace as envisaged by the prophets of Israel; it will ensure complete equality of social and political rights of all its inhabitants irrespective of religion, race or sex; it will guarantee freedom of religion, conscience, language, education and culture; it will safeguard the Holy Places of all religions; and it will be faithful to the principles of the Charter of the United Nations.

The State of Israel is prepared to cooperate with the agencies and representatives of the United Nations in implementing the resolution of the General Assembly of the 29th November, 1947, and will take steps to bring about the economic union of the whole of Eretz-Israel.

We appeal to the United Nations to assist the Jewish people in the building-up of its State and to receive the State of Israel into the comity of nations.

We appeal—in the very midst of the onslaught launched against us now for months—to the Arab inhabitants of the State of Israel to preserve peace and participate in the upbuilding of the State on the basis of full and equal citizenship and due representation in all its provisional and permanent institutions.

We extend our hand to all neighbouring states and their peoples in an offer of peace and good neighbourliness, and appeal to them to establish bonds of cooperation and mutual help with the sovereign Jewish people settled in its own land. The State of Israel is prepared to do its share in common effort for the advancement of the entire Middle East.

We appeal to the Jewish people throughout the Diaspora to rally round the Jews of Eretz-Israel in the tasks of immigration and upbuilding and to stand by them in the great struggle for the realization of the age-old dream—the redemption of Israel. Placing our trust in the Rock of Israel, we affix our signatures to this proclamation at this session of the Provisional Council of State, on the soil of the Homeland, in the city of Tel-Aviv, on this Sabbath eve, the 5th day of Iyar, 5708 (14th May, 1948).

Daniel Auster
Mordecai Bentov
Itzhak Ben Zvi
Eliahu Berligne
Fritz [Peretz] Bernstein
Rabbi Z'ev [Wolf] Gold
Meir Grabovsky
Itzhak Grünbaum
Dr. Abraham Granowsky [Granott]
Meir David Loevenstein
Zvi Lurie
Golda Meyerson [Meir]
Nahum Y. Nir [Nahum Ya'akov Nir-Rafalkes]
Zvi Segal
Rabbi Yehuda Leib Hacohen-Fishman [Y'huda Leb HaKohen Maimon]
David Zvi Pinkas
Aharon Zisling

Moshe Kolodny [Kol]
David Ben-Gurion
Eliyahu Dobkin
Meir Wilner-Kovner
Zerah Wahrhaftig
Herzl Vardi
Rachel Cohen
Rabbi Kalman Kahana
Saadia Kobashi
Rabbi Yitzhak Meir Levin
Eliezer Kaplan
Avrahm Katznelson
Felix Rosenblüth [Pinhas Rosen]
David Remez
Berl Repetur
Mordekhai Shattner
Ben Zion Sternberg
B'khor Shitrit
(Hayim) Moshe Shapira
Moshe Shertok [Sharett]

Concerning the Declaration of Independence of the State of Israel, cf. Alex Bein, *Israel's Charter of Freedom* (Jerusalem, 1949; translated into numerous languages). Regarding the background and proclamation of the Declaration, cf. Zeev Sharef,

Three Days (Jerusalem, 1962; Hebr. ed., 1959, 1965). The story of how the State came into being has been told by Harry Sacher in *Israel: The Establishment of a State* (London, 1952) and Ben-Gurion in *The Jews in Their Land*, ed. Ben-Gurion (London, 1966), 320ff.

411   TEL AVIV: The name of the city, which was founded in 1909 as a Jewish suburb of the coastal town Jaffa, comes from Theodor Herzl's programmatic novel *Alt-Neuland* (1902). Nahum Sokolow had translated *Alt-Neu*, the play on words that Herzl had derived from a reinterpretation of the name of the ancient *Altneuschul* in Prague, into Hebrew as Tel Aviv, a place in Babylonia mentioned in Ezekiel 3:15. Sokolow gave it a new interpretation in accordance with modern linguistic usage: *tel*-mound of ruins, *aviv*-spring—that is, a hill of ruins that awakens to new life.

412   JEWISH REFUGEE CAMPS IN EUROPE. IMMIGRATION. RESISTANCE: Victor Gollancz, *"Nowhere to Lay Their Heads": The Jewish Tragedy and Its Solution* (Brimpton [England], 1945); *Reports of the Political Department and of the Rescue Committee of the Jewish Agency for Palestine to the 22nd Zionist Congress* (Jerusalem, 1946); *American Jewish Yearbook* 49–50 (Philadelphia, 1948, 1949); Ephraim Dekel, *Bricha: Flight to the Homeland* (New York, 1973); Yehuda Bauer, *From Diplomacy to Resistance: A History of Jewish Palestine 1939–1946* (Philadelphia, 1970); idem, *Flight and Rescue: Brichah* (New York, 1970); Yitzhak Grünbaum, *Biymei Hurban V'shoah* (Hebr., In the days of destruction) (Jerusalem, 5706/1946); Hayim Barlas, *Hazalah Biymei Shoah* (Hebr., Rescue in the days of catastrophe) (Ghetto Fighters' House, 5735/1975); Martin Hauser, *Auf dem Heimweg: Aus den Tagebüchern eines deutschen Juden 1929–1945* (Bonn and Bad Godesberg 1976), 163ff. (about the encounter between the Palestinian Jewish soldiers who had come to Europe with British army and the Jewish refugees).

413   THE STRUGGLE WITH THE MANDATORY GOVERNMENT FOR THE IMMIGRATION AND THE INTERPRETATION OF THE TERMS OF THE MANDATE FOR PALESTINE: There are sections on this subject in all books about the history of Zionism and the building of Palestine. The pertinent articles in *EJJ* have been reprinted in *Immigration and Settlement*, Israel Pocket Library 6 (Jerusalem, 1973). The subject recurs in all reports of the mandatory government and the Jewish Agency for Palestine to the Permanent Mandates Commission of the League of Nations and in the minutes of their meetings, in the reports of the Jewish Agency and the mandatory government to the commissions appointed by the British government, and more recently by the United Nations, to investigate the situation and the problems following the riots in Palestine, as well as in the reports of these investigating committees. Of these reports the following are particularly instructive: *Memorandum Submitted to the Palestine Royal Commission, Report, Cmd. 5479* (London, 1937)—the so-called Peel Report (after the chairman, William Robert Wellesley, Earl Peel). This report, the most painstaking attempt at a relatively objective view of the Palestinian problem and therefore still worth reading, proposed for the first time that the land be partitioned into politically independent Jewish and Arab areas; Government of Palestine, *A Survey of Palestine*, prepared for the information of the Anglo-American Committee of Inquiry, 2 vols. (Jerusalem, 1946); British Government, *The Political History of Palestine under British Administration. Memorandum . . . to the United Nations Special Committee on Palestine* (Jerusalem, 1947); the Jewish Agency for Palestine, *The Jewish Case Before the Anglo-American Committee of Inquiry on Palestine: Statements and Memoranda* (Jerusalem, 1947); The Jewish Agency for Palestine, *Memoranda and Statements . . . to the United Nations Special Committee on Palestine* (Jerusalem, 1947).

LEGAL AND ILLEGAL IMMIGRATION: The Hebrew terms for this, which have become   414
part of general usage, are as follows: *aliyah*, actually "ascent," at first used in its
literal, physical-geographical meaning as ascent to the Jewish highlands and Jerusalem (800 meters high!), later as immigration to the Holy Land and also as a spiritual
ascent; since the beginning of the Zionist immigration it has been the general term
for Jewish immigration; *ha'apalah*, actually "daredevil mountain-climbing," later
applied to the "illegal" immigration that entailed much danger and hence was
perceived as a daring *aliyah*. Cf. also the Hebr. M.A. thesis by Yitzhak Avnery on the
development of the idea of *ha'apalah* (Jerusalem, 1969). A detailed contemporary
account of British policy and the Jews' struggle with it since the outbreak of World
War II, one that is based on the documents available at the time and the author's
experiences in the country, may be found in Daphne Trevor's book *Under the White
Paper: Some Aspects of British Administration in Palestine from 1939 to 1947* (Jerusalem, 1948). A fair presentation of the entire period of British mandatory rule over
Palestine is given by the British writer and historian Christopher Sykes in his book
Cross Roads to Israel: Palestine from Balfour to Begin (London, 1965; paperback ed.,
1967).

THE LEGAL IMMIGRATION AFTER THE FOUNDATION OF THE STATE: Between 1948   416
and 1979 the Jewish population of the State of Israel increased fivefold (from 650,000
to over 3 million). Immigration accounted for about half of this increase, and the other
half was due to the natural growth of the population. Thus an ever-increasing part of
the population was born in the country. The immigration took place in waves, and in
between there always were a certain number of emigrants. In some years of crisis,
immigration and emigration balanced each other, or emigration exceeded immigration. However, the statistics are never definitive, because frequently emigrants
return to the country after some years. Between May 1958 and the end of that year,
during the first and greatest wave of immigration, more than 686,000 immigrants
(*olim* in Hebrew) came to the country; of these about half were from Europe and the
other half from Asia and Africa. In many instances the Jewish communities settled in
Arab countries emigrate almost in their entirety, for the most part to Israel. Thus the
immigrants to Israel include about 10,000 from Syria and Lebanon, 129,000 from
Iraq, over 50,000 from Yemen, Aden, and Morocco, 727 from Algeria and Tunisia,
over 35,000 from Libya, and around 30,000 from Egypt and the Sudan. Around
50,000 Jews came from Iran and 21,000 from India. The number of immigrants from
Eastern European countries was always great when they were permitted to emigrate;
there ideological and political motives always played a role in the permission,
prohibition, and the limitation of emigration to Israel. In all about 100,000 Jews came
from the U.S.S.R., 162,000 from Poland, 240,000 from Rumania, about 40,000 from
Bulgaria, more than 22,000 from Czechoslovakia, 27,000 from Hungary, and over
8,000 from Yugoslavia. Forty thousand Jews immigrated from West European countries, around 30,000 from the United States and Canada, and an equal number from
South American countries.

THE MILITARY STRUGGLES: The most comprehensive book about these is Netanel   417f.
Lorch, *One Long War: Arab versus Jew since 1920* (Jerusalem, 1967). The author is
one of the greatest experts on the subject, having headed the army's department of
military history for some time; he later entered the diplomatic service and today is
First Secretary of the Knesset (the Israeli parliament) in Jerusalem. Concerning the
War of Independence, cf. his book *The Edge of the Sword* (Jerusalem, 1958).
Regarding the siege of Jerusalem, cf. Dov Joseph (at that time the civilian commander
of Jerusalem), *The Faithful City: The Siege of Jerusalem 1948* (New York, 1960).
Concerning the Six Day War, cf. Randolph S. Churchill and Winston S. Churchill,

The Six Day War (London, 1967). The attitude of young Israeli fighters toward the war and toward the Arabs is set forth in *The Seventh Day: Soldiers Talk About the Six Day War, Recorded and Edited by a Group of Young Kibbutz Members* (London: Penguin Books, 1971) (the original Hebr. edition appeared shortly after the war, in 1967, under the title *Siakh Lokhamim*). Cf. also the note in Part 1, p. 418. Concerning the history of the defense before the State, cf. the six-volume *Sefer Ha-Haganah* (Hebr.) (Tel Aviv, 1954–72). The 3-volume Hebrew anthology *Sefer Hagevurah* (Book of Heroism), edited by Israel Helprin (Tel Aviv, 1941–50) deals with Jews as fighters in the course of their history. It has been said that "success in war has for most peoples a magical prestige" (Brogan, *New York Times*, 15 October, 1944, quoted in *Forum* [Jerusalem], 3 November, 1944, 9); this, of course, was the case among the Jews and Israelis as well, and this "magical prestige: of the victorious fighters did not always turn out to be a good thing. Thus they have always opposed the transfiguration of combat and war out of bitter necessity into an ideal, as has happened in many countries. In Israel there is virtually no literature that idealizes war. However, this respect for the heroic martial type contributed a great deal to the prestige of the Israelis and the State of Israel, at least in the early years. During the past two decades, however, it has been distorted into a symbol of imperialistic conquest and capitalism that was identified with Zionism, the national movement of liberation. This was due to the problems created by the territories captured in the Six Day War, the influence of Arab propaganda (which was supported by an economic boycott and terrorist acts against the civilian population), and the ideological trappings of the "New Left" (whose slogans all too frequently conceal the anti-Semitic tradition).

422   THE JEW AS AGRICULTURIST: Concerning the Jews' construction work in the land and the State of Israel there is an enormous literature of all kinds, but only relatively few books are based on a thorough knowledge of the subject. The surveys and reference works given at the beginning of the notes for this chapter are the most dependable. In my book *The Return to the Soil* (Jerusalem, 1952) I attempted to present the history of the construction work up to the early 1950s; a second volume that concerns itself particularly with the period since the foundation of the state and its problems, appeared in Hebrew in 1982 under the title "Immigration and Settlement in the State of Israel."

The founding of the State of Israel was preceded by the far less noticed constructive work of two generations, pioneer work carried on under very difficult conditions, which the State was able to build on and without which its existence and the absorption and productive settlement of the mass of immigrants would not have been possible. The financial help of Western Jewry, which was given to an ever-increasing extent, also made a substantial contribution to the success of this work. No other people has given such comprehensive aid to its far-away members.

The work of building the country furnished irrefutable proof, if such proof was still needed, that the life of the Jews in the Diaspora was not the life of parasites, as the anti-Semites described it, convincing many others—both Jews and non-Jews. According to the definition of the biologist Caullery (cited in Part 2, pp. 715f.) a parasite is incapable of living independently and dies when it is separated from its host . . .

On the other hand, the life of the Jews among a great variety of nations, countries, and civilizations and the experiences and traditions acquired thereby contributed substantially to the dynamism and productivity of the work in the country. Thus every class of immigrants was able to make a singular contribution to it. As Herzl had already foreseen, the Jews' qualities, abilities, and customs were now applied productively to the building of their own country. To be sure, these different traditions frequently led to all kinds of conflicts—a phenomenon that is to be observed in all countries of immigration but is felt to be particularly hurtful in Israel because it seems to be in conflict with the community of origin and aims. (Cf. also the remarks about the Jewish consciousness of history in Part 1, chap. 11.)

"IDENTITY": The discussion of this concept has become so general and the essays 424f. published about it in books and all Jewish journals have become so numerous that here we cannot attempt to list even the most important references. The debate about what it means to be Jewish increasingly coalesces with the debates about the nature of the Jewish question and the tasks of the Zionist movement after the foundation of the State of Israel. Has Zionism completed its task with this founding, as some believe, or is it the beginning of a new task that is scarcely less important for the "solution" of the Jewish question—to educate the Jews of the world to a clear avowal of belonging to the Jewish people, one that goes beyond support of the State of Israel (which is given by many non-Zionist Jews as well)? In point of fact, in recent years a number of big Jewish organizations in America that had formerly rejected Zionism have embraced it and become members of the Zionist Organization, particularly the associations of Conservative and Reform congregations.

The problem of identity is discussed mainly among intellectuals who are not affiliated with one of the political or religious organizations. To be sure, this group is increasingly composed of the young generation of Jews, at least on the basis of their training at the universities. Concerning the freedom of decision and the normalcy which the founding of the State of Israel has given to the Diaspora in this regard, cf. the section "Exile *(Galut)* or Diaspora?" in Part 1, chap. 11, pp. 461ff.

Among the more recent attempts at a comprehensive presentation I shall mention André Neher, "The Dialectics of Jewish Identity: Beyond Religion and Secularism," in *Forum on the Jewish People, Zionism and Israel* (1975), 102–11; Albert Memmi, *Portrait of a Jew* (New York, 1962); William S. Schlamm, *Wer ist Jude: Ein Selbstgespräch* (Stuttgart, 1964). André Neher begins his essay with the following statement: "Jewish Identity is a concept that has been tossed about so much in the last years that it is now hardly more than a cliché."

THE ARAB QUESTION: So much has been, and is being, written and spoken every day 434ff. about the so-called Arab question, of late particularly as the problem of the Arab "Palestinians," that we can here give only a few guideposts to the literature. Actually, there are few writings that treat the history and problematical nature of this conflict knowledgeably and with a willingness to understand the various standpoints and interests, all of which have a certain justification. To my knowledge, there have been no serious attempts on the part of Arab authors (at least in languages I can read, which unfortunately do not include Arabic). On the Jewish side there have been a number of very penetrating investigations, and there are a considerable number of scholars who have specialized in this field. Among these there are quite a few who carry their fairness to the point of presenting the Arab or Arab-Palestinian standpoint with greater understanding than their own. The latter often seems suspect to them because they are afraid of making an unjust judgment or because they have been influenced by leftist or "new leftist" thinking that generally bears the stamp of Soviet Russian ideologies and has from the beginning equated Zionism with British imperialism and regarded it as the instrument of the latter's power. Of late this view has been transferred to American "imperialism" in an effort to hide the Soviet Russian imperialism which is furthering the imperialistic aims of Czarist Russia in geopolitical fashion, having replaced pan-Slavic Messianism with the Marxist-Leninist kind. Those observers and scholars who do not follow a party line are more inclined to understand the "normal" arguments of the Arabs and "Palestinians" than what appears from the usual viewpoints as the "abnormal" ones of the Jews and Israelis. They also find it easy to admonish the Jews to make compromises and renunciations, for haven't the bad experiences in their long history and their high cultural standards made them the "wise heads" that in case of doubt give in (to vary an old proverb)? In all this they tend to ignore the map, on which Palestine or Eretz Yisrael constitutes only a narrow strip of borderland (measured by larger countries), nor do they generally consider the fact that threats to the Arabs, to the extent that they exist in reality and not only in fearful fantasies, never mean a danger to their physical existence, as they do in the case of the Jews in the country.

Following these preliminary remarks and reservations I shall give some references in addition to those already cited:

Israel Pocket Atlas and Handbook, compiled by Hermann M. Z. Meyer (Jerusalem, 1961); James Parkes, *Whose Land: A History of the Peoples of Palestine* (London: Penguin, 1970); S. D. Goitein, *Jews and Arabs through the Ages* (New York, 1955, Paperback ed., 1964); George E. Kirk, *A Short History of the Middle East* (London, 1964); Shimon Shamir, *A Modern History of the Arabs in the Middle East* (Hebr.) (Tel Aviv, 1968); A. H. Hourani, *Syria and Lebanon: A Political Essay* (London, 1946); W. G. Smith, *Der Islam in der Gegenwart* (Frankfurt a. M.: Fischer Bücherei, 1963); *The Israel-Arab Reader: A Documentary History of the Middle East Conflict*, ed. Walter Laqueur (New York: Bantam Books, 1969) (a good compilation of basic documents and various views of the problem); *Israel, the Arabs and the Middle East*, ed. Irving Howe and Carl Gershman (New York: Bantam Books, 1972); *Israel and the Arabs: A Handbook of Basic Information*, ed. Julian J. Landau (Jerusalem: Ministry of Foreign Affairs, 1971); *The Historical Connection of the Jewish People with Palestine: Memorandum Submitted to the Palestine Royal Commission* (Jerusalem: Jewish Agency for Palestine, 1936); The General Council (Vaad Leumi) of the Jewish Community of Palestine, *Three Historical Memoranda* (Jerusalem, 1947); Susan Lee Hattis, *The Bi-National Idea in Palestine during Mandatory Times* (Haifa, 1970); Arthur Ruppin, *Memoirs, Diaries, Letters*, ed. and with an introd. by Alex Bein, afterword by Moshe Dayan (London and Jerusalem, 1971) (about the attempts to reach an understanding with the Arabs, the B'rith Shalom association founded for that purpose, etc.); David Ben-Gurion, *Talks with Arab Leaders* (Hebr.) (Tel Aviv, 1967); *To Make War or Make Peace—Proceedings: The International Symposium on Inevitable War or Initiatives for Peace* (Tel Aviv, 1969); Ori Steudel, *The Minorities in Israel: Trends in the Development of the Arab and Druse Communities 1948–1973* (Jerusalem, 1973); Saul Colbi, *Short History of Christianity in the Holy Land* (Jerusalem, 1965); Edward Atiyah, *The Arabs* (London: Penguin Books, 1955); Anthony Nutting, *Die arabische Welt, von Mohammed bis Nassar* (ca. 1965); George Antonius, *The Arab Awakening* (London, 1946; New York, 1965); T. E. Lawrence, *Seven Pillars of Wisdom* (New York, 1926; 1965); I. Zollschan, *The Arabian Race of Palestine*, offprint from *The Jewish Forum* (London), August 1946; P. A. Alsberg, *The Arab Question in the Politics of the Zionist Executive before the First World War* (Hebr.), offprint from hivat-Zion 4 (Jerusalem, 1957); Moldechai Nisan, *The Arab-Israeli Conflict: A Political Guide for the Perplexed* (Jerusalem, 1977); Herbert Parzen, *The Arab Refugees: Their Origin and Projection into a Problem*, offprint from *Jewish Social Studies* 31, no. 4(1969): 292–323; Walter Pinner, *How Many Refugees? A Critical Study of UNRWA's Statistics and Reports* (London, 1960); idem, *The Legend of the Arab Refugees* (Tel Aviv, 1967); Yehuda Z. Blum, *Secure Boundaries and Middle East Peace* (Jerusalem, 1971); *Secure and Recognized Boundaries* [maps with explanations] (Jerusalem: Carta, 1971); Moshe Maoz, *The Image of the Jew in Official Arab Literature and Communications Media*, (Jerusalem, 1976); *Arab Theologians on Jews and Israel*, ed. D. F. Green (Geneva, 1971): Y. Harkabi, *Fedayeen Action and Arab Strategy* (London, 1968); idem, *Arab Attitudes to Israel* (Jerusalem, 1972); idem, "The Palestinians in the Israel-Arab Conflict," in *Midstream* (March 1970), 3ff., 14: "The Palestinian (Arab) National Covenant," July 1968; idem, *Palestinians and Israel* (Jerusalem, 1974); Menahem Milson, *Medieval and Modern Intellectual Traditions in the Arab*

World (Hebr.) (Tel Aviv, 1973); Shlomo Avineri, *Modernization and Arab Society: Some Reflections* (Jerusalem, 1972); idem, *Zionism as a Movement of National Liberation* (Jerusalem, ca. 1976); Dan Yahalom, *File on Arab Terrorism* [maps with explanations] (Jerusalem: Carta, 1973); C. C. Aronsfeld, "The 'Protocols' Among Arabs," in: *Patterns of Prejudice* 9, no. 4 (1975): Marie Syrkin, "The Elders of Araby," in *Midstream* (April 1975); C. Luca, "Legal Discrimination Among Arabs," *Patterns of Prejudice* 10, no. 4 (1976): 1–14; Albert Memmi, *Who is an Arab Jew?* (Jerusalem, 1975); Haytham Al-Ayubi, *Future Arab Strategy in the Light of the Fourth War*, introduction and commentary by Y. Harcaby (Jerusalem: Israel Universities Study Group for Middle Eastern Affairs, 1974); David Gutmann, "The Palestinian Myth," *Commentary* 60, no. 4 (1975): 43–47; A. L. Tibawi, "Visions of the Return: The Palestine Arab Refugees in Arabic Poetry and Art," *Middle East Journal* 18 (1963): 507–26; Bernard Lewis [one of the greatest experts on the problem], "Settling the Arab-Israeli Conflict," *Commentary* 63, no. 6 (1977): 50–56; Y. Harkabi, *Temurot basichsuch Yisrael-Arav* [Hebr., *Changes in the Israeli-Arab Conflict*]. (Tel Aviv, 1978); Yehuda Z. Blum, "Grundzüge des arabisch-israelischen Konflikts," in *Aus Politik und Zeitgeschichte* B 17/77 (30 April, 1977); Christoph von Imhoff, "Des Orients längste Krise," in *Aus Politik und Zeitgeschichte* B 24/76 (12 June, 1976).

THE NEGOTIATIONS WITH THE ARABS, 1913–1914: Cf. the documents in the above-   435f. mentioned article by P. Alsberg.

AGREEMENT BETWEEN FEISAL AND WEIZMANN, JANUARY 1919: Reprinted in the   436 abovementioned *Israel-Arab Reader*, ed. W. Laqueur, 18–20. Two months afterward, on 3 March, 1919, Feisal wrote a letter to the American Supreme Court Justice Felix Frankfurter, who was participating at the Peace Conference in Paris as a member of the Zionist delegation, in which he expressly gave his consent to the Zionist endeavors and characterized the Zionist demands as moderate. In the Central Zionist Archives in Jerusalem I was able to verify the authenticity of the documents, which the Arabs have occasionally doubted or disputed.* I published a facsimile of Feisal's letter to Frankfurter in the report of the Central Zionist Archives to the 26th Zionist Congress. Cf. *Central Zionist Archives Report of Activities*, April 1960 to March 1964, Jerusalem, 1964 (the facsimile appears in the middle of the report). I shall reprint both documents here:

Agreement Between Emir Feisal and
Dr. Weizmann, January 3, 1919

His Royal Highness the Emir Feisal, representing and acting on behalf of the Arab Kingdom of Hedjaz, and Dr. Chaim Weizmann, representing and acting on behalf of the Zionist Organisation, mindful of the racial kinship and ancient bonds existing between the Arabs and the Jewish people, and realising that the surest means of working out the consummation of their national aspirations is through the closest possible collaboration in the development of the Arab State and Palestine, and being desirous further of confirming the good understanding which exists between them, have agreed upon the following Articles:

ARTICLE I

The Arab State and Palestine in all their relations and understandings shall be controlled by the most cordial goodwill and understanding, and to this end Arab and Jewish duly accredited agents shall be established and maintained in the respective territories.

*Ten years later Feisal (1855–1933), who became King of Iraq in 1921, had it proclaimed in his name that "His Majesty does not remember having written anything of that kind with his knowledge."

ARTICLE II

Immediately following the completion of the deliberations of the Peace Conference, the definite boundaries between the Arab State and Palestine shall be determined by a Commission to be agreed upon by the parties hereto.

ARTICLE III

In the establishment of the Constitution and Administration of Palestine all such measures shall be adopted as will afford the fullest guarantees for carrying into effect the British Government's Declaration of the 2nd of November, 1917.

ARTICLE IV

All necessary measures shall be taken to encourage and stimulate immigration of Jews into Palestine on a large scale, and as quickly as possible to settle Jewish immigrants upon the land through closer settlement and intensive cultivation of the soil. In taking such measures the Arab peasant and tenant farmers shall be protected in their rights, and shall be assisted in forwarding their economic development.

ARTICLE V

No regulation nor law shall be made prohibiting or interfering in any way with the free exercise of religion; and further the free exercise and enjoyment of religious profession and worship without discrimination or reference shall forever be allowed. No religious test shall ever be required for the exercise of civil or political rights.

ARTICLE VI

The Mohammedan Holy Places shall be under Mohammedan control.

ARTICLE VII

The Zionist Organisation proposes to send to Palestine a Commission of experts to make a survey of the economic possibilities of the country, and to report upon the best means for its development. The Zionist Organisation will place the aforementioned Commission at the disposal of the Arab State for the purpose of a survey of the economic possibilities of the Arab State and to report upon the best means for its development. The Zionist Organisation will use its best efforts to assist the Arab State in providing the means for developing the natural resources and economic possibilities thereof.

ARTICLE VIII

The parties hereto agree to act in complete accord and harmony on all matters embraced herein before the Peace Congress.

ARTICLE IX

Any matters of dispute which may arise between the contracting parties shall be referred to the British Government for arbitration.

Given under our hand at London, England, the third day of January, one thousand nine hundred and nineteen.

CHAIM WEIZMANN
FEISAL IBN-HUSSEIN

Reservation by the Emir Feisal

If the Arabs are established as I have asked in my manifesto of January 4th addressed to the British Secretary of State for Foreign Affairs, I will carry out what is written in this agreement. If changes are made, I cannot be answerable for failing to carry out this agreement.

FEISAL IBN-HUSSEIN

FEISAL-FRANKFURTER CORRESPONDENCE
Emir Feisal to Felix Frankfurter
Delegation Hedjazienne, Paris, March 3, 1919.

Dear Mr. Frankfurter: I want to take this opportunity of my first contact with American Zionists to tell you what I have often been able to say to Dr. Weizmann in Arabia and Europe.

We feel that the Arabs and Jews are cousins in race, having suffered similar oppressions at the hands of powers stronger than themselves, and by a happy coincidence have been able to take the first step towards the attainment of their national ideals together.

We Arabs, especially the educated among us, look with the deepest sympathy on the Zionist movement. Our deputation here in Paris is fully acquainted with the proposals submitted yesterday by the Zionist Organization to the Peace Conference, and we regard them as moderate and proper. We will do our best, in so far as we are concerned, to help them through: we will wish the Jews a most hearty welcome home.

With the chiefs of your movement, especially with Dr. Weizmann, we have had and continue to have the closest relations. He has been a great helper of our cause, and I hope the Arabs may soon be in a position to make the Jews some return for their kindness. We are working together for a reformed and revived Near East, and our two movements complete one another. The Jewish movement is national and not imperialist. Our movement is national and not imperialist, and there is room in Syria for us both. Indeed I think that neither can be a real success without the other. People less informed and less responsible than our leaders and yours, ignoring the need for cooperation of the Arabs and Zionists have been trying to exploit the local difficulties that must necessarily arise in Palestine in the early stages of our movements. Some of them have, I am afraid, misrepresented your aims to the Arab peasantry, and our aims to the Jewish peasantry, with the result that interested parties have been able to make capital out of what they call our differences.

I wish to give you my firm conviction that these differences are not on questions of principle, but on matters of detail such as must inevitably occur in every contact of neighbouring peoples, and as are easily adjusted by mutual goodwill. Indeed nearly all of them will disappear with fuller knowledge.

I look forward, and my people with me look forward, to a future in which we will help you and you will help us, so that the countries in which we are mutually interested may once again take their places in the community of civilised peoples of the world.

Believe me,
    Yours sincerely, (Sgd.) FEISAL

Felix Frankfurter to Emir Feisal 5th March, 1919

Royal Highness:
Allow me, on behalf of the Zionist Organisation, to acknowledge your recent letter with deep appreciation.

Those of us who come from the United States have already been gratified by the friendly relations and the active cooperation maintained between you and the Zionist leaders, particularly Dr. Weizmann. We knew it could not be otherwise; we knew that the aspirations of the Arab and the Jewish peoples were parallel, that each aspired to reestablish its nationality in its own homeland, each making its own distinctive contribution to civilisation, each seeking its own peaceful mode of life. The Zionist leaders and the Jewish people for whom they speak have watched with satisfaction the spiritual vigour of the Arab movement. Themselves seeking justice, they are anxious that the just national aims of the Arab people be confirmed and safeguarded by the Peace Conference.

We knew from your acts and your past utterances that the Zionist movement—in other words the national aims of the Jewish people—had your support and the support of the Arab people for whom you speak. These aims are now before the Peace Conference as definite proposals by the Zionist Organisation. We are happy indeed that you consider these proposals moderate and proper , and that we have in you a staunch supporter for their realisation. For both the Arab and the Jewish peoples there are difficulties ahead—difficulties that challenge the united statesmanship of Arab and Jewish leaders. For it is no easy task to rebuild two great civilisations that have been suffering oppression and misrule for centuries. We each have our difficulties we shall work out as friends, friends who are animated by similar purposes, seeking a free and full development for the two neighbouring peoples. The Arabs and Jews are neighbours in territory; we cannot but live side by side as friends.

Very respectfully, (Sgd.) FELIX FRANKFURTER

437 FRENCH ANTI-SEMITIC INFLUENCES: W. Laqueur, *History of Zionism* (New York, 1972), chap. 5 ("The Unseen Question"), 212. Cf. also A. Ruppin, *Dreissig Jahre Aufbau in Palästina* (Berlin, 1937), 84ff.

439f. ORIGIN OF STATES THROUGH CONQUEST AND SETTLEMENT: This favorite argument against the historical connectedness of the Jewish people with the Land of Israel is always forgotten where the West Jordan areas occupied by Israel as a result of the Six Day War of 1967 are concerned. In the heated debates one often gets the impression that the existing states have forgotten their own history and are living on the areas peacefully apportioned to them at the beginning of the world without ever having fought a war for them, let alone having made conquests for the enlargement of their ancestral territories.

445 THE SPECIAL STATUS OF JERUSALEM: Even Rome does not have as close a connection with Christianity as Jerusalem does with Judaism as a religion and as a people, in actuality and reality and as a symbol.

11
Retrospect and Prospect

Prefatory Note: The remarks in this chapter, with their recapitulation of the material presented in the preceding chapters and an attempt at a prognosis for the future, must of course be limited to what was typical and decisive for Jewry as a whole. It would be fascinating to demonstrate these typical elements in the variations of Jewish life and the Jewries of different countries, in their stratifications and currents—that is, to show the common features in this multifarious variety. But this would require another book—if one does not wish to get entangled in the jumble of the dazzling, "brilliant" formulations which in reality are frequently only stylized commonplace opinions in "intellectual" vogue language or in scholarly jargon. (This, of course, is not meant to indicate that there are no ingenious, profound, spirited, and elegantly presented essays about these problems.)

LITERATURE: Here I must refer principally to the well-known encyclopedias and the literature given there, as well as in the preceding chapters. In addition to these I shall list a number of books and articles that I found particularly useful or that supplement and extend what I have said in my presentation: David Ben-Gurion, ed. *The Jews in Their Land* (London, 1966) (Epilogue by Ben-Gurion, 374ff.); Yaacov Herzog, *A People that Dwells Alone: Speeches and Writings,* ed. M. Louvish (London, 1975); Isaiah Berlin, *Jewish Slavery and Emancipation* (New York, 1961); Jochanan Bloch, *Das anstössige Volk: Über die weltliche Glaubensgemeinschaft der Juden* (Heidelberg, 1964); Hermann Greive, *Theologie und Ideologie* (Heidelberg, 1969); Theodor Filthaut, *Israel in der christlichen Unterweisung* (Munich, 1963); Charles Y. Glock and Rodney Stark, *Christian Belief and Anti-Semitism* (New York, 1969); Hayim Yachil et al., *The Israel-Diaspora Relationships: A Starting Point about the Future of Israel,* ed. Gabriel Shefer (Hebr.) (Jerusalem, 1974); Moshe Davis, ed., *Publications of the Study Circle on Diaspora Jewry* (Hebr.), Series 1–7 (Jerusalem, 1966–75); Ehud Ben Ezer, ed., *Unease in Zion* (New York and Jerusalem, 1974) (interviews of the author with leading personalities with a great variety of views and orientations); Michael Selzer, ed., *Zionism Reconsidered: The Rejection of Jewish Normalcy* (London, 1970); Nathan Rotenstreich, *Tradition and Reality: The Impact of History on Modern Jewish Thought* (New York, 1972); M. J. Berdyczewski, "Zur Klärung," in *Die Stimme der Wahrheit,* ed. Lazarus Schön (Würzburg, 1905), 279–87; J. L. Talmon, *Israel Among the Nations* (Jerusalem, 1970); Joachim Prinz and Louis A. Pincus, *Israel and the Diaspora* (Geneva, 1973); Simon Rawidowicz, "Jerusalem and Babylon," *Judaism* (Spring 1969), 131–42; Simon A. Herman, *Israelis and Jews: The Continuity of an Identity* (Philadelphia, 1971); Horace M. Kallen, *Utopians at Bay* (New York, 1958); Richard N. Juliani, "The Use of Archives in the Study of Immigration and Ethnicity," *American Archivist* 39 (1976): 469–77 (and the bibliography there); Eran Laor, *Orientalische Renaissance: Ein Brief an die Juden* (Geneva, 1956); Joseph L. Blau, ed., *Modern Varieties of Judaism* (New York, 1966); Uri Avnery, *Israel without Zionism: A Plan for Peace in the Middle East* (New York, 1968),

1971; Meir Kahane, *Never Again! A Program for Survival* (New York, 1971); Eliezer Livneh, *Israel and the Crisis of Western Civilization* (Hebr.) (Tel Aviv, 1972); Hugo Bergmann, "Pluralistischer Zionismus," *MB* (Tel Aviv), 5 September, 1975; Nahum Goldmann, *Israel muss umdenken: Die Lage der Juden 1976* (Hamburg, 1976); Oscar I. Janowski, ed., *The American Jew: A Reappraisal* (Philadelphia, 1964); Moshe Davis, *The Emergence of Conservative Judaism* (Philadelphia, 1963); Julian Morgenstern, *As a Mighty Stream: The Progress of Judaism through the Ages* (Philadelphia, 1949); Yehuda Bauer, *My Brother's Keeper: A History of the Joint Distribution Committee* (Philadelphia, 1974); E. J. James, ed., *The Immigrant Jew in America* (New York, 1907); Ben Halpern, *The American Jew: A Zionist Analysis* (New York, 1956); C. Bezalel Sherman, *The Jew within American Society: A Study in Ethnic Individuality* (Detroit, 1965); *Dispersion and Unity. Journal on Zionism and the Jewish World*, no. 15/16, Jerusalem 1972; *Jerusalem Quarterly* (1976 ff.); Yehuda Bauer, *The Holocaust in Historical Perspective* (Washington, 1978); Alice and Roy Eckard, "The Theological and Moral Implications of the Holocaust," in *Christian Attitudes on Jews and Judaism* 52, (February 1977); Arthur Hertzberg, *Being Jewish in America: The Modern Experience* (New York, 1979); Ernst Vogt, *Israel—Kritik von links: Dokumentation einer Entwicklung* (Wuppertal, 1976); *Holocaust: Materialien zu einer amerikanischen Fernsehserie über die Judenverfolgung im Dritten Reich*, compiled by W. van Kampen, (Düsseldorf; Landeszentrale für politische Bildung, 1978). The concluding quotation from Goethe (1:472) is drawn from the chapter on the poet in Friedrich Meinecke's *Die Entstehung des Historismus* (Munich and Berlin, 1936), 2:606.

Chronology

Ca. 1900–1700 B.C.E.	Age of the patriarchs (Abraham, Isaac, Jacob).
Ca. 1300–1200 B.C.E.	"Exodus from Egypt." Moses. Revelation on Mt. Sinai. Monotheism. Conquest of Canaan as the "Promised Land" by the Israelite tribes under Yehoshua bin-Nun.
Ca. 1020–930 B.C.E.	Kingdom (Saul, David, Solomon).
8th century B.C.E.	The Jewish prophets Amos, Hosea, Isaiah, Micah.
722 B.C.E.	Conquest of Samaria by the Assyrians: end of the Northern state Israel. The state Judah under the hegemony of Assyria and (626) Babylonia.
586 B.C.E.	Conquest of Jerusalem by Nebuchadnezzar. Destruction of the First Temple. Mass deportation of the Judean population to Babylonia ("Babylonian Exile"). The prophets Jeremiah and Ezekiel. Establishment of the Egyptian Diaspora by Jewish refugees from Judea.
538–332 B.C.E.	Persian rule over Babylonia (Mesopotamia) and the Near East. Return of part of Jewry from Babylonia. Building of the Second Temple and the Judean state.
332 B.C.E.	Conquest of Jerusalem by Alexander the Great.
332–141 B.C.E.	Greek (Hellenistic) hegemony (213–198 rule of the Ptolemaic dynasty, after 198 of the Seleucids). Greek translation of the Bible (Septuagint).
167–141 B.C.E.	Struggle for liberation of the Maccabees (Hasmoneans).
141–37 B.C.E.	Hasmonean dynasty.
63 B.C.E.	Capture of Jerusalem by Pompey. Roman rule. Deportation of Jewish prisoners of war and first Jewish settlements in Rome.
37 B.C.E.–70 C.E.	Herodian dynasty.
30 C.E.	Crucifixion of Jesus under the Roman procurator Pontius Pilate.
47–64 C.E.	Missionary activity of the apostle Paul (Saul of Tarsus).
66 C.E.	Beginning of the Jewish uprising against Rome.
70 C.E.	Conquest of Jerusalem and destruction of the Second Temple by Titus. Establishment of the Sanhedrin in Jabneh by Johanan ben Zakkai.

73 C.E.	Fall of Masada, the last fortress.
132–135 C.E.	Bar Kochba rebellion.
210	Redaction of the Mishnah.
212	Granting of Roman citizenship to all freemen in the empire, including the Jews.
313	Milan edict of Constantine the Great for the protection of Christians.
325	Council of Nicaea.
354–430	The Doctor of the Church Aurelius Augustinus.
405	Completion of the translation of the Bible into Latin by Jerome (Vulgate).
425	Abolition of the Jewish patriarchate in Palestine.
438	Codex Theodosianus: The anti-Jewish laws are made part of the official Roman legal code.
Ca. 500	Completion of the Babylonian Talmud, which becomes the foundation of Jewish life.
528–536	Justinian's Corpus Juris: Adoption and expansion of the anti-Jewish legislation—the legal basis for the Roman empire and the European successor states.
589	Spanish-Visigothic Council of Toledo: Jews are forbidden to hold public office.
622	Mohammed's flight to Medina (Hegira).
638	Conquest of Jerusalem by Moslem Arabs.
711	Beginning of the Arab-Islamic conquest of Spain.
Ca. 740	Conversion of the Khazars to Judaism.
10th–12th century	Jewish center in Moslem Spain.
1084	Bishop Rüdiger of Speyer secures privileges for the local Jews.
1090	Emperor Henry IV grants privileges to the Jews in the Reich.
1096–1215	Period of the Crusades.
1096–1099	First Crusade: 1096, Jews are murdered in Rhenish cities, Regensburg, Bohemia, and elsewhere. 1099, capture of Jerusalem and murder of the Jews there.
1144	Charge of ritual murder in Norwich (English).
1146–1147	Second Crusade: Jews are persecuted in the Rhenish cities and Southern Germany.
1171	Blood libel at Blois (France), the first ritual-murder charge on the European continent.
1179	Third Lateran Council: Christians forbidden to charge interest.

1215	Fourth Lateran Council: Introduction of distinctive signs for Jews (the "yellow badge").
1238	Documentary establishment of the imperial "Kammerknechtschaft" for the Jews.
1249	Bull of Pope Innocent IV condemning blood libel.
1290	Expulsion of the Jews from England.
1306	Expulsion of the Jews from most of France.
1348–1349	The Black Death. Mass murder of Jews and expulsions from many countries (France, Spain, and especially Germany). Immigration of German Jews to Poland.
1356	The "Golden Bull": Jurisdiction over the Jews is transferred from the emperor to the princes.
1368	First documentation of a *Leibzoll* (body tax) on Jews (in Thuringia).
1391	Religious persecutions with forced mass baptisms of Jews in Christian Spain. 1413–1414 Disputation of Tortosa with forced baptisms. Problem of the baptized Jews ("Nuevos Christianos," Marranos).
1400ff.	Expulsion (and occasional burning) of Jews from many cities of the German Reich (1400: Prague; 1421: Vienna; 1424: Cologne; 1438: Mainz; 1400: Augsburg; 1452: Bavaria; 1453: Franconia; 1499: Nuremberg; 1519: Regensburg; etc.)
1453	Conquest of Constantinople by the Ottoman Turks.
1473	"Desecration of the Host" at Trent.
1480	Establishment of the Inquisition in Spain.
1483	Tomás de Torquemada becomes Grand Inquisitor.
1492	Expulsion of the Jews from Spain. Discovery of America by Columbus.
1496–1497	Mass baptisms and expulsion of the Jews from Portugal.
1516	Establishment of the ghetto in Venice. Conquest of Palestine by the Turks.
1517	Luther posts his Ninety-Five Theses.
1540	Papal ratification of the Society of Jesus.
1543	Luther's polemical writings against Judaism and the Jews.
1545–1563	Council of Trent: The Counter Reformation.
1555	Pope Paul IV decrees that the Jews should be segregated in ghettos.
1567	Joseph Caro of Safed publishes the *Shulhan Arukh*, which will become the standard Jewish judicial code.
1569–1572	Isaac ben Solomon Luria (Ha-Ari) in Safed: Renewal of the kabbalah.

Ca. 1590	Marranos settle in Amsterdam.
1600	First printing of Shakespeare's *The Merchant of Venice* ("with the extreame crueltie of Shylocke the Iewe").
1602	First printing of the chapbook about Ahasuerus the "Wandering Jew" (after 1694 also called "Eternal Jew").
1618–1648	Thirty Years' War.
1648–1649	Chmielnicki's Cossack uprising with massacres of the Jews in the Ukraine and Poland. As a consequence, westward emigration of the Jews from Poland.
1654	Establishment of the first Jewish settlement in New Amsterdam (later New York).
1656	Excommunication of Baruch Spinoza from the Portuguese-Jewish community of Amsterdam. The Jews are readmitted to Cromwell's England.
1665	Sabbatai Tzevi proclaims himself as the Messiah in Smyrna.
1666	Sabbatai Tzevi converts to Islam.
1670	Expulsion of the Jews from Vienna.
1671	Limited admittance of Jews to the Mark Brandenburg.
1700	Judah Hasid and his group immigrate to Palestine (first organized group immigration to Palestine in modern times).
1711	Publication of Eisenmenger's *Entdecktes Judentum*.
1738	Execution of the Court Jew Joseph Süss Oppenheimer ("Jud Süss") in Stuttgart.
1753	Jewish Naturalization Act (Jew Bill) passed by the British parliament and repealed because of excessive public opposition.
1755	First publication of Moses Mendelssohn (1729–86).
1770	Mendelssssohn's first public championship of the Jews (response to Lavater's missive.).
1772	First partition of Poland.
1776	Declaration of Independence by the American colonies of Britain, which leads to the founding of the United States of America.
1779	Lessing's play *Nathan der Weise* (first performed in 1783).
1781	Dohm's *Über die bürgerliche Verbesserung der Juden*.
1782	Edict of Tolerance issued by Emperor Joseph II.
1783	Mendelssohn's *Jerusalem, oder Über religiöse Macht und Judentum*.
1789	French Revolution. Declaration of the Rights of Man.
1791	The French National Assembly decrees equality of rights for the Jews. In Russia a limited Pale of Settlement is established for the Jews.

1799	Napoleon's campaign from Egypt to Acre. His proclamation to the Jews about the reestablishment of their state (April 20).
1804	Napoleon becomes emperor.
1806	On 29 July, opening of the assembly of Jewish notables convened by Napoleon.
1807	From 9 February to 9 March, meeting of the Great Sanhedrin convened by Napoleon in Paris.
1808	Equal rights for the Jews of Westphalia. Prussian Jews receive local citizenship on 27 January and are recognized as citizens of Prussia on 12 March.
1811	Equality of rights for the Jews of Frankfurt am Main.
1812	On 11 March the Jews of Prussia are officially emancipated.
1813	Battle of the Nations at Leipzig, 17–19 October. Napoleon is overthrown.
1814–1815	Congress of Vienna: Article 16 of the Act of the German Confederation concerning the continued validity of the civil rights granted the Jews by (instead of "in") the German states makes their rescission possible (e.g., in Frankfurt).
1819	"Hepp-Hepp" movement in Germany with violent acts against the Jews.
1829	The "emancipation law" for Catholics is debated and passed in England (March–April). The word *Emanzipation* enters common usage in Germany to denote the efforts for civil rights for the Jews.
1830	3 February: International guarantee of legal equality for members of all religions in Greece (London Protocol). July: Revolution in Paris, followed by revolutionary movements and uprisings in other countries.
1832	Abolition of slavery in England.
1840	Blood libel in Damascus. First public defense of the Jews by Moses Montefiore (together with Adolphe Crémieux).
1842	The discussion of Bruno Bauer's *Judenfrage* disseminates this word and concept.
1848	February: Revolution in France. March: Revolutions in Germany, Austria, etc. Riots against Jews in Germany. 5 December: Constitutional charter in Prussia with general equality.
1850	January 31: A revision of the Prussian constitution gives the Christian religion a preferential position.
1858	23 July: Full equality for the Jews in England, including seats in parliament. (The compulsory Christian oath is abolished.)
1860	Founding of the Alliance Israélite Universelle in Paris.

1862	Slavery is abolished in the United States of America (Abraham Lincoln's Emancipation Proclamation). Moses Hess publishes his book *Rom und Jerusalem*.
1866	War in Prussia.
1867	The constitutions of the North German Confederation and the state of Austria guarantee equal rights to members of all religious faiths.
1870	Unification of Italy with Rome as the capital. Abolition of all religious limitations of the ghetto in Rome. As French Minister of Justice, Adolphe Crémieux grants French citizenship to the Jews of Algeria. Charles Netter founds the Mikveh Israel Agricultural School (south of Jaffa) on behalf of the Alliance Israélite Universelle.
1871	Founding of the German (imperial) Reich. The equality of rights of the North German Confederation is extended to Bavaria as a law of the Reich.
1873	An economic crisis in Germany following the *Gründerjahre* (period of rapid industrial and commercial expansion).
1874	The Swiss federal constitution guarantees equality for members of all religious faiths.
1875	Introduction of civil marriage in Germany (in Bismarck's *Kulturkampf* with the Catholic Church).
1876	Heinrich Graetz completes his 11-volume *Geschichte der Juden*.
1878	Berlin Congress (after the Russo-Turkish War) decrees equality for all religions in Rumania. In Germany, anti-socialist laws and beginning of a policy of protective tariffs.
1879–1881	Political organization of the anti-Jewish movements under the new concept *Antisemitismus*.
1881	Eugen Dühring's work *Die Judenfrage als Rassen-, Sitten- und Culturfrage*. Pogroms in Russia; beginning of the Jewish mass emigration to Western Europe and America.
1882	Beginning of organized Jewish immigration to Palestine (First Aliyah). Leon Pinsker publishes his book *Autoemancipation*. Ritual murder charge at Tisza Eszlár (Hungary).
1884	Kattowitz Conference of the Hovevei Zion (Friends of Zion).
1890	First use of the word *Zionismus* by Nathan Birnbaum in his weekly *Selbstemancipation*.
1891	Baron Maurice de Hirsch founds the Jewish Colonization Association (ICA) for the mass settlement of Russian Jews in Argentina. Accusation of ritual murder in Xanten (Rhineland).
1894–1895	First Dreyfus trial in Paris. The Jewish captain Dreyfus is wrongfully sentenced, publicly degraded, and taken to Devil's Island to serve a life term.

1896	February: Herzl publishes his book *Der Judenstaat: Versuch einer modernen Lösung der Judenfrage.*
1897	August: Meeting of the First Zionist Congress. Founding of the Zionist Organization with the Basel Program.
1905	Revolution and pogroms in Russia.
1908	Beginning of systematic settlement work in Palestine by the Zionist Organizatioal under the direction of Arthur Ruppin.
1909	Founding of the first collective settlement (Kvutzah, Kibbutz) Degania in the Jordan valley.
1914–1918	First World War.
1917	Bolshevik revolution in Russian. Balfour Declaration of the British government favoring "the establishment in Palestine of a national home for the Jewish people."
1919	Pogroms in the Ukraine and in Poland.
1920	The San Remo Conference affirms the Balfour Declaration and awards the mandate for Palestine to Great Britain for its implementation. Arab unrest in Palestine. Beginning of the dissemination of the *Protocols of the Elders of Zion* in Central and Western Europe and in America despite proof that the work is a forgery.
1922	Assassination of Walther Rathenau.
1925	Opening of the Hebrew University in Jerusalem.
1929–1933	World economic crisis.
1929	August: Sixteenth Zionist Congress. Founding of the expanded Jewish Agency for Palestine. Arab unrest jeopardizes the Jewish work of construction in Palestine.
1933–1945	Hitler regime in Germany.
1933–1939	The so-called Fifth Aliyah to Palestine with 50,000 Jews from Germany.
1933	1 April: Boycott of Jewish businesses throughout Germany. 4 April: Robert Weltsch's editorial in the *Jüdische Rundschau:* "Tragt ihn mit Stolz, den gelben Fleck!" 7 April: Law restoring the permanent civil service; dismissal of all Jews from government positions. 11 April: Letter of protest by the writer Armin T. Wegner to Hitler—the only known public protest by a German against the Jewish policy of the National Socialists in Germany.
1935	15 September: Law defining citizenship in the Reich. Law for the protection of German blood: racial anti-Semitism becomes the law of the land.
1936–1939	Arab uprising against the Jews and the British mandatory government in Palestine.
1938	13 March: Annexation (Anschluss) of Austria to the German Reich and extension of the anti-Jewish laws to Austria.

July: Unsuccessful conference at Evian about the admittance of Jewish refugees.

August: Adolf Eichmann becomes director of the central office for Jewish emigration in Vienna.

28 October: Deportation of 15,000 to 17,000 Jews with Polish passports to a no man's land at the Polish-German border.

7 November: Hershel Grynszpan, a young Polish Jew, assassinates the German legation counselor vom Rath in Paris by way of revenge for the deportation of his parents.

9–10 November: Centrally organized "spontaneous" acts of violence against the Jews throughout Germany ("Reichskristallnacht"): Burning of the synagogues, destruction of shops and dwellings, arrest of 26,000 Jews.

12 November: The German Jews are fined one billion marks as "atonement" and their elimination from German economic and cultural life is decreed.

1939	15 March: Occupation of Czechoslovakia. Introduction of the anti-Jewish laws and decrees in force in the Rhineland.

17 May: British white book with severe limitations on Jewish immigration and settlement in Palestine.

1 September: German troops invade Poland. Beginning of World War II.

12 October: First deportations of Jews from Austria and the "protectorate" Bohemia and Moravia to the "Generalgouvernement" Poland.

1940 30 April: The first guarded ghetto is established at Lodz.
10 May: Beginning of the German Western offensive.

1941 22 June: The Germans attack the Soviet Union.
31 July: Göring orders Heydrich to evacuate all European Jews ("Final Solution")

1942 20 January: Wannsee Conference to organize and systematize the extermination of European Jewry (implementation of the "Final Solution").
June: Beginning of the mass gassings in Auschwitz and the deportation of German Jews to Theresienstadt. Closing of the Jewish schools in the Reich.
July: Establishment of the Treblinka extermination camp.
3 November: Battle of El Alamein; retreat of Rommel's Africa Corps which had posed a threat to Palestine.

1943 19 April to 16 May: Warsaw ghetto uprising.
June to December: "Liquidation" of the Polish and Russian forced ghettos.

1944 April: Beginning of the mass deportations of Greek and Hungarian Jews to Auschwitz.
6 June: Landing of the Allies in Northern France.
Late October: Last gassing in Auschwitz.

1945 8 May: Unconditional surrender of the German army.

1946 Intensified struggle of the Jewish population of Palestine against the British emigration policy.

29 June: "Black Sabbath"—arrest of Jewish leaders in Palestine by the British.

1947   29 November: United Nations resolution calling for the establishment of a Jewish and an Arab state in Palestine, including stipulations about an economic community between them. This was accepted by the Jews, but the Arabs resisted it by force of arms.

1948   14 May (5th of Iyar): Founding of the State of Israel. Beginning of mass immigration to Israel and the war of the Arab states against Israel.

1949   February–July: Armistice treaties with the defeated Arab states Egypt, Lebanon, Jordan, and Syria.

1956   October–November: Sinai War.

1967   June: Six Day War. Occupation of the Sinai peninsula and the West Jordanian areas Judea and Samaria. Reunification of Jerusalem (hitherto divided).
22 November: Resolution 242 of the United Nations.

1973   October: Yom Kippur War. First use of oil boycott by the Arab states against the Western powers. United Nations Resolution 338.

1977   19 November: Official visit of the Egyptian president Anwar Sadat to Jerusalem.

1978   September: Agreements of the Camp David conference between Israel, Egypt, and the United States about a peaceful settlement of the conflict.

1979   26 March: Signing of a peace treaty with Egypt.

Index

753

DUE